cal tissues]: histology, histone, histamine, antihistamine, histolytic

homo-, homeo- [Gk. *homos*, same; Gk. *homios*, similar]: homeostasis, homeothermy, homogeneous, homogenized, homologous, homologue, Homoptera, homozygote

hydro- [Gk. *hydor*, water; now, confusingly, pertaining either to water or to hydrogen]: hydrogen, hydrate, dehydration, hydraulic, carbohydrate, hydrolytic, hydrophobia, hydrocarbon, hydrochloric acid, hydroxide

hyper- [Gk. *hyper*, over, above, more than]: hyperacidity, hypertension, hyperthermia, hyperthyroid, hypertonic

hypo- [Gk. *hypo*, under, below, beneath, less than]: hypochondria, hypocotyl, hypodermic needle, hypoglycemia, hypophysis, hypotension, hypothalamus, hypothermia, hypothesis, hypothyroid, hypotonic

in-, im- [L. *in*, in]: imprinting, inbreeding, instinct, insulin

inter- [L. *inter*, between, among, together, during]: interaction, interbreed, intercellular, intercostal muscles, interior, interphase, interspecific, interstitial

intra-, intro- [L. *intra*, within]: intracellular, intracranial, intramolecular, intrauterine, intravenous, introduced

-itis [L., Gk. *-itis*, inflammation of]: arthritis, bronchitis, dermatitis

leuko-, leuco- [Gk. *leukos*, white]: leukocyte, leukemia, leukoplast, leukocytosis

-logue, -logy [Gk. *-logos*, word, language, type of speech]: analogue (analogy), homologue (homology), dialogue, monologue, travelogue

-logy [Gk. *-logia*, the study of, from *logos*, word]: anthropology, biology, cytology, embryology, histology

-lysis, lys-, lyso-, -lyze, -lyte [Gk. *lysis*, a loosening, dissolution]: lyse, lysogeny, lysozyme, paralysis, hydrolysis, phosphorolysis, analysis, analyze, catalysis, catalytic, electrolyte

macro- [Gk. *makro-*, now "great," "large"]: macrocyte, macromolecule, macromutation, macronucleus, macroscopic, macrospore, macrophage

mega-, megalo-, -megaly [Gk. *megas*, large, gr..., megaspore, mega..., bomb], acromeg...

-mere, -mer, mero... part]: blastomer..., chromomere, dim..., polymer

meso-, mes- [Gk. *mesos*, middle, in the middle]: mesencephalon, mesentery, mesoderm, mesomorph, mesophyll, Mesopotamia, mesothelium, Mesozoic

meta-, met- [Gk. *meta*, after, beyond; now often denoting change]: metabolism, metacarpal, metamorphic, metastasis, metatarsal, Metazoa

micro- [Gk. *mikros*, small]: microbe, microbiology, microcephalic, micrometer, micronucleus, micropyle, microscope, microspore

myo- [Gk. *mys*, mouse, muscle]: myocardial infarction, myocardium, myoglobin, myoma, myosin

neuro- [Gk. *neuron*, nerve, sinew, tendon]: neurasthenia, neuroanatomy, neuroblast, neurofibril, neuron, neurosis, neurotransmitter, neurula

oligo- [Gk. *oligos*, few, little]: Oligocene, oligochaete, oligotrophic

-oma [Gk. *-oma*, tumor, swelling]: carcinoma, glaucoma, hematoma, lipoma, sarcoma

oo- [GK. *oion*, egg]: oogenesis, oogonium, oophyte

-osis [Gk. *-osis*, a state of being, condition]: arteriosclerosis, cirrhosis, halitosis, metamorphosis, tuberculosis

osteo-, oss- [Gk. *osteon*, bone; L. *os, ossa*, bone]: ossicle, ossification, ossified, Osteichthys, osteoblast, osteoclast, osteomyelitis, osteopath, periosteum

para- [Gk. *para-*, alongside of, beside, beyond]: paradigm, paralysis, paramedic, parameter, parasite, parathyroid, Parazoa

patho-, -pathy, -path [Gk. *pathos*, suffering; now often disease or the treatment of disease]: pathogen, pathology, pathological, osteopath

peri- [Gk. *peri*, around]: pericardial, pericarp, pericycle, periderm, perimeter, periosteum, photoperiod, peripheral, peritoneum

phago-, -phage [Gk. *phagein*, to eat]: phagocyte, phagocytosis, bacteriophage

plasm..., plasm, -plast, -plasty [Gk. ...mething molded or ...k. *plassein*, to form or ...asma, plasma membrane, ...smid, plasmasol, plasmolysis, cytoplasm, ...sm, neoplasm; plastid, ...roplast, chromoplast, leucoplast, protoplast; dermoplasty, plastic surgery

-pod [Gk. *pod*, foot]: anthropod, cephalopod, gastropod, pseudopod, podiatrist

poly- [Gk. *poly-, polys*, many]: polychaete, polycotyledonous, polydactyly, polygenic inheritance, polymer, polymorphism, polypeptide, polyploid, polysome

-rrhea [Gr. *rhoia*, flow]: amenorrhea, diarrhea, gonorrhea

septi-, -sepsis, -septic [Gk. *septicos*, rotten, infected]: septic, septicemia, aseptic, antiseptic

-some, somat- [Gk. *soma*, body; Gk. *somat-*, of the body]: somatic cell, psychosomatic, centrosome, chromosome, ribosome, polysome

-stat, -stasis, stato- [Gk. *stasis*, stand]: metastasis, thermostat, electrostatic, hydrostatic

stoma-, stomato-, -stome [Gk. *stoma*, mouth, opening]: stoma, cyclostome, cytostome, deuterostome, protostome

sym-, syn- [Gk. *syn*, with, together]: symbiont, symbiosis, symmetry, sympathetic nervous system, symptom, synapsis, synaptonemal complex, synchrony

taxo-, -taxis [Gk. *taxis*, to arrange, put in order; now often referring to ordered movement]: taxonomy, syntax, ataxia, chemotaxis, geotaxis, phototaxis

tomo-, -tome, -tomy [Gk. *tome*, a cutting; Gk. *tomos*, slice]: atom [you can't cut it], anatomy, dichotomy, lobotomy, appendectomy

tropho-, -troph, -trophy [Gk. *trophe*, nutrition]: trophic level, trophoblast, atrophy, autotroph, heterotroph

trop-, tropo-, -tropy, -tropism [Gk. *tropos*, to turn, to turn toward]: tropism, tropical, entropy, geotropism, phototropism

ur-, -uria [Gk. *ouron*, urine]: uracil, urea, uremia, ureter, urethra, uric acid, urine, phenylketonuria

uro-, -uran [Gk. *oura*, tail]: urochordate, anuran

BIOSPHERE

The Realm of Life

BIOSPHERE
The Realm of Life

Robert A. Wallace
University of Florida

Jack L. King
University of California, Santa Barbara

Gerald P. Sanders

SCOTT, FORESMAN AND COMPANY
Glenview, Illinois   London, England

Cover and part openers by Jean Helmer and Dick Smyth.

Library of Congress Cataloging in Publication Data

Wallace, Robert Ardell, 1938–
    Biosphere: the realm of life.
    Includes index.
    1. Biology.   I. King, Jack L.   II. Sanders, Gerald P.
III. Title.
QH308.2.W355   1984   574   83-20381
ISBN 0-673-16603-1

3456-VHJ-8887868584

To Lisa,
with nosniborg
      RAW

To William and Thomas,
new and welcome members
        GPS

To Mom and the memory of my father
      JLK

Preface

It may seem a bit unusual, but we will begin the preface of this book by mentioning another book, *Biology: the Science of Life*. In it, we attempted to break new ground in introductory texts for science majors: we intended for it to be inclusive, more challenging, and more readable than the texts then available. We learned a great deal from the success of that book, and agreed to attempt to reach even more students with a different, shorter text that would be again challenging and readable, but with integrated pedagogy, less emphasis on technical terminology, and a concentrated effort to make the material not only "relevant" (an overworked term), but *interesting*. We wanted to generate a measure of sheer *enthusiasm* in the minds of biology majors and nonmajors alike. So, again, we find ourselves on unbroken ground. However, we feel a certain familiar exuberance, ourselves, at the opportunity to describe the fascinating world of life to a new and different readership.

This text is intended for one- or two-term introductory courses that may include science majors, nonmajors, or both. We must admit that it was not an easy task to attempt to write engagingly without yielding to the impulse to tell *all* the stories about biology that seem, to us, so engaging. We hope the anecdotes lend an air of friendliness to the book, as well as provide another pedagogical device. It would please us if the book were regarded as friendly and comfortable, if this helped to create a compelling affec-

tion toward the world of biology on the part of the reader.

The text is organized into seven sections and comprises 47 short chapters. Instructor flexibility is built into the sequence of material, and was constantly considered as we developed our structural rationale. The first part focuses on energy and universal principles of life. It covers the scientific method, basic chemistry, cell biology, energetics, metabolic pathways, and mitosis and meiosis.

Part II, *Genetics and Evolution*, affirms our theme of adaptiveness. This is deliberately a rather thorough section: Mendelian principles lead to the identification of genes and chromosomes; then we move to gene action, protein synthesis, and the constantly surprising frontiers in molecular genetics. This is followed by three chapters covering fundamental evolutionary concepts: principles of natural selection, population genetics, and speciation.

Part III covers the evolution and physiology of bacteria, protists, fungi, and plants. The origin of life as it is currently being considered in scientific circles is given ample coverage. Five chapters are devoted to plant diversity and physiology.

Part IV, *Animal Adaptations*, integrates principles of diversity, physiology, and evolution. Invertebrates are described in two chapters; vertebrates (fishes, amphibians, reptiles, birds, and most mammals) are then discussed in depth, until primates, including humans, become the focus of chapter 30.

Chapters 31–41 (Parts V and VI) involve vertebrate physiology with pertinent comparisons to invertebrate and prokaryotic systems. The nervous system is covered in three concise chapters, followed by chapters on hormones and homeostasis. Recent advances in immunology highlight Part VI, which also includes chapters on digestion and nutrition, gas exchange, circulation, reproduction, and development. In this section, too, comparative overviews from the animal world are followed by observations on the human condition.

Part VII, *Behavior and Ecology*, was a delight for us to write. Who is not intrigued by how animals behave in the kind of world in which they find themselves? Behavior is discussed in two chapters, the first discussing the roots of behavior, the second, the usefulness of various acts. Four chapters then describe the earth's biomes, the more theoretical areas of ecological structure and population ecology, and the remarkable story of human populations.

We have made a special effort to attend to pedagogy, in order to make the material easier to learn (and to teach). Key terms appear in bold type throughout the text and are defined when first mentioned. Color has been employed both to clarify the illustrations and photographs and to make the book more attractive to the student. Each chapter concludes with a summary of its major concepts, a list of key terms in the order of their appearance, and a brief set of review questions.

Special essays are used to amplify certain points or to provide interesting asides. Other essays focus on the relevance of biological science in today's society, and yet others are intended to bring home what may have seemed to be academic abstractions, to show that biology has a real and powerful influence at all levels.

Not surprisingly, appendices are found at the end of the text. We have provided a geological timetable, an outline of the classification of living things used in the text, and a special section on careers in biology. The latter is intended to help students who are considering a science major or who want to specialize within their major; it briefly ties the study of biology to real-world possibilities in a wide array of professional fields. Metric conversions appear inside the back cover of the text.

Suggested readings follow the appendices. They have been selected for their accessibility, clarity, brevity and, of course, relevance. The glossary includes pronounciation guides, and definitions, as you will see, are simple and direct. A biological lexicon appears in the front of the book to explain the roots of many biological terms and thereby assist the student in learning the host of new words that must be mastered in any unfamiliar field. Finally, we round out our pedagogical assistance by providing a carefully created Instructor's Manual, a Student Study Guide, transparency masters, and what we believe to be a particularly useful selection of 225 slides, taken from text art, and packaged with a guide that suggests alternative arrangements for use in comparing or reinforcing basic concepts.

Finally, let us say that we are happy we accepted this challenge, that we really didn't know the task would be so hard, that we are deliriously happy that this edition is finished, and that we look forward to doing it all again for the next edition.

RAW • JLK • GPS

Acknowledgements

Books have a way of being orphans. In a sense they are the offspring of no one; the authors traditionally get the credit, but they almost never bring successful books to fruition alone. A host of others work just as hard, are just as creative, and deserve just as much credit. So we, as the authors, would like to name a few of the people who share the credit for this book.

First, the book would have never gotten off the ground if it had not been for the sheer, unbridled confidence of Jim Levy, the general manager of the college division. His organizational skills are undoubtedly the most creative we've ever seen in this business. Richard Welna, working in close cooperation with Levy and "the people upstairs," gave us critical support when we needed it most. We apologize to Dick for the frequency of those times, but we are grateful to him.

We are proud of the unflagging support of Jack Pritchard. He knows the ropes in this business and never failed to give us an honest, straightforward assessment of any situation (and there are "situations" in publishing). We often needed his clear-eyed evaluations.

Jerry Westby, as editor, shepherded this book through most of its development. He wore many hats in those long months and wore each one well. He is responsible for much of what you see here. Rebecca Strehlow could not have known what she was getting into when she assumed first the development, then the overall editorial management of this book. Her intelligence and diligence saw us through one phase after another. Her ability and "can-do" attitude is largely responsible for bringing this book to completion. Susan Moss kept it all together for us in a tight and organized fashion until it became too much and she dropped out, pretending to have a baby. The slack was taken up by Patricia Schmelling, whose depth of experience in book production proved to be precisely what we needed—and at just the right time.

We also wish to express our strong appreciation to our designer, Lucy Lesiak; design manager, Barbara Schneider; photo editor, Mary Goljenboom; freelance editors Judith Gallagher Turpin and L. Sue Baugh; production liaison, Jeanne Schwaba; layout artist Mary Grenning; production coordinator, Victoria Moon; indexer, Brenda Matson; typists Donna Pompa, Spicea Bergman, Susan Portugal, Angel Brashear, Lois Rudloff, Lisa Chapman, and Alex Savino; and researchers Jim Cook and Kim Kendall.

Our illustrators, we think, have done a superb job. We wish to thank Jean Helmer—whose work included the cover and section openers; William Peterson; Sandra McMahon; ETC Graphics; Precision Graphics; Robin Brickman; and Kathie Langwell.

In particular, we must thank our families and friends for putting up with us through the years. We would gladly make an apology, and we will, immediately upon thinking of one.

• • •

We've all heard it said that time changes things, but this happens to be an old saying based on a very real, and sometimes saddening, truth. Things have indeed changed since the days that Susan Smith shepherded us as our production editor. But whatever we've done here is largely due to her relentless and loving efforts to get things rolling. Finally, we are privileged to mention again our friend and editor Clay J. Stratton. From the day he woke Wallace up from a desperate nap in Austin, Texas, things haven't been the same. It's Clay's fault. We owe him a great deal.

Special Note

Jack King died while working on the final stages of this book. We want to say something about Jack's life and his death, but words do not come trippingly on tongue or pen. Jack was an unusual man. He was probably the most brilliant man any of us has ever known. Few people come up with a single original idea throughout their professional lives, but Jack can be credited with at least two and maybe three. He enjoyed his mind immensely and was curious about everything. He was bemused even at the nattering of lesser academicians who criticized him for taking time out to explain biology through these books. But he thought biology was great fun and wanted to tell about it. In fact, he wanted to tell so much that it was a job just holding him within limits. He could exasperate anyone with his cheerful enthusiasm.

On a more personal note, Jack was a good friend, in the purest sense of the phrase. In spite of his prodigious abilities, or because of them, he could never learn the social graces; he told the truth, he never doubted a friend, he could not manipulate people and never seemed to even be trying to get the hang of it. He was loving and he was happy. (He even loved the word, *happy*.) He was gentle, abrupt, comprehending, and klutzy. We remember all sorts of unusual things about this singular man. He was known to show up wearing some strange hat. He knew the words to hundreds of songs but could not carry a tune. His jokes were awful and always followed by a proud grin. He wasn't exactly great at pool. He loved the beach. He is irreplaceable in our hearts and in our work.

Reviewers

The authors and publishers would like to express their appreciation to a number of biologists who have greatly assisted in the development of this book. Biology is a diverse and evolving discipline, and we owe a great deal to the specialists who reviewed our material.

Robert A. Anderson, *DePaul University*

Vernon Avila, *San Diego State University*

William Barstow, *University of Georgia*

Melvin Beck, *Memphis State University*

Robert A. Bender, *University of Michigan*

John P. Bihn, *Fiorello H. LaGuardia Community College*

Richard Boohar, *University of Nebraska*

Raymond Bower, *University of Arkansas*

Gilbert Brum, *California State Polytechnic University, Pomona*

Charles Daghlain, *University of Oklahoma*

Donald J. Defler, *Portland Community College*

Douglas Fratianne, *The Ohio State University*

Merrill L. Gassman, *University of Illinois at Chicago*

Walt Halperin, *University of Washington*

John J. Heise, *Georgia Institute of Technology*

Thomas Kantz, *Sacramento State College*

Jerry L. Kaster, *University of Wisconsin—Milwaukee*

Harris Linder, *University of Maryland*

Virginia Maiorana, *University of Chicago*

James Menees, *San Diego State University*

John Minnich, *University of Wisconsin—Milwaukee*

Darrel Murray, *University of Illinois at Chicago*

William O'Dell, *University of Nebraska*

Comer O. Patterson, *Texas A & M University*

Kathryn S. Podwall, *Nassau Community College*

William Presch, *California State University, Fullerton*

Robert Romans, *Bowling Green State University*

Orlando Schwartz, *University of Northern Iowa*

Marjorie Sharp, *University of Texas at Arlington*

Yvonne Singh, *University of North Carolina at Greensboro*

Roger Sloboda, *Dartmouth College*

Thomas Terry, *University of Connecticut*

Richard W. VanNorman, *University of Utah*

Thomas Wynn, *North Carolina State University*

Ronald P. Zeutschel, *North Seattle Community College*

John Zimmerman, *Kansas State University*

Contents in Brief

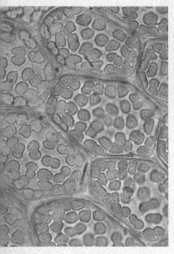

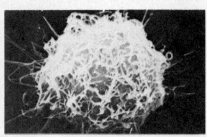

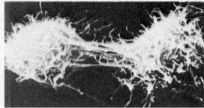

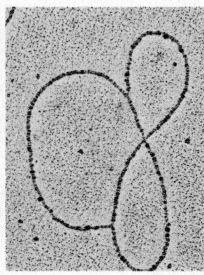

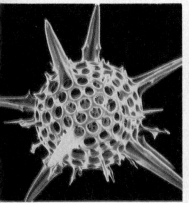

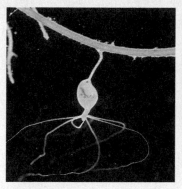

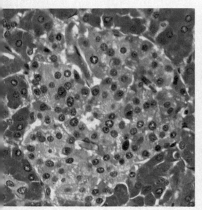

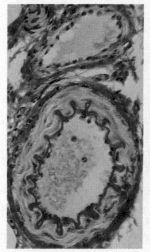
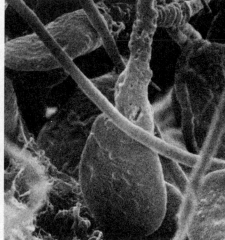

Contents

SCIENCE, CELLS, AND ENERGY
The Ongoing Flow of Life
1

PART
II

GENETICS AND EVOLUTION
History and Horizons
147

PART III

FROM PROKARYOTES TO PLANTS
273

PART IV

ANIMAL ADAPTATIONS
385

PART
V

VERTEBRATE REGULATION
455

PART VI

VERTEBRATE MAINTENANCE AND REPRODUCTION
537

PART
VII

BEHAVIOR AND ECOLOGY
Interrelationships in a Complex Biosphere
615

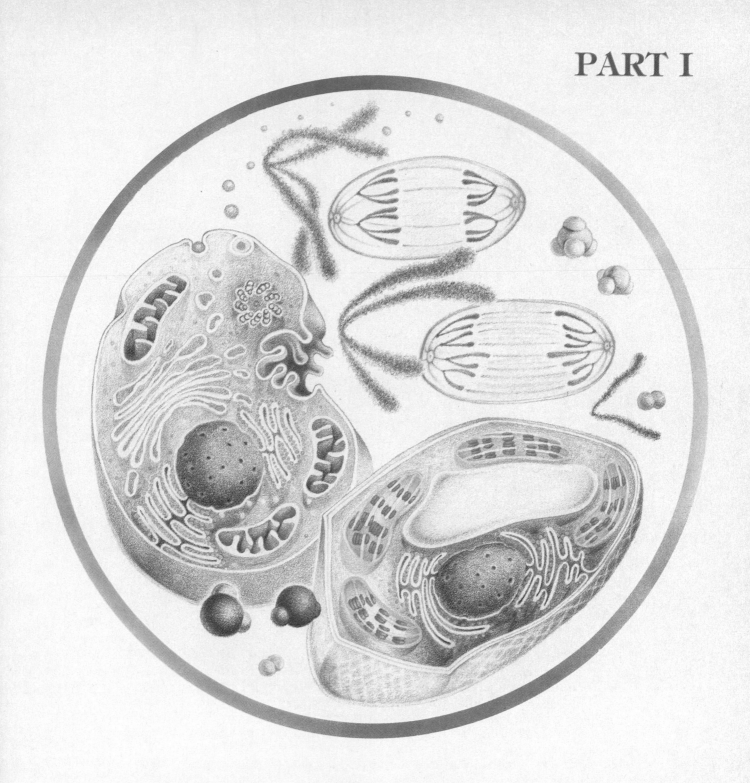

PART I

Science, Cells, and Energy:
The Ongoing Flow of Life

Science

The old man was clearly wrong. Any educated person of his time could easily point out the error in his logic. And he was a heretic as well. The Church taught that all the heavenly bodies revolved around a central, unmoving earth. Galileo Galilei, however, believed in a bold new idea that had been put forth by the Polish astronomer Copernicus, the idea that the earth and the planets revolved around the sun. The Churchmen hadn't stopped Galileo from teaching Copernicus' *heliocentric theory*, as long as it was presented as merely an interesting idea; but Galileo had overstepped those bounds. He had tried to prove the theory with his own astronomical observations. That was his mistake.

Now, in 1633, as he stood before the court of the Papal Inquisition in Rome, his bald head was bowed in forced obedience, humiliation, and rage. He was 69 years old (Figure 1.1).

Recant! he was ordered. The Inquisitors handed him a sheet of paper on which were written the words that he was required to say: that he "objured, cursed, and detested" his erroneous claim that the earth moved around the sun. Galileo reluctantly mouthed the words. He was given a prison sentence anyway, based on a forged document purporting to show that he had previously been expressly forbidden to publish his ideas. Later his sentence was to be commuted to lifelong house arrest. As he left the tribunal, Galileo was heard to mutter, "Nonetheless, it moves."

What had been Galileo's error? First, he had confronted the powerful Church. But he had also chosen an unaccepted method of attempting to establish truth.

The scholars of the middle ages had developed a time-tested method for determining truth, a method that was based on the teachings of Aristotle, heavily interpreted by medieval theologians such as Aquinas and Abélard. This was the formal method of deductive reasoning known as *Aristotelian logic*. In Aristotelian logic, one starts with a few established truths and deduces from them other, less obvious truths. The chain of reasoning is presented in the form of a *syllogism*, a series of connected statements of the *"if. . . then. . . therefore"* variety. The formal proofs of plane geometry were (and are) the finest products of this approach. And the Church, which controlled the schools and the universities, still taught in Galileo's time that Aristotelian logic was the only acceptable method of determining truth. In particular, the philosophers taught that the senses were not to be trusted. And here was Galileo trying to determine truth by looking through a telescope.

Observation? Why? Observation was clearly unnecessary. Observations depend upon our senses, and our senses can mislead us. Only rigorous, abstract logic could rise above the meaningless distractions of the imperfect, rough-and-tumble world to reveal the truths that lay beneath. At least this was what educated men believed in Galileo's time.

Thus, for example, two accepted truths were that *the heavens are perfect*, and *the moon is in the heavens*. Therefore, *the moon is perfect*. Another supposedly self-evident truth was *a sphere is the only perfect shape*. From this it followed that the moon must be a perfect sphere. Never mind that Galileo, with the telescope that he had invented, saw mountains on the moon. Logic had proven that there were no mountains there, and it was agreed that logic was superior to the senses. Galileo had begged the members of the Papal Court to look through his telescope and see the mountains for themselves, but they refused. The mountains were not there; the matter was closed.

But Galileo had persisted. The old man belonged to the coming modern age, not the fading medieval age that still held the minds of the philosophers of the Church. And he was curious about the real world. The old astronomer and mathematician had spent his life devising ways of measuring and weighing things, and inventing tools of measurement and calculation. He had measured the speed of sound, for instance, and had even attempted to measure the speed of light. He had measured the speed and acceleration of falling weights. He had applied mathematics to the real world; he had boldly proclaimed that "The book of Nature is written in mathematical characters." But he was most interested in the heavens.

Galileo had been a convinced Copernican since his youth, though by his own account he had kept his belief a secret to avoid ridicule. But with his invention of a reliable telescope, he believed he saw a way to test the Copernican theory. He could make a prediction based on the heliocentric theory. A *prediction*, of course, is a statement of something that is going to happen in the future, or that has already happened but hasn't yet been observed. Thus the Copernican theory was *testable*. One prediction that Galileo could make was that if the earth and planets revolved around the sun, the planet Venus should have phases like those of the moon: that is, it should always be illuminated on the side facing the sun. This prediction could be tested by observation.

So Galileo pointed his long, skinny telescope toward Venus. And he did so at various times of the year for several years. Sure enough, he found that the planet was illuminated on the side that should be facing the sun, according to Copernican calculations. Galileo thought he had proved the heliocentric theory.

The inquisitors and the scholars didn't think so. Because of their formal training, they could understand Galileo's argument only if they put it into the form of one of their own syllogisms. And so it was expressed:

1. *If the planets and the earth circle the sun, Venus should have phases like those of the moon.*
2. *Venus does have phases like those of the moon.*
3. *Therefore, the planets and the earth circle the sun.*

Preposterous, they sniffed. What kind of proof was this? By the conventions of Aristotelian logic,

1.1

Galileo's firm conviction that the earth, along with the planets, revolved around the sun brought him into conflict with Church dogma. Eventually he was brought before the Inquisitors and forced to recant.

it was a classic example of a well established type of erroneous, faulty, and invalid reasoning! Obviously the old man, with his strange machines and cantankerous spirit, simply did not understand how real science was done. His astronomical observations may have been *consistent* with his hypothesis, but they in no way *proved* it. There were any number of explanations that could just as easily account for Galileo's observations—especially if the observations themselves were to be taken seriously, and they were not. More importantly, it was the *form* of his reasoning, as his contemporaries saw it, that was in error. Some said that one could just as well argue:

1. *If the world is an illusion designed to deceive us, Venus should have phases like those of the moon.*
2. *Venus does have phases like those of the moon.*
3. *Therefore, the world is an illusion designed to deceive us.*

This "proof" had the same logical flaw that the scholars had perceived in Galileo's reasoning. But its conclusion was actually a more acceptable one: the idea of an illusory world had been taught by many of the early philosophers (who, living in what they firmly believed to be an illusory world, were usually on time for dinner just the same). The idea of the earth revolving around the sun was, by comparison, much more strange. It violated both philosophy and common sense—because as much as the senses were not to be trusted, they clearly seemed to indicate the sun arcing across the sky over the unmoving land.

In a sense, the exasperated Church fathers had asked for trouble. Years earlier they had told Galileo that he could publish a book on his ideas if he agreed to state that the Copernican theory was merely an unproved idea, and if he would *agree in advance* to conclude that "man cannot presume to know how the world is really made because God could have brought about the same effects in ways unimagined by man, and because no one must put limits on God's power." The problem was that when Galileo's book came out, his arguments for the Copernican theory were so strong that they made the dictated conclusion of the Church look weak and foolish. So Galileo's real crime was not to disagree with the Church over whether the sun or the earth was at the center of the universe: his crime was more insidious, and the Inquisitors correctly saw that it struck at the very roots of medieval beliefs. Galileo's crime was that he dared to test the real world with a new and dangerous tool. His crime was being a scientist.

Actually, the refusal of the Papal Court to look through Galileo's telescope was a credit to their own intellectual integrity. But they were fighting a doomed battle. They kept Galileo under house arrest until his death eight years later, but in the end, the world became convinced of the heliocentric theory. Today the Church agrees that the earth revolves around the sun (although a convocation in Rome recently decided *against* pardoning Galileo for what he did).

How did the world become convinced? By the same kind of evidence and reasoning that Galileo had offered. Measurement after measurement supported the theory that the earth and the planets revolve around the sun. Prediction after prediction had been tested and had supported the Copernican hypothesis. As a final and dramatic stroke, men have stood on the moon and watched the earth spinning silently in space (Figure 1.2). But who can say what truth is? Perhaps the astronauts were deceived; the world may yet turn out to be an illusion, but for now we are convinced that it is not. We are convinced, not by formal proofs and deductive logic, but by the weight of the evidence. Galileo's way of looking for truth—hopelessly flawed by ancient standards—has since been called many things, among them the **scientific method.**

1.2

Observations that support Galileo's theories are commonplace in the space age; anticipating and plotting the movement of the planets is critical to the success of space exploration.

TESTING HYPOTHESES

Galileo alone did not invent the scientific method, but he discussed and clarified it in his writings and surely was among its first and greatest modern practitioners (the ancient Chinese and Islamic worlds have their own just claims to priority on the scientific method). Partly through his work, the scientific method was firmly established in Europe by the end of the 17th century. By that time the mathematical laws that govern the movements of the earth and planets had been worked out by Kepler and Newton, and the conviction began to grow that the universe was governed not by divine whim, but by fixed laws.

Were those philosophers and scholars who had challenged Galileo's logic wrong? They were not. A basic tenet of modern science is that one indeed can never *prove* anything to be true by observation. Mathematicians can prove their theorems, but natural scientists live in a hazier, less precise world of relative probability. They can't prove anything is true, but they may be able to demonstrate that one thing is more likely to be true than another, and they can even prove that something is false. That "something" is some statement about the real world, a statement that may or may not be true. The statement may take the form of a *hypothesis*.

A **hypothesis** is a provisional conjecture that can then be used to form predictions, which can be tested. The results of the testing may support or refute the hypothesis. If the event that was predicted is, in fact, observed, we can say that the new observation is *consistent* with the hypothesis and thus tends to support it. That is, the observation increases our confidence in the likelihood that the hypothesis is true. This is because the hypothesis was tested and it passed a test that it might have failed. On the other hand, if the predicted event is not observed, the new findings are *inconsistent* with the hypothesis, and thus weaken or even destroy it. At the very least, the original hypothesis will have to be reformulated to take account of the new observation.

For instance, Einstein's theory of relativity led to the prediction that light would be bent by gravity. More specifically, it predicted that the apparent position of a distant star would change when a closer, massive star came between it and ourselves—that is, the light would be bent by the gravity of the massive star. Soon after the prediction was made, there was an opportunity to test it. Special observatories were set up. The moment came; the astronomers' photographic plates were analyzed and, sure enough, light had been bent just as Einstein had predicted. Thus the theory of relativity was supported, but still it was not *proven*. In fact, it remains unproven to this day, although it has passed a number of such tests. And although it is now generally accepted by physicists, it is still subject to further testing, and might still be disproven or modified in the future.

So we see that a scientific observation (or a thousand scientific observations) can support a hypothesis, but cannot prove it to be true. On the other hand, a single, repeatable observation can prove a hypothesis to be false.

Some hypotheses generate predictions that are more difficult to test, such as the prediction that continued cigarette smoking causes lung cancer. Both healthy octagenarian smokers and young, cancerous abstainers exist, so the hypothesis has to be modified to state that cigarette smoking has a *significant tendency* to cause lung cancer—which it almost certainly does. Such a hypothesis can be tested only by using massive numbers and sophisticated statistical analysis to show that the connection does indeed exist. But statistical hypotheses are testable too, and are potentially disprovable. So scientific "facts" are provisional at all times, and in the best of times they stand in danger of being defrocked.

In fact, it's amazing to see how many generally accepted "facts" of 20 years ago—that is, hypotheses that seemed then to be reasonably well supported—have failed further tests and have been discarded. There are undoubtedly many authoritative-sounding statements in this book that eventually will be proven to be patently untrue, perhaps by people who are only now encountering them for the first time.

How does an idea get to be a provisionally accepted "fact" in the first place? When there are several conflicting explanations for a phenomenon, each must be attacked until one simply cannot be disproven. This remaining hypothesis is then regarded provisionally as established—until another possible explanation is put forward. Always, in the background, lurks the possibility that there is some other explanation or fact of nature that no one has even conceived. But, as Sherlock Holmes said, "When you have eliminated the impossible, whatever remains, however improbable, must be the truth."

Some hypotheses simply are not subject to being disproven. An *untestable* hypothesis may be disprovable in principle, but the actual means of testing it are unavailable. An *unfalsifiable* hypothesis is worse—it is not disprovable even in principle. An example of an unfalsifiable hypothesis is the notion that the world is an illusion. Scientists may yawn rudely and sneak glances at their wristwatches when presented with an unfalsifiable hypothesis. Real science is fun and exciting—it is the fun and excitement of formulating and testing ideas that attracts the efforts of some very bright people into scientific research. For them, untestable and unfalsifiable hypotheses are no fun at all; there is simply nothing to be done with them. (Not everyone has this attitude, of course. More than a few people get a kick out of the predictions generated by the unfalsifiable premises of astrology, biorhythm charts, Chinese fortune cookies, and psychoanalysis.)

Ways of Doing Science

Calling something *The Scientific Method* might lead someone to believe that there is only one way of doing science. But there are many, and it would be difficult to define any single method. Science often seems to be more of a game or contest, a grand puzzle with many contending players. One prominent scientist has defined *The Scientific Method* as "doing one's damnedest with one's mind no matter what." There are rules of play, however (Essay 1.1).

ESSAY 1.1
HOW SCIENTISTS SPREAD THE NEWS

The process of scientific discovery knows no unbreakable rules, and is dominated by intuitive, creative eccentrics "doing one's damnedest with one's mind no matter what." The conventions of communication between scientists, however, are as formal and intricate as an English country dance. It's not enough just to unravel the universe's little secrets. If new discoveries are to be taken seriously by other scientists, certain rigid criteria must be met. This means, among other things, that the experiments must be done right. Often, as it happens, the discovery comes first, not infrequently by (educated) accident. Still, before the new finding can be published and accepted, the experiment must be repeated and verified according to accepted procedures.

New findings are almost always communicated through a formal **scientific paper** or **journal article.** Scientists may write books, book reviews, and review articles, but these are all based on the all-important research articles. The article may appear in any one of several thousand **scientific journals**—usually one devoted to the narrow specialty of the investigator. The most important new findings may appear in a journal of general interest to all scientists, such as *Science* or *Nature.*

In either case, the article will not be published until it has undergone the scrutiny of the journal's editor and of two or three anonymous volunteer referees. This is one of the extensive safeguards of formal science. The referee system, however, is not without drawbacks. The most important new ideas in science are those that break with established paradigms (world views) to permit fresh, unfamiliar perceptions, but referees may not be ready for fresh, unfamiliar ideas. Many of the most important landmark papers in any scientific field have had to withstand an initial rejection by suspicious referees. Of course, these referees have also prevented the publication of innumerable allegedly grand ideas and supposed paradigm shifts that were, in fact, pure hokum.

Scientific papers are frequently presented as lectures, usually illustrated with slides, given at scientific meetings. Scientists attend these meetings to exchange news and, often, **preprints**—photocopied manuscripts that have not yet been published. (Preprints are also sent through the mail by the hundreds, but they are supposedly privileged communications between friends and are *not* to be formally cited.) The papers presented at a scientific meeting sometimes are published together in a **symposium volume.**

A standard scientific article consists of six parts: the summary; introduction; methods and materials; results; discussion; and literature cited. The **Summary** includes the principal finding, or conclusion, of the experiment being reported. A reader can rapidly skim through a whole pile of journals, reading just the titles and summaries and delving into the rest of an article only if the summary seems interesting.

A short **Introduction** reviews any previous relevant work and explains the reasons for proposing

Science and Problem Solving. When you get right down to it, *science* just might be an extension of everyday, common sense approaches to problem solving. We human beings are all scientists in part—we are constantly dealing with ideas and possibilities that may or may not be true, and with observations that may or may not be reliable. When the car won't start or the soufflé falls or brown spots appear on the lawn, we do all the things scientists do: we formulate hypotheses about the source of trouble, and we try to test our hypotheses. If we're desperate enough, we may look for the answer in an auto repair manual or a cookbook or a gardening column—scientists search the literature, too. If we can't find a solution

to our problem there, we're on our own—we try a little of this or a little of that, check the spark plugs (on the hypothesis that they might be fouled); use less milk (on the hypothesis that we have been using too much); or try a little bug killer on one section of the lawn (on the hypothesis that there may be cutworms). If one of these approaches doesn't work, we tentatively reject that particular hypothesis and try to formulate a new one (Figure 1.3).

Replicas and Controls. You may have noticed that the world is a complex place, full of confounding **variables** (that is, nonconstant factors that affect our observations). Despite all of our technology, we often can't get a reliable weather

---

the hypothesis that is to be tested. The writing style here, as throughout the article, is usually quite impersonal—maddeningly impersonal to anyone not thoroughly familiar with scientific presentation. One usually learns very little about the investigator's actual thought processes, hunches, dreams, or lucky accidents by reading scientific journals. The experiments themselves are the focus of scientific writing.

The **Methods and Materials** section tells exactly how the experiment was conducted. It is written with enough detail and clarity that anyone who is sufficiently interested can repeat the experiment. Repeatability is the only guarantee that the findings are legitimate.

The **Results** section is the key part of most papers. It includes the observations made and experimental data compiled, along with any statistical analysis required to clarify the data. The investigator must accumulate enough data until it becomes extremely unlikely that the results could be due to chance. If the investigator cannot

show this, no reputable journal will publish the paper, and other scientists won't take the results seriously.

In the **Discussion** section, the author may be a little less formal, and can even indulge in speculation, comparisons, and suggestions for future research. Here ambiguities in the data can be accounted for and potential objections explored, and persuasion and argument are allowed. After all, it doesn't do much good to make a new discovery if you can't convince the rest of the world. To a surprising degree—given the austere formality and pretended impartiality that good scientific manners demand—the ultimate impact of a work of science depends on the skillful presentation of ideas, on the ability to be interesting, and on just plain good writing. Good writing will not make a dull experiment interesting or render an unimportant discovery important; still, our greatest scientists have often been not only great experimentalists and theorists, but great writers as well.

Every scientific paper is sprin-

kled with numerous parenthetical notes or footnotelike numbers referring the reader to the **Literature Cited,** a list of other journal articles that concludes the presentation. Each item on the list includes the name of the author or authors, year of publication, journal title, volume, and page number, and, sometimes, the title of the cited work. These references alert the reader to other important work in the field, in case he or she wishes to pursue the subject. Just as importantly, they give credit to workers who have made previous contributions. The first person to make a discovery has an eternal claim on all who follow. All humans hunger for recognition, appreciation, approval, and understanding from their peers, and most take pleasure in giving recognition where recognition is due. The formality of scientific citation is a humble acknowledgment that science is a cumulative, cooperative, and, above all, human venture. ●

Applying the "scientific method" is not necessarily a formal, somber business, restricted to the confines of laboratories. Its logical elements are often applied in less dignified circumstances: "The car won't start. I've kicked the tires, checked the radiator, and slammed the hood three times, but nothing happened. I wonder if the problem is the ignition switch? Let's see . . . . if I hot-wire the ignition and jump the starter, it should start right up!"

report. In the science of biology, in particular, all living organisms are complex, interact with their environments in complex ways, and are in a permanent state of metabolic change and activity. Any one of a large number of variables might be responsible for modifying the observations we are interested in.

So how do we go about testing the effect of this or that particular variable in a tangled web of interactions? One useful approach is to repeat the experiment a number of times—*replica tests*—because a single result might always be a fluke (an unexpected, rare occurrence that catches us by surprise). Another important approach is to hold *constant* as many factors as possible, changing other potentially confounding factors in regular, *controlled* ways. The factor that is of greatest significance to the hypothesis being tested is varied in a precise way so that its effect alone can be measured (Figure 1.4). If we want to know why the soufflé falls, we won't find out by adding less milk *and* turning up the oven *and* leaving out the celery, all at once.

Reductionists and Synthesists. Reducing any problem to its simplest level and studying the effect of a single factor is called *reductionism*, and scientists who emphasize this approach are called *reductionists*. Sometimes this powerful principle is itself described as being "the" scientific method. But the reductionist approach, as valuable as it is, is not the only way of doing science.

In every scientific field there are not only experimentalists but theoreticians, not only reductionists but *synthesists*. Any active scientist can be all of these things at different times, of course, and many are. Theorists and synthesists are people who generate new ways of looking at old observations—an "old observation" being anything that has already been published. A grand idea or theory usually is formulated from a large body of seemingly unrelated data, usually with the stimulus of some new, at first inexplicable, finding. Copernicus, as we have seen, was one such theorist. Einstein was another.

Inductive and Deductive Reasoning. Making connections and scientific sense out of various existing observations is called **inductive reasoning.** Inductive reasoning is not the exclusive province of armchair philosophers; many of the grand, unifying theories of science have been developed by hard-working scientists whose lifelong experience in collecting, observing, and experimenting has given them the necessary intuition or "feel" that is a major ingredient of inductive reasoning.

Inductive reasoning, then, goes from the specific to the general: that is, the large idea is based on an accumulation of data, derived from asking small questions and tied together by insight. A whole new array of small, specific questions can then be *deduced* from the newly proposed general principle. These new questions can then be explored and tested. **Deductive reasoning** is the process that generates new small questions and specific predictions from general principles. Deductive reasoning, then, goes from the general to the specific. For example, the idea that Venus should be lit on the side facing the sun was deduced from the Copernican theory.

REVOLUTIONS AND PARADIGMS

The sorts of questions scientists ask and the way they go about answering them depend on a set of encompassing views called *paradigms*. A **paradigm** is a general, accepted, and internally consistent view of the world. When an existing paradigm is replaced, the effect may be shattering to the scientific community, and the replacement may meet with stiff resistance. We saw this in the case of the Copernican revolution: Galileo's critics really couldn't understand the point he was trying to make. The medieval Church's way of looking at the world is almost as inpenetrable to us now.

It would be hard to list all of the major scientific revolutions and new paradigms that have come and gone. There are many. Physics, for instance, has seen two major revolutions in thought—relativity and quantum mechanics—in just this century. The science of geology was rocked to its foundations by the new idea of continental drift. But what is a major paradigm change in one field of science may be only a minor ripple in another field: physicists were only mildly interested in the earth-shattering paroxysms of reorganized thinking their geologist colleagues were experiencing. Biology has had its share of intellectual revolutions, too.

VITALISM AND MECHANISM

In the 17th and 18th centuries, two quite different notions developed regarding the nature of life: *vitalism* and *mechanism.* **Vitalism** maintains that living organisms have special properties and are governed by special laws that are not applicable to inanimate objects or to the chemistry of non-living substances. These special properties have been termed *vital forces.* What is the difference between a man and a corpse, it was argued, except for the presence or absence of a vital force? Unfortunately, the "vital force" hypotheses usually fell into the realm of the untestable and the unfalsifiable, and, in fact, have never led to any interesting discoveries.

The other school of thought was **mechanism,** the notion that a living body was a machine, subject to physical and chemical laws and depending only on those laws. Understand the laws and you will understand life, it was held, for life has no laws of its own.

The mechanist point of view was slow in taking hold, however. The question came to a crisis point in the 19th century, over the question of *spontaneous generation.* Many vitalists believed that the maggots, molds, and bacteria that could always be found in rotting meat, spoiled broth, or other decaying material were generated by the material itself—in other words, that lower forms of life were constantly being created by the vital forces of nature. But in a famous series of experiments,

1.4

This experiment is intended to determine the effect of an herbicide (plant killer) on bird development prior to its use on plants. The first procedure **(a)** includes piercing the fertile egg (under sterile conditions) and injecting a specific concentration of herbicide into the air space below the shell. The herbicide must be dissolved in alcohol. Following incubation, the embryo is studied for defects at a desired stage.

The experiment contains several sources of potential error, as listed. In any case, it is difficult to draw a meaningful conclusion from one embryo. To correct these errors, a controlled experiment must be devised.

In the controlled experiment **(b),** four large groups of fertile eggs are prepared. The first group is treated in the manner described above. The second group is treated identically, except that the injection is a prepared alcohol solution that does *not* contain the herbicide. The third group has been pierced and sealed only, and the fourth group has received no treatment, but is incubated along with the others. Now the results of the four groups can be compared, and any difference in results can be attributed to the presence of the herbicide.

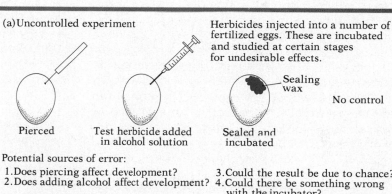

(a) Uncontrolled experiment

Herbicides injected into a number of fertilized eggs. These are incubated and studied at certain stages for undesirable effects.

Pierced   Test herbicide added in alcohol solution   Sealing wax   Sealed and incubated   No control

Potential sources of error:
1. Does piercing affect development?
2. Does adding alcohol affect development?
3. Could the result be due to chance?
4. Could there be something wrong with the incubator?

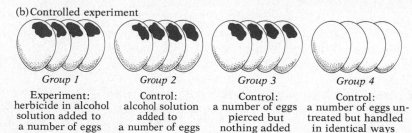

(b) Controlled experiment

Group 1   *Group 2*   *Group 3*   *Group 4*

Experiment: herbicide in alcohol solution added to a number of eggs

Control: alcohol solution added to a number of eggs

Control: a number of eggs pierced but nothing added

Control: a number of eggs untreated but handled in identical ways

All four groups are treated alike in all other ways

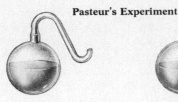

Pasteur's Experiment

Broth sterilized and stored in curved flask

Broth remains free of microbes

Flask tilted so broth touches dust particles in flask

Broth becomes cloudy with microbes

1.5

The question of the spontaneous generation of life has a long history in science. For example, it was once held that maggots (fly larvae) in carcasses were generated by the decaying flesh of the animal. Francesco Redi, a 17th-century physician, thought not. He conducted a simple, yet classical, experiment, and his conclusion was inescapable. Redi placed meat into two sets of jars; one set was sealed, while the other was left open. Flies laid eggs on the meat in the open jars, but no maggots grew on the meat in the sealed containers. Then on June 22, 1864, spontaneous generation was dealt a fatal blow. Louis Pasteur, the brilliant French biologist, was convinced that decay bacteria were simply carried from place to place by air currents and did not arise spontaneously. He also knew from past experiments that by boiling a rich broth and sealing the container, he could preserve the contents indefinitely. But this wasn't enough, for his chief antagonist, F. A. Pouchet, quite logically pointed out that without the presence of air—which is essential to life—spontaneous generation could not occur. Pasteur met the challenge. He created a flask in which broth could be sterilized by boiling, and air safely admitted. At last, the debate was over.

Louis Pasteur showed that these organisms had simply grown from preexisting life, present in the form of dormant but living spores (Figure 1.5). Thus, biologists are convinced that life *today* does not arise spontaneously, but comes only from preexisting life. Confidence in this conclusion is strong enough for the statement to be codified into what is called the *biogenetic law*. The key term above is "today," since life must have originated spontaneously at least once, but under far different circumstances (see Chapter 20).

time (for the last 3.8 billion years, to be precise). That's a pretty big family tree. Not only are all men our brothers, but whales, redwoods, lice, and mold are our relatives, too.

Almost as important as Darwin's proposed fact of evolution was his hypothesis for the mechanism of evolution, which Darwin called **natural selec-**

DARWINISM

In 1859, Charles Darwin (Figure 1.6) published a theory of evolution that implied that humans evolved from apes, and some people haven't forgiven him for that yet. Those who have accepted the evidence that suggests such humble ancestry may now find it hard, in this post-Darwinian age, to appreciate how much Darwin changed our thinking.

The Darwinian revolution was based on two related but different ideas: *evolution* and *natural selection*. It's important to distinguish between the two ideas. First there is the idea of **evolution**—the concept that all organisms are related to one another by common ancestry, and that all forms of life have diverged from a single ancestral form over eons of

1.6

Charles Darwin at age 27.

tion. Populations or organisms change over time, and become *adapted* to their environment, because random, heritable variations (mutations) occur by chance, and some of these heritable variations allow some individuals and their offspring to survive and reproduce more successfully than others. The organisms that outsurvive and outreproduce others of their own kind propagate those very mutations as they do so. An **adaptation** is the development of any trait that increases an organism's likelihood of success in its environment. Success may be defined not only as individual well-being but by reproductive output. Individuals that are better adapted, for whatever reason, become the ancestors of future generations, which in turn will share those adaptations (Figure 1.7).

Other people had hypothesized evolution before Darwin, but without a mechanism to explain its workings the idea had never been widely believed. In Darwin's time, by his own account, all serious biologists believed that *species* (specific kinds of plants and animals, such as pineapples and dogs) were fixed and unchanging. But *On the Origin of Species by Means of Natural Selection*, Darwin's great work, changed all of that. The Darwinian revolution was the greatest paradigm shift in the history of biology, and it greatly changed the way that ordinary men and women viewed their own place in the world.

The Darwinian revolution swept away a lot of age-old assumptions. The most painful loss, of course, was Darwin's dispensing with the neces-

1.7

The giraffe's neck has long been a source of evolutionary speculation. The neck is apparently a feeding specialization for browsing on lofty tree foliage that is unavailable to most other plant eaters. How did this unusual specialization come about? Applying the principle of natural selection, we can speculate that the giraffe's mammalian ancestors had relatively short necks, and probably had to compete for food and avoid predators along with many similar primitive browsing, hooved herbivores. Variants—mutants with slightly longer necks—probably arose from time to time, but until long necks became important, the variants' impact on the giraffe population was minimal. Certainly, chance favored such variants. The longer-necked giraffes found untapped food sources in the higher branches. Because of their competitive edge, the longer-necked oddities thrived, and thus were able to pass their novel genes on to more descendants than their shorter-necked contemporaries could.

sity of assuming a wise, foresightful creator. Also dispensed with, as unproven and unnecessary, were other deeply held assumptions. The theory of evolution challenged the previously accepted idea that each species was a permanent, fixed entity; that idea had to go. Gone was the idea of *perfection* in nature. Naturalists had always assumed or proclaimed that biological organisms were perfectly adapted to their environments; Darwin showed that the adaptations of nature, no matter how admirable or wonderful, were not perfect but were always open to change and improvement. Gone was the assumption that nature was full, that there was a place for every creature and that every creature was in its place. Gone was the idea of the "balance of nature," the deep-seated, almost mystical belief that all creatures interacted in a harmonious way that ensured that all would prosper. Gone was the idea that some organisms existed for the benefit of others—the lamb for the wolf, for instance, or the flower for the bee. Swept away, in fact, was the more recent, hard-won conviction that biology, like physics, was governed by fixed laws, and that all of nature was predictable if only the laws were known. In the place of these comforting ideas, Darwin offered only chance, competition, survival, and reproduction.

Now, Darwin did not disprove or even challenge the existence of an all-wise and all-powerful being. He didn't really have anything to say on the subject; it's merely that God was unnecessary to the theory of evolution and natural selection. Religious beliefs, by definition, are unfalsifiable hypotheses, and therefore are outside of the realm of science. It would seem that we are free to believe or not, as we choose.

What Is Darwinism?

From earliest times, everyone had considered each *species* (each kind of organism) to be a fixed, perfect entity. A robin is a robin, a wren is a wren, a monkey is a monkey, and a man is a man. The idea that new species could arise from old ones was literally not conceivable to minds caught up in the old paradigm. The human mind seems predisposed to organize the world into discrete categories, and is uncomfortable with ambiguities and transitions. The notion of the "fixity of species" was in perfect keeping with the teachings of the ancient Greek philosopher Plato, that objects of the real world were only imperfect manifestations of perfect, permanent, abstract ideas (*eidos*, Greek). The individuals of the species may vary—some cows had short horns, some were piebald, some gave more milk that others—but they were still "cows" and, it was believed, all of this variation was just the unimportant noise of the real world, only partly obscuring the abstract, Platonic *idea* of "cow."

Darwin argued that the species had no reality other than that of the individuals composing it, and that the *idea* of a species was just a category invented by the human mind, an idea created because people needed to group organisms that were very similar. In fact, the members of a species *are* very similar, but this is because they are closely related by recent common descent and continuing interbreeding.

Darwin claimed that *races*, *varieties*, and *strains* were categories that were just as "real" as species. He pointed out that departures from the alleged species ideal—that is, the variations within a group—were just as real (and at least as important)

1.8

The *H.M.S. Beagle* was one of many British vessels whose primary mission was to chart the oceans and collect oceanographic and biological information. The *Beagle* was a small vessel, just under 100 feet in length, but her fearless captain James Fitzroy, an expert navigator, guided her unerringly through a five-year voyage around the globe. Among her 74 voyagers was a young, very seasick divinity student, the ship's naturalist. There was little in his manner to suggest that his seagoing experiences would forever change the course of science.

as the constant characters that defined the species. Differences between individuals were what made evolution possible and even inevitable.

He also knew that a species could not be a fixed, perfect entity, because the obvious relatedness of different organisms required that, from time to time, an ancestral species must have given rise to two or more distinct species. He believed that this event, called *speciation,* could happen only if different members of a species became isolated from one another by geography, and then each isolated group adapted differently to its environment.

The Sources of Darwin's Ideas

Young Charles Darwin was something of a problem to his wealthy family. He had already failed at medical school, and would not be following the footsteps of his father and grandfather, both successful and famous physicians. So he had trained for the clergy, but he showed little inclination for ecclesiastical pursuits. He was mostly interested in collecting beetles and in gathering rocks. Natural history and amateur geology were acceptable hobbies for a young gentleman, and the family had plenty of money, but Charles was 22 and his father felt that he should have a job.

The opportunity came just before Charles had to decide whether to enter the clergy. Meanwhile, another young, wealthy, and rather more successful young man, Captain James Fitzroy of the Royal Navy, needed a companion of his own social class to accompany him aboard the *H.M.S. Beagle* (Figure 1.8) on a five-year expedition around the world (1831–1835). The Captain's companion would have the official position of Naturalist, and was expected to collect and study the exotic fauna of that little-known continent. The position was to be without pay, of course; only gentlemen need apply. One of Darwin's professors had recommended young Charles to Captain Fitzroy.

While in South America, Darwin had observed that many distinctly local mammals and birds were doing the same things in the same ways as similar mammals and birds in other parts of the world. For instance, the Pampas grasslands were the home of the mara (Figure 1.9), a mammal that looked like a rabbit and behaved like a rabbit; it was not a rabbit, however, but a rodent, related to other South American rodents such as the guinea pig. Why should this be? Other naturalists, if pressed, might have said that the Pampas was the right place for this creature, just as Europe was the right place for rabbits. But Darwin concluded that there must once have been an empty place in nature, an opportunity for a rabbit or rabbitlike creature to survive and flourish. However, there being no way for European or North American rabbits to cross the ocean, this empty *ecological niche* was exploited by a South American rodent, whose descendants became increasingly adapted, over time, to the grassland habitat—that is, increasingly rabbitlike. This is an example of what is now called **convergent evolution,** in which unrelated animals or plants evolve similar adaptations to similar environments.

It became increasingly clear that *chance* plays a large role in the history of life. Evolution depends not only on the chance occurrence of heritable variations, on which the mechanism of natural selection depended, but on such chance events as what kinds of plants and animals happened to be available to exploit opportunities in nature, or what kinds of geographic features or barriers might arise

1.9

The mara, or Patagonian hare *(Dolichotis patagonum),* is South America's version of the rabbit. Any resemblance this rodent has to a rabbit is coincidental. Its rabbitlike appearance is a product of *convergent evolution,* in which widely separated and unrelated animals take on physical similarities as they adapt to similar environmental conditions and modes of life.

While they are now considered separate species, evidence from many studies clearly indicates that the Galapagos finches evolved from a common finch ancestor.

to prevent (or facilitate) the spread of organisms from one place to the next.

For instance, the Galapagos islands rose as volcanos from the Pacific Ocean floor off Ecuador in fairly recent geological times (a hundred thousand years or so ago). The animals and plants that live there now are the descendants of a chance assemblage of random migrants that floated or were blown there, and found a variety of new opportunities. Each island had unique species of land birds, each adapted to a different and particular way of life. When Darwin collected them, he assumed that they were an unrelated motley collection of blackbirds, finches, and wrens. But upon analysis by experts, it turned out that all of these ecologically very different birds were finches, and were rather closely related to one another. It is clear from Darwin's journal that this belated revelation—two years after the *Beagle's* return—was the shock that suddenly opened his mind to the idea of evolution. He realized that all of the Galapagos land birds had probably descended from a pair of mainland finches that had been storm-blown to the islands tens of thousands of years previously. The descendants of these pioneers moved from island to island and eventually diverged into a number of quite distinct species (Figure 1.10).

Darwin the Experimentalist

Some of the implications of Darwinism are easy to test and some are not. The formation of two species from one is a slow process; we can see that it has

occurred, but so far no one has been able to make it occur experimentally. Other implications could be tested more readily. As one small example, oceanic islands are inhabited by species that are strictly terrestrial on the mainland. The question arose: if they were not able to cross the water, how did they reach the island?

Perhaps their ancestors floated in, or were brought in on the feet or in the crops of migrating birds. Darwin noted that salt is notoriously lethal to land snails; experimentally, however, he found that hibernating land snails could float for weeks in salt water, then later wake up and crawl away. He found viable seeds in the crop of a dead pigeon that had floated for weeks on the sea, and he observed tiny land plants sprouting from the droppings of birds. He suspended a duck's foot in an aquarium, and observed that a variety of freshwater larval forms immediately clung to the foot and could not be easily dislodged; later they would voluntarily dislodge themselves. He found other organisms and seeds in the mud on the feet of wild ducks, and concluded that ducks may be a major, if unwitting, force in the spread of freshwater species (Figure 1.11). This was the scientific method at work. First, evidence was accumulated (perhaps preceded by a hunch). And based on the evidence, an explanatory hypothesis was formed. Then the hypothesis was tested by vigorous experimentation. The species eventually inhabiting an island, it appeared, depended to an astonishing degree on the vagaries of chance dispersal.

It was this element of chance in Darwinism that bothered Darwin's Victorian contemporaries the most. Since Galileo's and Newton's time, physicists and chemists had uncovered an impressive array of *natural laws*—concise mathematical relationships that predicted the properties of matter and energy. The study of biology had not uncovered such laws, but it was assumed that the phenomena of life were as they were because of unknown but potentially knowable laws—in other words, that *the way things were was the way things had to be.* It was not easy to accept the notion that the nature of living organisms depended on volcanos, past storms, chance landings, and whether or not rabbits can swim across the ocean.

Unity and Diversity in Biology

The principle of the "unity of life" is manifest in countless ways. For example the genetic mechanisms of all living things are remarkably similar. Inherited traits are passed along in much the same way in such diverse groups as bacteria, dandelions, and real lions. All living things tend to utilize similar sorts of molecules as food and to shuffle them along very similar sorts of routes as they are drained of their energy. That energy is then used in very similar ways. Obviously, these sorts of similarities imply a rather narrow range in the chemical makeup of quite diverse species.

We also find that the membranes covering the cells of living things are likely to be quite similar from one group to the next. A shark searching the ocean floor has cells bounded by membranes that are similar to those surrounding the cells of a desert mouse. If one were to examine the cells of a shark and a mouse, one would find similar tiny structures within the cells of these two very different kinds of animals. It is clear that most of the life on this planet bears many of the common stamps that suggest relatedness. Furthermore, the notion of relatedness implies common ancestry. That is, even very different forms of life on the planet today may well be descended from the same distant ancestor. (The more related the life forms, the less distant the ancestor.)

Although there are common threads running through the realm of life, one is particularly struck with life's great diversity. The diversity, as we will see, is largely due to the great winnowing effects of natural selection. The opportunism of life has allowed the environment to shuffle, massage, enhance, and eliminate various traits of living things in such a way as to take advantage of whatever opportunities the environment affords. As life has probed every nook and cranny of our planet, each habitat has placed certain demands on its denizens, and as life has changed to meet these demands, variation has increased. Evolution has been described as *descent with modification.* The "descent" implies a certain unity, and the "modification" has produced the diversity of life.

We should add that a knowledge of the unity and diversity of life has quite useful applications. For example, when we realize just how a four-chambered heart functions in birds and mammals, we can utilize information gained from other species in drawing conclusions about how our hearts operate. Medical research has taken advantage of the critical similarities between humans and other animals. (We have all sorts of animals serving as guinea pigs that, in turn, serve as cheap, ex-

1.11

Darwin is best known as a synthesist—one who spends his or her time theorizing about the larger meaning of observations and data—but he was also an excellent reductionist. Among the many smaller issues he investigated was the question of island colonization. Could living things such as the seeds of plants, land snails, and the like survive submersion in sea water long enough to make it to isolated islands?

ESSAY 1.2
THE GALAPAGOS ISLANDS

The Galapagos Archipelago includes habitats ranging from dry, lowland deserts to wet, species-rich highlands. The islands are home to a bizarre collection of life, from grazing lizards and giant tortoises to a variety of bird life and shore dwellers. Darwin, who despised the place, was to make it famous because he saw it as an experiment of nature in progress. ●

Compare the lush vegetation of the Santa Cruz highlands to the more arid regions of the lowlands.

The flightless cormorant, *Nannopterum harrisi*, uses its wings to keep its balance as it walks.

Tidal pool and dry terrain near Topocra Bay on Isabela Island.

(above) The swallow-tail gull *(Creagus furcatus)* is a nocturnal bird unique to the Galapagos.

(left) The male frigate bird *(Fregata magnificens)* inflates its chest during sexual display.

(left) Desert vegetation
along the coast of Hood Island.

(below left) Blue-footed boobies
(Sula nebouxii) establish pair bonds.

(below) Colorful Sally Lightfoot
crabs *(Grapsus grapsus)*.

(above) The land iguana *Conolophus
subcristatus* is a herbivore.

The predatory Galapagos Hawk,
Buteo galapagoensis.

(left) Galapagos tortoises:
these represent just one of 13 species.

17

pendable humans.) Most heart surgery was first performed on dogs or baboons—species with structural similarities to ours. On the other hand, fish and reptiles have different metabolic and circulatory needs, and their hearts have taken developmental routes quite different from our own (Figure 1.12).

Of all the sciences, biology is, perhaps, the least subject to rigid laws. It has a fascinating and frustrating element of unpredictability, perhaps even unruliness. Part of the reason lies in the constantly changing realm of life—always shifting, adapting,

and modulating. But part of the problem (with apologies to our philosopher friends) also must lie in the phenomenology of biological explanations. Phenomenology encompasses the notion of the interpretation of observations, and biology is an interpretive science. Just as bread is flavored by the peculiar flora of the baker's own hands, so the essence of the biologist enters into his or her own explanations of the world of life. The biologist also has the problem of an eye trying to see itself because, after all, we are indeed a part of the realm of life.

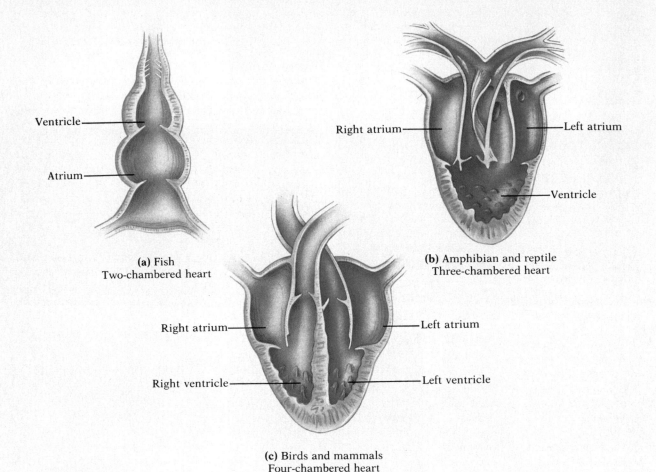

(a) Fish
Two-chambered heart

(b) Amphibian and reptile
Three-chambered heart

(c) Birds and mammals
Four-chambered heart

1.12

The hearts of vertebrates reveal certain structural and functional similarities, yet an inescapable trend—a progressive evolutionary change—is seen when the hearts are arranged in a series from the simplest to the most complex. Each basic change is believed to be closely related to the evolutionary direction followed by each of the vertebrate groups. The earliest vertebrates were the fishes, with their two-chambered hearts. Amphibians evolved from one line of fishes; and from the primitive amphibians, the reptile line arose. Most amphibians and all reptiles are air breathers, using the lungs for gas exchange. The hearts of

these cold-blooded amphibians and reptilians are three-chambered (except for the crocodile line, which boasts a four-chambered heart). The three-chambered heart—a great evolutionary success, having persisted over millions of years—still exists in these groups today. Birds and mammals trace their ancestry to the early reptilians, but both have evolved as warm-blooded creatures who are able to survive quite well in the coldest terrestrial environments. Part of their adaptive success can be attributed to the four-chambered-heart, which meets the increased oxygen demands of an elevated metabolic rate.

Summary

Introduction

Aristotelian logic was one of the first systematic methods used to determine the truth or falsity of statements or ideas. Galileo attempted to establish truth on the basis of theory and prediction, tested by observation—concepts that eventually replaced Aristotelian logic and led to the development of the scientific method.

Testing Hypotheses

It is a basic scientific tenet that nothing can be *proved* true by observation. However, natural scientists can use a hypothesis to make predictions about the world. These predictions can be tested, and the test results can be used either to support or disprove the hypothesis. While it often takes many tests to support a hypothesis, a single, repeated observation can prove it false. Hypotheses predicting that something has only a *significant tendency* to be true must be tested using massive numbers of observations and statistical analysis. An untestable hypothesis can be disproven only in principle, while an unfalsifiable hypothesis cannot be disproven at all.

Scientists observe some basic principles when testing hypotheses and conducting experiments. They attempt to hold as many variables constant as possible, manipulate only the factors they are observing, and replicate their tests to confirm their results.

In problem solving, reductionists try to reduce a problem to its simplest level, while synthesists attempt to look at old observations in new ways. When analyzing data or observations, scientists use both inductive and deductive reasoning.

Revolutions and Paradigms

Paradigm refers to an encompassing, accepted, and internally consistent way of looking at the world or its parts. New paradigms generally create a revolution in current thinking.

Vitalism and Mechanism

Two prominent paradigms in the 19th century were vitalism and mechanism. Vitalism stated that living organisms had vital forces and were governed by laws that did not apply to nonliving objects. Mechanism maintained that the living body was a machine subject to physical and chemical laws. Once the laws were understood, the mysteries of life could readily be solved. Today, biologists are convinced that life comes only from life, a paradigm known as the biogenetic law.

Darwinism

According to Darwin's theory of evolution and natural selection, populations of organisms develop new traits over time as they adapt to their environments. Successful organisms pass on these traits to their offspring. Thus, chance, competition, survival, and reproduction give rise to species, as well as to races, varieties, and strains within species. Darwin believed that speciation can occur only if different members of a species develop in isolation from one another, as on the Galapagos islands. The concepts of ecological niches and convergent evolution also help to explain the appearance of certain species.

Biological research may reflect the views and social milieu of the scientist. However, two principles can be stated with some certainty: common descent underlies the unity of life, and evolutionary change accounts for much of life's diversity.

Key Terms

scientific method	paradigm	natural selection
hypothesis	vitalism	adaptation
variables	mechanism	convergent evolution
inductive reasoning	Darwinism	
deductive reasoning	evolution	

Review Questions

1. Compare Galileo's approach to scientific questions with the more traditional Aristotelian approach, favored by philosophers of his day. (pp. 2–4)

2. Specifically, which of Galileo's many convictions was most directly in conflict with the teachings of the Church? (p. 4)

3. Criticize the following: Once a scientist has proposed a hypothesis or theory, his or her next task is to prove it through experimentation or observation. (p. 5)

4. What is the real value of a hypothesis? Are all hypotheses testable? What do scientists generally do with untestable hypotheses? (pp. 5–6)

5. What is a controlled experiment, and why is this a desirable procedure to follow wherever possible? (pp. 7–8)

6. List an example of synthesism and one of reductionism. Why are both essential to science? (p. 8)

7. Define inductive and deductive reasoning and provide an example of each. (p. 8)

8. Compare the approach of vitalists and mechanists, and support one or the other as the best approach to problem solving. (pp. 9–10)

9. Prepare a definition of natural selection, one you will want to keep in mind throughout your reading of the text. Use an outline form to emphasize its propositions, if you wish. (pp. 10–12)

10. Describe the traditional, preDarwinian, view of species, and explain how Darwin's concept of species differed. (pp. 12–13)

11. Some historians believe that Darwin's thinking about evolution suddenly solidified when his Galapagos finch collection was analyzed. With this event, many of his other observations fell into place. What was there about the finches that might have been the key, and what did Darwin finally decide? (p. 14)

12. What does "chance" have to do with evolution through natural selection, and why did this bother the Victorian scientists and philosophers? Does it bother you? (pp. 13–15)

The Basic Chemistry of Life

2

Since biology is the study of life, it can occupy the attentions of all sorts of scientists. Some wear muddy boots and ask where ducks go; others wear pristine lab coats and wonder about the molecules that compose us all. So let's begin by seeing what those scientists called molecular biologists can tell us.

THE ELEMENTS

They would start by defining elements, atoms, and molecules. An **element** is a substance that cannot be divided into simpler substances by chemical means. There are 89 naturally occurring elements, and 17 more have been made in the laboratory. Of the naturally occurring elements, just six—*S*ulfur, *P*hosphorus, *O*xygen, *N*itrogen, *C*arbon, and *H*ydrogen—make up about 99% of living matter. Notice that these initials spell SPONCH.

The smallest unit of any element is the **atom** (*atom* is Greek for "can't cut it"). Expressed another way, any element is composed of one kind of atom.

ATOMS AND THEIR STRUCTURE

Atoms comprise three kinds of particles: **neutrons, protons,** and **electrons.** Protons and neutrons are similar to one another in terms of mass (**mass** is defined as a measure of inertia).* Both protons and neutrons are much more massive than electrons; therefore, they make up most of the mass of an atom. (If you weigh 150 pounds, your body is made up of about an ounce of electrons and about 149 pounds, 15 ounces of protons and neutrons.)

At the center of the atom lies the **nucleus,** a dense cluster of protons and neutrons. Outside, spinning around the nucleus in **orbitals,** are the electrons. The protons have positive electrical charges, while the neutrons have no charge at all. Each tiny electron, on the other hand, has a negative charge equal to the proton's positive charge. Since *like* charges repel each other and *unlike* charges attract, the positively charged protons tend to hold the negatively charged electrons and, under the most stable conditions, the electrons remain in their orbitals. If the number of electrons equals the number of protons, the atom is electrically balanced and bears no net charge.

The smallest atom, hydrogen, consists of a single proton, with one electron revolving around it. The number of protons in a nucleus determines its **atomic number,** so the atomic number of hydrogen is 1. The largest naturally occurring atom, on the other hand, is uranium 238, the nucleus of which

---

*Mass should not be confused with *weight. Weight* is the force of gravity pulling on a body. On the surface of the earth, however, the weight of an object (measured in grams) is equal to its mass (also measured in grams).

contains 92 protons and 146 neutrons (Figure 2.1). The number of protons plus neutrons approximately determines the **atomic mass** of an atom. (The atomic numbers of the six SPONCH elements are 16, 15, 8, 7, 6, and 1, respectively. Notice that the letters are arranged in order of decreasing atomic number.) Table 2.1 lists the atomic numbers and atomic masses of SPONCH and some other elements that are important to life.

Isotopes

The atomic mass (or atomic weight) of an element is determined by simple addition. Hydrogen has one proton and no neutrons, so its mass is 1. Carbon has six of each, so its mass is 12; and oxygen, with eight protons and eight neutrons, has a mass of 16. But the atomic mass of most elements can vary because the number of neutrons can vary. Thus, for a given element our table of atomic masses usually just reflects an average number. Atoms with a specific number of neutrons are called **isotopes** of the element.

Of the more than 320 known natural isotopes, about 60 are unstable, or *radioactive*. In addition, about 200 more radioactive isotopes, or *radio-isotopes*, have been created in the laboratory. *Unstable* refers to an isotope's tendency to spontaneously

Nucleus of hydrogen
1 proton
0 neutrons

Nucleus of uranium-238
92 protons
146 neutrons

2.1

The lightest and heaviest atomic nuclei. The atomic mass of uranium is approximately 238 times that of hydrogen.

explode, or decay, releasing radiation in some form—either as a subatomic particle, a highly energetic photon (gamma ray), or some combination of these. In the process of decay, the radioactive isotope usually changes from one element to another. (Such a change is brought about by altering the number of protons in the nucleus, since this number actually defines elements.) The new element may or may not be radioactive.

Table 2.1

Some of the elements essential to the processes of life

Element	Symbol	Atomic Number	Atomic Mass	Example of Role in Biology
Calcium	Ca	20	40.1	Bone; muscle contraction
Carbon	C	6	12.0	Constituent (backbone) of organic molecules
Chlorine	Cl	17	35.5	HCl in digestion and photosynthesis
Cobalt	Co	27	58.9	Part of vitamin B_{12}
Copper	Cu	29	63.5	Part of oxygen-carrying pigment of mollusk blood
Fluorine	F	9	19.0	Necessary for normal tooth enamel development
Hydrogen	H	1	1.0	Part of water and of all organic molecules
Iodine	I	53	126.9	Part of thyroid hormone
Iron	Fe	26	55.8	Hemoglobin, oxygen-carrying pigment of many animals
Magnesium	Mg	12	24.3	Part of chlorophyll, the photosynthetic pigment; essential to some enzyme action
Manganese	Mn	25	54.9	Essential to some enzyme action
Molybdenum	Mo	42	95.9	Essential to some enzyme action
Nitrogen	N	7	14.0	Constituent of all proteins and nucleic acids
Oxygen	O	8	16.0	Essential to aerobic respiration; constituent of water and nearly all organic molecules
Phosphorus	P	15	31.0	High-energy bond of ATP
Potassium	K	19	39.1	Generation of nerve impulses
Selenium	Se	34	79.0	Essential to the workings of many enzymes
Silicon	Si	14	28.1	Diatom shells; walls of arteries; grass leaves
Sodium	Na	11	23.0	Salt balance; nerve conduction
Sulfur	S	16	32.1	Constituent of most proteins
Vanadium	V	23	50.9	Oxygen transport in tunicates
Zinc	Zn	30	65.4	Essential to the workings of several enzymes

The time required for half of the atoms of any radioactive material to decay is its **half-life.** Half-lives can vary considerably and depend on which isotope of which element we are examining. Most naturally occurring radioisotopes are extremely durable; some half-lives are billions of years long. Uranium 238 has a half-life of about one billion years, during which half of the atoms decay to form an isotope of lead called lead 206. On the other hand, some artificial radioisotopes have a fleeting half-life of only seconds.

The longer-lived isotopes often are used in determining the age of fossil-bearing strata from the earth's crust. In medicine, radioisotopes are used to destroy cancer-ridden tissues. And, especially since World War II, scientists have been vitally interested in the destructive effects of radiation.

In other instances, shorter-lived radioisotopes are used as *tracers* to determine the role of certain chemicals in living cells. This is possible because their chemical behavior is identical to nonradioactive atoms. The radioactive isotopes, however, can be traced by their telltale radiation as they move through living systems. Tracking radioisotopes of carbon, phosphorus, and hydrogen has helped unlock the secrets of photosynthesis, the process whereby plants use sunlight energy to convert carbon dioxide and water into sugars. And the use of radioactive phosphorus, hydrogen, and indirectly, sulfur, has been vital in determining the structure and function of DNA, the gigantic molecule that determines inheritance.

Depicting the Atom. An atom is too small to be seen, even with the most powerful electron microscope; therefore, much of what we know is derived deductively, from circumstantial evidence. The evidence is very impressive; it is, in fact, possible to make some very positive statements about atomic structure. However, any diagram of an atom is bound to be simplistic at best. Some notions of how atoms must look have been with us a long time, and most have been proven to be completely wrong, but in their time, they were useful indeed (Figure 2.2).

Atoms are sometimes described in terms of a model developed by the great physicist, Niels Bohr. In the *Bohr atom,* the nucleus is shown being circled by electrons (much as the planets circle the sun). Bohr's model suggests that electrons move in a single plane, but this is not the case. Electrons can move in any plane and at various distances from the nucleus. They tend to travel at specific distances, however, and the region in which there is a high probability of finding an electron at any given time is called an *orbital.* The electrons paths

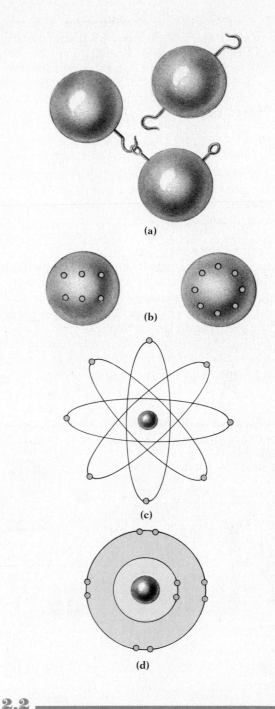

2.2

Four models of atomic structure. **(a)** An early attempt to explain the bonding of atoms into molecules. **(b)** The "watermelon" model, an attempt to show that atoms contain electrons (depicted as the seed). **(c)** A later model showing electrons orbiting around a central nucleus, much as planets orbit around the sun. **(d)** The concentric circles of the Bohr atom, indicating energy levels or electron shells; here, also, the electrons are depicted as moving around a central nucleus in flat, circular orbits.

may also be thought of as **electron shells,** or energy levels, each a specific distance from the nucleus. Electrons may move from one shell to another. Electrons farther from the nucleus contain more energy. Distant electrons are more reactive and may become so excited that they actually fly away from their atom.

Electron Shells

Two, eight, eight—this simple triplet might help explain a great deal about how atoms interact. For now, though, just keep in mind that these are the maximum numbers of electrons that can exist in the first three orbitals: two in the innermost, and eight each in the next two.

Atoms with full electron shells are termed *saturated*. This statement, you notice, implies that atoms can sometimes be *unsaturated*. That is, the outer shell contains fewer than the maximum number of electrons (fewer than two in the first shell, or fewer than eight in the second or third). As an atom fills its shells, it begins with the inner ones and works outward (Figure 2.3). For example, oxygen has a

total of eight electrons; since the first two fill the innermost shell, the next six do not fill the second shell, and the third shell is empty. As another example, sodium has eleven electrons; two fill the first shell, eight fill the second, and a single electron occupies the third shell. We will soon see the importance of such an arrangement.

Obviously, many atoms have more than 18 protons and electrons. So we know that there are yet other shells and that each of these accommodates only a specific number of electrons. However, the first three shells accommodate the electrons of all of the SPONCH elements as well as most other atoms of biological importance, so we will consider only these three for now (Table 2.2).

There are a number of ways to diagram atoms. Each is useful in its own way, depending on the point of the discussion. For example, the orbitals that we have shown as lines or referred to as statistical abstractions can also be depicted as hazy clouds that indicate where there is a certain probability that an electron *might* be at any given point in time. These are called **electron cloud models** (Figure 2.4). Remember that, in such depictions, the

2.3

Bohr atom diagrams of 12 common elements. Note the regular progression in which the first, second, and third electron shells are filled. Also note that helium and neon are in a saturated condition.

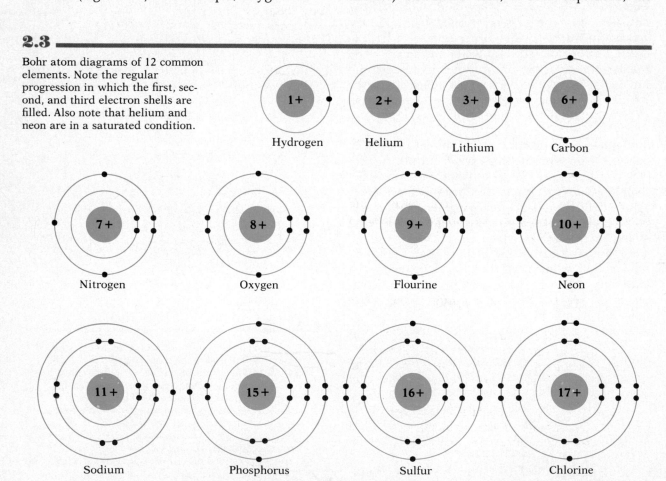

Table 2.2

Electron arrangements of SPONCH and other selected elements (note shell saturation numbers)

| Element | Atomic Number | Electrons in Each Shell | | |
| | | First Shell | Second Shell | Third Shell |
		(2)	(8)	(8)
Hydrogen	1	1	0	0
Helium	2	2	0	0
Carbon	6	2	4	0
Nitrogen	7	2	5	0
Oxygen	8	2	6	0
Sodium	11	2	8	1
Phosphorus	15	2	8	5
Sulfur	16	2	8	6
Chlorine	17	2	8	7
Neon	18	2	8	8

orbitals may appear hazy and indistinct, but they have definite shapes, each a precise distance from the nucleus.

Sometimes it is useful to clarify the electron cloud model a bit by representing the orbital of each electron as a solid, three-dimensional shape that indicates the volume within which an electron can be found 99% of the time (Figure 2.5). Note that each orbital has a particular shape. These shapes are important in understanding how atoms behave.

We can see that the innermost electron shell is spherical and holds one pair of electrons. (Electrons are usually found in pairs.) The second shell is occupied by four pairs of electrons, one whose orbital is spherical, and three pairs with dumbbell-shaped orbitals (see Figure 2.5). The four pairs of electrons in the third electron shell move in the same spherical and dumbbell-shaped orbitals as those in the second shell.

MOLECULES AND COMPOUNDS

SPONCH atoms are almost never found singly; nor are the atoms of most other elements. In fact, atoms may be joined in all sorts of combinations to form *molecules*. A **molecule** is two or more chemically joined atoms.

Consider a simple molecule, atmospheric oxygen. Oxygen in the air does not exist as single atoms. Instead, two oxygen atoms join to form *molecular oxygen*. Atomic oxygen is written as O, whereas molecular oxygen is O_2, the subscript indicating that two oxygen atoms are joined chemically. Gaseous nitrogen in the air is designated N_2

for the same reason. Three such molecules would be written $3N_2$.

Some molecules are composed of different elements. Thus, whereas an element is a substance comprising only one kind of atom, a **compound** is made up of a single kind of molecule, with each molecule consisting of atoms of different elements. Another example from the air is carbon dioxide (CO_2). Each CO_2 molecule consists of one atom of carbon and two atoms of oxygen. Carbon dioxide, with only three atoms in each molecule, is still a very simple compound. Some molecules of interest to biologists may consist of thousands or even millions of atoms. We will encounter some of these in Chapter 3.

As atoms join together to form molecules, their orbitals may change shape, and shape can be very important in terms of how molecules interact. For instance, Figure 2.6a shows electron orbitals of a simple molecule, methane gas (CH_4). The four hydrogen atoms center on the carbon atom. Note that their orbitals project outward in different directions, each the farthest possible distance from the others. Thus the molecule has the shape of a caltrop (Figure 2.6b). A *caltrop* is an ancient military device formed from a metal ball with four spikes placed so that if the thing were thrown on the ground, it would always rest on three spikes with the fourth pointing straight up. (Retreating Greek and Roman troops used them effectively to impede

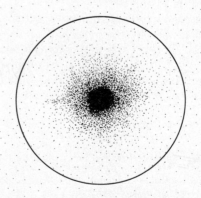

2.4

Electron density cloud model. In this hydrogen atom, which has only one electron, the density of the dots indicates the expected frequency of the electron in that region over a period of time. The circle represents an imaginary sphere that would be expected to contain the electron 99% of the time.

enemy cavalry.) The four tips of the caltrop, or the four tips of a methane molecule, form the corners of a perfect *tetrahedron* (Figure 2.6c). A number of molecules have this shape.

Molecular Bonds

One may wonder, what forces would cause atoms to join together to form molecules, anyway? The answer is deceptively simple: atoms form molecules because molecules are in a *lower energy state*. Thus the atoms can settle to lower energy states as parts of molecules, lower than they could as free, uncombined atoms. We will see, again and again, that physical systems tend to move toward their lowest energy states, the states at which they are most stable.

In order for atoms to reach this stable molecular state, they must be able to form *chemical bonds*. We will consider a few of the most important kinds of bonds shortly, but for now we should keep two generalizations in mind regarding making and breaking bonds.

1. *Energy is released when chemical bonds form.* This makes sense if we remember that atoms existing singly are at a high-energy state and that the molecule they help form is at a lower energy state. Thus, as they change from a high- to a low-energy state, some of their energy is released. When hydrogen and oxygen gas join to form water, the energy is released as heat. Hydrogen and oxygen moving to a lower energy state caused the hydrogen-filled Hindenburg to explode that fateful day in New Jersey (see Chapter 6).

2. *Energy is required to break a bond.* Remember that molecules are more stable than their constituent atoms. This means that, if two atoms of a molecule are held together by a chemical bond, they will tend to stay together. Some outside force is required to separate them. Separation, of course,

means that the two atoms must be boosted to their former high-energy level.

Now let's consider the various ways that molecules can behave, particularly the traits that lend themselves to the interactions that make life possible. We'll see that even atoms have to compromise.

INTERACTION AND SHIFTING ENERGY

Traits that cause atoms to interact with other atoms are called **energetic tendencies.** Let's consider three of the most basic of these tendencies. Although they are indeed simple, they form the basis of whatever is going on in your mind this instant and give you the strength to scratch your head as you ponder a sentence like this. The three basic energetic tendencies are:

1. Negative and positive charges of atoms and molecules tend to balance, usually simply by equalizing the numbers of protons and electrons.
2. Electrons within atoms and molecules tend to pair.
3. Electron shells of atoms and molecules tend to become filled.

These three principles are called energetic tendencies because to counteract or violate them requires a known and precise amount of energy. Thus it takes a certain amount of energy to remove an electron from a balanced atom, or to remove one electron from an electron pair. Such violations, by the way, permit chemical changes—changes such as the formation, disruption, and interaction of molecules, the sorts of changes that permit life.

The different energetic tendencies of an atom are sometimes in conflict. For example, the tendency of an atom to balance its electrical charges usually leaves the outer shell unfilled. And when

2.5

The first shell of the atom **(a)** can contain two electrons, which occupy a spherical orbital. The second shell contains as many as four orbitals, each with two electrons; the first **(b)** is spherical and the other three are dumbbell-shaped **(c).** The axes of the three dumbbell-shaped orbitals are at right angles to each other, and where their axes intersect we find the nucleus.

(a)

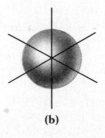
(b)

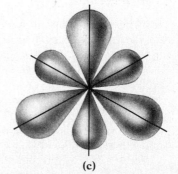
(c)

The electron orbitals of atoms assume different shapes when the atom becomes part of a molecule. **(a)** In the carbon atom of a methane (CH_4) molecule, the outer four carbon electrons pair with the four hydrogen electrons and move within four symmetrical, pear-shaped orbitals. The four orbitals form a figure similar to an ancient caltrop **(b)**; their tips coincide with the four corners of an imaginary tetrahedron **(c)**. The hydrogen nuclei are embedded within these four electron orbitals.

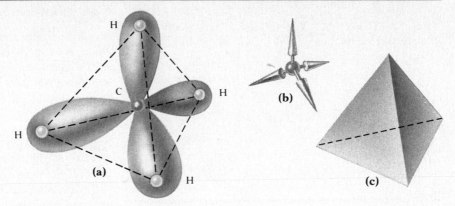

the outer shell is filled, the protons and electrons are usually not in balance.* Oxygen, for example, has eight protons. Thus, it is balanced when it has eight electrons. But note that after the first shell is filled with two electrons, there are only six electrons left for the next shell, though eight are required. Therefore, the outer shell of a charge-balanced oxygen atom lacks two electrons. If the oxygen atom were to fill its outer shell with electrons, it would have 10 electrons and only eight protons, and so it would have lost the balance between protons and electrons. How are competing energetic tendencies accommodated? We'll see that chemical reactions often involve a compromise.

CHEMICAL BONDING

An atom can fill its outer shell in one of three ways: (1) it can gain electrons from another atom; (2) it can lose all of the electrons in its outer shell to another atom, exposing the underlying filled shell; or (3) it can share electrons with another atom. (That is, the same electron or electrons can fill the outer shells of two atoms at once.)

The Ionic Bond

Let's first see how atoms can gain or lose electrons (Figure 2.7). Sodium (Na) has 11 protons. It also has 11 electrons: two in the first shell, eight in the

*Atoms that simultaneously fill all three energetic tendencies include the *noble gases*—helium, argon, neon, krypton, xenon, and radon. Noble gas elements are electrostatically balanced; they have even numbers of electrons and full electron shells. Because they rarely participate in chemical reactions, they have few roles in living systems.

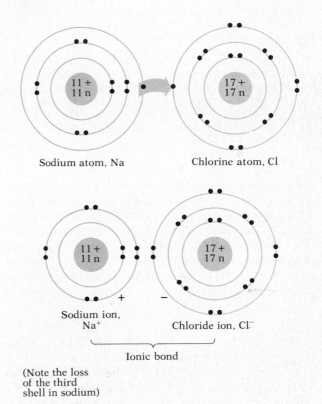

Sodium atom, Na   Chlorine atom, Cl

Sodium ion, Na⁺   Chloride ion, Cl⁻

Ionic bond

(Note the loss of the third shell in sodium)

Sodium *(left)* has only one electron in its outer shell, while chlorine *(right)* has seven. The outer shells of both atoms can be filled if sodium loses its lone electron to chlorine. If this should happen, the sodium atom will have more protons than electrons and a net positive charge, while the chlorine atom will have an extra electron and, thus, a net negative charge. In its ionic form, chlorine is called *chloride*.

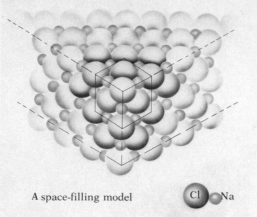

A space-filling model   Cl Na

2.8

A sodium chloride crystal. Sodium and chlorine form ionic bonds, but not as individual molecules. Because of the distribution of their charges, sodium and chloride ions attract each other, forming regular crystalline formations of alternating sodium and chloride ions. A salt crystal forms a perfect cube. (Other ionic crystals may have different shapes.) Water molecules are more attracted to the sodium and chloride ions than the sodium and chloride are to each other. Thus salt dissolves in water.

second shell, and only one in the third. So, the outer shell is seven electrons short (see Table 2.2). It is not energetically possible for an atom (in this case, sodium) to gain seven electrons, but if it can get rid of one electron, then the full second shell will become the outer shell. Chlorine (Cl), on the other hand, has 17 protons and 17 electrons. Thus, its third shell has seven electrons—one short. Also, one of the seven in that outer shell is an unpaired electron. Chlorine, therefore, can complete two of its three energetic tendencies by accepting just one more electron.

Because of their particular structures, sodium and chlorine react easily—and swiftly. In this reaction, sodium is called **electron donor,** and chlorine, an **electron acceptor.** In its pure state, each element is a deadly chemical, but together, they form table salt (NaCl) (Figure 2.8).

In the process of filling their outer shells, both become ionized, that is, electrostatically imbalanced. (An **ion** is any atom or molecule that has a net electrical charge, either negative or positive.) The sodium now has only 10 electrons and 11 protons, so it now has a net positive charge of $+1$. Chlorine now has 18 electrons and only 17 protons; it takes on a net negative charge of -1. Because of their opposite charges, they are attracted to each other, and they join in what is called an **ionic bond.**

The Covalent Bond: Sharing Electron Pairs

We know that one way an atom can fill its outer electron shell is by sharing electrons with other atoms. Two atoms sharing electrons form a molecule by what is called a **covalent bond.**

Consider hydrogen gas (H_2), formed from two hydrogen atoms. Each atom comprises one proton and one electron. Since electrons tend to travel in pairs, the two hydrogen atoms can pool their single electrons and satisfy this requirement. The shared pair of electrons form a new *molecular orbital* that includes both atomic nuclei. In this way, not only are the two electrons paired, but both atoms also satisfy the requirement of their electron shell. Furthermore, they still maintain the balance between protons and electrons (Figure 2.9).

THE PECULIAR QUALITIES OF WATER

We are generally aware that water is necessary for life, but we may not know that much of its magic lies in its peculiar molecular bonding. (You may recall that our hopes for discovering life on Mars faded when our interplanetary probes failed to find significant amounts of water there. Let's see why this finding bred such discouragement.)

The Molecular Structure of Water

The first thing to know is that a water molecule is made up of two hydrogen atoms covalently bonded to one oxygen atom. All three atoms fill their outer shells by sharing electrons. The two hydrogen atoms and one oxygen atom have, among them, 10 protons and 10 electrons; and so the internal charges of water are balanced.

The four electron pairs in the outer shell of the oxygen atom move in orbitals with the same tetrahedral shape that we saw in methane. In the water molecule, however, only two of the four molecular orbitals surround the hydrogen nuclei; the other two do not (Figure 2.10). This makes the water molecule strangely and magnificently lopsided. Furthermore, the hydrogen nuclei enclosed by the two orbitals give these orbitals a slight positive charge relative to the other two orbitals. This means that although the positive and negative charges of the molecule are balanced numerically, they are not evenly distributed—the water molecule is *polar*. In essence, a water molecule has a positive side and a negative side. This simple configuration had a great deal to do with the appearance of life on this planet.

The Hydrogen Bond. Because water molecules are polar, with positively and negatively charged regions, they are able to interact not only with each other, but with a variety of molecules when there is an electrical imbalance of almost any sort. Water molecules bond with each other because of the very slight attraction between the positively charged hydrogen-bearing orbitals, or *lobes*, of one molecule and the slightly negative lobes of another. It is this weak attraction that tends to hold two water molecules together in what is called a **hydrogen bond,** even if just for an instant. The magic of the hydrogen bond, in fact, lies in its weakness, as it is very easily broken. But just as it

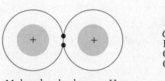

Checklist:
Electrons paired? ✔
Charges balanced? ✔
Outer shells filled? ✔

Molecular hydrogen, H₂

(a)

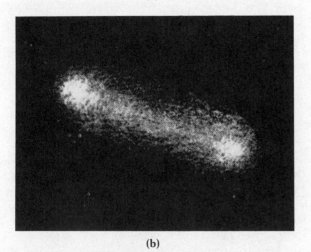

(b)

2.9

A molecule of hydrogen gas consists of two covalently bonded hydrogen atoms. **(a)** Each hydrogen contributes one electron, and the pair of electrons is shared. The electrons thus become paired and the electron shell of each atom is filled simultaneously. Covalent bonds are considerably stronger than ionic bonds because covalent bonding satisfies all the requirements of both partners. **(b)** The shared electrons form a molecular orbital, as shown in this electron density cloud model. (Photo from *Chemistry*, by Linus Pauling and Peter Pauling. Copyright © 1975 by W. H. Freeman and Company. All rights reserved.)

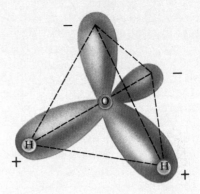

2.10

Uneven distribution of electrical charges in a water molecule. The four pairs of electrons in the outer shell of the oxygen atom have the same familiar tetrahedral shape, but only two of the four orbitals contain protons. The two orbitals enclosing protons have a slight positive charge; the two that do not, a slight negative charge.

breaks easily, it can also immediately form again. The bonds between molecules of water build and break with dazzling speed; and despite the weakness of the bonds, water molecules cling together with surprising tenacity.

Water, Temperature, and Life. One of the most important qualities of water is its temperature stability. Whoever was watching the proverbial pot that gave rise to the adage was probably amazed by the enormous amount of heat it takes to raise the temperature of water.

Specific heat is the amount of heat required to raise, to some specified amount, the temperature of some substance. If that substance is water, the specific heat is very high indeed. Water's high specific heat is caused by the hydrogen bonding of water molecules. Heat is produced by the movement of molecules, but so much heat is required to keep apart the molecules of water that little is left over to increase the movement of any molecules that happen to be free at the time.

The resistance of water to changing temperatures means that creatures composed largely of water, like ourselves, have a certain built-in temperature stability. It also means that organisms that live in water are buffered, to some degree, by the resistance of water to changes in temperature.

Anyone living near the seacoast knows that the weather there is much milder—cooler in the summer and warmer in the winter—than the weather of less fortunate communities only a few miles inland. The sea serves as a great heat reservoir, absorbing heat in summer and releasing it in winter.

Water also freezes slowly because ice is a crystal (Figure 2.11) and the busy water molecules are likely to shift before they can fuse into the regular structure that identifies any crystal. Since ice forms slowly (and melts slowly), it acts as a buffer in those delicate seasons between summer and winter by stabilizing temperatures.

As water cools, its molecules move closer and closer together, and it becomes heavier. Thus, cold water sinks, as expected. Its density is greatest at 4°C. But then as it cools further, it gets less dense again, and a more open latticework is formed between the molecules. The colder, lighter water rises and, as the temperature falls still further, ice forms on the lake surface, which makes skating much more pleasurable.

Water the Solvent.   Water is well known as a cleaning agent, partly because it is not expensive and partly because it is one of the best solvents known. Water's properties as a solvent lie, once again, in its polarity. Because of the imbalance of its charges, it has an affinity for a number of kinds of molecules, such as salt (NaCl), with its positive and negative parts, and sugars, with their own areas of positive and negative charges.

Ionic compounds such as sodium chloride dissolve in water by *ionizing* (that is, by separating into ions), with water molecules clustering around the resulting ions (Figure 2.12). This happens because negative chloride ions attract the positive parts of polar water molecules; and positive sodium ions attract the negative parts of the water molecules. Other molecules, such as sugar, may be electrostatically balanced, but they may also be polar, with slightly negative and slightly positive regions. Therefore, water will form hydrogen bonds with the appropriate regions of polar molecules, which is why sugar dissolves almost as readily as salt. Such qualities of water are important to living things because delicate internal balances require that many kinds of molecules be easily transported in fluids.

Nonpolar molecules, those without charged or even partially charged regions—such as oils, petroleum products, and certain fats—do not interact with the charged areas of water and, therefore, they do not dissolve. Instead, the affinity of water molecules for each other causes the excluded molecules to cluster into their own masses. That's why you have to keep shaking Italian dressing.

A different and generally stronger force is *hydrophobic interaction*. **Hydrophobic** means "fear of water" or, in this case, "avoidance of water." Hydrophobic interactions account for the fairly strong apparent attraction between nonpolar molecules, or between the nonpolar portions of molecules that occurs in the presence of water. For instance, if melted chicken fat is mixed with water, the fat will form into globules and the globules will merge with one another. It looks as if the fat molecules had a strong affinity for one another. In reality, however, the principal active force is one we have already encountered; namely, the attraction of the water molecules for one another.

2.11

As water approaches 0°C (32°F), the dynamic sliding lattice of its liquid state shifts to the rigid, expanded, crystalline array known as ice. In this expanded state, its density is less than that of liquid water, which explains why ice floats to the surface.

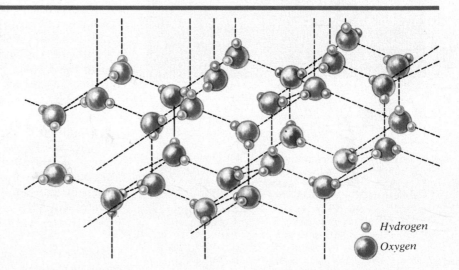

Hydrogen
Oxygen

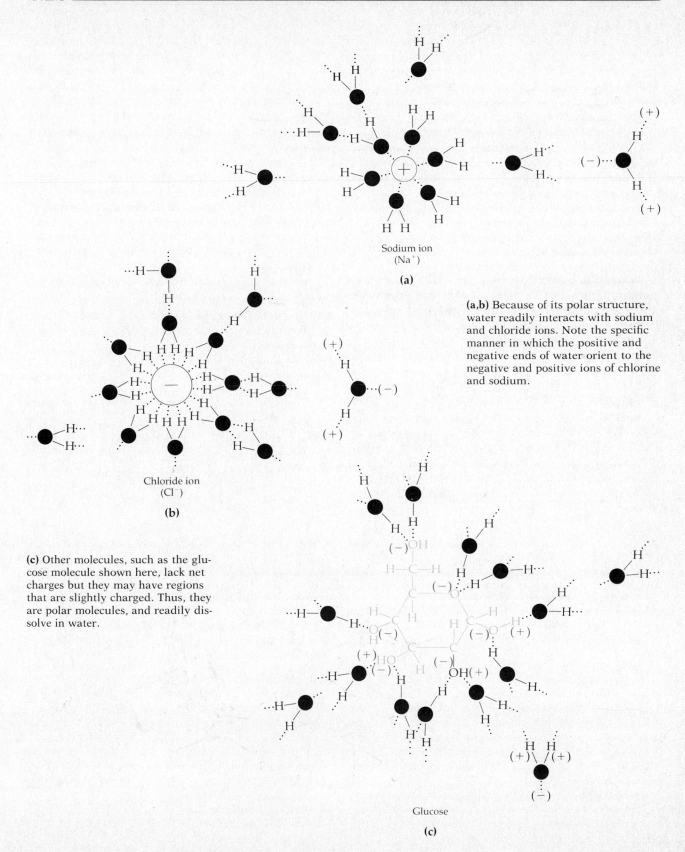

Sodium ion
(Na⁺)

(a)

Chloride ion
(Cl⁻)

(b)

(a,b) Because of its polar structure, water readily interacts with sodium and chloride ions. Note the specific manner in which the positive and negative ends of water orient to the negative and positive ions of chlorine and sodium.

(c) Other molecules, such as the glucose molecule shown here, lack net charges but they may have regions that are slightly charged. Thus, they are polar molecules, and readily dissolve in water.

Glucose

(c)

ACIDITY AND pH

Most of the chemical reactions of life take place in water. Such reactions can be affected by whether the solution in which they occur is *acidic, basic,* or *neutral*. Some reactions require specific levels of acidity.

The acidity of a solution is described according to its hydrogen ion (H^+) concentration. Lemon juice has a very high hydrogen ion concentration, a solution of baking soda has a low concentration, and tap water is somewhere in the middle.

In describing hydrogen ion concentrations, a simple shorthand is used, called the **pH scale.** The pH of a solution simply refers to its hydrogen ion concentration, expressed as the number of places to the right of the decimal point.* Thus lemon juice, with a hydrogen ion concentration of 0.1 (or 10^{-1}) has a pH of 1. A baking soda solution with a hydrogen ion concentration of 0.00000000001 (or 10^{-11}) has a pH of 11 and so on. So, the more acidic a solution is, the lower its pH. Note that one unit of the

pH scale indicates a tenfold change in the hydrogen ion concentration (see the table).

An **acid** is any substance that releases hydrogen ions in water— lemon juice, for instance, is a mixture that contains citric acid. Correspondingly, a **base** is any substance that removes hydrogen ions from water, as does baking soda. Pure distilled water has a pH of 7 (very close to neutral), which means that it has a hydrogen ion concentration of 0.0000001 (or 10^{-7}). ●

pH values of common solutions

Molar Concentration of Hydrogen Ions		pH	Example	Molar Concentration of Hydroxide Ions
1.0	$= 10^{-0}$	0	Concentrated	[OH]
0.1	$= 10^{-1}$	1	nitric acid	10^{-14}
0.01	$= 10^{-2}$	2	Gastric juice	10^{-13}
0.001	$= 10^{-3}$	3	Coca-Cola	10^{-12}
0.000001	$= 10^{-6}$	6	Vinegar	10^{-11}
0.0000001	$= 10^{-7}$	7	Saliva	10^{-8}
0.00000001	$= 10^{-8}$	8	Distilled water	10^{-7}
0.000000000000001	$= 10^{-15}$	15	Sea water	10^{-6}
			Drain opener	10^{+1}

*Technically, **pH** is defined as the negative logarithm (base 10) of the molar concentration of hydrogen ions in a solution. A **mole** of any pure substance is the mass in grams that equals the molecular mass of each molecule. Thus, since the molecular mass of a single hydrogen ion is 1, a mole of hydrogen ion weighs 1 gm. The molecular mass of a hydroxide ion is 17, so one mole of hydroxide weighs 17 gm. The **molar concentration** of any substance in solution is the number of moles of the substance per liter of solution.

Summary

Elements, Atoms, and Molecules
Elements are substances that cannot be broken down into simpler substances by chemical means. Only six elements make up about 99% of all living matter.

Atoms and Their Structure
Elements are made up of atoms, which contain neutrons, protons, and electrons. The number of protons determines the element's atomic number, while the number of protons plus neutrons determines its atomic mass. Electrons orbit the nucleus in shells, filling the inner shells first and moving outward. Atoms whose outer shells are unsaturated (not filled) can interact with other atoms.

An isotope is a particular form of an element that may have fewer or greater numbers of neutrons than average. Many isotopes are radioactive; their half-lives may range from a few seconds to millions of years.

Molecules and Compounds
Atoms that join chemically to form molecules shift from higher to lower energy states. Molecules, in turn, can join to form compounds. Atoms in these forms may assume the shape of a caltrop or a perfect tetrahedron.

Interaction and Shifting Energy
The energetic tendencies that cause atoms to interact with one another include the following: (1) negative and positive charges of atoms and molecules tend to balance; (2) electrons within atoms and molecules tend to pair; and (3) electron shells of atoms and molecules tend to become filled. Precise amounts of energy are required to violate these tendencies, which permit chemical changes to take place.

Chemical Bonding
Atoms can fill their outer shells by gaining electrons from other atoms, losing all their outer-shell electrons to

other atoms, or sharing electrons. Ions are atoms or molecules that carry an electrical charge. Ionic bonding occurs between ions of opposite charges, while covalent bonds are formed when atoms share electrons.

The Peculiar Qualities of Water

Water molecules, formed by two hydrogen atoms covalently bonded to one oxygen atom, are attracted to one another by weak hydrogen bonds. While the internal charges of water molecules are balanced, their uneven distribution means that the water molecule is polar, having a negative side and a positive side. The hydrogen bonding that occurs between these polar regions gives water its relatively great temperature stability. For or-

ganisms living in or near bodies of water, this temperature stability can act as a resistant buffer, protecting them from both sudden and seasonal environmental temperature changes.

Water is also a well-known solvent. Because of its polarity, water can form hydrogen bonds with a variety of other molecules, an important characteristic for life processes since many organisms depend on the transport of molecules in fluids.

Most of the chemical reactions of life take place in water. The pH scale is a shorthand method of measuring the hydrogen ion concentration in a solution. Acids release hydrogen ions in water, while bases remove hydrogen ions from water.

Key Terms

element	isotope	ion
atom	half-life	ionic bond
neutron	electron shell	covalent bond
proton	electron cloud model	hydrogen bond
electron	molecule	specific heat
mass	compound	hydrophobic
nucleus	energetic tendencies	pH scale
orbital	electron donor	acid
atomic number	electron acceptor	base
atomic mass		

Review Questions

1. Define the term *element* and list the six elements that make up most living matter. (p. 21)

2. List the three parts of an atom. Which of the particles contributes most of the mass? Which contributes negative electrical charges? Which contributes positive charges? (p. 21)

3. In what way do the isotopes of an element differ from each other? In what two ways are radio-isotopes useful to biologists? (pp. 22–23)

4. Sketch Bohr diagrams of atoms of helium (no. 2), oxygen (no. 8), and chlorine (no. 17). Which of the elements is saturated? Unsaturated? (pp. 23–24)

5. Clearly distinguish between the terms *molecule* and *compound* and cite examples of each. (p. 25)

6. Briefly explain how energy is involved in both the making and breaking of chemical bonds. (pp. 26–27)

7. What is the basic difference between the behavior of electrons in the formation of ionic bonds and that in the formation of covalent bonds? (pp. 27–28)

8. Briefly explain why water molecules form hydrogen bonds, and describe how these bonds behave in the three physical states of water (ice, liquid, and gas). (pp. 28–30)

9. List three important qualities of water and briefly explain how each is important to life. (pp. 29–30)

The Molecules of Life

3

Our planet is essentially a hostile place, its very nature disruptive to the processes of life. Life exists not because of the earth's benevolence, but in spite of its constant problems, dangers, and frustrations. Life forms have been able to succeed only by overcoming perils and challenges. Furthermore, life's success is inextricably linked to the behavior of the molecules of the earth's biosphere, the realm of many lives. The molecules that exist here (and, in fact, make up the "here") are able to interact with each other in such ways to evade, ignore, conquer, and even utilize the hostile elements that otherwise would destroy them.

We are here, in large part, because of such mundane facts as the number of electrons surrounding the nucleus of an element called carbon. We are here because chemical bonds store energy. We are here because some molecules have fatty tails that hate water. We are composed of molecules and we owe our existence to the precise and predictable behavior of molecules. To try to understand them as best we can is our privilege and our responsibility.

CARBON: THE BACKBONE OF THE MOLECULES OF LIFE

Carbon is indeed a fascinating molecule and has even prompted chemists, not known for their poetry, to refer to its "magic." (We will assume that learning about its specific properties in no way diminishes its magic.) Carbon is found in just about every molecule important to living things. In fact, it is the backbone, or framework, upon which organisms build a range of essential molecules. It is important not just because it can form covalent bonds, but because it forms four covalent bonds at once.

Carbon is quite versatile in the way it forms bonds. While it forms four single covalent bonds with hydrogen to become methane, it can also form double bonds, in which two pairs of electrons are shared. Carbon dioxide, in fact, contains two sets of double bonds, with the carbon in the middle and double-bonded oxygens on either side: $O\!=\!C\!=\!O$. Carbon can even form triple bonds, as it does in deadly hydrogen cyanide: $H\!-\!C\!\equiv\!N$.

In addition, carbon atoms can be linked, forming long chains; they can also form rings, chains of rings, and a whole range of other complex structures. There seems to be no limit to how large an organic (carbon-bearing) molecule can be. (Some, for instance, contain 50 billion atoms.)

Most such large molecules are **polymers.** Composed of chains of repeating units, they often obey the familiar rules of small molecules, which makes them seem easier to describe and predict. Most of the important macromolecules (*macro*, "large") of life fall into one of four classes: carbohydrates, lipids, proteins, and nucleic acids. Let's consider some traits of each.

THE MACROMOLECULES

The Carbohydrates

The empirical formula for most **carbohydrates** is $(CH_2O)_n$. (Empirical formulas refer to composition rather than size or structure.) The *n* means carbohydrates are composed of any number of multiples of CH_2O units. Here, we will concentrate mainly on 6-carbon carbohydrates, primarily because they can be linked together to form such important molecules as starch, glycogen, and cellulose.

Monosaccharides and Disaccharides. The basic unit of most carbohydrates is simple sugar, that is, a **monosaccharide** (*mono,* "one"; *saccharide,* "sugar"). There are many kinds of simple sugars, but the most familiar is the 6-carbon sugar called **glucose.**

A monosaccharide is formed of only a few, say, 5- or 6-carbon atoms, linked by covalent bonds. (However, 3-, 4-, 7-, and 8-carbon sugars exist.) Notice that, although we're now referring only to carbon atoms, the formula $(CH_2O)_n$ indicates that there are one oxygen atom and two hydrogen atoms present for each carbon. The oxygens and hydrogens branch off the carbon chain as **side groups.** There are three major kinds of side groups in a simple carbohydrate (Figure 3.1).

Disaccharides are molecules comprising two simple sugars. The most familiar disaccharide is *sucrose,* or common table sugar. It is composed of the two simple sugars glucose and fructose, joined by a *dehydration linkage*. In this type of linkage, a hydrogen atom is removed from one molecule and an —OH side group is removed from the other molecule (Figure 3.2), forming H_2O.

In biochemical processes such as a dehydration linkage, highly specialized proteins called **enzymes** are required. Enzymes are essentially biological **catalysts,** and a *catalyst* is a substance that speeds up a reaction (see Chapter 6).

The new bond between glucose and fructose is called a 1-2 linkage, since it involves the number 1 carbon of glucose and the number 2 carbon of fructose. The carbons of sugars are traditionally numbered for convenience.

Polysaccharides. Polysaccharides ("many sugars") are long chains of monosaccharides. The simplest polysaccharides are polymers of glucose, joined by dehydration linkages. Such polysaccharides include starches such as *amylose* and *amylopectin* (storage products in plants), and *cellulose,* a carbohydrate that lends strength to plants. Animals also assemble polysaccharides such as *gly-*

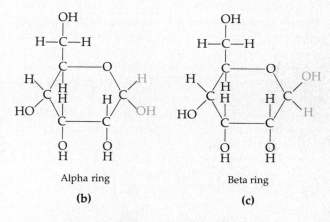

(a)

(b) Alpha ring   (c) Beta ring

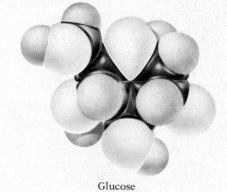

Glucose

(d)

3.1

The side groups of glucose include a hydrogen side group, a hydroxyl side group, and an aldehyde side group. Glucose spontaneously changes back and forth between its straight-chain form **(a)** and its two ring forms **(b, c)**. **(d)** A "space-filling" model of alpha glucose. The dashed line in the straight chain form indicates the carbons that will become linked to form the ring (the aldehyde group is then lost). The alpha and beta ring forms have a minor difference in the orientation of one **OH** group, but this becomes very significant when the glucose monomers are assembled into polymers.

cogen (animal starch) and *chitin*, a major structural material in some animal groups. Starches traditionally have formed a large part of our diet. Even today, in most primitive tribes, starchy plants make up the greater part of the diet. Starches are important storage materials because they are so easily converted to energy (Figure 3.3).

Cellulose, like starch, is composed of long chains of glucose molecules. However, there are important differences between the two that are based on whether alpha or beta glucose units are used in the polymer (see Figure 3.1). Because of these differences, starch is fairly soluble, while cellulose is not; cellulose has great tensile strength that starch lacks; starch is easily digested, but cellulose is completely indigestible to almost all organisms. Figure 3.4 shows the structure of cellulose and its organization into plant fibers.

Chitin is one of the major materials of the exoskeletons (outer coverings) of arthropods, the group that includes insects, lobsters, and crabs. Although chitin is soft and leathery, it can harden when impregnated with calcium carbonate or certain proteins. Chitin is similar in many ways to cellulose, except that the basic unit is not glucose, but a similar molecule that contains nitrogen. Chitin is indigestible to most animals.

The Lipids

The **lipids** are a diverse group of molecules, defined not by their structure but by their solubility. That is, they are fat- rather than water-soluble. Lipids may be very small molecules, large complex molecules, or large polymers of simple repeating subunits. They function as energy storage reservoirs, heat insulators, nerve insulators, lubricants, and even as hormones. Also, they are an important part of the membranes that surround cells. Lipids include animal fats, vegetable oils, waxes, steroids, and an interesting group called the *phospholipids*. Your own brain (as perhaps your parents have told you) consists largely of fat—more accurately, it contains large amounts of fat-soluble phospholipids.

Triglycerides and Their Subunits.   Animal fats (such as beef tallow) and vegetable oils (such as corn oil) are familiar lipids. Generally, the two are distinguishable because fats are solid at room temperature, while oils are liquid. At the animal's own normal body temperature, however, fats are usually liquids also.

Both fats and oils are **triglycerides**—compounds with three *fatty acid* chains covalently bonded to one molecule of *glycerol*. Triglycerides

3.2

Dehydration linkage. Glucose and fructose unite to form sucrose with the net loss of a molecule of water (color).

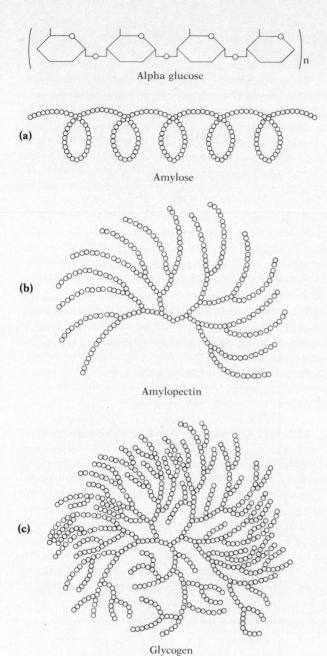

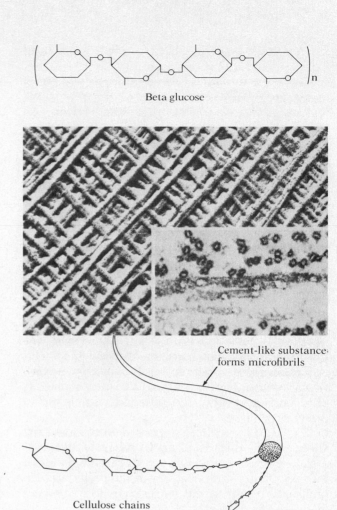

Alpha glucose

Beta glucose

(a)

Amylose

(b)

Amylopectin

(c)

Glycogen

Cement-like substance forms microfibrils

Cellulose chains

3.3 ━━━━━━━━

Three starches. **(a)** Amylose, a straight-chain plant starch. **(b)** Amylopectin, a branched-chain plant starch. **(c)** Glycogen, the animal starch, a branched-chain storage carbohydrate. All starches are polymers of alpha glucose rings. The chains of glucose subunits tend to form helical coils in all three starches.

3.4 ━━━━━━━━

Cellulose is a structural polysaccharide formed from repeated beta glucose units. It forms a tough wall around nearly every cell in the plant body. Its strength and flexibility make it an extremely valuable material to both plant and human consumer. Unlike other polysaccharides, cellulose forms lengthy microfibrils. These consist of cellulose chains embedded in cementlike substances. This combination forms the "wood" of woody plants. The microfibrils can be easily resolved by the electron microscope. Rows of microfibrils are laid down in laminated form, which explains the strength of cell walls.

are important as storage lipids, so let's take a close look at their subunits.

Glycerol is a small 3-carbon molecule with three hydroxyl (—OH) side groups. Glycerol provides the base, or the backbone, for all triglycerides. The differences between various triglycerides depend on what kinds of fatty acid chains are attached to that backbone. These chains can be of different lengths, but the most common are even-numbered chains of 14, 16, 18, or 20 carbons. A fatty acid molecule consists of a *hydrocarbon chain* with a *carboxyl group*, —COOH, at one end.

A fatty acid can be *saturated* with hydrogen, able to hold no more, or it can be *unsaturated*, which means that it is capable of accepting additional hydrogen atoms (Figure 3.5). Health advocates have long urged us to switch to unsaturated fats, although recent research has caused some scientists to question this belief (Chapter 37). In general, plant triglycerides are likely to be more unsaturated than those found in animal fat.

Triglycerides are produced through dehydration linkages (Figure 3.6), which means that, as each fatty acid joins the glycerol, a molecule of water is released.

Triglycerides contain a great deal of stored energy. In fact, they yield about twice as much energy per gram dry weight as do carbohydrates or protein. Plants store triglycerides in seeds, and animals may build up fat as reserves to be used in lean seasons ahead.

Humans also tend to store fat under their skin and around their internal organs. The tendency to build fat reserves may have been advantageous to our hunting ancestors, but improvements in agriculture, food storage, and efficient transportation have largely exempted us from the rigors of seasonal food depletion. Still, many of us seem to be taking no chances.

Phospholipids. **Phospholipids** are structurally similar to the triglycerides. However, the two differ in one important respect. While triglycerides contain three fatty acids covalently linked to one glycerol, phospholipids contain only two fatty acids. In place of the third is a negatively charged phosphate group that forms a link between the glycerol and one of several types of end groups. In cell membranes, for instance, the end group is usually *choline*, a nitrogen-containing, positively charged group. Because of their charged groups, phospholipids are polar or *hydrophilic* ("water-loving") molecules. This means that the end of the molecule that has the phosphate group can dissolve in water, and can also form ionic bonds with certain other charged molecules. The end of the phospholipid with the fatty acid chains is uncharged, hydrophobic, and nonpolar. Because of this peculiar arrangement of charges, phospholipids placed in water form spherical clumps, the nonpolar "tails" pointing in and the polar phosphate "heads" pointing out (Figure 3.7).

Detergents and Mayonnaise. Molecules that have polar (water-soluble) parts and nonpolar (lipid-soluble) parts can simultaneously form hydrogen bonds with water and hydrophobic ("water-fearing") interactions with their nonpolar parts. For instance, laundry detergents are composed of molecules with long nonpolar hydrocarbon "tails" and ionized "heads." In practical terms, the hydrocarbon tail forms hydrophobic interactions with gravy on shirts, while the ionized head forms strong bonds with water. Thus the

3.5

The difference between saturated and unsaturated fatty acids, shown through a comparison of stearic and linoleic acid. Each carbon in stearic acid is attached by single bonds to its neighbors and each is bonded to the maximum number of hydrogen atoms. Thus stearic acid is saturated with hydrogen. Linoleic acid, by contrast, has two double bonds in its carbon chain. Obviously it contains fewer hydrogen atoms than it otherwise might, and so linoleic acid is *poly*unsaturated since it has more than one carbon-to-carbon double bond.

Stearic acid

Linoleic acid

Glycerol +   3 Fatty acids   A triglyceride
Enzymes

3.6

Triglyceride synthesis. Triglycerides such as animal fats consist of a backbone of glycerol joined to three fatty acids by dehydration linkages. Note the three water molecules that form in the process.

detergent-gravy complex dissolves into the water.

Lecithin, a natural detergent, is a phospholipid of egg yolk. Like laundry detergent, it can, to some degree, dissolve fat in water. In fact, the lecithin in egg yolk can make salad oil dissolve in vinegar. The result is mayonnaise.

The dual personality of phospholipids recommends them as excellent building materials for the membranes surrounding living cells. As we will see in Chapter 4, these membranes are made up of two layers of phospholipids, along with several types of protein. Their nonpolar, fatty acid "tails" point in toward one another, forming a water-resistant core. Their charged phosphate heads face out, where they interact with charged regions of proteins (Figure 3.8).

Other Important Lipids. Other lipids include *waxes* and a peculiar group called the *steroids*. Waxes contain one fatty acid, but instead of being bound to glycerol, it is bound to a long-chain molecule with a single hydroxyl group. Waxes have powerful water-repellent properties, so they are common in organisms that must conserve water. Insect bodies generally are covered by a waxy layer, and many plants—especially those in drier areas—have waxy leaves.

Steroids are structurally quite different from fatty acids, but since they are either partly or wholly hydrophobic, they fall within the lipid category. All steroids have a basic structure of four interlocking rings. The differences in their biochemical activities are a function of the side groups that protrude from the rings. Some steroids are

very hydrophobic, some less so. We will see later that many of those regulatory chemicals circulating in the blood, the ones called hormones, are steroids, including those influencing sex.

We're all aware of something called **cholesterol** because food manufacturers don't hesitate to boast that their products don't contain any. But why should we care? Cholesterol, we are told, creates *arterial plaques,* abnormal thickenings of the walls of arteries, which can raise blood pressure dangerously (Figure 3.9). It cannot be denied that people with high levels of cholesterol in the blood have a greater risk of some circulatory disease.

However, recent findings suggest that cholesterol is not all bad. We need it for a number of vital functions, such as the development of cell membranes. Some forms of blood cholesterol—in the form of *high-density lipoproteins*—are actually beneficial in warding off bacterial disease. Also, *bile salts*, which are necessary for fat digestion, are modified cholesterol. When irradiated with ultraviolet light, cholesterol becomes vitamin D, which is necessary for normal bone growth. The human sex hormones—as well as the material that gives lustre to your hair—start out as cholesterol. Finally, sports physicians now suspect that women runners need cholesterol to maintain normal menstrual periods.

So we see that not only are lipids important in cell construction, they are also able to store great amounts of energy. As waxes, they help both plants and animals to conserve water. And they even contribute to those vital chemical messengers we call hormones.

(a) Phospholipids dispersed in water tend to aggregate with their fatty-acid "tails" clumped together by hydrophobic interaction, and their charged polar "heads" interacting with water. (b) The structure of a phospholipid from a cell membrane.

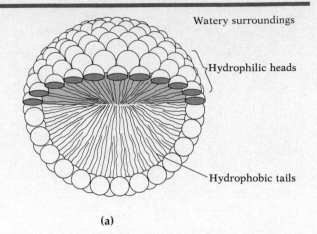

Watery surroundings

Hydrophilic heads

Hydrophobic tails

(a)

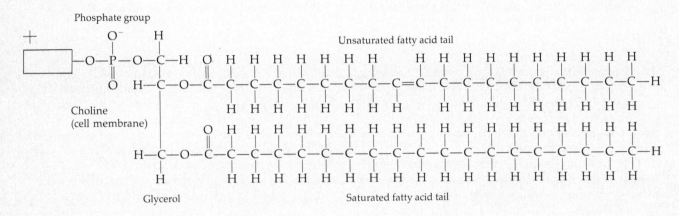

Phosphate group

Unsaturated fatty acid tail

Choline
(cell membrane)

Glycerol

Saturated fatty acid tail

(b)

Phospholipids make up the principal component of cell membranes. Their hydrophobic "tails" dissolve into one another, their polar "heads" facing the watery medium both inside and outside the cell. The po-

lar heads interact with polar regions of some proteins while their hydrophobic tails interact with hydrophobic regions of proteins.

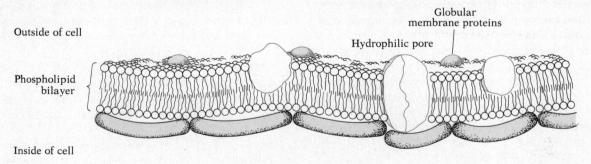

Outside of cell

Globular
membrane proteins

Hydrophilic pore

Phospholipid
bilayer

Inside of cell

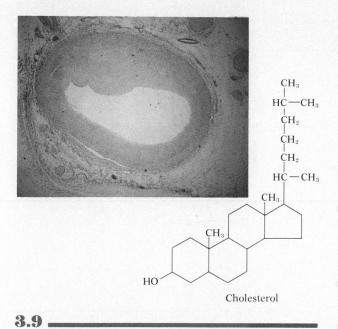

Cholesterol

3.9

Cholesterol and arterial disease. Accumulation of cholesterol in plaques on the interior of arteries greatly reduces the inside diameter of the artery and increases the pressure of the blood flowing through it.

The Proteins

Now let's consider those huge, twisted, and fascinating molecules called **proteins.** As you might suspect, regarding any kind of molecule with such important and varied responsibilities, there are many kinds of proteins. However, they all have certain common features that define the group.

Proteins can assume varied roles, functioning as structural molecules, as food reserves, and even as hormones (just as can carbohydrates and lipids). But other proteins form enzymes, those chemical catalysts that speed up certain chemical reactions in the cell.

Like the simpler carbohydrates and lipids, even these giants have a consistent and understandable organization. First, we should understand that all proteins are essentially long chains of simple **amino acids.** Let's take a closer look at these critical building blocks.

Amino Acids. There are 20 different naturally occurring amino acids used in the assembly of proteins. Like the subunits of carbohydrates and lipids, the amino acids form proteins by linking together through covalent dehydration linkages. There are about 150,000 different proteins in the human body alone, all of which function in important ways. No matter how complex they are,

they are all formed from the 20 amino acids. (But then, all of the elegantly arranged words in this book are formed from only 26 letters.)

The 20 amino acids clearly differ from each other, but they all have a few critical traits in common (Table 3.1). For example, every amino acid has at least one *carboxyl* group and one *amino* group (Figure 3.10). The presence of the two groups causes amino acids to behave in an interesting way in water. A carboxyl group (—COOH) can ionize in water, liberating a proton (H+) and becoming —COO⁻. Anything that releases protons (that is, positively charged hydrogen ions) in water is an *acid* by definition. The amino group, on the other hand, acts in an opposite manner. It tends to bond with any loose proton and, in so doing, takes on a positive charge. The amino group, —NH$_2$, then becomes —NH$_3^+$. (The dash at the left, by the way, merely represents the covalent bond between nitrogen and the adjacent carbon.) By accepting a proton from water, the amino group identifies itself as a *base*. Because an amino acid in water can simultaneously liberate a proton from its carboxyl group and accept a proton in its amino group, it has two oppositely charged side groups.

Each amino acid has one carbon atom (the alpha carbon) linking the carboxyl and amino groups. Attached to one side is a hydrogen atom, and to the other, making up the remainder of the amino acid, is what is called an *R group*. The "R" is simply shorthand for any of the 20 side groups that make

3.10

An amino acid. There are 20 or more distinct R groups (see Table 3.1); the rest of the molecule always has the same configuration (except for a minor variation in proline). **(a)** The un-ionized form of the amino acid. **(b)** The ionized form. Normally, both the carboxyl group and the amino group of a free amino acid will be ionized.

TABLE 3.1

The twenty amino acids* commonly found in proteins

Amino Acids with Nonpolar R Groups

Alanine (Ala)

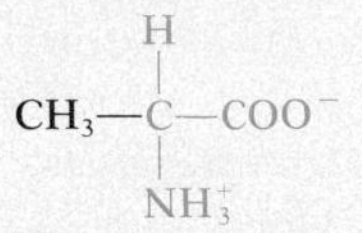

$$CH_3—C—COO^-$$ (with H above, NH_3^+ below)

Isoleucine (Ile)

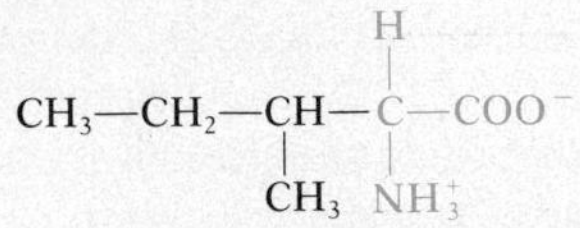

$$CH_3—CH_2—CH—C—COO^-$$ (with H above, CH_3 and NH_3^+ below)

Leucine (Leu)

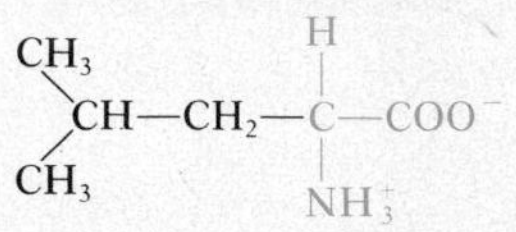

$$CH_3$$
$$CH—CH_2—C—COO^-$$
$$CH_3$$ (with H above, NH_3^+ below)

Methionine (Met)

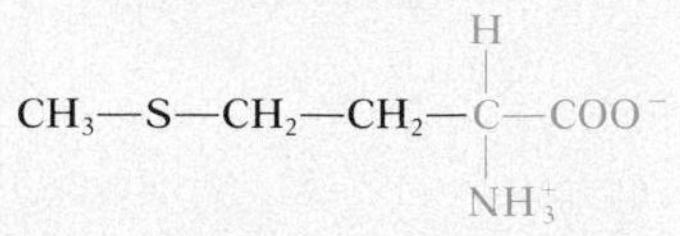

$$CH_3—S—CH_2—CH_2—C—COO^-$$ (with H above, NH_3^+ below)

Proline (Pro)

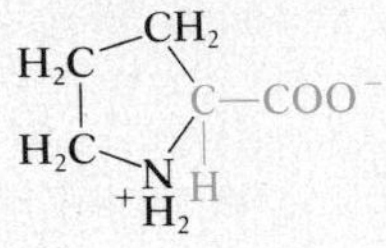

$$H_2C—CH_2$$
$$H_2C—C—COO^-$$
$$^+N—H_2$$ (with N and H)

Phenylalanine (Phe)

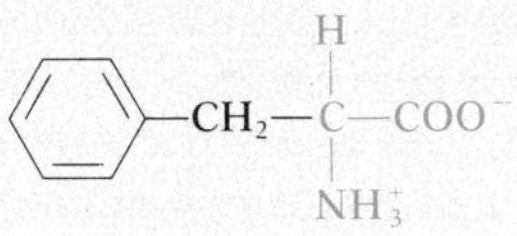

$$\bigcirc—CH_2—C—COO^-$$ (with H above, NH_3^+ below)

Tryptophan (Trp)

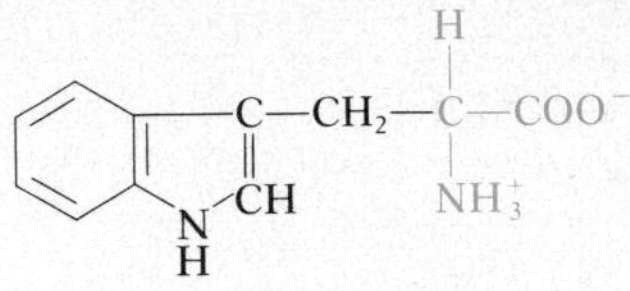

indole ring—$C—CH_2—C—COO^-$ (with H above, NH_3^+ below), ring with CH and N—H

Valine (Val)

$$CH_3$$
$$CH—C—COO^-$$
$$CH_3$$ (with H above, NH_3^+ below)

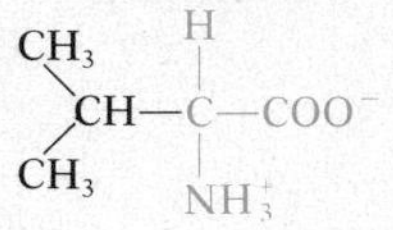

Amino Acids with Uncharged Polar R Groups

Asparagine (Asn)

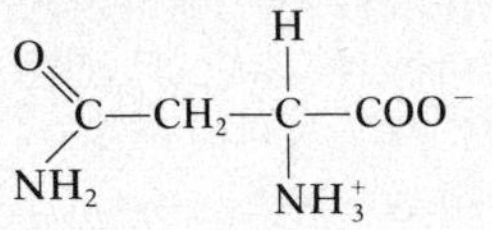

$$O$$
$$C—CH_2—C—COO^-$$
$$NH_2$$ (with H above, NH_3^+ below)

Cysteine (Cys)

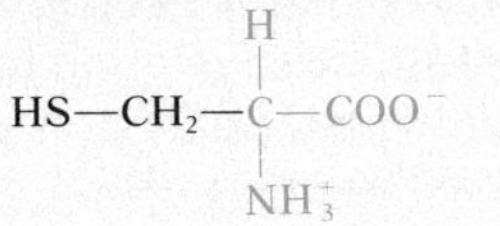

$$HS—CH_2—C—COO^-$$ (with H above, NH_3^+ below)

Glutamine (Gln)

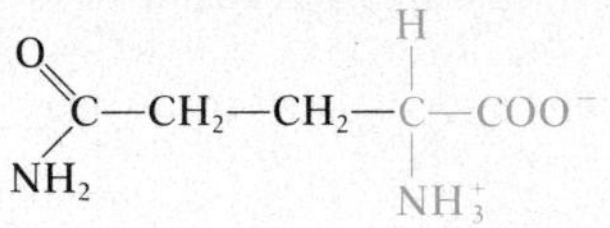

$$O$$
$$C—CH_2—CH_2—C—COO^-$$
$$NH_2$$ (with H above, NH_3^+ below)

Glycine (Gly)

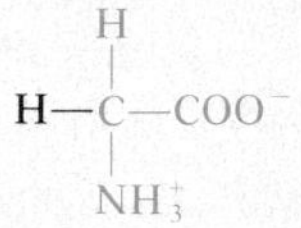

$$H—C—COO^-$$ (with H above, NH_3^+ below)

Serine (Ser)

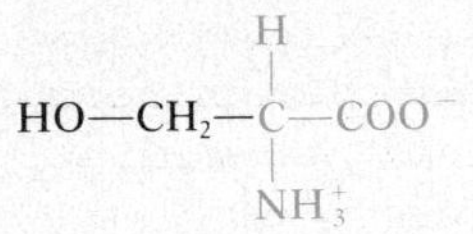

$$HO—CH_2—C—COO^-$$ (with H above, NH_3^+ below)

Threonine (Thr)

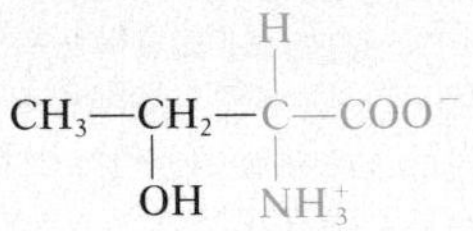

$$CH_3—CH_2—C—COO^-$$ (with H above, OH and NH_3^+ below)

Tyrosine (Tyr)

$$HO—\bigcirc—CH_2—C—COO^-$$ (with H above, NH_3^+ below)

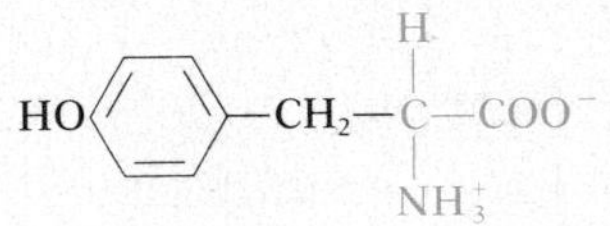

Amino Acids with Acid R Groups (Negatively Charged at pH 6.0)

Aspartic acid (Asp)

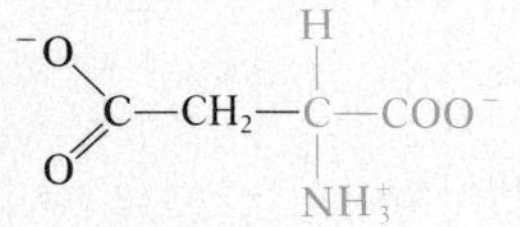

$$^-O$$
$$C—CH_2—C—COO^-$$
$$O$$ (with H above, NH_3^+ below)

Glutamic acid (Glu)

$$^-O$$
$$C—CH_2—CH_2—C—COO^-$$
$$O$$ (with H above, NH_3^+ below)

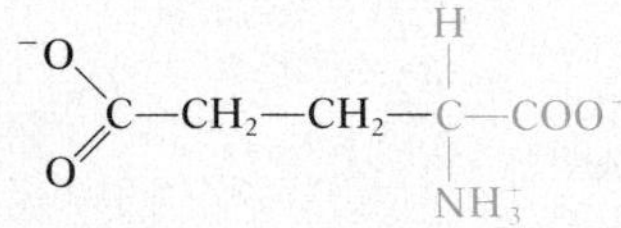

Amino Acids with Basic R Groups (Positively Charged at pH 6.0)

Arginine (Arg)

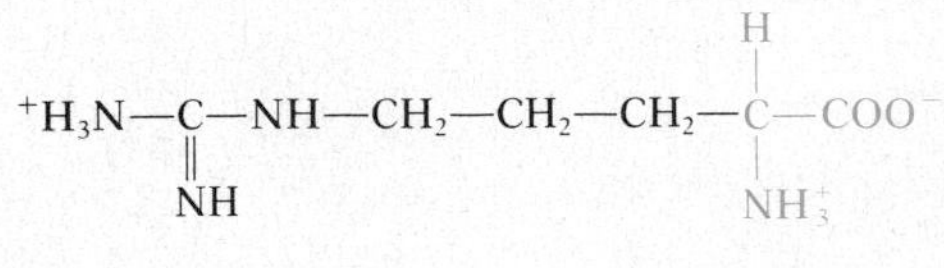

$$^+H_3N—C—NH—CH_2—CH_2—CH_2—C—COO^-$$
$$NH$$ (with H above, NH_3^+ below)

Histidine (His)

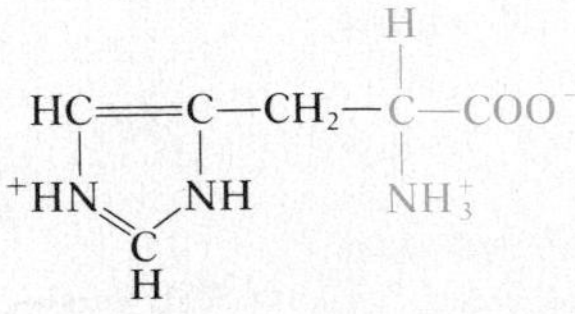

$$HC=C—CH_2—C—COO^-$$
$$^+HN\quad NH$$ (ring with C—H, with H above, NH_3^+ below)

Lysine (Lys)

$$^+H_3N—CH_2—CH_2—CH_2—CH_2—C—COO^-$$ (with H above, NH_3^+ below)

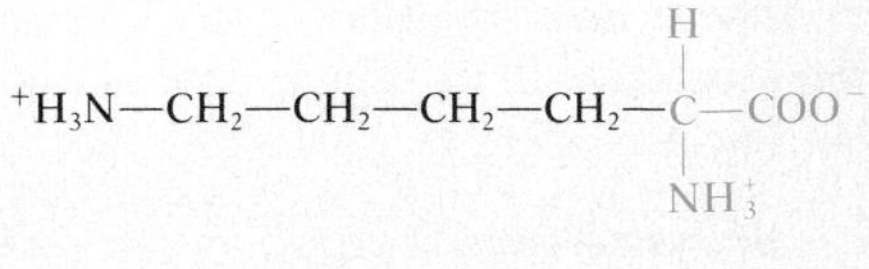

*The portion of the amino acid that is common to all is colored. Note that some of the amino acids contain more than one amino or acid group, giving them greater basic or acid qualities than the others. Cysteine contains a sulfur-hydrogen group at its R-terminal. This has special importance in determining the shapes of proteins. The abbreviations given in parentheses are used for convenience in writing protein formulas.

one amino acid different from the next (see Table 3.1).

Peptide Bonds and the Polypeptide. The covalent bond between two amino acids in a protein is called a **peptide bond,** so called because the enzyme *pepsin* breaks this bond in the process of digesting proteins. The bond is formed by a kind of dehydration reaction. Thus, the formation of each peptide bond yields one molecule of water (Figure 3.11).

It is through peptide bonding that amino acids form chains known as **polypeptides.** The polypeptide chain is the first step in protein synthesis. Proteins are biologically functional and complex, and they may contain one or several polypeptide chains. The specific kinds of amino acids used and the sequence in which they appear give proteins their special qualities. That is, the order of the amino acids along the polypeptide chain can determine where the chain will bend or fold, and where various lengths will be attracted to each other.

The Shapes of Proteins. The final shape of a protein has a great deal to do with its functions. In general, the shapes fall into two categories: *fibrous* and *globular*. In their final form, fibrous proteins contain lengthy, linear units, although some form sheetlike structures. The most common fibrous protein is *keratin*, an insoluble material found in hair, fur, nails, claws, hooves, and the outer skin. Muscle tissue also contains fibrous protein. Globular protein, as its name suggests, often forms irregular "globs" or spheres. It is usually water-soluble, very heavy, and it occurs in highly folded,

irregular masses. Examples are most enzymes, such blood proteins as hemoglobin, such storage proteins as the *albumen* of egg white, and the proteins embedded in membranes (see Figure 3.8). Globular proteins, which often consist of two or more polypeptides, may have four levels of structural organization (Figure 3.12).

Nucleic Acids: RNA and DNA

Our final category in the molecules of life includes the **nucleic acids, RNA** *(ribonucleic acid)* and **DNA** *(deoxyribonucleic acid)*, the largest of all biological macromolecules. DNA molecules are immensely long polymers. We have referred to genes as hereditary units and noted that they are, in most organisms, composed of DNA. We will soon see just how genes operate. In particular we will see their role in the formation of proteins. The precise ordering of the subunits within a DNA molecule specifies the order and number of amino acids in a protein—DNA and RNA are both involved in the synthesis of all biological proteins, including the all-important enzymes. DNA is not directly involved in protein synthesis, but serves as a storehouse of genetic information that is transferred to the RNA. Actually, there are several types of RNA, each with its own specific role in protein synthesis. With the help of certain enzymes, DNA prepares replicas of itself prior to the time when a cell divides into two, as happens repeatedly in growth and development.

As we've seen in all of the large molecules of life, DNA and RNA are composed of repeated subunits, in this instance, known as **nucleotides.** Despite the immense length of nucleic acids, the organization of their nucleotides is surprisingly simple. In fact, it was DNA's deceptive simplicity that, until the early 1950s, kept biologists in the dark as to the chemical nature of the gene. While proteins can contain as many as 20 different amino acid subunits, there are only four different subunits, or nucleotides, in DNA and RNA. These nucleotides are very much alike in most ways. Each contains a 5-carbon sugar, a phosphate group, and one of four different ringlike *nitrogen bases* (Figure 3.13a). In the assembly of a DNA polymer, the nucleotides are linked, one atop the other, into two opposing strands. The two strands are wound around each other in such a way as to form the well-known *double helix* (Figure 3.13b). In the assembly of RNA, nucleotides are also linked one atop the other, but the finished polymer is single-stranded, so the helix does not form.

3.11

Amino acids are joined by peptide bonds (dehydration linkages) in the formation of proteins.

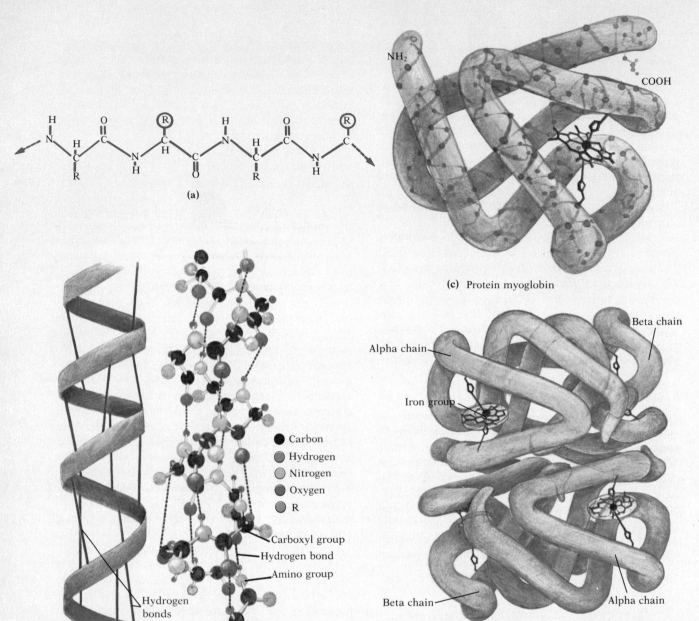

(a)

Carbon
Hydrogen
Nitrogen
Oxygen
R

Carboxyl group
Hydrogen bond
Amino group

Hydrogen bonds

(b) Alpha helix with hydrogen bonds between carboxyl and amino group of amino acids

(c) Protein myoglobin

NH₂

COOH

Beta chain
Alpha chain
Iron group
Beta chain
Alpha chain

(d) Protein hemoglobin containing four polypeptides, two alpha chains, and two beta chains, along with four iron-containing groups.

3.12

Proteins may have as many as four levels of organization and most have at least three. The first or *primary level* **(a)** is determined by the number, kind, and order of the amino acids joined together by peptide bonds to form a simple polypeptide strand. The *secondary level* **(b)** of organization forms spontaneously, as soon as the polypeptide has been synthesized. The chain of amino acids coils, forming what is called an *alpha helix* (right-handed coil). Coiling is brought about by numerous weak hydrogen bonds that form between oxygen and hydrogen in the carboxyl and amino groups of every fourth amino acid in the chain. The individual hydrogen bonds are weak, but so many form that the alpha helix is fairly stable. The *tertiary level* **(c)** of organization occurs when the alpha coil is coiled once more, and then folded back on itself in specific ways. It is particularly important

to the structure of globular proteins such as enzymes and albumin (egg-white protein). Tertiary coiling and folding are brought about by several kinds of interactions among amino acid R groups. Included are disulfide linkages, bridges that form between molecules of the sulfur-containing amino acid, cysteine. Some of the globular proteins reach the *quaternary level* **(d)** of organization. In this level, two or more polypeptides join to form the finished protein. Needless to say, quaternary proteins are giants. Among the proteins with quaternary structure is the oxygen-carrying blood protein, hemoglobin. It contains two pairs of interacting polypeptides (known as *alpha* and *beta chains*) attracted together by forces similar to those of the tertiary level. Also present are four very special iron-containing groups, the actual sites of oxygen transport.

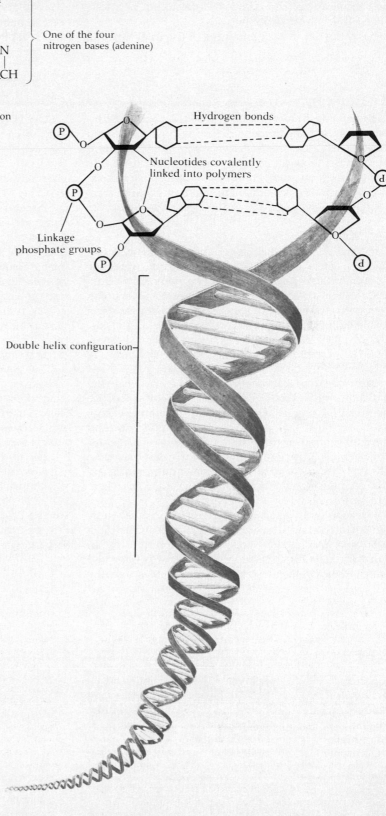

Phosphate {

OH

O=P—OH

One of the four nitrogen bases (adenine)

A nucleotide

5-carbon sugar

(a)

Hydrogen bonds

Nucleotides covalently linked into polymers

Linkage phosphate groups

Double helix configuration

DNA consists of two very long polymers of nucleotides coiled into a double helix configuration. Each nucleotide **(a)** contains a phosphate or phosphoric acid group, a 5-carbon sugar, and one of four different nitrogen bases. The one seen here is known as adenine. When assembled into the polymer **(b)**, each nucleotide is covalently bonded to the next via the phosphates and sugars, which form the backbone of the molecule. The nitrogen bases face inward, where weak but numerous hydrogen bonds attract those of one polymer to those of the other. The combined forces produce the familiar helical configuration.

This brief discussion of DNA and RNA has no doubt left you with many questions, and understandably so. In later chapters you'll find a great deal more about the complex interaction between DNA, RNA, and proteins.

Now that we have some idea of the qualities and properties of various molecular structures, we will see how their critical interactions function in living systems. Keeping these molecules in mind, since they relate both to our beginnings and our present successes, let's move on to explore other realms of the biosphere.

Summary

Carbon: The Backbone of the Molecules of Life

Carbon is the basic framework for the construction of a range of essential molecules. Carbon atoms can form four covalent bonds at once and can be linked into chains, rings of chains, and other complex structures. Most large molecules of life fall into four classes: carbohydrates, lipids, proteins, and nucleic acids.

The Macromolecules

Carbohydrates form such important molecules as starch, glycogen, and cellulose. Six-carbon sugars, which are monosaccharides, can be joined (via dehydration linkage) to form disaccharides and polysaccharides. Cellulose, unlike starch, is not water soluble, possesses great tensile strength, and is indigestible to most organisms. Chitin, a polysaccharide, is also indigestible and constitutes one of the primary materials in the exoskeletons of arthropods.

Lipids are a group of fat-soluble molecules that vary widely in complexity. They are an important part of the membrane that surrounds cells, and function as energy reservoirs, heat and nerve insulators, lubricants, and hormones. Lipids include animal fats and vegetable oils (triglycerides), waxes, steroids, and phospholipids. Glycerol forms the base for all triglyerides, which are produced through dehydration linkage and contain considerable amounts of stored energy.

Phospholipids, similar to triglycerides, contain only two fatty acids and an ionized phosphate that links them to an end group. Their polar and nonpolar parts can simultaneously form hydrophilic bonds with water and hydrophobic interactions with other molecules, a quality that makes them excellent building materials for cell membranes.

Lipids also include waxes and steroids. Waxes enable organisms to conserve water, while steroids help regulate activity at the cell surface. Cholesterol, long associated with circulatory disease, is now known to be necessary for the development of cell membranes, normal bone growth, and many other vital bodily functions.

Proteins act as structural molecules, food reserves, enzymes (catalysts), and hormones. All proteins contain one or more chains of amino acids known as polypeptide chains. Every amino acid contains one carboxyl group, one amino group, and an R group that determines the specific qualities of the amino acid and the final shape of the protein. When the carboxyl group ionizes in water, it acts as an acid, releasing a proton. The amino group acts as a base in attracting such protons. The covalent or peptide bond between amino acids is formed by a type of dehydration reaction.

The final shape of a protein, which is generally fibrous or globular, has a great deal to do with its functions. Keratin is a common fibrous protein. Globular proteins, such as hemoglobin, may have four levels of structural organization: primary, secondary, tertiary, and quaternary.

The nucleic acids, DNA and RNA, are the largest of all biological macromolecules. Both are involved in the synthesis of proteins, and most kinds of genes are made up of DNA. DNA and RNA are each composed of four repeated subunits called nucleotides. The nucleotides are linked together to form strands, which then wind around one another to create the double helix.

Key Terms

polymer	catalyst	amino acid
carbohydrate	polysaccharide	peptide bond
monosaccharide	lipid	polypeptide
glucose	triglyceride	nucleic acid
side groups	phospholipid	RNA
disaccharide	cholesterol	DNA
enzyme	protein	nucleotide

Review Questions

1. Distinguish between the terms *monosaccharide, disaccharide,* and *polysaccharide* and give an example of each. (pp. 35–36)

2. Using two molecules of glucose as an example, briefly describe the process of dehydration synthesis. (What is the product? What is the role of the enzyme in dehydration synthesis?) (p. 36)

3. Where would one look to find the polysaccharides amylopectin, cellulose, and glycogen? What is a primary difference between cellulose and the others? (pp. 35–36)

4. List the components of a triglyceride. How does one kind of triglyceride differ from another? (pp. 36, 38)

5. Briefly discuss the phospholipids. How do their structure and electrical charge differ from those of triglycerides? In what structure are they commonly found, and in what manner are they arranged there? (p. 38)

6. Cholesterol has received a lot of bad press in the past. What kinds of problems does it cause? Is cholesterol of any value to the body at all? Explain. (p. 39)

7. List four biological roles of proteins. (p. 41)

8. Using the terms *amino group, carboxyl group,* and *dehydration synthesis,* describe the manner in which amino acids are joined to form polypeptides. (pp. 41, 43)

9. List the four organizational levels in the large globular proteins, and explain briefly how each level is attained. (p. 44)

The Structure and Function of Cells

4

Robert Hooke realized that he had a problem. He had just been appointed Curator of Experiments for the prestigious Royal Society of London, and one of his first tasks was to devise some sort of demonstration for the next weekly meeting. He wanted something that would enlighten, entertain, and impress. He also wanted to make the Society members aware of his own abilities. Neither would be easy. The problem was, these were some of the brightest, crustiest, most argumentative, skeptical, and jaded people in all of 17th-century England—the elite of British science.

Hooke considered a number of possibilities, working and fretting until he struck upon a solution. Obviously, he had to show them something new, and the most exciting new technology of his day was curved and polished glass. He would demonstrate the lens.

The scientific world was buzzing with talk of lenses. With their ability to magnify, they revealed an entirely new world. Things no one had suspected existed were suddenly visible. Through new eyes, people could again see things long forgotten. With a pair of lenses held in a frame, people who had been nearly blind were able to see again—a miracle come true. Old men who had been unable to read had their books and letters returned to them. Of course, magnification by lenses was not a new idea. Earlier in the century, Galileo had pointed a lens toward the sky and had drawn some conclusions, as well as the wrath of the Church. Hooke, however, had a different intellectual appetite. He wanted to see things that were too small to be seen without a lens. He was so fascinated with the idea of using the lens to explore the world of the miniscule that he built his own microscope, one of the first in the world (Figure 4.1). Obviously, it is difficult to impress people if you're standing on *their* turf; but microscopy was *Hooke's* turf. So he decided to use his lens in some novel way. But what should he arrange for them? What would they like to see? Maybe cork. Cork was a mystery, appearing to be solid, yet able to float. Perhaps it was not so solid after all. Hooke aimed his microscope at a cork, and what do you think he saw? Wrong. He saw nothing. This is because microscopes do not work very well with reflected light. So with a penknife he cut a very thin sliver of cork from the bottom, and shined a bright light upward through it. This time, what he saw puzzled him and was sufficiently interesting to please the Society members. Hooke wrote that the cork sliver seemed to be composed of "little boxes." These, he surmised, were full of air, accounting for the ability of corks to float. Hooke called the little boxes *cells* because they reminded him of the rows of monks' cells in a monastery. And from this modest beginning, a new scientific field was born.

CELL THEORY

The birth, however, was slow. What was one to do with such knowledge? The group that week was pleased, but a full century would pass before the scientific world would understand the importance of Hooke's cells.

One of the first to try to put to use the knowledge was the German naturalist Lorenza Oken, who focused his primitive microscope on just about everything he could think of. Finally, in 1805, he wrote, "All organic beings originate from and consist of vesicles or cells." This simple statement became known as the **cell theory.** Then, in 1838, two other Germans, the botanist Matthias Jakob Schleiden and the zoologist Theodor Schwann, independently published the conclusion that all living things are composed of cells. (Schleiden and Schwann usually get the credit for the idea, even today.) Almost 20 years later, another German, Rudolf Virchow, added the very simple and very important statement, "omnis cellula e cellula." Anything written in Latin is, of course, very important—even if it only means "all cells come from cells." That was, in fact, not a bad try based on the available data.

Biology being biology, there are exceptions—see Essay 4.1. But let's ignore theory and sweeping generalizations for a moment. Microscopes are fun. Once Hooke had described his little boxes, the art of microscopy blossomed. Everyone in science wanted a microscope. And nothing—literally nothing—remained sacred. Everything was a fair target. Curious souls were anxious to be the first, the very first to see . . . whatever. At first, most of these efforts were prompted by sheer curiosity.

In time, however, the more serious among them used microscopes to answer questions. They noticed certain common themes and differences. They began to make generalizations. For example, they suggested that although organisms may be vastly different, certain cells and tissues could be nearly identical. For example, muscle, nerve, and reproductive cells in most animal species are quite similar. Thus people began to think of cells and tissues in terms of function.

The cell theory was gaining acceptance, and more and more researchers were drawn to these strange little boxes. In time, the cell theory expanded.

What is a Cell?

You may have heard that cells are defined as the basic units of life. However, this really doesn't tell us much. What are they? Such a simple question, such critical implications.

Cells are bodies surrounded by membranes containing those inclusions necessary for the many basic functions of life. Let's also say that many forms of life are composed of many specialized cells, although some organisms are composed of only one cell. Cells virtually carry out all the processes that make life possible. Thus it should be no surprise that they are not simple structures. They

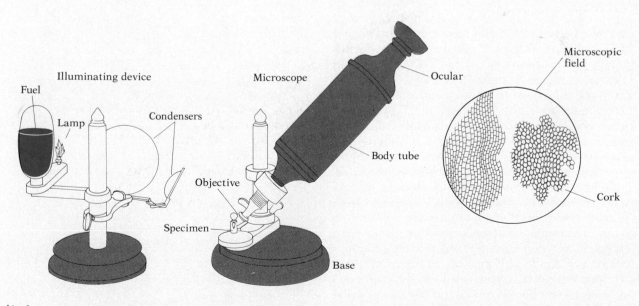

4.1

Hooke's primitive microscope consisted of two convex lenses at either end of a body tube some six inches in length. Focusing was done by twisting the body tube along its spiral threads. The subjects were simply stuck on a pin attached to the base of the microscope. The light source was a flame, and its light was focused by a lens. The cork cells shown here are from a drawing by Hooke.

TABLE 4.1

A comparison of some cell sizes

The range of cell size is enormous, extending from the bacterium to the meter-long nerve cell, a difference of about a millionfold. Yet most plant and animal cells are about 90 micrometers (μm) across. The smallest known cells, those of mycoplasma, sometimes are not visible through the light microscope. Viruses can be seen only with an electron microscope.

Abbreviations used in table: m = meter; mm = millimeter = 0.001 meter; μm = micrometer = 0.000001 meter; nm = nanometer = 0.000000001 meter.

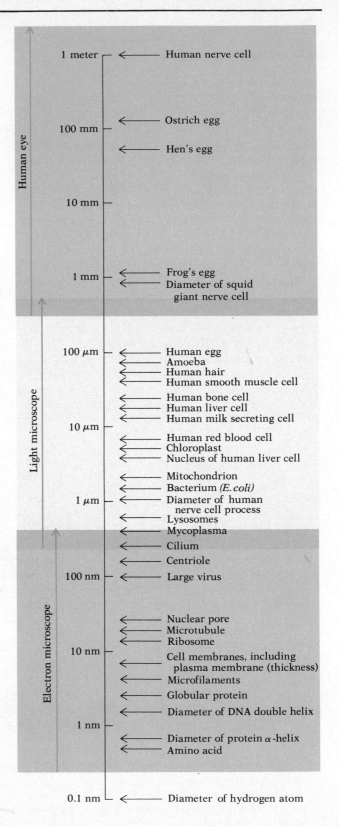

are filled with a number of tiny structures, bounded by membranes and called *organelles,* each with its own role to play. In some cases we know what those roles are. In other cases we don't.

In summarizing what we do know we can say that certain organelles specialize in synthesizing complex molecules such as proteins. Others convert food stored in the cell into energy. Still others store waste products, either permanently or temporarily. And some organelles may transport materials to the membrane, where they can be released to the outside. Later we will see that almost all cellular activities are directed by yet another membrane-bounded organelle, the *cell nucleus.*

Cell Size

Can cells be seen with the naked eye? They can if the naked eye can see a chicken egg yolk, which is a single cell, but most are far too small to be seen without some sort of magnification. It is very difficult to generalize about cell size and shape because there are so many kinds of cells, each specialized for a particular function. For example, there are cells invisible to the human eye that are over a meter long, such as the nerve cells that run down a giraffe's leg, but they are still too thin to be seen. So there is great variation in cell size. In spite of this, most plant and animal cells are about 90 micrometers (μm) long. Almost none are smaller than 10 μm in diameter, and only a few are larger than 100 μm. A micrometer is one millionth of a meter—Table 4.1. To give you an idea of this size, about fifty 10-micrometer cells set end-to-end would just reach across the period at the end of this sentence. Plant cells tend to be somewhat larger than animal cells, perhaps because they contain water-filled cavities—structures called *vacuoles.* In general, the amount of cytoplasm (living material) in the two types of cells is about the same.

Confronted with such information, biologists are likely to wonder what determines cell size. Why are most of them so small? Why do they first go through a rapid growth phase, then slow down as some critical size is reached, divide in half, and then start over? One way to phrase the question is to ask what the advantage is of having small cells?

The Surface-Volume Hypothesis. The generally accepted explanation for the small size of cells is that size strongly affects the ratio of the surface area to the volume. Specifically, smaller cells have larger surface areas in proportion to their volume.

In biology, there always seems to be a next question. This time the next question is, why is a large surface area necessary? The answer centers on a simple fact. The surface area of cells is covered by a regulatory membrane. The larger the membrane, the greater the regulation over what enters and leaves the cell. Oxygen and nutrients must be able to enter the cell easily, and other materials such as wastes, as well as functional products such as hormones, must leave.

A large membrane covering a small cell ensures that the material within is never far from the cell's exterior and, thus, the cell is more likely to be able to carry on transport in an efficient manner (Figure 4.2).

The next question is, why aren't cells even smaller? And the answer? No one really knows.

"Cube cells"

Surface: 6 square inches
Volume: 1 cubic inch
Ratio 6:1

Surface: 24 square inches
Volume: 8 cubic inches
Ratio 3:1

4.2

Surface-to-volume ratio. In two bodies of similar shape, the larger one has more mass (bulk) for its surface area. If the bodies are dependent on materials moving through the covering surface, the smaller body will be at an advantage since it has a comparatively large surface area to service its interior.

ESSAY 4.1

LIFE WITHOUT CELLS

Life on our small planet presents few opportunities for those who like tidy categories. There are few pigeonholes in the real world of adaptive, changing, opportunistic life. In fact, life is so diverse that there are exceptions to virtually every rule. (This is probably among the most reputable of the rules.) Exceptions to the cell theory are found, for example, in the kingdom Protista, the so-called single-celled creatures. (If they are cells, they are large cells.) These are sometimes large enough to be visible to the naked eye. The length of one common protist, the *Paramecium*, may reach 0.3 mm, and even it is dwarfed by another single-celled organism, the giant amoeba, whose length often measures 5 mm (about 3/16 of an inch). Compared to the typical animal cell, these giant single-celled organisms are 50 times longer, with 625,000 times more volume. Protists, it seems, are constructed along very different lines than are the cells of multicellular organisms. Because of this, some scientists prefer the term *acellular* when describing the protists. The implication is that they are not single-celled organisms, and that they simply are not organized along cellular principles. There are also organisms such as some flatworms and some fungi that undergo a strange sort of division in which the nucleus may divide, perhaps many times, but the total cell does not. The result is a very large "cell" with many nuclei.

At the other end of the size spectrum, far too small to be seen with the light microscope, are the viruses. Viruses are believed to be the smallest living things, although many scientists do not consider them to be alive.

Viruses lack most cell-associated traits, so perhaps they shouldn't be compared with cells. (But then what could we compare them with?) To begin with, what are viruses? Structurally, they are very simple, consisting of a protein container with a supply of enzymes surrounding a core of genes. In essence, they are self-reproducing, capable of making more self-reproducing material.

So although the cell theory applies quite well to most organisms, life has a disconcerting way of not allowing easy generalizations. We can see that some forms of life have found it advantageous to take another route. The result is the vast array of kinds of life on this planet. ●

CELL STRUCTURE

Now that we have some idea of the size and variation of cells, let's take a closer look at their structure. For convenience, we can consider the cell as three parts. The outermost part includes the cell membrane and, in plants, the **cell wall.** The next region is the **cytoplasm,** the incredibly active area between the membrane and the **nucleus**—the inner part. (**Nucleoplasm** is the jellylike substance inside the nuclear membrane.)

First we will consider the structure of the *eukaryotic* cell, the more advanced type that makes up plants, animals, fungi, and protists. Later we will compare the eukaryotic cell to the *prokaryotic* cell, that of bacteria and cyanobacteria (formerly called blue-green algae), with its much simpler structural organization. Let's begin with the eukaryotic cell membrane (Figure 4.3).

ESSAY 4.2

HOW CYTOLOGISTS SEE CELLS

Cytologists, the biologists who study cells, use an arsenal of highly sophisticated devices and precise techniques in their efforts to develop exact descriptions of cells. Their most venerable tool is the direct descendant of Hooke's primitive apparatus. It is the *compound light microscope* (see the illustration). Developed in the 19th century, it is still very useful and marvelously precise, but it is limited by the nature of the energy it uses: light. Any two objects closer together than 250 nm merge as a single, blurred image, because of the properties of visible light itself. The limitations of any microscope are, therefore, defined as *resolving power*—the ability to distinguish close objects as being separate from one another. In practice, this limitation is half the wavelength of visible light.

Fortunately, we need no longer be limited by the resolving powers of the light microscope. We now have the *transmission electron microscope* (TEM). This remarkable tool was conceived in the early part of the 20th century, but was not perfected until the 1950s. With the TEM, electrons—not light—are the energy source. The electrons are emitted from a heated coil and are focused so that they pass through the object. Their great advantage is that their oscillations (wavelengths)

are substantially smaller than the wavelengths of light. They can pass between the most finely separated objects in the cell. As they pass through matter of different densities, they cast an image on a screen or photographic film. The magic of the TEM lies in the fact that its resolving power is practically unlimited as far as cells are concerned. The TEM can magnify an object up to 1,000,000 times. In more understandable terms, consider that while the finest light microscopes can produce clear outline images of a single bacterium, the TEM can produce a detailed image of its inner structure.

Despite its great advantages the TEM initially met strong resistance among traditional cytologists. This is because the preparation of cells for the TEM involves extremely harsh, disruptive steps that could easily alter the material so drastically that no one could be sure what he or she was actually seeing. (Since that time the structures

Light microscope and transmission electron microscope.

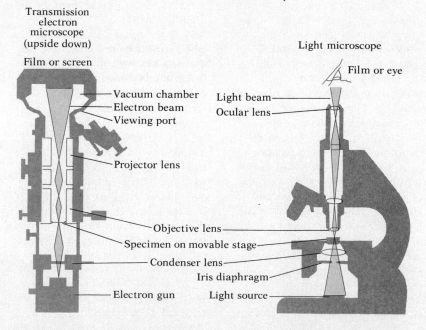

Transmission electron microscope (upside down)

Film or screen

Vacuum chamber
Electron beam
Viewing port

Projector lens

Objective lens
Specimen on movable stage
Condenser lens

Electron gun

Light microscope

Film or eye

Light beam
Ocular lens

Iris diaphragm
Light source

The Cell Membrane

The cell membrane (or plasma membrane) is simply the membrane that surrounds each cell. Now let's see if "simply" is a good choice of words. We learned earlier that the basic function of the membrane is to control the movement of materials into and out of the cell. It should be quite obvious, since the processes of life must be tightly regulated, that the cell membrane must be selective about what it allows to pass in and out. It must freely accept some substances and utterly reject others. It may do this passively, like a sleeping doorman, as it does with water and gases; or it may take an active part in transporting materials, alertly and with great discrimination using cellular energy to force other more reluctant substances across. Because of such discrimination, cell membranes are described as **selectively permeable.**

Regarding the structure of the cell membrane, its

Heavy metal shadow casting.

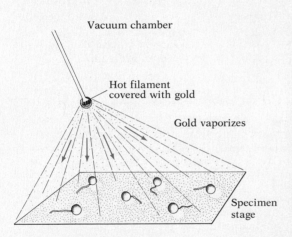

identified have been verified in many ways.)

First, bits of tissue are "fixed" by permeating them with heavy metal salts that solidify the cell's protein. If the material to be viewed is tiny, as are virus particles, the metallic salts are sprayed on at an angle in what is known as *shadow-casting* (see the illustration). This treatment increases the tendency of cell structures to absorb electrons, making their images darker and sharper.

One of the early techniques has continued to yield particularly valuable information. The technique is called *freeze-fracturing.* Quick-freezing the tissue produces natural fracture lines wherever two lipid regions meet. Because of this, membrane-bounded structures within cells become clearly visible (see photograph).

Today an entire family of electron microscopes has emerged, each demanding its own sophisticated techniques. One recent innovation, the *scanning electron microscope* (SEM), has produced rather startling three-dimensional images of whole subjects. A shower of electrons sweeps back and forth across the subject, scattered in different ways from the subject's surface depending on the nature of that surface. They land on image-producing plates, where they are detected and analyzed electronically. Focused on a screen, the results can be quite unsettling.

An even newer way to probe the incredible and unseen sea of minutiae around us is the *high-voltage electron microscope.* Its penetrating power is so great—1,000,000 volts—that it is not even necessary to slice the cell in order to see inside it. This three-story-high tool also produces three-dimensional images, revealing incredible details not even visible with the best standard EM techniques. Only a few of these gigantic microscopes exist at present, and there is a long line of cytologists—eager to probe more deeply into the world of the cell—waiting their turn to use them. ●

Freeze fracture showing nuclear membrane *(right).*

No one cell of either plant (a) or animal (b) actually shows all the characteristics shown in these composite drawings. These are both *eukaryotic* cells, which means each has a *nucleus*—the more or less spherical body with the double membrane, inside of which the genetic material (here, barely seen as a diffuse *chromatin net*) and the dense *nucleolus* are separated from the rest of the cell. Inside its cell membrane is a semifluid mass called *cytoplasm* in which there are numerous *inclusion bodies* and internal membranes. Both plant and animal cells have *mitochondria* in which food molecules are oxidized, *Golgi bodies* in which manufactured cell materials are collected, *ribosomes* on which proteins are synthesized, and an *endoplasmic reticulum* of variable internal membranes that communicate with both the nucleus and the cell membrane.

But plant cells and animal cells are not alike. One of the most prominent features of the plant cell is its huge vacuoles filled with cell sap, a clear, often pigmented fluid. (Vacuoles occur in animal cells less frequently and are usually small.) Plant cells are encased in a thick, semirigid cell wall. The animal cell, in contrast, owes its more variable shape to a shifting, dynamic fibrous *cytoskeleton* of *microfilaments* and *microtubules*. (Plant cells may have micro-filaments and microtubules at some stages of growth.) Typical animal cell inclusions are *secretion granules* and the complex *centriole*; typical plant cell inclusions are the *plastids*, including the photosynthesizing *chloroplasts* and the *leukoplasts*, in which starch grains are stored; and membrane-bound *peroxisomes* that seem to be involved in protecting the cell from toxic byproducts of photosynthesis. The cell surface of the animal cell may be thrown up into absorbing *microvilli* or grasping *pseudopods*; some animal cells have motile, complex *flagella* or *cilia* with their associated *basal bodies*. Higher plants lack cilia or flagella, although ferns and lower plants have motile sperm cells with flagella. Organelles found exclusively in animal cells are *lysosomes* and *secretion granules*, small membrane-bounded sacs in which powerful enzymes or other materials are stored. By definition, plant cells do not have lysosomes, although some plant cell vacuoles may perform the same functions.

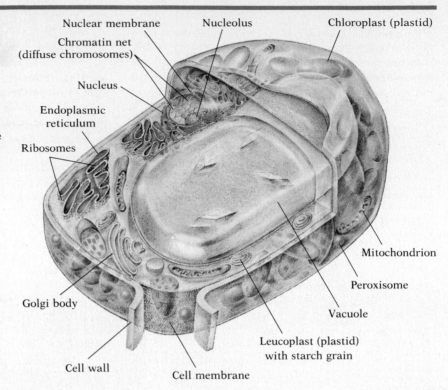

(a) Higher plant

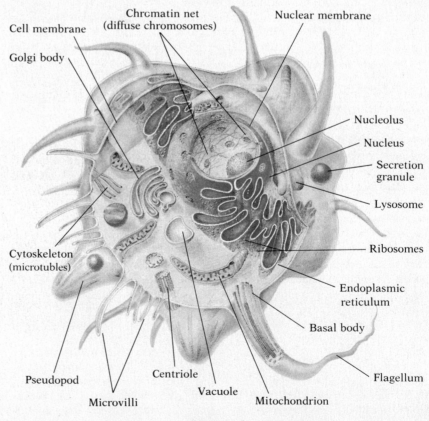

(b) Animal

two major components are proteins and phospholipids. The phospholipids exist in a double layer, with all the uncharged fatty acid tails directed inward. Under the electron microscope, the membranes look like two dark lines separated by a clear area about 5 nm wide (Figure 4.4; see Table 4.1).

The Fluid Mosaic Model.   We have been able to deduce the structure of the cell membrane by pulling together everything known about it and developing a model that accounts for all the facts. It is called the **fluid mosaic model** (described by S. J. Singer). In this model (Figure 4.5a) the phospholipids are visualized as small spheres composed of glycerol, phosphate, and perhaps other organic groups. Each head has two hydrocarbon tails that point inward. This arrangement therefore forms a water-resistant barrier that excludes molecules that are not lipid-soluble. (Recall from Chapter 2 that the polar or charged heads of phospholipids interact with water, which is also polar. The tails, however, are nonpolar or uncharged, and these tend to cling together and repel water.) Large, globular proteins are embedded in this membrane, and are believed to be penetrated by channels, through which water-soluble materials can be passed.

The fluid mosaic model is supported by freeze-fracture preparations (Figure 4.5b and c). When frozen cells split precisely between the tails of phospholipids, the membrane proteins remain on one of the surfaces, while the other surface is pitted with indentations where the proteins had been.

Smaller proteins may be embedded in only the inner or outer membrane layer, and others just lie against one of the layers, not passing through it at all. Some of the proteins associated only with the outer membrane layer are able to interact with hormones, and some membrane proteins may help cells recognize cells of their own type.

The proteins associated only with the inside membrane layer may play some role with the proteins floating in the cell fluid. Some of them are believed to form bridges between the cell membrane and the tiny filaments of protein (microtubules and microfilaments) that help maintain the cell's shape (see Figure 4.6).

Special Molecules of the Membrane Surface. The membrane is composed not only of lipid and protein, but also carbohydrates that, with certain proteins, form *glycoproteins* (sugar proteins). Other carbohydrates may form part of the outer cell membrane in ways that are not well understood, but that may influence how cells interact with each other.

Let's return to a point just mentioned: cells apparently recognize one another on the basis of the carbohydrates and proteins of the membrane. That recognition is important in many processes. Cells must be sensitive to foreign cells to build immunity against them. Also, as an embryo develops, recognition of various cell types assists in the coordinated and orderly development of the different body parts. One startling experiment shows the remarkable ability of cells types to recognize each other. If cells from different tissues are mixed together and allowed to grow on a nutrient medium, the cells will slowly begin to move about until each has found others of its own type. The result is distinct masses of specific tissue types. Such specificity of cell membranes plays a part in blood groupings, cancer defense, and the rejection of transplanted organs.

The Plant Cell Wall

One of the most obvious structures in all plant cells is the cell wall, a rigid, nonliving layer just outside the cell membrane and composed primarily of cellulose and other polymers (see Figures 3.4 and 4.2). Cell walls are composed of tiny fibers (microfibrils) of cellulose chains arranged in layers. Each layer lies at an angle with respect to the one below it, forming a laminated, strong, and porous covering for the cell. Its basic structure is strengthened as it becomes impregnated with hardening substances such as pectin.

Other substances may be added to the cellulose and pectin matrix, depending on the function of

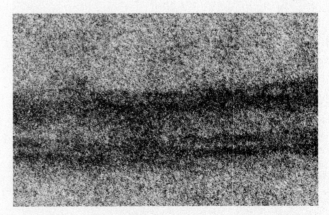

4.4

Electron micrograph of cell membranes. The dark parallel lines are the dense heads of the phospholipids, while the lighter core between represents the fatty acid tails between them.

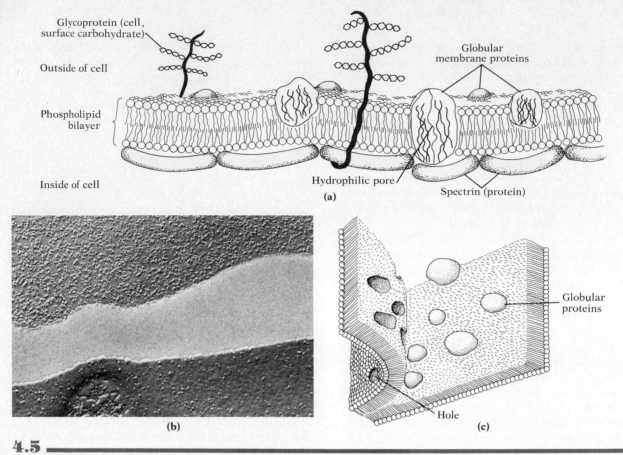

Glycoprotein (cell, surface carbohydrate)

Outside of cell

Phospholipid bilayer

Inside of cell

Globular membrane proteins

Hydrophilic pore

Spectrin (protein)

(a)

(b)

Globular proteins

Hole

(c)

4.5

(a) Fluid mosaic model of a cell membrane. The basic structure includes the phospholipid bilayer with the polar heads on the outside and the double nonpolar tails pointing inward. Numerous globular proteins are embedded throughout the membrane. Hydrophilic pores occur in some. Glycoproteins project their branched heads above the surface and attach to subsurface proteins below. Other subsurface structures, including the microfilaments and microtubules, attach below. (b) Freeze-fracture studies help substantiate the globular protein component of the membrane. These are clearly seen in the illustration where the upper lipid layer is torn away. (c) Note the holes left by the transmembranal proteins as the lipid layer is raised.

the cell. For example, *lignin* is continually secreted into the cellulose of cells in the stems of woody plants, forming a hard, thick, decay-resistant wall. *Suberin*, a waxy substance, is secreted into the outer layer of some plant cells, forming a protective, waterproof layer. The cells of the upper surface of leaves, on the other hand, are waterproofed by another waxy secretion called *cutin*.

The Skeleton of a Cell

Cytology presents one of the clearest areas in which our knowledge is dependent almost directly on advances in technology. For example, by the early 1900s, most of the cell structure visible through the light microscope had been described. With the advent of the TEM, a whole new dimension of the cell, its *ultrastructure*, was revealed. We could see things we never imagined existed.

Even with the new microscope, however, we didn't know much about the cytoplasmic fluid in which the organelles seem to float. We could only vaguely refer to "cytoplasmic matrix" or "ground substance," labels that seemed to convey information, but actually didn't. The problem was that cells had to be sliced into ultrathin sections to permit the electrons from the TEM to pass through, and this procedure demolished any details of the matrix that might have been present.

Technology saved the day again. With the high-voltage electron microscope (see Essay 4.2) we could see a whole new realm of cytoplasmic structure. It was no longer necessary to open the cell to see its contents. Furthermore, we can now see cell contents in three dimensions. So with our new device, we have found within the cell a fascinating and peculiar structural network. Because of its spongy appearance, it has been dubbed the *microtrabecular lattice* (Figure 4.6).

The Microtrabecular Lattice. The **microtrabecular lattice** appears as a mazelike network of hollow fibers, extending throughout the cell, connecting and suspending the organelles in a kind of three-dimensional web. Researchers are already hard at work unlocking the secrets of this grand network, and have proposed both structural and metabolic roles for the lattice.

Some have suggested that certain enzymes may be suspended in a delicate framework. The spatial arrangement of these enzymes might increase the efficiency of those that operate in some special sequence. Thus, enzyme B would be suspended near enzyme A, so that it might more easily interact with the products of A. Enzyme C would be near B, and so forth. Such a structural organization presumably would be much more efficient than random enzyme movement through the cell, long believed to be the way in which enzymes encounter the molecules with which they interact.

Cell Organelles

We have taken a brief look at the cell membrane, the cell wall, the boundaries of the cell, and the microtrabecular lattice. The remaining structures of the cell are called the *organelles*. An **organelle** ("little organ") is any specialized cell structure. Organelles are suspended on the pervasive microtrabecular lattice. The assumption is that cells have

organelles just as more familiar multicellular animals have livers, kidneys, stomachs, and so on.

The Nucleus. The nucleus is not easily summarized because of its very complex functions. To begin, we should note that the nucleus is the most prominent organelle of the cell. It was also one of the first structures to be seen. In fact, the word *nucleus* ("kernel") was first used in 1831, about the time of the development of the cell theory. It is difficult to overestimate the importance of this structure. Since their discovery, nuclei have been found in virtually every type of eukaryotic cell.

The nucleus has two important functions. First, it contains the hereditary information of the cell, the genes. All genetic instructions for reproduction, development, metabolism, and behavior of the species are found within those coiled molecules that reside in the nucleus. In its role as the repository of genetic information, the nucleus has the capacity to produce duplicates of its genetic information and to transmit this set of genetic instructions to new generations of cells.

Second, the nucleus contains the directions controlling certain cellular activities. Its control rests in the fact that it dictates the specific nature of enzymes produced by the cell.

In most cells, there is a dark nucleus laden with the *DNA* of *chromosomes* (Figure 4.7a). In many cells, even darker bodies are seen inside the nuclei. These bodies are the **nucleoli** ("little nuclei"). The

4.6

The microtrabecular lattice is an extensive network of tubular elements that extends throughout the cell. Note that the major organelles of the cell are suspended in this lattice. Also, note the position of the microfilaments and microtubules, the organelles that help determine the cell's strength and shape. This structure can be seen only in micrographs produced by the sort of penetrating, high-voltage electron microscope that eliminates the need for slicing the cell and destroying the lattice.

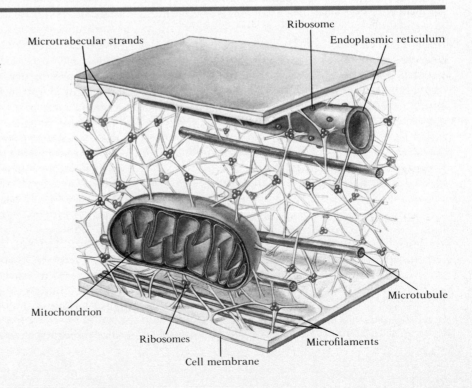

Microtrabecular strands

Ribosome

Endoplasmic reticulum

Mitochondrion

Ribosomes

Cell membrane

Microfilaments

Microtubule

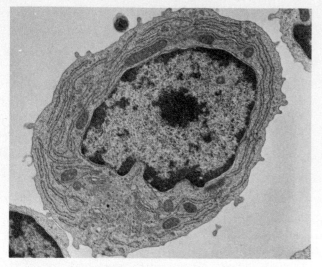 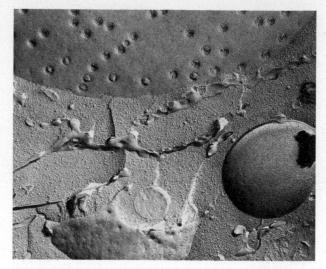

4.7

Electron microscope study of the nucleus. **(a)** The nucleus is the large central sphere with dark patches at its perimeter. The dark body is a nucleolus, a storage site for the RNA of ribosomes. Outside the nucleus we see a region of extensive rough endoplasmic reticulum. **(b)** In the freeze-fracture preparation, the outer nuclear membrane has been pulled away, revealing numerous nuclear pores. These are not simple holes, but are believed to be filled with hydrated proteins.

nucleoli are rich in the nucleic acid called *ribonucleic acid (RNA)*; each nucleolus is essentially a lump from which new ribosomes (small particles involved in protein synthesis) will be made at about the time of the next cell division (see Figure 4.3).

Nuclear structures generally are seen most easily in cells that are undergoing division. This is because the nucleus of a cell not actively dividing is rather featureless. Even then, however, its membrane is clearly visible. The nucleus is enclosed in a double membrane; that is, the nuclear envelope consists of two tightly adjoined membranes, each of which is the familiar lipid-protein bilayer. The two membranes pinch together in scattered places over the nuclear surface to form *nuclear pores*. The word "pore" implies hole, but these are merely pinched indentations that are filled with special proteins forming a semipermeable membrane. The electron microscope suggests that these pores communicate between the nucleoplasm inside the nucleus and the cytoplasm outside the nucleus (see Figure 4.7). Such pores are not unexpected, since we know that very large molecules can pass from the nucleus to the cytoplasm.

The Endoplasmic Reticulum. The **endoplasmic reticulum** (ER) was unknown in the days of the light microscope. In fact, those were the days when cell contents were believed to be a formless, soupy "protoplasm." But because of electron micrographs we now see a complex membrane system that takes up a large part of the cytoplasm of eukaryotic cells, especially those making proteins. We have known for 30 years that this reticulum is a dynamic, ever-changing structure.

The ER is a system of broad folded sheets and tubes that can form channels. The ER membrane is continuous with both the cell membrane and the outer membrane of the nucleus. This indirect contact suggests that the ER may help transport materials between the cell's environment and its nucleus (see Figures 4.3 and 4.8).

There are two types of ER: rough and smooth. Rough ER gets its name from the ribosomes, tightly adhered to one side of the membrane, making it look rough, like coarse sandpaper (Figure 4.8). The channels are formed by two sheets of this "sandpaper" lying side-by-side, their rough surfaces out. Rough endoplasmic reticulum is common in cells that manufacture proteins to be secreted outside the cell.

Smooth ER, on the other hand, lacks ribosomes, and is found primarily in cells that synthesize, secrete, and/or store carbohydrates, steroid hormones, lipids, or other nonprotein products. A great deal of smooth endoplasmic reticulum is found in the cells of the testis, oil glands of the skin, and some hormone-producing gland cells.

The Golgi Bodies. In 1898, Camillo Golgi, an Italian cytologist, discovered that when cells were treated with silver salts, certain peculiar structures appeared in the cytoplasm. The "reticular apparatuses" he described had not been noticed previously, and they didn't show up with any other stains. So for the next 50 years, cytologists argued over whether **Golgi bodies** were really cell structures or just artifacts caused by the silver treatment.

The electron microscope came to the rescue by showing that Golgi bodies are indeed real (Figure 4.9). Furthermore, they had a characteristic structure, regardless of the kind of cell they were found in. They always looked like a cluster of flattened, baglike, membranous sacs lying close to the nucleus and roughly parallel to each other. Naturally, another question arose: What do Golgi bodies do?

The answer was a long time coming, but now it is generally agreed that the Golgi body is derived from the endoplasmic reticulum and that it serves as a sort of packaging center for the cell. Such things in the Golgi bodies as enzymes, proteins, and carbohydrates accumulate in the closed membranous sacs (*vesicles*); and while isolated in this way, they cannot interact with the constituents of the cell fluid.

Lysosomes. **Lysosomes** are roughly spherical, membrane-bounded sacs (Figure 4.10) that contain powerful digestive enzymes, synthesized and packaged by the Golgi apparatus. If these digestive enzymes were released into the cell's cytoplasm, they would quickly digest the cell. Christian de Duve, who first described lysosomes, called them "suicide bags." His poetic fancy was not entirely

unwarranted, since lysosomes sometimes do destroy the cells that bear them. However, this is not necessarily disruptive to the organism. Cell death is a normal part of embryonic development. For example, as the fingers form from paddlelike tissue, the cells between them must die and disappear. In addition, lysosomes might rupture and release their deadly enzymes into a superfluous

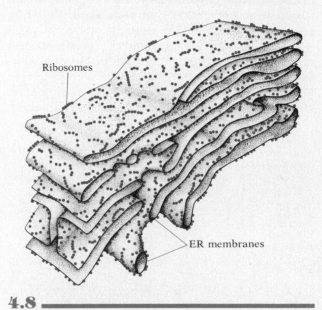

4.8

The rough endoplasmic reticulum (ER) consists of parallel rows of membranes surrounding deep channels. The three-dimensional view suggests the immense amount of folding in the ER. The small round bodies along the ER membranes are ribosomes. A cell containing rough ER is probably important in protein synthesis.

4.9

In this electron microscope view, the Golgi bodies appear as flattened stacks of membranes. The three-dimensional drawing suggests the function of the bodies. Note that the flattened membranous sacs, or *saccules*, seem to fill at either end and "bud off" to form true closed membranous sacs called *vesicles*. The vesicles may contain products originally produced in the ER, but modified and packaged in the Golgi bodies.

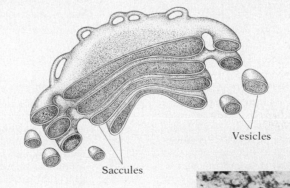

Vesicles

Saccules

cell, or one that is not functioning well. Lysosomes may also aid in digestion within the cell by releasing enzymes that help break down food particles.

Figure 4.11 summarizes some of the interrelationships among the membrane-bound organelles of the cell.

Peroxisomes.   The **peroxisomes** are small subcellular bodies, surrounded by membranes and found in a great variety of organisms, including plants and animals. (In animals, they are most common in liver and kidney cells.) Peroxisomes appear as very dense bodies with a peculiar crystalline core, somewhat resembling a cross-section through a honeycomb. The peroxisomes contain enzymes that, like those of the lysosomes, are important in certain chemical reactions. For example, the enzymes of peroxisomes are known to break down hydrogen peroxide into oxygen and water, protecting cells from its corrosive effect.

Chloroplasts.   Chloroplasts are large, green, round or oval organelles, easily seen through the light microscope. Most obvious in leaf cells, they are also present in all photosynthetic eukaryotes. (*Photosynthesis* is the process by which plants make food by using the energy of light.)

Like the nucleus, chloroplasts are surrounded by a two-layered membrane. Inside the double membrane are layers of flattened, membranous disks known as **thylakoids.** A stack of thylakoids is

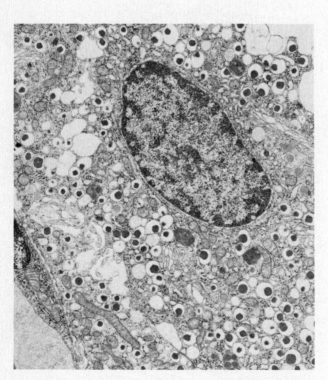

4.10

Lysosomes are storage bodies for powerful hydrolytic enzymes and hence their membranes are exceptionally strong. Their major function is in destroying or digesting. Their targets may include aging organelles within the cell or even the entire cell itself. They may also serve as storage places for unwanted and potentially dangerous substances that cannot be excreted.

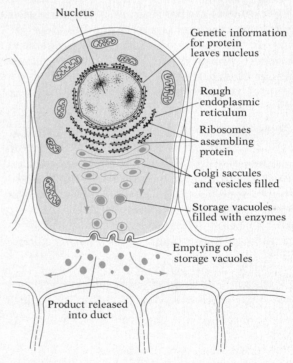

4.11

Secretory action in an exocrine cell: a suggestion for the relationship among rough ER, the Golgi complex, and enzyme secretion. The cell could be any secretory cell such as those from the pancreas or other gland of a mammal. Direct photographic evidence is meager, but the scenario suggests that protein synthesized by ribosomes first enters the membrane spaces of the ER. As the ER fills, it forms Golgi saccules in which the protein is modified into enzymes. As the saccules fill, vesicles bud off and become membrane-bound storage vacuoles. Finally, the vacuoles fuse with the cell membrane and dump their products into a channel, or duct, which will carry the products to the site of action.

Chloroplasts. **(a)** The chloroplasts in an intact plant cell appear as numerous minute, dark spheres. **(b)** At low electron microscope magnification, the inner structure becomes visible. The dark, neat stacks are made up of thylakoids, each stack forming a granum. The dense spheres are grains of starch that have been produced by photosynthesis. **(c)** This three-dimensional drawing shows a cross-sectional view of a chloroplast, with its stacks of disklike thylakoids.

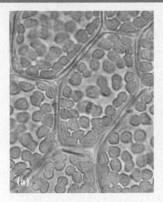

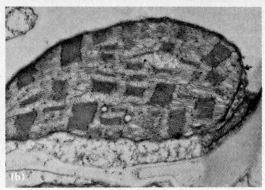

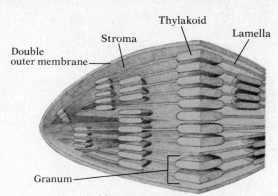

(c) Cross-section of a chloroplast

known as a **granum** (plural, *grana*). There are many grana in a chloroplast, each of which is connected to its neighbors by membranous extensions called **lamellae.** The clear fluid area surrounding the grana and lamellae is the **stroma** (Figure 4.12).

Obviously, the chloroplast is a complex, highly organized structure. As a general rule in biology, there is a close relationship between the structure and function of an organelle. In this case, the intricate process of photosynthesis depends so much on the chloroplast structure that if the structure is altered, the process cannot continue.

Chloroplasts are only one of a group of similar plant structures called **plastids.** Some of the others are not engaged in making food. For example, we find the whitish starch storage bodies known as *leukoplasts* and the brightly colored *chromoplasts* that lend their colors to flowers, fruits, and autumn leaves.

Mitochondria. Mitochondria (singular, *mitochondrion*) are complex, energy-producing organelles that are found in every eukaryotic cell. We will elaborate on this simplistic definition later. But first, we should note that, to an extent, chloroplasts and mitochondria are involved in somewhat opposite processes. This is because chloroplasts use energy to form carbon compounds and oxygen, while mitochondria use carbon compounds and oxygen to produce energy. (These processes are described in Chapters 7 and 8.)

Despite such differences, these two organelles are similar in important ways. Like chloroplasts, mitochondria are enclosed in double membranes. However, mitochondria are much smaller than chloroplasts, partly because the latter usually are somewhat spherical, whereas mitochondria tend to be long (Figure 4.13a). In electron micrographs, a mitochondrion usually appears as an oval structure, with the inner membrane curiously folded.

The folds of the inner mitochondrial membrane are known as **cristae,** and they greatly increase the inner surface area of the organelle. This is important since most of the mitochondrion's biochemical work is done on the cristae, as we will see in later chapters.

Although mitochondria are found in all eukaryotic cells, there are more in some cells than in others. This should be expected since mitochondria are involved in metabolism and since some cells are more metabolically active than others. As you might expect, mitochondria are abundant in muscle cells.

Vacuoles. The term **vacuole** means "empty cavity" in Latin, which impiies a body of nothing. In cytology, however, the term refers to a membrane-bound body with little or no inner structure. Of course, vacuoles are not empty; they hold something, but that something can vary widely, depending on the cell and the organism.

Plant cells generally have more and larger vacuoles than animal cells. In fact, the vacuoles of many types of plant cells dominate the central part of the cell, crowding the other organelles against the cell wall (see Figure 4.3).

The fluids within a plant vacuole may be solutions that include inorganic salts, organic acids, atmospheric gases, sugars, pigments, or any of several other materials. Sometimes the vacuoles are filled with a colorful sap containing blue, red, or purple pigments, some of which will grace the petals of beautiful flowers. Some plants store poisonous compounds in vacuoles. It has been suggested that this stored material helps protect the plant against grazing animals.

Microtubules and the Organelles of Movement. The earth varies from one place to another and, for any organism, some places are likely to be better than others at any given time. Many kinds of organisms are able to move about so as to place themselves in the most advantageous area. Some of these organisms move by cilia and flagella. These both contain peculiar structures called microtubules.

Microtubules, as the name implies, are very tiny tubes (Figure 4.14). They not only help maintain the shape of the cell, but for some, they are important to movement. We knew about them long before we knew of the microtrabecular lattice, but now it is assumed the two work together to maintain the cell's shape. Microtubules are also important parts of centrioles, cilia, and flagella— all organelles involved in certain types of cell movement.

Microtubules are made up of a common protein called *tubulin*. Each tubulin molecule consists of two spheres of slightly different polypeptides

ESSAY 4.3

THE HYPOTHETICAL ORIGIN OF CHLOROPLASTS AND MITOCHONDRIA

O The origin of the complex and highly organized structures that exist within cells has been a continuing puzzle for biologists. How did they evolve? And from what?

One suggestion has proven to be particularly difficult to discount, although it often appears to be an easy target, and is under a constant barrage of criticism that repeatedly falls short of its goal. The idea was conceived by Lynn Margulis, who contends that chloroplasts and mitochondria provide evidence that these energy-harnessing organelles may be the descendants of prokaryotic organisms that invaded other cells early in life's evolutionary history. This idea is known as the **symbiosis hypothesis,** and it is continually gaining support. The hypothesis is that chloroplasts and mitochondria are the descendants of once free-living prokaryotes. These distant ancestors were engulfed by ancient eukaryotic cells, but were not digested. Instead, the three kinds of cells developed a *mutualistic symbiosis*, which simply means that all parties benefited from living together. Eventually, the evolving chloroplasts and mitochondria became unable to exist outside their host cells, and the living-together arrangement evolved into a permanent marriage. Even their reproductive activities are precisely synchronized.

The proponents of the theory note that both chloroplasts and mitochondria are surrounded by a double membrane, very similar to the prokaryotic cell membrane. Also, both of these organelles contain their own DNA. Furthermore, this DNA occurs in simple, circular strands, as does the DNA of prokaryotes, and chloroplasts have their own ribosomes (tiny, protein-synthesizing bodies found in the cytoplasm of eukaryotes). The ribosomes of these two organelles are smaller than those of the eukaryotic cell; in fact, they are about the size and shape of bacterial ribosomes (remember, bacteria are prokaryotic).

There are, of course, other hypotheses to explain the strange relationship between these two organelles and the prokaryotic cells, but so far none is as intuitively satisfying as the symbiosis hypothesis. ●

4.13

The mitochondrion, a site of energy transformation in the cell. **(a)** Mitochondria are barely visible through the light microscope even at its highest magnification, but they appear clearly under low magnification in electron microscopy. In thin sections such as this, the long, tubular mitochondria appear as irregular ellipses and circles. **(b)** Each has two membranes. The inner one is folded repeatedly to form cristae.

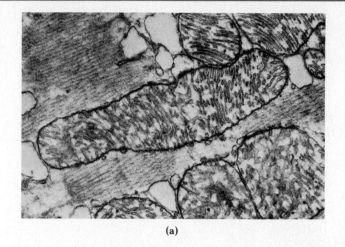

(a)

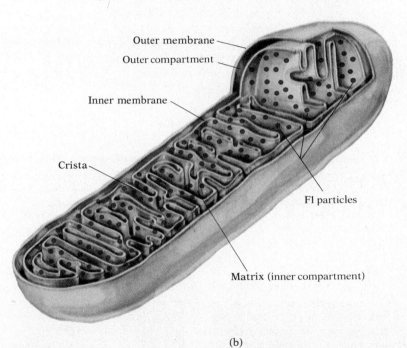

Outer membrane

Outer compartment

Inner membrane

Crista

F1 particles

Matrix (inner compartment)

(b)

4.14

Microtubules occur in many types of cells and apparently serve as a kind of cellular skeleton. With the electron microscope, they appear as long rods (vertical lines in the photograph), which, in cross-section, are found to be hollow. The tubes consist of spherical units of the globular protein tubulin.

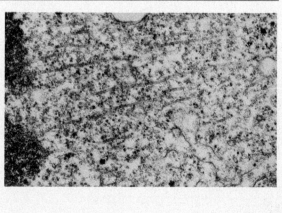

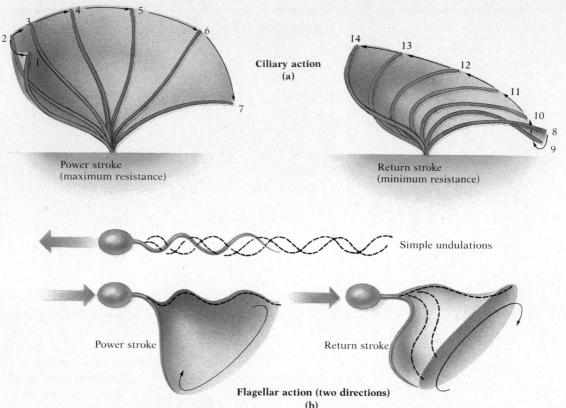

Ciliary action
(a)

Power stroke
(maximum resistance)

Return stroke
(minimum resistance)

Simple undulations

Power stroke

Return stroke

Flagellar action (two directions)
(b)

4.15

Patterns of motion. Cilia **(a)** move some single-celled organisms by a highly coordinated rowing action. Here a single cilium is shown executing both a power stroke (held away from the body for greatest resistance) and a return stroke (bent for the least body resistance). Flagella **(b)** can move in a variety of ways to propel the organism in different directions. An undulating flagellum pushes the cell body through the medium, but it can also pull the body by using a stroke similar to that used by cilia. Various combinations can produce wildly spinning and gyrating movements.

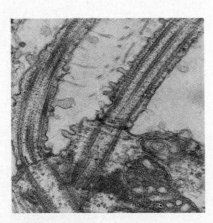
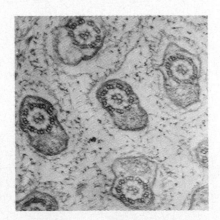

4.16

Three-dimensional view of a cilium as reconstructed through electron microscopy. The longitudinal view reveals the lengthy microtubules that extend to an anchoring base called the *basal body* (also believed to produce the cilium). The cross-section reveals the arrangement around the cilia. Note the nine-plus-two arrangement of microtubule pairs.

4.17

Centrioles. A thin section seen by the electron microscope across the central axis of one of the paired bodies of a centriole. Note the nine sets of triplet microtubules. Centrioles apparently organize the microtubules that help chromosomes separate in cell division.

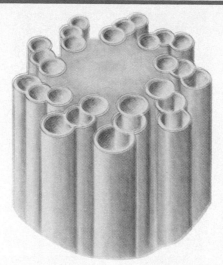

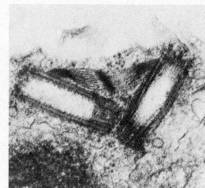

linked together into a figure-eight shape. In the microtubule, the tiny figure-eights join in a regular way to form a hollow tube. Microtubules have the remarkable ability to assemble quickly when needed, and just as quickly, to disintegrate when they are no longer required. They are associated with both structure and movement.

Cilia and Flagella. **Cilia** and **flagella** are fine, hairlike, and movable projections extending from the surfaces of some cells. Both the cilia and flagella appear, superficially, to be outside of the cell, but the cell membrane actually protrudes, covering each of them. Thus in reality the cilia and flagella are outpocketings of the cell.

Structurally, the cilia and flagella are almost identical to one another, differing only in length, numbers per cell, and patterns of motion. Cilia are short, numerous, and move in a characteristic rowing pattern (Figure 4.15). The cilia of all eukaryotes that have cilia—from protists to humans—are identical in size, structure, and movement. Flagella are more variable, but they are always long, fewer in number, and move by undulation (in waves). Both cilia and flagella serve to move the cell through its environment or to move the fluid of the environment past the surface of the cell.

In cross-section, the internal workings of a cilium or a flagellum is seen to consist of a regular array of microtubules. Two microtubules run down the center of the shaft; these are surrounded by nine pairs of microtubules. This universal arrangement is called the "nine-plus-two" pattern. The microtubules in each pair are connected by short arms, and the bending movements of the cilium or flagellum are the result of coordinated sliding movements between microtubule pairs.

Basal Bodies. Beneath each cilium or flagellum, in the cytoplasm of the cell, is a **basal body.** The two central microtubules do not extend into the basal body. The nine paired microtubules do, and each pair is joined by yet a third short microtubule; in cross section, therefore, the basal body shows a ring of nine triplets of microtubules (Figure 4.16), called the "nine-plus-zero" arrangement.

Centrioles. **Centrioles** have the same appearance, in cross-section, as basal bodies. But centrioles are found deep within the cytoplasm and have a very different function: they apparently organize the microtubules that serve to separate chromosomes during cell division (Figure 4.17). Each centriole actually consists of two short "nine-plus-zero" cylinders, held somehow at right angles to one another.

The cells of higher plants have no cilia, flagella, basal bodies, or centrioles. They manage to organize their chromosome-separating fibers perfectly well all the same.

WHY ARE THERE SO MANY KINDS OF CELLS?

Cells come in many sizes and shapes, each with its own limits and abilities. This is not surprising, since we would not expect the cells of a carrot to be identical to those of a clam, or those of a muscle the same as those of a nerve (Figure 4.18).

Not surprisingly, cells with different appearances may also behave differently. For example,

4.18

Diversity in plant and animal cells. These cells are from multicellular organisms, and each is well adapted to a specific role. (Plant cell photo courtesy Carolina Biological Supply.)

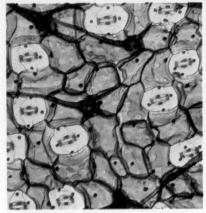
Leaf epidermis cells (covering)

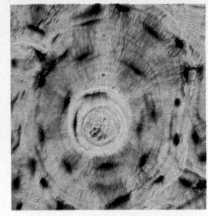
Compact bone cells (support)

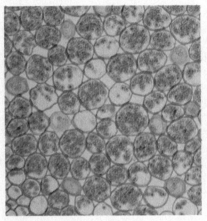
Plant root cells (storage)

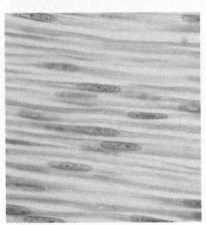
Smooth muscle cells (movement)

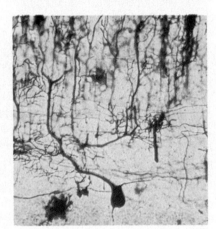
Nerve cells (impulse conduction)

4.19

Prokaryotes **(a)** lack the membrane-surrounded organelles of eukaryotes **(b).** Nevertheless, all of the life functions, including self-replication, are carried on in these simpler cells.

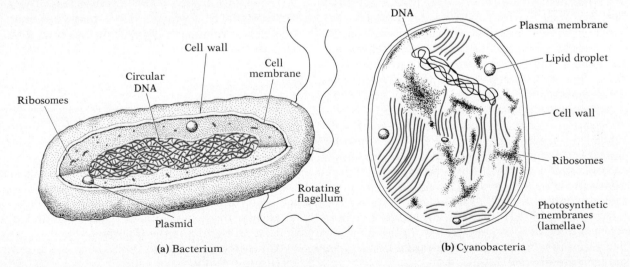

(a) Bacterium

(b) Cyanobacteria

some are highly irritable—that is, they respond quickly to environmental changes. Some can contract, others secrete fluids, and still others have long tails and can swim. Such variety indicates the great advantage of multicellularity: **specialization.** An organism living in a complex environment is better equipped to meet different demands if it comprises different kinds of cells, each with its own special abilities. Imagine the advantage of having some cells that can react to light, others that can distinguish pain, and yet others that can contract and therefore move you toward the light and away from the pain. Evolutionarily, we could expect groups of cells to become highly specialized for very specific functions, increasingly adapting the organisms they compose to better exist in a competitive world.

The Prokaryotic Cell, A Different Matter

Now let's consider simpler kinds of cells, the kinds believed to be more similar to the ancestral types. These are the prokaryotic cells. **Prokaryotes** ("before the nucleus") have a simpler cellular organization than do the eukaryotes but, since they are represented solely by single-celled bacteria this should not be unexpected. The prokaryotes are particularly interesting because they are believed to be similar to the earliest forms of cellular life on Earth, the forms that probably gave rise to today's life.

Characteristics of the Prokaryotic Cell. The prokaryotes are unquestionably cellular, but in most instances their cells are smaller and quite unlike those of eukaryotes. Like plant cells, they are surrounded by a cell wall, but the walls of the two groups are of quite different chemical composition. Also, the organelles of the prokaryote cell are not likely to be surrounded by membranes, and there is no nucleus. The DNA (genetic material) of a eukaryotic cell is found in numerous linear, protein-rich *chromosomes*, whereas the genetic material of a prokaryotic cell forms a single, continuous circle of nearly naked DNA. That is, the long DNA molecule is connected at the two ends to form a loop. Some prokaryotes have flagella, but these, too, are quite different structurally from those of the eukaryotes. To illustrate, prokaryotic flagella do not contain microtubules, but, instead, are solid and crystalline. What's more, they rotate. This may be the only rotary structure in any form of life. There are other differences between prokaryotes and eukaryotes (Figure 4.19), some of which we will mention later, but we can already see just how distinctive the prokaryotes are. Table 4.2 compares prokaryotes to plant and animal cells.

TABLE 4.2

Key differences among the cells of prokaryotes, plants, and animals

Feature	Prokaryotic Cell	Higher Plant Cell	Animal Cell
Cell membrane	External only (two, separated by periplasmic space)	External and internal	External and internal
Supporting structure	None seen	Protein cytoskeleton	Protein cytoskeleton
Nuclear membrane	Absent	Present	Present
Chromosomes	Single, circular, DNA only	Multiple, linear, complexed with protein	Multiple, linear, complexed with protein
Membrane-bounded organelles	Absent except for mesosome	Many, including mitochondria, large vacuoles, and chloroplasts	Many, including mitochondria, lysosomes
Endoplasmic reticulum	Absent	Present	Present
Ribosomes	Smaller, free	Larger, some membrane-bound	Larger, somewhat membrane-bound
Cell wall	Peptidoglycan	Cellulose	None
Flagella or cilia (when present)	Solid, rotating	Never present*	Microtubular (nine-plus-two pattern)
Ability to engulf solid matter	Absent	Absent*	Present, extensive movable membranes
Centrioles	Absent	Absent*	Present

*Although absent in higher plants, these features are found in more primitive plants. Apparently they have been lost in the course of evolutionary change.

Summary

Cell Theory

According to the cell theory, nearly all organic beings originate from and are composed of cells. All processes necessary to life are carried out by cells. The cell's regulatory membrane enables oxygen and nutrients to enter, and waste products to be expelled easily. Cell size seems to be related to the ratio of surface area to volume, a ratio that appears to favor smaller-sized cells. The structure and function of cells are studied by cytologists, who use a variety of microscopes.

Cell Structure

Cells are composed of a cell membrane, cytoplasm, and nucleoplasm. The fluid mosaic model describes the function and structure of the cell's selectively permeable membrane. Cells recognize one another on the basis of the carbohydrates and proteins in their membranes.

Plant cells have a rigid, nonliving cell wall composed of tiny fibers of cellulose chains arranged in layers. Substances such as pectin, lignin, suberin, and cutin strengthen and waterproof the cell wall.

The cytoplasm of the cell contains the microtrabecular lattice, a network of hollow fibers that extends throughout the cell. Organelles are suspended and connected in this network. The lattice organization appears to increase the efficiency of enzyme activity within the cell.

Cell organelles are specialized structures that play specific roles. The most prominent organelle is the nucleus, which contains the cell's genetic material and directions for controlling cell activities.

The endoplasmic reticulum, a system of broad, folded sheets and tubes forming channels, is a complex membrane system continuous with the cell membrane and the outer membrane of the nucleus. This organelle may be either rough or smooth and seems to help transport materials from the cell's environment to the nucleus. Golgi bodies are derived from the endoplasmic reticulum and serve as a type of storage center for enzymes, proteins, carbohydrates, and the like. Lysosomes, formed by Golgi bodies, contain powerful enzymes that destroy inoperative cells. Peroxisomes, small cellular bodies surrounded by membranes, seem to be a special class of lysosomes.

Chloroplasts and mitochondria are essential for synthesizing and metabolizing nutrients in cells. Both plant and animal cells contain vacuoles, membrane-bound bodies with little or no inner structure, which assist in capturing food particles and expelling wastes. According to the symbiosis hypothesis, such organelles as chloroplasts and mitochondria are descendents of symbiotes that entered primitive cells long ago.

The organelles of movement include centrioles, cilia, and flagella; microtubules are an important component of these structures. Cilia move in a rowing pattern, while flagella move by undulation. Beneath each cilium or flagellum is a basal body. Centrioles look like basal bodies, but are found deeper in the cytoplasm, and serve to organize the microtubules that function in cell division.

Why Are There So Many Kinds of Cells?

Cell specialization permits multicellular organisms to adapt in ways unavailable to one-celled types. Prokaryotes (bacteria) are small, single cells, lacking membrane-bounded organelles. Their DNA is circular without protein, and cell walls are of peptidoglycan.

Key Terms

cell	endoplasmic reticulum	cristae
cell theory	Golgi body	symbiosis hypothesis
cell wall	lysosome	vacuole
cytoplasm	peroxisome	microtubule
nucleus	chloroplast	cilia
nucleoplasm	thylakoid	flagella
selectively permeable	granum	basal body
fluid mosaic model	lamellae	centriole
microtrabecular lattice	stroma	specialization
organelle	plastid	prokaryote
nucleoli	mitochondria	

Review Questions

1. State the two basic propositions of the *cell theory* and list the contributions of Hooke, Schleiden, Schwann, and Virchow. (p. 49)

2. Describe what happens to the surface-volume relationship as cells (or any three dimensional objects) get progressively larger. Of what significance to the cell is its surface area? (p. 51)

3. Prepare a simple drawing of the cell membrane, indicating the arrangement of the phospholipid bilayer, surface proteins, and transmembranal proteins. (pp. 55–56)

4. What, essentially, is the microtrabecular lattice, and how was it discovered? (pp. 56–57)

5. What are the two principal roles of the nucleus? What well-known nuclear macromolecule is actually responsible for these roles? (p. 57)

6. List the functions of rough and smooth endoplasmic reticulum, Golgi bodies, lysosomes, and peroxisomes. (pp. 58–60)

7. Briefly describe the functions of the chloroplasts and mitochondria. In what way are their functions opposite? How does their complexity compare with that of other cellular organelles? (pp. 60–61)

8. What structural and functional characteristics do centrioles, cilia, and flagella have in common? (pp. 62–65)

9. List four ways in which prokaryotic cells differ from eukaryotic cells. (p. 67)

Cell Transport

5

The living cell is a changing, sensitive, and responsive structure. But it is important to realize that it changes, senses, and responds according to the balance and coordination of the substances and organelles within the cell. Thus, because of the complex arrangement of the internal cell structure, it has the ability to adapt to a wide range of environmental variables, and part of its rapid adjustment to changing conditions is due to the efficiency of the surrounding membrane. The nature of the cell's interior is largely dependent upon what is and is not allowed in and out of the cell. The importance of being covered by a selective membrane becomes increasingly clear.

In this chapter we will see how material enters and leaves cells, and how critical molecules move from one cell to the next.

MOVEMENT ACROSS THE CELL MEMBRANE

The cell membrane is exquisitely adapted to its function of accepting some substances while rejecting others. The membrane performs its gatekeeper tasks in a variety of ways that generally fall within two categories: (1) passive transport and (2) active transport.

These two categories are essentially very different because they involve different energy sources. One is expensive; the other is not. In passive trans-
port, thermal (heat) energy of the cellular environment, alone, provides the energy—much of it quite random in nature. Active transport, however, requires work on the part of the cell, and it costs something in terms of the precious energy the cell has stored.

Passive Transport

Passive transport involves four distinct kinds of movement of substances, none of which require an energy expenditure on the part of the cell. The four processes are diffusion, facilitated diffusion, bulk flow, and osmosis.

Diffusion. **Diffusion** is the *net* movement of ions or molecules from regions of higher concentration to regions of lower concentration (down a **concentration gradient**). In biological systems, it is an especially important way for ions and small molecules to get around. Diffusion enables substances to cross cell membranes, and to move within the cytoplasm.

Diffusion occurs because the molecules of any liquid or gas move constantly and randomly, bumping into each other and rebounding into new paths. The warmer the gas or liquid is, the faster its molecules move. Thus, the diffusion rate increases with the addition of heat. The movement of individual molecules is still random, but if the molecules are concentrated in one place, heat accelerates the net movement of those molecules—always in accord with the same physical principles, from the region of higher concentration to regions of lower concentration. This *net* movement continues (by pure chance) until the distribution of molecules is random. Once the molecules are randomly dispersed, there will be no further *net* movement in any direction. Diffusion, then, is a random process by which molecules move away from their place of higher concentration by their own thermal energy until equilibrium is reached.

In living systems highly dependent on diffusion as a means of transporting critical molecules, a number of factors can influence the system's efficiency. Such factors are heat, the steepness of the gradient (relative concentrations), and the size and charges of the ions or molecules (Figure 5.1).

Facilitated Diffusion. Facilitated diffusion is similar to simple diffusion in that it involves thermal energy, and the net movement of molecules is always from regions of higher concentration to regions of lower concentration, particularly across membranes. However, it differs from simple diffusion in that certain kinds of molecules move more easily than others. The types of molecules that move across such barriers at this accelerated rate are helped by special carriers called *permeases*. These carriers are embedded in the cell membrane, but just how they work remains a mystery. We do know that certain molecules and ions are quickly ushered across the membranes in which the permeases are found.

The Movement of Water.   The development of life on this planet is intimately associated with the abundance of a simple molecule, H_2O. Water is, indeed, important to both the development and sustenance of life. So you can imagine that the various life forms have devised ways of moving it around, shifting it to places where it will be of greatest advantage. Sometimes energy is expended in such movement but, often, since life is essentially opportunistic, it simply exploits the natural tendencies of water to move of its own accord.

Let's now consider two specific processes by which water is moved: *bulk flow* and *osmosis*. These are not necessarily isolated and mutually exclusive processes—they may interact with one another in very precise and coordinated ways.

Bulk Flow. Bulk flow refers to the mass movement of fluids. The amount of water and the speed with which it is moved cannot be accounted for by diffusion or facilitated diffusion alone. Instead, the bulk flow of water is caused by differences in *water potential*. **Water potential** is simply the potential ability of water to move or, more precisely, to do work. Let's consider a familiar example. A great

deal of water can accumulate behind a dam, and it is higher than the river bed below the dam. Thus, compared to the river, it has a greater water potential. It can, indeed, do a great deal of "work" on villages downstream. In this case, we know that, because of gravity, the water will move from a region of greater water potential (behind the dam) to one of lesser water potential (the river bed below). Gravity, however, is not the only energy source that can increase water potential.

Simple *pressure* also can increase water potential. For example, when water is pumped to an elevated holding tank, a mechanical pump creates greater water potential than the water in the elevated tank.

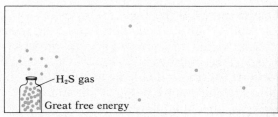

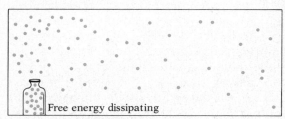

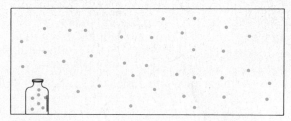

Equilibrium:
no free energy, no net movement in any direction

5.1 ▬▬▬▬▬▬▬▬▬▬

Diffusion of a gas. A container of hydrogen sulfide (H_2S) has been uncorked in one corner of a room. The container contains a higher concentration of molecules than the room. Thus, the gas has great free energy. Molecular motion is in all directions, but the greatest movement in any direction is toward areas where there are fewer molecules of H_2S. As movement continues, a concentration gradient is established, with the greatest concentration still in the container. Finally, a state of equilibrium is reached when the distribution of molecules is random throughout the bottle and the room.

Bulk flow also can be influenced by *substances in solution* (*solutes*). When comparing solutions of different strengths, remember that pure water has the greatest water potential, while water containing molecules or ions in solution has lower water potential; the more solute, the less water potential. This means that the bulk flow between two solutions is toward the water that has more substances in solution. The principle point to remember about bulk flow is that water always moves from regions of greater water potential to regions of lesser water potential. The concept of bulk flow is important to biologists because it helps them predict the direction in which water will move in living systems. Now let's consider a special case of how solutes can influence water potential.

Osmosis: A Special Case. Osmosis is one of those words that has been borrowed from science and then twisted and misused beyond recognition. The next time you hear the word in cocktail conversation, ask the speaker to define it. You may make a lifelong enemy if you smirk and say, "No, osmosis is the bulk flow of water across membranes, from an area of greater water potential to one of lesser potential." Instead, try explaining this way: "You see, when two solutions are separated by a selectively permeable membrane—that is, a membrane that allows only water to pass—the water will move from the solution with the greater concentration of water molecules through the membrane to the solution with the lesser concentration of water molecules. The concentration of water molecules is *lower* on the side of the membrane that contains the *higher* solute concentrations. Further, it doesn't really make any difference what kind of ion or molecule is in solution; it could be sugar, amino acids, or any other soluble substance. The water moves only according to the relative number of water molecules on either side of the membrane." (Figure 5.2.) This way, you will make fewer enemies, because your audience will have left.

But in case anyone should stay around, you should be prepared to answer questions, since osmosis is a very simple principle that, at first, may seem hard to understand. So, let's ask, how long does osmosis go on? Theoretically, it continues until the water potential (water concentration) on both sides of the membrane is equal. This equilibrium rarely occurs in cells; metabolism demands constant change and there is a constant ebb and flow of molecules across any living membrane. In the system shown in Figure 5.2, equilibrium can never be reached because the solutes cannot cross the membrane. Of course, this means that there will always be greater water potential on the side

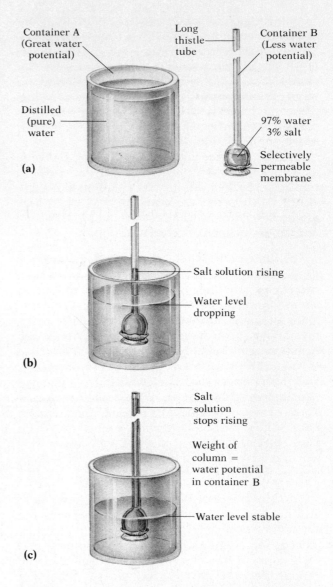

5.2

Osmosis. Container A holds distilled water, the fluid with the highest water potential. A second container, a thistle tube, holds a solution of 3% table salt and 97% distilled water. The tube has proportionately less water, so its water potential is lower. A semipermeable membrane covers the mouth of the test tube. (Water can pass through it but salt cannot.) When the tube is immersed in the distilled water, the salt solution rises in the tube as distilled water flows in. The water level rises until the water potential on either side of the membrane equalizes.

However, such an equilibrium can never be reached in this experiment. As long as the membrane is impermeable to salt, the water potential of the salt solution will be less than that of distilled water. However, when the weight of the solution equals the water potential, the net movement of water ceases.

with the distilled water. So does osmosis simply continue until that side goes dry? Remember, forces other than solute concentration can influence bulk flow. And, here, one of those other forces comes into play. The sheer weight of the rising column of solute becomes so heavy that its pressure finally equals the water potential of the distilled water. The net movement of water then stops. At this point we are able to measure **osmotic pressure,** the amount of force necessary to equal the water potential. This may seem a bit roundabout, so let's go back to the real world, and consider an example from plant cells.

Turgor and Wilting. The large central vacuoles of plant cells contain water and various solutes called *cell sap.* Each vacuole is surrounded by a semipermeable membrane and so is subject to osmosis. Thus, when water potential outside the cell is greater than that in the vacuole, water enters. This causes the vacuole to swell, pressing the rest of the cell contents against the cell wall. Animal cells lack cell walls and, if one is subjected to such conditions, it would simply swell and burst. But the plant cell wall is extremely strong, so it holds. As the size of the vacuole continues to increase, it meets increased resistance until, finally, the pressures are equalized and no more water can enter. This special kind of osmotic pressure is called **turgor pressure,** the force of water from within the cell. Turgor pressure is the force that holds leaves and soft stems of plants erect. Should turgor pressure decrease because of a reduction of water within the vacuole, the result is wilting.

Cells and Solute Conditions: Tonicity. The osmotic environment of cells is described in terms of **tonicity.** Biologists use specific terms to describe the osmotic conditions surrounding cells. For example, environmental conditions are **isotonic** (*iso,* same; *tonic,* tension) when the relative concentrations of water and solutes on either side of the cell membrane are equal, which, of course, means the water potential is equal. In isotonic systems, there is no net movement of water molecules across a membrane.

On the other hand, when the water outside a cell contains less solute than does the water inside (meaning the water potential outside is greater), the environment is called **hypotonic** (*hypo,* low). Cells immersed in hypotonic solutions tend to swell. For example, blood cells in tap water will swell and rupture, leaving limp "ghosts" of their membranes.

When the water outside the cell contains more solutes than that on the inside (resulting in the water potential outside being lower), the condition is called **hypertonic** (*hyper,* more or above). Cells in a hypertonic solution tend to lose water. Note that the terms *isotonic, hypotonic,* and *hypertonic* refer to the solute. Furthermore, they refer to conditions outside the cell (Figure 5.3).

Active Transport

Since life is such a delicate and constantly adjusting process, it is not surprising to find cells moving, shifting, adding, and expelling molecules. Thus, we often find great accumulations of some molecule inside or outside a cell. For example, mammalian red blood cells move sodium ions out and accumulate potassium ions. Furthermore, they do it by working against the concentration gradient. In such cases, the substances do not move by passive transport. Similarly, many marine fish secrete sodium from their gills, even though they must work against a powerful concentration gradient, because the sea is much saltier than is their blood. It is important to understand the significance of so simple an act as molecules being moved against a concentration gradient. It might crudely be compared to rolling boulders uphill. Work must be done, and work requires the expenditure of energy. This is why this type of movement is called **active transport.** Let's take a closer look at how molecules are shifted around at an energy cost.

Membrane Pumps. We really don't understand many aspects of active transport. What is known, however, is that some substances are carried across membranes against a gradient by proteins embedded in the membranes. Many cells have *sodium/potassium exchange pumps,* membrane carriers that exchange sodium ions for potassium ions. The pump uses energy in the form of a high-energy fuel molecule called *ATP* (described in Chapter 6). With each molecule of ATP used, three sodium ions are pumped outward and two potassium ions are pumped inward. The system provides a higher concentration of potassium inside the cell and a higher concentration of sodium outside the cell. Figure 5.4 is an artist's conception of the exchange pump.

Active transport mechanisms like the exchange pump were once perceived as being rather unusual, but research has revealed so many pumplike mechanisms that active transport is now believed to be a basic activity of nearly all membranes.

Endocytosis and Exocytosis. Some forms of active transport are active indeed, with clearly visible movement of the cell membrane. One of these, *endocytosis,* was first observed in feeding amoebas. When the amoeba touches a particle of food, the

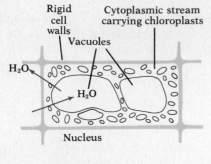

Rigid cell walls
Cytoplasmic stream carrying chloroplasts
Vacuoles
H₂O
H₂O
Nucleus

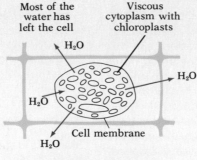

Most of the water has left the cell
Viscous cytoplasm with chloroplasts
H₂O
H₂O
H₂O
H₂O
Cell membrane

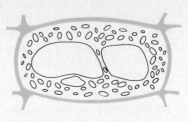

(a) Leaf in pond water, its normal hypotonic environment produces normal turgor pressure

(b) Leaf in 3% NaC1 solution, which is hypertonic to the cell (loss of turgor)

(c) Leaf in distilled water (increased turgor pressure)

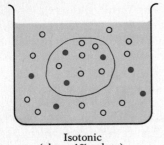

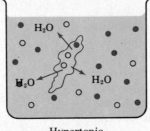

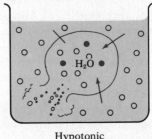

Isotonic (about 1% solute)

Hypertonic (3% solute)

Hypotonic (100% H₂O)

(d) Animal cell remains intact

(e) Animal cell shrinks as water leaves

(f) Animal cell swells up and bursts

5.3

Movement of water into and out of cells. The plant cell **(a)** contains two large central water vacuoles. In its normal watery environment the cell remains turgid, with its membrane-bound cytoplasm pressed against the cell wall like an inflated innertube in a truck tire.

(b) Placing the leaf in a 3% salt solution subjects it to a hypertonic environment and water, now in greater concentration inside the cell, will flow out. The result is that the vacuole empties and the cell membrane pulls free from the semirigid cell wall. Like a semirigid truck tire with a blown innertube, the cell wall doesn't collapse outright; but without pressure from within, it loses much of its strength and rigidity. The leaf wilts.

(c) If the plant cell is placed in distilled water, a hypotonic environment, the turgor pressure within it will rise as water flows inward. But the cell will swell only slightly, like a moderately overinflated truck tire. The cell wall is sufficiently strong to prevent the cell from bursting.

(d) Within a multicellular animal, the cell is bathed with isotonic tissue fluid, and its shape is determined by its flexible, internal cytoskeleton. **(e)** If placed in (hypertonic) 3% saline, the entire animal cell shrinks, much as the plant cell protoplast shrinks within its cell walls. **(f)** In (hypotonic) distilled water, the typical animal cell swells like a balloon and may burst.

cell membrane buckles inward. The depression continues until a vacuole is pinched off from the surface. It is now a membranous sac, with the inner surface of the vacuole membrane formed from the outer surface of the cell membrane. So, material that was outside the cell is now enclosed by the vacuole. Digestive enzymes are secreted into the vacuole and the food is broken down. The resulting nutrient molecules will be passed, by active transport, through the vacuole membrane and out into the cytoplasm (Figure 5.5).

Endocytosis is a general term that includes two

processes. If the vacuole engulfs solid material, the process is called *phagocytosis;* if it engulfs dissolved materials, such as proteins, it is called *pinocytosis.*

The exact opposite process is equally interesting. It is **exocytosis,** a process by which cells expel materials (see Figure 5.5). The material is enclosed in a vacuole that moves through the cytoplasm and fuses with the cell membrane, whereupon it is released to the outside. Many kinds of cells utilize such processes, from the single-celled amoeba to certain cells in humans that secrete hormones.

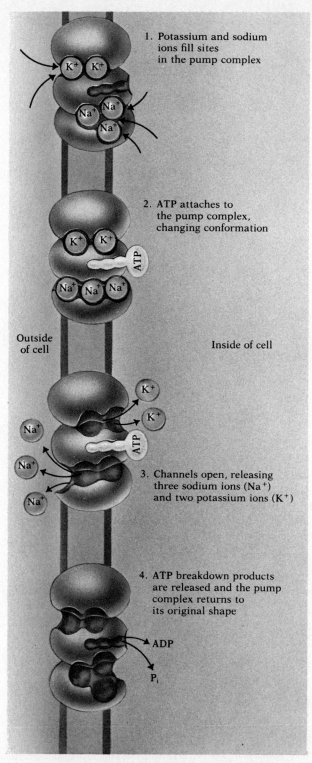

1. Potassium and sodium ions fill sites in the pump complex

2. ATP attaches to the pump complex, changing conformation

Outside of cell

Inside of cell

3. Channels open, releasing three sodium ions (Na⁺) and two potassium ions (K⁺)

4. ATP breakdown products are released and the pump complex returns to its original shape

ADP

Pᵢ

5.4

The sodium-potassium exchange pump uses one molecule of ATP (a cellular energy carrier) to pump three sodium ions out of the cell and two potassium ions into the cell (artist's conception).

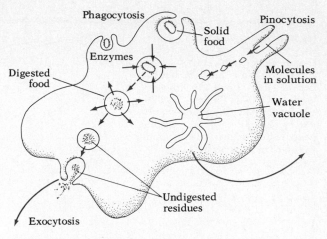

Phagocytosis — Solid food — Pinocytosis
Enzymes
Digested food
Molecules in solution
Water vacuole
Undigested residues
Exocytosis

5.5

Active transport and vacuoles. A very busy amoeba is demonstrating both endocytosis (phagocytosis and pinocytosis) and exocytosis in all their variations. At the upper region, it is engulfing a small ciliate protozoan by phagocytosis. At the right, a channel has surrounded a solution of large molecules by pinocytosis. Eventually, both processes will create a vacuole from the cell membrane. At the lower side of the amoeba, the undigested residue from a food vacuole is being expelled by exocytosis.

Gap Junctions

One problem in describing cellular processes piecemeal, as we are doing, is that it lends an artificial impression of simplicity. For example, it may seem that cells are isolated entities that simply shift for themselves and maintain independence from surrounding cells. This may be true for one-celled creatures, but in other organisms, it is not. For example, in multicellular organisms, the cytoplasm of adjacent cells is often in direct contact. This, of course, would enable one cell to quickly and effectively influence the next and encourage a rapid and precise adaptive response. The contact is made through special membranous passages called **gap junctions** (Figure 5.6).

At first these cellular passages were thought to be exceptional, existing in only very special cells. But they now have been found in so many kinds of tissues that they are believed to be the rule rather than the exception. For example, gap junctions have been found in human epithelial, hepatic, urinary bladder, pancreatic, and renal cells.

Perhaps gap junctions should not have been so unexpected. We have known for years that they exist in plant cells, where they are known as *plas-*

75

(a) Model of a *gap junction*, an organelle that allows the direct exchange of nutrients and other substances through channels that pass between cells. Each channel is created by a pair of "pipes," each pipe consisting of six dumbbell-shaped protein subunits. (b) Gap junctions make the cytoplasm of many multicellular tissues effectively continuous.

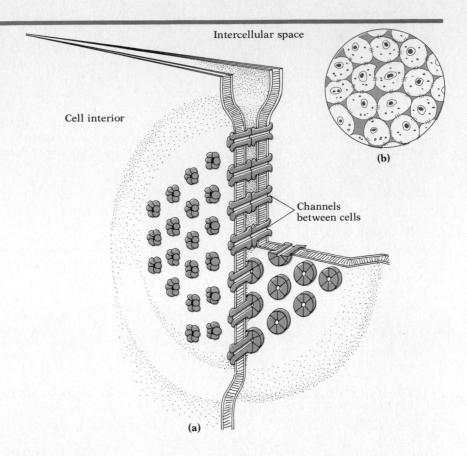

Intercellular space

Cell interior

Channels between cells

(b)

(a)

modesmata. Perhaps such lines of communication are more important in plant cells, since they are separated by the tough, nonliving cell walls. Plasmodesmata appear as thin strands of cytoplasm that pass from cell to cell through narrow holes in the cell walls.

We now know that many kinds of molecules pass through gap junctions. The growing list includes ions, steroid hormones, amino acids, simple sugars, vitamins, and even certain genetic materials called *nucleotides.* Obviously, the gap junction is important in moving molecules from one cell to the next in multicellular organisms.

We have seen, then, that even the simplest organisms must deal with the problem of moving molecules.

Summary

Movement Across the Cell Membrane

The cell membrane uses passive and active transport to allow some substances to move through the membrane freely while rejecting others. Passive transport involves the use of the cell's thermal energy, while active transport consumes some of the energy stored in the cell.

Passive transport involves four kinds of movement: diffusion, facilitated diffusion, bulk flow, and osmosis. Diffusion, which occurs in living and nonliving systems, is the net movement of ions or molecules down a concentration gradient toward random distribution. In facilitated diffusion, the diffusion of selected substances is accelerated by membranal carriers.

Bulk flow is the mass movement of fluids across a membrane due to differences in water potential. Gravity, pressure, and solutes can influence the rate and direction of bulk flow.

Osmosis is the bulk flow of water from an area of greater water potential to one of lesser water potential. It occurs when an unequal concentration of solutes produces a difference in water potential. Osmotic pressure is the amount of force necessary to stop the net flow of water. Leaves and soft plant stems are kept erect by osmotic or turgor pressure. The environment of cells is described as either isotonic, hypotonic, or hypertonic, depending on the relative concentrations of solute and solvent (water) inside and outside the cell.

Active transport is carried out at some energy cost to the cell, particularly since, in some cases, the cell must work against the concentration gradient by using membrane pumps. These pumps are proteins embedded in the cell membrane that act as carriers to alter concentrations of molecules.

Other forms of active transport involve movement of the cell membrane itself. In endocytosis, an organism such as an amoeba is able to bring food particles into the membrane via a food vacuole. In exocytosis, unwanted material is enclosed in a vacuole that moves through the cytoplasm and fuses with the cell membrane, whereupon the contents are ejected from the cell.

Gap junctions enable cells to communicate with one another through special membranal passages. In plant cells, plasmodesmata serve as gap junctions. A wide variety of molecules can pass through these junctions in all multicellular organisms.

Key Terms

passive transport	osmosis	hypertonic
diffusion	osmotic pressure	active transport
concentration gradient	turgor pressure	membrane pump
facilitated diffusion	tonicity	endocytosis
bulk flow	isotonic	exocytosis
water potential	hypotonic	gap junction

Review Questions

1. Compare (naming similarities and differences) the movement of ions or molecules in diffusion with their movement in facilitated diffusion. (pp. 70–71)

2. Consider the following situation and apply it to the related questions: A semipermeable membrane is stretched across a container, separating two sides. It is permeable only to water. On the left (side A) is distilled water. On the right (side B) is a 3.0% salt (NaCl) solution. (pp. 71–73)
   a. On which side do we find the greatest water potential?
   b. In which direction will there be a net movement of water?
   c. Will the system eventually reach equilibrium or randomness? Explain.
   d. Is this an example of bulk flow? Osmosis? Both?

3. What is turgor? How is it important to plants? (p. 73)

4. In question 2 above, on which side of the membrane do we find a hypertonic solution? Hypotonic? What would one have to do to make the system isotonic? (p. 73)

5. What two specific clues should we look for in determining whether cellular transport was occurring through an active process? (p. 73)

6. Briefly explain how the sodium/potassium exchange "pump" functions. (p. 73)

7. Using the terms *endocytosis*, *phagocytosis*, and *exocytosis*, explain how the amoeba makes use of its membrane in feeding, digestion, and waste elimination. (pp. 73–74)

8. What are gap junctions, and how do they facilitate transport within a dense layer of cells? (pp. 75–76)

Energy and the Cell

6

We humans often seem to enjoy maligning ourselves, being particularly fond of stressing our unusual savagery. But if humans did not walk the earth, would the planet be a gentler place? Probably not. After all, *life demands energy*, and many living things must derive energy from other living things. The problem is, if an organism wishes to harvest the energy stored in another organism's body, that body must be disrupted, hurt, and, very likely, killed. The unending search for energy can indeed be brutal. Those organisms seeking energy and those avoiding being exploited have developed many ways to carry out these tasks. Dainty plants growing silently on a flower-strewn hillside (Figure 6.1) may be relentlessly engaged in a battle for survival as they compete for the sun's rays and the earth's minerals. Yet after they have been blessed by the sun and are able to manufacture food, they must often yield that sequestered energy to some casual grazer. In turn, the grazers, as well as other plant eaters, fall prey to some sharp-toothed carnivore seeking the energy held in the grazers' bodies, energy previously derived from those hillside plants. Eventually, though, even those muscular creatures with the sharp teeth answer the ultimate call, and the energy they once stored becomes the salvation of small microbes as they break down a ponderous corpse.

The name of the game, of course, is energy. Energy is a far greater influence in our lives, our societies, and our politics than we know. Let's now see if we can justify that statement. We will first consider energy at the cellular level, keeping the larger picture in mind, so that the basic message does not escape.

ENERGY

The basic message is that the currency of life is energy. The primary tendency of matter is to become randomized, scattered, diffused, and disorganized. However, life depends upon a high degree of organization. It would appear, then, that the very processes of life fly in the face of basic physical laws. However, such is not the case. Life is able to exist within these laws because it can overcome the basic tendency toward disorganization by utilizing energy. And since organization is the hallmark of life, we are inevitably led to a consideration of the behavior of energy.

What are the characteristics of energy? How does it behave? The concept of energy is extremely elusive, so let's take a shortcut. *Energy is the ability to do work.* It is this work, this energy expenditure, that keeps the processes of life organized.

6.1

The bodies of many living things contain nutrients that are needed by other living things. The animal whose body is sought usually shows little empathy for the searcher and often may be reluctant to offer its body. Originally, almost all energy in living things came from sunlight energy that was captured by green plants. That energy is then passed from one organism to the next, usually through dramatic predator/prey interactions.

Potential and Kinetic Energy

The concept of energy—the ability to do work—is easiest to understand if we realize that it essentially exists in two states, **potential energy** (also called *free energy*) and **kinetic energy** (Figure 6.2). The two are generally quite easy to distinguish. The first really defines itself: potential energy is stored, not doing anything. For example, a man may notice a huge boulder on the hill above his house. This boulder, after all, represents a considerable store of potential energy (although he may describe the situation differently, especially if his house is paid for). It may have been raised to that level long ago by enormous geological upheavals. The difference between potential and kinetic energy is easy to visualize. Wait until whatever is restraining that rock gives way. By the time the boulder reaches the bottom of the hill, its potential energy will have been transformed into kinetic energy. (People generally choose not to deal with excessive kinetic energy if they can help it.)

Forms of Energy

Energy can take various forms. That may sound a bit esoteric, but it is a principle we all understand. For example, we are all aware of chemical energy,

heat energy, electrical energy, magnetic energy, and radiant energy, all of which are interchangeable. That is, one form of energy can become another.

Descriptions of energy have been divided a bit simplistically into time-honored categories known as the **laws of thermodynamics.** These physical principles also apply to living things. Let's see how.

6.2

Water in a reservoir has potential (free) energy that normally is depleted only when the water reaches sea level. As water passes through the dam and falls to a lower level, its potential energy becomes kinetic energy—energy in motion. The energy of the falling water is utilized as it begins its long path to the sea. At this stage, its kinetic energy turns electrical generators, transforming mechanical energy into electrical energy, which, in turn, will be transformed into light, heat, and other forms of energy.

THE LAWS OF THERMODYNAMICS

There are some basic scientific ideas that appear to hold up no matter how often they are tested. Therefore, we bestow upon them the label *laws*, and we like to think that these are natural laws that can't be broken under any circumstances. Laws, of course, are comforting, but because of the almost infinite variety of life, biology is actually rather short of laws. Since living systems involve matter and chemical processes, and because the laws of physics and chemistry usually are as valid in living systems as anywhere else, biologists are often forced to deal with concepts that are created, cultivated, and nurtured by physicists. One such group of concepts is called the laws of thermodynamics. Two of these laws are essential to our understanding the incredibly complex, delicate, and sensitive processes of life.

The First Law

The first law of thermodynamics is that *energy can neither be created nor destroyed*. This means, simply, that the total amount of energy in a "closed" system remains constant. A closed system is one in which matter and energy can neither enter nor leave. The earth, for example, receives energy from the sun and radiates some energy back into space. The total energy on the planet may remain relatively constant, but absolute constancy is only an assumption sometimes made by physicists to test some idea. The point here is that the energy that exists on the earth remains relatively constant. The earth, then, is in a *steady state*. But it is a dynamic steady state. All activity occurs because energy can change from one kind to another, because it can be stored and released, and because it ebbs and flows in countless directions, changing the face of the planet.

Let's see some of the ways energy can change in such a bewildering variety of ways. Energy in gasoline, when combined with oxygen inside an engine, can be transformed into the energy of heat, noise, and motion. The potential energy of the chemical bonds of gasoline can become kinetic energy, but the kinetic energy is at a lower energy level, so the sudden release of heat expands gases in the cylinder, forcing a piston to move a shaft that allows the engine to roll a machine over your foot. When this happens, electrical and chemical energy

changes occur in your body, and the sound you generate and later regret changes the chemical energy in your body to the mechanical energy of vibrating air.

Much of the energy in such an engine is uselessly dissipated as heat. This brings us to the next law.

The Second Law

The second law of thermodynamics is sometimes called the law of entropy. It states that *the free energy in any system constantly decreases*. Expressed another way, systems tend to become more random and disorganized as time goes on.

Thus the two laws make it clear that organized systems—that is, those with a complex molecular nature and great free (usable) energy—change, in

6.3

One way to define life is to describe death. Life is characterized by great molecular organization and abundant free energy. Its traits are maintained only through the receipt of energy from other sources. Death is marked by the inability to actively take in energy. Without energy, both molecular organization and the free energy state yield to the inexorable second law of thermodynamics. Entropy increases and the lifeless remains yield to the unpleasantries of decay.

time, to a simpler molecular organization and lower (less usable, or more random) state of free energy (Figure 6.3). The tendency toward disorganization is called **entropy.**

The concept of entropy can be illustrated by fuel in an engine. Gasoline molecules are long, combustible hydrocarbon chains, and they possess both great molecular organization and abundant free energy. As the motor alters those complex molecules, combining them with oxygen and releasing stored energy, those enormous molecular chains end up as simple carbon dioxide and water, their organization and free energy depleted. Essentially, the free energy is released as heat, but much of this heat is used to expand the gases that move the parts of the engine that turn your lawnmower blades and preempt your Saturdays. As for the wasted heat of the engine, it doesn't simply disappear, it just becomes more evenly distributed as it dissipates into the air, becoming part of a much simpler system that leaves little chance for its use as a creative force. One can say, then, that both matter and energy have reached a state of maximum entropy. Much of that free energy escaped as heat discharged uselessly into the air. There is no way to convert that heat to use potential energy again, so the increase in entropy, here, is irreversible.

The whole idea of entropy can yield a certain pessimism. But it does have its cheerful aspects. For example, in order for that engine standing on your foot to move off your foot, the ordered molecules of its gasoline *must* move to a lower energy state, releasing free energy (that turns shafts) as they do.

As available free energy diminishes, the ability to do work decreases. Generally, in chemical reactions some free energy is lost to entropy, so there is less and less available to do work.

This brings up an interesting point. No transfer of energy is totally efficient; with every change some energy is lost. Essentially, the loss occurs as molecules change from a higher to a lower energy state, releasing energy along the way.

Thermodynamics and the Delicate Process of Life

Consider two questions regarding the principles of thermodynamics. If matter tends to move toward entropy, how did the molecules of life come to be so complex? Do the laws governing entropy suggest that life on earth is headed toward disor-

ganization and oblivion? Remember, the laws of thermodynamics apply to closed systems. And although the universe may be a closed system, the earth is not. The earth receives a constant input of free sunlight. As long as this energy reaches the earth, living things will use that energy to remain organized and defy the laws of entropy. Energy can reorganize disorganized molecules into the complex and ordered systems of life.

CHEMICAL REACTIONS AND STATES OF ENERGY

We often find the laws of thermodynamics at work in very peculiar ways. Consider the case of the airship *Hindenburg*, the most famous of the giant zeppelins. It was filled with molecular hydrogen

6.4

The hydrogen-filled dirigible, the *Hindenburg*, exploded in 1937. Hydrogen is rarely encountered in its molecular form (H_2) because it reacts readily with many other chemicals and is nearly always found combined with something. Hydrogen production is always risky because of its reactivity. The smallest spark or flame can provide the impetus needed for a rapid chain reaction such as the one shown here. We will never know what created the spark responsible for the *Hindenburg* disaster, but today, the few remaining lighter-than-air craft are filled with heavier, but unreactive, helium.

gas—unfortunately. In the 1930s, Germany sent the *Hindenburg* to the United States as a dramatic effort to impress Americans with the Third Reich's technological advances. It did just that. Moments before landing in New Jersey, it exploded (Figure 6.4). The hydrogen gas combined with the molecular oxygen of the atmosphere to produce water. The speed with which the water was produced proved deadly.

Why was the water formed so explosively? Because of energy states. Water (H_2O) is at a lower energy state than an equivalent amount of H_2 and O_2. Thus, a mixture of molecular oxygen and hydrogen contains greater chemical free energy than does water, and when the *Hindenburg* burned, the chemical mix moved to a lower energy state, producing water and releasing the excess energy as heat and light.

The molecular reaction of such a tragedy may be written as

$$2H_2 + O_2 \rightarrow 2H_2O + Energy.$$

Oxygen and hydrogen will combine explosively to produce energy and water, but if you tried to demonstrate the principle by simply mixing oxygen with hydrogen, you would elicit one big yawn; nothing would happen. Molecular hydrogen and molecular oxygen will tend to just remain there, with their outer orbitals nicely filled. What now? Perhaps a spark of intuition.

With a tiny spark, the mixture will blow your hat off. But why didn't the mixture blow up without the spark? Molecular oxygen and molecular hydrogen do not combine with each other at room temperature because they must first be energized; the atoms making up each molecule must separate and then rejoin violently to be able to react. The spark provides the energy that forces them apart, allowing the reaction. The atoms separated from each other now have free electrons; that is, electrons no longer tied up in covalent bonds.

The energy of even a spark is all that is necessary to initiate the reaction. Once the first molecules are disrupted, they are able to enter into chemical reactions and release their own free energy. This free energy then provides the energy to separate the atoms of other molecules. Thus, the spark sets off a chain reaction and all of the molecules in the system quickly follow suit.

The energy required to break the original bonds and start the reaction is called the **heat of activation** (Figure 6.5). However, application of heat is only one way to initiate chemical reactions. *Catalysts* can achieve the same results with a lot less dramatic fanfare.

QUIETER CHANGES IN ENERGY STATES

Hydrogen and oxygen can combine to form water at room temperature under a variety of conditions, such as, if the reactions are initiated by a spark. The process also can be initiated by **catalysts**—substances that provide shortcuts between the higher and lower energy states of a molecule. Catalysts initiate chemical reactions, but emerge unchanged from those reactions. They work by lowering the heat of activation required to get things started. For instance, hydrogen and oxygen will combine readily, not only in the presence of a spark, but also if powdered platinum is present. (In the case of this catalyst, the hydrogen first combines with the platinum and then with the oxygen, leaving the platinum in its original state, unchanged by the reactions.)

In biological systems, catalysts are called **enzymes.** They are so vital to chemical reactions in the cell that they deserve a closer look.

ENZYMES: BIOLOGICAL CATALYSTS

If you were to leave hydrogen and oxygen gases together, a few of the molecules—but only a random few—could be expected to join together to form water. The spark, then, provides a form of energy to initiate processes that would have occurred anyway. However, in the highly orchestrated interior of a cell, intense heat would be a disruptive way to initiate biochemical processes. Instead, delicate, intricately coordinated, and vulnerable living systems depend on the gentler activity of enzymes.

Cells contain a great battery of enzymes, which are actually a special class of proteins. Each enzyme initiates only one kind of biochemical reaction. That is, each interacts with only one *substrate*. (A **substrate** is the specific substance with which an enzyme interacts.) Figure 6.6 illustrates the energy of activation in certain reactions that require enzymes, and in some that do not.

A Matter of Shape

Proteins are large molecules with precise shapes. These shapes are critical to the functioning of enzymes. The shape of the enzyme determines its

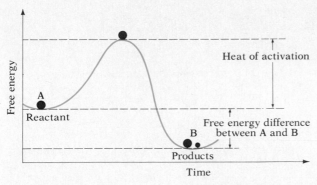

6.5 ━━━━━━━━━━━━━━━━━━━━━━━━━

The energy of activation (here, heat) is the energy required to initiate a chemical reaction. The reactant at point *A* will remain mostly inactive at its "resting" energy level until its energy level is raised. The reaction then proceeds. At point *B*, the products end up at a lower free energy level than the initial reactant.

active site, which is usually a groove or depression on the protein's surface. The bonding tendencies of functional groups at the active site enable an enzyme to interact specifically with only one kind of substrate. When an enzyme joins its substrate, the complex is called, appropriately enough, the **enzyme-substrate complex,** or **ES.** (Figure 6.7 illustrates the prevailing ideas about how enzymes actually work. Notice that the *product* is the result of interaction between an enzyme and its substrate.)

At this very moment, enzymes are at work in your body, carrying out harmonious interactions at dazzling speed. Each is believed to function in a unique way because of the prevailing notion that enzymes are not rigid molecules, but flexible ones that can bend or stretch to accommodate themselves to their specific substrates. The enzyme is able to attach to the substrate because the side groups of the substrate can join side groups (R) of amino acids that make up the enzyme. It has also been suggested that some enzymes operate by simply bringing two reactive substrate groups nearer to each other, so that they can react on their own.

After the enzyme has done its work, the product drifts away and the enzyme, unchanged, is fully capable of immediately entering into the same sort of reaction again.

Characteristics of Enzyme Action

It might seem that enzymes are in control of the cell. However, enzymes don't control anything; they are merely chemicals that themselves are controlled largely by the conditions within the cell.

The precise control of anything as influential as enzymes obviously is critical. Let's now look at the fascinating orchestration of cellular activities.

Rate of Reaction. The rate at which enzymatic products are produced depends on a number of controlling factors. For example, products may be formed faster when more substrate is present. There is no mystery about this, since an enzyme and its substrate join purely by chance collision. Naturally, when more substrate molecules are present, the chances of collision increase. But eventually, the enzymes become saturated with excess substrate. Increasing the substrate even further without increasing the enzyme concentration will not increase the rate of formation of the product (Figure 6.8).

When the substrate concentration is very low, not only will product formation be slowed, but in some instances, the reactions themselves can even be reversed, with the product now forming the substrate. This is possible because of what are called *the laws of mass action.*

The Laws of Mass Action: A Two-Way Affair. The delicate and responsive processes in a living cell involve a host of chemical interaction mediated by enzymes. To add to the complexity, most of these are reversible; the end products of such reactions can react with the enzyme to recreate the

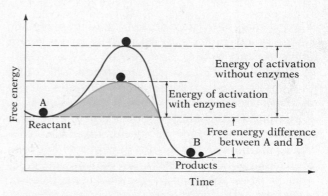

6.6 ━━━━━━━━━━━━━━━━━━━━━━━━━

The graph compares the activation energy requirement for a reaction with and without an enzyme. The reactant (*A*) is stable at ordinary temperatures. To form the product (*B*), the activation energy barrier must be overcome. Without an enzyme, this would usually mean a considerable amount of heat must be applied (*upper curve*). In ways that are not entirely known, enzymes provide the activation energy for biological reactions at considerably lower temperatures (*bottom curve*). Thus the energy barrier is much lower for an enzyme-catalyzed reaction.

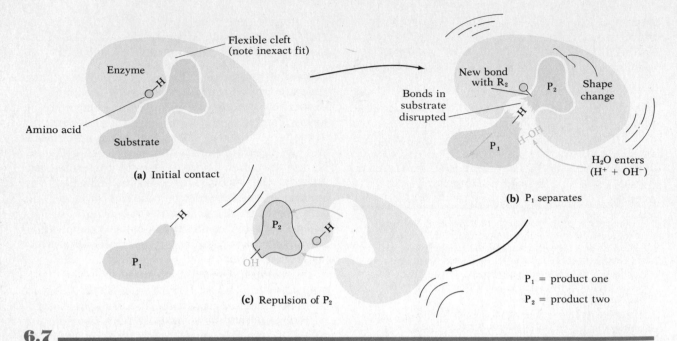

Enzyme

Flexible cleft
(note inexact fit)

Amino acid

Substrate

(a) Initial contact

New bond
with R₂   P₂   Shape
change

Bonds in
substrate
disrupted

P₁   H₂O enters
(H⁺ + OH⁻)

(b) P₁ separates

P₁

P₂

OH

(c) Repulsion of P₂

P₁ = product one

P₂ = product two

6.7

An enzyme "recognizes" and attaches to a specific substrate molecule. The substrate generally fits into an opening in the enzyme much as a missing piece might fit into a jigsaw puzzle (a three-dimensional one, if you can imagine it). The substrate is held in place by hydrogen bonds and other subtle forces. The enzyme itself is not inactive, but is a dynamic structure that is capable of movement. In most enzymes, the substrate fits into a flexible cleft that opens to accept the substrate, closes down on it to perform the catalytic reaction, and opens again to eject the products. Note that the initial fit between the enzyme and the substrate is not precise; this puts a mechanical stress on both molecules, creating places that are particularly vulnerable to chemical interaction. The reaction illustrated here is the hydrolytic cleavage of a bond, involving the addition of water and the use of its components in forming the products. Once its task has been completed, the enzyme is restored to its original state and is ready to act again.

starting material. The direction of such enzymatic reactions has nothing to do with what we might think the cell needs; the direction of the process simply follows the **laws of mass action.** Think of it this way: if a cell contains a lot of substrate but not much product, the reaction will proceed so as to form more of the product. When a lot of product is present but very little substrate, the reaction reverses itself, and the same enzyme will begin to cause the product to form the starting material. Finally, when substrate and product are in balance, there is no net accumulation of either—an equilibrium is reached.

Such reversibility is not always possible, for two reasons. First, if the product is immediately **metabolized** (changed chemically) by the cell, the reaction will tend not to reverse. Second, there are two major types of energy changes in chemical reactions. Some, called **endergonic reactions,** require energy input to proceed. Others (**exergonic reactions**) release energy as they proceed. The process can't be reversed if the reaction is highly exothermic. If the process were exothermic, with a

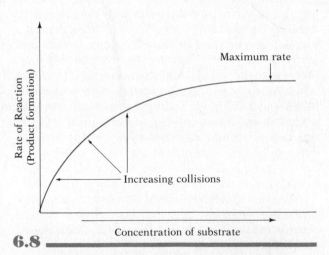

Rate of Reaction
(Product formation)

Maximum rate

Increasing collisions

Concentration of substrate

6.8

The shape of the reaction curve when the quantity of enzymes remains constant while the concentration of substrate is increased. Note that, up to a point, the reaction rate increases with the addition of substrates. The added concentration increases the probability of collisions with the enzyme. The reaction levels off because the enzyme system is saturated with substrate and is working at its maximum rate.

great deal of energy being lost in the process, the product would be left with very little free energy. The result is, a measurable amount of reversibility would be energetically difficult, if not impossible.

The Effect of Heat. Heat cannot only initiate chemical reactions, but it may also affect the functioning of enzymes. As a rule of thumb, an increase in temperature of 10° C doubles the rate of chemical reactions. Furthermore, the rule generally applies to enzyme activity (Figure 6.9). The effect of heat in such cases is not hard to understand. *Heat* is defined as molecular motion, and an increase in the movement of the molecules of substrate and enzyme increases the chances of their collision. (Of course, there is a limit to how much heat can be added to any system. After all, enzymes are made of protein, and heat can destroy the structure and function of any protein.)

The Effect of Acids and Bases. The pH (see Essay 2.1) within the cell can also influence enzyme activity. While a few enzymes perform best in strongly acidic surroundings, most require a more neutral condition (Figure 6.10). Apparently, improper levels of acidity can interfere with the proper folding of enzymes. In some instances, an enzyme's actions can even be reversed by changes in the acidity of a cell. For example, the same enzyme that helps synthesize glycogen from glucose at a high pH will reverse the process at a low pH, breaking glycogen down to glucose.

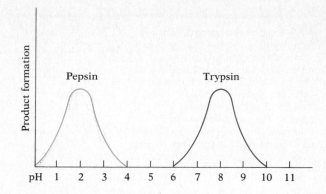

6.10

Enzymes are sensitive to the acidity or alkalinity of their surroundings. For example, pepsin, the protein-digesting enzyme of the stomach, is inactive in all but fairly strong acidic conditions (low pH). Trypsin, a protein enzyme of the small intestine, requires a slightly alkaline environment. Most enzymes work optimally at near neutral (pH 7) conditions.

Teams of Enzymes: Metabolic Pathways

Any enzymatic reaction is likely to be only one simple link in a long sequence of reactions that, together, keep the cell alive and functioning. This sequence is called a **metabolic pathway.** In such chains, each product becomes the starting material for the next reaction. Such an interdependent system must be very organized.

Some metabolic pathways involve the breakdown of large, complex molecules. Such processes are called **catabolic.** Those that build large molecules by joining smaller ones are called **anabolic.**

Now, let's consider the processes of energy transfer in cells, or how cells come up with the energy to complete the work required. Here, we will be introduced to a fascinating molecule called *adenosine triphosphate* (*ATP*). In this simple molecule reside many of the secrets of the cell.

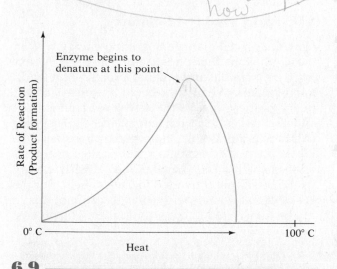

6.9

As thermal energy (heat) is added to an enzyme-substrate mixture, the rate of the reaction increases, due to accelerated molecular motion which increases the chance of collision. However, heat can also denature an enzyme, altering its properties and rendering it inactive. At this point the reaction rate suddenly drops.

ATP: THE ENERGY CURRENCY OF THE CELL

Adenosine triphosphate has been called the cell's "energy currency." This is because ATP can be saved or spent to get things done. The more energy that is required, the more ATP must be present. Let's consider the ATP molecule in more detail and see what role it plays in the life of a cell.

ATP is particularly interesting because it is used

Adenosine triphosphate (ATP) is a trisphosphate nucleotide, identical to that found in RNA. It consists of adenine covalently bonded to the number 1 carbon of ribose. Ribose, in turn, is covalently bonded at its number 5 carbon to three phosphates. The last two contain phosphate-to-phosphate bonds that readily release energy when broken. (*Below*, simplified representation of ATP.)

by all forms of life; it is a nearly universal molecule of energy transfer. Energy produced by virtually any cellular process, such as photosynthesis or respiration, is stored in ATP. When that energy is needed, it is released by ATP. You may recall that cells can store energy in molecules such as carbohydrates, lipids, and proteins. But before energy can be retrieved from such molecules, it must first be transferred to ATP.

The Molecular Structure of ATP

The secret of ATP's abilities lies in its structure (Figure 6.11). The molecule consists of three parts, the most obvious part being a double ring of carbon and nitrogen (*adenine*). In addition to adenine, each ATP molecule contains a simple, 5-carbon sugar (*ribose*). Ribose forms a link between the adenine and three phosphate (triphosphate) units that form a kind of tail. The phosphates are linked together by oxygen atoms.

The Phosphate-to-Phosphate Bond

Notice in Figure 6.11 that the phosphates forming the tail are linked by bonds shown as curved lines. These curved lines simply indicate the so-called *high-energy bonds*. This does not mean that the bonds themselves contain energy, but only that energy is released when the phosphate returns to its much more stable state as an inorganic phos-

phate ion (P_i). Such bonds can be formed only by an enormous energy input; and furthermore, a great deal of energy is released when those bonds are broken. (When we discuss precise quantities of energy we will describe it in terms of *kilocalories*. We will also at times describe substances in terms of *moles*.*)

ATP and Cellular Chemistry

How does a cell manage to get the energy held in those phosphate-to-phosphate bonds? It breaks them by a simple and familiar process—the addition of water. When a molecule of water is added to one of these bonds, the ATP loses a phosphate and the cell is left with **adenosine *di*phosphate (ADP)** plus a molecule of inorganic phosphate (P_i). When the bond breaks, a great deal of energy is released in the cell. Unattended, all that energy would be simply converted to useless heat. But the P_i still carries some energy, and, because of this, it can be transferred to other molecules. The process

---

*A **calorie** (cal) is the energy it takes to raise the temperature of 1 milliliter (ml) of water 1° C. A calorie is 0.001 kilocalories (kcal)—the units dieters count. A kcal is the energy it takes to raise the temperature of 1 liter of water 1° C. A **mole** of a substance is the combined atomic weights of all its atoms, expressed in grams (gm). Therefore, to calculate one mole of glucose ($C_6H_{12}O_6$) we find the atomic weight (mass) of carbon, hydrogen, and oxygen and multiply each by the number of atoms in the molecule. Thus, 1 mole of glucose = $12 \times 6 + 1 \times 12 + 16 \times 6 = 180$ gm.

of adding P_i is called **phosphorylation.** Whatever sort of molecule accepts the P_i thereby gains a portion of its energy. That energy can then enable a number of the phosphorylated molecules to interact more easily in chemical reactions. Because these interactions are not completely efficient, some energy is lost as heat. This is the source of the ''body heat'' of animals.

Phosphorylation works by increasing the chemical reactivity of the molecule that accepts the phosphate (P_i). This is because the molecule will readily trade the phosphate for some other kind of molecule. So, the P_i, a high-energy phosphate, simply makes the substitution more energetically favorable (Figure 6.12).

The ATP Cycle

So, we see that ATP can lose one P_i and become ADP (or lose even two and become *adenosine monophosphate* or *AMP*). The ADP or AMP molecules are simply recycled; that is, they regain their phosphate molecules, becoming ATP again, ready to supply the cell's energy.

The problem here is obvious: breaking those phosphorus bonds *releases* a great deal of energy, so making the bonds *requires* a great deal of energy.

Where can this energy be found? Most ATP is formed in tiny cellular structures, the mitochondria and the chloroplasts. And where do they get their energy for such a formidable task? The mitochondria utilize products from the food we eat, particularly glucose. The chloroplasts, a component of plant cells, utilize the energy of sunlight (Figure 6.13).

We have taken a look at two kinds of molecules that are important to cellular energetics—enzymes and ATP. Their roles are closely linked, since enzymes are catalysts for chemical reactions, and ATP can provide the energy for these reactions. Now let's consider another group of molecules, the *coenzymes.*

THE COENZYMES: AGENTS OF OXIDATION AND REDUCTION

Coenzymes, as their name implies, work in close association with enzymes. In particular, they help make ATP from ADP and P_i. Unlike enzymes, coenzymes are not proteins. (They are much smaller than proteins and, in fact, they look more like

6.12

Interaction between ATP, a substrate molecule, and a phosphorylating enzyme results in transfer of ATP's terminal phosphate to the substrate. The energy of the phosphate molecule increases the free energy in the substrate molecule. It can now enter into cellular reactions. As usual, the enzyme emerges unchanged.

ATP.) The two most common coenzymes are **nicotinamide adenine dinucleotide** and **nicotinamide adenine dinucleotide phosphate,** or **NAD** and **NADP** (usually pronounced "nad and nad-phosphate"). The third most important coenzyme is **flavin adenine dinucleotide (FAD).**

The Molecular Structure of Coenzymes

Molecules of both NAD and NADP contain the nitrogen base adenine, as well as ribose sugars and some phosphates. In addition, they include a compound known as **nicotinic acid** (Figure 6.14). The nicotinic acid group is the chemically active part of NAD and NADP. Note that NADP has one more phosphate than NAD. Another difference is that NADP operates in the chloroplast, while NAD is active in the cytoplasm (cell fluid) and the mitochondrion. FAD is structurally similar to NAD and NADP, but its active group is **riboflavin.**

In general, the three coenzymes have similar functions. They are all associated with enzymes that are involved with the fascinating and critical processes called *oxidation* and *reduction* reactions.

Oxidation and Reduction Reactions

Oxidation and reduction are such common chemical reactions that we may sometimes neglect to consider just how important they are. In terms of their role in cellular energetics, oxidation and reduction are often the mechanisms associated with energy transformations in the cell.

Oxidation is defined as the removal of electrons

6.14

The coenzymes NAD and NADP are very similar. But note the third phosphate of NADP (color). Both NAD and NADP contain the nitrogen base, adenine; a ribose sugar that is linked to a second ribose by two phosphates; and the active group, nicotinic acid, shown at the right. As nicotinic acid is reduced, it accepts a hydrogen ion and two electrons.

from a substance; and the opposite reaction, **reduction,** is the addition of electrons to a substance. Electrons normally don't exist unattached, so when something is oxidized (loses electrons), something else is reduced (gains electrons). In some cases, when an electron is shifted around, a proton tags along. In these cases, oxidation may

6.13

The ability of ATP to cycle ensures a constant supply of energy for the cell. ADP and P_i enter the mitochondrion or chloroplast where energy (cellular fuel in respiration and sunlight in photosynthesis) is used to join the two to form ATP. Many cellular processes utilize the energy released as ATP is again broken down into ADP and P_i.

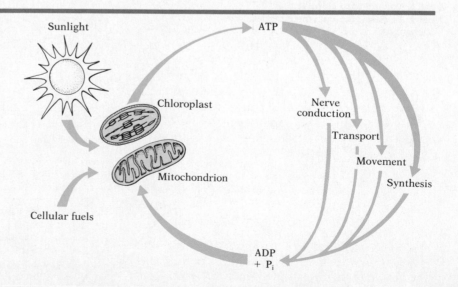

involve the removal of entire hydrogen atoms (a proton and electron together) and reduction may involve the addition of hydrogen atoms. So, in some cases we may refer to the transfer of electrons; in other cases, to the transfer of hydrogens. For our purposes, however, the processes are effectively equivalent. Thus, oxidation is the removal of electrons or hydrogen, and reduction is the addition of electrons or hydrogen.

Let's now return to the coenzymes and their role in oxidation and reduction.

Coenzymes in Action

Although enzymes emerge from reactions unchanged, coenzymes do not. For example, in an oxidation-reduction reaction, nicotinic acid (the active part of both NAD and NADP) accepts a hydrogen ion (proton) and two electrons from some substrate (Figure 6.15). In their reduced state, NAD and NADP are written as NADH and NADPH. The respective oxidized forms are NAD^+ and $NADP^+$ (note the charge change). Oxidized and reduced FAD are written FAD^+ and $FADH_2$. The chemical equation showing the reduction of NAD would be:

$$\text{Reduced substrate} + NAD^+ \xrightarrow[\substack{\text{(Oxidizing} \\ \text{enzyme)}}]{}$$

$$\text{Oxidized substrate} + NADH + H^+.$$
$$\substack{\text{(Reduced} \\ \text{NAD)}}$$

By tradition, the enzyme is shown under the arrow, since it is not changed in the oxidation reaction. In this text, the "H^+" is shown in the equations, but is assumed in the text discussion.

But this is only part of the story. Reduced NAD—that is, NADH—has taken on a hydrogen, but something else has happened as well. The NADH has substantially increased its free (or potential) energy. As a general rule, any time a coenzyme becomes reduced it becomes more reactive. Usually it reacts by passing its proton and electron (or hydrogen) along to a molecule at a lower energy state. We call the tendency to pass protons and electrons to another molecule **reducing power.** A simple reduction of substrate by NADH might be written:

$$NADH + H^+ + \text{Substrate} \xrightarrow[\substack{\text{(Reducing} \\ \text{enzyme)}}]{}$$

$$NAD^+ + \text{reduced substrate.}$$

So, the role of these coenzymes is to accept electrons (sometimes accompanied by protons) and then pass them along to some other molecule. This is why coenzymes are an important part of a group of molecules called **electron carriers.** In coupled oxidation-reduction reactions, these molecules pick up electrons or hydrogen from one molecule and pass them to another. Now let's take a look at one more aspect of oxidation and reduction reactions, and then see how all this fits into a cellular context.

Oxidation-Reduction Sequences and Stationary Carriers

The process of passing electrons (and their bond energy) along can get rather involved, especially when the electrons must be passed precisely and sequentially, as is often the case in cells. The coenzymes we have discussed so far are small molecules that are able to move about rather freely in the cell. However, some electron carriers are large molecules that are held immobile, actually embedded in membranes. We will shortly see why this must be, but first let's take a look at oxidation-reduction reactions when they occur sequentially.

Reducing power has been defined as the ability

6.15

NAD^+ or $NADP^+$ reduction. In the oxidized (unreduced) nicotinic acid group, the upper carbon is attached to one hydrogen group. A double bond extends down to the right of the top carbon. Compare this part of the molecule with the reduced form (*color*). Note that the oxidized nitrogen (N) group at the bottom is positively charged.

to add electrons or hydrogens to a substrate, and we know that NADH, as well as other reduced coenzymes, has great reducing power. Now imagine a series of molecules arranged in a row, each with slightly less reducing power than the next. The first molecule in line might be reduced by NADH. Another molecule in the vicinity has lower reducing power (that is, a greater ability to *be* reduced), so it receives the electron. So carrier number one has reduced carrier number two. In the transfer, some energy is lost, so number two doesn't have enough to return the electron to number one, so it reduces number three—then three reduces four—and so on down the line. So, electrons can be passed sequentially, as in a bucket brigade, down the line of carriers. *Down* is the correct word, since the sequence is energetically downhill (Figure 6.16).

Suppose such a sequence of carriers were embedded in a membrane. This would not only provide a way for electrons to be passed from one to the next, but the energy given up by such electrons could be used to accomplish work. In this instance, that work would be the active transport of protons from one side of the membrane to the other. Such transport mechanisms in mitochondria and chloroplasts are known as electron and proton transport systems. Strange as it might seem, this capability of such systems in mitochondria and chloroplasts

makes it possible for the energy locked in chemical bonds of cellular fuel to help restore the phosphate-to-phosphate bonds of ATP.

To tie this all together into an orderly and understandable framework, several important principles should be kept in mind, particularly what we've just learned about cellular energetics. But we also need to have an idea of how the membranes of the mitochondria and the chloroplasts are constructed. These things fall together in what is called the **theory of chemiosmotic phosphorylation.**

ATP PRODUCTION BY CHEMIOSMOTIC PHOSPHORYLATION

Both the chloroplast and mitochondrion are able to produce ATP, or, more specifically, they are able to phosphorylate ADP. Although their energy sources are different, the general mechanisms they use are similar. Both depend on small mobile carriers as well as the large carriers embedded in their membranes.

Back to Membranes

Now let's see how the membranes enclosing these tiny structures play a role in the ebb and flow of energy in the cell. We'll confine our discussion to the mitochondrion here, since we will discuss chloroplasts extensively in the next chapter. You may recall that the mitochondrion has two membranes, the inner one being highly folded and enclosing a space called the matrix. On one side of the membrane surface (the side facing the matrix) are a number of enzyme-rich bodies—the **F1 particles.** Because of the two membranes, the space within the mitochondrion is divided into two regions, an *outer compartment* and an *inner compartment*, or *matrix* (see Figure 4.13). Embedded in the inner membrane of the mitochondrion are a group of molecules that make up the electron transport systems. These are the molecules that pass electrons (sometimes accompanied by protons, sometimes not) along in a precise sequence to lower and lower energy levels, with each transfer releasing energy that will ultimately be used to restore ATP. As the electrons and hydrogens tumble down their precise and measured molecular stairway, the protons that sometime accompany them are all the while setting the stage for the next scenario, a fascinating sequence with an imposing name, *chemiosmosis.*

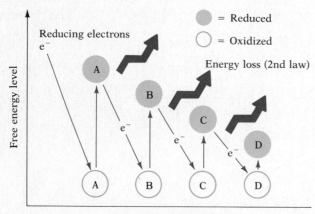

6.16

The electron transport system. When an electron carrier becomes reduced (gains a hydrogen), its free energy level is raised considerably. As it, in turn, reduces the next carrier in the sequence, that carrier's free energy level is also increased, and so on. But no energy transfer is totally efficient, so each transfer results in a loss in free energy of the previous carrier.

Chemiosmosis

Chemiosmosis is a process whereby hydrogen ions (with their positive charges) are pumped across membranes between isolated compartments. Their accumulation on one side of a membrane sets up a **chemiosmotic differential** (a concentration gradient which, in cells, always represents a great store of free energy). As you will recall from our discussions of diffusion, substances tend to move down concentration gradients until random movement (equilibrium) is restored.

In chemiosmosis, highly concentrated hydrogen ions that have accumulated on one side are then passed back across the membrane through rigidly controlled mechanisms, and the energy released in their passage is used to form more ATP. This is a relatively new and surprising discovery. Let's see how it happens.

In the mitochondrion, membranes separate reservoirs of positively charged hydrogen ions on one side and negatively charged ions on the other. The negative charges stem from hydroxyl (OH^-) ions. Since such concentrations can exist only if diffusion is not allowed to operate, we can assume that the separation of the two ions requires an expenditure of energy. In this case, the electron transport system provides that energy.

We are aware that the electron transport system can move either electrons alone, or electrons accompanied by protons. In this case, the protons do not just tag along; they will have a critical role. In fact, the electrons expend energy that will be used to move the protons (Figure 6.17). Electrons released from NADH are passed to the special molecules of an electron transport system embedded in the membrane. Each electron actually crosses the mitochondrial membrane several times, ferrying a proton with each crossing in one direction, then returning alone to pick up another proton. When the electrons are passed to the last carrier molecule, they are spent and do not cross the membrane. Instead, they are added to oxygen and to yet another proton to form water. Their energy has been used to pump the protons.

Thus, the selective transport produces a reservoir of protons (H^+) on one side of the membrane and negative ions on the other side, a most unnatural and highly charged condition. This is now a system of great free energy. The free energy exists because the protons have a strong tendency to rush back through the membrane, reestablishing the dynamic equilibrium that is so characteristic of living systems. Not only is there a great deal of free energy because of the chemiosmotic differential, there is also free energy produced by the resulting electrical charge difference and the osmotic gradient. Now let's see what all this potential energy does.

Phosphorylation and the F1 Particles

There is only one way that the highly energetic protons can escape their isolation—that is, they must pass through special channels. Behind each F1 particle is a tiny channel that opens into the proton reservoir. Moving and bumping around at random, the protons finally blunder into these channels and follow the energy gradient to increasingly lower levels until they end up in these particles. They do not simply rejoin their negative

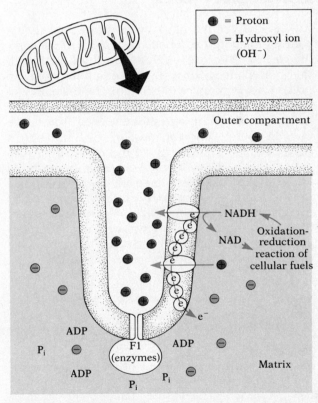

6.17

The chemiosmotic differential in the mitochondrion results from protons (hydrogen ions) crossing the membrane by energy expended as electrons are passed sequentially along to the electron transport system. Utilizing this energy, protons accumulate in the mitochondrial outer compartment. With the loss of protons, the matrix becomes alkaline because it is left with a preponderance of hydroxyl ions (OH^-). Thus, both a charge difference and an osmotic gradient form across the mitochondrial membrane. As the differential increases, the free (potential) energy level also increases. That energy will be used to reconstitute ATP.

counterparts, however. That would be an unfortunate waste of their great free energy, so natural selection has provided something else in store for them. Waiting in the particles are phosphorylating enzymes, along with supplies of ADP and P_i—everything needed to make ATP, except for energy such as the protons possess (Figure 6.18).

At this point our tidy story becomes shrouded in unknowns. We know that ADP is phosphorylated in the F1 particles, but no one has been able to figure out just how the passing protons yield their energy to form phosphate-to-phosphate bonds as they move through the particles.

ENERGETIC LIFE

In this chapter we have been introduced to the concept of energy and have seen some of the ways life can put it to use. We've seen that the laws of thermodynamics can apply to living things and can predict how energy will behave. The instability of molecules warns us that living systems can be maintained only by energy generated from some outside energy, and for most of earth's creatures this energy comes, directly or indirectly, from sunlight. In the evolution of life on earth, both simple and complex organisms have adapted marvelously to physical laws, constantly finding new ways to use these laws in their own interests. Life, then, in its simplest terms, is an interruption of entropy, an energy-demanding reversal in the inexorable trend toward randomness and equilibrium.

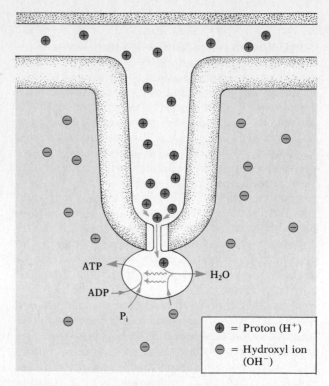

ATP

ADP

P_i

H$_2$O

⊕ = Proton (H$^+$)

⊖ = Hydroxyl ion (OH$^-$)

6.18

Chemiosmotic phosphorylation, the conversion of ADP and inorganic phosphate to high-energy ATP, occurs when protons drift into a channel in the membrane of the F1 particle, and then into the head of the particles.

Summary

Energy
Energy, whether potential or kinetic, is defined as the ability to do work. Such forms of energy as chemical, heat, electrical, magnetic, and radiant energy are interchangeable.

The Laws of Thermodynamics
The first law of thermodynamics states that energy can neither be created nor destroyed. While the total amount of energy available in a system remains relatively constant, it can be transformed into light, heat, noise, and the like. The second law of thermodynamics, also known as the law of entropy, states that free energy in any system constantly decreases. Entropy is the tendency for systems to become randomized. However, energy can reorganize disorganized molecules into the complex and ordered systems of life.

Chemical Reactions and States of Energy
A change from a lower energy state to a higher one can be explosive and involves the heat of activation, which breaks molecular bonds and initiates chain reactions.

Quieter Changes in Energy States
Catalysts are substances that provide shortcuts between higher and lower energy states, lowering the heat of activation needed to start the chain reaction. Catalysts are not changed by the chemical reactions they facilitate.

Enzymes: Biological Catalysts
Each enzyme acting as a biological catalyst is highly specific, interacting with only one kind of substrate. With some exceptions, many enzyme reactions can be reversed according to the laws of mass action. The rate of enzyme reactions depends on the amount of substrate

and enzyme products present, the temperature, and levels of acidity. Sequences of enzymatic reactions, or metabolic pathways, can be either catabolic or anabolic.

ATP: The Energy Currency of the Cell

Adenosine triphosphate (ATP) is a transport molecule used by nearly all forms of life. Cells can free the energy held in ATP's bonds by breaking those bonds with water, releasing a phosphate. When another molecule accepts the phosphate, phosphorylation occurs, increasing the chemical reactivity of the accepting molecule. While enzymes act as catalysts for chemical reactions, ATP provides the energy for those reactions.

The Coenzymes:
Agents of Oxidation and Reduction

Unlike enzymes, coenzymes are changed in the chemical reactions they facilitate. Coenzymes are able to accept and pass on electrons, and are involved in oxidation-reduction reactions. Coenzymes are among the molecules in cell membranes that serve as electron carriers,

which, in sequences called electron transport systems, provide a means of restoring the phosphate-to-phosphate bonds of ATP.

ATP Production by
Chemiosmotic Phosphorylation

Both mitochondria and chloroplasts can produce ATP through chemiosmotic phosphorylation. Electron transport systems pump protons (H^+) across membranes and hydroxide ions (OH^-) accumulate on the other side, creating a chemiosmotic differential of great free energy. Phosphorylation occurs when energetic protons pass down the chemiosmotic gradient into F1 or CF1 particles, where phosphorylating enzymes use the energy to form the high-energy bond between ADP and P_i.

Energetic Life

Energy can be put to use in a variety of ways. We can use the laws of thermodynamics to predict how energy will behave. The organisms living on our earth continually adapt to the physical laws of energy.

Key Terms

energy
potential (free) energy
kinetic energy
laws of thermodynamics
entropy
heat of activation
catalyst
enzyme
substrate
active site
enzyme-substrate complex
laws of mass action
metabolize
endergonic reaction

exergonic reaction
metabolic pathway
catabolic
anabolic
adenosine triphosphate (ATP)
calorie
mole
adenosine diphosphate (ADP)
phosphorylation
coenzymes
nicotinamide adenine dinucleotide
    (NAD)
nicotinamide adenine dinucleotide
    phosphate (NADP)

flavin adenine dinucleotide   (FAD)
nicotinic acid
riboflavin
oxidation
reduction
reducing power
electron carriers
electron transport system
theory of chemiosmotic
    phosphorylation
F1 particles
chemiosmosis
chemiosmotic differential

Review Questions

1. Using your car—its fuel and operation—as an example, distinguish between potential and kinetic energy. Then describe the changes of energy states (chemical, electrical, heat, and motion) you might expect as you start your car, accelerate for a time, and then, using the brakes, bring it to a stop. (pp. 79–81)

2. If, as the second law of thermodynamics states, "the free energy in any system tends to decrease," how is it that the earth maintains so many living creatures, each in a highly organized, great free-energy state? (p. 81)

3. Briefly summarize the events of the Hindenberg disaster, explaining the changes in the energy states of oxygen and hydrogen, and how the reaction started in the first place. (pp. 81–82)

4. Using the following characteristics as a guide, comment on the enzyme: type of molecule, peculiarities of shape, general role in chemical reactions, and specificity. (pp. 82–83)

5. List three factors that affect the rate at which enzymes act, and draw simple graphs representing the effects. (pp. 83–85)

6. Describe the ATP molecule, its basic structure, where its so-called high-energy bonds are located, and how their energy compares with that of ordinary chemical bonds. (pp. 85–86)

7. Construct a simplified ADP-ATP cycle, showing examples of how ATP is used, what happens after its use, and how ATP is regenerated. (pp. 86–87)

8. List three important coenzymes, and state their basic role in cellular reactions. (pp. 87–89)

9. Explain how an electron moves from one end of an electron transport system to another. What apparently controls the direction of movement? (p. 90)

10. Electron/hydrogen ion transport systems in the mitochondrion and chloroplast are used to establish a chemiosmotic gradient or differential. Briefly explain how they do this and how such systems are used to produce ATP. (pp. 91–92)

Photosynthesis

7

Recent interest in solar power as an energy source to replace fossil fuels has an almost touching naivety about it. We seem to view solar power as a new concept. In fact, however, the sunlight bathing the earth has long provided us with our most fundamental source of energy. Such fossil fuels as oil, gas, and coal simply are releasing solar energy stored away in the bodies of long-dead plants and algae. So while we continue to wander in the maze of engineering problems associated with harnessing the sun's energy to produce electricity, perhaps we should turn to the real experts—which are likely to be green (Figure 7.1).

The major process by which living things can make food from simple molecules such as carbon dioxide and water is called **photosynthesis.** This process is powered by the delicate but powerful energy of sunlight. Our goal in this chapter will be to consider specifically how **autotrophs**—organisms that can make their own food, such as plants, algae, cyanobacteria, and some other bacteria—are able to use something as ethereal as sunlight to make food. What we will see is that the energy of sunlight is used to form molecules that themselves contain high amounts of energy. These molecules can then be used to propel other reactions in which carbon dioxide and water are joined to form food molecules. In the process, the oxygen is released. Thus:

$$6 \ CO_2 + 6 \ H_2O \xrightarrow{\text{Energy of sunlight}} C_6H_{12}O_6 + 6 \ O_2.$$

Carbon dioxide — Water — Food molecule (here, glucose) — Oxygen

The energy of sunlight falling on a plant is trapped by chlorophyll and other pigments. Each kind of pigment absorbs light of only certain wavelengths in the visible spectrum (Essay 7.1). The rest is reflected, and this is the color we see. Since we live surrounded by green plants, it can be assumed that they have little use of the energy contained in the green wavelengths.

The photosynthetic pigments are contained within tiny bodies inside the cell called **chloroplasts** (Figure 7.2a). The fluid inside the chloroplast (called the **stroma**) is laden with batteries of enzymes that aid in assembling food molecules. Also inside the chloroplasts are stacks of membrane-bound disks called **thylakoids** (see Figure 7.2a). Each stack is a **granum** (plural, *grana*). The disks are connected by membrane-bound channels (Figure 7.2b, c, d). Where the membranes diverge, they form minute cavities. Each cavity is called a *lumen*. The thylakoid membranes are very complex, containing the *light-harvesting antennas* (green pigments), the *electron transport systems* with *proton (hydrogen ion)* carriers, and the *CF1 particles*. Each plays a specific role in energy capture, ATP production, and the reduction of NADP.

Light-Harvesting Antennas. The **light-harvesting antennas** of the thylakoid are actually molecules of three light-absorbing pigments: **chlorophyll *a*, chlorophyll *b*,** and a group of pigments known as the **carotenes.** Each antenna contains hundreds of these molecules, most of which are devoted to absorbing the elusive photons that make up light and shunting their radiant energy

7.1

Photosynthetic organisms are undoubtedly the dominant forms of life on earth. Nearly all of the earth's creatures depend on their ability to capture the sun's energy and store it in the chemical bonds of their myriad molecules, releasing life-sustaining oxygen in the process.

to a *reaction center*. A **reaction center** consists of one molecule of chlorphyll *a*, closely associated with a large protein, whose structure isn't fully known (Figure 7.2d). There are two kinds of light-harvesting antennas in the thylakoid membrane, known as **photosystem I** and **photosystem II.** The reaction centers of photosystems I and II absorb light of slightly different wavelengths—700 nm and 680 nm, respectively. For that reason, the reaction centers are called *P700* and *P680.*

In terms of their molecular structure, chlorophylls *a* and *b* are quite similar to each other, but very different from the carotenes (Figure 7.3). Because of the differences among them, each pigment absorbs wavelengths in its own way. Chlorophyll *a* absorbs primarily in the violet and red regions of the visible spectrum, while chlorophyll *b* absorbs more in the blue and lighter red regions. The carotenes absorb light primarily in the blue region. As you can see, this covers most of the spectrum, except for green, which is largely unabsorbed. It is reflected green light that gives leaves and green algae their color. (For more on this subject, see Essay 7.1.)

Electron Transport System and Proton Pumps. Also embedded in the membrane of the thylakoid are the **electron transport system** and **proton** (hydrogen ion) **pumps.** As discussed in Chapter 6, these systems use the energy of electrons to pump

protons across their membranes, producing concentration differences of these ions on either side of the thylakoid membrane. This action establishes the chemiosmotic differential, whose great free energy can be used to generate ATP as the ions move to reestablish an equilibrium.

The CF1 Particles. ATP is actually produced in the **CF1 particles,** spherical bodies embedded in the thylakoid membrane, but separate from the other membrane elements (see Figure 7.2 a & b). These bodies contain the all-important *phosphorylating* (phosphate-adding) enzymes for forming the energy-rich ATP bonds. The way in which these particles are oriented is essential to their function.

THE PHOTOSYNTHETIC PROCESS

Gentle sunlight falling peacefully on a green leaf can't even begin to suggest what is going on inside that leaf. It's a process that has occupied the minds of scientists for years. The search to understand it has finally begun to provide fascinating insight into the mechanisms and evolution of our silent partners on this planet. For simplicity, scientists have divided the process into two parts: the **light-dependent reactions** (or the *light reactions*), and the **light-independent reactions** (or the *dark reactions*). We can consider the light-dependent reactions as a way of increasing free energy in the chloroplasts, and the light-independent reactions as a way of using that free energy to produce glucose (Figure 7.4).

Let's first consider the processes that activate, or charge, the system, the light-dependent reactions. Then we'll see how that energy is actually used to make food in the light-independent reactions. The light-dependent reactions are divided into *cyclic photophosphorylation* and *noncyclic photophosphorylation.*

THE LIGHT-DEPENDENT REACTIONS

Cyclic Photophosphorylation

We will first consider how light is used to add inorganic phosphate (P_i) to ADP, forming ATP. There are two major processes involved in this step. The first of these, **cyclic photophosphorylation,** probably evolved eons ago by means of an-

Within the leaves of green plants **(a)** that feed us and lend grace to our lives lies an incredibly complex sub-order of organization. Tissues within the leaf contain vast numbers of photosynthetic cells, each with numerous chloroplasts. Within the chloroplasts are membranous grana, stacks of thylakoids in which the sunlight's energy first interacts with the biological realm. Surrounding the thylakoids are the clearer regions of the fluid stroma, where the final, carbohydrate-synthesizing events (light-independent reactions) occur. Each thylakoid **(b)** is bounded by two complex membranes that are alternately pressed together to form the *lamellae* and bulged outward to form the inner compartments, or *lumena* (singular, *lumen*). Studding the outer wall of the lumena are numerous CF1 particles, their bulbous heads containing phosphorylating enzymes. Each membrane **(c)** contains many light-harvesting antennas and associated electron/hydrogen carriers. Note the minute but vital channels in the CF1 particles, forming a communicating link between the lumen and stroma. An imaginative glance into one light-harvesting antenna **(d)** reveals numerous molecules of chlorophyll and accessory pigments, whose roles are to capture photons and shunt the captured light energy into a central reaction center.

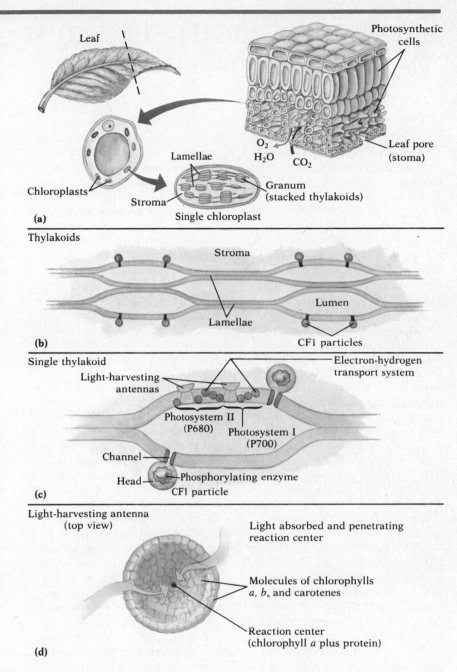

cient bacteria and cyanobacteria. The process is now activated only when a plant undergoes unusual kinds of stress.

Cyclic photophosphorylation, which involves only photosystem I, begins when its chlorophyll *a* molecule is activated by a photon of light energy. (This pigment primarily absorbs light of 700 nm wavelength.) As each photon of light energy is absorbed, an electron in the chlorophyll *a* becomes so excited that it jumps from the chlorophyll *a* mol-

ecule to an **acceptor molecule.** The acceptor molecule, in turn, transfers it to an electron transport system.

As electrons are passed through this electron transport system, from one molecule to the next (each at a lower energy level than the previous one), they gradually lose their energy. That energy is used to pump hydrogen ions across the membrane into the lumen, building the chemiosmotic differential. The free energy of the differential will

THE VISIBLE LIGHT SPECTRUM AND PHOTOSYNTHESIS

The earth is constantly bathed in radiation emanating not only from the sun, but from a host of other celestial bodies. Part of the radiation that reaches us is *visible light*. Visible light, however, is only part of an **electromagnetic spectrum** that includes (in increasing order of energy) radio waves, microwaves, infrared radiation, visible light, ultraviolet radiation, x-rays, and gamma rays.

At the low-energy end of the spectrum are very long waves; the very short waves are extremely high in energy, and visible light is in between. Visible light is visible because it interacts with special pigments (light-absorbing molecules) in our eyes. It also interacts with pigments such as chlorophyll, which are the molecules that absorb the energy of light and provide power for photosynthesis.

Light is very hard to describe in technical terms. One reason is that it can be considered in two ways: as particles called **photons,** or as a wave. Arguments have raged over these two concepts for years. So we will assert that light is composed of photons that move like waves. This side step will enable us to describe the energy of a photon in terms of its wavelength.

Infrared light is dissipated as heat, and its best role might be to warm our bodies. Visible light, of course, interacts with the retinas of our eyes, but it also provides the energy that enables green plants to grow. More energetic wavelengths are usually too powerful for most of life to utilize, since they tend to disrupt molecules, especially proteins and DNA. Ultraviolet light (UV), for example, burns our skin

and damages the retinas of our eyes. Even more penetrating radiation, such as gamma rays and man-made x-rays, is called **ionizing radiation,** because it can break up the water molecules within cells. This can be quite serious since the pieces are very active and enter into random and potentially harmful reactions. If such molecular fragments should disrupt the genetic material of a cell, the result may be a *mutation.* Fortunately for the earth's creatures, most of the more energetic and dangerous wavelengths of the sun are filtered out by the *ozone* molecules in the stratosphere.

So infrared warms us and ultraviolet burns us, and we can see many of the wavelengths in between. Obviously, there are no sharp dividing lines between visible and invisible rays. Both reds and violets become dully visible as they enter our range of sensitivity. It is interesting that different organisms may see different parts of the electromagnetic spectrum. For instance, bees and hummingbirds can see ultraviolet, but bees cannot see red. People who have had the lenses of their eyes removed because of cataracts can see ultraviolet light that is invisible to the rest of us. Light of different wavelengths interacts differently with color-sensitive cells in our eyes, and thus we are able to perceive different colors.

The specific light-absorbing qualities of the chlorophylls and carotenes can be determined by using a device known as a **spectrophotometer.** First, the pigments are extracted and dissolved in a solution. Next, light of a known wavelength is passed through the

solution and measured on the other side. The wavelength of the entering light can be varied to see which wavelength is most absorbed by the solution. Finally, the data are usually plotted on a graph to form what is called an **absorption spectrum.** Note the absorption spectrum for chlorophylls *a* and *b* on the graph shown here. The peaks represent light that is absorbed by the pigment, while the valleys represent light that passes through. As you can see, the green and yellow hues are least absorbed. Thus, these are the colors that we see when we look at a chlorophyll solution—or a leaf.

Certain wavelengths, such as violet-blue and orange-red, are strongly absorbed by chlorophyll. This indicates that these wavelengths are utilized in the light reactions, but the evidence is circumstantial. It is possible, however, to get more direct evidence. One way is to discover the rate at which some product of photosynthesis is produced when a plant is subjected to *monochromatic light* (light of one color only). Since photosynthesis produces oxygen, we can measure the rate of production of this gas. First the rate can be measured with one color of light, and then with other colors. The amount of oxygen produced is carefully calculated in each case.

With these data we can plot what is known as an **action spectrum** (as shown here), which is very similar to the absorption spectrum. As a result, we can be much more confident in the proposition that the light absorbed by the chlorophylls is the light that drives photosynthesis. ●

Electromagnetic spectrum

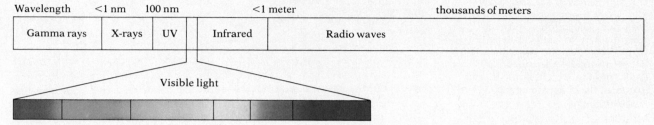

| Wavelength | <1 nm | 100 nm | | <1 meter | thousands of meters |

| Gamma rays | X-rays | UV | Infrared | Radio waves |

Visible light

Absorption spectrum

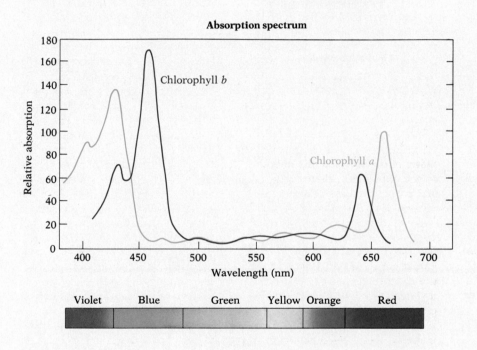

Chlorophyll *b*

Chlorophyll *a*

Relative absorption

Wavelength (nm)

| Violet | Blue | Green | Yellow | Orange | Red |

Action spectrum

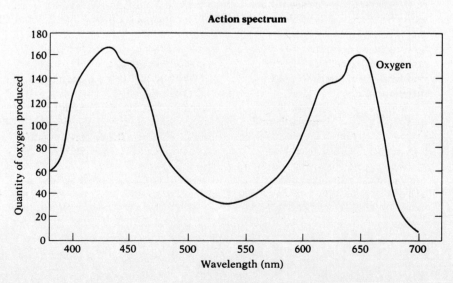

Oxygen

Quantity of oxygen produced

Wavelength (nm)

Structural differences among three light-absorbing pigments. The chlorophylls consist of a complex head (*above*), containing a multiple carbon-nitrogen ring structure with a single magnesium atom at its center. The lengthy tail is a lipid-soluble hydrocarbon chain. The difference in chlorophyll *a* and *b* is seen at the top, where the structure of each is indicated. The carotenes are represented here by beta-carotene (β-carotene). Its two rings of carbon are separated by a hydrocarbon chain. In both the chlorophylls and carotene, the rings are active in absorbing light.

(Chl *a*) H–C–H   C (Chl *b*)

Variable group

Magnesium-nitrogen containing head

Mg

Lipid-soluble tail

Chlorophyll

β-Carotene

In a general sense, the light reactions act to charge the system up—increasing its free energy state. The light-independent events are essentially downhill, with the decreasing free energy used to accomplish work. The second law of thermodynamics reminds us that transitions in energy states are always accompanied by energy losses. Thus glucose, while at a higher free energy state than H_2O and CO_2, is at a lower energy state than the products of the light reactions.

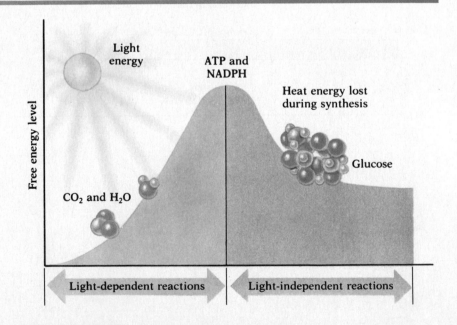

Light energy

ATP and NADPH

Heat energy lost during synthesis

Glucose

Free energy level

CO_2 and H_2O

Light-dependent reactions   Light-independent reactions

be used to add inorganic phosphate to ADP, producing ATP, the energy-charged molecule that is used to perform a variety of kinds of work. We'll look at phosphorylation in more detail in the next section. When the electrons reach the last acceptor in the electron transport chain, they are passed back to the chlorophyll *a* molecule—the origin of their journey (Figure 7.5). Therefore their cycle is completed, and light energy is transformed into ATP.

Cyclic photophosphorylation, itself, cannot lead to glucose production, since there is no reduction of NADP$^+$ to NADPH. It is believed to occur only when most available NADP$^+$ is already tied up as NADPH. In noncyclic photophosphorylation, the electrons are not returned to the chlorophyll molecule from whence they started. Instead, they are passed to the dark reactions to produce glucose. Photosystem I must be resupplied with electrons. It gets them from an entirely separate system (photosystem II) which, in turn, extracts its electrons from a readily available source—the water molecule.

Noncyclic Photophosphorylation

In **noncyclic photophosphorylation,** the light passing through the leaf also activates the light-harvesting antennas of the thylakoids. In this case, both photosystem I and photosystem II are utilized.

Stage 1. The activities in photosystems I and II occur simultaneously, but for clarity we will consider them sequentially, beginning with activities in photosystem II. As in cyclic photophosphorylation, an electron of chlorophyll *a* becomes excited and moves to an orbit farther from the nucleus; instead of returning to its lower energy orbital, it is passed to an acceptor molecule in the thylakoid membrane. The electron is then carried to the inner surface of the membrane and passed to molecules called *cytochromes* in the electron transport chain, then to the next cytochrome, and so on, with energy being released at each step. The energy of the light-energized electron is used in transporting hydrogen ions across the membrane, into the lumen, as we saw in cyclic photophosphorylation. The

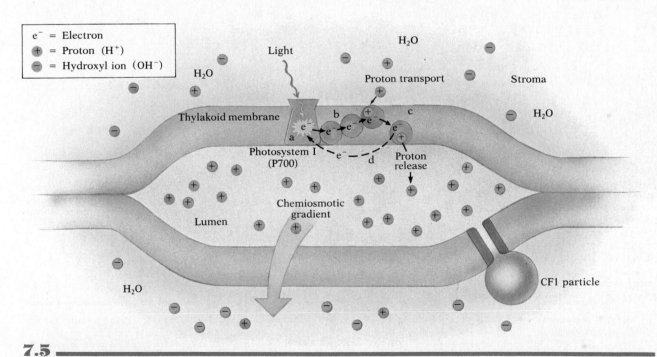

7.5

Cyclic photophosphorylation begins **(a)** when light is absorbed by P700 (photosystem I) and an energized electron is ejected from chlorophyll *a*. The electron passes through electron carriers in the membrane **(b)** until reaching a hydrogen carrier. There it is joined by a proton from the watery stroma **(c)**. The proton is released into the lumen, while the electron, now energetically spent, returns to chlorophyll *a*, completing its cycle **(d)**. Such events, occurring over and over, help in building the chemiosmotic gradient in the thylakoid, thereby providing a source of free energy for ATP synthesis.

electrons continue to be passed along the chain in the membrane, to a very specific destination (Figure 7.6a).

Stage 2. The energized electrons are passed from photosystem II to photosystem I, which has also been actively absorbing photons (Figure 7.6b). Just as in photosystem II, when light is captured by a pigment in photosystem I, electrons become excited and leave the pigment. Two of these eventually are passed to the molecule NADP$^+$. The two electrons are joined by a hydrogen ion (H$^+$) from spontaneously dissociated water molecules of the

stroma. NADPH is thus formed. This molecule contains a great deal of reducing power that will be useful later. The process leaves photosystem I short two electrons, which, as mentioned above, will be replaced by the two electrons leaving photosystem II (Figure 7.6b).

Stage 3. As you may have noticed, we have left the photosystem II requiring two electrons. The oxidized chlorophyll there will be reduced by electrons from water. This is an important but complex part of the light-dependent reactions, which can be represented by the following equation:

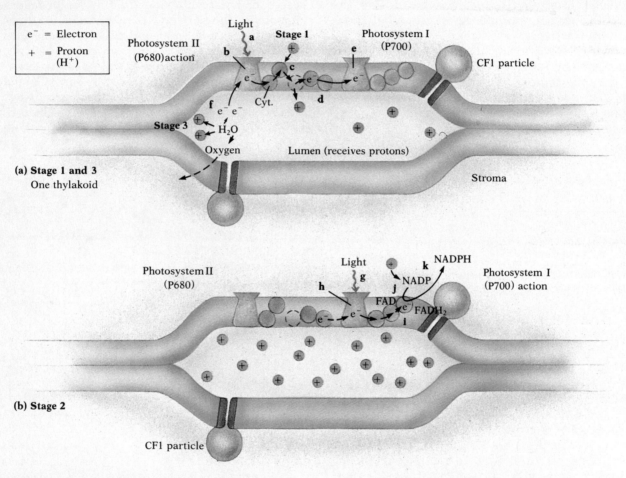

7.6

Stage 1 of noncyclic photophosphorylation. In this time-lapse scenario, the light reactions begin in photosystem II (P 680). **(a)** Light is absorbed by the P680 chlorophyll. **(b)** An excited electron leaves the reaction center. **(c)** The electron arrives at an H$^+$ carrier that **(d)** attracts one proton from the stroma, passes its electron to the next carrier, and releases its proton to the lumen. **(e)** The electron arrives at photosystem I (P700). **(f)** In a separate reaction (which occurs simultaneously with a), water is broken down. An electron reduces (restores) photosystem II, while hydrogen ions

are released into the lumen and oxygen escapes (as O$_2$ when two water molecules react).

In Stage 2, attention is focussed on photosystem I. **(g)** Light is absorbed by the P700 chlorophyll, and **(h)** an excited electron leaves the reaction center. (It is replaced by the spent P680 electrons.) **(i)** The electron passes through the electron transport system. **(j)** Coenzyme FAD receives the electron (and collects a second one), attracts two protons from the stroma, and is reduced to FADH$_2$. **(k)** FADH$_2$ then reduces NADP to NADPH, which then becomes available to the light-independent reactions.

Chemiosmotic phosphorylation involves using the free energy of the osmotic gradient to produce the terminal energy-rich bond of ATP. It occurs as protons escape from the thylakoid lumen. Protons entering the CF1 particles encounter hydroxyl ions, phosphorylating enzymes, ADP, and P_i. In this hypothetical scenario, the phosphorylating reaction is driven by energy released as the protons and hydroxyl ions join and lose their free energy, thereby becoming water. Some of this energy can be used to form ATP.

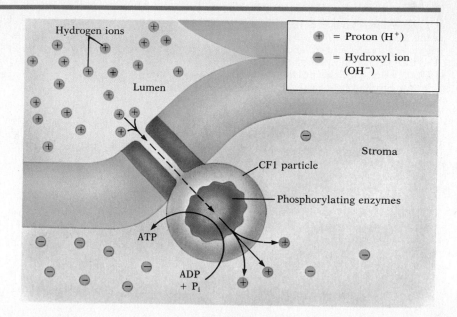

$$H_2O \longrightarrow 2 e^- + 2 H^+ + 1/2 O_2.$$

(to photo-   (released   (to
system II)   to lumen)   atmosphere)

The disruption of water molecules also releases hydrogen ions and oxygen. As you can see in the formula, not only are electrons made available to photosystem II, but the hydrogen ions released are added directly to the chemiosmotic gradient. As the noncyclic process continues, an enormous reservoir of hydrogen ions accumulates in the lumen. This difference in concentrations across the thylakoid membrane produces an important supply of free energy (see Figure 7.6b).

CHEMIOSMOSIS

Because of the continual pumping of hydrogen ions inward, there is eventually more than a thousand times the concentration of hydrogen ions inside the lumen of the thylakoid as there is in the stroma outside. Therefore, the lumen is highly acidic. As we know, molecules tend to move from places of higher concentration to those of lower concentration. In this case, the movement of these hydrogen ions through the membrane provides the energy to make ATP from ADP and P_i. Let's see how they move.

Embedded in the thylakoid membrane are tiny channels through which the hydrogen ions can pass. However, upon reaching the outer surface of the thylakoid membrane, they must pass through the all-important CF1 particles, which contain enzymes necessary to form ATP (Figure 7.7). That ATP, and the NADPH formed earlier, will provide the energy necessary to juggle molecules in the light-independent stage so that nutrient molecules such as glucose can be synthesized.

THE LIGHT-INDEPENDENT REACTIONS

The light-dependent reactions have left us with high-energy ATP and NADPH, so now the light-independent reactions can actually begin to make glucose. The glucose is synthesized in the unstructured region of the chloroplast known as the stroma. What happens can be summarized in the general formula:

$$6 CO_2 + 12 NADPH + 12 H^+ + 18 ATP + 18 H_2O \rightarrow$$

$$C_6H_{12}O_6 + 12 NADP^+ + 18 ADP + 18 P_i + 6 H_2O.$$
(glucose)

(The 18 water molecules on the left side of the reaction go into the hydrolysis of ATP; the six water molecules on the right come from glucose synthesis.)

The second half of photosynthesis involves incorporating (*fixing*) inorganic carbon dioxide into an organic molecule that is useful to the plant. This shouldn't seem too difficult, since CO_2 is everywhere and essentially all that needs to be done is to

An abbreviated version of the Calvin cycle. Five reactions occur between ribulose phosphate (RuP) and PGAL. The RuP is first phosphorylated by ATP **(1)**, after which its product ribulose bisphosphate (RuBP) is carboxylated (CO_2 added), a vital step **(2)**. The 6-carbon product **(3)** cleaves to produce two 3-phosphogylcerates, the first 3-carbon compounds of the cycle. A second phosphorylation by ATP occurs **(4)**, producing diphospho-glycerate (DPG). Finally **(5)**, NADPH + H^+ enters, reducing the DPGs to PGAL. PGAL is the starting compound of several pathways but most (10 of 12) recycles to RuP, thus keeping the cycle going. It requires six turns of the Calvin cycle to produce one glucose molecule.

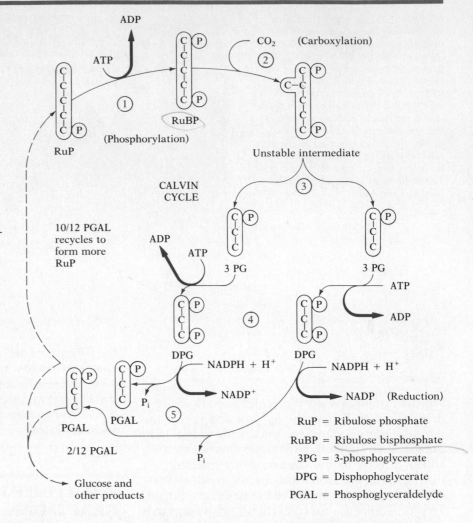

RuP = Ribulose phosphate
RuBP = Ribulose bisphosphate
3PG = 3-phosphoglycerate
DPG = Disphophoglycerate
PGAL = Phosphoglyceraldelyde

join the molecules to form glucose. But biochemistry is never that simple—the energetics of such straightforward events would be simply too costly. Instead, CO_2 molecules are ushered in one at a time, to be combined enzymatically with partially completed compounds. This all happens in a repeating pathway called the *Calvin cycle*, after its discoverer (Figure 7.8). In this cycle, as we saw in the preceding formula, six CO_2 molecules are needed to form one glucose molecule ($C_6H_{12}O_6$).

The **Calvin cycle** takes place in the structureless fluid of the stroma, where there are a number of carbon-containing molecules. One of these is a 5-carbon compound called *ribulose bisphosphate* (RuBP). The cycle is initiated when a molecule of RuBP is enzymatically linked to a molecule of CO_2 (from the air), producing a transient, highly unstable 6-carbon molecule. This molecule quickly breaks apart, forming two 3-carbon molecules of *phosphoglycerate* (PG). Thus, for every six CO_2 mol-

ecules that are combined with RuBP, 12 PG molecules are formed.

It is at this point that the energy of ATP and NADPH formed in the light reactions first comes into play. Twelve of each of these molecules are required to reduce the 12 molecules of PG to *phosphoglyceraldehyde* (PGAL). Through a complex process, the 3-carbon PGAL is altered so that two of the 12 molecules join to form the 6-carbon molecule, glucose. The other 10 PGAL molecules, with the energy provided by six more ATP molecules, are reassembled into six molecules of RuBP, which can then join with CO_2 . . . and so on.

We see, then, a process that recovers the RuBP it used, in addition to producing one glucose molecule for each six turns of the cycle. The ATP and NADPH molecules are now spent, and the resulting ADP, P_i, and $NADP^+$ are made available again to the light reactions, where they can be re-energized and used again.

What Does a Plant Do With Its Glucose?

Photosynthesis is a carefully orchestrated and precise sequence, but we may have neglected an important point. The process is indeed complex, but it occurs with dazzling speed and repetition in the chloroplasts of countless cells simultaneously. This efficiency results in a great deal of glucose production. So what happens to it? Most plants link the glucose molecules together and store them as starches—either in the cells that produced them, or elsewhere after being transported through the plant. The potato, for example, stores excess starch in swollen underground tubers that many humans have been known to eat. Other plants may convert glucose to other sugars, such as *fructose*. Most fruits, for example, are sweet because they are laden with sucrose or fructose. Sugar beets store sugar as sucrose in fleshy storage roots. Humans have been known to extract this sucrose, package it, and sell it to each other. We are indeed highly dependent on the ability of plants to make and store carbohydrates, one of our primary food sources.

Plants can make other sorts of molecules from glucose as well. For example, using PGAL, they can fashion a number of lipids and amino acids. The lipids are necessary for the construction of cell membranes and are stored in great quantities; and amino acids, of course, can be joined to make proteins.

C4 PLANTS: AN EVOLUTIONARY SUCCESS STORY

In the Calvin cycle, CO_2 is fixed to yield certain 3-carbon molecules, notably 3-phosphoglycerate (3PG) and PGAL. All plants use the Calvin cycle, but it was not known until the mid-1960s that some plants also fix CO_2 by an alternate pathway.

Working in Australia with these plants M. D. Hatch and C. R. Slack worked out the details of the alternate pathway. They determined that CO_2 enters certain leaf cells where it combines with a 3-carbon compound (*phosphoenolpyruvate* or *PEP*) to form a 4-carbon intermediate (*oxaloacetate*). Later, in other cells, the CO_2 is released to enter the Calvin cycle. Plants with the ability to carry out this process are called **C4 plants** (those that can fix carbon only into 3-carbon compounds, logically enough, are called **C3 plants**). C4 plants are found in over 100 genera, and they include Bermuda grass, crabgrass, and corn—the sorts of plants that have evolved in hot, dry climates (Figure 7.9). The C4 pathway is more efficient at utilizing CO_2 than is the C3 route. Why should this be? And what does an arid climate have to do with it?

The answer lies in the difficulty of fixing carbon dioxide into the developing glucose molecule. The Calvin cycle requires a relatively high concentration of CO_2 to work at all (the laws of mass action again). In C3 plants, most of the CO_2 that enters

7.9

Sugarcane, a C4 plant that thrives in brilliant tropical light, is more efficient at capturing light energy than any other terrestrial plant studied.

Sugarcane captures 8% of all photon energy reaching its leaves. The worldwide average is well below 1%.

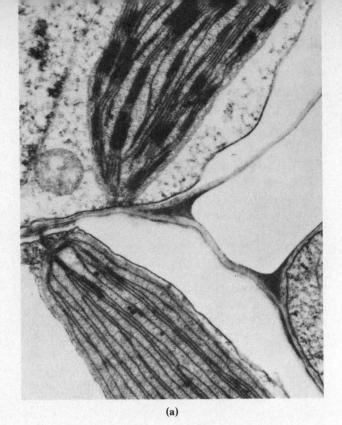

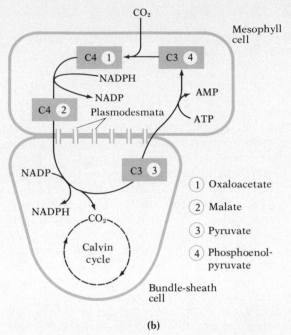

CO₂

Mesophyll
cell

C4 ①   C3 ④
NADPH
NADP   AMP
C4 ②   Plasmodesmata   ATP

NADP

NADPH
CO₂   C3 ③

Calvin
cycle

① Oxaloacetate
② Malate
③ Pyruvate
④ Phosphoenol-
pyruvate

Bundle-sheath
cell

(a)   (b)

7.10

(a) Electron micrograph of green maize chloroplasts. There is a startling difference between C4 bundle-sheath chloroplasts and those of ordinary mesophyll cells. The mesophyll chloroplast (*above*) contains the densely stacked thylakoids that make up the grana. The larger, bundle-sheath chloroplast (*below*) lacks grana but maintains the lamellae. The region between is principally the cell wall between the mesophyll and bundle sheath wall. Tubular plasmodesmata (*upper right*) penetrate the cell wall. **(b)** The purpose of this special C4 pathway is to concentrate carbon dioxide in the vicinity of the carboxylating enzyme of the Calvin cycle. This makes it possible for plants to incorporate carbon dioxide rapidly, improving their photosynthetic efficiency.

the pores of the leaf simply drifts right back out again. But in hot climates, plants must guard against desiccation. Therefore, much of the time the pores of the leaf remain closed or partially closed to keep in the moist internal air. If no air were allowed to enter the leaf, a plant could run short of CO_2, so some have evolved a way to increase the rate of utilization of any CO_2 that they encounter.

The C4 pathway utilizes an enzyme called *PEP carboxylase* that forms oxaloacetic acid from PEP. This enzyme has a very high affinity for CO_2 and will bind to it even at very low concentrations. Thus CO_2 is rapidly removed from the air that enters the leaf. The result is an increased difference in the concentration of CO_2 outside and inside the leaf. As the principle of diffusion would then suggest, there would be an increased tendency for atmospheric CO_2 to move along the diffusion gradient and into the leaf whenever the pores were open. Because of the high efficiency of CO_2 usage in such a system, the C4 plant would have a distinct advantage in dry climates where the pores would be closed much of the time.

The 4-carbon compound is formed in mesophyll cells (see Figure 7.2). The carbon dioxide is later released in the bundle-sheath cells, where it is finally fixed in the usual C3 Calvin cycle (Figure 7.10). The C4 cycle, then, is for a method of bringing CO_2 to the cells where the Calvin cycle is operating.

Thermal Efficiency Reconsidered

Although the Calvin cycle normally is very efficient, with about 38% theoretical thermal efficiency,* this rate drops in practice to nearly 1.0% at times. Such dramatic losses, which are most pronounced on warm bright days, can be attributed to *photorespiration*, during which the components of photosynthesis appear to be functioning, but without producing glucose or ATP—a most peculiar phenomenon.

---

*Thermal efficiency is calculated as the total free energy of the reaction products (ADP, NADP, and glucose) divided by the total free energy of the starting materials (ATP, NADPH, and CO_2), when all of the molecules are abundant.

106

Photorespiration occurs when carbon dioxide levels diminish. In bright sunlight, photosynthesis occurs rapidly and carbon dioxide is quickly depleted in the Calvin cycle, until the demand exceeds the supply. Concentrations of CO_2 in the stroma fall below a critical level, and, oddly enough, oxygen, rather than CO_2, is added to ribulose bisphosphate, and the products are then broken down to CO_2, which the plant gives off. The hard-won products of the light reactions, ATP and NADPH, thus are simply wasted.

RuBP

C3 plants can survive this trauma, but their metabolism and growth are slowed by it. Although photorespiration plagues C3 plants, it is almost totally absent in C4 plants. As you might have surmised, C4 plants are particularly well adapted to the bright sunlight of tropical and desert climates, where they often have a competitive advantage over their C3 rivals. The difference is that the plants are far more efficient in utilizing CO_2. Because of this pathway for concentrating CO_2 for use in the Calvin cycle, very little of the carbon dioxide entering the leaf pores of a C4 plant escapes fixation in the formation of glucose molecules. C3 plants have no similar way of concentrating carbon dioxide when conditions demand it, so they are more at the mercy of environmental circumstances.

So while C3 plants, growing under brilliant sunlight, are struggling to avoid photorespiration, C4 plants maintain a steady supply of CO_2 for their Calvin cycles. You might keep this in mind the next time you notice bermuda grass encroaching on your lawn and threatening to strangle your expensive C3 greenery.

HAVE YOU THANKED A PLANT TODAY?

Nearly all life on this planet depends on capturing the energy radiating from its nearest star. Energy is essential to living things because there is a strong tendency for systems toward entropy. Life, on the other hand, is highly organized and needs energy to maintain that level of organization. Deep in the ocean floor there are organisms that derive all of their energy from sulfurous compounds emitted from volcanic vents. Perhaps on other worlds, the energy to sustain life comes from different sources, such as heat emanating from the planet's core. Here, most of our energy comes from our sun and can only be captured by organisms that are often rudely or cavalierly treated by the other species. But if plants did not turn solar energy into food, this would be a far, far different place.

Let's add one more parting thought. Photosynthesis is an energetically costly process. Its molecular reactants, water and carbon dioxide, are in a low free-energy state—that is, they are stable—and are quite reluctant to participate in any chemical events. Fortunately for life as we know it, sunlight is plentiful and evolution has provided some organisms with the ability to use it. With this enormous and seemingly inexhaustible energy source, photosynthesizers can power their elaborate biochemical machinery without much concern for fuel economy. In our own energy-hungry world, we have much to learn from plants.

Summary

The Photosynthetic Process
Photosynthesis is the process by which some autotrophs use sunlight to make food from simpler molecules such as carbon dioxide and water. The energy of sunlight is trapped by pigments, such as chlorophyll, contained in chloroplasts. Enzymes aid in assembling more complex, high-energy molecules, releasing oxygen in the process.

Inside the chloroplasts are stacks of membrane-bound disks—thylakoids. The thylakoid membrane contains light-harvesting antennas (photosystems I and II), a group of pigments (chlorophyll *a* and chlorophyll *b* and carotenes), the electron transport system, proton pumps, and CF1 particles in which ATP is produced.

The Light-Dependent Reactions
Photosynthesis can be divided into light-dependent and light-independent reactions. In the light-dependent events, sunlight aids in ATP production through the processes of cyclic and noncyclic photophosphorylation. Cyclic photophosphorylation, which occurs only in photosystem I, is most likely to occur when carbon dioxide is in short supply or when the light-independent events are not occurring. In noncyclic photophosphorylation, light activates both photosystems in the thylakoids. As the process continues, an enormous reservoir of hydrogen ions accumulates in the lumen, producing an important supply of free energy.

Chemiosmosis
As hydrogen ions accumulate inside the lumen, they move through channels embedded in the thylakoid membrane to the CF1 particles. These particles contain enzymes necessary for the production of ATP.

The Light-Independent Reactions
In this part of photosynthesis, inorganic carbon dioxide is incorporated into an organic molecule of glucose, a process known as the Calvin cycle which takes place in

the stroma of the chloroplast. The cycle uses the ATP and NADPH molecules formed in the light-dependent reactions. When glucose is produced, ADP, P_i, and NADP are again made available to the light cycles, where they are reenergized.

Most plants store their excess glucose in the form of starches or sugars. Plants can also use PGAL in other pathways to produce lipids and amino acids.

C4 Plants: An Evolutionary Success Story

C4 plants utilize a 4-carbon pathway and an efficient enzyme system to assure a steady supply of CO_2 for the Calvin cycle. Because of these factors, C4 plants do not experience photorespiration, a common problem of C3 plants in bright sunlight. In photorespiration, the rate of photosynthesis exceeds the availability of CO_2, and carbon dioxide is quickly depleted in the Calvin cycle. Eventually, the C3 plant gives off CO_2, and ATP and NADPH are wasted. Because of their CO_2-concentrating pathways, C4 plants can also avoid water loss by keeping their leaf pores closed much of the time, an adaptation that permits them to thrive in the sun in dry regions.

Have You Thanked a Plant Today?

Photosynthesis provides the only known way of capturing the energy of sunlight and using it to synthesize glucose, a molecule essential for life. The abundance of sunlight as a source of fuel enables autotrophs to use this energy-costly process.

Key Terms

photosynthesis	photosystem I (P700)	ionizing radiation
autotroph	photosystem II (P680)	spectrophotometer
chloroplast	electron transport system	absorption spectrum
stroma	proton pumps	action spectrum
thylakoid	CF1 particles	noncyclic photophosphorylation
granum	light-dependent reactions	Calvin cycle
light-harvesting antennas	light-independent reactions	C4 plants
chlorophyll *a*	cyclic photophosphorylation	C3 plants
chlorophyll *b*	acceptor molecule	photorespiration
carotenes	electromagnetic spectrum	thermal efficiency
reaction center	photon	

Review Questions

1. Write a general equation for photosynthesis, making sure that the numbers of atoms of each element balance on both sides of the equation. (p. 95)

2. List four important elements of the thylakoid membrane, and state the general function of each. (pp. 95–96)

3. Absorption spectra of the chlorophylls reveal that light in the violet-blue and orange-red wavelengths is absorbed. What does this tell us about light used in photosynthesis and the apparent color of leaves? (p. 98)

4. Photosynthesis is usually organized into two major parts. Name these parts, state where in the chloroplast they occur, and make a general statement about what goes on in each. (p. 96)

5. Outline the events of noncyclic photophosphorylation, from light striking photosystem II to electrons reaching photosystem I. What is accomplished as far as the chemiosmotic gradient is concerned? What is the role of water in this part of the noncyclic reactions? (pp. 101–102)

6. Continue to follow the light reactions, starting with light striking photosystem I. What is the most important accomplishment in this part of the light reactions? (p. 102)

7. At what point in the light reactions is the phosphorylation of ADP (production of ATP) possible? How does this step occur? (p. 103)

8. What contributions do the light reactions make to the light-independent reactions? How will these products be used? (p. 102)

9. List the events of the Calvin cycle, from the uptake of carbon dioxide to the production of PGAL. What are the two directions PGAL may go in the Calvin cycle? (pp. 102–103)

10. Explain why it is necessary for six turns of the Calvin cycle to occur before a single molecule of glucose is produced. (pp. 102–103)

11. In general, what happens to carbon dioxide in the C4 plants? Under what conditions is the method of carbon dioxide utilization more efficient than what we find in C3 plants? (pp. 105, 107)

Cell Respiration:
Turning Food into Energy

The vast array of living things that walk, run, creep, crawl, or simply stand on earth must have ways of obtaining the critical 6-carbon glucose molecule, and they must also have ways of using it. They must be able to break it down and release its stored energy. However, if that energy were released all at once, there might be a brief blast of light and heat and a sizzle of cytoplasm followed by the silence of death. Living things generally could not withstand the trauma of the sudden release of the energy of glucose. So the power-laden molecule is handled in elaborate ways that release its energy in a stepwise process, a little at a time. The overall process is called **cell respiration.** For convenience, we will divide the process into three parts: *glycolysis*, the *Krebs cycle*, and *chemiosmotic phosphorylation* (Figure 8.1).

AN OVERVIEW OF GLYCOLYSIS

The first step in the breakdown of glucose, which requires no oxygen, occurs in the cytoplasm of the cell. The process is called **glycolysis** (*glyco*, sugar, *lysis*, breakdown). In this process, the 6-carbon glucose molecule is destabilized by the addition of phosphate and is quickly broken down into two 3-carbon fragments (Figure 8.2). The two fragments of glucose, each now containing three carbon atoms, undergo several enzymatically catalyzed rearrangements. With each rearrangement,

of course, the 3-carbon fragment changes its chemical name. The final product is called *pyruvate*. During the process of turning glucose into pyruvate, some of the energy bound up in the structure of the original molecule is used to make ATP from ADP and phosphate. The energy of the ATP bond can then be used for the cell's various energetic needs.

In the process, the 3-carbon fragment is partly oxidized. **Oxidation** is the removal of electrons. Specifically, two electrons (and two protons) are removed from each 3-carbon fragment, or four electrons (and four protons) are removed from the original starting glucose molecule. In the process, the electrons (and protons) reduce two molecules of NAD^+ to two molecules of NADH. This is the overall reaction of glycolysis:

$$C_6H_{12}O_6 + 2\ NAD^+ + 2\ ADP + 2\ P_i \longrightarrow$$
(Glucose)
$$2\ C_3H_3O_3^- + 2\ NADH + 2\ H^+ + 2\ ATP.$$
(2 Pyruvate)

What happens next depends on which of several different metabolic pathways the cell is utilizing. In any case, for the system to continue breaking down glucose, the two NADH must be oxidized; that is, their electrons and protons (H^+) must be removed. If oxygen is available to the cell, the electrons and protons can be used to produce more ATP, as we shall see. If oxygen is not readily available, the cell will have to get rid of the electrons and recycle its NAD in some other way. We'll first consider two of those other ways—called **anaerobic fermentation** (*anaerobic* means "without air"). One anaerobic pathway is **alcoholic fermentation,** which produces carbon dioxide and alcohol as waste products; the other anaerobic pathway is **lactic acid fermentation,** in which the waste product is lactic acid (Figure 8.3).

Yeasts can metabolize glucose either aerobically or anaerobically (that is, either with or without air). When they have access to oxygen and their food resources are limited, yeasts metabolize glucose just as we do, breaking it down all the way to carbon dioxide and water. But when glucose is abundant, yeasts break it down only partially,

whether oxygen is available or not. How do they get rid of their excess NADH? First, they break the pyruvate molecule apart, producing a molecule of carbon dioxide gas and a 2-carbon molecule called acetaldehyde. Then an enzyme called *alcohol dehydrogenase* adds the electrons (and two protons) to acetaldehyde to form ethyl alcohol, also known as ethanol. The overall reaction of alcoholic fermentation is:

$$C_6H_{12}O_6 + 2\ ADP + 2\ P_i \longrightarrow$$
(Glucose)

$$2\ CO_2 + 2\ C_2H_5OH + 2\ ATP + 2H_2O.$$
(2 Ethanol)

8.1

The three parts of cell respiration include glycolysis, the Krebs cycle, and chemiosmotic phosphorylation (which includes electron-hydrogen transport). *Part I* occurs in the cytoplasm, without oxygen, and yields a small amount of ATP. *Part II* is a cycle of oxidation reactions occurring in the mitochondria, where hydrogens are removed to drive the reactions of *Part III*. In the final part, the energy of electrons from hydrogen is used to power most of the ATP production of cell respiration via chemiosmosis.

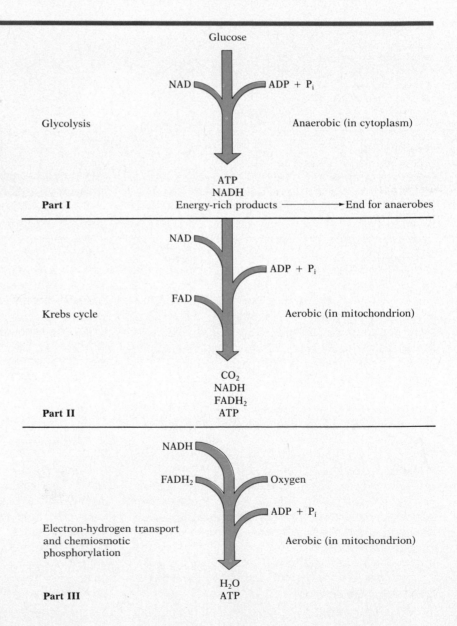

Glycolysis. **(a)** A specific enzyme is required for each step in glycolysis. Two ATPs must be invested (reactions 1 and 3), but the outcome of the first three reactions is that the fuel is made more reactive. Following the double phosphorylation, the product, fructose – 1, 6 – diphosphate, is split into two fragments (reaction 4). **(b)** In the first of two vital reactions (reaction 5), the two PGALs are oxidized, and 2 NADs are reduced to 2 NADHs. In addition, the PGALs are phosphorylated by inorganic phosphate (P_i). This sets up the two products, two 1,3 – DPGs, for the first energy yield (reaction 6) as two phosphates are transferred to 2 ADPs, charging them up to ATP. Thus, the earlier investment of 2 ATPs is repaid. Producing ATP directly from fuels in this manner is referred to as *substrate level phosphorylation.* **(c)** In the final phase of glycolysis, the two 2 – PGs are dehydrated (reaction 8), forming PEP, an unstable product that will react readily. Then in the last reaction (9), destabilized molecules again react with ADP, and two more ATPs are produced. This represents a net gain of 2 ATPs in glycolysis, along with two other energy rich products—the two NADHs from reaction (5) and two molecules of pyruvate, the final product of glycolysis.

(a)

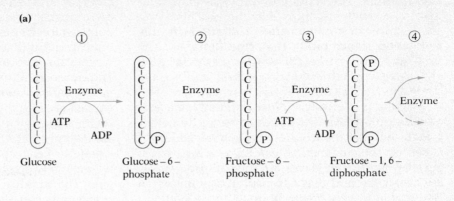

(b)

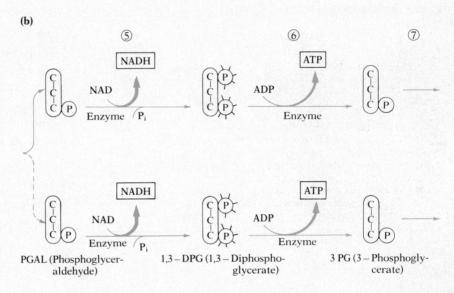

(c)

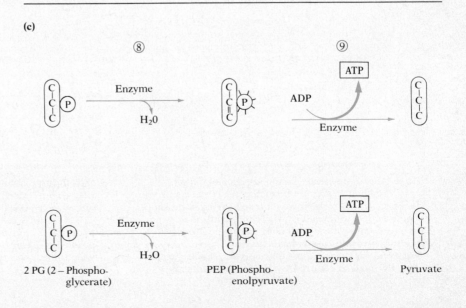

The process of making wine is simple: add yeast to grape juice. The grape juice provides ample glucose and the yeast provides the machinery to change most of it into ethanol. The carbon dioxide is allowed to escape as the wine ferments. The process continues until the yeast is poisoned by the increasing concentration of alcohol, and usually stops when the alcohol content reaches about 13%.

(Making beer is only slightly different. Here, the glucose comes from the starch of barley and other grains—malt, or sprouting barley, is added to speed up the enzymatic breakdown of the starch; hops are added for flavor. Carbon dioxide makes the beer acidic and gassy: fermentation stops when the alcohol level reaches about 4%).

In the second anaerobic pathway, pyruvate produced during glycolysis is converted to *lactate* (lac-

tic acid). Lactate fermentation is seen in many microorganisms, and, during heavy exercise, in our own muscle tissue. We generally think of anaerobic metabolism in terms of simpler forms of life, but the fact is that during heavy muscular activity we rely on the ATP generated during glycolysis and subsequently build up sizeable quantities of lactate in our own bodies. Although we take in oxygen and our muscles can make use of the more ATP-productive process of oxidative respiration during light activity, the supply of oxygen is inadequate to keep up with heavy ATP demands. So we must rely on glycolysis, which requires no oxygen. The buildup of lactate in muscle is closely associated with the familiar fatigue we feel after heavy exertion. The formula of the lactate pathway can be summarized in two parts as:

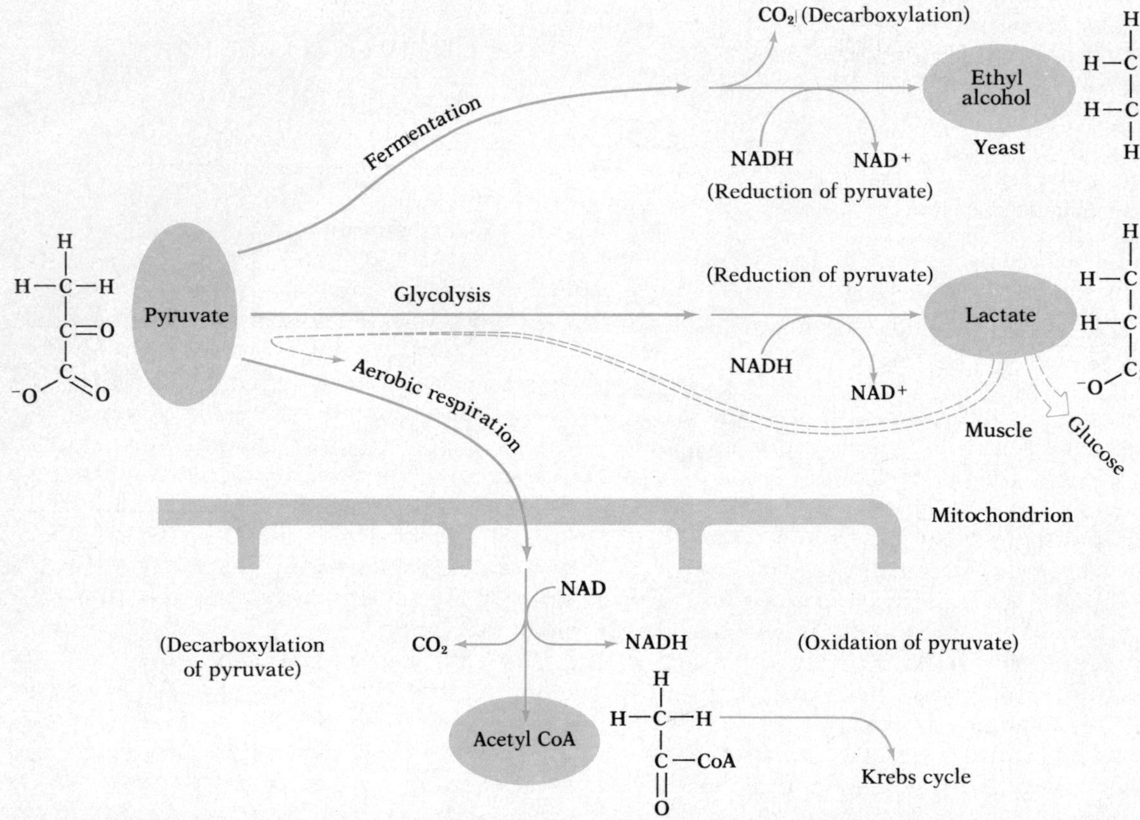

8.3

Three fates of pyruvate. In the absence of oxygen, some organisms carry on fermentation. Pyruvate is reduced by NADH (which was formed earlier), and carbon dioxide is removed by a decarboxylating enzyme. Two molecules of ethyl alcohol are formed for each glucose molecule that is fermented.

Glycolysis during muscular activity is also anaerobic. Pyruvate is reduced by NADH to lactate. Al-

though large quantities of lactate accumulate, eventually all of it will be sent through aerobic pathways or converted back to glucose.

Under fully aerobic conditions in mitochondria, pyruvate is oxidized by NAD, and CO_2 is removed, producing 2-carbon acetyl-coenzyme A (acetyl CoA), which then enters the Krebs cycle.

1. $C_6H_{12}O_6 + 2\ NAD^+ + 2\ ADP + 2\ P_i \longrightarrow$
   (Glucose)

   $2\ ATP + 2\ Pyruvate + 2\ NADH + 2\ H^+.$

2. $2\ Pyruvate + 2\ NADH + 2H^+ \longrightarrow$

   $2\ CH_3CHOHCOO^- + 2\ NAD^+.$
   (2 Lactate)

As you can see, NADH is oxidized, and as in alcohol fermentation, it is used to form the end product—which, in this case, is lactate. This frees the NAD for use again in glycolysis.

Lactate must be cleared from the muscles for them to recover. In our bodies, lactate is carried by the bloodstream to the liver, where it is converted to pyruvate once more. Some of the pyruvate can even be run through a backward version of glycolysis, and with an investment of ATP from oxidative pathways, is converted back to glucose. Glucose is then stored in the liver or in the muscle in the form of glycogen ("animal starch").

Now let's see what happens when pyruvate enters pathways in which oxygen is utilized. It is here that most of the great free energy of glucose is finally released to do work.

THE KREBS CYCLE

The **Krebs cycle,** first described by Sir Hans Krebs, is referred to as a cycle because it begins and ends with the same molecule. (Since citric acid is always formed first, it is often called the *citric acid cycle.*) It is here that pyruvate from glycolysis is completely oxidized to carbon dioxide. Again, however, not much ATP is formed (only two molecules). The main function of the Krebs cycle is to make electrons available for transport through an electron transport system that will use its energy to establish a chemiosmotic differential in the mitochondrion. Before the electrons (and protons) begin their journey, they are temporarily stored in two acceptor molecules, NAD^+ and FAD, reducing these molecules to $NADH + H^+$ and $FADH_2$.

The process begins when pyruvate loses a carbon, which is then released as carbon dioxide. More importantly, the pyruvate is *oxidized.* That is, another pair of electrons is removed. In the process, NAD^+ is reduced to NADH, and a hydrogen ion is liberated. The former pyruvate is now changed to a 2-carbon molecule that joins with a coenzyme (called *coenzyme A,* or *CoA*) to form acetyl CoA. This 2-carbon molecule then joins with a 4-carbon molecule (oxaloacetate) produced in the cycle itself, thereby forming citric acid. The CoA is released to accompany another pyruvate fragment into the cycle. So we see, the products of glycolysis enter the cycle as part of a citric acid molecule. You can follow the subsequent steps in Figure 8.4, noting that the main role of the cycle is to attach (temporarily) hydrogens to the acceptors NAD^+ and FAD so that they may be used in the next stage. As shown in Figure 8.4, for each glucose metabolized (2 pyruvates), six NADH and two $FADH_2$ are generated in the cycle proper, and to this we can add two NADH from glycolysis and two more from the acetyl CoA step.

CHEMIOSMOSIS IN THE MITOCHONDRION

Once NAD^+ and FAD have been reduced in the Krebs cycle, the final events of respiration can begin. NADH crosses the matrix of the mitochondrial inner compartment to reduce the first carriers of the inner membrane. $FADH_2$ has less reducing power than NADH, so it reduces a carrier further along in the system. The carriers then go about their usual task of reducing the next in line, and simultaneously transporting protons across the membrane into the outer compartment. We have covered this ground before (see Chapter 6); the details of electron and hydrogen ion transport are presented in Figure 8.5. As you know, this sequestering of protons produces the chemiosmotic differential, and the free energy of the differential is used in producing ATP. But before we look into this last event, let's follow the electrons to their final destination.

Electrons passing through the carriers of the electron transport system reach the last carrier in an energy-depleted condition. Their fate is interesting to all of us air breathers. You have probably been wondering what oxygen has to do with respiration, since we have yet to mention it. Let's mention it now: the final electron acceptor is oxygen, which combines with the electrons, along with protons from the matrix, to form H_2O (water). The oxygen, then, in its role as a final acceptor, serves as an electron dump. And that is why we breathe: to provide a receptacle for spent electrons that were once part of high-energy food molecules (see Essay 8.1).

The Krebs cycle involves 10 major reactions, each with its own specific enzyme. In the initial step, 4-carbon oxaloacetate joins 2-carbon acetyl CoA to produce 6-carbon citrate. As the cycle turns, two decarboxylations (reactions 5 and 6) occur, yielding two carbon dioxides and a 4-carbon product. Four critical oxidation steps (reactions 4, 6, 8, and 10) produce reduced NAD (NADH) and reduced FAD ($FADH_2$), the most important products of the cycle. In reaction 7, a substrate-level phosphorylation occurs, eventually yielding one ATP. Note the use of guanosine diphosphate (GDP) and guanosine triphosphate (GTP) as intermediates. These are energy carriers similar to ADP and ATP used in this specific step to hand off high-energy phosphate to ADP. Finally, in reaction 10, oxaloacetate (the only permanent acid in the cycle) emerges, ready to begin again. To relate the Krebs cycle to each glucose going through cell respiration, we must multiply the products by two, thus accounting for the two pyruvates produced in glycolysis.

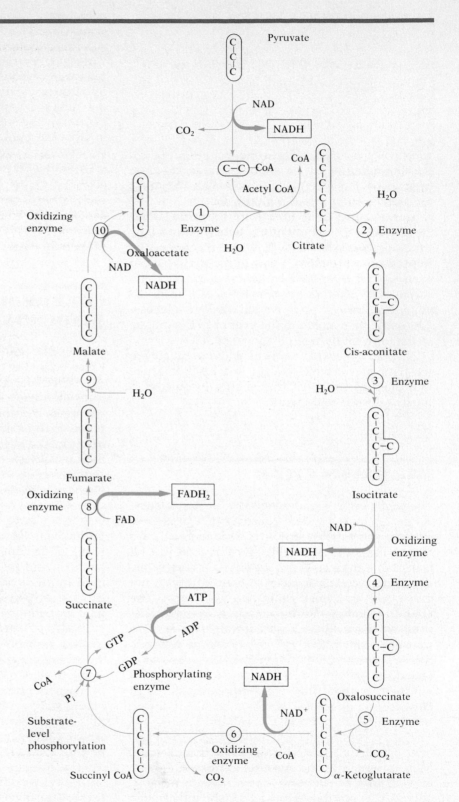

Chemiosmotic Phosphorylation

A look at the final events, the phosphorylation of ADP in the mitochondrion (Figure 8.6), reveals a general similarity with what we have seen in the thylakoid (see Chapter 7). Of course, the orientation of compartments in the two structures is somewhat opposite. In the thylakoid, protons were transported into an inner compartment, the lumen; while in the mitochondrion, protons are transported from an inner compartment into an outer compartment. But the orientation of the F1 particles in the mitochondrion indicates that the phosphorylating mechanisms are the same. Once the chemiosmotic gradient is established, all that remains is for the protons to pass down their gradient, through the F1 particles. As you recall, it is

within these particles that phosphorylating enzymes somehow tap the free energy of the chemiosmotic system to produce ATP.

Oxidative phosphorylation in the mitochondrion is far more ATP-productive than anaerobic respiration (glycolysis). While the latter produces a net gain of only 2 ATPs per glucose, the oxidative process nets somewhere between 25 and 36 ATPs. That is, organisms that run their fuels through the mitochondrion extract much more of the energy available in glucose. Aerobic respiration utilizes glucose far more efficiently when glucose is scarce and oxygen is abundant. When glucose is abundant and oxygen is rare or absent, as in a wine cask or within stressed muscle tissue, anaerobic fermentation may offer the most effective way of turning available resources into energy.

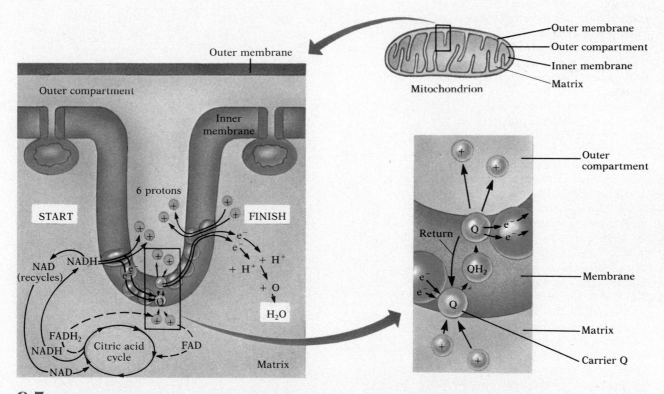

8.5

When NADH interacts with the electron-hydrogen transport system, it reduces the first carrier by passing its two hydrogens along. NAD then recycles. The first carrier then releases two protons into the outer compartment and reduces the next carrier with the two electrons. The pathway of the two electrons is indicated by the paired arrows. At carrier Q, protons are picked up from the matrix and carried to the outer compartment where they are released *(see inset)*. The

electrons continue through the carriers to the final one, which uses the remaining free energy to pass two more protons into the outer compartment. The electrons, now depleted, join protons and oxygen in the matrix to form water. Thus each NADH provides the energy required to pump six protons across the membrane. When coenzyme FADH$_2$ interacts with the system, it reduces carrier Q directly, resulting in only four protons pumped across.

ESSAY 8.1
THE MOLECULES OF FUEL

O We have followed the course of glucose molecules through their metabolic pathway, but it is important to realize that the body can use other types of molecules as well. This is obvious because we know that fats and proteins are good food. Lipids and proteins in the diet may be channeled through the respiratory processes that produce ATP, or their parts simply may be reassembled into the organism's own lipids and proteins. Fats, for example, may be broken down and reassembled as part of cell membranes; and amino acids from food protein may become part of structural materials such as bone, skin, or muscle, or used to make enzymes or more cells.

Both fats and proteins, however, can be altered in such a way that they can enter the Krebs cycle and be oxidized for energy. Fats, in fact, can produce a great deal of energy. Digestion breaks down fats into three fatty acids and glycerol (see Chapter 3). The fatty acids can be converted to acetyl CoA and enter the Krebs cycle. Several of the more common fatty acids contain 18 carbons, so they can produce nine acetyl CoAs and thus 108–147 ATPs. Fats are very high in energy because of the three fatty acid chains in each molecule.

Proteins are broken down to amino acids by digestion. These amino acids are often used as starting materials to make new proteins. If they are to be used as fuel, the nitrogen that they contain must be removed by a process called *deamination* (actually involving the removal of an amino group, NH_2). In higher animals,

this process occurs mainly in the liver. The waste amino groups are excreted from the cell and finally expelled from the body (in humans, as a component of urine). The resulting deaminated acid can enter the respiratory process as pyruvate or one of the other Krebs cycle acids (see figure).

The ATP energy that can be derived from an amino acid depends upon how much NADH it generates. Logically, amino acids that are converted to pyruvate and complete all steps in the Krebs cycle have the most to offer. Those entering at steps beyond produce less ATP. ●

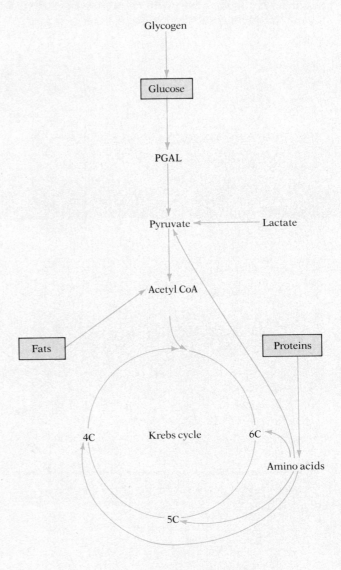

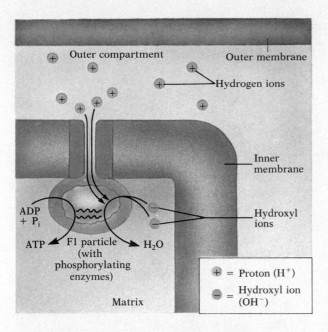

Outer compartment   Outer membrane

Hydrogen ions

Inner membrane

ADP + P$_i$

ATP   F1 particle (with phosphorylating enzymes)   H$_2$O

Hydroxyl ions

Matrix

+ = Proton (H$^+$)

− = Hydroxyl ion (OH$^-$)

8.6

Chemiosmotic phosphorylation occurs when protons pass through the F1 particles. The actual energy transfer is believed to occur as two protons (hydrogen ions) meet two hydroxyl ions to form water. The difference in free energy between the ions and water is enough to produce a new high-energy bond between ADP and P$_i$ as it is captured in a coupled reaction.

The Efficiency of Respiration

The oxidative respiratory yield of 25 to 36 ATP sounds like a ball-park figure—and it is. Some sources may pinpoint the figure to an exact amount, but exact numbers are based on older theories of phosphorylation. Supporters of the chemiosmotic theory (or "mitochondriacs," as some traditionalists like to call us) point out that things aren't that clear cut. One problem is that membranes tend to leak, reducing the chemiosmotic differential. Furthermore, some of the energy of the system may be used for other purposes, such as the active transport of ADP into the mitochondrion. For those with a fascination for numbers, we can determine an efficiency range for respiration.

If glucose is completely oxidized experimentally (by burning), the energy yield is 680 kcal per mole (see Chapter 6). The caloric value of the terminal energy-rich bonds of ATP is 8 kcal per mole. The total energy stored in 38 ATPs (36 plus two from glycolysis) is 304 kcal per mole. So under ideal conditions, respiratory efficiency is about 45% (304 ÷ 680 × 100). Under less than ideal conditions —at the lower end of the range—the efficiency is about 32%. All things considered, a fuel efficiency of 32% to 45% isn't bad. A well-tuned auto engine has a fuel efficiency of less than 25%.

Summary

An Overview of Glycolysis
Cell respiration involves the gradual release of energy from glucose. Glycolysis, the first step, occurs in the cytoplasm, where glucose is broken down to pyruvate, producing a net yield of 2 ATPs. Pyruvate enters one of three different pathways: alcoholic fermentation, lactic acid fermentation, or the Krebs cycle.

Fermentation pathways are anaerobic and are used by simple organisms such as certain yeasts. Alcoholic fermentation occurs when sugars are metabolized in an oxygen-scarce environment. Lactic acid fermentation is used by muscle cells as a source of ATP energy. The end product, lactate, is converted back to pyruvate that can then be sent through the Krebs cycle.

The Krebs Cycle
In the Krebs cycle, pyruvate from glycolysis is completely oxidized to carbon dioxide. The main function of the cycle is to make electrons and protons available for the establishment of a chemiosmotic differential. In the end, the cycle generates six NADH and two FADH$_2$, to which we can add two NADH from glycolysis and two from the acetyl CoA step of the cycle.

Chemiosmosis in the Mitochondrion
NADH and FADH$_2$ pass electrons to the electron transport system and the energy released is used to move protons across the membrane to the outer compartment, building a chemiosmotic differential. Protons then pass through the F1 particles. Some of the energy of their movement is used to form ATP (25 to 30 ATPs per glucose). Spent electrons at the end of the transport chain join protons and oxygen in the stroma to form water.

Other types of molecules, such as fats and proteins, are also used in metabolic processes. Proteins are broken down into amino acids, and fats are broken down into fatty acids and glycerol. Fatty acids can be converted to acetyl CoA, and amino acids can be converted to pyruvate or other acids, which then enter the Krebs cycle.

Key Terms

cell respiration
glycolysis
oxidation
anaerobic fermentation

lactic acid fermentation
Krebs cycle

Review Questions

1. Write the general equation representing cellular respiration, making sure to balance the number of atoms of each element on both sides of the equation. Compare the equation to the one representing photosynthesis. (Chapter 7)

2. Summarize the process of glycolysis by answering the following: (p. 109)
   a. Why must ATP be used to start the process?
   b. What role does NAD^+ play?
   c. What is the net yield of ATP?
   d. What is the final product of glycolysis? Does this represent an energy-depleted molecule? Explain.

3. What is the final product of glycolysis in muscle? How is it cleared from the body? (pp. 112–113)

4. What is the overall purpose of the Krebs cycle? How do NAD and FAD fit into the reactions of this cycle? (p. 113)

5. Explain how $NADH + H^+$ is able to contribute more protons to the chemiosmotic gradient than $FADH_2$ can. (p. 115)

6. Explain how the chemiosmotic differential is used in phosphorylating ADP. (p. 115)

7. What, precisely, is the role of oxygen in cell respiration? (p. 113)

8. Compare the efficiency of glycolysis with the efficiency of oxidative respiration (that is, kcal of energy available in glucose vs kcal of energy stored in ATP bonds). (p. 115)

Mitosis

9

Even as you sit quietly reading this book, your body is changing at a dazzling rate. Certain cells are being created, others are dying, and yet others are being altered. Your body is literally different now than it was when you started this paragraph. Let's concentrate on just one of those changes. Let's see how all those millions of new cells you've acquired in the past few seconds came to be.

We've known for centuries that cells come from other cells. In this chapter, we will investigate how one cell divides to form two virtually identical daughter cells. Keep in mind that some cells reproduce at an incredibly rapid rate (such as those on the palms, which may be subjected to intense friction), while others (such as nerve and muscle cells), once formed, do not reproduce at all. The processes we will consider here are characteristic only of the eukaryotes. The prokaryotes divide by a much simpler process (as we will see in Chapter 20).

Why does cell division occur at all? There are several answers. In some cases, cell division is simply a way to replace damaged and aging cells. In others, it serves as a means of reproduction. For example, single-celled organisms may multiply by dividing. Cell division is also important in the formation of eggs and sperm, as we will see in the next chapter.

Cell division is not the same as mitosis. **Mitosis** is, technically, a very precise division of the nuclear material, especially the chromosomes. Mitosis ensures that each *daughter cell* has the same genes and capabilities of the cell from which it arose; the DNA of the daughter cell will be identical to that of the *mother cell*.

After mitosis has taken place, the cell itself is ready to divide. Cell division is referred to as *cytoplasmic division*, or *cytokinesis*. **Cytokinesis** divides the cell membrane, the organelles, and the cell fluids so that the daughter cells are more or less identical in these respects.

Chromosome Replication

A human cell grown in tissue culture divides about every 20 hours. For convenience, this period is divided into several stages (Figure 9.1). The first and longest stage of the **cell cycle,** known as Gap One (G_1), lasts about eight hours. During this time, the cell grows to about twice its original size. Then DNA replication begins. The DNA replication process (S) takes about six hours. The next stage (G_2) marks the period of protein synthesis, which continues until the last stage, when mitosis and cell division occur (M).

Let's see how the cell prepares for DNA replication. You may recall that each DNA molecule is a double strand; and each strand is composed of

Typical cell cycle.

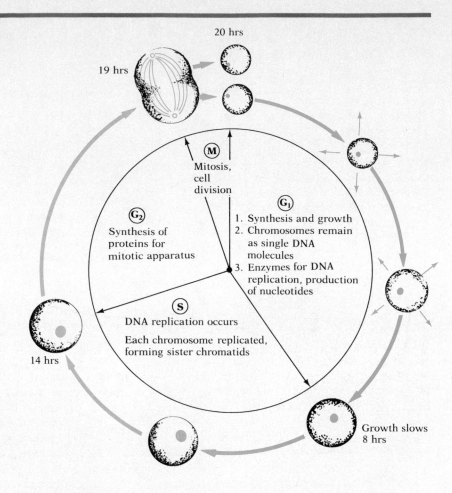

- 20 hrs
- 19 hrs

M Mitosis, cell division

G₂ Synthesis of proteins for mitotic apparatus

G₁
1. Synthesis and growth
2. Chromosomes remain as single DNA molecules
3. Enzymes for DNA replication, production of nucleotides

S DNA replication occurs

Each chromosome replicated, forming sister chromatids

14 hrs

Growth slows 8 hrs

DNA replication, occurring between hours eight and 14 of the typical cell cycle. **(a)** The double polymer is opened from its helical configuration by specific *unwinding proteins*, exposing its nitrogen bases. **(b)** Along each polymer, two new strands are synthesized according to the specific coding of the preexisting strands. **(c)** After replication, two double polymers, exact replicas of the first, have formed.

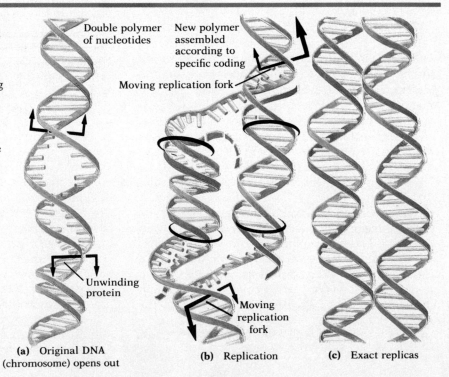

Double polymer of nucleotides

New polymer assembled according to specific coding

Moving replication fork

Unwinding protein

Moving replication fork

(a) Original DNA (chromosome) opens out

(b) Replication

(c) Exact replicas

nucleotide chains and held together by hydrogen bonds. Sections of these long chains are roughly equivalent to what we call *genes.*

DNA replication involves a DNA molecule duplicating itself by "unzipping" the strands or *polymers* (*poly*, many; *mer*, part) and allowing each strand to make a new complementary strand. Unzipping takes place when hydrogen bonds break apart, thereby exposing the nucleotides of each strand. These nucleotides are then free to join other specific nucleotides floating in the cellular fluids. They join by hydrogen bonds, and thus new strands of DNA are formed (Figure 9.2). The process requires many specialized enzymes and a large input of energy. (We will say more about this in Chapter 14.)

So now there are two DNA molecules where there was one, each composed of two twisted strands. These two very long DNA molecules are attached by the **centromere,** a structure that is a bonding site and more. Centromeres hold together two **chromatids** (Figure 9.3). Held together, the two chromatids form a **chromosome** and later, when the centromere divides and the chromatids separate, each of the resulting structures will also be called a chromosome. Another way to say all of this is that you can count chromosomes by counting centromeres.

The cell has now completed the first requirement for division: it has replicated its DNA so each daughter cell has identical chromosomes.

A CLOSER LOOK AT THE CHROMOSOME

Before going on to the mitotic process itself, let's take a closer look at chromosomes, because they are complex and interesting. We have indicated that chromosomes are essentially individual DNA molecules, but that's actually only true in the prokaryotes, where the DNA molecules are "naked" (not associated with protein). The chromosomes of eukaryotes are more complex.

The core of each eukaryotic chromosome is a DNA molecule that is associated with several important proteins. One group of these proteins, the *histones*, seems to serve merely as packaging material—cores of protein around which the DNA winds itself. Other chromosomal proteins, wittily called *nonhistone chromosomal proteins*, are believed to be involved in controlling the genes lying along the DNA strand. That is, they are able to control whether any individual gene along the chromosome is turned "on" or "off." The DNA and protein together are called **chromatin.**

9.3

Following replication, a chromosome consists of two chromatids joined at the centromere. The centromere will divide during mitosis and each chromatid will then be a fully qualified chromosome.

The Chromatin Net

If we examine the nucleus of an **interphase** cell—that is, a cell not in the process of mitosis—we find the chromatin in a *diffuse* (spread-out) condition. Diffuse chromatin resembles a bundle of yarn subjected to the attention of a demented kitten, but in reality has a precise structure. The diffuse chromosomes are firmly attached, at intervals, to latticelike strands of the *nuclear matrix.* The **nuclear matrix** consists of interlocking thin strands of protein and includes most of the enzymes of DNA function. The whole nuclear matrix gives the nucleus some rigidity during interphase; it is dismantled for mitosis and is reconstituted afterward.

Diffuse chromatin often is referred to as the **chromatin net** because of its netlike appearance (Figure 9.4). Some parts of the chromatin net are more diffuse than others, and apparently only the more diffuse areas are actually involved in the principal activity of DNA: the synthesis of RNA.

Mitotic Chromosomes

One would be hard-pressed to distinguish an individual chromosome in its diffuse state, but as mitosis begins, each separate chromosome will gather itself together, condense, and be quite distinguishable. Then each chromosome becomes attached at intervals to a protein **chromosomal scaffold** that gives shape to the mitotic chromosome. Long loops of the chromosome coil tightly around themselves and hang off the sides of the scaffold like overwound rubber bands. The structure of the tightly condensed chromosome is essentially a system of coils within coils (Essay 9.1).

THE SUPERCOILED MITOTIC CHROMOSOME

The organization of the mitotic chromosome is mostly a story of coils within coils. *Supercoil* is the term used when the structure that is being coiled already consists of a coil.

(a) At the lowest level, the DNA molecule itself is a coil, the famous double helix (2 nm in diameter). **(b)** In the eukaryotic cell, DNA is tightly wound around spheres of histone protein at all times to form *nucleosomes* about 10 nm in diameter. **(c)** The nucleosomes, in turn, become coiled into a structure known as a *solenoid* (30 nm in diameter). **(d)** The solenoid forms a fiber that also coils. In this case, it folds back on itself to form a double supercoil. In mitosis, the double supercoil, about 200 nm in diameter, is anchored at its base to the protein chromosomal scaffold. **(e)** The chromosomal scaffold is long and straight in the first stages of condensation in mitosis, but as mitosis proceeds **(f)**, the scaffold itself is thrown into coils—and sometimes into further supercoils. **(g)** Finally, the highly condensed scaffold forms a discrete chromosome, from which side loops of supercoiled DNA can still project. This is a scanning electron micrograph. **(h)** Under the light microscope, the two chromatids of a chromosome may look like two dark-staining sausages held together by a tight napkin ring—the still undivided centromere. ●

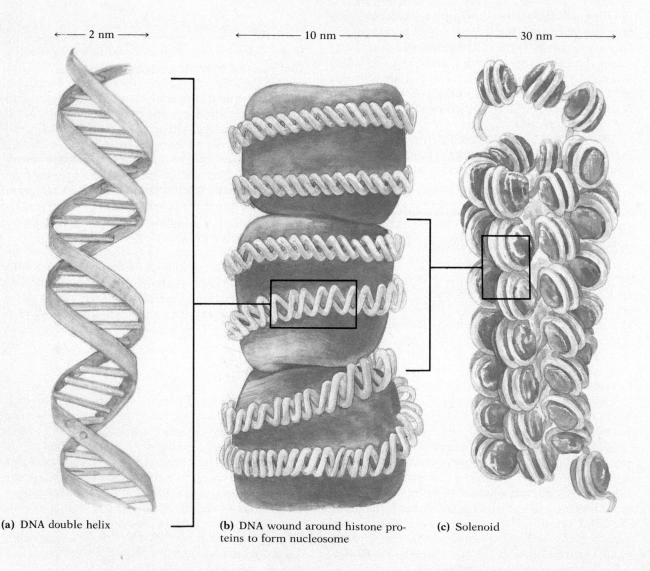

← 2 nm →   ← 10 nm →   ← 30 nm →

(a) DNA double helix

(b) DNA wound around histone proteins to form nucleosome

(c) Solenoid

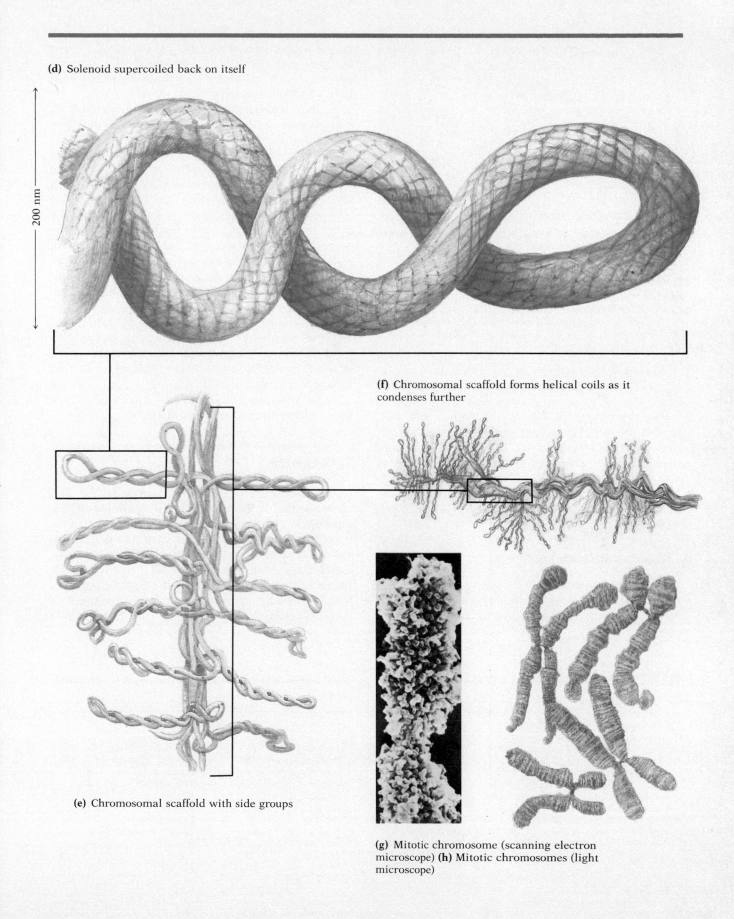

(d) Solenoid supercoiled back on itself

200 nm

(f) Chromosomal scaffold forms helical coils as it condenses further

(e) Chromosomal scaffold with side groups

(g) Mitotic chromosome (scanning electron microscope) **(h)** Mitotic chromosomes (light microscope)

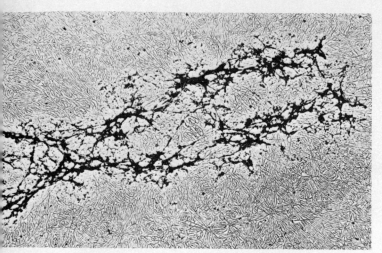

9.4

The chromatin net is composed of diffuse and partially condensed chromatin. DNA must be in a diffuse condition to produce RNA. The larger, dense areas in the nucleus represent nucleoli—RNA processing centers.

Mitotic condensation is the ultimate in packaging. For example, the length of DNA double helix in a human *x* chromosome, one of the larger of our complement of 46 chromosomes per cell, would presumably be about 13 cm (5 in) long if fully stretched out. In its fully coiled and condensed state, however, it is reduced to a dense body some 30,000 times shorter. This tight package can be readily moved about the cell; without this condensation, mitosis would demand far too much space to be feasible.

Chromosome Pairs

Chromosomes come in pairs; in other words, for every DNA molecule in the nucleus, there is another one virtually identical to it. The paired chromosomes of plants and animals result from each parent's contribution of one of each type. Thus, our own paired chromosomes can be traced to our parents, each of whom contributed one of each type of chromosome on conception.

Each of a given pair of chromosomes is called a **homologue,** with each chromosome being constructed of the same linear sequence of genes as is its homologue. However, genes at the same location on homologous chromosomes may not give rise to identical traits. For example, although genes on one homologue may direct the body to produce brown eyes, the genes in the same position on the other homologue may code for blue eyes. It's the same for all of the genes at the same positions on homologous chromosomes: they may or may not code for precisely the same expression of any trait.

Each species has a precise number of chromosomes in normal members of the population (Table 9.1). For example, humans have 46 (23 pairs), but the lowly amoeba has 50 and Rover, sleeping at your feet through all this, has 78. (For a view of the entire human chromosome complement and how *karyotyping* is done, see Essay 9.2.)

Now let's turn to the process of mitosis and see how chromosomes behave during cell division.

MITOSIS

In the last hours of interphase, prior to the first visible signs of mitosis, the cell completes DNA replication. It is now time to devote most of its energy to another activity: synthesizing **tubulin,** spherical proteins that serve as building blocks of the slender, hollow microtubules (see Chapter 4). These microtubules will form the **mitotic spindle,** which will later be involved in the movement of chromosomes during mitosis. The spindle is a

TABLE 9.1

Chromosome numbers

There is no apparent significance to chromosome number as far as biologists can determine. If you feel good about your 46 (see human being), check the turkey, amoeba, cattle, and tobacco. Note the variation in some plant and animal species. Plants undergo spontaneous doubling and tripling of chromosome number, so their numbers may vary.						
	Alligator	32	English holly	40	Opossum	22
	Amoeba	50	Fruit fly	8	Penicillium	2
	Brown bat	44	Garden pea	14	Pheasant	82
	Bullfrog	26	Goldfish	94	Pigeon	80, 79
	Carrot	18	Grasshopper	24	Planaria	16
	Cat	32	Guinea pig	64	Redwood	22
	Cattle	60	Horse	64	Rhesus monkey	42
	Chicken	78	House fly	12	Rose	14, 21, 28
	Chimpanzee	48	Human	46	Sand dollar	52
	Corn	20	Hydra	32	Sea urchin	40
	Dog	78	Lettuce	18	Starfish	36
	Earthworm	36	Marijuana	20	Tobacco	48
	Eel	36	Onion	16, 32	Turkey	82

KARYOTYPING

A **karyotype** is a graphic representation of the chromosomes of any organism, in which individual chromosomes are systematically arranged according to size and shape. Each species has its particular karyotype, and so we know the number and kinds of chromosomes found in carrots, fruit flies, and people. Karyotyping in humans is done by a simple and straightforward method.

A blood sample is drawn and the white cells are separated and transferred to a culture medium. The medium contains not only nutrients, but also chemical agents that first induce mitosis and then stop the process when the chromosomes are at their maximal condensation (the stage at which the chromatids are seen most easily). The cells are then put on microscope slides and stained.

Cells that show all of the individual chromosomes are photographed through a light microscope. A large, glossy print is made from the negative. The jumble of chromosomes is hard to in-terpret and count, so here comes the most technically sophisticated trick of all: cutting out, with scissors, each chromosome from the photograph. Next, the cut-out images of the chromosomes are sorted by size and shape. The homologous pairs are matched up, and the chromosomes are arranged in one or more lines, from the largest to the smallest. Finally, the chromosomal arrangement is mounted with rubber cement. (By convention, pair number 23, the sex chromosomes, is set aside as shown.) This is the karyotype. ●

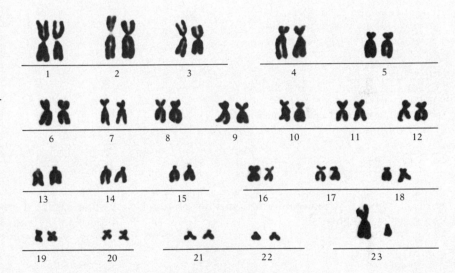

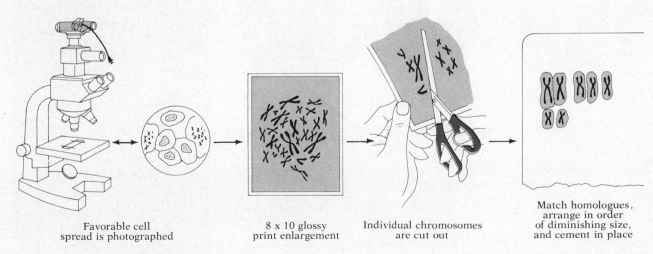

Favorable cell
spread is photographed

8 x 10 glossy
print enlargement

Individual chromosomes
are cut out

Match homologues,
arrange in order
of diminishing size,
and cement in place

125

(a) Mitosis and cytokinesis in animal cells, as illustrated by micrographs and interpretive drawings of mitosis in pancreatic cells of a rat kangaroo. Little of the impending action is suggested in *interphase* (1), but the cell is actively synthesizing protein that will be used in the mitotic apparatus (the centrioles, spindle, spindle fibers, and asters). In *prophase* (2), the chromosomes and mitotic apparatus are clearly visible. Two prominent asters surround the centrioles and the spindle extends across the nucleus region. In this view, the chromosomes are moving to the metaphase plate. When aligned on the plate, (3) a lull in activity characteristic of *metaphase* begins. At *anaphase* (4), the centromeres have divided and the former chromatids move to opposite poles. Then, during *telophase* (5) the mitotic apparatus is dismantled as the chromosomes gather in a dense mass and the daughter cells begin to take shape. The line passing between the daughter cells represents a cleavage furrow that forms as cytokinesis ensues. (Photos courtesy Carolina Biological Supply.)

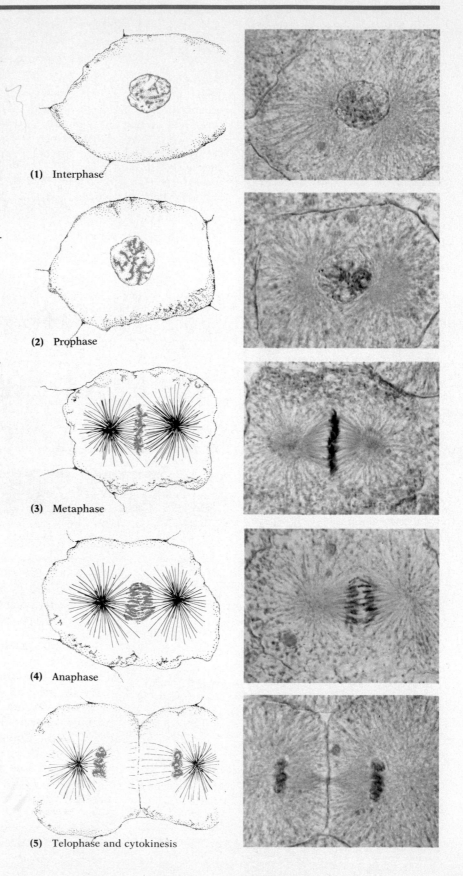

(1) Interphase

(2) Prophase

(3) Metaphase

(4) Anaphase

(5) Telophase and cytokinesis

(b) Cytokinesis as viewed through the scanning electron microscope. The sequence begins prior to cytoplasmic division at the upper left. The first sign of cytokinesis is an elongating cell, upper right, marking the telophase stage. Cytokinesis continues, middle left, and is finally completed at the middle right, although these cells still cling through their sticky cytoplasmic extensions (bottom).

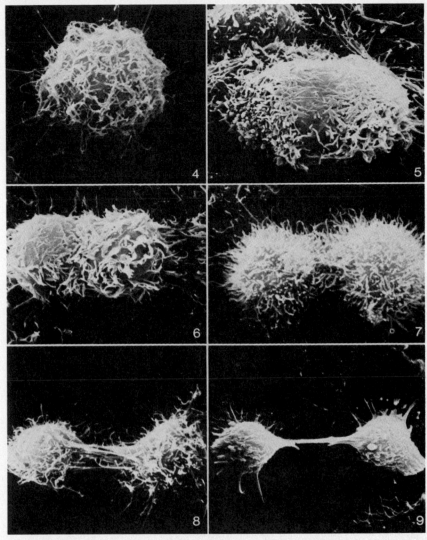

From *Scanning Electron Microscopy in Biology: A Student's Atlas on Biological Organization,* by R. G. Kessel and C. Y. Shih. Copyright © 1974 Springer-Verlag.

peculiar structure that behaves tenaciously and with precision during cell division, but at the same time is of such a delicate constitution that it quickly disintegrates if touched, thereby making it extremely difficult to study. Also, the spindle forms anew for each cell cycle and is dismantled after each use, so at times it can't be studied at all.

The Phases of Mitosis

Mitosis begins at the end of interphase. The process is customarily divided into four phases: *prophase, metaphase, anaphase,* and *telophase*. Mitosis is a gradual process and the distinctions between the stages are blurred, so the naming of any stage is often open to debate. The mitotic events of plants and animals differ slightly, as shown in Figures 9.5 and 9.6. Mitosis in animals will be discussed here.

Centrioles and the Mitotic Apparatus. Even as the chromosomes are condensing, the mitotic apparatus is forming in preparation for chromosome movement. At the onset of mitosis, in early **prophase,** the paired centrioles that lie near the nucleus separate and migrate to opposite sides of the nucleus. Once in place at the **spindle poles,** they begin organizing the microtubules to form three remarkable structures (Figure 9.7). The first structures to form are the **asters** (stars), which radiate out from each centriole. These structures occur in animals but not usually in plants; microscopists have watched them for years, but to date any function they may have remains a mystery.

Mitosis and cytokinesis in plant cells. Here the tissue is from the African globe lily. Little activity is apparent in *interphase* (1), but in *prophase* (2), the chromosomes are clearly visible. Note the absence of centrioles and asters. The spindle is visible at *metaphase* (3), where the chromosomes have become aligned on the metaphase plate. The centromeres divide and the chromosomes move apart as usual during *anaphase* (4). During *telophase* (5) there is no cleavage furrow, but a new cell wall develops between the new daughter cells as the events of mitosis end. The photos are of nonsupportive embryonic cells. Thus the development of a new cell wall between the daughter cells is not apparent.

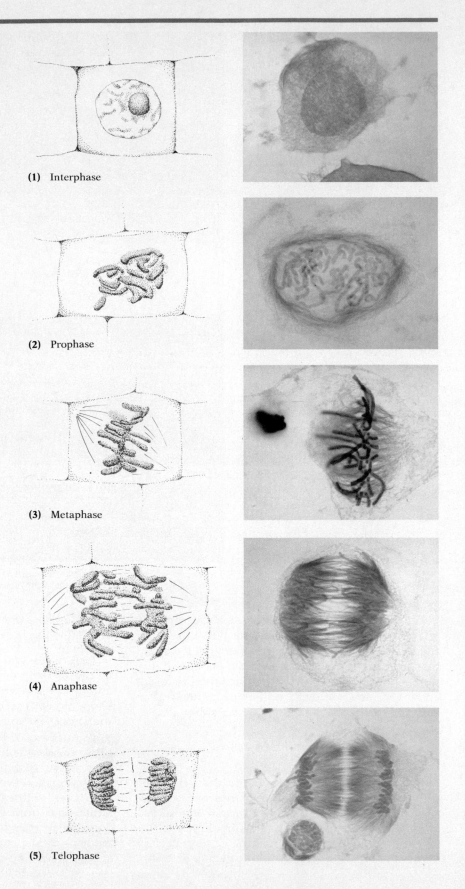

(1) Interphase

(2) Prophase

(3) Metaphase

(4) Anaphase

(5) Telophase

(They possibly make the surrounding cytoplasm more rigid, firming it up for events to come.)

The mitotic spindle comprises two types of microtubules. One type, the *continuous spindle fibers,* begin their assembly at each centriole in the region of the spindle poles. The fibers at each pole then extend across the chromosomes toward the opposite pole, stopping randomly somewhere short of this goal, but not before they have slid past each other so that they overlap.

The second type of microtubules, called *centromeric spindle fibers,* behave even more strangely. These also extend out from the centrioles, but they link up with the centromeres of the chromosomes. The result is that each centromere is attached to fibers that are joined to each pole. In case you are wondering how the mitotic spindle gets through the nuclear membrane, it doesn't. As the mitotic apparatus is assembled, the nuclear membrane seems to disappear.

Final Events of Prophase. Once the centromeric spindle fibers have reached out from each pole and attached to the centromeres (much like roping a horse from both sides), the movement of the chromosomes becomes more precise. Now captured by opposing spindle fibers, they are pulled along, finally to line up across the middle of the spindle. There they form a ragged single file that is called the **metaphase plate,** and then metaphase itself begins.

Metaphase

In **metaphase,** individual chromatids are easily seen. Although the chromatids lean out in all directions, the centromeres are held in position along the metaphase plate, which can be regarded as the cell's equatorial plane since it lies midway between the poles.

Up to this point, the two chromatids of each chromosome have been held together by a single centromere, and the centromere has been held rigidly in place by the centromeric spindle fibers. The next event, which helps make sense out of previous events, signals the onset of **anaphase.** This stage is marked by centromere division. When each centromere divides to become two centromeres, the two chromatids are no longer held together—in fact, they are no longer called chromatids. They are now called *daughter chromosomes,* each with its own centromere.

Anaphase

With the division of the centromeres, the identical daughter chromosomes quickly separate. One daughter chromosome moves toward one pole, while its identical counterpart moves toward the other. But while this elegant ballet is satisfying to watch, it raises an obvious question: how do the chromosomes move?

The Spindle and Chromosome Movement. When the daughter chromosomes begin to separate, the role of the mitotic spindle becomes apparent. The chromosomes are pulled along at their centromeres with the "arms" of the chromosomes trailing behind. Each centromere is attached to its centromeric spindle fibers, which, in turn, are attached to the spindle poles. Therefore, the centromeres are dragged away from the metaphase plate

9.7

The mitotic apparatus in a whitefish embryo cell. Large asters are characteristic of these cells. We can see here the three ways microtubules are assembled. Some form the aster, while others form the overlapping continuous spindle fibers, and yet others form the centromeric spindle fibers that extend from the centrioles to the centromeres.

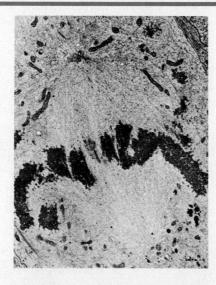

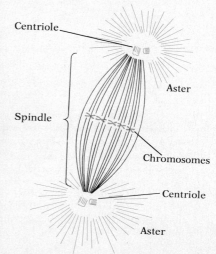

Centriole

Aster

Spindle

Chromosomes

Centriole

Aster

by the pull of the centromeric spindle fibers. But how?

Hypothetically, two mechanisms are involved (Figure 9.8). First, the spindle lengthens, so that the opposite poles move apart. Daughter centromeres, being attached to opposite spindle poles, also separate. The overlapping continuous spindle fibers appear to be involved in this spindle lengthening. The mechanism seems to be a form of *sliding filament action*, wherein the continuous spindle fibers actively pull at each other, shortening the zone of overlap.

The second mechanism of chromosome movement in anaphase involves the centromeric spindle fibers, which are able to shorten and to pull on their attached centromeres. The shortening occurs by a process known as *subunit disassembly*, which simply means that the spindle fiber microtubules are broken down piecemeal into their subunit tubulin molecules. As this occurs the shortening fibers somehow remain firmly attached at both ends.

Telophase

Telophase, which begins after the chromosomes have been pulled to their poles, is like prophase in reverse. The chromosomes uncoil, reversing the condensation process. The mitotic apparatus is disassembled and the nuclear membrane—now actually two nuclear membranes, one around each clump of chromosomes—is reassembled. In animals, the centrioles may replicate at this time or later. Telophase also marks the time of actual cell division (cytokinesis). Cytokinesis progresses differently in animals and plants.

Animal Cytokinesis

In animals (and many protists), cytokinesis begins with a furrow along the cell's equator. The furrow eventually becomes a deep groove. Finally, the cell is pinched in two, forming two daughter cells. The entire sequence is often referred to as *cleavage* (see Figure 9.5).

Plant Cytokinesis

Cytokinesis in plants must occur within the confines of a cell wall. Because the wall is rigid, cleavage cannot occur. Thus the plant cell simply produces a new wall between the telophase nuclei (Figure 9.9).

The new wall begins with the formation of a number of tiny vesicles originating from Golgi bodies (see Chapter 4), which form in the plane of the metaphase plate. The vesicles fuse to form a *cell plate,* which extends to the original cell wall. The cell plate fills with pectin, a carbohydrate, to form the *middle lamella.* This is a gummy layer that will come to lie between the mature cell walls of adjacent plant cells. New cell membranes assemble over the middle lamella, and cellulose is deposited on either side of it to form a new *primary cell wall.* (For further details, see Figure 9.9.)

Metaphase

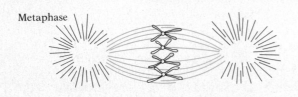

Spindle elongates, chromosomes pulled apart

Anaphase

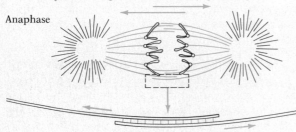

Continuous filaments sliding

(a) Sliding filament hypotheses (continuous fibers)

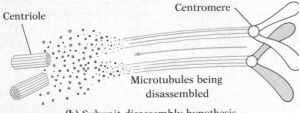

Centriole

Centromere

Microtubules being disassembled

(b) Subunit disassembly hypothesis (centromeric fibers)

9.8

The sliding filament-microtubular disassembly hypothesis suggests that the spindle is elongated as anaphase begins. Elongation is produced as the continuous microtubules or filaments "ratchet" past each other. Simultaneously, the centromeric microtubules pull the chromatids along, somehow disassembling themselves in the process.

Summing Up Cell Division

We've seen that cell division involves two distinct parts—mitosis and cytokinesis. The primary objective of mitosis is to divide the products of DNA replication—the chromatids—equally between the two daughter cells. Mitosis is followed by cytokinesis, which involves a less precise division of cytoplasm. Its mechanisms differ greatly in plants and animals, but in both the result is two daughter cells.

The primary function of mitosis in single-celled eukaryotes is in reproduction. In multicellular organisms, mitosis is principally involved in growth and repair. Mitosis in multicellular organisms begins at conception, and from then on provides a continuous supply of cells to be molded into the embryo's structures. In animals, mitosis continues rapidly until maturity, at which time it occurs much less frequently, except in areas where cells can be expected to wear out quickly. Since plants grow continuously throughout their life spans, new cells are continuously needed for that growth, and mitosis occurs at a relatively constant rate.

9.9

In plants, cytokinesis begins as a new cell wall is constructed between daughter cells. In the sequence shown here, evidence of a cytoplasmic division is first seen as the formation of vesicles at the middle of the cell. These coalesce and extend across the cell, forming the *cell plate*. The completed plate is known as the *middle lamella*; from this structure, the primary cell wall will emerge.

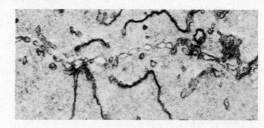
(a) Microtubules form bundles and vesicles form

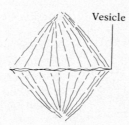
Vesicle
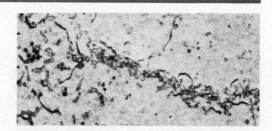
(b) Later telophase—cell plate forming

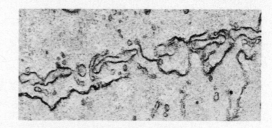
(c) Middle lamella (fused vesicles accumulate pectin)

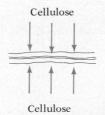
Cellulose
Cellulose

(d) Primary cell wall (cellulose deposited in middle lamella forms first cell wall)

Summary

Introduction

Cell division occurs in two distinct stages: mitosis and cytokinesis. Mitosis is a precise division of nuclear material, especially the chromosomes. The DNA molecule replicates by separating its polymers, which exposes the nucleotides of each strand. The nucleotides are then joined by free nucleotides to form two new strands of DNA that are attached to each other by a centromere. When the replication process is completed, the DNA of each daughter cell is identical to that of the mother cell. After mitosis, or nuclear division, cytokinesis divides the cell membrane, organelles, and cell fluids into two distinct cells.

A Closer Look at the Chromosomes

Each eukaryotic chromosome is a DNA molecule associated with several important proteins. The DNA and protein together are called chromatin. Histone proteins act as packaging material, while nonhistones are involved in controlling the genes. In an interphase cell, chromatin is diffuse, forming the chromatin net. Diffuse chromosomes are attached at intervals to the nuclear matrix, and it is this diffuse DNA that is active in RNA synthesis. As mitosis begins, chromosomes condense and attach to a protein chromosomal scaffold. The chromosomes coil tightly around themselves and become more condensed.

Chromosomes exist in pairs. Each chromosome, or homologue, contains the same linear sequence of genes as its partner. However, genes at the same position on the homologous chromosomes may not code for exactly the same expression of a trait. Each species has a precise number of chromosomes and a particular karyotype (the arrangement of chromosomes according to size and shape).

Mitosis

In preparation for mitosis, the cell completes DNA replication and begins to synthesize tubulin, which serves as the building material for the microtubules of the mitotic spindles.

Mitosis proceeds through four phases: prophase, metaphase, anaphase, and telophase. In early prophase, paired centrioles near the nucleus separate and migrate to opposite sides of the nucleus. At the spindle poles, the centrioles organize the microtubules to form asters, continuous spindle fibers, and centromeric spindle fibers. In late prophase, opposing centromeric spindle fibers attach to centromeres; the chromosomes move to form a metaphase plate across the middle of the spindle. In metaphase, individual chromatids can be easily seen.

When anaphase begins, the centromeres divide, releasing the two chromatids, which are now called daughter chromosomes. The daughter chromosomes, each with its own centromere, travel to opposite poles, pulled along by one of two hypothetical mechanisms—the sliding filament action or subunit disassembly mechanism—of the spindle fibers.

Telophase begins when the daughter chromosomes reach their poles. The chromosomes uncoil, the mitotic apparatus disassembles, and the nuclear membrane forms around each group of daughter chromosomes. Telophase marks the time of actual cell division, or cytokinesis.

Cytokinesis in animal cells is referred to as cleavage. In plants, cytokinesis takes place when a new cell wall forms between telophase nuclei. Mitosis in animals occurs rapidly during early growth and slows as the organism matures. In plants that grow continuously, mitosis occurs at a fairly constant rate.

Key Terms

mitosis	nuclear matrix	prophase
cytokinesis	chromatin net	spindle poles
cell cycle	chromosomal scaffold	asters
centromere	homologue	metaphase plate
chromatids	karyotype	metaphase
chromosome	tubulin	anaphase
chromatin	mitotic spindles	telophase
interphase		

Review Questions

1. List several purposes of mitosis and cell division. (p. 119).

2. Briefly describe the process each chromosome must go through prior to mitosis. Why is this necessary? (pp. 119–121)

3. Explain what constitutes a eukaryotic chromosome, and how it is condensed prior to mitosis. (p. 121)

4. List the three main structures of the mitotic apparatus. Of what protein are they composed, and which permanent cellular structure appears to be responsible for their organization? (pp. 124, 127–129)

5. List the stages of mitosis, and briefly explain what happens in each. (pp. 126–130)

6. Explain how the sliding-filament hypothesis and subunit disassembly hypothesis account for chromosome movement. (p. 130)

7. Describe cytokinesis in plants, including the steps in cell wall formation. How does cytokinesis differ in animals? (p. 131)

Meiosis and Shuffling Chromosomes

10

As we live out our lives on this planet, whether climbing the earth's great peaks or "meditating" in a hammock, our bodies are undergoing constant changes as, each instant, millions of cells die, while new ones take their place. But while our cells are in rapid turnover, our bodies maintain a remarkable constancy. The constancy is due, of course, to the precise mechanisms of mitosis that ensure the similarity of cells descended from a single line. However, some cells produce daughter cells that are not alike. These are specifically, the cells that give rise to eggs and sperm. (In fact, the odds of two sperm or two eggs being genetically identical have been calculated at 13 billion to one.) The process by which such genetically diverse cells arise is called **meiosis**.

In meiosis, the mother cell produces daughter cells that not only are genetically different, but that also have only half the normal genetic complement. As we will see, it is from these "halved" cells that eggs and sperm (and spores in plants) are formed. This should not be surprising if you think about it. Eggs and sperm combine their genetic material at fertilization, forming **zygotes** (fertilized eggs). If the normal complement of chromosomes were added together at each occasion, the number of chromosomes in each new generation would double. Obviously that wouldn't do.

The basic process of meiosis is outlined in Figure 10.1. (Here we have simplified the scheme by showing only two pairs of homologous chromosomes, rather than our own 23, and by omitting

such complications as crossing over. We'll get to these later.) As shown, meiosis consists of two divisions, so that each *diploid* meiotic cell eventually produces four *haploid* daughter cells. (**Diploid** means that there are two copies of each chromosome in the cell, and **haploid** means that there is just one copy of each.)

The reason that meiosis requires two divisions is that the meiotic cell begins the first division with its chromosomes already doubled by DNA replication, so that there are actually *four* copies of each kind of gene—two identical strands from the mother and two identical strands from the father. These four DNA molecules eventually will be parcelled out to the four cells that are the products of meiosis.

The two divisions are called **meiosis I** and **meiosis II,** although they are parts of just one process: In the first division, meiosis I, the centromeres do not divide as they do in mitosis; instead the homologous *chromosomes* of each pair separate, moving to opposite poles. Centromere division and the separation of chromatids is delayed until the second division, meiosis II (Figure 10.2).

If you find yourself confusing meiosis and mitosis, you will not be the first person in history to have done so. The processes have much in common, but they also have some crucial differences. To begin with, homologues do not separate in mitosis. In mitosis, in fact, the two members of each pair—the one from the father and the one from the mother—behave as if they had never been intro-

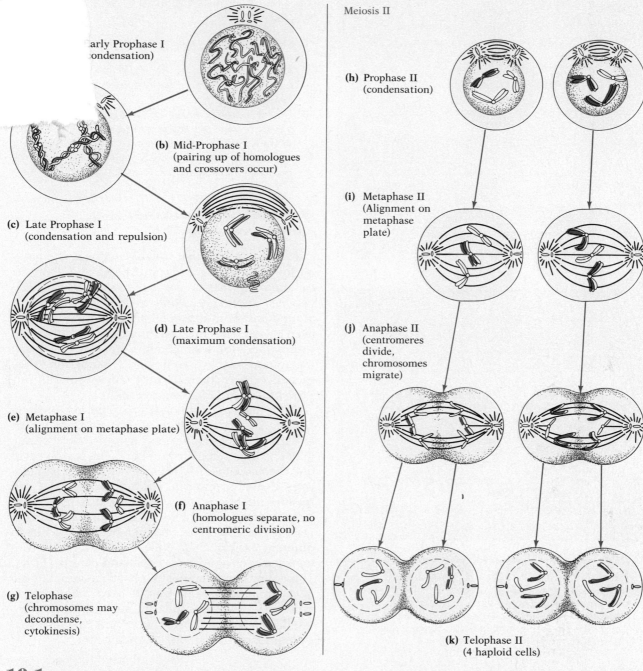

Meiosis II

(a) Early Prophase I (condensation)

(b) Mid-Prophase I (pairing up of homologues and crossovers occur)

(c) Late Prophase I (condensation and repulsion)

(d) Late Prophase I (maximum condensation)

(e) Metaphase I (alignment on metaphase plate)

(f) Anaphase I (homologues separate, no centromeric division)

(g) Telophase (chromosomes may decondense, cytokinesis)

(h) Prophase II (condensation)

(i) Metaphase II (Alignment on metaphase plate)

(j) Anaphase II (centromeres divide, chromosomes migrate)

(k) Telophase II (4 haploid cells)

10.1

Prophase in **meiosis I (a–d)** is a lengthy stage. Individual chromatids become visible very late in the stage, after genetic recombination through crossing over has occurred. At *metaphase* (e), the homologous chromosomes move together to the metaphase plate. Unlike what occurs in mitosis, only one centromeric spindle fiber attaches to each centriole. As a result, when *anaphase* (f) occurs, the homologues separate, each with its chromatids still intact. In *telophase* (g), the chromosomes may unwind, depending on the species.

In **meiosis II**, the events proceed in a manner simi-lar to those in mitosis as far as chromosomal movement is concerned. Condensation occurs in a brief *prophase* (h), with random alignment of chromosomes on the metaphase plate as *metaphase* (i) begins. Note that this time the centromeric spindle fibers attach to each side of the centromere. When *anaphase* (j) begins, the centromeres divide and the chromatids finally separate. In *telophase* (k), each of the four resulting cells is haploid, containing unpaired chromosomes. However, because of crossing over in meiosis I, each chromosome consists of a mix of maternal and paternal genes.

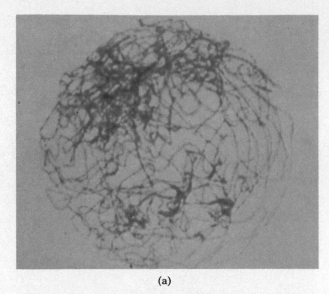

(a)

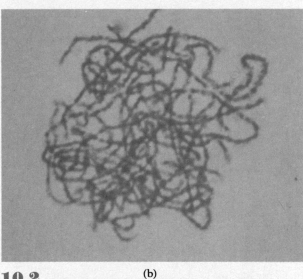

10.2 _____ (b)

In earliest prophase **(a)**, the chromosomes are only partially condensed, appearing as long, spindly strands. The chromosomes begin to move, the homologues finding each other and fusing **(b)**, permitting crossing over to occur. (Each strand now represents two fused homologues.)

duced. In mitosis, each homologue divides independently. The resulting identical chromatids are separated and equally distributed to the daughter cells. It's different in meiosis: there, for the first time, the chromosomes from the father and mother join one another side by side—in preparation for a strange, intimate event called *crossing over.*

How Mitosis and Meiosis Differ. Now let's see if we can briefly clarify some of the differences between mitosis and meiosis and rid ourselves of

this small plague. We'll have to keep three things in mind:

1. *Meiosis requires two divisions,* whereas mitosis is completed in one.
2. *At the completion of meiosis, the chromosome number is reduced by one-half,* while in mitosis the number remains constant.
3. *During meiosis, crossing over and genetic recombination occur*—a breaking and rejoining of DNA resulting in the creation of chromosomes with new combinations of genes. In mitosis, by contrast, the chromatids remain intact, exact copies.

Recombination and the Chromosome Shuffle

We've mentioned that meiosis reduces the chromosome number in eggs and sperm to prepare for the doubling that occurs in fertilization. But meiosis has another function also: it shuffles genes around and produces combinations that never existed before. The chromosomes from the father and the mother don't simply line up side-by-side in metaphase I—they pair up and scramble, and they exchange parts to create new chromosomes. This process is called **crossing over.**

After the two homologues have paired, the long DNA molecules of each chromatid are broken apart at various places along their lengths, and become joined to their opposite numbers. The fragments of one chromosome may then fuse with the homologous chromosome. The controlled breakage and rejoining happens in such a way that, generally, both chromatids end up with the same amounts of genetic material (none having been lost), but in different assortments. Now each chromatid contains portions of both maternal and paternal DNA. These new combinations of genetic material, these new chromosomes, are unique to each haploid cell produced. Therefore meiosis, in contrast to mitosis, does *not* produce daughter cells that are exact genetic duplicates of the original cell.

THE FIRST MEIOTIC DIVISION

Premeiotic Interphase

A cell preparing for mitosis grows, forms spindle material, and replicates its DNA. The same thing happens in a cell preparing for meiosis. This means that a human cell entering the first prophase of meiosis is a G_2 cell with 92 molecules of chromosomal DNA. This is because each of the 46 chromosomes consists of two identical chromatids, and each chromatid is a molecule of DNA with its associated proteins. By the time meiosis is over, each *gamete* (egg or sperm) will be haploid and in G_1, with just 23 chromosomes each. Decreasing from 92 to 23 obviously requires two divisions; let's see how they occur.

Prophase I

As the meiotic cell begins to change in preparation for **prophase I,** the chromosomes begin to condense, just as we would expect. But in meiosis, the process occurs with agonizing slowness (Figure 10.3a). We are eventually able to detect the long, spindly chromosomes as they first begin to shorten, but we may also see that they are moving—almost as if searching for something.

That "something" is each other. Each chromosome must find its counterpart, its homologue. The meiotic cell nucleus slowly begins to roll or tumble in such a way that the chromosomes within are moved randomly about. When two homologues finally bump into each other in the right way, homologous *regions* of the chromosomes will adhere, side-by-side. The regions of side-by-side fusion grow as the two homologues come together much like the two halves of a zipper.

The structure responsible for this zipperlike pairing is a complex nucleoprotein organelle called the **synaptonemal complex.** It is synthesized on the chromosomes before they actually pair, and forms a bridge between homologues. In some electron micrographs, the synaptonemal complex looks surprisingly like—well, a zipper, of all things (Figure 10.3a).

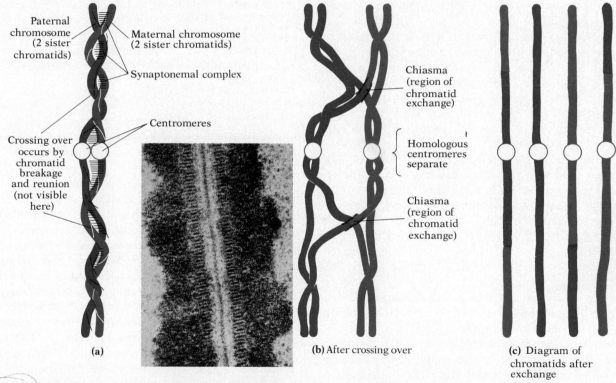

(a) (b) After crossing over (c) Diagram of chromatids after exchange

10.3

Crossing over and chiasma formation. **(a)** Following the zipperlike pairing of homologous chromosomes, the maternal and paternal chromosomes are intimately associated and bound together by the synaptonemal complex. Each of the two chromosomes consists, in turn, of two sister chromatids, which are even more intimately associated and cannot be distinguished even under the electron microscope. Thus the whole complex consists of four strands. In some cases the DNA strands may break and reunite. **(b)** In a later stage, the homologous maternal and paternal chromosomes separate. The visible evidence of crossing over is the cross-shaped chiasma. Here two chiasmata are shown. **(c)** If the four chromatids could be unwound and separated, and the regions of maternal and paternal origin indicated, they would look like this. Actually, the four chromatids will separate in later stages of meiosis. Any one exchange involves only two of the four chromatids, but ordinarily there are many exchanges between each pair of homologues, and all four chromatids become scrambled. The synaptonemal complex is clearly visible in the electron micrograph.

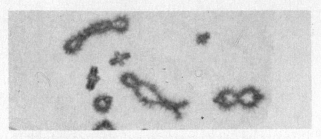

10.4

After pairing-up and crossing over in prophase I, the formerly intertwined homologues begin a repulsion process. The regions still clinging together at this time represent the previous crossover points.

It is within the synaptonemal complex that crossing over—the actual shuffling of genes—takes place (Figure 10.4). In human meiosis, there is an average of about 10 exchanges per chromosome pair. How does it happen? The details are still a subject of intense scientific investigation. The most important thing to realize about crossing over is that it is in no way an accident or a byproduct of other processes. It is such an important process that at least 50 genes and their enzymes are responsible for seeing that it happens. What does crossing over accomplish? We'll approach this problem in Chapter 12.

After crossing over, things begin to happen a bit more rapidly. The chromosomes continue to shorten and condense, and then at some point the synaptonemal complex breaks down. The homologues lose their affinity for each other, and they move apart in a process appropriately called **repulsion.**

Repulsion doesn't occur as rapidly as it might because the homologues persist in clinging together at scattered points called **chiasmata** (singular, *chiasma*). They mark the places where crossing over had taken place earlier (see Figure 10.3).

As the first metaphase of meiosis approaches, the chiasmata slide to the ends of the chromosomes, much like a ring being pulled off two napkins. Finally, the chromosomes are joined only at their tips. They continue to touch for this last moment as they move together to the metaphase plate where they prepare to be separated forever.

Metaphase I and Anaphase I

At **metaphase I,** when the chromosomes arrive at the metaphase plate, there is a brief pause in activity. Then the chromosomes completely disengage,

and **anaphase I** has begun. But, unlike what happens during mitotic anaphase, *the centromeres do not divide.* Instead, joined chromatids move together, homologues being drawn toward opposite poles of the cell. Once they have gathered at their respective poles, telophase I can begin.

Telophase I

Telophase I is similar to mitotic telophase. The chromosomes uncoil (sometimes only partially), the nuclear membrane forms around them, centrioles replicate, and cytokinesis occurs. Of course, the daughter cells are unlike any produced by mitosis, since chromosome pairs no longer exist. Remember, the maternal and paternal centromeres were separated forever at the metaphase plate.

After telophase I, the daughter cells enter their **meiotic interphase,** the period before the second stage of meiosis begins. In this interphase there is no DNA replication, so the chromosomes entering meiosis II will appear exactly as they did at the end of meiosis I. Each chromosome will be composed of two scrambled chromatids still attached by a centromere.

MEIOSIS II

Meiosis II is a bit easier to follow since it proceeds much as does mitosis (see Figure 10.2). Both daughter cells from meiosis I enter **prophase II** (with a few exceptions we will discuss later). At this stage, the centromeric spindle fibers from each pole attach to either side of the chromosomal centromeres, just as they do in mitosis. However, these two chromatids are not identical sister strands. Instead, they are composed of different combinations of maternal and paternal genes. Nonetheless, they line up on the *metaphase II* plate in preparation for being separated. When **anaphase II** begins, the centromeres finally divide, and the chromatids, now daughter chromosomes, are drawn to opposite poles. After **telophase II,** the two daughters of meiosis I are divided into four cells.

The final four daughter cells of meiosis each contain half the chromosome number of the original cell. In other words, they are now haploid. In addition, each is unique, having a different combination of the genes from the original maternal cell.

Figure 10.5 sums up the differences between mitosis and meiosis.

Summing Up the Meiotic Mechanism

We see, then, that meiosis precisely reduces (halves) the number of chromosomes in cells that will become eggs and sperm (or spores, in the case of plants). Meiosis II is very similar to mitosis, as we see the chromatids separate to be divided among the daughter cells. Although we have emphasized the precision of meiosis, such a complex mechanism must often fail. There is too much room for error and, in fact, errors in chromosome and chromatid separation do occur. Sometimes, for example, the centromeres may not release the chromosomes. The results can be tragic should such an abnormal gamete enter into fertilization.

Such an error, known as *nondisjunction*, occurs all too frequently in our own meiotic mechanisms (Essay 10.1).

WHERE MEIOSIS TAKES PLACE

In multicellular organisms, meiosis usually takes place in the *germinal tissues*. In animals, the organs in which germinal tissues are found are the *ovaries* (in females) and the *testes* (in males). In flowering plants, the equivalent structures are the flower's *ovaries* and *anthers*. Curiously, the germinal tissues of animals begin to form early, while the individual

---

ESSAY 10.1

WHEN MEIOSIS GOES WRONG

Meiosis is much more complicated than mitosis. Considering all the phases of chromosome pairing, crossing over, and double divisions, one shouldn't be surprised to learn that something frequently goes wrong. In humans, for instance, about a third of all pregnancies spontaneously abort within the first two or three months. When the expelled embryos can be examined, most of them turn out to have the wrong number of chromosomes. Failure of the chromosomes to separate correctly at meiosis is termed **nondisjunction.**

Not all meiotic failures result in early miscarriage. There are late miscarriages and still births of severely malformed fetuses. Even worse, about one live-born human baby in 200 has the wrong number of chromosomes, a condition often accompanied by severe physical and/or mental abnormalities.

With the exception of its occurrence in a special pair called the *sex chromosomes* (Chapter 12), any condition of abnormal chromosome number is almost always fatal, resulting in spontaneous abortion or death in infancy. There is

one important exception. People can survive with three copies of one certain chromosome. About one baby in 600 has this condition. Such infants may grow to adulthood, but have all kinds of abnormalities. This condition is known as **trisomy-21** (because the condition was believed to be caused only by triplicates of chromosome number 21), or **Down's syndrome,** after the 19th century physician who first described it. Other characteristics of the syndrome are general pudginess, rounded features (a rounded mouth in particular), an enlarged, often protruding tongue, and various internal disorders. Trisomy-21 individuals also have a characteristic barklike voice and unusually happy, friendly dispositions. The "happiness" apparently is a true effect of the extra chromosome, rather than a result of their (usually) extremely low IQs.

Trisomy-21 occurs most frequently among babies born to women over 35 years old, affecting up to 2% of such births. The age of the father apparently is much less influential than that of the mother. We can guess that the

much-prolonged prophase I of the human egg might have something to do with this. Since infant girls are born with all their eggs in prophase I, the egg would have been arrested in this stage for 35 years. ●

Mitosis and meiosis compared. The differences between mitosis and meiosis become apparent when they are compared stepwise. In **mitosis,** homologous chromosomes have no particular interest in each other and arrange themselves randomly in the nucleus, while in meiosis, the homologues pair up.

At *metaphase*, the alignments are also different. Mitotic chromosomes align randomly with the spindle fibers attached on both sides. In meiotic metaphase I, attachments form on one side only.

At mitotic *anaphase*, the centromeres divide and chromatids separate, while in anaphase I of meiosis they do not. Sister chromatids remain attached and homologous chromosomes, still doubled, move apart.

Mitosis terminates with *telophase*. The cell enters interphase and its DNA will be replicated in the S phase. In addition, the manner of division at anaphase ensures that each daughter cell will have the same number of chromosomes as the mother cell. The meiotic daughter will not enter an S phase and no DNA replication occurs.

In **meiosis,** a second division will occur with centromeres now dividing and sister chromatids (now chromosomes) moving to opposite poles, just as happened in mitosis. Unlike mitosis, however, the four daughter cells will be haploid, with exactly half the chromosome number of the mitotic daughter cells.

Mitosis

1. Interphase
Chromosome not visible; DNA replication.

2. Prophase
Centrioles migrated to opposite sides; spindle forms; chromosomes become visible as they shorten; nuclear membrane, nucleolus fade in final stages of prophase.

3. Metaphase
Chromosomes aligned on cell equator. Note attachment of spindle fibers from centromere to centrioles.

4. Anaphase
Centromeres divide; single-stranded chromosomes move toward centriole regions.

6. Daughter cells
Two cells of identical genetic (DNA) quality; continuity of genetic information preserved by mitotic process.

5. Telophase
Cytoplasm divides; chromosomes fade; nuclear membrane, nucleolus reappear; centrioles replicate (reverse of prophase).

These cells may divide again after growth and DNA replication has occurred.

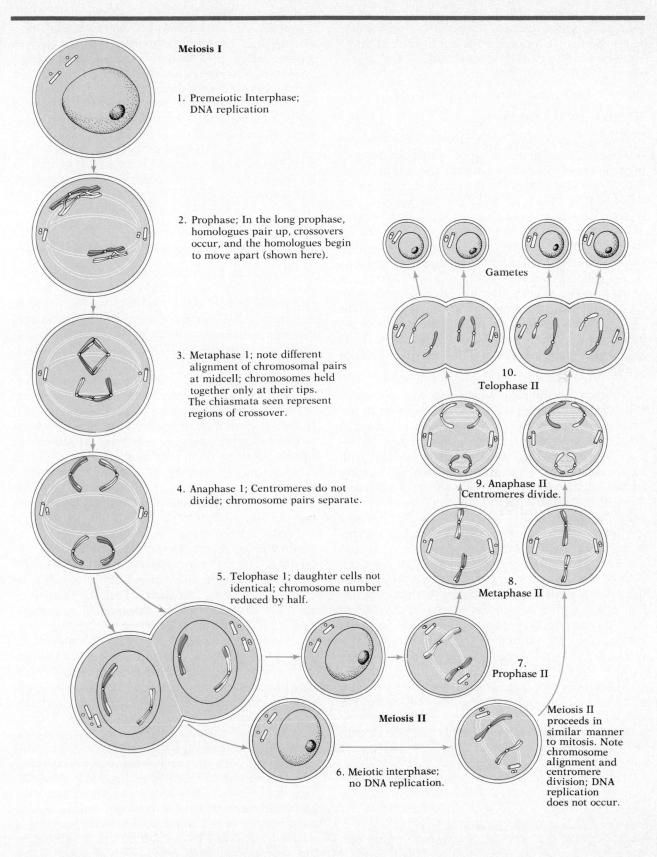

Meiosis I

1. Premeiotic Interphase; DNA replication

2. Prophase; In the long prophase, homologues pair up, crossovers occur, and the homologues begin to move apart (shown here).

3. Metaphase 1; note different alignment of chromosomal pairs at midcell; chromosomes held together only at their tips. The chiasmata seen represent regions of crossover.

4. Anaphase 1; Centromeres do not divide; chromosome pairs separate.

5. Telophase 1; daughter cells not identical; chromosome number reduced by half.

6. Meiotic interphase; no DNA replication.

Meiosis II

7. Prophase II

Meiosis II proceeds in similar manner to mitosis. Note chromosome alignment and centromere division; DNA replication does not occur.

8. Metaphase II

9. Anaphase II Centromeres divide.

10. Telophase II

Gametes

is still an embryo. Flowering plants, however, maintain regions of uncommitted tissues, which begin to change following an environmental cue, some breaking out of the usual cycling and developing into the floral parts.

Meiosis in Humans

In humans, as well as most other animals, the gonads (ovaries and testes) are formed during embryonic development. In males, the germinal tissue forms the lining of the long, highly coiled tubules that make up most of the mass of the testes. However, once these tissues are formed, activity ceases until puberty—when the cells begin dividing again. Some of the new cells produced in these divisions will begin to undergo meiosis, while others continue with mitosis, forming a ready reserve supply (for the sperm). Male meiosis, or **spermatogenesis,** holds no surprises. In each complete meiotic event, four haploid cells are formed. Each of these will become a sperm. However, meiosis in females is quite different (Figure 10.6).

Meiosis in Women.   In women (and in females of other vertebrate species as well), the cells in the ovaries that will give rise to eggs take a somewhat unexpected developmental route. Meiosis in females, or **oogenesis,** is well under way during the embryonic stage. In fact, a newborn girl already has all the developing eggs she will ever have; and most are already in prophase I, where they will stay until puberty.

When a girl reaches puberty, one or two **oocytes** (eggs, ova) resume meiosis each month, in preparation for ovulation (release of the egg from the ovary). This process will be repeated throughout the reproductive life of a woman. Although an infant girl is born with several thousand developing eggs in her ovaries, only about 400–500 actually mature. So, although sperm are produced continuously after puberty in men, women are born with all the oocytes they will ever have.

There are other significant differences between meiosis in males and females. The end product of meiosis in males is four sperm, but the result of meiosis in females is only one potential egg cell. What happens to the other three cells one would expect from the division process?

The answer lies in the position of the cleavage plane in female meiosis. Although in males the size of the cells produced by each division is similar, in females one daughter cell is large and the other is small. In fact, the cleavage plane is far off to one edge, just below the cell surface. Thus, at each

division, one daughter cell gets nearly all of the cytoplasm while the other, known as a **polar body,** acts only as a receptacle for the unused chromosomes. Once a polar body is pinched off, it undergoes no further divisions. The larger cell will divide again, however, producing a large cell and a small polar body. Thus there are actually only three cells formed in meiosis in human females—one huge egg cell and two tiny, doomed polar bodies. In human egg cells, meiosis II isn't completed unless fertilization occurs. Meiosis II begins at the time of ovulation, but no second polar body is formed unless a sperm penetrates the egg.

Gametes in Plants, a Different Matter

We have seen that gamete production in animals (humans being rather typical examples) is the direct result of meiosis. However, this isn't true in most plants. For example, in flowering plants, meiosis in the anthers is followed by mitosis, so that there are two haploid cells in each pollen grain. However, only one of the two cells in pollen is a potential sperm cell. Another peculiarity of flowering plants is that just before fertilization, the sperm cell will enter mitosis again, producing two sperm. In the ovary of flowering plants, meiosis proceeds as usual, but only one of the haploid products will survive. Rather than becoming an egg, it enters three rounds of mitosis, producing eight nuclei. One produces two, which produce four, which produce eight, only one of which will become an egg cell (see Chapter 23).

Ferns are stranger still. Like a number of nonflowering plants, ferns live double lives. The familiar, graceful plant we admire does not itself engage in sex, although it does carry on meiosis. Its meiotic products, millions of tiny, dust-sized spores containing haploid chromosomes, are carried away by wind and water. Should they find themselves in a favorable situation, the spores will begin to grow and divide, producing tiny (but independent) plants. The primary role of each plant is to produce sperm and egg cells by mitosis. Once fertilization occurs, a new, graceful, but celibate individual will emerge—to produce more spores.

What does meiosis accomplish? Meiosis and fertilization are part of a cycle that allows genes to come together to form one individual, and to separate again to form other individuals. *Meiosis facilitates evolution* by allowing every gene to be, in a sense, an interchangeable plug-in module, which must survive or fail on its own merits. The merit of meiosis is defined by the advantage it confers on the reproducing organism. Asexual species that

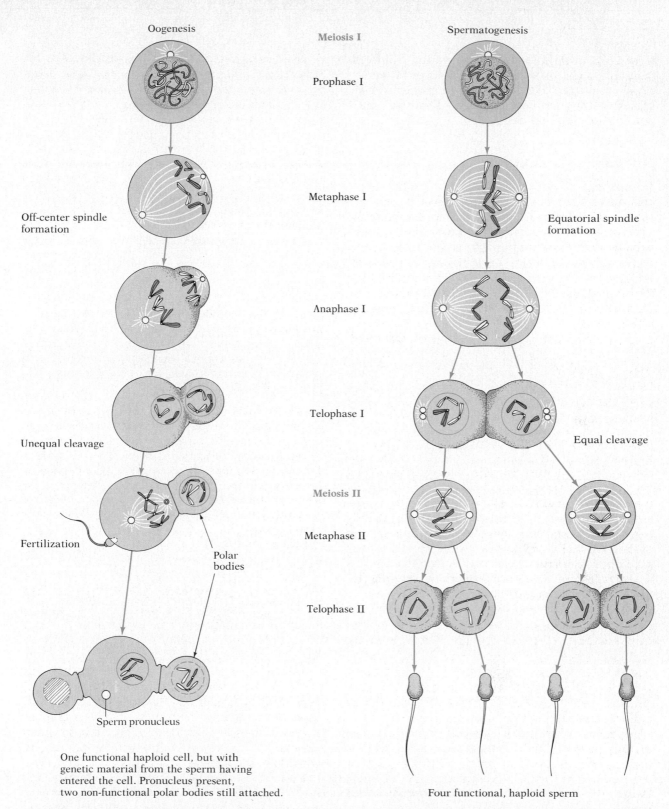

Oogenesis

Meiosis I

Prophase I

Spermatogenesis

Off-center spindle formation

Metaphase I

Equatorial spindle formation

Anaphase I

Telophase I

Equal cleavage

Unequal cleavage

Meiosis II

Fertilization

Metaphase II

Polar bodies

Telophase II

Sperm pronucleus

One functional haploid cell, but with genetic material from the sperm having entered the cell. Pronucleus present, two non-functional polar bodies still attached.

Four functional, haploid sperm

10.6

Although meiosis occurs in both oogenesis and spermatogenesis, the end result of the two processes is quite different. Although spermatogenesis results in four functional sperm, oogenesis produces one functional cell and two smaller, nonfunctional polar bodies. The unusual arithmetic of oogenesis can be explained by the off-center alignment of the chromosomes and meiotic apparatus at metaphase, and the highly unequal division of the cytoplasm at telophase. Meiosis II does not occur in the human egg unless fertilization has taken place.

have lost the ability to undergo meiosis and fertilization do exist, producing generation after generation of identical descendants, seemingly forever. But, in fact, such species face a relatively short tenure on our small planet. Their sexual relatives, by contrast, adapt—through genetic recombination—to an ever-changing world, and survive time and again to face new challenges.

Summary

Introduction

Meiosis is the process by which gametes and spores are formed. In meiosis, each diploid meiotic cell eventually produces four haploid daughter cells. Meiosis occurs in two divisions: meiosis I, in which homologous chromosomes separate, moving to opposite poles of the cell; and meiosis II, in which the centromeres divide and chromatids separate, reducing the number of chromosomes by one half. This reduction allows for the doubling that occurs in fertilization.

One of the main functions of meiosis to create new combinations of genetic material. In this process, chromosomes from the mother and father cross over and exchange parts.

The First Meiotic Division

In the premeiotic interphase, the cell enlarges, forms spindle material, and replicates its DNA. As meiosis moves into prophase I, the separated homologues condense and find their counterparts. They pair through the synaptonemal complex, where crossing over takes place. In late prophase I, the chromosomes continue to shorten and condense, the synaptonemal complex breaks down, and the homologues begin to separate in repulsion, joined only by chiasmata.

In metaphase I, the homologues disengage and enter anaphase I. Since the centromeres do not divide in this phase, the chromatids move together as the homologues are drawn toward opposite poles of the cell.

Telophase I begins as the chromosomes uncoil, the nuclear membrane forms around them, and the centrioles replicate. The phase ends when cytokinesis occurs. The daughter cells now enter the meiotic interphase. There will be no DNA replication.

Meiosis II

In prophase II, centromeric spindle fibers from each pole attach to either side of the chromosomal centromeres. After lining up on the metaphase II plate, the centromeres finally divide as anaphase II begins, and the chromatids are drawn to opposite poles. When telophase II is complete, the two daughter cells of meiosis I have divided into four haploid cells, each with a different combination of the genes from the original maternal cell.

Chromosomes do not always separate correctly. Nondisjunction of chromosomes, for example, can result in birth defects and miscarriages.

Where Meiosis Takes Place

Meiosis usually takes place in germinal tissues—ovaries and testes in animals, and ovaries and anthers in flowering plants. In humans, germinal tissues form as the embryo develops, then cease activity until puberty. Spermatogenesis is continuous in males. In females, oogenesis begins in the embryo but each oocyte is arrested in prophase I; meiosis is only continued after the onset of puberty.

Each meiotic division in males produces four sperm, while in females only one egg is produced, with two smaller polar cells that serve as receptacles for unneeded chromosomes. In human egg cells, meiosis II is completed only when fertilization occurs. Flowering plants use a combination of meiosis and mitosis to reproduce.

Key Terms

meiosis	repulsion	anaphase II
zygote	chiasmata	telophase II
diploid	metaphase I	nondisjunction
haploid	anaphase I	trisomy-21 (Down's syndrome)
meiosis I	telophase I	spermatogenesis
meiosis II	meiotic interphase	oogenesis
crossing over	prophase II	oocytes
prophase I	metaphase II	polar body
synaptonemal complex		

Review Questions

1. Meiosis occurs for one purpose alone. Name that purpose and explain why it must happen. (p. 134)

2. What are homologous chromosomes? What happens to homologues if the meiotic process is successful? (pp. 134, 136)

3. One of the most significant developments during meiosis is crossing over. Explain what this is and how it affects the content of what were originally maternal and paternal chromosomes. (p. 136)

4. List the events of prophase I of meiosis, and include the terms *homologue, synaptonemal complex, crossing over, repulsion,* and *chiasma.* (pp. 137–138)

5. Anaphase I of meiosis differs from anaphase of mitosis in one very essential way. Describe this difference and how it affects the daughter cells. (p. 138)

6. Describe the events of anaphase in meiosis II. What long-awaited event finally occurs? (p. 138)

7. What are the characteristics of Down's syndrome? Using a diagram showing nondisjunction, explain how Down's syndrome might arise. (Essay 10.1)

8. Meiosis in human males and females differs in several respects, including when it occurs, how the cytoplasm is divided, and number of products per event. Elaborate on each of these points. (p. 142)

9. Explain how the events of meiosis may be of significance to the long-term survival of a species. (pp. 142, 144)

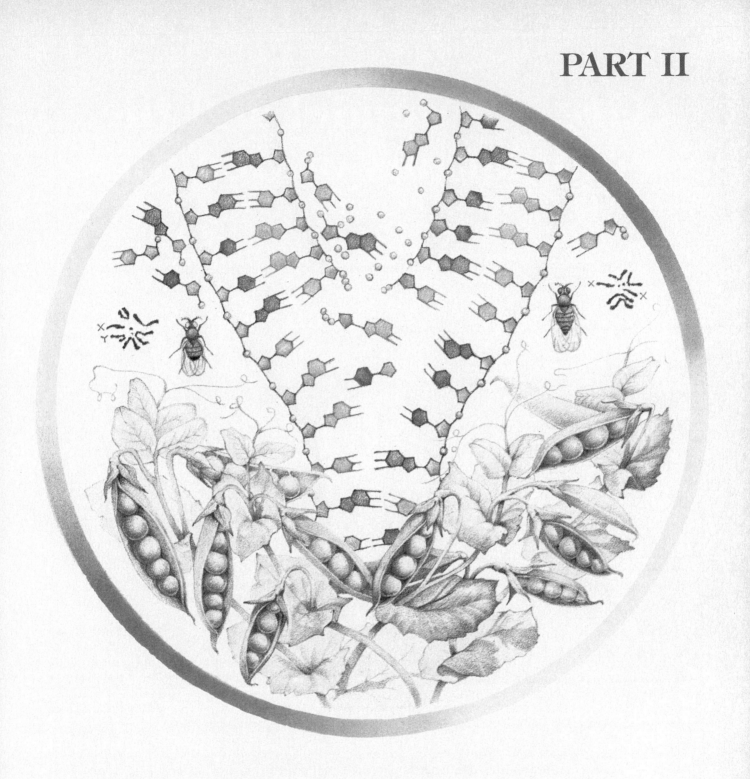

PART II

Genetics and Evolution:

History and Horizons

Gregor Mendel and the Foundations of Genetics

11

Charles Darwin was the 19th century's greatest biologist. Even so, he was a terrible geneticist, and most of his ideas about heredity were wrong! Darwin's chief mistake was to accept the only intellectually respectable theory of his day, which was that of *blending inheritance*. According to this theory, the "blood" or hereditary traits of both parents blended in the offspring, just as two colors of ink blend when they are mixed. The blending hypothesis appeared superficially to work reasonably well for some traits—such as height or weight, where there is a continuous gradation of possible values—but it couldn't account for others.

It's always surprising, in hindsight, to recognize the degree to which a strongly held belief will blind its proponents to obvious contradictions. The blending theory would predict that the offspring of a white horse and a black horse should always be gray, and that the original white or black should never reappear if gray horses continued to be bred. In reality, of course, the offspring of a white horse and a black horse are not always gray, and black or white descendants do appear. Something was obviously wrong with the theory, but no one seemed to notice—or if they did, they tried to ignore it.

Darwin had become embroiled in the aftermath of his new book, *On the Origin of Species by Natural Selection* (1859). His most trying problem was to counter the arguments of his sharper critics, who logically pointed out that natural selection and blending inheritance are antagonistic concepts; any new traits that might arise would be swamped by existing traits and simply be "blended away." Darwin was never able to answer this criticism adequately. But across the channel, deep in the European continent, a bright and dedicated monk was setting the goundwork for a new revolution by crossing strains of garden peas. He was also answering Darwin's most vexing questions. But Darwin would die ignorant of the monk's work.

The monk, Gregor Johann Mendel (Figure 11.1), was a member of an Augustinian order in Brunn, Austria (now a part of Czechoslovakia). Early in his life Mendel began training himself, and he became a rather competent naturalist. To support himself during those early years, he worked as a substitute high school science teacher. The professors at the school, noting his unusual abilities, suggested that he take the rigorous qualifying examination and become a regular member of the high school faculty. Mendel took the test and did reasonably well, but he failed to qualify, so he joined a monastic order.

In 1851 his superiors, confident of his abilities, sent him to the University of Vienna for two years of concentrated study in science and mathematics. There he learned about the infant science of statistics. He was to use this information when he returned to his old hobby of plant breeding. This time, though, he had specific questions in mind and he thought he knew how to go about finding the answers.

MENDEL'S CROSSES

Mendel began by trying to find the effects of crossing different strains of the common garden pea. But he carried out his research with more precision than any casual curiosity would call for. To begin with, he based it on a very carefully planned series of experiments and, more importantly, he would attempt to analyze the results statistically. The use of mathematics to describe biological phenomena was a new concept. Clearly, Mendel's two years at the University of Vienna had not been wasted.

Mendel was able to purchase 34 true-breeding strains of the common garden pea for his experiments. These strains differed from each other in very pronounced ways, so that there could be no problem in identifying the results of a given experiment. Mendel decided to work with seven different pairs of traits:

1. Seed form—round or wrinkled
2. Color of seed contents—yellow or green
3. Color of seed coat—white or gray
4. Color of unripe seed pods—green or yellow
5. Shape of ripe seed pods—inflated or constricted between seeds
6. Length of stem—short (9–18 inches) or long (6–7 feet)
7. Position of flowers—axial (along the stem) or terminal (at the end of the stem)

MENDEL'S FIRST LAW: THE SEGREGATION OF ALTERNATE "FACTORS"

What we will discuss here is something we already know; the point is that we learned it from Mendel. Remember that in meiotic division, gene pairs are separated from each other, one going to each of the two daughter cells. Mendel didn't know anything about meiosis or genes (he called them "factors"), but somehow, he concluded that these "factors" came in pairs and that they separated into different gametes. He called this separation *segregation*, and the segregation of alternate factors became known as **Mendel's first law.** Mendel was truly operating at the frontier of science, with little to go on except his own intuition and creativity.

To see how he started, first we must know something about peas. Each pea in a pod is essentially a unique plant, with its own genes and traits, or, in the language of genetics, its own *genotype* and *phenotype*. (The total combination of an organism's genes is called its **genotype,** and the combination of its visible traits is called its **phenotype.**) Therefore, the first three traits in Mendel's list of pea traits can be categorized by simply examining the peas in their pods.

The Experimental Procedure

Mendel's approach, a novel one at that time, was to cross two *true-breeding* strains that differed in only one characteristic. (**True-breeding strains** are those that consistently [generation after generation] yield progeny—offspring—with the same

11.1

Gregor Johann Mendel (1822–1884), the first mathematical biologist. Bringing together an innate curiosity, keen observational powers, and mathematical training, Mendel developed the basic laws of heredity. His work, published in 1866, went unnoticed for many years until it was rediscovered about the turn of the century. Once his ideas were understood, they opened the door to 20th-century genetics.

traits.) Mendel began by asking simply questions, such as: What will happen if I cross a true-breeding yellow-seed pea plant with a true-breeding green-seed pea plant?

Pea breeding, by the way, is extremely tedious work. To carry out a cross, Mendel first had to select and plant his seeds, and then wait for them to grow and flower. That gives one plenty of time to read, file one's nails, and practice accents. But later things become a bit more hectic. A garden pea plant, if left alone, generally will self-pollinate, its pollen fertilizing its own ovules (Figure 11.2). In this way, garden peas go on happily producing their own true-breeding kind. But Mendel was interested in crosses. To cross two strains, he had to open the flowers early in their growth and cut off the pollen-producing anthers of particular plants. Then, using a fine brush, he had to transfer pollen from other flowers—a laborious task. The plants selected for the cross would be called the P_1 (first parental) generation and their offspring the F_1 (first filial) generation. The offspring of the F_1 would be called the F_2, and so on.

F_1 Generation and the Principle of Dominance.
When Mendel crossed his original P_1 plants, he found that the characteristics of the two plants didn't blend, as prevailing theory said they should. When plants grown from yellow seeds were crossed with those grown from green seeds, their F_1 offspring were not intermediate seeds. Instead, all of them were yellow seeds, indistinguishable from the yellow seeds of the true-breeding parental strain. Mendel termed the trait that appeared in the F_1 generation the **dominant** trait, and he described the one that had failed to appear as the **recessive** trait. But he was left with a vexing question. What had happened to the recessive trait?

Mendel had quite a puzzle on his hands. But he was apparently quite good at puzzles. His next step, a stroke of intuition, was to allow his F_1 plants to self-pollinate. In this second filial generation (the F_2 generation), Mendel found that roughly 1/4 of the peas were green and that about 3/4 were yellow. The recessive trait had reappeared (Figure 11.3)! He repeated the experiment with other pea strains, with comparable results. When he crossed a round pea strain with a wrinkled pea strain, all of the F_1 peas were round; but in the F_2 generation, about 1/4 of the peas were wrinkled again. The constancy of the ratios did not escape the tenacious Mendel, who was determined to keep tackling the problem until he could make some sense of it.

Two Kinds of Yellow Peas: Homozygous and Heterozygous.
From his experiments thus far, Mendel realized that there were two kinds of yellow peas: the true-breeding kind, like the original parent stock, which would grow into plants that would bear only yellow peas; and another type, which—when grown and self-pollinated—would produce pods containing both yellow and green peas. Two kinds of yellow peas: one pure-breeding, one not. So, he wondered, were there

11.2

The unusual petals of the garden pea generally ensure self-pollination. To cross-pollinate a plant, Mendel had to open the young flower and remove the pollen-bearing anthers. Then he transferred pollen from another flower to the stigma (female receptive structure) to accomplish the cross he wanted.

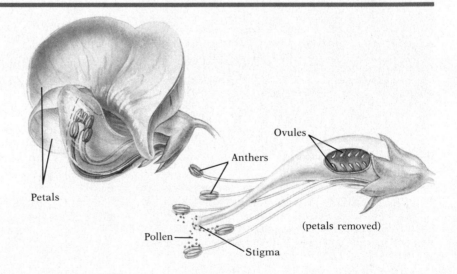

Petals

Ovules

Anthers

(petals removed)

Pollen

Stigma

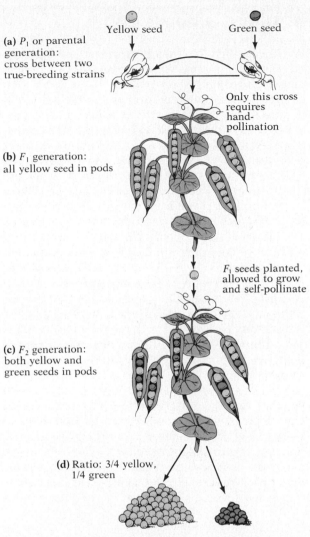

(a) P_1 or parental generation: cross between two true-breeding strains

Yellow seed

Green seed

Only this cross requires hand-pollination

(b) F_1 generation: all yellow seed in pods

F_1 seeds planted, allowed to grow and self-pollinate

(c) F_2 generation: both yellow and green seeds in pods

(d) Ratio: 3/4 yellow, 1/4 green

11.3

In his P_1 generation, Mendel crossed true-breeding yellow peas with true-breeding green peas **(a)**. When the P_1 bore pods, all of the seeds within, representing the F_1 generation **(b)**, were yellow. These seeds were planted and, when grown, were allowed to self-pollinate, producing an F_2 generation of pea seeds within the pods of the F_1 plant. F_2 seeds included both yellow and green peas **(c)** in a ratio of 3/4 to 1/4, or 3:1 **(d)**. The green trait had disappeared in the F_1, only to reappear in the F_2.

one trait (such as green color in peas); **heterozygous** means that the organism bears genes for different traits, regardless of its appearance. Thus a yellow pea *could* be carrying unexpressed genes for green color.

Clearly, some factor determining the recessive form was passed down from the true-breeding recessive P_1 parental strain, through the hybrid (offspring of crossbreeding) F_1 generation to the true-breeding recessive F_2 generation; whatever it was, however, it was not being expressed in the F_1 generation. Mendel, at that time the world's only mathematical biologist, thought he could use algebraic symbols to express his dilemma.

He let a capital letter, say **Y**, represent the factor that determines the dominant form, and let a lower-case letter, say **y**, represent the factor that determines the recessive form. The F_1 hybrid, he concluded, must have both factors present, and could be represented as **Yy**. Since there are two parents, Mendel figured that in the hybrid **Y** comes from one parent, and **y** from the other. (If this sounds simplistic, considering what you know about chromosomes, remember that Mendel didn't know about chromosomes.) Using reciprocal crosses, Mendel determined experimentally that it didn't matter which parental strain bore the peas and which provided the pollen.

If heterozygous plants get a **Y** from one parent and a **y** from the other parent, and are symbolized **Yy**, it makes sense that the true-breeding dominant forms get two **Y** factors—one from each parent—and can be symbolized **YY**. In the same way, the true-breeding recessive forms get **y** factors from both parents and can be symbolized **yy**. We can use **YY** to symbolize the *dominant homozygote* (when the factor from each parent is identical), **yy** to symbolize the *recessive homozygote*, and **Yy** to represent the *heterozygote* (when the factor from each parent is different). Let's use these symbols to take a closer look at Mendel's first crosses.

Mendel had by now deduced:

True-breeding P_1:	**YY**	×	**yy**
F_1 progeny:	All		**Yy**
F_1 inbreeding cross:	**Yy**	×	**Yy**
F_2 progeny:	**YY**	**2Yy**	**yy**

The genotypic ratio expressed in the F_2 is 1:2:1, or

1/4 round **(YY)**	=	Homozygous yellow
1/2 round **(Yy)**	=	Heterozygous yellow
1/4 wrinkled **(yy)**	=	Homozygous green.

What would be the phenotypic (visible) ratios here? Actually, there is a simpler way of represent-

also two kinds of green peas? There were not. When green peas were cultivated and allowed to self-pollinate, they always bore only green peas. This kind of experiment is now called **progeny testing.**

And we now call the true-breeding peas *homozygous* and the other kind *heterozygous*. **Homozygous** means that the organism bears the genes for only

ing the results, using what is known as a Punnett square, developed by Reginald Crandall Punnett, an early 20th-century fan of Mendel (Figure 11.4).

Summing up Mendel's First Law

Mendel wasn't so presumptuous as to name anything after himself, but his discoveries from the crosses described so far have been brought together into what we call *Mendel's first law*, the law of segregation. This law states:

1. Any trait is produced by at least a pair of factors. The pair may be homozygous or heterozygous. These factors segregate during pollen and ovule formation.

2. A gamete receives one of a pair of factors.

3. For each trait, offspring receive only one factor from each parent. If one parent's factors are heterozygous, the offspring has an equal chance of receiving either factor.

4. Where dominance is found, the dominant factor will be expressed over the recessive, and the recessive trait will appear only in the offspring when in the presence of another recessive trait.

These statements are not in Mendel's words, except for the term *factor* which, in more modern terminology, would be *gene*. Most of what the first law contains actually is attributable to simple meiosis, but remember that Mendel had no knowledge of that phenomenon. He arrived at his conclusions through sheer logic.

SCIENCE AND MODELS

We have called Mendel a mathematical biologist not just because he was trained in both mathematics and biology, or because he was the first biologist to use statistical analysis in his work, but because of the way he arrived at his conclusions. What does a mathematical biologist do? Usually, he or she starts with a set of observations. In Mendel's case, it was the dominance of one trait in the first generation and the reappearance of the recessive trait in a subsequent generation. Through a mental process involving both intuition and logic, the mathematical biologist then constructs a *model*. The model is an imaginary biological system based on the smallest possible number of assumptions, and it is expected to yield numerical data consistent with past observations. New experiments are then performed to test further predictions of the model. If the new data don't fit the predictions, the model is discarded or adjusted to fit the new observations so that further experiments can be done. A **model,** then, is a biological hypothesis with mathematical predictions.

Models and hypotheses cannot be proven with experimental data. We can only say that the data are *consistent* with the model. Mendel did not prove his first law, but its simplicity and consistent usefulness in verifying predictions enabled him to make and test new predictions. His success came very close to a formal proof, at least as far as he was concerned. However, others were unconvinced

11.4

Punnett squares are useful for keeping track of the gametes produced and for carrying out the multiplications necessary to show the possible outcomes of a cross. The gametes are placed outside the box as shown, and the new combinations are written inside where the letters intersect. In this example, each square represents 1/4 of the offspring. Adding up the squares reveals a 1:2:1 genotypic ratio and a 3:1 phenotypic ratio.

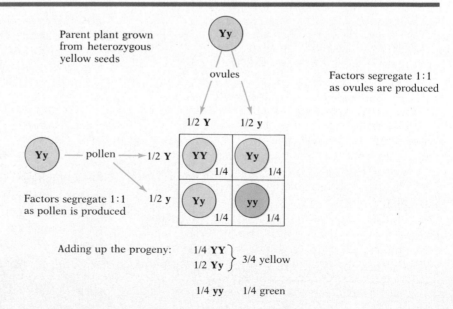

TABLE 11.1

Mendel's F_2 generations

The dominant and recessive traits analyzed by Mendel are shown, along with the results of F_1 and F_2 generations. Note the large numbers he worked with. How does a large sample size (large numbers) improve the validity of the conclusions? How well do his numbers in the last two columns agree with what we should expect in the crosses (see Essay 11.1)? The proportion of the F_2 generation showing recessive forms is in the far-right column.

	Dominant form	Number in F_2 generation		Recessive form	Number in F_2 generation	Total examined	Ratio	Proportion of F_2 generation
⬤	Round seeds	5,474		Wrinkled seeds	1,850	7,324	2.96:1	0.253
 ⬤⬤	Yellow seeds	6,022	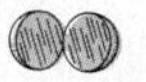	Green seeds	2,001	8,023	3.01:1	0.249
⬤	Gray seed coats	705		White seed coats	224	929	3.15:1	0.241
	Green pods	428		Yellow pods	152	580	2.82:1	0.262
	Inflated pods	882		Constricted pods	299	1,181	2.95:1	0.253
	Long stems	787		Short stems	277	1,064	2.84:1	0.260
	Axial flowers (and fruit)	651		Terminal flowers (and fruit)	207	858	3.14:1	0.241

until after the discovery of chromosomes and meiosis. Have you noticed how well Mendel's findings fit with what you already know about meiosis? Imagine how elated Mendel would have been if meiosis had been discovered in his own lifetime!

We've mentioned that Mendel extended his crosses to all seven selected traits. How well did his results fit the mathematical model? Table 11.1 shows that in each cross, his results were amazingly close to the 3:1 phenotypic ratio predicted by his models (see Figure 11.4). The closeness between Mendel's expectations and observations did not escape the attention of certain skeptical statisticians. In 1936, R.A. Fisher, a noted statistician and geneticist, concluded that Mendel's data were literally too good to be true. Did the good abbot fudge his data? Or did he simply see what he had ex-

pected to see, an all-too-human trait? The question has generated great controversy, but we will leave all that to the historians. Whatever is the case, Mendel's first law was found to apply to animals as well as plants, and has held up under the most rigorous scrutiny.

MENDEL'S SECOND LAW: INDEPENDENT ASSORTMENT

We have noted Mendel's success in breaking his problem down to its smallest parts, partly by studying only one characteristic at a time. His next step was to consider two characteristics at a time. So he crossed a true-breeding strain that bore

153

round, yellow peas with another true-breeding strain that bore wrinkled, green peas.

The F_1 offspring (which, remember, could be categorized and counted while still in the pod) were all round and yellow. We can symbolize this as follows:

$$RRYY \times rryy \longrightarrow RrYy$$

We will now begin considering two factors, and from now on we will refer to factors as *alleles*, a more modern term. **Allele** means "a particular form of a gene at a locus." The term *locus* derives

from our present knowledge that each gene occupies a specific place, or locus, on the chromosome (plural, *loci*). **R** and **r** will be symbols for the two alleles of the round-or-wrinkled locus, and **Y** and **y** will be the symbols for the two alleles of the yellow-or-green locus.

Now let's see what happened in the F_2 generation when Mendel crossed plants that were different in two ways (called a *dihybrid cross*) (see Table 11.1). Remember that the F_1 peas were uniformly round and yellow. In the F_2 generation—the offspring of $F_1 \times F_1$ (**RrYy × RrYy**)—Mendel found

ESSAY 11.1
GENES, COINS, AND PROBABILITY

Suppose someone flips a penny and says, "call it." If the penny is a real one and your friend is too, you can assume that there is a statistical probability of 1/2 that the coin is "heads." This can be written in algebra as follows: $P(H) = 1/2$; that is, the probability of heads = 1/2.

If you didn't know anything about coins and tried to generalize from the single toss, and the coin came up tails, you might assume that coins *always* come up tails, but the more times you toss the coin the closer the number of tails would be to 1/2. That's why a large sample size (large numbers) is better in the statistical game.

Predicting the results of simple Mendelian crosses has a lot in common with flipping coins. For example, we begin Mendelian crosses by determining what types of gametes are possible. Obviously, there's no chance involved when a homozygote produces gametes, so it's like flipping a two-headed coin. Heterozygous individuals, however, have two different alleles for a trait, say **A** and **a**. So an **Aa** individual forms two kinds of gametes, **A** and **a**, in equal numbers. The probability that any given gamete will carry the **A** allele is 1/2. Alternately, the probability that a gamete will carry

a is also 1/2. All of Mendelian genetics is based on this 50–50 segregation of alternate alleles.

But so far we have only seen how flipping a penny can represent segregation in the gametes. Let's see how it applies to a cross between two gamete-forming individuals. For this, you need a partner and two coins. Since each penny has two sides, a head **(H)** and a tail **(T),** the result of:

$$HT \times HT$$

will be any of four *possible outcomes:*

1. both coins come up heads **(HH);**
2. both coins come up tails **(TT);**
3. your coin is *heads*, your partner's is *tails* **(HT);** or
4. your coin is *tails*, your partner's is *heads* **(TH).**

All four of these possible outcomes are equally likely; each has a probability of 1/4. Why is this? It's an example of the **multiplicative law of probability,** which states that *the probability of two independent outcomes both occurring is equal to the product of their individual probabilities.* (*Independent outcomes* are outcomes that don't influence one another; we assume that the way your coin lands has no influence

on the way your partner's coin lands, and vice-versa.) So the law states that the probability of **HH** equals the probability of your coin landing heads, *times* the probability of your partner's penny landing heads, which is $1/2 \times 1/2 = 1/4$.

The third and fourth possible outcomes are more interesting and can be used to illustrate another law. First, let's see how their probabilities are determined. The probability of:

- your penny landing heads and your partner's landing tails is $1/2 \times 1/2 = 1/4$;

- your penny landing tails and your partner's landing heads is $1/2 \times 1/2 = 1/4$.

So, what is the probability of heterozygous offspring **(Aa)** in our cross? To determine the answer, the probabilities of the last two possible outcomes are simply added together $(1/4 + 1/4 = 1/2)$. Or, there is a 1/2 chance that the two pennies will come up one head and one tail.

This basic law, called the **additive law of probability,** states that *the probability that any one of two (or more) mutually exclusive outcomes will occur, is equal to the sum of their*

and classified 556 peas. He was able to divide them into four groups:

315 round and yellow	**R–Y–**
101 wrinkled and yellow	**rrY–**
108 round and green	**R–yy**
32 wrinkled and green	**rryy**

Note that a total of 133 peas were wrinkled and 140 peas were green. In either case, this comes close to 139, which is 1/4 of 556. The dashes mean that either allele could exist there without altering the phenotype.

So about 1/4 of the F_2 peas were wrinkled and 1/4 were green, while 3/4 were round and 3/4 were yellow, which demonstrates Mendel's first law in both cases. But the data indicated more than that. Mendel now suspected that the two pairs of contrasting characters were inherited *independently*. Another way of stating this is: the two pairs of alleles illustrate the principle of **independent assortment**. This means that a gamete's receipt of an **R** or an **r** has nothing to do with its receipt of a **Y** or a **y**. How did Mendel arrive at that? He looked at the numbers (Essay 11.1).

---

individual probabilities. Mutually exclusive outcomes means that if one happens, the other can't; for instance, if the outcome is: your coin, *heads*; your partner's coin, *tails*; then this excludes the possibility of the outcome being the other way around.

Now, what is the probability that at least one head will be showing? Here, we combine the three mutually exclusive outcomes (1), (3), and (4). The probability that at least one head will come up is 1/4 + 1/4 + 1/4 = 3/4.

The multiplicative and additive laws can be applied to independent assortment, where over two traits are considered simultaneously (the dihybrid cross). It's like tossing two pennies and two quarters at the same time. If you toss two pennies and two quarters simultaneously, what is the probability of seeing both Lincoln and Washington (at least once each)? The probability of seeing Lincoln is 3/4; the probability of seeing Washington is also 3/4; the chance of seeing both is 3/4 × 3/4 = 9/16. The chance of seeing Abe and *not* seeing George is 3/4 × 1/4 = 3/16, the same as for seeing George and not Abe; and the probability of seeing neither president is 1/4 × 1/4 = 1/16. Of such simple stuff are Mendelian ratios made. ●

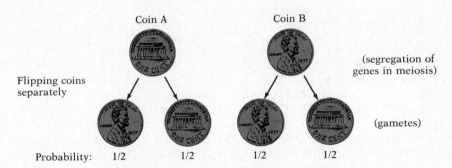

(segregation of genes in meiosis)

(gametes)

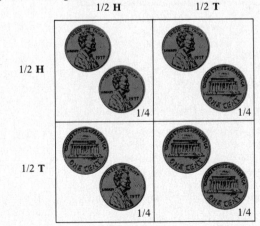

The Punnett square keeps track of all possible combinations and their frequency of occurrence

Results: 1/4 **HH**
1/2 combination **HT** + **TH**
1/4 **TT**

(This is the genotypic ratio Mendel found in his F_2)

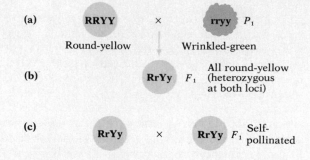

(a) **RRYY** × **rryy** P_1

Round-yellow   Wrinkled-green

(b)   **RrYy** F_1 All round-yellow (heterozygous at both loci)

(c)   **RrYy** × **RrYy** F_1 Self-pollinated

R, **r**, **Y**, and **y** assort independently into all possible combinations

R, **r**, **Y**, and **y** assort independently into all possible combinations in the pollen

	RY	Ry	rY	ry
RY	RRYY	RRYy	RrYY	RrYy
Ry	RRYy	RRyy	RrYy	Rryy
rY	RrYY	RrYy	rrYY	rrYy
ry	RrYy	Rryy	rrYy	rryy

F_2

(d) Analysis of results

Round and yellow (like the F_1)	9	(9/16)
Round and green	3	(3/16)
Wrinkled and yellow	3	(3/16)
Wrinkled and green	1	(1/16)
Total	16	

11.5

Independent assortment of two pairs of alleles. Mendel developed his second law by crossing pea plants for two traits simultaneously. The scheme here illustrates the crosses from P_1 through F_2, using the Punnett square to show the results of the F_1 self-pollinated cross. The traits being considered are round and wrinkled shape and yellow and green color, both characteristics of seeds. When true-breeding round-yellows (**RRYY**) are crossed with true-breeding wrinkled-greens (**rryy**) (a), the F_1 is heterozygous round-yellow (**RrYy**), since these are the dominant traits (b). Inbreeding the F_1 individual produces four different types of gametes. The F_2 generation is diagrammed in the Punnett square (c). It comprises four distinct phenotypes, which include every possible color and shape combination. These occur in a 9:3:3:1 ratio (d). Mendel determined this ratio by counting and classifying 556 pea seed offspring.

As Figure 11.5 reveals, two pairs of alleles assort independently, producing four kinds of gametes in both the pollen and the ovules. The chances of any particular combination of alleles occurring in any of the progeny is equal to that of any other combination. Therefore, we have to multiply the four kinds of male gametes by the four kinds of female gametes to predict the outcome of independent assortment. Again, the Punnett square comes to the rescue, helping us keep track of the products.

The 9:3:3:1 Ratio

When Punnett squares are used, the gametes possible from both individuals must be determined first. Where two traits are being considered in plants and both individuals being crossed are heterozygous for both traits, there will be four kinds of pollen and four kinds of ovules. Should a parent individual be homozygous for one of the traits, only two types of gametes will occur. We can use this information to sum up a cross between plants differing in two traits. The phenotypic results are 9/16, 3/16, 3/16, and 1/16. These readily convert to the ratio 9:3:3:1, which is as familiar in genetics as $E = mc^2$ is in physics.

As we saw in Figure 11.5, when Mendel classified his 556 peas according to the four possible phenotypes and counted the peas in each group, the ratio was remarkably close to 9/16:3/16:3/16:1/16, as would be expected if two gene loci were segregating independently, each with a 3/4:1/4 phenotypic ratio.

But the monk wasn't finished yet. A good scientist is never satisfied with explanations that merely account for observations that have already been made. To be useful, an explanation must lead to new predictions that can then be tested. Mendel's theory predicted that while there were four phenotypes in a 9:3:3:1 ratio, there should be a total of nine genotypes in a 1:1:1:1:2:2:2:2:4 ratio. Mendel knew that he could determine the genotypes of his peas by letting them grow to adult plants and examining their progeny; so the 556 peas went into the soil, and Mendel waited another year. 529 of the resulting plants fertilized themselves and produced a new crop of peas, the F_2 generation. Now their genotypes could be determined; the results are shown in Table 11.2. Mendel was elated—his prediction had held.

The Test Cross

Although Mendel had carried out numerous progeny tests for determining whether a dominant indi-

TABLE 11.2

Mendel's predictions and results for the F_2 genotypes (529 pea plants classified by progeny test).

Genotype of F_2	Fraction expected	Number according to the hypothesis	Number actually observed by progeny testing
RRYY	1/16	33	38
RRYy	2/16	66	65
RRyy	1/16	33	35
RrYY	2/16	66	60
RrYy	4/16	132	138
Rryy	2/16	66	67
rrYY	1/16	33	28
rrYy	2/16	66	68
rryy	1/16	33	30

NOTE: Keep in mind that Mendel had to progeny test each of the 529 F_2 peas in order to learn their genotype. There is no other way to prove the genotype of a heterozygote.

vidual was homozygous or heterozygous, he soon devised a much simpler procedure, the **test cross.** The subject was simply crossed with a recessive individual. Recessives are always homozygous, so the predictions were straightforward. Let's use the traits round and wrinkled as an example:

1. If the dominant round individual in question is homozygous, then the test cross becomes **RR × rr,** and all of the progeny will be round **(Rr).**

2. If the dominant round individual is heterozygous, then the test cross becomes **Rr × rr,** and, statistically, half the offspring will be heterozygous round **(Rr)** and half will be wrinkled **(rr).**

The test cross is often applied today to test the pedigrees of plants and animals in agriculture (see Figure 11.6).

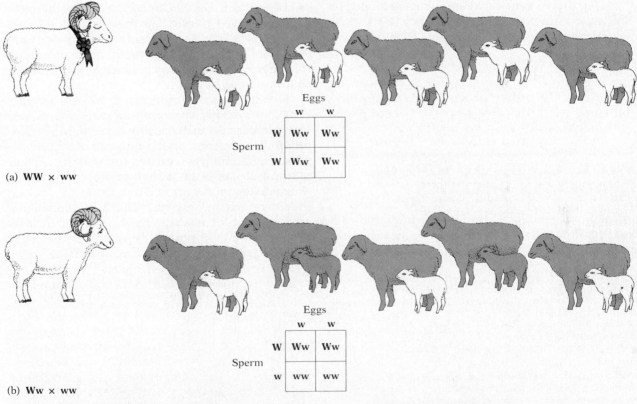

(a) **WW × ww**

(b) **Ww × ww**

11.6

The test cross. Sir Beauregard Thickfuzz is a prize ram by all ram-judging standards. He will be useful for breeding, but only as long as we are sure he is homozygous for white wool. White is dominant over black in sheep. The genotypes for color are **WW** = white, **Ww** = white, and **ww** = black. To test our prize white ram, we mate it with some homozygous black ewes. **(a)** If Sir Thickfuzz is homozygous, all of his sperm will carry the dominant **W** allele. All of the eggs of the black ewes will carry the recessive **w** allele, but the offspring will be white lambs. If he passes the test, our prize ram will probably father hundreds of lambs. **(b)** However, if he is a heterozygote, half of his sperm will carry the allele **w** for black wool and about half of the test progeny will be black. Just one black sheep in the family will be enough to condemn Sir Beauregard Thickfuzz to a life of celibacy!

Summing up Mendel's Second Law

Mendel's own statement of the law of independent assortment, in translation, is as follows:

> The behavior of each pair of differing traits in a hybrid association is independent of all other differences between the two parental plants.

A more modern version of this statement is:

> If an organism is heterozygous at two or more unlinked loci, each locus will assort independently of the others.

Note that a new word—"unlinked"—has been inserted. This just reminds us that Mendel didn't know everything. Most pairs of gene loci follow his second law, but some don't. The ones that do are called *unlinked*, and the ones that don't are called *linked*. Mendel's second law, as important as it is, is true only some of the time. As you may have guessed, **linked genes** are genes that are located on the same chromosome so that they are usually passed along together. Linkage will be discussed further in Chapter 12.

The impact of Mendel's laws on science is almost incalculable, yet new ground is broken by dissenters. The source of new ideas in genetics, we'll find, was in the dogged pursuit of exceptions to Mendel's laws.

THE DECLINE AND RISE OF MENDELIAN GENETICS

In 1866, after seven years of experimentation (at the very time Darwin was pondering the enigma of heredity), Mendel presented his results to a meeting of the Brunn Natural Science Society. His audience of local science buffs sat there politely, probably not understanding a word of what they were hearing. The minutes of the meeting, which still exist, record that not a single question was asked. Instead, the restless audience launched into a discussion of the "hot" topic of the time—Darwin's *Origin of Species*.

Mendel's single paper was published in the society's proceedings the following year, and was distributed widely. The learned scientists of the day were just as baffled and uninterested as Mendel's original audience. Historians have come up with a small, sad, but remarkable piece of information. In Darwin's huge library, which is also still intact, a one-page account of Mendel's pea work appears in a German encyclopedia of plant breeding. Some relatively obscure work is described on the facing page, and it is covered with extensive notes in Darwin's handwriting. The page describing Mendel's work is clean. Darwin must have seen the paper that could have clarified his theory of natural selection, saving him years of agony and uncertainty. But even Darwin was not ready for mathematical biology, and he too failed to grasp Mendel's simple but profound ideas.

Mendel's work continued to be ignored until 1900, the year his work was suddenly revived with great fanfare. In that year, three biologists in three different countries, each trying to work out the laws of inheritance, searched through the old literature and came up with Mendel's paper. They immediately recognized its importance. Science had changed in 35 years. The 20th century had arrived, and the obscure monk, dead for 16 years, became one of the most famous scientists of all time.

Summary

Mendel's Crosses

Until Mendel's work, heredity was thought to be the result of parents' traits "blending" in the offspring. Mendel approached the problem by setting up controlled experiments to cross different strains of the common garden pea. He used statistical methods to analyze the results and developed the first laws of genetics.

Mendel's First Law: The Segregation of Alternate "Factors"

Mendel selected seven pairs of traits for his experiments and proceeded to cross true-breeding pea strains that differed in only one trait. Each pea in a pod contained its own phenotype and genotype. As he observed the results, he discovered that some traits were dominant and others recessive. Through repeated progeny testing, Mendel developed the principles of his first law, the law of segregation: (1) any trait is produced by a pair of either homozygous or heterozygous factors; (2) a gamete receives only one of a pair of factors; (3) offspring receive only one factor from each parent for each trait; and (4) a dominant factor will be expressed over a recessive one, which will only appear in the presence of another recessive trait.

Science and Models

Models such as Mendel used can be thought of as biological hypotheses with mathematical predictions. While they cannot be proven with experimental data, models are useful in verifying predictions and testing new ones. Mendel's results fit his mathematical model remarkably well.

Mendel's Second Law: Independent Assortment

In the next stage of his experiment, Mendel studied two characteristics at a time. He found that two pairs of alleles ("factors") assort independently; that is, the appearance of one has nothing to do with the appearance of the other. Using the multiplicative and additive laws of probability to calculate the likely outcomes of independent assortment, Mendel predicted four phenotypes in a 9:3:3:1 ratio and nine genotypes in a 1:1:1:1:2:2:2:2:4 ratio. His results confirmed his predictions.

The impact of Mendel's laws on science is almost incalculable, yet new ground is broken by dissenters. The source of new ideas in genetics, we'll find, was in the dogged pursuit of exceptions to Mendel's laws.

Key Terms

Mendel's first law	progeny testing	independent assortment
genotype	homozygous	multiplicative law of probability
phenotype	heterozygous	additive law of probability
true-breeding strain	model	test cross
dominant	Mendel's second law	linked genes
recessive	alleles	

Review Questions

1. Using the traits *tall* and *short* for height in peas, carry out a P_1 and F_1 cross. Use Punnett squares and assume that *tall* is dominant and that the P_1 individuals are true-breeding. List the phenotype(s) of the F_1 and the phenotypes and their ratio in the F_2. (pp. 150–152)

2. Mendel's first law is actually a description of meiosis (even though meiosis deals with whole chromosomes rather than "factors"). To illustrate this point, prepare a simple diagram of one pair of chromosomes going through meiosis, but mark the homologues with the letters Y (yellow) and y (green), and carry the "markers," along with the chromosomes, through meiosis I and meiosis II. (p. 152 and Ch. 10)

3. Briefly explain the meaning of the term *mathematical model* and explain how such models are used by scientists. What is another term for *model?* (p. 153)

4. An experimenter crosses a number of plants that produce red flowers. In observing the offspring, the experimenter counts 289 plants with red flowers and 112 with yellow flowers. What, most likely, was the genotype of the parent plants? Prove this. If your hypothesis is correct, how many red-flowered plants and how many yellow-flowered plants should one expect in the offspring of such a cross? How can we explain any difference between what was predicted and what was actually observed? (pp. 150–153)

5. Two of the traits Mendel worked with were inflated versus constricted pods (**I** vs **i**) and axial versus terminal flowers (**A** vs **a**). Consider these traits in the dihybrid (two pairs of factors) cross: **IiAa × IiAa.**

   a. List the different gametes possible with respect to the factors.

   b. Using a Punnett square, show the cross.

   c. Determine the phenotypic ratio. (pp. 154–157)

6. Where dominance is expressed, it is often impossible to tell by simply looking whether an individual is homozygous or heterozygous. Explain how you would apply a test cross to determine whether the genotype of a tall pea plant (dominant) was **TT** or **Tt.** (p. 157)

7. An experimenter carries out a dihybrid cross of pea plants and finds the following in the offspring:

   32 have yellow, round seeds
   27 have yellow, wrinkled seeds
   14 have green, round seeds
    9 have green, wrinkled seeds

   Working back through the cross and using a little intuition, determine the most probable genotypes of the individuals crossed. Prove your answer. (*Hint:* before you start drawing Punnett squares, pay close attention to the numbers.) (pp. 155–157)

Genes and Chromosomes

12

Long, idyllic days of thoughtful puttering in a Moravian monastery once marked the leading edge of the field that would be called *genetics*. The coming of warm spring days would, year after year, signal new growth, new experiments, and new ideas by the careful abbot, Gregor Mendel. He was almost ignored in those days. Science itself was not ready for him, but didn't know it. Other scientists read his work but couldn't grasp its importance.

Nevertheless, even in Mendel's final years there were rapid improvements in the microscope and in various techniques for studying cells. Biologists were beginning to be able to watch the puzzling pageant of mitosis and meiosis. They watched those strange, twisted molecules go about their slow dances. They decided that chromosomes must be important, but they had no idea why. The closing years of the 19th century marked a very busy and exciting time for cell biologists.

The stuff of genes, DNA, was isolated and characterized in Mendel's own lifetime, although a more precise understanding of the chemical nature of the gene was 50 years away. But by the first year of the 20th century, the world was at last ready for Mendel. After years of obscurity, Mendel's work burst upon 20th-century science. Biologists of the time were keenly interested in heredity, and some were experimenting with plants. It was inevitable that dominance and 3:1 ratios would occur. Then the inevitable happened. Three researchers inde-

pendently rediscovered the old monk's findings. In the 16 years since his death science had grown. These three investigators at last understood the meaning of Mendel's ratios. The Mendelian revival was followed by an era of intense activity, in which 3:1 and 9:3:3:1 ratios dominated the conversations of turn-of-the-century geneticists.

LOCATING THE GENES

Mendel, we have mentioned, referred to the units of inheritance as *factors*, or what we now call *genes*. The genes, as you are well aware by now, carry the instructions for producing specific kinds of proteins, among them the various enzymes. The genetic message is encoded in the linear sequence of the DNA nucleotides. One gene follows another, with ample "spacer DNA" between, along this single informational molecule—rather like a series of coded messages in a punched tape.

Mendelism and Meiosis

The phenomenon of pairing and separation of homologous chromosomes in meiosis wasn't worked out until 1900, the year of Mendel's rediscovery. Some microscopists already suspected that chro-

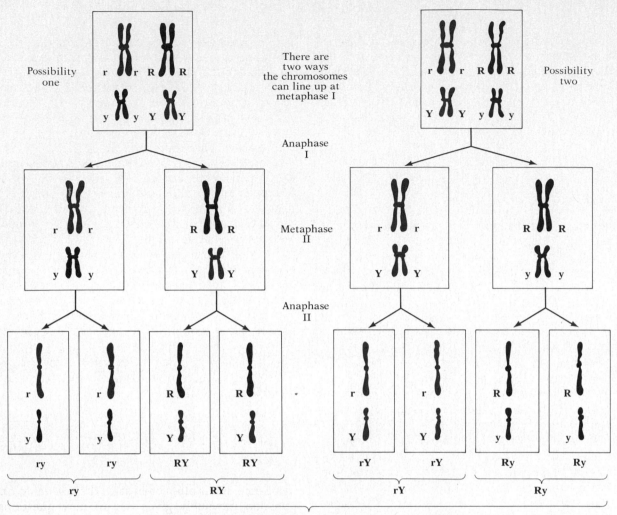

Possibility one

There are two ways the chromosomes can line up at metaphase I

Possibility two

Anaphase I

Metaphase II

Anaphase II

ry ry RY RY rY rY Ry Ry

ry RY rY Ry

These are the gametes possible from genotype **RrYy** when meiosis occurs in two or more cells without crossing over

12.1

Mendel's second law, independent assortment, also describes the behavior of chromosomes in meiosis. The cell entering meiosis with two pairs of genes on two different chromosome pairs has two alternatives at metaphase of meiosis I. The homologues can align themselves in either manner (possibility one or two in the diagram), with a 50:50 chance of either. Of course, once a meiotic cell goes to either alternative, that's all for that cell. Actually, large numbers of meiotic cells must be considered for the independent assortment to be tested. Following the alternatives as each continues through meiosis reveals that there are four equally likely combinations of chromosomes and genes in the gametes.

mosomes were the carriers of inheritance; and soon after Mendel's work was republished, Theodor Boveri in Europe and Walter Sutton in America published influential papers pointing out the relationship between Mendelism and meiosis.

It isn't hard to follow their thinking. Suppose a pair of alternate alleles (for instance, **R** and **r**) are carried on a pair of homologous chromosomes. When the homologous chromosomes separate during the first division of meiosis, exactly half of the haploid cells will receive one of the alleles (**R**), and exactly half will get the other (**r**). And that, quite simply, is the physical basis of Mendel's first law.

The interpretation of Mendel's second law—the law of independent assortment—is almost as clear. (Recall from Chapter 11 that the second law involves alleles, or factors, that are located on different chromosome pairs.) Suppose one pair of homologous chromosomes carries one pair of alternate alleles—**R** and **r**—and a second pair of chromosomal homologues carries another pair of alleles—**Y** and **y** (Figure 12.1). When the chromosomes line up on the metaphase plate, either of two things can happen. In one possible way of lining up, **R** and **Y** will go to one pole of the dividing cell, and **r** and **y** will go to the other pole. In the second way of lining up, **R** and **y** move to one pole and **r** and **Y** move to the other. There is exactly the same chance of one possibility as of the other. The overall result, when many such cells undergo meiosis, is that the genotypes of the haploid cells formed will be **RY, Ry, rY,** and **ry** in equal numbers—just as Mendel claimed.

Chromosomes Determine Sex: Support for the Chromosome Theory of Inheritance

The theory that chromosomes were the carriers of genetic information was strengthened, in the early years of this century, when it was shown that chromosomes could determine sex. In mammals and fruit flies (and many other insects), there are two *heteromorphic* (*hetero*, "different"; *morph*, "shape") sex-determining chromosomes named *X* and *Y*. The X and Y chromosomes can readily be distinguished under the microscope (Figure 12.2). The important thing is that even though they have very different appearances, they are obviously homologous. One line of evidence is that they pair with one another during meiosis.

Let's review the essentials of X and Y chromosomes. Males of some species have one of each of the two chromosomes called X and Y in every cell. This is because every male gets an X chromosome from his mother and a Y chromosome from his father. Females of these species have no Y chromosome at all, but have two X chromosomes in every cell. Every female gets an X chromosome from her mother and another X chromosome from her father, and so she is designated XX.

Since females have only the two X chromosomes, every gamete produced must carry a single X. In spermatogenesis (meiosis in males), the X

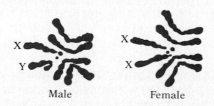

X
Y
Male

X
X
Female

12.2 ▬▬▬▬▬▬

Drosophila melanogaster (the fruit fly) has four pairs of chromosomes. In females, each pair contains typical homologues, with identical pair members. (Note the extremely tiny pair.) In males, however, only three pairs are truly homologous. The fourth pair consists of an X chromosome, similar to that in the female, and a peculiar J-shaped Y chromosome. The Y is almost devoid of loci, and those present deal with male fertility only. By contrast, the X chromosome has about 1,000 loci.

and Y chromosomes pair and then separate in the first anaphase, so that half of the sperm produced will bear an X and half will bear a Y. The sex of the offspring will depend on whether the fertilizing sperm is X-bearing or Y-bearing. A Y-bearing sperm fertilizing an X-bearing egg will produce a son, and an X-bearing sperm fertilizing an X-bearing egg will produce a daughter.

Watching a heteromorphic X and Y chromosome pair segregate during meiosis supported Mendel's law of alternate segregation, but it was necessary to watch *two* pairs of chromosomes in action to verify his law of independent assortment. This wasn't long in coming. An insect species was found that had a pair of homologous but heteromorphic *autosomes* (an **autosome** is any chromosome that isn't a sex chromosome); one member of this pair had a big, dark-staining knob of extra chromatin. Tracking the heteromorphic X and Y and the heteromorphic autosomes in the same cell soon established that the pattern of segregation in one pair had nothing to do with segregation in the other pair. Thus, the cellular basis of Mendel's second law was established.

LINKAGE

In science, it has often been said, the answer to one question inevitably gives rise to new questions. And this was the case with both Sutton's and Boveri's findings. Both had decided that chromosomes bore hereditary factors and that many such factors (genes) were contained on each chromosome. The problem they encountered, however, was that Mendel's principle of independent assortment didn't work with all genes. This, they decided, was because genes on the same chromosome should stay together during assortment, moving with the chromosomes as part of a *linkage group*. **Linkage group** came to be defined as any group of genes on the same chromosome.

Any such linkage, of course, would refute the law of independent assortment. Soon enough, some exceptions to the law began to surface. William Bateson and R. C. Punnett, trying to reconfirm Mendel's findings, got some puzzling results. They started with two sweet pea strains: one with blue flowers **(BB)** and long pollen grains **(LL)**; the other with red flowers **(bb)** and round pollen grains **(ll)**. The offspring of this cross had blue flowers and long pollen grains, so "blue" and "long" were Mendelian dominants. This is their original cross:

BBLL × bbll ⟶ BbLl

Following Mendel, they tried to reconfirm the law of independent assortment by crossing the double heterozygote **BbLl** back to the double recessive **bbll** parental strain (a test cross):

$$BbLl \times bbll$$

Mendel's law said that they should get equal numbers of all four possible combinations of phenotypes. However, if the two genes were on the same chromosome, one might predict that only two types should result. In other words, two separate hypotheses led to two different predictions. Bateson and Punnett observed neither of these predictions. Instead, they found:

Offspring		Expected Frequency		
Phenotype	Genotype	*	†	Observed Frequency
Blue, Long	**BbLl**	25%	50%	44%
Blue, round	**Bbll**	25%	0	6%‡
red, Long	**bbLl**	25%	0	6%‡
red, round	**bbll**	25%	50%	44%

* = Hypothesis I: Mendel's independent assortment; † = Hypothesis II: Sutton's complete linkage; ‡ = These demanded explanation.

Neither hypothesis was confirmed! Mendel's law didn't hold for these two pairs of genes. Mendel would have predicted equal numbers of the four phenotypic combinations. The *parental* phenotypes (blue, long and red, round) were, in fact, more frequent than the unexpected phenotypes (blue, round and red, long). On the other hand, if the markers were on the same chromosome, Sutton would have predicted that the nonparental combinations would not appear at all. But although they were fewer in number, there they were. These plants with nonparental phenotypes were called **recombinant progeny** since they had a different genetic combination after meiosis than did the chromosomes entering meiosis. But it's worth noting that the results also didn't seem, at first, to be consistent with Sutton's idea that the two genes could be on the same chromosome. Of the entire test cross progeny, 12% were recombinants, and how could genes on the same chromosome possibly move to a new chromosome? Bateson and Punnett never did figure out what was going on. A new, unexpected result requires the formulation of a new hypothesis. They were stumped. They dimly suggested that the haploid pollen and ovules with the parental combinations somehow underwent proliferation before fertilization. But the real explanation turned out to be even more bizarre. It seems that chromosomes regularly break apart and rejoin in new patterns.

GENETIC RECOMBINATION

The **recombination** of two different genes that are physically part of the same chromosome—in modern terms, linkage groups, or two regions of the same DNA molecule—requires the actual breaking of the chemical bonds of two chromosomes at the same loci and their rejoining in a new pattern. This is the complex meiotic process of *crossing over* (see Chapter 10). The early geneticists had a hard time of it, but they managed to work out the concept of crossing over using only their crosses, test crosses, and progeny counts (Figures 12.3 and 12.4).

It was confusing at first. Only some pairs of genes deviated from the law of independent assortment, but each of these pairs seemed to have its own deviation. Two genes that tended to assort together in a test cross (that is, **B** and **L**, **b** and **l**) were called *linked*. But some gene pairs showed stronger tendencies to link than others. In Figure 12.4, 12.6% of the test cross progeny were recombinant (**B** and **l**, **b** and **L**); but in other crosses, the recombinant progeny might represent only a fraction of a percent. Gene pairs that had very low percentages of recombination were described as *tightly linked*, and those with higher percentages of recombination were described as *loosely linked*. These test cross numbers had none of the appeal of Mendel's wonderfully precise ratios. If the terms "loosely" and "tightly" linked genes sound vague, consider the dilemma of the geneticists. A considerable time would pass before they would be able to equate linkage groups with the linear structure of DNA.

Linkage Groups and Genetic Maps

Eventually, some patterns began to emerge. Two mutant genes, *Bar eye* and *scalloped wings* in the fruit fly (*Drosophila melanogaster*) were linked. In addition, *Bar eye* and *garnet eye* also were found to be linked. A number of such mutually linked genes formed a linkage group. The inference, as mentioned previously, was that all members of a linkage group were on the same chromosome.

Working with fruit flies, A. H. Sturtevant eventually reasoned that the more tightly linked gene pairs (those more likely to stay together in crosses) were very close together on a chromosome, while the loosely linked gene pairs (those staying together less frequently) were spaced farther apart on the same chromosome. The farther apart two genes were, Sturtevant reasoned, the greater was the chance that the length of chromosome separating them would break and rejoin in a crossover.

The idea of genes being beads on a string, that is, all arranged on a line in any given chromosome, began to win acceptance.

The numbers began to make some sense, too. For instance, in the example given, Bar eye and scalloped wings showed 6% recombination in a test cross; scalloped wings and garnet eye showed 7% recombination; and in another test cross, Bar eye and garnet eye showed just slightly less than 13% recombination progeny. (According to our calculations, 6% plus 7% equals 13%.)

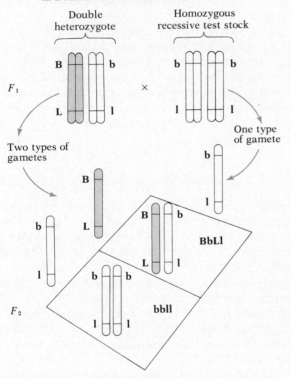

Assumption:

Two pairs of alleles linked on the same chromosome pair will not segregate in a Mendelian fashion thus

Double heterozygote

Homozygous recessive test stock

F_1

Two types of gametes

One type of gamete

BbLl

F_2

bbll

Results = 1:1 ratio

with no new combinations appearing

12.3

In this situation, genes **B** and **L**, and genes **b** and **l**, are permanently linked together on their chromosomes without crossing over. As such, they are passed as a unit to the gametes. In the test cross seen, a heterozygous individual is crossed with a homozygous individual. Since the genes are passed as units, only two phenotypes are possible in the offspring, and these occur in a 1:1 ratio. This situation may represent the exception rather than the rule.

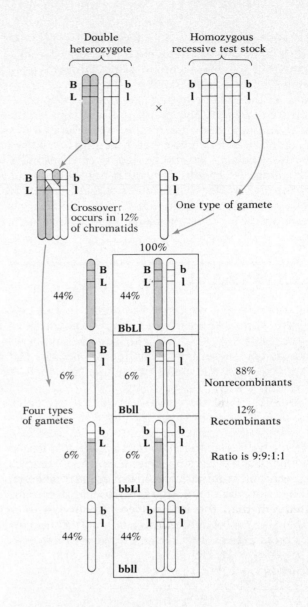

Double heterozygote

Homozygous recessive test stock

Crossover occurs in 12% of chromatids

One type of gamete

100%

Four types of gametes

44% 44% BbLl

6% 6% Bbll

6% 6% bbLl

44% 44% bbll

88% Nonrecombinants

12% Recombinants

Ratio is 9:9:1:1

12.4

Now let's reconsider the test cross seen in Figure 12.3, this time allowing for a limited amount of crossing over between the two loci. We will be using Bateson and Punnett's cross as an example. Here, 12% of the chromatids undergo reciprocal exchange between the two genes for flower color and pollen shape. The remaining 88% of the chromatids do not undergo exchange. There are two kinds of *recombinant* chromosomes produced and two kinds of *nonrecombinant* chromosomes produced. The results might suggest, at first, that the genes were not really linked after all, and are undergoing independent assortment. But the numbers tell us otherwise. There is no 1:1:1:1 ratio; it is more like a 7:1:1:7 ratio. Of the total, 12% will be equally divided between the two kinds of recombinant progeny and the remainder equally divided between the two kinds of nonrecombinant progeny.

Sturtevant believed that these data meant not only that all three genes were on the same chromosome, but that they were in a line, with scalloped wings in the middle (Figure 12.5). He made maps of all of the linkage groups, with each "map unit" being equal to 1% recombination. Each site on the gene map was henceforth called a *gene locus*, and a given gene locus could be occupied by one of two or more alleles on homologous chromosomes. Genetic maps eventually were made of all of the *Drosophila* chromosomes, and included hundreds of known genes (Figure 12.6). The technique was soon used for other organisms.

SEX LINKAGE

Before genetic mapping techniques were perfected, chromosomes were already known to be responsible for sex, but the sex chromosomes themselves presented a continuing puzzle. Did they, too, contain genes? Even the tiny male Y chromosome?

In 1910, T. H. Morgan showed that one gene, the one determinant of white eyes in *Drosophila*, was located on the X chromosome (Figure 12.7). Thus it followed that the trait was not inherited independently of sex, but showed a complex pattern of inheritance known as **sex linkage**. Morgan eventually received the Nobel prize for his achievement.

Of the two sex chromosomes X and Y, the X is the more interesting, because it carries thousands

Separate test crosses indicate

13% recombination between bar eye and garnet eye
7% recombination between garnet eye and scalloped wings
6% recombination between scalloped wings and bar eye

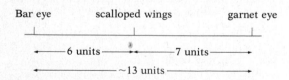

12.5

Gene maps are developed through studies of the crossovers between genes located on the same chromosomes. Each percent of recombination is equal to one map unit. In this example, the locus of scalloped wing was determined to be between Bar eye and garnet eye, all mutant characters of *Drosophila*. The percent recombined was determined by test crosses between heterozygous individuals and homozygous recessives.

of genes that affect all aspects of the phenotype. Also, its pattern of inheritance is the more complex, since it is present in both sexes. But before we try to understand the genetics of the X chromosome, we should take a brief look at its smaller partner, the Y chromosome.

The Y Chromosome

The Y chromosome's pattern of inheritance is simplicity itself: it is passed from fathers to sons, period. If you are a man, your Y chromosome was inherited intact from your father, from your father's father, and from your father's father's father and so on, right back to the first mammalian Y chromosome. And unlike all other human chromosomes, the Y chromosome never undergoes crossing over.

In XY species, such as flies and mammals, the Y chromosome is nearly devoid of identifiable genes. The few genes that are present on the Y chromosome include several genes for sperm function. In humans, the Y chromosome also has genes that influence height. In humans and all other mammals, the Y chromosome carries the determinant of sex itself.

The X Chromosome and X-linked Genes

In earlier chapters, we've emphasized that diploid organisms have two copies of every gene—one from the father, and one from the mother. This is perfectly true for women, who get two X chromosomes, but it is not true for men. About 10% of all human genes are carried on the X chromosome, and for each of these gene loci, a man (XY) gets one copy from his mother, period. From his father he gets (in addition to one of each of the 22 human autosomes) only the genetically impoverished Y chromosome.

This means that human males are effectively haploid for approximately 10% of their estimated 40,000–50,000 genes. The lone copies of a mother's X-linked genes in her son therefore can be referred to as neither homozygous nor heterozygous; geneticists have coined a special term for them: **hemizygous** (which means that they have no allelic counterparts).

Both in theoretical terms and in terms of human experience, the implications of this are enormous—especially when it comes to harmful, recessive mutant genes. This is because diploid organisms usually are protected from the effects of recessive genes since such alleles usually are "cov-

12.6

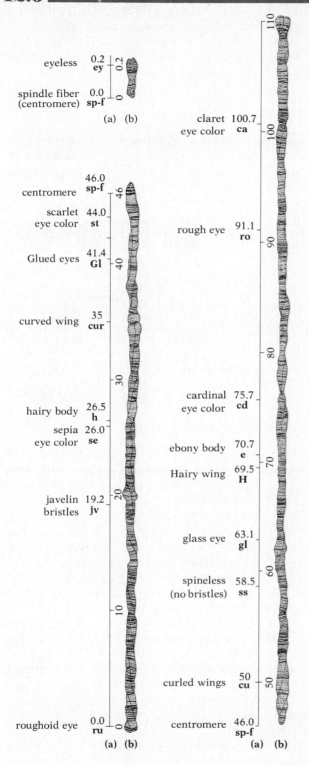

eyeless — 0.2 **ey**

spindle fiber (centromere) — 0.0 **sp-f**

(a) (b)

centromere — 46.0 **sp-f**

scarlet eye color — 44.0 **st**

Glued eyes — 41.4 **Gl**

curved wing — 35 **cur**

hairy body — 26.5 **h**

sepia eye color — 26.0 **se**

javelin bristles — 19.2 **jv**

roughoid eye — 0.0 **ru**

(a) (b)

claret eye color — 100.7 **ca**

rough eye — 91.1 **ro**

cardinal eye color — 75.7 **cd**

ebony body — 70.7 **e**

Hairy wing — 69.5 **H**

glass eye — 63.1 **gl**

spineless (no bristles) — 58.5 **ss**

curled wings — 50 **cu**

centromere — 46.0 **sp-f**

(a) (b)

Seen here are recombination maps (vertical ruler lines with loci indicated) of two of *Drosophila's* chromosomes, and reproductions of the actual chromosomes. (Included is the tiny fourth chromosome and the right and left arms of the long third chromosome.) Recombination map distances and relative loci are seen on the left of the vertical ruler lines, along with the names of mutant traits. The numbers on the right of the vertical lines are the actual loci as visually determined through the study of the distinct bands seen on the chromosomes themselves. This second method of loci identification, called *cytological mapping*, is based on a very different methodology. Actually the cytological determination of loci has been remarkably consistent with recombination mapping. In the preparation of cytological maps, fruit-fly larvae are bombarded with X rays, and changes in phenotype are equated with observable changes in the chromosomes.

ered'' and rendered harmless by a normal dominant allele on the homologous chromosome. This protective effect of dominance still works for X-linked recessives, but only in females. If a woman (XX) has received a detrimental recessive X-linked gene from one parent, she still has a good chance of receiving a normal dominant allele from the other parent. But when a man (XY) receives a detrimental recessive X-linked gene *from his mother*, it will always be expressed. His Y chromosome will be of no help.

This is not to say that women cannot express sex-linked traits. They can and do, but the probability is quite reduced. Thus men get the dubious distinction of being the ones who are most often affected by X-linked genetic pathologic conditions. The list of these is long and depressing, and includes three kinds of muscular dystrophy, two kinds of hemophilia (bleeder's disease), the Lesch-Nyhan syndrome, three types of hereditary deafness, pituitary dwarfism, testicular feminization, and several kinds of congenital blindness, in addition to such less life-threatening conditions as color blindness (Figure 12.8).

The Lyon Effect

The ''saliva test'' is sometimes used in women's athletic competitions as proof that a competitor is, in fact, a woman. This is because a swab of the person's mouth cavity will carry with it a few cells from the lining. When these cells are stained, sex differences can be detected. The cell nucleus in females shows a dark-staining body, the *Barr body*,

12.7

 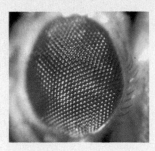

The mutation white eye in *Drosophila* was discovered early in the 20th century by Thomas H. Morgan. From crosses carried out with the mutant, Morgan was able to determine that the allele responsible was recessive and sex-linked—carried on the X chromosome. That is, it is most often expressed in males, where only one white eye allele is needed to produce the trait. Females can be white-eyed, but for this to happen, they must have white-eyed fathers and mothers that are at least carriers of the white eye allele. As we see in the crosses, Morgan began his analysis with his discovery, a white-eyed male. His F_1 flies were all red-eyed, indicating typical dominance as Mendel would have predicted. Surprises began to show up when the F_1 sons and daughters were inbred. White eyes showed up only in males, and then just half of them were white-eyed. Morgan then crossed his now geriatric white-eyed male with its heterozygous F_1 daughters. More surprises! Half the males and half the females were white-eyed. The others were red-eyed. Courtesy Carolina Biological Supply Company

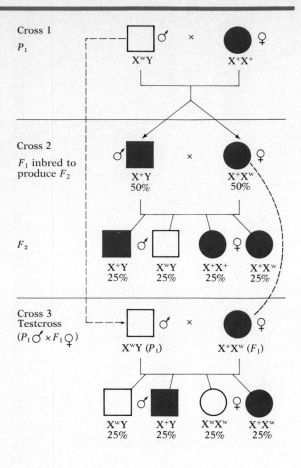

12.8

The defective color blindness allele *(solid color)* in this family tree has been traced through four generations. Can you determine the genotypes in the three *normal* individuals (indicated with question marks)? What are the clues that sex linkage is involved?

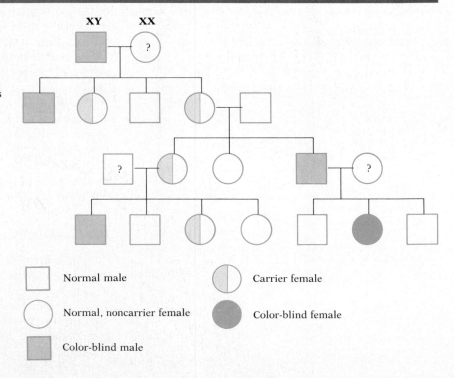

Normal male

Normal, noncarrier female

Color-blind male

Carrier female

Color-blind female

168

absent in normal male cells. The Barr body is actually a condensed X chromosome (Figure 12.9a).

Every female cell has twice as many X-linked genes as are present in a male cell. Presumably, there would be a physiological imbalance if both X chromosomes were activated. In any case, evolution has solved the problem by permanently inactivating one of the two X chromosomes in each XX cell during embryonic development—each cell, that is, except for the germ line cells (those that form gametes). Which of the two X chromosomes is inactivated—the one from the father, or the one from the mother—seems to be a matter of chance. Every tissue in the adult female is a mosaic of patches in which one or the other X has been put to sleep, as it were. However, the suppressed and condensed X is replicated normally and is passed from cell to daughter cell. It is only inactive with regard to genetic function. For instance, the muscle tissue of women who are heterozygous carriers of X-linked muscular dystrophy is made up of patches of normal muscle and of degenerate muscle. The normal cells expand in size and strength, so such women appear to be normal. This effect was first established by an English geneticist, Mary Lyon, for whom it is named.

The condensed X chromosome also can be viewed microscopically in certain white blood cells, where it forms a characteristic projection from the cell nucleus called the *drumstick*. Although the Barr body was named after Murray L. Barr, its discoverer, the drumstick got its name because it reminded someone of a chicken leg (Figure 12.9b). Studies of Barr bodies and drumsticks are used in the clinical determination of X-related nondisjunction (see Essay 10.1), a fairly common problem. The presence of a condensed X chromosome in males or extra X's in females is a positive indicator.

MUTATION

Although DNA is a relatively stable molecule, it is nonetheless subject to wear, tear, and disruption by such influences as heat, radiation, or destructive chemicals. Any random, permanent change in the DNA molecule is called a **mutation.** We have mentioned mutations before, and as we will find later (Chapter 18), they occur with a predictable regularity. We all carry them, and experts can even tell us how many we can expect.

A mutation can be harmless, in which case it is called a *neutral* mutation. Some human blood group differences are probably due to neutral mutations. If a mutation destroys a vital genetic function, it can kill the organism outright—a *lethal* mutation. In between are all sorts of *harmful* mutations that can be passed from generation to generation, resulting in whole families with, say, crooked teeth or a tendency to acne. Much rarer are *beneficial* mutations, but they do exist. All of our normal, functioning genes were beneficial mutations when they first showed up in our ancestors.

All kinds of mutations can occur spontaneously, sometimes while DNA is being replicated, but more often when it is just sitting around minding its own business. For example, a nucleotide might become changed, or the DNA chain broken, by an encounter with an energetically active *free radical* that occurs spontaneously in the nucleus when a water molecule breaks apart into an uncharged hydrogen and an uncharged but very reactive OH radical. Most such changes in DNA are promptly and correctly repaired by *DNA repair enzymes*. It is the ones that are not repaired, or that are incorrectly repaired, that become recognized as mutations.

12.9

Condensed and inactive chromatin is seen in the Barr body **(a)** and the drumstick of cells from women **(b).** Barr bodies are visible in specially stained cells, while the drumstick is seen in stained white blood cells.

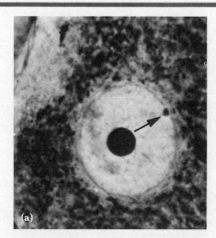

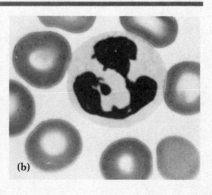

ESSAY 12.1
THE DISEASE OF ROYALTY

Because ruling monarchs consolidated their empires through marriage alliances, hemophilia was transmitted throughout the royal families of Europe. **Hemophilia** is a sex-linked recessive condition in which the blood does not clot properly; any small injury can result in severe bleeding—and if the bleeding cannot be stopped, in death. Hence, it has sometimes been called the *bleeder's disease*.

The hemophilia allele has been traced back as far as Queen Victoria, who was born in 1819. One of her sons, Leopold, Duke of Al-

bany, died of the disease at the age of 31. Apparently, at least two of Victoria's daughters were carriers, since several of their descendants were hemophilic. Hemophilia played an important historical role in Russia during the reign of Nikolas II, the last Czar. The Czarevich, Alexis, was hemophilic, and his mother, the Czarina, was convinced that the only one who could save her son's life was the monk Rasputin—known as the "mad monk." Through this hold over the reigning family, Rasputin became the real power behind the disintegrating throne. ●

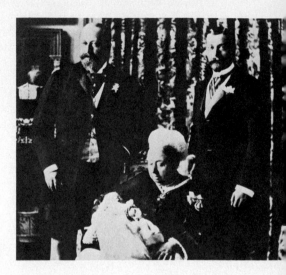

□ Normal male

○ Normal female

■ Hemophilic male

◐ Carrier female

? Possible carrier female

? Male died in infancy, possible hemophilic

Generations

I — Albert ☐—◐ Victoria

II — Victoria Empress Frederick, Edward VII, Alice of Hesse, Leopold Duke of Albany, Eugenie wife of Alfonso XIII, Beatrice

III — Kaiser Wilhelm II, George V, George VI, Fred William, Irene Princess Henry, Alix Tsarina Nikolas II, Alice of Athlone, Leopold, Maurice

IV — Duke of Windsor, Earl Mountbatten, Waldemar, Prince Sigismund of Prussia, Henry, Alexis, Lady May Abel Smith, Rupert, Alfonso, Gonzalo

V — Princess Margaret, Queen Elizabeth II, Prince Phillip, Sophia, Juan Carlos of Spain

VI — Princess Anne, Prince Charles, Prince Andrew, Prince Edward

A mutation must occur in a germ line cell in order to be passed to the next generation. But mutations in other cells can be serious, too, because such changes can transform a normal cell into a cancerous one.

The probability of such changes can be increased by certain chemicals that can interact with DNA to cause mutations. Of even greater concern is *ionizing radiation*, which drastically increases the rate of mutations (and cancer) because it greatly increases the production of deadly free radicals. Overall, for any exposure to radiation there is a far greater risk of cancer than of a heritable mutation. Perhaps this is because even one cancerous cell, arising among our body's trillions of cells, can grow into a cancer that kills us.

Point Mutation and Mutant Alleles

A mutation can be limited to a single nucleotide or to a small region of DNA, affecting a single gene. Thus, a new mutant allele is produced that could be dominant or recessive, lethal or harmless, X-linked or autosomal. This is called a **point mutation** to distinguish it from gross, large-scale shifts in entire sections of chromosomes. The hemophilia mutation that must have occurred in a gamete of one of Queen Victoria's parents is an example (Essay 12.1).

Chromosomal Mutations

Whole chromosomes can mutate, sometimes in comparatively spectacular and bizarre ways. Chromosomal mutations are better known as **chromosomal rearrangements** because they all involve the breaking of one or more DNA molecules and their rejoining in unusual and abnormal ways. There are two ways that this happens: (1) actual breakage followed by fusion repair, and (2) errors in crossing over that result in new spatial relationships of loci because the process of normal, controlled breaking and rejoining at precise points fails. The results are about the same. But since breakage followed by fusion repair is probably easier to understand, let's take a closer look at this sort of change.

Breakage and Fusion Repair. **Breakage** is just that: both of the phosphate-sugar backbone strands of a double-stranded DNA molecule will sometimes break, and the chromosome will fall into two pieces. You'd think that this would be fatal to the cell, because only one of the pieces would have a centromere and the other surely would be lost in the next mitotic division. But, in fact, chromosome breakage seems to happen frequently, usually with no permanent effect. The two broken ends simply rejoin and are healed, as good as new, by the same repair enzymes that heal other kinds of DNA damage. Under the microscope, it looks as if the two broken ends were sticky. Careful studies have demonstrated that more than 99.9% of all such breaks in *Drosophila* sperm chromosomes are healed by such a process.

Problems arise when two chromosome breaks occur in the same nucleus at the same time. *Two* breaks means *four* sticky, unhealed, broken ends. The fusion repair enzymes aren't choosy and will rejoin any two ends, sometimes correctly and sometimes incorrectly. If they are rejoined in new ways, the results can be disastrous.

Consider what happens when two breaks occur in the same chromosome. This means that there will be three fragments, one of them with two sticky ends. In such a case, the two fragments with one sticky end may rejoin and leave out the middle fragment, resulting in a **deletion** of genetic material. A small deletion affecting only one or a few genes may be passed on to the next generation, but most large deletions are immediately lethal.

Another interesting thing can happen with such breakages. The middle fragment with the two broken ends can eventually form into a ring. If this fragment is large and contains a centromere, it may become an abnormal **ring chromosome.** There are reasonably healthy people walking around today with ring chromosomes in every one of their cells; however, ring chromosomes can also be associated with hereditary mental retardation. Another possible outcome of such breakages is that the middle fragment may flip end-over-end before being rejoined to the two end fragments, resulting in a chromosome with an **inversion,** or inverted segment (Figure 12.10).

If the two breakpoints occur in separate but homologous chromosomes or chromatids, and in different positions on the two homologues, abnormal fusion repair can result in one too-short chromosome and another too-long chromosome. The short chromosome will have a deletion and the long homologue will have a **duplication** of genetic material: it will have an extra copy of all of the genes that occur in the duplicated region. Surprisingly enough, such duplications are sometimes beneficial and have played an important role in evolution. For example, because of such duplication, we have multiple genes for manufacturing hemoglobin, the protein that carries oxygen in our blood.

Translocations.   As a final example of a chromosomal rearrangement, consider what can happen when two nonhomologous chromosomes break in the same nucleus at the same time. An incorrect fusion repair results in a **translocation** of genetic material from one chromosome to the other (Figure 12.11). If both chromosomes break approximately in the middle, such misrepair can result in two reciprocal translocation chromosomes. When the breaks happen to be close to the ends in both chromosomes, the tiny end fragments may become lost and the only surviving chromosome will be a **fusion chromosome** containing most of the genetic material of both chromosomes. A fusion chromosome is responsible for one form of Down's syndrome (see Figure 12.11). Most incidents of Down's syndrome (trisomy 21) are products of spontaneous nondisjunction (see Essay 10.1), where maternal age is the important factor. Translocation Down's, which accounts for about two percent of all cases, is inherited and has no relationship to the mother's age. Karyotyping of the Down's child reveals the normal chromosome number (23 pairs), but with close examination, the extra twenty-first chromosome is visible.

Translocations and other chromosomal rearrangements aren't always bad. Like mutations of individual genes, most are harmful or lethal, but those rare harmless or beneficial ones are the stuff of evolution. Even closely related species *as a rule* show substantial chromosomal differences that must have originated as mutations. For instance, while normal humans do indeed have 46 chromosomes per cell, our closest relatives—the chimpanzees, gorillas, and orangutans—have 48 chromosomes per cell. A close study of the chromosomes of the four species indicates that one of our treasured human chromosomes arose as a fusion translocation mutation in some ancient ancestor.

12.10

When two breaks occur in a single chromosome **(a)**, repair enzymes can heal any two sticky ends. (Here the letters *a* through *k* represent gene loci.) **(b)** The original chromosome can be reconstituted. **(c)** The middle segment can flip end-over-end before repair to produce an inversion chromosome. **(d)** The other possibility is that the middle segment will join its own two ends to form a ring chromosome, while the two end segments join to form a deletion chromosome. In the case illustrated here, the centromere is in the middle segment, so the deletion chromosome is an *acentric fragment*.

(a) When two breaks occur in the same chromosome, there will be four sticky ends (1–4). Repair enzymes can join any two sticky ends. There are three possible outcomes:

(b) 1 joins 2
3 joins 4

(c) 1 joins 3
2 joins 4

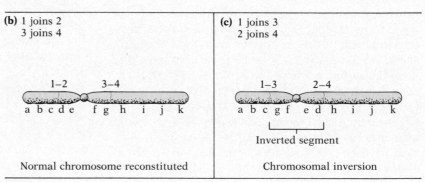

Normal chromosome reconstituted

Chromosomal inversion

(d) 1 joins 4
2 joins 3

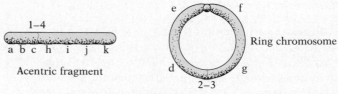

Acentric fragment and ring chromosome

12.11

Unlike nondisjunction Down's syndrome (simple trisomy-21), translocation Down's syndrome is brought about through an inherited chromosomal mutation. The translocation and fusion of chromosomes 14 and 21 are found in a carrier mother **(a)**, but have no effect on her since the correct number of homologues are present. The problems begin during meiosis in her oocytes, where there are two possible ways for the chromosomes to align in metaphase I **(b)**. From these alignments, four kinds of eggs are possible **(c)**. After oocyte fertilization **(d)**, four kinds of zygotes can result **(e)**. One will have a normal chromosome complement. A second will be a 14/21 translocation carrier, just like the mother. A third results in a deletion of chromosome 21, so the embryo will fail. Finally, the fourth alternative results in a trisomy, with three number 21 chromosomes present in the offspring. This will be the Down's syndrome child.

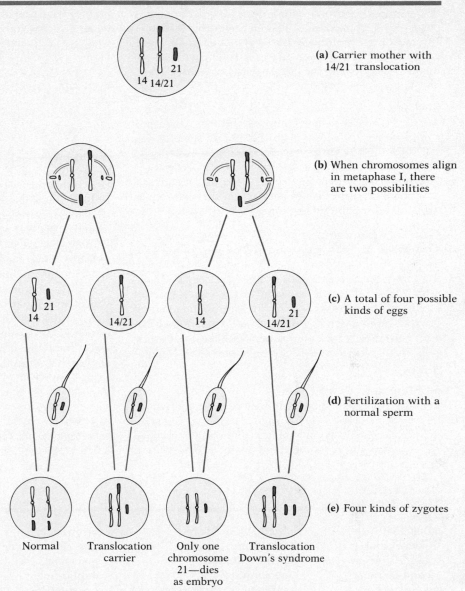

(a) Carrier mother with 14/21 translocation

(b) When chromosomes align in metaphase I, there are two possibilities

(c) A total of four possible kinds of eggs

(d) Fertilization with a normal sperm

(e) Four kinds of zygotes

Normal   Translocation carrier   Only one chromosome 21—dies as embryo   Translocation Down's syndrome

Summary

Locating the Genes
Mendel's "factors" are what we now call genes. All genetic messages are encoded in the linear sequence of the DNA nucleotides. Early in this century, researchers reasoned that the separation of homologous chromosomes during the first division of meiosis provided the physical basis of Mendel's first law. They also noted that, when many cells undergo meiosis, four types of haploid cells will result, which supported Mendel's law of independent assortment. These facts revealed the connections between Mendelism and meiosis, and explained the mechanism by which traits are passed on to offspring.

Chromosomes Determine Sex: Support for the Chromosome Theory of Inheritance
Mammals, and many other organisms, contain two heteromorphic sex-determining chromosomes, X and Y. These chromosomes are homologous and pair with one another during meiosis. Since males have XY chromo-

some pairs, while females have XX pairs, male gametes (X-bearing or Y-bearing sperm) determine the sex of the offspring. The separation of heteromorphic X and Y chromosomes supports Mendel's law of alternate segregation, and when they were observed along with heteromorphic autosomes, the cellular basis of Mendel's second law was established.

Linkage

A linkage group is any group of genes on the same chromosome that moves with the chromosome during cell division. Linkage groups provide for an exception to the law of independent assortment. Test crosses of the F_1 with homozygous recessives produce unusual ratios and new combinations of genes in offspring that can only be explained through crossing over.

Genetic Recombination

Two genes in a linkage group recombine through the process of crossing over. Tightly linked genes are less likely to recombine than loosely linked genes, which are farther apart on the chromosome, increasing the chances of chromosome breakage and crossover. When linkage groups were mapped by researchers, it was found that each gene locus or site on the map could be occupied by only one of two or more alleles on homologous chromosomes.

Sex Linkage

In some experiments, traits showed complex patterns of inheritance known as sex linkage. The XY combination in males leaves them vulnerable to detrimental recessive genes, since the recessive traits are not covered by a normal dominant allele on the homologous chromosome (as they would be in females). The Y chromosome never undergoes crossing over and contains only a few genes, while the X chromosome carries about 10 percent of all human genes.

In female cells, one of the X chromosomes is inactivated in regard to genetic function, a phenomenon known as the Lyon effect. The suppressed and condensed X chromosome is replicated normally and passes from cell to daughter cell.

Mutation

A mutation is any random, permanent change in the DNA molecule. Most mutations are either harmful or neutral; only a few are beneficial. Mutations often occur spontaneously when energetically active free radicals alter the DNA chain. Mutations occurring in gamete-forming cells are passed on to future generations. Heat, radiation, and chemical agents can increase the rate of spontaneous mutations.

Point mutations are confined to a single nucleotide or small region of DNA affecting a single gene. Chromosomal mutations, or rearrangements, happen when one or more DNA molecules break and rejoin in abnormal ways. Improper fusion or inadequate repair of broken DNA parts can result in the deletion of genetic material, a ring chromosome, an inversion within a chromosome, duplication of genetic material on the same chromosome, or translocation of material from one chromosome to another. Most of these mutations are harmful; however, some have played an important role in the evolution of species—including our own.

Key Terms

autosome	Lyon effect	deletion
linkage group	mutation	ring chromosome
recombinant progeny	point mutation	inversion
recombination	hemophilia	duplication
sex linkage	chromosomal rearrangement	translocation
hemizygous	breakage	fusion chromosome

Review Questions

1. Using two pairs of chromosomes, and the markers **A** and **a** on one pair and **B** and **b** on the other, carefully illustrate how events in meiosis explain how independent assortment produces four types of gametes. (Figure 12.1)

2. Explain why it was necessary for early geneticists to find two pairs of heteromorphic chromosomes in order to clearly establish the relationship between meiosis and Mendel's second law. (p. 163)

3. To illustrate the effect of gene linkage on gametes, revise your illustration for question 1, this time using one pair of chromosomes and adding the markers **A**, **a**, **B**, and **b**, so that each chromosome has both markers present:

   A   **a**
   B   **b**

   Determine the number of genetically different gametes possible, and compare this to what we expect during independent assortment. (pp. 164–165)

4. In a certain test cross, F_1 individuals with the genotypes **AaBb** are crossed with the corresponding recessives, **aabb.** The offspring occur in the following ratio: 45% **AaBb,** 45% **aabb,** 5% **Aabb,** and 5% **aaBb.**

   a. Can independent assortment explain these results? Explain.

   b. If the two pairs of alleles were "tightly linked," what might we expect?

   c. What percent of the time was crossing over occurring?

   d. Construct a simple diagram to illustrate the cross. (pp. 164–166)

5. In the text example of recombination mapping, *Bar eye* and *garnet eye* showed 13% recombination, while *Bar eye* and *scalloped wings* showed 6%, and *scalloped wings* and *garnet eye* showed 7%. Explain how these data enable one to determine the relative order of the three genes on the chromosome. How do we know they are even on the same chromosome? (pp. 165–167)

6. Using a simple cross showing the X and Y chromosomes (XY × XX), explain why the sex ratio in human births is about 1:1. (p. 166)

7. Explain the statement: human males are effectively haploid (hemizygous) for about 10% of the total human gene complement. (p. 166)

8. In establishing the origin of sex-linked conditions in males, such as color blindness, the father's genotype is irrelevant. Explain this statement in terms of the X and Y chromosomes. (pp. 168–169)

9. Explain specifically why the spontaneous breakage of two chromosomes, or the breakage of one chromosome in two places, is potentially more dangerous to an individual than a single break. In what cells must such events occur in order for them to be genetically significant? (pp. 170, 172–173)

How Genes Express
Themselves in
Higher Organisms

13

Small but critical differences in the sequence of DNA bases along a chromosome can result in blue or brown eyes, in sick or healthy people, in round or wrinkled peas, and, for that matter, in round or wrinkled people. But the pathway between the DNA in the cell nucleus (the genotype) and the physical characters that can be seen and measured (the phenotype) is often complex and indirect. Genes act through intricate developmental processes that may involve feedbacks, loops, branches, interactions, and built-in corrections. Also, the expression of every gene is influenced by tens of thousands of other genes, as well as by the other genes' products and developmental pathways. Genetic expression also may be influenced, directly or indirectly, by environmental factors.

Mendel frankly attributed his success to his deliberate decision to work only with "factors" that always produced large, dramatic effects with clear and distinct phenotypes. He examined such traits, one or two at a time, in highly inbred, genetically unvarying pure strains. Only in such simple systems could he have worked out his famous ratios. However, not all genetic variation is so simple. Mendel's discoveries were valuable because nearly all genes have proven to be Mendelian in their meiotic behavior and in their transmission from

generation to generation—that is, on a genotypic level. But most genetic variation is not Mendelian at the level of the phenotype because of the complexities of development and gene expression that Mendel had so cleverly sidestepped.

NORMAL AND ABNORMAL ALLELES

Normal alleles are those that have accumulated in the population because they have withstood the test of natural selection. Thus, there is a high probability that they are adaptive. That is, they, in some way, help the organism survive and reproduce. However, we will also see that the simple presence of a gene does not mean that it is adaptive. Some quite common genes that confer no benefit or harm at all can be carried from one generation to the next. Harmful, but often rather common, genes may also be passed along. Then there are the so-called "abnormal" genes, which not only are not beneficial, but do harm in some way. These are generally the result of recent mutations that simply are not in harmony with the rest of the genotype or with the organism's environment.

Geneticists tend to be interested in abnormal alleles for a variety of reasons. For one thing, they may be able to help people with genetic disabilities, or, through genetic counseling, to help families avoid bringing more such disabilities into the world. From an academic point of view, abnormal mutant alleles are interesting because they often meet Mendel's requirement of having an easily classified phenotype. This characteristic is very useful in many kinds of genetic studies, such as linkage mapping.

But this narrow focus misses most of the real genetic variety of nature. In truth, most genes do not have a single normal or "wild-type" allele, but a whole range of slightly different wild-type alleles, all of which are functional, normal, and adaptive. This falls within the realm of normal genetic variation. Most of the genetic differences we see in our friends—differences in height, weight, body build, skin color, temperament, facial features, athletic ability, intelligence, and hairiness—are due to normal allelic variation. These normal phenotypic differences, which add so much to human interest, seldom follow Mendelian ratios (although their underlying genotypes may follow Mendelian laws). Even blue and brown eye color, a popular example of Mendelian inheritance in humans, turns out to be quite complex and unpredictable, in fact: people do not merely have blue or brown eyes but may have grey, light blue, deep blue, hazel, flecked, or green eyes, as well.

GOING BEYOND MENDEL

The actual expression of genes into phenotypes in natural populations is influenced or determined by many kinds of complications that Mendel deliberately avoided. Whole courses in genetics are devoted to these complications, but we can list the major categories and then give some examples of each. The question might be: Why don't we find Mendel's simple 3:1 ratios everywhere? And the answers are:

1. *Dominance relationships:* the interactions between two homologous alleles. Mendel considered only **complete dominance,** in which the effect of one allele completely masks the effect of the other. Actually there is a whole range of ways in which two homologous alleles can interact, producing intermediate effects.

2. *Multiple alleles.* Up to a point, we have considered only two alleles at each gene locus. But there actually may be many different functional alleles that can occupy a specific gene locus—and, for that matter, many different kinds of mutants of the same gene.

3. *Gene interactions.* The genes at one gene locus may affect the expression of genes at another locus.

4. *Polygenic inheritance.* Many different gene loci may affect the same phenotypic trait, especially if the trait is one that varies continuously, like height or weight. The phenomenon is called **polygenic inheritance** (from the Greek roots for "many origins")—that is, many genes interact to determine a single trait.

5. *Other sources of variability* include environmental interactions (the same genotype may be expressed differently in different environments), sex influences (the same trait may be expressed to different degrees in males and females), and effects of development and aging (some genes begin to exert their effects only in adulthood or old age).

Dominance Relationships: The Interactions Between Homologous Alleles

Mendel's first empirical discovery was *dominance;* in all of his original crosses, one form of the trait (one allele) was completely dominant over the other. He had no idea why this should be, but there it was. Later, when he stopped crossing peas and turned to string beans, he was greatly puzzled by his new discovery of partial dominance and polygenic inheritance.

A diploid organism can have two different alleles at the same locus on homologous chromosomes (that is, in fact, the definition of *heterozygous*). The various ways in which two different alleles interact to form a phenotype are called **dominance relationships.** The basic advantage of diploidy is that it provides, among other things, a backup system in case one of the genes isn't working properly.

What really happens when the gene from one parent and the corresponding gene from the other parent give conflicting directives? Say an allele for blue eyes comes from one parent and an allele for brown eyes comes from the other. What then? Actually, many things can happen, but one of the most common results is that one of the two sets of instructions will appear to be ignored completely. In that case, as we've seen, the other allele is dominant. That's what Mendel observed in the heterozygous pea plants for his seven pairs of contrasting traits.

But so far we have given only observations and definitions, not explanations. What *really* happens when two different alleles occur together? How is one suppressed? And how does the organism "choose" between two sets of information?

The Inoperative Allele.   Usually, dominance simply involves one allele fulfilling some biological function while the other allele doesn't do anything. For instance, many genes make enzymes. A mutant allele of an enzyme-making gene may simply make no enzyme, or it may make a bogus protein with no enzymatic activity. This problem is clearly observed in some rare medical disorders in which the absence of an enzyme can have a severe or even lethal effect. In a relatively benign example, an **albino** organism lacks any one of the enzymes necessary to make *melanin*, the normal black, red, and/or brown pigments of animals and plants. Albinos do not receive a functioning gene from either parent, so their melanin-producing mechanism is defunct: they are recessive homozygotes. Human albinos of the most extreme variety have white hair and pinkish skin; the absence of pigment from the retina and iris makes the eyes appear pink or red, as in albino rabbits. Less severe forms of albinism—where the mutant allele is not totally inoperative, but retains a small measure of enzymatic activity—may have pale yellow hair and pale blue eyes.

Heterozygotes for albinism or other enzyme deficiencies, on the other hand, have one working allele and one nonworking allele. They produce only half the normal amount of the enzyme in question, but this is usually enough to produce a normal phenotype.

Inhibiting Dominants.   In some cases, the dominant and recessive alleles interact in another way. The gene locus may be involved in the *control* of some biochemical or developmental function. In other words, it can act as a kind of switch. For example, in some albinos a controlling gene may turn off a normal function, such as the synthesis of melanin. Although most human albinos are homozygous for recessive alleles, there are albinos that are *hetero*zygous for a dominant *inhibiting* allele.

Partial Dominance.   Sometimes the conflicting instructions of two alleles are compromised in what is called **partial dominance**. Partial dominance occurs whenever the phenotype of the heterozygote is somewhere between the two contrasting phenotypes of the two homozygotes.

In snapdragons, a cross between a true-breeding red-flowered strain (say **RR**) and a true-breeding white-flowered strain (say **rr**) results in a

uniform F_1 generation **(Rr)** in which the flowers are neither red nor white, but pink. This is partial dominance (Figure 13.1).

Codominance.   In other cases one homozygote will show one trait, the other homozygote will show a different phenotypic trait, and the heterozygote will show both traits. The interaction is called **codominance:** there is no compromise as

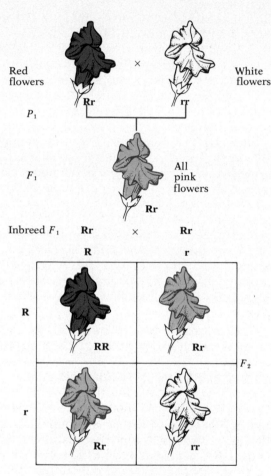

1. What colors appear in the F_2 generation?
2. What is the phenotypic ratio?

13.1 ━━━━━━━━━━━━━━━━━━━━━

Snapdragons represent a good example of *partial dominance*. When (in the P_1) white-flowered snapdragons are crossed with red-flowered snapdragons, the F_1 offspring are pink, as shown in the first cross. In the second cross, pink heterozygotes have been crossed, resulting in red, pink, and white in the F_2 progeny. The ratio of the three colors is 1:2:1. Since we can identify the heterozygous progeny by their color, we have derived both the phenotypic and genotypic ratios. Is it possible to produce a true-breeding strain of pink snapdragons?

there is in partial dominance, because both alleles are fully expressed (see Figure 13.5b).

The most familiar example of codominance is found in the ABO blood group system. One allele, **A,** codes for an enzyme that, in turn, synthesizes a cell-surface sugar called the *A antigen*. Specific antibodies can recognize and bind to this sugar on the surface of human red blood cells. An alternate allele, **B,** codes for an alternate enzyme that, in turn, synthesizes an alternate cell-surface sugar called the *B antigen*. In heterozygous persons, **AB,** there is neither dominance nor compromise. Both antigens are expressed, and the red blood cells react to both antibodies. Such persons are said to have the blood type AB.

Multiple Alleles and Blood Groups

The ABO blood group system also illustrates the effect of *multiple alleles*. The term **multiple alleles** simply refers to systems in which three or more alleles exist at a specific locus. There are several alleles responsible for blood types, with A, B, and O being the most common. (For a discussion of Rh blood types and the incompatibility problem, see Essay 13.1.)

To recapitulate, persons who are homozygous for the **A** allele express one kind of cell-surface antigen and are said to be *type A*. Persons who are homozygous for the **B** allele express a different kind of cell-surface antigen and are said to be *type B*. Heterozygotes, **AB,** carry both alleles, express both kinds of cell-surface antigens, and are said to be *type AB*.

Persons who express neither the A antigen nor the B antigen belong to a fourth type—*type O*. Type O people are more common than any of the other blood types. It seems that O is a third allele at the same gene locus, one that has neither enzymatic activity. It is recessive when paired with either B or A. With three different possible alleles, there are six different possible genotypes:

Genotype	A Antigen	B Antigen	Blood Type
AA	present	absent	type A
AO	present	absent	type A
BB	absent	present	type B
BO	absent	present	type B
AB	present	present	type AB
OO	absent	absent	type O

So although **A** and **B** are codominant with respect to each other, they are simply dominant with respect to the **O** allele. Note that although there are

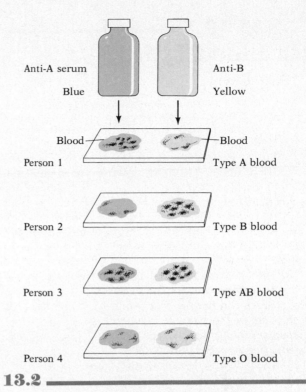

13.2

ABO blood typing. The presence of A and B antigens in one's blood can be determined in a simple test using anti-A (blue) and anti-B (yellow) antisera. (These antisera are commonly extracted from plants and color-coded for convenience.) A positive reaction (agglutination) is characterized by a distinct graininess occurring in the mixture. The red cells eventually form a patchwork pattern in the serum. Where there has been a negative reaction (no agglutination), the texture of the blood remains homogeneous.

three alleles of this gene locus in the human species, no one individual can have all three alleles at once. Diploid organisms like ourselves are limited to two at a time.

Blood typing—that is, the determination of an individual's blood type—is simply done. Two drops of the individual's blood are placed on a slide. To one drop is added a small amount of *anti-A antiserum;* to the other drop is added a small amount of *anti-B antiserum*. The antisera interact only with their appropriate antigens: the anti-A antiserum, for instance, will cause type A cells to *agglutinate* (clump). This clumping (not to be confused with clotting, a different process) is readily visible after a few minutes. The anti-B antiserum will clump type B cells, and either antiserum will clump type AB cells. If neither drop agglutinates, the person is type O (Figure 13.2). Such information is critical in blood transfusions. It wouldn't do to infuse a person's veins with a type of blood that

ESSAY 13.1

Rh Blood Types

When an Rh negative woman is made pregnant by an Rh positive man, the fetus she carries may be Rh positive—if the man is an Rh positive homozygote **(RR)**, the fetus will certainly be Rh positive; if he is a heterozygote **(Rr)**, the probability is 50%. In either case, if the baby is Rh positive, it is sure to be a heterozygote.

A serious incompatibility sometimes occurs between an Rh negative woman and her Rh positive child, resulting in a severe and sometimes fatal anemia in the newborn infant. This immunological incompatibility does not occur in the first pregnancy, because the Rh negative woman does not build up antibodies against the Rh positive antigen until Rh positive red blood cells enter her bloodstream during delivery.

At the time of delivery, small quantities of the baby's blood cells may enter the mother's bloodstream. If the baby is Rh positive, the mother is at risk of building up antibodies against the Rh positive antigen.

Before preventative treatment became standard for Rh negative **(rr)** mothers of Rh positive **(Rr)** babies, fetal Rh positive red blood cells in the mother's circulation would eventually trigger the buildup of antibodies against the Rh positive antigen, giving the mother a permanent "immunity."

It is now standard practice to treat the Rh negative **(rr)** mothers of Rh positive **(Rr)** babies with a single injection of antibodies against the Rh positive antigen. This destroys the Rh positive cells before they can trigger the immune response.

A subsequent pregnancy with another Rh positive baby can end in disaster, because the mother's anti-Rh positive antibodies enter the baby's bloodstream and destroy its Rh positive red blood cells.

In the treated mother, the injected antibodies soon dissipate. Subsequent pregnancies are as normal as the first, because the mother has no anti-Rh positive antibodies. ●

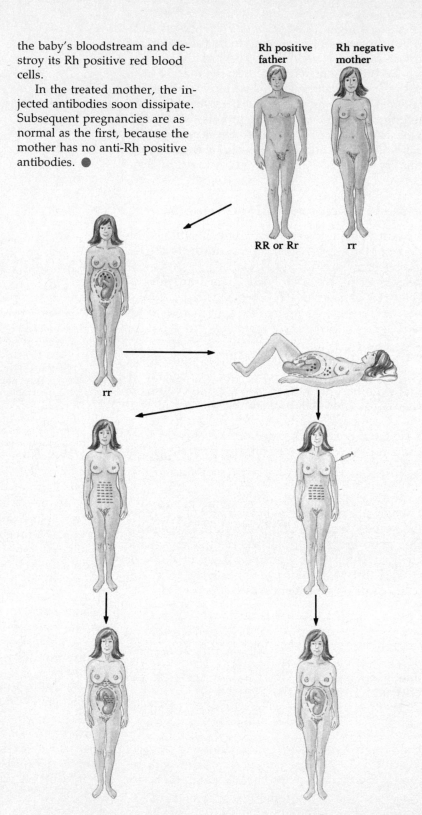

Rh positive father   Rh negative mother

RR or Rr   rr

rr

180

would clump there. There are also other uses for such information. Could a man with type O blood father a child with AB blood? Could an AB man be the father of a type O child?

Gene Interactions and Epistasis

When Mendel crossed true-breeding round, yellow peas with true-breeding wrinkled, green peas, you'll recall, the F_2 generation yielded 9/16 round and yellow, 3/16 round and green, 3/16 wrinkled and yellow, and 1/16 wrinkled and green. Such ratios are possible only in straightforward situations in which the genes do not influence each other. When two different gene loci do interact, the tidy 9:3:3:1 ratio doesn't show up.

Mouse coat color, for instance, would have driven Mendel up the wall. Consider two gene loci that affect the coat color of mice. In one case, black **(B)** is dominant to brown **(b)**. If a true-breeding black strain **(BB)** is crossed with a true-breeding brown strain **(bb)**, the F_1 generation will all be heterozygous and black **(Bb),** and the F_2 will show a 3:1 ratio of black to brown. No surprises there.

But at yet another gene locus there is another pair of alleles that can also affect coat color. These are the alleles at the albino locus. The recessive homozygote **(cc)** is a snow-white albino mouse. The dominant homozygote **(CC)** and the heterozygote **(Cc)** have normal pigment, although it can be black or brown, depending on the first gene locus, as we've seen. The recessive albino gene **c,** of course, is defective and does not supply one of the enzymes necessary for the production of pigment.

Now consider a mating between an albino mouse from a true-breeding white strain and a mouse from a true-breeding brown strain. What would you expect? You might *not* expect the litter to be entirely black. But here is the cross:

CCbb (brown) × **ccBB** (white) ⟶ **CcBb** (black)

The dominant **B** alleles were carried by the white strain, completely hidden. The masking of the effects of one gene locus by the effects of another gene locus is called **epistasis.** Here the recessive albino genotype is epistatic to the brown/black genotype.

In the cross above, the only possible outcome of the cross between the two kinds of *double homozygotes* is the *double heterozygote* offspring **CcBb.** Since there is an active allele for pigment formation and an active allele that makes the pigment black, the entire litter is black.

Now consider crosses among a number of those

double homozygote mice **(CcBb × CcBb).** Will you get a 9:3:3:1 ratio? No. The F_2 generation—providing you raise enough of them—will approximate a 9:3:4 ratio: 9/16 black, 3/16 brown, and 1/4 albino. Figure 13.3 confirms that the two gene loci assort independently, just as Mendel would have predicted. But because of epistasis, the last two terms of the 9:3:3:1 ratio are combined to produce the 9:3:4 ratio. After all, once a mouse is albino, it doesn't much matter whether the other gene locus specifies brown or black.

Polygenic Inheritance

Many Small Effects Added Together. Many of the phenotypic traits that are most important to biologists, and especially to plant and animal breeders, do not fit into "either-or" categories. Instead, these traits occur in a gradient of phenotypes, a situation known as **continuous variation.** Differences among individuals are still caused by

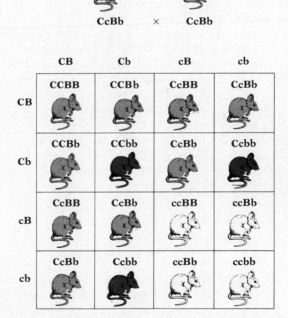

13.3 ━━━━━━━

In this diagram we follow the path of two pairs of genes that influence mouse coat color. The **B** (black) and **b** (brown) alleles occur at one locus, and the **C** (color) and **c** (albino) alleles occur at another locus. The two pairs assort independently in typical Mendelian fashion, but produce strange ratios when heterozygous F_1 are inbred **(CcBb × CcBb).** The resulting ratio is 9:3:4 because of an epistatic interaction.

different alleles at specific gene loci on chromosomes, and these alleles segregate and assort according to the usual Mendelian laws. But in these cases, many different gene loci will determine a single phenotypic trait, with each individual gene having a very small effect. This is called **polygenic inheritance.** Common examples of continuous variation in humans are height, skin color, shoe size, nose size, weight at birth, and, even, aspects of intelligence. At first glance, continuous variation may seem to lend belated support to the old notion of blending inheritance, but it can be explained quite satisfactorily in Mendelian terms.

A great many gene loci determine height, but for simplicity we'll assume that height is determined by only three loci. Also, in reality there may be multiple alleles possible at each gene locus, but in our example we'll assume only two alternatives are available: "short" alleles and "tall" alleles.

Now let's assume that the presence of a "tall" allele rather than a "short" allele increases adult height by 5 cm (about two inches). People with only the "short" genes (six in all) will then grow to be about 160 cm (five feet, three inches), while those with only the "tall" genes (again, six) grow to 190 cm (six feet, three inches). In the middle, with three short alleles and three tall alleles, are individuals about 175 cm tall (five feet, nine inches). Table 13.1 summarizes the seven height categories possible in this model. We've added the relative frequencies of the seven predictable height categories in the F_2 generation of a hypothetical cross between a short race and a tall race. Note that the distribution approximates the "bell-shaped curve" or *normal distribution* that is, in fact, observed in real populations for adult height and for nearly every other kind of continuous variation. That is, most people are of intermediate height; few are very tall or very short (Figure 13.4).

Other Kinds of Variability

It may have occurred to you that the polygenic model of the genetic control of adult height can't possibly explain everything. For one thing, men (as a group) tend to be taller than women (as a group). And what about diet, general health, and other environmental factors? Modern-day humans are taller than their medieval and 19th-century ancestors (have you noticed how small the suits of armor in museums are?), and young Japanese adults are noticeably taller than their own parents because of rapid improvements in the Japanese standard of

TABLE 13.1

Polygenes controlling height: a model of three loci

Genotypes	Number of "Tall" Alleles	Number of "Short" Alleles	Height (cm)	Distribution
AABBCC	6	0	190	1/64 (1.6%)
AaBBCC, AABbCC, AABBCc	5	1	185	6/64 (9.4%)
aaBBCC, AAbbCC, AABBcc, AaBbCC, AaBBCc, AABbCc	4	2	180	15/64 (23.4%)
aaBbCC, aaBBCc, AabbCC, AaBBcc, AaBbCc, AAbbCc, AABbcc	3	3	175	20/64 (31.3%)
aabbCC, aaBBcc, AAbbcc, AaBbcc, AabbCc, aaBbCc	2	4	170	15/64 (23.4%)
aabbCc, aaBbcc, Aabbcc	1	5	165	6/64 (9.4%)
aabbcc	0	6	160	1/64 (1.6%)

living. Furthermore, don't we all get shorter in our old age? We do, indeed. The point is that nongenetic effects have very marked influences on many genetic traits.

Environmental Interactions. Environmental interactions may be very direct or very subtle. Let's consider a straightforward example: the Siamese cat. One of the enzymes in its pigmentation pathway has mutated so that it is now sensitive to temperature; the enzyme won't function above a certain temperature. As a result, Siamese cats are darker in their cooler extremities: the nose, ears, tail, and feet (Figure 13.5a).

Incomplete Penetrance. Incomplete penetrance refers to a condition in which an individual may bear genes for some abnormal condition, but may have a normal phenotype anyway. Sometimes a Mendelian dominant gene appears to skip a generation entirely, only to express itself among the offspring of later generations. For instance, a rare dominant gene in humans causes **polydactyly,** a condition characterized by extra fingers or toes, or

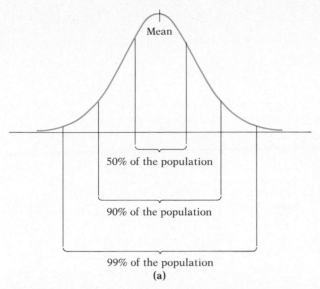

(a)

(b)

13.4

The normal distribution. **(a)** Polygenic genetic traits, when plotted by phenotypes gathered from large samples, tend to form curves approximating the idealized distribution shown here. **(b)** The accompanying photograph shows a good example. The

World War I soldiers are arranged in rows according to height. Although the curve thus formed at the top of each row is not perfectly symmetrical, there is an apparent cluster around a *mean*, with rapidly tapering tails.

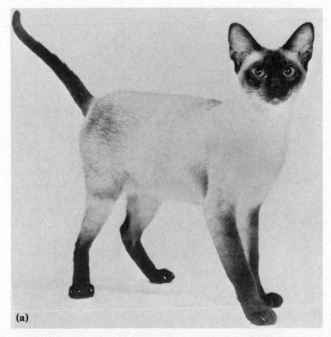

(a)

(b)

13.5

(a) Coat color in the Siamese cat is an example of the influence of environment on gene expression. Where the skin is coolest, in the extremities, dark pigment is produced in the hair. **(b)** All three-color

cats are heterozygous for orange and black coat-color genes. Since both alleles are expressed, three-color cats show codominance for this trait.

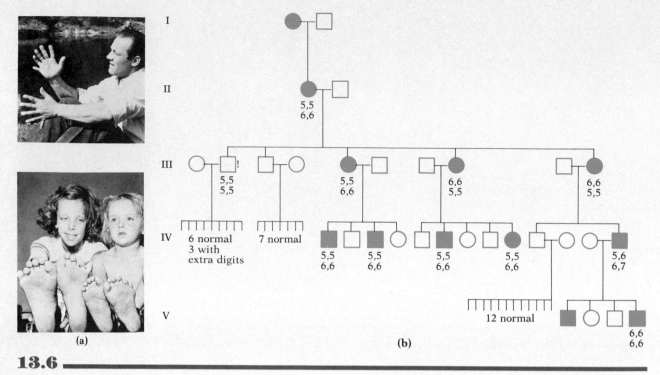

13.6

Polydactyly and incomplete penetrance. **(a)** The individuals shown here have inherited a dominant gene that expresses itself in the development of extra fingers or toes, or both. Although the gene is dominant, its expression is somewhat incomplete. Some individuals carry—but do not express—the gene. Their children, however, may not be so lucky. The variables involved in polydactyly are unknown. **(b)** In the family portrayed in the chart, the numbers represent the number of digits on the left and right hands *(top set of figures)* and left and right feet *(bottom set of figures)*. The dominant gene expressed itself in either the hands or feet of every carrier except for the first male in the third generation *(exclamation mark)*. Although he was phenotypically normal, three of his children were afflicted. For some reason, his dominant gene did not *penetrate* during his embryological development.

both. Persons who have this gene show variable expression. All four extremities may be affected, with six or seven digits on all hands and feet; or only the feet may be affected; or only the hands; or perhaps only one hand or foot (Figure 13.6). This expression appears to be entirely a matter of chance. Occasionally someone will receive the defective gene from a polydactylous parent, but, by chance, will have normal hands and feet. In such a case, fortune has smiled four times and the person would be unaware of carrying the polydactyly gene at all, if it weren't for the fact that about half of his or her children will probably have extra fingers or toes. In some cases, a dominant gene simply isn't expressed.

Sex-Limited and Sex-Influenced Effects. A dominant gene is known to be responsible for a rare type of cancer of the uterus. This is a **sex-limited** trait since, needless to say, it has no influence on men. On the other hand, the most common kind of middle-aged baldness is also due to a dominant gene, which doesn't usually affect women. Some genetic conditions affect one sex more often, or more severely, than the other and are said to be **sex-influenced.** For instance, *pyloric stenosis*, a common and serious congenital malformation of the digestive tract, runs in families but affects five times as many boy babies as girl babies.

Variable Age of Onset. Baldness due to a dominant gene, in addition to being sex-limited, also has a variable age of onset. Even among brothers, presumably carrying the same dominant gene, one man may lose his top hair in his 20s, while the other loses it in his 40s or even later. A more serious example of a dominant gene with a late, variable age of onset is that for *Huntington's disease*. This disease is characterized by a severe neuromotor condition that begins with subtle personality changes and progresses through tremors and paralysis to death. The dominant gene does not even begin to show its effects until sometime in adulthood. The average age of onset of symptoms is about 40, but it can begin affecting heterozygous men or women as early as age 15 or as late as age

60. Usually, the victim learns that he or she has the disease—and the defective gene—only after it is too late to make a decision as to whether to risk having children.

Many of the more common diseases of old age are believed to have a genetic basis, at least in part.

The genes for "old-age disorders" may be considered to have a delayed and variable age of onset. At some point, it is impossible to tell what is genetic and what is environmental, but we do know this: some folks are old at 40, while others are surprisingly young at 70.

Summary

Normal and Abnormal Alleles
Normal alleles are the product of natural selection, while abnormal alleles are more often produced by random mutation. Many genetic diseases, nonadaptive—even lethal—phenotypes, and loss of normal functions are the results of abnormal alleles. The ease with which abnormal alleles can be studied is useful, however, in gene mapping and in pinpointing genetic disabilities. A range of slightly "wild-type" alleles are found in most organisms and account for many of the normal, adaptive phenotypic differences among individuals.

Going Beyond Mendel
There are a number of factors Mendel did not consider when studying phenotypes. Dominance relationships, for example, describe how two different alleles at the same locus interact to form a phenotype. One set of genetic instructions may be either inoperative, inhibited, or partially dominated while the other set of instructions is expressed. In codominance, both alleles are expressed in the phenotype.

There may be more than two alternative alleles for a specific locus, although each individual receives only two. An example is the ABO blood system, where three alleles (A, B, and O) combine in pairs to produce six possible genotypes and four phenotypes (blood types). A and B produce antigens and are codominant to each other and dominant over O, which does not produce an antigen.

Rh factors in blood types can cause serious problems if a mother is Rh negative and the baby is Rh positive. The mother may build up antibodies against the Rh positive antigen, endangering the fetus of a second pregnancy. Modern treatment can eliminate the problem, however.

Epistasis occurs when two different gene loci interact so that one masks the effect of the other. These interactions yield much more complex results than Mendel's 9:3:3:1 ratio.

Many traits occur in a gradient of phenotypes, a situation known as continuous variation. In polygenic inheritence, many different gene loci will determine a single phenotypic trait, such as height. Generally the results of such genetic expression are distributed in a bell-shaped curve throughout a population.

Environmental factors can favor one trait over another and thus affect genetic expression. In incomplete penetrance, abnormal or dominant genes are suppressed or skip a generation. Phenotypes are also influenced by sex-limited and sex-influenced traits. Some dominant genes, such as those for Huntington's disease, have a variable age of onset and appear only later in an individual's life.

Key Terms

complete dominance	partial dominance	continuous variation
polygenic inheritance	codominance	incomplete penetrance
dominance relationships	multiple alleles	polydactyly
inoperative allele	gene interaction	sex-limited trait
albino	epistasis	sex-influenced trait
inhibiting dominants		

Review Questions

1. Albinism provides us with a relatively clear-cut example of Mendelian dominance. How should we classify this form of dominance, and what, biochemically speaking, is the recessive allele doing? (pp. 177–178)

2. Flower color in snapdragons is a good example of partial dominance. True-breeding red, when crossed with true-breeding white, produces pink. Is it possible to produce a true-breeding pink strain? Prove your answer. (p. 178)

3. Explain how ABO blood represents three genetic concepts: codominance, the inoperative allele, and multiple alleles. (p. 179)

4. What ABO blood types can one expect in the children of a couple whose blood types are AB and O? (p. 179)

5. List the four reactions possible and explain what they would mean when a person of unknown blood type is tested with anti-a and anti-b sera. (pp. 179, 181)

6. Carry out this version of the epistatic cross involving mouse coat color: **CcBb × ccBb.** Remember that **BB, Bb,** and **bb** represent black, black, and brown phenotypes, respectively, but for color to show up, at least one **C** (**CC** or **Cc**) must be present. State the phenotypic ratio of the offspring. (pp. 179, 181)

7. Consider the following example of continuous variation. Color in a certain variety of tomato plants is controlled by two independently assorting loci: two pairs of genes, each of which has a dominant and recessive form—**R** or **r,** and **P** or **p.** When only dominants are present **(RRPP)** a deep red color is produced. Alternatively, when only recessives **(rrpp)** are present, the color is a pale yellow. Other genotypes produce intermediate colors. In all, how many phenotypes (colors) are possible in this variety? Suggest colors for each and list the genotypes that would produce each color you mentioned. Verify your list of genotypes and their frequency by carrying out a heterozygous cross **(RrPp × RrPp)**. Finally, develop a graph where the frequency of each color (phenotype) from the cross is plotted, and describe the resulting curve. (pp. 181–183)

8. Explain how sex-limited, sex-influenced, and sex-linked traits differ. (pp. 184–185)

What Is DNA and How Does It Work?

14

Mendel and the early Mendelians dealt with genes as abstract entities, but they knew that, at some level, genes must have a physical reality. As William Bateson put it in 1906: "But ever in our thoughts the question rings, what are these units (genes)? How the pack is shuffled and dealt, we are beginning to perceive; but what are they—the cards? Wild and inscrutable the question sounds, but genetic research may answer it yet."

Simply counting kinds of offspring has proven to be a powerful technique for discovering the nature of the gene and how it mutates, recombines, and interacts with other genes. But there are other equally valid ways to study the gene, such as isolating and analyzing both the gene and its products. We are now at the point where we can begin to merge, with success, such diverse techniques as progeny counts and biochemistry. This expanding and exciting field is called **molecular biology.** Since the inception of molecular biology, what have geneticists and molecular biologists learned about the gene? More than they expected. They have learned, for example, that genes have two fundamental functions: to be preserved and transmitted from generation to generation, and to control such biological processes as cell chemistry, development, and differentiation. They also have shown that genes are involved in the synthesis of all proteins, and that some of these proteins influence the expression of other genes.

In this chapter and the next we'll review some of the scientific experiments that led to the modern concept of the gene. We'll take a close look at the biochemical structure of the gene and at how genes direct the synthesis of proteins. Finally, we will consider how the genes themselves are controlled and how accidental changes in DNA (mutations) can affect gene function.

Historically, genetics consists of two stories that finally merge: the story of gene function, and the story of gene structure (that is, the story of DNA). The story of gene function begins with Mendel. The story of gene structure begins with Miescher.

DNA: THE STUFF OF GENES

It seems incredible, but DNA was isolated and characterized in Mendel's lifetime. In 1869 Johann Friedrich Miescher, a Swiss chemist, first isolated the nuclei of pus cells (concentrated, dead white blood cells), and then chemically dissolved the nuclear membrane and most of the remaining protein. This left a phosphorus-rich material he called *nuclein*, which we now call **chromatin** (DNA and its associated proteins were discussed in Chapter 9). That same year he also found nuclein in a number of other cell types. He speculated that the material might simply serve as a way for the cell to store phosphate, and he also suggested that it might have something to do with heredity. In a letter to a friend, he even mused that the subunits of large biological molecules might be arranged linearly to spell out some kind of biological information, just as the letters of the alphabet are arranged linearly to spell out messages. (Miescher was thinking of proteins, rather than of his own nuclein, but it is eerie how close he was to the truth as we now perceive it.)

By 1889, other European biochemists, who had further purified nuclein by removing the last traces of protein, found that they were left with a gummy, acidic substance, which they renamed **nucleic acid.** Researchers eventually determined that there are two kinds of nucleic acid, which we now call *DNA* (deoxyribonucleic acid) and *RNA* (ribonucleic acid).

Geneticists began to lose interest in DNA after Miescher's time and began testing other kinds of molecules, looking for the stuff of genes. We'll soon see how interest in DNA was revived by a remarkable set of experiments, and how its role was finally nailed down by two brilliant young scientists. But first let's see how the story of gene function slowly developed.

GENE FUNCTION

In 1908 an English physician, A. E. Garrod, published a book called *Inborn Errors of Metabolism.* Interested in genetic breakdowns in the biochem-

ical process of life, Garrod had noticed that certain diseases tend to run in families, some of which appeared to be caused by Mendelian recessive alleles. Furthermore, some of the diseases could be diagnosed by abnormal products in the blood or urine.

In phenylketonuria, for example, the amino acid phenylalanine accumulates in the blood and, in large amounts, causes severe mental retardation. Garrod suggested that the excess levels of the amino acid were caused by an absence of the enzyme that breaks it down. He also believed that phenylalanine was a normal intermediate product in a long metabolic pathway (Figure 14.1). Imagine an assembly line in which a worker is absent. Half-completed products (phenylalanine) pile up at that station while other workers (enzymes) further down the line sit idly, contributing nothing.

Phenylketonuria is a rare disease because it is caused by a recessive gene. In a sense, the diploid condition provides the system with a backup, so that two assembly lines are available with a low probability that the same worker will be missing from each.

Garrod had shown that genes can act directly on biochemical metabolism by dictating whether specific enzymes are or are not present. In retrospect, this might have helped remove some of the early haziness about the gene concept, but alas, Garrod was ignored in his own time. Geneticists of

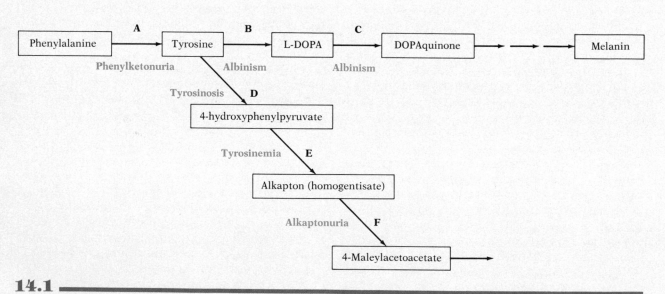

14.1

A branched biochemical pathway in human metabolism. The enzymes (A–F), working in teams, are responsible for the proper formation of their products. When enzymes fail, as they do when the genes that produce them are faulty, problems arise. The substrate of such an enzyme (at its left) will accumulate, appearing in the blood and urine in toxic quantities and producing a metabolic disorder (listed in color).

his day were interested primarily in doing controlled crosses for such variables as eye color and seed shape, rather than in the chemical composition of urine.

One Gene, One Enzyme

The slogan "one gene, one enzyme" was an electrifying bit of public relations in its day, 30 years after Garrod's work. It referred to the Nobel Prize-winning studies of George Beadle and Edward Tatum, who once again applied Mendelian analysis to metabolic pathways. But instead of drawing inferences from human abnormalities or from crosses of mutant flies, Beadle and Tatum imaginatively chose what was until then a very unusual experimental organism: the fungus *Neurospora*, which is a relative of the green mold that can ruin oranges. *Neurospora* was to be the first in a series of important microorganisms that would be used in the upstart field of molecular biology.

Microorganisms like *Neurospora* have two great advantages over such organisms as mice, flies, peas, and humans: (1) they can be grown cheaply, quickly, and in abundance, and (2) they are haploid, so the complications of dominance interactions can be avoided altogether and the effects of mutation can be seen immediately.

Beadle and Tatum irradiated (x-rayed) *Neurospora* spores to produce random mutations. They then grew the irradiated spores and screened for biochemical mutations; that is, they looked for strains that could not grow unless certain simple biochemical compounds were added to the medium (the food on which the fungus was grown). These simple compounds were the metabolites (intermediate products) that are routinely present in biochemical pathways under normal conditions. Their idea was that if a mutant gene was not producing a certain enzyme, then the enzyme's usual product would not be produced and the biochemical pathway would be brought to a lethal halt. The biochemical pathway could be said to be *blocked* at a critical step. So, by adding the missing product of the blocked step, the scientist would be able to unblock the pathway and allow it to proceed to completion, and the fungus would thrive (Figure 14.2).

Once the "nutritional mutants" had been identified, mutant strains of the fungus could be maintained and genetic crosses could be made. All of the enzyme deficiencies turned out to follow the rules of Mendelian genetics; hence the slogan "one gene, one enzyme." Garrod's idea had been rediscovered: biologists now knew that specific genes were responsible for the presence or absence of specific enzymes.

Transformation

In 1928 Fred Griffith, a British bacteriologist, conducted what seemed at first to be an oddball experiment, but it proved to be a classic. He studied the virulence (disease-producing capacity) of two strains of the bacterium that includes the agent of pneumonia. One strain was dangerous and the other was harmless. The virulent strain formed a smooth, gummy polysaccharide coating that apparently protected it from the host's defenses. The harmless strain lacked a gummy coat. When grown in the laboratory, the virulent strain produced smooth, glistening colonies, whereas the harmless strain (which lacked the proper enzymes to make a jelly coat) produced rough colonies.

When Griffith injected the dangerous smooth-strain bacteria into mice, the mice died, as expected. When he injected the harmless rough-strain bacteria into other mice, the mice did not die. But then Griffith mixed dead smooth-strain bacteria with live rough-strain bacteria—both of which had earlier proved to be harmless—and injected the mixture into a fourth group of mice. These mice died. What had happened?

Autopsies showed that the dead mice were full of virulent, living, smooth bacteria! Where did they come from? Apparently the genetic material of the harmless living, rough-strain bacteria had somehow been *transformed* by something in the dead smooth-strain bacteria, something that made them deadly also. Moreover, the rough-strain's progeny were all smooth (Figure 14.3).

Sixteen years later, O. T. Avery and his colleagues set out to learn more about transformation. After finding that the phenomenon could take place in test tubes as well as in living mice, they decided to try to discover just what substance was causing it. Various substances derived from the dead smooth bacteria were isolated and purified to see whether they might be the mysterious "transforming substance." In 1944, they finally found it. In that very year, Avery and his colleagues discovered that purified DNA from the deadly smooth-strain bacteria could transform a rough-strain pneumococcus bacterium, giving it the ability to synthesize the necessary enzymes for making the protective smooth coat.

Although they now knew that pure DNA had some kind of transforming capability, its role in

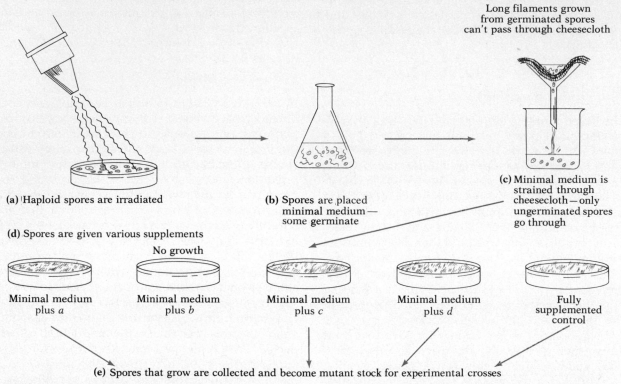

(a) Haploid spores are irradiated

(b) Spores are placed minimal medium — some germinate

Long filaments grown from germinated spores can't pass through cheesecloth

(c) Minimal medium is strained through cheesecloth — only ungerminated spores go through

(d) Spores are given various supplements

No growth

Minimal medium plus *a*

Minimal medium plus *b*

Minimal medium plus *c*

Minimal medium plus *d*

Fully supplemented control

(e) Spores that grow are collected and become mutant stock for experimental crosses

14.2

Beadle's and Tatum's experimental procedure began **(a)** with the irradiation of *Neurospora* spores, producing mutations. To locate the spores with nutritional mutations, they first eliminated those with normal metabolism by **(b)** growing them in a "minimal medium" (food that could be used only by normal individuals). These normal individuals, now in the form of growing filaments, were strained out and discarded, and the suspected mutant spores collected from the filtrate below **(c)**. Then, Beadle and Tatum prepared a series of culture dishes **(d)**, each with a different nutritional supplement (vitamins, amino acids, or their metabolites) added to a minimal medium. Samples of spores were placed in each dish, and those that were able to grow were designated by the supplement they required. They then used these in crosses to determine the hereditary patterns of the deficient strains.

heredity was still unclear. DNA was a rather simple molecule and genes had very complex roles, so many geneticists were convinced that the hereditary material itself also had to be very complex, as proteins were known to be. After all, enzymes were proteins, and enzymes were the most complex molecules known; so it would seem that the genes that made enzymes would have to be at least as complex.

Informational Macromolecules. We see, then, that the idea of *informational macromolecules* was beginning to take hold. Certain chromosome-associated molecules obviously contained information that somehow directed the cell's biochemical processes. Avery's work pointed to DNA as being an informational molecule, though most scientists of the day favored proteins. No one knew much about DNA, but proteins were not well understood either, so the problem was compounded. Proteins

had always been regarded as fairly structureless entities, possibly made up of repeating subunits or, perhaps, an untidy conglomeration of amino acids. Scientists believed they couldn't understand any role of proteins as informational molecules until they could ascertain their structure. It was not until 1955 that Frederick Sanger was able to analyze precisely the structure of a simple protein—the hormone insulin—and to prove, for the first time, that it had a highly specific, unvarying, linear sequence of amino acids. By this time, the eyes of the scientific community were already beginning to focus on DNA.

Sickle-cell Anemia: A Molecular Disease. Let's continue the historical course of events. In 1949 Linus Pauling, the great theoretical chemist, investigated and compared purified **hemoglobin** (the oxygen-carrying protein of blood cells) from certain sick and healthy persons. The sick people had the genetic disease called **sickle-cell anemia,** which is characterized by strangely misshapen red blood cells that are inefficient at carrying oxygen (Figure 14.4). Pauling found that the net electrical charge of purified hemoglobin from affected homozygotes was slightly different from that of the healthy people. The difference in charge was due to a difference of one amino acid out of 287! Heterozygous carriers of the sickle-cell gene had both kinds of hemoglobin. Pauling thus demonstrated that the alleles of a gene were not merely responsible for the presence or absence of a protein, which is all that Garrod and Beadle and Tatum had shown; but that different alleles could specify *qualitative differences;* namely, changes in the amino acid sequence of a protein.

Pauling's finding also demonstrated that very

small molecular shifts could be responsible for large-scale phenotypic effects. This one small change in an amino acid sequence produces extremely destructive effects and has initiated one of the most intense research efforts in medical history. The condition is generally lethal in homozygotes, since the sickled cells cannot efficiently bind oxygen and they tend to form clots within the blood vessels. The heterozygotes bear both normal and sickled genes, and their blood may have only about 70 percent of the hemoglobin content of normal blood. For this reason they tend to suffer from anemia.

Sickle cell anemia is most common in East Africa and in the Gold Coast of West Africa. It would seem that its obvious disadvantages would result in its continual decline in the population; however, it continues because of a peculiar biological twist to the story. Persons heterozygous for the condition are highly resistant to malaria, a disease that kills many people who are normal for the condition. The people with affected cells are protected because it turns out that the malarial parasite cannot live within these abnormal cells. With natural selection favoring the heterozygotes, it is apparent how the sickled condition is able to persist in the population. In fact, in some of the more severely stricken malarial regions, over 40 percent of the population are carriers of the sickle-cell gene.

It is at about this point that the story of gene function begins to merge with the story of DNA. Let's see how this happened.

Hershey and Chase: The Great Kitchen Blender Experiment

Progress in molecular biology often follows the development of new technology. Given a new tool, researchers can expect new information. In this case, the new technology was provided by Fred Waring, a popular band leader of the 1950s. When he was not leading his group in song, he was busy inventing the kitchen blender. The blender, of course, whips food into a mush. The gourmet cook probably is not interested in the fact that, in so doing, it disrupts cells. But biologists happened to need a good way to disrupt cells, and so they crept away with their kitchen blenders and installed them in their laboratories.

In 1952, Alfred Hershey and Margaret Chase, who had followed Avery's work with interest, performed a crucial experiment. Their work firmly established that DNA was the only genetic material of at least one organism: the *bacteriophage* (or *phage,* for short). The **bacteriophage,** a virus that attacks bacteria, was a new tool for genetic analysis. If you

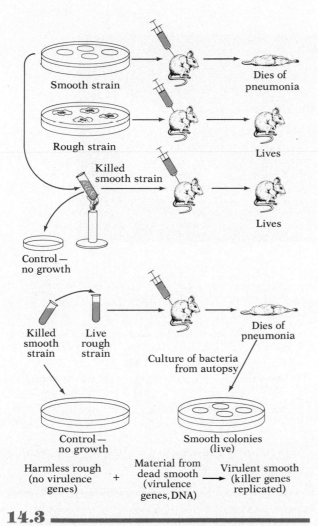

14.3

Transformation (1928). Twenty-five years before the function of DNA was finally resolved, Griffith's experiments clearly laid the groundwork for the idea that DNA was the genetic material.

have ever wondered whether a germ can get sick, you will be glad to learn that it can. It can become infected with a bacteriophage that can even kill it.

The bacteriophage that Hershey and Chase used is composed of a small DNA chromosome inside a juglike body made of protein. This particular one attacked *Escherichia coli*, the common colon bacterium. The phage resembles a hypodermic needle both in form and function (Figure 14.5). When it touches down on the surface of its bacterial host, tail (needle) first, it pierces the bacterial cell and injects its entire complement of DNA. Then a peculiar thing happens. The phage DNA takes over the synthesizing machinery of the host cell. The genes and enzymes that once directed the metabolism of the bacterium are now in the service of the parasite. Thus the bacterial host begins to make a hun-

dred or so new, complete viruses. It manufactures their DNA, proteins and all. The burgeoning new viruses then rupture the cell, and are free to infect other cells.

It is important to note that only the DNA is injected into the host cell. The original empty protein body stays outside like a discarded overcoat. Hershey and Chase didn't know this ahead of time, of course; they had to discover it for themselves through experimentation (Figure 14.6). They did this by growing bacteriophages on bacteria that had been fed radioactive sulfur (^{35}S) and radioactive phosphorus (^{32}P). They knew that proteins contained sulfur and no phosphorus, whereas nucleic acid contained phosphorus and no sulfur; so they had simultaneously and uniquely "tagged" both kinds of molecule.

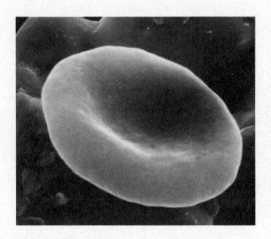

(a)

Phenotype	Genotype	Hemoglobin electrophoretic pattern	Hemoglobin types present
		Origin ⟶ +	
Normal	**AA**		A
Sickle-cell trait	**AS**		S and A
Sickle-cell anemia	**SS**		S

(b)

14.4

(a) Sickle-cell victims go through periodic crises during which the normally circular red blood cells *(left)* take on the sickled form *(right)*. When subjected to an electrical field (passing through a tray of starch pudding in a procedure called *gel electrophoresis*), sickle-cell hemoglobin separates from the normal protein and can be identified in both homozygous (SS) and heterozygous (AS) individuals. Note in the analysis **(b)** that approximately half the hemoglobin of heterozygotes matches hemoglobin of normal (AA) individuals. This indicates that both the normal and sickle-cell alleles in heterozygotes are functional. In spite of this, heterozygotes (carriers) rarely suffer the symptoms of sickle-cell anemia.

14.5

The bacteriophage consists of a head ("hypodermic syringe") and a narrow, hollow tail ("needle") ending in several tail fibers. The head contains viral DNA protected by its protein covering. When the phage lands on a bacterium, as we see in the electron micrograph of *E. coli*, it attaches via its tail fibers, and injects its DNA into the host.

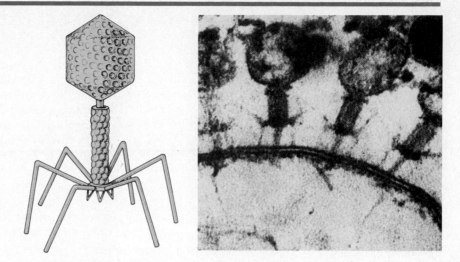

Hershey and Chase infected bacteria with these "hot" (radioactive) bacteriophages and allowed enough time for them to attach themselves and inject their DNA, but not enough time for the production of new bacteriophages. Then they put the mixture into their Waring blender.

The empty viral coats, which were pure protein, were broken loose from the bacterial surfaces and could be separated from them by centifugation. That is, the whole mixture, consisting of infected bacteria and loose empty viral coats in liquid, was put into a high-speed centrifuge. The whirling force settled the bacterial cells at the bottom of the centrifuge tube, leaving the viral coats suspended in the remaining liquid. All of the radioactive sulfur was found in the liquid with the empty protein coats, and *all of the radioactive phosphorus was found inside the infected bacteria.* Since the infected bacteria could still produce complete, virulent virus particles, Hershey and Chase had shown that all of the genetic information of the tiny organisms resided in its DNA—and only in its DNA.

Chargaff's Rule. Thus DNA was shown to be the stuff of genes. Attention was at last turned to this key molecule: how was it formed? How did it work? And how was it able to make precise copies of itself?

Erwin Chargaff tried to answer such questions with analytical biochemistry. He broke down purified DNA into its constituents: the four nucleotides of **adenine** (A), **thymine** (T), **guanine** (G), and **cytosine** (C). He carefully measured the exact quantity of each of these four subunits. Up to that time, the four nucleotides A, T, G, and C were believed to exist in equal amounts. But by about 1953, Chargaff reported that it wasn't so; the relative amounts of the four bases varied from species

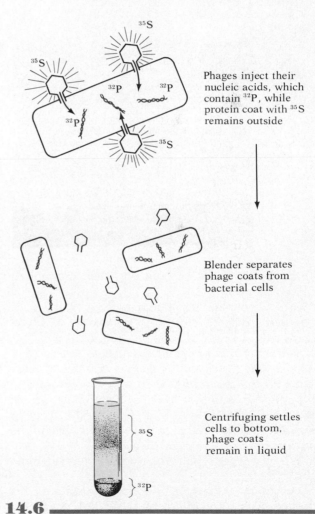

Phages inject their nucleic acids, which contain ^{32}P, while protein coat with ^{35}S remains outside

Blender separates phage coats from bacterial cells

Centrifuging settles cells to bottom, phage coats remain in liquid

14.6

Hershey-Chase experimental procedure. Hershey and Chase were able to grow phage particles that had their DNA labeled with radioactive phosphorus (^{32}P) and their protein coats labeled with radioactive sulfur (^{35}S). They were later able to show that only the phage DNA enters the cell to carry out its genetic activity.

TABLE 14.1

Chargaff's rule (1949–1953)*

| | Base Composition (mole percent) | | | |
	A	T	G	C
Animals				
Human	30.9	29.4	19.9	19.8
Sheep	29.3	28.3	21.4	21.0
Hen	28.8	29.2	20.5	21.5
Turtle	29.7	27.9	22.0	21.3
Salmon	29.7	29.1	20.8	20.4
Sea urchin	32.8	32.1	17.7	17.3
Locust	29.3	29.3	20.5	20.7
Plants				
Wheat germ	27.3	27.1	22.7	22.8
Yeast	31.3	32.9	18.7	17.1
Aspergillus niger (mold)	25.0	24.9	25.1	25.0
Bacteria				
Escherichia coli	24.7	23.6	26.0	25.7
Staphylococcus aureus	30.8	29.2	21.0	19.0
Clostridium perfringens	36.9	36.3	14.0	12.8
Brucella abortus	21.0	21.1	29.0	28.9
Sarcina lutea	13.4	12.4	37.1	37.1
Bacteriophages				
T7	26.0	26.0	24.0	24.0
λ	21.3	22.9	28.6	27.2
φX174, single strand DNA†	24.6	32.7	24.1	18.5
φX174, replicative form	26.3	26.4	22.3	22.3

*By determining the composition of nitrogen bases in the DNA of a variety of organisms, Chargaff and his contemporaries were able to provide vital information as the central dogma emerged. Pay close attention to the relative quantities of A and T, and G and C here. (But note that the values are not exactly equal due to experimental error.)

†Note that this virus has single-stranded DNA, which does *not* follow Chargaff's rule. Why not?

Adapted from A. L. Lehninger, *Biochemistry*, 2d ed. (New York: Worth, 1975).

to species (Table 14.1). So it was clear that not all DNA was alike.

In spite of this, a peculiar pattern emerged in Chargaff's data that came to be known as **Chargaff's rule.** In each species studied, he found that *the amount of adenine was always equal to the amount of thymine, and the amount of guanine was always equal to the amount of cytosine.* There are various ways to state this. In addition to A = T and G = C, one could also state A + G = T + C = 50%. That is, regardless of the source of DNA, exactly half of the nucleotide bases are **purines** (adenine and guanine) and exactly half are **pyrimidines** (thymine and cytosine).

Although Chargaff naturally thought his finding was very interesting, he did not really know what to make of it. But his work was being watched very closely by James Watson and Francis Crick, who were trying to work out DNA structure in England. Eventually they saw the physical reality behind Chargaff's rule.

WATSON AND CRICK AND THE MOLECULAR MODEL OF DNA

X-ray crystallography is a technique that helps to determine the structure of crystals. It involves shooting a narrow beam of x-rays at a crystal and noting how the rays are diffracted (bent) before reaching a target of photographic film.

Crystals can be made of biological as well as geological substances. Hemoglobin, for instance, forms good crystals. But such large molecules are far more complex than the simple inorganic molecules that form rock crystals, and the problems of interpreting biological x-ray diffraction patterns were enormous (Figure 14.7). By the early 1950s, only a few organic substances had been studied this way. DNA was much on everyone's mind, and a few laboratories were beginning to look at DNA crystals.

Among those engaged in such work were Maurice Wilkins (who was to share the Nobel prize with Watson and Crick) and Rosalind Franklin (who died before her work was fully appreciated). Their studies revealed a few repeating distances within the molecules of DNA: 0.34 nm, 2 nm, and 3.4 nm. We'll see what these numbers mean later; at the time they were just mysteries. But Wilkins and Franklin also saw a pattern indicating that DNA was a *helical* (corkscrew-shaped) molecule. Franklin had even argued that there were probably two strands in each molecule of DNA, not one or three. These two workers had the data and had

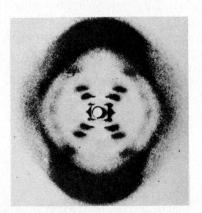

14.7

To many (including most biologists), the product of x-ray crystallography—the *diffraction pattern*—may be interesting, but it is quite meaningless. But to Wilkins and Franklin, patterns like these held a great deal of information about the DNA crystal. From them they perceived a helical structure and measurable repeated subunits in the lengthy polymer.

almost figured out what the DNA molecule was like, but they couldn't nail it down. The problem was to be solved by the young researchers Watson and Crick. They did no crystallography of their own, but relied instead on Wilkins' and Franklin's data.

Just what did Watson and Crick accomplish? Before we get to that story, it will help to review some of the basic features of the DNA molecule from the standpoint of today's knowledge. Then we can go back and see where that knowledge came from.

What Is DNA?

DNA is a **polymer,** that is, a chain of repeating subunits. The repeating subunits are called *deoxynucleotides* (or, simply, **nucleotides**). The DNA molecule itself consists of two strands wound around each other in a **double helix,** resembling two wires twisted around each other. Each of the two strands of a DNA molecule is forged of strong covalent bonds between adjacent nucleotides. There are four different kinds of nucleotides in DNA, as we have seen before, but a closer look at their structure at this point will be helpful.

The DNA Nucleotides

The diagram represents one of the four nucleotides of DNA—the adenine nucleotide (or, more properly, deoxyadenosine 5-phosphate). The pentagon-shaped portion in the lower center is deoxyribose, a sugar. Attached to the sugar are both a phosphate ion and a two-ring structure, adenine (a nucleotide base). Also, notice that the five carbons of the sugar molecule have been numbered, and that the numbers have primes [']. Thus the five deoxyribose carbon atoms have names, 1' through 5' (pronounced *one-prime through five-prime*). This standard nomenclature will be useful as we proceed.

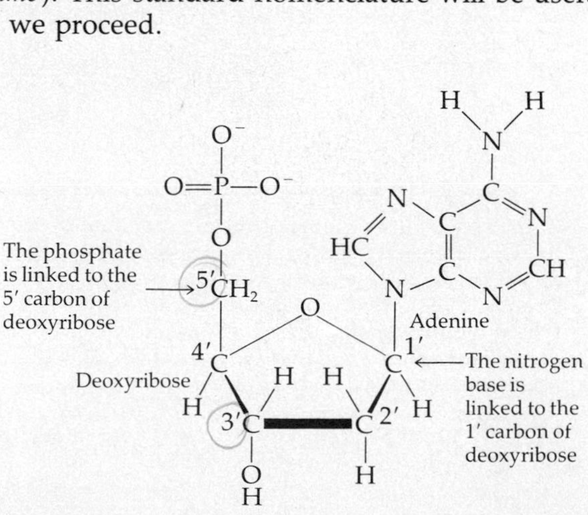

The deoxyribose molecule serves as a link holding together the other parts of the DNA molecule. Its important bonding points are the 1', 3', and 5' carbons. The nucleotide bases are always covalently bonded to the 1' carbon of deoxyribose, as shown in the diagram. In free-floating nucleotides, the phosphate is linked to the 5' carbon only; but when the nucleotides are joined together to make a strand of DNA, the 5' phosphate of one nucleotide is joined to the 3' carbon of the next nucleotide. The alternating phosphates and sugars form what is called the *backbone* of the DNA strand; the nucleotide bases hang off the sides of the molecular backbone.

All four of the DNA nucleotides follow this organization, with only the identity of the nucleotide base portion being different. The four DNA bases, as we have seen, are adenine, thymine, guanine, and cytosine (A, T, G, and C, respectively). The purines (guanine and adenine) consist of two attached rings: one ring with five sides, and one with six sides, the two rings sharing a common side. The pyrimidines (thymine and cytosine) each consist of a single six-sided ring. (Note that the smaller molecules have the larger names—this might be useful if you are asked to recall the structures.)

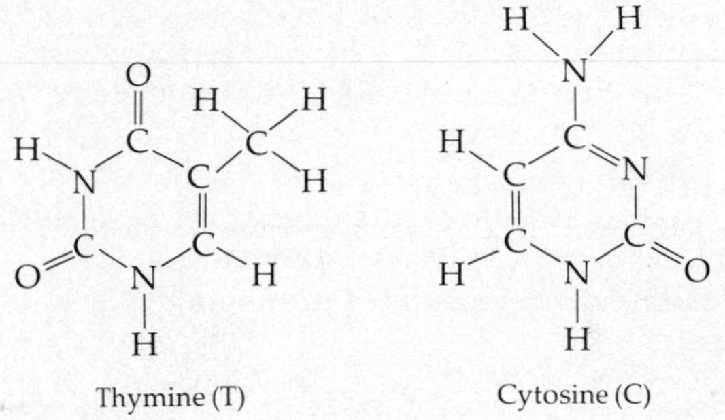

Thymine (T)

Cytosine (C)

Pyrimidines
(single ring)

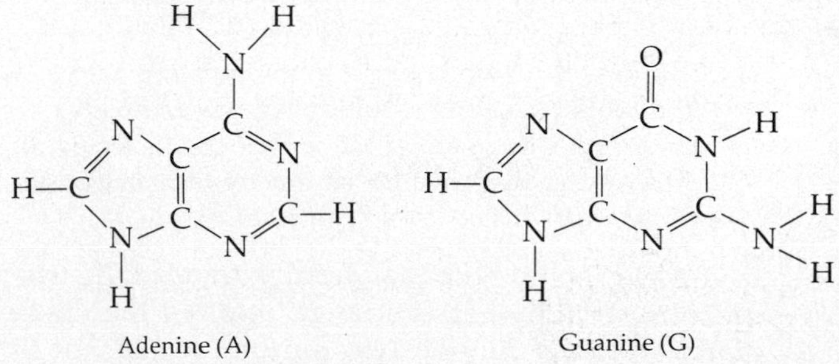

Adenine (A)

Guanine (G)

Purines
(double ring)

The two halves of DNA—the two strands of the double helix—fit together in an interesting way. But that's Watson's and Crick's story; let's return to them and see how they finally figured out the structure of DNA.

The phosphate is linked to the 5' carbon of deoxyribose

Deoxyribose

Adenine

The nitrogen base is linked to the 1' carbon of deoxyribose

The Watson and Crick Model

Consider first what Watson and Crick knew when they tackled the DNA problem in 1953. They knew: (1) that DNA was a polymer consisting of four different nucleotides; (2) the chemical structures of the nucleotides; and (3) that the deoxyribose and the phosphate alternated in long chains, with the nucleotide bases hanging off the sides of each chain like signal flags on a single rope. From Wilkins' and Franklin's work they knew that DNA formed some kind of a helix, with three intramolecular distances: 0.34 nm, 2.0 nm, and 3.4 nm. Finally, they knew Chargaff's rule: the number of adenines somehow had to equal the number of thymines, and the number of guanines had to equal the number of cytosines. *That* was where everything came together.

Chargaff's Rule and Base Pairing. Watson's and Crick's experimentation was based on real models made of wire, sheet metal, and (literally) nuts and bolts. These models were designed to provide a graphic representation of the DNA molecule and its constituent parts. They began to fiddle with these models, to see how the parts might fit together. Sometimes the fingers can grasp what the mind cannot.

Biological intuition and fitting the pieces this way and that seemed to indicate that there might be two strands wrapped around one another, with the phosphate-sugar backbone on the outside and the nucleotide bases inside, facing one another. But how were the bases arranged inside?

Wilkin's and Franklin's numbers began to make sense:

- 2 nm: their molecular model was consistent with the entire double helix being just 2 nm wide.
- 0.34 nm: the nucleotide bases were just about 0.34 nm thick, and perfectly flat. If the bases were stacked one on top of the other, like pennies in a roll, the layers would be 0.34 nm apart.
- 3.4 nm: with a gentle slope to the twisting helix, the double backbone would make one complete turn every 3.4 nm along the axis of the molecule; in other words, there would be exactly ten nucleotide pairs in each helical turn (Figure 14.8).

It was Watson who insightfully grasped the true meaning of Chargaff's strange rule. In the sheet metal and wire model, two purines would not fit opposite one another within the 2-nm confines of the double helix; and two pyrimidines would leave a gap. But one purine and one pyrimidine *could* fit opposite one another. Watson saw that adenine (a purine) and thymine (a pyrimidine) in a flat plane would form two hydrogen bonds with one an-

other; guanine (a purine) and cytosine (a pyrimidine) would similarly form three hydrogen bonds in a plane (Figure 14.9). And this was the *only* way the DNA molecule would hold together. Opposite every adenine in one strand there had to be thymine in the second strand; every guanine in the one strand could be firmly hydrogen-bonded to a cytosine in the second strand, and so on. This— **base pairing**—was Watson and Crick's major finding. The linear order of nucleotides in any one strand might be perfectly arbitrary, but whatever

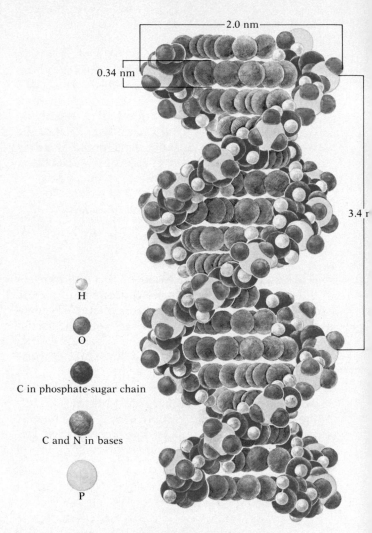

H

O

C in phosphate-sugar chain

C and N in bases

P

14.8

In the space-filling model of the DNA double helix we can clearly distinguish the sugar-phosphate backbone of the two intertwining strands. The pairs of nitrogen bases are represented by lines of spheres lying stacked within the helix. Each base pair is 0.34 nm thick, and 10 such pairs, found in each full turn of the helix, measure 3.4 nm. The overall width of the DNA helix is 2 nm. Each measurement was determined through x-ray crystallography studies.

Base pairing in DNA always occurs between adenine and thymine and between cytosine and guanine. The pairs are joined by hydrogen bonds *(dashed lines)*, and as you see, the bonding is very specific. Hydrogen bonding will not readily occur when bases are mismatched.

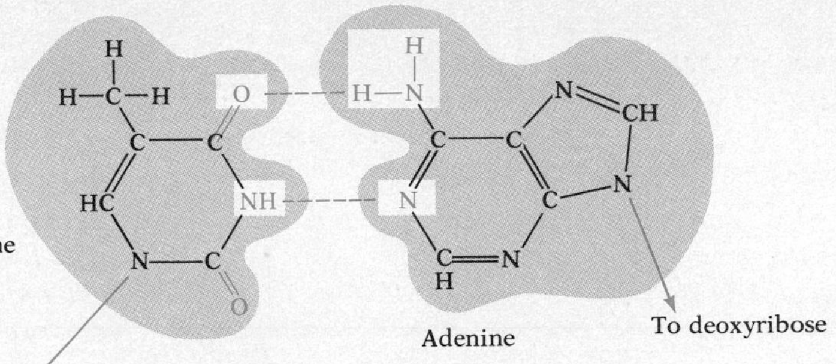

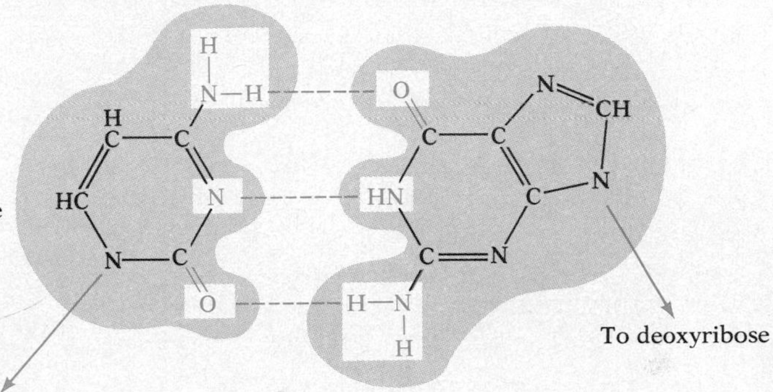

Thymine

To deoxyribose

Adenine

To deoxyribose

Cytosine

To deoxyribose

Guanine

To deoxyribose

nucleotides were in one strand rigidly fixed the sequence of nucleotides in the other strand. Thus Chargaff's empirical rules suddenly made logical sense: every A with a T, every T with an A, every G with a C, every C with a G. From this belatedly obvious conclusion sprang a whole new era in science, the era of molecular biology.

Base Pairing. The paired bases lie perfectly flat, as we have seen, and are stacked one on another. The thickness of the layers and the molecular distances along the sugar-phosphate backbone produce the characteristic coiling of the molecule. The flat base pairs are not quite aligned with the one below, but are slightly offset, like the steps in a winding staircase.

The two chains of the DNA molecule run in opposite directions. That is, if you pictured a DNA molecule vertically on a page, one of the chains would appear upside-down relative to the other (Figure 14.10). So if one strand has its 3' end at the top of the page and its 5' end at the bottom of the page, the other strand will have its 5' end at the top and its 3' end at the bottom.

DNA molecules can be quite long. The average chromosomal DNA molecule in a human cell nu-

cleus consists of about 140 million nucleotide pairs (two strands of 1.4×10^8 nucleotides each). However, because atoms are so small, a stretched-out DNA double helix of that size would only be about 5 cm long. The 46 DNA molecules in each human cell nucleus (prior to chromosome replication) total some 6.4 billion nucleotide pairs (6.4×10^9 pairs) which, stretched out end-to-end, would measure a little more than 2 m.*

Crick Solves the Riddle of DNA. DNA is fairly simple stuff, with only four subunits arranged in a simple, repetitive way. Crick, at the height of his intellectual powers, made the leap from DNA structure to DNA function. But how does DNA work? How could it be responsible for the incredibly complex role of the hereditary material? Crick solved the puzzle for us. He deduced how the perfectly matched strands of DNA could unwind, and how each half of the original double helix could direct the synthesis of a new, perfect,

---

*A nanometer is 10^{-9} meters, and the distance between one nucleotide pair and the next is 0.34 nm. So $6.4 \times 10^9 \times 0.34 \times 10^{-9} = 2.176$ m. Imagine all this coiled up into a microscopic cell nucleus.

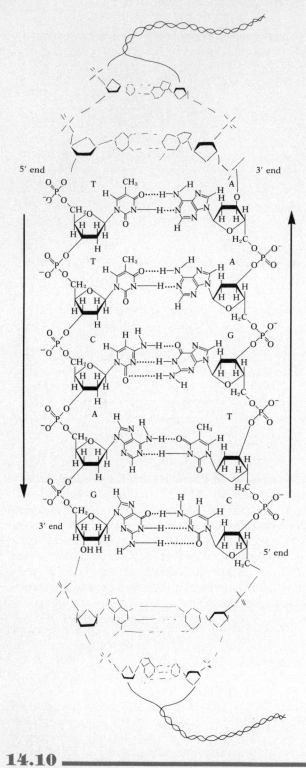

14.10

In the fully assembled DNA polymer, one strand appears upside down to the other. Note the covalent bonds of the sugar-phosphate backbone and the hydrogen bonds between pairs of bases. In this view the bases have been turned up 45° to show their structure and bonds, but in the actual molecule, only their edges would be seen.

identical double helix. He also was among the first to propose that a short sequence of DNA nucleotides along the DNA molecule could somehow specify a single amino acid in the construction of a protein. But how, he wondered. His mind was forced to race ahead of the available data. How was he to get around the fact that, in eukaryotes, proteins are synthesized *only* in the cytoplasm, while the DNA (which directed the synthesis) occurred *only* in the nucleus? Crick had only the flimsiest of circumstantial evidence with which to work. He knew that RNA moved from the nucleus to the cytoplasm; perhaps RNA was copied from DNA. Next, he proposed the existence of an "adapter molecule." This molecule, he suggested, could join with a particular amino acid and then be able to recognize a particular RNA sequence, possibly a sequence only three nucleotide pairs long.

Later, as we shall see, something like Crick's adapter molecules were found and were named *transfer RNA*. Before the decade was over, Crick, whose awesome intellect had come to dominate molecular biology, was able to formulate what he called "the central dogma." Let's take a closer look at Crick's bold synthesis.

THE CENTRAL DOGMA

Since we're discussing science, you may be surprised to see the word *dogma*. **Dogma** usually refers to something that can't be questioned, and the term is usually reserved for matters of religion and politics. In a sense, the only dogma in science is that there can be no dogma—everything and anything can and should be questioned and tested. Crick's term originally was meant as a kind of self-deprecating joke, but it stuck. It is amusing that his idea was so powerful that many people accepted his little joke with not even a raised eyebrow.

In any case, the **central dogma** has been a landmark finding, in spite of the fact that there are, even now, important details to be worked out and intriguing mysteries to be solved. Some of these questions perhaps may never be answered; furthermore, each answer begets new questions. But still, with the working out of DNA function and the central dogma, the essence of the life process becomes better understood. But we're getting ahead of ourselves. Just what is the central dogma? Simply stated, it is as follows:

1. All DNA is copied from other DNA (a process called **replication**).

2. All RNA is copied from DNA (a process called **transcription**).
3. All proteins are synthesized from RNA in such a way that three sequential RNA nucleotide bases code for (direct the placement of) one amino acid in a protein chain, using a genetic code that is the same for all organisms (a process called **translation**).

Hardly the stuff, it would seem, for an earth-shattering intellectual revolution. Perhaps it seems that way only because the revolution has already happened, and we live in a world where the central dogma is accepted. (There are some interesting exceptions to these three absolute statements, requiring a couple of amendments to the dogma that will be discussed in the next chapter.) Let's restate the central dogma in more general terms.

All *biological information* (here, "information" refers to the coded directions needed for the organism to develop, function, and reproduce) is contained in linear sequences of nucleic acid bases in DNA; is retained when these sequences are copied into newly synthesized DNA; is also capable of being copied into ribonucleic acid sequences; and uniquely determines the linear sequences of amino acids in protein synthesis. Finally, the linear sequence of amino acids in a protein uniquely determines the shape and function of the protein itself (see Figure 3.12).

You may have decided that the rules and statements of the central dogma can be terribly befuddling; our task here is to unfuddle them so that they make sense. So let's go directly to the first rule of the dogma—DNA replication.

DNA Synthesis and Replication

Synthesis means to make something, and *replication* means to make an exact copy of something. With very few exceptions, DNA synthesis and replication are the same thing, because DNA molecules are made by copying other DNA molecules. Watson and Crick immediately grasped the significance of the special properties of DNA structure. In fact, they ended their classic 1953 paper by stating, "It has not escaped our notice that the specific pairing we have postulated immediately suggests a possible copying mechanism for the genetic material." Their suggestion was soon shown to be correct.

The complementary pairing of nucleotide bases in DNA suggests the analogy of a positive and a negative photographic film. The same information is present in both; one can make a positive print

from a negative and a negative film from a positive. And, of course, to reproduce a positive print from a positive print one has to go through the intermediate step of developing a negative. Similarly, a DNA "Watson" strand can be produced from a "Crick" strand. (A little in-joke; a Watson strand or a Crick strand can be either one of the two halves of a DNA molecule.) So in DNA replication, the Watson and Crick strands unwind, a new Crick strand is produced from the information in the Watson strand, and a new Watson strand is made from the information in the Crick strand. Thus there are two complete DNA molecules where before there was only one.

We still don't know all the details of DNA replication; this remains an active area of research in molecular biology. For example, biologists would like to have a better idea of just what initiates the process or of why DNA is duplicated only once in the cell cycle; but at least we know the essentials of the process.

Note in Figure 14.11 that the first step in DNA replication is the unwinding of the double helix. This involves breaking the weak hydrogen bonds holding the two strands together. The process requires energy and special **unwinding enzymes.** Then another set of enzymes called **DNA polymerase** goes to work, matching each exposed nucleotide with a new complementary nucleotide. As the new nucleotides are added, they are joined to one another in a new chain or strand. Replication is always in the 5'-to-3' direction of the new chain being synthesized.

DNA replication requires a great deal of energy. ATP provides the energy for unwinding, whereas energy for the synthesis of new bonds comes primarily from the raw deoxynucleotides themselves. In the reserve pools of the nucleus, the building blocks of DNA are present as deoxynucleotide 5' triphosphates: dATP, dTTP, dGTP, and dCTP. The two terminal phosphates are broken off, and the one remaining 5' phosphate of one nucleotide is bonded to the 3' position of the next nucleotide in the line.

Interestingly, the trailing ends of both of the new strands are set down in short sections of a couple of hundred nucleotides; these are called **Okazaki fragments** after their discoverer. The Okazaki fragments are eventually joined together by another enzyme called *ligase.*

DNA Replication in Bacteria. In prokaryotes, most or all of the cell's DNA is in a single, circular molecule of DNA. (It is not nearly as long a molecule as a typical eukaryotic chromosome. For example, humans have about 1400 times more DNA per cell than the average bacterium.) Although a circle has neither a beginning nor an end, replication—at least in the common intestinal bacterium *E. coli*—always begins at a single, specific initiation point, or **origin of replication** (Figure 14.12). A pair of **replication forks** then move away from the origin in opposite directions, forming a bubble of newly replicated strands. The two replication forks continue to travel around the enlarging bubble. Eventually they meet each other at a **termination point** halfway around the circle.

DNA Replication in Eukaryotes.

The principal difference between eukaryotic and prokaryotic replication is that each long eukaryotic chromosome has hundreds of different origins of replication. Eventually the replication forks back into each other as the bubbles (duplicated regions) expand, so that the entire linear DNA molecule is finally doubled. This replication takes place in the S phase of the cell cycle of cells that are preparing for division.

We've described the process in terms of the replication complexes moving along the chromosomes. The process is easier to visualize that way, and it's correct enough. But movement is relative, and, in fact, the replication complexes are firmly fixed to the interlocking strands of the nuclear matrix. So as replication proceeds, it is the chromosomes that move; as they are reeled through the fixed replication complexes, the bubbles of newly replicated DNA form larger and larger loops, and the still unreplicated DNA forms smaller and smaller loops.

The replication of DNA is only one aspect of the central dogma. Replication prepares the chromosomes for cell division, and the precision of the process ensures that each daughter cell will receive identical strands of DNA. The other thing that the genes on chromosomes do is to function in cellular processes, primarily through directing the synthesis of specific proteins. For this task the DNA must make copies of its genetic information in the form of messenger RNA, which is then translated into protein structure in the cytoplasm. This intricate and amazing story is the subject of the next chapter.

14.11

In DNA replication, two replication complexes (unwinding proteins and DNA polymerase) move in opposite directions along the double helix. As they proceed, the strands "bubble out," separating and exposing the nitrogen bases. Then short segments (Okazaki fragments) are assembled by pairing new nucleotides with those in the strands, and these are joined together by the enzyme *ligase*. Replication in each strand occurs simultaneously, but in opposite directions (always in the 5' to 3' direction). The two newly replicated strands will be identical.

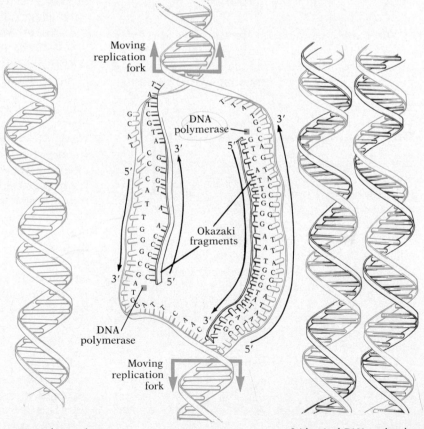

Original strand   2 identical DNA molecules

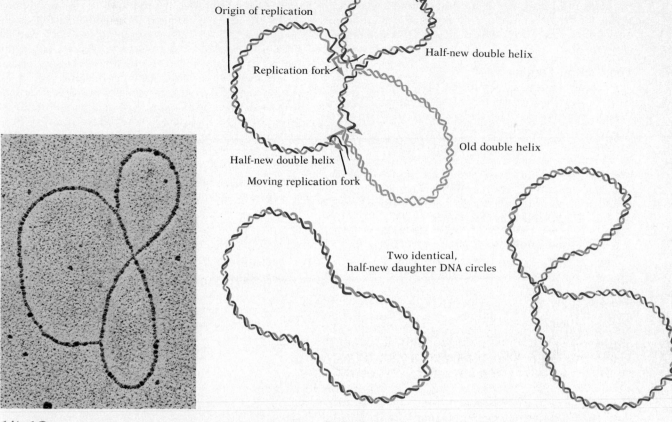

Origin of replication

Replication fork

Half-new double helix

Old double helix

Half-new double helix

Moving replication fork

Two identical,
half-new daughter DNA circles

14.12

Replication in a circular chromosome from *E. coli*, the intestinal bacterium. This particular chromosome is known as a *plasmid*, one of several types of minute circular chromosomes that accompany the large main chromosome of the bacterium. The replication principle is the same, however. Two replication forks are seen traveling in opposite directions, each spinning off the replicas of the original chromosome.

Summary

DNA: The Stuff of Genes
There are two types of nucleic acid—deoxyribonucleic acid (DNA) and ribonucleic acid (RNA). DNA was first isolated in a substance called nuclein (now called chromatin) and was not initially linked to heredity.

Gene Function
Genes were found to act directly on biochemical metabolism by determining the presence or absence of specific enzymes. Further experiments gave rise to the "one gene, one enzyme" slogan. In yet other studies, the process of transformation was investigated. Such knowledge supported the idea of informational macromolecules directing the cell's biochemical processes. Work with sickle-cell anemia showed that alleles could specify qualitative differences in the amino acid sequence of a protein. Researchers soon discovered that DNA was the only genetic material in the bacteriophage.

Erwin Chargaff separated DNA into its four nucleotides: adenine, thymine, guanine, and cytosine. From this information came Chargaff's rule that A = T and G = C; half of the nucleotide bases are purines and half are pyrimidines.

Watson and Crick and the Molecular Model of DNA
The DNA molecule is a polymer consisting of two strands of nucleotides, with alternating phosphates and sugars forming the backbone of each strand. The strands are wound into a double helix. There are two types of DNA nucleotides. The purines consist of two attached rings which share a common side, while the pyrimidines consist of a single six-sided ring each. Using data from x-ray crystallography and Chargaff's rule, Watson and Crick determined the double-stranded, helical, and base pairing characteristics of DNA. They suggested that be-

cause of base pairing, the order of nucleotides in one strand fixes the sequence of the other, providing a mechanism for DNA replication. Furthermore, the order of nucleotides determines the arrangement of amino acids in a protein.

The Central Dogma

The central dogma, as formulated by Crick, states that: (1) all DNA is copied from other DNA (replication); (2) all RNA is copied from DNA (transcription); and (3) all proteins are synthesized from RNA (translation). In other words, all biological information is contained in the linear sequences of nucleic acid bases in DNA. It is retained when replicated, and can be copied into RNA sequences. This information determines the linear sequences of amino acids in protein synthesis, and the sequence dictates the shape and function of each protein.

DNA synthesis and replication generally are the same process, requiring ATP energy and special unwinding enzymes. An enzyme called DNA polymerase joins exposed nucleotides with new complementary nucleotides. The new DNA strands form Okazaki fragments that are eventually joined together by the enzyme ligase.

In prokaryotes, most DNA takes the form of a single, circular molecule. Replication begins at a specific origin, with a pair of replication forks moving in opposite directions to form a bubble of newly replicated strands. These replication forks eventually meet at a termination point.

For eukaryotic cells, each chromosome can have hundreds of different origins of replication. The replication process prepares chromosomes for cell division, assuring that the genetic message of DNA will be identical from one generation of cells to the next.

Key Terms

molecular biology	Chargaff's rule	transcription
chromatin	purines	translation
nucleic acid	pyrimidines	synthesis
hemoglobin	polymer	unwinding enzymes
sickle-cell anemia	nucleotides	DNA polymerase
bacteriophage	double helix	Okazaki fragments
adenine	base pairing	origin of replication
thymine	dogma	replication forks
guanine	central dogma	termination point
cytosine	replication	

Review Questions

1. In a few words, summarize the contributions of Miescher, Griffith, and Avery to our understanding of the nature of the gene. Why did it take so long for biologists to shake off the erroneous idea that genes were enzymes? (pp. 187, 189)

2. Explain how Garrod managed to make the connection between abnormal substances in the urine and gene function. How did he know that such abnormalities were hereditary in the first place? (p. 188)

3. Briefly review the experimental procedure of Beadle and Tatum and explain how they made use of the nutritional mutants they created. What conclusions did they reach? Explain how their choice of *Neurospora* follows an important dictum in science: "reduce the problem to its simplest terms." (pp. 189–190)

4. The work of Hershey and Chase with the bacteriophage provided important information on the nature of the gene. Summarize their procedure, and state their conclusion. (pp. 191, 193)

5. While Watson and Crick are credited with the final resolution of DNA structure, they relied heavily on the experimental work of others such as Wilkins, Franklin, and Chargaff. In general, what information did these researchers provide and how did Watson and Crick put it to use? (pp. 193–195)

6. Beginning with the molecular units, the nucleotides, describe the structure of DNA. List the parts of a nucleotide, explain how they are assembled into single strands, and then explain the role of base pairing and hydrogen bonding in the formation of the double polymer. (pp. 195–198)

7. List the three primary tenets of the "central dogma." (pp. 198–199)

8. Describe the steps in the replication process, including in your description such terms as unwinding enzymes, Okazaki fragments, base pairing, and DNA polymerase. What specific mechanism assures that the two replicas will be identical to the original DNA polymer? (pp. 199–200)

DNA in Action:
Transcription, Translation, and Control

15

We have followed the history of science's long, tedious search for the stuff of heredity. We have seen the search move first in one direction and then another, as various kinds of molecules were proposed. Finally, we have seen the hereditary material. We have seen it unveiled as DNA and have seen that the key to its signals to the cell is the sequence of the nucleotides along the length of the long DNA molecule. We have also found how the DNA replicates, and that the precision of the replicating mechanism explains the constancy of the DNA from one generation to the next. So let's now see how this fascinating molecule dictates the business of the cell by directing the synthesis of specific enzymes and other proteins.*

First, it should be clear that in eukaryotes, at least, the genes control protein synthesis in an indirect manner. Whereas the genes are enclosed in the nucleus, the proteins that they direct are formed in the cytoplasm. This means that the genes must act through intermediaries. Copies of the instructions are passed from the nucleus to the cytoplasm through pores in the nuclear membrane. The actual carriers of the genetic message are molecules of *ribonucleic acid*, or *RNA* for short. There are several different kinds. Our first task here will be to learn about the chemical characteristics of RNA. Then we'll consider the different kinds and describe how they all function.

THE RNA MOLECULE

The things you've learned about the structure of DNA should help you here, because DNA and RNA are very similar. Both DNA and RNA are lengthy polymers of nucleotide subunits that are held together by covalent bonds between phosphates and sugars. The nucleotide bases hang off the familiar sugar-phosphate backbone like signal flags on a line. But there are several important differences between DNA and RNA that are significant to their different roles.

1. In RNA, the 5-carbon sugar is ribose instead of deoxyribose. As you see in the molecules shown below, the 2' carbon of deoxyribose of DNA contains two hydrogen side groups. This same carbon in the ribose of RNA has a single hydrogen side group, but opposing it is a hydroxyl (OH) side group.

---

*Note: Throughout the chapter, the term *protein synthesis* is often used in a general sense. Actually we will be describing polypeptide synthesis. A protein is biologically functional, containing one or more polypeptides that have assumed their final functional form (Chapter 2).

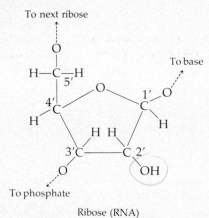

To next deoxyribose

Deoxyribose (DNA)

To next ribose

Ribose (RNA)

2. While both RNA and DNA contain adenine (A), guanine (G), and cytosine (C), the thymine (T) of DNA is replaced in RNA by a base called *uracil* (U). Uracil is structurally very similar to thymine and base-pairs with adenine in the same way:

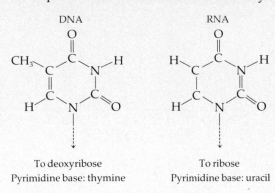

DNA

To deoxyribose
Pyrimidine base: thymine

RNA

To ribose
Pyrimidine base: uracil

3. DNA almost always occurs as a double-stranded helix with a very regular structure. RNA almost always occurs as a single-stranded molecule, and usually has complex *secondary* and *tertiary* levels of structure, as we have often seen in proteins, twisting and folding on itself into a precise three-dimensional shape.

4. DNA molecules are typically much longer than RNA molecules. DNA molecules are millions

15.1

(a) In transcription, the DNA helix unwinds and the double strand opens, as in replication. But the active enzyme is RNA polymerase, which goes to work base-pairing RNA nucleotides to the transcribing strand of the DNA. The other strand remains idle. Notice that every A (adenine nucleotide) in DNA becomes opposed by a U (uracil nucleotide) in the RNA strand. (b) As is often the case, the simultaneous transcription of RNA occurs. Transcription complexes move along the DNA molecule, each unwinding the helix as it moves, and rewinding the helix behind itself.

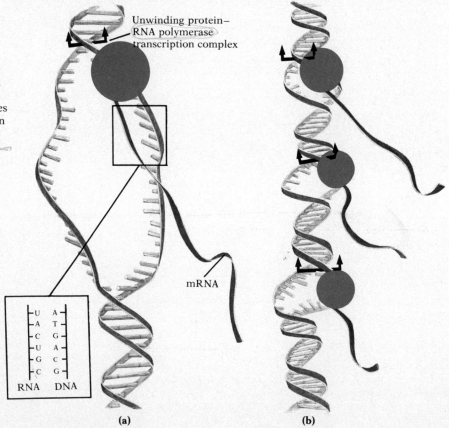

Unwinding protein–RNA polymerase transcription complex

mRNA

RNA	DNA
U	A
A	T
C	G
U	A
G	C
C	G

(a)

(b)

of nucleotides long, while the nucleotides in RNA molecules only number in the hundreds.

5. DNA is more stable than RNA: that is, it is more resistant to chemical breakdown.

6. There are several different classes of RNA molecules, each with different functions, whereas all DNA functions in information storage and transmission.

TRANSCRIPTION: THE SYNTHESIS OF RNA

RNA synthesis, more specifically known as *transcription,* is reminiscent of DNA replication. In **transcription** (Figure 15.1), DNA is unwound and its bases are exposed, just as if it were about to begin replication. Instead of each strand of DNA making a complementary strand, however, one strand lies dormant while short sections of the other act as a template for the formation of RNA. And as we mentioned above, uracil replaces thymine in RNA. During RNA synthesis, uracil pairs with DNA's adenine, all along the strand being transcribed. After the copying is over, the RNA **transcript** drifts free and the DNA rewinds.

Just as the replication complex of DNA synthesis consists of an unwinding protein and the enzyme DNA polymerase, transcription is accomplished by a **transcription complex** consisting of an unwinding protein and the enzyme **RNA polymerase.** The length of DNA along which a single RNA molecule is transcribed is called a **unit of transcription,** which in eukaryotes is roughly equivalent to a gene.

As soon as the first few bases of an RNA sequence have been formed, the DNA and RNA strands begin to separate and the growing RNA chain or transcript begins to dangle off to the side. The DNA to which it was attached is then free for further transcription. Many RNA molecules can be transcribed in a very brief time from the same DNA transcription unit. This is known as **simultaneous transcription** (Figure 15.2).

DIFFERENT KINDS OF RNA

While transcription accounts for the synthesis of RNA, the immediate product is only the raw material for further chemical modification of the transcripts. As we mentioned above, there are several functional types of RNA. Three of these will be of special interest to us, because they are necessary for protein synthesis: *messenger RNA (mRNA), ribosomal RNA (rRNA),* and *transfer RNA (tRNA).* Each has a specific role in the synthesis of enzymes and other proteins. Let's begin with mRNA (messenger RNA), and find out what its message is all about.

Messenger RNA and the Genetic Code

Messenger RNA (mRNA) carries the specific information that has been stored in the sequence of nucleotides in DNA. In DNA, that information is coded in the form of nucleotide base sequencing—the linear order in which A, T, C, and G are arranged in DNA strands. The equivalent sequence is copied into RNA, with U replacing T.

Raw mRNA starts out as a transcript, a complete copy of a transcription unit. At this stage it can be called *pre*-messenger RNA. Before this RNA transcript can be considered mRNA, and before it can move out into the cytoplasm, it must undergo *tailoring.* Tailoring implies cutting and stitching, and the term is apt. Long pieces are cut out of the original RNA transcript, while the remaining intact nucleotides join together again to form functional mRNA. The pieces that are cut out are disassembled into free nucleotides, which can then be recycled.

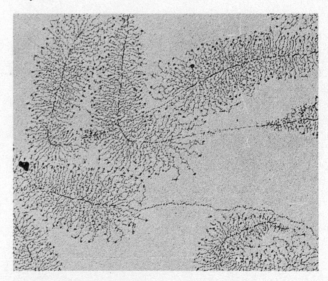

15.2

Evidence of simultaneous transcription is seen in chromosomes from an amphibian egg as the cell builds its protein reserves. Although the "bubbling out" of the DNA is not visible, the direction of transcription can be determined. The shorter, feathery strands of RNA are just starting, while the longer ones are well along in the transcription process.

The parts of the transcription unit that are ultimately discarded are called **intervening sequences,** or *introns* for short. The sequences that actually end up in the mature mRNA molecule are called **expressed sequences,** or *exons*. As of this writing, no one knows why nearly all eukaryote genes have intervening sequences (bacteria get along just fine without them), but there they are. In fact the introns are usually much larger than the exons, and the original transcript is typically many times larger than the mature mRNA.

After tailoring, the mature mRNA consists of three regions: a *5' leading region*, a *cistron* in the middle, and a *3' following region*. Only the cistron is *translated*. That is, **cistrons** are the portions of mRNA that direct the sequencing of amino acids in the developing protein. In essence, cistrons are the "message."

The Message Is Written in the Genetic Code.

The cistron of the messenger RNA molecule carries its message in the form of **codons,** which are nucleotides in groups of three. Each codon specifies one of the 20 different amino acids commonly found in proteins. For example, the three-nucleotide sequence GAG (guanine-adenine-guanine) is a codon, and it specifies *glutamic acid,* one of the 20 common amino acids. The 64 codons (representing all of the ways in which four kinds of nucleotides can be arranged in a sequence of three) are shown in Table 15.1, together with the amino acids they specify. This is the famous *genetic code,* a major discovery of 20th-century science.

To better understand how the code works, let's consider the **principle of colinearity** (Figure 15.3), a concept that Francis Crick so elegantly proposed long before much was known about RNA. DNA, RNA, and protein are each linear molecules consisting of repeated subunits, and there is a clear relationship among the units. The linear ordering of nucleotides in DNA specifies the order of codons in mRNA, and the linear ordering of codons in mRNA specifies the linear ordering of amino acids in the protein.

It is now well established which amino acids are specified by which codons, but working out the genetic code required the efforts of some of the best minds in molecular biology, and a great deal of painstaking experimental verification. Once the genetic code table was finally worked out, the genetic code proved to be exactly the same for such diverse groups as humans, *Escherichia coli,* and yeast—underscoring the basic relationships and unity of life—and so it was known for decades as the "universal genetic code."

The idea of the universal genetic code fit well with the idea of the universality of all life. It seemed that every form that is alive today still

TABLE 15.1

The genetic code

		SECOND LETTER							
		U		*C*		*A*		*G*		
FIRST LETTER	U	UUU, UUC } Phe; UUA, UUG } Leu		UCU, UCC, UCA, UCG } Ser		UAU, UAC } Tyr; UAA STOP; UAG STOP		UGU, UGC } Cys; UGA STOP; UGG Trp		U C A G
	C	CUU, CUC, CUA, CUG } Leu		CCU, CCC, CCA, CCG } Pro		CAU, CAC } His; CAA, CAG } Gln		CGU, CGC, CGA, CGG } Arg		U C A G
	A	AUU, AUC, AUA } Ile; AUG Met (Start)		ACU, ACC, ACA, ACG } Thr		AAU, AAC } Asn; AAA, AAG } Lys		AGU, AGC } Ser; AGA, AGG } Arg		U C A G
	G	GUU, GUC, GUA, GUG } Val		GCU, GCC, GCA, GCG } Ala		GAU, GAC } Asp; GAA, GAG } Glu		GGU, GGC, GGA, GGG } Gly		U C A G

THIRD LETTER

Amino acid abbreviations: alanine, Ala; arginine, Arg; asparagine, Asn; aspartic acid, Asp; cysteine, Cys; glutamic acid, Glu; glutamine, Gln; glycine, Gly; histidine, His; isoleucine, Ile; leucine, Leu; lysine, Lys; methionine, Met; phenylalanine, Phe; proline, Pro; serine, Ser; threonine, Thr; tryptophan, Trp; tyrosine, Tyr; valine, Val.

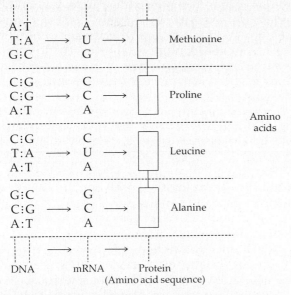

A:T   A
T:A → U → Methionine
G:C   G

C:G   C
C:G → C → Proline
A:T   A

C:G   C
T:A → U → Leucine
A:T   A

G:C   G
C:G → C → Alanine
A:T   A

DNA   mRNA   Protein
(Amino acid sequence)

Amino acids

15.3

The colinearity concept illustrates the relationship between DNA, mRNA, and protein. The triplet nucleotides of DNA are transcribed into the codons of mRNA, which in turn specify the order and kind of amino acids to be inserted into protein. (Omitted is the role of tRNA in protein synthesis.)

shared, by inheritance, the unchanged genetic code that must have been laboriously achieved by our universal common ancestor, at least three and a half billion years ago. Alas, the great diversity of life, which results from myriads of species wheedling out their own existence, each trying to gain an edge on the others, affords biology few blanket statements. So now we must modify even this grand notion. Mitochondria, those cellular organelles responsible for oxidative respiration, have their own protein-synthesizing machinery. It has now been shown that our very own mitochondria use a genetic code that is slightly different from the "universal" code used both by bacteria and by eukaryote nuclear chromosomes. Furthermore, yeast mitochondria have yet other slightly different codon assignments. So there are several dialects of the genetic language, and the code isn't quite so universal after all.

A Closer Look at the Genetic Code. You have probably wondered why there are 64 codons to code for only 20 amino acids; some of the amino acids must obviously be coded for by more than one codon. Different codons that specify the same amino acid are called **synonymous codons.** As you can see in Table 15.1, most (but not all) synonymous codons come in blocks and differ only in the third position.

We also now know that three of the 64 codons do not specify amino acids at all but instead indicate STOP. These are UAA, UAG, and UGA; they are, in effect, punctuation marks, and translate into "this is where to end the polypeptide." There is also a START codon, AUG; in addition to specifying START, it specifies the amino acid *methionine*. This means that all newly synthesized polypeptides have to start with methionine. If a methionine in the first position of a protein doesn't suit the needs of the organism—and apparently it often doesn't—then it will have to be removed enzymatically later on. Since AUG is the only codon for methionine, when it occurs in the middle of a cistron it is ignored as a START codon and is simply read as a methionine-specifying codon. Only the very first AUG to occur in a mRNA molecule means START.

We've seen that the genetic message is transcribed from DNA into mRNA, which, in turn, carries the message to the cytoplasm. There, as we will see, *translation* will occur. **Translation** is the conversion of the coded message into the arrangement and assembly of amino acids into polypeptides. The polypeptides will become functional, three-dimensional proteins. Before we can understand how the sequence of codons in mRNA is translated into a sequence of amino acids in a polypeptide, we'll have to back-track and look at the other two types of RNA involved in protein synthesis: ribosomal RNA and transfer RNA. Each has its role to play.

Ribosomal RNA and Ribosomes

Ribosomal RNA (rRNA) is found in ribosomes. The ribosomes, large enough to be seen with the electron microscope (see Chapter 4), contain about 100 proteins in addition to two large and two small RNA molecules. Ribosomes are the vital organizing centers where the messenger RNA and transfer RNA assist in assembling polypeptides. Ribosomes have been likened to gigantic enzyme complexes, or to workbenches in a factory, but really they are like no other molecular complex or cellular organelle in all of biology.

Each ribosome is made up of two subunits, called the *large subunit* and the *small subunit*. Each subunit has a characteristic shape: the large subunit looks startlingly like a hand puppet, and the small subunit looks remarkably like a rubber duck (Figure 15.4).

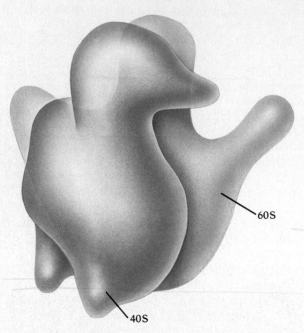

15.4

The ribosome's two subunits are not actually spherical. In point of fact, the intact ribosome looks startlingly like a hand puppet (the large subunit) grasping a rubber duck (the small subunit).

If we rotate the figure of the hand puppet grasping the rubber duck, to view the ribosome from the top, we can visualize three important functional sites in the intact ribosome. Figure 15.5 is a simplified diagram of the ribosome from this viewpoint. One of the functional sites is the groove formed where the two subunits join. The messenger RNA will fit into this groove during protein synthesis. The other two sites are pockets in the larger subunit, one along each arm of the hand puppet. The pockets will be important to the third type of RNA: transfer RNA.

Transfer RNA

What is the physical link between a codon—a sequence of three RNA nucleotides—and its specific amino acid? The physical link is **transfer RNA.** One end of tRNA becomes temporarily joined to a specific amino acid, and the other end can become temporarily joined to a specific mRNA codon. Yet other parts of this versatile molecule interact with the ribosome.

Transfer RNA has three tasks in the assembly of amino acids into polypeptides. First, each tRNA molecule must become *charged*. That is, it must seek out and bind to its own specific amino acid. Then, each tRNA must be able to bind to a ribosome where a polypeptide is being assembled. And finally, it must recognize a specific codon in mRNA, and insert its specific amino acid into the proper position in the growing polypeptide. As you might suspect, the ribosomal binding and amino acid insertion are closely interrelated events.

The specific charging of tRNAs suggests that there must be at least as many specific tRNAs as there are different amino acids. Actually, there are usually several tRNAs for each amino acid because of the synonymous codons.

The proper connections are made by *charging enzymes*. There is a highly specific charging enzyme for each variety of tRNA. The charging enzyme has a binding site for the amino acid, a binding site for the tRNA, and another binding site for ATP. It uses the energy from the terminal ATP bond to fasten the amino acid to the stem of the tRNA molecule. Let's turn now to the structure of tRNA, since its structure is closely related to its roles.

Transfer RNA is formed from a linear strand of about 100 nucleotides, whose sequence is transcribed from tRNA genes just as mRNA sequences are transcribed from other genes. After tailoring, the strand becomes twisted and folded into a definite three-dimensional shape, forming three "loops" and a "stem." In its finished form the whole molecule takes on sort of an L shape (Figure 15.6).

The different loops and the stem of the tRNA molecule play their own roles in the three aspects of its function:

1. The stem, with its 3' terminal sequence of CCA, is the attachment site of the specific amino acid.

2. One of the side loops forms base-pairing attachments to ribosomal RNA nucleotides in the tRNA binding sites.

3. Most interesting to us is the anticodon loop, which contains a three-base sequence known as the **anticodon.** The anticodon fits its base-pairing counterpart, the codon, in the mRNA. The three anticodon bases, then, must be able to pair with the three mRNA codon bases. For example, the mRNA codon GCC, according to the genetic code table, specifies alanine. One of the alanine-specific tRNA molecules has the anticodon CGG, which makes the proper base pairing with GCC (Figure 15.7).

15.5

(a) Ribosomes, minute bodies of rRNA and protein, contain two subunits designated 40S and 60S (a measure related to their density). They join to form an 80S body (the numbers are correct: density units are not to be added). The groove between the subunits fits over mRNA, while the two pockets accommodate two tRNAs. (b) Ribosomes, as seen in the electron micrograph, often appear in clusters.

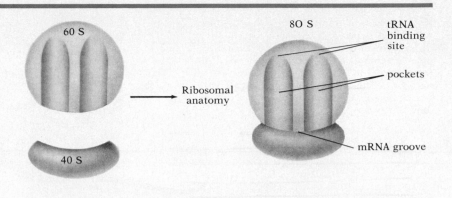

Ribosomal anatomy

(a)

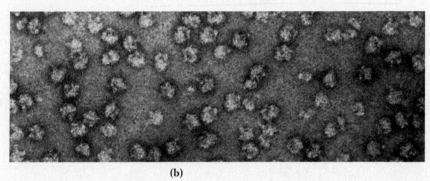

(b)

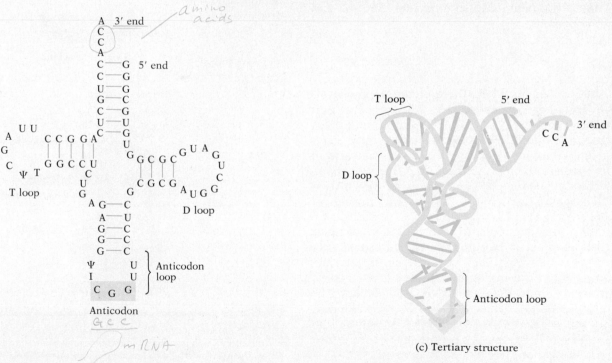

(c) Tertiary structure

15.6

Transfer RNA molecules contain about 90 nucleotides and are transcribed similarly to mRNA. (a) In its secondary form, the nucleotides of tRNA base pair to produce a multi-looped figure. The 3′ CCA end is the attachment site for an amino acid, while one of the side loops interacts with rRNA on the ribosome. The lower, or anticodon, loop holds three nitrogen bases that pair or match up with codons in mRNA. (ψ = various modified bases.) (b) In its final or tertiary form, tRNA twists and folds into the shape of an inverted L.

If, somewhere along the mRNA, the codon GCC appears, it will code for the placement of the amino acid alanine. Glycine-tRNA contains the anticodon CGG, which will pair up with GCC. This is but one step in the translation of genetic code into protein.

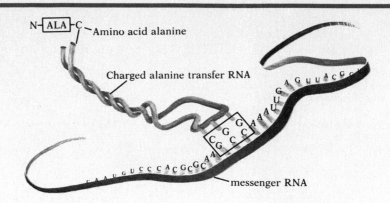

N—ALA—C Amino acid alanine

Charged alanine transfer RNA

messenger RNA

PROTEIN SYNTHESIS: TRANSLATION OF THE GENETIC MESSAGE

We now have all of the elements needed for a step-by-step description of protein synthesis. The process will be divided into three parts: *initiation, elongation,* and *termination*. These terms refer respectively to the beginning, the middle, and the end of the process.

Initiation

Initiation begins when three elements known as the **initiation complex** are brought together: mRNA (with its AUG START codon), the ribosome, and a charged tRNA molecule (Figure 15.8). Since methionine is always the first amino acid in any protein being synthesized, this will be a methionine-charged tRNA. Its anticodon—UAC—will match the codon—AUG—on messenger RNA.

All three elements of the initiation complex must be present before the two ribosome subunits can join together to form an intact ribosome. When the initiation complex is assembled, the methionine-charged tRNA will occupy the left-hand pocket of the larger ribosome subunit, and the AUG codon of the mRNA will fit into the ribosomal groove. All is now ready for the next step, elongation.

Elongation

With the initiation complex in place, **elongation,** the addition of amino acids, can proceed. Recall that the left-hand pocket of the ribosome was oc-

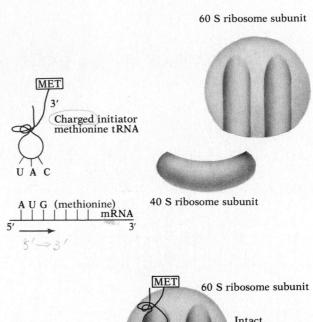

60 S ribosome subunit

MET

3'

Charged initiator methionine tRNA

U A C

A U G (methionine)
mRNA
5' ——————— 3'

40 S ribosome subunit

MET

60 S ribosome subunit

Intact, functional 80 S ribosome

U A C
A U G G G C

5' ——————— 3'

40 S ribosome subunit

The elements of an initiation complex include methionine-charged tRNA, the leading (AUG) end of mRNA, and the two ribosomal subunits. As the codon-anticodon match is made, the smaller subunit joins the complex. Only then can the larger subunit join. Note that methionine-charged tRNA is in the ribosome's left-hand pocket. The right pocket is empty, but in the groove below lies the second mRNA codon, ready for a charged tRNA with a matching anticodon.

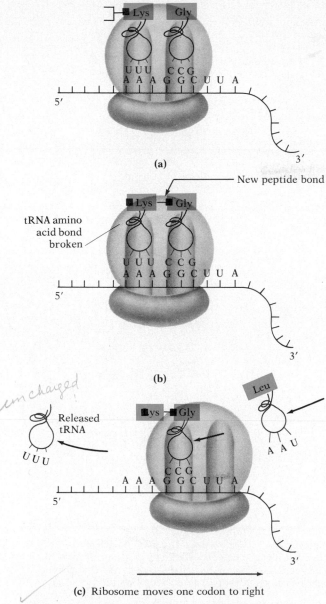

(a)

New peptide bond

tRNA amino
acid bond
broken

(b)

unchanged!

Released
tRNA

(c) Ribosome moves one codon to right

15.9

Elongation. **(a)** Two charged amino acids lie in the two pockets of the large ribosome subunit. On the left, lysine (Lys) is also attached to the growing end of the polypeptide being synthesized. The next amino acid that will be added to the polypeptide is glycine (Gly), which is already in place. Note that the anticodons of the lysine and glycine tRNA molecules match the corresponding codons of the mRNA. **(b)** A new peptide bond is formed, between lysine and glycine. The entire growing polypeptide, now one unit longer, is transferred to the glycine. **(c)** The now-uncharged lysine tRNA diffuses out of the left-hand pocket. The critical step is *translocation*, in which the glycine tRNA, attached to the polypeptide, moves from the right pocket to the left pocket. At the same time the ribosome moves along the mRNA, from left to right, the distance of one codon. A charged leucine (Leu) tRNA is about to drift into the right-hand pocket, where it will bind. Then elongation will be repeated.

cupied by methionine-charged tRNA and the right-hand pocket was empty. Below the right pocket, however (as seen in Figure 15.8), was the next mRNA codon waiting for a charged tRNA with a matching anticodon. Many charged tRNA molecules, in random motion, may bounce in and out of the empty pocket, but only one with the correct anticodon will bind. When the match occurs, the right-hand pocket will be filled.

Once the second charged tRNA is in place, the two amino acids above will join, producing the first of many covalent **peptide bonds.** And when this linkage has formed, the tRNA in the left-hand pocket, now uncharged and freed, will drift away to be recycled.

With the left-hand pocket empty, a crucial step called **translocation** can occur. The ribosome moves one codon to the right and the second charged tRNA lands in the left pocket. Emptying of the right pocket permits a third codon to enter and a third charged tRNA to pair up, so that the cycle can be repeated. Figure 15.9 picks up the action about half way through elongation. A number of amino acids have been joined to produce the growing polypeptide and yet another is about to be added.

Thus the action continues, with the ribosome clumping along its mRNA in short jumps of one codon at a time. There is a constant arrival of charged tRNA molecules as the right hand pocket keeps emptying. With every translocation step, the polypeptide grows one amino acid longer. You can see how the ribosome plays its essential role in keeping things organized. By moving along the mRNA strand exactly one codon at a time, it ensures the accurate translation of the code (Figure 15.10).

How long does all of this take? The translocation step occurs in microseconds. The fastest time known for the completion of an entire good-sized polypeptide is six seconds (in *E. coli*).

Termination: Derailing the Ribosome

As the ribosome moves along its mRNA to the end of the cistron, it runs into one or another of the three STOP codons: UAA, UAG, or UGA. Sometimes there are double stops (for example, UAAUAG), just to be sure that the ribosome gets the message.

The next step is the **termination** of the building process. There are no tRNAs with anticodons that correspond to any of the STOP codons. Instead there are specific *terminating proteins* that move into position when the STOP codon is on the ribosome. There they seem to clog the works, and bring about

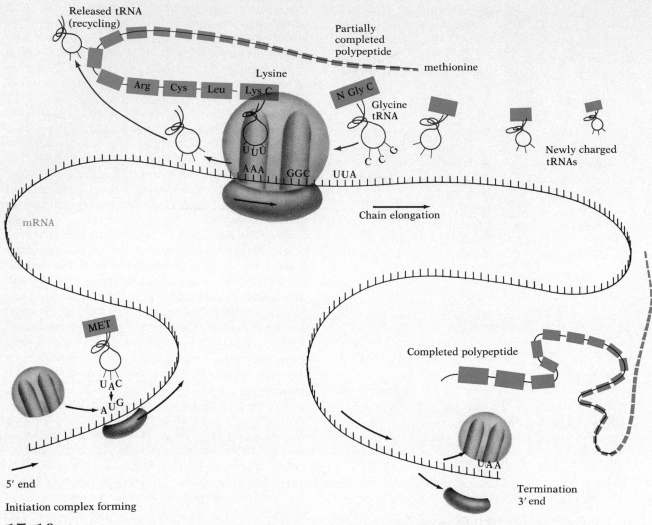

15.10

An overview of polypeptide synthesis: on the left, a ribosome assembles at the start codon and begins translation with the amino acid methionine. Elongation continues the process, and the ribosome moves from left to right, one codon at a time. With each translation event the polypeptide grows one amino acid longer. At termination, the polypeptide is released and the ribosome falls apart into its two subunits.

the release of the last tRNA, which is then removed enzymatically from the end of the now-completed polypeptide. Finally, with no charged tRNAs in place, the ribosome separates into its large and small subunits, which drift away from the messenger to recycle for another run.

The polypeptide, now a free chain of amino acids at the primary level of protein structure, has its own fate. It will automatically form its secondary structure, and may join other polypeptides, reaching the tertiary and quaternary levels of protein structure (see Chapter 3). Some will form the enzymes that are the link between the coded genes of DNA and the metabolic activities of the cell.

Polyribosomes

During active protein synthesis ribosomes generally occur in small clusters, with perhaps two to ten ribosomes per cluster. Each cluster is called a *polyribosome* (or, sometimes, *polysome*). A **polyribosome** is actually a strand of messenger RNA with a group of attached ribosomes, like pearls on a string

(Figure 15.11). Each ribosome will travel the whole length of the cistron, from the START codon to the STOP codon, then each will fall apart and drop off, as others assemble at START. Thus several ribosomes can be producing copies of the same protein at the same time, each working on a different portion of the message.

The polysomes can be free in the cytoplasm, or they can appear to be bound to the membranes of the endoplasmic reticulum. The bound ribosomes produce proteins that will be secreted by the cell at some later time. Actually the polysomes themselves are not directly attached to the membrane, but are held there by the growing polypeptides that are moving into and through the endoplasmic reticulum. The polypeptides are able to penetrate the membrane of the endoplasmic reticulum because their leading ends contain lipid-soluble amino acids.

MUTATION: ERRORS IN THE GENETIC MESSAGE

The DNA molecule is well adapted to its function as a repository of genetic information. After all, it is the product of eons of evolution. It is the descendant of generations of similar molecules that withstood the relentless process of natural selection. Since it is a "proven" molecule, it should be somewhat stable. Any changes are not likely to be beneficial. Most of the time its nucleotide bases are all safely tucked inside and tightly hydrogen-bonded to one another. Also, in eukaryotes, DNA is tightly bound to protective histone molecules and packaged into beadlike nucleosomes (see Chapter 9).

The most important protection that DNA has against random chemical change, however, is not strictly chemical; this protection exists because of the specific A:T and G:C base-pairing rules. The specific ordering of bases in one chain uniquely determines the specific ordering of bases in the other, so there are actually two copies of the coded information in each DNA molecule. It's something like keeping both a photographic negative film and a positive print in your files. If you have one, you can always make the other. In the cell, if one of the two DNA strands is accidentally altered, say by ultraviolet light or x-rays, the organism is able to throw out the damaged strand and to make a new, perfectly good double helix by using the other strand as a template. But disruptions can occur, despite the protection given the DNA molecule.

DNA Repair Systems

Sometimes spontaneous changes—known as *primary lesions*—occur in DNA. Fortunately, most of the primary lesions are quickly eliminated by *DNA repair systems* (Figure 15.12). **DNA repair systems** are enzyme complexes that rove along the DNA strands, uncovering irregularities such as broken phosphate bonds and nucleotide bases that are not paired according to the Watson and Crick rules. When such irregularities are encountered, a section of perhaps 100 nucleotides may be cut out of the offending strand and a new, correct sequence is synthesized.

DNA repair systems are very efficient, but even so, they occasionally fail. When a primary lesion is not healed, or if it is healed improperly, the genetic message in that area is changed permanently. The changed message will be copied faithfully during the next round of DNA replication, and will be passed on to new generations of cells, including gametes. We refer to such a permanent, accidental change in DNA as a **mutation.** Mutations can be caused by chemicals, ultraviolet light, or higher energy radiation. Any agent that causes mutations is called a **mutagen.**

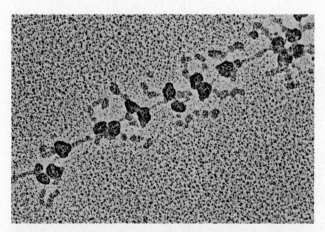

15.11

Polyribosomes are seen lying along a strand of mRNA (just visible) in this highly magnified view through the electron microscope. Each ribosome moves along the mRNA translating the code into polypeptides. Such simultaneous translation greatly speeds the process of protein synthesis.

Mutation at the Molecular Level

We noted in Chapter 12 that one kind of mutation involves the rearrangement of chromosome pieces, as in the case of translocation Down's syndrome. We've also described the effects of nondisjunction, mutations that involve entire extra or missing chromosomes. For the most part, such gross chromosomal abnormalities spell the death of the cell, so the genetic change is not passed on to future generations. Mutations involving minor changes in the DNA sequence—ones that geneticists call **point mutations**—are far more subtle, less destructive, and stand a better chance of being passed on from generation to generation. The effects may be neutral or even beneficial (see Chapters 12 and 13). Point mutations fall into three general categories:

1. *Base substitution:* the number of nucleotide base pairs is unchanged, but one of the four nucleotide bases is replaced by another in each DNA strand. This is the most common type of spontaneous DNA mutation.

2. *Insertion:* one or more base pairs are added into the DNA molecule, changing the total number of nucleotides.

3. *Deletion:* one or more base pairs are lost, also changing the total number of nucleotides.

Such changes will, of course, have an impact on the amino acid sequences in polypeptides when translation occurs.

Base substitution. Single base changes in a coding region alter a codon from one of the 64 possible types to another. If the old and new codons happen to be synonymous—that is, if they code for the same amino acid—there will be no change in the polypeptide synthesized, and the mutation is likely to be perfectly neutral and therefore not acted upon by natural selection. As you can see, synonymity in the codons has certain advantages.

Other base substitutions may actually alter the code, causing single amino acid substitutions in the proteins produced by the genes. A change from GAA to GUA, for instance, would substitute valine for glutamic acid (Figure 15.13). Such a change may have no measurable effect at all, may be lethal, or may have an effect anywhere in between.

For instance, in the genetic disease **sickle-cell anemia,** a single base substitution changes glutamic acid to valine in the sixth amino acid of one of the polypeptides of human hemoglobin; this small change causes the molecule to crystalize in the cell. The long, slightly bent crystals distort red blood cells into a sickle shape, and also reduce the ability of the hemoglobin to carry oxygen. The damaged cells cause painful and, eventually, fatal blood clots to form in small blood vessels (see Chapter 14).

If the new codon caused by a base substitution happens to be one of the three STOP codons, the mutation is called (not surprisingly) a **chain-terminating mutation.** If a ribosome encounters one, it will fall off its mRNA at a new place, resulting in an abnormally short polypeptide. Unless the new STOP codon is very close to the end of the coding sequence, the protein will be totally nonfunctional. The great majority of lethal point mutations, in experimental microorganisms at least, are chain-terminating mutations.

Insertions and Deletions.   What would you expect to happen when extra nucleotides are inserted into or deleted from the coding region of a gene? The usual effect of inserting or deleting a single nucleotide is to cause a **frame-shift mutation.** Ribosomes can only read mRNA molecules three nucleotides at a time. Thus if the normal sequence were, say,

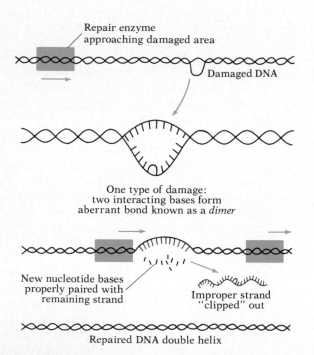

Repair enzyme approaching damaged area

Damaged DNA

One type of damage: two interacting bases form aberrant bond known as a *dimer*

New nucleotide bases properly paired with remaining strand

Improper strand "clipped" out

Repaired DNA double helix

15.12

DNA repair systems are teams of roving enzymes that travel along the strands somewhat like railroad repair crews. When a damaged portion is encountered, the faulty section is removed and a new strand is assembled by matching the nucleotide bases in the remaining strand. In this case, two bases in the same strand had joined, forming an abnormality called a *dimer*.

U
↓
5' ⟶ UGG GAG AAA AAA UUU AAG ⟶ 3'
Tryp — Glu — Lys — Lys — Phe — Lys

and a U were inserted at the point indicated by the arrow, the new sequence would be translated:

5' ⟶ UGU GGA GAA AAA AUU UAA G ⟶ 3'
Cys — Gly — Glu — Lys — Ile —STOP

The translated protein in this instance would have a large number of amino acid changes and would be nonfunctional. Not surprisingly, frame-shift mutations, when homozygous, are usually lethal to organisms.

Retroviruses and Transposable Elements. There is one special class of insertions and deletions that deserves special attention. Biologists have recently discovered that the DNA of most or all higher organisms is heavily infected by **retroviruses** and **transposable elements.** Both are DNA sequences that have the ability to insert themselves

15.13

A base substitution in DNA can have serious implications. In the upper half is seen the proper coding for a short segment of one of the poly-peptides of hemoglobin. A simple substitution of A (adenine) for T (thymine) in the DNA *(below)* changes the corresponding codon in mRNA from GAA to GUA. Instead of glutamic acid appearing in the corresponding position in the polypeptide, we now see valine. The chemical structure in the R groups of valine and glutamic acid is quite different, and the R groups of amino acids often help determine the shape of a protein. This particular change sets up a chain of events leading to sickle-cell anemia.

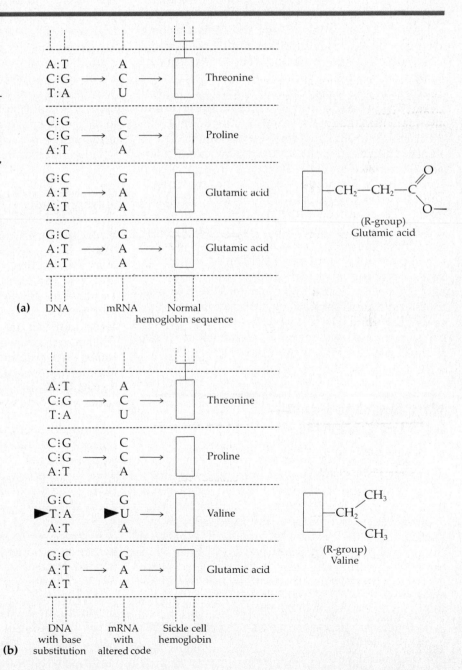

randomly into a chromosome and to remove themselves later. They also have another quite amazing ability: they can make RNA copies of themselves *which can then be recopied into DNA,* to be once again inserted randomly into the chromosome. The copying of RNA into DNA is done by enzymes called *RNA-dependent DNA polymerase* or **reverse transcriptase.** Note that this is a new addition to the central dogma: we now know that *DNA can be copied from RNA.*

Both the transposable elements and the retroviruses can be passed along from generation to generation through the gametes, and both can spread from one chromosomal location to others. The principal difference between the two is that retrovirus RNA can also leave the cell (wrapping itself in a bit of cell membrane) and be transmitted as a free, infectious virus. Some especially unpleasant retroviruses also contain *oncogenes* that cause infected cells to become cancerous.

What has this to do with mutations? You can imagine what happens when a transposable element or a retrovirus inserts itself into the middle of a gene: the gene won't work anymore. To the surprise of every geneticist, it has recently been shown that many of the alleged "point mutations" and chromosome rearrangements that have been studied so intently over the last eight decades have in fact been due to gene-wrecking by transposable elements. Included are T.H. Morgan's famous white-eye fruit fly mutant of 1910 (see Chapter 12), and most of the other well-studied mutants of mice and *Drosophila.* And while it has long been known that x-rays cause mutations, it now appears that one of the things the x-rays do best is to induce the cell's dormant transposable elements to move around and cause their own havoc.

MECHANISMS OF GENE CONTROL

Although it has been modified through the years, the central dogma answered many difficult questions. Biologists finally knew the chemical structure of the gene and the basic mechanism by which it expresses its information. But even with all this knowledge, a major question remained. What controls transcription? In other words, how is DNA turned on or off? This question has proven difficult indeed, partly because there are in fact numerous mechanisms. Also, different organisms, it turns out, control their genes in different ways.

Human chromosomes carry an estimated 40,000 to 50,000 pairs of protein-coding genes (for the record, *E. coli* carries about a tenth that number of genes on about 1/1400 as much DNA as is in the human genome). Obviously all of these genes are not active at the same time. If they were, all the cells in the body would look the same and be doing the same things. In order for specialization to occur, some genes must be active while others are shut down.

How do the genes of eukaryotes become turned off or on in the course of cell specialization and in response to environmental stimuli? There is no one answer, because for one thing we know that there are many different, competing mechanisms of gene control, and, for another thing, we also know that we don't understand most of them. Answers are beginning to take shape, however, For instance, it is known that some genes are activated by hormones, and a fair amount is known about hormone action. But the overall picture of gene control in eukaryotes is hazy at best. The mechanisms of gene control in bacteria are much better understood, so we must turn once again to our smaller and simpler contemporaries.

Gene Organization and Control in Prokaryotes: The Operon

About the time Crick was putting together the idea of the central dogma, and while molecular biologists were still trying to work out the genetic code and the mechanism of protein synthesis, two French microbiologists were concluding a long experimental program of their own. In 1961 François Jacob and Jacques Monod unveiled their model of bacterial gene organization and control. They called their system, which included a set of genes and the systems that influenced them, the **operon.** Molecular biology suddenly took a huge leap forward.

Inducible Enzymes in *E. coli.* Jacob and Monod knew that some of the enzymes of *E. coli* were produced constantly, while other enzymes were under some kind of control. The tiny bacterium could make these enzymes when it needed them and could stop production when it didn't.

For instance, if *E. coli* is grown on a medium that does not contain lactose (milk sugar), it will not bother to produce the specific enzymes that are needed for lactose metabolism. That makes perfectly good sense from the standpoint of evolution and energetics; protein synthesis is expensive, and producing unneeded enzymes would be wasteful. *E. coli* is nothing if not practical.

On the other hand, if these same bacteria are placed into a medium that does contain lactose, they will almost immediately begin to produce enzymes that break the lactose down into its constituents, glucose and galactose. These lactose-metabolizing enzymes are said to be *inducible*, because their production can be induced or stimulated by an appropriate substrate.

It turns out that there are three enzymes that are induced by the presence of lactose. These are *beta galactosidase, galactose permease,* and *thiogalactoside transacetylase*; but Jacob and Monod found it easier to refer to them simply as enzymes *z, y,* and *a,* letters that also refer to the cistrons or *structural genes* that code for the three enzymes. Jacob and Monod's question was an ambitious one: just how did lactose in the medium activate them? That is, how are genes turned off and on?

The Lactose Operon. The inducible **lactose operon** was found to consist of five specific genes (Figure 15.14). The three structural genes, *z, y,* and *a* are located in a row on the *E. coli* chromosome. When transcription occurs, all three are transcribed into messenger RNA together; that is, all three genes are in one transcription unit, which makes a single mRNA containing three cistrons. (*Polycistronic messenger RNA* is a feature found only in bacteria. We eukaryotes never have more than a single cistron on one mRNA molecule.)

A fourth gene, dubbed the **operator,** is a relatively short segment of DNA lying near the beginning of the *z* cistron. The operator gene is transcribed into mRNA, but it doesn't make enzymes as structural genes do. Instead, it helps control the structural genes. The operator gene is, in a sense, the switch that determines whether the structural genes will be turned off or on.

The fifth element of the lactose operon is an **inhibitor** gene. The inhibitor gene is the key to the control process. In all cells, induced or not, it is constantly (but very slowly) transcribed into mRNA. The mRNA codes for a **repressor protein,** which is produced in very small quantities, about ten molecules per cell. It is called a repressor protein because it has a high affinity for the operator gene, binding to it and preventing transcription from occuring in the rest of the operon. While the repressor protein is bound to the operator DNA, the RNA polymerase transcription complex cannot move past it. In effect the structural genes are turned off as long as the repressor protein is present and active in the cell.

However, the repressor protein has an even greater affinity for lactose, so when lactose molecules are present in the cell, some of them will bind to the ten repressor protein molecules, rendering them incapable of binding to the operator. Soon the operator gene is free, and the entire unit of transcription becomes operational, transcribing messenger RNA which, in turn, becomes translated on the bacterial ribosomes into the three enzymes. This, then, is the way lactose acts as an *inducer* of gene action.

Perhaps it will help to consider a fanciful analogy. Suppose RNA polymerase is a train that must run along a DNA track. The repressor protein is an elephant that has a penchant for sitting on the track. However, when peanuts are available, the elephant lumbers off to eat the peanuts, and the train may at last proceed. So the availability of peanuts controls whether the train will run or not.

But enough about elephants. As you see, this scheme leaves us with the problem of shutting the system down again when the enzymes are no longer needed. When the enzymes hydrolyze the lactose molecules into glucose and galactose, the repressor protein (which is still being slowly produced) is once again free to bind the operator gene. Thus transcription of the three structural genes is shut down once again. The lactose operon, and other like it, utilize *negative control*; the inducer molecule, lactose in this case, makes something happen by repressing a repressor.

Other Operons. Other operons have been found that function in different ways. For instance, the second operon to which Jacob and Monod turned their attention was the *tryptophan operon,* which controls a series of enzymes that are needed for the synthesis of the amino acid tryptophan. They were interested because tryptophan is always needed by the cell for protein synthesis. They found that the tryptophan operon functions continually *except* when there is ample free tryptophan already in the medium. Again, the adaptive function of such control is obvious: there's no sense in putting cellular resources into making tryptophan when tryptophan is available at no cost.

Jacob and Monod learned that the tryptophan operon is also under negative control: in this case the repressor protein will not bind to its operator unless it first binds to a tryptophan molecule. So the tryptophan operon is a **repressible operon** and tryptophan is its **repressor.**

Many other operons have been discovered since 1961. Alas, each seems to operate according to its own principles. Some operator sequences, for example, have multiple binding sites for repressor molecules, allowing for graduated responses: that

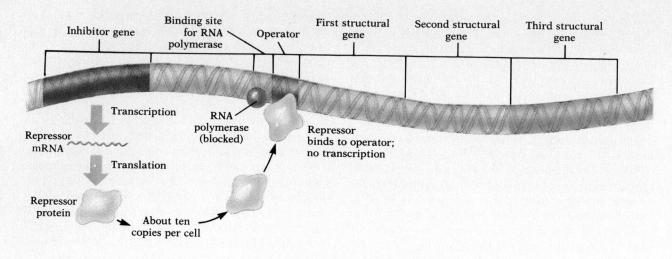

Inhibitor gene | Binding site for RNA polymerase | Operator | First structural gene | Second structural gene | Third structural gene

Transcription

Repressor mRNA

Translation

Repressor protein

About ten copies per cell

RNA polymerase (blocked)

Repressor binds to operator; no transcription

(a) Lactose absent—no enzyme produced

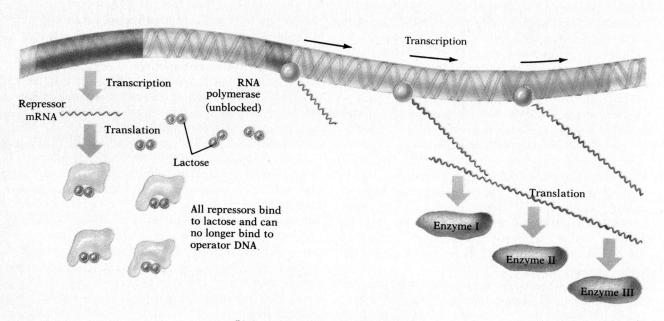

Transcription

Repressor mRNA

Translation

RNA polymerase (unblocked)

Lactose

All repressors bind to lactose and can no longer bind to operator DNA.

Transcription

Translation

Enzyme I

Enzyme II

Enzyme III

(b) Lactose present—enzymes produced

15.14

(a) The five genes making up the lactose operon include the inhibitor, the operator, and three structural genes coding for enzymes. In the absence of lactose sugar (the inducer in this operon), the operator and structural genes are shut down. Repressor proteins, whose synthesis is directed by the inhibitor gene, coat the operator. When lactose is present **(b)**, it binds with the repressor protein, freeing the operator **(c)**. This permits RNA polymerase to transcribe RNA, which leads to the synthesis of the three lactose-metabolizing enzymes. The system will shut down again when the enzymes have hydrolyzed all of the lactose into glucose and galactose. Repressor protein, produced continually in small amounts, soon coats the operator gene again.

is, the gene doesn't necessarily have to be either "turned on" or "turned off," but is, in effect, controlled by a dimmer switch.

Gene Control in Higher Organisms

For the most part, gene control systems in higher organisms tend to be quite different from those in bacterial systems, and from each other as well. In recent years, however, experimenters have found some control systems in higher organisms that are similar in some ways to gene control in bacteria. For example, steroid hormones can control gene activity rather directly.

The oviducts of baby chicks have been found to be responsive to the steroid *estrogen*, the female sex hormone. In the presence of estrogen the chick oviduct will begin to produce albumin and other egg-white proteins. Radioactively labeled estrogen molecules have been found to enter the cell, where they are bound by a specific cytoplasmic receptor protein. The protein-steroid complex then passes into the nucleus, where it binds tightly to a non-histone chromosomal protein. This complex then initiates mRNA transcription through positive control (Figure 15.15).

The steroid-hormone system is similar in some ways to that of a bacterial operon. But even this, the simplest of all known eukaryote gene control systems, is still much more complex than the lactose operon. To illustrate, estrogen doesn't induce the synthesis of egg-white proteins in any other kind of chick cell; apparently only the chromosomes of oviduct cells have the specific chromatin receptors. Also, estrogen may have very different effects on different genes and different tissues. For example, it can suppress the synthesis of some proteins as it induces the synthesis of others. Estrogen also has well-documented effects on behavior.

We have come a long way since Francis Crick presented the "central dogma" to a bemused world. The euphoria that swept the scientific community in those days, when a surprisingly simple system of genetic coding was first unveiled, has been dampened by the realization that the system is not so simple after all. But the very complexity of life that discourages some people stimulates others. They see the complexity and the variety of life as providing not just challenges, but opportunities. Some of the greatest opportunities lie before us now. We are on the verge of being able to manipulate genes, to turn them on, to turn them off, to move them about, and to make them work for us in very critical and specific ways, as we will see in the next chapter.

15.15

When the steroid hormone estrogen is introduced into baby chicks, it sets albumen (egg-white protein) production in motion. Estrogen enters the cell to join a protein receptor. This steroid-receptor complex enters the nucleus and binds with a specific gene-controlling chromosomal protein. This induces the albumen gene or genes to begin transcribing RNA and albumen production begins.

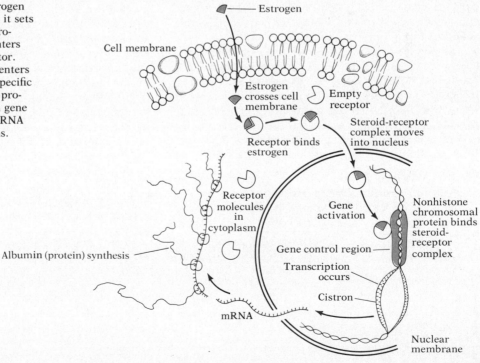

Summary

The RNA Molecule
RNA is a polymer of nucleotide subunits, usually single-stranded. It contains the sugar ribose, has uracil instead of thymine as the fourth nucleotide base, possesses complex secondary and tertiary levels of structure, is shorter and less stable than DNA, and occurs in different classes that have different functions in the cell.

Transcription: The Synthesis of RNA
RNA is synthesized as the DNA strands unwind and nucleotide bases are exposed. One strand lies dormant while short sections of the other serve as a template for RNA formation. When copying is complete, the RNA transcript separates and the DNA rewinds. Many RNA molecules can be transcribed from the same DNA transcription unit (simultaneous transcription).

Different Kinds of RNA
Messenger RNA carries the specific information that has been stored in the sequence of DNA nucleotides. Mature messenger RNA, which must be tailored from its initial stage as a single-stranded copy of a transcription unit, consists of a leading region, a cistron, and a following region. However, only the cistron is translated.

The cistron carries codons (nucleotides in groups of three), each specifying a specific amino acid commonly found in protein. The linear ordering of codons determines the order of amino acids in the polypeptide being synthesized. Synonymous codons specify the same amino acid; other codons indicate stop and start orders in the genetic code.

Ribosomal RNA is found in ribosomes, the cell organelles involved in protein synthesis. The ribosome consists of two subunits, which are connected during synthesis to hold mRNA and tRNA.

Transfer RNA plays three roles in assembling amino acids into polypeptides: (1) it covalently binds to a specific amino acid; (2) it binds to a ribosome; and (3) it recognizes a specific codon in mRNA and inserts its amino acid into the proper position in the polypeptide chain. The structural pattern of transfer RNA, consisting of three loops and a stem, plays its own role in transfer RNA functions, including base pairing with mRNA.

Protein Synthesis: Translation of the Genetic Message
The process of protein synthesis is divided into initiation, elongation, and termination. In initiation, mRNA, the ribosome, and methionine-charged tRNA are required to start translation. Elongation, the addition of amino acids, occurs through peptide bond formation and translocation. With each addition, the ribosome moves one codon along the mRNA. At termination, the ribosome reaches a STOP codon, the final tRNA is released, and the polypeptide separates. Polyribosomes are clusters of ribosomes attached to a single mRNA, translating it simultaneously. Some are located along the endoplasmic reticulum, into which the polypeptide is released.

Mutation: Errors in the Genetic Message
When spontaneous changes occur in DNA strands, repair systems cut out defective parts or rejoin broken chains. If the repairs are incorrect or incomplete, a mutation may occur.

Chromosomal mutations are changes in whole chromosomes, while point mutations involve nucleotide base substitutions, insertions, and deletions in DNA. In base substitutions, one amino acid in a polypeptide may be changed, or the change may produce a new STOP codon in mRNA, ending polypeptide synthesis too soon. Insertions and deletions change the message from their point of occurrence on, resulting in a faulty polypeptide. Transposable elements and retroviruses insert themselves randomly into a chromosome, causing heritable genetic change.

Mechanisms of Gene Control
In studies of *E. coli* it was found that some enzymes were produced constantly while others were inducible, or made when needed. Inducible lactose enzymes are coded for by three structural genes. In the lactose operon, an operator gene directs the structural genes, and an inhibitor gene directs the production of repressor proteins. When lactose is absent, repressor proteins impede the operator gene's functions. In the presence of lactose, the repressor proteins cannot bind to the operator, and the transcription unit becomes active. When lactose is hydrolized, the repressor protein is again free to bind to the operator and inhibit activity.

Most operons utilize negative control in genes, although many have been discovered that function more gradually. Gene control is not completely understood in higher organisms, although the control processes involving steroid hormones are similar to gene control in bacteria.

Key Terms

transcription
transcript
transcription complex
RNA polymerase
unit of transcription
simultaneous transcription
messenger RNA (mRNA)
intervening sequence (intron)
expressed sequence (exon)
cistron
codon
principle of colinearity
synonymous codon
translation
ribosomal RNA (rRNA)

transfer RNA (tRNA)
anticodon
initiation
initiation complex
elongation
peptide bond
translocation
termination
polyribosome
DNA repair system
mutation
mutagen
point mutation
base substitution

sickle-cell anemia
chain-terminating mutation
insertion
deletion
frame-shift mutation
retrovirus
transposable element
reverse transcriptase
operon
lactose operon
operator
inhibitor
repressor protein
repressible operon

Review Questions

1. Explain how each aspect below differs between DNA and RNA: 5-carbon sugar, nitrogen bases, helical configuration, length, stability. (pp. 203–205)

2. Briefly describe the transcription process. (p. 205)

3. List the three types of RNA, and briefly summarize the role of each in protein synthesis. (pp. 205–209)

4. Using a simple diagram, explain the principle of colinearity: what is the relationship between codons of DNA, codons of mRNA, and the various amino acids? (pp. 206–207)

5. List the three elements of an initiation complex, and explain what each must do for translation to begin. (p. 210)

6. Using simple diagrams, explain how translocation occurs. (pp. 210–212)

7. List three ways in which DNA is protected against spontaneous change. How are most primary lesions corrected once they do occur? (p. 213)

8. Compare the potential effect of a base substitution mutation with that of a base insertion or deletion. How does the organization of the genetic code itself negate the effects of most base substitutions? (pp. 214–215)

9. Briefly explain how introducing lactose into a bacterial cell induces that cell to begin producing lactose-metabolizing enzymes. Why are such systems important to the cell, and how does the system shut itself down? (pp. 216–218)

New Frontiers in Molecular Biology

16

Some scientists are disturbed—and others elated—by our newly emerging abilities to manipulate genes. The grounds for the disagreement are apparent, considering the possibilities that may lie before us. No one is morally indignant because we can insert rat growth hormone genes into developing fertilized mouse cells to produce giant mice. And probably few would object to our ability to make human hormones out of a bacterial soup. But dare we try, not just to bring abnormal people to normality, but to make normal people "better"? Taller? Stronger? Smarter? Let's take a look at the promise and threat of our expanding ability to manipulate genes.

Over the years, different organisms have tended to dominate the study of genetics. First there were Mendel's true-breeding pea plants, followed by the hardy, prolific, and amazingly versatile fruit fly. Later, the cutting edge of genetic research focused on the corn plant, *Zea mays*; next, Beadle and Tatum brought the mold *Neurospora crassa* into the spotlight. Then, in the late 1940s, a surprising organism became in vogue: an invisible microbe. Geneticists began to focus on *Escherichia coli*, the common colon bacterium, and the viruses that infect it.

Perhaps the emergence of *E. coli* should not have been so surprising. After all, the thrust of molecular biology has been to reduce problems to their simplest terms, and bacteria, when all is said and done, are much simpler than fruit flies, corn, or even mold. The viruses that infect bacteria are simpler still, since they consist of only a DNA or RNA molecule, a protein coat and a few enzymes.

Investigators decided that the wisest move would be to try first to understand these simple organisms and then to progress to more complex ones.

E. coli organisms did, indeed, offer a number of advantages as experimental subjects. Not only were they genetically simpler, but bacterial cells have little internal structure, and are easily broken open so that their cellular machinery can be isolated and analyzed biochemically. More importantly, bacteria and viruses can be grown in enormous numbers in very short periods of time—*E. coli* can double in number in 20 minutes—so experiments can be done quickly. Billions of such organisms can be grown in a drop of fluid, so statistical sampling is never a problem, and even very rare events (such as the occurrence of specific mutations) will occur dependably and reproducibly.

GENETIC RECOMBINATION IN BACTERIA

From Mendel's time on, genetic analysis had always depended on genetic recombination. And genetic recombination, it seemed, depended on meiosis and sex. This is the main reason why bacteria such as *E. coli* had originally been of little interest to geneticists: like other biologists, they believed that bacteria were confirmed celibates, capable only of asexual reproduction.

It's true that bacteria have never mastered the processes of meiosis, fertilization, and sexual reproduction that together constitute a crucial aspect of the life cycles of most higher organisms. But *E. coli* and many other bacteria do exhibit some rudiments of genetic recombination. What passes for sex in bacteria is incomplete, bizarre, and infrequent—*so* infrequent that the odds of its occurrence are about one in a million. Fortunately for the geneticist, however, something that happens to one or two out of a million cells still occurs with dependable frequency when billions of cells are grown and tested.

In 1946, Joshua Lederberg and Edward Tatum (the same Edward Tatum, who, with George Beadle, developed the notion of "one gene, one enzyme") performed an imaginative experiment that provided the first evidence of genetic recombination in bacteria. Following the lead of Tatum's own *Neurospora* research, they chose two mutant bacterial strains that had different enzyme deficiencies. Neither strain, by itself, could grow on the usual bacterial *minimal medium* (food) that consists of glucose, glycine, and minerals in a jelly-like matrix of *agar*. To grow, each *nutritional mutant strain* required the addition of one or more specific metabolites that their own enzymes could not synthesize. In a simple but ingenious experiment, Lederberg and Tatum combined the two strains and spread the mixture on minimal medium agar. They reasoned that any bacteria that could grow on this minimal medium would represent new genetic recombinants: that is, they would be the descendants of bacteria that had somehow managed to combine the *functional* enzyme genes from both parental strains.

The two strains were:

Strain A: met−, bio−, thr+, leu+, thi+
Strain B: met+, bio+, thr−, leu−, thi−

The abbreviations represent *methionine, biotin, threonine, leucine,* and *thiamine,* respectively. A minus sign after an abbreviation indicates that the strain could not grow unless that specific metabolite was provided; a plus sign indicates that the strain was able to manufacture that particular metabolite on its own.

Lederberg and Tatum found that about one in every 10 million of the bacteria they had spread on the minimal medium plate had survived and had given rise to a *colony* of healthy descendents. These **recombinant colonies** were all wild type (that is, normal), and so had the following genotype (Figure 16.1):

met+, bio+, thr+, leu+, thi+

Lederberg and Tatum needed only to spread a nor-mal amount of *E. coli*—that is, about a billion cells—on a dish of agar medium to be able to observe about 100 recombinant colonies.

Encouraged by this, they repeated their experiment, crossing the same two strains but plating them out on partially supplemented agar. For instance, if the agar plate had minimal medium plus added biotin and threonine, they would get a mixture of four kinds of surviving recombinant colonies:

met+, bio+, thr+, leu+, thi+
met+, bio−, thr+, leu+, thi+
met+, bio+, thr−, leu+, thi+
met+, bio−, thr−, leu+, thi+

In this case, methionine, leucine, and thiamine were **selected markers,** since only plus-strain bacteria with the corresponding functional enzymes could survive. The biotin and threonine genes were **unselected markers** because both plus and minus strains could grow on the partially supplemented medium. Lederberg and Tatum counted the numbers of colonies for each possible combination of unselected markers. From the recombination frequencies, they tried to make a genetic map, using the techniques that had proven so useful for fruit flies and corn. They had a terrible time! The worst problem was the strange nature of bacterial "sex" itself. The rules of recombination and crossing over that had been worked out for peas and *Drosophila* clearly did not work for bacteria.

The Sex Life of *E. coli*

Other investigators picked up Lederberg's and Tatum's promising lead, and as new data came in, a strange and confusing picture began to emerge. One discovery was that bacterial strains could be divided into two groups, which were promptly (perhaps too promptly) dubbed "male" and "female." Males mated only with females and females mated only with males; a mixture of two male strains, or two female strains, never once produced recombinant progeny.

What distinguished "male" from "female" bacteria was that gene transfer always occurred in a single direction, from male to female as the two individuals joined in a process called **conjugation** (Figure 16.2). The surprising thing was that the male usually transferred only a few genes each time. This is a very different situation from that of the truly sexual group, the eukaryotes, in which fertilization involves the essentially equal mixing of two entire genomes. (A *genome* is one entire set of the genes of an organism.)

Lederberg and Tatum uncovered the first firm evidence of genetic recombination in bacteria. Two strains **(a)** whose nutritional deficiencies and sufficiencies complemented each other were grown together **(b)** in a fully supplemented food medium, and their descendants recovered. The young cells were then plated onto minimal media **(c)** that neither parental strain could have utilized. Any colonies emerging **(d)** had to originate from cells that had undergone genetic recombination.

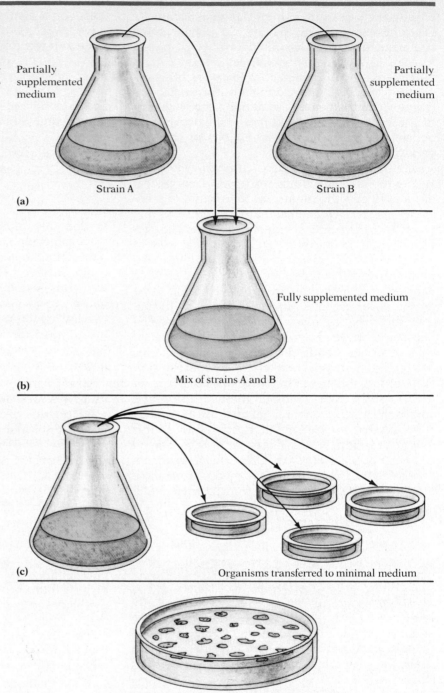

Partially supplemented medium

Partially supplemented medium

Strain A

Strain B

(a)

Fully supplemented medium

Mix of strains A and B

(b)

(c)   Organisms transferred to minimal medium

Growth indicates genetic recombination has occurred

(d)

In the early 1950s, William Hayes came up with some unnerving observations. In separate experiments, he treated either the male or the female strain of *E. coli* with streptomycin (an antibiotic that prevents cell division, but does not prevent bacterial conjugation or gene transfer) before mixing the two together. A mixture of untreated males and streptomycin-treated females produced no viable progeny; the females could not divide, and the males received none of the female strain's necessary wild-type genes. But crippled, streptomycin-treated males were still capable of leaving viable progeny of their own, by transferring some of their genes into receptive, untreated females.

Contagious Masculinity and the F Plasmid. Then Hayes showed that the "maleness" of the male strains was *catching!* He mixed male and female bacterial strains together, spread the mixture on fully supplemented medium, and then tested the resulting colonies for maleness or femaleness. The male-strain bacteria were all still male, but now about a third of the female-strain bacteria had also become male! Unlike genetic recombination, this infection of maleness was not at all a rare event. Hayes thought that this was a curious kind of sexuality; maleness seemed to be a disease—and contagious at that.

Much later, to jump ahead of our story, bacterial maleness was actually found to be a contagious and, in some ways, diseaselike state. Maleness in *E. coli* is due to the presence of a tiny genetic parasite called a **plasmid,** a small circle of DNA that contains only a few genes, usually all dedicated to

its own survival. In the case of the male-determining plasmid, the plasmid also includes genes responsible for bacterial conjugation and for the construction of a small, hollow *conjugation tube* that extends from the male cell to the female cell (see Figure 16.2). Also included in the DNA of the sex-determining plasmid is a gene that makes the infected cell unreceptive to the advances of any other male cell. A mixture of infected (that is, male) and uninfected (that is, female) cells results in widespread conjugation, with the passage through the hollow conjugation tubes of copies of the plasmid from infected to receptive cells.

Electron microscopes were not well enough developed in the 1950s for anyone to know about bacterial conjugation, but because both genetic recombination and contagious masculinity required direct physical contact, Hayes had a pretty good idea of what was going on.

Hayes knew that something was being transferred from male to female bacteria. That "something" was originally called the *fertility factor.* But soon, the male strains were renamed **F+ strains** (short for *fertility-positive*), and the female strains were renamed **F− strains,** (short for *fertility-negative*). As we've mentioned, the fertility factor itself was identified as a plasmid. The **F plasmid** was the first plasmid to be discovered, and it wasn't until many years later that scientists realized that it was only one of a large number of similar parasitic bacterial plasmids that ensure their own survival by inducing the formation of conjugation tubes, and then transferring copies of themselves to susceptible hosts. So now we see that the F plasmid is responsible for the genetic recombination that Lederberg and Tatum had observed in *E. coli.*

Although the F plasmid is usually a closed circle of DNA during normal replication, the DNA that squeezes through the thin conjugation tube must be linear. Once the tube has made a connection with a receptive host cell, the plasmid DNA begins to replicate at a particular position in its sequence. One of the newly replicated strands remains in the usual circular form, and stays behind in the infected donor cell. The new strand is linear, and it is this strand that passes through the tube and into the recipient cell. Once the entire linear copy of the F plasmid DNA has passed safely through the narrow tunnel and into the F− cell, it becomes a circle again and the newly infected host becomes male, or fertility-positive (Figure 16.3).

What about the transfer of the bacterial genes themselves? After all, that's what made the F plasmid so special in the first place. The F plasmid

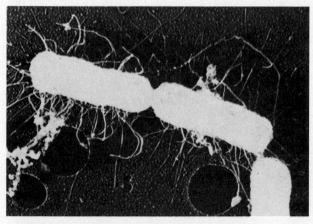

16.2

The slender conjugation tube between the two bacteria of different strains provides a passageway for the transfer of a plasmid.

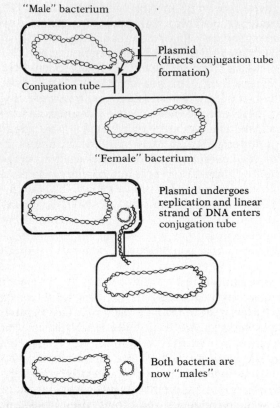

"Male" bacterium

Plasmid (directs conjugation tube formation)

Conjugation tube

"Female" bacterium

Plasmid undergoes replication and linear strand of DNA enters conjugation tube

Both bacteria are now "males"

16.3

Sex can be catching in bacteria. For bacterial conjugation to occur, a conjugation tube must be extended from a "male" cell to a "female" cell. The formation of the conjugation tube is directed by a specific plasmid inside the male cell. Following this, the plasmid DNA replicates, and a copy is sent through the tube. The recipient cell then contains the genes for producing a conjugation tube and thus becomes a "male."

occasionally—very rarely, but occasionally—becomes inserted into the main circular chromosome of its bacterial host as a linear sequence in the larger circle. The plasmid can show up anywhere in the host chromosome. After such an insertion, the F plasmid DNA is replicated right along with the host DNA, and can be passed on to all of the bacterial progeny. But later, when the plasmid attempts its usual transfer to a susceptible F− bacterium, strange things begin to happen.

First, the F plasmid begins its special round of linear replication, just as it always does when attempting a transfer. But since it is now part of a larger circle, the entire structure—host chromosome and all—attempts to pass through the conjugation tube as a linear DNA molecule. Because the chromosome is very long, it takes 89 or 90 minutes for the whole thing to get through. In fact, the

conjugation tube usually breaks apart before the transfer is completed, so ordinarily only part of the host chromosome and only one end of the F plasmid sequence enter the recipient bacterial cell. So the recipient cell isn't transformed into an F+ cell, but the bacterial DNA that has made the journey can recombine, through a kind of crossing over, with the main chromosome of the recipient cell (Figure 16.4).

As an evolutionary aside, since the F plasmid doesn't survive the process of host gene transfer, the phenomenon of bacterial "sex" is clearly not adaptive as far as the plasmid is concerned. This suggests that the process did not evolve by natural

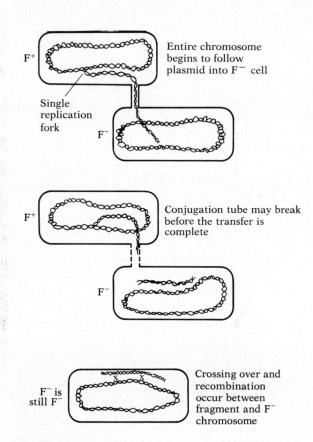

F+

Single replication fork

F−

Entire chromosome begins to follow plasmid into F− cell

F+

F−

Conjugation tube may break before the transfer is complete

F− is still F−

Crossing over and recombination occur between fragment and F− chromosome

16.4

Where the F plasmid has inserted itself into the main bacterial chromosome, plasmid transfer from an F+ cell to an F− runs into problems. Upon conjugation, a conjugation tube forms in the usual manner, but DNA replication includes the entire chromosome, plasmid and all. Part of the F plasmid replica starts through the tube, dragging the lengthy chromosome behind it. Quite often the tube breaks before the entire plasmid sequence completes its transfer. The portion making it through is incorporated into the F− chromosome through crossing over and recombination, but because of the incomplete transfer, the F− recipient remains F−.

selection. It has never been observed except in the descendants of Lederberg and Tatum's original strain. Perhaps it is merely a happy accident, but it has been a useful one for geneticists.

It wasn't long before Hayes and others were able to develop pure strains of bacteria in which *every* individual had the F plasmid integrated into the main chromosome at precisely the same place. Such strains are a thousand times more efficient at transferring normal bacterial genes than are ordinary F+ bacteria. The new ones were called **Hfr strains,** for "high frequency of recombination."

Gene mapping in *E. coli* is done somewhat differently from gene mapping in higher organisms. The breakthrough was an ingenious approach pioneered by François Jacob and Elie Wollman. They noted that when the Hfr strain conjugated, the genes closely behind the leading part of the F plasmid were transferred efficiently, but that the trailing genes made it less frequently since the conjugation tube was more likely to break before they made it through. They reasoned that they could control this process—and once again Fred Waring's versatile blender made its impact on molecular biology. They mixed the Hfr strain with a recipient F− strain, and poured the mixture into a kitchen blender. After allowing the bacteria to con-

jugate for a prescribed length of time, they turned the machine on. This rudely broke apart the mating bacteria.

They found that when the genetic transfer was interrupted after just a few minutes, some of the genetic markers would make it across, while others always remained behind. As the periods of mating were extended, more and more markers were transferred and could be recovered in the progeny. The markers that appeared with greater frequency obviously were nearer the leading end of the length of DNA. The frequency of appearance fell off for those that were more distant. In this way, the gene sequence could be mapped (Figure 16.5).

Plasmids and Plasmid Genes

The F plasmid is only one of many kinds of bacterial plasmids that have been discovered. None of the rest can transfer the host's chromosomal genes to other bacteria, but they do have roles in bacterial genetics, with genes of their own. Most have genes for making conjugation tubes, as well as those for coating the cell surface to protect the host (and the plasmid) from infection by other plasmids. In addition, some have genes that protect their hosts (and

ESSAY 16.1
ONCOGENES AND HERITABLE CANCER

For most of this century, the research spotlight focused on viruses as the cause of some cancers. While continuing research has ruled out viruses as a major cause of human cancer, today they are being used to help find certain genes that are implicated in some kinds of cancer.

Researchers discovered that some cancerous cells contain genes that can be incorporated into viruses and then transmitted to normal cells, in which they can cause cancer. Then it was discovered that those same genes are found in normal cells. In normal cells, however, these *oncogenes* (cancer-causing genes) are inoperative. So far about 20 oncogenes have been identified in normal cells.

Because oncogenes are so com-

mon, it is possible that they have a useful function in normal cell division. Apparently, however, they can be activated inappropriately, causing the rapid and unrestrained growth of tissue—the hallmark of cancer. The problems with oncogenes being transmissible by viruses are that they may also transmit the DNA sequence that can activate the uncontrolled cell proliferation, or may transmit the oncogenes into healthy cells *without* also passing along the DNA segment that inhibits them from being activated inappropriately. Thus, with oncogenes residing in our cells, viruses can indeed pose the risk of cancer.

The mechanism of triggering cancer suggested by viral research could also account for the way that

chemical carcinogens (cancer causers) and ultraviolet rays operate. They might stimulate the activity of oncogenes directly, or they might activate the control region of the DNA sequence (the operator gene) that would in turn activate the oncogene. Carcinogens that are able to move around sections of DNA could conceivably shift the oncogene so that it would fall under the control of an operator gene that could activate it.

Such findings are promising, but final answers are not around the corner. For example, the notion of oncogenes as a primary mechanism of cancer is incompatible with the long lapse between exposure to a carcinogen and development of the disease. ●

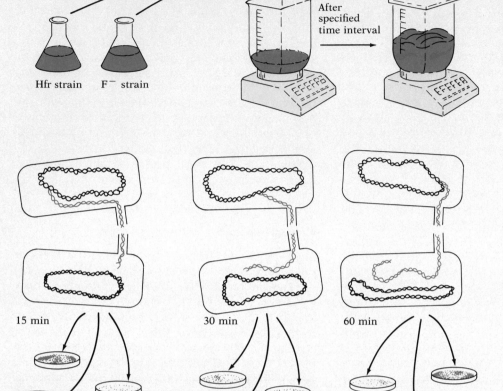

Conjugation tubes disrupted

Length of time determines number of markers transferred

15 min

30 min

60 min

Test for recombination determines which markers have made it through.

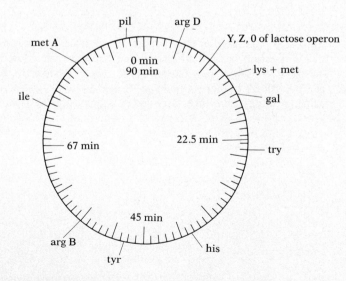

pil

arg D

met A

Y, Z, 0 of lactose operon

0 min
90 min

lys + met

ile

gal

67 min

22.5 min

try

45 min

arg B

his

tyr

Circular "clock" recombination map of *E. coli* showing a few markers (symbols are amino acids)

16.5

Jacob and Wollman used Hfr *E. coli* strains to develop recombination maps. The lengthy chromosome transfer from the Hfr cells to the F− cells was disrupted at increasing time intervals between 0 and 90 minutes in sequential cultures. Then the cells representing each time interval were studied for evidence of genetic recombination. In this manner, the linear arrangement of gene loci along the circular chromosome was finally determined. In future years, more and more markers (selected loci) became known and the same procedure utilized to determine their relative locations.

thus themselves) in other ways. For example, a plasmid is responsible for the deadly toxins produced by the diphtheria bacterium.

Some plasmids even carry genes that make their hosts resistant to antibiotics. One plasmid, known as the **multiple-resistance plasmid,** endows its host with resistance to six important antibiotics. This plasmid can also be transferred between distantly related species of bacteria. We previously noted that plasmids were a kind of parasite, and that plasmid infection resembled a disease infection in some ways; we have to modify that now and admit that life is not so simple. Some plasmids protect their hosts (and thus themselves).

Now that we know about infectious antibiotic resistance, some mysteries have been cleared up. Time and again physicians have nearly defeated some bacterial infection with antibiotics, only to find that the same disease erupts again and is no longer susceptible to the same antibiotic. What has happened is that natural selection has been at work, and our very success at battling microbes has given rise to new, more potent strains. Fortunately, the drug industry has kept up with the challenge by continually developing new or modified antibiotics.

Indiscriminate overuse of antibiotics is a controversial issue in health science today, due to the resistance phenomenon. Antibiotics are used routinely in livestock feed to accelerate growth rates and to protect against disease, and those antibiotics can be transferred to the carnivorous consumer. It is also clear that physicians routinely prescribe antibiotics for all types of minor ailments—in part to guard against secondary infections, but mainly to satisfy their patients' demands that something dramatic be done to end the sniffles.

It is now believed that this indiscriminate overuse of antibiotics has given rise to monstrous, superresistant bacterial strains. On the other hand, there is good evidence to support the opposite view, which is that the indiscriminate overuse of antibiotics by American and European physicians can be good. It has been pointed out that such usage has almost accidentally managed virtually to eliminate rheumatic heart disease and salmonellosis in those parts of the world. (Rheumatic heart disease, which is due to *Streptococcus* infection, until recently was a leading cause of death among young and middle-aged adults. Until recently, salmonellosis was a major debilitating disease. Both diseases are still raging in less developed parts of the world). Antibiotics have also greatly reduced the prevalence of syphillis, once a leading cause of insanity. But resistant strains of the syphillis organism are on the loose, and some

strains of *Salmonella typhimurium*, the agent of salmonellosis, have picked up the multiple-resistance plasmid, and are showing resistance to antibiotics.

Plasmids have recently taken on new significance in molecular biology. Many of the most recent advances in *genetic engineering* and *gene cloning* have involved plasmids. Their small genomes are readily isolated and manipulated, and they are widely used as carriers of spliced genes in recombinant DNA experiments. Let's take a closer look at these advances.

GENETIC ENGINEERING

Molecular biology has recently become interesting to big business. The reason is simple: there are now opportunities in **genetic engineering,** or the application of some of this technology to practical ends. (Or, in the dim view of some critics, molecular biology is about to be perverted because there are now lucrative opportunities available.)

A new generation of molecular biologists has learned to manipulate genes with amazing ease. A specific segment of DNA can routinely be removed from cells (including human ones) and inserted into a tamed plasmid which can then be grown in large quantities. The specific gene can be removed again, analyzed for its nucleotide sequence, perhaps altered to some new specification, and inserted into bacterial or yeast cells. There it can produce unlimited quantities of its protein product. Already, *human insulin, human growth hormone,* and several types of a promising antiviral substance called *human interferon* are produced this way. Such capabilities stagger the imagination. We may soon have the ability to manufacture any of the body's chemicals with ease and at low cost.

Gene Splicing

When the idea of using plasmids for **gene splicing** (also called *gene cloning* or *recombinant DNA technology*) was introduced by Paul Berg and others in the late 1970s, the possibilities were so dramatic and so bizarre that the new technology immediately spawned a raging controversy. Trouble started when the very people who invented the techniques called for a research moratorium while any possible dangers could be evaluated. Did they say *possible dangers?* The scare was on.

Supporters of the new gene-splicing technology claimed that it held great promise for humanity, and that some of our more pressing problems soon might be met. They spoke glowingly of cancer cures and of a possible end to all genetic disease. Some even visualized a possible end to hunger with the synthesis of new plants that combine, say, the productivity and photosynthetic efficiency of maize with the nitrogen-fixing ability and protein production of peanuts.

In the minds of genetic engineering proponents, the principal benefit is that scientists like themselves will be able to do more experiments and to learn things faster—and that's nothing to scoff at. There are also more practical benefits, some of which have been realized and some of which are on the horizon. For example, there are thousands of growth hormone-deficient people who, with the help of human growth hormone, can attain normal height. In the past, growth hormone had to be extracted from the pituitaries of human cadavers, and was extremely expensive. Even though the glands of 50 cadavers are needed for only one dose, a few thousand seriously undersized adolescents have been treated to some extent—as well as one man who grew to normal height after having been only four feet tall until the age of 35. Very soon, no one will have to be any shorter than he or she wants to be. Does that seem to you like a blessing, or like cavalier tampering with nature?

One enormously valuable feat has already been accomplished: engineered *E. coli* now grows the antigen for hoof-and-mouth disease, for the first time making possible a relatively inexpensive vaccine against that costly disease. (That bit of genetic engineering alone might save the economy of Mexico).

Alarmed critics of the new techniques, on the other hand, saw nothing but disaster ahead. Their fears ranged from the possible release of newly created disease organisms—genetic monsters capable of creating uncontrollable plagues—to new kinds of cancer, to constructing new kinds of humans. Nonsensical scare fiction began to appear. Some critics accused the new biologists of "playing God," of messing around with primal forces, or of seeking demonic new power. Politicians tried to capitalize on the scare; the city fathers of Cambridge, Massachusetts passed an ordinance prohibiting recombinant DNA research within the city limits (which include Harvard University and the Massachusetts Institute of Technology). The National Institutes of Health set up rigid guidelines as to what kinds of research were to be allowed and what precautions were to be taken.

Then, just as suddenly, the controversy died. Interestingly, this happened at about the time that gene splicing became big business, with new developments being offered for sale to the highest bidder. One would hope we never find out whether there was ever any real basis for the scare. In any case, Cambridge relented and the NIH guidelines were relaxed. No new epidemics have been unleashed and no new forms of cancer have been created (so far). And the promises have begun to be realized.

How Gene Splicing Is Done. Gene splicing depends on the availability of **restriction enzymes,** which are a normal part of the bacterial cell's defenses against the foreign DNA of viruses and plasmids. Restriction enzymes have the ability to cut DNA at specific places along its length. Commercial companies now purify dozens of kinds of restriction enzymes and sell them by the bottle. Each variety recognizes a certain short DNA sequence and cuts wherever it is found along the molecule.

For example, a restriction enzyme called *Eco-R1* recognizes the following sequence in double-stranded DNA, and cuts it at a particular place (X stands for any nucleotide):

$$\downarrow$$
$$-X-X-X-C-T-T-A-A-G-X-X-X-$$
$$-X-X-X-G-A-A-T-T-C-X-X-X-$$
$$\uparrow$$

Note that the two strands are not cut directly opposite each other, but that the cuts are offset *(arrows)*. This leaves new free ends of complementary, single-stranded DNA:

$$-X-X-X-C-T-T-A-A- \qquad -G-X-X-X-$$
$$-X-X-X-G- \qquad -A-A-T-T-C-X-X-X-$$

The free, single-stranded ends will recognize and base-pair with one another, given the opportunity and the right conditions. For this reason, they are called *sticky ends.* After such base-pairing, the DNA can be *healed* again with another enzyme called **ligase.** Specific sequences, such as the one shown above, are found in many life forms. The same restriction enzymes will break any of these. If the DNA of one life form, broken in this way, should encounter the DNA from another life form, the two forms of DNA can heal together, mixing the genes of two species (Figure 16.6). Do you want an organism that combines bacterial genes with genes from, say, a chicken? It's been done. If you think a genetic cross between a chicken and a bacterium is amusing, you'd better ponder the implications very carefully. Techniques are improving so rapidly that any combination of genes is technically possible.

The gene splicers' favorite trick is to use a restriction enzyme to cut open the circular DNA of a plasmid and then to splice in a fragment of DNA from some other organism. After they heal, the

Through the use of gene splicing techniques, donor DNA from nearly any source can be inserted into a bacterial plasmid where it will be transcribed and translated along with the bacterial DNA. **(A)** Bacterial plasmids and segments of eukaryotic DNA are obtained, and **(b)** using the same specific restriction enzyme, sections are cleaved out. The enzyme ligase is then used to fuse the matching sticky ends of the donor DNA segment to those of the plasmid. Next **(c)**, the altered plasmid is taken in by a new bacterial host, where it is replicated and passed along through many rapidly arising generations of cells **(d)**. The donor DNA is routinely transcribed and translated in the host cell and eventually its protein product can be collected.

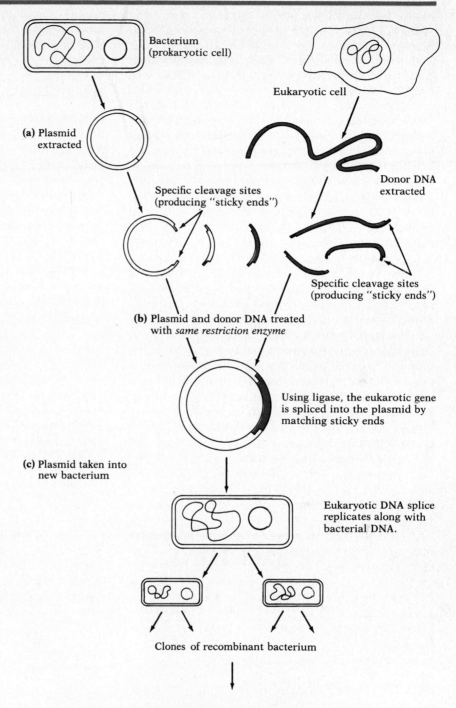

Bacterium (prokaryotic cell)

Eukaryotic cell

(a) Plasmid extracted

Donor DNA extracted

Specific cleavage sites (producing "sticky ends")

Specific cleavage sites (producing "sticky ends")

(b) Plasmid and donor DNA treated with *same restriction enzyme*

Using ligase, the eukarotic gene is spliced into the plasmid by matching sticky ends

(c) Plasmid taken into new bacterium

Eukaryotic DNA splice replicates along with bacterial DNA.

Clones of recombinant bacterium

(d) Eukaryotic gene product isolated and collected in large amounts

plasmids with foreign DNA inserts are allowed to infect susceptible bacteria. As the newly infected bacteria are allowed to multiply rapidly in their usual fashion, copies of the altered plasmid and its new insert are passed on to all descendants (see Figure 16.6).

If the altered bacteria are infused with genes that make human insulin, the bacteria will make human insulin. And bacteria multiply so rapidly that it isn't long before significant amounts of this hormone can be recovered.

Do you see why some people were alarmed? It's possible to put the gene for botulism toxin into *E. coli,* a bacterium that is already adapted for thriving in your gut. Who would do such a thing? Perhaps the same folks who brought us binary nerve gas, cruise missiles, cluster bombs, and napalm. It's also possible to clone the entire genome of a cancer-causing virus, or the specific cancer-causing genes. Unlikely, you think? This, too, has been done. That was one of the scare items, but now that it's actually happened, the isolation of cancer-causing genes (**oncogenes**) has been hailed as the research breakthrough that may lead science to a final understanding of the cancer process, and possibly from that to a dependable cure (Essay 16.1). Not that anyone can afford to be careless: we mustn't forget that the last two minor epidemics of smallpox in Europe—including the very last death ever caused by this virus—were due to es-

caped laboratory strains (the deadly smallpox virus, which only two decades ago infected millions of people, is now extinct except for laboratory cultures).

Gene Sequencing

Other new techniques, based on plasmid transfer, have permitted molecular biologists to determine the exact nucleotide sequence of any piece of DNA or RNA they can isolate—and they can isolate just about any piece they want to. The entire base sequences of DNA in bacteriophages, plasmids, polio viruses, and human mitochondria have now been determined. They run pages and pages filled with A, T, C, and G; for example, there are exactly 5315 in the case of the first bacteriophage sequence to be discovered. Your own DNA sequence of some 6.4 billion nucleotide pairs, if it were ever determined, would fill a thousand volumes the size of this one. And, incredible as it sounds, the task is already well underway. Tom Maniatis, a Harvard molecular biologist, has chopped human DNA into fragments a few tens of thousands of nucleotides long, has inserted them into the DNA of a bacteriophage, and is maintaining three million separate clones of cultured human DNA. Such a collection is called a **DNA library.** Sequencing is now fully automated, and any DNA sequence can be quickly "read" and recorded (Essay 16.2).

ESSAY 16.2
THE GENE MACHINE

If you aren't convinced of the almost bizarre possibilities of scientific technology, consider one of the latest additions. The **gene machine,** a device whose name has definite Madison Avenue overtones, is now available for about $30,000, and it does just what it says. An operator can create any DNA sequence he or she wants simply by imagining it and typing it out. The computerized machine does the rest. For instance, one might have a protein amino acid sequence, but be unable to isolate the corresponding mRNA. From a knowledge of the genetic code, the investigator can

predict what a short segment of the gene might be, type it into the gene machine, and have a *probe* that can be used to locate the rest of the gene from a DNA library consisting of cloned chromosome segments of the species in question. If all one has is a tiny amount of protein, a highly sensitive protein-sequencing accessory is available. Samples of protein placed in the *automatic sequenator* are dismantled chemically, one amino acid at a time from one end of the polypeptide. These fragments are identified automatically and the amino acid sequence is printed out.

Once a probable nucleotide sequence is determined, it is typed into the gene machine. The gene machine goes through all the steps of DNA synthesis. In about a day's time, a small quantity of the artificial gene is available. In order to get a sufficient quantity of absolute purity, sticky ends are included in the synthetic sequence and it is cloned in a bacterial plasmid, which is then taken up by a receptive bacterium. Standard biological gene cloning methods then take over. Potentially, any enzyme the experimenter can imagine or any other kind of protein or gene can be made to order. ●

Summary

Genetic Recombination in Bacteria

Many bacteria, besides reproducing asexually, have also been found to exhibit some form of genetic recombination. Certain strains of bacteria grown under experimental conditions were found to occur in "male" and "female" types. During conjugation, gene transfer always occurred from male to female. Only a few genes were transferred at a time, rather than an equal mixing of two entire genomes, as occurs in truly sexual eukaryotes.

Maleness was found to be "contagious" in the bacteria, caused by a genetic parasite known as a plasmid. Genes in this plasmid were responsible for conjugation and the construction of conjugation tubes through which the plasmid could pass. The F plasmid is usually a circular DNA molecule. A replicated portion of the plasmid becomes linear when passing through the conjugation tube, but resumes a circular shape once inside the new host, where it can again be replicated and passed on to bacterial progeny. While this type of sexual transfer is usually not efficient, Hfr strains developed in the laboratory showed a high level of efficiency in this process. By interrupting bacterial conjugation at different time periods, researchers could detect the presence of various genetic markers and thus map the gene sequence.

While other types of plasmids cannot transfer the host's chromosomal genes to other bacteria, their genes govern the formation of conjugation tubes, the coating of cell surfaces, the production of various toxins, and cell resistance to antibiotics. Indiscriminate use of antibiotics has given rise to new, more resistant bacterial strains.

Genetic Engineering

Genetic engineering involves the manipulation of genetic material. Segments of DNA can be removed and inserted into a plasmid, which can then be grown in large quantities. Substances produced using this technique include human insulin, growth hormone, and interferon.

Gene splicing technology depends on the availability of restriction enzymes, which can cut DNA at specific sites. The sticky ends are base paired and healed with ligase. Using this procedure, researchers can splice together the genes of two species. While the process has certain risks, it also has been helpful in isolating oncogenes—as cancer-causing genetic material.

Gene sequencing, based on plasmid transfer, enables molecular biologists to determine the exact nucleotide sequences of any isolated piece of DNA or RNA. A DNA library contains the collection of clones of cultured human DNA. With a "gene machine," researchers can create any DNA sequence that can be imagined.

Key Terms

recombinant colonies
selected markers
unselected markers
conjugation
plasmid
F+ strain

F− strain
F plasmid
Hfr strain
multiple-resistance plasmid
genetic engineering
gene splicing

restriction enzymes
ligase
oncogenes
DNA library
gene machine

Review Questions

1. Lederberg and Tatum tried to apply the standard techniques of chromosome mapping to *E. coli*, the colon bacterium. What were two significant reasons for their failure? (p. 223)

2. Hayes found that the ability of *E. coli* to transfer genes during conjugation depends on the presence of a certain plasmid. What, specifically, is a plasmid, and why is it essential to successful conjugation? (p. 225)

3. Explain how the F plasmid brings about the transfer of all of the bacterial genes during conjugation. How did Jacob and Wollman make use of this process in bacterial gene mapping? (pp. 225–228)

4. Briefly summarize the antibiotic controversy and explain how the multiple-resistance plasmid is thought to fit into the problems of disease control. (p. 229)

5. List four steps used in carrying out gene splicing and cloning. Be sure to include the role of restriction enzymes, plasmids, "sticky ends," and ligase in your answer. (pp. 230–232)

6. List four products now available through genetic engineering, and two possibilities for the immediate future. (pp. 229–230)

7. Genetic engineering is controversial. What are some of the fears people have about this new tool of molecular biology? (pp. 229–230, 232)

8. What is a "gene machine"? Suggest how such an innovation might be of future use in the cure of genetic diseases. (Essay 16.2)

Evolution In Populations

17

Living things reproduce; at least living things today are the offspring of predecessors that reproduced, and among the offspring of sexual reproducers we will always find variation. Each individual will be different from all the others. Look your little brother directly in the eye and you might develop a new appreciation for this principle. Biologically, the differences between you and your brother may be your parents' way of ensuring that at least one of you will be able to cope with the unpredictable world in which you find yourselves. One of you is simply likely to be more suited than the other to the prevailing environment. But keep in mind that there are biological implications of the differences between you and him. For instance, your little brother's close-set eyes, receding chin, prominent brow, sloping forehead, and the tendency to snort may interfere with his success in the world of fraternities. But his unusually long arms may prove beneficial if things should change so that climbing and throwing became more important. The prevailing environment, then, can "select," or favor, the traits of one of you over the other. The process, as described in earlier chapters, is called **natural selection.** It is dintinguished from **artificial selection,** the process by which a breeder chooses which traits to perpetuate in his stock. A dairy farmer, for example, might wish to breed only those cows that yield more milk (Figure 17.1).

Let's now take a close look at natural selection to see how nature goes about winnowing out those traits that are least compatible with the environment. We will see that the principle of natural selection is very powerful, requiring only (a) reproducing organisms, (b) heritable (genetic) differences between them, and (c) that these heritable differences influence the likelihood of survival and/or reproduction. And for natural selection to be maintained over a reasonably long period of time, there must also be (d) a source of new heritable variation: that is, genetic mutation.

NATURAL SELECTION WITHOUT SEX

Some organisms reproduce without sex (*asexually*) by such means as budding, fission, or shedding spores. In such cases, the offspring are likely to be genetically identical to each other and to the parent. Thus, natural selection in asexual groups would seem to be a matter of competition among **clones,** that is, among genetically identical organisms. However, natural selection cannot occur among identical organisms, since one can never have the edge over the others. Natural selection implies the existence of differences among individuals.

The rates of mutation in asexual groups can be very low—in fact, among dividing bacterial populations, only about one gene in one hundred million will show mutation. But such low rates of mutation are enough to give natural selection something to work on, since wherever there are bacteria (which is practically everywhere), there are likely to be billions of them. As a result of their huge numbers, there will be a great deal of mutation in the group—hopeful genes awaiting their evaluation by nature.

NATURAL SELECTION IN MENDELIAN POPULATIONS

Since variation in asexual populations is largely caused by random mutations, evolution must proceed slowly. In sexual reproducers, though, mechanisms are established that ensure variation and so natural selection can proceed more rapidly.

Natural Selection with Sex

The principle of natural selection is so compelling, logical, and powerful that Darwin was able to make a good case for it even though he did not understand the mechanisms of genetics. Imagine the principle's strength when we add what is now known about meiosis, genetic recombination, and sex. We now know that meiosis—that complex dance in which chromosomes pair, exchange, and segregate—has an important function in selection. Genetic recombination, or the shuffling of genes,

can account for much variation. And now that we know how sex provides the variation that allows natural selection to work more efficiently, some people can't take their minds off it. These processes, then, greatly increase the amount of heritable, genetic difference among individuals, giving natural selection something to work on.

In addition, combining genes from different parents is important if a population is to adapt to several different aspects of the environment simultaneously. Thus if one parent has one genetic advantage and the other parent has a different advantage, some offspring might end up with both beneficial traits. Of course, this doesn't work with asexual organisms. If one bacterium has a mutation that gives it better temperature tolerance, for example, and another has a mutation that gives it, say, a more efficient glucose metabolism, their offspring will just have to compete with one another until one strain eliminates the other.

In a sexual (also called Mendelian) population, the first principle is *every gene for itself*. If an allele increases the **fitness** (reproductive success) of the organism in its environment *on the average*, the frequency of that allele will increase in the population, and it will increase at the expense of less beneficial alleles. On the other hand, a mutant allele that makes the organisms that carry it less fit *on the average* will rapidly be lost from the population.

Keep in mind that evolution implies differences in genes as they are passed from one generation to the next. Individuals do not evolve in this sense. Sexually reproducing organisms are rather temporary creatures, but genes are potentially immortal in that they pass exact or nearly exact copies of

17.1

Today's dairy cows are the product of generations of artificial selection. Each breed produces milk with certain characteristics desirable to the dairy industry. Although the quantity and quality of milk are prime factors in the management of pedigrees, other traits, such as disease resistance and reproductive success, are equally important.

themselves from generation to generation. It has been suggested rather irreverently that we are simply lumbering robots devised by our genes to enable them to pass themselves along. In his brilliant book *The Selfish Gene*, Richard Dawkins states that:

> Individuals are not stable things, they are fleeting. Chromosomes too are shuffled into oblivion, like hands of cards soon after they are dealt. But the cards themselves survive the shuffling. The cards are the genes. The genes are not destroyed by crossing-over, they merely change partners and march on . . . They are the replicators and we are their survival machines. When we have served our purpose we are cast aside. But genes are the denizens of geological time: genes are forever.

Robert Wallace, in *The Genesis Factor*, makes the point in a different way. He suggests that whatever we do, are, or hope to be in life is irrelevant as long as we obey our "reproductive imperative." There is no such actual directive, of course, but we tend to behave as if there were. People tend to pass along genes into those noisy and endearing repositories we call children. And of course, in order to make that effort worth it, we must then see them through to their own reproductive stages.

The Population and How It Evolves

Evolution is defined as descent with modification. We can see, then, that genes evolve: that is, they persist and yet they change. But we should keep in mind that *populations* also evolve. That is, the characteristics of a population change over time, usually for the good. And, of course, species evolve. These are referred to as *levels of evolution.* Now let's take a closer look at evolution at the population level.

A **Mendelian population** is a group of interbreeding individuals of a single species. All of the genes found in such a population make up the **gene pool** (Figure 17.2). Here we are interested in how the ratios of the various alleles to one another change over time in that pool. As one allele in the population becomes more frequent, the DNA of the gene pool changes. Such changes are the subject of a field called **population genetics.**

The Hardy-Weinberg Law

G. H. Hardy, an eminent mathematician, had few professional interests in common with R. C. Punnett, the young Mendelian geneticist, but they fre-

17.2

Each of these populations represents a gene pool. The degree of variability we find depends, to a great extent, on the size of the population and whether new input is restricted. In the larger population, new members are constantly incorporated, adding their alleles to the pool. In smaller, more restricted populations, such as the Amish, membership from the outside is strongly discouraged. As a result, variability is limited, and certain alleles that are low in frequency in other populations are common among the Amish.

TABLE 17.1

Idealized random mating of 32,000 hypothetical people when two alleles **B** and **b** are equally frequent

When 16,000 men of three genotypes mate randomly with 16,000 women of three genotypes, there will be nine kinds of matings. In each type of mating, the offspring will occur in Mendelian proportions. Here the parents are already in the Hardy-Weinberg frequencies. When the numbers of the offspring are added up, they too will be in the Hardy-Weinberg distribution, in this case 25% **BB**, 50% **Bb**, and 25% **bb**.

Type of Mating		Number of Mating Pairs in Thousands	Relative Frequency	Genotypes of Offspring and Their Expected Numbers in Thousands		
MALE	FEMALE			BB	Bb	bb
BB	× BB	1	$1/4 \times 1/4 = 1/16$	1	—	—
BB	× Bb	2	$1/4 \times 1/2 = 1/8$	1	1	—
BB	× bb	1	$1/4 \times 1/4 = 1/16$	—	1	—
Bb	× BB	2	$1/2 \times 1/4 = 1/8$	1	1	—
Bb	× Bb	4	$1/2 \times 1/2 = 1/4$	1	2	1
Bb	× bb	2	$1/2 \times 1/4 = 1/8$	—	1	1
bb	× BB	1	$1/4 \times 1/4 = 1/16$	—	1	—
bb	× Bb	2	$1/4 \times 1/2 = 1/8$	—	1	1
bb	× bb	1	$1/4 \times 1/4 = 1/16$	—	—	1
Total (thousands)		16		4	8	4

quently met for lunch and tea at the faculty club of Cambridge University. One day in 1908 Punnett was telling his colleague about a small problem in genetics. Someone had noted that there was a rare dominant gene for abnormally short fingers, while the allele for normal fingers was recessive. In view of the famous 3:1 Mendelian ratio, shouldn't short fingers become more and more common with each generation, until no one in Britain had normal fingers at all? Punnett didn't think this argument was correct, but he couldn't explain why.

Hardy thought the problem was simple enough, and wrote a few equations on his napkin. He showed that the relative numbers of people with normal fingers and people with short fingers ought to stay the same for generation after generation, as long as there were no outside forces—such as natural selection—to change them.

Punnett was excited. He was amazed that his friend had solved so complex a puzzle so casually and wanted to have the idea published (on something besides a napkin) as soon as possible. But Hardy was reluctant. He felt that the idea was so simple and obvious that he didn't want to have his name associated with it and risk his reputation as one of the great mathematical minds of the day. But Punnett prevailed, and the relationship between genotypes and phenotypes in populations quickly became known as *Hardy's law*. As fate would have it, Hardy, who was indeed one of the great mathematical minds of the day, is now best known for his reluctant contribution to biology.

In Germany, Hardy's law was known as *Weinberg's law*, since it had been discovered independently by a German physician by that name. Wein-berg, in fact, published his version within weeks of the publication of Hardy's short paper. Eventually the formula became known as the **Hardy-Weinberg law,** and it is now the basis of the population genetics of sexual organisms. (Table 17.1.) Later, it was discovered that both had been scooped by an American, W. E. Castle, who had published a neglected paper on the relationship in 1903. Some people now refer to the *Castle, Hardy, Weinberg law*. But we will follow convention and also neglect our compatriot for now.

The Implications of the Hardy-Weinberg Law. To rephrase the problem of the Mendelians, brown eyes are dominant over blue eyes in humans, so why doesn't everyone have brown eyes by now? From basic Mendelian genetics we know what happens in a cross between a homozygous blue-eyed person and a homozygous brown-eyed person. But in population genetics, we must consider not just one cross, but large numbers of matings and all their outcomes taken together, so imagine thousands of blue-eyed homozygotes **(bb)** mating with thousands of brown-eyed homozygotes **(BB).** The several thousand children resulting from such festivity will all be brown-eyed, since all the offspring will be **Bb** heterozygotes. Blue eyes have disappeared, as feared by the early Mendelians.

Now imagine that all these genetically identical F_1 heterozygotes grow up, choose mates, and manage to reproduce. Now it becomes apparent that the blue-eye alleles didn't disappear after all. In fact, about one fourth of their children will have blue eyes. Now if we let the F_2 generation grow up and choose mates, things start to get complicated.

But why? They weren't so complicated in Mendel's pea plants, which were entirely self-fertilizing. But humans are not self-fertilizing. And, despite songs and poems to the contrary, we can assume that people don't care all that much about blue or brown eyes, but will essentially mate at random in so far as eye color goes. So let's take a look at our F_2 generation. We find blue-eyed males, blue-eyed females, brown-eyed males, and brown-eyed females. And, in fact, there are two kinds of brown-eyed individuals of each sex—homozygotes and heterozygotes. We end up with six genetically distinct kinds of humans in our population: three genotypes of males and three genotypes of females. This means that there can now be *nine* kinds of matings.

Now, we let these types wander off into the sunset and begin pairing off. In due time the F_3 generation will appear. When we look them over we see that once again one-fourth of the children will be blue-eyed and three-fourths will be brown-eyed (Figure 17.3). And so it will continue for generation after generation.

We see, then, that the gene for blue eyes didn't disappear at all. What did happen? Since the heterozygotes harbored hidden blue-eyed genes, the actual frequency of the blue-eyed allele remained at 50%, just as at the start. The idea is, whether genes are expressed in homozygotes or hidden in heterozygotes, they are distinct physical entities that don't just go away without some reason.

An Algebraic Equivalent

In the example above, the two alleles start out at the same frequency—half **B** and half **b.** The Hardy-Weinberg law also works in populations in which the alleles have different frequencies. For those burning with a fierce love of mathematics, let's put it into algebra. First, let p be the allele frequency of allele **B,** while q is the allele frequency of allele **b.** If there are only two of these alleles, then $p + q = 1$.

The Hardy-Weinberg law says that the expected genotype frequency of **BB** is p^2, the expected genotype frequency of **Bb** is $2pq$, and the expected genotype frequency of **bb** is q^2. The Hardy-Weinberg formula is written: $p^2 + 2pq + q^2$. New generations will show these same frequencies (with exceptions). We can show this by listing the nine possible matings, the frequencies in which they should occur, and the distribution of alleles among the offspring. Remember that the ratio of the total genotype frequencies of the offspring, which was 1/4, 1/2, and 1/4 in the numerical example, will be p^2, $2pq$, and q^2, according to the rules of algebra.

B = brown eyes
b = blue eyes

F_3 offspring

17.3

In the crosses between homozygous brown- and blue-eyed individuals, the F_2 contained the genotypes **BB, Bb,** and **bb.** Their frequency was 1/4, 1/2, and 1/4. To determine the genotype frequencies of an F_3 generation, all nine possible matings of the F_2 are considered. The results of each are seen in the heavily lined boxes *(color).* By simply adding up each of the genotypes we find that nothing has changed. The frequencies remain 1/4 **BB,** 1/2 **Bb,** and 1/4 **bb.** Adding up the individual alleles, we find that the allele frequencies of 1/2 **B** and 1/2 **b,** introduced in the F_1, are also present in the F_3, as we would predict for an F_4, F_5, etc. This reminds us that recessive genes do not disappear and, barring selection against them, their frequencies do not change.

The Random Association of Gametes. The Hardy-Weinberg law is easier to understand if we think of it in terms of the *random association of gametes* (Figure 17.4), which is really the same as the random mating of diploid individuals.

After all, when an egg and sperm meet—either in the open sea, as with sea urchins, or in the dark confines of an oviduct, as with our species—the parents' diploid genotypes no longer really matter. All that matter are the haploid genotypes of the two gametes. Now, let's ask, what is the probability that a zygote will be **BB?** It is a *product* of the probability that the egg will be **B,** (we call that probability p) and the probability that the sperm will be **B** (which we also call p). So the probability that any given zygote will be **BB** is p^2.

On the other hand, the probability that a zygote will be heterozygous, **Bb,** is the *sum* of two probabilities: the probability that the egg will be **B** and the sperm will be **b,** which is $p \times q = pq$, and the probability that the egg will be **b** and the sperm will be **B,** which is also pq. So the probability that any given zygote will be a heterozygote **(Bb)** is $pq + pq$, or $2pq$.

Albinism: People and the Algebraic Equivalent. The Hardy-Weinberg law is not just a mathematical exercise. It has implications that could affect such diverse areas as politics, law, and sociology. For example, if we know the prevalence in the population of persons affected with a recessive condition such as albinism—the absence of normal melanin pigment (Figure 17.5)—we can predict, within limits, the probability that a couple will have an albino baby. Here's how this would work. Normal skin and eye pigment in humans is dominant over the albino condition; thus albinism is associated with a recessive allele, **b.** And normal

17.5

The recessive allele for albinism, when homozygous, reveals itself in the absence of pigment in the hair, skin, and eyes. In this photograph, an albino of the Coral Islands (near New Guinea) attends a feast with his dark-skinned brothers. Albinism is estimated to occur in about one in 20,000 persons, which translates into a gene frequency of one in 140.

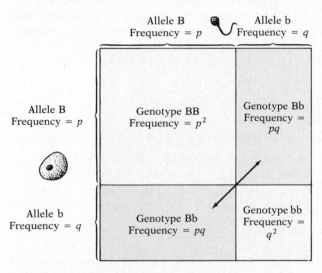

Allele B
Frequency = p ⎫⎧ Allele b
Frequency = q

Allele B
Frequency = p

| Genotype BB
Frequency = p^2 | Genotype Bb
Frequency = pq |

Allele b
Frequency = q

| Genotype Bb
Frequency = pq | Genotype bb
Frequency = q^2 |

17.4

Gametes and the Hardy-Weinberg equilibrium. If there are two alleles, **B** and **b,** occurring in relative frequencies p and q, and mating is random, a proportion of p of the sperm will carry the **B** allele, and p of the eggs will also carry the **B** allele. For each zygote formed, the probability that the egg and sperm will both carry **B** alleles is $p \times p$ or p^2. Similarly, the probability that both of the uniting gametes will carry **b** alleles is q^2. There are two ways that a **Bb** zygote can be formed: **B** sperm uniting with a **b** egg, and a **b** sperm uniting with a **B** egg. The total probability of these two events occurring is $pq + qp$, or simply, $2pq$. (The arrow connects two boxes that represent the same **Bb** genotype.) The relative frequencies of the three kinds of genotypes in the population will be equal to the individual probabilities of each kind of event: p^2, $2pq$, and q^2 will be the frequencies of genotypes **BB, Bb,** and **bb,** respectively.

pigmentation is associated with the corresponding dominant allele **B.** The homozygous recessive genotype **(bb)** occurs in about one of every 20,000 people. According to the Hardy-Weinberg law, this frequency would be given by q^2, so

$$q^2 = 1/20,000.$$

The frequency of the allele **b** has to be the square root of this, or

$$q = \sqrt{1/20,000} = 1/141.$$

The frequency of the dominant allele **B** would then be $p = 1 - q$, or

$$p = 1 - 1/141 = 140/141.$$

The heterozygous condition **Bb** would occur in the population with a frequency of $2pq$:

$$2pq = 2 \times 140/141 \times 1/141 = 1/70,$$

or about 1.4%. Therefore, about one person in 70 is a *carrier* for this fairly rare condition. Since 1/70 of 20,000 is 280, about 280 people are heterozygous carriers **(Bb)** for everyone who is a homozygous, affected albino **(bb).**

We might note that there are actually several different kinds of albinism, due to different mutant alleles at different gene loci. That makes this kind of analysis very difficult unless the initial diagnosis is completely accurate; for the Hardy-Weinberg law to be of use, only one gene locus at a time can be considered.

A Closer Look at the Model

If it has occurred to you that mathematical models are often a little short on realism, you're right. In fact, the Hardy-Weinberg law has a number of stringent restrictions:

1. The alleles in question must segregate according to Mendel's first law. This eliminates, for example, sex-linked alleles.

2. The model applies only to loci that have two alleles (or two classes of alleles). However, most gene loci have multiple alleles, and more complex forms of the Hardy-Weinberg law must be used.

3. The model applies only to the genotypes of the zygotes. If some zygotes survive better than others because of natural selection, the law may no longer hold for adults.

4. Mating must be completely random.

5. The model is valid only within single, interbreeding populations, and not if samples are taken from different populations.

6. The model only applies if there is no migration either into or out of the population.

7. The expectations are exact only if the population and the sample are infinitely large.

Of these restrictions, the last is the least realistic, since no populations and no samples are infinitely large. But statisticians are willing to assume that smaller samples are representative of an infinite population.

Obviously, it's easy to violate the assumptions of the Hardy-Weinberg law. So is it of any real use? What happens when the assumptions of the Hardy-Weinberg law are violated? In physics you might quite casually study some problem by making similarly absurd assumptions: frictionless surfaces, falling bodies without air resistance, mass concentrated at a single point, and so on. Just because these things don't really happen doesn't mean that the formulations you derive aren't any good. Once the simple model is derived, it can be decorated by adding new terms to take care of such complications. Mathematical laws are always compromises between the simplicity that our minds can grasp and the complications of nature. Similarly, the expectations of the Hardy-Weinberg law are based on a set of idealized circumstances that may seldom occur in nature, but the expectations they generate are useful all the same because they give us a platform that can then be modified to fit the real world.

Summary

Natural Selection Without Sex
In asexual reproduction, offspring tend to be clones, that is, genetically identical to one another and the parent. Natural selection works only when individuals differ (or mutations introduce different traits); although mutation in asexual populations occur at a low rate, the sheer numbers of organisms in, for instance, a bacterial population allow for a range of mutations within the group.

Natural Selection in Mendelian Populations
The mechanisms of sexual reproduction ensure variation among individuals and can speed up the pace of natural selection. Meiosis, genetic recombination, and sex greatly increase the number of heritable, genetic differences among organisms in a population, enabling them to adapt to environmental changes. In sexual reproduction, a successful allele will increase in frequency at the expense of the less beneficial or successful allele.

Evolution implies differences in genes as they are passed from one generation to the next. While individuals are transitory, genes are potentially immortal, since they pass on nearly exact copies of themselves from generation to generation.

Evolution is defined as descent with modification. A Mendelian population is a group of interbreeding individuals of a single species. Population genetics involves the study of changes in the ratios of various alleles to one another in a population's gene pool.

The Hardy-Weinberg law is a mathematical model that predicts, in the absence of natural selection, that gene frequencies will remain unchanged generation after generation. Using this law, one can predict what percentage of the population will carry or express a recessive gene for such characteristics as albinism. While a number of restrictions limit the usefulness of the Hardy-Weinberg law in real-world situations, the model still provides a basic framework for genetic studies of populations.

Key Terms

natural selection	**fitness**	**gene pool**
artificial selection	**evolution**	**population genetics**
clones	**Mendelian population**	**Hardy-Weinberg law**

Review Questions

1. What is the difference between natural and artificial selection? Cite an example of the latter. (p. 234)

2. List the four requirements of natural selection. (p. 234)

3. List three mechanisms in sexual reproduction that help increase variability in populations. Why is variability so limited in asexual populations? (pp. 234–235)

4. Explain this phrase in your own words: "On the average, the fitness of any allele will determine whether its frequency increases or decreases." Be sure to explain the terms *fitness* and *frequency*. (p. 235)

5. Evolutionary theorists tell us that it is the gene that evolves, not the individual. What does this mean? Of what importance to evolution, if any, is the individual? (p. 236)

6. If the ratio of dominant to recessive alleles in the P_1 of a Hardy-Weinberg population was 1:1, what ratio would one expect to find in the F_2? F_3? F_4? Prove your answer. (pp. 238–239)

7. Assume that tongue rolling is made possible by the presence of a dominant allele **(T)**. Recessive individuals **(tt)** cannot "roll" their tongues no matter how hard they try. A population sampling reveals that recessives make up 36% (0.36) of the individuals. What portion of the population is homozygous dominant? Heterozygous? (pp. 238–239)

8. Application of the Hardy-Weinberg law to real populations has several important restrictions. List three of these that seem unrealistic. In view of these, how can the law be of any practical value? (p. 240)

Evolution and Changing Genes

18

The **gene pool** is the reservoir of genetic information of any population. This pool, though, should not be likened to a still pond. Its apparent stillness is deceptive; these waters change. As some flows over the dam to be lost, new genetic waters join the pool through myriad tributaries. The point is that although some gene pools change slowly and others change rapidly, they do change. Let's see now how the gene frequencies in such a pool can change and what this means in the evolution of living things.

There are three major forces that can change gene frequencies: natural selection, mutation, and genetic drift. None of these forces acts alone, but together they direct the course of evolution. Of the three, the most intriguing is natural selection.

GENE CHANGES UNDER NATURAL SELECTION

Natural selection can act in rather extreme ways, as we see in the case of certain *lethal* alleles. Lethal genes can kill you outright. Thus, the death removes the individual (and the allele) from the gene pool. Let's consider an unusual implication of this seemingly straightforward effect—the case of the Manx cats (Figure 18.1).

Manx cats are peculiar animals, having rather large hind legs and practically no tails. No one has ever been able to develop a strain of true-breeding Manx cats for the simple reason that the tail-less animals are all heterozygotes. Normal cats, with tails, are **TT** homozygotes; Manx cats, without tails, are **Tt** heterozygotes. The problem is, the homozygous **tt** genotype is an embryonic lethal; that is, these cats die while still embryos. So already we see a strange thing. The **t** allele is dominant for one trait, and recessive for another. It is dominant for the absence of a tail, and it is recessive for the absence of a kitten. So when two Manx **(Tt)** cats mate, 1/4 of the offspring will be normal cats, 1/2 will be Manx cats, and 1/4 will be dead cats. The dead ones are reabsorbed by the mother's body as embryos, so the only litter you would see from such a cross would be 2/3 **Tt** Manx and 1/3 **TT** alleycat.

Now suppose that someone should populate a remote island with a shipload of Manx cats, turning them loose to run wild, yowling and scratching and mating randomly, in the fashion of cats. What would happen? We know that the frequency of the Manx allele, **t**, starts out at $q = 1/2$. But then we find that, in one generation, it is reduced to $q = 1/3$. What happens then? With random mating, the third generation of *zygotes* will be $p^2 = 4/9$ **TT**, $2pq = 4/9$ **Tt** (Manx), and $q^2 = $ **tt** homozygous lethal. (See Chapter 17 for a review of the algebra.)

But when the recessive homozygotes are removed by natural selection, 1/2 of the remaining cats are now Manx and 1/2 are alleycats. The frequency of the recessive lethal **t** allele has gone from 1/2 to 1/3 to 1/4 in three generations, and in succeeding generations it will fall further to 1/5, 1/6, and so on. Meanwhile, the proportion of homozygous lethal **tt** zygotes will also follow the Hardy-Weinberg distribution: 1/4, 1/9, 1/25, 1/36, and so on. As you can imagine, Manx cats will become increasingly rare on our fair island. On the other hand, the severe selection against the **t** allele will diminish. Figure 18.2 plots the course of the genotypes over 70 generations. Note that the allele frequency of **t** has fallen to 1.37% (1/70) by the end of the 70 generations, and that about 2.8% of the cats will then be Manx. It would take another 70 generations to bring the recessive allele frequency down to 0.7%.

Selection doesn't have to be so severe, of course. As a general rule, the rate of change in gene frequency in a population is proportional to the amount of selection against some genotype. For instance, in the case of Manx cats, suppose that the recessive genotype **tt** wasn't lethal, but merely reduced the individual cat's reproductive ability by 1/10. Then it would take 700 generations, rather than 70, to go from $q = 50\%$ to $q = 1.37\%$.

You might wonder why there are any Manx cats at all. It's because people tend to be impressed by anything bizarre in cats (and goldfish) and tend to keep Manx kittens while disposing of the alley-kittens. So artificial selection keeps the Manx gene going.

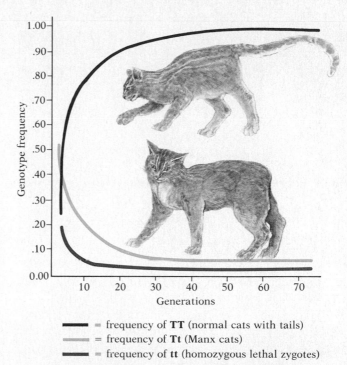

= frequency of **TT** (normal cats with tails)
= frequency of **Tt** (Manx cats)
= frequency of **tt** (homozygous lethal zygotes)

18.2

If an isolated population of Manx cats were permitted to breed indiscriminately, the "Manx allele" would readily decrease in the gene pool. The rate of decrease would be rapid, since all homozygous Manx individuals fail to survive. By the 70th generation the tail-less cats would be reduced to a rarity, their frequency dropping below 2%. Why doesn't the allele simply vanish from the population?

18.1

The Manx cat, a genetic oddity originally bred on the Isle of Man, lacks a tail. All adult Manx cats are heterozygous for the tail-less condition, since the homozygote embryos fail to survive. Obviously, the association of mutant genes producing the odd condition affects far more than the production of a tail.

The Peppered Moth

The British peppered moth, *Biston betularia,* occurs in two forms, or *morphs* (Figure 18.3). One morph is light and mottled (or peppered), and the other is black. The British, who have a long tradition of collecting butterflies and moths, have kept excellent records on the peppered moth for two centuries. The black morph, whose color is controlled primarily by a single dominant gene, originally showed up in 18th-century collections as a rare, highly prized variant, or mutant.

In the early days of the industrial revolution (in the 1840s), the black morph began to appear more and more often, especially near cities. In fact, the black morph became so common in industrialized areas that it eventually outnumbered the light peppered morph. (In Manchester, England's industrial center, the black morph came to compose 98% of the population.) Meanwhile, the light peppered morph remained the predominant form in rural areas.

18.3

The protective coloration of the peppered moth *Biston betularia* reduces predation by birds. The ancestral form has a salt-and-pepper pattern that allows it to blend visually with the lichen-covered trees of rural England **(top).** Over the last century and a half, pollution from burning coal has blackened trees throughout much of the industrial midlands, rendering the peppered-white form highly visible against the sooty background **(bottom).**

What had happened? It seemed clear that the species was adapting to some environmental change. That change was due to burning coal in the factories of heavy industry. Industrial England in the 19th century was quietly submitting to a dark cloak of carbon. As the countryside darkened and the mottled lichens began to disappear from the bark of trees, the frequency of black moths increased in the population. It was hypothesized that this was because the black moths were harder for predatory birds to see against the soot, while the peppered moths stood out in sharp contrast and were quickly taken.

From the historical data, J.B.S. Haldane calculated that the black moths survived and reproduced twice as well as the peppered moth in the industrial environment. Then a British naturalist, H.B.D. Kettlewell, performed the crucial experiment that validated the hypothesis. Kettlewell released known numbers of marked black and light peppered moths in unpolluted woodlands and two similar groups in polluted, soot-blackened woodlands. Later, he recaptured a portion of the released moths. The following are some of Kettlewell's mark-and-recapture data:

Dorset, England (unpolluted woodland)	Peppered morph	Black morph
Marked and released	496	473
Recaptured after predation	62	30
Percentage recaptured	12.5%	6.3%
Relative survival	1.00	0.507

Birmingham, England (soot-blackened woodland)	Peppered morph	Black morph
Marked and released	137	447
Recaptured later	18	123
Percentage recaptured	13.1%	27.5%
Relative survival	0.477	1.00

In the first set of moths, released in the unpolluted woodland, over twice as many light forms survived as black forms. In the second set, selection favored the black morph and acted against the light peppered morph. About twice as great a percentage of the favored black type survived long enough to be recaptured.

Incidentally, England has been doing rather well lately in its battle against pollution. The woodlands near the cities are once again becoming covered with lichens and the soot is disappearing. And, as one might predict, the black morphs of *Biston betularia* are beginning to become scarce again.

MUTATION: THE RAW MATERIAL OF EVOLUTION

If the environment is to select the best types from a group of organisms, the group must be variable. Individuals must differ. Variation, of course, can arise from a number of factors such as meiosis and crossovers, but the original source of variation in both sexual and asexual species must still be mutation, the chance alteration of DNA. Earlier, we saw how mutations arise through rare, unrepaired changes in base sequences and through chromosome breakage and rejoining. Now we are interested in the *fate* of mutations after they appear in the gene pool of populations.

Mutation Rates: Constant Input of New Information

Any given gene in a population is bound to mutate at one time or another (usually with neutral or harmful results). In fact, each gene undergoes mutation in a statistically regular and predictable manner, producing a constant and measurable input of new genetic information into the gene pool. Typically, mutations arise at the rate of one per gene locus per 100,000 gametes. The most severe and harmful of these are likely to go unnoticed, however, because no offspring are produced. In fact, it has been estimated that 1/3 to 1/2 of all human zygotes fail to develop because of the drastic changes produced by mutations! The potential parents are usually quite unaware that anything untoward has happened, as the lethal gene carries the embryo into oblivion.

Whereas these drastic changes are usually caused by dominant alleles, most of the mutations that end up being transmitted from generation to generation are recessive. This is because recessive alleles either fail to function at all or they function at a reduced level. Recessive mutations can be lethal, but only when they occur in the homozygous state, and double recessives are not likely to happen until many generations after the mutations first enter the gene pool. (Recessive lethal mutations that kill early in development are virtually impossible to detect in human populations, but they can be counted accurately in such experimental organisms as yeasts and fruit flies.)

The easiest mutations to study, of course, are dominant mutations that cause *visible* changes. An invisible change might be an alteration in some enzyme that had little or no effect. One example of a visible change might be dwarfism. A peculiar type of human dwarfism, known as **achondroplasia,** occurs in one out of about 12,000 births to normal parents (Figure 18.4). In achondroplasia, the person's head and trunk are of normal dimensions, but the arms and legs are stunted or fail to grow at all. Since the condition is dominant, each new incident represents a newly mutated gene. So the mutation for achondroplasia is one per 24,000 gametes. When achondroplastic dwarfs mate with normal individuals, about half of their children are afflicted by the condition.

Consider this: with an average mutation rate of

18.4

Each occurrence of achondroplasia (dwarfism) in the children of normal people can be traced directly to a new mutation in their fathers or mothers. The allele or alleles responsible are dominant, so they cannot be hidden by a heterozygous condition. Most are recessive. We know that the trait is dominant since half of the children resulting from unions between achondroplastic dwarfs and normal individuals are achondroplastic. What might we expect if the allele were recessive? (Milwaukee Journal Photo)

about one mutation per gene locus per 100,000 gametes, and with an estimated 80,000 genes per human zygote, *everyone* is likely to be carrying a newly arising mutation. The beneficial or neutral mutations, of course, will readily be passed on. If the mutation is harmful it is more likely to be transmitted if its effects are minor. Some of the more common of less-than-ideal genetic conditions are nuisances such as missing teeth, dental malocclusion, near-sightedness, and deviated nasal septum.

But, as we've seen, some genetic conditions are severe, and to achondroplasia, hemophilia, albinism, sickle-cell anemia, and phenylketonuria we can add schizophrenia, manic-depressive syndrome, early-onset diabetes, hereditary deafness, cystic fibrosis, Tay-Sachs disease, and literally thousands of other known genetic disorders. In spite of such devastating potential, however, you should remember that mutation is one of the reasons you are not an amoeba—or, for that matter, a random collection of carbon dioxide, hydrogen, and mud.

The Balance Between Mutation and Selection. We've learned that natural selection can cause the frequency of a beneficial mutation to increase in a population. But we've also learned that this phenomenon is extremely rare. After all, most mutations can't be expected to make a gene work better than it did before. The great majority will make the gene work less well or not at all. It's as if you raised the hood on your Mercedes and let your neighbor's kid randomly bang the internal workings with a hammer. He may make precisely the adjustment needed to make the car run better; all in all, though, you may not want to take the chance.

It is important to realize that, genetically, a mutation that proves lethal at the embryonic stage will have about the same effect on its bearer as a mutation that allows him to be born but kills him before he reproduces, or one that renders him sterile. That person's genes are not passed along; they die with him.

So although lethal alleles are constantly fed into the gene pool by mutation, they remain rare because they are not passed along. However, if the mutant allele is only *partially* limiting in its effect, and the afflicted individuals reproduce, but at a reduced level, then the mutant form may become much more common. From the known frequencies of recessive genetic diseases, it can be calculated that the average person carries about seven recessive alleles for serious genetic diseases.

The Genetic Future of Humans

This brings us to a philosophical and moral question about genetic variation in future human populations. The question inevitably arises: if better medical and social care saves the lives of persons with adverse genetic conditions, thus allowing them to reproduce, what is to become of us?

It's not hard to find examples that illustrate the problem. One genetic condition, *pyloric stenosis*, an abnormal overgrowth of a stomach valve muscle, was once invariably fatal in infancy. Since the 1920s a simple surgical procedure has saved the lives of nearly all affected infants in developed countries (Figure 18.5). But about half of the offspring of the saved people are also affected, and they also need surgery. And since there are just as many new mutations as ever, the condition constantly appears anew, so the genes that cause it have actually increased in frequency. Where will our species be in 10,000 years?

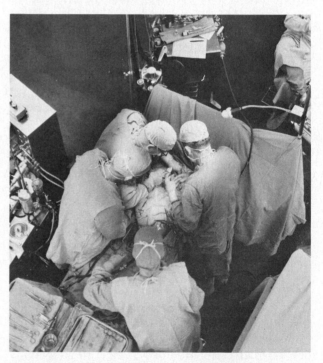

18.5

Modern medicine, particularly as applied to the correction of genetic abnormalities, has a definite effect on the frequency of aberrant alleles in the human gene pool. Under less sophisticated conditions, such alleles are controlled by natural selection—afflicted individuals simply would not reproduce. Yet no one in modern society is prepared to seriously suggest this alternative to corrective surgery.

What has happened, in effect, is that a *severe* genetic condition for "certain death in infancy by intestinal obstruction" has been transformed to a relatively *mild* genetic condition for "simple abdominal surgery needed in infancy." Suppose that the remaining risk of the condition, including possible delayed diagnosis and surgical mishap, are such that now about one affected infant in 20 fails to survive. The mutant genes for the condition will continue to increase until, many millenia from now, there will be exactly 20 times as many affected individuals as there were before the operation was developed. In the meantime, many lives will have been saved, and many new people—with slightly aberrant genotypes—will have joined the human population. Is that good or bad?

This sort of thing has already happened repeatedly in a variety of cultures. For example, in primitive hunting and gathering tribes, *myopia* (nearsightedness) must be a nearly lethal condition. Presumably, nearsighted aborigines can't even find roots and berries efficiently, let alone a zebra. But long before the invention of corrective lenses, the stable social conditions that came with villages and agriculture allowed myopics to survive. In some cases they may have even benefited. For example, male myopics would have been of no value in hunting or in war, and might have stayed safely home to make tools, weave baskets, tell stories, and help the women around the hut. In any case, myopia is much more common among people with a long history of agriculture, writing, and urban civilization than among groups that have more recently given up nomadism or the hunting-gathering life. American Indians and American blacks are blessed with much better visual acuity, on the average, than are Americans of European or Oriental ancestry.

POLYGENIC INHERITANCE AND NATURAL SELECTION

The stories of the Manx cats on imaginary islands and peppered moths in polluted woodlands are instructive, but they can also be misleading. To be sure, evolution does proceed sometimes by the rapid sweep of a dramatically advantageous allele through a population. But most of the genetic differences between individuals in a population are not caused by a few genes with great effects, but by numerous genes with small, individual effects. A trait controlled by more than one gene is said to be under the influence of **polygenic inheritance** (see Chapter 13). For example, many genes may influence a simple trait such as height. This is why people don't come in only two sizes, tall and short (*dimorphic*), or several sizes (*polymorphic*). Instead height varies along a continuum, producing a gradation. Many other traits—such as weight, blood pressure, length of limbs, skin color, and swiftness of foot—are also largely controlled by the cumulative action of many different gene loci, each gene with a vanishingly small effect. The cumulative effect of polygenic inheritance on the phenotypic variation in a population is enormous, and it is on this sort of variation that natural selection usually works. The individual gene obediently follow Mendel's rules, but there are so many effects of gene interaction and other complications that the response of a population to natural selection is not simply one of allele increase and replacement. Let's take a look at how natural selection works with such continuous and graded traits.

Three Patterns of Natural Selection

To approach this problem, we should first be aware that most individuals will be about average for most traits. Thus, for any given measurement, there will be relatively few individuals with extremely high or low values. If we group all of the individuals in a population according to a single trait, when placed on a graph, they will almost always form a bell-shaped curve—the statistician's **normal distribution** (Figure 18.6). In considering the effects of natural selection, the question is, how do the individuals in the middle of the distribution thrive compared with those on either extreme? Depending on how they fare, we can find three trends: *directional selection*, *stabilizing selection*, and *disruptive selection*.

Directional Selection. Directional selection favors one extreme of the phenotypic range—one end of the curve. This is the kind of selection practiced by dairy breeders who want only the offspring of the cows that give the most milk. In nature, directional selection may be a response to a change in the environment that begins to favor individuals at one extreme. For example, a small population may find itself in an unfamiliar territory, a new place offering new challenges. Or the species may suddenly lose a competitor and have new food sources open to it. In such cases, the formerly aberrant individuals at one tail of a curve may be better adapted to the new conditions than are those at the center of the curve. Their pre-

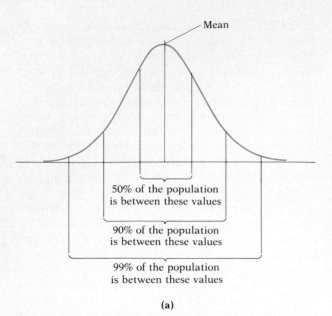

Mean

50% of the population
is between these values

90% of the population
is between these values

99% of the population
is between these values

(a)

(b)

18.6

Normal distributions, when translated into graphs, produce bell-shaped curves **(a)**. We find such distributions common in polygenic traits such as height and coloration. **(b)** The World War I soldiers are arranged in rows according to height. Although the curve formed is not perfectly symmetrical, there is an apparent cluster about the *mean*, with rapidly tapering *tails*. If we understand the genetics of body height, we can predict that a much larger number would form a more symmetrical, bell-shaped curve.

viously unfavored traits may then become the new optimum. Subsequent evolution can be rapid, as the population quickly adapts to its new environmental demands. Giraffes present a classic case of directional selection, as shown in Figure 18.7.

Stabilizing Selection. Stabilizing selection usually is associated with a population that has become well adapted to its particular surroundings. These surroundings usually are rather stable. Any genetic change in the population, therefore, is likely to be harmful. Although genetic variability still exists, selection tends to favor the mean, or average, individual. Actually, most populations are well adapted to their environments most of the time, so stabilizing selection is the most common kind of natural selection.

Consider the giraffe, for instance. As far as necks and legs go, giraffes are now well adapted to their environment, and are no longer subject to directional selection. And they haven't, in fact, changed much at all in 20 million years (Figure 18.8).

Perhaps the best-studied example of selection for an intermediate condition is that of birth weight in human babies. The data are readily available from hospital obstetric wards. If we plot survival rate against birth weight, we find that abnormally small babies have relatively low rates of survival, a fact that is not too surprising. But abnormally large babies also have lower survival rates (Figure 18.9). The highest survival rate is for babies around 3.4 kg (7.4 lb). In this case, the *optimal* birth weight (as determined by survival rate) is almost exactly the *average* birth weight. Selection works against genes for both high and low birth weight. In essence, the average tends to be the best, and "survival of the fittest" becomes "survival of the most mediocre."

Disruptive Selection. In **disruptive selection,** the direction of selection may shift back and forth, or cycle, in the environment. As the environment changes, what was formerly the optimal phenotype now feels the force of selection as a new optimal type is favored. In one dusty year, say, alleles for many nose hairs may have a selective advantage over alleles for few nose hairs, but in the next damp year the direction of selection may be reversed. In effect, the gene pool attempts to "track" the shifting and unpredictable environment. This sort of disruptive selection is believed to be an important cause of genetic variability in populations.

Disruptive selection may also produce *bimodal* (or two-humped) distribution curves for certain

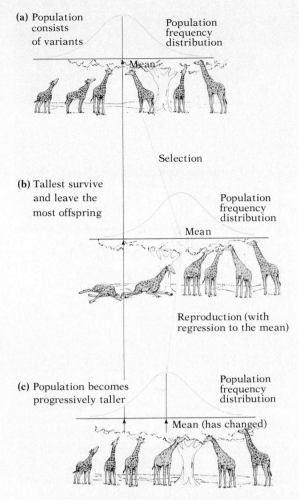

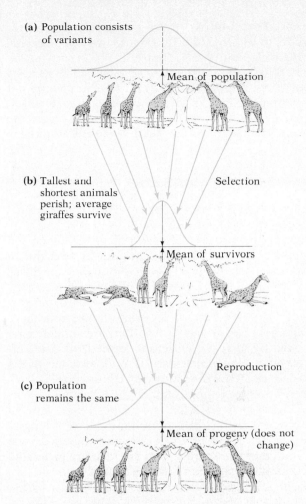

18.7

Directional selection favors phenotypes at one extreme of the distribution. In this example we consider the *past* evolution of the giraffe, an animal that browses on tree leaves. Along with each drawing is a population frequency distribution, which characterizes the mean and spread of the population with respect to an important giraffe characteristic, height. **(a)** Among the antelopelike ancestors of the giraffe, height is variable, as is any other characteristic (bell-shaped distribution). **(b)** The tallest individuals with the longest necks are best able to reach the foliage of trees on the African veldt; these individuals survive or reproduce more offspring, or both, than shorter animals. The average height of the surviving/reproducing individuals is greater than that of the population as a whole, as can be seen in the frequency distribution. **(c)** The offspring of the survivors tend to resemble their successful parents, although there is some regression to the mean. The average height increases over the course of one generation (exaggerated here). Over many generations, giraffes become taller and taller. (And so, incidentally, do the trees, as only the tallest trees escape defoliation by giraffes.)

18.8

Stabilizing selection. Phenotypes are usually already well adapted to the needs of the organism and are not under directional selection. **(a)** In this scheme, we assume that the giraffe population is already at its optimal tallness—on the average. But there is still some variation, with some giraffes being too short to browse well, and some being too tall for their own good. (The tallest giraffes may have trouble drinking efficiently, or perhaps may be too tall for the trees, or may be subject to high blood pressure or enormous sore throats.) **(b)** The most successful giraffes are no longer the tallest individuals, but the most average ones, and these leave the most offspring. **(c)** The population mean is not expected to show any further change under these conditions. Because of genetic recombination, the distribution (spread) of phenotypes also remains the same from generation to generation *(curves a and c)*.

traits. For example, it may be advantageous for males to be large and females to be small, as is the case in elephant seals (Figure 18.10). In such a case, individuals of intermediate sizes would be weeded out of the population. That is, selection would not favor very small males and very large females. When bimodality results from differences in the sexes, the condition is called **sexual dimorphism.**

Punctuated Equilibrium

It would seem, from what we know of directional selection, that evolution would generally be a slow and gradual process. However, Niles Eldredge and Stephen Jay Gould at the American Museum of Natural History have pointed out that the fossil record does not support this position. In fact, they say that just the opposite is true—that organisms seem to remain about the same for thousands or even millions of years, and then are suddenly replaced by a clearly different form. Thus, they argue, evolution proceeds not gradually, but in fits and starts. This theory is called **punctuated equilibrium.** Rapid and drastic changes supposedly occur when a population establishes a new kind of ecological niche. Then nothing happens as long as the environment remains the same. Not everyone is convinced, however, and the idea has generated a great deal of argument in scientific circles.

18.10

Plotting the range of body weights for male and female elephant seals produces a decidedly bimodal curve. In these mammals, natural selection apparently favors large males and comparatively small females, an example of disruptive selection at work.

Genetic Drift, Population Bottlenecks, and the Founder Effect

Genetic drift refers to *random* changes in gene frequency, when certain genes accumulate by chance—not because of the effects of selection. The phenomenon is seen most easily in small populations. For example, should some catastrophe, such as a flood or a plague, suddenly wipe out most of a population, the survivors would then begin to reproduce. However, the frequency of alleles in this small population might be different from that of the former, larger group. Thus, the gene frequency in the renewed population would depend on just which harmful recessive genes happen to have been carried by the few survivors (remember, we all carry our share). In the jargon of genetics, the population would have gone through a **bottleneck.** Thus, the harmful alleles, which were once rare, may now be not so rare. Similarly, if one or a few individuals stray out of their normal habitat and establish a successful colony in a new place, any rare genes they happen to carry would become common among their descendants. This special kind of bottleneck is referred to as the **founder effect.**

There are many examples of genetic bottlenecks and founder effects in human history. The Afrikaaners of South Africa are all descended from some thirty 17th-century families (Figure 18.11). (Remember, all humans carry their share of harmful, recessive genes, but they are very rare, and so they are seldom expressed in homozygotes.) The

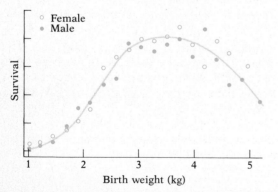

18.9

Plotting the survival rate of babies of different birth weight clearly indicates that there is an optimal weight of about 2.7 to 3.8 kg (6 to 8 lbs). Of course, babies making up the left side of the curve represent premature births, where developmental deficiencies are an important factor. On the other hand, a baby in the 5-kg (11-lb) range might well experience birth difficulties, which could also contribute to a lower survival rate.

18.11

Afrikaaners, the hardy decendants of 30 original European families that colonized South Africa, represent a population that has experienced a genetic bottleneck. As chance would have it, the original colonists carried a larger-than-usual number of certain abnormal recessive alleles. Today the frequency of the conditions these alleles produce is greater than that found in the regions from which the colonists came.

Afrikaaners' genes, having gone through a bottleneck of only 30 families, cause present-day Afrikaaners to suffer from a unique set of recurrent, recessive genetic diseases that are seldom seen in other populations. Among these is a version of **porphyria,** a metabolic disease that results in liver damage and bright red urine. Conversely, Afrikaaners are almost completely free of other recessive genetic diseases. The 30 families obviously

did not carry those genes to Africa. Similarly, Jews of Eastern European ancestry harbor a different but equally distinctive array of recessive genetic diseases, one of which is the tragic Tay-Sachs disease—an enzyme deficiency that leads to blindness, mental deterioration, and death in infants. These high gene frequencies can be taken as circumstantial evidence for one or more population bottlenecks in the history of this group.

Evolution Without Natural Selection?

We've built a strong case for natural selection as *the* molding force of evolution, and most biologists would agree with this position. We have seen, however, that evolutionary change can occur in the absence of selection, as in the Afrikaaners and in the Eastern European Jews. In these cases, genetic change exists that is clearly nonadaptive. Other genetic changes may be neither harmful nor beneficial, but completely neutral with regard to natural selection. The question of just how significant nonselective evolution is has led to raging arguments.

Neutralists Versus Selectionists. In recent years, there has been some controversy over to what degree natural variation is due to **neutral mutations** and **random drift. Neutralists** say that much variation on the molecular level is simply incidental and nonadaptive. For example, there are frequently several slightly different forms of any enzyme in a population. These enormous molecules may differ from each other by only one or two amino acids. Neutralists hold that most of this kind of variation has no effect on the function of the enzyme. They believe that the responsible alleles are equivalent and appear by chance mutation, and that the allele frequencies ''drift'' meaninglessly. **Selectionists,** on the other hand, contend that virtually all variation is caused by natural selection and has some adaptive basis, even if we don't happen to know what it is.

Summary

Gene Change under Natural Selection

The gene pool of a population contains all the genetic information of that population. Gene frequencies can be changed by natural selection, mutation, and genetic drift.

Natural selection can work several ways. Lethal alleles may kill off certain individuals, so the alleles are removed from the gene pool. In general, however, the rate of change in gene frequency is proportional to the amount of selection against some genotype. Such changes may take from a few generations to several hundred to complete. In some cases, such as that of the peppered moth, changes in gene frequency reflect the survival advantage a particular trait bestows.

Mutation: The Raw Material of Evolution

Mutations provide a constant flow of new genetic information into a species. Most mutations that are transmitted from generation to generation occur as recessive traits in nearly every individual. Beneficial or neutral mutations are usually passed on, while harmful ones are likely to be transmitted only if their effects are minor. However, in the case of many hereditary diseases, the disorder can be severe and still be passed on to future generations. For any mutant form—beneficial, neutral, or harmful—to become more common, it must be reproduced in the descendants of a population.

Polygenic Inheritance and Natural Selection

Most differences among individuals in populations are caused by the influence of polygenic inheritance, in which a trait is controlled by more than one gene. Thus, most of the time, natural selection is at work on highly variable phenotypes.

Usually, the appearance of phenotypes for any given trait in a population will follow a normal distribution curve. Directional selection favors one extreme of the phenotypic range. It may be a response to changes in environment that favors individuals in the extreme range. Stabilizing selection usually applies to a population that has become well adapted to relatively stable surroundings. Because stabilizing selection usually favors the average individual, any genetic change is likely to be harmful to the group. In disruptive selection, the direction of selection shifts in response to changing pressures on the population, often from cyclic changes in the environment. This type of selection may produce bimodal (or two-humped) distribution curves for traits. Sexual dimorphism occurs when bimodality is the result of differences in the sexes.

The theory of punctuated equilibrium states that organisms remain the same for long periods and then are suddenly replaced by a clearly different form. Evolution thus supposedly proceeds in fits and starts, as when an organism invades a previously empty ecological niche. This theory is controversial.

Genetic drift refers to random, nonselective changes in gene frequencies brought about by chance when a small population is suddenly reduced (bottleneck effect), or specifically when a group of individuals becomes separated from the main population (founder effect).

Evolutionary change can occur in the absence of selection, but some controversy exists regarding to what degree natural variation is due to neutral mutations and random drift. Neutralists say that many variations on the molecular level are simply incidental and nonadaptive. Selectionists believe that nearly all variations are caused by natural selection and have some adaptive basis.

Key Terms

gene pool	disruptive selection	porphyria
achondroplasia	sexual dimorphism	neutral mutations
polygenic inheritance	punctuated equilibrium	random drift
normal distribution	genetic drift	neutralists
directional selection	bottleneck	selectionists
stabilizing selection	founder effect	

Review Questions

1. Summarize the effects of selection in the Manx cat population. (pp. 242–243)

   a. At what period does selection have its most dramatic effect on the gene frequencies? Its slowest effect?

   b. Suggest a simple explanation for the change.

   c. Will the Manx gene eventually disappear?

2. The case of the peppered moth is often cited as an example of natural selection and evolution in action. What were Haldane's observations? His hypothesis? Explain how Kettlewell tested Haldane's hypothesis. (pp. 243–244)

3. What is the rate of mutation? Why is it that we do not see more evidence of genetic mutation in humans than we do? (p. 245)

4. In what ways do modern societies counter the usual effects of natural selection? Cite a specific example. How might this affect the frequency of harmful alleles? (pp. 246–247)

5. Using simple graphs, depict the effects of directional, stabilizing, and disruptive selection. Suggest environmental conditions that might favor each type. (pp. 247–250)

6. Describe genetic drift and cite two examples. How does genetic drift differ from natural selection? (pp. 250–251)

Evolution and the Origin of Species

19

One of the most interesting things about biology, and probably other sciences as well, is that although a great deal of attention is given to working out details, many of the larger, more basic questions remain unanswered. For example, some biologists may peer endlessly at the pattern of bristles on a fruit fly's back, while others stroke their chins and ask, *where do new species come from*? And if that question weren't basic enough, others point out that we still don't even know what a species *is*. No definition of the term is fully satisfactory to everyone. So let's look into some of these most fundamental questions. First, let's see how species arise (a process called **speciation**) and then let's look at some other aspects, including the problem of defining species.

It is important to realize that speciation is not the same as evolution, but that it is an important *result* of evolution. Keep in mind that speciation has occurred time after time in the past and is continuing today—just as natural selection continues to exist today.

NAMING NAMES

First, we should explain how species are named and some of the problems of naming. The science of naming new species is called **taxonomy.** The first modern taxonomist of note was a Swede by the name of Karl von Linne (1707–1778), or Linnaeus, as he preferred to call himself. Linnaeus took upon himself the incredible task of naming all the plant and animal species known. He also introduced the system of **binomial nomenclature**—the practice of giving species two Latin names.

You might expect that taxonomists would have named all the earth's species by now. But there are so many species on the earth that most of them, to this day, are undescribed and unnamed, and the taxonomists are still hard at work. There are estimated to be hundreds of thousands of unnamed mites; one of your authors discovered a new species of roundworm that lives only in the heads of woodpeckers.

When presented with a strange beetle or jungle flower, the taxonomist must first determine whether anyone else has already described and named it. This is no easy task, and taxonomists spend as much time wandering in the musty archives of libraries as they do tromping around exotic locales or hunched over their microscopes.

The second task of a taxonomist who has found a new species is to describe it. The description includes the physical appearance, the internal anatomy, the place where the organism was found, and as much about its range, ecology, behavior, and physiology as can be managed.

19.1

Today's humans all fall within a single genus and species, *Homo sapiens*. We share our genus with two extinct species—*Homo habilis* and *Homo erectus*. We share many traits with these two, but the differences are sufficient to warrant individual species designations.

Homo erectus

Homo habilis

Homo sapiens neanderthalensis

The next problem is to make up a name, a *scientific* name. This is a very formal procedure, involving international commissions whose job it is to keep track of all such names and to ensure that all of the rules of nomenclature are followed. These rules are complex and detailed. The first of such rules is that each species receives two names: a *generic name* and a *specific name*. The generic name is the name of the **genus,** or group of closely related and ecologically similar species; and the specific name identifies the **species** within the genus. Long-standing tradition and international regulations state that (1) both names must be in Latin or at least latinized; (2) both are to be written in italics; and (3) the first (generic) name is to be capitalized, while the second (specific) name is never capitalized. Once assigned, this combination of names may never be used again. Also, the genus name is generally a noun, while the specific name should be an adjective—these rules are bent a little to allow the latinized adjectival version of the name of a friend, colleague, or authority figure (the rules prohibit anyone naming a species after himself or herself). Thus do taxonomists seek to impose order on a disorderly world.

As an example, we humans are called *Homo sapiens*. *Homo* is our generic name, and *sapiens* is our specific name. *Homo* means "man," while *sapiens* means "wise" or "discerning." (Make of this what you will.) Other species in the genus are *Homo*

habilis (*habilis* means "able to do or make") and *Homo erectus* ("upright"), both extinct (Figure 19.1).

When necessary, the binomal nomenclature is extended to a third Latin term, the **subspecies,** or variety. Thus contemporary humans are sometimes referred to as *Homo sapiens sapiens*, to distinguish us from our recently departed cousins, *Homo sapiens neandertalensis*. And one race of apes is called *Gorilla gorilla gorilla*. (Using the same name for genus and species is acceptable in zoology, but not in botany. A botanist friend was once heard to ask disparagingly, "Really, now, what kind of information is conveyed by a name like *Gorilla gorilla gorilla*?" To which a zoologist present muttered "all you need to know.")

BUT WHAT DO YOU MEAN BY "SPECIES"?

You can rattle a graduate student preparing for a doctoral examination in biology by asking, "Quick, what is a species?" This may be surprising because the question seems simple enough at first. But the simplicity is deceiving.

There usually isn't much difficulty in telling one species from another when you are out in the field—on a safari, for instance. A giraffe is quite

The organisms seen here are readily identifiable as different species. This is true of most species within a specific locality where each species type is represented by a local population of interbreeding individuals. The problem of distinguishing among species gets more difficult when totally separated populations of similar types are compared.

distinguishable from a lion. A tree fern clearly belongs to one species, and an African violet clearly belongs to a different species. For field work, then, a simple definition of species is adequate—*a species is a distinct and recognizable group of organisms* (Figure 19.2). This definition may not be very intellectually satisfying, but in truth it is usually adequate—except for evolutionary and biogeographic studies of sexually reproducing populations. For those, a more exacting definition will be needed.

Perhaps *interbreeding* is the critical criterion. Two groups clearly belong to the same species if they interbreed and produce viable, healthy offspring on a regular basis. But what about groups that are *capable* of interbreeding, but are simply separated by geography? Now the issue becomes sticky. Animals that interbreed successfully when confined together in zoos (Figure 19.3) may ignore one another in their own less stressful (and, perhaps, less boring) natural environments. Plants that set seed when pollinated by hand may depend on their own insect pollinators in the wild, and so wouldn't necessarily cross-fertilize without our help. So the interbreeding criterion is generally useful, but far from absolute. It doesn't help at all, for instance, in the task of identifying species in asexual organisms. The criterion of interbreeding isn't much more help in defining species among plants, where hybridization between species is a common event.

One of the basic problems of defining the word

Some crossing of species lines can occur, as we see in this unusual member of the cat family, when animals are in captivity. This is a *tiglon*, produced in a cross between a male tiger and a female lion. This hybrid is never seen in the wild, since African lions and Siberian tigers would be unlikely to meet. If they did, their relationship would be unpredictable and, most likely, would not involve mating. Such hybrids are probably sterile. (© Jungle Larry's Safari Land, Inc.)

species is determining whether two seemingly geographically isolated groups are different populations of a single species, or whether they are two separate species (Figure 19.4).

Another question is, when (in evolutionary time) do two diverging groups start to qualify as separate species? It obviously can't happen suddenly, since the process is continuous. However, the human mind seems to love categories and hates having to make difficult decisions. So, perhaps the best working definition, at least for the animal species, is one by the zoologist Ernst Mayr:

> "A *Species* is a group of actually or potentially interbreeding natural populations that is reproductively isolated from other such groups."

Reproductive isolation means that two populations are unable to interbreed successfully. Organisms can be reproductively isolated in a number of ways. If they live on separate continents, they are not likely to interbreed. If they can reach each other, they may not recognize each other as being sexually attractive. If they should attempt to mate anyway, their reproductive organs may not be compatible so that copulation can occur. And, even if copulation should occur, the chromosomes may be different in number or kind, resulting in a misalignment at meiosis resulting in infertility.

THE MECHANISMS OF SPECIATION

There has been a great deal of interest in recent decades over just how new species are formed. The arguments have been rather vigorous and have followed some rather distinct trends. Let's examine a few of the findings now, beginning with the influence of geography.

ESSAY 19.1
CONTINENTS ADRIFT

In 1912, Alfred Wegener published a paper that was triggered by the common observation of the good fit between South America's east coast and Africa's west. Could these great continents ever have been joined? Wagner coordinated this jigsaw-puzzle analysis with other geological and climatological data, and proposed the theory of **continental drift.** He suggested that about 200 million years ago, all of the earth's continents were joined together into one enormous land mass, which he called Pangaea. In the ensuing millennia, according to Wegener's idea, Pangaea broke apart and the fragments began to drift northward (by today's compass orientation), to their present location.

Wegener's idea received rough treatment in his lifetime. His geologist contemporaries attacked his naiveté as well as his supporting data, and his theory was neglected until about 1960. At about that time, a new generation of geologists revived the idea and subjec-

ted it to new scrutiny based on recent findings. These findings buttressed Wegener's old notion and breathed new life into it.

The most useful data have been based on magnetism in ancient lava flows. When a lava flow cools, metallic elements in the lava are oriented in a way that provides a permanent fossil of the earth's magnetic field at the time, recording for future geologists both its north-south orientation and its latitude. From such maps it is possible to determine the ancient posi-

tions of today's continents. We now believe that not only has continental drift occurred, as Wegener hypothesized, but that it continues to occur today.

Geologists have long maintained that the earth's surface is a restless crust, constantly changing, sinking and rising because of incredible, unrelenting forces beneath it. These constant changes are now known to involve large, distinct segments of the crust known as *plates.* At certain edges of these masses, immense ridges

END OF
MESOZOIC ERA

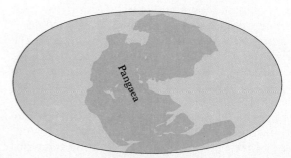

Lower Triassic period
225 million years ago

Ranges and Clines

The geographic area over which a population may be found is called its **range.** A range may be limited and compact, as in a vacant lot for field mice or a pond for fish; or it may be quite extensive, covering entire continents. We see large ranges in some bird populations. The larger ranges, of course, may encompass many different kinds of habitats, and in such cases it is possible to see the effects of natural selection as the population changes from one kind of place to another—for example, from cooler northern climates to warmer southern ones.

Natural selection will have predictable effects where such climatic differences exist across a range. For example, among the warm-blooded species, those in cooler areas tend to be larger (resulting in relatively less surface area compared to mass, ensuring a reduction in the rate of heat loss)

than those in warmer areas. They can also have shorter extremities, since longer extremities dissipate body heat (Figure 19.5).

The results of such differential selection *within* a species will depend ultimately upon the amount of *gene flow* throughout the range. **Gene flow** occurs when an organism's genes move where they are likely to be mingled with allele frequencies different from those at the point of origin. That is, the genes move—either as the organism itself moves, or as its pollen, gametes, or seeds disperse.

If there is a great deal of gene flow throughout the species range, the species is likely to have a uniform appearance. But when species do not tend to mate freely across a range, subpopulations may become closely adapted to their own habitat. In this case, two possibilities may arise. If the environment is "patchy," varying sharply from one area to the next, polymorphism may result as organisms tend to adapt to the particular patch they

---

are being thrust up, while other edges sink lower. Where plates are heaved together, the buckling at the edges has produced vast mountain ranges. When such ridges appear in the ocean floor, water is displaced and the oceans expand. (Astoundingly precise satellite studies reveal that the Atlantic Ocean is 5 cm wider each year.)

In addition to its fascinating geological implications, an understanding of continental drift (or **plate tectonics**) is vital to the study of the distribution of life on the

planet today. It helps to explain the presence of fossil tropical species in Antarctica, for example, and the unusual animal life in Australia and South America.

As the composite maps indicate, the disruption of Pangaea began some 230 million years ago, in the Paleozoic era. By the Mesozoic era, the Eurasian land mass (called Laurasia) had moved away to form the northernmost continent. Gondwanaland, the mass that included India and the southern continents, had just begun to divide.

Finally, during the late Mesozoic era, after South America and Africa were well divided, what was to be the last continental separation began, with Australia and Antarctica drifting apart. Both the North and South Atlantic Oceans would continue to widen considerably up to the Cenozoic era, a trend that is continuing today. So we see that although the bumper sticker "Reunite Gondwanaland" has a third-world and trendy ring to it, it's an unlikely proposition. ●

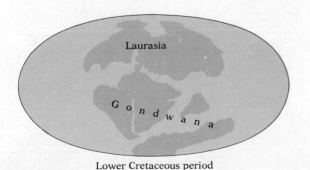

Lower Cretaceous period
90 million years ago

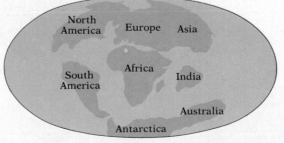

Paleocene epoch 65 million years ago

call home. If the habitat changes gradually from one type to the next, the species may also form **clines,** or graded changes, across its range.

Should a mountain range arise or a new river form, subgroups may become isolated, resulting in a halt in gene flow across the barrier. Such isolated groups, subjected to different selective factors, are commonly the raw material of speciation. Eventually, such **geographic isolation** could lead to physiological or behavioral reproductive changes, as the isolated organisms became more and more different. Ultimately, should the opportunity even arise, interbreeding becomes impossible. Thus we have the formation of two species where before there was one (Figure 19.6).

Allopatry and Speciation

The formation of new species through the geographic isolation of populations that were once continuous is known as **allopatric speciation.** Aside from the formation of such local barriers as rivers or mountains, large-scale geological changes can divide a previously continuous range. The most fundamental changes of the planet's surfaces occurred some 230 million years ago, when the worldwide process of *continental drift* began; and

again about 65 million years ago, when Africa and South America parted company. The uniqueness of species communities in the world's present-day continents, particularly those of Australia and South America, has been the result of millions of years of allopatric speciation made possible by continental drift (Essay 19.1).

There are other ways that populations of a species might become geographically isolated. One possibility is illustrated by a seed, an inseminated female, or a group of individuals finding themselves—by some happy accident—in a new, yet hospitable, place. Ocean islands, for instance, are occasionally populated by the descendants of unwilling, drenched, and thoroughly disgusted passengers on driftwood logs. Birds and flying insects may be blown to some island by particularly violent storms. Migrating birds may make an error in navigation.

The Galapagos Islands and Darwin's Finches. The finches of the Galapagos islands (Figure 19.7) provide the best known example of allopatric speciation (involving separated populations). Compared to the giant tortoises, strange flightless cormorants, and impish sea iguanas living there, the finches are not particularly interesting—that is, until the saga of their evolution is revealed.

19.4

The red-shafted flicker, *Colaptes cafer*, of the western United States and the yellow-shafted flicker, *Colaptes auratus*, of the midwest and east, are considered two distinct species. For the most part they are geographically isolated, but their ranges come together in several states. Where they meet, they may mate. So are they of different species?

◼ Red-shafted flicker
◻ Yellow-shafted flicker
◼ Hybrid flicker

19.5

As a rule, the length of extremities (such as limbs and ears) in related animals varies with the temperature of a range, as seen in these two species of foxes. The arctic fox **(a)** has short extremities, permitting exposure of minimal body surface to cold temperatures. The kit fox **(b),** who has the opposite need (to cool its body in its warm environment) has longer extremities.

The principle is referred to as *Allen's rule*. Another rule, called *Bergmann's rule*, is based on the tendency of organisms living in colder areas to be larger than their counterparts in sunnier climates. This is also a mechanism to conserve heat. House sparrows, introduced into the U.S. in recent centuries, have already established clines of body size.

19.6

Geographical isolation is an important aspect of speciation. The Grand Canyon, with the Colorado River at its floor, effectively isolates many populations. The ancestors of the Abert squirrel **(a)** and the Kaibab squir-

rel **(b)** are believed to have been one species prior to the canyon's formation. Once isolated, the populations followed their own evolutionary paths and today are normally unable to interbreed.

19.7

Darwin's finches. The darker birds on the ground and standing on the low cactus are ground finches (9–14); those in the tree are tree finches (1–8). Are there similarities within each group? Can you account for this? What conclusions can you draw about the diets of different species by looking at the size and shape of their bills? The different species presumably arose from a single stock that gradually spread across the Galapagos islands. The finches have a strong attachment for their home areas and are reluctant to fly across water. Once a group reached an island, it was likely to remain there and be isolated, so it was left to follow its own evolutionary pathway. Eventually, groups differed so much that they could not interbreed.

The tree finches are: 1, *Camarhynchus pallidus* (the woodpecker finch); 2, *C. heliobates*; 3, *C. psittacula*; 4, *C. pauper*; 5, *C. parvulus*; 6, *C. crassirostris*; 7, *Certhidea olivacea* (the warblerlike finch); and 8, *Pinaroloxias inornata* (the Cocos Island finch). The ground finches are: 9, *Geospiza magnirostris*; 10, *G. fortis*; 11, *G. fuliginosa*; 12, *G. difficilis*; 13, *G. conirostris*; and 14, *G. scandens*.

All of the finches, also called Darwin's finches, are 10 to 20 cm long, and both sexes are drab-colored browns and grays. Six are ground species, feeding upon different, appropriately sized seeds or cactus, and eight are tree finches. In such species, the bill has become modified for a specific diet. (In one case, the behavior, rather than the bill, has become modified. The woodpecker finch lacks the long, piercing tongue of the woodpecker, so it uses long cactus spines to pry insect grubs out of cracks and crevices in the trees.)

On the *Beagle's* historic visit to the Galapagos islands, Darwin collected everything he could find or catch, including these ordinary little brown finches. He took no special interest in them. But a London bird taxonomist examined the specimens and noted that the inhabitants of different islands—though they were very similar to one another—were clearly different species. Ordinarily, birds living in one locale tend to be very different from one another. These birds were all clearly finches, and, indeed, they were South American finches. But Darwin had seen many of them doing things that finches don't ordinarily do.

Darwin concluded (and his conclusions are supported by ensuing years of careful research by others) that the different species of birds were all descended from the same stock (Figure 19.8). Long ago (about 10,000 years ago, by current estimates) the then-newly formed volcanic islands were colonized by South American finches that were probably blown out to sea by a storm. Apparently, conditions on the island were favorable and the "castaways" flourished. Their descendants eventually populated all the islands by their occasional island-hopping. However, the island hopping was rare enough to ensure the virtual isolation of each group. What followed then is referred to as **adaptive radiation.**

The little birds had the islands to themselves, as far as they were concerned. They found food of all sorts everywhere. They were already well adapted for foraging for small seeds on the ground, but now there were other plentiful, unutilized food resources—food not ordinarily eaten by finches.

Soon enough, the expanding populations were demolishing the supply of available small seeds. Thus, natural selection began to favor birds that could also cope with larger seeds, as well as other types of food. In time, the birds' bill sizes began to change as each population began to adjust itself more closely to the food found on its island. Not only were bill sizes changing, but so were gene frequencies. Natural selection (undoubtedly influenced by genetic drift and the founder effect) was having its way. Eventually the isolated birds of the different islands differed genetically to the extent

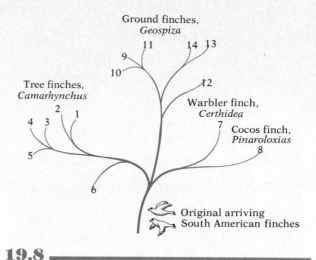

19.8

Studies of Galapagos finches have led biologists to suggest a phylogenetic scheme that indicates the origins and relatedness of four groups of these birds. (See also Figure 19.7).

that any island hoppers would find themselves to be reproductively incompatible with the residents of other islands. In this way, new species were formed.

Even if some species invaded an island and found a genetically incompatible species already there, they might be able to coexist with the residents if the two groups tended to utilize different resources. This, of course, would mean the pressure for further change was on. With two species of finches trying to survive on one small island, natural selection would favor the individuals in *each* population that were as different as possible from those in the other population (and so would be less affected by competition from them). There would be a tendency toward further separation and divergence of the two groups as each became a specialist in utilizing the environment in a particular way. The tendency for differences in competing species to become exaggerated as each specializes is called **character displacement.**

After thousands of years of occupying these dismal islands and separating, changing, specializing, and rejoining, the different populations are now totally unable to interbreed. Today, several of the species exist side-by-side on every island. Each species utilizes the resources of the island in its own unique manner, in some cases filling niches that are occupied by other kinds of birds on the mainland.

Darwin's finches are not an isolated example. Exactly the same kind of adaptive radiation is seen in the birds of another archipelago—the honeycreepers of Hawaii.

Sympatry and Speciation

While allopatric speciation—that is, the formation of new species in geographically isolated groups—is by far the most common route of speciation, it is not the only one. Speciation within a single habitat (**sympatric speciation**) can indeed occur. The best examples are found among plants.

Hybridization: Meiosis and the Sterile Hybrid. Plants, unlike most animals, regularly undergo sympatric speciation. Among the flowering plants in particular, there are many examples of new species arising by the hybridization of existing species. This may be surprising, since hybrids between animal species are usually infertile.

In the case of the mule, for example, we find a vigorous hybrid that is completely sterile. The reason is simple: a mule is a cross between a donkey and a horse; however, the chromosomes of a donkey and a horse are so different that they cannot pair in meiosis (see Chapter 10). As you know, this pairing up is essential for the proper alignment and separation of homologous chromosomes if normal gametes are to be produced.

Why don't plants suffer from this problem? Primarily because species with very different appearances sometimes may be genetically similar enough to allow the hybrids between them to undergo normal or nearly normal meiosis. Where such species overlap there may be extensive **hybrid swarms**—essentially, large hybrid populations. (Fertile hybrids, of course, stretch the traditional working definition of *species.*) Such hybridization between plant species is common and, surprisingly enough, it doesn't seem to result in the breakdown of either species or cause them to merge into a single species. This could be because hybrid swarms occasionally find their own niche to fill, becoming a new, distinct species.

Polyploidy: Autotetraploids and Allotetraploids. Another more dramatic way in which plant species can hybridize successfully involves **polyploidy,** where whole sets of chromosomes become doubled. This happens spontaneously from time to time in the mitotic divisions of a growing plant. The chromosomes double in preparation for cell division, but for some reason the cell fails to divide. Later, the cell will again double its chromosomes, as if nothing were unusual, and proceed with normal mitosis. Thus all of its progeny will have four complete sets of chromosomes. The abnormal cell is called a **tetraploid** cell, and its progeny may form tetraploid tissue and, even, tetraploid flowers.

When this happens in an ordinary diploid plant, the resulting plants or tissues are called **autotetraploids** ("self-tetraploid" or "self-four-genomes"). Meiosis in autotetraploid flowers is, once again, abnormal. The chromosomes will still try to pair two-by-two, but there are now four of each type of chromosome. So clumps of homologous chromosomes form and meiotic segregation becomes a real mess. Perhaps a few balanced seeds will be produced, but autotetraploids are usually infertile, and probably have an extremely limited role in evolution.

On the other hand, spontaneous tetraploidization in *hybrid* plants is different. You'll recall that the reason most hybrids fail in meiosis is that the chromosomes from the parental species fail to find partners to line up with at metaphase I. This is because the hybrid cell has two different haploid chromosome sets. But when spontaneous tetraploidization occurs, there will suddenly be two different complete diploid chromosome sets. Such a tetraploid is called an **allotetraploid** ("other-tetraploid"). When flowers form in the allotetraploid hybrid, there is no longer a compatibility problem in meiosis, since every chromosome now has a homologue and meiosis can proceed normally (Figure 19.9).

The allotetraploid plants are fertile only when crossed with themselves and with each other; if they are crossed with either parental species, with its haploid pollen and ovules, they produce only *triploid* seeds, which are infertile. This reproductive isolation means that the new allotetraploid plant constitutes, in fact, an "instant" species. The new species will soon fail, of course, unless it happens to fill a new niche or unless it can outcompete another plant species—perhaps one of its parents. This has been known to happen.

Polyploidy can happen repeatedly. Thus, we can have *hexaploids* (six genomes, or three doubled copies of three different parental genomes), *octaploids,* and so on. (The term *polyploid* covers any level of chromosome doubling higher than diploid.) Strange as it seems, polyploidy is common among many wild and domestic flowering plants. Wheat, for example, is actually an allohexaploid, a genetic combination of the chromosome complements of three entirely different Middle Eastern species of wild grasses. **Triticale** (Figure 19.10) is a human-engineered application of the tendency of wheat and rye grasses to form *allopolyploids*.

For reasons not fully understood, polyploid species often have much greater tolerance for harsh climatic conditions. In one study, for instance, only 26% of the plants sampled in lush tropical regions

19.9

Although a plant hybrid may readily be produced in nature, it is often sterile. Sterility arises when, during meiosis, unmatched chromosomes fail to find their homologues. Here, species A is successfully pollinated by species B, producing a hybrid. Since there is no match in the chromosome complement, the hybrid cannot carry out meiosis and is therefore sterile. However, should a spontaneous doubling of chromosomes occur, as it sometimes does, normal pairing-up and meiosis occurs and normal gametes are produced. Following self-fertilization, a new viable species is produced.

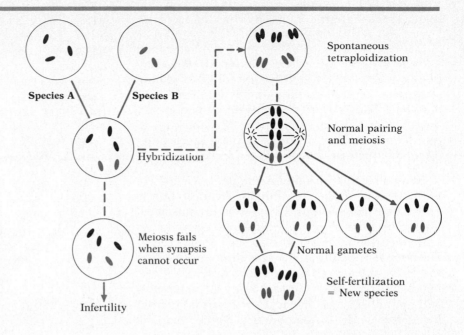

Species A   Species B

Hybridization

Spontaneous tetraploidization

Normal pairing and meiosis

Normal gametes

Self-fertilization = New species

Meiosis fails when synapsis cannot occur

Infertility

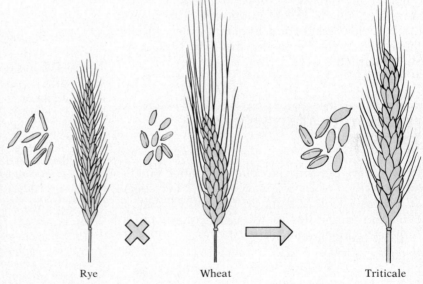

Rye   Wheat   Triticale

19.10

Triticale is a hybrid grain produced by crossing wheat and rye (the name is a combination of *Triticum* and *Secale*, the genus names of the two). Actually, the hybrid formed is sterile, because of the usual chromosome incompatibility. But agricultural scientists solve the problem by treating the hybrid with *colchicine*, a mitosis inhibitor that causes a doubling of chromosomes—synthetic tetraploidy. Following this treatment, the treated plant will carry out a normal meiosis and produce viable gametes and viable subsequent generations. Triticale combines the vigor of rye with the high-grain yield of wheat. Also, the genes of the rye add the amino acid lysine to the usual high quality of wheat protein, resulting in a more nutritious product.

were polyploids, while 86% of all the flowering plant species in the raw environs of northern Greenland were polyploid.

So hybridization followed by polyploidization creates instant, sympatric species of flowering plants, ready to be tested by the forces of natural selection. This versatility helps explain how flowering plants arose abruptly in evolution and how they quickly spread out over the landscape to create the incredible diversity of plant species that dominate our world.

Sympatric Speciation in Animals.   While there are polyploid species of animals, hybridization is not as likely in species that have sex chromosomes. This is because in polyploid meiotic cells, the Xs tend to pair with Xs and the Ys with Ys, instead of the normal XY pairing. The resulting gametes are therefore unbalanced for sex chromosomes. Polyploidy is frequently found among fish, reptiles, and amphibians; sex in these groups is influenced by factors such as temperature, rather than by chromosome ratios.

Evolutionary theorists argue over whether sympatric speciation could occur in animals in ways other than through polyploidy, but nowhere among the animals is the situation as clear-cut as in the polyploid plants and hybrid swarms. In fact, there is little solid evidence that sympatric speciation in animals ever occurs.

MAJOR EVOLUTIONARY TRENDS

How can we put the concept of speciation into the larger context of evolutionary history? Let's begin by taking a look at some of the major trends in evolution as revealed by the fossil record, and by comparing living animals.

Divergent Evolution

We used the term *adaptive radiation* to describe the manner in which speciation occurred in the Galapagos finches. The finches developed new ecological niches, and in the process of adapting to their niches, they became less similar to one another. Thus adaptive radiation is dependent upon *divergence* or **divergent evolution,** which simply means that newly emerging species tend to become increasingly different from each other over time (Figure 19.11).

19.11

Divergent evolution. The long-range outcome of divergence in evolutionary history can be visualized through the analogy of the phylogenetic tree. The outermost green twigs represent species that are alive today, while the branches from which the twigs originate are their last common ancestors—the ones that founded the different genera. Moving inward, we find older branches, which themselves have originated from previous divergences. All branches, with the exception of the green twigs, represent ancestors that no longer exist—both the ones that have speciated into more advanced forms and the dead-end species that have produced no living descendants. Such tree analogies are commonly used to represent specific evolutionary hypotheses about the origin of species and of higher taxonomic groups.

Such changes proceed more slowly under some conditions than others. If ecological demands in different areas are severe and narrow, evolution will proceed rather rapidly. Change may also be accelerated by competition. This can happen, for example, when one species forces another into a more restricted, narrower niche.

The idea of divergence has strong ecological overtones, since becoming different is often associated with finding some new way of utilizing the environmental resources—in Darwin's words, a new "place in the polity of nature." The opening of new niches is greatly encouraged by natural selection, since it relieves the unrelenting competition for resources. Such divergence has suggested a scheme called the *phylogenetic tree*.

Convergent Evolution

We may be struck with the tendency toward divergence in long-term evolution, but it is not the only possible trend. In some cases, species may grow more alike. This should not be unexpected in different species that are adapting to similar environments and establishing similar niches; that is, ways to exploit those environments. The process is called **convergent evolution.**

Darwin was impressed by the evidence of convergent evolution in his lengthy travels. He recorded in his journal that the South American mara or Patagonian hare, *Dolichotis patagonum*, was quite similar, in both appearance and ecological niche, to the European rabbit. Close examination of the mara revealed that it was not a rabbit at all, but a rodent. Thus, despite its resemblance to a rabbit, it is actually more closely related to the guinea pig (Figure 19.12).

Convergence is dramatically evident in comparisons between placental mammals and the distantly related marsupial (pouched) mammals of Australia. Marsupials and placental mammals have established very similar niches. Through a long period of isolation, selection, and adaptation, unrelated species have often taken on a striking resemblance to one another. In Australia we find the rabbit bandicoot, the marsupial mouse, the marsupial mole, the flying phalanger, and the banded anteater. All of these have a placental counterpart on other continents (Figure 19.13).

Coevolution

Quite often the direction of evolution in one species is strongly influenced by what is happening in the evolution of another species, particularly if either is dependent on the other. The most obvious examples of this sort of change are seen in predator-prey relationships. As natural selection improves the predator's skill, it also favors the de-velopment of behavior that will improve the prey's ability to escape. As the predator population gets better, so does the prey population. This two-way tracking by natural selection is called **coevolution.**

The great array of flowering plants on the earth has been so influenced by the coevolution of insect pollinators that today many flowering plant species are selectively pollinated by only one kind of insect. For example, yucca is entirely dependent on the yucca moth for pollination; the yucca moth, in turn, is entirely dependent on the yucca flower, where it lays its eggs and where its larvae grow on a diet of yucca seeds. The yucca moth goes to a considerable amount of trouble to ensure pollination, since only properly pollinated flowers will produce the seeds the moth larvae need.

As a remarkable example of herbivore-plant coevolution, consider the relationship between passion flower vines and a butterfly *(Heliconius),*

19.12

Convergent evolution. The mara (or Patagonian hare) is South America's "rabbit," although it is not a rabbit at all. The ecological niche it occupies is very similar to that of the rabbit, and behavioral and structural similarities have evolved as well.

whose caterpillars specialize in eating them (Figure 19.14). This plant has succeeded in manufacturing poisons that prevent most other insects from devouring its leaves and young shoots, but these butterflies have evolved the ability to detoxify the poisons. The butterfly lays bright yellow eggs on the young leaves, which act as a warning to other female butterflies that it would be wiser for them to find their own leaves. The other butterflies avoid laying eggs where there are already eggs, since this cuts down the competition their own larvae will face. Through natural selection, the plant has taken advantage of this behavior and now has perfected rather good mimic eggs, little round lumps of bright yellow tissue scattered randomly on the leaves and shoots. These also tend to persuade the butterfly to hunt elsewhere. Furthermore, the same vines have mimicked the shriveling of leaves that usually accompany larval infestations.

Homology and Analogy

One of the ways in which evolutionary origins can be traced is by comparing the physical structures of different species and noting their similarities. Thus, on close examination, the fin of a whale

19.13

The concept of convergent evolution is well supported by observations of Australian mammals. Although phylogenetically unrelated to their counterparts in other continents, they bear a striking resemblance to many. Some of these animals are marsupials—pouched mammals, whose young complete their development in the pouch. Notably absent in Australia is a marsupial bat—there's no such animal. The niche is filled by the giant placental type, clearly related to bats in other continents. Unlike other terrestrial mammals, bats are not easily isolated by water barriers, and apparently they made an island-hopping migration from Asia sometime in the past.

A marsupial cuscus *(left)* and a placental sloth *(above)*

Marsupial rabbit bandicoots *(left)* and a placental arctic hare *(above)*

turns out to be rather similar to the arm of a man or the wing of a bat (Figure 19.15). Additionally, the bones of the forelimbs of these disparate creatures form embryologically in similar ways. Therefore, the bones are said to be **homologous.** Since homologous structures are similar in appearance and embryology, they can be very useful in constructing family trees.

Similarity of general appearance can be deceiving, however. Can we consider the dorsal fin of a shark as being homologous with that of a whale? The superficial resemblances of fin structure and the similarities in how the fins are used by each animal are deceiving. They are *not* evolutionarily related. Such structures with similar functions but very different evolutionary histories are called **analogous.** They are not very useful in constructing phylogenetic trees.

We see, then, that although the notion of evolution is one of the most pervasive themes in biology, we are still far from solving some of the most fundamental questions. For example, we really haven't made much progress over the years in defining the term *species*. Also a virtual barrage of problems in phylogenetic organization exists even at the kingdom level. But with the small army of researchers now attacking these problems, new and exciting ideas are in store.

A marsupial sugar glider *(top)* and a placental flying squirrel *(above)*

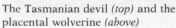
The Tasmanian devil *(top)* and the placental wolverine *(above)*

The marsupial numbat *(top)* and the placental giant anteater *(above)*

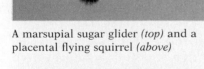
Short- and long-nosed bandicoots *(above, right)* and the placental Norway rat *(far right)*

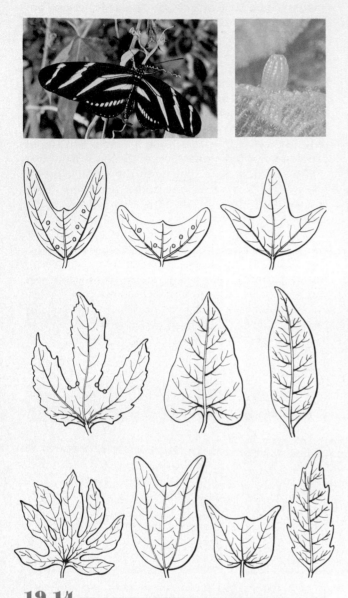

THE PRODUCTS OF EVOLUTION: THE KINGDOMS

Until recently, most biologists accepted the organization of species into five large categories known as *kingdoms*. But it has been shown that there are two very different kinds of bacteria, so now we categorize living organisms into six kingdoms. We have loosely used the term from time to time, so let's now be more precise. **Kingdoms** are the broadest taxonomic category, each containing organisms that share basic features of cell structure.

If we were describing political organization, kingdoms would be the equivalent of nations. They are generally subdivided into what taxonomists call **phyla** (singular, *phylum*)—equivalent, roughly, to our own states, if we continue the political analogy. Each phylum is itself subdivided into **classes** (counties), and so the subdivisions continue. It is easier at this point to look at the total organization as we make our way down to the species level (Figure 19.16). The increasingly finer divisions are as follows:

	And one socially acceptable mnemonic device is:
Kingdom	King
Phylum*	Philip
Class	Came
Order	Over
Family	From
Genus	Greece
Species	Singing
Subspecies (race)	Songs

19.14

Coevolution. The passion flower vine *(Passiflora)* continues to evolve new strategies to resist the parasitic activity of the *Heliconius* larvae. The yellow spots, randomly arranged on some leaves, are actually displaced nectar glands that resemble the butterfly's eggs. Their presence discourages females from laying eggs on leaves so adorned. In addition, the passion flower produces a variety of leaf shapes, imitating those of other nearby forest plants. Such mimicry may fool the butterfly into continuing her search for the right plant. These defenses could limit the *Heliconius'* success and, conceivably, lead to its extinction, since it is highly specific for the type of plant food eaten by its larvae. However, predators are also subjected to selection, and it wouldn't be surprising to learn of behavioral countermeasures evolving in the butterfly populations.

We will find that there is no single "correct" way to place an organism into a scheme such as this. In fact, there is often a great deal of argument over such placement. Obviously, however, the smaller the group into which two kinds of organisms are placed, the more similar they must be. Those placed in the same species are likely to be so similar that they can interbreed. Those in the larger categories may be quite different. For example, it is apparent that humans and sponges are not alike at all (your opinion of your next-door neighbor not withstanding).

---

*In botanical terms, the phylum is replaced by the *division*.

The Six Kingdoms

The organization of life into the six-kingdom scheme is as follows:

1. *Archebacteria:* prokaryotes, mostly restricted to anaerobic environments; includes chemosynthetic and photosynthetic types with bizarre and unusual metabolic pathways and cell walls.

2. *Eubacteria:* prokaryotes, chiefly aerobic, some chemosynthetic and some photosynthetic, many heterotrophic, including saprobes and parasites. Peptidoglycan cell walls. All cyanobacteria and probably all disease bacteria are included.

3. *Protista:* various simple, mostly single-celled eukaryotes, including both protozoa (animal-like protists) and some photosynthesizing algae.

4. *Fungi:* mostly multicellular; parasitic, mutualistic, and scavaging organisms; long tubular cells or cell-like structure. Cell walls.

5. *Plantae:* mostly multicellular photosynthetic organisms. Includes some of the algae. Cellulose cell walls.

6. *Animalia:* multicellular animals, including sponges (parazoa) and other animals (metazoa). No cell walls.

There are obviously some problems here. You may have noted that there is no mention of the viruses. They should probably have their own kingdom since they are unlike anything else (see Chapter 20), but since kingdoms should be based on evolutionary relationships, we can't justify this step. We simply don't know their evolutionary origin.

Within the six-kingdom scheme there are further problems, specifically with regard to the protists. Kingdoms are supposed to be cohesive units with all of their members traceable to a common evolutionary ancestor. Such descent is called *monophyletic.* Yet there is no evidence that the various protozoa and algal protists are descended from a single line. In fact, they are definitely *polyphyletic,* having evolved from different ancestors. However, they will be lumped together provisionally until their evolutionary origins can be sorted out.

19.15

Homologous structures. The forelimbs of several representative vertebrates are compared here with those of the suggested primitive ancestral type. In each case, individual bones have undergone modification, although they can still be traced to the ancestor. Since they all have the same embryological origin and they can be traced to the ancestor, they are said to be homologous. The most dramatic changes can be seen in the horse, bird, and whale. In these animals, many individual bones have become smaller and some have even fused. Another interesting modification is seen in the greatly extended finger bones of the bat.

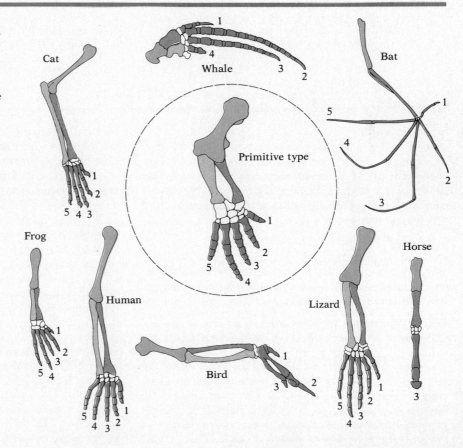

Kingdom	Animalia	Kingdom	Plantae	Kingdom	Animalia
Phylum	Chordata	Division	Tracheophyta	Division	Chordata
Subphylum	Vertebrata	Subdivision	Pterophyta	Subdivision	Vertebrata
Class	Mammalia	Class	Angiospermae	Class	Mammalia
		Subclass	Dicotyledoneae		
Order	Cetacea	Order	Sapindales	Order	Insectivora
Family	Mysticeti	Family	Aceraceae	Family	Soricidae
Genus	*Balenoptera*	Genus	*Acer*	Genus	*Suncus*
Species	*B. musculus*	Species	*A. rubrum*	Species	*S. etruscus*

19.16

Classification of two mammals and a flowering plant. The two animals whose classifications are listed here represent the largest and smallest members, respectively, of a diverse class, the mammalia. The great blue whale grows to about 100 feet long, can weigh over 150 tons, and devours eight tons of food per day. The shrew weighs only about 4 gm (0.14 oz). Relatively speaking, shrews eat far more than whales. In fact, a shrew eats the equivalent of its body weight each day in an effort to keep up with its record-breaking metabolic rate. Both of these animals have hair, are warm-blooded, suckle their young, and nourish their embryos through a placenta. Neither species is divided into subspecies. The red maple is a flowering plant of considerable size and is closely related to other species that are also called maples.

Summary

Naming Names
Speciation refers to the process by which species arise; taxonomy is the science of naming new species. Linnaeus introduced binomial nomenclature, a system in which a species is given two Latin names. An organism's formal scientific name identifies its genus, species, and subspecies, if any.

But What Do You Mean by "Species"?
A "species" is a group of actually or potentially interbreeding organisms that is reproductively isolated from other such groups because of geography, infertility, or some other incompatible trait.

The Mechanisms of Speciation
The effects of natural selection can be seen across the various ranges that populations inhabit. Changes within species depend on the amount of gene flow, which determines the general appearance of the population. If the environment tends to vary sharply, populations will tend to be polymorphic. An environment that changes gradually may cause a species to form clines across its range. If the gene flow is halted because of geographic isolation, allopatric speciation will give rise to two or more species where only one existed before. Continental drift, based on the theory of plate tectonics, has fostered the development of many species that were once part of the same group. Darwin's finches on the Galapagos islands are among the best illustrations of allopatric speciation. The finches developed into various species through adaptive radiation and character displacement as they adapted to specific island environments or sought to coexist within the same environment.

Speciation also can occur within a single habitat. Many plants undergo sympatric speciation through hybridization, which may produce hybrid swarms and result in a new species. Plants hybridize successfully through polyploidy, where sets of chromosomes double, giving rise to cells that are tetraploid, hexaploid, and so on. Autotetraploids are usually infertile; however, spontaneous tetraploidization in hybrid plants will produce allotetraploids, which reproduce normally when crossed with themselves and one another. As a result, allotetraploids may explain the sudden appearance of new, "instant" plant species, but these species rarely persist.

Hybridization and polyploidization are thought to be the reason flowering plants were able to spread so rapidly and in such diversity over the planet.

While some polyploid animal species exist, hybridization is not likely, since meiosis fails in those species with X and Y sex chromosomes. No sympatric speciation in animals has ever been found in nature.

Major Evolutionary Trends

In divergent evolution, newly emerging species become increasingly different from one another as they adapt to their own ecological niches. In convergent evolution, species grow more alike. Even those that differ in many ways, such as marsupial and placental mammals, may fill the same niches in their respective environments and bear a remarkable resemblance to one another.

At times two species will coevolve, the evolution of one influencing the evolution of the other. Such relationships often occur between predators and prey, or between insects and plants.

Evolutionary origins of species can also be traced through the comparison of physical traits, such as bone structure, among various species. Homologous structures are evolutionarily related, while analogous structures are not.

The Products of Evolution: The Kingdoms

Species are organized into six kingdoms: Archebacteria, Eubacteria, Protista, Fungi, Plantae, and Animalia. Kingdoms are subdivided into phyla (or divisions, in botany), classes, orders, families, genera, species, and subspecies. However, viruses do not fit neatly into any kingdom, and the various protists cannot be traced to a common evolutionary ancestor.

Key Terms

speciation	allopatric speciation	allotetraploid
taxonomy	continental drift	triticale
binomial nomenclature	plate tectonics	divergent evolution
genus	adaptive radiation	convergent evolution
species	character displacement	coevolution
subspecies	sympatric speciation	homologous
reproductive isolation	hybrid swarm	analogous
range	polyploidy	kingdoms
gene flow	tetraploid	phyla
cline	autotetraploid	classes
geographic isolation		

Review Questions

1. Using an example of a scientific name, explain how the binomial system is applied to species. List three rules followed in assigning a scientific name. (pp. 253–254)

2. What is the usual criterion for designating a species? Is it foolproof? Explain. (pp. 254–256)

3. Define allopatric speciation and describe two major ways in which it can come about. (p. 258)

4. Using the Galapagos finches as an example, explain how adaptive radiation can come about. (pp. 258, 260)

5. Why might sympatric speciation be far less common in animals than allopatric speciation? (p. 264)

6. Why do most hybrids fail? How is this problem overcome in allotetraploids? (p. 262)

7. Cite two examples of convergent evolution, and state the theory behind it. (p. 265)

8. Using the passion flower and its infesting butterfly as an example, explain how coevolution occurs. (pp. 265–266)

9. Distinguish between homologous and analogous structures, and cite examples of each. (pp. 266–267)

10. List the six kingdoms, and state a general characteristic and an example of each. (p. 269)

PART III

From Prokaryotes to Plants

Bacteria, Viruses, and the Origin of Life

20

It's difficult to ponder the complexities of evolution for long without arriving at the ultimate question: how did life begin? The question is as old as humanity. The ancients throughout the world were absorbed by this mystery, and their conclusions have formed the bases for practically all religions.

But science is fettered with all manner of restraints, and faith in an idea is only a starting point. How does one legitimately investigate an improbable event that may have happened only once, several billion years ago? It's clear that we can never prove how life really first came to be on this planet. We can, however, examine any number of seemingly plausible notions of how life *might* have arisen. Most speculations about the possible origin of life involve suppositions. These suppositions lead to predictions, and some can be tested. Many such speculations have been trotted out, many of the predictions based on their suppositions have been tested, and the answer is reasonably clear. Most of the proposed schemes of how life might have originated couldn't possibly have worked; they have depended on suppositions about nature that have proven to be untrue.

THE ORIGIN OF LIFE

Although Darwin speculated that life might have arisen in a warm, phosphate-rich pond, the first serious proposals concerning the spontaneous origin of life (those that were based on sound biochemical and geological information) began to ap-pear some 50 years ago. Similar schemes were presented by J.B.S. Haldane, a Scottish biochemist, and by A.P. Oparin, his Soviet counterpart. They proposed that shortly after the earth's formation, under conditions quite different from those of today, a period of chemical synthesis occurred in the warm primeval seas. During this era, the precursors of life's molecules—amino acids, sugars, and nucleotide bases—formed spontaneously from the hydrogen-rich molecules of ammonia, methane, and water. Such synthesis was possible because there was no destructive oxygen in the atmosphere, and there was an abundance of energy in the form of electrical discharges, ultraviolet light, heat, and radiation. Since there were no organisms to degrade the spontaneously formed organic molecules, they accumulated until the sea became a "hot, thin soup."

Haldane and Oparin suggested that continued synthesis and increasing concentrations led to the formation of polypeptides from amino acids, and, eventually, to a diversity of molecules, including the first enzymes. Proteins—especially enzymatic ones—catalyzed more synthesis, producing more interactive proteins. Collections of these new catalysts then became enclosed by simple, water-resistant protein or lipid shells that allowed certain molecules to pass through them. These collections thus perpetuated themselves by making use of the energy-rich nutrients of the sea.

At first (to continue with Oparin and Haldane's scenario), these conglomerates divided when they reached a certain critical size. But eventually the increasingly specialized droplets, or **coacervates** as Oparin called them, broke up into molecules that in some way induced the formation of molecules like themselves. The accidentally successful first **protocells** persisted and increased in numbers. The development of a crude mechanism of molecular duplication may have been an accident, but the presence of "genetic" mechanisms assured faithful preservation of the chemical traits of successful droplets, and set the stage for the forces of natural selection. The success principle of life—the survival of the fittest—was underway. From these early protocell successes, the forces of evolution would produce the first true, if simple, cellular life.

Haldane's and Oparin's hypothetical scheme remained a neglected intellectual curiosity for more than a quarter of a century. But in 1952, Nobel laureate Harold Urey and Stanley Miller, a younger colleague, began testing some of the assumptions in earnest.

The Miller-Urey Experiment

The crucial supposition of the Haldane-Oparin hypothesis was that *organic* (carbon-containing) molecules would form spontaneously in the primitive atmosphere. Urey and Miller created a laboratory apparatus at the University of Chicago that attempted to simulate what were then believed to be some of the primitive conditions of the earth (Figure 20.1). They introduced a small amount of water

20.1

In the classic Miller-Urey experiment, the heated gases of the theoretical primitive atmosphere were subjected to electrical discharges in a sealed, sterile environment. Residues were collected in the lower chamber and analyzed. Results indicated that some of the simple monomers of life could be produced spontaneously under test conditions.

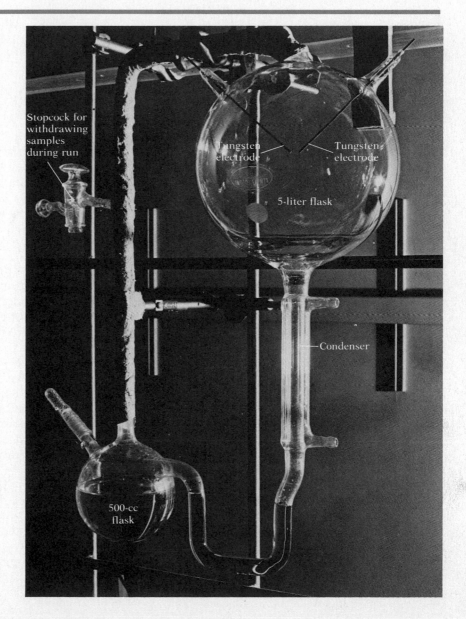

and a mixture of gases including methane, ammonia, water vapor, and hydrogen—but no free oxygen—into the apparatus. Energy was provided in the form of repeated electrical discharges (lightning?) through the atmosphere of the upper flask. After a week-long run, analyses of the sediments that collected in the lower flask revealed the presence of aldehydes, carboxylic acids, and, most interestingly, amino acids. All of these are common products of cellular activity.

Although these small molecules were a far cry from anything alive, their production under the simulated primitive conditions provoked a lively revival of interest in the Haldane-Oparin hypothesis. Before we look any further into the work that has followed Urey and Miller's breakthrough, we should review what scientists today accept as probable conditions on the primitive earth.

The Early Earth

The best estimates suggest that the earth took form about 4.6 billion years ago, along with the sun and the other planets of our solar system. Prior to this, the precursor of the solar system was a vast, flattened cloud of gases, dust, and other debris. Recent theories maintain that the cloud was cold, but that as the sun and planets coalesced, a great deal of heat was released from gravitational energy, supplemented with heat from radioactivity. The earth was a molten fireball 4.6 billion years ago, and 600 to 800 million years were to pass before its crust solidified.

When the crust cooled to less than the boiling point of water, torrential rains marked the formation of the oceans. Along with the seas, an atmosphere was forming from volcanic emissions. The makeup of the early atmosphere was quite unlike that of our own atmosphere. Volcanic gases consist largely of water vapor, methane, carbon monoxide, carbon dioxide, ammonia, hydrogen, and hydrogen sulfide. This is a highly *reducing* mixture; it has a tendency to add hydrogen or electrons to substances. This mix contrasts greatly with the atmosphere of today, which consists principally of nearly inert molecular nitrogen (N_2) and of that active, highly oxidizing gas, molecular oxygen (O_2) (our atmosphere also contains a little argon, variable amounts of water vapor, and traces of carbon dioxide).

Until recently, atmospheric scientists were convinced that the highly reducing constituents of volcanic emissions also characterized the atmosphere of the primitive earth. This belief was the rationale for the Miller-Urey experiment. However, computer simulations now show that methane, ammonia, and hydrogen sulfide would be rapidly broken down by ultraviolet radiation, and that most of the hydrogen liberated would be lost to outer space. According to current theory, the principle constituents of the early atmosphere were water vapor, carbon dioxide, carbon monoxide, molecular nitrogen, and possibly some free hydrogen. Recent repeats of the Miller and Urey experiment, this time using the revised version of the probable primitive atmosphere, happily give even greater yields of appropriate small organic molecules. Included among these are the nucleotide bases of RNA and DNA.

Energy sources abounded in the primitive atmosphere. Although the sun was not as bright as it is now, ultraviolet light was plentiful, since the ozone layer, which today screens out much of this energy, had yet to form. Forms of energy were plentiful in lightning, heat, volcanic eruptions, and what geologists call shock energy. So the major requirements of chemical evolution—reactive gases and available, concentrated energy—were abundant (or at least that is the consensus of scientists today).

The Hypothesis Today

The spontaneous generation hypothesis is vigorously pursued today, but much of the effort is concentrated on its troublesome aspects. While the continued clarification of conditions on the primitive earth goes on—aided by NASA's planetary probes—and the spontaneous formation of monomers offers few problems, there are difficulties at the higher levels of the scenario.

Polymers. The polymerization of monomers into the familiar macromolecules of life—proteins, carbohydrates, lipids, and nucleic acids—without the assistance of enzymes presents many difficult problems. It is here that the original hot, thin soup hypothesis is weakest. All biological polymerizations involve *dehydration linkages* between the monomers—that is, water is removed to produce the linkage. Researchers agree that, because of mass action laws, such reactions would not have proceeded in the right direction—from monomer to polymer—in the primitive seas, or, indeed, in any watery medium. Biological polymers in water slowly dissociate back into monomers, and heat just accelerates the process. The reaction moves in the direction of spontaneous polymerization *only* when the concentration of monomers is very high and the concentration of water is very low.

How can this be achieved? There have been many suggestions. Carl Woese has proposed that life began not in the sea, but in the hot, extremely dense atmosphere of the *very* early earth!

Experimentally and theoretically, the best results have come from the work of Sidney Fox of the University of Miami. Fox has demonstrated that polymerization of amino acids occurs readily under hot, drying conditions such as might be found along the edges of volcanos or even on the hot beaches of ancient seas. Pools of organic precursors, rich in amino acids, could have been concentrated by evaporation and heated to allow the spontaneous formation of polypeptides. Fox has succeeded in producing polymers of 200 or more amino acids under very dry conditions. Fox calls these spontaneously generated polymers **proteinoids** (Figure 20.2). The search goes on. In Israel, biochemists have concentrated and polymerized amino acids on the surfaces of clay particles, and the suggestion has been made that the first living, successfully reproducing organisms were mostly made of clay!

The successful spontaneous polymerization of nucleotides is another matter. In the hope of proving something, investigators have boiled and dried concentrated solutions of energy-rich nucleotide triphosphates in the presence of single strands of DNA, loading all the dice toward the successful production of a second DNA strand. But without

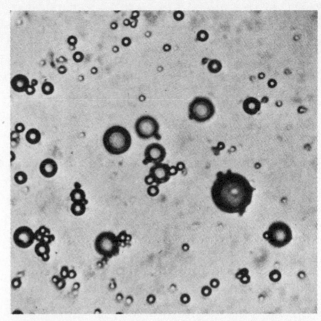

20.3

When proteins or other polymers are introduced into water, they tend to cluster together into distinct droplets called coacervates. The coacervate surrounds itself with a boundary layer that tends to be selective in admitting kinds of molecules. When coacervates reach a critical size, they divide spontaneously.

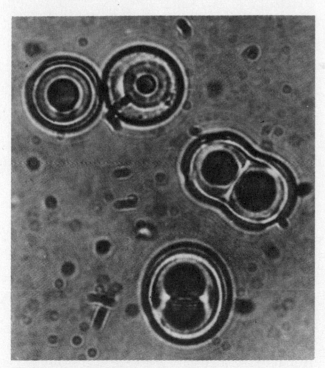

20.2

Proteinoids are polypeptides that polymerize spontaneously from amino acids concentrated by evaporation.

the appropriate enzymes, no recognizable polymers are formed. Spontaneous linkages can be forced, but they occur in the wrong places. Supporting evidence for the spontaneous formation of nucleic acids remains to be found.

The Active Droplets: Coacervates and Proteinoids. After presenting his hypothesis in the 1920s, Oparin spent most of the next 50 years experimenting with versions of coacervate droplets (Figure 20.3). What are the properties of such simple, cell-like structures? Oparin and his coworkers experimented with great numbers of different combinations of proteins, nucleic acids, and other substances to produce the coacervate droplets. Some simple versions of metabolism were simulated. For instance, coacervate droplets containing simple nucleic acids and nucleic-acid replicating enzymes, immersed in a medium containing energy-rich nucleotides, would "grow," "divide," and "replicate" themselves. But, of course, we have to keep these experiments in proper perspective. Coacervate droplets are not living entities, and their more spectacular feats depend upon their being supplied with biological enzymes that have previously been extracted from living organisms. The experiments may tell us something about a critical stage in the origin of life, however, and it's worth noting that Fox's spontaneously polymerized proteinoids have also been found to form coacervate-like encapsulated spheres in water.

The Earliest Cells

Having presumptuously taken the giant step between metabolically active aggregates to self-reproducing protocells—leaving huge gaps for future theorists to deal with—we can apply some informed speculation about early cellular life. What were the earliest cells like? What were their energy sources? How do we get from this earliest stage—which could have occurred no earlier than 3.8 billion years ago—to cyanobacteria known to exist 3.5 billion years ago?

The earliest cells are believed to have been primitive versions of today's anaerobic fermenting bacteria, such as *Clostridium*, a soil bacterium that is rapidly killed by oxygen. These first living beings probably relied heavily upon the comparatively simple process of anaerobic fermentation (see Chapter 8). Oxidative respiration was a long way away, and there was no available oxygen in any case. Originally, their energy supply probably came from the abiotically produced monomers that were still available in the ocean. We can surmise that expanding populations of the new, living cells soon began to use up the available resources, and increasing competition caused natural selection to favor those cells able to exploit new energy sources or to exploit old ones more efficiently. Cells could prey on one another, but this just redistributed the limited and dwindling supply of organic nutrients. The necessary, big advance was to break out of this limited food chain altogether. The cell that could do this, even just a little bit at first, would quickly evolve to take over the world.

The Early Autotrophic Cells.   Autotrophs are of two main types: chemotrophs and phototrophs. Both require carbon dioxide as a source of carbon for their own cell structures, and simple, inorganic molecules, such as water or hydrogen sulfide, as a source of hydrogen to reduce the carbon dioxide. They also need a source of energy.

The most primitive living phototrophs obtain their hydrogen from dissolved hydrogen sulfide, and it's a good bet that the earliest successful phototrophs also utilized this source, using light energy in the simplest of photosystems to pry the hydrogen away (see Chapter 7). But the number of places in the world that provide both hydrogen sulfide and abundant sunlight are severely limited.

At some point, some ancestral cyanobacterium began to obtain its photosynthetic hydrogen supply from an energetically less favorable—but far more abundant—source: water. This step required more complex photosystems, as discussed in detail in Chapter 7. But the accomplishment was a success, and it was to change the earth forever.

The waste product of the photosynthetic oxidation of water is molecular oxygen. As these early cyanobacteria flourished, exploited new niches, and multiplied, they must have colored the primeval ocean green. Their release of oxygen gradually became significant, poisoning the water

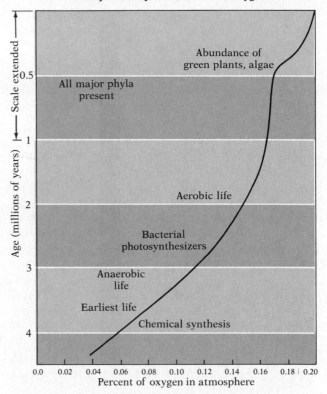

Today's atmosphere: about 20% oxygen

20.4

The accumulation of oxygen in the atmosphere of the early earth was a slow process at first, requiring about 2 billion years to approach the concentration that now exists. Although photosynthesis liberated oxygen, cellular respiration used it up almost as fast. Furthermore, in the early earth there were many *oxygen sinks* that absorbed photosynthetic oxygen as fast as it could be produced. The elemental iron, elemental sulfur, and abundant iron sulfide of the early earth's crust absorbed enormous amounts of oxygen as they were transformed into iron oxide and various sulfates. Only when these oxygen sinks were finally saturated could free oxygen increase in the air. By this time, organisms of a new kind—the eukaryotes—were already present.

for their anaerobic competitors (Figure 20.4). At first, the regions of oxygen poisoning would have been local—just a thin layer of oxygenated water in the sea or in a shallow pond.

All life is capable of change, and although many oxygen-sensitive organisms undoubtedly became extinct—or were literally driven into the mud—new forms were to emerge through mutation and natural selection. The first step was to develop means of detoxifying oxygen. Later, ways were developed to harness the corrosive power of oxygen in order to extract the maximum amount of energy from organic foodstuffs, and oxidative respiration came into being in the biosphere.

New modes of nutrition arose, too. The burgeoning cyanobacteria themselves represented an abundant new source of food for any heterotroph that could engulf prey; thus the world saw the emergence of the first herbivores. The remaining anaerobes were soon relegated to a backwater in the progression of life, hidden away from poisonous oxygen in pockets of the earth's crust, in nutrient-rich muds, and in deep recesses of stagnant waters.

In this imaginative scenario, we have seen two metabolic forms of life emerging: the photosynthetic, oxygen-producing green phototroph and the aerobic, oxygen-using heterotroph. This is all we require to make the transition from the unknown to the known, for we have arrived at the time of the first fossil evidence of early life on our planet.

Much of the origin of life, therefore, remains unexplained, and what explanations we do have are based on conjecture and on our imperfect knowledge of what the primitive, inorganic earth was like. But this is the way of science, and whether current theory thrives and grows or dwindles into oblivion ultimately will depend on imaginative experiments and observations still to come.

THE PROKARYOTES

We will now begin our survey of life as it exists today. It might seem that since we are moving to things that are alive and observable, we should be able to speak in more certain terms and that we should no longer be forced to deal with conjecture and hypothesis. However, solid observations often seem merely to give biologists more raw material with which they simply create more guesswork. With the guesswork, of course, comes argument, but many biologists believe that such disagreements are an important part of advancing science.

We will now consider some of the more basic arguments about what may seem to be simple kinds of life.

As recently as 1980, most biologists accepted the classification of prokaryotes into two major groups: the *bacteria* and the *cyanobacteria* (the cyanobacteria, in fact, were previously not considered to be bacteria at all, and were called *blue-green algae*). These two kinds of prokaryotes were grouped together into one kingdom called **Monera**. As you are well aware, however, notions about how things should be grouped can change rapidly in biology. Intensive research, using new molecular techniques for establishing phylogenetic relationships, has changed the way we classify microorganisms. The prokaryotes (Figure 20.5) are now perceived by some as distinct kingdoms—the **Archebacteria** and the **Eubacteria** ("first or ancient bacteria,"

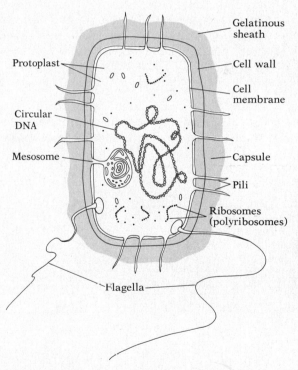

Gelatinous sheath

Protoplast

Cell wall

Cell membrane

Circular DNA

Mesosome

Capsule

Pili

Ribosomes (polyribosomes)

Flagella

20.5

The prokaryotic cell is quite small compared to the eukaryotic cell, and lacks membrane-bounded organelles. In the rodlike eubacterium, one of several known shapes, the DNA is naked and circular, lacking the protein complex of eukaryotic chromosomes. A dense cell wall, quite different chemically from eukaryotic cell walls, surrounds the membrane, and is often itself surrounded by a slimy sheath. Free-floating ribosomes and polyribosomes are common, as are tubelike, cytoplasmic projections called *pili*. The membranous mesosome is believed to be important in cell division.

and "true bacteria," respectively). Both groups are definitely prokaryotic, but they differ in enough ways to suggest, if not prove, that they went their separate ways very early in the evolution of life (Figure 20.6). Under the microscope, the two kinds of bacteria look very much alike, and even their cellular organizations are similar. On the biochemical level, however, the Archebacteria and Eubacteria are as different from one another as either group is different from eukaryotes like ourselves. Before we consider the two kinds of prokaryotes, we should review some of the differences between prokaryotes and eukaryotes (Table 20.1, and see Figure 20.5).

The Origins of the Prokaryotes

There is no longer any doubt that the prokaryotes preceded all other modern forms of life. They are indeed ancient, since there are clear indications of their presence in deposits 3.5 billion years old. The most widespread evidence of their antiquity is seen in strange, columnlike deposits known as **stromatolites** (Figure 20.7). These are highly laminated deposits of sedimentary rock, each layer having been produced by dense populations of bacteria (or cyanobacteria) that deposited mineral particles around their cells.

Some paleontologists (those who study fossils) doubted that these strange geological formations were true evidence of early life forms, until it was found that there are still stromatolite-forming mats of cyanobacteria living on this planet. Living stromatolites can be seen, for instance, in Yellowstone national park in the United States and on the shores of Shark Bay, Australia.

The Archebacteria

The Archebacteria, which are not very easy to grow in the laboratory, are not as familiar to bacteriologists as are the Eubacteria. As more has become known about them it has become clear that they are very peculiar, indeed. Because of their peculiarities, the Archebacteria were assumed to be rare, "primitive," and possibly relics of the earliest form of bacterial life. This impression was reinforced by two findings: (1) that the best-studied Archebacteria are obligate anaerobes (that is, they cannot survive in the presence of oxygen), and (2)

20.6

Newly developed biochemical evidence has led biologists to reconsider existing concepts of prokaryote taxonomy. It is now suggested that the old prokaryotic kingdom (Monera) be renamed as two kingdoms: the Archebacteria and the Eubacteria. The division is based on important differences in very basic specializations of the two groups. According to this scheme, all of life is divided into three main categories: Eubacteria, Archebacteria, and eukaryotes.

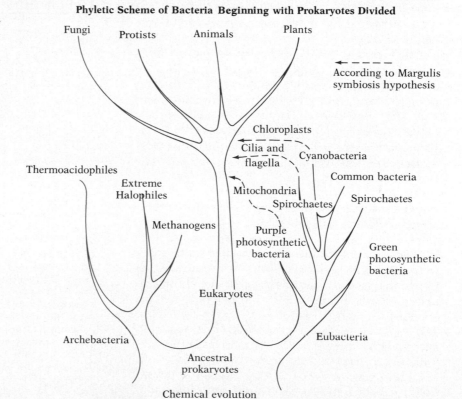

Phyletic Scheme of Bacteria Beginning with Prokaryotes Divided

TABLE 20.1

Differences between prokaryotes and eukaryotes

	Archebacteria	Eubacteria	Eukaryotes
Cell wall	Variety of substances, often proteinaceous	Peptidoglycans	Cellulose, pectin; absent in animals and some protists
Cell membrane lipids	Modified branched fatty acids	Straight-chain fatty acids	Straight-chain fatty acids
Nuclear membrane	Absent	Absent	Present
DNA	Naked, circular	Naked, circular	Associated with chromosomal protein
Membrane-bounded organelles	Absent	Absent (except for mesosome and thylakoid in some)	Present
Ribosomes	30S, 50S subunits; structural similarity to eukaryotic	30S, 50S subunits; unlike archebacteria and eukaryotic	40S, 60S subunits (30S, 50S in chloroplasts and mitochondria)
Flagella	?	Solid, rotating (protein flagellin)	Microtubular undulating (protein tubulin)
Photosynthetic pigments	Bacteriorhodopsin	Bacteriochlorophyll (a and b)	Chlorophyll a, b, c
Cell division	Fission	Fission	Mitosis and meiosis

that others survive in strange and improbable places, such as near-boiling hot springs, ammonia-rich habitats, and salt marshes. But the Archebacteria are also the predominant form of life in such widespread habitats as swamp mud and lake bottoms. Furthermore, they are the principal inhabitants of our own large intestines (sharing their home with the better-known but less numerous *Escherichia coli*).

Microbiologists have now abandoned the notion that the Archebacteria are the oldest form of bacterial life. The two groups of prokaryotes are now believed to be about equally ancient; they probably diverged from one another billions of years ago, when the world was a place without oxygen. (Many Eubacteria are also obligate anaerobes, but most can use oxygen in their metabolic processes.)

The largest group of Archebacteria, the **methanogens** (methane-generators), are found in habitats where carbon dioxide and hydrogen are readily available, but where there is little or no oxygen (Figure 20.8). Among these habitats are anaerobic marshes, sewage treatment plants, mucky, anaerobic sea and lake bottoms (such as in the Black Sea), and the airless bowels of animals, including humans. There they ferment carbohydrates and reduce carbon dioxide, producing a mixture of methane gas (CH_4), or "marsh gas" as it was first called, and hydrogen gas (H_2). Well-designed sewage treatment plants can supply their own energy by utilizing the methane gas produced by methanogenic Archebacteria.

Other Archebacterial types include the so-called *extreme halophiles* (salt-lovers) and *extreme thermophiles* (heat-lovers), both names suggesting rather

20.7

Fossilized stromatolites are believed to represent the most ancient evidence of life on the earth. They arose on rocky ledges in the tide pools of shallow preCambrian seas. Their peculiar layered construction was the product of constantly growing populations of bacterial cells—probably cyanobacteria—that were continually infiltrated by tide-carried sand particles. As new populations arose at the surface, their predecessors beneath became fossilized. As a remarkable example of evolutionary conservatism, recognizable descendents of these forms are living today.

281

drastic living conditions. The halophiles thrive in the Great Salt Lake, in the Dead Sea, and in salt-evaporation facilities, where they carry on a unique version of photosynthesis. Instead of the usual chlorophylls, the halophiles use a pigment called *bacteriorhodopsin* to harness the sun's energy. Some inhabitants of deep-sea volcanic vents flourish in temperatures above 104°C—the water is kept from boiling by the extreme pressure of the ocean depths. And then there are the *thermoacidophiles* that live under even harsher conditions; they thrive in strong acids and sea-level temperatures of 90°C (194°F, close to boiling!).

The Eubacteria

The Eubacteria are the more familiar prokaryotes, and include species that tend to live under less drastic conditions than those that support the Archebacteria. Although many are heterotrophs—requiring organic nutrients—three groups are phototrophs (using light to make food), and a number fall into a category known as **chemotrophs.** The phototrophs all utilize some sort of chlorophyll, although it is somewhat different than that found in algae and plants. The chemotrophs are bacteria that utilize inorganic substances, such as iron and sulfur compounds from the earth's crust, in their metabolism. Of the heterotrophs, many are pathogens—disease-causing parasites—of plants and animals (including humans). The remainder fall within the category of soil and water bacteria. These are the important recyclers that convert dead organisms to useful elements.

The eubacterial cell is unique in a number of ways. Most are small, as cells go, about one-tenth the size of most eukaryotic cells, and their internal

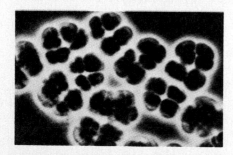

20.8

Methanogens are a diverse group of Archebacteria that are capable of producing methane gas from carbon dioxide and hydrogen.

structure is also much simpler (see Figure 20.6). As you learned earlier (Chapter 4), membrane-bounded organelles are absent. An exception is the *mesosome,* membranes that may act in transport or in cell wall formation. There is no organized nucleus. The chromosome is essentially a naked, circular strand of DNA, lacking the protein complexes of eukaryotic chromosomes. Bacteria also lack the microtubular mitotic or meiotic apparatus, and following DNA replication, the cell divides by a little-understood process called *fission.* You may recall from Chapter 16 that some bacteria have a primitive form of sexual exchange called conjugation.

Eubacterial cell walls are also unique, chemically different even from those of Archebacteria. The molecular unit of structure is the **peptidoglycan,** a molecule containing two *glucosamine* units and a short tail of amino acids. **Glucosamine** is basically glucose, but it also contains a nitrogenous side group at its number 2' carbon. Penicillin, the familiar antibiotic, interferes with peptidoglycan synthesis and is therefore lethal to many Eubacteria. The eubacterial flagellum is also quite different. Unlike the microtubular, undulating eukaryotic flagellum, it is solid and rotates (Figure 20.9).

Eubacterial Diversity.   For years, the first criterion for classifying bacteria has been *shape.* The three primary shapes—rod, sphere, and spiral—are known, respectively, as **bacillus, coccus,** and **spirillum** (Figure 20.10a).

The bacillus forms occur as single cells and in chains (Figure 20.10b). Some chain-formers are enclosed in sheaths. Many bacilli are also known for their ability to form highly resistant, thick-walled **endospores** (Figure 20.11) in response to unfavorable conditions. These dehydrated bodies contain the cellular components in a state of dormancy, ready to reabsorb water and resume their metabolic activities when conditions improve. The spherical or coccoid forms occur singly (coccus), in pairs (diplococcus), in beadlike chains (streptococcus), or in grapelike clusters (straphylococcus) (see Figure 20.10b). The spiral-shaped cells, or **spirochaetes,** occur singly. Many of these have lengthy flagella.

Bacterial Villains.   We have all heard that bacteria can be both helpful and harmful, but since people are understandably more concerned with the harmful ones, let's take a closer look at some of these. They can be responsible for some relatively temporary problems as well as some horribly painful, debilitating diseases.

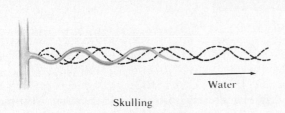

Skulling

Water

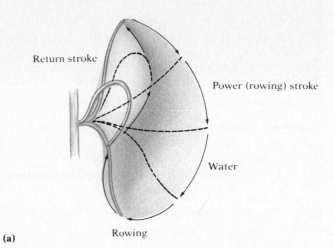

Return stroke

Power (rowing) stroke

Water

Rowing

(a)

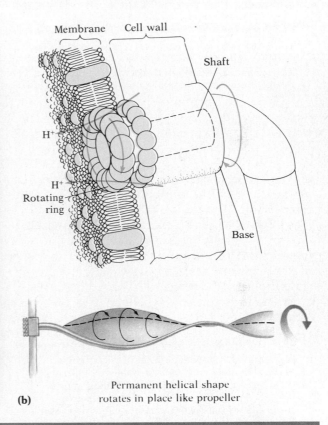

Membrane Cell wall

Shaft

H⁺

H⁺
Rotating
ring

Base

(b)

Permanent helical shape
rotates in place like propeller

20.9

Prokaryotic and eukaryotic flagella appear similar when viewed through the light microscope, but intensive EM and biochemical studies reveal vast differences in both their structure and movement. Eukaryotic flagella and cilia **(a)** undulate in whiplike fashion, owing to sliding microtubules composed of the protein *tubulin*. They originate in basal bodies and have the common 9 + 2 microtubular arrangement. Prokaryotic flagella **(b)** are solid structures, permanently bent into a helical configuration and composed of the protein *flagellin*. Unlike any other known cellular organelle, the bacterial flagellum rotates. High EM magnification reveals that the flagellum is anchored to a hooklike shaft that penetrates the cell wall and is anchored in two ring-shaped bases. The innermost ring, composed of 16 spherical proteins, rotates; the outer, similarly constructed ring is fixed in place. Movement is believed to be powered by an influx of protons generated in a chemiosmotic gradient.

283

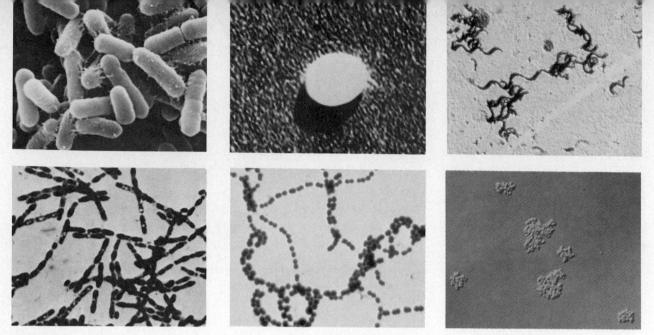

20.10

The three common eubacterial forms—the bacillus (rods), coccus (spherical), and spirillum (corkscrew). The spirillum form occurs singly with great variation in size. Each form is useful in identification. The three forms of bacteria occur in different, recognizable aggregations. All occur singly, but bacilli may occur in chains and cocci may occur as pairs, chains, or grapelike clusters.

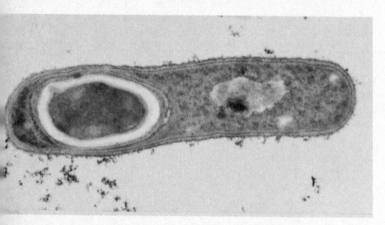

20.11

Endospores. Many bacteria, particularly those in the soil and water, survive unfavorable conditions by forming tough-shelled, resistant spores. Within each spore is a naked, spherical chromosome—and a bit of dehydrated cytoplasm. Under more promising conditions, the spore will take in water and the cell will resume activity. Bacterial spores are found everywhere, and some are so heat-resistant that they can survive boiling temperatures. Where sterile conditions are vital, spores can be killed by successive boilings, by heat and pressure, or, where practical, by the use of chemical agents called *bactericides*.

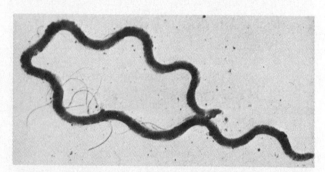

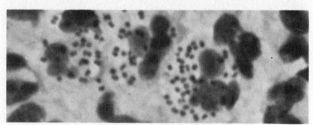

20.12

Two common agents of veneral disease are *Neisseria gonorrhoeae* and *Treponema pallidum*, the Eubacteria of gonorrhea and syphilis, respectively. Gonorrheal bacteria are diplococci, occurring in pairs within a capsule. The agent of syphilis is a spirochaete. Both gonorrhea and syphilis are transmitted through sexual contact, although both can occur in the newborn. Infant gonorrhea is contracted (particularly in the eyes) during the birth process, and the eyes of newborn babies are routinely treated with an antibacterial agent, whether gonorrhea is suspected or not. The spirochaetes of syphilis can cross the placenta after the 18th week of development, infecting the baby and causing traumatic, often fatal defects.

The pathogenic bacilli include the agents of such dread diseases as leprosy, typhus, black plague, diphtheria, and tuberculosis. These conditions are so dangerous that they have been the focus of much research attention and effective means of combating them have been developed. However, we are still threatened by some not-uncommon bacteria such as two anaerobic organisms, *Clostridium tetani* and *Clostridium botulinum.* The first thrives in the soil, where it decomposes dead organic material. Unfortunately, it can also thrive in deep puncture wounds, where there is little oxygen. It brings on the symptoms of *tetanus*— excruciatingly painful, prolonged muscle contractions—when its powerful toxins spread to the nervous system. The toxins of *C. botulinum* cause the symptoms of *botulism* (a severe form of food poisoning), and are among the most powerful poisons known. Even minute amounts are fatal. This bacillus thrives in oxygen-free pockets of the soil, but occasionally finds its way into improperly prepared canned foods, most frequently into those prepared in the home. (*C. botulinum* managed to put one soup company out of business several years ago, and occasionally a canned product will be swept from grocers' shelves by federal agencies when there is even a suspicion of contamination.) Fortunately, botulism toxins are extremely heat-sensitive, and are readily destroyed by cooking.

Most coccoid pathogens are not quite as life threatening as those two bacilli, but they can also cause serious problems. Staphylococci, for example, are commonly involved in minor skin infections, boils, and pimples. One notorious group of staphylococcus, called "hospital staph," crops up occasionally in hospitals. The virulent strain may sweep through infant wards and cause numerous deaths before it can be contained.

The familiar **strep throat** can be brought on by streptococci. Because of the widespread use of antibiotics, strep throat isn't nearly as serious a health threat in the United States today as it was early in this century, or as it still is in less developed parts of the world. The body's own reaction to the streptococcus is the real threat: allergic reactions produce scarlet fever, rheumatic heart disease, and kidney inflammation. All can be fatal.

One highly persistent coccoid bacterium that is increasingly reported today is *Neisseria gonorrhoeae,* the diplococcus of gonorrhea (Figure 20.12a). At one time, gonorrhea was readily cured with antibiotics, but bacteria evolve to adapt to the challenges of their environment, and now we have to deal with new and highly resistant strains.

The most notorious of the spirillum form of bacteria is *Treponema pallidum,* the corkscrew-shaped spirochaete of **syphilis,** another common venereal disease (Figure 20.12b). In its more progressive stages, syphilis has been called the "great pretender" since its effects on the body are widespread and since it mimics the symptoms of a wide range of diseases. If the disease is allowed to go untreated, the spirochaetes eventually will enter the central nervous system, permanently damaging brain tissue and bringing on blindness, insanity, and death. Before the development of antibiotics, syphilis was indeed a threat, and a great number of people died of the disease.

The Biology of Phototrophic and Chemotrophic Eubacteria

Phototrophs: the Cyanobacteria. The best known of the photosynthetic bacteria are the cyanobacteria, which are mostly aquatic organisms that live singly or in colonies (Figure 20.13). Although the most ancient fossils, the 3.5 billion-year-old stromatolites, may have been produced by cyanobacteria, the cyanobacteria are nevertheless considered to be *advanced* (highly evolved) organisms. This is because they are more efficient than other photosynthetic bacteria. Like plants, cyanobacteria contain chlorophyll and utilize the energy of light and the hydrogen of water to reduce carbon dioxide to carbohydrate. In addition, the cyanobacteria are among the few organisms that can utilize atmospheric nitrogen for their metabolic needs. Let's see what this means.

Cyanobacteria, along with some soil bacteria and certain bacteria that live in association with certain flowering plants, are **nitrogen fixers.** That is, they take in nitrogen gas (N_2) from the atmosphere and reduce it to ammonia (NH_3) and ammonium ions (NH_4^+) for their own use. Some of these products are released into the environment; and once in the environment, ammonia, organic nitrogen, and nitrates become the sources of nitrogen for other organisms. Except for the action of lightning (and human activities such as automobile exhaust pollution and fertilizer production), nitrogen fixing is the only source of new nitrogen for living organisms. (Human activities now fix more atmospheric nitrogen throughout the world than do bacteria and cyanobacteria). This nitrogen, of course, is necessary for the synthesis of amino acids, nitrogen bases of DNA and RNA, and other essential molecules. Without continued nitrogen input, the activities of plants and algae would cease. Their deaths, of course, would be followed by the demise of herbivores, carnivores, and decomposers. (The nitrogen cycle is discussed in greater detail in Chapter 45.)

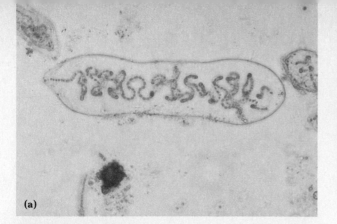
(a)

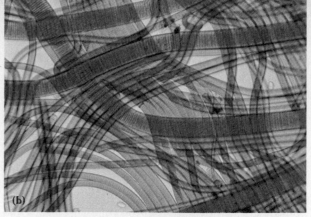
(b)

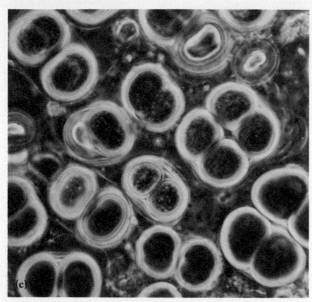
(c)

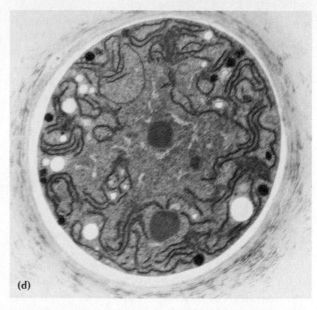
(d)

20.13

The diverse cyanobacteria include the beadlike *Nostoc* **(a)**, the quietly undulating, filamentous *Oscillatoria* **(b)**, and the spherical *Gleocapsa* **(c)**, enclosed in its gelatinous wall. All are inhabitants of stagnant fresh water. The larger cells of *Nostoc* are known as *heterocysts*, which specialize in nitrogen fixation. Electron microscope studies of cyanobacteria **(d)** reveal that their cellular organiza-tion can be quite complex. Un- like other Eubacteria, they do have some membranous structure in the cytoplasm. Numerous chlorophyll-containing lamellae form a prominent part of the cytoplasm. This is where the light reactions of photosynthesis occur. Although the lamellae are not organized into grana, as we find in the chloroplasts of eukaryotes, their complexity suggests that photosynthesis in cyanobacteria is a highly evolved process.

20.14

Among the newly discovered chemotrophic bacteria are those that form the base of a short food chain in the deep oceanic rifts. These are chemotrophic sulfur bacteria that thrive around heated vents in the ocean's floor. The bacteria cloud the vent areas in populations as high as 1,000,000 per cm^3 (cubic centimeter), metabolizing hydrogen sulfide as it escapes from the earth's bowels. The bacterial population, in turn, is fed upon by a number of other rift inhabitants. These include tiny pink fish, giant clams, and other filter feeders.

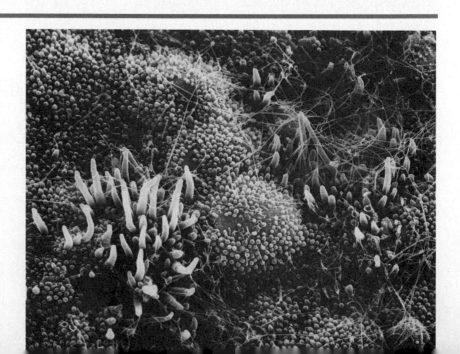

Bacterial Chemotrophs. Chemotrophic bacteria obtain their energy from the oxidation of inorganic compounds in the earth's crust (Figure 20.14). One group plays an essential role in the cycling of nitrogen compounds. This group oxidizes ammonia, producing nitrates and nitrites (NO_3^- and NO_2^-), which helps make nitrogen available to plants. Another group breaks down sulfur, producing sulfuric acid, which becomes ionized in the soil to form hydrogen ions (H^+) and sulfate ions (SO_4^{++}). Plants require sulfate ions for the manufacture of certain amino acids. And we need the plants' amino acids.

We see, then, that the prokaryotes are an ancient group, and that one or more prokaryote lines were to give rise to the first eukaryotes. There are some intriguing clues as to how this might have happened. One theory, the symbiosis hypothesis, even adds a totally new dimension to how we perceive evolution (see Chapter 21).

VIRUSES

We must now take a conceptual leap, because viruses really don't fit in any organizational scheme of living organisms. (Some argue that since they can crystallize, they aren't even truly alive.) Viruses are a mixed bag of unrelated entities, sharing only a few features, such as their extremely small size.

All **viruses** are parasites that invade cells and utilize the metabolic machinery of their hosts. They are well-known agents of disease in virtually all forms of life. Human viral miseries include rabies, polio, smallpox, encephalitis, and yellow fever— each of which can be fatal. Less severe, but still dangerous, are the many forms of influenza, as well as the common cold, measles, chicken pox, and herpes. Viruses are also implicated in some cancers.

Outside their host, they consist of a core of nucleic acid and a coat of protein. Many viruses are either cylindrical or polyhedral. Bacteriophages ("bacteria eaters") are more complex, with polyhedral heads and cylindrical tails (see Figure 20.15). The infective form of a virus carries on no metabolism and has no cytoplasm, and can usually be crystallized. Viruses seem to fit somewhere between a very large molecule and a very small organism, but they are really neither.

The Structure of Viruses

No one knows for sure where viruses came from, but it seems probable that they originated from aberrant genetic material of normal cells. Different kinds of viruses must have arisen independently of one another, since their basic mechanisms are so different. For example, in some viruses the genetic material is standard, double-stranded DNA, just as it is in all metabolizing organisms. But in other viruses the genetic material varies, and we find

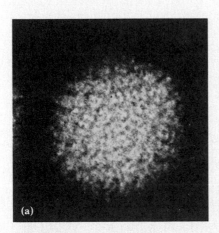
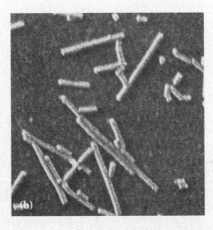
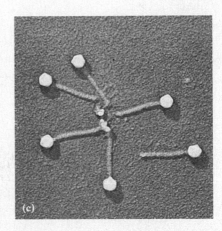

20.15

(a) The 20-sided polyhedron (or icosahedron) *animal* shape is characteristic of the viruses of colds, polio, chicken pox, warts, and fever blisters. Each sphere represents a protein subunit. A core of DNA lies within the polyhedron. (b) The tobacco mosaic virus, a plant patho- *plant virus* gen, is a cylinder of protein subunits containing a core of RNA. (c) Bacteriophages commonly have a hexagonal head of protein containing a core of DNA. A cylindrical contractile sheath surrounds the core of protein.

(1) single-stranded DNA, (2) double-stranded RNA, (3) a single large molecule of single-stranded RNA, or (4) several small strands of RNA. The nucleic acid can be circular or linear, and the single-stranded nucleic acid can be either the transcribed strand or the nontranscribed strand. Furthermore, once the virus is inside its host cell, it may even change the kind of nucleic acid it uses: the RNA viruses often make DNA copies of their own genomes. Viruses are complicated things, indeed.

How Viruses Behave—or Misbehave

Most viruses contain one or more specialized enzymes that facilitate attachment to and penetration of a host cell. In some viruses, notably the bacteriophages, only the nucleic acid enters the host cytoplasm; but in other viruses, some enzymes are carried in as well. Once inside the host cytoplasm, the virus can make a more or less permanent home for itself in the cell. Alternatively, it can take over the cell's metabolic apparatus, using it for its own ends, and produce hundreds of offspring—killing its host in the process.

When a host-killing virus captures a cell, it acts quickly, stopping all of the host's normal protein synthesis and destroying the host's DNA. Then it utilizes the cell's own ribosomes and protein synthesizing machinery to make viral enzymes and protein coats. The virus may use either its own enzymes or its host enzymes to manufacture new viral nucleic acids. The new infectious viral particles are assembled, and viral enzymes lyse (dissolve) the remains of the host cell, liberating new viruses. In the case of some mammalian viruses, the new viruses are not assembled inside the cell. Instead, the viral-coat proteins merge with the host cell membrane, and new viruses are then budded off the surface of the cell (Figure 20.16).

Events are even more bizarre in viruses that, rather than killing the host, make a semipermanent home in the host cell. A virus does this by physically incorporating a copy of its genome (its total genetic material) into its host's DNA. This trick was first observed in bacterial viruses, but human viruses do the same thing. You probably have some viral genomes inserted into the DNA of your own cells right now.

Some viruses that contain RNA, called **retroviruses,** infect humans in a remarkable way. They contain an enzyme (*reverse transcriptase*) that can transcribe the viral RNA sequence into double-stranded DNA. The double-stranded DNA is then inserted into one or more of your chromosomes.

As the infected cell proliferates, the virus proliferates right along with it. It may even be passed down through the generations in eggs and sperm. Some retroviruses even ensure the rapid proliferation of their host cells by *transforming* them into cancer cells!

At some later time, the incorporated viral DNA cuts loose from the host chromosome and reverts to the other strategy—taking over the cell and making more infectious virus particles, thereby killing the cells. They will switch to this behavior whenever something goes wrong with normal host cell DNA replication. It is as if this is a sign that the host is in trouble and that it is time for the virus to jump ship, as it were.

We can usually mount immunological defenses against our virus parasites and, in fact, we are seldom infected twice by the same strain of virus. So why do we get so many colds? And why do we come down with the flu time after time? The answer is that the short-lived, numerous viruses evolve at a terrific rate. The same virus strain won't infect us more than once, but it can change to a slightly different strain through mutation, so that our antibodies no longer recognize it.

One human virus deserves to be singled out: the *Herpes simplex* virus. It is "the" disease of the 80s (the 60s had ulcers; and in the 70s, it was high blood pressure). Strain I herpes causes cold sores, but strain II causes the famed genital herpes. So what is herpes all about? The herpes virus resides in nerve cells, but usually doesn't kill them. When the host's defenses are down, perhaps because of stress, the virus buds off from its sanctuary, perhaps deep in the spinal cord, and infects surface cells of mucous membranes, killing them and liberating numerous infectious virus particles. Time and again the host builds up his or her antibodies, causing the virus to become quiescent and retreat into the nerve cells, where it is safe from the antibodies. Then the antibody level falls, and sooner or later herpes strikes again. As if the pain and temporary disfigurement were not enough, there appears to be a direct relationship between early type II herpes infections and many cases of cervical cancer, which may develop years afterward. Herpes infections last a lifetime, and are currently incurable, although intensive research is underway that may soon lead to at least a partial remedy.

We have begun our survey of life in the biosphere with an introduction to the simpler forms. It should be apparent, however, that the simpler forms are not so simple after all. Life at any level is complex, and our understanding of it is riddled with unknowns that, for some, translate into exciting challenge.

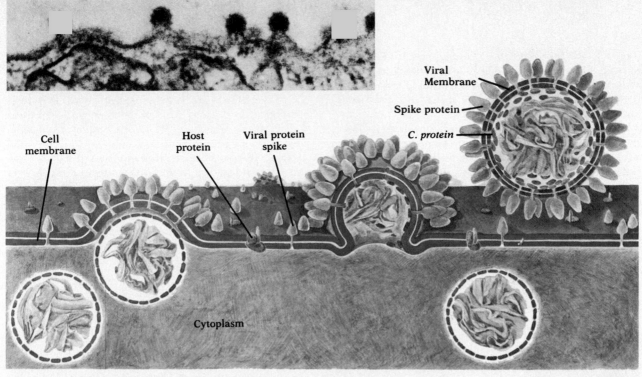

Cell
membrane

Host
protein

Viral protein
spike

Viral
Membrane

Spike protein

C. protein

Cytoplasm

20.16

Many mammalian viruses produce proteins that integrate into the host's cell membrane. A viral-coat protein binds to a viral-spike protein in the cell membrane, becoming anchored to the membrane and allowing more proteins to bind. When the virus is mature, it buds off from the host membrane but is covered with a regular array of spikelike viral proteins. The virus is then free to infect other cells.

Summary

The Origin of Life

The Haldane-Oparin hypothesis concerning the spontaneous origin of life suggests that chemical synthesis could have occurred on the very early earth, where destructive oxygen was absent and energy sources abounded. Conglomerates of proteins, or coacervates, might have taken in new types of molecules and given rise to the first self-reproducing protocells. The Miller-Urey experiment tested the assumptions behind this hypothetical scheme, illustrating that amino acids and other cellular constituents could be created when energy was applied to mixtures approximating the atmosphere of the ancient earth.

The current parts of the hypothesis of the spontaneous generation of life are: (1) continued verification of the physical conditions of the early earth; (2) production of essential monomers under primitive conditions; (3) spontaneous formation of polymers from monomers; (4) spontaneous formation of active cell-like bodies; and (5) the resulting production of simple, self-replicating systems. Experiments have resulted in the production of many monomers. Although one researcher has produced clusters of protein polymers called proteinoids, the production of nucleotide polymers is still the weakest part of the hypothesis. Supporting evidence for the spontaneous formation of nucleic acids remains to be found.

The earliest cells were probably primitive versions of today's anaerobic fermenting bacteria. The earliest autotrophs were most likely phototrophic. Soon some bacteria also began to use water as an energy source. Photosynthetic, oxygen-producing phototrophs arose, as did aerobic, oxygen-using heterotrophs. Anaerobes were relegated to environments that did not include oxygen, where we still find them today.

The Prokaryotes

Prokaryotes, among the oldest life forms on earth, are separated into two distinct kingdoms: Archebacteria and Eubacteria. Archebacteria are obligate anaerobes and survive well in such harsh environments as hot springs, ammonia-rich habitats, and salt marshes. The best-known group of Archebacteria are the methanogens; other types include the extreme halophiles, the extreme thermophiles, and the thermoacidophiles.

Some Eubacteria are heterotrophs, three groups are phototrophs, and a few are chemotrophs. Many heterotrophs are pathogens while others, such as soil and water bacteria, recycle material within the environment.

The eubacterial cell is unique in many ways. With few exceptions, all Eubacteria make cell walls of peptidoglycan, which is inhibited by antibiotics as they attack and kill the bacteria. Scientists traditionally have classified Eubacteria by shape: rod (bacillus), sphere (coccus), and spiral (spirillum). Bacilli exist as single cells or in chains, and form endospores to protect themselves against hostile environments. The coccoid forms occur in pairs, chains, or clusters, while spirilla (or spirochaetes) exist as single cells.

Pathogenic bacilli can cause serious illnesses, even death, in many organisms. Also, the body's reaction to some bacteria such as streptococcus can result in severe health problems. Pathogens often respond to antibiotics by producing new, more resistant strains.

Phototrophs such as cyanobacteria are considered highly evolved because they are more efficient than other photosynthesic bacteria. As nitrogen fixers, they are a source of new nitrogen in the environment, which is used in the synthesis of amino acids, nitrogen bases of DNA and RNA, and other essential molecules. Most bacterial phototrophs are marine aquatic organisms.

Chemotrophs oxidize inorganic compounds to obtain their energy. Some are involved in cycling nitrogen; others break down sulfur, a process that is vital to the production of some amino acids by plants.

Viruses

Viruses are parasites that invade and use the metabolic processes of cells. Outside the host, they consist of a core of nucleic acid and a coat of protein, and many have a cylindrical or polyhedral shape. Infectious forms carry on no metabolic processes on their own. The composition of DNA and RNA strands in viruses differs widely, suggesting that viruses may have arisen independently of one another.

Most viruses use specialized enzymes to invade cells, and may reside permanently within the host or take over its metabolism and produce hundreds of offspring. By destroying the host's DNA, the virus can use the cell's ribosomes and protein synthesizing mechanisms to manufacture new viral protein coats. Some viruses can even incorporate their genomes into the host's DNA.

Retroviruses can transcribe viral RNA into double-stranded DNA, which is then inserted into the host's chromosome. When the infected cell multiplies, so does the virus. At some point, the viral DNA may take over the cell and make more infectious particles, killing the host.

Generally, the immune system of the body can fight off viruses. However, viral infections such as *herpes simplex* may lie dormant in cells until triggered into action whenever the immune system is weakened.

Key Terms

coacervate droplet	methanogen	endospore
protocells	chemotroph	spirochaete
proteinoids	peptidoglycan	strep throat
Monera	glucosamine	syphilis
Archebacteria	bacillus	nitrogen fixer
Eubacteria	coccus	virus
stromatolite	spirillum	retrovirus

Review Questions

1. What did the Urey-Miller experiments prove about the spontaneous generation of life? (pp. 275–276)

2. Describe the current status of the hypothesis of the spontaneous generation of life, and cite the most problematic area still being tested. (pp. 276–287)

3. Name and describe the formation of the oldest known undisputed fossils. (p. 280)

4. Give two examples of Archebacteria and describe the conditions under which they grow. (pp. 280–281)

5. List and define the three nutritional categories of eubacterial life. (pp. 281–282)

6. Eubacterial cells occur in three major forms. List these and cite a common example of each. (pp. 282–285)

7. Cyanobacteria are of great ecological importance because they are among the few organisms that can "fix" nitrogen. Explain what this means and why nitrogen fixation is a vital activity. (p. 285)

8. Describe the organization of viruses. What about them makes biologists reluctant to consider them living organisms? (pp. 287–288)

9. Summarize the two alternatives some viruses follow once they successfully invade a host cell. (p. 288)

10. Describe the peculiar behavior of retroviruses. (p. 288)

11. Describe the manner in which the herpes simplex virus brings on the flow and ebb of symptoms in infected persons. (p. 288)

Simpler Eukaryotes:

Protists and Fungi

21

The story of evolution, as we now understand it, is punctuated by notable features of two sorts. First, there are the tidy stories that provide us with clear textbook examples of the evolutionary march in terms that we can understand. We love the story of the descent of the modern horse from the ancient little "dawn horse," *Eohippus*. And then there are those perplexing cases that we keep trying to explain. Why did our early vertebrate ancestors shift from filter-feeding to biting? How did reptiles come to fly? Are wings a modification of some reptilian gliding apparatus, or have they descended from some scaly reptile's sexual display? In this latter group of tough questions we must include the one at hand: how did the prokaryotes give rise to the eukaryotes? The question's seeming simplicity is deceptive.

THE SYMBIOSIS HYPOTHESIS

The evolutionary transition from the prokaryotic cell to the much more complex and elaborate eukaryotic cell has perplexed biologists for some time. One hypothesis proposes that eukaryotic membrane-bounded organelles evolved when infoldings of the cell membrane pinched off and enclosed various cellular functions. Hypotheses such as this often seem reasonable enough, but they simply can't be tested readily.

In 1967, a totally different hypothesis was proposed by Lynn Margulis. Using information from a wide variety of fields, Margulis concluded that the primitive eukaryotic cell developed in at least three separate stages that involved the union of four different prokaryotic lines. Her conclusion has become known as the **symbiosis hypothesis. Symbiosis** is a fairly common biological phenomenon involving the close physical association of two or more organisms, which are referred to as **symbionts.** Parasitism is one form of symbiosis, but it is not the only kind. **Mutualistic symbiosis** is a close physical relationship that benefits both partners, and there are thousands of such relationships among organisms living today. Margulis proposed that mitochondria, which are found in all eukaryotic cells, are the descendants of once free-living bacteria that long ago formed such a mutualistic symbiosis with a host cell. She also proposed that chloroplasts and cilia are the descendants of other bacteria that also entered the eukaryotic cell in what began as mutualistic symbioses (Figure 21.1).

Margulis' symbiosis hypothesis was testable: specifically, it allowed her to predict that mitochondria, chloroplasts, and cilia should be biochemically and genetically more similar to certain free-living prokaryotes than they are to other parts of the eukaryotic cell. So far these predictions have held up remarkably well for mitochondria and for chloroplasts, but not for eukaryotic cilia.

Schematic diagram of the symbiosis hypothesis, in which symbiotic events occur between the earliest eukaryote—called a protoeukaryote—and a number of prokaryotes. According to Margulis' hypothesis, line A cells had already developed the organized nucleus. Then some line A cells engulfed primitive aerobic prokaryotes (line B), digesting them at first, but eventually retaining them and utilizing their mitochondrionlike organization. The next event included incorporation of flagellated cells (line C), which provided a new means of propulsion for the early eukaryote. Some descendants of this latest line may have been ancestral to the first animal-like protists. Other descending lines incorporated phototrophic bacteria (line D), perhaps cyanobacteria, developing a motile, aerobic, photosynthetic line which could have been ancestral to the algal line of protists.

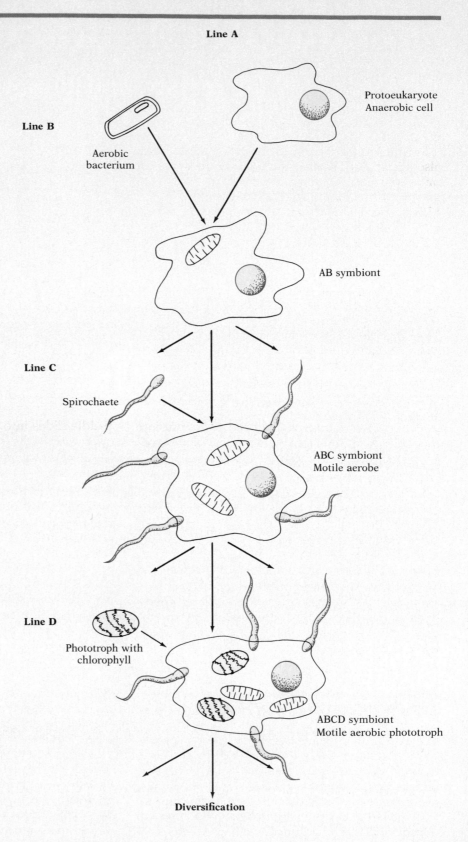

Line A

Protoeukaryote
Anaerobic cell

Line B

Aerobic
bacterium

AB symbiont

Line C

Spirochaete

ABC symbiont
Motile aerobe

Line D

Phototroph with
chlorophyll

ABCD symbiont
Motile aerobic phototroph

Diversification

We've seen that all living organisms can be placed into three grand categories, the Eubacteria, the Archebacteria, and the eukaryotes (see Chapter 20). One of the lines of evidence for this is that the small ribosomal subunit has a different characteristic shape in each group: in the eukaryote cytoplasm, it looks like a rubber duck with two tiny legs (see Figure 15.4); in the Archebacteria, the tiny legs are missing; in the Eubacteria, both the legs and the duck's bill are missing. The legs and bill are also missing in the small subunits of ribosomes in mitochondria and chloroplasts. Thus these two eukaryotic organelles have ribosomes with the characteristic size and shape of eubacterial ribosomes; this is probably one of the strongest single pieces of evidence for the symbiosis hypothesis.

THE KINGDOM OF PROTISTS

The kingdom **Protista** consists of all eukaryotic organisms that are not plants, animals, or fungi. This negative definition encompasses quite a grab-bag of disparate creatures, but most of them consist either of single cells or of simple colonies of identical cells (Figure 21.2).

For practical purposes, the protists are put into two categories: the photosynthesizing, plantlike *algal protists*; and the nonphotosynthesizing, animal-like *protozoa*. As far as evolutionary relationships go, however, the categories aren't so clear-cut. Some photosynthetic, chloroplast-containing protists seem to be related much more closely to protozoans than to other algal protists, while some non-

photosynthetic protists are clearly algal protists that have lost their chloroplasts and have taken up other ways of making a living. There is also an enigmatic group of creatures poetically called the *slime molds*, which are sometimes classified among the fungi.

The Algal Protists

There are about 10,000 named species of **algal protists.** In the oceans, many live in dense floating populations, and are referred to as **phytoplankton.** Other algal protists live as mutualistic, photosynthesizing symbionts within the cells of corals, giant clams, sea slugs, and protozoa. Altogether, marine algal protists fix more carbon by photosynthesis than does the entire plant kingdom—more than all of the land plants and all of the seaweeds combined. But not all algal protists are marine; some live in fresh water, and others live on land, either independently or in mutualistic symbiotic partnerships.

Dinoflagellates.   Visitors to tropical waters are often surprised and delighted as they are rowed in the evening between ship and shore. Each time the paddle slides into the water, the sea seems to explode with iridescent light. Even the wake of the canoe is aglow. The tiny, twinkling lights are the magic of minute living creatures, the microscopic **dinoflagellates.**

However, when conditions are favorable, their numbers can increase explosively, and these same little creatures can be responsible for another,

 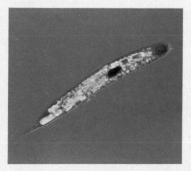 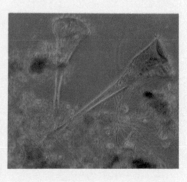

21.2

The kingdom Protista includes widely diverging groups of single-celled and colonial organisms. Some are autotrophic photosynthesizers with organized chloroplasts. Others are heterotrophic, with nutritional requirements similar to those of animals. All are eukaryotic, with many of the organelles found in plants and animals. Protists are wide-ranging organisms, inhabiting most of the marine and fresh water aquatic environments, and a few are terrestrial.

equally dramatic, and far more dangerous phenomenon: the **red tide.** Teeming trillions of dinoflagellates turn the sea to a bloody color, and fish, subjected to deadly toxins, die by the thousands. Clams, oysters, and mussels survive, but accumulate the poisons as they filter-feed on the dinoflagellates. At these times—generally, from May through August—the poisoned mollusks can prove fatal to humans who eat them.

Dinoflagellates are flagellated, photosynthetic protists, covered with plates of cellulose and quite unlike anything else alive. Each typically has two flagella, one trailing and one confined to a groove that encircles its waist (Figure 21.3). Details of their cell structure seem "primitive" to systematists—for instance, dinoflagellate chromosomes are massive, permanently condensed, and permanently attached to the nuclear membrane in a way that is reminiscent of the attachment of the circular DNA in bacteria to the bacterial cell membrane.

Although most dinoflagellates are photosynthetic, a few are nonphotosynthetic heterotrophs or parasites. Most photosynthetic dinoflagellates are free living, but a variety live most of their lives as photosynthetic symbionts in the cells of marine protozoa or animals, often imparting a peculiar green color to their larger symbiotic partners.

The Chrysophytes: Golden-brown Algae and Diatoms. The **chrysophytes** are single-celled or colonial algae of both marine and fresh waters. Their golden-brown colors are derived from several bright pigments, but usually the dominating pigment is carotene, an accessory pigment of photosynthesis (see Chapter 7). The chrysophytes are an important part of ocean life, since they are among the creatures that turn sunlight into food.

The **diatoms** produce cell walls of silicon dioxide, which is to say, of glass. These glassy cell walls can be intricately sculptured in a variety of patterns (Figure 21.4). The designs are produced by the arrangements of tiny perforations, through which water and dissolved gases pass (even glass houses need windows). The cell walls form tiny boxes, each with an inner part and an outer, overlapping lid (the two parts fit together a lot like the halves of the covered petri dishes that microbiologists use for growing colonies of bacteria). This arrangement presents some interesting problems when the diatom grows and reproduces (Figure 21.5).

The diatoms are not an ancient group, as protists go. They show up suddenly in the fossil record in the Cretaceous era, but they do not become numerous until the beginning of the Cenozoic era, about 65 million years ago.

The Euglenoids. *Euglena gracilis* (see Figure 21.2b) is one of about 800 species of euglenoids. Most **euglenoids** thrive in fresh, preferably nutrient-enriched water—polluted water, by our standards. The group has always been a taxonomic enigma to biologists. In those that have chloroplasts (one-third of the genera—the rest are heterotrophic), the chloroplasts closely resemble those of plants; but in all other regards, the euglenoids seem to be flagellate protozoa. Like animals and protozoa, they have no cell walls and instead have

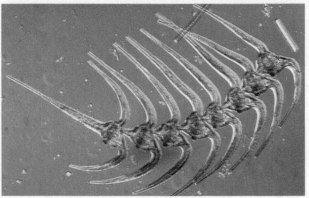

21.3

Among the marine phytoplankton are the dinoflagellates, rather primitive single-celled photosynthesizers.

The most spectacular chrysophytes are the 5000 or so species of diatoms. Their glassy walls contain numerous types of finely etched patterns so regular and clear that mounted specimens are used to test the quality of microscope lenses. Their populations change seasonally. At their peak they may produce 35 million cells per cubic meter of water.

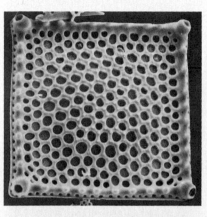

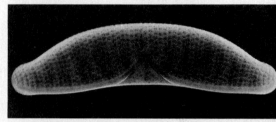

a flexible, proteinaceous *pellicle*. Animals, protozoa, and euglenoids also share a list of essential vitamins and amino acids that must be provided in their diets, whereas plants and fungi manufacture their own vitamins and amino acids. These nutritional requirements help explain the euglenoids' preference for polluted water.

Euglena gracilis moves its flexible body through the use of a single, massive flagellum. It has a *photoreceptor* at the base of its flagellum. A bit of pigment shields the photoreceptor on one side, which allows the organism to orient itself toward the source of light. Euglenoids have no known sexual activity, but instead reproduce asexually by mitosis and by cell division (cytokinesis) along the long axis of the cell.

The Animal-like Protists

The **protozoa** are clearly similar to animals. They are heterotrophic, which means that they derive their energy and carbon from the efforts of other organisms, in the form of ready-made organic molecules. As we have seen, the protozoa need to have essential vitamins and amino acids in their diet. And like animals, they show a wide range of feeding specializations. Many protozoa are parasites: some are decomposers that feed on nonliving materials, and others capture and engulf living prey. Most protozoa belong to this last group, and ingest food by **phagocytosis;** that is, the cell surrounds a solid food particle and encloses it within a digestive vacuole that moves through the cytoplasm.

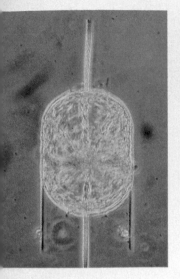

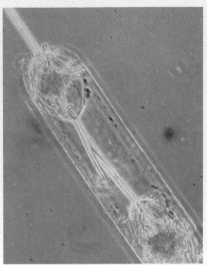

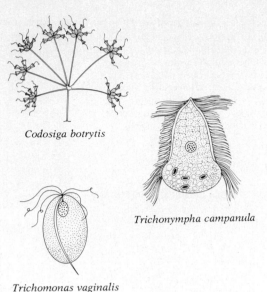

Codosiga botrytis

Trichonympha campanula

Trichomonas vaginalis

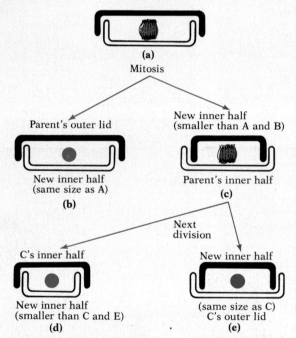

(a)
Mitosis

Parent's outer lid

New inner half
(smaller than A and B)

New inner half
(same size as A)
(b)

Parent's inner half
(c)

Next
division

C's inner half

New inner half

New inner half
(smaller than C and E)
(d)

(same size as C)
C's outer lid
(e)

21.5

Diatoms are among the most beautiful, delicate, and fascinating species on earth. They are also among the most peculiar. The life cycle of diatoms has some strikingly peculiar aspects. In their asexual reproduction, which occurs through mitosis and cell division, one daughter cell gets the upper lid of the glassy box, while the other gets the lower, smaller lid. For some unknown reason, diatoms manufacture only lower lids after division. As you can see, the arithmetic of lid size leads to an interesting problem. Some diatoms get smaller and smaller. The diatom's answer to this vexing problem is to stop mitosis and enter a sexual phase. Meiosis occurs with one flagellated gamete produced per diatom. The gametes fuse, becoming diploid again, and then produce a full-sized set of lids. Then the shrinking begins again.

21.6

The flagellates are animal-like protists with single, paired, or multiple flagella. Otherwise the many species may bear little resemblance to each other, as we see here. Flagellates such as *Codosiga botrytis* are sessile, attached to stalks, with their flagella extending out of collarlike feeding structures. Others, such as *Trichonympha campanula*, a wood-digesting symbiont of the termite, use their many flagella to move freely about. One species, *Trichomonas vaginalis*, inhabits the human vagina, where it can cause severe discomfort.

The Flagellate Protozoans. The **flagellates** are often vase-shaped. All move about by means of one or more whiplike, undulating flagella (Figure 21.6), although we hasten to add that not all protists with flagella necessarily belong to this group. A flagellum can either push or pull, depending on the organism—some protozoa have both pushing and pulling flagella. This organelle of locomotion may occur singly, in pairs, or in greater numbers, but each flagellum has the characteristic eukaryotic 9 + 2 arrangement of microtubules within the membrane (see Chapters 4 and 20).

All protists are capable of asexual reproduction, and the flagellates are no exception. Mitosis is followed by duplication of the flagella and then by cleavage along the long axis of the cell. Sexual reproduction is infrequent among the flagellates, but where it has been observed, there are no gametes or sex cells; two cells simply fuse together to form a zygote. This fusion is not even preceded by meiosis—there is no need for chromosome reduction beforehand, since flagellates, like many protists, are haploid (with a half-number of chromo-

21.7

In the flagellate *Trypanosoma*, the lengthy flagellum is attached to an undulating membrane along the cell, tapering down at the cell's leading edge. In Africa, certain species of trypanosomes are transmitted by the bite of the tsetse fly, causing a potentially lethal disease called African sleeping sickness. The trypanosomes are shown among bloodcells at the right; the tsetse fly is shown at the far right.

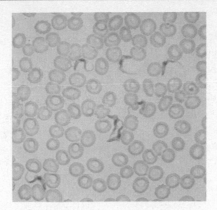 

somes) throughout most of their lives. Following the fusion of two cells, a brief diploid state (full number of chromosomes) exists, but the new zygote soon undergoes meiosis, forming four new haploid individuals. As you know, we animals (and some of the protists) are diploid throughout nearly all of our life cycles; our only haploid cells are our gametes.

Some parasitic flagellate protozoans cause severe diseases in humans. Among them are the **trypanosomes,** members of the genus *Trypanosoma*. A trypanosome can be identified by an undulating flap—actually a modified flagellum—that runs the length of its spindly body (Figure 21.7). *Trypanosoma gambiense* is the cause of African sleeping sickness. The bite of the infamous tsetse fly injects the parasite into the bloodstream of a mammalian host. Multiplying trypanosomes eventually enter the central nervous system of the unfortunate mammal. Control of the disease is very difficult, since nearly all large mammals in tropical Africa harbor the parasite and serve as reservoirs of reinfection. Through coevolution, the native animal hosts aren't particularly affected by the parasite, but infection often leads to death in humans and in domestic cattle.

Amoeboid Protozoans—The Amoebas and Their Relatives. The **amoeboid protozoans** (phylum *Sarcodina*) are fascinating creatures. Some of them are quite large as protists go. (Some amoebas grow so large that they are able to engulf humans, and even whole restaurants, in science fiction movies such as *The Blob*.) In all reality, there are amoebas that are capable of engulfing animals, such as struggling crustaceans (Figure 21.8). Other amoebas are nastier—*Entamoeba histolytica*, for example, feeds on the cells that line human colons and causes amoebic dysentery.

Some amoeboid protozoa produce flagellated gametes, and some even bear flagella throughout their entire life cycles. But all amoeboid species move about by the use of *pseudopods*. **Pseudopods** ("false feet") are temporary, formless, lobelike projections of the cell membrane and the cytoskeleton. These projections can extend in any direction, and the amoeba moves by extending a false foot and then flowing into it. With pseudopods, an amoeba can walk along the bottom of a pond or squeeze its way through soil or living tissue. The pseudopods

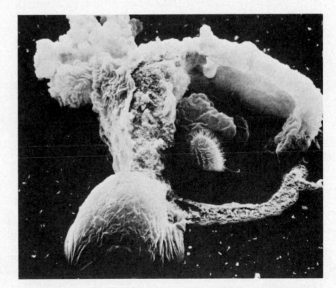

21.8

Amoebas feed by surrounding their prey and taking it into food vacuoles by phagocytosis. After this, enzymes enter the vacuole, digest the prey, and the products of digestion enter the cytoplasm. Any remaining residue is carried to the membrane and is released through exocytosis.

are also used to capture prey: they can become cuplike and flow around a food item.

The dramatically beautiful **heliozoans** or "sun animals" (Figure 21.9a) live in fresh water and are partially encased in glassy capsules of silicon dioxide. The radiating rays consist of lengthy pseudopods of motile cytoplasm, stiffened with long, straight bundles of microtubules. The microtubule bundles can quickly dissolve and reform later as they are needed. **Radiolarians** of the open sea (Figure 21.9b) have a similar body plan, and their glassy corpses litter the ageless ocean floor with deposits known as *radiolarian ooze.*

Foraminiferans belong to another group of planktonic amoeboid protozoans. They produce chalky, not glassy, skeletons, sometimes in shapes remarkably reminiscent of the shells of garden snails (Figure 21.9c). The calcium carbonate skeletons bear multiple *foramina* ("little windows") through which slender pseudopods can be extended. The pseudopods branch and rejoin to form a net that serves as a prey-capturing device. But foraminiferans get most of their energy and carbon needs from photosynthetic symbionts that live within their cells. The fabled white cliffs of Dover, England are chalky deposits of ancient foraminiferan shells.

The Ciliate Protozoans.

Among the most complex cells on earth are those of the **ciliates** (Figure 21.10). Ciliates range in size from about 10 μm to 3 mm, which is about the same relative difference that exists between a shrew and a blue whale. The ciliates' most obvious characteristic is that they are covered with cilia, in longitudinal or spiral rows. Like flagella, cilia can move, but they are so numerous that it wouldn't do for each cilium to beat wildly, independent of the rest. Their movement is highly coordinated by a network of connecting fibers that run beneath the surface of the cell. Under the microscope, the coordinated beating of cilia gives the appearance of a field of wheat bending before gusts of wind. The beating of the cilia produces an organized rowing action that speeds free-swimming ciliates along, often in a spiralling, corkscrew path.

Cilia are also used in feeding. Some ciliates live firmly anchored to a solid base; in the stationary ciliates, the cilia move a current of water over the cell, directing bacteria and other organic matter into a mouthlike opening called the **cytostome.** (Rows of cilia similarly sweep food into a cytostome in swimming species such as *Paramecium.*) At the cytostome, a fixed place on the surface of the cell, particles of food are phagocytized and taken into a newly formed **food vacuole** for digestion (Figure 21.11). Wastes are discharged from the cell at another specific location known as the **cytopyge,** a sort of cellular anus.

Freshwater ciliates have to deal with osmotic problems. Water moves to follow its own concentration gradient, which means it tends to move from the environment (where its concentration approaches 100%) into the cytoplasm (where the concentration of water is reduced due to other cellular constituents). So inflowing water must somehow

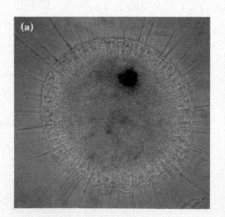
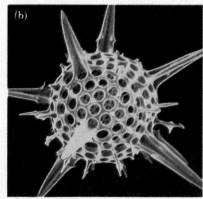

21.9

Unusual sarcodines include the heliozoan, *Actinosphaerium* **(a),** which has a covering of fine spines. Each spine is surrounded by streaming (circulating) cytoplasm that engulfs minute food particles, carrying them into the cell. Radiolarians **(b)** from the marine environment are typically spherical, with highly sculptured glassy skeletons, reminiscent of vintage Christmas ornaments. The skeletons of marine foraminiferans **(c)** are often coiled in snail-like fashion, but unlike the radiolarians, are composed of calcium carbonate. Both radiolarians and foraminiferans contribute their skeletons to the thick ooze that is so common on the ocean bottom.

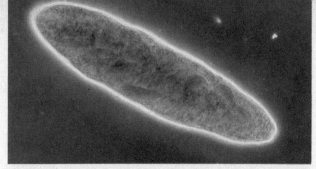

S. ambiguum

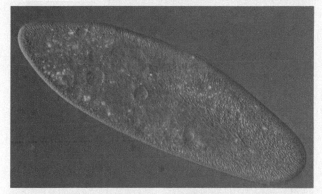

P. mutimicronucleatum

 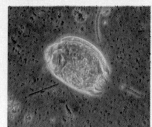

V. campanula, D. dentatum

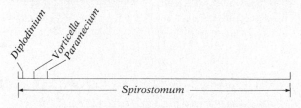

21.10

Ciliates are an extremely diverse group and some of them are the most structurally complex protists known. Their size range is comparable to that of mammals (from the shrew to the blue whale), but on a much different scale. The protistan giant, *Spirostomum ambiguum*, reaches 3000 μm (3 mm) and is easily seen with the unaided eye. Even the larger species of *Paramecium*, such as *P. multimicronucleatum*, are comparative midgets, growing to only 350 μm. Some ciliates, such as *Vorticella campanula*, are attached to contractile stalks that quickly draw the cell inward when disturbed. *V. campanula* feeds through the action of rows of beating cilia about the mouth, which create the vortex (whirlpool) for which it is named. One of the smallest ciliates, *Diplodinium dentatum*, only 20–40 μm long, lives as a symbiont in the cow's stomach. There, along with other microorganisms, it digests cellulose, something the cow cannot do on its own.

be pumped out again. The answer for freshwater ciliates, and for many other freshwater protists, is the **contractile vacuole.** This is a specialized organelle, a hollow chamber that is surrounded by organized, mobile elements of the cytoskeleton. Expansion of the contractile vacuole produces negative pressure inside, which allows water to flow from the cytoplasm into the vacuole. A subsequent contraction of the vacuole empties the watery contents through a pore to the outside. Both the filling and the emptying of contractile vacuoles require the ATP-powered contractions of microfibrils in the cytoskeleton.

It is the short, beating cilia that identify members of this group. All ciliates have cilia on their body surfaces at some stage in their lives. The cilia of some species are quite specialized, such as the cilia of *Euplotes*, which are fused into spinelike projections.

Paramecium is the best-known ciliate. This slipper-shaped creature gains its fame because it is so often used as a laboratory subject. Other species, however, are rarely used this way because they are so dangerous. *Balantidium* is one of the few parasitic species. It invades the colon of humans and can cause the entire lining of the large intestine to erupt in great, hemorrhagic ulcers. The victim is notified by violent and persistent diarrhea. This species also moves in quick swirling motions by use of its cilia.

Most ciliates do not become sexually mature until they have divided asexually a number of times— 40 or 50 times is typical. Then they go into a sexual

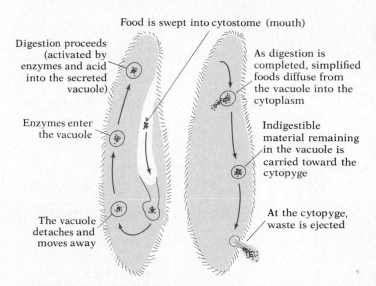

Food is swept into cytostome (mouth)

Digestion proceeds (activated by enzymes and acid into the secreted vacuole)

As digestion is completed, simplified foods diffuse from the vacuole into the cytoplasm

Enzymes enter the vacuole

Indigestible material remaining in the vacuole is carried toward the cytopyge

The vacuole detaches and moves away

At the cytopyge, waste is ejected

21.11

Digestion in *Paramecium*, as in many protozoans, occurs in food vacuoles.

cycle, and become receptive to appropriate mates. There are no males or females, but there are different *mating types*. *Paramecium*, for instance, has eight different mating types, any two of which can mate. Matings are always between members of such different strains, and never between members of the same, asexually produced clone.

Mating occurs by **conjugation.** The two mating individuals fuse in the region of their cytostomes. Meiosis occurs during conjugation, and four haploid nuclei are formed within each partner. Typically, three of these products of meiosis disintegrate and the fourth undergoes replication and mitosis. Then each partner keeps one nucleus and sends the other across a cytoplasmic bridge. This swapping of haploid nuclei accomplishes fully reciprocal fertilization. The traveling nucleus fuses with the stationary nucleus in each partner, which restores the normal diploid condition. The partners separate, and each then proceeds with asexual reproduction until it has produced its own genetically unique clone of descendants.

SLIME MOLDS: A DIFFERENT KIND OF PROTIST

Now let's consider that romantic group of organisms called the **slime molds.** No one is quite sure how to classify them, since they have traits in common with both the protists and our next kingdom, the Fungi. In some respects, they are even animal-like. In fact, it seems that the slime molds live double lives. Part of the time they multiply and grow over their food supply (often a rotting log), each cell behaving like some amoeba. But when their food source dries up, they change drastically. The individual cells crawl together and coalesce, forming a single body called a *slug*. The slug wanders blindly about like a mindless worm. Eventually, it stops and vertical stalks begin to arise from this peculiar mass of protoplasm, bearing fruiting bodies that give rise to airborne spores, just like any respectable mold might do (Figure 21.12).

Actually, there are two distinct groups of slime molds—the *cellular slime molds*, as just described, and the *acellular slime molds*. The two groups may not be closely related to one another, although they both have a bizarre, double lifestyle. Acellular slime molds form huge multinucleate masses, forming what looks like a giant amoeba—large enough to engulf an entire log. The mass, however, may be only a millimeter thick.

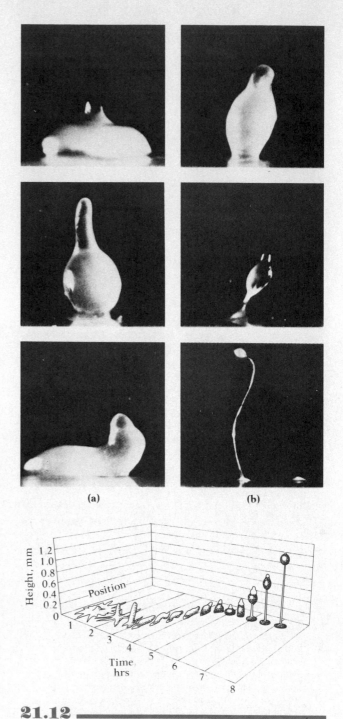

(a)   (b)

21.12

(a) Cellular slime molds live as independent, unicellular amoebas, phagocytizing soil bacteria and reproducing asexually during the vegetative part of their life cycle. In the sexual phase, individual cells coalesce into a heap, which differentiates into a motile, nonfeeding "slug." (b) Eventually the slug stops crawling; a stalk appears, first as a bump which then lengthens, lifting a ball of cells to its tip. The ball (sporangium) develops spores as it rises higher with the further elongation of the stalk. Eventually the spores are released into the wind.

THE FUNGI

The **fungi** are a strange lot, in many ways quite unlike other organisms. Most are stationary and multicellular, and all are heterotrophs, living as parasites, symbionts, or reducers. In their reducing or decomposing activities they join with the bacteria in recycling essential molecules. We are, perhaps, most familiar with fungi that are reducers, decomposers of nonliving organic material, appearing as mold on leftover sandwiches. These are indeed the most commonly seen fungi. The majority of fungal *species*, however, live in association with other organisms, either as parasites or, even more commonly, as symbionts. There are thousands of species, for example, that live in association with algae to form lichens. The **mycorrhizae**, an association of fungi and plant roots, aid the plants in obtaining soil nutrients and moisture in exchange for a modest amount of organic food energy.

Fungi spread over the world by forming tiny **spores** that can be carried by air currents. Under favorable conditions—when there is adequate moisture, food, and warmth—the spores germinate, and a *vegetative* (feeding) *stage* emerges. In most fungal species, the vegetative stage is marked by an extensive, spreading **mycelium**, which consists of numerous branching, threadlike growths called **hyphae.** Individually, the hyphae are minute tubes of cytoplasm, surrounded by a cell wall that is usually composed of the complex carbohydrate **chitin** (the same tough, flexible material that is also found in the skeletons of insects and their relatives). In some fungi, the cytoplasm is not organized into cells, but is continuous and contains many nuclei. Other fungi exhibit a typical cellular state, with one nucleus per cell.

Some hyphae penetrate food (which may or may not be a living host). Each tiny projection secretes digestive enzymes into the food and then simply absorbs the products by cellular active transport. Other hyphae grow upward to produce large, spore-forming bodies that will eventually liberate the spores, which then lend themselves to be wafted great distances on the winds of fate. The system works well, as we all know, since molds often help us decide what to do with "leftovers" or send us scurrying to our physicians.

The fungi are haploid throughout nearly all of their vegetative and reproductive states. Some reproduce sexually, restoring the diploid state. This state is of the briefest duration because the zygote immediately enters meiosis and the haploid state is resumed. The structures in which fertilization and meiosis take place are often huge and elaborate, and include the familiar shelflike growths seen on rotting logs and the mushrooms that sprout almost overnight in our lawns. However, fungi are so strange and varied that there are exceptions to practically every generality that can be made about them.

The fungal kingdom includes several minor groups and four major groups: The **oomycetes,** or water molds; the **zygomycetes,** or bread molds; the **ascomycetes,** or sac fungi (which include the familiar yeasts and citrus molds); and the **basidiomycetes,** or club fungi (which include mushrooms, puffballs, and shelf fungi). An additional group, the *deuteromycetes*, or so-called *Fungi Imperfecti*, is a mix of species whose classification is unresolved.

Oomycetes: The Water Molds

The water molds are most familiar as the ugly, furry growths that plague the fish in our aquariums. Others are parasites of insects and plants, and one caused the famous Irish potato famine of the 1840s. Water molds can reproduce both sexually and asexually. They are cellular and develop flagellated, swimming spores. (No other fungus produces motile cells.) The water molds are biochemically and physiologically so unlike other fungi that most mycologists (fungus experts) believe the water molds are actually protists that have achieved membership in the kingdom Fungi spuriously, by convergent evolution.

Zygomycetes: The Bread Molds

Let's now consider three phyla in the subkingdom Eumycota (the "true fungi"). The common bread mold, *Rhizopus stolonifer*, is bound to turn up in everyone's refrigerator at one time or another. *Rhizopus* actually grows vigorously on many foods, preferably starchy types (Figure 21.13). The mycelium develops long, horizontal hyphae called *stolons* that send branching rhizoids down into the food. The tiny black dots on moldy bread are the **sporangia,** producers of many tiny haploid spores that will be dispersed in the asexual reproduction of the fungus. Such spores are spread over great distances.

Although there are no true sexes in the zygomycetes, there are different mating strains designated as "plus" and "minus". Sexual reproduction occurs when a plus strain meets a minus strain. The hyphae of the two types connect, permitting the haploid nuclei from each strain to join. Their

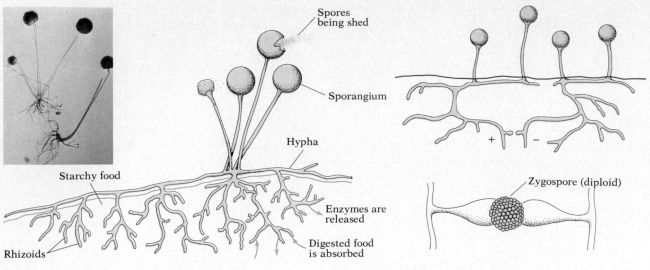

Spores being shed

Sporangium

Hypha

Starchy food

Enzymes are released

Digested food is absorbed

Rhizoids

Zygospore (diploid)

21.13

Rhizopus stolonifer, the common black bread mold, grows well on any starchy medium. Its spreading mycelium forms a tangled mat on the food, sending feeding hyphae into the interior. There digestive enzymes are secreted into the food, and the products of digestion are taken in. Asexual reproduction begins when erect hyphae develop black sporangia. Numerous spores are produced through mitosis (the mycelium is already haploid), and are released to be carried away by air currents. The few that land in favorable places germinate to form a new mycelium. *R. stolonifer* can reproduce sexually when plus and minus strains are present. Nearby hyphae form bridges in which the haploid plus and minus nuclei meet, fusing to form diploid zygospores. As in most fungi, the diploid state is brief, followed almost immediately by meiosis and the growth of a new mycelium. (Photo courtesy of Carolina Biological Company.)

union brings about the development of a tough, black, diploid **zygospore.** The brief diploid state ends as soon as meiosis occurs in the zygospore. When the zygospore germinates, the hyphae that emerge are once again haploid.

Ascomycetes: The Sac Fungi

The ascomycetes (and the basidiomycetes) have an essentially cellular structure, with *septa* (cross-walls) isolating each nucleus in the tubelike hyphae. The septa have large pores, through which the nuclei are free to migrate. The names *ascomycetes* and *sac fungus* both refer to a characteristic, microscopic, saclike reproductive structure, the **ascus** (plural, *asci*), in which sexual spores are produced.

The sac fungi include such familiar members as the powdery mildews and the blue and green molds of blue cheese and citrus fruit (Figure 21.14), as well as edible truffles and morels. Baker's and brewer's yeasts belong in this group, as well as the yeast that sometimes causes troublesome vaginal infections.

One sac fungus that holds rather ghastly implications for humans is *Claviceps purpurea*, a fungal parasite that causes a disease called *ergot* in rye and other grasses. When ergotized rye flour is eaten, it has the strange property of causing hallucinations and burning sensations in the hands and feet, where blood vessels become constricted. Historically speaking, there is some reason to believe that the hysterical girls who testified against Salem's famous witches were suffering from ergot poisoning. Severe ergot poisoning, called "St. Anthony's fire" or "holy fire," can eventually produce gangrene and painful death. (An outbreak occurred in France in the late 1960s.) The hallucinogen LSD is derived from the fungus.

The sac fungi reproduce both asexually and sexually. The latter is characterized by a strange kind of delayed fertilization and an elaborate sexual structure, the *ascocarp* (Figure 21.15).

Basidiomycetes: The Club Fungi

The basidiomycetes, or club fungi, include the common forest mushroom, the shelf fungus, the puffball, and other fleshy species, along with the parasitic wheat rusts and corn smuts. The names *basidiomycetes* and *club fungi* both refer to a characteristic microscopic reproductive structure

21.14

The green mold *Penicillium* (from which penicillin is derived) is commonly seen on the surface of citrus fruits. *Penicillium* reproduces asexually by the continuous production of spores in an assemblyline fashion. There is no known sexual stage in this species.

Conidiospores

Conidiophores

Penicillium

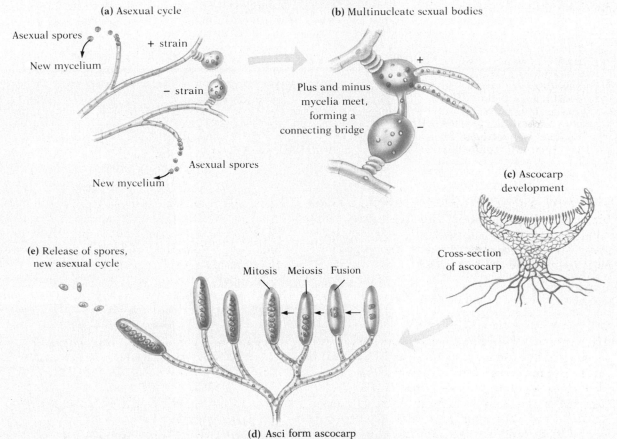

(a) Asexual cycle

Asexual spores

New mycelium

+ strain

− strain

Asexual spores

New mycelium

(b) Multinucleate sexual bodies

+

−

Plus and minus mycelia meet, forming a connecting bridge

(c) Ascocarp development

Cross-section of ascocarp

(e) Release of spores, new asexual cycle

Mitosis Meiosis Fusion

(d) Asci form ascocarp

21.15

Asexual reproduction in the sac fungi **(a)** occurs through simple spore formation. The spores germinate and produce new mycelia. Sexual reproduction requires the presence of plus and minus strains. When such strains meet in some species, they produce bulbous sexual bodies containing many haploid nuclei. A bridge forms between the plus and minus bodies **(b)**, and nuclei migrate from one strain to the other. However, the plus and minus nuclei do not fuse, but remain separated. New hyphae emerge, with each cell containing the two types of nuclei (called a *dikaryotic state*). These hyphae and the older uncombined hyphae join together to produce a cup-shaped ascocarp **(c)**. The bulk of the ascocarp's mycelium is formed from older hyphae, while the sexual structures within **(d)** are formed from the dikaryotic hyphae. Fusion of plus and minus strain nuclei finally occurs in the asci. The ensuing diploid state is brief, with meiosis immediately following. The four haploid products formed have undergone genetic recombination, so each may contain a mix of genes from both strains. They enter into one round of mitosis each and eight ascospores are formed. Upon their release **(e)**, the ascospores germinate to begin a new asexual cycle, as seen in **(a)**.

from which the sexual spores are budded off: the **basidium** ("little pedestal"). To some, the same structure also resembles a club (Figure 21.16).

The familiar mushroom growing on the forest floor is only a part of the organism. Below the soil surface lies an extensive, unseen mycelium, silently secreting enzymes, digesting organic matter, and absorbing nutrients. The mycelium may also form the mycorrhizal relationship with plant roots, as was described earlier. The mushroom's above-ground portion—the part sold in supermarkets—is known, technically, as the **basidiocarp.** It is produced after mycelia of plus and minus strains have united below ground (Figure 21.17). And, just as we found in the sac fungi, each cell produced after the union contains two separate haploid nuclei, one contributed by each strain. The plus and minus nuclei remain separate in all cells except those des-

tined to form spores. Fusion of plus and minus nuclei takes place in the numerous basidia that line the thin **gills** found on the underside of the umbrella-shaped **cap.** The diploid state is brief, followed immediately by meiosis and the formation of haploid spores. People who are dedicated to counting such things tell us that a single mushroom can produce billions of spores in this manner—a sizable investment in the mushroom's future.

The Fungi Imperfecti.   **Imperfect** is a botanical term referring to the presumed absence of sexual reproduction. There are thousands of poorly understood species of *Fungi Imperfecti* (phylum Deuteromycetes), which apparently will occupy the energies of taxonomists for decades to come. Undoubtedly, many of these species will eventually

21.16

Some club fungi can become quite large and are often colorful. The common mushrooms and bracket fungi obtain their nourishment from digesting dead organisms and organic matter in the soil. Bracket fungi **(a)** can also cause the death of living trees by penetrating and digesting the nonliving core of woody cells, thereby weakening the plant and opening it up for other infections. Mushrooms that look like *Lepiota* **(b)** can be edible or dangerously poisonous, as is *Amanita* **(c).** These are clearly different, but sometimes edible and deadly mushrooms can appear distressingly similar. Some club fungi, such as the common corn smut **(d),** are devastating parasites that are capable of causing huge crop losses if not controlled.

The familiar mushroom is a fruiting body, technically known as a *basidiocarp*. It is the product of sexual reproduction. The initial event is hidden from sight within the soil, where plus and minus hyphal strains met. Nuclear fusion is delayed **(a)**, as seen previously in the sac fungi. After this, the familiar basidiocarp grows, rapidly emerging from the soil **(b)**. When the cap opens, numerous gills become visible on its undersurface **(c).** Each gill is lined with many tiny basidia, and it is within the basidia that fertilization finally occurs. As usual, fertilization is immediately followed by meiosis and the production of haploid spores.

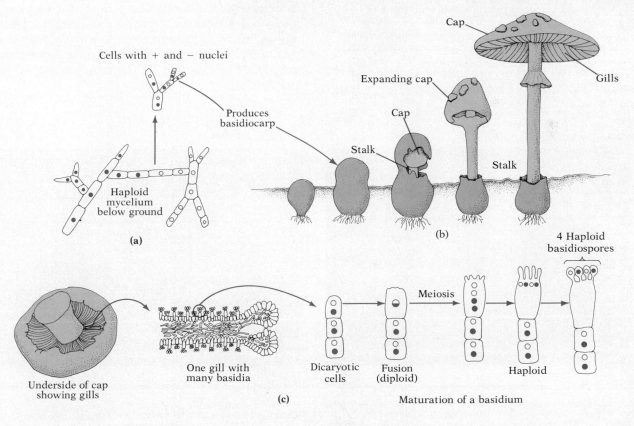

Cells with + and − nuclei

Produces basidiocarp

Haploid mycelium below ground

(a)

Cap

Expanding cap

Cap

Stalk

Stalk

Gills

(b)

4 Haploid basidiospores

Underside of cap showing gills

One gill with many basidia

Dicaryotic cells

Fusion (diploid)

Meiosis

Haploid

(c)

Maturation of a basidium

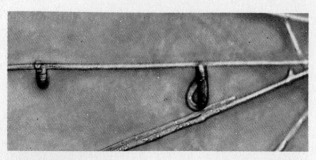

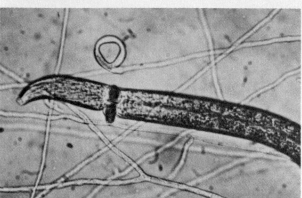

21.18

Among the *Fungi imperfecti* is the bizarre, predatory species, *Dactylaria*. Its mycelium contains many looplike snares, each capable of swelling rapidly upon touch, to close the loop on anything passing through. Soil nematodes, moving through the soil water, are its usual victims. Once captured, they are penetrated by fast growing fungal filaments that secrete digestive enzymes.

be placed among either the sac or club fungi. The *Fungi Imperfecti* include a number of human parasites such as *Trichophyton mentagrophytes*, which causes athlete's foot. Another causes ringworm. A fascinating but presumably unrelated species, *Dactylaria*, is a predator that catches certain roundworms that live in the soil (Figure 21.18).

THE LICHENS

We include **lichens** among the fungi, but they are actually composed of a symbiotic association of a fungus and a green alga or a cyanobacterium. A number of fungi may be involved in such associations, but the most common are the sac fungi. Whatever the species, however, the association is mutual; both partners benefit. The fungus provides moisture, mineral nutrients, and strong attachment to the substrate. The alga or cyanobacterium provides food produced through photosynthesis. This unique partnership permits the lichen to grow in unusual places where there is little competition from other organisms. We commonly find them on rocky outcrops, where, because of their erosive effects on the rocks, they may begin soil formation. Lichens also grow on trees and as luxurious ground cover in the frigid tundra (Figure 21.19). They rarely live in cities, since they are highly susceptible to the toxic effects of air pollution.

21.19

Lichens are perhaps the best known example of mutualistic symbiosis. The lichen consists of two organisms, a fungus and an alga or cyanobacterium, living in an intimate association from which both benefit. Lichens are sometimes found on decaying stumps (the green, frilly growth above left). They are often found on rocky surfaces, where they initiate the process of soil-building through their erosive effects and their own decomposition (above right).

Summary

The Symbiosis Hypothesis

The symbiosis hypothesis suggests that eukaryotic cells developed in at least three separate stages that involved the union of four prokaryotic lines. Symbiosis in this case was mutualistic, with one cell living inside another. The similarity of ribosomes in mitochondria and chloroplasts to those in bacteria supports the hypothesis.

The Kingdom of Protists

Protists include all eukaryotic organisms that are not plants, animals, or fungi. Most consist either of single cells or colonies of identical cells. Algal protists are photosynthesizing and plantlike, while protozoa are nonphotosynthesizing and animal-like. Algal protists comprise thousands of marine, freshwater, and land-dwelling species. Marine algae, which include dino-flagellates and chrysophytes, produce vast quantities of new living material.

Euglenoids resemble both plantlike and animal-like protists. They can absorb some nutrients from their surroundings, but also have chloroplasts and can manufacture their own food. Euglenoids reproduce asexually.

Protozoa are clearly more like animals, as they are heterotrophic and show a wide range of feeding specializations. Most protozoa obtain their food through phagocytosis. Flagellates are propelled by undulating flagella that occur singly, in pairs, or in great numbers. While most flagellates reproduce asexually, some use sexual reproduction. Certain species can cause serious diseases in humans.

Amoebas, members of the phylum Sarcodina, use pseudopods to move about and, often, to obtain nutrients. The sarcodines also include heliozoans, radiolarians, and foraminiferans.

Ciliates contain some of the most complex cells on earth. Their numerous cilia can be coordinated for movement, and can keep a current of water flowing over them, directing food and bacteria into their cytostomes. Freshwater ciliates have contractile vacuoles that act like miniature pumps, which function to help regulate osmotic conditions. Some ciliates, such as *Paramecium*, can reproduce sexually by conjugation. Different mating types represent different genetic strains, ensuring genetic recombination.

Slime Molds: A Different Kind of Protist

Slime molds have traits similar to protists and fungi, and even possess some animal-like characteristics. Slime molds are able to reproduce and grow over their food sources; but when food sources disappear, they come together to form a slug. The slug produces spores similar to those released by molds. Both cellular and acellular slime molds carry on this double lifestyle.

The Fungi

All fungi are heterotrophs and live as parasites, symbionts, or reducers. Reducer fungi help recycle essential molecules of organic material. Fungi reproduce through spores, which germinate into a vegetative state that is usually marked by a spreading mycelium. Fungi are haploid throughout most of their vegetative and reproductive states; they become diploid only when reproducing sexually. They consist of four major groups: water molds (oomycetes), bread molds (zygomycetes), sac fungi (ascomycetes), and club fungi (basidiomycetes). *Fungi Imperfecti* are species that are not easily classified, including a number of human parasites.

The Lichens

Lichens are composed of a symbiotic association between fungi and a green alga or a cyanobacterium. As a result of this association, lichens are able to flourish in unusual habitats where there is little competition from other organisms.

Key Terms

symbiosis hypothesis	amoeboid protozoan	mycelium
symbiosis	pseudopod	hyphae
symbiont	heliozoan	chitin
mutualistic symbiosis	radiolarian	oomycete
protist	foraminiferan	zygomycete
algal protist	ciliate	ascomycete
phytoplankton	cytostome	basidiomycete
dinoflagellate	food vacuole	sporangia
red tide	cytopyge	zygospore
chrysophyte	contractile vacuole	ascus
diatom	*Paramecium*	basidium
euglenoid	conjugation	basidiocarp
protozoa	slime mold	gill
phagocytosis	fungi	cap
flagellate	mycorrhizae	*Fungi imperfecti*
trypanosome	spore	lichens

Review Questions

1. How does Margulis explain the presence of chloroplasts, mitochondria, cilia, and flagella in eukaryotic cells? (pp. 291–293)

2. List four characteristics of dinoflagellates, including one that is life threatening. (pp. 293–294)

3. Briefly explain why the euglenoids, as a group, have been a taxonomic puzzle to biologists. (pp. 294–295)

4. List the three major groups of protozoans and their methods of movement. (pp. 295–299)

5. Briefly describe two examples of human parasites among the protozoans. (p. 297)

6. Describe the water regulatory problem of freshwater ciliates, and explain how it is solved. (pp. 298–299)

7. Summarize the manner in which sexual reproduction takes place in *Paramecium*. (pp. 299–300)

8. Describe the fungal method of feeding. (p. 301)

9. Review the life cycle of a sexually reproductive fungus, noting where the haploid and diploid states begin and end. (pp. 301–304)

10. List three fungi that create severe problems for humans, and briefly summarize these problems. (pp. 301, 306)

Plants:

Evolution and Diversity

22

We humans sometimes take delight in wondering aloud just who has inherited the earth: cockroaches, rats, houseflies, or us. Of course, it's a nonsensical question, but it is interesting that we never consider our silent partners, the plants. Everywhere we look we see green. Not only are plants the most prominent form of land life on our planet, but they also form the base of nearly every terrestrial **food chain.** In other words, they manufacture the organic molecules that are eventually passed along through both plant eaters and predators, the creatures that roam the earth in search of the food that is stored in the bodies of other individuals.

What makes members of the plant kingdom special? The answers seem obvious at first. For example, plants are multicellular photosynthesizers, and their cells are enclosed by cell walls composed of cellulose. Typically, their cells and tissues are organized into roots, stems, and leaves, and the individuals are more or less stationary.

So far so good, but now we have a problem: these traits really apply best to such familiar plants as the oaks, pines, grasses, turnips, orchids, and ferns. There are other plants that cannot be characterized this way. The plant kingdom, as it is presently defined, is an unruly group that also contains mosses, liverworts, and a number of algae. Some of these are not multicellular, and some are not even related very closely. In fact, the plant kingdom is a *polyphyletic* group—that is, it includes different kinds of organisms that independently achieved plant status after having evolved from different protist ancestors.

The algal members of the plant kingdom fall into three unrelated groups, or *divisions* (botanists prefer the term *division* to its zoological equivalent, *phylum*): the red algae, the brown algae, and the green algae. Most algae are aquatic—either freshwater or marine. In addition to these three algal divisions, the plant kingdom includes two groups of terrestrial plants: the nonvascular *bryophytes* (mosses, liverworts, and hornworts) and the vascular plants (also called *tracheophytes*). (The vascular plants have specialized conductive tissues and true leaves, stems, and roots.) The terrestrial plants appear to have evolved from the green algae.

In spite of their lack of evolutionary relatedness, the varied members of the plant kingdom do have many things in common, such as cell walls, multicellularity (in all *groups* if not in all species), and the ability to photosynthesize. And no matter how uneasily any species resides in the plant kingdom, its life cycle (with few exceptions) will have two stages: a haploid *gametophyte generation* and a diploid *sporophyte generation*—a major characteristic called the **alternation of generations.**

THE ALTERNATION OF GENERATIONS

In the plant life cycle, two kinds of multicellular plant bodies follow one another sequentially. One is diploid and produces **spores** by meiosis; the other is haploid and produces **gametes** by mitosis. These are known respectively as the **sporophyte generation** and the **gametophyte generation,** which we will refer to simply as the sporophyte and the gametophyte (Figure 22.1). Nothing in the animal kingdom fully compares to this situation in plants, for, as you know, meiosis in animals leads directly to the development of haploid gametes, which fuse to form a diploid *zygote*. But plants do things differently: in all but a few algae, both haploid and diploid cells undergo mitosis to form multicellular structures. The full life cycle of a plant, starting at an arbitrary point in the cycle, is: (1) fusion of haploid gametes to form a diploid zygote; (2) mitosis and growth to form a multicellular sporophyte; (3) meiosis to form haploid spores; (4) mitosis and growth to form a multicellular haploid gametophyte; (5) mitosis within the gametophyte to form haploid gametes; and then a return to (1), since this is an endless cycle.

Most of the familiar plants around us, from the larger shrubs and shade trees gracing our homes to the potted geranium on the window sill, are in the sporophyte generation of their life cycle. Their gametophyte generations are not at all obvious, since they are hidden away within specialized sporophyte tissue such as flowers or cones. Within these reproductive structures, the gametophytes occur as haploid cells in the ovules and pollen.

In the less familiar plants, this might not be the case at all. In the ferns, for example, the familiar leafy plant is also the sporophyte, but the gametophyte grows as a tiny, separate individual that emerged from a dust-sized fern spore, shed sometime previously. Separate sporophyte and gametophyte generations are also common in the algae, but in some instances it is the gametophyte that is prominent while the sporophyte is highly reduced.

As you can see, there is a great deal of variability in how the alternation of generations is expressed in plants. Actually, prominent gametophytes and separated generations are considered to be primitive traits, those most like the ancestral condition. We will soon look into the evolutionary status of each of the plant groups, but be prepared for surprises.

A QUICK SURVEY OF THE PLANT KINGDOM

Now that we know something about the basic principle of the alternation of generations, let's take a closer look at the fascinating diversity of the plant kingdom. We've already seen that the kingdom is divided into several divisions. Since people are especially interested in what we like to call the "higher" plants, we can also conveniently divide the kingdom into two groups: the **vascular plants** and the **nonvascular plants** (Table 22.1). The term *vascular* refers to specialized conducting tissues that move water and food through the plant. Most nonvascular plants are aquatic or are restricted to moist places, and most are small. With few exceptions, the vascular plants—the tracheophytes—are terrestrial, a point to keep in mind since the presence of conducting tissues is apparently one of the prerequisites for success in drier regions.

THE NONVASCULAR PLANTS: ALGAE AND BRYOPHYTES

The Red Algae

The **red algae** (division *Rhodophyta*) are primarily seaweeds, multicellular marine organisms that live along rocky coasts (Figure 22.2). (There are a few unicellular red algae.) Red algae are able to survive in rather deeper water than other photosynthetic organisms. About 4000 named species exist, including a few tiny, simple, terrestrial red algae and some freshwater forms. The seaweeds attach themselves to the rough sea floor, or to rocks, with fingerlike structures known as **holdfasts.** (The holdfasts are not roots; their name describes their function.) While some red algae really are red, others are green or black, and some are even blue

22.1

The life cycle of plants alternates between a diploid sporophyte generation and a haploid gametophyte generation. One generation may dominate the life of a plant, or the two may be roughly equivalent in duration. The sporophyte generation begins with fertilization and ends with meiosis and spore production. The gametophyte generation begins with spores and ends with gametes joining in fertilization.

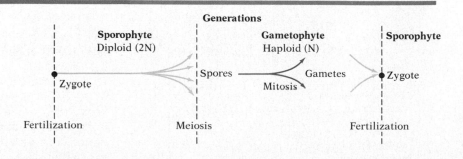

TABLE 22.1

Divisions of the plant kingdom

Division, Examples, and Number of Living Species	Common Characteristics	Life Cycle
Red algae (division Rhodophyta) *Polysiphonia* (4000 named species)	Mostly marine; some freshwater; photosynthetic pigments are like those of cyanobacteria: green chlorophylls *a* and *c*, blue phycobilin, red phycoerythrin; no flagella or centrioles	Separate generations; variable dominance; nonflagellated sperm
Brown algae (division Phaeophyta) Giant kelps *(Fucus), Sargassum* (1000 named species)	Marine; chlorophylls *a* and *c*; fucoxanthin pigment; laminarin starch reserves; flagella and centrioles; phloemlike conducting tissue in giant kelps	Separate generations, or gametophyte embedded in sporophyte; swimming sperm and stationary egg. In some gametophyte generations, is reduced to gametes only
Green algae (division Chlorophyta) *Chlamydomonas, Volvox, Ulva* (sea lettuce), *Chlorella* (7000 named species)	Marine, freshwater, terrestrial, often found in mutualistic symbiosis. Photosynthetic pigments like those of higher plants; typical plant starches; centrioles generally present	Separate generations; isogametes in most; gametophyte often predominates; in some, sporophyte generation is reduced to zygospore
Bryophytes (division Bryophyta) Mosses, liverworts, hornworts; *Riccia, Marchantia* (7000 named species, mostly mosses)	Terrestrial; multicellular, with considerable tissue specialization; no true roots or leaves, but rhizoids and leaf scales; can resist drying; typical plant starches; carotene, chlorophylls *a* and *b*; centrioles absent or rare; xylemlike conducting tissue in some moss sporophyte stalks	Gametophyte predominant; swimming sperm. Egg develops within archegonium; sporophyte emerges from gametophyte
Vascular plants (270,000 named species)	Have xylem (water-conducting tissue) and phloem (food-conducting tissue); true roots and leaves in most; terrestrial; centrioles absent or rare	Sporophyte is dominant form, but separate gametophyte present in some groups

22.2

A rhodophyte, more commonly known as red algae. Most species are marine and are found in warm waters, usually attached to rocks by their holdfasts. The branched bodies are usually frilly and delicate, but some form the widened, flat blades seen here.

or violet. Most are small, with lengths ranging from a few centimeters to perhaps a meter. Lovers of Japanese *sushi* are familiar with the thin, greenish-black, edible red alga that is used to wrap the portions of raw fish and sticky rice.

Red algae store a carbohydrate called **floridean starch.** Some species also produce the structural polysaccharide *agar*, which can be extracted and boiled to form the jelly-like material that is used by biologists to grow bacterial cultures, and by Southeast Asians to thicken soup. One species of red algae, *Irish moss*, is harvested for its literally indigestible polysaccharide **carrageenan,** which is used to give chocolate-flavored dairy drinks their fake creaminess.

Red algae are not recognizably related to any other kind of organism. Their chloroplasts resemble cyanobacteria and have the same kinds of photosynthetic pigments. Analysis of the molecular structure of red algae supports the hypothesis that their chloroplasts are unrelated to the chloroplasts of protists, higher plants, or other algae, but, rather, evolved separately as the result of an independent symbiotic union of an ancestral host species and a cyanobacterium. Red algae lack flagellated cells; the sperm cells (male gametes) move like amoebae. In some species, the gametophytes and the sporophytes are of equal size and identical appearance, except for the reproductive structures.

The Brown Algae

The **brown algae** (division *Phaeophyta*), including kelps, other seaweeds, and certain microscopic filaments, are all marine organisms. They owe their color to a brown pigment called **fucoxanthin,** which is found only in this group. One of their structural polysaccharides, **algin,** is used commercially to thicken ice cream and frozen custards.

Most of the 1000 or so named species of brown algae live in cold coastal waters, but one genus, *Sargassum,* grows in shallow tropical and subtropical waters. Storms regularly break *Sargassum* bodies from their holdfasts, and the broken plants are washed to sea, where they continue to photosynthesize and grow, although they can no longer successfully reproduce. In the middle Atlantic, vast tangled masses of *Sargassum* form the Sargasso sea, which has spawned many salty legends about trapped ships and sea monsters.

The giant kelps can grow to 30 m (100 ft) in length (Figure 22.3). Their large, flattened, leaflike **blades** can be close to the sunlit surface and their tangled, elaborate holdfasts can anchor them far below. Connecting the two ends of the plant are stemlike **stipes,** and the blades are kept near the surface by the buoyancy of hollow **floats.** Although they are listed among the nonvascular plants, kelps actually have evolved food-conducting tissues very similar to those of higher plants. These conducting tissues allow photosynthetic products to be transported to the dark sea bottom to nourish the holdfasts.

In some brown algal species, the gametophyte develops completely within the sporophyte body. This is considered to be an *advanced* trait (that is, a trait that is greatly modified from the ancestral condition). In the prominence of the diploid sporophyte generation, as in the development of vascular tissue, the kelps show convergent evolution with land plants. They have large, stationary eggs and tiny, flagellated, swimming sperm (*heterogametes*)—another advanced trait.

22.3

Giant kelps such as *Nereocystis* thrive in cold oceans. *Nereocystis* is a common sight along the beaches of the Pacific coast, particularly after storms, when its holdfast is torn from the ocean floor. Kelp beds form refuges for a variety of marine organisms.

The Green Algae

The **green algae** (division *Chlorophyta*) make up the largest division of the algal plants, with about 7000 named species. Most live in fresh water, but a sizeable number are marine. Some are even terrestrial, living in the soil, on trees, and even in snow banks. A few have given up the independent life to live within the cells of such other organisms as ciliates and invertebrate animals. Terrestrial green algae are often found living successfully in a mutualistic symbiosis with certain fungi, to form the rock-encrusting lichens (see Chapter 21).

Many of the green algae look more like members of the protist kingdom than those of the plant kingdom, and, in fact, they would be perfectly good protists if it weren't for the fact that they have relatives in high places. The simpler green algae are included with the plants not because of their appearance, but because of their biochemistry. Like higher plants, the green algae utilize chlorophyll *a*, chlorophyll *b*, and carotenes; they store their carbohydrates as starch (amylose and amylopectin); and they make their cell walls of cellulose—all characteristics of higher plants.

The green algae are a highly diverse group. They may be tiny, single-celled organisms; they may form simple colonies of nearly identical cells; or they may be complex and multicellular. One group of green algae falls into none of these categories, but forms large, multinucleate, noncellular structures. In all this diversity one can choose no "representative" species, since each group has its own bizarre specializations and complexities; but a random sampling of species will give some notion of what green algae are all about.

Single-celled Green Algae. Single-celled green algae may be nonflagellated, such as *Chlorella*, or flagellated. One of the best-known flagellated forms is *Chlamydomonas reinhardi*, which has been studied extensively by geneticists. Each tiny, oval cell has two anterior (pulling) flagella, a red, light-sensitive **eyespot**, and a single cup-shaped chloroplast that takes up much of the cell's volume. For most of its life cycle *Chlamydomonas* is haploid, and reproduces asexually by mitosis and cell division.

Sexual reproduction in *Chlamydomonas reinhardi* involves the formation and fusion of identical-appearing cells of distinct (plus and minus) mating types. The fusing cells are actually gametes—**isogametes** because they are of same size and shape (as compared with eggs and sperm, which are of different sizes and shapes). They are similar in appearance to the asexual haploid cells, which can acquire the ability to fuse when asexual reproduction is not possible. Following fusion, metabolic activity slows and a tough, resistant covering forms around the zygote, producing a **zygospore**. When conditions become favorable again, the zygospore becomes active, undergoes meiosis, and breaks open to release four haploid spores. Each spore will then germinate into an active, flagellated cell, and the cycle goes on. Here the sporophyte generation is reduced to a single diploid cell, which never undergoes mitosis; and the haploid gametophyte generation, the photosynthetic generation, is also capable of undergoing extensive asexual reproduction (Figure 22.4). Other species of the genus *Chlamydomonas*, by the way, may have flagellated spores of different size. Some species have

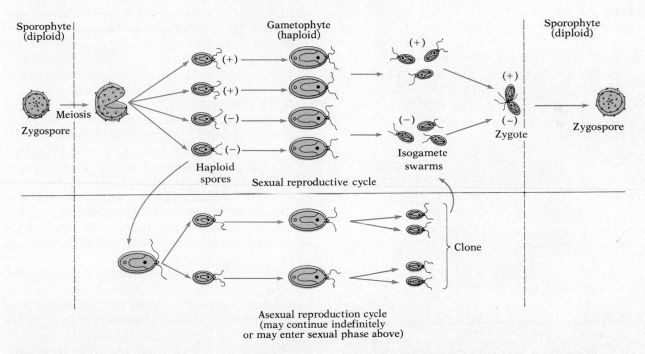

22.4

Life history of *Chlamydomonas reinhardi*. The sporophyte is a brief interlude in an otherwise lengthy gametophyte phase. Zygospores go through meiosis to produce flagellated haploid spores. These can then enter either a sexual phase, producing many isogametes, or an asexual phase, producing enormous cloned populations through repeated mitotic divisions. Sexual reproduction can occur when different plus and minus mating strains meet. Flagellated isogametes fuse, producing a diploid zygospore once again.

even evolved a large, nonmotile *egg* gamete and a tiny, motile *sperm*.

Colonial Green Algae. *Volvox*, a rather remarkable green algae, is composed of an unusually organized spherical colony of flagellated cells (Figure 22.5). In a sense, *Volvox* is a community of cells behaving as a single organism—but then, in a sense, so are humans. Although *Volvox* is not directly related to any truly multicellular higher plant, nor even to truly multicellular green algae, its organization does suggest something about how multicellularity itself *might* have begun.

Multicellular Green Algae. Many green algae are multicellular. Some form thin filaments of cells, and others exist as bladelike or leaflike structures. *Ulothrix*, a common freshwater *filamentous* alga (Figure 22.6a), is characterized by a predominant gametophyte generation that, like *Chlamydomonas reinhardi*, produces motile, flagellated isogametes. The isogametes fuse to form a diploid zygospore—the sporophyte—which immediately enters meiosis to liberate haploid spores that will produce new gametophytes. Another multicellular green alga, *Ulva* or "sea lettuce" (Figure 22.6b), is quite different. Its sporophyte and gametophyte generations are both multicellular, in the form of large,

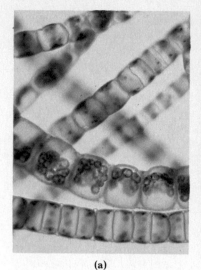

(a) (b)

22.6

(a) The filamentous body of the freshwater green alga *Ulothrix* is the gametophyte, the prominent generation. (b) *Ulva* is a familiar sight in tide pools and shallow coastal waters. Unlike many other green algae, *Ulva* has identical sporophyte and gametophyte generations.

leaflike blades that are two cells thick. Except for their respective diploid and haploid chromosome numbers, the sporophytes and gametophytes are identical. Like *Ulothrix*, the *Ulva* gametophytes produce flagellated, motile, haploid isogametes by mitosis, while the sporophyte produces flagellated, motile, haploid spores by meiosis.

We've lingered with the green algae for two reasons. First, they are interesting and diverse. More importantly, we are interested in the relatives that they have in high places. At some time in the dim past (perhaps in the middle of the Paleozoic era, 400 million years ago), one or more of these delicate but adventurous water plants made the first successful transition to multicellular terrestrial life (Table 22.2). It was from these algae that today's great array of terrestrial plant life is believed to have arisen.

Just how this happened is still a matter of controversy among botanists. There are two widely held hypotheses. One is that the bryophytes and the tracheophytes arose independently from different filamentous green algae; the other is that only the tracheophytes arose from the green algae, and that the bryophytes are simplified descendants of early tracheophytes. A third possibility, namely that the bryophytes evolved from green algae and that the tracheophytes then evolved from the bryophytes, does not seem to be taken seriously by any botanist today.

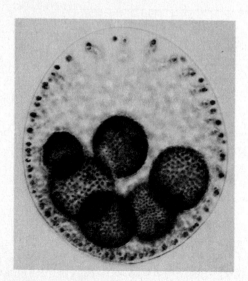

22.5

Volvox, a spherical colony of tiny, interconnected, flagellated cells. There is enough differentiation in the colony to suggest a trace of tissue-level organization. Some individuals move their flagella in a coordinated manner, moving the colony about. The cells are immersed in a gelatinous sheath and are interconnected by strands of cytoplasm. The larger concentration of cells visible in the colony is specialized for sexual reproduction.

TABLE 22.2

Geological history of plants

Era	Period(s)	Conditions	Plant History	
Cenozoic	(Millions of years ago)	Glaciation, mountain building, cooling	Extensive grasslands	**AGE OF ANGIOSPERMS**
	— 65 —		————— Asteroid collision —————	
Mesozoic	Cretaceous	Rocky mountains / Extensive lowlands	Flowering plants	
	— 135 —		Conifers	**AGE OF GYMNOSPERMS**
	Jurassic	Lowlands, inland seas	Cycads	
	— 197 —			
	Triassic	Mountains, drying		
	— 225 —		———— Continental drift begins ————	
Paleozoic	Permian	Glaciers / Inland seas dry up	Earliest brown algae fossils Gingkos	
			Earliest conifer fossils	
	— 280 —		Earliest fern fossils	**GREAT PALEOZOIC FORESTS**
	Carboniferous	Mountain building	Sphenophytes	
			Earliest bryophyte fossils	
	— 345 —			
	Devonian		Lycophytes	
	— 405 —			
	Silurian	Extensive shallow seas, mild climate	Earliest vascular plant fossils (Rhyniophytes)	Plants invade land **AGE OF ALGAL PLANTS AND PROTISTS**
	— 425 —			
	Ordovician		Red and green algae	
	— 500 —			
	Cambrian			
	— 570 —			
Precambrian			Red algae Green algae	

The Bryophytes

The **bryophytes** (division *Bryophyta*)—the mosses, liverworts and hornworts—are all multicellular terrestrial plants with specialized tissues that efficiently divide the tasks of life. There are about 23,000 named species, most of which are mosses. Most bryophytes are distinguished from other terrestrial plants by their lack of specialized vascular tissue; they must move water and nutrients through their bodies by the tedious process of cell-to-cell transport. They also lack the supporting tissue of higher plants, and so they are generally small and hug the ground. While they have no true leaves, their thin, flattened, leaflike *scales* contain chloroplasts and are the sites of photosynthesis (Figure 22.7).

Bryophytes anchor themselves in the soil by rootlike **rhizoids.** Unlike true roots, the rhizoids are not involved in water transport; the entire organism must absorb and retain moisture from rain and condensation. In spite of this need for direct moisture, mosses can get by in fluctuating environments because they can survive a temporary drying out. The deprived mosses become dry and brittle, and all metabolic activity ceases, but the plants revive and begin metabolizing again when moist conditions return. There are even some successful mosses in deserts and high mountains.

Despite their reasonable successful transition to terrestrial life, the mosses and their relatives have some of the same requirements for reproduction as did the ancient green algae from which they ultimately descended. Their sperm have flagella, and must swim in order to reach the egg, which lies protected within the parent gametophyte in a vase-like structure called the **archegonium.** In some bryophytes swimming to the egg is not much of a trick, because the egg and sperm are produced on the same gametophyte. In other cases the sperm must travel from one gametophyte to the archegonium of another gametophyte. It generally accomplishes this more frequently by being splashed by falling raindrops than by its own flagellar activity, but it is a perilous trip all the same.

22.7

The gametophytes of *Polytrichum* **(a)** form the green leafy carpet we generally think of as moss. Emerging from gametophytes are the sporophytes, consisting of a stalk and capsulelike sporangia. The capsules will open to scatter the haploid spores. The liverwort

gametophyte **(b)** is a flattened, ground-hugging growth. The erect bodies that look like miniature palms are egg-producing structures, while those that resemble toadstools produce the sperm.

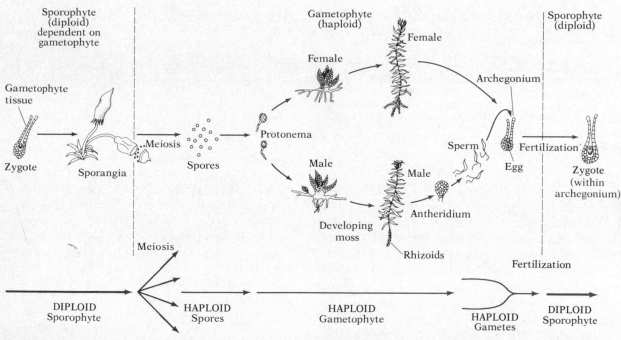

22.8

Alternation of generations in mosses. The haploid gametophyte generation dominates the moss life cycle. The diploid sporophyte, which consists of a stalk and a capsule, grows out of the gametophyte tissue and is dependent upon it for nourishment. Within the capsule, a sporangium produces dry, haploid spores by meiosis and cell differentiation. The spore is borne by the wind to a suitably moist spot, where it germinates to produce a slender thread of tissue, the protonema. This develops into the familiar, carpetlike moss game-

tophyte. Gametophyte tissues specialize as antheridia and archegonia, which respectively produce flagellated sperm and stationary eggs by mitosis. Rainwater splashes the sperm into a receptive archegonium, where it swims down to fertilize the egg. Fertilization produces a diploid zygote, which begins the sporophyte generation. The zygote divides and develops within the archegonium, to produce a new stalk and capsule.

The Alternation of Generations in Mosses.
The gametophyte generation is predominant in the moss life cycle—which is just to say that most of the plant's physical bulk is gametophyte tissue, and most, though not all, of the photosynthesis occurs in gametophyte tissue. The velvety green carpet we think of as moss is the haploid gametophyte. The sporophyte is only a slender stalk growing from the archegonium, topped by a spore-producing capsule. It is nourished and supported by gametophyte tissue, but it is green and does some of its own photosynthesizing. And once again we find that the categorization of moss as *nonvascular* is stretching the truth a bit, because the core of the sporophyte stalk, in some moss species at least, is composed of cells that seem to be specialized for water transport. Whether the presence of this conducting tissue is due to convergent evolution, or is evidence that the mosses are really specialized tracheophytes, is still being debated.

The gametophyte generation begins within the capsule at the tip of the sporophyte when haploid spores are produced through meiosis (Figure 22.8). When the capsule is mature, it bursts open, releasing the spores to disperse in the wind. Those that land in a suitably moist habitat will germinate to form a thin, green filament. This filament—reminiscent of a filamentous green alga—then develops into the familiar moss gametophyte. There may be extensive growth through mitosis and cell division. Sexual reproduction can occur after specialized sex organs, the **antheridia** and the archegonia, produce sperm and eggs respectively. In a good rain, the flagellated sperm makes its way into the archegonium, and ferilization occurs. The diploid zygote undergoes mitosis within the archegonium to produce the slender, stalked sporophyte, and the cycle continues.

THE VASCULAR PLANTS

The vascular plants (tracheophytes) comprise the vast majority of today's plant species. The tracheophytes have two types of specialized conducting tissues: **xylem,** which transports water and minerals, and **phloem,** which distributes organic food from one part of the plant to another. The xylem often has an important secondary function: it provides support for the plant body. *Wood* consists primarily of xylem. Xylem and phloem are discussed in detail in Chapter 25.

The tracheophytes are quite diverse. Included are ferns as well as various *lower* (or allegedly more primitive) tracheophytes, such as the club mosses and horsetails. The lower tracheophytes and the ferns have separate, photosynthetic gametophyte and sporophyte generations, much as do the bryophytes. The *higher* tracheophytes are the seed plants; throughout their evolution, the tendency seems to have been toward a predominating sporophyte generation at the expense of the gametophyte generation.

The earliest tracheophytes appear in the fossil record some time before the earliest bryophytes. These early vascular plants belong to an extinct group, called the Rhyniophytes, a group that flourished in the marshes of the early Paleozoic era (see Table 22.2). They were simple plants that lacked leaves and roots. A main **rhizome** (underground stem) produced vertical branches and simple, anchoring rhizoids (Figure 22.9). Within their stems lay a system of crude tubules, true xylem elements specialized for water conduction. With this inno-

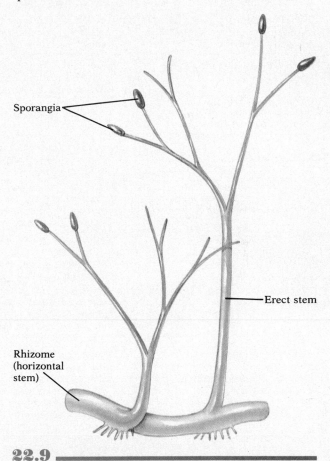

Sporangia

Erect stem

Rhizome (horizontal stem)

22.9

Rhynia is the oldest known fossil vascular plant. It flourished some 350–400 million years ago. It lacked leaves and true roots, but had photosynthetic stems that grew up from an underground stem, or rhizome. Spore-producing sporangia developed on the tips of the erect stems. True conductive tissue is evident in the fossil traces. This is the sporophyte; the gametophyte is unknown.

TABLE 22.3

Diversity among the vascular plants

Group, Examples, and Number of Living Species	Common Characteristics	Life Cycle
I. Lower vascular plants (12,000 named species, mostly ferns)	Terrestrial; stem tends to be underground (rhizome); fruit and seeds lacking	Meiosis produces haploid windborne spores; swimming sperm carried by water to eggs in archegonia; sporophyte begins development in archegonium
Psilophytes (Psilophyta) *Psilotum* (4 extant species)	Terrestrial, tropical; mostly fossil forms; primitive vascular tissue; no true leaves	Minute, nonphotosynthetic but free-living gametophyte; swimming sperm
Ground pine or club moss (Lycophyta) *Lycopodium* (1000 named species)	Terrestrial, widespread; well-developed vascular tissue in some; true leaves, resemble pine seedlings superficially	Separate generations; gametophyte is minute and nonphotosynthetic
Horsetails (Sphenophyta) *Equisetum* (12 named species)	Terrestrial, widespread; most are marsh dwellers; 10 cm to 10 m tall; photosynthetic side branches, reduced leaves; rhizomes; aerial stems hollow, silicon-rich; vascular tissue well developed	Separate generations; gametophyte is minute and nonphotosynthetic; swimming sperm. Vegetative and reproductive stems of sporophyte separate
Ferns (Pterophyta) Boston ferns, tree ferns (11,000 named species)	Terrestrial, widespread, shade; underground stem (rhizome); large divided leaves; well-developed xylem and phloem	Dominant sporophyte, but free-living gametophyte is photosynthetic; swimming sperm
II. Higher vascular plants: the seed plants Gymnosperms and flowering plants (approximately 251,000 named species)	Terrestrial; sporophyte embryo develops within a seed; dispersal of seeds by various means; extensive root, stem, and leaf development; secondary growth common; tracheids in all groups	Gametophytes develop within sporophyte tissue; male gametophyte becomes dry, easily dispersed pollen grain, germinates near female gametophyte
IIA. Gymnosperms	Seeds not enclosed in fruit; all with xylem tracheids, but xylem vessels absent except in one	Pollen is captured in fluid exuded from gametophyte
Ginkgo (Ginkgophyta) 1 extant species *Ginkgo biloba*, the maidenhair tree	Native to China, now widespread by introduction; large tree with typical secondary growth pattern, broad, fan-shaped leaves with parallel veins	Sporophytes dioecious (i.e., separate sexes); flagellated sperm swims in fluid produced by gametophyte
Cycads (Cycadophyta) (100 named species)	Tropical and subtropical; thick, partly subterranean stem; palmlike foliage; very large pollen cones and seed cones	Swimming sperm utilizes fluids produced by gametophyte
Gnetophytes (Gnetophyta) *Gnetum, Welwitschia, Ephedra* (71 named species)	Warm and temperate regions, deserts; some have features resembling angiosperms: bladelike leaf with central vein and net of veinlets; two cotyledons; xylem vessels in one species; pollen cones resemble flowers in structure	Nonflagellated sperm
Conifers (Coniferophyta) Pines, redwoods, firs, junipers, larches, cypress, hemlock (500 named species)	Widespread, but most common in temperate and subarctic; most have needle-shaped leaves; most are trees with single, straight trunk; most are evergreen (nondeciduous); multiple embryonic leaves (cotyledons)	Seeds and pollen borne on separate cones; pollen wide-dispersed; sperm nonflagellated, but becomes embedded in fluid produced by female gametophyte
IIB. Flowering plants (Anthophyta) Monocots and dicots (about 250,000 named species)	Flowers; seeds develop completely enclosed by fruit (surrounding sporophyte tissue); pollination by insects or wind; xylem vessels present	No flagellated sperm; pollen tube enters ovule; double fertilization by sperm nuclei; polyploid endosperm formed
Dicots (class Dicotyledonae) Orchard trees, bushes, herbs, cacti, potatoes (about 200,000 named species)	Worldwide; many cultivated; net-veined leaf with central rib; flower parts in 4, 5, or multiples of 4 or 5; two cotyledons (embryonic leaves); secondary growth in most	Mainly insect-pollinated
Monocots (class Monocotyledonae) Grasses, palms, orchids, lilies, tulips, onions, corn, wheat, yucca (50,000 named species)	Worldwide; many cultivated; leaves with parallel veins; single cotyledon; floral parts in 3 or multiples of 3; secondary growth absent except in one group	Both insect- and wind-pollinated

22.10

The heyday of the psilophytes, lycophytes, and sphenophytes was hundreds of millions of years ago, but a few of their descendants still survive. (a) *Psilotum* produces an erect, highly branched stem with scattered sporangia. (b) The lycophytes are known as *ground pine* or *club moss*. They are, of course, neither pines nor mosses, but they do rather resemble carpets of pine seedlings. They have true roots, upright stems, and needlelike leaves, and produce complex, conelike sporangia. (c) *Equisetum* (the name means horsetail) has rather different photosynthesizing and reproductive shoots rising out of a single rhizome. Note the multiple sporangia at the tip of the reproductive shoot.

vation, the evolutionary future of the tracheophytes was assured.

Vascular plants now inhabit every terrestrial part of the earth except for Antarctica, and a few forms have even reinvaded the sea. Their ancestors radiated out over the earth, adapting to new environments in many different ways (Table 22.3). Early tracheophytes evolved various sorts of leaves, stems, and root systems, meeting their specific needs, and the most advanced group evolved seeds for efficient dispersal and reproduction. With the development of the hardy seed, the transition to land was nearly complete. The finishing touch was the development of a means of sexual reproduction that did *not* require water.

The living vascular plants can be divided into six major groups, which are sometimes called classes, and sometimes called divisions:

1. The psilophytes (*Psilophyta,* or "naked plants")
2. The club mosses or ground pines (*Lycophyta,* or "spider-like plants")
3. The horsetails (*Sphenophyta,* or "wedge plants")
4. The ferns (*Pterophyta,* or "winged plants;" the name derives from the appearance, not the function, of the fern frond)
5. The gymnosperms ("naked seeds"): this category is made up of four groups—the cycads (*Cycadophyta*), the ginkgos (*Ginkophyta*), the *Gnetophyta*, and the familiar conifers (*Coniferophyta,* the "cone-bearing plants")
6. The flowering plants (*Anthophyta,* or "flowering plants"); they are often called *angiosperms,* which means "enclosed seed types"

The last two groups, the gymnosperms and the flowering plants, are sometimes grouped together as the *Spermophyta,* or seed plants. Now that we've covered all of these Latin names, we'll try to use the English equivalents wherever possible.

The first three of these groups were once an important part of the earth's flora. They were the giants of the Paleozoic forests. Evidence of the incredible size and numbers they achieved in the Carboniferous period is with us today, in the form of the earth's enormous coal deposits. But the heyday of these groups is over, and only a few stragglers remain (Figure 22.10). In fact, of the estimated 261,000 names species of vascular plants, these groups account for only about 1000, and of these all but 16 are club mosses—which are not mosses at all, but tiny forest-floor plants that look like miniature Christmas trees.

The Ferns

The ancient Paleozoic forests were graced with another common plant, the **fern.** Ferns are interesting botanically because they have survived in great numbers and have adapted more easily to changing environments, and to competition from seed plants, than have other primitive vascular plants (Figure 22.11). Some of the 12,000 or so named species are adapted to desert conditions, and many hanging varieties appear to thrive in the dim recesses of smoky bars.

The sporophyte is definitely the prominent gen-

22.11

Although many ferns are restricted in size and make up part of the forest ground cover, these tree ferns compete with flowering trees for bright sunlight. They thrive chiefly in tropical climates, where they may reach a height of 15 m (50 ft).

eration among ferns. The fern sporophyte typically consists of a thick rhizome (underground stem) that gives rise to a profusion of fine, hairy roots that absorb water and minerals, and a succession of fronds (leaves) that function in both photosynthesis and reproduction. As the plant grows, the fronds first appear as the familiar coiled **fiddleheads,** each of which then unrolls into a large leaf, subdivided into leaflets (Figure 22.12a). Spores are produced on the underside of the leaves in structures known as **sori.** Each sorus is a group of **sporangia** (spore-forming organs) hidden under a scalelike cover (Figure 22.12b). You have undoubtedly seen sori on the underside of fern fronds. They sometimes occur in rows as black, red, white, or (most commonly) brown dots, and may be mistaken for insect or fungal invasions.

Tiny windborne spores are released when the wall of the mature sporangium ruptures. When the spore germinates, a small, soft, heart-shaped, photosynthetic fern gametophyte, the **prothallium,**

22.12

(a) Anatomy of a fern. Below the soil, an extensive underground rhizome produces root growth and sends leaves above ground to form the cluster shown here. The leaves emerge from the rhizome as tightly curled fiddleheads, which gradually open. (b) Fern sporangia occur in a variety of forms and patterns, but the sorus shown here is common. Spores are produced meiotically in the sporangia, and remain there until the sporangium splits and the spores are ejected.

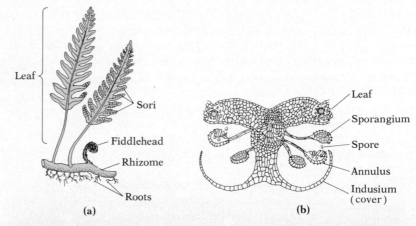

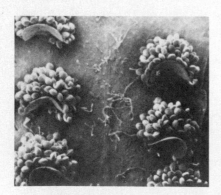

320

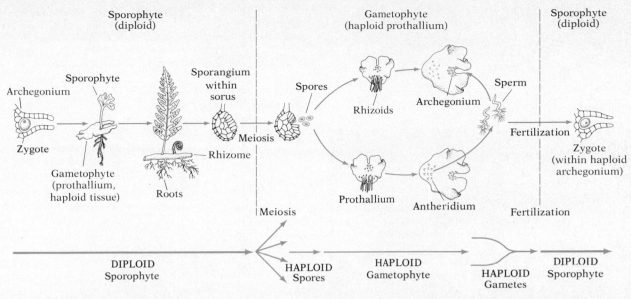

22.13

Alternation of generations in a fern. In ferns, the sporophyte is highly dominant and the generations are represented by separate plants. After fertilization, the young diploid sporophyte begins its growth from the archegonium, soon producing its own roots and photosynthetic tissue as the tiny, soft gametophyte withers

and dies. The sporophyte produces spores meiotically in great numbers, suggesting a low probability of success for any individual spore. Spores that succeed produce a heart-shaped gametophyte, which bears antheridia and archegonia.

develops. This inconspicuous plantlet, typically about a centimeter across, lies close to the soil and is anchored to the ground by tiny rhizoids. On the prothallium's upper surfaces, antheridia and archegonia give rise to flagellated sperm and protected eggs respectively, as in the mosses. After fertilization, the fern sporophyte grows from the nurturing tissue of the gametophyte archegonium, but soon sends its own roots into the soil and becomes an independent entity (Figure 22.13).

The Mesozoic Era: The Time of the Gymnosperm

The primitive vascular plants, including some inconspicuous seed plants, persisted through the Devonian, Carboniferous, and Permian periods—roughly from 400 million to 225 million years ago, or the last half of the Paleozoic era (see Table 22.2). Then, toward the close of the Permian period and the Paleozoic era, the plant life of the earth experienced a dramatic change.

Throughout the Paleozoic era, the earth was a rather smooth globe, and the low-lying continents were largely covered with warm, shallow seas. With the beginning of the next major era—the Mesozoic—the surface of the earth itself began to

shift, as the drifting continents slammed together. Soggy lowlands began to rise, eventually becoming vast mountain ranges separated by great valleys and trenches. The monotonous warm climate began to cool and to fluctuate between extremes, as ice ages came and went and great deserts formed in the shadows of newborn mountain ranges. Great changes were afoot; in the animal kingdom, it has been estimated, more than 90% of the species, and some major groups, died out within a fairly short period of time—around 225 million years ago. These extinctions marked the end of the Permian period (the last period of the Paleozoic era) and the beginning of the Triassic period (the first period of the Mesozoic era). The Permian-Triassic extinction event was the greatest mass extinction of life on earth, and the reasons for it are not fully known. We do know that most of the great plants of the Paleozoic era perished, leaving behind only scattered remnants.

With the demise of the ancient forests, the competitive edge passed to the seed plants, which had resided inconspicuously on the forest floors. The new, changed earth presented untried opportunities, and the extinction of the older giants opened up new ecological niches. (An *ecological niche* refers to the nature of the interrelationship of an organism and its environment.) Soon the

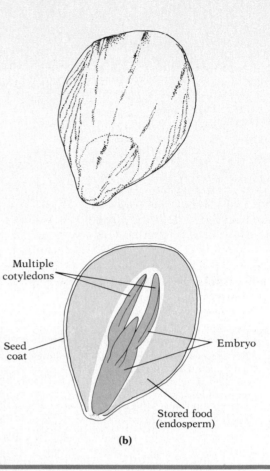

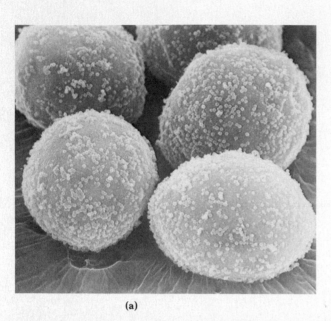

(a)

Multiple
cotyledons

Seed
coat

Embryo

Stored food
(endosperm)

(b)

22.14

Two reproductive developments helped the gymnosperms adapt to the new conditions. The pollen grain carried the entire male gametophyte safely to the female gametophyte in a tough, resistant case. The sporophyte embryo came to be protected in an equally tough container of its own, the seed. **(a)** The pollen shown here in the scanning electron micrograph is from the northern white cedar. **(b)** The seed (pine) contains the embryo of the plant, some stored food, and a surrounding seed coat, which is hard and water-resistant.

seed plants appeared everywhere over the Mesozoic landscape. These were primitive *gymnosperms*, the forerunners of today's conifers.

Why were the gymnosperms so successful? One likely reason is that they had evolved extensive root systems that could draw water from the earth and transport it, through the increasingly well-developed xylem tissue, upward to the leaves. Both the root and the stem were capable of extensive *secondary growth*—growth in diameter by the addition of rings of vascular tissue. Earlier tracheophytes did not have this ability.

Second, the male gametophyte had evolved into the dry, windblown *pollen grain*, which could travel for miles and withstand severe drying to remain viable for years (Figure 22.14a). Furthermore, fertilization did not require water, since the windblown male gametophyte could now release its flagellated sperm directly into fluid produced by the female gametophyte. One group of gymnosperms, the conifers, evolved even further, so that the growing gametophyte formed a *pollen tube* that could deliver the nonflagellated sperm directly into the female gametophyte.

Third, and perhaps most importantly, there was the evolution of the **seed** itself (Figure 22.14b). The female gametophyte came to remain within the parental sporophyte tissue, where it could be supported, protected, and nourished. Then, after fertilization, the seed itself developed and could be released for dispersal and propagation. The gymnosperm seed consists of a tough, nearly water-proof covering of parental sporophyte tissue, surrounding a mass of succulent, well-protected, haploid gametophyte tissue, which in turn surrounds and nourishes a dormant, partly formed, diploid **plant embryo**—the next sporophyte generation. Seeds, like pollen grains, can survive harsh conditions and can remain dormant for years before germinating.

Four Types of Living Gymnosperms

Gymnosperms ("naked seeds") are seed plants that do not have flowers or fruit. Four groups of gymnosperms survive today; they are not closely related to one another. These are the **ginkgos,** the **cycads,** the strange **gnetophytes,** and the familiar **conifers.** The ginkgo, or maidenhair tree, qualifies as rare because there is only one surviving species, *Ginkgo biloba* (Figure 22.15). Until recently, individuals of this single species were rare even in its native China. Now, however, it has become a common decorative tree throughout the world—partly because it is quite pretty, partly because of its unusual appearance, and partly because it is relatively resistant to insects, disease, and even air pollution. The large, rather smelly seed is considered a great delicacy by some gourmets.

The cycads have done a little better than the ginkgos; about 100 species of cycads are alive in the world today. Most of these are native to the tropical and subtropical regions of the world. In hothouses and botanical gardens, cycads are often mistaken for palms, which they superficially resemble, just as ginkgos superficially resemble ashes or sycamores. But ashes, sycamores, and palms are all flowering plants, unrelated to either cycads or ginkgos. Palms produce flowers, while cycads produce massive cones (see Figure 22.15).

The 70 or so named species of gnetophytes are a bizarre, diverse lot. Some botanists believe that the flowering plants evolved from this group, or at least that the two groups are related. The evidence is sparse but interesting. For example, plants of the genus *Gnetum* have leaves with netlike veins, rather resembling the leaves of a cherry tree. Another gnetophyte, the rare and totally weird *Welwitschia mirabilis* (see Figure 22.15) has xylem *vessels.* Vessels are specialized xylem cells that are common in flowering plants (see Chapter 25), but do not exist in the xylem of any other gymnosperm.

The Conifers. The conifers are made up of about 500 named species—not very many species, considering the vast coniferous forests of the

22.15

(a) To a casual observer, the ginkgo *(Ginkgo biloba)* looks like almost any broad-leaved tree, such as an ash or a sycamore. However, the ginkgo is a gymnosperm, albeit a strange one. It has separate sexes. **(b)** Cycads grow in the tropical and subtropical regions of most continents. Cycads also have separate sexes; note the bright yellow pollen cone of this male cycad sporophyte. Both ginkgo and cycad pollen germinate to produce flagellated sperm, which swim in fluid produced by the small female gametophytes. **(c)** *Welwitschia mirabilis*, perhaps the strangest of all gymnosperms, grows in the remote Kalahari desert. Its upright stem is only a few centimeters tall, but may be more than 1 m in diameter; throughout its long life it produces exactly two ragged, splitting, continuously growing leaves. Seed cones grow on the edges of the leaves.

world. Many conifers thrive in the cold climates of the earth (Figure 22.16), but some are also doing quite well in warm regions. Typically, they produce *needles:* narrow, tough leaves with thick, water-resistant cuticles. This is an adaptation to arid conditions, whether the habitat is simply dry or the water is periodically bound up as ice. The needles are produced in the spring, as are the leaves of deciduous (leaf-shedding) trees, but since the conifer needles stay green and each one stays on the tree for several years (so that several generations of leaves overlap one another) the conifers stay green throughout the year. And that, presumably, is why they are called *evergreens.*

The conifers include the pines, firs, spruces, redwoods, hemlocks, junipers, and larches. Of these, the most common and best-known group is the pine family, *Pinaceae.* Pines have separate male (pollen-bearing) and female (ovule-bearing) *cones,* and each tree is bisexual (that is, each sporophyte bears both male and female cones). The shapes and sizes of the cones are usually the most distinctive features of the different pine species. The seeds—*pine nuts*—remain in the female cones for about two years as they slowly mature (Figure 22.17). During this period, the seeds of many pines develop a winglike structure that will catch the wind, so that when the cone opens and they are released, they will float far from the parent tree. In some pines, the cones will not open to release their seeds until they first are scorched by fire and then cool off; each new generation of such pines must await its own forest fire.

In ancient Mesozoic times, the dominance of the gymnosperms and that of the dinosaurs were strangely intertwined, and both groups fell from prominence toward the end of the Mesozoic era. The giant reptiles—except for the alligators and crocodiles—were to pass into oblivion, while the conifers managed to survive, although their numbers decreased drastically. The Cenozoic era, which followed the Mesozoic era and began 65 million years ago, was the time of the *flowering plants.* The flowering plants came to dominate the landscape from the tropics to the temperate regions, leaving mainly the colder northern regions to most of the surviving gymnosperms. The conifers were well on their way to being rare, archaic relics, like the gnetophytes and the ginkgos, but in the Pleistocene period, which began only two million years ago, they began an amazing comeback. In these relatively recent times both their geographic range and the number of individuals, if not the number of species, have greatly increased.

The Cenozoic Era: The Time of the Flowering Plants

When did the flowering plants evolve? Were they inconspicuously sprinkled among the dominant, if primitive, conifers, cycads, and ginkgos of the Mesozoic era, or were they absent altogether in those days? What kinds of conditions promoted their rather sudden explosion to dominance?

One theory is rather simple: the flowering

22.16

Coniferous forests are found chiefly in the cold regions of the earth. They form a continuous belt across Northern Asia, North America, and Europe. Such forests also extend southward along mountain ranges. Some conifers thrive in more temperate or even subtropical regions.

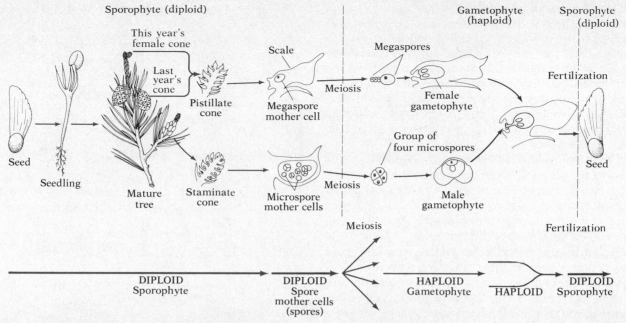

Sporophyte (diploid)   Gametophyte (haploid)   Sporophyte (diploid)

DIPLOID Sporophyte → DIPLOID Spore mother cells (spores) → HAPLOID Gametophyte → HAPLOID → DIPLOID Sporophyte

22.17

Alternation of generations in a conifer. With the exception of cells hidden in their reproductive structures, and an occasional yellow cloud of windborne pollen, all of the conifer we see is the sporophyte. The conifers have no truly separate gametophyte generation. Cells in the male cones, known as *microspore mother cells*, enter meiosis and form haploid *microspores*. These microspores form a winged pollen grain, and later, the male gametes. Cells in the female cone, the *megaspore mother cells*, enter meiosis and produce haploid *megaspores*. These produce the female gametophyte, with two archegonia. When pollen (the male gametophyte generation) lands on the female cone, a *pollen tube* grows into the tissue surrounding the egg cell within an archegonium. Fertilization occurs when a sperm from a pollen tube reaches an egg cell.

plants had evolved two advantages, *animal pollination* and *seed dispersal*. Insects had been around for a very long time, but the gymnosperms had depended on wind pollination alone. It is generally agreed that the earliest flowering plants were animal pollinated, and probably insect pollinated. Most are dependent upon insects for pollination today, although a number of groups of flowering plants have reverted to wind pollination. But this efficient and rather specific mode of sexual reproduction may have given the early flowering plants a decided advantage in the Darwinian struggle. As for seed dispersal, the key event was probably the emergence of birds. Birds were attracted to the fleshy, tasty, sugar-laden tissue encasing resistant seeds, and seeds passed through their digestive systems in viable condition, often after being carried to distant but suitable locations. This again was a major advantage to early flowering plants, as it is to many flowering plants today.

Other theories abound. Some investigators believe that the relatively rapid emergence of the flowering plants can be explained on the basis of geological and climatological changes; temperatures of the Cenozoic era were colder than those of the Mesozoic era, for instance. The end of the Mesozoic era, 65 million years ago, also was marked by the final drifting apart of the continents.

There is good evidence that the Cenozoic era started abruptly and dramatically with a major catastrophe, an event of nightmarish proportions—the impact upon the earth of a huge asteroid or comet, some 10 km (six mi) in diameter. The dust this cosmic body raised, according to some calculations, must have blocked out the sun's rays and caused massive weather changes, including subzero temperatures even at the equator. This event marked the second mass extinction of animal species (we noted the first in discussing the gymnosperms), including the dinosaurs, ichthyosaurs, plesiosaurs, and pterosaurs; and in the sea, it coincided with the disappearance of most coral-dwelling cyanobacteria, most foraminiferans, and certain other protists. Of course, the extinction of these groups permitted the expansions of other species, which were now free to establish new ecological niches formerly occupied by the extinct animals. Thus the early Cenozoic era was marked by rapid proliferation and adaptive radiation of the mammals on the land and of the diatoms in the sea, as the ecological opportunities vacated by reptiles and various plankton were filled by newly evolving groups. The change was sharp, dramatic, and permanent.

How does all of this bear upon the origin of the flowering plants? We're not really sure. It's clear that the flowering plants were already established by the end of the Mesozoic era; that is, before there was any hint of an asteroid impact. And the fossil species of seed plants did not seem to be directly affected by the event; there was no sudden, mass extinction of land plants coinciding with the essentially instantaneous mass extinctions of the animals. This makes sense, because those groups that came through the cataclysm intact were precisely those organisms that had developed long-lived, resistant, dormant cysts, spores, or seeds, which could last out a few years of dark skies and bad weather. But all of the great changes in the world, whether extraterrestrial in origin or otherwise, ultimately changed the landscape enough so that innumerable interlocking balances were shifted, and some groups flourished while others declined.

The Angiosperms Today.   All we need to do is to look around us to see that the **angiosperms**—the flowering plants—have inherited the earth, at least for the time being. No one knows how many kinds of flowering plants there are, but about 250,000 different species have already been named.

In spite of such diversity, the flowering plants can all be divided into two great groups. These are the *Monocotyledonae* ("monocots," for short) and the *Dicotyledonae* ("dicots," for short). The first group is in the minority, since there are only about 50,000 named species of monocots. Among them are all of the grasses—including corn, wheat, and all the other cereal grains we depend upon—and palm trees, orchids, tulips, lilies, yuccas, and many other familiar plants. Most other common plants are dicots. Monocots and dicots are rather distantly related, and although they share many key features, they also differ from each other in several important aspects. The most obvious differences are in their leaf patterns, seeds, floral arrangement, and the pattern of their vascular systems, as we see in Figure 22.18. The life cycle of the flowering plants is the topic of the next chapter.

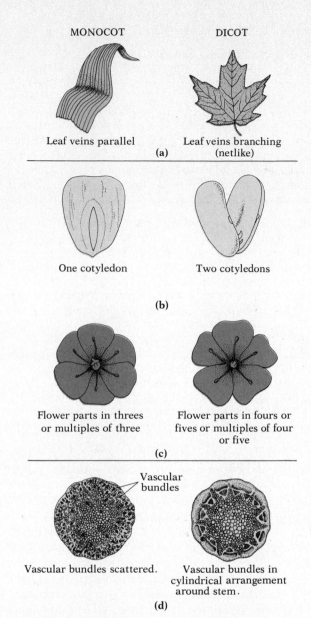

22.18

Angiosperms are divided into monocots and dicots according to four major structural differences. **(a)** The most obvious difference is in the pattern of veins in the leaf, which is netlike in the dicot (such as a sugar maple) and parallel in the monocot (such as corn). **(b)** The seeds also differ in that two *cotyledons* (seed leaves) are seen in the dicots, while only one is present in the monocots. **(c)** The flowers of dicots have four or five floral parts, or multiples of these numbers (when the floral parts are divided). Monocots have three floral parts, or multiples of three. **(d)** The vascular system of dicots is generally a neat ring of vascular bundles arranged in a circle around the stem. In the monocots, the vascular system commonly occurs in scattered bundles.

Summary

The Alternation of Generations

Plants have two alternating stages in their life cycles: the diploid, sporophyte (spore-producing) generation and the haploid, gametophyte (gamete-producing) generation. The two may occur in separate individuals (for example, in many algae) or within one individual (as with higher vascular plants). Either generation may predominate, although the gametophyte is greatly reduced in higher plants. The sporophyte generation always begins after fertilization, while the gametophyte always begins after meiosis.

A Quick Survey of the Plant Kingdom

The plant kingdom is divided into nonvascular and vascular plants. Nonvascular plants, algae and bryophytes, do not have conducting tissues; they are flat or small enough that substances move through them by diffusion. Vascular plants are mainly terrestrial, and water and nutrients move through their conducting tissues.

The Nonvascular Plants

Red and brown algae, which include most seaweeds and kelps, store foods in the form of special starches and attach themselves to the sea floor with holdfasts. Most red and brown algae have separate sporophyte and gametophyte individuals, although the gametophyte develops completely within the sporophyte body in some species of brown algae.

Green algae live on land and in fresh and salt water, at times in symbiosis with other organisms. They produce chlorophylls, starches, and cellulose. Some green algae are single celled, while others are multicellular or are organized into colonies. Terrestrial plant life may have arisen from the many varieties of green algae.

The bryophytes—the mosses, hornworts, and liverworts—are multicellular plants with specialized tissues. They lack vascular tissues, however, and fluids and nutrients must move through their bodies by cell-to-cell transport. In bryophytes, the egg is protected in the archegonium, to which the sperm must swim. The gametophyte generation is dominant in the mosses, with the sporophyte generation often represented by a simple stalk topped by the sporangium. The spores are released and germinate to form a thin filament that develops into the moss gametophyte. The sexual reproduction cycle then begins, culminating in the zygote that produces the sporophyte.

The Vascular Plants

Vascular plants have evolved xylem for support and water transport and phloem for the distribution of photosynthetic products. There are six categories of vascular plants: psilophytes, club mosses, horsetails, ferns, gymnosperms, and flowering plants. The first three were dominant in earth's early history. Ferns have survived in great numbers and have adapted to many environments.

Gymnosperms arose in the Mesozoic era, their success based on the development of extensive root systems, pollen grains, and seeds. Four groups survive today: the rare ginkgo, the cycads, the gnetophytes, and the familiar conifers. Conifers are well adapted to many climates, and typically bear separate male and female cones. During the Cenozoic era, geological events brought about dramatic changes in climate that eventually favored many angiosperm species. Flowering plants, divided into monocots and dicots, are now the dominant plant form on earth.

Key Terms

food chain	algin	rhizome
alternation of generations	blade	fern
spore	stipe	fiddlehead
gamete	float	sori
sporophyte generation	green algae	sporangia
gametophyte generation	eyespot	prothallium
vascular plants	isogamete	seed
nonvascular plants	zygospore	plant embryo
red algae	bryophyte	gymnosperm
holdfast	rhizoid	ginkgo
floridean starch	archegonium	cycad
carrageenan	antheridia	gnetophyte
brown algae	xylem	conifer
fucoxanthin	phloem	angiosperms

Review Questions

1. Using a simple diagram, explain alternation of generations. (pp. 309–310)

2. Describe the chief difference between non-vascular and vascular plants, and explain the evolutionary significance of the latter. (pp. 310, 319)

3. The body length of some marine kelps approaches that of a tall tree, yet the alga gets along without xylem—water-transporting and supportive tissue. Explain. (p. 312)

4. Give an example of an alga that produces iso-gametes, and an example of one that produces heterogametes, and explain the difference. (pp. 312 and 313)

5. Why are the green algae believed to be more closely related to higher plants than the red or brown algae? (p. 314)

6. Review the life cycle of a moss, describing the gametophyte and sporophyte generations and the main events in each. (pp. 315–317)

7. What did vascular tissue permit plants to do that was not possible for bryophytes? (pp. 317–319)

8. Summarize the major events in the fern life cycle, point out the primary difference between ferns and mosses, and name an important similarity. (pp. 315–317, 319–321)

9. Relate the rise of gymnosperms to changing geological conditions, and list three characteristics that helped ensure their success. (pp. 321–322)

10. List four groups of gymnosperms. Which of these is the most prominent today? (pp. 323–324)

11. Summarize two theories offered as explanation for the rise of flowering plants. (pp. 324–326)

Reproduction in the Flowering Plants

23

The flowering plants, the angiosperms, began with a rich heritage. By the time their great invasion of the earth's varied habitats began, they were already well prepared for the rigors of terrestrial life. Their vascular systems were well developed, permitting great increases in size as they pushed their leaves toward the sun. Their massive but delicate roots were able to draw water from the soil. They produced pollen, and fertilization no longer required water. The embryo was protected by a hardened seed coat that could resist most environmental rigors. But one problem remained: how to get the sperm to the egg.

Early in their evolutionary history, seed plants had to rely primarily on the winds to carry the male gametophyte to the female gametophyte. But because plants were so successful at invading virtually every nook and cranny of the earth's habitats, wind pollination was no longer enough. It wasn't long before some of these new kinds of plants were employing other forms of assistance—the earth's insects were pressed into service. But insects were not in the business of raising plants. What was in it for them? How did plants, through the opportunism of natural selection, enlist their little six-legged partners?

The earliest angiosperm insect lure was probably a device that oozed a sugary plant fluid, at least enough to interest some crawling Mesozoic beetle. Once the trend was established, the race was on as new insect-tempting devices arose to be tested against the forces of natural selection. As a result, plants developed ever more attractive and efficient ways of making use of the wandering insects. At the same time, the insects were also undergoing changes that would enable them to exploit more efficiently whatever it was the plant was offering them. In time, many insects had evolved remarkably efficient sensory devices for detecting flowers and long tubular mouthparts for sucking up nectar. Plants, of course, competed among themselves for the attention of these creatures. Some even began a garish form of advertising that attracted insects—those remarkable displays we call *flowers*, but Darwin referred to as "contraptions."

THE ANATOMY OF THE FLOWER

A woodland stroll in the spring makes it clear that there are many kinds of flowers. All of the flowers, from tiny quivering bells in a meadow to giants that boldly stand taller than a man, are all variations on one theme.

TABLE 23.1

Animal pollinators and floral adaptions

Animal Vector	Beetles	Bees	Flies
Visual Cues	Not significant, flowers dull colored, or white	Bright colors: yellow or blue (ultraviolet perception) Highly divided floral parts with uneven outline	Large flowers, dull, flesh-colored
Chemical Cues	Strong odors: fruity, spicy, or foul	Odors very significant	Musky to rotting odors

Because flowers boast such great variety, we must rely on generalizations that may only leave us with a convenient fiction, but perhaps an instructive one. First, our generalized flower is composed of four regions, arising from a widened base called the **receptacle.** Each region in the flower represents a *whorl* (or circle) of highly mofified leaves. The whorl closest to the stem is the **calyx.** It is formed of leaflike **sepals.** In the mature flower the sepals are flattened, usually triangular blades; their most important role is performed a little earlier: they form a protective cover over the developing bud. The second whorl is the **corolla,** composed of **petals.** In plants that must attract insects or birds, the petals are usually very conspicuous and often attractively colored and fragrant; and *nectaries,* glands at the flower's base, exude sugary nectar. There is a great deal of variation in the way flowers attract their pollinators, some of which are summarized in Table 23.1.

The third and fourth whorls of the flower, going from the edge toward the center, contain the reproductive organs, including the **stamens,** or the male parts; their female counterpart is called the pistil (made up of one or more **carpels**). Each stamen consists of a slender stalk called the **filament** and a terminal **anther,** where, following meiosis, the male gametophyte is produced. The carpels are sometimes rather complex structures, consisting of three parts: the ovary, style, and stigma. Carpels are often fused, either at their bases or throughout their lengths. In older terminology, carpels are often referred to as **pistils** (Figure 23.1).

carpels = pistils

The **ovary** is the widened base of the pistil or carpels. It will later form the fruit. In its early developmental stages, the ovary contains the cells that will undergo meiosis to produce the female gametophyte and, after fertilization, the growing seed and its developing embryo. The **style** is the narrow stalk that arises from the ovary, its tip bearing the **stigma,** a sticky or hairy structure that receives the pollen. Some of the more common variations in floral anatomy are described in Essay 23.1 (p. 334).

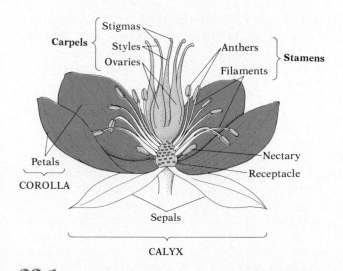

23.1

The generalized flower.

TABLE 23.1 (continued)
Animal pollinators and floral adaptions

Butterflies	Birds	Bats
Bright colors: red, orange, yellow, blue	Bright colors: red and yellows	Large, dull-colored flowers, color not significant (Bats are night flyers.)
Strong, sweet odor	Copious sugary nectar, little odor	Copious nectar, fruity and fermenting odors

THE SEXUAL LIFE OF THE FLOWER

As a flowering plant prepares for sexual reproduction, changes begin in both the ovary and the anther. Certain of these diploid tissues contain special cells that will undergo meiosis in order to usher in the inconspicuous gametophyte generation (Figure 23.2).

Inside the Ovary: Ovule and Embryo Sac

Within the soft tissues of the flower's young ovary, tiny but complex bodies called **ovules** develop. Although the term *ovule* means "little egg," ovules are technically not eggs. In their early state, they contain sporophyte cells that have the ability to produce the female gametophyte. Each ovule consists of a *megaspore mother cell* surrounded by nutritive and protective tissues.

The **megaspore mother cell** is a large diploid cell that will produce the female gametophyte. This cell will undergo meiosis in the usual fashion (see Chapter 10) and produce four haploid cells. Three of these will disintegrate, leaving one large cell, the **functional megaspore** that then begins three rounds of mitosis and produces eight haploid nuclei (one round produces two nuclei, which produce four, and the four produce eight). The eight-nucleate structure is the mature female gametophyte, now called the **embryo sac** (see Figure 23.2).

Eventually, cell walls form and isolate all but two of the eight nuclei. At one end, one of the isolated cells changes to become the **egg cell,** which is the female gamete. As we will see, both the egg cell and the binucleate cell will enter into fertilization.

Inside the Anthers: Pollen Formation

While the embryo sac has been developing in the ovary, changes have been occurring in the anthers that will produce the male gametophyte (Figure 23.3). The anthers typically contain four chambers known as **pollen sacs.** Within the pollen sacs are numerous diploid cells, the **microspore mother cells.** It is these cells that undergo meiosis. Each meiotic event forms four haploid cells called **microspores.** Each of these cells then doubles by mitosis—just once—to produce the two-celled male gametophyte. Each of these two cells has its own role and name. One is called the **sperm cell** and the other is called the **pollen tube cell.** The sperm cell becomes completely enclosed within the cytoplasm of the pollen tube cell. Each gametophyte produces a tough, resistant coat and matures to become a small, light **pollen grain.** Most pollen is lost in this uncertain world, but some grains will land on the stigma of a receptive flower. In the angiosperms, the gametophyte generation (which was so prominent in the more primitive plants) is represented only by the pollen grain and the embryo sac.

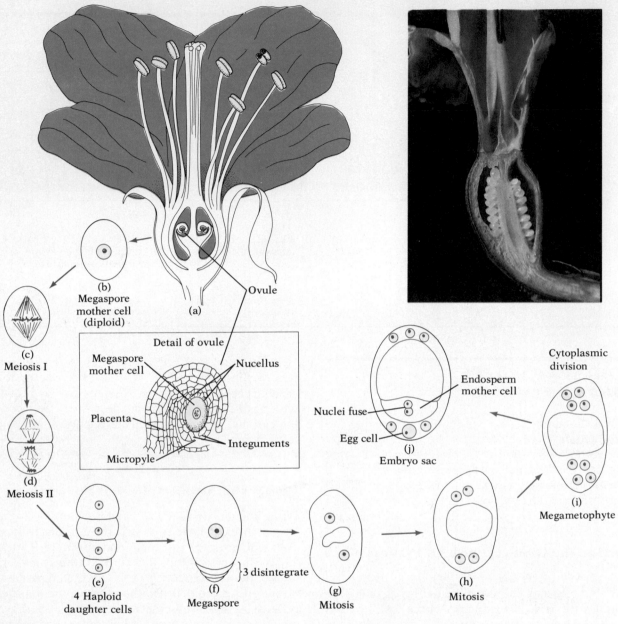

(b) Megaspore mother cell (diploid)

(a)

Ovule

(c) Meiosis I

(d) Meiosis II

Detail of ovule

Megaspore mother cell

Nucellus

Placenta

Micropyle

Integuments

(e) 4 Haploid daughter cells

(f) Megaspore   } 3 disintegrate

(g) Mitosis

(h) Mitosis

(i) Megametophyte

Cytoplasmic division

Endosperm mother cell

Nuclei fuse

Egg cell

(j) Embryo sac

23.2

The female gametophyte generation begins after meiosis in the megaspore mother cell **(a–e)**. One of the haploid megaspores goes through three rounds of mitosis, eventually forming the seven-celled embryo sac

(g–j). The embryo sac includes an egg cell and a central binucleate cell, both of which will participate in fertilization and embryo formation.

Pollination and Fertilization

Technically, pollination occurs when pollen is deposited on a receptive stigma, but actual fertilization occurs somewhat later, by the fusion of the sperm with certain nuclei of the embryo sac (Figure 23.4). The events leading to fertilization begin when pollen on the moist stigma germinates (emerges from dormancy). After the hard coat

breaks open, a **pollen tube** emerges and grows through the stigma and down the style. The growing tube, under the direction of the pollen tube nucleus, produces enzymes that actually digest the soft tissues ahead of the tube. The tube nucleus remains near the tip as it grows downward. During this growth the single sperm nucleus undergoes one round of mitosis, producing two genetically identical, haploid **sperm.**

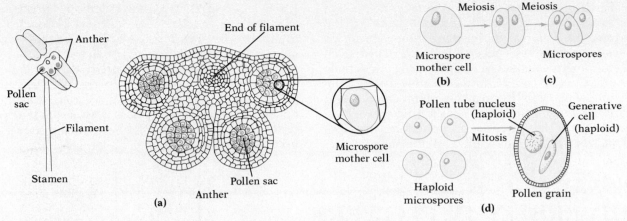

23.3

The male gametophytes develop in pollen sacs within the anthers **(a)**. Meiosis in a microspore mother cell produces four haploid microspores **(b, c)**, each of which goes through one round of mitosis, producing a two-celled gametophyte. The tiny gametophyte secretes a thick, resistant wall and matures to become a pollen grain **(d)**.

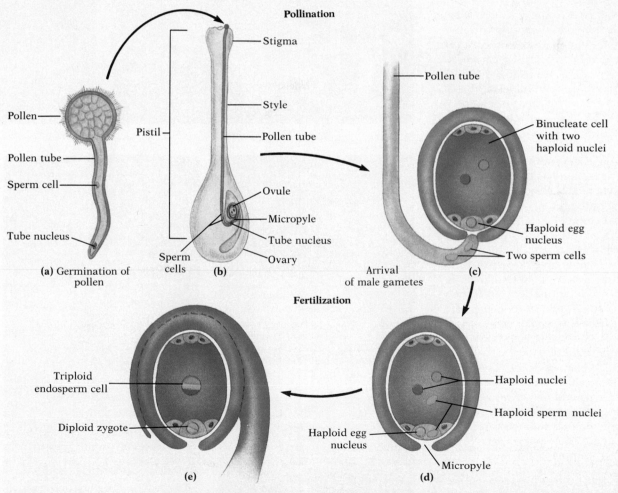

23.4

Upon contacting the stigma, the pollen grain produces a pollen tube that grows down through the style into the ovary **(a–b)**. As it nears its objective, the sperm cell within the pollen tube cell undergoes mitosis, producing two sperm cells. One fertilizes the egg cell and the other fertilizes the binucleate cell **(c–e)**.

Fertilization and Fusion. Finally the pollen tube penetrates the ovule at a tiny opening, the **micropyle.** The two sperm then enter the embryo sac. One fertilizes the egg cell. The sperm cell membrane breaks down and the male and female haploid nuclei fuse to form the new zygote. The zygote will develop into the plant embryo and eventually form the plant body of the sporophyte generation. The other sperm penetrates the large binucleate cell in the center of the embryo sac, where it also loses its plasma membrane and fuses with the two nuclei there to form a **trinucleate (triploid) cell.** This unusual cell will undergo numerous mitoses to form a special nutritive tissue called the **endosperm.** The starchy triploid endosperm usually forms the food reserves of the seed.

The simple plant endosperm has played a critical role in human affairs. This is because the starchy endosperm provides the flour and meal produced from wheat, corn, rice, rye, millet, and oats.

ESSAY 23.1
DIVERSITY IN FLOWERS

Natural selection has molded, warped, changed, hidden, and amplified flower parts to a remarkable degree. To begin, there is a basic difference between flowers of *monocots* (a) and those of *dicots* (b). The floral parts (sepals, petals, etc.) of dicots are arranged in fours and fives or in multiples of these numbers, while those of monocots appear in threes or multiples of threes. In both groups the basic arrangement may become highly modified depending on how much specialization has occurred.

When all the basic parts of a flower are present, the flower is called **complete (c),** as opposed to the **incomplete** flower (d), which is missing some parts. If the missing parts include only the sepals or petals, or both, then the flower is incomplete but **perfect (e).** If, however, either or both of the sexual parts (the stamens or carpels) is absent, the flower is incomplete and **imperfect.**

Such plants as corn have imperfect (and incomplete) flowers, but both male and female flowers appear on the same plant (f). Other plants, such as the holly and date palm, are *either* male or female (g). In fact, commercial date-palm growers usually plant one male tree per grove to pollinate the female (date-bearing) trees.

In some instances, flowers are grouped together into clusters, as in daisies, marigolds, sunflowers,

(a) Lillies (monocots)

(b) Geranium (dicot)

(c) Water lily (complete)

(d) *(above)* Pussy willow (incomplete)

(e) *(left)* Anthuriums (incomplete, perfect)

EMBRYO AND SEED DEVELOPMENT IN A DICOT

Soon after the triploid cell is formed, it repeatedly undergoes mitosis, thus forming the endosperm. While the endosperm grows, the embryo undergoes rapid cell division. Later, the embryonic cells will begin to differentiate (undergo changes leading to specialization) in preparation for different roles in the life of the plant. Among its first efforts, the young embryo will give rise to one or two wings of tissue called **cotyledons.** An embryo will thus reveal at an early stage whether it is *monocotyledonous* (a monocot) or *dicotyledonous* (a dicot). The cotyledons in the two plant groups function differently. In monocots, the single cotyledon will often absorb food from the surrounding starchy endosperm, while in dicots, the two cotyledons will actually contain the food.

and dandelions. This means that a single sunflower is really a whole bouquet of flowers **(h).** Composite flowers are produced only by dicots, and each individual flower bears *five* fused stamens around the fused pistil. Each of these tiny flowers produces a single seed. In the daisy, marigold, and sunflower head, the outer rows of flowers (petals) are imperfect and sexless, serving only to attract pollinators.

Finally, flowers are not always the colorful, fragrant attractors of insects that the word brings to mind. Some insect-pollinated flowers **(j)** smell awful, and a bat-pollinated flower may actually be ugly and smell like a bat (see Table 23.1). Many flowers scatter their pollen to the wind and thereafter depend completely on chance. Grasses (including grains) and most temperate-zone trees (including gymnosperms) are wind-pollinated. You may have noticed that some broad-leaf trees produce clusters of drably colored flowers before the first spring leaves appear. This permits pollen to be blown about without interference. Wind-pollinated plants do not need to advertise or to manufacture nectar, but since the wind is not selective, they need to produce enormous amounts of pollen and must grow in fairly dense stands **(i).** Their usually inconspicuous flowers contain branched, feathery, or sticky stigmas and rather conventional-looking stamens. ●

(f) Tan bark oak flower (incomplete, imperfect) **(g)** *(right)* Holly (incomplete, imperfect)

(h) Subalpine daisy (composite) **(i)** Red maple (wind-pollinated) **(j)** Goldenrod (insect-pollinated)

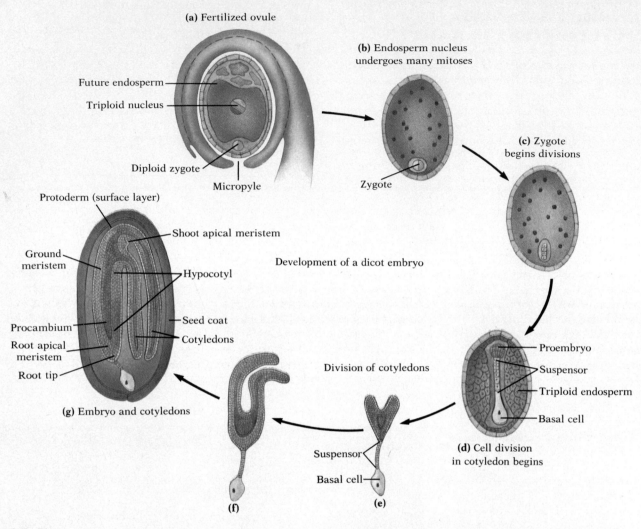

(a) Fertilized ovule

Future endosperm
Triploid nucleus

Diploid zygote
Micropyle

(b) Endosperm nucleus
undergoes many mitoses

Zygote

(c) Zygote
begins divisions

Protoderm (surface layer)

Shoot apical meristem

Ground
meristem

Hypocotyl

Procambium

Seed coat

Root apical
meristem

Cotyledons

Root tip

Development of a dicot embryo

(g) Embryo and cotyledons

Division of cotyledons

Proembryo
Suspensor
Triploid endosperm
Basal cell

(d) Cell division
in cotyledon begins

Suspensor

Basal cell

(f)

(e)

23.5

Development of the embryo in the dicot *Capsella bursa-pastoris*, the shepherd's purse. After fertilization, the ovule contains a diploid zygote and a triploid endosperm **(a)**. The endosperm nucleus undergoes numerous mitoses **(b)**, followed soon by mitosis in the zygote **(c)**. As the endosperm lays down cell walls, the embryo is relegated to a ball of cells at its upper end, connected by a stalk to the suspensor, a large bulbous cell below **(d)**. As the embryo begins to differentiate, two masses of cells grow from the embryo and form the developing cotyledons **(e, f)**. As the cotyledons continue, they turn and enlarge to fill the endospermal space, absorbing the nutrients of the endosperm. Differentiation in the embryo proper **(g)** results in the emergence of regions: the protoderm, ground meristem, and the procambium. Patches of simple, undifferentiated tissue persist that will form the shoot and root apical meristems. Most of the embryo consists of the enlarged cotyledons and the lengthy hypocotyl.

The Embryo Proper

The developmental history of one dicot embryo, the *shepherd's purse*, is seen in Figure 23.5. As this embryo completes its development, the two cotyledons characteristic of dicots are quite prominent. Below the cotyledons, some cells in the embryo begin to reveal signs of differentiation, while others remain simple and undifferentiated. The latter make up regions known as **meristem**, which include the **shoot apical meristem**, the **root apical meristem**, and the **ground meristem**. Each region will later participate in growth and development.

Partially differentiated cells include the **protoderm** and the **procambium**. The protoderm surrounds the embryo, later giving rise to the **epidermis** (outer skin), while the procambium, the more centrally located group, contributes to the plant's vascular system. Most of the embryo at this time is designated as the **hypocotyl**. In many dicots, upon

336

seed germination the hypocotyl undergoes rapid growth, its upper region drawing the seed upward to break the soil surface and its lower region forcing the young root downward. The root tip is protected by a layer of expendable cells called the **root cap,** a product of the root apical meristem.

Seed Coats and Dormancy

After its initial differentiation and development, the embryo becomes dormant. It will undergo no further changes until germination, the metabolic awakening process in the seed. At that time, cell division and differentiation will resume. Until then, the embryo lies protected by a hardened seed coat. In its dormant state, the seed will lose water, becoming dry and hard.

Interestingly, seeds can lie dormant but viable for a long time. Most seeds can sustain at least several years of dormancy; certain lotus seeds, found in a peat deposit near Tokyo, germinated after 2000 years of dormancy. The record, though, is held by a delicate flower of the Yukon, *Lupinus arcticus,* which grew into a fine plant after having lain in the frozen soil for over 10,000 years!

Fruit

In all angiosperms, the fruit develops along with the seed. **Fruit** is actually the mature ovary that surrounds the seeds. You may be surprised to learn that some foods you know as vegetables are, technically, fruits. Among these are squash, eggplant, cucumbers, and pumpkins, as well as corn, wheat, rye, and beans (if we count the pods). Essay 23.2 discusses the varieties of fruit.

Seed Dispersal

It is advantageous for any plant to be able to disperse its seeds—first, so as not to be forced to compete with its own seedlings, and second, in order to be able to invade new habitats. However, it is often the fruit, rather than the seed itself, that brings about seed dispersal. Such dry fruits as peas and beans pop open and expel seeds forcefully, projecting them at least a few meters away (probably even a few gardeners have witnessed this). Other fruits may use wind, water, or birds and foxes to scatter the seeds even more widely (see Figure 23.6).

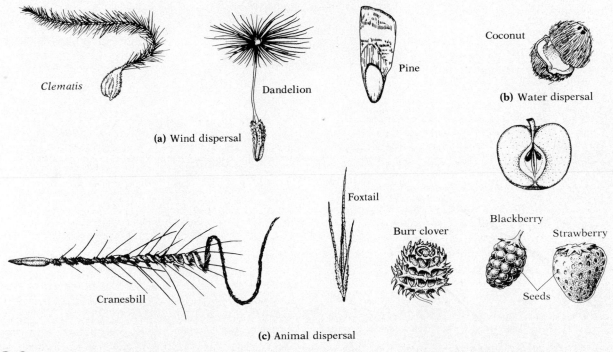

23.6

Plants have developed a variety of means of dispersing seeds. **(a)** The wind-dispersed fruits have plumes or wings that help in sending them aloft. **(b)** The coconut can be carried long distances by ocean currents. **(c)** The cranesbill, foxtail, and bur clover fruits are adapted for clinging to the fur of mammals. The cranesbill fruit has the ability to screw itself into the ground. The seeds of berries may be carried for a while in an animal's digestive tract.

FLOWERS TO FRUITS

A fruit is a ripened ovary that sometimes exists in association with certain floral parts. There are three basic types of fruits: *simple, aggregate,* or *multiple,* depending on the number of ovaries in the flower or the number of flowers in the fruiting structure.

Simple fruits may be derived from a single ovary or, more commonly, from the compound ovary of a single flower. They can be divided into two groups according to their consistency at maturity: *simple fleshy fruits* and *simple dry fruits.*

Simple fleshy fruits include the *berry, pome,* and *drupe.* The **berry** has one or several united fleshy carpels, each with many seeds. Thus the tomato **(a)** is a berry, and each of the seed-filled cavities is derived from a carpel. Watermelons, cucumbers, and grapefruit are also berries (but, oddly enough, blackberries, raspberries, and strawberries technically are *not* berries). **Pome (b)** means "apple,"

(a) Flower of tomato

Young, simple fleshy fruit (berry) of the tomato with only sepals remaining.

Mature fleshy berry of the tomato. A cut at right angles to its axis reveals five fused carpels, each containing the seed-bearing, fan-shaped parts of the ovary.

(b) Apple flower

The organization of a pome becomes apparent in the young fruit, as the bases of corolla and calyx form the *floral tube* surrounding the ovary.

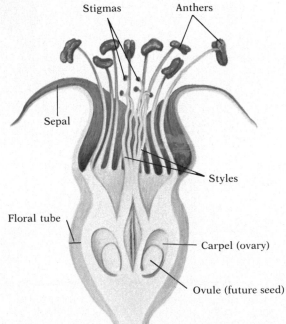

Young fruit of the apple

and the group includes apples, pears, and quinces. In the pome, only the inner chambers (roughly, the "core") are derived from the ovary, and most of the flesh comes from the calyx and corolla. A **drupe**—what a wonderful word—is also derived from a compound

ovary, but only a single seed develops to maturity. The ripened ovary consists of an outer fleshy part and a hard, inner *stone*, containing the single seed. Peaches and cherries are drupes.

There are many kinds of simple dry fruits, but they are neatly cate-

gorized as follows: (1) those with many seeds, which split open and release their seeds, and (2) those with few seeds, which do not split open or release seeds. The first group is called **dehiscent (c),** from the verb *dehisce,* to split or to open, and includes poppies, peas, beans,

Mature fruit. Most of the floral parts have withered away, but the floral tube has greatly enlarged, producing the sweet, edible portion of the fruit that contains the ovary (core). In the cross section we see the remnants of the flower, including the united carpels. The small ovals and circles represent the former vascular system of the flower.

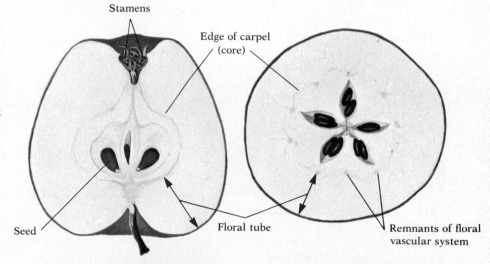

Stamens

Edge of carpel (core)

Seed

Floral tube

Remnants of floral vascular system

(c) Flower of poppy

The dry dehiscent fruit takes the form of a capsule surrounding the maturing seeds.

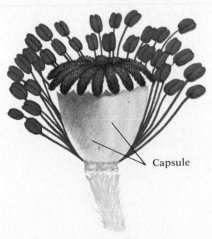

Young fruit

Capsule

Capsule splitting

Seeds

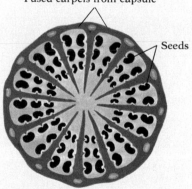

Fused carpels from capsule

Seeds

Mature fruit. The capsule, free of other floral parts, becomes a seed-dropping machine as it splits. In cross section, the united carpels are visible in this simple fruit. Each carpel contains numerous seeds in rows along its length.

FLOWERS TO FRUITS

milkweed, snapdragons, and mustard. The second group is called **indehiscent (d)** (nonsplitting). Its members include sunflowers, dandelions, maples, ash, corn, and wheat.

Aggregate fruits (e) are derived from numerous separate carpels of a single flower. Blackberries, raspberries, and strawberries are aggregate fruits. Aggregate fruits consist of many simple fruits clumped together on a common base.

Multiple fruits (f) are formed from the single ovaries of many flowers joined together, as seen in the mulberry, fig, and pineapple. The pineapple starts out as a cluster of separate flowers on a single stalk, but as the ovaries enlarge, they coalesce to form the giant multiple fruit. (The commercial variety, the kind we most commonly see, is a seedless hybrid.) ●

Individual flower of sunflower

Individual sunflower fruits
at two different stages

(d) The sunflower, a composite form, consists of many individual disk flowers, making up the *head*. Each flower is simple, consisting of one carpel that will hold a single seed. As the dry indehiscent fruit matures, it will become surrounded by the familiar hardened "shell" or capsule.

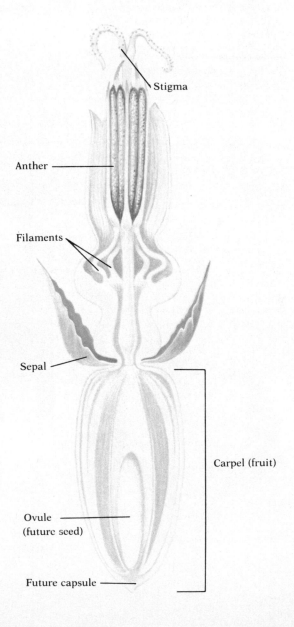

Stigma

Anther

Filaments

Sepal

Carpel (fruit)

Ovule
(future seed)

Future capsule

(e) Flower of the blackberry

Each of the small spheres, the carpels of this aggregate, is actually a simple fleshy fruit (drupes, in this case) containing a hard seed.

Maturing aggregate fruit of the blackberry

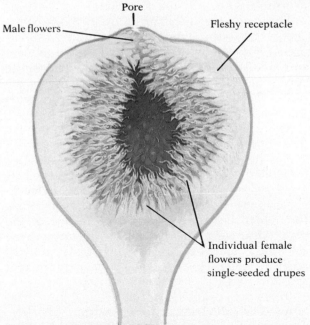

Individual carpels aggregated on a single receptacle

(f) Female flowers of the edible fig are produced within a fleshy receptacle. The receptacle has a pore through which a fig wasp enters in an attempt to lay her eggs. In this way, the wasp pollinates the flowers within. Each of the many female flowers matures into a simple drupe, but these occur in a single mass characteristic of multiple fruits. To see the flowers of a fig, the entire receptacle must be turned inside out.

341

Wind-dispersed fruit or seeds have plumes or wings that help in lofting them in breezes from the parent plant to some distant place. The winged maple seed tends to drop straight down at first, but as its speed increases, it begins to spin horizontally away from the parent. The buoyant, water-borne coconut fruit or *husk* contains one huge, hollow seed, the edible part. The coconut is tough and can float, so even the loneliest Pacific atoll is likely to boast a coconut tree. The cranesbill, foxtail, and clover burr are dry fruits adapted for clinging to the fur of animals. Burrs may be carried for miles before they split open and release their seeds. The cranesbill fruit is remarkable in that it lodges itself into the ground once it has been dropped. As the humidity rises and falls, the spiral fruit opens and closes, turning and ratcheting itself into the ground. Other fruits are fleshy, red, sweet, and tasty, and pass through the digestive tracts of traveling animals.

Germination and Early Seedling Development

In most plants, germination is triggered by the presence of adequate water, proper temperature, and oxygen. But some species require some rather surprising conditions. For example, in some seeds, germination must be triggered by fire or the grinding action of running water (see Chapter 22).

Some seeds won't germinate at all unless they have been subjected to an animal's digestive processes. On the island of Mauritius in the Indian Ocean, there are only 11 huge trees of a species found nowhere else. All of the trees are about 300 years old. Every year they produce a crop of fruit containing huge seeds with thick seed coats. But the seeds never germinate. In this species, germination cannot occur unless the seed is passed through the crop of a bird native to the island— *Raphus cucullatus*, better known as the dodo. The problem is, the trusting and helpless dodos were killed in great numbers by 17th-century Europeans, and the last one died 300 years ago. So year after year the seeds just lie around waiting for the bird that will never come. (This tragic tale may yet have a happy ending, as the naturalist who discovered this curious phenomenon recently managed to get several of the seeds to germinate by passing them through a turkey.)

The Seedling

Let's now consider the early growth of two kinds of seedlings: the green bean, a dicot, and corn, a monocot. Since there is so much diversity, even within dicots and monocots, our descriptions cannot be taken to represent even most of the members of each major plant group.

The Bean Seed and Seedling.   The bean seed (Figure 23.7a) contains an embryo with two large cotyledons. When the bean absorbs enough water, the seed coats soften and split. The cotyledons open slightly as the embryo expands.

Growth in the bean embryo begins as the hypocotyl forms a loop and elbows its way up through the soil (Figure 23.7b). As the loop continues to reach above the soil, it draws the cotyledons along until they are free. Then the hypocotyl straightens, exposing them to the sunlight. Just below the plumule (embryonic leaves), a rapidly elongating region (the **epicotyl**) pushes the shoot tip further upward. At the other end of the hypocotyl, the rapidly growing primary root penetrates the soil, anchors the plant, and absorbs water.

As the food reserves in the cotyledons begin to dwindle, the plumule enlarges, producing leaves that unfold to the sun. Soon the little plant becomes independent, producing its own foods through photosynthesis. The cotyledons wither and fall, as food reserves diminish.

The Corn Grain and Seedling.   Corn germinates in a different way. Corn (a monocot) has only one cotyledon (Figure 23.8a). It takes the form of a digestive structure called the **scutellum.** Surrounding the scutellum is the starchy endosperm. When corn germinates, it immediately produces enzymes, and the starches are digested. The products are absorbed by the scutellum.

The corn embryo contains roughly the same tissues as the bean embryo, with significant differences. Both the embryonic leaves and roots are surrounded by protective sheaths: the **coleoptile** covers the leaves and the **coleorhiza** covers the roots. These sheaths will remain and grow throughout the early part of germination.

The corn's cotyledon and endosperm, unlike those of the bean, remain in the soil when growth begins (Figure 23.8b). The young shoot emerges from the soil while still within the coleoptile, but as the first leaf grows, pushed up by rapid cell division in the shoot apical meristem below, it breaks through to become the first true foliage of the plant. Meanwhile, the root has broken through the coleorhiza and begun its downward growth, pushed along by the rapid cell division in the root apical meristem.

In the next chapter, we will see just how drastically cells can change, how they can specialize, act in concert, and even die to meet the challenges faced by plants on earth.

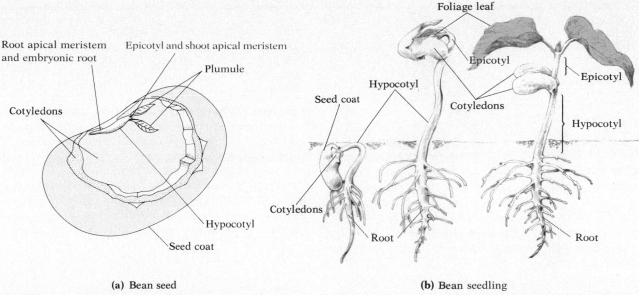

(a) Bean seed

(b) Bean seedling

23.7

The bean seed **(a)** consists mainly of two large cotyledons that contain stored food. The embryo itself already resembles a miniature plant. Its principal parts are the lengthy hypocotyl, the root tip, and the plumule. When the seed germinates **(b)**, the hypocotyl grows rapidly, forming a prominent curve. It pushes its way out of the soil, drawing the cotyledons with it. Meanwhile the expanding root penetrates the soil. Eventually the plumule escapes the cotyledons and expands, lifted away by the epicotyl. When the food reserves of the cotyledons diminish, they wither and fall.

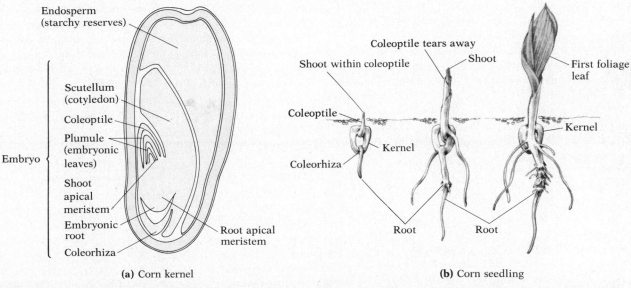

(a) Corn kernel

(b) Corn seedling

23.8

The corn kernel **(a)** is actually a fruit containing starchy food reserves. The embryo consists of the large single cotyledon, the scutellum, and the embryo proper. The embryonic leaves and root of the embryo form early, but are covered by sheaths (the coleoptile and coleorhiza). As the corn fruit germinates, its shoot **(b)**, still within the coleoptile, emerges from the soil. Eventually, the first leaf will burst through its sheath and open to the sunlight. New foliage will be added by cell division in the shoot apical meristem. Simultaneously, the root lengthens through rapid cell division in the root apical meristem.

Summary

The Anatomy of the Flower

In general, flowers are composed of four regions arising from the receptacle: (1) the calyx, formed of sepals; (2) the corolla, composed of petals; (3) the stamens, consisting of the filament and anther; and (4) the carpels, containing the ovary, style, and stigma. Pistils are carpels that are completely fused.

Natural selection has resulted in the basic differences in flower parts, such as those between the flowers of dicots and monocots. The floral parts of dicots appear in fours, fives, or multiples of these numbers, while those of monocots appear in threes or multiples of three. Flowers can be incomplete or complete, and perfect or imperfect. Composite flowers are produced only by dicots. Some plants depend on insects or other organisms for pollination, while others are pollinated by wind and water.

The Sexual Life of the Flower

Each ovule of a flowering plant consists of a megaspore mother cell surrounded by nutritive tissues. Meiosis results in four haploid cells, only one of which survives as the functional megaspore. The megaspore produces eight haploid nuclei that together form the eight-celled embryo sac; one of these cells becomes the egg cell.

Anthers typically contain four pollen sacs holding many diploid microspore mother cells. Each of these mother cells produces four haploid cells called microspores, which undergo mitosis to produce binucleate male gametophytes. One nucleus is the sperm cell, the other the pollen tube cell. Each gametophyte becomes a pollen grain.

Pollination takes place when pollen is deposited on a receptive stigma, but fertilization occurs only when the sperm fuses with the nuclei of the embryo sac. One sperm nucleus fertilizes the egg cell, forming the new zygote, while the other sperm nucleus fuses with the two nuclei in the center of the embryo sac, forming a trinucleate cell. This cell eventually develops into the endosperm.

Embryo and Seed Development in a Dicot

As the endosperm develops, the dicot embryo undergoes rapid cell division and, later, differentiation, giving rise to cotyledons and other tissues. The protoderm will give rise to the epidermis; the procambium will become the vascular system. Much of the embryo is composed of the hypocotyl, whose rapid growth lifts the embryo out of the soil and sends the first root into the soil. Until germination, the embryo lies dormant, protected by a hard seed coat.

In angiosperms, fruits and seeds develop together. Fruits are mature ovaries and exist in three basic forms: simple, or those derived from a single ovary or from the compound ovary of a single flower; aggregate, or those derived from numerous separate carpels of a single flower; and multiple, or those formed from the single ovaries of many flowers. The fruit often brings about seed dispersal.

Germination is triggered by a variety of environmental conditions. The cotyledons of the bean (a dicot) seeds nourish the seedlings as they grow. After the hypocotyl pushes above the soil, the plumule enlarges and the first leaves appear to begin photosynthesis. The embryonic root grows and produces the primary root. Corn (a monocot) has only one cotyledon, or scutellum, surrounded by the starchy endosperm. Embryonic leaves and roots must break through the coleoptile and coleorhiza, respectively, in order to grow. The cotyledon and endosperm remain in the soil as growth begins.

Key Terms

receptacle	complete flower	pollen tube	root cap
calyx	perfect flower	sperm	fruit
sepal	imperfect flower	micropyle	simple fruit
corolla	ovule	trinucleate cell	berry
petal	megaspore mother cell	endosperm	pome
stamen	functional megaspore	cotyledon	drupe
carpel	embryo sac	meristem	dehiscent
filament	egg cell	shoot apical meristem	indehiscent
anther	pollen sac	root apical meristem	aggregate fruits
pistil	microspore mother cell	ground meristem	multiple fruits
ovary	microspore	protoderm	epicotyl
style	sperm cell	procambium	scutellum
stigma	pollen tube cell	epidermis	coleoptile
incomplete flower	pollen grain	hypocotyl	coleorhiza

Review Questions

1. Summarize the coevolution of insects and flowering plants. How might this relationship have encouraged diversification in both groups? (pp. 329–331)

2. List the parts of a flower and state a function of each. (p. 330)

3. Review the events in the ovule and anther that lead to the formation of an embryo sac and pollen grain, respectively. (pp. 331–333)

4. Beginning with pollination, list the events that result in fertilization. What is unusual about fertilization in plants? (pp. 332–334)

5. Describe the sequence of events in the growth of a dicot embryo. (pp. 335–337)

6. List four adaptations for seed dispersal, and explain how each works. (pp. 337, 342)

7. Compare the emergence of the bean seedling (dicot) with that of the corn seedling (monocot). (pp. 342–343)

Growth and Organization in Plants

24

Now that we have launched the tiny seedling on its way, we can turn to the growth and organization of the mature plant. We will consider the angiosperms—in particular, the dicotyledonous plants (the dicots). By comparing these with the monocotyledonous plants (the monocots), some fundamental differences will be brought into focus. But first, a few general points about plant life cycles should be mentioned.

OPEN GROWTH AND INDETERMINATE LIFE SPAN

Many of the familiar angiosperms are **annuals,** short-lived species that germinate, mature rapidly, reproduce, and die, all within a single season. Others, the **biennials,** complete their life cycle in two seasons, with the second reserved for flowering and seed production. However, gymnosperms such as the conifers, along with many angiosperm shrubs and trees, are **perennials,** with **indeterminate life spans.** Barring injury, infection, consumption by animals, and many other death-dealing circumstances, they live, theoretically, forever.

There are arguments over which tree holds the record for longest life. Certainly, one of the oldest is a gnarled bristle-cone pine from the White Mountains in California. Its age has been determined to be 4900 years. In any case, we can be sure that some tree, somewhere, is the oldest living thing on earth.

The most logical explanation for the long life of a plant lies in its potential for continuous growth or *open growth.* **Perennial** (long-lived) plants never completely mature. The continuous production of immature and undifferentiated cells in both the root tip and the shoot tip characterizes all of these plants. In addition, some plant cells that have differentiated and begun to function in specific roles are often able to turn back the clock and "dedifferentiate." Having returned to their immature state, they can then begin to differentiate again, perhaps into cells of a totally different type (see Essay 24.1).

The plant's meristem, or meristematic tissue, is composed of undifferentiated and immature tissues. Some of these tissues are always held in reserve—in a sense, they are the plant's investment in its own immortality. When new growth occurs, some of the meristematic cells simply divide mitotically. Some of the daughter cells remain as meristematic tissue, while others proceed to enlarge and differentiate, producing a variety of new tissue.

TOTIPOTENCY IN PLANT CELLS

In some ways, plants are ideal subjects for studying cell growth. Some plants have the ability to generate roots from stem cuttings, stems from bits of root, and even entire plants from leaves. These phenomena have been invaluable in agriculture through the ages, and for biologists it offers clues to the puzzle of differentiation.

From regeneration studies, we have learned that many, perhaps most, plant cells are **totipotent**—that is, they have all the ability to produce the entire organism from which they come. Unlike most animal cells, their differentiation is often reversible. The question arose: Can *individual* plant cells duplicate the regenerative feat we see in cuttings?

Some 50 years ago it was discovered that carrot tissue could be grown from individual cells of the carrot embryo. Once separated, they were cultured in a medium made from coconut milk (which contains critical nutrients and hormones). Then, in the 1950s, mature *phloem* (food-conducting) cells from carrots, cultured in a similar medium, grew into rootlike structures that, when planted, produced entire carrots. More recently, there has been progress in culturing redwood trees and orchids in a similar manner. In addition, botanist James Shepard of Kansas State University has dissolved the walls of mature potato cells, leaving behind the naked cells. He has grown individual cells in a nutrient medium and produced plants, proving again that mature plant cells have lost none of their genetic potency.

Although such work is in its early stages, the potential benefits are encouraging. An obvious outcome would be the use of **cloning** (the production of genetically identical individuals from a single cell) to produce selected crop plants. But even more in keeping with the new era of genetics would be the use of these techniques in gene splicing and recombinant DNA programs. Scientists have already succeeded in producing a potato-tomato hybrid by joining the nuclei from these plants. This capability is important because it lends itself to the ongoing search for ways to improve the resistance of crop plants to disease, drought, cold climates, and other agricultural problems. It is interesting and sobering to try and imagine just how far such techniques could conceivably take us in the future. ●

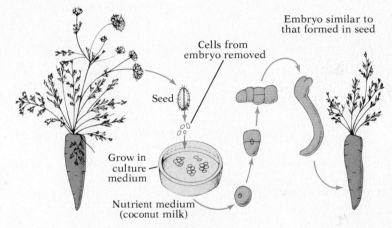

Experiment 1

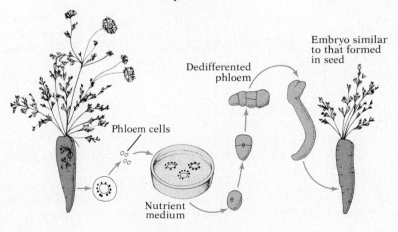

Experiment 2

Primary and Secondary Growth

Essentially, **primary growth** increases the length of a plant, while **secondary growth** increases its girth or thickness. More specifically, primary growth occurs when cells contributed through mitosis in the shoot and root apical meristems elongate and mature. Some of the specific products of primary growth are young roots, shoots (including new branches), leaves, and flowers. (Figure 24.1 shows the body of a "generalized" plant and illustrates the functions of these systems.) Primary growth is, of course, responsible for the emergence of the young plant from the seed. Some of the cells pro-

duced through primary growth remain simple and unspecialized, capable of resuming activity later. Such tissue, in some plants, will contribute to secondary growth.

Secondary growth generally originates in two sources, *vascular cambium* and *cork cambium,* both of which emerge from the unspecialized reserves of tissues mentioned earlier. They produce a variety of tissue types (these will be discussed later). Although all plants carry on primary growth, secondary growth is not universal. The most obvious examples of secondary growth are seen in the woody dicots, such as trees. Most monocots and many short-lived dicots show only primary growth.

24.1

The generalized plant and its two organ systems.

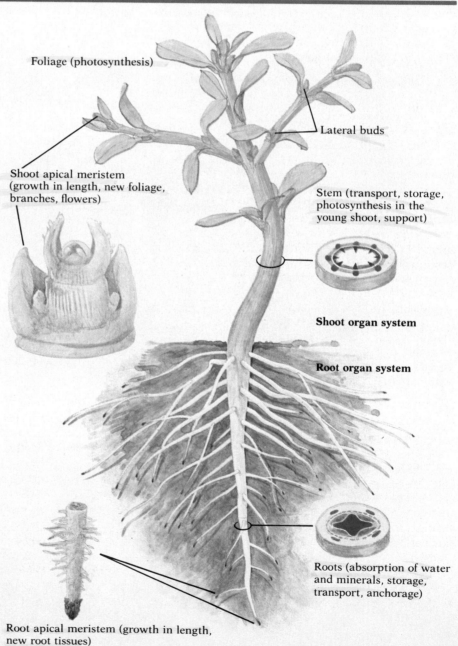

Foliage (photosynthesis)

Lateral buds

Shoot apical meristem (growth in length, new foliage, branches, flowers)

Stem (transport, storage, photosynthesis in the young shoot, support)

Shoot organ system

Root organ system

Roots (absorption of water and minerals, storage, transport, anchorage)

Root apical meristem (growth in length, new root tissues)

TISSUE ORGANIZATION

Plants, maintaining their passive vigils, may seem to be simple, inactive organisms, but this appearance is deceptive. In fact, they are often highly organized, dynamic organisms that interact with their environments in very complex ways. Some of this complexity is revealed in their many kinds of tissues. In the last chapter, we described the early formation of three types, the protoderm, meristem, and procambium (see Figure 23.5g). It is from these three that the many types of plant tissue are derived. Table 24.1 summarizes tissue types and their derivations. The tissues are organized into organs that comprise two major systems: the **root** (usually underground) and the **shoot** (usually above ground). (Their functions were shown in Figure 24.1.) For now, our discussions will concentrate on vascular tissue—the xylem and phloem.

Since terrestrial plants are not bathed in life-sustaining waters, as were their ancestors, they have had to develop the means to transport the necessities of life within their bodies, primarily in tissues called the *xylem* and *phloem*. Let's take a look at these fascinating, fluid-filled channels.

The Vascular Tissues

Xylem. Xylem, which is the water- and mineral-transporting tissue, contains several types of cells, each with a specific role. Those most directly involved in transport are the **vessels** and **tracheids.** Vast numbers of these cells, laid end-to-end in the vascular system, form minute tubes through which water can pass from root to stem and leaf.

As young xylem cells mature, they die and their cytoplasm disappears, leaving them essentially hollow. At this time they are referred to as *elements*. In their mature form, both vessels and tracheids are elongated elements with thick, pitted side walls. The *pits* are indentations containing only the thin primary wall, so water readily passes through. The end walls of tracheids contain thin-walled pits, while those of vessels tend to be entirely absent or are highly perforated (Figure 24.2).

Phloem. Whereas xylem moves water, phloem moves dissolved nutrients, the food made by photosynthesis. Although the principal food substances are sugars, amino acids and even hormones are also carried in the phloem stream. Unlike the xylem, phloem must remain alive to be functional.

Phloem is also a complex tissue, comprising **sieve tube members** and **companion cells** (Figure 24.3). The cells that actually carry out transport are

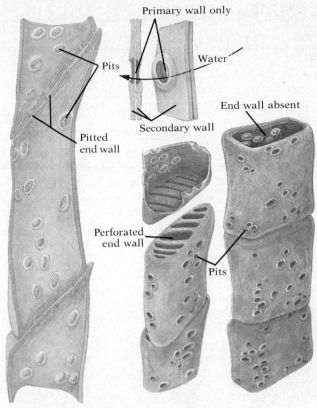

(a) Tracheids (cutaway view)   **(b)** Vessels

24.2

The conducting elements of xylem include tracheids **(a)** and vessels **(b)**. Tracheids are long, slender elements with pitted side and end walls. The pits are not actually openings, but regions where only the primary wall exists; thus water easily passes through them. Vessels also have pits, but their end walls are completely perforated or altogether absent. Vessels are also considerably larger in diameter than tracheids, permitting a more rapid flow of water. For these reasons, they are generally considered to be more efficient in water transport than are tracheids.

the sieve tube members. The term *sieve* comes from the prominent pores that pock the walls of sieve tubes. They occur in both the side walls and the end walls. Actually, they are enlarged *plasmodesmata* (see Chapters 4 and 5), through which the cytoplasm of one sieve tube member is continuous with that of the next. Anything in the cytoplasm, then, can move from one member to the next. The largest pores, occur in the *sieve plates*, located in the end walls.

As we noted earlier, phloem is living. This may be stretching the definition a bit, however, since the cytoplasm of sieve tubes lacks a nucleus. How does a cell—that is, a sieve tube member—survive

TABLE 24.1

Meristem and its tissue derivatives in primary growth

In primary growth, meristematic tissue produces:

Protoderm

Protoderm differentiates into covering tissues, including the epidermis of roots, stems, and leaves. More specialized examples include guard cells, leaf hairs, and root hairs.

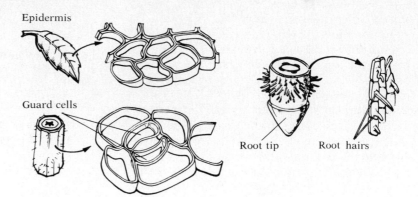

Epidermis

Guard cells

Root tip   Root hairs

Ground meristem

Ground meristem differentiates into three basic tissue types:

Parenchyma is widely distributed in the stem and root and makes up the photosynthetic tissues of the leaf. The cells are large and thin-walled, often involved in storage.

Collenchyma is primarily involved in support. Its thick-walled cells form tough strands of tissue below the epidermis, within vascular tissue, and in the supporting portions of the leaf.

Sclerenchyma, in its *fiber* form, strengthens young shoots. In its *sclereid* form, it provides hardness for seed coverings and shells.

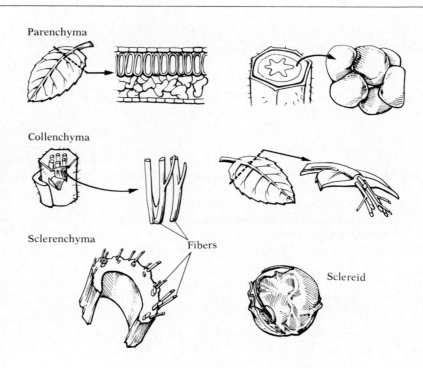

Parenchyma

Collenchyma

Sclerenchyma

Fibers

Sclereid

Procambium

Procambium differentiates into xylem and phloem, the conducting (vascular) tissue of roots, shoots, and leaves. Xylem specializes in water and mineral transport; phloem, in food transport.

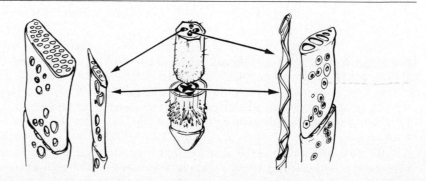

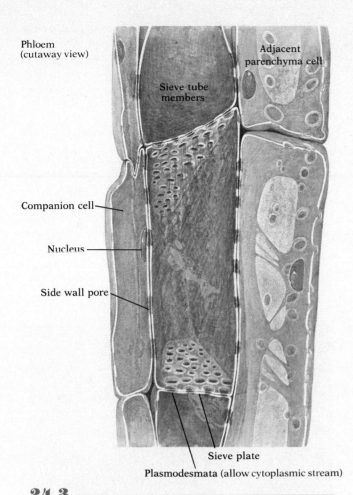

Phloem
(cutaway view)

Adjacent
parenchyma cell

Sieve tube
members

Companion cell

Nucleus

Side wall pore

Sieve plate

Plasmodesmata (allow cytoplasmic stream)

24.3

The major constituents of phloem tissue are the sieve tube members and their companion cells.

without a nucleus? In the case of phloem, each sieve tube member lies against a nucleated *companion cell,* and the cytoplasm from one can move into the other. Since sieve tube members lack ribosomes as well as nuclei, it is believed that most metabolic activities are carried out in the companion cells. We do know that the death of a companion cell signals the immediate death of its sieve tube member.

THE ROOT SYSTEM

A walk through a forest convinces us of the great diversity of plant shoots, stems, leaves, and so on. But far from obvious is the forest beneath our feet, a hidden growth of vast root systems that are just as diverse as what we see above ground. Different kinds of roots boast their own special properties,

and different parts of roots have their own important functions.

In plants that are capable of secondary growth, a root can be divided into two parts. The **primary root** includes the young roots that are constantly being crowded forward by activity in the root apical meristems. As older regions of the primary root mature, changes and rearrangements in its tissues produce the secondary growth.

The Primary Root

The Root Tip.   The primary root (Figure 24.4) is marked by areas of intense activity in the root apical meristem, which is located near the very tips. These areas are dense regions of tiny,

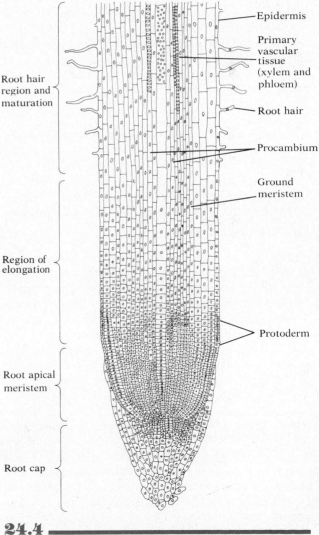

Epidermis

Primary vascular tissue (xylem and phloem)

Root hair region and maturation

Root hair

Procambium

Ground meristem

Region of elongation

Protoderm

Root apical meristem

Root cap

24.4

The root tip.

undifferentiated cells that continually divide and redivide, producing cells that contribute to the protoderm, the ground meristem, and the procambium. Protoderm will produce the epidermis, while procambium matures into vascular tissue. The ground meristem will later contribute to the cortex. Some of the cells replace those lost by the **root cap,** a cluster of cells at the very end of the root tip. They are worn away as the root pushes through the abrasive soil.

Push is the right word, since root tips are literally forced through the soil. As cell division in the root apical meristem continues, the new cells left behind grow rapidly in length, and their elongation pushes the root tip along. Elongation is brought about by the absorption of water into the cells, which stretches the elastic primary walls and lengthens the cells in the direction of the root axis. Soon, firmer secondary walls will be laid down, and elongation will stop in those cells. In the meantime, a new generation of cells will elongate, and the pushing continues.

While the elongation process takes place, other changes occur in the root tip. Tiny **root hairs** emerge from the epidermal cells that cover the roots. Root hairs grow in great profusion and provide an enormous surface area through which water can move into the plant (Figure 24.5).

Finally, at the uppermost region of the root tip, the vascular tissue begins to differentiate. At the very center of the young root procambial cells (those that will give rise to the vascular system), the **primary xylem** and **primary phloem** begin to form. These will develop in the form of a cylinder of tissues called the *stele*.

The Stele.   The **stele** is a remarkable example of plant differentiation and reorganization (Figure 24.6). In cross sections of some roots, the primary xylem forms a kind of star. The smaller, thinner-walled primary phloem lies between the arms of the star. Surrounding the primary xylem and phloem is a final cylinder of cells called the **pericycle,** which will be important to growth later on.

Just outside the pericycle lies the **endodermis**— a kind of "inner skin" that is actually a part of the cortex. The endodermis is important to water transport because its cell walls contain a waxy layer of **suberin**—the **Casparian strip.** The waxy regions are so arranged as to direct incoming water through the endodermal cytoplasm, instead of along porous cell walls, the usual route. Since cytoplasm can act to increase or decrease its own osmotic potential (see Chapter 5), it can exercise some control over water uptake.

Outside of the stele are large, thin-walled parenchyma cells, often swollen with stored starches. Together with the endodermis they make up the **cortex.** Around the cortex lies the root's **epidermis,** or outer skin.

The Roots of Dicots and Monocots

We have stressed that monocots and dicots are fundamentally distinct and more distantly related than it might seem at first. This point can be clearly illustrated by a comparison of their roots.

Most dicots produce a single primary root, the *tap root*, from which branches a profusion of *lateral roots*. As lateral roots mature, they produce their own side branches, which, in time, produce their own, and continue to do so as long as the root

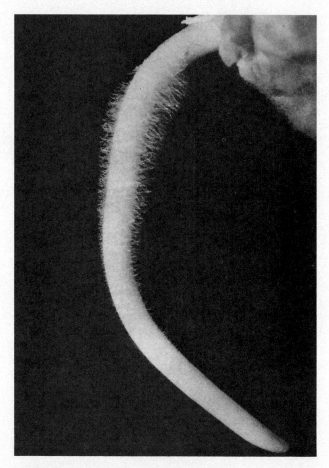

24.5

When germinated in a moist chamber, the seedling produces an enormous number of root hairs. Each is an extension of an epidermal cell. Their combined area provides the root with a great absorbing surface.

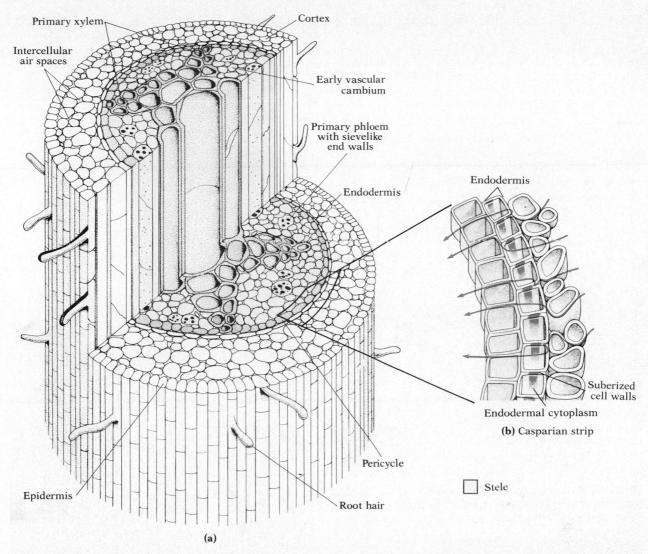

Primary xylem

Cortex

Intercellular
air spaces

Early vascular
cambium

Primary phloem
with sievelike
end walls

Endodermis

Endodermis

Suberized
cell walls

Endodermal cytoplasm

(b) Casparian strip

Pericycle

☐ Stele

Epidermis

Root hair

(a)

24.6

(a) The tissues of the primary root become established in regions just above the root tips. In their final arrangement, the tissues form concentric cylinders. The inner one, the stele, is surrounded by the endodermis. Within this cylinder lies a ring of uncommitted cells known as the pericycle. The vascular tissue in some plants takes on a definite arrangement as the thick-

walled primary xylem forms a four-armed star, with the primary phloem nestled between the arms. Outside the stele lies a region of storage parenchyma called the cortex. It is bordered by the epidermis. **(b)** The Casparian strip, the suberized cell walls between endodermal cells, directs water through the endodermal cytoplasm before it enters the stele.

grows. Lateral roots originate in the pericycle of the stele some distance above the root tip (Figure 24.7).

In monocots, by contrast, the original embryonic root tip is very temporary. It is quickly replaced by other roots that, strangely enough, grow outward from the base of the *stem*. Roots that originate in this way are called *adventitious roots*. Adventitious roots form a great mass of *diffuse (fibrous) roots* (Figure 24.8). In corn, a monocot, adventitious roots arise from the part of the stalk

just above the ground, arching downward and forming *prop roots*, essentially flying buttresses that keep the heavy, rapidly growing plant erect.

It should be noted that some dicots also form adventitious roots. The adventitious roots of Algerian ivy, for example, hold it to the sides of aging college dormitories. And many dicots—as well as monocots—can be propagated by cuttings that sprout adventitious roots when suspended in water.

24.7

Lateral or branch roots are initially produced by the pericycle of tap roots. Cells in the pericycle undergo repeated divisions. The mass of cells produced breaks through the endodermis and begins to digest its way through the cortex.

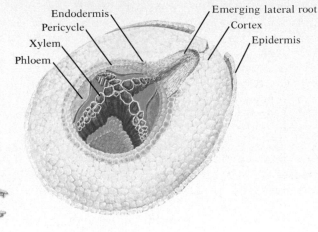

Endodermis
Pericycle
Xylem
Phloem
Emerging lateral root
Cortex
Epidermis

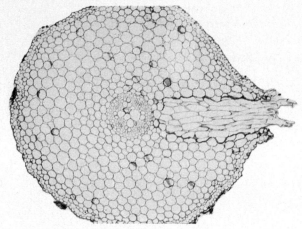

24.8

In contrast to the dicot's tap root system, monocots (such as the bluegrass seen here) produce a diffuse root system. Diffuse roots are of the adventitious type, emerging directly from the stem in large numbers to form a vast network of individual roots.

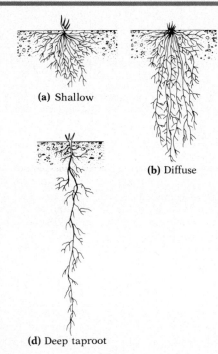

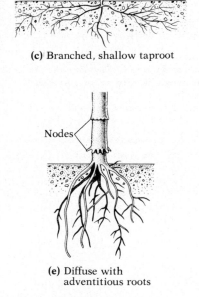

(a) Shallow

(b) Diffuse

(c) Branched, shallow taproot

(d) Deep taproot

Nodes

(e) Diffuse with adventitious roots

Secondary Growth of a Root

Secondary growth begins in older regions of the root after the primary organization has been completed. It starts in the stele and is first seen as mitotic activity in the procambium, which lies between the primary xylem and phloem (Figure 24.9). The cells in the isolated patches divide and begin to grow toward each other until they join, forming a continuous ring within the stele. This ring is known as the **vascular cambium** (a secondary cambium). Once the ring is formed, the vascular cambium continues to divide and its thickness increases. This tissue is quite remarkable because, on its outer edge, its mitotic activity produces **sec-**

ondary phloem. This crowds the primary phloem outward and away from the primary xylem. On its inner border, the vascular cambium produces **secondary xylem,** a most intriguing developmental situation.

Continued mitosis of the vascular cambium begins to crush the primary phloem and to push the thin ring of secondary phloem outward so that it lies just below the root's surface cells. The primary xylem remains and even retains its old cross shape. The secondary xylem becomes the **wood** of the root, eventually consisting chiefly of dead, water-conducting xylem walls. It is because of this tough old thick-walled xylem that dynamite is sometimes required to remove a stump.

24.9

Secondary growth in the root begins with activity in the residual procambium between the primary xylem and the primary phloem **(a).** As the cells grow they eventually reach between the primary xylem and phloem **(b).** Now matured into a vascular cambium, the active cells begin to produce secondary xylem on their inner side and secondary phloem on their outer side. The growing vascular cambium pushes outward to form a complete circle, eventually crushing the primary phloem **(c).** The secondary xylem and phloem enlarge, with only remnants of the primary cells remaining **(d).** In the older root, the xylem has expanded into a large woody region of the root, and the vascular cambium and phloem are found only near the perimeter **(e).**

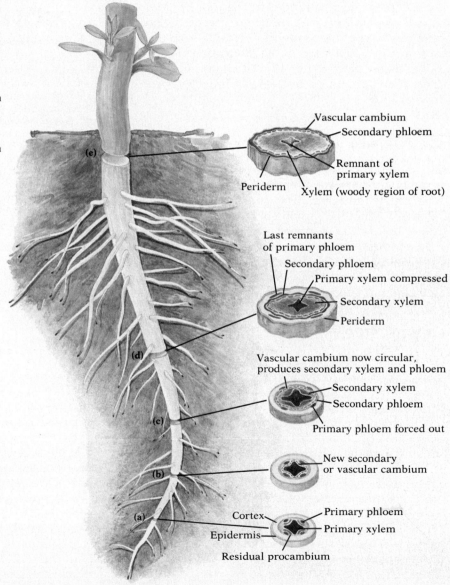

The Periderm (Cork). The epidermis of the young root is destroyed during secondary growth and is replaced by a new tissue, the **periderm.** The periderm is several cell layers thick. The outer layers of dead cells are the cork, which is impregnated with waterproof suberin. The inner cork cambium remains active, continuing to divide, and replacing the aging outer cells. Because of the waxy layer of suberin in the periderm, water cannot enter or leave. For this reason the mature root can only conduct water; for the uptake of water, the plant must rely on its young root tips.

THE SHOOT SYSTEM

Growth at the shoot tip continues throughout the life of a plant, just as it does in the root tip. New tissues arise from apical meristem and then elongate, resulting in stem growth. But aside from this, there are few similarities in the development of the root and the shoot. After all, the shoot must produce such structures as leaves, branches, and flowers.

The Primary Shoot

The shoot apical meristem (Figure 24.10) is somewhat dome-shaped and is covered by a protective layer called the *tunica.* The shoot meristem does not simply lengthen, leaving behind differentiating tissue. Instead, as it grows, it leaves behind both differentiating tissues and patches of various kinds of meristem. One of these kinds of patches, the **leaf primordia,** gives rise to leaves, while others, called **lateral bud primordia,** produce branches.

Behind the Shoot Meristem. Tissues behind (or below) the shoot meristem remain undifferentiated for a time, but strands of procambium, dispersed in the cortex, mark the sites of future xylem, as well as phloem and certain large parenchyma cells called **pith.** The outer cells of the young shoot, still green with chloroplasts and carrying on photosynthesis, have begun differentiating into the young epidermis (see Table 24.1).

In dicots, as the young tissues left behind by the apical meristem mature, they reorganize into specific patterns quite unlike those of the monocots. Bundles of vascular tissue are often scattered in the monocots, but they tend to form ringlike patterns in the dicots (Figure 24.11). Also, in many dicots (but not in the monocots), a small region of

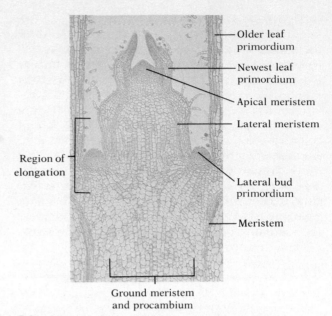

Older leaf primordium

Newest leaf primordium

Apical meristem

Lateral meristem

Region of elongation

Lateral bud primordium

Meristem

Ground meristem and procambium

24.10

The shoot tip contains the second region of apical meristem *(center).* It is located in a dome-shaped mass. The two small projections rising from the meristem are the newest leaf primordia. Older, much larger leaf primordia now rise up to cover the entire structure. In their axes, two patches of dark tissue mark the location of lateral bud primordia. These buds can produce branches. Further down on the shoot are two older lateral bud primordia. Note how the cells increase in size below the apical meristem, as they take water into their vacuoles. Most of this tissue is simple, but further down are the islands of procambium that will later form the primary xylem and phloem.

procambium (a tissue that is important to secondary growth) is retained between the xylem and phloem.

Secondary Growth of the Shoot

Secondary growth begins as the primary shoot matures; however, it does not occur in all species of plants. Primarily it is a trait of large, woody dicots and is largely responsible for the great size of many trees. However, some monocots, such as palms, grow quite large even without secondary growth. This is because a palm tree spends the first part of its life as a low-lying rosette of leaves. Then, when its stem becomes thick enough, its enormous apical meristem begins a surge of growth and the tree shoots upward. This growth eventually produces a trunk of almost the same diameter from top to bottom.

Secondary Growth in Transition. As we know, about the time that primary growth ends in the dicot stem the vascular system begins to become organized into a ring of bundles or cylinders. We also know that, in many dicots, a tiny region of procambium remains between the xylem and phloem. Secondary growth originates from this small area in stems as well as in roots (Figure 24.12).

When this procambium becomes active, it links up with cortical cells between the vascular bundles, forming a circle that becomes the vascular cambium. As these cells continue to divide, the ring thickens and differentiates into secondary phloem and xylem, as it did in the root. In this way the vascular system changes from the bundle to the cylinder form.

As the activity continues, the new phloem and xylem merge with the old, soon obliterating the primary organization of the shoot. Only residual portions of the primary xylem remain in the pithy center of the stem to mark the passing of these events (see Figure 24.12e). As the newly produced xylem matures, it grows and pushes outward on the vascular cambium and the phloem beyond. Likewise, the new phloem can only grow outward, crushing the older, more fragile tissue. The growth in girth, then, is due to an expanding ring of dividing and growing cells.

The Older Woody Stem. Older regions of the stem, those that have gone through several seasons of secondary growth, now are mostly composed of woody xylem tissue. The vascular cambium, the phloem, and the periderm all lie outside the xylem, or "wood," and together they form a rather thin ring of living material.

The growth rate of the xylem tissue is highly dependent on environmental conditions. For example, it may slow down drastically during winter seasons. A cross section of an older stem or trunk reveals a definite pattern in trees that undergo seasonal growth. During periods of rapid growth, the xylem tends to consist of large, relatively soft cells. As growth slows, the differentiating xylem cells do not expand as much, and remain smaller and denser. The differences in seasonal rates of growth produce the familiar **annual rings** of trees (Figure 24.13).

A second growth pattern seen in the older stem takes the form of radiating spokes that extend through the wood and secondary phloem. These are known as **vascular rays** or, simply, **rays**. They consist of sheets of thin-walled parenchyma cells and their thicker-walled descendants called **collenchyma** (a supportive tissue—see Table 24.1). Both are produced by the vascular cambium. Vascular rays provide a means of transporting nutrients laterally, a trait required in younger stems, in which much of the tissue is still alive. In older stems, the growth of rays is essential in relieving the forces created by the expanding cylinder of xylem inside the trunk.

24.11

After primary growth, the vascular system in the young shoot is organized into bundles or cylinders. In the dicot **(a)**, the bundles are arranged in an orderly circle, just below the epidermis. Each bundle contains xylem and phloem, separated by a patch of procambium, along with supporting fibers. Most of the stem consists of soft pithy parenchyma. In the monocot corn **(b)**, the vascular bundles are scattered in the stem. Each bundle contains xylem, phloem, and some tough supportive fibers. Procambium is absent, and the large open circles that resemble a nose and two eyes are actually air spaces. (Photos courtesy Carolina Biological Supply)

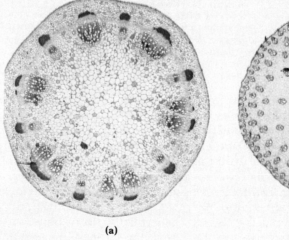

(a)

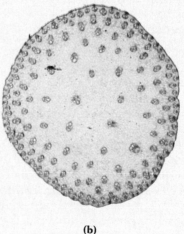

(b)

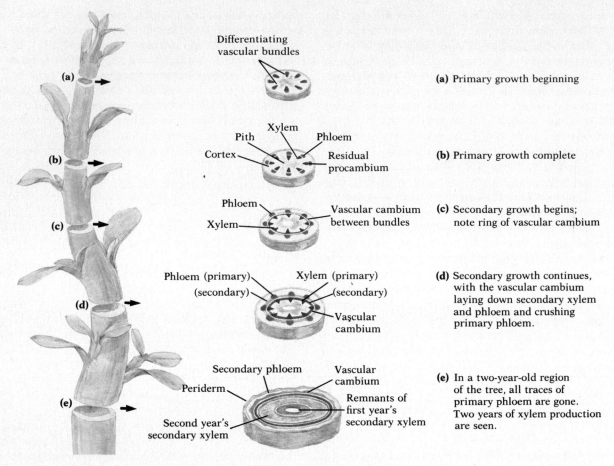

Differentiating
vascular bundles

(a) Primary growth beginning

Xylem
Pith   Phloem
Cortex   Residual
                      procambium

(b) Primary growth complete

Phloem   Vascular cambium
Xylem   between bundles

(c) Secondary growth begins;
note ring of vascular cambium

Phloem (primary)   Xylem (primary)
(secondary)   (secondary)
                    Vascular
                    cambium

(d) Secondary growth continues,
with the vascular cambium
laying down secondary xylem
and phloem and crushing
primary phloem.

Secondary phloem   Vascular
                    cambium
Periderm   Remnants of
                    first year's
                    secondary xylem
Second year's
secondary xylem

(e) In a two-year-old region
of the tree, all traces of
primary phloem are gone.
Two years of xylem production
are seen.

24.12

It is possible to observe different growth stages in the same plant since growth is a continuous process. In primary growth, the vascular system of the dicot shoot matures (**a and b**) into distinct vascular bundles forming a ring about the central pith. Secondary growth begins with the formation of a ring of vascular cambium from the residual procambium (**c**). The vascular cambium produces secondary xylem on its inner side and secondary phloem on its outer side. This growth begins to push the primary xylem and phloem away (**d**), with the vascular tissue becoming a continuous ring. In an older region (**e**) the results of continued activity in the vascular cambium are seen as an enlarging region of secondary xylem with the vascular cambium and phloem making up the perimeter. Secondary growth has also replaced the epidermis with a new tissue, the periderm.

Secondary Growth at the Perimeter. Secondary growth in the vascular tissues is accompanied by changes in the shoot epidermis. As occurs in the root, cells in the cortex near the epidermis now take on a new role. They begin to divide rapidly, producing what is known as the *cork cambium* (see Figure 24.13). The cork cambium produces layer upon layer of cells that are continually pushed outward, rupturing and replacing the old epidermis. These new tissue layers constitute the shoot periderm. The outer layer of the periderm becomes impregnated with suberin, producing a waterproof covering. In this way, the plant has begun to produce **cork.** Cork is often mistakenly called bark, but technically, **bark** is everything outside the secondary xylem, so bark also includes the vascular cambium, the living and dead phloem, and the cork cambium—far more than the rough outer layers of cells.

The corks in wine bottles are true cork. But such cork does not occur naturally. Cork growers remove the periderm of the cork oak, causing the tree to respond to the injury by obligingly forming a new, smoother cork cambium. The new tissue is removed and cut into cylinders. (These cork cylinders are then placed into wine bottles in such a way that they split or crumble at any attempt to remove them.)

THE LEAF:
A PHOTOSYNTHETIC ORGAN

Leaves are so much a part of our lives that we tend to take them for granted, except perhaps when they signal a change in season. A leaf is primarily devoted to the conversion of sunlight energy into chemical bond energy in foods. The leaf is one of the original solar energy devices, perfected long before we humans found the idea fashionable. As such, leaves are amazingly complex and efficient.

The development of even the simplest of leaves necessitates contributions from several basic tissues. Protoderm contributes to the highly specialized epidermis, which slows water loss and admits air. The layers of light-trapping, photosynthetic parenchyma cells within owe their presence to ground meristem, while the vascular tissues, so vital in bringing water and carrying sugars out of the leaf, form from the versatile procambium.

Leaf Anatomy

The typical dicot leaf is a flattened **blade** attached to a stem by a stalklike **petiole.** The vascular system of the stem passes into the leaf through the petiole, and into the blade along a large central vein called the **midrib.** In typical dicots, the midrib supplies a network of smaller branches, or *veins*, that carry fluids through the blade. Within the blade, each smaller vein is covered by specialized cells that form the **bundle sheath.** Anything entering or leaving the veins must pass through these cells.

The organization of the monocot leaf is quite different. Such monocots as the grasses have no petioles. The leaves emerge from a tough sheath around the stem (which is why it is so frustrating to try to tear off a corn leaf). In most monocots the veins do not branch from a central midrib; they lie in parallel rows, interconnected by short, smaller veins (Figure 24.14).

The Organization of the Leaf. A cross-section of a dicot leaf (Figure 24.15) reveals outer layers of cells of the **upper epidermis** and **lower epidermis.** The upper epidermis, the part most often exposed to light, consists of fairly large, flattened cells whose outer walls are coated with a layer of a wax called **cutin.** Most epidermal cells lack chloroplasts and are transparent.

Within the leaf there are several layers of parenchymal cells that contain chloroplasts. Those nearest the upper epidermis are arranged in one or more tightly packed layers and, because of their elongated shape, they are called **palisade parenchyma.** They are the first to receive incoming light. Below this lie less orderly layers of cells that are more rounded, and scattered in such a way that spaces form between them into which air can move. This layer is the **spongy parenchyma,** aptly named for its appearance. The air spaces are important avenues of the carbon dioxide diffusion that is so essential to photosynthesis. Air enters the leaf through minute openings called **stomata,**

24.13

A photomicrograph of a cross section through a three-year-old woody stem clearly reveals regions of different tissues. The outermost tissue is the protective cork, a suberized layer of cells produced by the cork cambium lying just inside. The conducting tissue consists of a circle of phloem divided by rays. Just inside the phloem is a thin cylinder of vascular cambium, which seasonally produces phloem and xylem. Inside the vascular cambium and making up most of the stem tissue is the xylem, or wood. At the very center, a small region of pithy parenchyma remains. Note the definite annual ring pattern in the xylem, produced by slowing fall and winter growth and rapid spring growth.

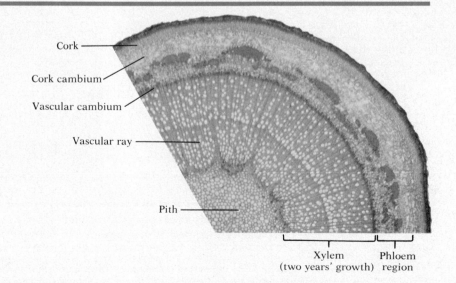

Cork
Cork cambium
Vascular cambium
Vascular ray
Pith
Xylem (two years' growth)
Phloem region

24.14

(a) Dicot leaves are typically net-veined, with a central midrib giving rise to numerous smaller, branching veins. A leaf petiole forms the attachment to the stem. (b) Monocot leaves, on the other hand, contain parallel veins and the leaves attach to the stem by a sheathlike arrangement.

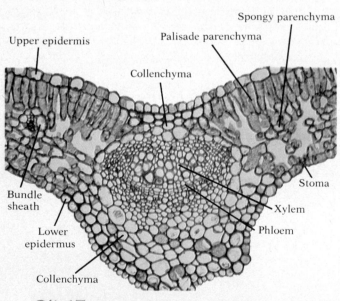

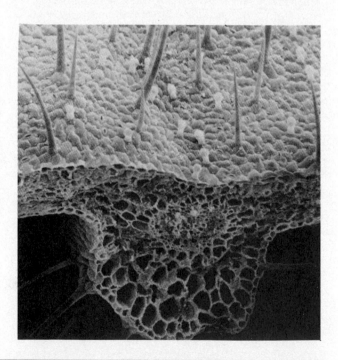

24.15

The cross-sectional view of a leaf reveals its complex tissue organization. The midrib contains the flattened layers of xylem and phloem, supported by regions of dense collenchyma. The upper epidermis is relatively simple, with flattened, irregularly shaped cells. Below this are the rows of palisade parenchyma, containing numerous chloroplasts. Below the palisade layer is the spongy parenchyma, a less orderly tissue with intra-cellular air spaces. A small vein, penetrating the spongy layer, contains xylem and phloem and is surrounded by cells of the bundle sheath. The lower epidermis contains flattened cells and guard cells whose curved borders form stomata. Many leaves have epidermal leaf hairs as well, as seen in the scanning electron micrograph. (*Left*, courtesy Carolina Biological Supply.)

which are found primarily in the lower epidermis—the underside of the leaf. Each stoma (singular) is formed by a pair of kidney bean-shaped *guard cells* (Chapter 25).

The undersides of leaves are often covered with fine **leaf hairs,** each of which arises from a single epidermal cell. Some leaf hairs are soft and downy, but some are sharp and hooked and can be lethal to insect larvae. Leaf hairs also have another function: they impede the movement of air over the leaf's surface, slowing the evaporation of water.

Plants are highly organized and complex organisms. This complexity is revealed in the many specialized tissues of a single plant, as well as in the evident array of diversity when species are compared. Still, there are common themes: the general similarity of tissue types, primary growth mechanisms, and systems of transport. In the next chapter we will take a penetrating look at these transport systems, and we will discover that the xylem and phloem are uniquely adapted to their vital tasks.

Summary

Open Growth and Indeterminate Life Span

The indeterminate life span of some plants is primarily a function of open, or continuous, growth. Plant cells are totipotent, containing all the genetic information they need to produce the entire organism, even from leaf or stem cuttings. Plants can reverse the differentiation of their cells or generate new plants from immature cells, a fact that enables scientists to clone selected species.

Primary growth occurs in all angiosperms, originating in root and shoot apical meristem and producing growth in length. Secondary growth occurs primarily in perennial dicots, arising in vascular and cork cambiums and producing growth in girth.

Tissue Organization

In general, plant bodies consist of the root system and the shoot. The meristemic reserve continuously gives rise to new tissue, with new cells changing first into protoderm, ground meristem, and procambium tissues. Vascular tissues—xylem and phloem—transport food, water, and gases through the plants. In xylem, vessels and tracheids carrying water from the roots to the stem and leaves act as a pipeline system. In phloem, sieve tube members permit the transport of fluids from cell to cell.

The Root System

In primary roots, cells behind the meristemic tissue elongate, pushing the root tip through the soil. Tiny root hairs greatly increase the plant's ability to absorb water. Vascular tissue forms in the upper region of the root tip, with the procambial cells giving rise to the primary xylem and phloem. These eventually occupy the stele.

Most dicots produce a single tap root that branches out into lateral roots. In monocots, the original embryonic root tip is replaced by adventitious roots that grow outward from the stem. These branch to form diffuse roots. Prop roots keep rapidly growing plants such as corn upright.

Secondary root growth begins in the stele, where a ring of vascular cambium forms that produces secondary xylem and phloem. The epidermis of a young root is destroyed during secondary growth and is replaced by the periderm.

The Shoot System

Growth continues at the shoot tip throughout the plant's life. New tissues arise from the shoot apical meristem and are protected by the tunica. Behind the shoot meristem are differentiating tissues and various kinds of meristem, which will produce leaves and branches. Secondary growth in shoots is mainly a trait of large, woody dicots and accounts for the great size of many trees. As secondary growth continues in the dicot, the vascular system develops rapidly and soon merges with primary xylem and phloem. Seasonal differences in growth rates produce the annual rings in trees. A second growth pattern in the older stem develops the vascular rays that extend through the wood and move fluids laterally. Secondary growth also produces cork cambium and cork, or bark, impregnated with suberin.

The Leaf: A Photosynthetic Organ

Leaves are composed of an epidermis, photosynthetic cells, and vascular tissues, which arise from protoderm, ground meristem, and procambium. Dicot leaves are attached to the stem by petioles and possess a central vein, or midrib, with many branches that transport nutrients, fluids, and gases. Monocot leaves have no petioles but emerge from a sheath around the stem and contain veins running in parallel rows. While leaf epidermal cells lack chloroplasts, the layers of parenchyma cells receive the incoming light, with spongy parenchyma permitting carbon dioxide diffusion. Leaf hairs protect plants against some insects and help leaves to resist water loss.

annual	primary xylem	annual ring
biennial	primary phloem	vascular ray
perennial	stele	collenchyma
indeterminate life span	pericycle	cork
totipotent	endodermis	bark
cloning	suberin	blade
primary growth	Casparian strip	petiole
secondary growth	cortex	midrib
root	epidermis	bundle sheath
shoot	vascular cambium	upper epidermis
vessel	secondary phloem	lower epidermis
tracheid	secondary xylem	cutin
sieve tube member	wood	palisade parenchyma
companion cell	periderm	spongy parenchyma
primary root	leaf primordia	stomata
root cap	lateral bud primordia	leaf hairs
root hair	pith	

Review Questions

1. What is the cellular basis for open growth and the indeterminate life span of some plants? (p. 346)

2. List the three types of meristematic tissue, and name one specific type of mature tissue derived from each. (Table 24.1)

3. Name and compare the two types of xylem elements. What is the general function of xylem? (p. 349)

4. Prepare a rough sketch of the root tip, showing the following regions: root cap, root hairs, zone of maturation, zone of elongation, apical meristem, and procambium. (pp. 351–352)

5. Starting with the epidermis of the mature primary root, list the tissues that would be encountered as you proceed toward the center of the root. Which of these tissues constitute the stele? (pp. 352–353)

6. Compare the tap root system with the diffuse root system. How has each adapted differently for the same general functions? (pp. 352–354)

7. Prepare a rough sketch of the growing shoot, showing the leaf primordia, lateral bud primordia, procambium, and developing vascular system. (p. 356)

8. In plants capable of secondary growth, the vascular cambium becomes very significant. What specific tissues does it produce? (p. 355)

9. List the tissues one would encounter in a young woody stem, beginning with the cork and working inward to the pith. (pp. 355–358)

10. Using a simple sketch of a dicot leaf cross section, illustrate the tissue organization. Your drawing should include upper and lower epidermis, palisade and spongy parenchyma, stomata, and one small vein. (pp. 359–360)

Mechanisms of Transport in Plants

25

The leaves of a tall tree may discharge enormous amounts of water into the air. And, in certain seasons, they do this day after day, dampening the forest air and lending authority to that glorious smell of the woodlands. Those leaves may be hundreds of feet from the ground, but the water they lose comes from the roots, deep in that same ground (Figure 25.1). How does the water, pouring into millions of tiny root hairs, reach those lofty leaves? The question is a good one. But water is not the only fluid that moves through plants.

Many trees are girdled with a series of small holes, the work of a migratory little woodpecker called the *sapsucker*. The holes are shallow, but they penetrate the phloem and fill with sap that is intercepted on its way downward from the leaves. The sapsucker laps at the sugary fluid before it continues on its way down the tree. The movement of nutrient-bearing sap through the tree raises as many questions as does the movement of water, and the answers to some of the more basic ones have yet to be clarified.

THE MOVEMENT OF WATER AND MINERALS

Let's begin with water transport, which is the responsibility of xylem, those lifeless vessels and tracheids that carry water and minerals from the root

to the foliage. It will be useful to first review some of the properties of water discussed much earlier (see Chapters 2 and 5). In a real sense, the vascular plant has evolved around the behavior of water.

Water Potential

Earlier, we used the term **water potential** in reference to the various forces that can cause water to move. These forces can account for such behavior as the swelling of cells due to osmotic pressure, and the downward flow of water due to gravity. Essentially, water potential describes the *free energy* of water (see Chapter 5).

To illustrate our definition, consider water potential in a cell, where it is dependent upon how dilute the cell's fluid is. Dissolved solutes within a cell *reduce* the cell's water potential. You may recall from our discussion of osmosis (see Chapter 5) that water tends to move through a semipermeable membrane from regions of lower solute concentration (higher water potential) to those of higher solute concentration (lower water potential). We can simplify this by remembering that the transport of water within the plant body always occurs from regions of higher water potential to lower water potential. Water thus moves from cell to cell along a **water potential gradient.** Since we know that water moves from the roots to the leaves, we can infer that the roots have a higher water

Water escapes because of evaporation, and is constantly replaced by water moving upward from the roots. The loss of water from the leaf is known as **transpiration.**

Energy for Transpiration. So the movement of water through a plant begins with transpiration in the leaf. The amount transpired daily is enormous (Figure 25.2), and all of it must be replaced if the plant is to remain active and healthy. This movement requires the expenditure of large amounts of energy. Fortunately for plants, they do not have to provide this energy; the energy of evaporation is provided by the sun and the wind, and it is absolutely free. The sun's energy powers transpiration and subsequent water transport. But other mechanisms are also at work; let's look at these.

As water evaporates from the moist air spaces in

25.1

This towering giant sequoia, *Sequoiadendron giganteum*, is one of the world's tallest trees 83 m (272 ft). It is truly awe-inspiring to stand in one of the remaining groves of such giants. If you are aware of the problems of water transport, the marvel of it all increases.

potential than the leaves. And now we come to some basic questions regarding this phenomenon. Why should a leaf cell have the lower water potential? Where does the water go? If you are thinking that the water is used up in photosynthesis, think again. Only a small portion is used.

The Transpiration-Cohesion-Tension Hypothesis

The Problem of Water Loss. The problem is that leaves leak—they have to. As you know, plants use carbon dioxide from the air in photosynthesis. It diffuses through the stomata into the leaf's moist air spaces as a gas, but must be dissolved before it can move into cells. This means that plants must continually bathe their leaf cells in water. However, plants have not evolved a way to let carbon dioxide in without letting water escape.

25.2

Plants transpire far more water than they use in photosynthesis. The amounts can be staggering. During the growing season, each wheat plant in this field transpires about 100 liters of water.

the leaf parenchyma, it is replaced by water from surrounding cells (Figure 25.3). Essentially, this increases the concentration of solutes in the cells and therefore lowers their water potential. The leaf parenchyma cells react to changes in water potential more or less as a unit. Their cell walls are very porous and their cytoplasm is connected by numerous plasmodesmata, so a rapid interaction occurs among the cells. That is, the cell walls and plasmodesmata permit water to move rapidly from cell to cell along a water potential gradient to the site of transpiration. Of course, for water movement to continue in the leaf, there must be a constant supply of water, and this supply comes from the xylem of the leaf vascular system. As we've mentioned, the xylem elements are lengthy, water-filled tubes. But in the xylem, the mechanisms of water movement change.

Tension and Cohesion in the Xylem. To understand what happens next, we must visualize the xylem as containing an unbroken *column* of water, extending from leaf to root. As water evaporates through the stomata, its responding movement through the leaf cells exerts a pull, or **tension,** on the column. Any pull at the top of the column raises the entire column, permitting water to enter the leaf. The pull is substantial enough to raise a column of water to the foliage of the tallest trees. It is interesting that water in an ordinary hose or pipe cannot be lifted more than 10 m by any amount of suction, since suction is dependent on the force of atmospheric pressure *pushing* a heavy column of water upward. Yet transpiration can *pull* water 10 times higher than that. But let's look more closely at the notion of water being pulled through the vascular system, since it raises an important question. You are probably wondering why the column of water doesn't simply break up.

The mechanism described, often referred to as **transpiration pull,** works quite efficiently, but it wouldn't work at all if it were not for the extremely small diameter of the xylem elements and the cohesive quality of water. Water molecules, you may

25.3

Water potential in leaf tissues occurs as a result of a gradient between the xylem and the air surrounding the leaf. The gradient is established by water evaporating from the leaf, which lowers the water potential in the air spaces within. This decrease in water potential starts a chain of events resulting in a constant flow from the xylem to the outside.

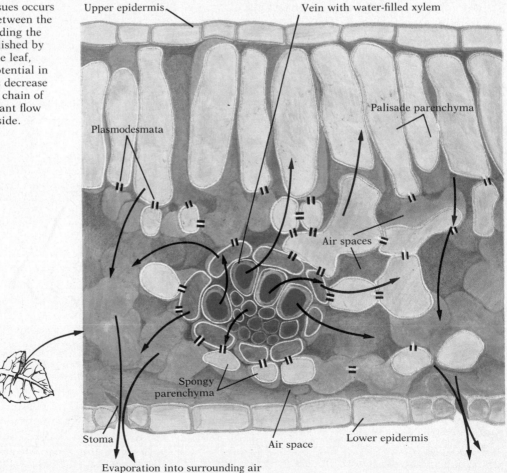

Upper epidermis

Vein with water-filled xylem

Palisade parenchyma

Plasmodesmata

Air spaces

Spongy parenchyma

Stoma

Air space

Lower epidermis

Evaporation into surrounding air

recall (see Chapter 2), cling together because of hydrogen bonding—the attraction between positively and negatively charged ends of adjacent molecules. This tendency among molecules is called **cohesion.** The cohesive forces in water would be ineffective in a large tube, but xylem is microscopic, so the water molecules within cling together tenaciously. In fact, the tensile strength of water in such a thin column approaches that of surgical steel wire of the same diameter!

In addition to these factors, water exhibits another characteristic known as **adhesion**—the tendency of water molecules to stick to certain surfaces. If the end of an extremely fine glass tube many feet in length is immersed in water, the water will move quickly up the tube completely on its own. This happens because water adheres to the confining walls, producing a sort of "molecular creeping" action. The column stays together because of cohesion; the significance of adhesion to water transport is still being argued.

The tension exerted on water in the xylem through transpiration pull is not hypothetical. It can be demonstrated through the use of a sensitive instrument known as a *dendrograph* (Figure 25.4). Precise measurements of tree trunks over 24-hour periods have revealed that trunk diameters decrease significantly at midday, when transpiration is most intense. This clearly indicates that the tension within the trunk is both real and enormous.

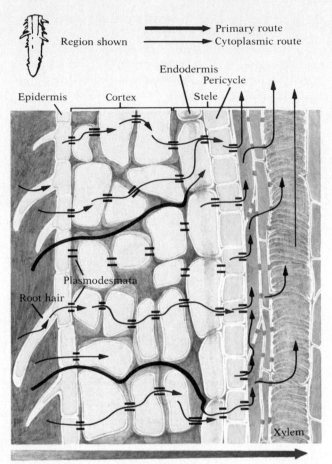

25.5

In the root, as in the leaf, water moves from regions of greater water potential to those of lesser water potential. Thus, the gradient that brings water into the stele of the root extends from the soil water to the xylem. Water moving through the cortex mainly passes along porous cell walls, as well as in cell-to-cell fashion through plasmodesmata.

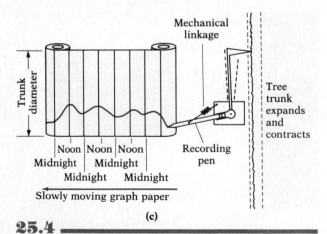

25.4

Changes in the diameter of a tree over several days can be registered on a drum recording. D. T. MacDougal, testing the hypothesis that transpiration pull places enough tension on columns of water within the stem to compress the trunk, found that his intriguing data support the hypothesis. The 12-hour variations in trunk diameter correspond nicely with measured transpirational activity. Plants transpire most at midday and least at night. Thus the transpiration pull hypothesis is supported.

Of course, with water transpiring from the leaf and being pulled out of the xylem for replacement, the root must be able to meet the demands. As long as the water potential in the surrounding soil water is greater than that in the root cells, there will be an inward gradient (Figure 25.5). However, the root is not simply passive in the transport of water: it assists the process by actively transporting minerals inward. This increases the solute concentrate in the root cells, decreasing water potential and encouraging the inward movement of water by osmosis. Plants can create a substantial **root pressure** in this manner, enough to force water right up through special openings on the tips of the leaves of ground-hugging plants such as strawberries and lawn grasses. This exudation of excess water is called **guttation,** an event most commonly seen at night when root pressure exceeds evaporation.

To sum up the **transpiration-cohesion-tension hypothesis,** the energy needed to power water transport is provided by the sun and expressed in evaporation or transpiration. As transpiration occurs at the leaf, the loss is translated into a water potential gradient there. Water moving along the gradient exerts a substantial pull or tension on water in the xylem elements. The cohesive (and adhesive) qualities of water keep the moving column intact, but this water must be continually replaced by uptake in the root (Figure 25.6).

Turgor and Guard Cell Operation

Some water loss through transpiration is critical if water is to be pulled upward through the xylem. However, the plant also regulates the size of the stomatal openings, which helps to reduce water loss. This is done by numerous, paired guard cells that regulate the size of the stomatal opening by their own swelling or shrinking.

Guard cells (Figure 25.7) are somewhat sausage-shaped with thin walls, except for the walls that form the stomatal opening. These are quite thick—a significant fact. When the **turgor pressure** (the pressure exerted by a water-filled vacuole) in the

25.6

Transpiration results because of what is essentially a water potential gradient between soil water and the air surrounding the leaves. As water evaporates from the leaf surface, it is replaced by water from the tissues within and, eventually, from the leaf xylem. The outward movement from the xylem creates a pull on the water within the xylem that draws the column of water up through the entire vascular system. The deficit produced in the xylem causes soil water to move along the established gradient. (Different intensities of blue are used in the drawing to indicate water concentrations.)

Guttation

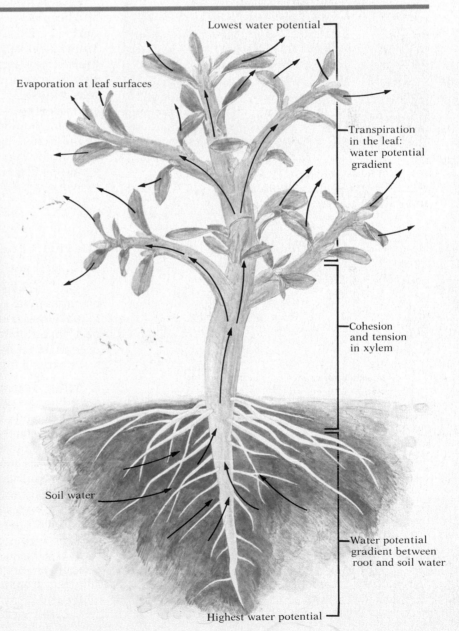

Lowest water potential

Evaporation at leaf surfaces

Transpiration in the leaf: water potential gradient

Cohesion and tension in xylem

Water potential gradient between root and soil water

Soil water

Highest water potential

guard cell is low, the spring-like, thickened region tends to straighten out and the stomatal opening becomes a mere slit. When turgor pressure increases, the thickened part of the guard cell walls bends in such a way that the stomata open (as seen in Figure 25.7).

The stomata also are light-sensitive, and tend to open during the day and to close at night. Thus, carbon dioxide is allowed to pass into the plant mostly when the plant is actively involved in photosynthesis. Naturally, there are exceptions. The cells of a plant wilting for lack of water will lose turgor and close their stomata, conserving precious fluids even at the expense of being unable to carry on photosynthesis. In some plants, the stomata close in the early afternoon to prevent excessive water loss in the heat of the day. In the desert, where excessive water loss is unacceptable, some plants have evolved biochemical answers to the problem. Their stomata open only at night, admitting carbon dioxide that is incorporated into organic compounds until daylight. Then the stomata close, the biochemical reactions are reversed, and carbon dioxide is released for photosynthesis.

Several mechanisms for guard cell control have also been proposed. It is known, for instance, that during periods of water shortage, a plant hormone known as *abscisic acid* accumulates in the leaf. Does the hormone affect the guard cells? It is known that abscisic acid, applied to the plant, causes the guard cells to close. It now seems that guard cells may be controlled by a number of factors. Under experimental conditions, guard cells of some plants respond to blue light by actively transporting potassium ions into their cytoplasm. The increased solute concentration results in the uptake of water by osmosis and the swelling of the cell.

(a)

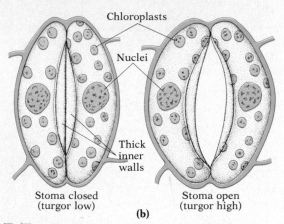

(b)

25.7

Guard cells must allow gases to pass through and yet prevent excessive water loss. These cells are distributed over the lower epidermis of leaves and along green stems. **(a)** The scanning electron micrograph shows a guard cell in the epidermis of a leaf. **(b)** The guard cells in the drawing look like twin sausages, with their curved shapes surrounding the stomata. Note the presence of chloroplasts in the cells: they are not found in any other epidermal cells. Note also that the inner walls of each guard cell are thicker than the rest of the cell wall. These thickened walls apparently resist stretching, and when turgor pressure is reduced, they close the stomatal opening.

Mineral Uptake by Roots

For most plants, the only sources of mineral nutrients are the ions dissolved in soil water. Since the plant has to take a great deal of water from the soil to make up for transpiration losses, you might expect that it would simply passively extract its needed minerals from the water. However, plants must expend energy to obtain mineral nutrients.

Active Transport. Some of the nutrients required by the plant are found in very low concentrations in soil water, so the plant must selectively move these minerals from the water into its tissues. They are taken into the root by active transport, with ATP as the energy source. Once inside the root, the nutrients can move from cell to cell by way of plasmodesmata (Figure 25.8) until they reach the root xylem. They can enter the conducting tissue only with the further expenditure of ATP. From there they are rapidly distributed upward and throughout the plant in the transpiration flow. Interestingly, in many cases the plant gets a little help from a friend.

The Role of Fungi and Bacteria in Mineral Uptake. The roots of most vascular plants form a peculiar association called *mycorrhizae* with fungi (Figure 25.9; see also Chapter 21). The fungus either surrounds the root or sends its fingerlike mycelia right into the root cortex. There it can and does help itself to the plant's sugars and other nutrients. But the relationship is mutualistic—both parties benefit. The extensive fungal mycelium outside concentrates mineral ions, particularly phosphate, along with water. These are delivered to the root cells. In this manner the mycorrhizae act as a second root system, and incidentally ensure their own survival.

Nearly all plants are dependent on the activities of bacteria for nitrates and ammonium ions, forms of nitrogen needed in the synthesis of proteins, nucleic acids, and other essential molecules. Bacteria (and fungi) decompose the wastes and the

25.9

Three nine-month-old sweetgum seedlings grown in fumigated soil of moderate fertility. The fumigation killed the mycorrhizal fungi that live symbiotically with the plants. The fungi were restored in the two larger plants on the right. The stunted plant on the left developed without the fungi. The experiment illustrates the importance of such associations in the development of some plants.

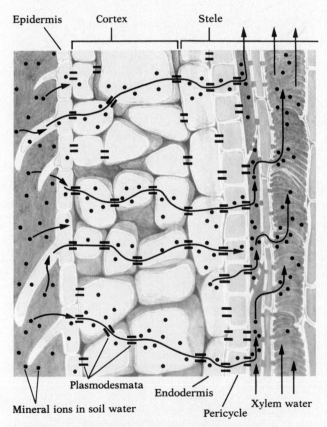

25.8

The ion pathway through the root begins with the absorption of ions by root hairs. From there they move, cell-by-cell, via plasmodesmata into the stele. Compare this to the pathways of water shown in Figure 25.5.

Epidermis Cortex Stele

Plasmodesmata Endodermis

Mineral ions in soil water Pericycle Xylem water

corpses of all forms of life, releasing the nitrogen ions as waste products. In addition, some bacteria and cyanobacteria are able to convert atmospheric nitrogen (N_2) into nitrates and ammonium ions through nitrogen fixation (see Chapters 20 and 45). In some instances, nitrogen-fixing bacteria actually invade the root, which responds by forming a confining nodule (cystlike growth) around the colony. As in the mycorrhizae, this association is mutualistic, with the bacteria obtaining food and water and the plant getting the usable nitrogen. Nodules are common in the roots of such legumes as alfalfa, beans, peas, and clover.

Mineral Requirements

Plants require many kinds of minerals (Table 25.1). These minerals can be divided into two groups: the macronutrients and the micronutrients. The

TABLE 25.1

Elements and nutrients essential to plant growth

Element	How Taken In	Examples of Use
Macronutrients		
Calcium	Calcium ion (Ca^{2+})	Cell wall, membrane, coenzyme activity
Carbon	Carbon dioxide (CO_2)	Proteins, lipids, carbohydrates
Hydrogen	Soil water (H_2O)	Proteins, lipids, carbohydrates
Magnesium	Magnesium ion (Mg^{2+})	Chlorophyll molecule
Nitrogen	Nitrate ion (NO_3^-), Ammonium ion (NH_4^+)	Amino acids, purines, pyrimidines, protein
Oxygen	Atmospheric oxygen (O_2)	Cell respiration
Phosphorus	Phosphate ion ($H_2PO_4^-$)	Nucleic acids, phospholipids, ATP
Potassium	Potassium ion (K^+)	Cell membrane, enzyme activity, guard cell mechanism
Silicon	Silicate ion ($HSiO_3^-$)	Cell walls
Sulfur	Sulfate ion (SO_4^{2-})	Proteins, coenzyme A
Micronutrients		
Boron	Borate ion (BO_3^-), Tetraborate ion ($B_4O_7^{2-}$)	Cell elongation, carbohydrate translocation
Chlorine	Chloride ion (Cl^-)	Accumulates as HCl in chemiosmotic photosynthesis
Copper	Cupric ion (Cu^{2+})	Enzyme activity
Iron	Ferrous ion (Fe^{2+}), Ferric ion (Fe^{3+})	Enzyme activity, chlorophyll synthesis
Manganese	Manganese ion (Mn^{2+})	Enzyme activity
Molybdenum*	Molybdenum ion (Mo^{3+})	Enzyme activity, including N-fixation
Zinc	Zinc ion (Zn^{2+})	Hormone activity

*Indirectly important in the nitrogen cycle

macronutrients are required in large amounts. They include carbon, hydrogen, nitrogen, oxygen, and sulfur—elements important in synthesizing the molecules of life (see Chapter 3). Potassium is also needed in fairly large quantities. The **micronutrients** are needed in smaller amounts and generally play more subtle roles, working in concert with enzymes, coenzymes, and hormones. Many of the micronutrients are required in trace amounts only, perhaps a few parts per million. In fact, if they are overly abundant, they may even kill plants.

FOOD TRANSPORT IN THE PHLOEM

Now that we have considered the movement of water and minerals through the plant, with a brief look at the roles of the minerals, let's see how food moves through the phloem.

We learned earlier that plants use the energy of evaporation and the cohesive property of water in moving it from root to foliage. We found that the pull produced by transpiration creates great tension on the water column within the tracheids and vessels.

Things are different in the phloem. The **phloem sap** is under positive internal hydrostatic pressure, so the sap pushes outward. Aphids take advantage of the hydrostatic pressure of phloem sap by using

their long, hollow mouthparts to drill tiny holes in individual sieve tubes (Figure 25.10). Then they just let the nutrient-laden phloem sap flow into their bodies as if from an artesian well. Researchers use aphids to obtain pure samples of phloem sap.

Sap is actually a rather thick fluid, especially

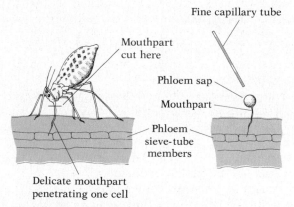

Fine capillary tube

Mouthpart cut here

Phloem sap

Mouthpart

Phloem sieve-tube members

Delicate mouthpart penetrating one cell

25.10

An ingenious method of obtaining pure phloem sap involves the use of aphids, insects that suck out the fluid of sieve tubes. After the aphid has pierced the phloem, it is anesthetized and the mouthpart is removed. When the operation is successful, the mouthpart remains in place and sieve tube fluids continue to flow out. This technique produces a higher quality of sap than any mechanical means known.

when the plant is actively metabolizing and photosynthesizing. Nonetheless it moves rapidly through the phloem, up to a meter per hour. Sucrose makes up about 90% of the solutes in sap, but it also carries other sugars, inorganic nutrients, hormones, and amino acids.

Flow from Source to Sink

Sugars and other nutrients originally produced in the leaf are widely distributed in the plant, moving to the actively growing regions, into the root, into maturing fruit, and to storage regions. This transfer, or **translocation,** as it is known, is multidirectional; it can occur in different directions in the same tissue at different times. We will refer to areas where nutrients are to be used or stored as **sinks,** and to areas where they originate as **sources.**

The flow of sap is *from source to sink:* nutrients are actively transported into the sieve tubes at the source, and are actively transported from the sieve tubes at the sink (Figure 25.11). The active transport at both sites requires an expenditure of ATP.

The Pressure Flow Hypothesis

Active transport loads nutrients into the sieve tubes at the source and unloads them at the sink, but what accounts for the flow between the two? There have been many hypotheses to account for this mechanism, but the one currently favored, the **pressure flow hypothesis,** is an older one, first proposed in 1927. It is based on the differences in water potential and osmotic pressure between the xylem and the phloem.

The idea is this: the active transport of sugars from the source into the phloem greatly decreases its water potential in comparison to the high water potential in the nearby xylem. The result is that water leaves the xylem and moves into the phloem sieve tubes, raising the hydrostatic pressure there. (**Hydrostatic pressure** is the pressure that is exerted in all directions by a fluid at rest. In this case, it might help to consider it as being similar to blood pressure in our vessels.) The increased hydrostatic pressure then forces the sap to move as a stream through the phloem tubes.

Meanwhile, at the various sinks, solutes are being unloaded, increasing the water potential within the sieve tube above that of surrounding cells. Because of this, water leaves the sieve tube, entering the sink tissues or moving back into the

xylem. Within the phloem, water (and the nutrients dissolved in it) follows the gradient in water potential that is created by active transport at both ends of the pipeline—that is, at the sink and at the source (see Figure 25.11).

So, as you now see, the simple tree, standing among other simple trees, is not so simple after all. It is quietly and efficiently engaged in processes that dedicated scientists are only now beginning to understand.

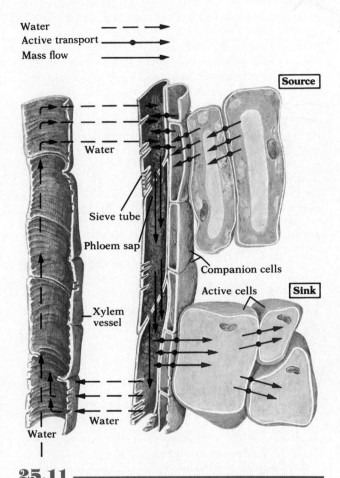

Water - - - →
Active transport ————→
Mass flow ————→

Source

Water

Sieve tube

Phloem sap

Companion cells

Active cells

Sink

Xylem vessel

Water

Water

25.11

Pressure flow is initiated when sugars and other foods produced in the leaf cells—the source—are actively transported into the phloem. Water from nearby xylem, with a much higher water potential, moves into the sieve tube member, creating great hydrostatic pressure there. Mass flow begins as the pressure forces the sap downward through the phloem system. At nearby cells that make up the sink, active transport again moves the sugars and other foods, this time out of the sieve tubes. With the loss of solutes, the water potential in the phloem increases and water moves out, recycling back to the xylem.

Summary

The Movement of Water and Minerals

Water potential refers to the various forces that cause water to move. Water always moves from regions of lower solute concentration (higher water potential) to regions of higher solute concentration (lower water potential) along a water potential gradient.

The movement of water in plants follows a water potential gradient from the soil water around the roots to the air surrounding the leaves. As water is transpired by the leaf, it is replaced by water from the xylem, moving along a gradient in the leaf cells. The leaf gradient produces a tension-creating pull on water columns in the xylem, where water is held together by cohesion. Water moving through the xylem is replaced by water entering the root and moving along the water potential gradient there. The gradient in the root is established through the active uptake of minerals by root cells.

Plants exert some control over water loss by regulating the size of the stomatal openings. The guard cell walls that form the stomatal openings bend and straighten in response to turgor pressure. In most plants, stomata tend to open by day and close at night to maximize the intake of carbon dioxide during photosynthesis. In desert environments, plants open their stomata at night and close them by day to conserve fluids.

Plant absorb mineral nutrients from ions dissolved in soil water. The minerals reach the root xylem through plasmodesmata. In most vascular plants, mineral absorption is facilitated by symbiotic relationships (mycorrhizae) with various fungi. Plants require large amounts of macronutrients as nitrogen, and only small amounts of micronutrients.

Food Transport in the Phloem

Phloem sap, composed primarily of sucrose, moves under positive internal hydrostatic pressure from various sources to various sinks in the plant, nourishing new growth. The pressure flow hypothesis suggests that changes in water potential and hydrostatic pressure at the plant's sources and sinks account for the flow of phloem sap between these sites.

Key Terms

water potential
water potential gradient
transpiration
tension
transpiration pull
cohesion
adhesion

root pressure
guttation
transpiration-cohesion-tension
    hypothesis
guard cells
turgor pressure
macronutrients

micronutrients
phloem sap
translocation
sink
source
pressure flow hypothesis
hydrostatic pressure

Review Questions

1. Water transport in a plant requires great energy. What is the source of that energy, and how is it applied to the leaf? (pp. 364–365)

2. In terms of water potential, describe conditions in the plant that cause water to move from the soil into the root, then into the vascular system, the leaf, and finally into the surrounding air. Under what conditions might all of this fail? (pp. 363–366)

3. Water movement through a plant involves a process called *transpiration pull.* What creates the "pull," and what keeps the xylem water column together? (p. 365)

4. Explain how water entering a pair of guard cells can cause the opening of the stoma. (pp. 367–368)

5. What is the role of mycorrhizae in ion uptake? (p. 369)

6. The flow of nutrients in plants is from "source to sink." Explain what this means, and provide examples of sources and sinks. (p. 371)

7. Summarize the pressure flow hypothesis, making sure to mention the role of active transport, hydrostatic pressure, and water potential. (p. 371)

Response Mechanisms in Plants

26

You have probably noticed that plants tend to be a little short on personality, which is probably why many people have switched to hamsters. However, perhaps a few very patient people with time on their hands have learned that plants can and do respond to their surroundings in many ways. A plant, like any other organism, responds continuously to a variety of cues, signals both from within itself and from its environment. But a plant's responses are usually gradual and based on time-consuming chemical changes.

Regulation through chemical mechanisms frequently involves certain molecules known as **hormones**. Hormones are essentially chemical messengers that are manufactured in one part of an organism and are transported to another part, where they can cause some sort of change. The cells in which the change takes place have specific receptor sites that recognize and respond to the hormones.

In addition to being very specific, hormones are effective in minute amounts, and they are almost always short-lived. They do not accumulate in cells and tissues, but are rapidly broken down.

Plant hormones are important in a number of ways. They are involved in growth, cell division, seed germination, flowering, tissue differentiation, dormancy, and other vital activities. You may recall from our earlier discussions, for example, that primary growth itself occurs through cell division and cell elongation, both of which require the presence of certain hormones. Let's now consider a few specific plant hormones and see how they function to regulate and coordinate the activities of the plant.

PLANT HORMONES AND THEIR ACTIONS

Auxin

Auxin is a class of very small molecules with far-reaching effects. The principal naturally occurring auxin is *indoleacetic acid*, or *IAA*. Auxin was chemically identified about 50 years after its presence was suspected (Figure 26.1).

Auxin is best known as a growth hormone. It affects nearly every aspect of growth, from root tip to foliage. It doesn't cause plants to grow by increasing the rate of mitosis, but by promoting cell enlargement in stems, particularly by elongation of cells behind the apical meristem (see Chapter 24). Although we still don't completely understand just how auxin works, it seems that, among other things, it promotes cell elongation by going to work on the soft primary cell walls of newly divided cells before they have reached their final, hardened state (that is, before they are impregnated with pectin and other wall hardeners). Auxin promotes the loosening of closely bound filaments of cellulose near the ends of the young cell walls, thus permitting turgor pressure to expand the cells in those areas. The increased turgor is due to enlarged central vacuoles, rather than to added cytoplasm.

Auxin often works in concert with other hormones—in some cases, it begins to act with certain hormones after it has stimulated their synthesis. Auxin interacts in a number of ways with other hormones, such as by influencing cell differentiation and affecting the growth of vascular cambium and fruit. It is also known to play a role in leaf fall. This versatile hormone is also involved in the way plants react to such environmental cues as light and gravity.

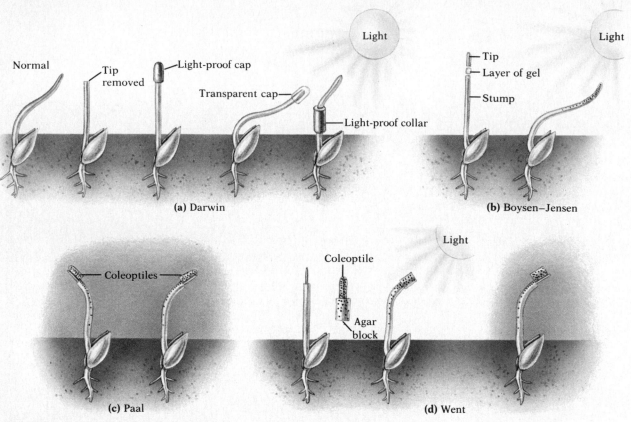

(a) Darwin

(b) Boysen–Jensen

(c) Paal

(d) Went

26.1

Experimentation leading to the discovery of auxin has had a long and interesting history. Surprisingly, Charles Darwin and his son Francis made the early attempts. Using canary grass seedlings treated in five different ways **(a)**, the Darwins tried to determine why plants bend toward the light. The young shoot of the canary grass and the shoots of other grasses are covered by a sheath known as the *coleoptile*. The Darwins found that the coleoptile does not bend if light cannot reach its tip. They also concluded that the agent causing the bending passed down to regions below the tip. In later experiments, P. Boysen-Jensen **(b)** determined that the agent proposed by Darwin was a diffusible substance, capable of passing through gelatin. A. Paal had a different approach **(c)**. He carefully removed the coleoptile tip, exposing the slender leaf within, and re-placed it on one side or the other. Growing his subjects in the dark as shown, he found that they simply responded to the greatest concentration of the agent in the coleoptile tip. His results suggested that, under normal conditions, light somehow determined where the greatest concentrations of the agent would be located. The work of F. Went **(d)** combined the techniques of Boysen-Jensen and Paal. He removed the coleoptile tips, and placed these tips on minute blocks of agar for about an hour. He then used the agar blocks in his experiments, which were carried out in the dark. With the agar blocks simply replacing the tips, the shoots responded to light in a normal manner. His results were similar to those of Paal. Went proposed the name "auxin" for the diffusible agent, and his techniques are still employed in auxin studies.

Gibberellins

The **gibberellins,** a family of some 57 known molecules, received their name from the fungus in which they were first found, *Gibberella fujikuroi.* This fungus, which once threatened rice harvests in Japan, causes the rice plant stem to elongate strangely and does not permit the plant to produce normal flowers. Between 1926 and 1935, Japanese botanists isolated and purified the active substances (gibberellins) that were produced by the fungus, but it wasn't until the 1950s that biologists in other nations began to take an interest in these strange molecules.

Gibberellins are now believed to be present in all plants, and have been found in all plant structures, with greatest concentrations in immature seeds. Experiments with gibberellins have produced some peculiar results (Figure 26.2). However, the power of gibberellins has been illustrated most dramatically in experiments with genetic dwarfs. Some varieties of dwarf corn, for instance, can be induced to grow to normal height after the application of gibberellins. Such experiments suggest that the dwarf corn is short only because of a lack of a hormone, its presence genetically controlled. Obviously, the dwarf corn always had the potential to grow tall. Further, the degree of growth in a dwarf plant depends on the quantity of gibberellins applied. Gibberellins also have other roles. For example, these hormones stimulate the synthesis of an enzyme called *alpha-amylase* in some seeds, including barley and corn. As the grains germinate, the embryo secretes gibberellins, which move to the cell layer (the *aleurone*) that surrounds the starchy endosperm. The cells of the aleurone, apparently stimulated by gibberellins, begin to produce the enzyme alpha-amylase, which breaks down starch and makes glucose available to the growing plant. Gibberellins also stimulate pollen germination and pollen tube growth. In addition, they can inhibit seed formation, and so they have been applied in agricultural research as a means of producing seedless fruits.

Cytokinins

Most of what we know about the **cytokinins** springs from work begun in the 1950s, when plant growth was found to be influenced by a substance in corn kernels. In 1964, the first of the molecules, **zeatin,** was isolated. Others also were soon isolated and described.

Before the isolation of zeatin, botanists could only suspect from circumstantial evidence that something in plants stimulated cell division. But what was it? Biologists soon began to isolate chemicals from corn and from coconut milk that stimulated cell division. They named this group of chemicals the cytokinins. They soon found that cytokinins alone cannot stimulate cell division or other plant activities; they must function with other plant hormones. Figure 26.3 shows how critical the ratio of auxin to cytokinins is in determining the direction of plant differentiation.

Cytokinins also are important in preventing aging in plants. For example, just before leaves fall from deciduous trees (those that shed seasonally), they grow "old." Their organic constituents break down, and sugars and mineral nutrients are returned to other plant tissues. Also, if leaves are

26.2

Gibberellins have a dramatic effect on stem growth, as seen in these plants. The plants at the left were grown normally, while the ones at the right were treated with gibberellins.

The effects of cytokinins on differentiation. This unseemly mass of tissue (*top*) is an undifferentiated and unorganized mass of tissue known as *callus*. In this experiment the callus is formed from tobacco parenchyma subjected to a combination of auxin and cytokinin. At top, right, a specific ratio of this combination produced a normal stem shoot, which is esen emerging from the callus. By varying the ratio of auxin to cytokinin, specific growth patterns, including roots and shoots, can be produced.

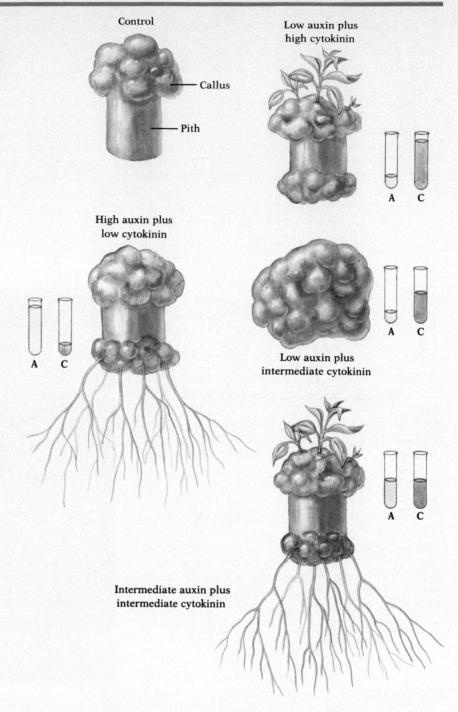

Control

Callus

Pith

Low auxin plus high cytokinin

A   C

High auxin plus low cytokinin

A   C

Low auxin plus intermediate cytokinin

A   C

Intermediate auxin plus intermediate cytokinin

A   C

picked while in the prime of life, they too go through an aging process before they die. But when picked leaves are treated with cytokinins, death comes far more slowly—programmed aging is retarded. For example, chlorophyll does not disintegrate (so the leaves stay green), protein synthesis continues, and carbohydrates do not break down. Synthetic cytokinins have been applied to such harvested vegetable crops as celery, broccoli, and other leafy foods to extend their storage life. (Unfortunately, cytokinins have no such effect on humans.)

Ethylene

Ethylene is a real lightweight among the plant hormones—light enough to escape from the plant as a gas. Ethylene is a hormone whose development is promoted by auxin, and it often operates in concert with auxin. It is important in the ripening of fruit. Picked fruit will ripen much more rapidly if it is kept in an enclosed space, such as a paper bag, where the ethylene produced by the fruit itself is concentrated.

In plants that bear separate male and female flowers, ethylene may help to determine the sex of the flowers. In some plants, when young buds are treated with ethylene, they change into female *(pistillate)* flowers. In contrast, high levels of gibberellins seem to produce male *(staminate)* flowers. Ethylene is also involved, along with another hormone, *abscisic acid*, in the falling of leaves. In this case, the two hormones stimulate the production of enzymes that dissolve the specialized cell walls that hold the petiole to the stem.

Ethylene may be important in maintaining the curved hypocotyl that acts as a bumper when seedlings make their way out of the soil (Figure 26.4). It also prevents the hypocotyl from straightening until it breaks through the soil surface. Once this happens, light apparently inhibits the production of ethylene, so that the stem straightens and the leaves unfold to begin photosynthesis.

As you might expect, ethylene has agricultural applications. Such fruits as tomatoes, grapes, and bananas can be shipped in a well-ventilated, unripened state to reduce the risk of spoilage. Then, before their final point of distribution, a synthetic ethylene gas can be released over them to hasten the ripening process. Such sophisticated advances in the transport and handling of food has had tremendous social and economic impact in areas able to utilize such techniques.

Abscisic Acid

Let's take a closer look at a hormone already mentioned, **abscisic acid (ABA).** The molecule is named for its role in leaf *abscission*, or separation.

After it was discovered that there were such things as hormones that promoted growth in plants, physiologists began to search for other kinds of hormones that might retard growth or impede cell function. In the 1960s several researchers reported finding a number of substances that accelerated the abscission of leaves and fruits. Later the substance was found to be identical to another chemical called *dormin* that had been discovered in the dormant buds of potatoes and in certain trees. The chemical inhibitor was renamed *abscissic acid*. Today the chemical is collected from the ovaries of fruits, particularly those of the cotton

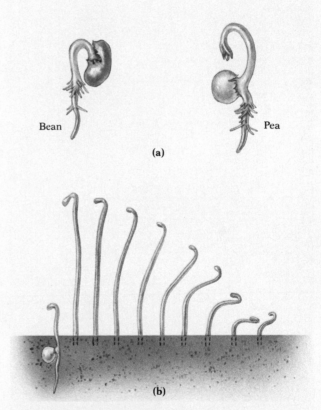

Bean   Pea

(a)

(b)

26.4

Ethylene is associated with shoot curvature in the seedling. **(a)** Note the typical curvature of seedlings as they emerge from the soil. The curved hypocotyl in the bean is thought to act as a protective "bumper." **(b)** The pea seedlings have been grown in increasing concentrations of ethylene gas. As the concentration is increased, the curvature also increases.

plant. One possible new use for abscissic acid is to close the stomates of plants, enabling new kinds of crops to be grown in arid parts of the earth.

Leaf fall may be a seasonal event, or it may follow wind damage, animal browsing, or drought. Since the vascular system of plants extends directly into the midrib of the leaf (see Chapter 24), the fall of a leaf could produce an open area that must be closed as rapidly as possible. So, in a complex interaction with other plant hormones, especially ethylene and auxin, abscisic acid causes the cells where the leaf is attached (the abscission zone) to die and harden, preferably *before* the leaf falls naturally (Figure 26.5) or after the leaf has been damaged or eaten.

Abscisic acid also induces winter dormancy by retarding the plant's growth. It does this by inhibiting the growth-promoting hormones, auxin and gibberellin. Only dormancy can save many species that are exposed to winter's freezing temperatures and the water shortages resulting from frozen ground. In a sense, then, abscisic acid works in an opposite manner to the cytokinins. Abscisic acid may also play an important role in the response of roots to gravity, a point we will return to shortly.

ARTIFICIAL AUXINS AND PLANT CONTROL

As humans have learned more about plant hormones, we've increasingly utilized these chemicals to cause plants to behave in the ways we want—such as to grow, to die, and to bear fruit. We've also looked for cheaper and better ways to control plants. One way has been through the production of synthetic or artificial hormones. For example, industry can now produce a number of inexpensive artificial auxins or other growth-promoters. Some of these have even greater effects than the natural auxin, because they are not rapidly broken down by the plants' enzymes. One growth promoter is the herbicide ("plant killer") 2,4-dichlorophenoxyacetic acid, known mercifully as *2,4-D*. 2,4-D promotes growth at very low concentrations, but it kills plants at higher concentrations. This compound is very commonly used in weed control because it is highly selective in that it is usually highly toxic to the dicotyledonous plants (such as clover, dandelions and certain other "weeds") and spares the monocotyledonous plants (such as grasses, wheat, and oats).

2,4-D is not exactly uncontroversial. There is some ominous evidence that it may interfere with the reproductive success of mammals, particularly by causing birth defects. Thus its value as a weed killer has to be measured carefully in terms of its risk.

Other artificially manufactured plant hormones used in agriculture (or to control the growth of unwanted flora) may have unexpected repercussions in organisms other than plants. Some of these effects may not appear until years after exposure. For example, contaminants in Agent Orange, a defoliant used during the Vietnam War, are now accused of being responsible for a horrible array of effects on the Vietnamese farmers and American veterans who were exposed to it.

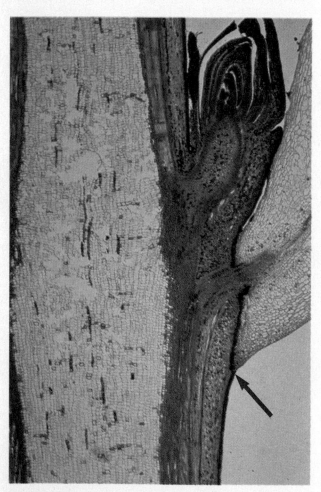

26.5

Abscisic acid and the leaf abscission layer. Before the leaf falls, the cells of the abscission zone (note the *dark vertical line* at the base of the diagonal petiole—arrow) die and harden under the influence of abscisic acid and auxin. Eventually, when the leaf breaks away and falls, the dead abscission zone will have already sealed the scar, reducing any danger of infection.

HORMONES AND THE PLANT TROPISMS

Since the environment varies over both time and space, it should be expected that plants would have evolved the ability to avail themselves of the most optimal environmental conditions. Since plants are fixed in place, the primary way they do this is by reacting to environmental cues through specific growth patterns.

The growth of plants in response to environmental factors is called a **tropism.** There are many kinds of tropisms. For example, plants respond to light through *phototropism*, and to gravity through *geotropism*. Tropisms can be either positive or negative—a plant bending toward the light shows *positive phototropism*. In general, root tips exhibit *positive geotropism* (growth toward the pull of gravity), and shoot tips show *negative geotropism* (growth away from the force of gravity). A plant's response to touch is known as *thigmotropism*, which is found in a number of plants, such as certain carnivorous ones that trap insects.

Hormones are usually involved in tropisms. For example, auxin is the growth hormone responsible for phototropism.

Phototropism

Phototropisms are a plant's responses to light, such as bending in the direction of light (see Figure 26.1). Obviously, something in the shoot tip must respond to light. But what is it? So far, no one has positively identified the specific mechanism, but plant physiologists are on the trail of a yellow-colored pigment, possibly one of the flavoproteins, that specializes in the absorption of light in the blue range. The receptor is believed to have an effect on the distribution of auxin as it is produced in the shoot tip. In one series of experiments, investigators learned that the total auxin production in the tip is the same under lighted conditions as it is in darkened conditions. But in the light, the distribution can be quite different. In plants exposed to light on the right side, for example, much of the auxin diffused or was transported to the left side. The cells on the left responded by elongating more rapidly, producing a curvature toward light (Figure 26.6). (This is the reason you have to keep rotating your window plants unless you favor the "windblown" look.)

This migration of auxin away from the light has been fully substantiated through the use of auxin labelled with carbon 14, a radioactive tracer. All of this suggests that the light receptor somehow produces selective changes in the permeability of cell membranes in the shoot, favoring the diffusion, or perhaps the active transport, of auxin away from the lighted side.

Now, if light brings about the changes in the distribution of auxin, one would expect that plants kept in the dark would grow straight and tall, at least until their energy reserves were depleted. And one would be right. For example, bean seedlings grown in a darkroom go through a surge of growth, becoming tall and spindly (as well as ghostly white, since the production of chlorophyll requires light). However, the photoreceptor is quite sensitive, and a mere pinpoint of light from any direction will initiate the phototropic response.

Geotropism

When a seedling is placed on its side, the shoot tip bends upward and the root tip bends downward (Figure 26.7). In the shoot, auxin moves away from the light, crossing the shoot and accumulating on the lower side. This side then elongates, causing the tip to bend upward toward the light. But what about the young root? What causes it to turn downward (a response referred to as **geotropism**)?

That question has left plant physiologists awash in a sea of contradictory hypotheses, but one theory is generally favored. First, investigators have not been able to establish the presence of natural auxin gradients in the root as they have in the shoot, so it is doubtful that auxin is the primary hormone of root curvature. More recently their attention has turned to abscisic acid. ABA is known to be produced in the core cells of the root cap; further, it is subject to distribution in the root tip in a manner similar to the way auxin is distributed in the shoot. However, unlike auxin, ABA acts as an inhibitor of cell elongation, so such gradients would have an opposite effect on root curvature. That is, ABA concentrating in cells on the underside of the young root would inhibit elongation, while the cells above would be free to elongate. The result would be a downward curvature. This hypothesis sounds quite reasonable, but like all such ideas, it must be subjected to further vigorous testing.

Thigmotropism

The ability of some plants to respond quickly to touch has presented an enduring problem to plant physiologists. They just can't figure out how the

Auxin is believed to promote cell elongation in the growing tips of stems. Cells in the apical meristem continually divide, producing cells which then elongate. **(a)** When light comes from all sides, elongation occurs equally around the entire stem. **(b)** But when light comes only from one side, only the cells on the unlighted side elongate. This is because auxin diffuses, or is transported to the unlighted side.

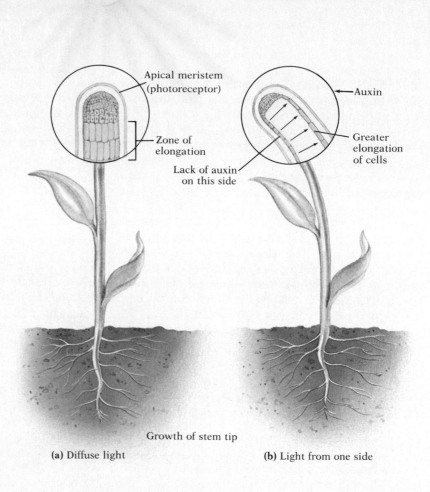

Light

Apical meristem (photoreceptor)

Zone of elongation

Auxin

Lack of auxin on this side

Greater elongation of cells

Growth of stem tip

(a) Diffuse light

(b) Light from one side

plants do it. However, the basic mechanism of rapid movement in plants is believed to be due to sudden changes in turgor in certain tissues.

As an example, touching or pressing the leaflets of the "sensitive plant," *Mimosa pudica* (Figure 26.8), causes the leaves to fold almost spasmodically as the petioles droop. Some theorists suggest this drooping response tends to discourage browsing animals, while others claim it helps the plant avoid excessive water loss when the leaves are stimulated by hot, dry winds.

Another example is the Venus flytrap, *Dionaea muscipula* (Figure 26.8b). The trap, a highly modified leaf, lies open when at rest. Each half of the trap has three tiny, hairlike triggers that, when brushed by a wandering insect, spring the trap, quickly closing the leaf. The toothed leaf presses the insect against the digestive glands on its inner

surface, and the plant gains nutrients, particularly nitrogen, from the insect's body.

It is known that both of these **thigmotropic responses** involve rapid changes in turgor, but they also involve a fascinating kind of electrical activity. The insect's touch may cause the rapid active transport of certain ions from cell to cell. The charges of these ions, theoretically, could generate significant electrical activity. A shift in ions within a cell could produce a change in the water potential which, in turn, would cause the movement of water and a subsequent change in turgor. This all seems logical enough, but it doesn't explain how the response occurs so quickly. There must be other factors at work, but they remain a mystery.

Incidentally, you may not be able to trigger the response of the Venus flytrap. Its leaves respond only to a special code: two hairs must be touched, in succession, or one hair must be touched twice. This means that a falling twig or other inert object brushing the trap probably also will have no effect. A wandering insect, on the other hand, is more likely to touch the leaf in such a way.

PHOTOPERIODISM AND FLOWERING PLANTS

The response of an organism to changing relative lengths of the day and night is known as **photoperiodism.** A clear example of photoperiodism in plants is the production of flowers during their reproductive season, a season also measured by

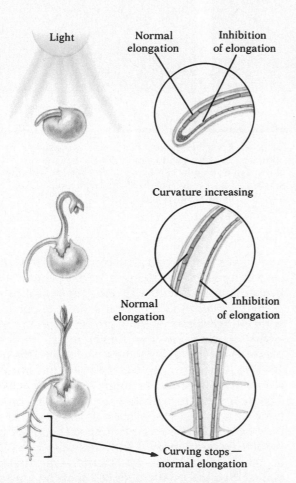

26.7

Geotropism. When a seedling is placed on its side, the shoot responds by curving upward, a positive phototropic response. The root, however, curves downward, a positive geotropic response. The geotropic response has not been explained satisfactorily, but it seems that cell elongation is inhibited on the lower side of the root.

26.8

Examples of thigmotropism, response to touch, are seen in the sensitive plant *Mimosa pudica* **(a)** and the Venus flytrap *Dionaea muscipula* **(b).** The responses may be due to active transport of ions that cause rapid changes in turgor.

the length of day. There are essentially three responses flowering plants may have to these changing day lengths, and depending on the species, the plants are called *short-day plants, long-day plants,* and *day-neutral plants.* The day-neutral plants can flower at any time of the year and so we won't bother with them.

Short-day plants begin to flower as the days

26.9

Three plants with specific photoperiod requirements for flowering. **(a)** The chrysanthemum is a short-day plant that produces flowers in the autumn. Flowering can be delayed if the plant receives an hour of light during the night. **(b)** Poinsettias are also short-day plants and will bloom when the night is longer than 13 hours. Their blossoming can be easily controlled by illuminating the greenhouses in which they are grown; thus, blooms can be made to coincide with the Christmas season. **(c)** The henbane requires long days (short nights) for flowering.

grow shorter. For example, chrysanthemums and poinsettias (Figure 26.9 a,b) typically begin flowering in autumn. **Long-day plants,** on the other hand, begin to flower when the days begin to last longer than a certain length of time prescribed by the rhythms of life. That time period varies for different species, and none will react to any day length shorter than is specifically required. Thus, long-day plants—like potatoes, spinach, and henbane (Figure 26.9 c)—flower at different times in summer. Spinach, incidentally, will not flower in tropical regions, because days are never long enough to exceed its 14-hour critical photoperiod.

Photoperiodism and the Length of Night

The long- and short-day terminology is unfortunately misleading. (And so, perhaps, is the notion we left you with in the preceding section.) This is because the terms *long-day* and *short-day* were already fixed in the scientific vocabulary before it was discovered that plant photoperiodism isn't determined by changes in day length at all. Instead, it's determined by the length of *night*.

Here's the situation as it's now understood: nights longer than a certain critical period are necessary to promote the flowering of short-day plants. But in long-day plants, the opposite is true. They require short nights, their length not to exceed a critical period of time. Again, the specific dark periods vary with the species. Based on this information, here's a question before you read any further: if a mixture of plant species is kept in a room that is uniformly lit 24 hours a day, what will be the effect on long-day plants? On short-day plants? You may have deduced that the long-day plants—freed from the inhibition of darkness—will soon flower, but none of the short-day plants, bereft of their needed stimulation, would ever flower.

How We Know. By raising plants in darkness and controlling the time they are exposed to light, investigators have found that the length of darkness controls flowering. When the *light* periods are changed drastically, the plants show no response at all. If the *dark* periods are changed in the same way, however, the plants respond.

Another interesting experiment has provided us with fascinating information. A long-night (short-day) plant can be fooled into behaving as if any night were short for flowering by being subjected to a flash of light in the middle of the night. The flash of light resets what has come to be called the plant's "dark clock." The dark clock behaves like a countdown timer that tells you when the roast is done. The timer of each species is set to go off when the required length of darkness is reached. This triggers the flowering process. So it is the extended darkness that influences the plant's reproductive behavior.

The flash of light or, more precisely, the red wavelengths in the light, sets the clock back to zero. The cool light of dawn soon comes and makes the night seem extremely short from the plant's viewpoint. Under natural conditions, of course, that same morning light will be sensed by the plant, and if the nights are too short to initiate flowering (in other words, if daylight comes before the clock runs out), the clock will be reset to zero and the timing process will begin again the next night.

This sort of tampering not only can be used to prevent a short-day (long-night) plant from flowering in autumn, but can also cause a long-day (short-night) plant to bloom in the dead of winter. Plants can therefore be made to produce flowers at any time. Those in charge of the Rose Bowl are well aware of this aspect of plant physiology.

Phytochrome: The Light Receptor

Plant physiologists have never been able to pin down the biochemical mechanisms of photoperiodism, although research has been intense and many major hypotheses have been proposed and discarded. Scientists have, however, established the nature of the light receptor involved in this phenomenon, and have named it *phytochrome*. **Phytochrome** is a protein associated with a light-absorbing accessory pigment that, like chlorophyll, absorbs light in the 660 nm range. Through several ingenious experiments, it has been conclusively shown that phytochrome is located in the leaves (Figure 26.10). There, it responds to the light stimulus by setting the flowering process in motion, probably through the release of a hormone. Although no such hormone has been isolated, botanists are confident enough that it exists to have tentatively named it *florigen*. In addition to its role in flowering, phytochrome has also been shown to be the receptor often involved in leaf growth, seed germination, and the lengthening and branching of stems.

It is apparent that plants are not only structurally complex, with a variety of very specialized tissues, but that they are also highly regulated and coordinated organisms. We are fully aware of our own complex adaptations to this world, but we must keep in mind that the plants also interact with the world, and their interactions and adaptations can be as complex as our own. In this chapter we have explored some of what has been discovered about the means by which plants respond to the environment, but we have taken only a glimpse at just how complex that interaction can be.

26.10

This experiment with the cocklebur, a short-day plant, establishes that the phytochrome photoreceptor is in the leaf. Only one leaf in this series of six grafted cocklebur plants is exposed to the proper photoperiod, yet all six plants produce flowers. It is likely that a hormone is being transferred from the exposed leaf to the other plants, but as yet no specific chemical messenger is known. For now, we can only conclude that the photoperiod effect is transferrable.

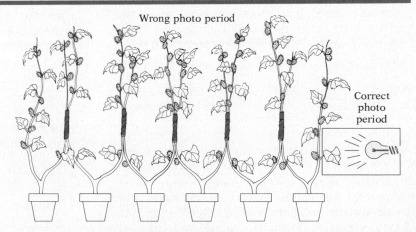

Wrong photo period

Correct photo period

All six plants produce flowers

Summary

Plant Hormones and Their Actions

Plant hormones are specific and effective, even in minute amounts. They control such activities as cell growth, germination, and flowering.

Auxin affects nearly every aspect of plant growth, particularly by promoting cell enlargement in stems, and often interacts with other hormones in cell differentiation, growth, and plant reactions to environmental cues. Gibberellins promote growth in stems and stimulate the synthesis of alpha-amylase. They also stimulate pollen germination and pollen tube growth, and can inhibit seed formation. Cytokinins, with other hormones, stimulate cell differentiation and retard aging in plants. Ethylene is important in the ripening of fruits, and is involved in determining the sex of flowers, facilitating the fall of leaves, and maintaining curved hypocotyls until they reach the soil surface. Abscisic acid, in conjunction with other hormones, has a role in leaf abscission and the induction of winter dormancy.

Artificial Auxins and Plant Control

Artificial hormones can be used to control plant responses for commercial or agricultural purposes. They can promote rapid growth or selectively kill some plants while sparing others. However, such hormones also can have toxic side effects on other organisms.

Hormones and the Plant Tropisms

A tropism is plant growth in response to various environmental factors. Phototropism, or a plant's response to light, may involve the stimulation of an absorbing pigment that affects the distribution of auxin in the shoot tip. Cells on the side away from the light receive the most auxin and elongate, bending the plant toward the light source.

Root tips are geotropic, appearing to bend downward in response to gravity. While it is known why shoots bend upward, it is not known what causes root tips to grow downward. One hypothesis is that abscisic acid inhibits cell elongation to produce the downward curvature. Some plants have fairly rapid thigmotropic (touch) responses. The rapid movement probably involves sudden changes in turgor and a type of swift active transport of ions from cell to cell, which affects water potential and, therefore, turgor.

Photoperiodism and Flowering Plants

Photoperiodism is the response of organisms to relative changes in the lengths of day and night. The length of night determines plant photoperiodism. Short-day plants flower as nights lengthen, while long-day plants flower when nights grow shorter. Day-neutral plants can flower at any time of the year. Light introduced during the dark period resets a plant's "dark clock" to zero, either inhibiting or inducing the development of flowers.

The light receptor involved in photoperiodism is called phytochrome; it consists of a protein associated with a light-absorbing accessory pigment. Phytochrome is also often involved in leaf growth, seed germination, and the lengthening and branching of stems.

Key Terms

hormones	ethylene	thigmotropic responses
auxin	abscisic acid (ABA)	photoperiodism
gibberellins	tropism	short-day plants
cytokinins	phototropism	long-day plants
zeatin	geotropism	phytochrome

Review Questions

1. What is the general effect of auxin on cells? (p. 373)

2. Briefly describe the action of gibberellins during seed germination. (p. 375)

3. List two metabolic roles of the cytokinins. (pp. 375–376)

4. In what way do fruit and vegetable shippers make use of one of the primary actions of ethylene? (p. 377)

5. In what way are the effects of abscisic acid (ABA) opposite those of auxin and gibberellins? (p. 378)

6. Summarize the action of auxin in phototropic responses, being sure to mention how light affects the distribution of the hormone. (p. 379)

7. Explain why plant physiologists suspect that abscisic acid is the primary agent of geotropism. How does its effect on cells differ from that of auxin? (p. 379)

8. In terms of periods of darkness, explain the response differences of short-day and long-day plants. (pp. 381–382)

9. Briefly discuss the experimental evidence suggesting that night length is the important factor in flowering response. (pp. 382–383)

10. Explain the action of phytochrome in flowering. (p. 383)

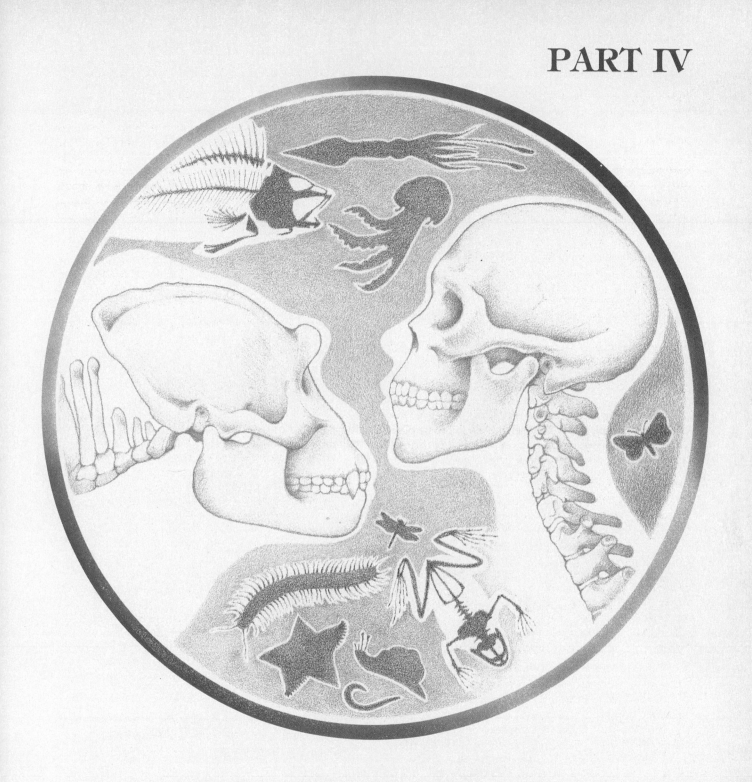

PART IV

Animal Adaptations

The Lower Invertebrates

27

What is an animal? This is one of those deceptively easy questions: almost anyone can come up with a quite useable answer, but probably no one can satisfy all of the experts. Animals are so varied that exceptions can be made to almost any proposed definition. For example, most animals move, have mouths, and eat things. If the trait of multicellularity were added, that would just about cover the animal kingdom. But, invariably, some creature would shout, "Not me!" One such exception is a very peculiar giant red tube worm that lives near the Galapagos islands. It lives near recently discovered vents in the ocean floor that spew mineral-laden water that is heated by the molten earth beneath (see Chapter 45). This creature has neither a mouth nor a gut, but derives its nourishment from bacterial symbionts living in its body. It doesn't move much; it just lies there, absorbing oxygen from sea water and hydrogen sulfide spewing forth from the vents. In almost every way, this creature is exempt from the animal kingdom. It's an animal, nevertheless.

Despite such exceptions, let's see if we can come up with a workable definition for the animal kingdom. We can probably cover *most* animals, at least for our purposes, with just seven criteria:

1. Animals are multicellular and eukaryotic.
2. Animals are heterotrophic; that is, they require food from other organisms.
3. Animals reproduce sexually, producing large, nonmotile eggs, and small, flagellated sperm.
4. Animals have a number of kinds of cells, tissues, and organs that carry out different functions.
5. Animals are essentially diploid throughout life. When meiosis occurs, the products develop directly into gametes. (Only the diploid cells undergo mitosis.)
6. Animals can respond rapidly to stimuli through well-organized nervous and muscular systems.
7. Animals hold themselves together with an extracellular connective-tissue matrix of *collagen*, a protein.

A PREVIEW OF THE MAJOR ANIMAL PHYLA

We are all generally aware of the major groups (or phyla) of the animal kingdom. The name of the phylum *Chordata* may have an unfamiliar ring to it, but it is our own. That's because the largest subgroup of this phylum is the **vertebrates**—animals with backbones. We share the phylum with a few **invertebrates** (animals without backbones) such as sea squirts and salps. It's perhaps a bit embarrassing to learn that you are rather closely related to species you've never heard of. But it may be even more disconcerting to learn that salps are tubelike, transparent, headless creatures of the open ocean.

We can find ourselves on more familiar ground with the insects, earthworms, and garden snails of the phyla *Arthropoda*, *Annelida*, and *Mollusca*, respectively. The roundworms that plague dogs are members of the phylum *Aschelminthes*, and should you ever host a tapeworm, it will be from the phylum *Platyhelminthes*.

If you have ever prowled a rocky coast, you may have looked into those fascinating little natural aquaria, the tidepools (pools left by a receding tide). Each is different, but any is likely to boast jellyfish (phylum *Coelenterata*); sea stars and sea urchins (phylum *Echinodermata*); and perhaps some lacy, branched bryozoans (phylum *Ectoprocta*). All of these abound in tidepools. Farther out at sea you might find a tiny transparent creature with rows of beating "combs" propelling it through the water. This would be a comb jelly (phylum *Ctenophora*). With that, we've named the 10 major animal phyla. (For a more formal listing of the animal phyla, see the Appendix.) Let's now learn how this amazingly varied kingdom got its start, and how it is being shaped by evolutionary forces.

ANIMAL ORIGINS

It seems clear that all existing plants, animals, and fungi sprang from the ancient protists. It is generally believed that the animal kingdom evolved from two different protist lines. One, a flagellate protozoan, produced the **Parazoa,** a subkingdom with only one phylum—*Porifera*, the sponges. The rest of the earth's animals (comprising the 10 major phyla just listed) are in the subkingdom **Metazoa,** all derived from a single ancestor which was, in turn, descended from a protozoan of some sort. There is a great deal of argument about the nature of this ancient creature. What was it like?

There are two leading hypotheses at the present time. One assumes that it was a flagellate protozoan, unlike any of those existing today. The other is that animals are derived from a ciliated protozoan, not unlike certain primitive multinucleate marine flatworms in the ocean today (Figure 27.1).

Unfortunately, we have no relevant fossil evidence at all—in fact, the oldest eukaryotic fossils (some 680 million years old) are clearly metazoans, jellyfish similar to those found today. Therefore, we now can only guess how the first multicellular

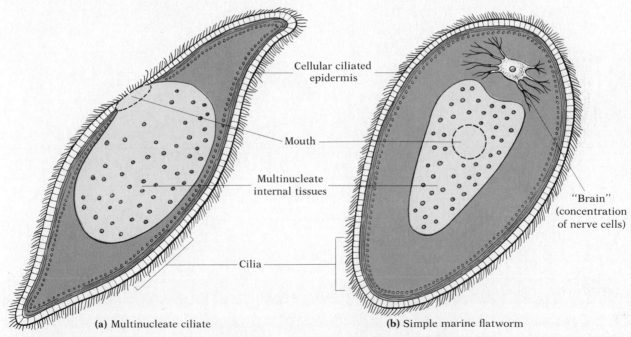

(a) Multinucleate ciliate   (b) Simple marine flatworm

27.1

According to one theory, the metazoans arose from multinucleate ciliates. One line of evidence is the similarity between **(a)** certain living multinucleate ciliates (protists) and **(b)** simple, ciliated, and multinucleate flatworms (metazoans). Much of the flatworm's body is noncellular, and it is also similar to the ciliate in feeding, food sources, behavior, physiology, and ecology. This is far from proof of the ciliate hypothesis of metazoan origins, but it is suggestive of how one phase of the transition might have occurred.

animal came to be. It is reasonable to assume that the transition to multicellularity was gradual, a continuum of small, sequential steps. Perhaps the key step was the aggregation of single-celled forms, with different individual cells becoming specialized for specific roles. The increasing coordination and interdependence of the cells eventually might have produced a sort of primitive multicellular animal.

Any such developments must have occurred in the ancient seas, among marine protozoans. Protozoans are already animal-like in that they engulf solid food particles, and all animals today have at least some cells with such ability. Protozoans and metazoans also have basically identical dietary requirements in terms of essential amino acids and vitamins, further evidence of a common ancestry.

The Early Fossil Record

The earliest known record, which appears to be fossil worm burrows, is estimated to be 700 million years old but the burrows' authenticity is still being debated. However, the oldest *unambiguous* animal fossil beds are found in rocks about 580 to 680 million years old. These rich beds, the *Ediacarian fauna* of southern Australia, include abundant fossils of jellyfish and worms (Figure 27.2). Interestingly, fossils in the extremely rich *Burgess Shale Formation* of western Canada represent all of the major living animal phyla and a number of extinct phyla as well (Figure 27.3). Yet the Burgess Shale Formation is estimated to be 570 million years old. This means that either the Ediacarian fauna is not representative of animals of that period, or most animal phyla

27.2

The fossil record indicates that Ediacarian fauna (animals) of the late Precambrian oceans probably was dominated by the thin-bodied coelenterates. Among these are **(a)** jellyfish—not unlike those seen today, and **(b)** stalked, featherlike corals, nearly identical to today's "sea pens." The bottom dwellers include several species of annelids **(c)**, the segmented worms, identified by lines crossing the body. Representatives from the jointed-legged animals, the arthropods **(d)**, are also present, as are a few shelled mollusks **(e)**. In addition, there are fossil animals of phyla that are now entirely extinct **(f)**. The egg-like mass at the left **(g)** is believed to be algae.

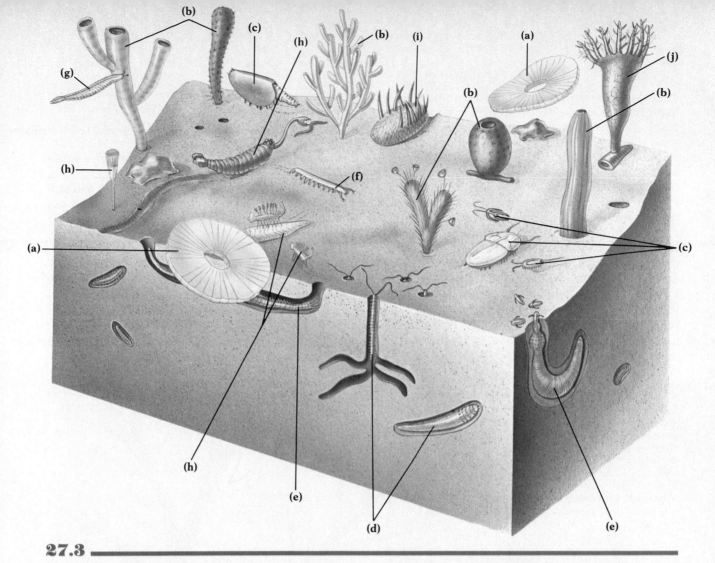

27.3

The Burgess Shale fauna includes some very familiar animals and others that are completely unfamiliar. The complexity of some forms suggests a long developmental period. The "pineapple slices" **(a)** are coelenterates, a group not as common here as in the earlier Ediacarian fauna. The large stalked animals are primarily filter-feeding sponges **(b)**, while the many-legged creatures scurrying across the ocean floor are obviously arthropods **(c)** (possibly ancestors of our crabs and lobsters). We also see tube-dwelling annelids **(d)**, the predecessors of today's marine worms and the familiar terrestrial earthworms. The large, wormlike creatures in the U-shaped burrows are pri-

apulids **(e)**, very similar to certain rare species that burrow in the ocean floor today. The appearance of the marine onychophoran **(f)** is almost indistinguishable from that of the very puzzling modern onychophorans, which are terrestrial species that have certain traits of two phyla—the annelids and the arthropods. Interestingly, the Burgess Shale fossils also include primitive chordates (our own phylum) that closely resemble today's *Branchiostoma* **(g)**. But there was a long road ahead. The first vertebrates appeared millions of years later. There are members of phyla not known today **(h)**, as well as a spiny mollusk **(i)** and an echinoderm **(j)**.

evolved at an incredibly fast rate—in no more than 10 to 100 million years.

There are still great voids in our knowledge of animal evolution. We have a tiny hypothetical ciliate representing the earliest animal, and then no real evidence until the relatively simple animals of the Ediacarian deposits, which were soon followed by the vast array of all existing phyla in the Burgess Shale Formation. And between these? Nothing. The Burgess Shale was a rare and lucky find, since the soft tissues of animals rarely fossilize. We can only await further discoveries.

PHYLOGENY OF THE ANIMAL KINGDOM

The history and relationships of animal phyla can be represented in what is called a **phylogenetic tree** that depicts one of several possibilities and shows the major milestones of animal evolution (Figure 27.4). Such trees are constructed from several kinds of information, including paleontology (the fossil record), and the comparative anatomy, physiology, and embryology of living animals.

The major branches of the tree represent the evolutionary events that produced the great variety of animals on earth today. The names shown in red reflect the two major divisions of animals: the **protostomes** ("first mouth") and the **deuterostomes** ("second mouth"). (These terms refer to the embryological origin of the mouth. We will cover these terms later, but for now, just keep in mind that such seemingly trivial embryological events as the development of the mouth can tell us a great deal about evolutionary history.) Notice that this sort of tree implies nothing about evolutionary *time*. However, nearly all of the major branches seem to have appeared rather suddenly (perhaps within tens of millions of years), at some time before the Burgess Shale deposits were formed.

LIMITED ORGANIZATION: THE PARAZOA

From an organizational viewpoint, most animals have achieved what is called the *organ system* level. Organ systems are collections of organs that carry out some major function or life process. Digestion, for example, occurs in the digestive system, a collection of various organs, including the mouth, gut (digestive tract), and liver. Such organs are, in turn, made up of various specialized tissues—groups of cells—performing specific tasks within the organs. For example, the tissues lining the gut specialize in secreting enzymes and absorbing digested food. So within most animals we have four levels of organization: cell, tissue, organ, and or-

27.4

One of several possible phylogenetic trees for animals. The tree does not reflect absolute durations of geological time, since all of the phyla are present in the richest Precambrian and early Cambrian fossil record. There is some disagreement as to whether the mesoderm-lined coelom originated once (a) or more than once (b).

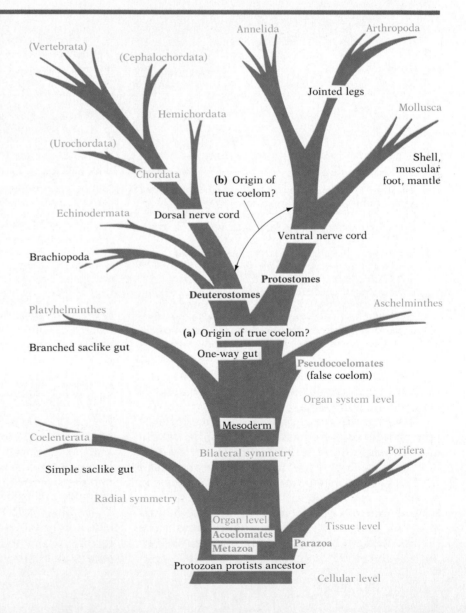

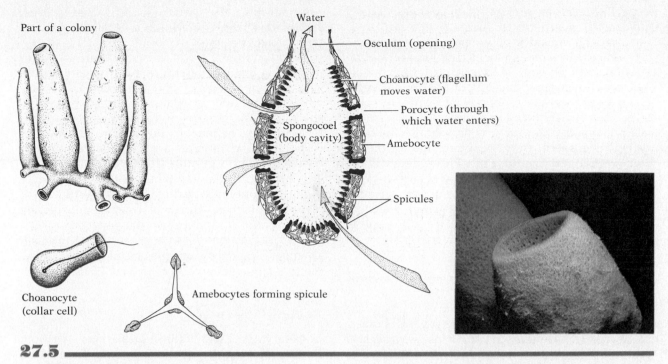

Part of a colony

Water

Osculum (opening)

Choanocyte (flagellum moves water)

Porocyte (through which water enters)

Spongocoel (body cavity)

Amebocyte

Spicules

Choanocyte (collar cell)

Amebocytes forming spicule

27.5

The vaselike sponges have reached a simple tissue-level organization. Thus, they lack organs or organ systems. The body wall is only two cell layers thick. The organism supported by calcereous (chalky) spic-ules. The vase sponge feeds by the choanocytes that line the body cavity, moving water. Currents of water, drawn in by the beating flagella, carry nutrients in the form of microorganisms and bits of organic debris.

gan system. One exception is the *Porifera*—the sponges. Essentially, they consist of just a few types of cells, loosely arranged into a tissue level of organization. But their very simplicity and limited organization make them interesting to compare with other animals.

Biology of the Sponges: Porifera

Sponges are primarily ocean dwellers, although a few species live in fresh water. They live unobtrusively, fastened securely to the ocean or lake bed, where they busily filter tiny food particles from the surrounding water. Sponges lack organized muscles and nerves, so they are incapable of rapid, whole-body responses. After a great deal of intense consideration, biologists have concluded that sponges are not particularly intellectual and probably are not even very aware of the nature of their surroundings (though, as with most species, they probably know all they need to know). Not surprisingly, early naturalists classified sponges as plants.

The simplest sponges are the **vase sponges** (Figure 27.5). Their hollow, vaselike bodies are just a few cell layers thick, and are composed of only four or five types of cells. Like all sponges, they feed by

filtering particles—mostly bacteria and other microscopic organisms—from the surrounding water. The food is carried past them by a current of water produced by the beating flagella of the *collar cells* (**choanocytes**) that line the inner body. (The water enters through pore cells called **porocytes**.) The *collar*, which gives the cell its name, consists of a ring of stiff cilia circling the base of the long flagellum. Food particles are trapped in mucus secretions on the collar cells, and are carried down to the base of the collar, where they are engulfed through phagocytosis and, later, digested in food vacuoles. The partly digested food is then transferred to wandering *amoeboid cells* (**amoebocytes**) that creep about the tissues, digesting the food further and distributing it throughout the body. The water that is brought in by the flagella also carries in oxygen. Carbon dioxide and waste products are carried away as the current exits through a large opening at the top, the **osculum**.

Sponges maintain their shape because of a kind of skeleton formed of **spicules**. Spicules are secreted by the amoeboid cells and, depending on the species, may be composed of chalk (calcium carbonate), glass (silicon dioxide), or *spongin*, a fibrous protein. The glassy sponge skeleton can be quite elaborate and beautiful. Some species with

391

spongin skeletons are the bath sponges, largely replaced by synthetic "sponges."

Now let's consider how an immovable animal reproduces. In some sponges, the sexes are separate. But other species are **hermaphroditic;** that is, the same animal produces both sperm and eggs. The eggs are stationary, lying just below the collar cells. They are fertilized by clouds of sperm from a neighboring sponge that are drawn into the body cavity. The sperm must penetrate the recipient's body wall to fertilize the eggs. The zygote will develop into a ciliated, swimming larva, which eventually will be carried away by ocean currents, finally to settle to the bottom, become attached, and mature into an adult.

THE METAZOANS

Metazoan animals have two basic types of bodies: those with *radial* symmetry, and those with *bilateral* symmetry. **Radial symmetry,** which is believed to have evolved earlier, is characterized by a cylindrical or spherical form. The body parts are arranged so that any radius extending from the center outward will pass through similar parts (Figure 27.6).

Only a few phyla today have radial symmetry. These include the **coelenterates** (the jellyfish, corals, hydroids, and sea anemones) and the **ctenophorans** (such as sea walnuts and comb jellies).

Echinoderms—the starfish (sea stars), sea urchins, and sand dollars—as adults, have a strange pentaradial symmetry (see Chapter 28).

All other animal phyla consist of bilaterally symmetrical animals. **Bilateral symmetry,** as its name suggests, creates right and left sides. The overwhelming number of bilaterally organized animal species may suggest to you that there are disadvantages in radial symmetry, but beware of such conclusions. Radial animals are well adapted to their niches and perform quite efficiently within them. The advent of bilateral symmetry in animal evolution undoubtedly led to the establishment of many new niches—different ways of utilizing existing resources. As you see, the key word is "different," not "better." As we proceed with the coelenterates, look for examples of how radial symmetry is quite suitable to their way of life.

Coelenterates

Coelenterates (also called **cnidarians**—phylum *Cnidaria*) barely rise above the tissue level of organization seen in the sponges, although some organ development is present. The coelenterate body is essentially a thin-walled sac, with an inner and outer tissue layer, each only one cell thick. Sandwiched between the two layers is an acellular, jelly-like *matrix*. The matrix may contain wandering amoeboid cells, nerve cells, and contractile fibers. The outer tissue layer is essentially protective,

27.6

The radially symmetrical body is essentially cylindrical. Thus, any sections that include the central axis are similar; that is, each radial division must cut through similar structures. Bilateral symmetry, on the other hand, indicates that the body can be divided in one plane only, one that produces mirror-image left and right halves. There are few examples of precise radial or bilateral symmetry. Thus, the designations are generalized and not to be interpreted too literally.

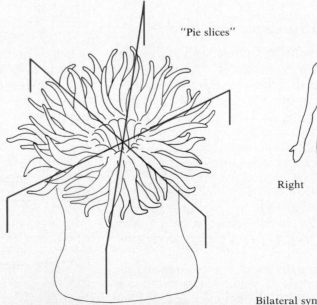

"Pie slices"

Right   Left

Radial symmetry in coelenterate (anemone)

Bilateral symmetry in the human, a chordate

Hydra, a freshwater coelenterate, feeds very much like its marine relatives. After paralyzing its prey **(a)**, its tentacles draw the victim into its gastrovascular cavity. Here, digestion commences **(b)**. Several kinds of cells line the gastrovascular cavity **(c)**. Various of these specialize in secreting enzymes, in engulfing particles through phagocytosis, or in moving currents of water with flagella. Digestion, then, begins in the cavity (extracellularly), and is completed after the food enters the vacuoles within. Wastes are expelled through the single opening.

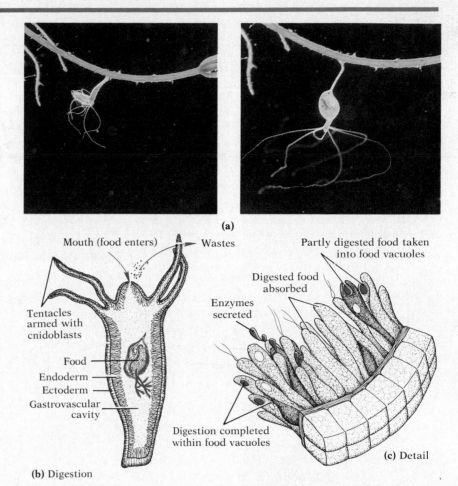

(a)

Mouth (food enters)

Wastes

Tentacles armed with cnidoblasts

Food

Endoderm

Ectoderm

Gastrovascular cavity

(b) Digestion

Partly digested food taken into food vacuoles

Digested food absorbed

Enzymes secreted

Digestion completed within food vacuoles

(c) Detail

while the inner one forms the lining of the saclike gut or **gastrovascular cavity.** (This cavity extends everywhere, even into the tentacles.) The body plan of *Hydra*, a freshwater coelenterate, will serve as an example (Figure 27.7).

Hydra, like most coelenterates, has tentacles that are armed with stinging cells called **cnidoblasts,** which are used in immobilizing prey and in defense. Cnidoblasts are curious structures. Each contains a **nematocyst,** a kind of coiled, poisonous harpoon at the end of a hollow thread.

Hydra are the terrors of their tiny world. Any small creature moving by triggers the *Hydra*'s stinging cells, and once it is immobilized, tentacles draw the stunned victim into the gastrovascular cavity. Since coelenterates are saclike, the opening serves both as mouth and as anus. Thus, the gastrovascular cavity serves as a two-way gut, since food and waste materials come and go through the same opening.

Once the victim is drawn inside the cavity, it will undoubtedly be impressed with the very specialized lining. Some gastrovascular cells produce digestive enzymes, others absorb digested food, some engulf whole food particles to be digested later in vacuoles, and still other cells have flagella with which they move particles around for greater ease of handling.

Hydra can move quickly and with coordination. If you touch it, it will immediately duck, drawing itself into a protective ball. Its rapid response and type of movement are made possible by contractile fibers that run both longitudinally and circularly.

A number of nerve cells control such responses. These nerve cells spread a netlike arrangement throughout the entire body. While there is no centralized nervous system or brain, the nerve cells are concentrated around the mouth and tentacles, with complex interconnections.

Other Coelenterates.   Two basic body patterns are found among the coelenterates, the **polyp,** or fixed and sedentary state (as in *Hydra*), and the **medusa,** a swimming jellyfish state. Interestingly, some groups alternate between the two body patterns, although one is usually the dominant or longer-lived state. In other groups, either the swimming medusa or the polyp state may be entirely absent. *Hydra,* for example, has the polyp state only. The organization of the coelenterates into their three classes is based principally on these factors.

Class Hydrozoa includes *Hydra,* along with many marine hydroids. The polyp is the dominant state. Typically, the tiny marine hydroids form highly branched colonies of polyps that feed on drifting plankton. Like *Hydra,* they produce new polyps on the sides of their bodies through an asexual process called *budding.* In sexual reproduction, the hydroids bud off tiny swimming medusae that produce gametes and release them into the water. Upon fertilization, the zygote develops into a swimming larva that later fastens to a rock on the ocean floor. It then goes through a period of development, emerging as a polyp (Figure 27.8).

The dominant stage in the second class, *Scyphozoa,* is the swimming jellyfish (medusa). It also releases its gametes into the water and produces a swimming larva. But this larva grows into a small, inconspicuous polyp that fastens to the underside of a rocky ledge and buds off young jellyfish that grow into adults.

Sea anemones and corals are in the third coel-

enterate class, *Anthozoa.* In this class, the polyp is dominant and the medusa state is entirely absent. Some anthozoans have a direct method of reproduction whereby the swimming larva grows right into an adult polyp. The anemones, common both in tidepools and in deeper waters, can live alone or in clusters that form through budding.

Many corals form massive colonies, constantly secreting limestone and forming awesome and beautiful coral reefs. Interestingly, although corals capture food with their tentacles, as is expected of a coelenterate, most of their food comes from photosynthetic organisms (usually dinoflagellates) living within their cells. (Representatives of classes Scyphozoa and Anthozoa are seen in Figure 27.9.)

The Comb Jellies

The ctenophorans ("comb carriers") should be mentioned because they appear to be closely related to the coelenterates. They differ in that all comb jellies are free-swimming, and their tentacles lack stinging cells. Instead, their tentacles are coated with sticky secretions from what are known as **glue cells.** These are used to trap plankton. Some ctenophorans produce an intriguing—and sometimes eerie—luminescence that makes their

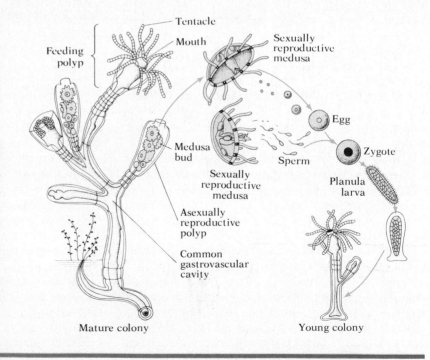

Feeding polyp — Tentacle — Mouth — Sexually reproductive medusa — Medusa bud — Sexually reproductive medusa — Sperm — Egg — Zygote — Planula larva — Asexually reproductive polyp — Common gastrovascular cavity — Mature colony — Young colony

27.8

Obelia, like many other hydroids, at some time forms polyps. These can specialize in either feeding or reproduction. The asexually reproductive polyps form swimming medusae, which quickly disperse. Mature medusae produce eggs and sperm that are released into the surrounding water, where fertilization occurs. The zygote develops into a ciliated larva called a *planula.* Eventually, the planula settles to the ocean bottom and begins its transition into adulthood. Then the cycle will be repeated.

27.9

(a) The jellyfish (class Scyphozoa) are free-swimming, trailing their stinging tentacles. A fish brushing against these will be stung until it is senseless, and then digested. (b) Jellyfish larvae enter a brief polyp state, where they bud off numerous young jellyfish.

(c) Coral polyps (class Anthozoa) are also colonial, with the many individual polyps secreting hardened calcareous walls around themselves. (d) The anemone (also class Anthozoa) is a polyp frequently found in shallower waters.

watery home actually glow. Some are quite large. In fact, one species, *Cestum* ("Venus' girdle"), looks like a glowing ribbon, nearly a meter long.

THE BILATERAL TREND AND THE VERSATILE MESODERM

The radial, hollow-bodied coelenterates with their two layers of cells may strike you as being quite different from what you expected of animals. If you feel this way, your thinking is right on track. In the groups to come we will not only encounter bilateral symmetry, but we will see vast changes in internal structure. Bodies become dense, true muscle tissue appears, and soon we will come to those metazoans who can boast of skeletons that hold them

erect, muscular hearts that pump blood, and centralized brains that integrate sensations and coordinate responses.

We can trace these more animal-like characteristics to important differences in the embryo. In the development of coelenterate embryos, only two types of embryonic tissue ever form. These tissues, or **germ layers,** as they are known, are the *endoderm* and the *ectoderm*. During development, the **endoderm** (inner skin) forms many internal linings, while the **ectoderm** (outer skin) is primarily involved in forming outer linings. But in the animals to come, we find a very important middle germ layer, the **mesoderm** (middle skin). And it is from the mesoderm that muscle, blood, and skeleton are derived. We see some evidence of the importance of mesoderm in our next phylum of animals, the group that includes flatworms.

Platyhelminthes: The Flatworms

With the **platyhelminthes,** or flatworms, we finally find animals with definite organ systems, and we can see how the mesoderm has increased their complexity (Figure 27.10). There are three major groups of flatworms, and we can't guarantee that you will be thrilled to learn about all of them. You may feel okay about the free-living Turbellaria, but the other two groups are parasites, including some that attack humans. They are the tapeworms (Cestoda) and the flukes (Trematoda).

Let's start on a cheerful note. Most streams and ponds are inhabited by **planarians,** fascinating little worms just a few millimeters long. Planarians, like other flatworms, have flattened, bilateral bodies. The planarian moves slowly by means of cilia on its ventral (belly) side, and it steers with well-coordinated and well-defined muscles. The nervous system of this creature is rather simple and

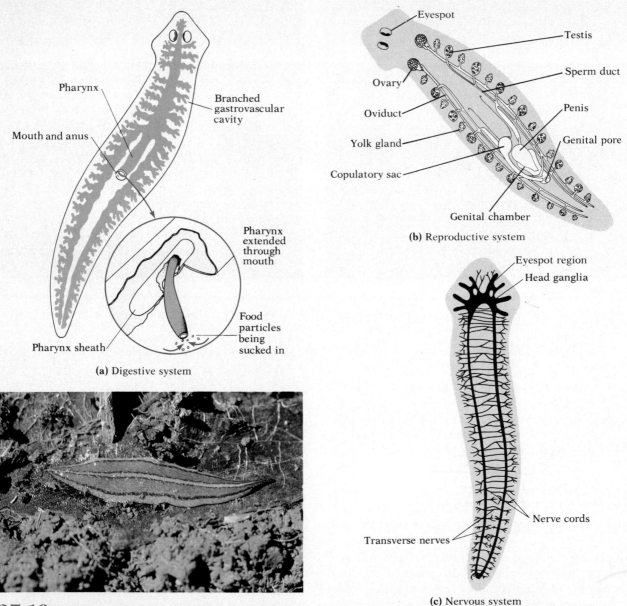

(a) Digestive system

(b) Reproductive system

(c) Nervous system

27.10

The apparent simplicity of a free-living planarian is highly deceptive. Within its tiny, flattened body are a number of complex organ systems that permit the animal to respond to stimuli, digest food, and reproduce. Digestion **(a)** occurs in a gastrovascular cavity, which, unlike the gastrovascular cavity of the coelenterates, is highly branched and includes a complex, muscular pharynx. The reproductive system **(b)** includes well-defined testes and ovaries, along with related ducts and yolk glands. Since it is hermaphroditic, it has both penis and vagina. Light-sensitive eyespots detect the direction of a light source, and the flatworm moves away, a ladderlike nerve network **(c)** coordinating its movement.

ladder-shaped, but here we see a major new evolutionary development. Most of the *neural ganglia* (masses of nerve cell bodies) are concentrated at the anterior (head) end. Two "eyespots" detect the presence and direction of light. This enables the vulnerable creature to remain in the darker and safer regions of its domain.

The planarian's digestive system is a highly branched gastrovascular cavity. But it is still a sac-like structure, with one opening. Nonetheless, it is rather specialized, with a protrusible pharynx (which means that the worm can extend its tube-like mouth out of its body). It uses its muscular pharynx like a vacuum cleaner hose, sucking up the juices and soft body parts of its prey.

The flatworm lacks a circulatory system, so oxygen and carbon dioxide must be exchanged through the skin. The thin, flattened body provides enough surface area for an efficient cell-to-cell exchange.

Although some systems in the flatworm are very simple, the reproductive system is surprisingly complex. Planarians are hermaphroditic. They all have well-defined testes and ovaries, as well as long ducts through which gametes travel. The penis can extend from the chamber in which it rests, and a *genital chamber* acts as a vagina. Planarians usually don't self-fertilize; instead, they democratically exchange sperm.

The Parasitic Flatworms

The parasitic flatworms—the tapeworms and flukes—are quite unlike the planarians. As is true of most successful internal parasites, their evolutionary specialization has led to a sometimes startling emphasis on some systems, while other systems have become reduced or have even disappeared. For example, the tapeworm, commonly found in its host's small intestine, has no gut whatsoever, but has a very complex and specialized head with suckers and grasping hooks that ensure a firm hold on the host's intestinal wall. It absorbs predigested food over its entire body surface, which is covered with tiny projections that increase the absorptive area. In a sense, the worm is inside out, with what amounts to a gut lining the outside.

With so many of life's daily problems solved, the tapeworm can devote much of its energy to reproduction. Its body, which may be several meters long, is composed of segments called **proglottids** that contain both ovaries and testes. The proglottids are continually produced just behind the creature's tiny head, or **scolex.** Each proglottid may contain thousands of eggs, and following fertilization (tapeworms can self-fertilize) the proglottids break off and are passed out with the feces. When they rupture, the eggs are released, ready to initiate a complex life cycle (Figure 27.11).

27.11

The tapeworm, a common intestinal parasite. The beef tapeworm of humans can grow to about 7 m (23 ft) in length, but the record is probably held by the broad (or fish) tapeworm of humans, which can exceed 18 m (60 ft).

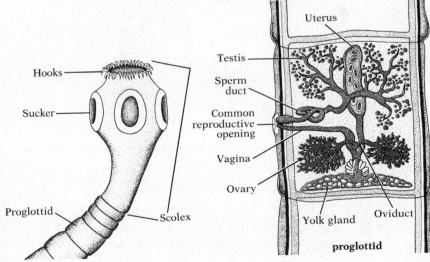

proglottid

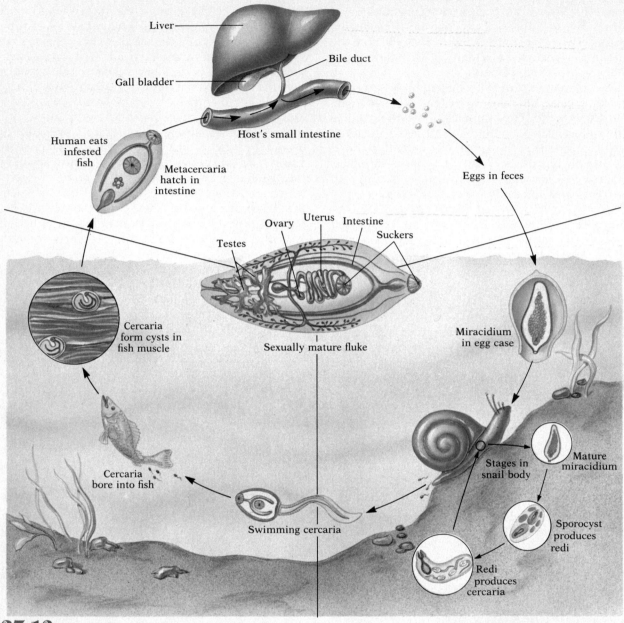

Liver

Bile duct

Gall bladder

Host's small intestine

Human eats infested fish

Metacercaria hatch in intestine

Eggs in feces

Testes

Ovary   Uterus   Intestine

Suckers

Cercaria form cysts in fish muscle

Sexually mature fluke

Miracidium in egg case

Cercaria bore into fish

Swimming cercaria

Stages in snail body

Mature miracidium

Sporocyst produces redi

Redi produces cercaria

27.12

The human liver fluke *(Chlonorchis sinensis)*, common in many Asian regions, lives in the bile passages of the liver, where heavy infestations can bring on cirrhosis and death. Its life cycle is one of the most complex known, requiring three separate hosts: human, snail, and fish. Its primary or sexual stage occurs in humans **(a)**, where the eggs are fertilized and the first of several intermediate stages, the *miracidium*, forms. The egg cases then pass into the intestine and out of the host with the feces. When the miracidia are eaten by a freshwater snail **(b)** (in rice paddies or other polluted waters), they hatch from the egg case and bore into the snail's tissues, forming *sporocysts*. The sporocyst then enters an asexual phase, producing numerous *redia*, each of which, in turn, produces many

swimming *cercaria*. The cercaria escape from the snail to seek out the next host, the fish **(c)**, whereupon they bore into its muscles and secrete protective capsules (cysts) around themselves. The encysted cercaria (or *metacercaria*) remain there until some hapless human eats the fish—raw or partially cooked. The digestive enzymes of the human host weaken the capsules and the young flukes emerge and make their way up into the bile duct to the bile passages of the liver. The cycle then repeats. You can probably see several ways in which the chain of infestation could be broken, the most obvious being to cook the fish. But customs of hundreds of generations of rural Asians are not so easily changed.

The life cycles of many parasites are extremely complicated. They may go through a number of physical changes and may inhabit a number of hosts. The timing and sequence of the changes must be precise, and a great deal is left to sheer luck. The odds against making it to that final host are so great that natural selection has dictated that each worm maximize the number of eggs it produces, leaving the rest to chance. For example, consider the life cycle of the human liver fluke, as portrayed in Figure 27.12.

BODY CAVITIES, A ONE-WAY GUT, AND A NEW BODY PLAN

Now let's review a few of the important evolutionary events that have proven to be key developments—changes that made possible new trends and directions, and altered life on this planet forever.

With the development of bilateral symmetry, a significant and probably simultaneous trend in body organization arose. Animals developed a leading, or head, end and a trailing, or tail, end. At first, the head may well have been simply a concentration of muscles, an adaptation for burrowing in the soft sea beds of ancient oceans, which is where the oldest fossils of bilateral animals are found. But leading ends soon became equipped with sensory structures for the detection of food, light, sound vibrations, and other stimuli. Such structures require neural support and integration, so, as we might expect, clusters of nerve cells were located close by in what would become the brain.

With the bilateral plan well established, newer, far-reaching evolutionary developments were in store. Two of these were to go hand-in-hand. One was the complete, tubelike, one-way digestive tract with a mouth, gut, and anus. So, with a gut inside a body wall, the body plan of these animals took on a tube-within-a-tube organization. Between the gut and the body wall—between the tubes—emerged a body cavity, known in its final form as the **coelom**. Apparently this organization was a huge success, paving the way for numerous modifications. Today, the vast majority of animals have retained the tube-within-a-tube plan.

Pseudocoeloms and the Roundworms

We have used the term *coelom* to refer to the space between the intestine and the body wall. Technically, a coelom must meet certain other criteria.

For example, a true coelom is lined entirely with mesoderm. However, in the roundworm this space only partly meets the usual criteria. Therefore, the roundworm's cavity is referred to as a **pseudocoelom** ("false coelom"). The body cavity of the roundworm develops from the space between two layers: the mesoderm and the endoderm. Furthermore, although the gut in roundworms is complete (that is, has both mouth and anus), it lies free in the fluid-filled pseudocoelom; also, its wall is not muscular and is usually only one cell layer thick, all conditions not typical of true coelomates. Let's consider a few of the pseudocoelomate phyla and the implications of their development.

The Biology of Roundworms and Rotifers (Phylum Aschelminthes)

Phylum Aschelminthes includes two important groups of pseudocoelomates that are vastly different: the **nematodes** (roundworms) and some tiny, almost microscopic animals that seem to have wheels, the **rotifers**.

The Nematodes. It's hard to believe that roundworms are either important or interesting, but they are both, as we shall see. The word *nematode* means "threadlike," a description that applies to most of the species. There are many species of roundworms and, surprisingly, they are all monotonously cylinder-shaped and tapered at both ends. Taxonomists have already described 10,000 of the estimated half-million species of nematodes, many of which are efficient predators, winnowing their way among moist soil particles, paralyzing prey with their saliva, or piercing them with mouth parts to suck their bodily juices (Figure 27.13).

Virtually all plants or animals are parasitized by one or more kinds of nematodes. Some of these parasites, in fact, have been devastating to agriculture, and at least 10 species are dangerous to humans. On the other hand, about 50 species live in or on our bodies without doing us apparent harm. But let's take a brief look at a particularly dangerous species, the giant *Ascaris lumbricoides*, which parasitizes humans (Figure 27.14).

Ascaris is an unusually large roundworm, often becoming longer than 20–35 cm (8–14 in). It is one of those repulsive parasites whose habits could be considered the stuff of nightmares. Its powerful sucking mouth, with which it grasps the host's intestinal wall, leads to a flattened, ribbonlike, but very simple gut, a tube that extends from the mouth to the anus. Thousands of these creatures can live in the intestine of one person.

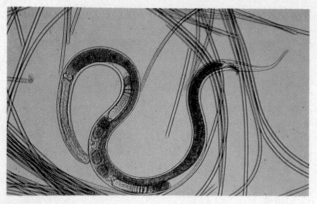

27.13

Nematodes are common in most soil, but abound in moist, fertile places. Many are scavengers or predators of soil organisms and are considered free-living, but a great number are agricultural parasites. Because of their minute size, the plant parasites can readily move throughout plant tissues, where they consume food reserves.

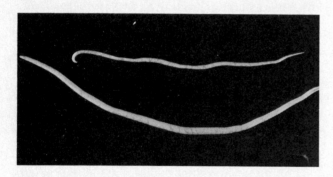

27.14

Ascaris lumbricoides, male and female. Female ascarid worms grow to 35 cm (14 in) in length, while the males are shorter and more slender. Males can immediately be distinguished from females by the presence of a curled tail with fine bristles emerging from the tip. The adults are commonly found in the small intestines of infected people and hogs. The *A. lumbricoides* of humans and *A. suum* of hogs are identical in their physical features, but they are apparently physiologically distinct species. They do not develop well in the wrong host.

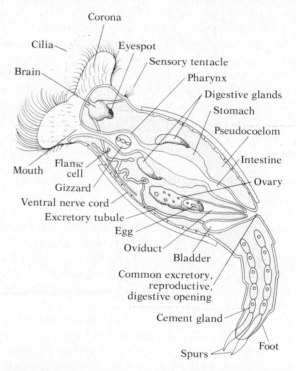

27.15

The rotifers are extremely common in fresh water. Although they are only about the size of many protists, the rotifers are far more complex. The digestive system is well developed, with definite organ specialization. Unique to the rotifers is the gizzard, a set of grinding structures in the pharynx. The nervous, excretory, and reproductive systems of these animals are also quite complex. Many rotifers have cement glands at the base of the body that secrete a sticky substance, permitting the animal to fasten itself, temporarily, to an underwater surface.

Like other parasitic worms, *Ascaris* is a prodigious reproducer, with mature females producing up to 200,000 eggs per day. The eggs pass out of the body with the feces, and new infestations occur when the eggs are accidentally swallowed. If you can't imagine this, it's probably because you haven't lived in places without toilets and haven't eaten vegetables from a garden fertilized with untreated "night soil." However, many of the earth's billions are parasitized by these creatures.

The Rotifers.   The rotifers are not parasites. But they are microscopic, and are often confused with the protists whose watery environment they share. They are interesting because in spite of their tiny size, they are distinctly more complex than other Aschelminthes (Figure 27.15).

Rotifers feed in a most unusual way. The double rings of cilia that circle their heads in a wheel-like manner (*rotifer* means "wheel bearer") sweep food into a grinding gullet, or gizzard. The rotifer's digestive system is unusually complex for such a small animal. Who would suspect that it has a muscular, grinding pharynx, a stomach, two digestive glands, an intestine, and an anus?

The reproductive system of the rotifer is even more unusual. Sexual reproduction is common among some rotifers, but usually they engage in an asexual process called **parthenogenesis**—the development of eggs without being fertilized by sperm. In some rotifers, such eggs are diploid, not having undergone meiosis, and the offspring produced are female—*exact* genetic replicas of their mothers. Environmental conditions seem to determine whether the daughters will reproduce asexually or sexually. Apparently, under stressful conditions such as drought, rotifers produce fertile males and females. If fertilization occurs, the zygotes lose water and form *cysts* (extremely resistant bodies). When the rains come, the cysts begin to develop. The world of rotifers is distinctly distaff; the males only occasionally add some genetic variability to an otherwise all-female population. It appears that many species lack males altogether.

We've learned something about the lives of a few of those often-neglected animals, the invertebrates. We may have also gained a new respect for their complexity, their life histories, and their place in the scheme of life. Such creatures sometimes are referred to as "primitive," but organisms cannot be classified in this way; only a particular trait can be described as *primitive* (retaining the ancestral condition of the group) or *advanced* (changed by evolutionary adaptation). We will soon see that there is no orderly progression toward "advanced" forms of life. Each type of animal is uniquely adapted to its role; it is likely to be very good at doing those things necessary to its own existence. It may survive quite well with traits we find trivial or unnecessary, and it may have no use whatsoever for ours. We will now proceed to other species, but these are only different—not necessarily more advanced or "better."

Summary

A Preview of the Major Animal Phyla

Animals are multicellular and eukaryotic; have various cells, tissues, and organs for specific functions; remain essentially diploid throughout their lives; possess well-organized nervous and muscular systems; and possess a connective-tissue matrix of collagen. They are heterotrophic and reproduce sexually. The animal kingdom is grouped into ten major phyla: Chordata, Arthropoda, Annelida, Mollusca, Aschelminthes, Platyhelminthes, Coelenterata, Echinodermata, Ecotoprocta, and Ctenophora.

Animal Origins

The animal kingdom probably arose from two protist lines: the Parazoa include only the sponges; the Metazoa include all other animals. Multicellularity may have developed from the aggregation of single-celled forms that, over time, developed specialized cells. Early fossil records in Australia and Canada suggest that, after the emergence of Ediacarian fauna, animal phyla evolved rapidly.

Phylogeny of the Animal Kingdom

A phylogenetic tree can be used to represent the evolutionary history and relationships of animal phyla. The two major divisions of animals are the protostomes and the deuterostomes, whose names refer to the embryological origin of the mouth.

Limited Organization: The Parazoa

Sponges (phylum Profera—the only phylum in the subkingdom Parazoa), while classified as animals, have attained only the tissue level of organization. They have no organized muscles or nerves and feed by filtering particles from water. They are hermaphroditic and can reproduce sexually or asexually.

The Metazoans

Metazoan animals such as coelenterates, ctenophorans, and the adult echinoderms possess radial symmetry, which is characterized by a cylindrical or spherical form. Animals with bilateral symmetry have distinct right and left sides in their body plans.

Coelenterates consist of three classes: Hydrozoa, Scyphozoa, and Anthozoa. They usually have stinging tentacles, two-way guts, polyp and medusa body patterns, and sexual and asexual reproductive capabilities. The ctenophorans, related to the coelenterates, have sticky tentacles rather than stinging ones.

The Bilateral Trend and the Versatile Mesoderm

Early metozoans develop from two types of embryonic tissue: the endoderm forming internal structures and the ectoderm forming protective outer layers. However, the other metazoans have a third layer—the mesoderm—that gives rise to muscle, bone, and blood tissue.

Flatworms possess true organ systems. Planarians are hermaphroditic and have a relatively organized neural ganglia, eyespots that detect light, and rather specialized gastrovascular cavities. Their flattened bodies are bilateral, with well-coordinated muscles. Tapeworms and flukes are parasitic flatworms that have poorly developed nerve, muscle, digestive, and circulatory systems but do possess highly complex reproductive systems.

Body Cavities, a One-Way Gut, and a New Body Plan

Animals with bilateral body plans have head ends that are equipped with sensory structures that detect stimuli. The development of head and tail ends includes a one-way digestive tract with mouth, gut, and anus. The gut is a tube within the larger tube of the body wall itself; in its final form, the area between the tubes is called the coelom.

Nematodes and rotifers are both pseudocoelomates but are vastly different. The numerous species of parasitic nematodes attack both plants and animals. Rotifers, on the other hand, are not parasitic. The microscopic organisms have a complex digestive system with pharynx, stomach, digestive glands, intestine, and anus. Rotifers can reproduce sexually, but more often use an asexual process known as parthenogenesis, in which eggs develop without being fertilized by sperm.

Key Terms

vertebrates	amoebocytes	gastrovascular cavity	platyhelminthes
invertebrates	osculum	cnidoblast	planarian
Parazoa	spicules	nematocyst	proglottids
Metazoa	hermaphroditic	polyp	scolex
phylogenetic tree	radial symmetry	medusa	coelom
protostomes	coelenterates	glue cells	pseudocoelom
deuterostomes	ctenophorans	germ layers	nematodes
vase sponges	echinoderms	endoderm	rotifers
choanocytes	bilateral symmetry	ectoderm	parthenogenesis
porocytes	cnidarians	mesoderm	

Review Questions

1. List seven characteristics of animals and note which, if any, are unique to this kingdom. (p. 386)

2. What is the theoretical basis for the division of animals into Parazoa and Metazoa? (pp. 387–388)

3. Make a general comparison between the Ediacarian fauna and Burgess Shale fossils. What do the estimated ages of these two fossil beds indicate about the rate of early metazoan evolution? (pp. 388–389)

4. List the four levels of organization seen in animals and cite examples of organisms that are limited to the three lowest levels. (pp. 390–391)

5. Describe the general body plan of sponges, listing the main types of cells and their functions. (pp. 391–392)

6. Using *Hydra* as an example, describe the general body plan of a coelenterate. Mention symmetry, body regions, and any specialized tissues and their functions. (pp. 392–393)

7. Describe the hydroid life cycle; mention feeding and asexual and sexual stages. (p. 394)

8. As a group, the flatworms exhibit three primary evolutionary innovations not seen in the coelenterates. Identify these, using the free-living planarian as an example. (pp. 396–397)

9. Briefly discuss the organization of the nervous, digestive, and reproductive systems in the planarian. Which system seems to have the most specialized structures? (pp. 396–397)

10. Briefly describe the basic body plan of the roundworm. Which of its characteristics do we see in the more complex animals? (pp. 399–401)

11. List three ways nematodes feed, and summarize the life cycle of *Ascaris*. Would you call the nematodes a successful group? Explain. (pp. 399–401)

The Coelomate Invertebrates

28

"Human beings are the most complex, the most advanced, and the most nearly perfect organisms on earth, just one cut above the majestic Indian elephant. Other animals are, by degrees, less advanced, less complex, and less perfect—which is to say, less and less human. Higher forms, such as birds and mammals, are more advanced—closer to perfection—than such lower forms as reptiles, fish, crabs, and worms."

We hope nothing so far has been touched by the reader's yellow marking pen. These were the basic notions of an ancient idea called the *scala naturae*, or the natural scale. Of course, they haven't a grain of truth in them, but somehow the idea has been subtly preserved, as is evident in the almost inescapable notion of "higher" and "lower" species, the higher ones being the ones that have more traits in common with humans. In actuality, each species of life on this earth is continually adapting to better utilize its own niche, and that niche may be quite different from our own.

We will now consider a second group of invertebrates. These are the ones that traditionally have been referred to as the higher invertebrates, but you already know our opinion on this. At the same time, it can probably be assumed that these species have a greater number of advanced traits than those discussed in the preceding chapter. An "advanced" trait is one that is considered to be more unlike those of ancestral organisms than a "primitive" trait (so a primitive trait more closely resembles those of the animal's evolutionary forebearers).

EUCOELOMATES AND A SEGMENTAL ORGANIZATION

The species we will consider here all have a true coelom, and so are referred to as **eucoelomates** (*eu*, true) (see Figure 27.4). The eucoelomates have a complex gut that is lined with digestive and absorptive tissue, surrounded by muscles, and covered by a smooth epithelium that permits free movement of the gut within the coelom. In most eucoelomates, the gut has specialized regions along its length. For instance, there are regions whose primary functions are grinding, swallowing, digesting, and absorbing food; there are others for the temporary storage of food, and yet others for the concentration of wastes. Such linear specialization permits food to be continuously processed, since, during a given time, food in different regions will be undergoing different stages of digestion (Figure 28.1). This arrangement is quite

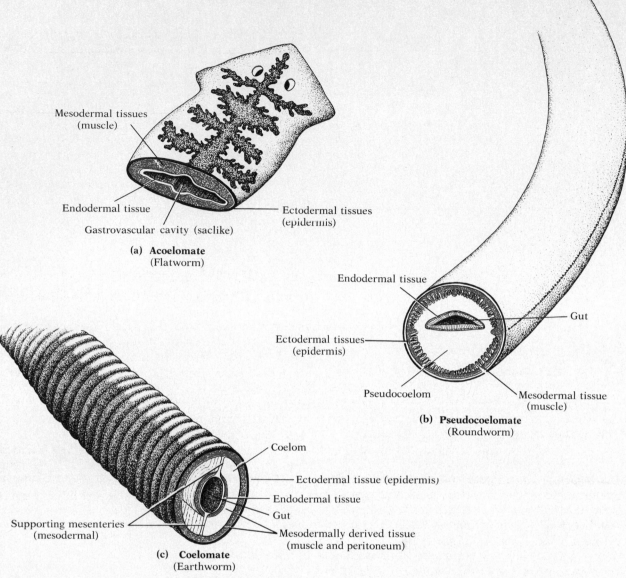

(a) Acoelomate
(Flatworm)

Mesodermal tissues (muscle)

Endodermal tissue

Gastrovascular cavity (saclike)

Ectodermal tissues (epidermis)

Endodermal tissue

Gut

Ectodermal tissues (epidermis)

Pseudocoelom

Mesodermal tissue (muscle)

(b) Pseudocoelomate
(Roundworm)

Coelom

Ectodermal tissue (epidermis)

Endodermal tissue

Gut

Supporting mesenteries (mesodermal)

Mesodermally derived tissue (muscle and peritoneum)

(c) Coelomate
(Earthworm)

28.1

The coelom is a mesoderm-derived and -lined body cavity between the gut and the body wall. Since it is lacking in the flatworms **(a)**, they are referred to as *acoelomates*. An extensive body cavity is present in the roundworms **(b)**, but it is designated as a pseudocoelom, since it does not contain the complete mesodermal linings found in the true coelom. In eucoelomates such as earthworms **(c)**, the body cavity is fully lined by mesodermally derived tissue, including the gut, which usually contains layers of muscle. The true coelom may have evolved independently more than once.

different from the saclike gastrovascular cavities of the flatworms and coelenterates.

Two Ways of Producing a Gut

The eucoelomate animals are divided into two groups according to the sequence of the embryonic development of the mouth and anus. We learned earlier that this embryonic distinction characterizes a great split in animal evolution that led to the formation of two major animal groups: the protostomes and the deuterostomes. We can translate the term protostome to "mouth first," and the term deuterostome to "mouth second." In both groups, the early embryo goes through a stage called the *blastula*, which resembles a hollow ball of cells. Soon, a small ingrowth of cells begins and the embryo progresses to its next stage, the *gastrula*. As the ingrowth—a process called *gastrulation*—continues, it produces a depression that deepens to

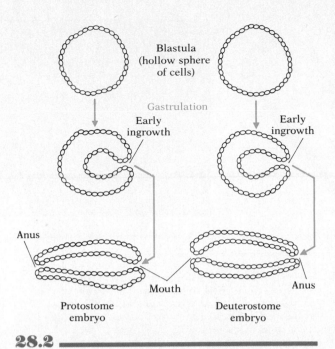

Blastula
(hollow sphere
of cells)

Gastrulation

Early
ingrowth

Early
ingrowth

Anus

Mouth

Anus

Protostome
embryo

Deuterostome
embryo

28.2

Gastrulation. During embryonic development, an ingrowth of cells occurs through a process called gastrulation, producing the first outlines of the gut. In the protostomes, the initial site of gastrulation becomes the mouth; in deuterostomes, this early ingrowth marks the future site of an anus.

form, this means that the body was organized into serially repeated units or segments, as seen in the centipede and earthworm. Each segment is divided from the next by transverse **septa** or cross walls, and the structures within each are more or less repeated. In some cases, the basic segmentation has been modified to such a degree that it may be difficult to see (or absent). For example, the segmentation in humans is relegated to repeated vertebrae, ribs, spinal nerves, and trunk muscles. Actually, many zoologists believe that segmentation arose independently in the protostomes and deuterostomes.

SEGMENTED WORMS: THE ANNELIDS (PHYLUM ANNELIDA)

Earthworms are commonly considered representative of the **annelids,** but that's only because they're easy to catch. The vast majority of annelids are **polychaete worms** that live in the sea. Typical polychaetes (Figure 28.3) are the sedentary, filter-feeding *fan worm* and the active, predatory *clam worm.* Both marine and terrestrial annelids have highly segmented bodies.

The earthworms are **oligochaetes** ("few-bristled ones"), which are land-dwelling worms. Another group of annelids are the **hirudinians** (leeches), external blood-sucking parasites that inhabit moist or swampy environments.

The Earthworm

Most of the organ systems are well developed and complex in the earthworm (Figure 28.4). The segmented body contains well-developed muscle layers, the coelom is fluid-filled, and the fluid is under pressure, which provides a firmness that helps with movement and maintenance of body form. As in all protostomes, the nervous system includes a **ventral nerve cord** that extends along the entire body, below the intestine. Two large **ganglia** (nerve cell clusters) make up the brain—which, as in all annelids, arthropods, and mollusks, is above and below the esophagus.

The earthworm's muscular, tubelike digestive system includes several unusual specializations. For example, the **typhlosole,** a large fold in the gut wall, aids digestion and absorption by greatly increasing the surface area. The excretory system, which is responsible for removing nitrogenous wastes and for water regulation, consists of paired, funnel-shaped **nephridia** that clear the wastes

form a saclike gut. In order for the tube-within-a-tube arrangement to develop, a second opening forms much later. In the protostomes, the first depression marks the future location of the mouth, and the second opening becomes the anus. However, in the deuterostomes things are reversed. The first opening marks the future anus, and the second opening marks the mouth (Figure 28.2). Because of this significant difference in development, biologists are reasonably certain that the two groups evolved quite independently from different, sac-gutted ancestors.

The protostomes primarily include the annelids, arthropods, and mollusks, which together make up the vast majority of today's named animal species. The deuterostomes include the numerous, successful echinoderms, plus a few minor phyla such as the chaetognaths, lampshells, and bryozoans, and the group that includes humans: the chordates.

The Segmented Body

Along with the development of the coelom and the linearly specialized digestive system, some eucoelomates achieved a third evolutionary milestone: the **segmented body plan.** In its simplest

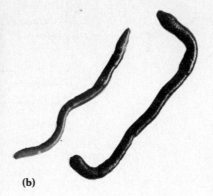

28.3

The most diverse and numerous of the annelids are the polychaete worms. Many, like the fan worms seen here **(a)**, are tube dwellers that use feathery devices in feeding and respiration, popping them in and out of their tube houses. The oligochaetes—terrestrial annelids—lack complex outer structures that would complicate their burrowing activities. Segmentation, a prominent annelid characteristic, is readily seen in the earthworm **(b)**. Hirudineans **(c)** specialize in ecto-parasitism (external parasitism), using their sucker devices to attach to the host animal. Their mouth-parts include three razor-sharp lancets, used in piercing the host's tissues, and salivary glands that secrete an anticoagulant. The stomach contains highly expandable pouches that become engorged with blood as the leech feeds. In years past, leeches were used in the archaic medical practice of "bleeding" the sick, and up to a few years ago, they were sold in pharmacies for the removal of such discolorations as black eyes and bruises.

from the coelomic fluid in each segment. Cell-by-cell diffusion of food and gases, which was quite sufficient in the smaller and simpler invertebrates, does not work in the comparatively dense body of the earthworm. Here we encounter, for the first time, an efficient circulatory system. Furthermore, it is a *closed* system, like our own. This means that blood remains within vessels rather than percolating through open cavities and sinuses, as it does in many other invertebrates. Since the blood contains hemoglobin, it is red, like ours. The blood is pumped through five pairs of "hearts" or **aortic arches,** which send it coursing through large blood vessels that branch into dense beds of finer vessels called **capillaries.** The capillaries, passing through the thin, moist skin, permit oxygen to diffuse into the blood and waste carbon dioxide to diffuse out. The capillaries also provide the deeper tissues with food and oxygen.

The earthworm's reproductive system is quite well developed. Although the sexes are separate in many of the marine annelids, earthworms are hermaphroditic, with each individual possessing both testes and ovaries. Earthworms mate by lying head to tail and exchanging sperm. The sperm are stored in **seminal receptacles** until the eggs become mature and ready to be passed over the receptacles.

A REMARKABLE SUCCESS STORY: THE ARTHROPODS (PHYLUM ARTHROPODA)

No one has any idea how many species of arthropods there are, but the most respected guesses range between 800,000 to 1,000,000. In any case, Arthropoda is the most successful phylum on earth.

What is an **arthropod?** *Arthropod* means "jointed foot," so arthropods have jointed feet. They are also segmented, but their segments are not the simple repeating units characterizing the earthworms. Instead, the segments may be specialized and modified for different tasks. Arthropods have exterior skeletons **(exoskeletons)** covering their bodies. The exoskeleton is made up of *chitin*, a dense, flexible carbohydrate. (In aquatic species, it is often hardened with calcium salts; while in insects, it is hardened with various organic substances.)

The Arthropods Today

Arthropods have been incredibly successful in their expansion over the earth, sometimes establishing very narrow ecological niches. (Consider

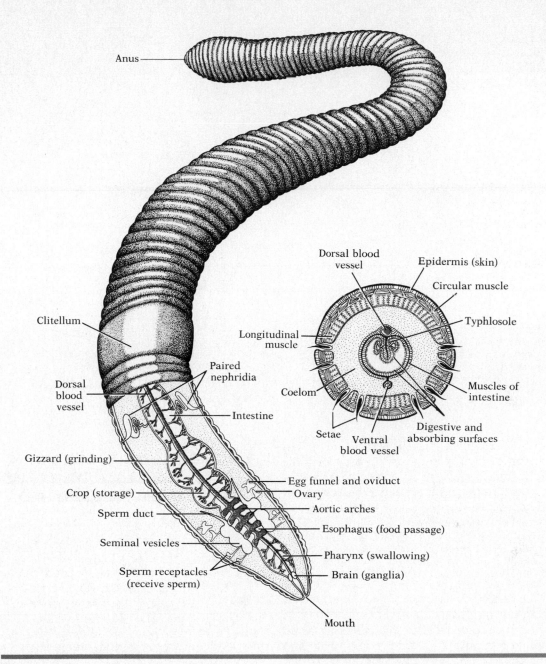

Anus

Clitellum

Dorsal
blood
vessel

Gizzard (grinding)

Crop (storage)

Sperm duct

Seminal vesicles

Sperm receptacles
(receive sperm)

Paired
nephridia

Intestine

Egg funnel and oviduct

Ovary

Aortic arches

Esophagus (food passage)

Pharynx (swallowing)

Brain (ganglia)

Mouth

Dorsal blood
vessel

Epidermis (skin)

Circular muscle

Longitudinal
muscle

Typhlosole

Coelom

Muscles of
intestine

Setae

Ventral
blood vessel

Digestive and
absorbing surfaces

28.4

Most organ systems in the earthworm are quite complex. Note the prominent segmented body plan. The
body wall contains circular and longitudinal muscle
groups that are used in extending and contracting the
body. The transport of food, oxygen, and carbon dioxide is carried out by a closed circulatory system that
includes five paired "hearts" and an extensive system
of blood vessels and capillaries. The muscular gut,
which is suspended in the coelom, contains several
specialized regions (the pharynx, esophagus, crop, giz-

zard, and intestine) for the continuous processing of
food. Earthworms are hermaphrodites. The copulatory
structures are simple, consisting of pores in the body
wall. Following fertilization, the eggs are enclosed in a
cocoon of slime, which is produced by the clitellum.
The nervous system consists of a pair of enlarged ganglia (clusters of neurons) above and below the esophagus, and a lengthy ventral nerve that gives rise to
ganglia in each segment (not seen here). Nearly all
segments contain paired nephridia.

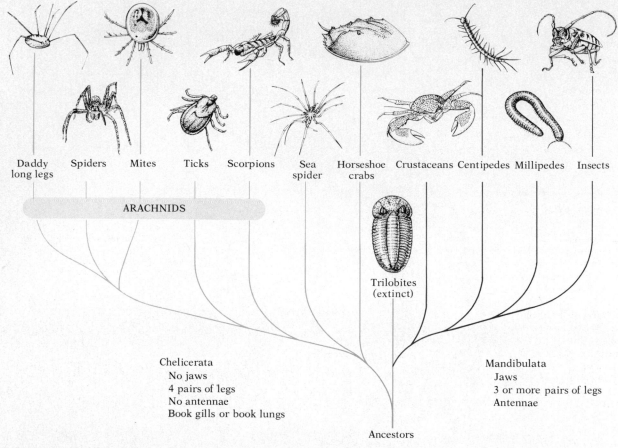

Daddy long legs Spiders Mites Ticks Scorpions Sea spider Horseshoe crabs Crustaceans Centipedes Millipedes Insects

ARACHNIDS

Trilobites (extinct)

Chelicerata
No jaws
4 pairs of legs
No antennae
Book gills or book lungs

Mandibulata
Jaws
3 or more pairs of legs
Antennae

Ancestors

28.5

The immense arthropod phylum contains two sub-phyla: the jawless *Chelicerata*, and the jawed *Mandibulata*. The jawless arthropods include horseshoe crabs and sea spiders, along with the several types of arachnids. Most have four pairs of walking legs, and lack antennas and compound eyes. The spiders bite with venomous, clawlike chelicerae. The man-

dibulates, outnumbering the chelicerates by far, include the familiar crustaceans and insects whose species number in the hundreds of thousands. Mandibulates are equipped with jaws (mandibles), and usually have three pairs of walking appendages, paired antennas, and compound eyes.

the mayfly, a delicate creature that emerges as an adult without mouthparts and must mate and leave offspring in the few precious hours of life allowed it; or strange green insects that live only on year-round alpine glaciers). In fact, arthropod niches are often so specialized that many species can live in very close association without seriously competing with each other.

Arthropods include omnivores, herbivores, filter feeders, carnivores, scavengers, ectoparasites, endoparasites, and even a few opportunistic cannibals. How did they become so successful? For one thing, the use of jointed limbs was an immediate evolutionary success. Limbs were subject to all sorts of modifications that could eventually permit crawling, burrowing, jumping, grasping, feeling,

and even hearing. The mouthparts themselves are derived from jointed appendages, and are also extremely specialized, modified for such actions as biting, chewing, sucking, stinging, or lapping.

Through such diversity the arthropods became able to exploit just about every resource on earth. The development of wings in the insects greatly increased their ability to disperse and to exploit previously unavailable niches. And we must not forget the phenomenal reproductive capabilities of this group. In addition, some species produced *larvae* whose diet was entirely different from that of the adults. This not only resulted in a subdivision of the niche, but also helped to preclude parent-offspring competition.

Arthropod Diversity

Since there is no concise way to deal with the enormous diversity of arthropods, we'll have to pick and choose a few examples. The living arthropods are traditionally divided into two huge subphyla, the **Chelicerata** and the **Mandibulata** (Figure 28.5). The Chelicerata include the *arachnids* (spiders, scorpions, and others), the *sea spiders*, and the *horseshoe crabs*. The Mandibulata include the *crustaceans*, *cen-tipedes*, *millipedes*, *insects*, and a number of minor groups (Figure 28.6). Some scholars claim that the remaining mandibulates are actually three unrelated phyla that are lumped together only because of convergent evolution. In any case, we'll concentrate on just three arthropod classes: the arachnids, the crustaceans, and the insects.

The Arachnids: Spiders and Their Relatives. Subphylum Chelicerata includes the **arachnids:**

28.6

Typical mandibulates. Crustaceans such as the Jonah crab **(a)** are primarily aquatic. Most mandibulates are insects. Wasps **(b)** are predators, while grasshoppers **(c)**, such as the large lubbers seen here, are strictly vegetarians. **(d)** Ants and aphids often live as commensals, a form of symbiosis in which both members benefit. Some aphid species **(e)** are unusual in that they sometimes lay eggs but at other times are live bearers, giving birth to developed young. Typically, the carnivorous mantis **(f)** remains motionless, blending into its surroundings while awaiting prey. The delicate, short-lived mayflies **(g)** spend most of their lives in a nymph state, living as adults for just a few hours.

spiders, scorpions, ticks, mites, and daddy long-legs. All arachnids have six pairs of appendages, the first being the **fangs** or **chelicerae**. These are followed by sensory **pedipalps,** and then by four pairs of legs.

Spiders are carnivores, but they lack jaws and must suck in their foods. Typically, a spider first injects venom into its prey's body to kill or paralyze it, then it pumps in digestive enzymes that liquify the prey's tissues. Spiders breathe by **book lungs,** essentially sacs with slits that open to the outside. The sacs are lined with flattened folds that resemble the pages of a book. Blood passing through the thin sheets exchanges gases with air in the sac.

Nearly all spiders have silk-producing glands connected to external appendages called **spinnerets.** The system is used to form both the web and cocoon (Figure 28.7). There are several kinds of silk, formed from a protein known as *fibroin.* Each kind of silk has a particular function: webs may have sticky, prey-snaring parts, and safe, dry parts along which the spider can run. (It wouldn't do to become entangled in one's own web.) The events that first led to snaring prey in a web of coagulated protein must have opened up an entirely new (and highly profitable) range of ecological niches which, by now, have been exploited and elaborated in every conceivable way.

The Crustaceans.   Most species of **crustaceans** are aquatic, and are common in both marine and fresh waters. This class includes crabs, shrimp, crayfish, and lobsters, as well as terrestrial wood lice (also called *sow bugs*). Crustaceans range in size from the microscopic freshwater *ostracods* to the gigantic *king crabs* of cold Pacific waters. As they grow, all arthropods must periodically discard their hardened exoskeleton through **molting,** replacing it with a larger one.

Typically, crustaceans breathe through gills that are covered by the tough exoskeleton. Blood continuously flows through delicate, feathery gills, releasing carbon dioxide and taking in oxygen. Crustaceans often have highly developed sensory structures. Interestingly, the general plan of the arthropod nervous system is similar to that of the earthworm and the mollusk: a "brain" surrounding the esophagus, and paired, solid, ventral nerve cords with paired ganglia at intervals.

Among the most specialized of the crustacean sensory structures are the **compound eyes,** which are often borne on flexible stalks. The crustacean eye is similar to that of an insect, composed of a large number of visual units called *ommatidia.* Each ommatidium has a tough, transparent lens, and pigmented, light-sensitive receptors (retinal cells) (Figure 28.8). With this arrangement, the animal obtains a nearly 360-degree view of its surroundings, though this "view" may be a shimmering mosaic of light and dark colors—quite different from the images we see.

The Insects.   The crustaceans are the dominant, or most prevalent, arthropods in the sea, but **insects** dominate the land, both in number and in kind. Insects are of such ecological and economical

28.7

Most spiders have silk glands that are associated with external appendages called spinnerets. Many, like the orb spider, produce several kinds of silk, including a sticky thread used in trapping prey, and a dry type, upon which the spider can safely walk. When alerted, the spider darts quickly across its web, each of its eight legs deftly avoiding its own sticky traps.

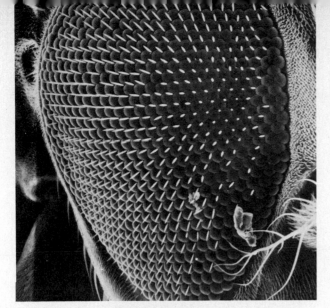

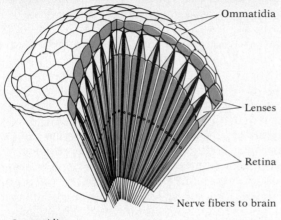

Ommatidia

Lenses

Retina

Nerve fibers to brain

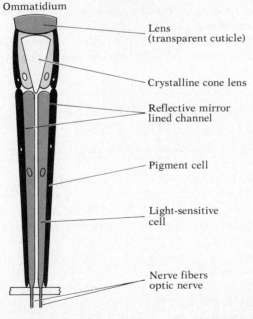

Ommatidium

Lens
(transparent cuticle)

Crystalline cone lens

Reflective mirror
lined channel

Pigment cell

Light-sensitive
cell

Nerve fibers
optic nerve

28.8

The compound eyes of crustaceans and insects consist of many individual light-receiving units called ommatidia.

importance that we literally could not have reached our own place in nature without understanding something about them. One reason is that we must continuously compete with them, and we don't always win. There are a great many humans who go hungry because their food is eaten or ruined by insects, and many live debilitated, shortened lives, victims of insect-borne diseases such as malaria, typhus, and African sleeping sickness. It is indeed a high price to pay to be able to share the planet with the butterflies.

The segmented body of insects as we know them today (Figure 28.9) has undoubtedly changed considerably from the ancestral form. For one thing, many of the segments have become fused. Segmentation in many adult insects is readily apparent only in the abdominal region. Typically, there are three body *regions:* the **head, thorax,** and **abdomen.** The sensory structures—the eyes, antennae, and sensory palps—are concentrated in the head region. The thorax gives rise not only to three pairs of legs, but commonly to two pairs of wings.

The wings of insects are thin, chitinous sheets, moved by powerful muscles in the thorax on elaborate, levered hinges. Wing movement in some insects is incredibly rapid. Fruit flies, for example, can maintain a continuous beat of 300 strokes per second for as long as two hours. And the 1000 wing beats per second of the tiny midge has animal physiologists stymied, since the neural impulses the midges generate travel far too slowly to support such rapid muscle contraction. Apparently the muscles can contract more than once when stimulated by a single neural impulse.

Insects exchange gases with the environment by admitting air into a complex system of tubes (the *tracheae*) that pass throughout the body, branching to produce ever finer passages that finally end blindly. The air enters through valvelike body openings called *spiracles*.

There is enormous variety among the specialized insect mouthparts. For example, the mouthparts of grasshoppers are suited for tasting, shearing, and chewing. Moths have long sucking mouthparts that they coil neatly when not in use. Mosquitos have piercing and sucking mouthparts, as we are all aware, while the crass housefly salivates on its food, stirs it with its bristled tongue, and then sucks up the resulting mess. Carnivores, such as the dragonfly and praying mantis, have strong tearing jaws with which they dismember any hapless insect they can catch. Female praying mantises regularly devour their lovers even while they mate.

411

28.9

The insect body (represented here by the grasshopper) consists typically of three regions: the head, thorax, and abdomen. While segmentation is prominent in the abdomen, it is obscured in the head and thorax, where a considerable amount of fusion usually is seen. Sensory structures on the head include both compound and simple eyes, paired antennas, and sensory palps (for tasting and detecting texture) in the mouthparts. The thorax region produces the three pairs of walking legs, and in the flying insects, usually two pairs of wings. Spiracles, located along the thorax and abdomen, admit air into the insect tracheal system. The last abdominal segments contain reproductive structures, which are often quite specific to each species. In the female grasshopper seen here, the ovipositor is used to dig into the soil where the eggs are laid.

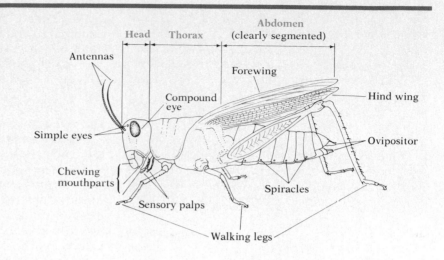

The insect digestive system includes three parts: the **foregut, midgut,** and **hindgut** (Figure 28.10). Food is digested in the midgut and then moves to the hindgut, where water is removed and fecal wastes are concentrated. The area where the midgut and hindgut join receives metabolic wastes from the excretory system, which consists of numerous hairlike structures known as *Malpighian tubules.*

Insects, like other arthropods, have an *open* circulatory system. The main dorsal blood vessel has several contractile areas called "hearts." Openings in the vessel allow blood to be drawn in from the surrounding spaces and then pumped along by the vessel's contractions. But the blood soon leaves the vessels and is pumped into sinuses and cavities. From here it sluggishly percolates through the tissue and back to the dorsal vessel.

The insects' reproductive adaptations contribute significantly to their success. The life span is typically short, but many species compensate by quickly producing incredibly large numbers of offspring. (A female housefly has the potential to leave over five trillion descendants in just seven generations, or one year's time!) In addition, each of the four parts in the life cycles of many insects has its own adaptive significance. The **eggs** are often well concealed and resistant. The **larva** and adult often utilize entirely different food sources, so they are not in direct competition. The **pupa,** quietly passing through its *metamorphosis* into **adulthood,** lives on food stored in the larval stage. Egg and pupa often survive the winter in dormant states.

Females of many insect species use an **ovipositor,** a hollow appendage used to dig or bore holes into which they lay their eggs. The reproductive appendages of insects are often quite complex. The penis, for example, may look a bit like an instrument of torture, with angles, hooks, and barbs. But the male's penis will fit the genital opening of females of only one species: its own. This would obviously discourage mating attempts between similar but different species.

SHELLS AND A MUSCULAR FOOT: THE MOLLUSKS (PHYLUM MOLLUSCA)

The earth is burgeoning with **mollusks.** In fact, we already know of about 100,000 species, which makes them third only after the arthropods and nematodes. And, like the arthropods, the mollusks are a highly diverse phylum (Figure 28.11). Some mollusks are minute—tiny, inconspicuous creatures huddled in fragile shells—but others are truly giant. The North Atlantic squid, for example, may reach a length of 18m (60 ft).

The fossil history of mollusks goes back to the Cambrian period. Interestingly, the earliest fossils include an ancestral form very similar to *Nautilus,* a living shelled cephalopod. In fact, it seems that the Cambrian fossils include at least twenty times the number of mollusk species that now exist. The presence of these and other complex invertebrates in the very oldest true fossil animal records demonstrates the total inadequacy of geological and paleontological evidence in tracing the dim origins of invertebrate phyla. We must assume that most of the important events in invertebrate history occurred in the millions of years preceding the Cambrian period.

In many ways, the mollusks are a phylogenetic puzzle. For example, they show little, if any, evidence of segmentation, and the size of the coelom is so reduced that some scholars deny that mollusks have ever been coelomate animals, and hold that the mollusks share very little of their evolutionary history with the other protostomes.

Many biologists, however, believe that the mollusks are simply highly specialized relatives of the annelids and the arthropods. They note strong similarities in the earliest embryonic stages of mollusks and annelids, and in the nervous systems of all three groups.

Modern Mollusks

There are four major classes of mollusks and several minor ones. The major classes are the *chitons*, the *gastropods* (snails), the *bivalves* (clams and their relatives), and the *cephalopods* (octopuses and squids). As would be expected, no class of living animals conforms entirely to any simplified, generalized mollusk body plan. But all mollusk classes include at least some species with the basic molluscan characters: a muscular **foot,** a **shell,** a **mantle** and **mantle cavity,** and featherlike external **gills.** Except for the bivalves, most mollusks have a highly specialized feeding device, the rasplike **radula,** which is found in no other phylum.

All of these basic parts, however, have been subjected to intense evolutionary modification, and they may differ greatly from one group to the next (see Figure 28.11). In some cases, a part may even be entirely absent. The shell of most mollusks is secreted by a soft, underlying mantle. These secretions produce the smooth, often iridescent "mother of pearl" inside the shell. Pearls themselves are secreted to cover grainy irritants lodged in the mantle.

Chitons. The **chitons** (see Figure 28.11a) are perhaps the least modified of the major groups of mollusks. That is, this class has changed relatively

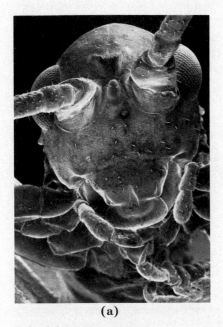

(a)

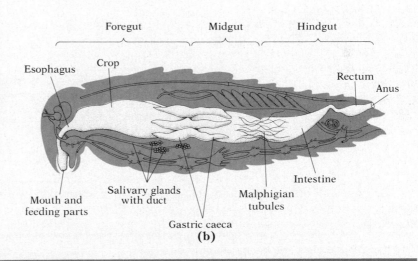

Foregut   Midgut   Hindgut

Esophagus Crop

Rectum

Anus

Mouth and feeding parts

Salivary glands with duct

Gastric caeca

Malphigian tubules

Intestine

(b)

28.10

(a) The grasshopper's chewing mouth is nicely adapted for eating foliage. The two sets of palps contain taste receptors for identifying food. Initial biting and tearing are done with large mandibles, while the paired maxillas do more delicate shredding and manipulating. The labrum and labium help in holding and positioning food. **(b)** The insect digestive system. The grasshopper's foregut contains an enlarged crop that stores food and grinds it through the action of its abrasive lining. The gastric ceca, fingerlike pouches, secrete digestive enzymes into food entering the midgut. Following digestion and absorption in the midgut, wastes are concentrated in the hindgut. Hairlike Malpighian tubules, which constitute the excretory system, remove nitrogenous waste from the coelomic fluid, convert it to uric acid, and deposit it into the gut for removal with the digestive wastes.

413

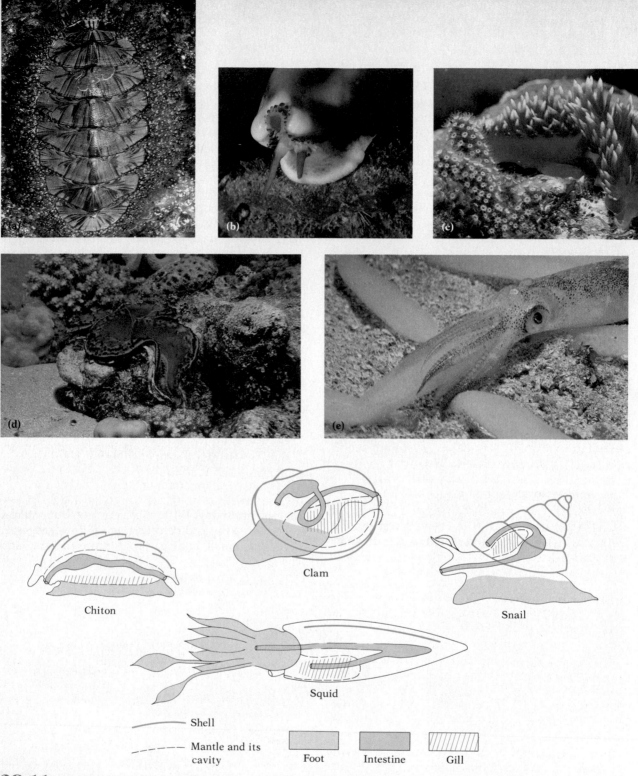

Chiton

Clam

Snail

Squid

Shell ———

Mantle and its
cavity — — — —

Foot   Intestine   Gill

28.11

Variations of the basic molluscan plan are seen in
these representatives. The body plan of the chiton (a),
with the simple foot, repeated gill structures, and
eight-part shell, is considered primitive. Snails (b)
have a relatively simple foot, but the body takes on a
helical form as the animal matures. Along with the
closely related slugs (c), they have adapted to marine
and freshwater environments and have successfully invaded the land. Clams (d) are sedentary bivalves that
dig into the bottom and filter their food from the water. The squid (e) and octopus are perhaps the most
highly specialized mollusks, having changed drastically from the ancestral type. The external shell is
gone, and the foot has been subdivided into eight tentacles. The mantle is modified into a propulsive device. They are comparatively big-brained predators,
with acute vision, rapid movements, and, often, complex behavior.

little from the ancestral condition. The chiton's eight-part shell and repetitious rows of gill structures may reflect an ancient heritage. Its powerful foot moves it slowly over the rocky ocean floor, and holds it securely there when the waters become turbulent. Just below the shell is a fleshy mantle, which covers the body like a cloak and encloses the rows of gills within the mantle cavity. Like most other mollusks, the chiton feeds with a rasplike radula.

Gastropods. The **gastropods** are more specialized than the chitons, and therefore have departed more from the ancestral line. For example, snails and slugs have retained the simple gliding foot, but have added the ability to retract it. They feed with a radula, but their shells, when present, are asymmetrical and quite different from the segmented shell of the chiton. Early in its development, the snail embryo undergoes extreme *torsion*, or twisting (180°), displacing the internal organs. Thus, the anus ends up over the head, if you can imagine that. In addition, the genitals end up on one side of the head, in about the position of what would be the right cheek, if gastropods had cheeks. This torsion is then followed by an equally severe spiralling in the shell. Many gastropods are hermaphroditic and have large penises with which they fertilize each other. The sight of the organ extending from the side of the head is remarkable. Even more remarkable is the habit of garden snails of injecting piercing "love darts" into the flesh of potential mates, just to get their attention.

Bivalves. The **bivalves** (class *Bivalva*—"two shells") include the clams, oysters, mussels, scallops, and their relatives. These species have followed yet another adaptive path: they have become **filter feeders**, filtering food from water, drawing the water through an *incurrent siphon* and directing it over and through their gills. The gills have been modified into sievelike feeding structures. Cilia covering the gill surfaces create the water currents that carry food particles to the simple mouth. The water then passes on through the gills and exits through an *excurrent siphon*.

The clam foot is modified for digging, and is quite retractable in most species. Powerful cylinders of muscle clamp the two halves of the shell closed when the clam is threatened.

Cephalopods. The **cephalopods** have diverged the most from the basic molluscan body plan. This class includes the octopuses, squids, and the chambered nautilus. The first two are swift predators, in which the foot has been modified into a number of grasping tentacles. The mantle can rapidly contract, forcefully expelling water and jet-propelling the animal along (see Figure 28.11). The shell of the chambered nautilus may appear snail-like at first glance, but it has a simple, symmetrical coil (Figure 28.12).

The cephalopods are undoubtedly among the most fascinating of all the invertebrates. They all have excellent image-producing eyes, remarkably like those of vertebrates. Since cephalopods are not at all closely related to vertebrates, this is a coincidence—an amazing example of convergent evolution. The nervous systems of these fascinating creatures reveal different evolutionary directions as well. For example, the cephalopod brain is quite large in comparison to the brains of other mollusks, and we know that cephalopods can learn certain things with surprising ease, and that they respond quickly and vigorously to external stimuli. People who own octopuses often boast that their pets have terrific personalities—but they are seldom believed.

To sum up, we have pointed out that the protostome line produced three great invertebrate phyla—Annelida, Arthropoda, and Mollusca—whose members make up the vast majority of animal species today. With relatively few (but notable) exceptions, the protostome line emphasized great diversity, small bodies, rapid reproduction, and dense populations. It can be argued that such characteristics more than compensate for their limited intelligence and learning ability.

THE DEUTEROSTOMES: THE ECHINODERM-CHORDATE LINE

The earliest deuterostomes were small and simple, with extremely limited nervous systems. And yet there was an unsuspected potential in these animals. No one could be too surprised that the deuterostomes were to produce the witless starfish, but who would have imagined that they would also give rise to the chordates, and that from the chordates would come the vertebrates—the largest and brainiest animals on earth? (However, the earth was to age hundreds of millions of years between the appearance of the first deuterostomes and the rise of the vertebrates.)

We've seen the differences in the development

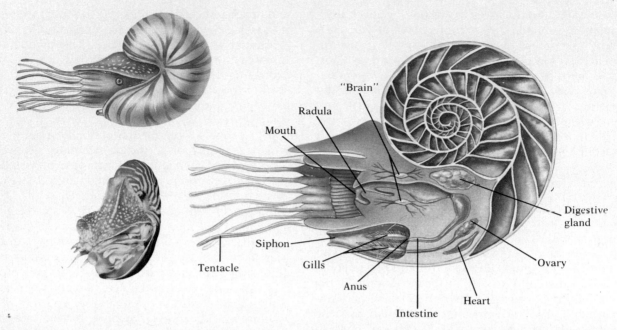

Labels on figure: "Brain", Radula, Mouth, Digestive gland, Siphon, Tentacle, Gills, Ovary, Anus, Heart, Intestine

28.12

The chambered nautilus *(Nautilus)*, in spite of its shell, is closely related to the octopus and squid, as its tentacles and prominent eyes attest. The tentacles (60 to 90 or more) lack suckers, but produce sticky secretions used in trapping prey. Its greatly partitioned shell is used in maintaining buoyancy. As each compartment is formed, fluids within are withdrawn and replaced by respiratory gases. The strength of the nautilus' shell is quite impressive, since it can resist pressures greater than 40 times the pressure of the air at sea level.

of the digestive tract in protostomes and deuterostomes, and we've considered some evolutionary implications. There are other differences in the two groups as well. Protostomes produce external supportive skeletons from epithelium (such as skin or covering membrane) that, itself, originates from ectoderm. On the other hand, the internal skeletons of deuterostomes generally are derived from mesoderm. Differences in these supportive structures could have accounted for the great size differences that were to come.

Minor Deuterostome Phyla

Before considering the echinoderms and chordates, we should acknowledge a few obscure phyla that seem to be related to our own. The first, definitely a deuterostome, includes the *Chaetognaths* ("bristle-mouths"), or arrow worms—free-swimming, transparent marine organisms that resemble simplified fish. A less certain deuterostome phylum is *Bryozoa* ("moss animals"), tiny colonial animals with frilly, branched structures resembling seaweed. One common bryozoan is dried, painted green, and sold in department stores as a "living air fern" that never needs water. Also questionable are the *Brachiopods* ("arm-feet"), or lamp shells. They are often mistaken for clams, since both are protected by two half-shells. The brachiopods filter water through a horseshoe-shaped loop of semirigid tentacles that somewhat resemble the teeth of a comb.

Spiny Skins and Radial Bodies: The Echinoderms

Echinoderms are exclusively marine animals, with many species living in the shallow waters of the continental shelves. Others are found in the deepest oceanic trenches.

There are five major classes of echinoderms (Figure 28.13), each with its own variation on the basic five-part body plan. Included are the familiar sea stars (class *Asteroidea*), brittle stars (class *Ophiuroidea*), and sea urchins and sand dollars (class *Echinoidea*), whose members are all quite spiny. The less familiar and rarer stalked crinoids (class *Crinoidea*) are considered primitive and more representative of fossil echinoderms, while the cylindrical, soft-bodied sea cucumbers (class *Holothuroidea*), with their scattered body plates, are vastly different from other echinoderms.

Echinoderms are unusual in many respects. Their radial symmetry, for instance, is not like that of the simple coelenterates, but is a modified form called **pentaradial symmetry** (*penta*, five). In other words, any "pie slices" could only be cut at certain places to produce nearly identical sections. However, the embryonic stages are not radially symmetrical at all. The larvae (and, indeed, the ancient fossilized adult echinoderms) are bilaterally symmetrical.

Even the spiny echinoderm skeleton is a true endoskeleton. That is, it is of mesodermal origin and actually it is located on the inside. Don't confuse the lengthy spines of many echinoderms with exoskeletons. They form inside the animal and emerge from bony (mesodermal) plates located below its skin.

One of the most unusual features of the echinoderms is the **water vascular system.** It is the principal mechanism of locomotion for some species (although some sea urchins also clamber about on their stiltlike, movable spines). The *madreporite* is the system's sievelike inlet. The major parts of the internal plumbing are the hardened *stone canal*, *ring canal*, and *radial canals*. The moveable parts are the *ampullas*, muscular "squeeze bulbs" that force water into the *tube feet*, thereby extending them. The mechanism and role of the water vascular system in the sea stars are described in Figure 28.14.

Other systems in the echinoderms are also strange, yet simple. Many are unique to this group. For example, respiration is carried out by **dermal branchiae,** simple ciliated extensions of the coelomic lining that stick out through the body wall and act in gas exchange. Dissolved gasses can also cross the thin membranes of the tube feet. The sea star's nervous system is a simple ring, with extensions reaching into each of its five arms. There is no sign of centralization, no clumps of ganglia, and no concentration of nerve cells. This may explain why

28.13

Five-part radial symmetry is a basic feature of echinoderm anatomy, but many variations of this theme are seen in the phylum. While this symmetry is obvious in starfish (**a**) and brittle stars (**b**), finding it in sea urchins (**c**) and silver crinoids (**d**) requires a much closer look. The soft-bodied sea cucumber (**e**), seemingly the strangest of all echinoderms, reveals little of the five-part plan. Its water vascular system is well developed, but the tube feet are modified into a large number of feeding tentacles.

(a)

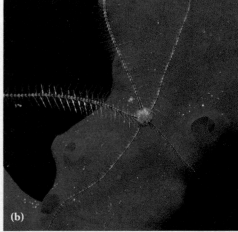
(b)

(c)

(d)

(e)

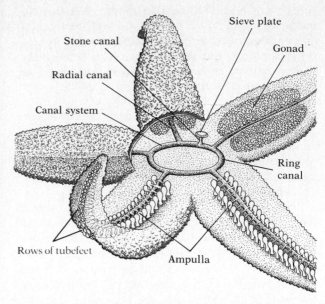

Stone canal

Sieve plate

Radial canal

Gonad

Canal system

Ring canal

Rows of tubefeet

Ampulla

28.14

In the sea star or starfish, the water vascular system consists of the sieve plate (an inlet), a canal system, and numerous tube feet. The tube feet are used in moving about and feeding. To accomplish this, the animal contracts its ampullae, forcing water into the tube feet and extending them. When the tube feet contact a surface, their terminal suckers fasten on. Then,

muscles in the tube feet contract, shortening them. As they shorten, water is allowed to escape back into the system, which has a number of check valves to regulate its flow. In this way, many tube feet, working in series, pull the animal along the ocean floor. The tube feet are used similarly to open the shells of bivalves, the sea star's favorite food.

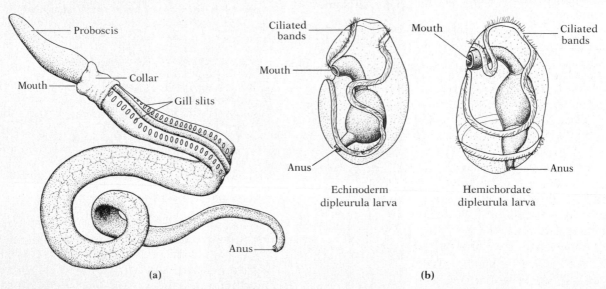

Proboscis

Mouth

Collar

Gill slits

Anus

(a)

Ciliated bands

Mouth

Mouth

Anus

Echinoderm
dipleurula larva

Ciliated bands

Anus

Hemichordate
dipleurula larva

(b)

28.15

The presence of gill slits and a dorsal hollow nerve cord are the only similarities acorn worms have with the chordates, but these are used primarily in feeding. Many acorn worms (a) spend their lives burrowing in salt water mud flats, where they feed through the use of a ciliated proboscis. The water currents generated guide bits of organic debris through the collarlike

mouth. Once inside, the food is taken into the digestive tract and the water leaves through the gill slits. The relationship of hemichordates and echinoderms is well established on the basis of larval forms (b), which are remarkably similar, right down to the arrangement of the ciliated bands. This larval type is known as a *dipleurula*.

418

the animal can move in any of five directions with equal ease and full coordination. The digestive tract is *complete*; that is, it includes a mouth, a gut, and an anus. The reproductive system is simple, consisting of testes or ovaries (sexes are separate) that lead to ducts. In most echinoderms the gametes are simply released into the water, where fertilization occurs.

The Hemichordates

The hemichordates (phylum *Hemichordata*) comprise a very peculiar group, including a few rather uninspiring aquatic creatures such as the *acorn worms*. The acorn worms of this minor phylum have two primitive chordate characteristics, *gill slits* and a *dorsal hollow nerve cord* (which we will discuss shortly). Equally significant, the acorn worm's larvae are startlingly similar to those of some echinoderms (Figure 28.15). If you didn't blossom with pride at the idea of being distantly related to a starfish, knowing about these even more closely related bottom dwellers has probably done little to boost your ego.

The Chordates

And now we come to the chordates (phylum *Chordata*), the group that includes humans. Some of the chordate traits may seem alien to you, but keep in mind that they may appear only briefly, at some embryonic stage.

Phylum Chordata includes three subphyla: *Urochordata*, *Cephalochordata*, and *Vertebrata*. In each chordate subphylum, the following characteristics are shared:

1. All chordates possess, at least at some time in their lives, a **notochord**—an internal, flexible, turgid rod that runs along the dorsal (back) side. The phylum derives its name from this structure.

2. All chordates possess, at some time in their lives, a number of **gill arches** (forming between them the **gill slits**). In primitive chordates, these become sieves used in filter feeding; in the fishes, they support the gills; but in other vertebrates, they appear only temporarily in the embryo.

3. All chordates have, at some time in their lives, a **dorsal hollow nerve cord.**

4. At some time (in an early embryonic stage, at least), all chordates possess **myotomes**—serially repeated blocks of muscle along either side of the notochord.

5. All chordates have a **post-anal tail** at some time in their lives.

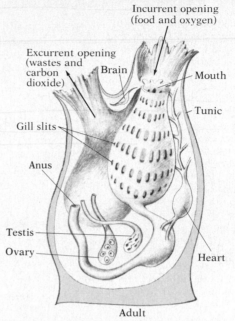

Incurrent opening (food and oxygen)

Excurrent opening (wastes and carbon dioxide)

Brain

Mouth

Tunic

Gill slits

Anus

Testis

Ovary

Heart

Adult

28.16

As an adult, the tunicate hardly represents what we expect in a chordate. The simple saclike body lacks nearly all of the typical chordate structures, except for the telltale chordate gill slits. The ciliated gill structure (called a *gill basket*) is used in gas exchange and for straining food particles from the sea water drawn into the incurrent opening of the tunic. Digestive wastes leave the anus to join water currents leaving through an excurrent opening in the tunic. Tunicates, or sea squirts, live quiet lives in the company of barnacles, mussels, and sea stars, firmly attached to rocks, wharf pilings, and boat hulls (which must be periodically scraped to get rid of the drag they create).

The **urochordates** include the ugly, stationary *tunicates* (sea squirts); the bizarre, transparent, free-swimming *salps;* and a minor, but highly significant group, the *larvacea,* planktonic forms with small, soft bodies.

Adult tunicates (Figure 28.16) have a hollow saclike body composed of a tough *tunic.* A casual observer could confuse them with coelenterates—especially since, like sea anemones, they squirt sea water out of their bodies when they contract. But

The chordate body plan is clearly seen in these three representatives. The tunicate larva (a), unlike the adult, is truely bilateral with an elongated body. While it lacks obvious sensory structures, the head is well defined and the gill slits, notochord, and dorsal hollow nerve cord are prominent. Similarly, the adult lancelet *(Branchiostoma)* (b) has a slender bilateral body with a well-defined tail. Also prominent are the gill slits, notochord, and dorsal hollow nerve cord. In both the tunicate larva and lancelet, the gill slits are openings in the gill basket, an important filter-feeding structure. We can draw many favorable comparisons between these chordates and the so-called *ammocoete* larvae of the sea lamprey, (c) a vertebrate, jawless fish. The ammocoete larva, like the other two, is a filter feeder, with feeding structures similar to those in the lancelet.

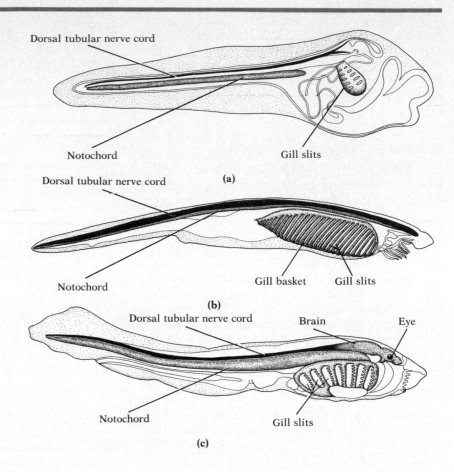

the larva of the tunicate unveils it as a chordate, with its bilateral form, a notochord, gill arches, myotomes, a dorsal hollow nerve cord, and a post-anal tail that permits vigorous swimming. (The adult larvacea retain this body form.) Larval tunicates are called *tadpoles*, and indeed do look and act a lot like the larvae of frogs and toads.

Cephalochordates have been found fossilized in the Burgess Shale deposits of the early Cambrian era. They are very similar to the living cephalochordates, the lancelets. They belong to the genus *Branchiostoma*, but are perhaps better known by their former scientific name, *Amphioxus*. They, at last, are clearly our own relatives. In fact, the

basic cephalochordate body plan seems almost like a simplified cartoon of the general vertebrate body plan. At the same time, it is similar in many ways to that of the urochordate larva (Figure 28.17), and, like urochordates, cephalochordates are filter feeders. These similarities have strongly suggested how chordates may have evolved. (Such a scenario is seen in Figure 28.18.) Much later in the Cambrian era, the cephalochordates gave rise to a new kind of animal in the oceans. At first it was an awkward, slow-swimming, jawless creature, sucking up its nutrients from the mucky bottom sediments. But it *was* the first vertebrate, a fishy ancestor to a group that would someday dominate and change the very face of the earth.

Summary

Eucoelomates and a Segmental Organization
Most eucoelomates have a complex linear gut with specialized regions for such functions as grinding, swallowing, digesting, and absorbing food. Many also possess a segmented body plan, in which septa divide the repeating units or compartments of the body.

Segmented Worms: The Annelids (Phylum Annelida)
Annelids include polychaetes and oligochaetes. Earthworms have a ventral nerve cord and a "brain" made up of two large ganglia; have well-organized digestive, excretory, and circulatory systems; and are hermaphroditic.

A Remarkable Success Story: The Arthropods (Phylum Arthropoda)

The success of arthropods is based on movement with jointed limbs, specialized mouthparts, and high rates of reproduction. Their body segments are often specialized for different tasks. An exoskeleton of chitin protects their soft body parts. The two major groups of arthropods are the Chelicerata and the Mandibulata.

Arachnids all have six pairs of appendages: chelicerae, pedipalps, and four pairs of legs. Spiders are unique in this group because of their ability to spin fibroin silk. Most crustaceans are aquatic and discard their exoskeletons by molting as they grow. They breathe through gills and often have highly developed sensory structures such as compound eyes. Insects, the dominant arthropod species on land, have three body regions: head, thorax (where wings are often attached), and abdomen. Insects exchange gases through a complex system of tubes, or the tracheae. While various species have widely different mouthparts, all insects possess an open circulatory system and a complex digestive system including a foregut, midgut, and hindgut, each with specialized functions. The insect reproductive cycle includes four stages: egg, larva, pupa, and adult. Females of many species use paired ovipositors to dig or bore a hole in which to lay their eggs.

Shells and a Muscular Foot: The Mollusks (Phylum Mollusca)

Segmentation and coelomic development in mollusks are questionable, so their relationship to other coelomates is not resolved. The major classes of mollusks are the chitons, gastropods, bivalves, and cephalopods. All classes include at least some species that share the same basic characteristics: a muscular foot, a shell, a mantle and mantle cavity, and external gills. Many mollusks feed with a radula. The chitons are the least modified group, having an eight-part shell and repeating gill structures. Gastropods are more specialized, with a retractable foot. Many gastropods are hermaphroditic.

Bivalves have two shells and are filter feeders. Cephalopods, including octopuses, squids, and the chambered nautilus, possess grasping tentacles instead of feet, mantles used for locomotion, relatively large brains, image-producing eyes, and the ability to respond quickly to external stimuli.

The Deuterostomes: The Echinoderm-Chordate Line

Because prostostomes and deuterostomes evolved along such different lines, it is possible that they were ecologically or geographically isolated from one another and did not compete for niches. Minor deuterostome phyla

28.18

Theoretical chordate evolutionary scenario. According to one theory, echinoderms, hemichordates, primitive chordates, and vertebrates arose from an ancestral arm-feeding deuterostome. Like so many of today's marine invertebrates that are fixed in place (sessile), these simple animals produced a swimming larva. From this ancestor arose the echinoderms and hemichordates, both of which still retain the free-swimming larva. Following these divergences, the deuterostomic line divided once more, but in a most unusual manner. One branch produced the urochordate line, today's tunicates and salps. The other was quite unusual. It arose from certain larvae that had somehow retained their juvenile body form while reaching sexual maturity. The best evidence of this strange capability is seen in *Larvaceae*, a group of living urochordates that remains permanently in a larval state. From this seemingly odd venture arose the cephalochordates and the vertebrates.

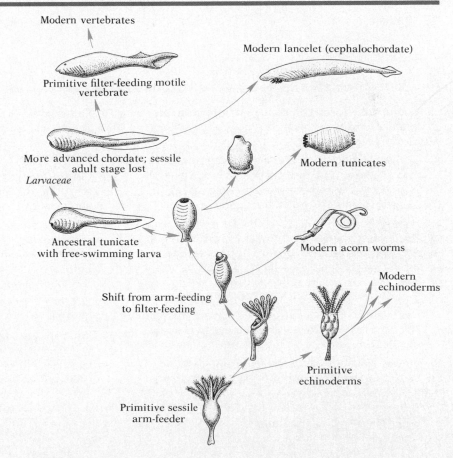

Modern vertebrates

Modern lancelet (cephalochordate)

Primitive filter-feeding motile vertebrate

More advanced chordate; sessile adult stage lost

Larvaceae

Modern tunicates

Ancestral tunicate with free-swimming larva

Modern acorn worms

Modern echinoderms

Shift from arm-feeding to filter-feeding

Primitive echinoderms

Primitive sessile arm-feeder

include the Chaetognaths, the Bryozoa, and the Brachiopods. Echinoderms, which are all marine, possess true endoskeletons, water vascular systems, dermal branchiae for respiration, and complete digestive tracts. The acorn worms of the phylum Hemichordata have two primitive chordate characteristics, gill slits and a dorsal hollow nerve cord.

All chordates, at some time in their life cycles, have a notochord, gill arches, a dorsal hollow nerve cord, myotomes, and a post-anal tail. Phylum Chordata is divided into the subphyla Urochordata, Cephalochordata, and Vertebrata. Urochordates are similar to coelenterates, but their larvae definitely possess chordate characteristics. Cephalochordates have a body plan similar to that of vertebrates, yet close enough to the urochordate larva to show their evolutionary link. Cephalochordates eventually gave rise to the first vertebrates.

Key Terms

eucoelomates	Mandibulata	egg	cephalopod
segmented body plan	arachnid	larva	echinoderm
septa	chelicerae (fangs)	pupa	pentaradial symmetry
annelids	pedipalps	adult	water vascular system
polychaete worm	book lungs	ovipositor	dermal branchiae
oligochaete	spinnerets	mollusk	notocord
hirudinian	crustacean	foot	gill arches
ventral nerve cord	molting	shell	gill slits
ganglia	compound eye	mantle	dorsal hollow nerve cord
typhlosole	insect	mantle cavity	myotomes
nephridia	head	gills	post-anal tail
aortic arches	thorax	radula	preoral gut
capillaries	abdomen	chiton	urochordate
seminal receptacles	foregut	gastropod	cephalochordate
arthropod	midgut	bivalve	
exoskeleton	hindgut	filter feeder	
Chelicerata			

Review Questions

1. Contrast the formation of the gut in protostomes and deuterostomes. List the major phyla in each category. (pp. 404–405)

2. Explain segmentation and cite examples of "segments" in annelids, arthropods, and vertebrates. How do theorists explain the presence of segmentation in both protostomes and deuterostomes? (pp. 404–405)

3. Briefly describe the anatomy of the earthworm's nervous, digestive, circulatory, excretory, and reproductive systems. In what ways does the anatomy and physiology of its circulatory system compare favorably with our own? (pp. 405–406)

4. Describe two types of structures that are characteristic of arthropods. How might these have led to the amazing success of this phylum? (pp. 406–408)

5. Briefly describe each of the following insect systems: digestive (gut only), respiratory, excretory, and circulatory. Which, if any, compares favorably with its counterpart in the earthworm? (pp. 411–412)

6. Summarize the reproductive potential and four-part life cycles of many insects and explain how these factors may have contributed to their success. (p. 412)

7. List the four major classes of mollusks, and describe the specific modifications of the foot, shell, and mantle in each. (pp. 413–415)

8. Echinoderms have a pentaradial form of symmetry and a unique water vascular system. Using the sea star as an example, explain what these are and how the water vascular system is used in feeding and locomotion. (pp. 416–417)

9. List the five major characteristics of chordates. (p. 419)

10. What are the suggested evolutionary links between echinoderms and hemichordates, between hemichordates and chordates, and between urochordates and cephalochordates? (pp. 419–420)

The Vertebrates:

Animals with Backbones

29

Now we come to the animals that we probably know the most about—the ones that cross our minds when we hear the word "animal." They have no ventral nerve cords; no open circulatory systems; no bodies growing from arms; no anuses above the eyes. These arc the ones most people can relate to: the **vertebrates** (subphylum *Vertebrata*).

Most vertebrates share certain traits in addition to the standard chordate characteristics. They each have a vertebral column (backbone), a centralized nervous system (brain), a closed circulatory system, a dorsal heart, gills or lungs, two pairs of limbs, two image-forming eyes, and a compact excretory system with paired kidneys. There are two distinct sexes in each species. These traits are characteristic of vertebrates, and although exceptions are inevitable, they are minor. Vertebrates, as a group, have distinct traits that leave little room for exceptions.

Taxonomists generally recognize eight classes of vertebrates. Of these classes, one is extinct, but it is important because it was the first to develop jaws. Most taxonomists today organize the vertebrates into the following groups:

1. *Agnatha:* jawless fishes, now represented by lampreys and hagfish.
2. *Placodermi:* the first jawed fishes, now extinct.
3. *Chondrichthyes:* those with cartilagenous skeletons, such as rays, sharks, and ratfishes.
4. *Osteichthyes:* the bony fishes.
5. *Amphibia:* frogs, toads, and salamanders.
6. *Reptilia:* turtles, snakes, lizards, and crocodilians.
7. *Aves:* birds.
8. *Mammalia:* mammals.

Here we will focus on the evolutionary relationships of vertebrates. This group, of course, includes a staggering array of animals and life styles. We will see that in spite of the great diversity among backboned animals, there are a number of underlying similarities that virtually all of them share. So, we'll begin where vertebrate evolution began—with the jawless fishes.

HUMBLE BEGINNINGS: THE JAWLESS AGNATHAN FISHES

The earliest vertebrate fossils ever found are of the **ostracoderms.** Their remains have been found in the sediments of the Ordovician period (500–425 million years ago—Table 29.1), the Silurian period (425–405), and the Devonian period (405–345). The earliest findings are about a half billion years old. The ostracoderms whose fossils have survived were slow, heavy, armor-plated fishes living on the ocean bottom. They lacked jaws and obtained their food by sucking up the bottom sediments and sorting out the nutrients. They were fearsome-looking creatures with large heads and huge gill chambers. Their bluff occasionally might have been called, however, because their appearance notwithstanding, they were only 10–15 cm (4–6 in) long.

Jaws may seem trivial, but they are not. They are an important development and, probably because of this, the agnathans now are represented by only a few species. Most agnathan species died out at the end of the Devonian period 345 million years

ago, possibly because they were displaced by the rapidly evolving jawed fishes. The only survivors are the eel-like *lamprey* and the *hagfishes*.

The *lamprey* (Figure 29.1) has changed little since the Devonian period, and today it is wide-ranging and quite successful. The success of the parasitic lamprey belies its ungainly features and unadmirable habits. After all, it clamps its round, jawless mouth onto the side of a larger fish, scrapes away the skin and flesh with a tough, rasping tongue, and sucks out the blood and juices of its living victim, dropping off only when gorged. Curiously, the nonparasitic lamprey does not feed as an adult, and dies soon after spawning. The larval lamprey almost seems to pretend that it is unrelated to the adult. A shy and retiring filter feeder, the larva retains both the ecological niche and most of the physical characteristics of its cephalochordate ancestors (see Figure 28.18).

29.1

The lamprey is believed to be descended from the ostracoderms, jawless fishes of the early Paleozoic era. Species found today include some that are parasitic, using their suckerlike mouths and rasping rows of teeth to attach to bony fish and draw their blood. Lampreys were accidentally introduced into the Great Lakes in 1932 by the deepening of the Wellend Canal connecting Lake Erie to Lake Ontario. Once established, they virtually destroyed the population of lake trout, even before industrial sites on Lake Erie had rendered the lake virtually uninhabitable.

THE FIRST JAWS: CLASS PLACODERMI

There is little doubt that the evolution of jaws was one of the most significant events in vertebrate history. It almost immediately changed the behavior of many species, broadened the feeding niche, and encouraged new variations, some of which have succeeded to the present. All sorts of bony creatures can bite the daylights out of you these days.

Figure 29.2 depicts one hypothesis regarding the evolutionary development of the vertebrate

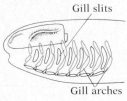

Gill slits

Gill arches

(a) Jawless ostracoderm
(unspecialized gill arches)

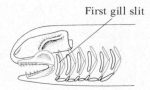

First gill slit

(b) Primitive jaw of placoderm
(gill arches modified into weak jaws)

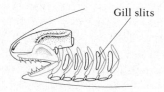

Gill slits

(c) Jaw of shark (gill arches modified into strong jaws and their supporting elements)

29.2

The forerunner of the jaw in the vertebrates was the primitive gill arch. In the jawless ostracoderms, the gill arches were all similar and unspecialized **(a)**. As jaws evolved in the placoderms **(b)**, the front gill arches became modified into very primitive upper and lower jaws. A great deal of muscle modification ac-

companied these developments. In the modern shark **(c)**, the modifications involve more of the gill arches devoted to other specialized structures. As we continue to mammals, including humans, we find that the original arches form the structures of the throat, inner ear, jaw, and tongue.

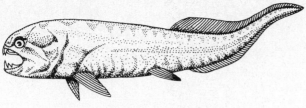

Dunkleosteus

29.3

Giant whale-sized placoderms such as *Dunkleosteus* retained some of the armor of their predecessors, but most of the creature's huge body lacked such protection. They apparently relied on newly acquired maneuverability, jaws, and large teeth for self-defense. Even with these advantages, they could not compete with the newly emerging bony and cartilaginous fishes.

jaw. Note that it is derived from the gill arches (the bony structures that support the gills) in embryonic development. For gills to give rise to jaws would, of course, require a great number of changes both in the position and in the strength of the arches, as well as in the surrounding muscles. However, just such changes are suggested by comparing the jaws of extinct placoderms with those of living sharks. In both groups, the jaws are formed from a crude, limited hinge. While the lower jaw is hinged to the upper jaw, the upper jaw—unlike ours—is not attached to the skull. But, as you may have heard, even such primitive jaws as those of a shark can be quite effective.

Placoderms apparently appeared in the Silurian period. Once established, their numbers increased rapidly and the group persisted for some 150 million years—an obvious success story. With the placoderms, we find the first evidence of paired pelvic and pectoral fins, which later gave rise to the four limbs of terrestrial vertebrates. One of the more fascinating placoderms was the gigantic *Dunkleosteus* (Figure 29.3), which was about the size of a modern gray whale, and one of the most fearsome predators that ever lived.

CARTILAGINOUS FISHES: CLASS CHONDRICHTHYES

The cartilaginous fishes, those with skeletons of **cartilage,** include the sharks, rays, and chimeras—a large and successful group of predators and scav-

engers. The protective armor and heavy skeleton of the ancient species have been replaced in the modern species by a tough skin, slight frame, powerful muscles, and, in some cases, great speed. According to the fossil record, they first appeared in the early Devonian period, dwindled during the Jurassic period, and then began to increase again up to the present time.

The Shark

In addition to having cartilaginous skeletons, sharks are unusual in other ways. Their body and tail shapes are unlike those of most bony fishes (Figure 29.4), and their skin is rough, covered with minute, toothlike growths known as *placoid scales*. The shark's true teeth are not anchored into the jaw. They begin to grow inside the mouth, move forward, and eventually fall out, to be replaced by new teeth from a seemingly inexhaustible supply. Some parts of the ocean floor are covered with discarded shark teeth.

The shark's short, cylindrical intestine has a curious structure called the **spiral valve** (also seen in agnathans and primitive bony fishes). It is essentially a twisted flap resembling a spiral staircase and consisting of absorbing tissue. The valve greatly increases the surface area of the intestine. The shark's digestive system ends in a structure common to most vertebrates, the **cloaca.** This is a chamber that serves as a common passageway for solid and metabolic wastes. It also functions as the reproductive opening of the body, and is used by male and female sharks in copulation and by females in egg-laying.

The male shark lacks a true penis, but it has paired *claspers* on its pelvic fins that are grooved on the inner sides. When the claspers are brought together, they form a channel through which semen can flow into the female cloaca.

Sharks have keen senses and can locate prey by smell, by sight, and by vibration and water-movement. Such patterns are detected in the **lateral line organ,** a sensory device found in bony fishes as well. The lateral line organ is composed of numerous sensory cells located in tiny canals that run along the head and body.

Sharks are also sensitive to variations in bioelectrical fields (which are present in all animals), and may detect their prey through this seventh sense. However, nothing in their evolutionary past has prepared them for encounters with such metal objects as boat propellers, oxygen tanks, and spear guns.

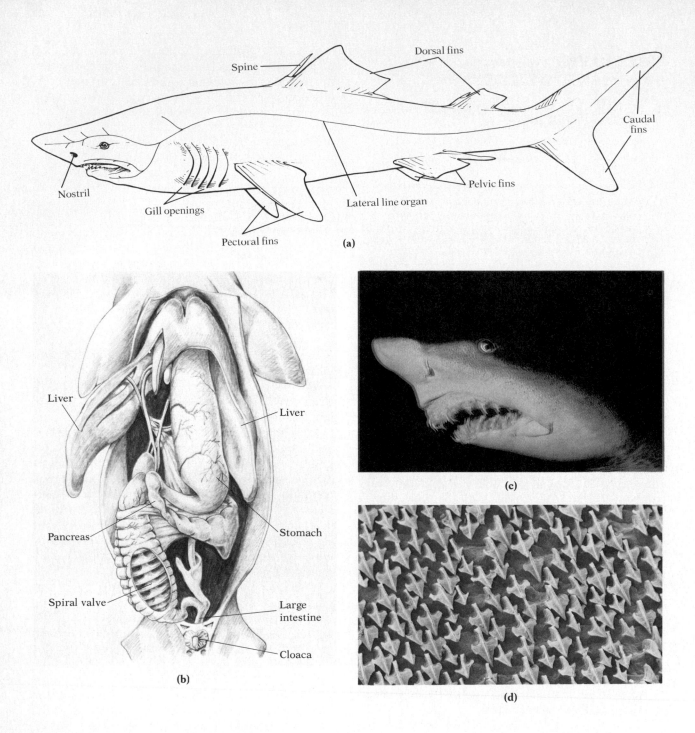

Spine

Dorsal fins

Caudal fins

Nostril

Gill openings

Pectoral fins

Lateral line organ

Pelvic fins

(a)

Liver

Liver

Pancreas

Stomach

Spiral valve

Large intestine

Cloaca

(b)

(c)

(d)

29.4

Sharks are often described as eating machines because of their ravenous appetites. There is no doubt about their success as ocean predators, and they show a number of adaptations to this mode of life. The body shape **(a)** is, in fact, a perfect example of streamlining. Their sensory structures include an extensive lateral line organ running along the sides of the head and body, along with keen olfactory and visual senses.

Within the intestine **(b)**, a flaplike spiral valve increases the surface area and slows the movement of any chunks of food the shark swallows whole. The powerful jaws, with row after row of razor-sharp, replaceable teeth, tell their own story **(c)**. The skin is tough and flexible, consisting of scales that resemble miniature teeth **(d)**.

THE BONY FISHES: CLASS OSTEICHTHYES

The bony fishes are categorized into two subclasses represented by the **lobe-finned fishes** and the **ray-finned fishes.** The ray-finned fishes are the ones that probably come to mind when you hear the word "fish," since the lobe-fin subclass contains only a few living species. Ray-fins include perch and bass, tuna and swordfish, catfish and sea-horses. They are a very diverse group (Figure 29.5); presently, more than 20,000 species have been identified.

Bony Fishes and Sharks Compared

The ray-finned bony fishes are not at all closely related to sharks. For example, their fins are generally much more delicate and movable, with fan-shaped supporting elements (thus the name, ray-finned). Such fins permit great maneuverability. The quick, darting movements of the bony fish are not possible in the shark.

Some bony fishes have a **swim bladder.** By controlling the gas volume in the bladder, the fish adjusts its buoyancy and is able to remain stationary at any depth. The swim bladder, surprisingly enough, is an evolutionary remnant of paired lungs, dating back to the time when the distant ancestors of modern bony fishes evolved in shallow, stagnant waters. Sharks apparently evolved under different conditions, since they lack swim bladders. They cannot adjust their buoyancy and must swim continuously or lie on the bottom. However, some buoyancy is provided by concentrations of lightweight lipids in the shark's huge liver.

The skin of most bony fishes is covered with scales and numerous mucus glands. The slimy mucus covering the body is quite important to swimming. Studies reveal that its presence reduces drag or water friction by up to 65%.

Gas exchange in nearly all fishes occurs in the gills, where oxygen dissolved in the water crosses the thin gill membranes to enter the moving bloodstream, and waste carbon dioxide diffuses out into the water (see Chapter 38). In bony fishes there are usually five pairs of gills. These are located in gill chambers, each of which is covered by a protective bony flap called the *operculum.* In sharks, the gill chambers open to the outside through separate gill slits with simple flaps.

Reproduction in bony fishes occurs in a variety of ways, from simple, brief acts of spawning—

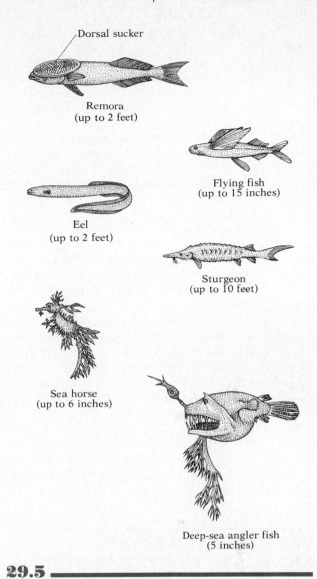

Dorsal sucker

Remora
(up to 2 feet)

Flying fish
(up to 15 inches)

Eel
(up to 2 feet)

Sturgeon
(up to 10 feet)

Sea horse
(up to 6 inches)

Deep-sea angler fish
(5 inches)

29.5

Most of the ray-finned fishes are similar in general body shape, with some variation in the fins. However, both the sea horse and angler fish of the deep appear to break some of the rules. This proves that, in spite of the strict requirements placed upon aquatic vertebrates, there will be divergence.

where males and females come together just long enough to release their gametes—to intricate pre-mating behavior, nest-building, internal fertilization (in some groups), and vigorous care of the eggs and young. As you might expect, the number of eggs released by the female fish generally reflects the degree of parental care that can be provided to each. The range is enormous, from millions in the simple spawners like the Atlantic cod, to perhaps a few dozen in highly protective species like the seahorses. The male seahorse holds the fertilized eggs, and later the growing hatchlings, in its mouth.

Development is also highly varied. In **oviparous** (egg-laying) fishes, such as the cod, the eggs are simply released to be fertilized, and the nutrients needed by the embryo are provided by the egg. In toothcarps (the family of the common aquarium guppy) and other **ovoviviparous** fishes, fertilization is internal—and the egg is retained within the female for development. The young emerge from the cloaca fully developed. However, in ovovivipary, nourishment is still provided by food stores in the egg itself. Other species of toothcarp provide rare examples of fish that are truly live-bearing or **viviparous,** a system usually associated with mammals. In viviparity, some or all nourishment is provided by tissues in the mother's uterus.

Sharks also exhibit all three modes of development, although viviparity is established more clearly in these fishes. The gray, smoothhound, and hammerhead sharks produce what is clearly a **placenta.** This is a soft mass of tissue containing an intimate association of blood vessels of both mother and embryo, through which the embryo takes in oxygen and nutrients and rids itself of metabolic wastes. We are not quite sure how to characterize the bizarre development of the sandshark. Sandsharks are technically ovoviviparous, but the source of food for the more mature embryos turns out to be a continuing supply of younger brothers and sisters.

VERTEBRATES INVADE THE LAND: THE TETRAPODS

According to fossil evidence, both bony and cartilaginous fishes evolved from placoderm ancestors, albeit different ones, in the Devonian period (see Table 29.1). The bony fishes then diverged into two separate groups: the ray-finned fishes and the lobe-finned fishes (Figure 29.6). The ray-finned fishes quickly became the predominant group in the bodies of waters around the world. The lobe-finned fishes didn't do as well. But some of their descendants were to find good jobs in the garment industry, while others have walked on the moon.

Lobe-Finned Fishes: A Dead End and a New Opportunity

Lobe-finned fishes have never been very abundant and are rare today. Their heavy, fleshy fins were probably best suited for resting on the bottoms of

TABLE 29.1

Geologic timetable

Eras (Years since Start)	Periods	Extent in Millions of Years
Cenozoic	Quaternary	
	Holocene (present)	last 10,000 years
	Pleistocene	.01–2
	Tertiary	
	Pliocene	2–6
	Miocene	6–23
	Oligocene	23–35
	Eocene	35–54
65,000,000	Paleocene	54–65
Mesozoic	Cretaceous-Paleocene discontinuity	65
	Cretaceous	65–135
	Jurassic	135–197
225,000,000	Triassic	197–225
Paleozoic	Permian	225–280
	Carboniferous	280–345
	Devonian	345–405
	Silurian	405–425
	Ordovician	425–500
570,000,000	Cambrian	500–570
Precambrian		570–4500

Origin of earth, 4.5 billion years

muddy habitats. In time, however, they diverged into two evolutionary lines, one of which includes today's bizarre **lungfishes,** sluggish, air-gulping oddities of shallow ponds in Australia, Africa, and South America. They are unusual because they have retained the air-breathing lung that, in most other fish, became the swim bladder. Thus they can live in muddy, stagnant water that would not contain enough oxygen for most animals.

The second line of lobe-finned fishes, the **crossopterygians** (translated as "the fringed-wing ones"), and their close relatives, the coelacanths, died out in the Cretaceous period—at least that's what scientists thought until recently. In 1939, a group of puzzled fishermen caught a live coelacanth—a species known as *Latimeria chalumnae*—in deep waters off of the east coast of South Africa. It was a startling find. Its line had held its own against competition from ray-finned fishes for 80 million years. Many more of these "living fossils" have now been found (Figure 29.7).

But the crossopterygians are most interesting because they were to give rise to another line—the terrestrial vertebrates. The first problem, of course, was the transition from water to land, but we know that some crossopterygians had lungs and could

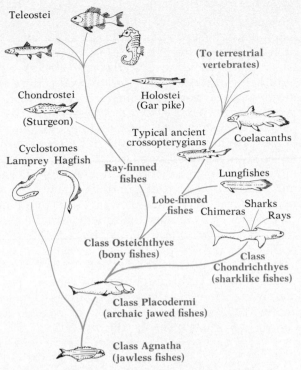

Teleostei

Chondrostei
(Sturgeon)

Holostei
(Gar pike)

(To terrestrial
vertebrates)

Cyclostomes
Lamprey Hagfish

Typical ancient
crossopterygians

Coelacanths

Ray-finned
fishes

Lungfishes

Lobe-finned
fishes

Sharks

Chimeras   Rays

Class Osteichthyes
(bony fishes)

Class
Chondrichthyes
(sharklike fishes)

Class Placodermi
(archaic jawed fishes)

Class Agnatha
(jawless fishes)

29.6

In the phylogenetic tree of fishes, modern species occupy three classes: Agnatha (the cyclostomes), Chondrichthyes (sharks, rays, and chimeras), and Osteichthyes (ray-finned and lobe-finned fishes). While ray-finned fishes include thousands of species, only seven species of lobe-finned fishes are known of today. Six of these are lungfishes, while the seventh is the coelacanth, believed for many years to be extinct, but now known to be still thriving in the waters off South Africa. While lobe-finned fishes are no longer of great numerical significance, one of their immediate ancestors gave rise to the first terrestrial vertebrates.

breathe air. From this came species that spent parts of their lives both on land and in water—the **amphibians.** There isn't much resemblance between fossilized lobe-finned fishes and existing amphibians, but there are important similarities between the early lobe-finned fishes and the first amphibians (Figure 29.8).

It's not easy to understand the evolutionary pressures that favored leaving familiar waters for inhospitable dry terrain. Terrestrial life is rigorous and fraught with the risk of desiccation (drying out). Perhaps the land was invaded because it offered new resources and few competitors. Obviously any such transition would take time to allow for adaptations to the new conditions, yet the process was very rapid in terms of geological time.

29.7

Coelacanths still exist off the coast of South Africa. *Latimeria*, a direct descendant of the crossopterygians, was long thought to be extinct. Of all the living fishes, *Latimeria* is the one most closely related to ourselves.

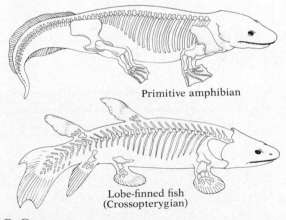

Primitive amphibian

Lobe-finned fish
(Crossopterygian)

29.8

By comparing ancient amphibian fossils and fossils of lobe-finned crossopterygians, we can see how the transition to land life might have occured. For example, the first use of lobe fins as walking appendages may have simply involved getting from pond to pond, or even as a brief respite from relentless aquatic predators.

TRANSITIONAL VERTEBRATES: THE AMPHIBIANS

Those first fishy attempts to crawl out of the water were undoubtedly rather awkward, but an awkward time on land must have offered some rewarding new opportunities, and some species were soon getting around with a certain ease (Figure 29.9). We can still see some of the problems in the modern salamander. Its frail upper limbs protrude nearly straight out to the side before angling down, and its body drags on the ground. (Try doing push-ups with your arms in this position.) It moves with an undulating, fishlike motion, its body first curving to the left and then to the right—an impressive show of vigor coupled with rather limited forward progress.

Amphibians reveal ancestral habits in other ways as well. For example, the thin, moist skin of amphibians contains dense capillary beds. This permits gases to be exchanged, augmenting the work of the limited, hollow lung. For this to work efficiently, the skin must be kept moist, so most amphibians must avoid dry places. (As we will see, there are exceptions.) In addition, many amphibians require water for reproduction. Such species fertilize the eggs externally, and the young develop in the water. Most frogs and toads go through a tadpole stage, using gills for gas exchange and a temporary, fishlike tail for swimming. As development continues, the tail and gills are absorbed, replaced by legs and lungs in the final transition.

The amphibian heart has three chambers, one muscular *ventricle* (lower pumping chamber) and two smaller atria (upper receiving and pumping chambers). This organization differs from the two-chambered heart of fishes. In the fish, blood is pumped from the single ventricle to capillary beds in the gills, where it is oxygenated. It then passes throughout the body, entering many capillary beds once more before returning to the single atrium for another trip. In amphibians, a second circuit is added for oxygenation (Figure 29.10).

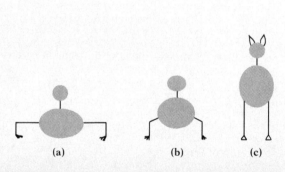

(a)　　　(b)　　　(c)

(a)

(b)

(c)

29.9

The adaptation to terrestrial life involves the positioning of limbs in the tetrapods. Amphibians **(a)** such as the salamander and the newt have thin, lightly muscled legs splayed out to the side so that the body weight is borne on flexed joints. Reptiles **(b)** retain the legs alongside the body, and the limbs remain flexed as they carry the body weight. The bodies of mammals **(c)**, the fastest moving land creatures, are raised above the ground, with the limbs essentially below them. The significance of this positioning is best seen in a comparison of such heavyweights as crocodiles and rhinoceri.

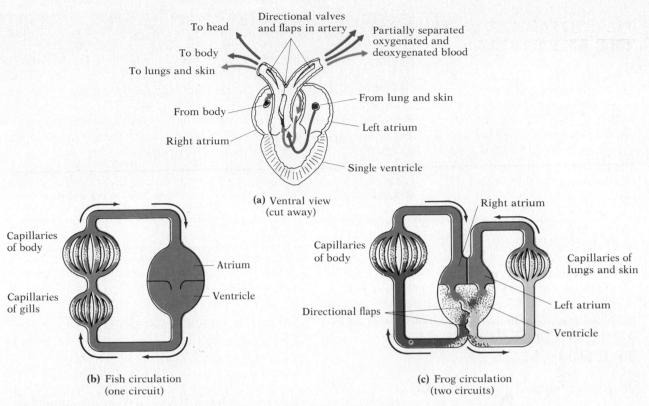

To head

To body

To lungs and skin

Directional valves
and flaps in artery

Partially separated
oxygenated and
deoxygenated blood

From lung and skin

From body

Right atrium

Left atrium

Single ventricle

(a) Ventral view
(cut away)

Capillaries
of body

Capillaries
of gills

Atrium

Ventricle

(b) Fish circulation
(one circuit)

Right atrium

Capillaries
of body

Capillaries of
lungs and skin

Directional flaps

Left atrium

Ventricle

(c) Frog circulation
(two circuits)

29.10

(a) The amphibian heart is three-chambered, with two thin-walled atria and one muscular ventricle. Oxygenated blood from the lungs and skin is received by the left atrium, while deoxygenated blood from the rest of the body is received by the right atrium. Both empty into the single ventricle. When the ventricle contracts, blood is forced out into arteries for another trip through the two circuits. At least a partial separation of oxygenated and deoxygenated blood is made possible by directional flaps in the arteries. A highly diagrammatic comparison of circulation in the fish **(b)** and amphibian **(c)** serves to emphasize the presence of the second circuit in the latter.

Modern Amphibians

There are three existing orders of amphibians. The first two have been mentioned: the *Urodeles* ("with tails"—the salamanders); and the *Anurans* ("without tails"—the frogs and toads). The third order is the *Caecilians*, an obscure group of legless, wormlike tropical amphibians (Figure 29.11). Some species of urodeles and anurans have evolved toward an increasingly terrestrial life, while others have returned completely to the water, where they spend their entire lives.

There are some remarkable examples of specialization among the amphibians. For example, the desert spadefoot toad survives in its dry habitat by burrowing into the soil and waiting for one of the infrequent rains, whereupon it crawls out, quickly locates a temporary pond, and immediately mates. The offspring must develop quickly before the usual drought returns. (Essay 29.1 reveals some of these developmental events in a toad called Couch's Spadefoot.) As another example, while most frogs and toads must mate in water, one species, *Pipa pipa*, the Surinam toad of South America, carries its fertilized eggs in moist pouches on its back, where the offspring completely develop.

Charles Darwin found a tiny frog in Chile that skips the tadpole stage altogether. *Rhinoderma* females deposit their eggs on moist ground, where the males fertilize them. Then the males sit and wait, apparently guarding the eggs, until the developing offspring begin to move within their globes of jelly, whereupon the males pop them into their mouths. The young develop in the enlarged vocal sacs of their patient fathers, until one day, tiny—but fully formed—froglets jump out.

Caecilians avoid the water problem altogether. Their gametes are not subject to desiccation, because the male has a copulatory organ and is able to deposit sperm directly into the female's cloaca. The eggs develop within the female, and the young caecilians are born fully formed.

29.11

The three modern amphibian orders. Salamanders **(a)** are probably the most primitive representatives because of their body shape and limbs; but their method of reproduction is quite advanced. Frogs and toads **(b)** are reproductively primitive, but their limb structure is advanced. Caecilians **(c)** are in the minority, comprising only 160 species. They are nearly blind and lack limbs, using their wormlike bodies to burrow into the soil. Reproductively, their adaptation to land life is more complete.

TRANSITION COMPLETED: THE REPTILES

Amphibians and reptiles evolved from the same common ancestor, and the first **reptiles** probably appeared soon after the amphibians developed. The reptiles, however, took up an entirely different lifestyle. While the amphibians continued to exploit the planet's aquatic niches, the reptiles simply left the moist environment for drier places, changing to an entirely terrestrial life.

One of the necessary adaptations was a tough, scaly, dry, water-repellent skin that controlled water loss and resisted wear. But this meant that the skin could no longer be used in gas exchange. Thus, a second adaptation included changes in the lung. Essentially, the lung's exchange surface was increased by the development of a spongy construction with many vascularized spaces, or *alveoli* (see Chapter 38). Reptiles have a thin *epidermis* (outer, dead skin) that is shed periodically to accommodate growth in the thick *dermis* (inner, live skin) below. Amphibians have a much more elastic skin, so growth doesn't produce such problems.

Some reptiles have advanced circulatory systems. *Crocodilians* (including the crocodiles and alligators) have four-chambered hearts like those of birds and mammals. The other reptiles, however, have three-chambered hearts similar to those of amphibians, except that they have partial walls dividing the ventricle.

On land, reptiles are swifter than salamanders because their legs do not act as simple pivots for the trunk muscles. Instead, reptile legs are very muscular. The muscles are necessary because reptile legs still tend to splay out to the side, bearing the animal's heavy weight at an awkward angle. But even large crocodilians can support their weight long enough for a remarkably quick dash to catch an unfortunate deer or dog—or human.

The greatest changes demanded of terrestrial reptiles were in their reproduction and development. External fertilization was not possible on the dry and hostile land, so, like the caecilians, the reptiles developed the capacity for internal fertilization. The male lizard or snake has two penises that can evert (like turning the fingers of a glove inside-out). Which one he uses depends on which side he is on as he lies partly across the female's back, but careful observations have shown that the male alternates sides in successive copulations— left, right, left, right.

A new, drastically modified cell—the *land egg*— first introduced by the early reptiles, was a vital adaptation to complete terrestrial life (Figure 29.12). The land egg was surrounded by a tough leathery shell (later replaced by a calcium shell in birds), which, while admitting air, protected the embryo against desiccation and mechanical injury. Included within the egg was a supply of water and food, everything necessary for the embryo's development.

A second and equally important developmental adaptation involved the embryo itself. The developing reptile (and bird) produces a number of supporting **extraembryonic membranes,** with vast networks of blood vessels. The **yolk sac,** an extension of the embryo's gut, brings in food; the **chorion,** a thin but extensive membrane, exchanges respiratory gases; the **allantois,** an extension of the urinary bladder, receives and stores solid nitrogenous wastes (later in development, it fuses with the chorion and aids in gas exchange); and the **amnion** encloses the embryo, providing a protective, water-filled environment. All of these extraembryonic membranes are left behind when the animal hatches and leaves the egg.

The Age of Reptiles

There are fewer reptiles than there once were, but they certainly had their day. In fact, the entire Mesozoic era, which lasted 160 million years (see Table 29.1), is referred to as the "Age of Reptiles." There were, indeed, many successful lines, each exploiting the planet in its own way. Some partly returned to the water, some became exclusively marine, and others learned to fly. But the ones that captivate our imagination stayed on the land and grew. Some became truly enormous beasts.

By the start of the Mesozoic era (225 million years ago), the trend toward large size was well underway, and as time went on, natural selection favored even larger species. Even the flying reptiles—the *pterosaurs*—produced a giant called *Pteranodon*, which was about the size of a small airplane. Some of the great beasts were carnivores, and they were well equipped with huge claws and teeth like steak knives. The most fearsome of great reptiles was *Tyrannosaurus rex* ("tyrant lizard"), probably the largest terrestrial carnivore that ever lived. However, even larger dinosaurs stalked the earth, but these were herbivores. Even the foliage of very tall trees did not escape *Diplodocus*, which was 30 m long (98 ft) and weighed about 30 metric tons (33 tons) (Figure 29.13).

We've deliberately concentrated on the spectacular beasts of the time. But we should remember that the bushes, grasses, and streams were alive with very wary and watchful little creatures that were also among the "ruling" reptiles. However, things have a way of beginning and ending in our world. And the age of reptiles was soon to end.

ESSAY 29.1
DEVELOPMENT IN THE SPADEFOOT TOAD

The Couch's Spadefoot Toad, in Arizona's Sonora Desert, breeds only one night a year. Eggs are fertilized in pools of rain water, then the adult frogs burrow into the ground. Bacteria in the warm pools provide food for the developing eggs, which become mobile toadlets in nine days. After consuming 11 months' worth of food and water, they too will burrow into the ground, waiting to reproduce during the next rainy season. ●

(a) The early stages of embryonic development

(b) In the first several hours, eggs undergo important developmental changes (see Chapter 41)

(c) 18–24 hours after fertilization, the embryos are recognizable as tadpoles

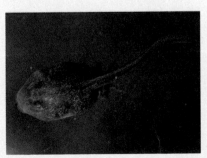

(d) After five days, the rear legs have begun to develop

(e) The toadlet, after only nine days of development, will emerge from the water to search for the nutrients it will use in its months underground

29.12

The reptilian egg represents the complete transition from amphibian reproduction to the terrestrial form of life. The egg provides the necessary environment for the embryo's development.

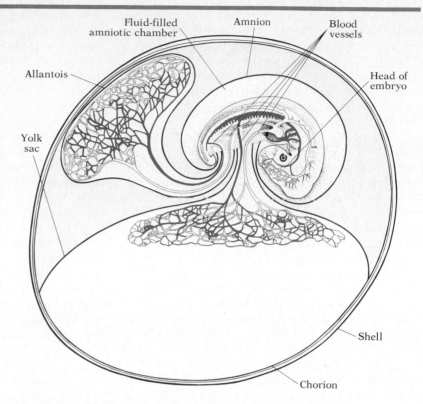

Fluid-filled amniotic chamber — Amnion — Blood vessels — Head of embryo — Allantois — Yolk sac — Shell — Chorion

29.13

The so-called ruling reptiles of the Mesozoic era included some of the largest animals ever to roam the earth. During the end of their time, the earth was the home of the legendary hunter, *Tyrannosaurus rex*, and the even larger *Diplodocus*, a herbivore. *Triceratops*, another herbivore, was smaller than these two, but was heavily armored. Great size was even apparent in flying reptiles such as the pterodactyls, where wingspans in some species reached 12 m (nearly 40 ft)! This beast lacked a tail, but some flight stability may have been provided by the keel-like crest on the head. The leading edge of the pterodactyl's wing was strengthened by an enormous fourth finger.

Exit the Great Reptiles

About 65 million years ago, at the end of the Mesozoic era, the great reptiles suddenly disappeared. The great beasts were gone—virtually all at once. The great flying reptiles and the giant sea reptiles disappeared at the same time.

The sudden passing of these reptiles has long presented a great puzzle. What could have caused such a massive extinction? Hundreds of hypotheses have been considered. For a time, the favored idea was that the dinosaurs were simply outcompeted by emerging numbers of smaller, more intelligent mammals of the time. Or perhaps, some thought, the little rascals ate so many reptilian eggs that this great vertebrate class eventually became eradicated. Other ideas involved drastic climatic changes at the close of the Mesozoic era. The problem is that none of the explanations could account for the dramatic *suddenness* of the mass extinction.

Perhaps the answers can be found in the rocks. After all, rocks can be formed by sedimentation, forming *strata* (layers) that may include clues suggesting the conditions on earth when each layer was formed. There are places where a stratum—a geological boundary—was formed 65 million years ago, marking the end of the Mesozoic and the beginning of the Cenozoic era. In the waters off Gubbio, Italy, the marine deposits are particularly well defined. Below this geological boundary, in the Mesozoic strata, are carbonate rocks containing many types of plankton skeletons, particularly very large foraminifera—early protists (Chapter 21).

But just above the boundary, in the rocks deposited in the early Cenozoic era, the life forms change drastically. In layer after layer of Cenozoic rocks, there are fewer and much smaller species. And there is something else in these rocks. At the boundary itself is a single layer of clay about a centimeter thick.

In 1980, paleontologist Walter Alvarez, along with his father, Luis Alvarez (a physicist and Nobel prize winner), noted that this thin layer of clay has peculiar concentrations of some unusual elements. There is about 50 times more iridium and platinum in the clay than one would expect. Now, iridium is extremely rare on earth, but it is a very common metal in meteors and asteroids. Why would iridium suddenly appear in the rocks being formed at the very time the dinosaurs were dying? The **Alvarez hypothesis,** as it has come to be known, is that an asteroid collided with the earth some 65 million years ago. Other research has since supported the Alvarez hypothesis.

Judging from the amount of iridium found in that thin layer, the Alvarezes calculated that the Mesozoic asteroid was about 10 km (six miles) in diameter. A rock six miles across could knock you down. It could also end the Mesozoic era, according to the hypothesis. Astronomers calculate that we can expect an asteroid of that size to hit our planet every hundred million years or so.

Computer simulations tell us that the dust thrown up by the impact of the asteroid blocked out much of the sun's rays, and the earth quickly darkened for about three months. With the darkness, photosynthesis could not occur, and all over the earth plants began to wither and die. Many of the earth's animals would have been unable to see well enough to take care of basic needs, and tropical species would have been subjected to subfreezing temperatures for the first time.

Obviously, many organisms survived the catastrophe. For example, marine plankton that could form resistant spores, or cysts, and the seeds of plants were apparently unaffected. Many bird groups somehow got through the event. Even some reptiles survived, although all species that weighed over 26 kg—about 60 lb—were eradicated. In any case, descendants of the smaller reptiles are still with us. At this point, let's step back and consider the survivors—the modern reptiles.

Modern Reptiles

The four orders of modern reptiles (Figure 29.14) probably descended from four general lines of ancient reptiles. One line produced the turtles and the side-necked turtles. A second line produced the crocodiles and alligators. A third led to the lizards, monitor lizards, and snakes. A final reptilian evolutionary line is represented by only one living species, *Sphenodon punctatus*, the tuatara of New Zealand, whose third eye, a crude light receptor (the *pineal eye*), on the top of its head makes it one of the world's strangest creatures.

AVES: THE BIRDS

The ancestors of modern birds can be traced back about 180 million years to the early Jurassic period (see Table 29.1). *Archaeopteryx*, the oldest known fossil bird, had feathers and presumably could fly (Figure 29.15). The skeleton of this early bird is, interestingly, almost indistinguishable from that of the **thecodonts**—the same reptilian stock that also produced crocodiles.

It takes a great deal of evolutionary change for a reptile to fly, and birds have certainly changed from their reptilian stock. However, beneath their

29.14

There are four orders of reptiles today, all descendants of the survivors of the great Mesozoic extinction. Most now live in tropical or subtropical regions, although a few survive the rigorous winters of temperate zones.

(a and b) Lizards and snakes are members of the same order. (c) Turtles represent a second order. (d) The crocodile is a third, and (e) the tuatara represents the fourth order of living reptiles.

29.15

Archaeopteryx, the earliest known bird—or is it? While most experts think it was just that, some claim that this feathered, winged creature was not a direct ancestor of today's birds, but merely a divergent side-branch in reptilian evolution. Note the numerous teeth, long tail, and clawed fingers. Whatever it was, this pigeon-sized, rather weakly muscled animal was abundant in the Mesozoic era. Numerous fossil finds of *Archaeopteryx* were identified as being examples of just another small thecodont reptile, until clear, fossilized impressions of feathers were found in a number of the best-preserved specimens.

obvious flight modifications lie many ancient reptilian traits. Their legs, for example, are still covered with reptilelike scales. And feathers, complex as they are in today's birds, can be traced back to reptilian scales. The upright, bipedal posture of birds was already established in their thecodont ancestors.

More interesting, perhaps, are the specializations for flight developed by birds (Figure 29.16). The wrists and fingers have undergone extensive fusion and elongation, supporting the important primary flight feathers. The skeleton is light and strong. Many bones are hollow, containing extensive air cavities, and are crisscrossed with netlike bracings for strength. Further weight reduction occurs in the gonads. The weight of the testes is drastically reduced between breeding seasons (some 1500 times in starlings). The females have but one ovary. The largest flight muscles are found in active flyers such as the pigeon, where they make up about half of the body weight. In soaring birds, these muscles may be greatly reduced, but the tendons and ligaments that hold the wings in position are considerably strengthened.

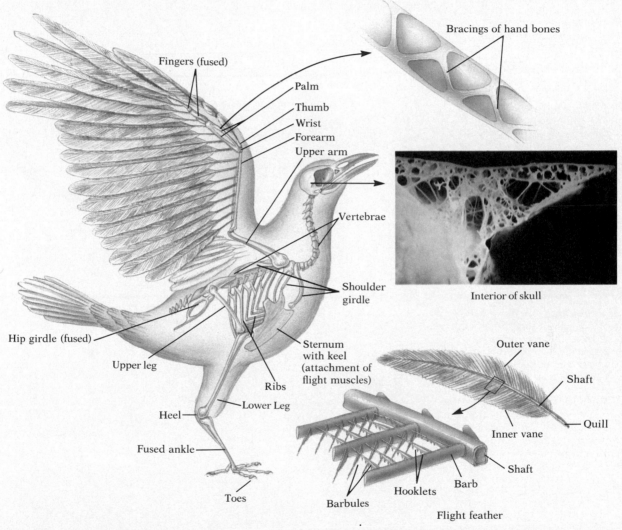

29.16

Modifications for flight are seen in nearly every aspect of the bird's anatomy and physiology, from the streamline form to the elevated metabolic rate. In spite of the demands placed upon it, the skeleton is extremely light. The frigate bird, for instance, has a wingspan of just over 2 m (7 ft), yet its skeleton weighs just 113 g (4 oz). In general, the slender, hollow bones of birds have a deceivingly delicate appearance; in fact, however, they are strong and flexible, containing numerous triangular bracings within (see x-ray image). Part of the skeletal strength is due to fusion, as is seen in the hip girdle, tail vertebrae, and, most spectacularly, in the long finger bones. Flight feathers, which can weigh more than the skeleton, owe their extreme strength and flexibility to numerous vanes. These have an interlocking arrangement of hooklike barbules.

29.17

The bird's respiratory system, which is quite extensive, includes posterior and anterior air sacs **(a)** that act as reservoirs and bellows for filling and emptying the lungs. The flow of air is essentially *through* the lungs **(b)** rather than *in and out*, as we find in other air-breathing vertebrates. The one-way passage permits a counter-current exchange of oxygen and carbon dioxide since the air and blood flow in opposite directions. Oddly enough, the bird lung contracts on inhalation and expands on expiration, but this is in response to expansion and contraction in the air sacs, rather than to air entering or leaving the trachea.

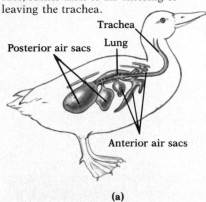

(a)

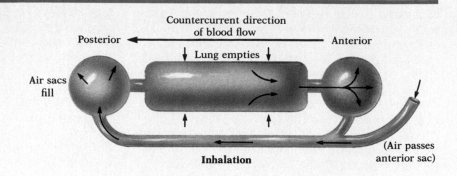

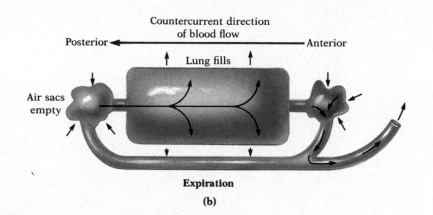

(b)

29.18

The mammals arose from the therapsids. The earliest therapsids retained many primitive reptilian traits, including scales, but in other ways they were already different in the Triassic period (197–225 million years ago). The limbs and stance of the therapsids, for instance, are not typical of reptiles. Raising the body off the ground was an adaptation for running and leaping, but it introduced new problems of balance and coordination—problems that required simultaneous adaptive changes in the brain.

The ancestral reptilian jaw has been drastically lightened, and teeth have been replaced with a light, horny bill. Bills vary enormously according to the feeding habits of the bird. The typical bird neck is long and flexible, and the bones of the trunk (pelvis, backbone, and rib cage) are fused into a semirigid unit. The breastbone is greatly enlarged, and has a *keel* (a flattened, vertical bone) from which the large flight (breast) muscles originate. The tail is reduced, consisting of only four vertebrae. Finally, the feet are specialized in various ways for digging, swimming, grasping, running, or perching.

There are less obvious internal modifications for flight. Like mammals, birds are *homeothermic;* that is, they can maintain a relatively constant and rather high internal body temperature. The constancy of temperature is maintained at a metabolic cost, but it has permitted them to adapt to virtually all climates. Helping to meet the oxygen requirements demanded by homeothermy is an efficient four-chambered heart that ensures that oxygenated and deoxygenated blood follow fully separated pathways in the circulatory system. The bird's respiratory system is unique in that the air moves in a one-way flow through the lung (Figure 29.17), as opposed to the in-and-out movement of air in other vertebrates.

The flow of air in the bird lung opposes the flow of blood, and so a *countercurrent exchange* is established. This results in a greater efficiency in the exchange of oxygen and carbon dioxide. Such efficiency is essential to flight at high altitudes where oxygen is less plentiful.

Birds continue the reptilian tradition of producing large, self-contained eggs. But as a rule, they produce fewer eggs than do reptiles, and tend to care for them more after laying them.

MAMMALS: ANOTHER SUCCESS STORY

The evolutionary history of mammals can be traced back to a group of reptiles known as the **therapsids.** Their branch arose early in reptilian history. The earliest therapsids made up a majority of reptile species throughout the Permian period (280–225 million years ago), but their numbers decreased with the rise and incredible increase of ruling reptiles at the beginning of the Mesozoic era (225 million years ago). The therapsids are said to have been doglike in size and appearance, but this is an exaggeration. You could clear out a bar if you walked in with one of these creatures on a leash (Figure 29.18).

29.19

Small, inconspicuous insect eaters, similar to the shrew shown here, may have given rise to the placental mammals. As long as reptiles were abundant, these animals remained in the background, gradually gaining in intelligence, evolving new reproductive strategies and improved sensory structures.

The earliest true mammals certainly were not very inspiring creatures. For the most part, they were very small carnivores that probably fed on insects, worms, and the eggs of reptiles. Some scientists accuse the modern shrew (Figure 29.19) of being very similar to these early mammals.

The Age of Mammals

The reptiles owned the Mesozoic era, but mammals inherited the Cenozoic era, perhaps with a little help from an asteroid. The survivors of that great extinction faced a new kind of world. When the air cleared and the dinosaurs were all dead, the mammals were greeted with countless new opportunities. They rapidly took advantage of what the new earth had to offer, filling niches vacated by the reptiles and establishing new niches for themselves.

Today, the surviving mammals are of three types (Figure 29.20): the **monotremes,** mammals that lay eggs; the **marsupials,** pouched mammals without true placentas; and the **placentals,** which constitute the great majority of mammals on all continents other than Australia. The placentals nourish their embryos through a well-developed placenta, and give birth to relatively advanced young.

All of the many different kinds of placental mammals—from shrews to whales—have evolved during the last 65 million years from just two (or possibly even just one) species that survived the great extinction. Either shortly before or shortly

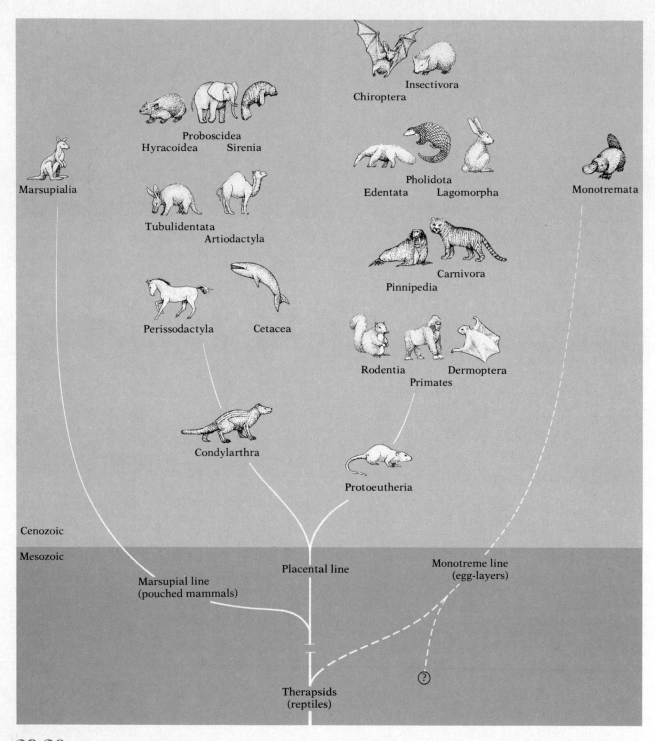

29.20

The 19 orders of modern mammals emerged from the Mesozoic in three primary lines of descent: the egg-laying monotremes represented by the duckbilled platypus *(right)*, the pouched marsupials of Australia and New Zealand *(left)*, and the placental mammals *(center)*, which include 17 of the orders. The fossil record of monotremes is scanty, but they do have mammalian traits suggesting a similar origin *(dashed line)*. The marsupials entered the Cenozoic in their own line, and were once widespread in North America. Except for the opossum they were displaced by placental mammals. The marsupials were limited first to South America, then to Antarctica, and finally to Australia. They were isolated there, free from placental competition, by the final events of continental drift. The placental mammals entered the Cenozoic in two groups, represented in the early Cenozoic fossil record by *Condylarthra* and *Protoeutheria*.

after the beginning of the Cenozoic era, the ancestors of today's placental mammals were represented by two species: *Condlyarthra* and *Protoeutheria*. *Condlyarthra* was eventually to give rise to most of the larger mammals existing today: horses, cows, giraffes, elephants, dugongs, and whales, as well as the small, hooved hyrax. Living descendants of *Protoeutheria* are the other placental mammals, including rodents, rabbits, bats, bears, seals, insectivores, anteaters, and our own group, the primates.

Modern Mammals

Why have mammals become so numerous and successful? They are not as numerous or successful as birds, but they do well enough. There is no explanation that can't be argued with, but it does seem that mammals have evolved a particularly well-matched group of critical traits and evolutionary adaptations that have enabled them to survive and flourish. If we concentrate on the placental mammals only, these traits include the following:

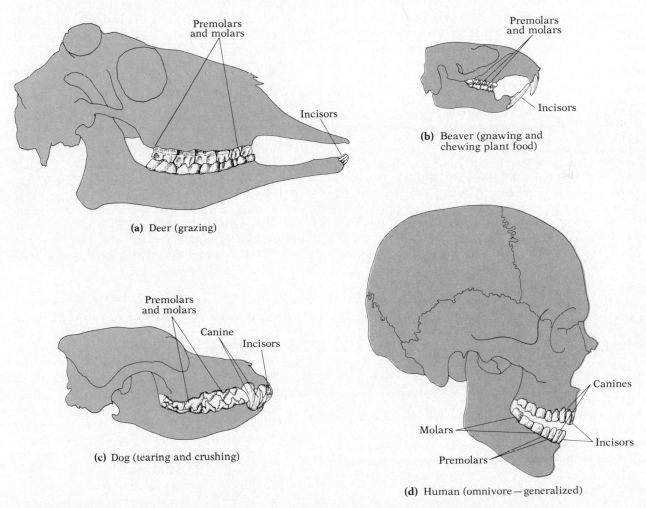

(a) Deer (grazing)

(b) Beaver (gnawing and chewing plant food)

(c) Dog (tearing and crushing)

(d) Human (omnivore—generalized)

29.21

Mammalian teeth are firmly socketed, with a covering of hard enamel. Any one mammal may have incisors for biting, canines for stabbing or tearing, and premolars and molars for crushing and grinding. In different species the teeth may be specialized according to the animal's diet. There are four general feeding specializations: herbivorous, carnivorous, omnivorous, and insectivorous types. Herbivores that graze on grasses often have large even incisors and large ridged molars (a), and those that gnaw on hardened plant parts (such as seeds and bark) have greatly enlarged incisors (b). In both, the canines are usually absent. Carnivores generally have large canines and sawlike molars (c), the former for killing and defense, and the latter for crushing bone. Human mouths (d) are not very specialized, and are a good example of adaptation for an onmivorous diet. Insectivores, ranging from shrews to bats, have fine, sharply pointed teeth with which they puree fragile prey.

1. A constant, high body temperature and high metabolic rate.
2. Internal development, with the embryo nourished through a placenta.
3. Mammary glands (in the female) for milk production.
4. Specialized teeth and efficient jaw (Figure 29.21).
5. A muscular diaphragm separating the chest and abdominal cavities.
6. Hair.
7. A large and versatile brain.

The Mammalian Brain. Above all, the hallmark of a modern mammal is its brain. Modern mammals are "smarter" than other vertebrates; they rely less on genetically programmed instincts, basing much of their behavior on parental guidance, individual experience, and learning. Not only is the brain much larger in mammals than in reptiles, but the mammalian brain has parts not found in other vertebrates, such as the *corpus callosum* that integrates the mental activities of the left and right halves of the brain.

Keep in mind that increasing learning capacity is simply one evolutionary alternative that provides an animal with a certain approach to survival. But there are other adaptive routes. It is not always best for a group to become smarter. For example, the insects are our chief competitors for the earth's resources, and they have a comparatively limited ability to learn. However, their alternative path of evolution obviously works well for them.

In the next chapter, we will consider the group that has the most highly developed ability to learn and takes great pride in this adaptation.

Summary

Introduction
In addition to having standard chordate characteristics, each vertebrate has a backbone, a centralized nervous system, a closed circulatory system, a dorsal heart, gills or lungs, two pairs of limbs, two image-forming eyes, and an excretory system involving paired kidneys. The vertebrate classes are Agnatha, Placodermi, Chondrichthyes, Osteichthyes, Amphibia, Reptilia, Aves, and Mammalia.

Humble Beginnings:
The Jawless Agnathan Fishes
Early jawless fishes, such as the ostracoderms, obtained food by sucking up bottom sediments. However, most agnathan species probably were displaced by the evolving jawed fishes. Hagfishes and lampreys are among the only living agnathans.

The First Jaws: Class Placodermi
The jaw represents an important evolutionary step in the development of vertebrates. The jaws of extinct placoderms are similar to those of living sharks. Placoderms appeared in the Silurian period, their paired pelvic and pectoral fins serving as the forerunners of the limbs of land vertebrates.

Cartilaginous Fishes:
Class Chondrichthyes
Cartilaginous fishes—sharks, rays, and chimeras—first appeared in the early Devonian period and proved to be highly successful predators and scavengers. The shark's tough skin is covered with placoid scales; its teeth can be continuously replaced; its intestine has a spiral valve; and it possesses a sensory device called the lateral line organ.

The Bony Fishes: Class Osteichthyes
Bony fishes are either ray-finned or lobe-finned. There are only a few living species of lobe-finned fishes. Ray-finned fishes have fins that permit rapid maneuvers; most have skin covered with scales and mucus glands, and have five pairs of gills. Some have swim bladders that are used to adjust buoyancy. Ray-fins have a variety of reproductive strategies and may be oviparous, ovoviviparous, or viviparous.

Vertebrates Invade the Land: The Tetrapods
Lobe-finned fishes diverged into lungfish and crossopterygians. The latter gave rise to terrestrial vertebrates, in the form of early amphibians.

Transitional Vertebrates: The Amphibians
Amphibians are characterized by thin, moist skin that contains dense capillary beds; three-chambered hearts; and several distinct stages of growth. Many amphibians require water for reproduction. Modern amphibians include Urodeles (salamanders), Anurans (frogs and toads), and Caecilians. Amphibians have adapted to a variety of climates.

Transition Completed: The Reptiles
Although amphibians and reptiles evolved from a common ancestor, reptiles took up an entirely terrestrial life. The development of water-repellent skin paralleled the development of improved lungs with alveoli. Reptiles possess either a four-chambered or three-chambered heart, muscular limbs, and the capacity for internal fertilization. Their eggs are protected by leathery shells that contain all the nutrients necessary for the embryo's de-

velopment. The developing embryo produces a number of supporting extraembryonic membranes.

During the Mesozoic era, some reptiles attained enormous size and diversity. At the end of this era, many reptilian species disappeared. The Alvarez hypothesis suggests that dust from the collision of a large asteroid with the earth blocked much of the sun's light, causing drastic climatic changes. The smaller reptiles that survived were the ancestors of modern reptiles, which are divided into four lines represented by turtles, crocodiles and alligators, lizards and snakes, and the tuatara.

Aves: The Birds

Birds, the oldest known fossil of which is *Archaeopteryx*, underwent several evolutionary changes that made flight possible, including the development of lightweight skeletons, flight muscles, horny bills, feathers, and specialized feet. Birds are homeothermic, possess a four-chambered heart, and have specially adapted respiratory and circulatory systems that allow for increased efficiency in the exchange of oxygen and carbon dioxide.

Mammals: Another Success Story

Mammals, descended from the therapsid reptiles, grew in number during the Cenozoic era. They are divided into monotremes, marsupials, and placentals. *Condylarthra*, an early placental mammal, is the ancestor of most large modern mammals, while *Protoeutheria* gave rise to many smaller mammals, as well as to primates. Evolutionary traits that enabled placental mammals to flourish on the earth include a constant high body temperature and metabolic rate, internal fertilization, mammary glands, specialized teeth and an efficient jaw, a muscular diaphragm, hair, and a large, versatile brain. The mammalian brain is capable of learning and adapting through experience.

Key Terms

vertebrates	ray-finned fishes	crossopterygians	amnion
ostracoderms	swim bladder	amphibians	Alvarez hypothesis
placoderms	oviparous	reptiles	thecodonts
cartilage	ovoviviparous	extraembryonic membranes	therapsids
spiral valve	viviparous	yolk sac	monotremes
cloaca	placenta	chorion	marsupials
lateral line organ	lungfish	allantois	placentals
lobe-finned fishes			

Review Questions

1. List the scientific names of the living vertebrate classes and provide an example (by common name) of each. (p. 423)

2. In what two principal ways did the ostracoderms differ from placoderms? (pp. 423–425)

3. Summarize the hypothesis presented regarding the origin of jaws in vertebrates. When did the first jawed vertebrates appear? From what structures did the jaws evolve? Where, in the living vertebrate, would one look for supporting evidence? (pp. 424–425)

4. Compare the following in the sharks and the bony fishes: skeleton, maneuverability, gill arrangement, and buoyancy structures. (pp. 427–428)

5. Compare the fins of ray-finned and lobe-finned fishes. Why are the lobe-fins of great interest to evolutionists? (pp. 427–429)

6. Discuss three amphibian traits that illustrate their close ties to the aquatic environment. (pp. 430–431)

7. Describe two reproductive adaptations found in reptiles that indicate successful evolutionary adaptations to the land environment. (pp. 432–433)

8. Explain how the skin, lungs, and limbs of reptiles represent further adaptations to terrestrial life. (p. 432)

9. List the extraembryonic membranes in the "land egg" and explain their functions. (p. 433)

10. Explain, briefly, how each of the following represents an adaptation for the requirements of flight in birds: bone structure, forelimbs, body covering, respiratory system, and heart. (pp. 437–438)

11. Summarize the Alvarez hypothesis, pointing out the supporting evidence and its significance to vertebrate history. (p. 435)

12. Briefly characterize each of the following in placental mammals: support of the embryo, feeding of newborn, regulation of body temperature, jaw and tooth structure, body covering, respiratory system, and learning ability. (pp. 439–441)

Human Evolution

30

The notion that humans evolve, as do other species, has provoked endless responses and arguments. Most scientists today, however, are not as interested in the validity of the notion itself as in the mechanisms and pathways of the evolutionary process. *Evolution* is a basic theoretical framework from which much of the biological sciences proceeds. This applies equally to research in human origins and to the origins of any other form of life. Lay people who accept this—and those who do not—are equally interested in what scientists think. Some questions that are currently being asked are:

> When did the first human appear?
> Did we really evolve from apes?
> Are we still evolving?

The answers are, respectively: *it depends on what you mean by human; probably not in the way you're thinking;* and *yes, but things have gotten very complicated.* If these answers seem arbitrary and vague, it's because we are now dealing with a subject that has a remarkable ability to draw out deep emotions, one with a long history of conflicting ideas.

PRIMATE ORIGINS

Humans are, of course, primates, so we might best begin to trace our origins by reviewing what we know about our taxonomic order. **Primate** fossils,

like those of most other placental mammals, first appear in the Paleocene deposits, formed about 60 to 65 million years ago, soon after the dinosaur extinction and the onset of the great mammalian expansion. The earliest primates, with their long snouts and claws, somewhat resembled modern tree shrews or even rodents. In fact, they may have occupied ecological niches similar to those of modern rodents, with some primate species living in trees and others scurrying about on the ground or living in burrows. People in technologically advanced societies may be a bit embarrassed to think of how many grubs our ancestors ate, although grubs still form a staple in the diet of many 20th-century humans.

By the beginning of the Eocene epoch (about 54 million years ago), primates began to resemble those existing today. They had become primarily fruit-eating and tree-dwelling; and there was a general shortening of the snout, a more forward location of the eyes, and a more definite primate tooth structure. Toward the middle of the Miocene epoch, only about 20 million years ago, lines that lead to all modern primate families (including Hominoidea—apes and humans) were well established (Figure 30.1).

Modern Primates

Primates differ from other mammals in a number of ways—for example, in their limbs. Most primates are well adapted for *arboreal* (tree-dwelling) life, as evidenced by their **prehensile** (grasping) hands and feet, long arms, and, in the case of the New World monkeys, prehensile tails.

But life in the trees had demanded other changes as well. As their eye sockets moved to the fronts of their faces, the primates acquired binocu-

lar, stereoscopic vision. With both eyes focused on an object, a fine, three-dimensional image could be produced that permitted more accurate estimates of distance. Coupled with this visual precision was an acute eye-hand coordination, which undoubtedly continued to develop as visual information

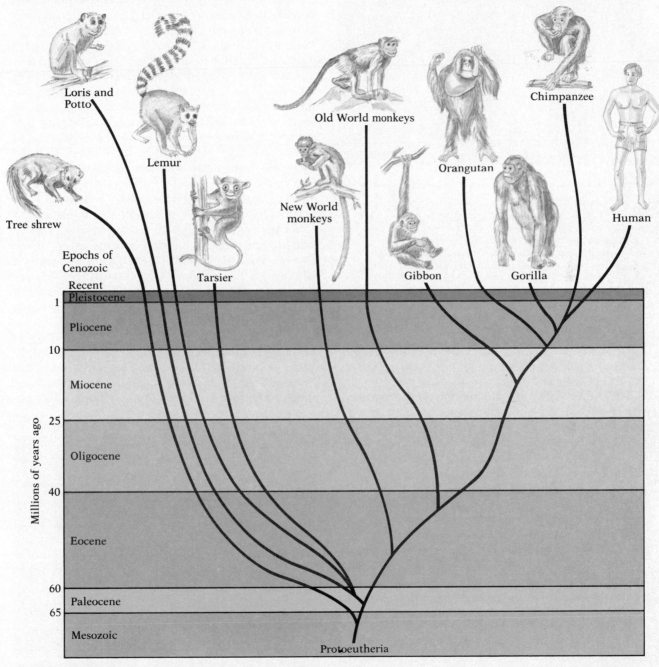

30.1

Primates are chiefly a product of the Cenozoic era. The evolutionary relationship between primate groups can be determined by noting where their ancestors diverged from the main stock. Thus *prosimians* and *New World monkeys* are quite distant from the others, their lines having diverged in the early Paleocene and

Eocene epochs, respectively. Old World monkeys and hominoids began their divergence much later, towards the close of the Eocene epoch, but the eventual separation of humans from apes is relatively recent, a product of the Pliocene epoch.

30.2

Prehensile hands and feet (and, sometimes, tails) help primates move through the tree canopy. The movement also requires keen hand-eye coordination and stereoscopic vision. Of the creatures with these traits, the agile howler monkey is one of the most talented at climbing and swinging. Its long limbs and tail are specialized for such movement, and the small thumb does not interfere with the strong, grasping fingers.

became more and more "informative." These traits are obviously important if one is to swing through the trees (Figure 30.2).

Such anatomical specializations would require a substantial degree of simultaneous brain development, with strong emphasis on brain centers dealing with coordination and vision. For example, we can propose that as the hand developed and became increasingly dexterous, its use would have gone beyond simply keeping the animal from falling out of trees. The hand could be used in other ways, but learning these would have demanded a correspondingly more complex (larger) brain. Such a brain might then discover new uses for the hand, but then an even more advanced brain would have been required.

Primates tend to be omnivores, eating all sorts of food, and their mouths are relatively unspecialized. However, with the exception of humans, primates—particularly the males—have rather large canine teeth. These are used primarily in aggressive encounters with other male primates and in defense against predators (Figure 30.3). Human canines have become reduced in size, probably an adaptation to a changing diet. Their loss has since been more than compensated for by the development of such tools as rocks, spears, knives, and missiles.

Human Specializations. It might be argued that human evolution has been markedly mental rather than physical. This is because many of our physical traits are those of a generalist—ones expected in a species with a high intelligence that tends to live an opportunistic existence. Our principal evolutionary achievements outside of the nervous system are our **bipedal gait** and our famous **opposable thumb,** which can touch the fingers of the same hand. The upright human posture is quite unlike that of any other living primate. Savannah chimpanzees sometimes stand to see over tall grass, and may walk bipedally a short way, but normally the apes are *quadrupedal,* walking on all fours (Figure 30.4). It is amusing to see an ape running on its rear legs, partly because it is so humanlike and yet so ungainly. Humans, however, are beautifully adapted to bipedal walking and running. We owe this ability to our enlarged *gluteus maximus* (buttocks) and, in part, to our uniquely specialized foot, and its springlike arched construction and broad first toe. Interestingly, a human sprinter can outrun a horse over 100 m (horses are slow getting started), and a marathon runner can outrun a horse in a 50 km race. Horses tire first. But on a 2 km (1.25 mi) run, bet on the horse. A primitive hunter can run down most game to exhaustion.

As for the human thumb, it is merely a refinement of a specialization that is possessed, to some degree, by other primates. Originally, the opposable thumb evolved as an adaptation for grasping branches. But in most primates it is rela-

30.3

The large canines of many primates are important defensive weapons. They are often displayed to potential adversaries as a warning. In chimpanzees, canines also are used in killing prey—often young baboons or baby gazelles—to supplement their vegetable diet.

446

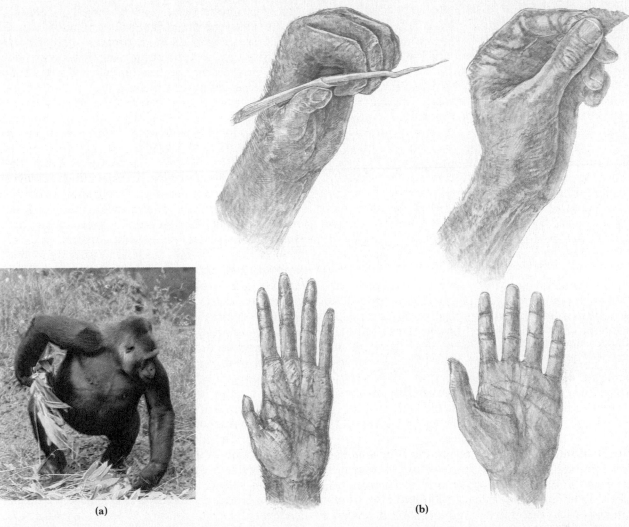

(a)

(b)

30.4

(a) While apes can assume a bipedal posture, neither their hip nor leg structure supports this very well. In bipedal walking, the weight is borne on the outer edge of the archless foot. (b) The hands of humans and chimpanzees appear generally similar, but there are important differences. Chief among these are the length and musculature of the thumb. In the chimpanzee, the thumb doesn't quite reach the base of the forefinger, while in humans the thumb extends nearly to the middle joint. This "out of the way" location in the chimp is important to a brachiator, but makes handling tools and other human objects far less precise than when handled by humans. Compare the precision grip in the two, noting that in using its thumb, the chimpanzee must flex its fingers. Try buttoning your shirt that way.

tively short, poorly muscled, and much less capable of precise movement. The human thumb has evolved special musculature and can be rotated much more readily. Apes can be trained to use simple tools and to open beer cans, but they are comically clumsy all the same. With our much greater manual dexterity, we can make precise tools, even from rocks and sticks if we must. Other animals have been reported to use or even make tools, although the definition of "tool" must be stretched to include such things as the stone upon which a sea otter smashes a clam, or the twig that a chimpanzee will use to probe termite nests and to extract the excited insects. But no other species can build a watch that works, or can make tools that are used just to make other tools. To worry about how much of this has to do with thumbs, and how much has to do with brains, is to miss the point— which is that our intelligence and our manual dexterity have evolved together.

Our intelligence has not evolved without costs. Like other mammals, we are born in a helpless state, but human infants seem to be particularly helpless, with fewer built-in adaptive responses than infants of many other species. A baby hare, for example, will lunge and hiss at an intruder. Newborn antelopes follow their mothers within minutes, and infant baboons quickly learn to ride on their mothers' backs. Virtually all baby primates will hold onto their mother's hair, so that she can move with ease. In comparison, our newborns seem witless. And in what other species do the offspring ask for help 21 years after parturition?

Even the extensive development (some say *over-development*) of the human brain merely extends a long-standing trend in mammalian and especially primate evolution. Over the millions of years, the consistent trend in most mammalian orders has been toward larger and larger brains. This is accompanied by a greater capacity for learning and for versatile behavior, at the expense of stereotyped, genetically based instinctive behavior.

The importance of intelligence to humans, coupled with our complex and highly interactive social system, has led to another unusual trait in our species: the development of language. Of course, wolves howl, birds sing, and bees relate the location of a new food source by complex dances. And there are controversial reports that apes or dolphins can learn various nonverbal means of communicating with humans. However, so far, it seems that humans can claim exclusive rights to the ability to communicate abstract ideas.

The evolutionary emphasis on both intelligence and language in such a highly social group as our own has resulted in another kind of change: *cultural evolution*. Cultural evolution involves transmitting traits through the generations by means other than genetic. Such descent may take the form of traditions, laws, or even superstitions. For example, many of our sexual codes are transmitted, at least partly, by cultural means. Our society (or family) makes it perfectly clear to us what is acceptable and what is not. We have been carefully taught by our predecessors, and we, in turn, tend to instruct our own immediate descendants. Of course, we are no longer restricted to influencing those within earshot. We have learned to read and write, and so our words can reach those who are born long after we die. With writing, it seems, we can expect traits transmitted culturally to be more uniform and more broadly distributed in the population. Any pattern transmitted by both cultural and genetic means would be powerfully buttressed in our society.

Humans also have an enormous capability for mathematics, some of us more than others. Why or how this ability evolved is not easy to fathom. Careful neurological measurements reveal that the human brain has a highly localized site for the pro-

cess of multiplication—and an entirely different, equally localized site that becomes active when the person is doing a division problem. What these specialized parts of the brain were doing just a few thousand years ago, before mathematics had been invented, is anybody's guess.

THE HUMAN LINE

In the early 1960s, comparisons of proteins clearly indicated that humans are related more closely to African chimpanzees and gorillas than to Asian orangutans. Researchers were aware that such molecules as these change at a constant and predictable rate, and thus are able to provide us with kind of a molecular "clock." This clock suggested that humans and African apes diverged from a common ancestor not more than five million years ago. The suggestion was startling at the time; anthropologists had always assumed that the separation had occurred much earlier. And so these findings were met with skepticism and, in cases, outright hostility. However, other data—both biochemical and paleontological—began to appear that supported the newer findings, and so we have adjusted our notions of human lineage.

The current theory is that, about three to four million years ago, humanlike forms lived in the relatively dry open grasslands of Africa. Their fossils suggest that there were four recognizable and distinct groups: *Australopithecus robustus, Australopithecus africanus, Australopithecus afarensis,* and *Homo habilis.* (The name *Australopithecus* means "southern ape," a misleading designation, since they are not apes.) Direct ancestry to the genus *Homo* has not been conclusively established, but it is clear that *A. robustus* and *A. africanus* were widespread and successful, persisting almost unchanged until at least a million years ago, long after the genus *Homo* was well established.

The Australopithecines

The **australopithecines** (members of the genus *Australopithecus*) were rather small-boned, light-bodied creatures, about 1–1.5 m (3.5–5 ft) tall. They had humanlike teeth and jaws with small incisors and canines, and they walked upright (Figure 30.5). They apparently hunted baboons, gazelles, hares, birds, and giraffes. The australopithecine cranial capacity ranged from 450 to 650 cc (a measure of brain size), as compared with 1200–1600 cc for modern adult humans.

The australopithecines were rather small, from 1 to 1.5 m (3.5 to 5 ft) tall. They were heavy-boned, suggesting strong muscularity and a weight of up to 68 kg (150 lb). Their heads appeared more apelike than humanlike, with a low cranial profile and little or no chin. However, the jaws were large and forward-thrusting. Their bodies were human-like. There is no evidence that they produced tools, although they may have made use of materials at hand, as chimpanzees are known to do.

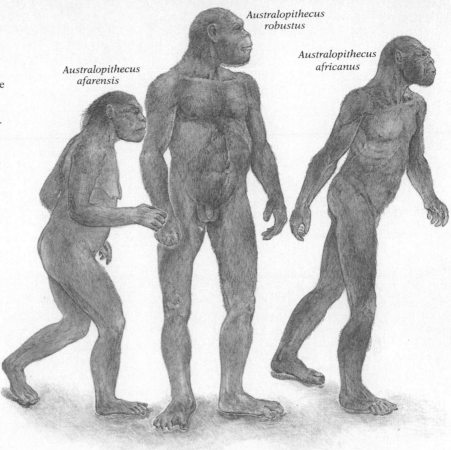

Australopithecus afarensis

Australopithecus robustus

Australopithecus africanus

A. robustus, as the name suggests, was larger-boned—though not taller—than *A. africanus*. Most strikingly, *A. robustus* had huge jaws, greatly expanded cheek bones to accommodate massive jaw muscles, and very large teeth. The teeth, however, were more humanlike than apelike, and the tooth wear suggests that these australopithecines were vegetarians. (Some anthropologists now question whether *A. robustus* and *A. africanus* were actually two different species, since there seems to be an array of intermediate forms, and it is likely that any such groups ate both flesh and plants.)

The first specimen of another australopithecine, *A. afarensis* (dubbed "Lucy" after a song recorded by the Beatles in the 1960s), was found in the northern Ethiopian desert region in 1974 by Donald Johanson. It consisted of a little more than half of a skeleton of an upright-walking female, calculated to be about three million years old. Then, the following year, Johanson unearthed the remains of 13 more "Lucy" types, all in one area. Johanson concluded that these australopithecines were more primitive than *A. robustus* and *A. africanus*, and tentatively placed them as a separate species in the main line of **hominid** (humanlike) evolution, suggesting that they were ancestors to both the australopithecines and the line leading to *Homo* (Figure 30.6).

Homo habilis

Homo habilis is the name given by the famed anthropologist Louis Leakey to the human relatives represented by certain fossils from the Olduvai Gorge in Tanganyika, Africa. As the generic name indicates, these fossils seemed to be close to the modern human form, and *H. habilis* is clearly associated with tool making. Critics have argued that the new find is simply a variant of the genus *Australopithecus*, and that Leakey was unjustified in trying to include his fossils within the genus *Homo*. For the moment, *H. habilis* is placed, phylogenetically, in the early *Homo* line (see Figure 30.6).

More recently, Leakey's son Richard and his widow Mary found a hominid skull of unusual interest at Koobi Fora, east of Lake Turkana, Africa (Figure 30.7). At 1.6 to 2.5 million years old, it is older than many *Australopithecus* fossils, but it appears to be much closer to the human line than *Australopithecus*. For one thing, it has a greater cranial capacity (775 cc) than either *Australopithecus* or the earlier *H. habilis* finds. The Leakeys, apparently fed up with the arguments over the assignment of species and genus names to hominid fossils, simply identified their unique find by its arbitrary field identification: "Fossil Skull 1470."

Homo erectus

More recently, fossil beds of the eastern shore of Lake Turkana have yielded fossils that are more similar to the modern human. The new species, called **Homo erectus,** is an extinct member of our own genus. The earliest African *H. erectus* skulls are known to be more than 1.5 million years old. What is most interesting about them is that they appear to be of the same species as some of the first hominid fossils ever found—those that were once called "Java Ape Man" and "Peking Man." The problem is that these fossils were only about half a million years old. Then some *H. erectus* fossils were found that may be even less than 200,000 years old. In other words, *H. erectus* flourished, relatively unchanged, for well over a million years. Furthermore, during its first 300,000 years it coexisted with other more primitive hominid species, including the australopithecines and, possibly, *Homo habilis*. During at least the final 100,000–200,000 years of its existence, *H. erectus* existed concurrently with

30.6

The known hominid history spans a period of nearly four million years. According to Donald Johanson, the most recent ancestor to the human line was *Australopithecus afarensis*. Johanson suggests that *A. afarensis* produced two lines of descent: the australopithecines and *Homo*, with *Homo habilis* possibly representing the earliest human, although not in the main line. *Homo erectus* had a rather long history, coexisting toward the end with the first *Homo sapiens*, an offshoot of the *H. erectus* line. The earliest *H. sapiens*, as far as we know, were the familiar Neanderthals, a diverse but successful group, finally replaced entirely by modern humans, only 40,000 years ago.

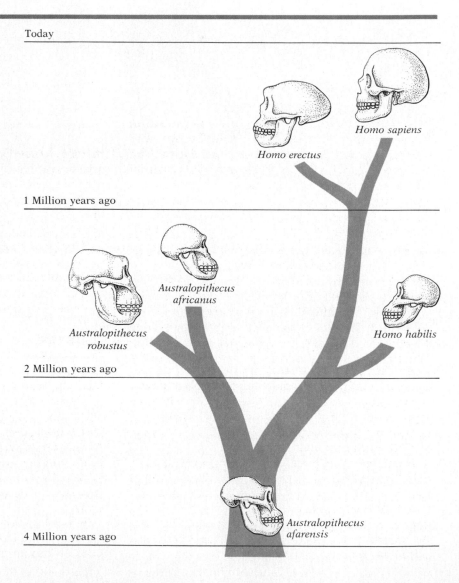

Today

1 Million years ago

2 Million years ago

4 Million years ago

Homo sapiens

Homo erectus

Australopithecus africanus

Australopithecus robustus

Homo habilis

Australopithecus afarensis

30.7

The richest australopithecine finds are located along Africa's Rift Valley in Ethiopia, Tanzania, and Kenya. *H. erectus* was far-ranging, with fossils recovered in eastern and southern Africa, Europe, China, and Indonesia. Neanderthal fossils have been unearthed throughout much of Europe, the Middle East, North Africa, and China.

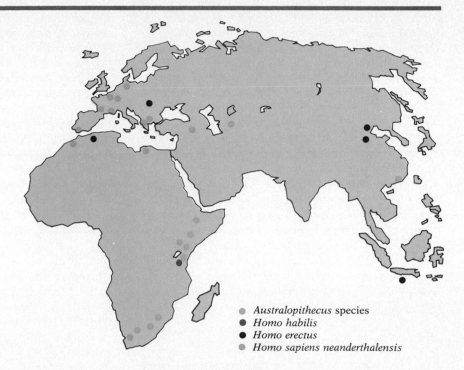

● *Australopithecus* species
● *Homo habilis*
● *Homo erectus*
● *Homo sapiens neanderthalensis*

yet another species, **Homo sapiens.** Now, fossils of *H. erectus* have been found in China, Europe, and southern Africa, and, of course, East Africa. The evidence left by *H. erectus* provides fascinating grist for the mills of our imaginations.

Recent findings at a well known site at Zhoukoudian, China reveal that one large cave was continuously inhabited by *H. erectus* for over 200 thousand years, and finally abandoned 230 thousand years ago. During this incredibly long period of residence, both the anatomy and the technology of *H. erectus* changed significantly. Skulls unearthed in the oldest debris of the cave revealed a cranial capacity of about 915 cc, while those in the most recent layers had reached 1,140 cc. The stone tools also progressed from large, crude, hastily fashioned choppers and scrapers in the oldest, deeper layers to smaller, much more refined tools in newer layers near the surface. These cave inhabitants used fire from the start, hunted both large and small game, and ate a variety of nuts, fruits, seeds, and other plant matter.

H. erectus was obviously successful, but their time also ended. Most passed from the earth just after the first glaciers of the Pleistocene epoch receded. At least one line of descendants are believed to have persisted, quietly changing and adapting. We are the product, but there is still one more link before we come to modern humans.

Neanderthals and Us

In 1856, while Darwin was puzzling over natural selection at his country estate, workmen in a steep gorge in the Valley of Neander (in German, *Neanderthal*) were pounding at a rock they didn't recognize. They finally saw that it was a skeleton, but by then it had been smashed to bits. Fortunately, they had left enough for researchers to study, and soon it was announced that there was clear evidence of a new and different kind of human. (Interestingly, a similar skull had been unearthed at Gibraltar a few years earlier, but had not created much of a stir.)

Scientists are rarely at a loss for words, so an explanation of this peculiar find was immediately forthcoming. Professor E. Meyer of Bonn examined the heavy-browed skull, cleared his throat, and proclaimed that the skull and bone fragments belonged to a Mongolian cossack chasing Napoleon's retreating troops through Prussia in 1812. An advanced case of rickets had caused him great pain, and his furrowed brow had produced the great ridges. Because he was so distraught he had crawled into a cave to rest, but, alas, had died right there.

However, this scenario has been rejected in favor of the idea that the bones were those of an early form of human that became extinct—the so-called

Neanderthal man (Figure 30.8). (Interestingly, the individual who originally owned that skeleton did indeed have rickets. Perhaps it was hard to get enough sunshine, what with living in a cave in Northern Europe during an Ice Age.)

Members of *Homo sapiens neanderthalensis* thrived, or at least survived, around 70,000 to 40,000 years ago. They left a rich record of fossil remains and some indication of their tools and culture. Their geographic range was large, extending at least from Portugal to Soviet Central Asia.

At first, Neanderthal fossils seemed to show exactly what anyone of the 19th century would expect of an "ape-man" (Figure 30.8). Neanderthals were depicted as being heavy-boned and heavy-browed, with low foreheads, wide faces, and little or no chin. "Reconstructions" drawn in the 19th and early 20th centuries always showed ugly, stooped, hairy, apelike bodies, although we now know that the Neanderthal body was virtually identical to our own—and we are not all ugly,

stooped, and apelike. It was an embarrassment to the Victorians that the Neanderthal had a greater cranial capacity than modern humans do. They got around this by arguing that the relatively sloping forehead of the "ape-men" meant that they were less than moral, and certainly not nearly as sophisticated as we are.

Later, it was found that, although the Neanderthals did indeed have large brow ridges, sloping foreheads, and small chins, their necks and bodies—when they didn't have rickets—were like ours (Figure 30.9). There is no way to know whether they had a spoken language, but we do know, from fossil pollens found with their remains, that Neanderthals sometimes covered their dead with flowers before burial. Whether or not that's sophisticated, it certainly is human—touchingly so.

Neanderthal-type fossils have not been found in rocks formed more recently than about 40,000 years ago. With a few exceptions, fossils from 30,000 years ago onward are all identical to those of modern human skeletons (including the once-celebrated *Cro-Magnon Man*, a European cave dweller who lived about 20,000 years ago).

Why did the Neanderthals disappear? One suggestion is that the classic (or more primitive) Neanderthal line and the line of modern humans diverged from each other as long as 250,000 years ago. For some reason, the Neanderthals flourished at the time the developing "sapiens" types were few in number. Then, about 40,000 years ago, the scarce *Homo sapiens sapiens* population suddenly burgeoned, and expanded its range. This was when Neanderthal became extinct, possibly from attacks by *H. sapiens sapiens*.

A second theory suggests that the differences between the two groups were insignificant, because *H. sapiens* in the Neanderthal age was a highly variable species that included both the classic Neanderthal types as well as individuals much like ourselves. This theory implies that the Neanderthals were squarely in the mainstream of human evolution. The upshot is that modern humans evolved from Neanderthal ancestors. Therefore, the theory states, the Neanderthals didn't die out, but merely changed—they changed into us.

Whatever the case, *Homo sapiens* became rather well established on earth, and, at the point record-keeping began, much of the rest of human evolution is called *history*. We will have more to say about ourselves later. We deserve the attention, not only from an egotistical view, but because of the impact we had—and are continuing to have—on other species and our limited planet as well. We will see much more of the effect of our impact in future discussions (see Chapter 46 and 47).

30.8

Traditional museum painting of the Neanderthal.

30.9

In a face-to-face confrontation **(a)**, a modern human and the Neanderthal reveal many general similarities and some striking differences. In the Neanderthal, note the sloping of the forehead, the large brow ridges, and the receding lower jaw. The angle of the jawbone itself is smaller where it curves upward to join the skull. The facial reconstruction **(b)** produces an image quite different from the traditional view of Neanderthal, long considered an apelike creature. With the exception of obvious differences in skull structure, Neanderthals had fairly modern skeletons. (Copyright © Jay H. Matternes—Courtesy Science 81.)

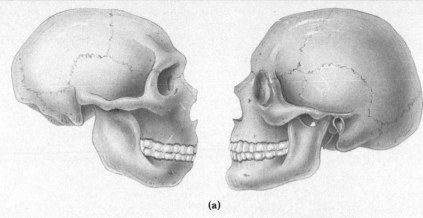

(a)

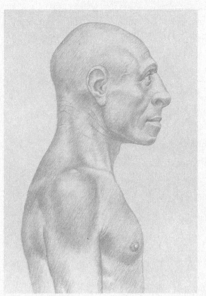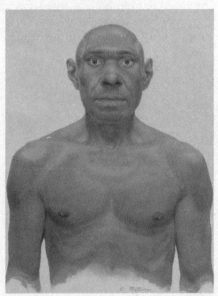

(b)

Summary

Primate Origins

Primate fossils first appeared in deposits of the Paleocene epoch and somewhat resembled rodents, living on the ground, in burrows, and in trees. Eocene primates looked more like modern species, and by the Miocene epoch, the lines that lead to modern primate families were well established.

Primates, unlike most mammals, possess prehensile hands and feet; binocular, stereoscopic vision; and a brain with strongly developed centers of coordination and vision. The hand-eye coordination needed by tree dwellers resulted in the increasingly complex development of both the hand and brain. Primates tend to be omnivores, and most have large canine teeth.

Human specializations include a bipedal gait and opposable thumbs. Humans are more helpless in infancy than other mammals, but have a considerably greater capacity to learn. We humans, with our capacity for language, are capable of cultural as well as genetic evolution.

The Human Line

By comparing human and primate proteins, researchers have linked humans more closely to African chimpanzees and gorillas than to other primates. Humans and primates diverged not more than five million years ago, with humanlike australopithecines probably living in African grasslands three to four million years ago. Recently discovered fossils of *A. afarensis* indicate that they were one of the earliest humanlike forms, ancestor to both the australopithecines and the humanlike lines.

Homo habilis, older than many australopithecines, is

clearly associated with tool making. *Homo erectus*, similar to modern humans, coexisted with both australopithecines and *Homo sapiens*. During their tenure on earth, the cranial capacity of *H. erectus* increased, and their tools became quite refined. The species disappeared during the Pleistocene epoch.

Homo sapiens neanderthalensis lived some 70,000 to 40,000 years ago. Their geographic range extended from Portugal to Soviet Central Asia. Neanderthals had large brow ridges, sloping foreheads, and small chins, and had greater cranial capacity than modern humans. As the *Homo sapiens sapiens* population grew, the Neanderthal species disappeared. One theory suggests that Neanderthals did not die out but changed into modern humans. Others contend that *H. sapiens sapiens* outcompeted the Neanderthals.

Key Terms

primates	*Homo habilis*
prehensile	*Homo erectus*
bipedal gait	*Homo sapiens*
opposable thumb	*Homo sapiens neanderthalensis*
australopithecines	*Homo sapiens sapiens*
hominid	

Review Questions

1. List the following primates in the order in which they are believed to have diverged from the original primate line: New World monkeys, lemurs, humans, gibbons, tree shrews, chimpanzees, Old World monkeys, and gorillas. (Figure 30.1)

2. Describe three characteristics of primates that make them different from most other mammals. (pp. 444–446)

3. Summarize the differences between modern humans and the modern chimpanzee or gorilla in terms of posture, walking gait, feet, buttock muscles, hands, and learning ability. (pp. 446–448)

4. Develop a time line for hominid evolution, listing the dates and order of appearance of *Homo erectus*, *Homo sapiens sapiens*, the three *Australopithecus* species, *Homo sapiens neanderthalensis*, and *Homo habilis*. (pp. 448–452)

5. Describe the three known types of australopithecines and suggest why they have been assigned to their own genus and species. Which of the group seems to fit more closely into the *Homo* line? (pp. 450–451)

6. Briefly describe the physical features and technology of *Homo erectus*. Suggest two different explanations for their demise. (pp. 450–451)

7. In what general ways do Neanderthal fossils differ from modern humans? Summarize what you believe to be the most logical explanation of their extinction. (pp. 451–452)

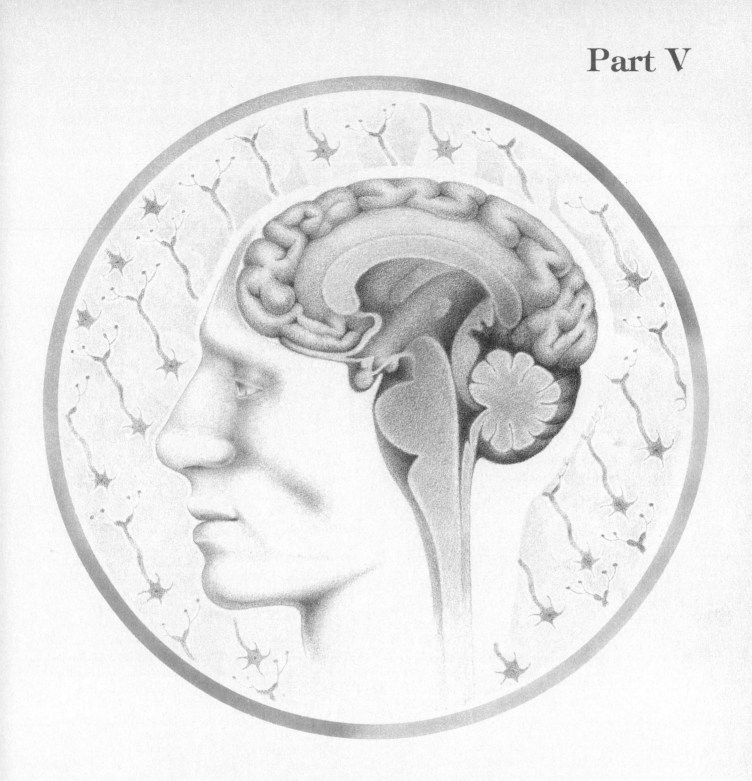

Part V

Vertebrate Regulation

The Vertebrate Body

31

Now we focus our attention on the vertebrate body. But we must begin with the niggling awareness that there is no such thing as "the vertebrate body." Vertebrates are a highly varied group with a wide range of appearances. The most skilled physician might have difficulty performing an appendectomy on a turtle. Where would one begin to look?

On the other hand, all vertebrates have many traits in common. For example, they all obviously have backbones. The sturdy column of bones is needed as support and as a place for the attachment of powerful muscles. The vertebrate head is always located at the anterior end of the body. In addition, we will see that the bodies of all vertebrates are composed of only a few types of tissues. The similarities continue even to the molecular level where we will find that the cell constituents of all vertebrates are remarkably similar, and even the chemical reactions that power the muscles reveal a common heritage.

VERTEBRATE TISSUES

A **tissue** is a group of specialized cells, together with their noncellular **matrix** (a *matrix* is a supporting substance—plural, *matrices*), that generally perform the same function. There are four major types of vertebrate tissue: *epithelium, connective tis-*

sue, muscle, and *nerve.* These tissues rarely act alone, but rather they are assembled in an integrated manner to form the organs and the organ systems of the body.

Epithelial Tissue

Epithelium, or *epithelial tissue,* forms the interior and exterior linings of most surfaces of the vertebrate organism. Wherever they are located, these tissues are commonly separated from other tissues below by a fibrous, noncellular *basement membrane.* Thus the **epidermis** ("outer skin") is epithelial, as are the linings of the mouth, the nasal cavities, the respiratory system, the coelom, the tubes of the reproductive system, the gut, and the interior of blood vessels. Some glands of the body are composed of thickened tissue called *glandular epithelium.* The cells there not only form the linings of the ducts, but produce the secretions that later will be released through the ducts to the exterior.

As you might expect, epithelial cells differ greatly from place to place, although there are only three main shapes: flattened, cylindrical or columnlike, and cubelike (Figure 31.1). In the epidermis, for example, we find an outer *stratified squamous epithelium,* containing many layers of flattened cells. The outermost cells are filled with the protein keratin and are hardened and dead. The innermost cells of the epidermis, a living layer of relatively cuboidal cells, repeatedly divide to provide new cells to the flattened layers above. This layer of living, dividing cells responds to friction and wear by speeding up cell division, often producing thickened callouses of dead keratinized cells. Stratified squamous epithelium also lines the mouth, esophagus, and vagina—all regions of potential frictional wear and rapid cell replacement.

In the nasal lining and other respiratory linings, the epithelium is more complex, containing glandular, mucus-secreting cells and ciliated cells, both of which occur in columnlike rows and are known as *columnar epithelium*. The respiratory cilia constantly sweep the passages clear (see Chapter 38), unless they have been killed by tobacco smoke—in which case the passages may be cleared by other means, such as hacking and coughing. Columnar epithelium also occurs in the uterine lining, in many glands, and in the lining of the gut. Cells lining the sweat glands, kidney tubules, and the surface of the ovary are cube-shaped and are thus known as *cuboidal epithelium*.

Connective Tissue

Connective tissue is found throughout the vertebrate body—which is probably a good thing, since it basically holds the body together. But some types of connective tissue have other roles, also. Essentially, connective tissue consists of cells plus their secretions, which together produce a noncellular **connective tissue matrix** (Figure 31.2). Familiar connective tissues are bone, cartilage, ligaments, tendons, and, perhaps surprisingly, blood.

The principal substance in most connective tissue matrices such as tendons, ligaments, basement membranes, and muscle coverings is **collagen,** a fibrous protein that accounts for at least a third of the total body protein in larger vertebrates. Collagen serves as the "glue" of the animal body, as it is responsible for binding various tissues together. It also forms such extremely tough structures as the cornea of the eye and the *intervertebral discs* (the cushions between the bones of the spine). Collagen is even the principal component of bone, excluding the minerals that account for its hardness. It is found in all animals.

Collagen is secreted by special cells known as **fibroblasts,** forming tough, lengthy fibers (Figure 31.3). Fibroblasts are vitally important to wound healing (they produce scar tissue), and are essential in the mending of broken bones. They fill the fracture site with tough fibers of collagen. This specialized collagen remains in place only until new bone forms and hardens, permanently fusing the break.

31.1

Epithelial cells vary depending on their location and tasks. Simple linings are formed by flattened or squamous cuboidal cells **(a)**, which may be a single layer thick or stratified. The latter are more common in regions of rapid wear and replacement. The respiratory linings—nasal passages, trachea, and bronchi—contain columnar cells **(b)**, commonly including glandular, or secretory, and ciliated cells. Glands may also be formed by epithelial, secretory cells **(c)** that empty their secretions into a common duct.

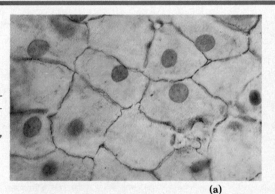
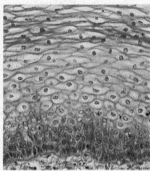

(a)

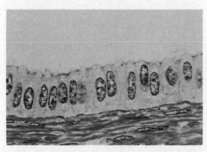

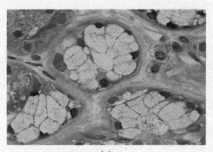

(b)

(c)

Elastin, another connective tissue protein, makes the skin elastic. Since ears are rich in elastin, you can reach over and tug your neighbor's ear and it will snap right back into place. (If it doesn't, feign innocence, say something about the weather, and leave.) Elastin loses its properties with age. The loss of elastic properties is responsible for the sagging of older faces.

Adipose tissue is a primary storage site of fats. These "fat cells" are found under the skin, between muscle fibers, in the breasts and buttocks, in intestinal membranes, and in other places in the body. Pinch tests provide one way to ascertain the amount and distribution of fat on your body. As a very simple test, if you can pinch up more than one inch of fat in any area (usually the waist, the shoulder blade, and the back of the arm), you may be eating too much. Some parents consider a fat infant a healthy infant. According to some theories, however, overfeeding in infancy can build a surplus of adipose cells that may sentence the baby to a lifetime of obesity or constant dieting.

Blood is also a connective tissue, according to the standard definition of the term. Its cells are suspended in a viscous fluid, the **plasma,** which is the connective tissue matrix. (The qualities of this peculiar fluid will be discussed in Chapter 39.)

Muscle Tissue

Muscle tissue is unique in that it has the peculiar ability to contract. This contraction, of course, is responsible for movement in vertebrates. Not only do the arms and fingers flex in a coordinated way, but some party goers can wiggle their ears. Aside from moving the skeleton, other muscular contractions, over which we have little control, are responsible for breathing, heartbeat, and digestion.

(a)

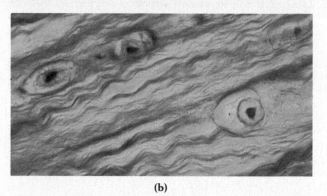

(b)

31.3

(a) Collagenous fibers form a tough binding material that literally holds the vertebrate body together. Logically enough, collagen is the primary material of tendons—strong, cordlike structures attached to bones. (b) Individual collagen fibers in tendons form a wavy pattern, with distinct cross-banding of dense protein. *(a: From TISSUES AND ORGANS: a text atlas of scanning electron microscopy,* by Richard G. Kessel and Randy H. Kardon, W. H. Freeman and Company, copyright © 1979.)

31.2

Connective tissues. In *loose* connective tissues **(a),** the fibroblasts lie scattered in a loosely arranged matrix of dense collagen fibers, interspersed with fine elastic fibers. Loose connective tissue occurs beneath the skin and epithelial linings, and surrounds blood vessels and nerves. *Dense* connective tissue (such as that forming tendons and ligaments) contains much more of the fibrous matrix **(b),** arranged in parallel rows, with the fibroblasts crowded among individual collagen fibers.

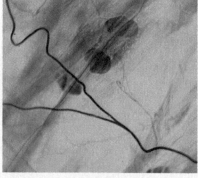

(a)

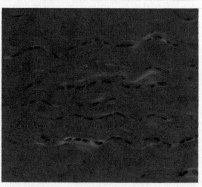

(b)

Nerve Tissue

Nerve tissue is excitable and irritable. These are not unpleasant traits, in this case. The statement simply means that nerve cells are responsive to external stimuli. Nervous tissue responds by sending *nerve impulses* along the nerve cells. The nerve cells, the functional units of nerve tissue, are called *neurons* (the basic parts of one kind of neuron are described in Figure 31.4). We will discuss the structure and function of these tissues in the next chapter.

THE VERTEBRATE SKELETON

The **skeleton** in nearly all classes of vertebrates is composed of hardened bone. Major exceptions are fish with cartilaginous skeletons, such as sharks. The usual bony skeleton has four major functions: (1) it supports the body; (2) it serves as an attachment for muscles; (3) it protects parts of the body; and (4) some bones produce red blood cells in their marrow cavities.

The Structure of Bone

Bones may be very different from each other, depending upon how they are formed. The flattened, platelike bones of the skull, for example, are formed differently from the long bones of the appendages and most of the skeleton. We will confine our discussion to the structure of the long bones.

In their general appearance, long bones have expanded *heads* and longer, narrower **shafts.** Except at the joints, the long bones are surrounded by a living layer of connective tissue called the *periosteum* ("around the bone"). Its cells are important in both bone formation and in the repair of broken bones. Most of the shaft is composed of **compact bone.** As the name suggests, it is thick and dense. Within the shaft is a cavity containing a fatty material known as *yellow marrow.* At first glance, compact bone appears to be too dense and rocklike to be living, but it is indeed alive. The heads of long bones contain **spongy bone,** so-called because the hardened matrix is weblike, rather than solid. The spaces within spongy bone are filled with soft tissue making up the *red marrow,* the site of red blood cell production.

The Microscopic Structure of Bone. Despite its stonelike appearance, compact bone contains many metabolically active bone cells as well as nu-merous nerves and blood vessels. Most of the bony mass (about 65%), however, consists of hardened mineral salts, such as calcium phosphate, which are set in a matrix of collagen.

Microscopic sections of compact bone (Figure 31.5) reveal intricate, repeated units of structure called **Haversian systems.** Such systems consist of a *Haversian canal* that contains blood vessels, and a

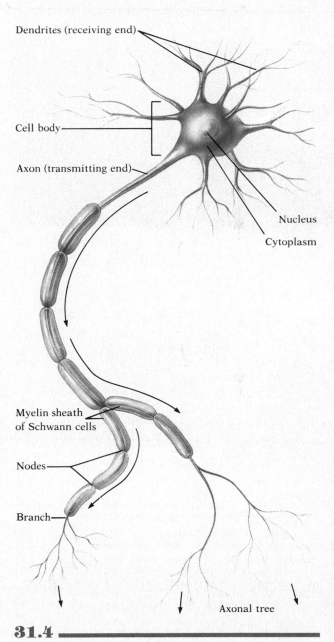

Dendrites (receiving end)

Cell body

Axon (transmitting end)

Nucleus

Cytoplasm

Myelin sheath of Schwann cells

Nodes

Branch

Axonal tree

31.4

Neurons are very reactive to stimuli and impulses through the body. The *cell body* contains the usual cellular organelles, while other parts are adapted to either receiving or sending signals. Neurons range from a few micrometers to a meter in length.

surrounding region of concentric cylinders **(lamellae)** of calcified bone. The cylinders impart great strength and resilience to the bone.

Within the lamellae are the **osteocytes,** the bone cells. The main body of each osteocyte resides in a tiny cavity—a *lacuna* (plural, *lacunae*). Tiny canals, the *canaliculi,* pass through the hardened bone from one lacuna to the next. The osteocytes touch each other with long extensions projecting through the canaliculi. Some of these projections reach the central canal, permitting the living bone cells to

exchange materials with the circulatory system. The osteocytes help deposit or withdraw calcium deposits, according to the body's needs and the normal processes of change. The Haversian systems are in a constant state of flux—they are broken down and rebuilt continually through life.

Organization of the Human Skeleton

The human skeleton, a complex and fascinating system, can be divided into two parts: the *axial skeleton* and the *appendicular skeleton*. The axial skeleton includes the skull, the vertebral column, and the bones of the *thoracic region* (chest). The appendicular skeleton includes the two *limb girdles*, that is, the pectoral girdle (shoulder) and pelvic girdle (hip), along with the *limbs* (the arms and legs). Movable bones may form a number of kinds of joints, such as splices, hinges, and pivots. In some joints, the bones simply slide past each other.

The Joints. Joints range from totally immovable bony unions, such as those in the skull (*sutures*), to the free-ranging, 360-degree *ball-and-socket* rotations of the shoulder and hip. In between are the *gliding joints* of the wrist, as well as joints of the pelvic bones, which move only slightly during childbirth. The construction of the more movable joints is often complex and quite elegant.

The *articulating* (contacting) surfaces of a joint are covered with a thin layer of very smooth, glistening cartilage. The bones are bound together at the joints by **ligaments** made up of tough, flexible connective tissue. A *sprain* usually involves a torn ligament, and because ligaments do not contain many cells or blood vessels, they heal slowly.

The ligaments at some joints are hollowed and contain a lubricant called *synovial fluid*. Synovial joints help account for the ease and range of movement at the hip, elbow, shoulder, and knee.

(a)   (b)

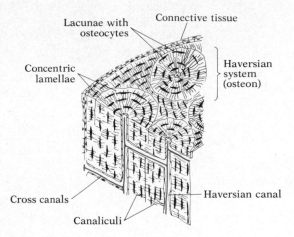

Lacunae with osteocytes
Connective tissue
Concentric lamellae
Haversian system (osteon)
Cross canals
Haversian canal
Canaliculi

(c) Compact bone

31.5

In long bones, the shaft consists of compact bone **(a),** while the head contains spongy bone **(b).** In a microscopic view, compact bone consists of units known as Haversian systems **(c).** Each of these units contains a central canal and concentric layers of bony deposition. Within the layers are entombed osteocytes that communicate via minute canaliculi. (*a:* From *TISSUES AND ORGANS: a text atlas of scanning electron microscopy*, by Richard G. Kessel and Randy H. Kardon. W. H. Freeman and Company, copyright © 1979.)

The Axial Skeleton

The **axial skeleton,** as its name implies, forms the central axis of the body. It is particularly interesting to anthropologists because it includes the skull and jaw, structures that fossilize well and have yielded a great deal of information about human evolution (see Chapter 30). The role of protection falls largely to the axial skeleton, since the skull offers protection to the brain, the rib cage surrounds the heart and lungs, and the vertebrae house the vulnerable spinal cord. The protective role of the skeleton is apparent in Figure 31.6.

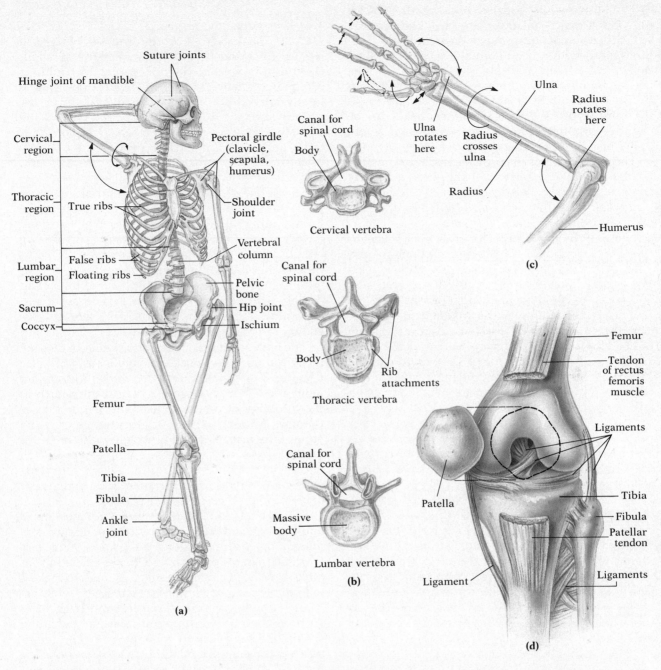

Suture joints

Hinge joint of mandible

Cervical region

Thoracic region

Lumbar region

Sacrum

Coccyx

True ribs

False ribs

Floating ribs

Femur

Patella

Tibia

Fibula

Ankle joint

Pectoral girdle (clavicle, scapula, humerus)

Shoulder joint

Vertebral column

Pelvic bone

Hip joint

Ischium

(a)

Canal for spinal cord

Body

Cervical vertebra

Canal for spinal cord

Body

Rib attachments

Thoracic vertebra

Canal for spinal cord

Massive body

Lumbar vertebra

(b)

Ulna rotates here

Radius crosses ulna

Ulna

Radius rotates here

Radius

Humerus

(c)

Femur

Tendon of rectus femoris muscle

Ligaments

Tibia

Fibula

Patellar tendon

Ligaments

Patella

Ligament

(d)

31.6

The human skeleton **(a)** is divided into the axial and appendicular portions. The skull contains many plate-like bones joined at sutures, and numerous openings accommodate nerves and blood vessels. The mandible, or lower jaw, forms a very mobile hinge joint at its socket in the temporal bone. Two large muscle groups on each side provide this joint with great crushing strength. The 33 vertebrae of the vertebral column are divided functionally into three regions, cervical (neck), thoracic (chest), and lumbar (lower trunk) **(b)**. Each vertebra has protrusions (processes) for the attach-ment of muscles, and thoracic vertebrae provide for rib attachment. Note the curve of the vertebral column, and the increasing size of the vertebrae from cervical to lumbar regions. The ball and socket shoulder joint is highly movable (arrows), and, coupled with the rotating ability of the forearm, the hinged and gliding wrist joint **(c)**, and versatile fingers, provides us with a remarkably useful appendage. The knee, a synovial joint, is one of the most interesting joints of the body. Note its highly complex ligament, muscle, and tendon arrangements **(d)**.

The human **skull** consists of 28 bones. Most of its volume makes up the **cranium** ("brain case"), which surrounds and protects the delicate and baffling organ within. The cranial bones of the skull do not fully meet until about 18 months of age, leaving a vulnerable soft spot on top of the baby's head. The resulting flexibility of the skull helps in the birth process, when the large head can be slightly compressed. The skull bones will eventually fuse by about age two.

The **vertebral column,** or backbone, forms the flexible axis of the skeleton. It supports the weight of the upper body, delivering its load to the pelvic girdle below. It may also represent a problem to modern humans, since so many of us—from sedentary office workers to muscled athletes—seem to suffer from back problems sooner or later. After all,it has only been four or five million years that our backbones have carried weight vertically, and we were much smaller most of that time.

Since bones often serve as attachments for muscles, they usually have **processes** protruding from them, places where the muscles can attach. The vertebrae, in particular, have rather pronounced processes. Each vertebra also has a dense, rounded **body** that is separated from its neighbors above and below by a cartilaginous disk. Most also have a *foramen* (opening) through which the spinal cord passes (see Figure 31.8a). Exceptions are the sacrum, the wedgelike group of fused vertebrae, and the *coccyx*, the fingerlike remnant of the tail, a persistant reminder of our humbler origins.

The third region of the human axial skeleton includes the 12 pairs of **ribs** and the shieldlike **sternum** (breastbone). The 10 upper pairs of ribs make their connections to the sternum through *costal cartilages*, while the two lower pairs (often called the "floating ribs") have no direct connection (see Figure 31.6). The flexible costal cartilages permit the range of motions needed for breathing. The rib marrow is one of the most important sources of red blood cells.

The Appendicular Skeleton

The *pectoral girdle*, the *pelvic girdle*, and the *limbs* make up the appendicular skeleton. The appendicular skeletons of vertebrates, from amphibians to primates, have become enormously modified as species have become increasingly adapted to the terrestrial environment. Also, since humans are the only truly bipedal primates, our skeletons have required additional modifications (see Chapter 30).

The **pectoral girdle** consists of the paired *clavicles* (the collar bones) and *scapulae* (shoulder blades). The seemingly loose formation of the arm socket, for instance, is what makes the shoulder the most mobile of all our joints, providing a 360-degree rotation (used by softball pitchers). The gently curved scapula glides smoothly over the rounded rib cage. This flexibility, coupled with the partially rotating, hinged elbow, the complex wrist, and the versatile hand, provides for a variety of motions characteristic of primates, but not found in many other vertebrates.

The **pelvic girdle** includes the end of the vertebral column and the three pairs of bones that make up the right and left halves of the pelvis. Each half includes a flattened *ilium* (hip bone), an *ischium* (sitting bone), and a *pubis* (pubic bone). The two pubic bones join in the front to form the *pubic joint*, whose flexibility allows the birth canal to expand during birth. Human male and female pelvic girdles have subtle but important differences, as shown in Figure 31.7.

The limbs of humans are quite similar to those of other primates, yet differ in significant ways (see Chapter 31). We described the versatile shoulder joint previously, but we might add that much of the flexibility of the lower arm and hand is made possible by arrangement of the two lower arm bones. The **radius,** which articulates with the wrist on the thumb side, can cross over the **ulna,** which rotates in response (see Figure 31.6b). The wrist itself cannot rotate, but can merely do "wig-wag" and "goodbye" motions.

The articulation of the **femur** with the hip is another ball-and-socket arrangement. A far more interesting, if unlikely, joint is the knee. While less versatile than the elbow hinge, the knee hinge does have some ability to rotate—just enough to make it vulnerable to football injuries. The knee, while essential to upright, bipedal posture and walking, is such a complex contraption that its evolution seems like the work of a committee. The femur perches on the upright **tibia** (the larger lower leg bone or shinbone), with some protection offered by the **patella** (kneecap). But, however flimsy it may seem, the knee has the toughest supporting capsule of any of the synovial joints. Additional strength is provided by a number of tough ligaments that bind bone to bone, and several muscles and tendons help to bind the joint externally. The patella itself is embedded in the tendon of a large thigh muscle (the *rectus femoris*) that passes over the knee to attach to the tibia below.

VERTEBRATE MUSCLE AND ITS MOVEMENT

Any movement of cells, whether the waving of cilia, the contraction of the mitotic apparatus, or the flexing of an arm, relies on a universal principle; it is due to some variation on the same mechanism. Certain long, filamentous proteins, by using ATP, are able to slide past each other. The result is an effective shortening of the filament pair. When a great number of such filaments are organized into a muscle, and that muscle is attached to a structure such as bone, it can move the structure.

Muscle Tissue Types

Vertebrate muscles can be classified into three types according to their physical appearance, their mechanisms of control by the nervous system, and their specific roles. First, *smooth muscle* is involuntary (not under conscious control) and, mainly, visceral (associated with the internal organs). *Cardiac muscle*, the muscle of the heart, is also involuntary. *Striated (skeletal) muscle* is voluntary (under conscious control), and primarily moves the bones of the skeleton. Although each muscle type is uniquely adapted to its principal function, all types utilize the same biochemical mechanisms.

Smooth Muscle. **Smooth muscle** cells are shaped like long spindles; that is, they are tapered at both ends. They may occur in sheets of muscle that often overlap (Figure 31.8a). A single nucleus lies near the center of each cell. Smooth muscle tissue is found in such diverse places as the walls of the digestive tract and of the blood vessels, at the base of each body hair, in the iris of the eye, and in the uterus, as well as in other parts of the reproductive system.

Cardiac Muscle. **Cardiac muscle** has traits in common with both smooth and skeletal muscle. For example, like smooth muscle, the heart is largely under involuntary control. And, like skeletal muscle, the cardiac muscle cells form cylindrical, striated (striped) fibers. On the other hand, cardiac muscle differs from both of these. The fibers of heart muscle are branched; and within those branching fibers, individual cells each contain one nucleus (separated by *intercalated disks*). The disks are formed by folded and compressed membranes, and they have the ability to transmit impulses easily (Figure 31.8b).

One important trait of cardiac muscle tissue is its intrinsic tendency to contract rhythmically. Cardiac cells removed and grown in a tissue culture will lie pulsing and beating until the tissue dies.

Skeletal Muscle. **Skeletal muscles** are largely under conscious, or voluntary, control, which means that usually they can be moved at will. The cells are cylindrical and striated, with many nuclei lying just underneath the membrane (Figure 31.8c). Because they are multinucleate, skeletal muscle cells are considered to be **muscle fibers** rather than cells, a distinction we will support.

31.7

The human pelvis. Some of the differences between male and female pelvises can be detected at a glance. Note in particular the difference in the size of pelvic inlets. In addition, the pelvic arch may be quite different. In women, the arch generally forms an angle greater than 90 degrees; in men it is generally less than 90 degrees. The wider angle in women, of course, provides room for the birth canal. Note also the difference in the shape and length of the sacrum and the flare of the ilium. The pelvic girdle is completed at the back by the sacrum (part of the vertebral column), forming the vulnerable *sacroiliac joint*.

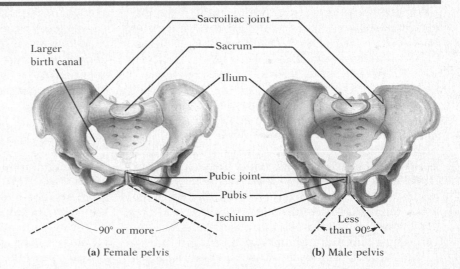

(a) Female pelvis   (b) Male pelvis

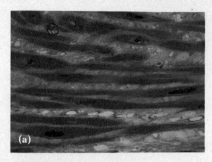 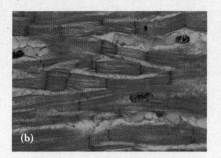 

31.8

Smooth muscle **(a)** is involuntary, consisting of long, spindly cells, each containing a single nucleus. Smooth muscle often occurs in sheets. Cardiac muscle **(b)** is also involuntary, but unlike other types, the tissue branches and rebranches, and is interrupted by in-tercalated disks. Like skeletal muscle, it is heavily striated (cross-banded). Skeletal muscle **(c)** is, of course, largely voluntary—moved at will. It is heavily striated and multinucleate.

The Organization of Skeletal Muscle

Muscle fibers are held together by connective tissue composed largely of extracellular material. Skeletal muscles are richly supplied with blood vessels that run between and within the bundles of fibers, supplying oxygen and nutrients and carrying away wastes. An efficient circulatory system is critical to the efficient functioning of muscle. (What happens when a working muscle does not receive enough oxygen? See Chapter 8.) Nerves also penetrate the bundles, their branches dividing ever more finely until individual neurons finally innervate each muscle fiber at what are called **neuromuscular junctions.** These nerves carry the messages that cause the fibers to contract. Other neurons carry messages to the brain that tell the position of the muscles in each part of the skeletal system. This is how we are able to have some idea of where our left foot is without actually seeing it.

The mass of aligned bundles constitutes the muscle *belly.* It is enclosed by the *fascia,* a tough casing of connective tissue. At both ends of the muscle, the fascia merges into increasingly denser collagenous tissue, forming cordlike **tendons** that attach muscle to bone. For muscles to move the skeleton in an organized manner, one end must be attached to a stationary base, with the other attached to the movable part. The stationary attachment is the muscle's **origin,** while the movable part is the muscle's **insertion.** The *rectus femoris* has its origin on the hip and its insertion down on the shin. Keep that in mind the next time you kick something. Examples of muscle origins and insertions are shown in Figure 31.9.

Not all skeletal muscles move bones. The muscles of your face, for instance, move your face. This produces all of your wonderfully varied and attractive expressions that help you to communicate. Tongue muscles also have complex origins and insertions, and you can move your tongue in an interesting variety of ways. Both smooth muscles and skeletal muscles may form rings around various passages or openings. These muscles, called *sphincters,* are found around the anus and in the gut, in the mouth, and even in many blood vessels. Other muscles form flattened sheets and have broad, thin tendons, such as the sheet of abdominal muscles that helps you pull in your stomach.

Opposing Muscle Groups. Muscles that move an appendage one way usually have opposing muscles that move it the other way. For example, the biceps flexes the arm and its opposing muscle, the triceps, straightens it. Such muscles with opposite actions are called **antagonists** (see Figure 31.9). The term suggests that they oppose or "fight" each other. In fact, however, they must cooperate in a highly coordinated fashion for most normal movements. Consider the many opposing muscles of the trunk that must coordinate their efforts to keep us upright (and what happens when a muscle cramp occurs on one side).

The Ultrastructure of Skeletal Muscle

A skeletal muscle, we have seen, is composed of fibers. Let's now take a closer look at the microscopic arrangement of muscle units to see how they actually work.

The electron microscope has revealed that skeletal muscle fibers are covered by a cell membrane, the **sarcolemma** (sarco, *flesh*, lemma, *husk*). The sarcolemma receives the endings of the nerve cells

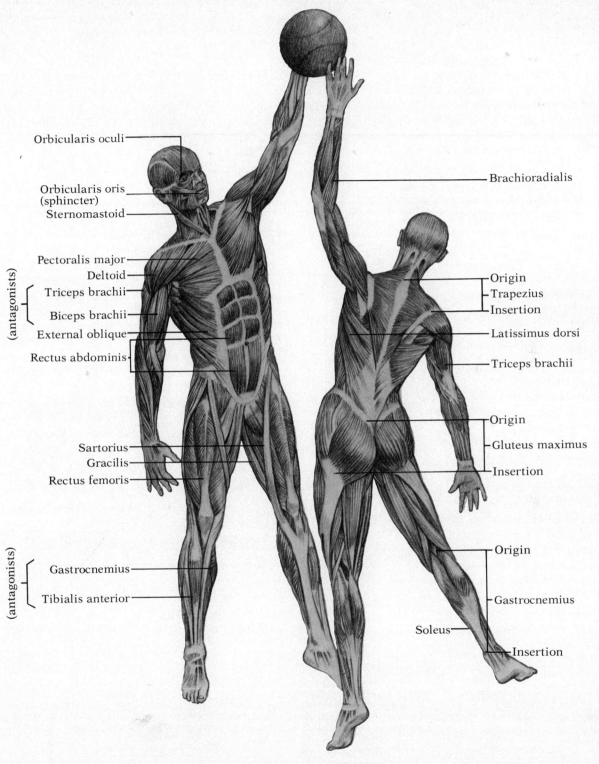

Orbicularis oculi

Orbicularis oris (sphincter)

Sternomastoid

Pectoralis major

Deltoid

(antagonists) { Triceps brachii

Biceps brachii

External oblique

Rectus abdominis

Sartorius

Gracilis

Rectus femoris

(antagonists) { Gastrocnemius

Tibialis anterior

Brachioradialis

Origin

Trapezius

Insertion

Latissimus dorsi

Triceps brachii

Origin

Gluteus maximus

Insertion

Origin

Gastrocnemius

Soleus

Insertion

31.9

The human muscles illustrate the various types and arrangements and give us some idea about origins and insertions. Only the major muscles have been named. By finding tendons of origin and insertion, and the general orientation of a muscle, you can determine just what it does. Although muscles can contract forcefully, they cannot extend with force; they, therefore, work in opposing units known as antagonists.

that stimulate muscle contraction. Just below the sarcolemma are a number of nuclei and many mitochondria (we would expect a heavy mitochondrial density in such active tissue as muscle). Just under the sarcolemma we also find a rich supply of glycogen and ATP, each ready to carry out its role in energy production. Also near the fiber's surface is a modified endoplasmic reticulum (see Chapter 4) called the **sarcoplasmic reticulum,** which not only functions much like any other endoplasmic reticulum, but also is important in muscle contraction.

The sarcolemma dips into the fiber, here and there, forming small tubules that actually touch the sarcoplasmic reticulum. Together, the tubules and the reticulum form a unit called the **T system** (Figure 31.10). We will see the role of the T system shortly.

The Sarcomere.   The further organization of the muscle fiber is complex, so it would be best to study Figure 31.10 as we proceed. Most of what we have described so far are surface structures. Actually, most of the muscle fiber is made up **myofibrils**—cylindrical units composed of long,

31.10

Ultrastructure of muscle. **(a)** Each muscle fiber is surrounded by a cell membrane called a sarcolemma. Within the sarcolemma, some of the unique cellular organization of muscle is seen. Each fiber contains numerous cylindrical myofibrils, which reveal the banding that gives skeletal muscle its other name, striated muscle. **(b)** Close-up of the myofibril. Each sarcomere, or contractile unit, is bordered by two Z lines. Within are I bands, A bands, and an H zone, all produced by the organization of the myosin and actin myofilaments.

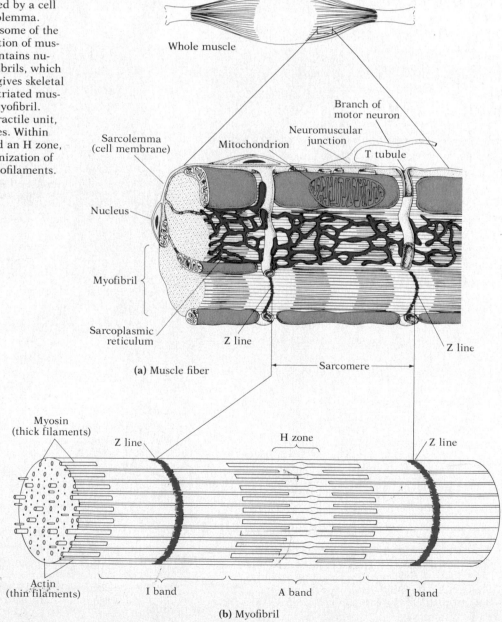

filamentous proteins known as **myofilaments** (or simply, *filaments*). The filaments produce the light and dark bands that give stained skeletal muscle (and cardiac muscle) its striated appearance under the microscope. The striations are due to the particular arrangement of two kinds of protein filaments—one thick and one thin.

Each thin myofilament is formed from twisted strands of the protein **actin,** while each thick filament is composed of many subunits of a larger protein called **myosin.** The thick and thin myofilaments are organized into contractile units called **sarcomeres.** The contractile property of muscle is dependent upon the arrangement of these two proteins in the sarcomere.

A sarcomere may be defined as the area between two dark lines, called **Z lines,** crossing the myofibril. The Z lines are actually disks, though they appear to be lines in cross section. The thin actin fibers are anchored in the Z lines and extend toward each other, but, when the muscle is inactive, the actin fibers do not meet. Because the actin fibers are so thin, any area where they exist alone appears light in density, and these areas make up *I bands.* The thick myosin filaments lie more centrally in the sarcomere. They are not permanently attached to anything, but partly overlap the actin filaments. The denser myosin forms the distinctive *A band* of the sarcomere, as seen in Figure 31.10. Since the actin filaments do not extend all the way through the myosin filaments, a somewhat lighter region, the *H zone,* is seen at the center. All this business of bands and zones may seem a bit overdone and confusing at first, but you will find that the terms will make the sequence of events in contraction easier to understand. So, with all the terms now completely understood and fresh in our minds, let's see how skeletal muscles contract.

The Contraction of Skeletal Muscle

Painstaking studies of electron micrographs of relaxed and contracted sarcomeres reveal that, during contraction, the actin filaments move toward each other, sliding through the stationary myosin filaments. This is now called the **sliding filament theory.** As seen through the electron microscope (Figure 31.11), the inward movement of actin from both sides brings the Z lines closer together and shortens the entire sarcomere. This movement continues until the actin filaments touch. At that time the H zone disappears and the A band is uniformly dense. This is not a local event in contracting muscle, but occurs simultaneously in each sarcomere, producing a rapid shortening of the en-

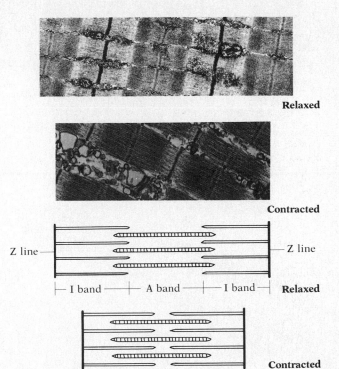

Relaxed

Contracted

Z line — — Z line

— I band — A band — I band — **Relaxed**

Contracted

31.11

These two electron micrographs clearly demonstrate what happens to the contractile unit when muscle contracts. Note the inward movement of the Z lines, the change in density of the A band, and changes in the H zone. Does the A band change in width? When a muscle is contracted, these reactions occur throughout its mass.

tire muscle (which explains the furrows that have been deepening in your brow as you have read this). However, to understand how the actin moves we will need to examine the molecular structure of both myosin and actin.

The sliding action is made possible by the presence of numerous minute projections—the *myosin heads*—along the myosin filament (Figure 31.12). In relaxed muscle, the myosin heads approach—but do not touch—the actin. In contraction, the heads bend back and attach all along the actin filaments, forming *cross bridges.* The bridges straighten, and in so doing, produce a "power stroke" that actually pulls the actin inward. As each myosin head completes its limited movement, it reattaches farther along and repeats its action. Therefore, the sliding of actin filaments is actually a ratcheting action.

So, you may ask, why do the myosin bridges attach only in contracting muscle? The answer is in the actin filaments, which contain three proteins: actin, *tropomyosin*, and *troponin.* In the resting muscle, conditions around the troponin site inhibit

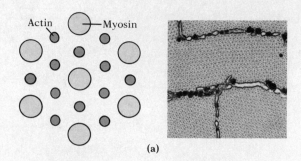

Actin — Myosin

(a)

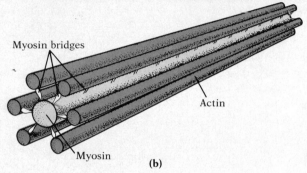

Myosin bridges

Actin

Myosin

(b)

31.12

The arrangement of myofilaments and the cross-bridges. (a) The electron micrograph of a cross-section through the myofibril; the accompanying illustration shows the arrangement of actin and myosin filaments in respect to each other. The three-dimensional drawing (b) shows the bridges between myosin and the surrounding actin.

myosin bridge formation. Bridge formation requires the presence of two substances: calcium ions (Ca^{++})—the key to muscle contraction—and ATP, which, as you would expect, provides the energy. When Ca^{++} is present, it alters the troponin site and the bridges attach. The attachment triggers the enzymatic hydrolysis of ATP: the phosphate bond energy is transferred to the myosin head, which responds by straightening and tugging on the actin filament. For a myosin head to reattach farther along on the actin, another ATP is required, and the ratcheting action continues until maximum contraction is reached. The roles of Ca^{++} and ATP are shown in Figure 31.13.

Actually, contraction can be maintained voluntarily, as long as Ca^{++} is present and the ATP holds out. ATP is directly restored by the breakdown of *creatine phosphate*, an energy-storage compound in muscle tissue, and glucose (from stored glycogen) must be metabolized in glycolysis for the restoration of creatine phosphate. (Muscle fatigue sets in as glucose reserves fail and lactic acid accumulates.)

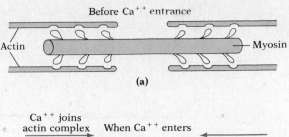

Before Ca^{++} entrance

Actin — Myosin

(a)

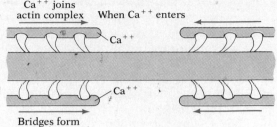

Ca^{++} joins actin complex   When Ca^{++} enters

Ca^{++}

Ca^{++}

Bridges form

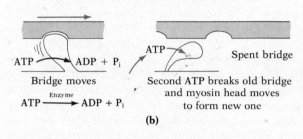

$ATP \longrightarrow ADP + P_i$

Bridge moves

$ATP \xrightarrow{\text{Enzyme}} ADP + P_i$

ATP   Spent bridge

Second ATP breaks old bridge and myosin head moves to form new one

(b)

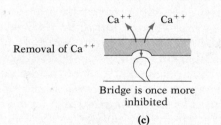

Ca^{++} Ca^{++}

Removal of Ca^{++}

Bridge is once more inhibited

(c)

31.13

(a) Without Ca^{++} in the sarcomere, the myosin bridges cannot form. (b) When a neural impulse reaches a muscle, the calcium Ca^{++} pumps cease and Ca^{++} diffuses into the contractile units. In the presence of Ca^{++}, the myosin bridges form, ATP transfers energy to the myosin bridges, and they contract and straighten, pulling the actin inward. ATP molecules continue to restore each bridge, permitting it to act again. (c) When Ca^{++} is removed, bridge formation is inhibited, and the muscle rests.

We have noted that calcium ions are a key factor in muscle contraction, so the real questions are as follows: where do the calcium ions come from? What controls their presence? How are they removed so that the muscle can relax? In the relaxed muscle, calcium ions are sequestered within the membranous sarcoplasmic reticulum (see Figure 31.12a). Continuous active transport is required to move the ions there, which involves a pumping action by elements in the membrane itself. This is how muscles relax.

The events leading to contraction begin when a motor neuron relays a message across the neuromuscular junction. This creates a sweeping *polarity* change—a shift of plus and minus charges—in the muscle fiber, which passes along the T system to the sarcoplasmic reticulum. The polarity shift drastically alters the permeability of the sarcoplasmic reticulum, permitting the rapid escape of Ca^{++}, which floods the sarcomeres. The presence of Ca^{++} permits myosin bridges to form throughout the muscle, and contraction begins. When the motor impulse ends, it is the active pumping of Ca^{++} back into the sarcoplasmic reticulum, and the restoration of that membrane's ability to hold the ions, that inhibits further bridge formation.

We now have some ideas on the basic tissue and skeletal organization in our representative vertebrate, and we know some of the intracacies of muscle contraction. Our introduction of nerve action was rather sketchy, but the next chapter will attend to this problem. There we will consider some of the startling new finds of *neurobiology*, one of the fastest growing fields of biology.

Summary

Vertebrate Tissues
A tissue is a group of specialized cells, together with their noncellular matrix, that generally perform the same function. The four major types of vertebrate tissues are epithelium, connective tissue, muscle, and nerve.

Epithelium forms the interior and exterior linings of most surfaces of the vertebrate organism. Glandular epithelium forms the lining of gland ducts and the gland's secretions. Epithelial cells can be flattened, columnar, or cuboidal. Connective tissue consists of cells plus their secretions, which together produce a noncellular connective tissue matrix. Bone, cartilage, ligaments, tendons, and blood are connective tissues. Muscle tissue is capable of contraction. Nerve tissue is excitable and irritable, and enables organisms to respond to stimuli.

The Vertebrate Skeleton
The bony skeleton supports the body, serves as an attachment for muscles, protects parts of the body, and produces red blood cells. Long bones have expanded heads made up of spongy bone, and shafts composed of compact bone. Microscopic sections of compact bone reveal Haversian systems that contain the osteocytes, or bone cells. The human skeleton is divided into the axial skeleton (skull, vertebral column, and bones of the thoracic region) and the appendicular skeleton (pectoral girdle, pelvic girdle, and limbs). Bones can form a number of kinds of joints. Bones are bound together at joints by ligaments, some of which form synovial joints.

The skull consists of 28 bones, most of which surround and protect the brain. The vertebral column forms the flexible axis of the skeleton, and supports the weight of the upper body. Vertebrae have rounded bodies and pronounced processes to which muscles can attach. Ribs and the sternum complete the axial skeleton.

The appendicular skeletons of vertebrates have become enormously modified as species have adapted over time. The pectoral girdle consists of the paired clavicles and scapulae, which permit a wide range of movement in the shoulders and arms. The pelvic girdle includes the sacrum and three pairs of bones (ilium, ischium, and pubis).

The variety of joints permits great versatility in movement, particularly in such joints as the elbow, wrist, hip, knee, and ankle.

Vertebrate Muscle and Its Movement
There are three basic types of vertebrate muscle: smooth muscle is involuntary (internal organs); cardiac (heart) muscle is also involuntary; and striated muscle is voluntary (movement of bones).

Muscle fibers are held together by connective tissue, are richly supplied with blood vessels, and are penetrated by nerves that carry messages to and from the brain and spinal cord. Aligned muscle bundles are enclosed in a tough casing of connective tissue that merges to form cordlike tendons, which are fastened to bone at origins and insertions. Some muscles form sphincters, while others are broad, flat sheets. Muscles that work with others of opposing action are called antagonists.

Skeletal muscle fibers are covered by the sarcolemma, which forms the T system where it touches the sarcoplasmic reticulum. Muscle fibers contain myofibrils that are composed of myofilaments, which are in turn of actin and myosin organized into sarcomeres. When muscles contract, actin filaments move toward each other through the stationary myosin filaments. A complex interaction of proteins, calcium ions, and ATP enables myosin filaments to attach to actin filaments to form cross bridges, which function in a ratcheting action to cause the muscle to contract. A contraction begins when a nerve impulse crosses a neuromuscular junction, causing a polarity change in the muscle fiber that allows calcium ions to enter the sarcomere.

Key Terms

tissue
matrix
epithelium
epidermis
connective tissue
connective tissue matrix
collagen
fibroblast
elastin
adipose tissue
blood
plasma
muscle tissue
nerve tissue
skeleton
shaft
compact bone
spongy bone
Haversian system

lamellae
osteocyte
ligament
axial skeleton
skull
cranium
vertebral column
process
body
ribs
sternum
pectoral girdle
pelvic girdle
radius
ulna
femur
tibia
patella
smooth muscle

cardiac muscle
skeletal muscle
muscle fibers
neuromuscular junction
tendons
origin
insertion
antagonists
sarcolemma
sarcoplasmic reticulum
T system
myofibrils
myofilaments
actin
myosin
sarcomere
Z lines
sliding filament theory

Review Questions

1. List the four types of vertebrate tissues and discuss the functions of each. (pp. 456–458)

2. How is collagen produced, and how is it used in the animal body? (p. 459)

3. With the help of a sketch, describe the appearance of a long bone, labeling spongy and compact bone and the two types of marrow. Add to your diagram the microscopic structure of a Haversian system, labeling canals, canaliculi, lamellae, osteocytes, and lacunae. (pp. 459–460)

4. Describe three types of movements possible in joints. Describe the synovial joint in detail, and give four examples of such joints. (p. 460)

5. List the three parts of the axial skeleton; describe the two girdles of the appendicular skeleton, including the joints they form with the appendages. (pp. 460–462)

6. Compare the general appearance, location, and function of the three types of muscle tissue. (p. 463)

7. List the typical cellular structures of an individual muscle fiber, and describe the functions of each. (pp. 464–467)

8. Prepare a simple drawing of a contractile unit, indicating the relationship between actin and myosin filaments and labeling Z lines, I bands, A bands, and the H zone. Indicate what happens to the four during contraction. (pp. 466–469)

9. Carefully explain how muscle contraction is inhibited in the resting muscle, and describe the role of calcium ions (Ca^{++}) in bringing on contraction. (pp. 468–469)

Neurons and How They Work

32

A browsing deer nips at tender buds and avoids toxic plants nearby. A cougar spots the deer and stealthily tries not to alert the deer to its approach. The cougar's nervous system is largely adapted to the detection of prey; and the deer's, to the detection of predators and plants. Each may ignore, or not even register, stimuli that are of no use to it. The earth is a variable and changing place, filled with opportunities and dangers. At a very basic level, animals' nervous systems are equipped to detect the nature of the immediate environment and enable them to respond in an appropriate manner (Figure 32.1).

The mechanism that permits animals—including humans—to react appropriately to a changing world is a network of highly specialized cells called *neurons*. Despite our understanding of the human nervous system, there are still many unknowns. What is *thought?* What is *memory?* What elicits feelings of jealousy in even the most generous of souls? Why are some of us so obsessed? How can a brain tumor cause constant rage?

These questions and many more like them have intrigued generations of biologists, and before them, intrigued philosophers and romantics alike. The human mind has always been considered to be a special thing, its qualities distinct from those of all other animals. Similar beliefs are held in science today, but as we will learn, there are important qualifications.

Even as we work to understand the most basic mechanisms of nerve impulses, we are trying to answer the larger questions, and we are making headway in some cases. We will begin our investigation of the human nervous system with a look at how neurons and nervous systems carry messages through the body.

THE NEURON

Neurons (Figure 32.2) exist in many sizes and shapes, but every neuron has a **cell body** and a number of processes extending from the cell body. Some of these processes can be extremely long, reaching from one part of the body to another some distance away. For example, a neuron can reach from your foot all the way to your spinal cord.

The cell body (Figure 32.3) contains the nucleus and most of the cell's cytoplasm. The cytoplasm includes such typical cell organelles as ribosomes, an endoplasmic reticulum, and numerous secretory bodies. In addition, the cell body produces **neurotransmitters,** which are chemicals that move to special sites in the neuron where they are secreted, thus stimulating an impulse in an adjacent neuron. Neurotransmitters may also stimulate an **effector** (a structure capable of a response) such as a gland or a muscle.

32.1

Animals generally respond rapidly to incoming environmental cues. The ability is important in finding food and in recognizing and avoiding danger. Specialized receptors detect events in the animal's surroundings. This "raw information" is directed to the animal's spinal cord and brain for *integration*, the processing that permits a coordinated response. The type of response will depend upon the animal's abilities, options, and environment.

Two major types of processes extend from the cell body (see Figure 32.2): the *dendrites* and the *axons*. The **dendrite** ("little tree") is the receiving end of the neuron. Each dendrite can receive impulses from its surroundings or from other neurons, and it then generally converts this information into a nerve impulse that is transmitted *toward* the cell body.

The **axon** transmits the neural impulse *away from* the cell body. It may communicate with other neurons or directly with an effector. A neuron often has many dendrites, but it usually has only one axon. The single axon, however, may branch at any point along its length. An axon commonly divides and redivides at its tip, forming a terminal *axonal tree*. The axonal tree releases the neurotransmitters formed in the cell body, thus chemically relaying the message to the next neuron or to an effector. At the point where the tips of the axons *innervate* a muscle fiber (supply it with nerves), they branch and spread over the muscle fiber, increasing the surface area at this *neuromuscular junction* (see Chapter 31).

The axon in Figure 32.2 is surrounded by a sheath of fatty material called **myelin.** Like any

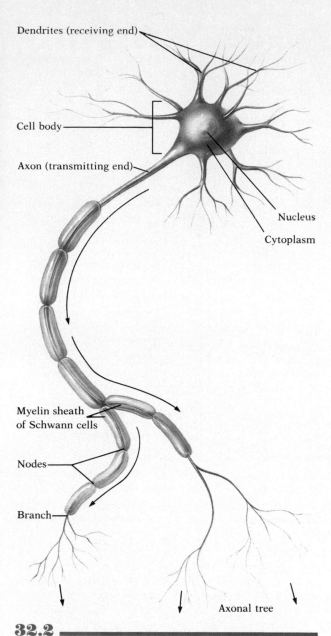

32.2

A motor neuron. The neuron is a highly specialized cell that can be stimulated and can produce waves of impulses. Each neuron is composed of an end adapted to receiving impulses at branched areas called dendrites. These join the cell body, an enlarged region that contains many typical cellular structures. The impulse travels along the long axon, that, like the dendrite, branches at its end. Both dendrites and axons may be enclosed in a fatty myelin sheath consisting of adjacent Schwann cells. The sheath contains minute gaps between these cells that are called nodes.

lipid, myelin has great electrical resistance, so it acts like an insulator. The myelin sheath outside of the brain and spinal cord is essentially composed of flattened *Schwann cells* wrapped around the neuron, and the sheath is interrupted at frequent intervals between these cells. These spaces create *nodes*, places where the axon is in direct contact with the surrounding intercellular fluid (Figure 32.4). This is important to neural conduction.

Types of Neurons

There are three basic kinds of neurons: *sensory neurons, interneurons,* and *motor neurons* (Figure 32.5). **Sensory neurons** carry impulses toward the spinal cord or brain, or both. They are activated by a stimulus—touch, light, temperature, odor, or some other environmental signal. Some sensory neurons are quite simple, but others—such as the light-sensitive cells in the retina of the eye—are very specialized. Sensory neurons tell us what's going on not only in the external environment, but in the internal one as well; we receive "status reports" from our internal organs. But regardless of

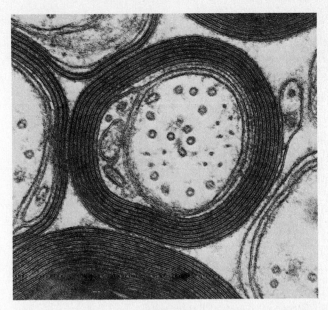

32.4

A cross-section through a myelinated axon shows the wrappings surrounding the axon itself. The wrappings are the membranes of a Schwann cell, whose cytoplasm and nucleus produce the enlarged region. The membrane wrappings produce an effective insulation that plays an important role in impulse propagation.

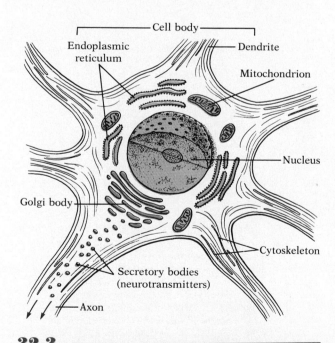

32.3

The neural cell body contains organelles typical of many cells. One of its primary functions is the production of neurotransmitters, specialized molecules that travel to the axonal tree where they are released to stimulate the next neuron in the sequence. Other organelles in the cell body include the nucleus, numerous mitochondria, and an extensive endoplasmic reticulum.

where the stimulus is perceived, incoming impulses travel along sensory (or *afferent*) neurons from the stimulated organ or cell to the brain or spinal cord, where they may meet a second kind of neuron.

Here, the stimulus is processed and shunted along the proper neural routes with the aid of interneurons. **Interneurons** are nerve cells that communicate only with other nerve cells. They receive input from neurons such as the sensory neurons, and are largely responsible for integrating the stimuli and responses in the nervous system. In the human nervous system, interneurons make up much of the spinal cord and brain. The interneurons may route an impulse to processing centers in the brain; they may also route impulses onward to the muscles and cause a specific reaction to the incoming stimulus. These outgoing (*efferent*) impulses travel over motor neurons.

The **motor neurons** are responsible for the body's final reactions to stimuli. They commonly receive impulses from the interneurons and transmit these impulses to effectors such as muscles and glands. Thus, activated motor neurons can make you yell, jump, blink, secrete, sweat, blush, squint, and perform any number of other actions.

While the neurons carry impulses in the nervous system, the brain and spinal cord contain other types of cells. One type, the **glial cells** (or *neuroglial cells,* as they are also known), outnumber neurons ten to one. Their functions are not well understood, but they serve some structural roles and provide metabolic support for the neurons. Neurobiologists have recently suggested possible information-processing roles for the glial cells as well.

Nerves

The axons and dendrites that extend throughout the body usually travel over the same routes, forming tracts called **nerves.** Thus, a spinal nerve, for example, might carry both afferent and efferent impulses. A nerve is somewhat like a telephone cable carrying many individual lines, each insulated from the other. Nerves appear as white, glistening cords, and are surrounded by their own coverings of tough connective tissue.

32.5

Nerve cells generally fall into three categories: sensory neurons, interneurons, and motor neurons. Vertebrate sensory neurons, particularly those of the skin, tend to have exceedingly long dendrites, since they must reach almost to the spinal cord. The sensory neurons that enter the cord meet the interneurons located there. Interneurons are the most variable of the three types. Some may be quite small, with numerous highly branched processes, as found in the cortex of the brain. Others may be found throughout the spinal cord. Motor neurons may originate in the spinal cord, sending out their axons over great distances to reach effectors such as muscles or glands.

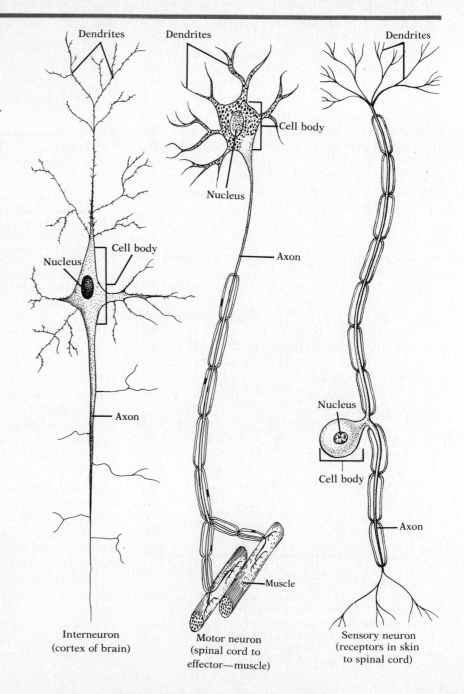

Interneuron
(cortex of brain)

Motor neuron
(spinal cord to
effector—muscle)

Sensory neuron
(receptors in skin
to spinal cord)

THE NEURAL IMPULSE

You're aware that nerves conduct impulses from one part of the body to another, but the word *conduct* can easily be misunderstood. This is because neurons are far more than simple conductors; each neuron *generates* its impulse and also conducts it. Although an electrical current in a copper wire diminishes with time and distance, neural impulses, once started, do not diminish along the length of the neuron. They are as strong at the farthest branch of the axonal tree as they were at their origin—in the dendrite.

Therefore, instead of being like a current of electricity in a copper wire, the nerve impulse is more like a line of falling dominoes. Each domino triggers the fall of the next, but once triggered, each domino falls with the same energy. The similarity doesn't end there. Before a line of dominoes can repeat its act, the line has to be set up again; that is, its potential energy must be restored.

To understand precisely how the neural impulse is generated and how it moves along, we must examine the special nature of the neural membrane and the role of certain ions.

Ions and the Neural Impulse

Impulses are transmitted differently in axons and in dendrites, but physiologists happen to know much more about the transmission of impulses in axons—so let's begin there, starting with the resting axon. *Resting* in this context means that there are no impulses moving past a particular point at a given moment. Actually, the resting axon, between impulses, is not resting at all; it is working hard pumping ions.

Work, in cells, usually involves the transfer of energy from ATP, and pumping ions is no exception. But what does it mean to pump ions? The nerve cell membrane is studded with enzyme complexes called **sodium/potassium ion exchange pumps** (Figure 32.6). For every molecule of ATP used, the ion exchange pump moves three sodium ions out of the cell and two potassium ions into the cell. Thus, it creates two opposite concentration gradients of ions: sodium ions (Na$^+$) become heavily concentrated outside the membrane (in the extracellular fluid), while potassium ions (K$^+$) accumulate in the cytoplasm inside the membrane. Such gradients, of course, are sources of potential energy, and it is this energy that the neuron will use to propagate a nerve impulse.

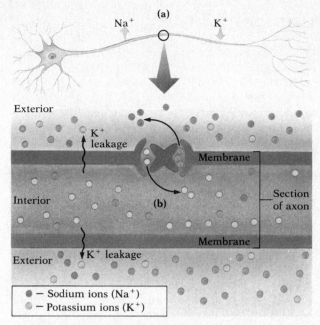

32.6

When not conducting neural impulses, a neuron maintains a high sodium ion (Na$^+$) gradient outside the axon and a lesser potassium ion (K$^+$) gradient inside **(a)**. This gradient represents a considerable amount of potential energy that will be released when a neural impulse is generated. The sodium/potassium gradients are produced by special membranal carriers known as sodium/potassium ion exchange pumps **(b)**. In each action of the pumps, three sodium ions are pumped outside and two potassium ions are pumped in.

The Resting Potential

The sodium/potassium ion exchange pumps, with their three-for-two rate of exchange, pump more positive ions out of the cell than they pump in. Furthermore, the nerve cell membrane is more permeable to potassium ions than it is to sodium ions; thus, many of the potassium ions that are pumped in leak right back out again. Because of these factors, the inside of the cell becomes *negatively charged* relative to the outside of the cell, and the cell is described as being **polarized**.

The use of a tiny electrode can show that this difference in charges causes an electrical potential difference of -60 millivolts (mV). (A millivolt is one thousandth of a volt.) This measurement, called the **resting potential**, represents a significant amount of potential energy (Figure 32.7a). The energy can be released when the different charges inside and outside the neuron rush together to establish an electrostatic equilibrium.

The Action Potential

These opposing electrical charges are able to join when an impulse passes down the axon. The impulse causes the cell membrane suddenly to become permeable to sodium ions. Therefore, the ion concentration gradient (which causes the resting potential) is suddenly lost as positively charged sodium ions rush into the cytoplasm of the axon. Then, for an instant, the inside of the axon becomes positively charged, producing a change from −60 mV to +40 mV (Figure 32.7b,c).

The rapid shift in charges is called an **action potential.** Action potentials last briefly. The inside of the neuron becomes positively charged only for microseconds. But as one area along the neuron experiences this shift in ions, it triggers the next area to do the same. So, once started, the shift in ions continues in a cascading manner—in a **wave of depolarization**—down the length of the axon.

32.7

Neural impulses are depolarizing waves that sweep along the highly polarized axon and are immediately followed by repolarization. During the impulse's passage, the resting potential of −60 mV changes to +40 mV, a shift called an action potential. The shift is caused by a sudden loss of the ion gradients established by the sodium/potassium pumps **(a).** It begins as the membrane changes its permeability, allowing a sudden inrush of sodium ions **(b).** The inrush continues **(c)** until equilibrium is reached (+40 mV), followed by a rapid recovery. Recovery or repolarization occurs as potassium ions rush outward, followed by sodium. The excess of positive ions outside produces a temporary overshoot **(d),** but the resting gradients are soon restored by the exchange pumps.

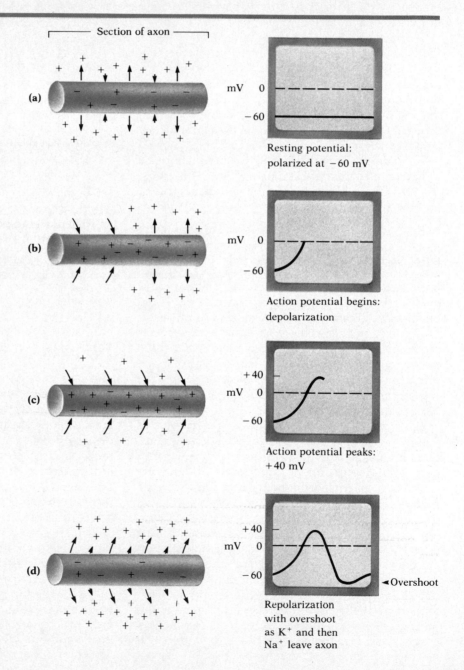

— Section of axon —

(a)   mV   0

−60

Resting potential: polarized at −60 mV

(b)   mV   0

−60

Action potential begins: depolarization

(c)   +40

mV   0

−60

Action potential peaks: +40 mV

(d)   +40

mV   0

−60   ◄Overshoot

Repolarization with overshoot as K⁺ and then Na⁺ leave axon

In its wake, an immediate recovery, or **repolarization,** begins and the resting potential of the neuron is quickly established (Figure 32.7d).

In repolarization, potassium ions leave the cell even before sodium ions can be pumped out. The outflow of both these positively charged ions from the axon renders the outside of the neuron excessively positive, a situation referred to as an *overshoot* or *hyperpolarization* (see Figure 38.7d). The voltage potential at this time can reach −70 mV or more. However, these overshoots are temporary; the axon instantly reestablishes its usual resting gradients and is ready to act again.

Biologists are only beginning to understand some of the mechanisms behind the transmission of neural impulses. Let's take a look at some of these new findings.

Ion Gates and Channels.   To begin, why does a nerve impulse make the nerve cell membrane permeable only to sodium ions? The cell membrane is studded with ion gates. **Ion gates** are special protein bodies that can allow the passage of specific ions across the membrane. There are several types of ion gates, but only the sodium and potassium gates concern us now.

The gates are selective, so sodium ions can't move through potassium gates, and *vice versa.* Each gate controls the entrance of a protein-lined pore in the cell membrane. In the case of sodium, there are two gates, both of which must be open before sodium can move passively across the membrane. However, both are seldom open simultaneously.

The two gates of each sodium channel are called the **voltage-dependent gate** and the **voltage-independent gate** (Figure 32.8). In the resting axon, the voltage-independent gate is open, but the voltage-dependent gate is closed. When an action potential causes a change in voltage, the voltage-dependent gate also opens. With both gates of the sodium channel open, the sodium ions rush into the cell.

At this point, the action potential peaks briefly. Then, just as the voltage-independent gates on the sodium channels close, the potassium gates open. As potassium ions rush out, with sodium ions blocked from moving in, the voltage differential reverses again. The sodium/potassium ion exchange pumps work doggedly, and the sodium ion concentration gradient is quickly reestablished. Until the voltage-independent gates open, the axon membrane is in a *refractory state*, during which it cannot respond to any further stimulus.

Myelin and Impulse Velocity

Axons in vertebrates are commonly surrounded by *myelin sheaths* that both insulate the neuron and help to speed up impulses. Myelinated neurons in humans, for example, can conduct impulses at a speed of up to 100 m per second, many times faster than the non-myelinated neurons found in many invertebrates.

Aside from myelination, the only other way to speed up impulses is by increasing the diameter of the axon. For example, the giant axons of the squid are several millimeters thick and can conduct impulses at 30 m per second—a rate that is fast for an invertebrate, but still far from vertebrate capabilities.

Myelin sheaths presumably evolved as a means of keeping the axons of vertebrates (with their extensive nervous systems) small. There are advantages to having small, insulated neurons that carry impulses rapidly. We can see how the fatty myelin sheaths would insulate nerves, but how do they increase impulse *velocity*? And, for that matter, how can an action potential be generated in an axon that is *insulated from* the surrounding sodium-rich fluid?

The answer to both questions is suggested in the arrangement of the myelin sheath. The domino effect involving a wave of depolarization actually describes an impulse traveling along a non-myelinated fiber. In the myelinated neuron, the action potentials only occur in the nodes, those gaps in the myelin sheath that occur at regular intervals (between the Schwann cells) along the axon. Thus, the neural impulse "jumps" from one node to the next, along the axon, in what is called **saltatory propagation** (Figure 32.9). This method not only greatly increases the speed of the impulse along the fiber, but also conserves energy. One experiment indicated that a non-myelinated axon required 5000 times as much energy to send an impulse as did a myelinated fiber of the same size. One reason is that the sodium/potassium pumps that use a great deal of ATP operate only at the nodes of myelinated axons.

NEURAL CODES

Aside from the differences between myelinated and non-myelinated fibers, action potentials in all neurons proceed in about the same way. This situation presents a puzzle. After all, we can sense

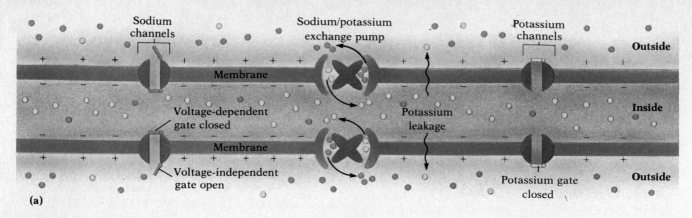

(a)

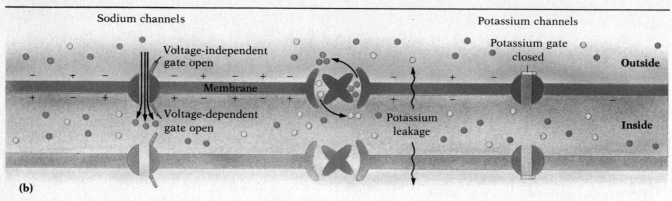

(b)

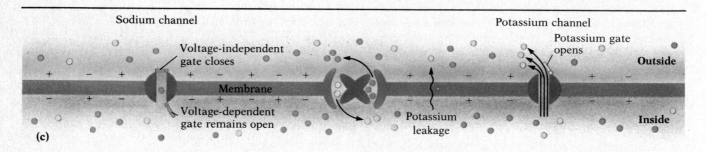

(c)

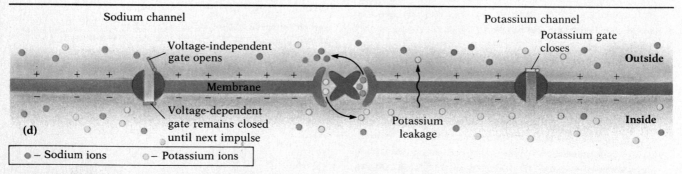

(d)

● – Sodium ions   ○ – Potassium ions

32.8

The rapid change in the axon's permeability to sodium during a neural impulse can be viewed in terms of sodium and potassium ion gates in the membrane. While the exchange pumps work constantly, the gates change with action potential. In the resting state **(a)**, the voltage-independent sodium gates are open, but the pore is still blocked by voltage-dependent gates. The single potassium gates are closed. The sudden in-rush of sodium ions accompanying a neural impulse occurs as the voltage-dependent sodium gates open **(b)**. As sodium reaches equilibrium and the action potential peaks, the sodium movement stops as the potassium gates open **(c)**, permitting potassium to leave. The exchange pump immediately begins to reestablish the sodium and potassium gradients **(d)**.

sweetness, light, noise, and heat. If all the neurons work alike, how can we distinguish among the sensations?

Receptors or sensory neurons, those structures that respond to stimuli, don't really sort anything out; they simply generate action potentials. The sorting, identifying, interpreting, and integrating is done in the interneurons that make up most of the spinal cord and brain. One way the brain can decode an incoming impulse is through its frequency. A mild stimulus, such as a light touch, might stimulate only a few receptors and produce just a few impulses per second, and might even be ignored by the brain. A much stronger stimulus, such as smashing one's finger with a hammer, produces a rapid barrage of impulses and stimulates many more receptors, making the stimulus difficult for the brain to ignore.

We can detect *kinds*—as well as *degrees*—of sensations. This is largely due to the arrangement of the sensory neurons and the integrating interneurons. If the interneurons shunt the impulse to one part of the brain, sound will be perceived; if they send it to another part, light will be perceived. Each part of the brain is capable of even finer discriminations. For example, sound may be evaluated so precisely that when alone after dinner, we immediately perceive the quiet testing of a doorknob in spite of our intense concentration on TV.

COMMUNICATION AMONG NEURONS

The place where the axon of one neuron activates the dendrite or cell body of another is called a **synapse.** Most neurons come very close, but do not touch one another; the tiny space between one neuron and the next is called the **synaptic cleft** (Figure 32.10). Thus, in a chain of neurons, one must stimulate the next across this cleft. It does this by releasing the chemicals called neurotransmitters. There are many different kinds of neurotransmitters, depending on the functions of the neurons involved. The most common are *acetylcholine* and *norepinephrine* (others are discussed in Chapter 33).

Action at the Synapse

At the tips of the axonal tree are many tiny bulbs, the *synaptic knobs.* These knobs are filled with tiny vesicles, or sacs, that contain the neurotransmitter. When the action potential reaches these synaptic knobs, calcium ions (Ca^{++}) enter the cytoplasm there through calcium gates. This shift causes the vesicles to rupture and empty their neurotransmitter molecules into the synaptic cleft. These molecules diffuse across the narrow cleft and attach to

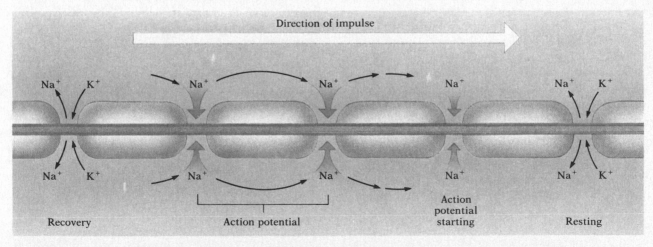

32.9

In myelinated neurons, action potentials occur only at the nodes—tiny gaps between the Schwann cells. The neural impulse leaps from node to node down the axon. This type of transmission, known as saltatory propagation, is considerably faster and requires less energy in terms of ATP than transmission in non-myelinated neurons. The current generated at one node depolarizes the next nodal region, and so on down the axon. Because of saltatory propagation, myelinated neurons transmit impulses up to 20 times faster than the fastest non-myelinated neurons.

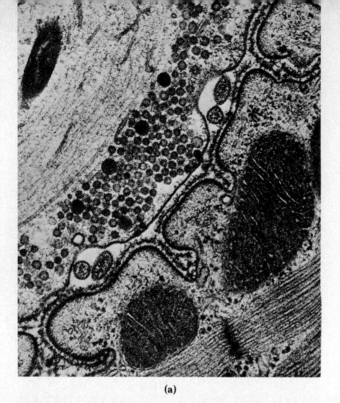

(a)

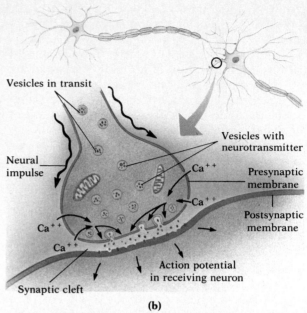

Vesicles in transit

Neural impulse

Ca++

Ca++

Synaptic cleft

Vesicles with neurotransmitter

Presynaptic membrane

Ca++

Ca++

Postsynaptic membrane

Action potential in receiving neuron

(b)

32.10

(a) The synaptic cleft, as viewed through the electron microscope, is a minute space between the axonal endings of one neuron and the receptor membrane of another. Each axonal ending is filled with saclike synaptic vesicles that contain neurotransmitter molecules such as acetylcholine. (b) Activity at a synapse begins when an action potential reaches an axonal ending. The depolarizing action opens calcium ion (Ca^{++}) gates in the ending, admitting the positive ions. The presence of calcium ions causes the synaptic vesicles to rupture, spilling neurotransmitter molecules into the cleft. If sufficient receptor sites in the postsynaptic membrane fill, a neural impulse—a depolarizing wave—will ensue and the impulse will travel along the second neuron. In the case of an effector, such as skeletal muscle, the depolarizing wave will cause a contraction.

specialized receptors on the membrane of the next neuron (see Figure 32.10b).

When a critical number of receptor sites have been filled, the receiving membrane opens its own calcium ion gates. As calcium ions rush into the cytoplasm of the dendrite or cell body, a new impulse is generated that quickly moves down the axon. The neurotransmitter released into the synapse is almost immediately destroyed by special enzymes. The destruction of the neurotransmitter means that the neuron does not continue to fire when it is no longer needed.

In *tetanus*, bacterial toxins block the action of these enzymes, so the neurotransmitter remains in the synaptic cleft. The next neuron keeps firing, releasing its own neurotransmitters at neuromuscular junctions and keeping the muscles contracted or causing spasms and convulsions. Certain powerful insecticides known as *organophosphates* work on this principle. They inhibit the neurotransmitter enzyme called *acetylcholinesterase* and cause insects to develop a form of tetanus.

Significantly, some neurons that receive neurotransmitters are not activated, but inhibited. Inhibitory neurons act in conjunction with other types of neurons to produce a finer and more coordinated control within animals. For example, they may work to increase the *threshold level* of a pathway—the threshold level is the amount of stimulation required for a pathway to react—at times screening out noises that might keep us from sleeping, or perhaps inhibiting us from jumping when a leaf falls.

THE REFLEX ARC

Now let's see how a system comprising many neurons might operate to produce a simple behavioral response. Consider the **reflex arc,** a phenomenon many of you may recognize. The anatomy of such an arc is shown in Figure 32.11.

The reflex arc is a complete reaction (encompassing detection, integration, and response) that does not directly involve the brain. A familiar ex-

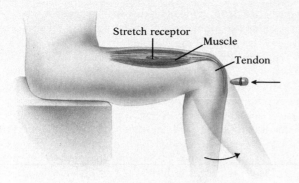

Stretch receptor
Muscle
Tendon

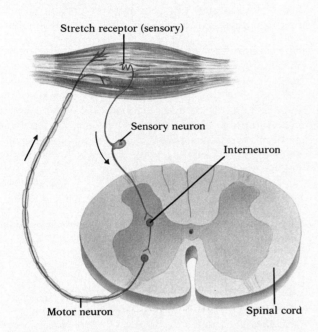

Stretch receptor (sensory)

Sensory neuron

Interneuron

Motor neuron

Spinal cord

32.11

In the knee-jerk reflex, striking the tendon causes the muscle above to extend slightly. Stretch receptors, specialized sensory neurons in the muscles, are stimulated. They then transmit impulses to the spinal cord, where the appropriate motor neurons are activated. The contraction in the muscle is accomplished without intervention by the brain. Such circuits are known as reflex arcs.

ample of the reflex arc is the "jumping" of your leg when a doctor taps the tendon below your knee (a test commonly used to rule out certain neurological disorders). Your leg jumps, or kicks, because the blow stretches the tendon, which also causes the muscle above to stretch. The change is detected by certain *stretch receptors*, specialized sensory neurons within muscles, that flash a message to the spinal cord. The impulse is immediately relayed through interneurons to nearby motor neurons whose axons pass back down to the same muscle. The reflexive response is sudden and involuntary, since the brain is not involved except as a passive and possibly surprised observer. The muscle contracts, and your leg kicks.

Stretch receptors are also responsible for your head snapping up as you doze off during lectures, announcing to everyone your opinion of the class. Such reflex systems are also essential to the delicate processes that enable you to maintain posture and limb position. Highly coordinated contractions in opposing muscles must be adjusted constantly by neural behavior, but this involves little conscious intervention. (When's the last time you thought to yourself, "I really must contract my left sterno-cleidomastoid; my head seems to be leaning to the right"?)

Reflexes are a particular and relatively simple type of neural response. In general, they are identified by a few special traits. Reflexes usually: (1) are involuntary; (2) are stereotyped (always performed the same way); (3) are adaptive; (4) involve relatively few neurons; and (5) are rapid.

Our nervous systems, then, are important to our adjusting to a complex and variable world. Neurons, the individual nerve cells, are highly sensitive, reactive, and complex structures that, when properly coordinated, allow us to make adaptive responses. In the next chapters, we will see how these neurons come to form incredibly complex systems—some of which are involved in conscious behavior, and some of which are not.

Summary

The Neuron

Neurons contain a cell body, axons, and dendrites, and can range from a few millimeters to over a meter in length. The cell body contains the nucleus and produces neurotransmitters. Dendrites receive impulses and transmit them toward the cell body, while axons transmit impulses away from the cell body. Axons are often surrounded by a myelin sheath, which is composed of Schwann cells interrupted by nodes.

The nervous system contains sensory neurons, interneurons, and motor neurons. Sensory neurons, activated by stimuli, carry impulses toward the brain and spinal cord. Interneurons communicate only with other nerve cells and help in the integration of stimuli and responses. Motor neurons receive impulses from interneurons and transmit them to effectors, enabling the body to respond. The brain and spinal cord contain glial cells in addition to neurons. Nerves are tracts of axons and dendrites traveling the same route.

The Neural Impulse

Neural impulses are depolarizing waves (action potentials) that proceed along a neuron, followed immediately by repolarization. The polarized, or resting, state (−60 mV) is maintained by sodium/potassium ion exchange pumps that produce the polarizing gradients. With neural stimulation, Na⁺ gates open, permitting an inrush of Na⁺ and a shift to +40 mV. Recovery occurs as the –Na⁺ gates close and the K⁺ gates open, with K⁺ ions rushing out. Then the K⁺ gates close and the sodium/potassium ion exchange pumps restore the resting gradients.

Myelin insulates the neurons and accelerates impulses, allowing the impulse to jump from one node to the next in saltatory propagation.

Neural Codes

Although action potentials in all neurons occur in roughly the same way, interneurons help us discriminate between one sensation and another. The brain can decode impulses according to their frequencies and by means of specialized centers.

Communication Among Neurons

Synapses are the points at which the axon of one neuron activates the dendrite or cell body of another. Neurons are separated by synaptic clefts, which are bridged by the release of neurotransmitters such as acetylcholine and norepinephrine. The action potential activates the synaptic knobs of the axon, where vesicles rupture to release neurotransmitters that attach to special receptors on the membrane of the next neuron. When enough receptor sites are filled, the receiving membrane opens its calcium ion gates, and a new impulse is sent down the axon. The neurotransmitter is destroyed shortly after release, so that the neuron does not keep firing. Some neurons are inhibited by neurotransmitters and act with other neurons to produce finely controlled coordination.

The Reflex Arc

In the reflex arc, specialized sensory neurons (such as stretch receptors) generate an impulse and immediately transmit it to the spinal cord. Interneurons relay the impulse to motor neurons that reach back to the source of the impulse. Reflex systems help maintain posture and limb position, and are usually rapid, involuntary, stereotyped, adaptive, involve relatively few neurons, and do not directly involve the brain.

Key Terms

neuron	motor neuron	repolarization
cell body	glial cell	ion gates
neurotransmitter	nerves	voltage-dependent gate
effector	sodium/potassium ion exchange	voltage-independent gate
dendrite	pumps	saltatory propagation
axon	polarized	synapse
myelin	resting potential	synaptic cleft
sensory neuron	action potential	reflex arc
interneuron	wave of depolarization	

Review Questions

1. Prepare a simple sketch of a motor neuron, label its parts, and indicate with arrows the way a neural impulse is received and transmitted. (p. 472)

2. List three types of neurons and discuss the general function of each. (p. 473)

3. Carefully describe the role of sodium/potassium exchange pumps in maintaining the "resting" state of a neuron. Explain what the term *potential* means in the case of resting potential. (p. 475)

4. State, in mV, the voltage change during an action potential, and draw a graph representing this. Explain the voltage shift in terms of the movement of sodium and potassium ions. (p. 476)

5. Explain the behavior of the sodium and potassium ion gates as an action potential begins, peaks, and

ends. What are the exchange pumps doing throughout this period? (p. 477)

6. Describe the arrangement of the myelin sheath in a myelinated neuron, and discuss how the sheath affects the speed of neural transmission. (p. 477)

7. If all neural impulses have the same characteristics, how can we distinguish among different stimuli? (p. 479)

8. Describe the specific organization of a synapse and explain the manner in which neurotransmitters function in the synaptic cleft. (pp. 479–480)

9. Using the "knee jerk" reflex as an example, explain how a reflex arc works. In what ways do such reflexes differ from other responses, and why is this important to us? (pp. 480–481)

The Central Nervous System

33

We now come to the part of biology where the brain discusses itself. We can only begin to guess at what lies ahead in this area of research, but we will get some very tantalizing glimpses as we concern ourselves with some of the work that has already been done. There are now people who are trying to understand the biochemical bases for schizophrenia, violence, passion, jealousy, and love. And at the same time, there are others trying to understand, more precisely, just how sodium enters a single neuron.

The field of neurobiology is, indeed, being approached on a broad front, by people with a variety of interests. So now that we've learned something about the anatomy of neurons and the chemistry of neural behavior, let's learn something about our highly regarded brain (are these the words of a brain complimenting itself?) and the great thick cord that communicates with it.

The vertebrate nervous system can be divided into two major parts: the **central nervous system** and the **peripheral nervous system** (Figure 33.1). The central nervous system comprises the brain and spinal cord. The peripheral nervous system includes the vast network of neurons and nerves outside the central nervous system. Neurons enter and leave the central nervous system through *cranial* and *spinal nerves*. The peripheral nervous system is divided functionally into two more systems. One is the *somatic system*, which includes sensory pathways (from sensory structures) and motor pathways (to skeletal muscle). The other is the *autonomic system*, which is chiefly motor and controls the internal organs—or *viscera*, as they are collectively known. It is important to note that the somatic and autonomic neurons often share the same cranial and spinal nerves. In this chapter we will be concerned with the central nervous system.

THE SPINAL CORD

The **spinal cord** (Figure 33.2a) serves as the primary link between the brain and other parts of the nervous system. Essentially, its outer areas consist of incredible numbers of myelinated axons running parallel to each other and forming **spinal tracts.** Myelin gives these tracts a white, glistening appearance. Inside this area is a butterfly-shaped gray region (the **gray matter**), which is composed not only of non-myelinated nerve tracts but of the non-myelinated cells bodies of all the spinal neurons (Figure 33.2b). (Myelinated fibers have limited powers of repair, but damaged gray matter cannot repair itself.)

The spinal cord begins as a narrow continuation of the brain, passing through the *foramen magnum* ("big hole") at the base of the skull. It lies sheltered

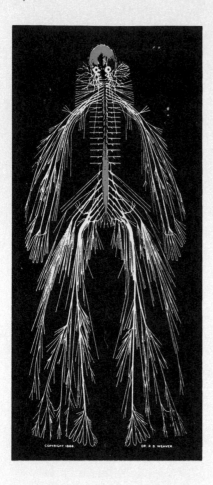

33.1

The central nervous system *(color)* includes the brain and spinal cord. The vast proliferation of branched sensory and motor nerves emerging from the brain and cord as cranial and spinal nerves makes up the peripheral nervous system.

within the **vertebral canal,** a continuous channel lying within the vertebral column. Paired **spinal nerves,** which are part of the peripheral nervous system, emerge from the cord through the spaces between adjacent arches. Each of these spinal nerves is formed from two roots in the cord, a *dorsal* (rear) sensory root and a *ventral* (front) motor root (see Figure 33.2b). The cell bodies of the motor neurons, like those of the tracts, lie in the gray matter of the spinal cord, with their lengthy axons passing out through the spinal nerves and onward to the effectors. On the other hand, the cell bodies of sensory neurons are clustered just outside the cord, where they form a number of mound-like **dorsal root ganglia.** The spinal cord is surrounded by a tough, three-layered sheath, the **meninges,** which contains a cushioning fluid, the **cerebrospinal fluid.**

THE HUMAN BRAIN

The human brain (Figure 33.3) is a fascinating structure. To this day, we know very little about the brain, but even the things that we do know are often hard to believe. For example, there is some evidence that every word you have ever said or heard is filed away in your brain, even though you will go to your grave having retrieved hardly any of that information. (Imagine what it would be like to be able to recall every word of our last conversation with a loved one.)

The human brain weighs in at about 1.4 kg (3 lb), has a volume of about 1200–1500 cc, contains over 100 billion neurons, and has about 10 times that number of supporting glial cells. Since each neuron may synapse with a number of other neurons, there are a number of alternative pathways for impulses, and the coordination necessary to produce even a simple response must be due to a veritable neural symphony.

The brain, which has a consistency somewhat like gelatin, is obviously fragile, but it is well protected. In addition to the surrounding skull, the brain—like the spinal cord—is directly enclosed by the tough, elastic meninges. The spaces within these membranes, and the cavities within the brain itself, are filled with the pressurized, shock-absorbing cerebrospinal fluid. The billions of delicate neurons themselves are embedded in the vast numbers of glial cells that make up much of the brain's mass.

The vertebrate brain consists of three regions: *hindbrain, midbrain,* and *forebrain.* In humans, the midbrain is not easily seen, since most of it is enclosed by the prominent forebrain (Figure 33.4).

THE HINDBRAIN

The **hindbrain,** which consists of the *medulla oblongata,* the *pons,* and the *cerebellum,* is continuous with the spinal cord. As a rough generality, the more unconscious, involuntary, and mechanical processes are directed by these more posterior parts of the brain. For example, the **medulla oblongata** (or, more simply, the **medulla**), which can be considered an enlargement of the spinal cord, controls such functions as breathing, digestion, and heartbeat. All communication between the brain and spinal column must pass through the medulla.

The **pons,** which lies just above (anterior to) the medulla, contains the ascending and descending tracts that run between the brain and spinal cord. It also receives tracts to and from large nerves that extend from the brain itself (primarily to regions of the head and face). These are called the **cranial nerves.** The pons also links the functions of the forebrain with those of the cerebellum.

The **cerebellum** is a paired, bulbous structure, about the size and general appearance of the two halves of a large walnut. It lies above the medulla and somewhat toward the back of the head. The cerebellum is concerned with balance, equilibrium, and muscle coordination. (Do you suppose, then, that the cerebellums of atheletes and nonatheletes might differ? It now appears that they do, but the differences are subtle.)

THE MIDBRAIN

Essentially, the **midbrain** connects the hindbrain and forebrain. All of the tracts between the two must pass through this area. Certain parts of the midbrain receive sensory input from the eyes and ears. All auditory (sound) input of vertebrates is processed here before being sent to the forebrain. In most vertebrates, visual input is first processed here also. But in mammals, the visual information is sent directly to the forebrain. While the midbrain is involved in complex behavior in fishes and amphibians, many of these functions are assumed by the forebrain in reptiles, birds, and mammals.

33.2

The spinal cord **(a)** extends from the base of the brain into the lumbar region of the spine, where it begins branching into many descending nerves. The spinal nerves are major branches that emerge from between vertebrae. A cross-section **(b)** reveals the spinal cord to be composed of two distinct regions. The gray double-winged region consists primarily of cell bodies and non-myelinated neural tracts, while the outer white region is largely composed of myelinated axons that form the major spinal tracts. The emerging spinal nerves contain motor and sensory neurons. Motor nerves emerge from a ventral (front) root; sensory nerves enter the cord through a dorsal (rear) root. The thickenings seen in the dorsal root are the cell bodies of numerous sensory neurons (the dorsal root ganglia).

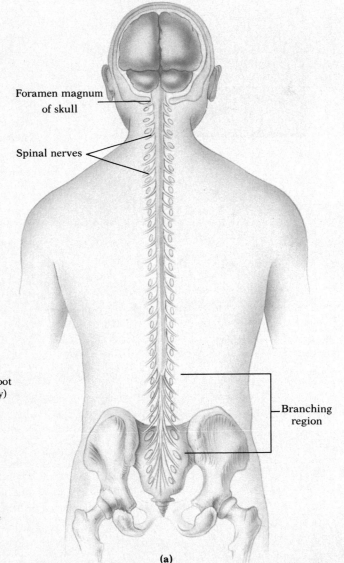

Foramen magnum of skull

Spinal nerves

Branching region

(a)

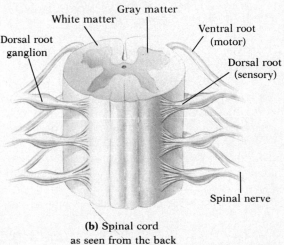

Dorsal root ganglion

White matter

Gray matter

Ventral root (motor)

Dorsal root (sensory)

Spinal nerve

(b) Spinal cord as seen from the back

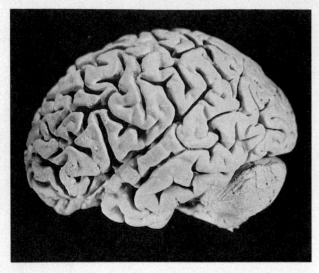

33.3

Under the wrinkled exterior of the human brain resides an incredibly complex array of neurons. We know very little about the precise mechanisms of brain functioning. The problem is compounded by the uncountable neurons, the innumerable neural tracts and neural bodies, and the maze of chemical and physical interactions among neurons.

THE FOREBRAIN

The **forebrain,** the largest and most dominant part of the human brain, is responsible for conscious thought, reasoning, memory, language, sensory decoding, and certain kinds of movement. The embryonic forebrain gives rise to such important structures as the *thalamus*, the *reticular system*, the *hypothalamus*, and the *cerebrum*.

The Thalamus

The **thalamus** is located at the base of the forebrain. It has been rather unpoetically called the "great relay station of the brain" (Figure 33.4). It consists of densely packed clusters of neurons, which provide connections between the various parts of the brain—between the forebrain and the hindbrain, between different parts of the forebrain, and between parts of the sensory system and the cerebrum.

The Reticular System

The thalamus also contains most of an extensive area called the **reticular system,** composed of interconnected neurons that are almost feltlike in appearance. These neurons run throughout the thal-

33.4

A brain divided along the midline from front to back. The dominant forebrain (thalamus, hypothalamus, and cerebrum) is obvious. The areas of the hindbrain (medulla oblongata, pons, and cerebellum) are also quite distinctive, but the midbrain that connects them is not well defined. The *corpus callosum* connects the two halves of the brain.

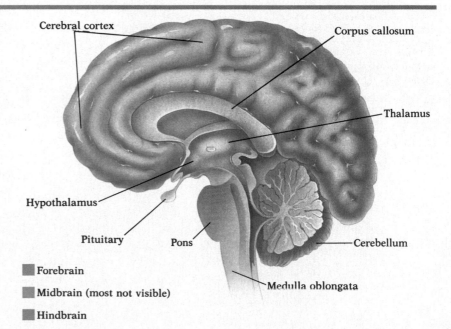

Cerebral cortex
Corpus callosum
Thalamus
Hypothalamus
Pituitary
Pons
Cerebellum
Medulla oblongata

■ Forebrain
■ Midbrain (most not visible)
■ Hindbrain

amus and into the midbrain. The reticular system is still somewhat of a mystery, but several interesting facts are known about it. For example, we know that it monitors the brain. Every pathway to and from the various portions of the brain sends side branches to the reticular system as it passes through the thalamus, so it virtually taps all incoming and outgoing communications to the brain. Also, reticular neurons appear to be rather unspecific. The same reticular neuron may be stimulated by impulse from the hand, foot, ear, or eye. As for its function, the leading hypothesis is that the reticular apparatus is something of an alarm system that serves to activate the appropriate parts of the brain upon receiving a stimulus. The more messages it intercepts, the more the brain is aroused (Figure 33.5).

The reticular system seems to function importantly in sleep. You may have noticed that it is much easier to fall asleep when you are lying on a comfortable bed in a quiet room with the lights off than under conditions with many incoming signals. With fewer stimuli, the reticular system receives fewer messages, and the brain is allowed to relax. Some people can sleep under almost any condition, perhaps because the system screens out sensory signals on their way to the cortex.

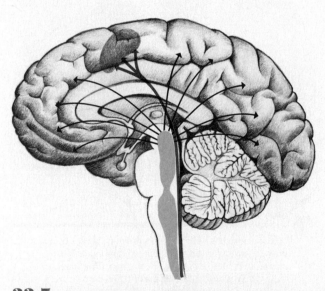

33.5

The reticular system is not a distinct structure, but rather a number of neural pathways that act as an arousal system for the higher brain centers. It apparently has the task of sorting incoming stimuli during sleep or concentrated effort, screening out minor irrelevant signals, and relaying significant messages.

The Hypothalamus

As the name implies, the **hypothalamus** lies below the thalamus (see Figure 33.4). It is densely packed with cells that help regulate the body's internal environment as well as certain aspects of behavior. The hypothalamus helps control heart rate, blood pressure, and body temperature. It is also involved in such basic drives as hunger, thirst, sex, and rage. Electrical stimulation of various centers in the hypothalamus can cause a cat to act hungry, sexy, cold, hot, benign, or angry. In humans it is known that a tumor pressing against the hypothalamus can cause a person to behave violently, or even murderously.

A major function of the hypothalamus is its coordination of the nervous system with the **endocrine (hormonal) system.** In fact, the hypothalamus has a certain monitoring control over the so-called "master gland," the pituitary (see Chapter 35). The hypothalamus may even be considered something of an endocrine gland itself, since the posterior lobe of the pituitary consists of axons whose cell bodies are in the hypothalamus. The hormones that are released by the posterior pituitary are actually manufactured in nerve cell bodies lying within the hypothalamus.

The hypothalamus and the thalamus, along with certain pathways in the cortex, are functionally part of what is called the **limbic system** (Figure 33.6). The limbic system links the forebrain and midbrain and is composed of a number of *nuclei* (sharply defined and specific areas usually associated with a single function) that are also centers of emotion. For example, the *amygdala* lying within the limbic system can produce rage if stimulated, and docility if removed. The *hippocampus*, another limbic structure, may figure importantly in the memory of recent events. Without the hippocampus, a person may be unable to complete a sentence, because he or she forgot how it began.

The Cerebrum

The word *brain* usually conjures up an image of two large, convoluted (wrinkled) gray lobes. Those lobes make up much of the **cerebrum,** the largest and most prominent part of the human brain. If we had to ascribe one prominent responsibility to the cerebrum, we would probably say it is *intelligence.* You are probably waiting for a definition of this word, but so far no two people (much less three) have agreed on what it means. What it may boil down to is simply the *potential* to devise new

33.6

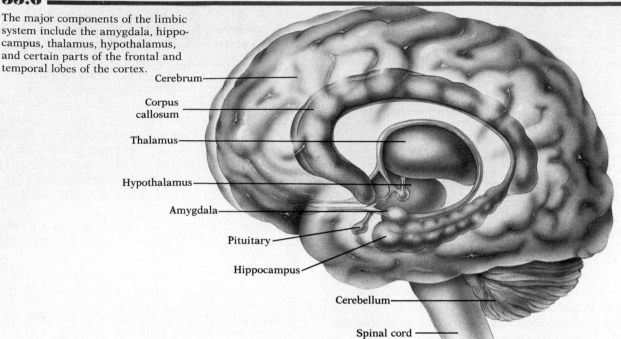

The major components of the limbic system include the amygdala, hippocampus, thalamus, hypothalamus, and certain parts of the frontal and temporal lobes of the cortex.

Cerebrum

Corpus callosum

Thalamus

Hypothalamus

Amygdala

Pituitary

Hippocampus

Cerebellum

Spinal cord

---

ways of coping with one's surroundings, but don't quote us.

The left and right halves of the cerebrum are the **cerebral hemispheres,** and the outer layer of gray cells is the **cerebral cortex.** (*Cortex* means "rind," and is a general biological term for the outer layer of any organ.) The cerebral cortex consists of a thin but extremely dense layer of about 15 billion nerve cell bodies and their dendrites. It overlies the whitish, more solid region of myelinated nerve fibers below (Figure 33.7).

Every vertebrate species has a cerebrum, but it differs markedly from one class to the next, especially in the degree of development of the cortex (Figure 33.8). In some animals, the cerebrum may only help to implement behavior that could be performed, at least to some degree, without it. These animals rely more on the genetically programmed behavior emanating from the "old brain"—the noncerebral part. In mammals, the cerebrum is more important and often takes over functions that were once the responsibility of lower, older, parts of the brain.

The evolution of the cerebrum may be reflected in traits other than size. For example, its convolutions may indicate its dominance. Con-

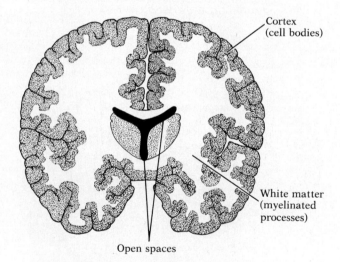

Cortex (cell bodies)

White matter (myelinated processes)

Open spaces

33.7

A cross-section of the cerebrum reveals an outer layer of gray matter, the cortex, that contains several very dense layers of neurons. The underlying white matter consists of immense numbers of myelinated neural processes. The overlying cortex is highly convoluted. Such folds and fissures increase the cortical surface area within a confined space.

volutions increase the surface area of the cortex without enlarging the braincase. The deep convolutions seen in the human brain are lacking in the brain of a rat. The highly touted and undoubtedly intelligent dolphin has a highly convoluted brain, but with fewer layers than the human cerebrum.

Hemispheres and Lobes. In humans, each cerebral hemisphere is divided into four lobes (Figure 33.9). At the back on each side is the **occipital lobe,** which receives and analyzes visual information. The *visual field* of the cerebral cortex is stimulated by the images formed on the retinas of the eyes. If the occipital lobe is injured, black "holes" appear in the part of the visual field that occurs in the injured area.

The **temporal lobes**—at the sides of the brain— roughly resemble the thumbs on boxing gloves. They help process visual information, but their main function is in hearing. The **frontal lobes** are right where you would expect to find them—at the front of the cerebrum. (This is the part of your head that you hit with the palm of your hand when you suddenly remember what you have forgotten.) Part of the frontal lobe regulates precise voluntary movement. Another part controls movements that produce speech.

The very front of each frontal lobe is called the **prefrontal area.** Its principal function is to sort out sensory information. In other words, it places information and stimuli into their proper context. The gentle touch of a mate and the sight of a hand protruding from the bathtub drain will both serve as stimuli, but each stimulus will be processed differently by the prefrontal area. In recent years, parts of the frontal lobes of aberrant persons were surgically removed in an effort to bring their behavior more into line with the norm. Fortunately, this surgery has been replaced by tranquilizing

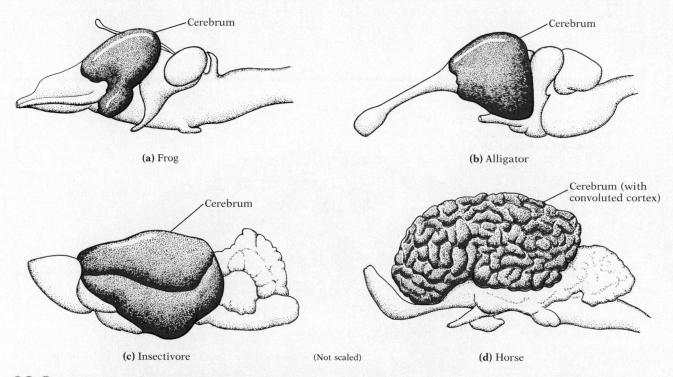

(a) Frog

(b) Alligator

(c) Insectivore   (Not scaled)   **(d)** Horse

33.8

Cerebral development in vertebrates varies from class to class, roughly in the order in which they evolved. In amphibians **(a)**, the first terrestrial vertebrates, the cerebrum is small relative to the other brain regions. The hindbrain and optic lobes are quite prominent. In advanced reptiles, such as the alligator **(b)**, the size of the cerebral region is increased, but the relative size of the hindbrain also remains great. The large bulbous extension is devoted to smell. In mammals, the cerebrum is proportionately large, but in the primitive insectivore **(c)**, the cerebrum is smooth and does not occupy the volume seen in the horse. In the horse **(d)**, the cerebrum contains a considerable amount of convoluted cortex, and the cerebrum is proportionately large compared to the hindbrain.

drugs that can accomplish the same end in a far less permanent manner.

The **parietal lobes**—located directly behind the frontal lobes—contain the sensory areas for the skin receptors, as well as the areas that detect body position. Damage to the parietal lobe may cause numbness, and can also cause grossly distorted visual perceptions.

By probing the brain with electrodes, investigators have determined exactly which areas of the cerebrum are involved in the body's various sensory and motor activities, and have mapped these functions on the cortex. Figure 33.10 shows the results of such mapping. The figures are distorted to demonstrate the relative area of the cerebrum devoted to each body part. The sensory areas of the cortex are largely devoted to integrating sensations from the face, tongue, hands, and genitals, while the motor areas are devoted primarily to the muscles of the tongue, face, and thumbs.

Right and Left Halves of the Brain.   Although the two cerebral hemispheres are roughly equal in size and in potential, they are quite different in function. Moreover, their differences apparently are accentuated by learning, because certain learned patterns are associated primarily with one hemisphere. One example of the difference between the hemispheres is seen in *handedness*.

It is interesting that species such as rats and parrots show right and left handedness. Furthermore, although only about 11% of humans are left-handed, rats and parrots are equally likely to be left- or right-handed. Because neural tracts cross from one side of the brain to the other, the right side of the body is controlled by the left side of the brain, and *vice versa*; thus in right-handed people, the left half of the brain is dominant. It is also slightly larger than the right half.

No one knows what causes left-handedness. In fact, apparently, there are two kinds of left-handedness. In the more common type, the left half of the brain is still dominant, in that it contains the speech center; but it also controls the left hand. These "left-handers" are the ones who write by crooking their left hand around, appearing to write upside down. In the rarer type of left-handedness, the *right* half of the brain is dominant and contains

33.9

The human cerebrum is divided into four prominent lobes: occipital, temporal, frontal, and parietal. Each has a specialized function, and together they represent the so-called higher centers of the brain.

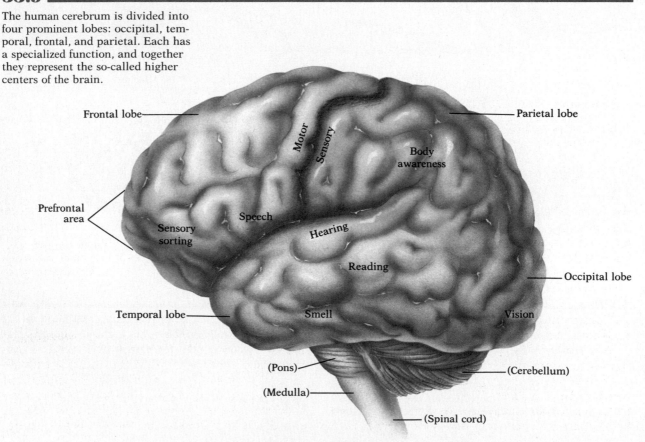

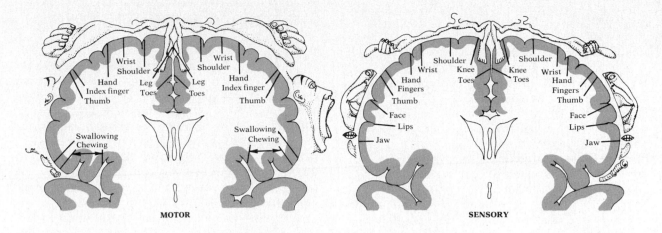

MOTOR　　　　　　　　　　　　**SENSORY**

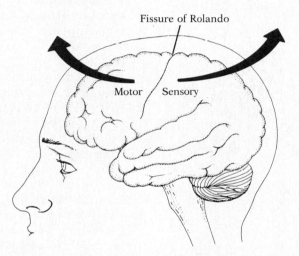

Fissure of Rolando

Motor　Sensory

33.10

Among the distinct regions of the cortex are the sensory and motor areas. The two are located on opposite sides of the *fissure of Rolando*, a prominent dividing line between the frontal and parietal lobes *(inset)*. The parts of the human body that lie over each region are emphasized according to how much brain tissue is de-

voted to that part. Thus the face—particularly the lips—is exaggerated in the figure overlying the sensory region, since sensory neurons abound in the face. Note that the size of the hand is similar to both, indicating that both sensory and motor functions are well developed in this organ.

the functional speech center, and it also controls the left hand. These people use a more conventional writing angle. A few people have both traits, a sort of double negative: their right hands are controlled by dominant right hemispheres, so they write with their *right* hands—held upside down!

Other functions, such as speech, perception, and different aspects of IQ test performance, are also more likely to be controlled by one hemisphere than the other. The primary speech center of all right-handed people (and most left-handed people as well) is located in the left hemisphere. The left hemisphere also seems to be the seat of analytical thinking, while spatial perception is a right-hemisphere function. Left-hemisphere brain dam-

age can result in *aphasia*—the inability to speak or understand language—while damage to the right-hemisphere of the brain may result in the inability to draw the simplest picture or diagram (but does not affect the ability to write letters and numbers, which is a left-hemisphere function).

In spite of these specializations, the right and left hemispheres operate as an integrated functional unit, connected primarily by the **corpus callosum** (Figure 33.11). If one side of the brain learns something—for instance, by feeling an object with just one hand—the information will be transferred to the other hemisphere. However, if the corpus callosum has been severed, the left side of the brain literally doesn't know what the left hand is doing.

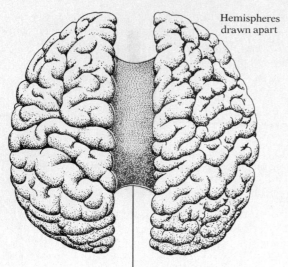

Hemispheres
drawn apart

Corpus callosum

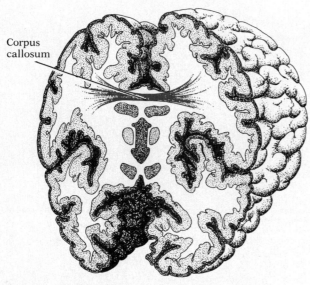

Corpus
callosum

33.11

The corpus callosum is a neural bridge between the cerebral hemispheres, relaying information from one half to the other. This connection can be severed without obvious ill effects. Some forms of epilepsy are treated by an incision of this sort. There are no apparent problems after such seemingly drastic treatment, but there is a reduction in the transfer of learning from one hemisphere to the other.

CHEMICALS IN THE BRAIN

We know that the brain contains billions of neurons and that these neurons interact in a delicate and coordinated manner, integrating and shunting information from one place to another. This interaction includes both the excitation and inhibition of adjacent neurons through very specific actions in the trillions of synapses. The brain has at least 50 neurotransmitters, with more being discovered all the time. This number probably shouldn't be too surprising, considering the specificity necessary in orchestrating the brain's vast network of cells.

The neurotransmitters are synthesized in the cell bodies of neurons (see Chapter 32). Generally, different neurotransmitters and different kinds of receptors are concentrated in different regions of the brain, so that the brain is organized chemically as well as anatomically.

The brain's neurotransmitters may be simple **monoamines,** such as norepinephrine, dopamine, histamine, and serotonin. Other neurotransmitters may be modified or unmodified amino acids. One more recently discovered class of transmitters, the **neuropeptides,** are short chains of amino acids varying in number from two to about 40.

Among the more interesting brain neuropeptides are the **enkephalins** and **endorphins.** These modify our perception of pain, and also have an elevating effect on mood. Anything acutely painful, such as running a marathon race or being shot in the foot, will stimulate the release of enkephalins. The "runner's high," the slight euphoria that may result after about a 10-mile run, is also attributed to the release of enkephalins (although some runners may simply be ecstatic at having covered that distance without dying in the process). These peptides are called *opioid* neurotransmitters because morphine and other opiates will also bind to the enkaphalin neuron receptors and mimic their action. Our rapidly expanding knowledge of the neurotransmitters is shedding some light on the action of certain drugs that affect the central nervous system. It is also being found that neurotransmitters are implicated in certain disease conditions (Essay 33.1).

ELECTRICAL ACTIVITY IN THE BRAIN

Each firing neuron in the brain creates impulses that generate a form of electrical activity. If, perhaps, a million neurons fire simultaneously, this electrical energy can be detected experimentally outside the body. The instrument used in such detection is called an **electroencephalograph,** and the record obtained is called an *electroencephalogram (EEG)*. Electrodes leading to the instrument are fastened at various places on the cranium, and the very faint currents they pick up (primarily from the cortex) are amplified and recorded.

The EEG is not very useful in determining specifically what is going on the brain, but it is useful in detecting certain abnormalities or changes in brain activity—certain kinds of brain damage, for example, or the differences between wakefulness and sleep. Figure 33.12 compares the EEG of a normal person with that of a person with *epilepsy*. As the recording shows, the brains of epileptics are subject to sudden, random bursts of electrical activity. In a few instances, this abnormality can be traced to physical defects, such as scars or lesions in the brain tissue, but most forms of epilepsy are simply not understood.

Sleep

Electrical activity in the brain does not cease with sleep—quite the contrary is true. EEGs reveal that sleep is accompanied by a considerable amount of activity. Sleep has four distinct phases (Figure 33.13). By far the most interesting of these is called **rapid eye movement (REM) sleep.** During this period, the skeletal muscles are very relaxed—except for the eyes, which dart about beneath the eyelids. The EEG recording at this time is similar to that

ESSAY 33.1
ALZHEIMER'S DISEASE

We are all unhappily aware that some people may become forgetful, foolish, and incompetent as they age. They may regress to reliving the distant past, no longer functioning in the present. Such people suffer from *senile dementia*, the most prevalent form of which is called *Alzheimer's disease*, a relentlessly progressive condition that afflicts 5–10% of all people over 65. (It can also be found in people younger than 65.) Many patients in nursing homes have been placed there because their cognitive abilities, and especially their memories, have deteriorated too far for family members to be able to care for them at home.

Alzheimer's disease first manifests itself as an inability to recall recent events. At this stage, afflicted people cannot remember what happened an hour or a week ago, but they can often remember childhood experiences in vivid detail. As short-term memory lapse continues, other cognitive functions begin to fail. In the second stage of the illness, victims gradually forget how to read or write or perform simple calculations, and their speech may become garbled and irrational. The impairment of these abilities is often accompanied by irritability, paranoia, and hallucinations. Yet afflicted people remain alert (and aware of their degeneration) until the final stages of the disease.

Whereas any form of senile dementia was once considered to be simply a natural part of aging—the mind deteriorating as the body does—researchers now recognize certain variables associated with Alzheimer's disease. For example, the disease seems to be strongly influenced by genetic factors. This is difficult to fully substantiate, since the disease appears so late in life that there is a strong possibility that the individual may die before the traits ever have the opportunity to be expressed. Another indicator of Alzheimer's disease is a reduction in the level of *choline acetyltransferase*, an enzyme that helps synthesize the neurotransmitter *acetylcholine,* in the brain cells of victims.

People suffering from Alzheimer's also show a marked decrease in the number of neurons in the cortex of the brain (the gray matter) and especially in the *nucleus basalis*, a structure in the base of the forebrain that has many neural extensions to the cerebral cortex. (If you point your finger directly at your temple, you will be pointing at this largely uninvestigated structure.) Alzheimer's affects large parts of the brain, causing dense abnormal growths and bizarre tangles of nerves.

Scientists continue to investigate the physiological causes of what was once thought to be a mental condition. Their discoveries regarding Alzheimer's disease's effects on the brain raise possibilities of counteracting these effects with medication or surgery, and offer new hope for treating this affliction of the elderly. ●

produced by wakefulness. If a person is awakened at this time, he or she will report vivid dreams (that will otherwise be forgotten if the person is allowed to waken naturally). REM sleep appears to be essential to restfulness, although no one really knows why, just as no one really knows why dreaming might be useful. Experimental studies have revealed that people deprived of REM sleep wake up tired, and in subsequent sleep periods the REM period will be extended (contrary to myth, you *can* make up for lost sleep). If the REM sleep deprivation is continued, the person experiences increased anxiety and concentration becomes difficult. Eventually, noticeable personality disorders may arise.

Psychologists and biologists generally agree that, for whatever reason, sleep appears to be essential, especially to mental concentration, and is somehow restoring. Theorists suspect that sleep (and REM sleep in particular) is a period of information sorting and storage, and may be essential to long-term memory storage. One amusing theory of

dreams is that they are the process by which all of the incorrect, whimsical, absurd, and meaningless mental associations of the day are sorted out and disposed of. (Don't we wish!)

MEMORY

Mammals have two distinct kinds of memory. *Short-term memory* lasts for just a few hours, whereas *long-term memory* is relatively permanent. The two apparently function together because the neural events that form memories must be encoded in the short-term memory first. These short-term memories may or may not be consolidated into long-term memory. No one knows just what physical form either kind of memory takes but experimental manipulation of rats suggests that short-term memory does not require protein synthesis, but that the consolidation into long-term memory does require it (see Essay 33.2).

33.12

(a) An electroencephalogram (EEG) is produced by fastening a number of electrodes on the patient's scalp and then recording differences in the electrical potential between or among the leads. (b) The normal electrical activity of the brain is seen at the left, showing several EEG tracings from different locations on the cranium. In an epileptic person, the brain may show normal electrical activity between seizures, but when these episodes do occur, the electrical disturbances are obvious.

(a)

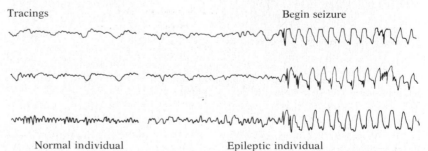

Tracings   Begin seizure

Normal individual   Epileptic individual

(b)

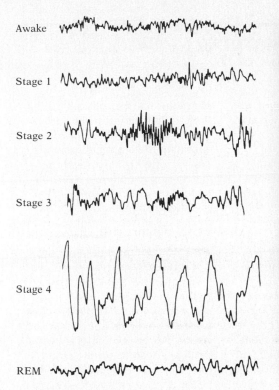

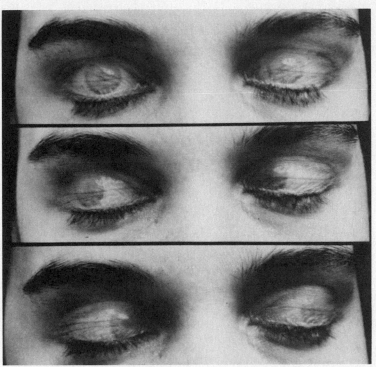

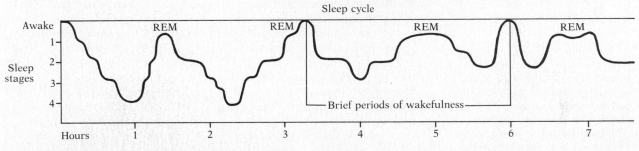

Sleep cycle

33.13

By studying the electrical activity of the brain and eye movement during sleep, researchers have identified four sleep stages: Stage 1, drowsiness; stage 2, light sleep; stage 3, intermediate sleep; and stage 4, deep sleep. Each has its own pattern of electrical activity, as seen in the EEG. Typically, sleep is interrupted by bursts of electrical activity whose patterns resemble wakefulness. Such sleep is associated with rapid eye movement, and is called REM sleep.

What we do know is that the **hippocampus** part of the limbic system (see Figure 33.6) is necessary for long-term memory consolidation. Rats with experimental lesions in the hippocampus must be taught the same maze every day, because they will have forgotten it by the next day. Humans with hippocampal lesions are in the same kind of a fix. They may be perfectly rational, intelligent people, with the ability to learn and with an unimpaired memory of events that occurred before their brain damage. But they will have no recollection whatever of anything that has happened to them since, unless it has happened within the previous several hours.

We now have some idea of the complex structure and function of the brain. We also are aware that the brain is an evolutionary product and that there is no universal progression toward "brain-iness." Some species do just fine with behavioral patterns dictated at a more instinctive level. In the complex, highly variable, and social world of an opportunistic species like *Homo sapiens*, however, the potential to learn and to deal with abstractions takes on a great adaptive importance.

THE ADVANTAGES OF FORGETTING

There are all sorts of strange abilities associated with memory in humans. *Idiot savants*, a special class of retardates, have very low IQs, but some are able to accomplish incredible mathematical feats, such as multiplying two five-figure numbers in their heads. Others can immediately tell you the day of the week on which Christmas fell in 1492—or any day in any year (although this is probably not a memory feat). A normally intelligent Russian man made his living as a *mnemonist*, giving stage performances in which he would memorize lines of 50 words. Once, in just a few moments, he memorized the nonsense formula:

$$N \cdot \sqrt{d^2 \cdot \frac{85^3}{vx} \cdot \sqrt[3]{\frac{276^2 \cdot 86x}{n^2v \cdot 264}} \cdot n^2b} = SV \cdot \frac{1624}{32^2} \cdot r^2s$$

Fifteen years later, upon request, he repeated the entire formula without a single mistake.

And what about people with "photographic memories"? They exist, and are called *eidetikers*. Proof of their abilities has been demonstrated with *stereograms*, apparently random dot patterns on two different cards that, when superimposed, produce a three-dimensional image. One person was asked to look at a 10,000-dot pattern on one card with her right eye for one minute. After ten seconds, she viewed another "random" dot pattern with her left eye. She then recalled the positions of the dots on the first card and conjured up the image of a "T."

If such abilities are possible in our species, why haven't they been selected for so that by now we could all, more or less, remember everything? On the surface, the advantages seem enormous, but the reason we can't is, in part, because there are serious drawbacks to having "total recall." Both the Russian mnemonist and the eidetiker could look at a barren tree, "recall" its leaves, and, when they looked away, be confused over whether the tree was leafy or not. Also, what about all those insignificant events that are of no advantage to remember? The energetically expensive neural apparatus would be wasted in retaining such information for recall (assuming that such retention takes more energy than the storage of information we normally can't recall). Another problem with remembering everything concerns times-lapse. The mnemonist recalled everything so well that it seemed as if every event of his life had just occurred. Forgetting, then, can give us a sense of time.

Obviously, the reason all humans can't remember things as well as the people in these examples is that we, as a species, have *not* found total recall necessary or useful. We generally don't need to recall every stone on the path to the place where we found food yesterday; we only need to remember the location of the path. In fact, remembering too much about our physical environment might cause us to relate to the environment on the basis of remembrances. Thus, any change in the environment might not be adjusted to as quickly as if we were never quite sure of what to expect. Instead, we operate under the assumption that we can't rely too strongly on our memories. ●

Summary

Introduction
The vertebrate nervous system is composed of the central nervous system (brain and spinal cord) and the peripheral nervous system (cranial and spinal nerves and their branches). The peripheral nervous system is divided into the somatic and autonomic systems.

The Spinal Cord
The spinal cord, running within the vertebral canal, is the primary link between the brain and other parts of the nervous system. Its outer area consists of myelinated axons that form tracts, and its inner area (gray matter) consists of nonmyelinated nerve tracts and cell bodies. Each paired spinal nerve is formed from a dorsal sensory root and a ventral motor root. The cell bodies of the motor neurons lie in the gray matter of the cord, and have long axons that pass through spinal nerves to effectors. The cell bodies of sensory neurons form dorsal root ganglia outside the cord. The spinal cord is surrounded by the meninges, which contains cerebrospinal fluid.

The Human Brain: Hindbrain and Midbrain
The human brain contains over 100 billion neurons and is composed of three parts: hindbrain, midbrain, and forebrain. The hindbrain—including the medulla oblongata, pons, and cerebellum—is continuous with the spinal cord and directs most unconscious, involuntary, and mechanical processes. The midbrain connects the hindbrain and forebrain; also, certain parts receive and process auditory input and some visual impulses.

The Human Brain: Forebrain
The forebrain consists of the thalamus, the reticular system, the hypothalamus, and the cerebrum. It is the larg-

est part of the brain and is responsible for conscious thought, memory, language, reasoning, sensory decoding, and certain types of voluntary movements. The thalamus provides connections between various parts of the brain and contains the reticular system, which monitors the activity of other parts of the brain. The hypothalamus helps regulate the body's internal environment and coordinates the nervous system with the endocrine system. The thalamus and hypothalamus are part of the limbic system, which also includes the hippocampus.

The cerebrum is the largest part of the forebrain, and is divided into right and left cerebral hemispheres; the outer layer of gray cells is called the cerebral cortex. In mammals, the cerebrum is responsible for "intelligence" and for numerous other functions. Each cerebral hemisphere in humans is divided into four lobes: the occipital lobe (visual processing); the temporal lobe (auditory and some visual processing); the frontal lobe (regulating voluntary movement and speech); and the parietal lobe (receiving sensory input and detecting bodily position).

Certain learning patterns, such as right or left handedness, are associated with each of the hemispheres. The corpus callosum, connecting the two hemispheres, enables information to be transferred from one side to the other.

Chemicals in the Brain

The brain is organized chemically as well as anatomically. Neural activity is facilitated by at least 50 neurotransmitters, which include simple monoamines and neuropeptides. Neuropeptides such as enkephalins and endorphins can modify perceptions of pain and induce a sense of euphoria.

Electrical Activity in the Brain

Neural impulses generate a form of electrical activity that can be detected and measured by electroencephalographs. Such electrical activity persists even during sleep, particularly when rapid eye movement sleep occurs. REM sleep appears to be essential to restfulness, and sleep may be a time when the brain sorts and processes information.

Memory

Memory can be short term, lasting only a few hours, and long term, which is relatively permanent. Short-term memories may or may not be consolidated into an individual's long-term memory. Long-term memory may require types of protein synthesis that short-term memory does not, and it is known that the hippocampus functions in long-term memory consolidation.

Key Terms

central nervous system	cranial nerves	temporal lobe
peripheral nervous system	cerebellum	frontal lobe
spinal cord	midbrain	prefrontal area
spinal tract	forebrain	parietal lobe
gray matter	thalamus	corpus callosum
vertebral canal	reticular system	monoamine
spinal nerves	hypothalamus	neuropeptide
dorsal root ganglia	endocrine (hormonal) system	enkephalin
meninges	limbic system	endorphin
cerebrospinal fluid	cerebrum	electroencephalograph
hindbrain	cerebral hemisphere	rapid eye movement (REM) sleep
medulla oblongata	cerebral cortex	hippocampus
pons	occipital lobe	

Review Questions

1. List the regions of the hindbrain and describe their general functions. (pp. 484–485)

2. Where is the reticular system of the brain, and what are its functions? (pp. 486–487)

3. List five specific functions of the hypothalamus. (p. 487)

4. Comment on the apparent evolutionary trend with respect to convolutions of the cerebral cortex. (pp. 488–489)

5. Which lobes of the cerebrum are most closely associated with each of the following: hearing, vision, voluntary movement, sensory input reception, and spatial relationships? (pp. 489–490)

6. In general, how do the right and left cerebral hemispheres differ functionally? Name the communicating tract between the two. (pp. 490–491)

7. Why is it logical to expect the brain to contain many different neurotransmitters? What is the role of enkephalins and endorphins? (p. 492)

8. List the phases of sleep-related electrical activity in the brain. Which of these seems most closely related to the restorative effects of sleep? (pp. 493–494)

The Peripheral Nervous System and the Special Senses

34

The contorted mass that is the brain and the great cord reaching down from it make up the central nervous system. It has been the focus of a great deal of research; but as is now apparent, there are still great gaps in our knowledge. We do know that the brain and spinal cord connect to an array of neural structures that branch throughout the body, an array collectively known as the *peripheral nervous system*. This system may be divided into two groups—the *somatic nervous system* and the *autonomic nervous system*. The former deals more with sensation and conscious control, the latter with less conscious reactions.

THE AUTONOMIC NERVOUS SYSTEM

The **autonomic nervous system** (ANS) is essentially a *motor system*. This means that it carries impulses from the brain and spinal cord to the organs it serves. In doing this, it works in concert with the central nervous system in regulating and sensing the activity of the **viscera**, the internal organs. These include not only the prominent contents of the chest and abdominal cavities (the heart, lungs, digestive tract, kidneys, and bladder), but also such body parts as the arteries, the veins, the irises of the eyes, the nasal lining, the sweat glands, the salivary glands, and the tiny muscles that cause our hair to stand on end (Figure 34.1).

The general function of the autonomic nervous system is to promote *homeostasis*, about which you will be hearing much more as other systems are discussed. Essentially, **homeostasis** is the maintenance of stability or constancy in the face of changing conditions. The ANS, under the direction of the central nervous system, constantly adjusts and coordinates the internal organs to meet changing demands. For such a system to function efficiently requires a considerable amount of sensory feedback from the organs served. This is carried out by sensory nerves of the somatic nervous system, which, by keeping the brain informed, also play an important role in homeostasis.

The autonomic nervous system is divided into two parts: the **sympathetic division** and **parasympathetic division.** These divisions usually have opposite effects, but they operate in a highly coordinated manner to produce an overall adaptive effect. One example of this is seen in the control of heart rate. The human heart, without outside influence, contracts about 70–90 times per minute. It speeds up when stimulated by a sympathetic *(cardioaccelerator)* nerve, and slows down on a signal from a parasympathetic *(vagus)* nerve (see Figure 34.1). How can neural impulses from two different nerves have opposing effects on heart rate? The answer has to do with the specific neurotransmitters released by those neurons. Most (but not all) of the sympathetic neurons secrete the chemical *norepinephrine* at their target organs, while neurons of the parasympathetic system secrete *acetylcholine* (as do motor neurons that move skeletal muscle). Norepinephrine accelerates heart rate, while acetylcholine slows it down.

(a) The organization of the human nervous system. (b) The organization of the autonomic nervous system, showing the various organs it serves.

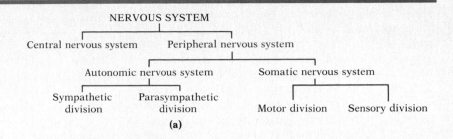

NERVOUS SYSTEM

Central nervous system — Peripheral nervous system

Autonomic nervous system — Somatic nervous system

Sympathetic division — Parasympathetic division — Motor division — Sensory division

(a)

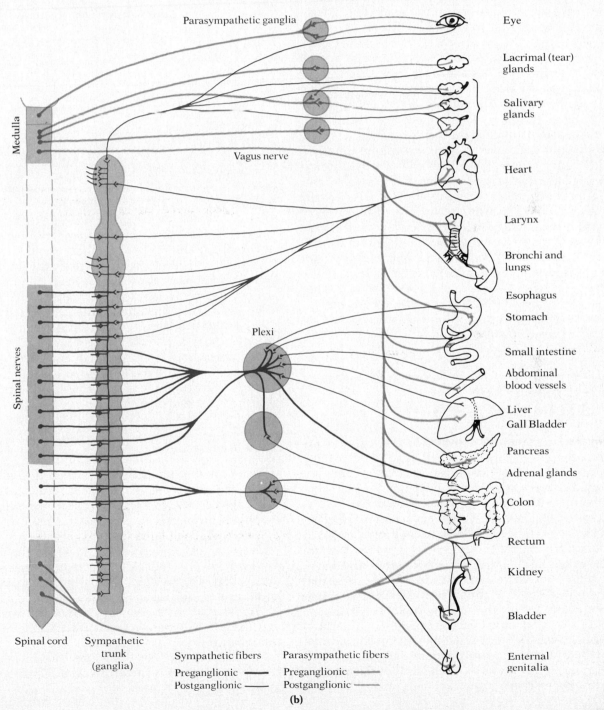

Parasympathetic ganglia — Eye

Lacrimal (tear) glands

Salivary glands

Medulla

Vagus nerve — Heart

Larynx

Bronchi and lungs

Esophagus

Stomach

Plexi

Small intestine

Abdominal blood vessels

Spinal nerves

Liver
Gall Bladder

Pancreas

Adrenal glands

Colon

Rectum

Kidney

Bladder

Spinal cord — Sympathetic trunk (ganglia) — Enternal genitalia

Sympathetic fibers	Parasympathetic fibers
Preganglionic	Preganglionic
Postganglionic	Postganglionic

(b)

An interesting example of how the two ANS divisions affect such changes in the viscera is seen in emergencies—the so-called "flight-or-fight" syndrome. In an emergency, the heart and breathing rates increase, accompanied by an increase in blood pressure, the shunting of blood from the digestive tract to the brain and skeletal muscles, and a general slowing of all functions not essential to immediate survival. After the emergency has passed, the parasympathetic nervous system takes over, and the internal situation reverses. The parasympathetic nervous system has a variety of effects on other organs as well (Table 34.1).

As you might expect, the divisions of the autonomic nervous system differ anatomically as well as physiologically. As shown in Figure 34.1, most of the parasympathetic nerves originate in the brain, with a few coming from the lower region of the spinal cord. Some go directly to their target organs; others end in external ganglia, where they relay their messages to nerves continuing toward the target organ. The sympathetic system originates only in the gray matter of the spinal cord. Furthermore, all of the sympathetic nerves leaving the cord pass through or synapse within rows of **sympathetic ganglia** just outside the cord. Some sympathetic nerves synapse once again in ganglia at various locations in the body. You may be familiar with one of these ganglia, or *plexi*, as they are known. The general area of the *celiac plexus*, better known as the *solar plexus*, is quite often the target of a boxer or a martial arts enthusiast who tries to land a breath-paralyzing blow.

THE SOMATIC NERVOUS SYSTEM

The **somatic nervous system** (*soma*, body) includes all of the sensory nerves plus the motor nerves that serve skeletal muscles and some glands. It is composed of *afferent* neurons (which sense and send stimuli) and *efferent* neurons (which respond to those stimuli by causing some reaction in the effectors). The cell bodies of somatic neurons are found exclusively within the central nervous system (brain and spinal cord) and its external ganglia, and extend outward to synapse with other neurons lying outside of it. Traditionally, the somatic system has been described as being "voluntary" (as opposed to the "involuntary" quality of the autonomic system). Actually, the voluntary and involuntary patterns are intimately associated, and their coordinated interactions produce the required adaptive response.

TABLE 34.1

Sympathetic and parasympathetic responses

Organ	Sympathetic Effect	Parasympathetic Effect
Pupil of eye	Dilates	Constricts
Heart	Accelerates	Slows
Intestine	Decreased movement	Increased movement
Salivary glands	Decreases secretion	Increases secretion
Stomach glands	Decreases secretion	Increases secretion
Lungs	Dilates air passages	Constricts air passages
Blood vessels		
Skin	Constricts	Dilates
Abdomen	Constricts	
General metabolism	Increases	Decreases

SENSORY STRUCTURES

The world is far more complex than we know. Our receptors are able to perceive only small parts of the world, parts that give us precisely the information that is important to our survival. The human sensory structures are therefore highly varied and, in addition, they are often quite specialized. For example, by specialized sensory detectors we can perceive those parts of our environment that produce information in the form of pressure, pain, touch, heat, cold, odors, flavors, sound, light, and position. Some of the simpler of these sensory structures are found in the skin.

Skin Receptors

Technically, the skin is an organ consisting of several specialized types of tissues. Its primary function is protective, essentially to keep the good in and the bad out, but the skin also constitutes one of our most sensitive systems. The sensory structures of the skin (Figure 34.2) include numerous *free nerve endings*, which often lie just under the surface and register pain. Deeper down are **mechanoreceptors,** including bulbous neural endings called *pacinian corpuscles*, which detect pressure, and *Meissner's corpuscles*, which are touch receptors. Touch receptors are more concentrated in some parts of the skin than they are in others; examples include the fingertips, lips, nipples, and genitals.

Thermoreceptors (heat and cold sensors) are also located in the skin. These receptors often detect relative temperatures, that is, they are sensitive to *changes* in temperature (so that a change from cold to cool might be registered as warmth). Their precise mechanism of detection remains a mystery.

Chemoreceptors: Taste and Smell

Chemoreceptors are stimulated by a broad range of chemicals. For the most part, substances must go into solution before they can be detected. Neurologically, our sense of taste is very closely related to our sense of smell (both are forms of chemoreception). In fact, what we think we are tasting is often mostly what we are smelling. (You've probably noticed that food is not so tasty when your nose is stuffed up by a cold.)

"True" taste receptors are found in the tongue. There are four recognized categories of taste: sweet, sour, salty, and bitter. The tongue's *taste map* (Figure 34.3) illustrates how certain areas of the tongue contain **taste buds** that specialize in sensing one taste or another.

Our sense of taste, a product of evolution, has had an important survival value. To illustrate, *bitter* is the taste of many alkaloid poisons, and we tend instinctively to avoid it. *Sweet,* on the other hand, is the taste of carbohydrates—the taste of ripened fruit. (Fruits lack this taste until they are ripe, when they have their highest nutritional value.) *Sour* is generally not a desired taste. It is, instead, often

the taste of unripened fruit—fruit that will be more nutritious if we wait until it has developed a "sweet" taste. The taste of *salt* is very appealing to most people—but only up to a point. We need salt, so we seek it, but we tire of it easily, since too much of it can throw off many delicate physiological processes. (For instance, we have seen the role sodium ions play in impulse conduction.) Preferences, then, are not just a matter of "taste," but of survival as well.

Olfaction, the sense of smell, is not nearly as well developed in humans as it is in some other mammals. Furthermore, there seem to be great differences among humans in the ability to taste and smell. But whatever the ability, human olfactory neurons (like those of other mammals) are located in the nasal epithelium, where stimulating molecules in the air are dissolved in the moist surface (Figure 34.4). The olfactory neurons send their signals to the olfactory bulb of the brain, where the information provided by the stimulating molecules is processed and interpreted.

Proprioception and the Sense of Coordination

Proprioceptors tell us the position of our body and our skeletal muscles. We partly perceive muscle position by stretch receptors that are located in muscles and tendons, where they are stimulated by tension.

The sense of body position and balance is detected not only by the stretch receptors, but also by a structure of the inner ear called the **vestibular**

34.2

The skin contains a variety of sensory structures, each specialized for detecting certain stimuli. Interestingly, the hair shaft itself is a sense organ: a slight bending of the hair causes it to discharge a very small electrical impulse, which is picked up by the nerve endings that surround the root of the hair.

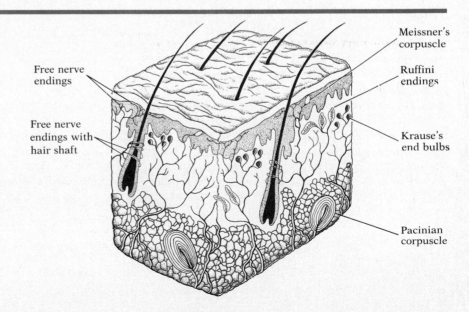

Free nerve endings

Free nerve endings with hair shaft

Meissner's corpuscle

Ruffini endings

Krause's end bulbs

Pacinian corpuscle

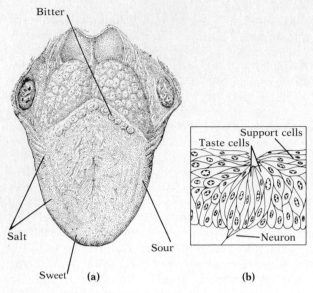

34.3

The arrangement of taste buds on the tongue **(a)** is such that certain regions specialize in detecting each of the four primary tastes: bitter, sour, sweet, and salty. Within the taste buds **(b)**, clusters of specialized neurons converge at tiny pits in which solutions form.

Individual taste buds, as seen in the micrograph **(c)**, are constantly being worn out and replaced. Their surfaces contain numerous pits that lead to the neural clusters.

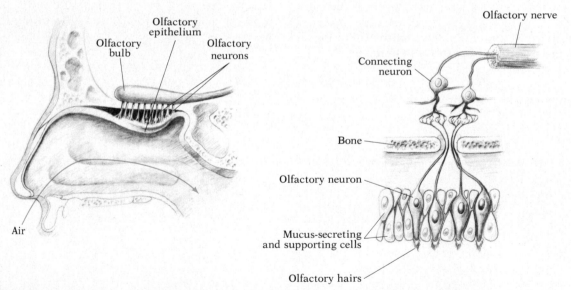

34.4

Olfactory neurons are scattered among the cells of the moist nasal epithelium. Odors are detected by olfactory hairs that emerge from the receptors. To be detected, the molecules we smell (like those we taste) must be in a solution on the surface of these neurons.

The olfactory neurons synapse with other neurons in the olfactory bulb located at the base of the brain. From there, impulses travel to the frontal region of the brain, which is responsible for their interpretation.

apparatus (Figure 34.5). The vestibular apparatus contains the bulbous **saccule** and **utricle,** and the three **semicircular canals,** all of which are fluid-filled. The saccule and utricle contain sensory hairs that are coated with fine granules of calcium carbonate. The weight of the granules pressing on the sensory hairs provides information about head and body position with respect to gravity. The semicircular canals contain uncoated sensory hairs that respond to movement (acceleration or deceleration) of the fluid within the canals. Since each canal is arranged in a different plane, a change of movement in any direction can be detected.

Some impulses from the vestibular apparatus travel only to the spinal cord, which can adjust body position reflexively. Others are sent to the cerebellum, where muscular coordination is orchestrated; yet others stimulate higher brain centers involved with delicate mechanisms, such as those controlling eye movement. The eyes are important in maintaining balance. (Try closing your eyes and standing on one leg.)

Some kinds of movement, such as continuous rotation or the movement of a ship at sea, can stimulate the medulla, bringing on dizziness, nausea, and vomiting. Why should this be? An interesting hypothesis is that vomiting due to dizziness may be adaptive. Many poisons also affect the vestibular apparatus, and the first indication that one has been poisoned is a feeling of disorientation and dizziness. The reflex vomiting reaction probably saved the lives of our ancestors time after time. (When at sea, you can try to convince your lower brain centers that your dizziness does not indicate a dangerous condition, but the lower centers don't take chances—or advice, either.)

Structures of Hearing

The human ear, like that of other mammals, consists of three basic regions: the *external, middle,* and *internal ear* (Figure 34.6). The **external ear** includes the *pinna,* the *auditory canal,* and the *tympanic membrane* (eardrum). The **pinna** directs sound waves inward, through the **auditory canal** to the **tympanic membrane,** which vibrates in response. Many mammals can move their ears to help maximize sound reception, but in humans, the ear muscles are largely undeveloped. With practice, some people can learn to move their ears, a remarkable feat that wins them great respect.

The **middle ear,** an air-filled cavity, contains three tiny and unusual bones: the **malleus, incus,** and **stapes.** Acting as a jointed lever, they transfer vibrations of the eardrum to the cochlea of the internal ear (*malleus, incus, stapes,* and *cochlea* translate, respectively, as *hammer, anvil, stirrup,* and

34.5

General body position and movement are monitored through neural information received from the vestibular apparatus of the inner ear.

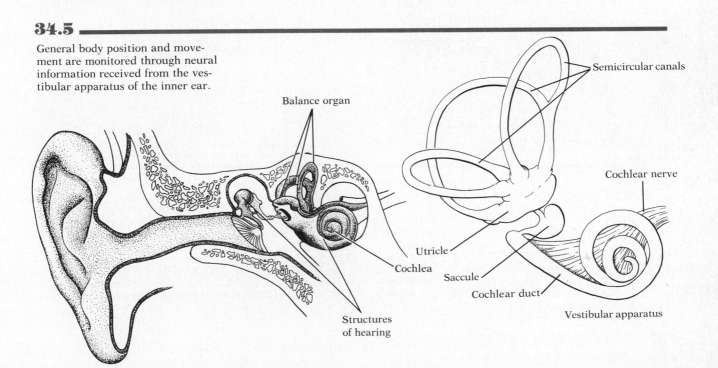

Balance organ

Semicircular canals

Cochlear nerve

Utricle

Cochlea

Saccule

Structures of hearing

Cochlear duct

Vestibular apparatus

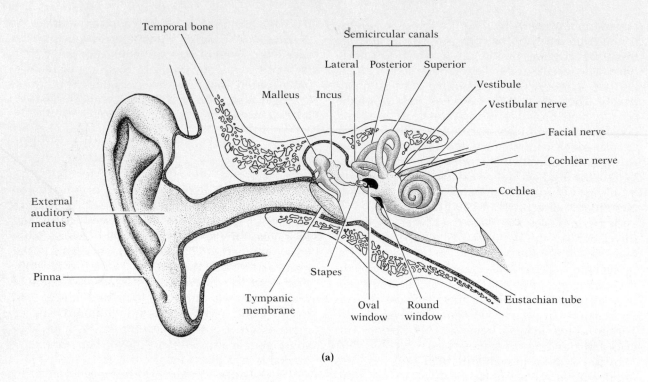

(a)

(b)

(c) Cross-section of vestibular canal

34.6

(a) When sound waves vibrate the human eardrum (tympanic membrane), they set in motion three tiny leverlike bones: the malleus, incus, and stapes. The stapes, attached to the oval window, sets fluids in motion within the snail-shaped cochlea. **(b)** The cochlea is actually a U-shaped tube, divided by the basilar membrane. **(c)** Sensory cells of the membrane are embedded in the gelatinous tectorial membrane. The two membranes and the sensory cells are called the organ of Corti. Sound impulses are transmitted by the middle ear bones from the tympanic membrane to the oval window of the fluid-filled cochlea. The sound impulses pass inward over one surface of the basilar membrane, turn a corner, and pass outward over the opposite surface of the membrane to be dissipated at the round window. Wherever incoming and outgoing sound waves are in phase (vibrating together) on the two sides of the basilar membrane, sympathetic vibrations in the membrane excite the sensory cells of the organ of Corti. Different regions of the basilar membrane are sensitive to different sound frequencies.

snail shell). The middle ear, therefore, transfers the energy of sound through an intricate lever system (via the bones of the middle ear) to the internal ear.

The **internal ear** consists of the *cochlea* and the *vestibular apparatus* (already discussed). The **cochlea** is a lengthy, fluid-filled tube that doubles back on itself and then coils like a snail in its shell. The coiling makes it hard to imagine how it works, but if we were to assume that it is straight (as it is, in fact, in birds), we can see a U-shaped tube containing the sensory neurons that are stimulated by the energy of sound (see Figure 34.6). One end of the U-shaped tube contains the *oval window*, to which the stapes is attached. The other end holds the flexible *round window*.

As sound waves strike the eardrum, it vibrates and moves the three middle ear bones that transfer the energy of sound to the oval window, causing it to vibrate rapidly. This vibration moves the fluid of the outer tube, and at its far end, it causes the round window to move back and forth. (The round window serves to dissipate the sound energy.) As the fluid pulsates within the tube, it moves what is called the **organ of Corti**. As shown in Figure 34.6c, the organ of Corti consists of a *basilar membrane*, from which arise sensory *hair cells* (actually modified cilia). The tips of these hair cells are embedded in the gelatinous *tectorial membrane*. As the basilar membrane moves, the sensory hairs are bent, creating impulses in the neurons. The impulses travel along the cochlear nerve, eventually reaching hearing centers in the cortex.

Sounds can vary in intensity and pitch. The perception of intensity seems to be due to the *number* of auditory neurons that fire, as well as the *frequency* of their firing. Differences in pitch (highness or lowness) depend on which auditory neurons are stimulated. The basilar membrane responds to high-pitched tones better at its thicker and wider beginning, while low-pitched tones stimulate the narrow apex of the snail-shaped chamber. Recall that the sound waves travel up one side of the U-shaped tube and down the other. Each particular sound frequency traveling up one side of the basilar membrane will be exactly in phase with the same frequency traveling down the other side of the basilar membrane only in one region. The in-phase resonance (or reinforced vibration) at that region vibrates the basilar membrane, producing the sensation of pitch.

Structures of Vision

Humans are very visual creatures. We rely on vision in nearly every aspect of life. Although much is known about the anatomy and physiology of vision, the answers to some particularly knotty questions remain to be found.

The **eyeball** (Figure 34.7), a spherical, fluid-filled structure, contains three tissue layers: the outermost, tough, white **sclera,** to which muscles

34.7

A cutaway view of the eye. The structure is multilayered, with two major fluid-filled chambers separated by the lens. Light entering the eye through the pupil is regulated by the iris, which is able to change the diameter of the pupil. The light is focused on the retina by changes in the shape of the pliable lens, as various degrees of tension are applied by the ciliary muscles. The retina contains light-sensitive cells (the rods and cones) that lie beneath two layers of associated neurons. The highest concentration of receptors is in the *fovea.* Neural impulses travel to the brain via the optic nerve.

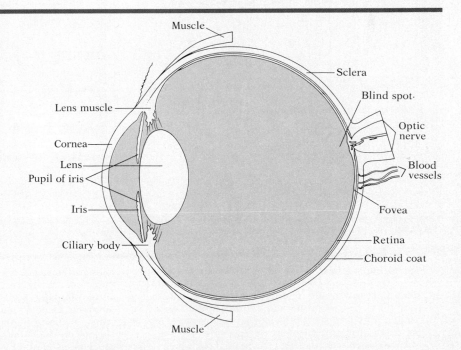

of eye movement attach; the middle *choroid coat*, rich in blood vessels; and the inner, light-sensitive *retina*. Light entering the eye first passes through the **cornea,** a transparent portion of the sclera that forms a slight bulge at the front of the eyeball. It then passes through the **iris,** an adjustable circle of pigmented tissue that controls the amount of light entering the **pupil.** Next, light enters the **lens** and is focused on the retina, but to reach this dense region of neurons it must cross the large, fluid-filled interior of the eye. We will return to a discussion of the retina, but first, let's see how the lens does its work.

A camera lens, as you may know, adjusts to distance by moving back and forth. Interestingly, sharks focus on objects in the same way. However, human eye lenses do not move back and forth; they adjust to varying distances by changing their shape. The changes are brought about by a ring of supporting muscles directly attached by ligaments to the flexible lens. Muscular contraction flattens the lens, and muscular relaxation allows it to become more nearly round. As humans reach their mid-forties, the lenses lose some flexibility. Thus, many of us end up with reading glasses in order to see the details of nearby objects (or in order to write this paragraph).

The Retina.   The **retina** consists of four layers of cells (Figure 34.8). The deepest layer, attached to the inner surface of the choroid coat, is pigmented. It absorbs light that might otherwise be reflected inside the eyeball, creating visual problems. Overlying the pigmented layer are the *rods* and *cones*, the actual light receptors. You might expect them to be in the direct path of light, but they are covered by two more layers of rather transparent neurons. When the rods and cones are stimulated by light, they send their impulses to the overlying *bipolar cells*; these, in turn, synapse with the *optic neurons* just above. Optic neurons gather from all parts of the retina to form the **optic nerve,** which carries visual impulses to the brain.

In many vertebrates, including cats and dogs, the absorptive pigment layer can be altered at night by movement of the pigment granules within the

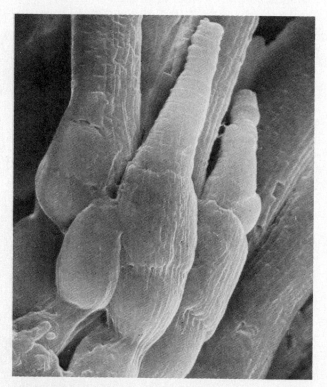

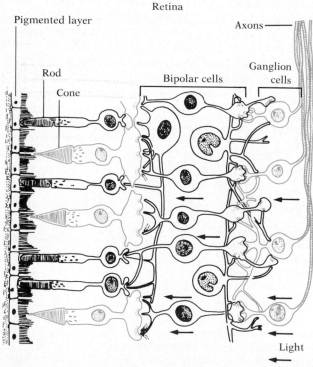

34.8

The retina is a field of two types of photoreceptor cells: the rods and cones. The rods especially react to shades of gray in dim light. Rods tend to be localized near the periphery of the retina, so most of us lose some ability to distinguish color at the periphery of our fields of vision. There are at least three types of cones, each with its own type of pigment which responds maximally to either red, green, or blue. If a red-sensitive and a blue-sensitive cone are stimulated, the colors are summed at their synapses and we see purple. Actually, a great deal of stimulus filtering, summing, blending, and inhibiting goes on in the retina, mediated by the bipolar and ganglionic cells. This means the brain receives preprocessed stimuli, which helps in rapid integration of the varied information arriving from the environment.

cells. This reveals another layer of reflecting crystals. The reflective layer bounces the excess light back through the layer of rods and cones, which doubles the sensitivity of the eye. This reflective layer in animals' eyes can be quite startling at night to human travelers on lonely highways.

The Rods and Cones.   **Rods** are slender cells; they are especially sensitive to dim light, but they react to all wavelengths (that is to say, all colors) of light between 430 and 750 nm. These wavelengths therefore make up what we call the *visible spectrum* (see Essay 7.1).

Cones, however, respond best to a narrower portion of the visible spectrum. Cones (which are actually cone-shaped) not only discriminately respond to colors, but they are capable of much finer discrimination of detail in bright light than are rods. They respond weakly to dim light, which is why we can see light at night, but not much color.

According to the prevailing theory of color vision, there are three types of cones: red-sensitive, green-sensitive, and blue-sensitive. With these, we can see many colors because these receptors overlap in their ranges of sensitivity. The sensitivities of the different types of cones to a given color depend upon what sorts of visual pigments (light absorbers) they contain.

The rods operate on an entirely different principle. Each rod contains a light-sensitive pigment called **rhodopsin.** When rhodopsin absorbs light, it loses its color and chemically breaks down into two subunits: *opsin*, a colorless protein, and *retinal*, a derivative of vitamin A. It is the chemical process itself that is believed to trigger neural impulses to visual centers in the brain. After their chemical breakdown, opsin and retinal enter into a chemical pathway where rhodopsin is restored. Apparently, dietary vitamin A must be continually supplied to keep the biochemical pathway going in the right direction. If the body is deprived of this vitamin, rhodopsin synthesis is curtailed, and severe night blindness can result.

Summary

The Autonomic Nervous System
The autonomic nervous system works in concert with the central nervous system to regulate and sense the activity of the viscera, and thus plays an important role in maintaining homeostasis. Its sympathetic and parasympathetic divisions oppose one another in a highly coordinated manner to produce an overall adaptive effect. Most sympathetic neurons secrete norepinephrine, while parasympathetic neurons secrete acetylcholine. The parasympathetic nerves originate in the brain and lower spinal cord; the sympathetic nerves originate in the spinal cord, and many pass through sympathetic ganglia before reaching their target organs.

The Somatic Nervous System
The somatic nervous system is composed of sensory (afferent) nerves and the motor (efferent) nerves that serve skeletal muscles and some glands. This "voluntary" system work closely with the autonomic system to achieve adaptive responses.

Sensory Structures
Highly varied and specialized, sensory structures perceive touch, temperature, taste, odor, sound, light, and position. The skin serves a protective function, but also contains many sensory structures, including free nerve endings that register pain, pacinian corpuscles that detect pressure, and Meissner's corpuscles that register touch. The skin also contains numerous thermoreceptors.

The senses of taste and smell are forms of chemoreception. The taste buds of the tongue detect sweet, sour, salty, and bitter tastes. The sense of smell (olfaction) is highly varied among individuals. Olfactory neurons in the nasal epithelium send signals to the olfactory bulb of the brain.

Proprioceptors tell us the position of our body and skeletal muscles. In addition to stretch receptors, the vestibular apparatus of the inner ear helps maintain body position and balance.

The human ear consists of the external, middle, and internal ear. The pinna of the external ear directs sound waves inward through the auditory canal to the tympanic membrane. The middle ear contains the malleus, incus, and stapes, which together transfer vibrations to the internal ear consisting of the coiled cochlea and the vestibular apparatus. Impulses travel along the cochlear nerve, eventually reaching hearing centers in the cortex.

Vision is important in self-protection, coordination, and equilibrium. The eyeball contains three tissue layers. Light first passes through the cornea, then through the pupil, finally entering the lens, where it is focused on the retina. Muscles change the shape of the lens to adjust for varying distances.

The retina of the eye consists of four layers of cells, the deepest of which is pigmented. It is covered by the rods and cones, which are covered by two more layers of rather transparent neurons. The optic nerve carries visual impulses to the brain. Rods are especially sensitive to dim light, but react to all wavelengths of the visible spectrum. Cones respond best to a narrower segment of the visible spectrum, and discriminate among colors and details in bright light. Light absorbed by the rods creates a chemical change, breaking down rhodopsin and initiating neural impulses. Vitamin A is required for the resynthesis of rhodopsin.

Key Terms

autonomic nervous system
viscera
homeostasis
sympathetic division
parasympathetic division
sympathetic ganglia
somatic nervous system
mechanoreceptors
thermoreceptors
chemoreceptors
taste buds
proprioceptors
vestibular apparatus

saccule
utricle
semicircular canals
external ear
pinna
auditory canal
tympanic membrane
middle ear
malleus
incus
stapes
internal ear

cochlea
organ of Corti
eyeball
sclera
cornea
pupil
lens
retina
optic nerve
rods
cones
rhodopsin

Review Questions

1. The autonomic nervous system functions in maintaining homeostasis. Explain what this means and give an example. (p. 498)

2. List the divisions of the autonomic nervous system, and compare their effects on the viscera. (pp. 498–500)

3. Compare the origins and pathways of the nerves of the two autonomic divisions. (p. 500)

4. List three specific sensory receptors in the skin and state their specializations. (pp. 500–501)

5. What are the four basic tastes, and where on the tongue are their receptors concentrated? (p. 502)

6. Describe the anatomy of the vestibular apparatus and discuss how each part relates to sensing gravity and movement. (pp. 501–503)

7. What is the effect of sound on the tympanic membrane, the middle ear bones, and the fluid-filled cochlea? How does the organ of Corti function to create neural impulses? (pp. 503–505)

8. List the structures through which light passes on its way to the retina, and describe the function of these structures in controlling the amount of light eventually perceived. (pp. 505–506)

9. Which cells specialize in color reception, and how are they able to distinguish among wavelengths? (p. 507)

10. Briefly summarize the chemistry of vision, including the role of vitamin A. (p. 507)

Chemical Messengers in Animals

35

Generally, people know just enough about hormones to both credit and blame them. We know that they ebb and flow in our bodies, and we may even admire some of the things that they do. And yet we may dread, despise, or even doubt some of their other activities. Hormones, of course, are responsible for the familiar changes of puberty. Hormones have also been blamed for initiating criminal behavior, and women have successfully argued in court that their hormone-based premenstrual tension drove them to commit violent crimes. We suspect athletes of ingesting steroid hormones to beef up their bodies and increase their strength. Male sex offenders are given drugs to reduce their hormone levels so that they can better adjust to society's expectations. Indeed, hormones may even be much more important than we think.

THE BODY'S CHEMICAL MESSENGERS

We have seen that the nervous system of animals adjusts to both internal and external environments very rapidly, if somewhat temporarily. In so doing, it has vital homeostatic roles. The other great regulatory system comprises a battery of hormones also of homeostatic significance. These adjust the body's internal environment, usually acting more slowly than neural responses, but often having a longer-lasting impact.

Hormones are often called *chemical messengers*: they are produced in one part of the body and then travel through the bloodstream to other parts, where they cause changes. A number of hormones are released throughout the body, but not always by special hormone-producing glands. For example, one cell may secrete substances that affect an adjacent cell. Other hormones are released by the brain, bone, intestine, and even by wounds. Their regulatory role helps the body behave in a coordinated manner. Thus hormones, like the autonomic nervous system, function in maintaining homeostasis.

Hormones are effective in minute quantities—often in *trace* amounts that are difficult to detect experimentally. Their highly specific **target tissues** (the tissues they change) have specific **receptor sites,** usually located on the cell membrane, that respond only to a certain hormone. Once a hormone has activated its target, it is rapidly altered or destroyed. The characteristics of hormones are essential to their usefulness as chemical messengers.

The range of hormonal effects is wide. Some hormones promote growth while others retard it; some increase the body's metabolic rate while others slow it; and some cause the release of other hormones. In vertebrates, most of the more familiar hormones are produced in bodies known as **endocrine** (ductless) **glands.** (The system is called the **endocrine system,** and the study of these hormones is called *endocrinology.*) The best-known hormones fall into several major classes according to their basic structures—the **steroids, peptides** (including polypeptides and proteins), **modified amino acids,** and **prostaglandins** (Figure 35.1).

In invertebrates, the close and coordinated interaction of hormones and neurons is accentuated.

Dopamine
(amino acid derivative)

Testosterone
(steroid)

Prostaglandin E₁
(fatty acid derivative)

Oxytocin
(polypeptide)

35.1

Hormones are composed of a wide variety of molecular structures. There are some basic categories, however. Dopamine is one of those hormones derived from an amino acid (here, tyrosine), while testosterone, the male sex hormone, is one of the many steroid hormones. The prostaglandins, such as E₁, are highly modified fatty acids. Oxytocin is a polypeptide containing nine amino acids.

Among the vertebrates, hormonal systems operate in very similar ways, so let's consider, once again, that brainy mammal with the rather unspecialized mouth and the very talented thumbs.

ANATOMY OF THE HUMAN ENDOCRINE SYSTEM

The human endocrine system consists of nine distinct glands plus numerous other tissues scattered throughout the body (Figure 35.2 and Table 35.1). The endocrine glands are often called the *ductless glands* because their secretions pass from the glands or cells directly into the bloodstream without passing through ducts. By contrast, there are glands with ducts (called *exocrine glands*) that secrete substances other than hormones. Examples are the salivary glands, the sweat glands, the liver and pancreas, the scent glands, and the lubricating mucus glands. However, even this time-honored distinction is fading as we find new evidence that the secretions of some ducted glands may also carry hormones.

The Pituitary

The **pituitary** has long worn the undeserved title of the "master gland." To the degree that it does rule, it is sensitive to its constituents through a system of checks and balances that operates by way of the general biological process called **negative feedback control.** The hormones of the pituitary activate other glands, which in turn send messages back that moderate the pituitary. The pituitary is also quite responsive to signals from other parts of the brain; in particular, the hypothalamus (see Chapter 33).

The pituitary's size belies its importance. It is a tiny, two-lobed structure about the size of a kidney bean (Figure 35.3). If you point your left index finger directly between your eyes and point your right index finger straight at your ear, the lines described will intersect at about the location of the pituitary. It lies protected in a pocket of bone and is suspended by a stalk that emerges from the base of the brain, just below the hypothalamus. The connections between the hypothalamus and the pituitary run through the stalk that supports the pituitary. Thus, this pathway is one of the main connections between the nervous system and the endocrine system.

The Pituitary and the Hypothalamus. Both lobes of the pituitary, under the influence of the brain's hypothalamus, release important but very different hormones (since the lobes are actually different glands). The **posterior pituitary** *(neurohypophysis)* is actually part of the nervous system; embryologically, it arises from the central nervous system. The posterior lobe doesn't manufacture its own hormones; it simply stores and releases three

The major human endocrine glands, as traditionally identified. A number of other tissues and organs produce chemical messengers that can be considered hormones (a few of these are indicated in parentheses).

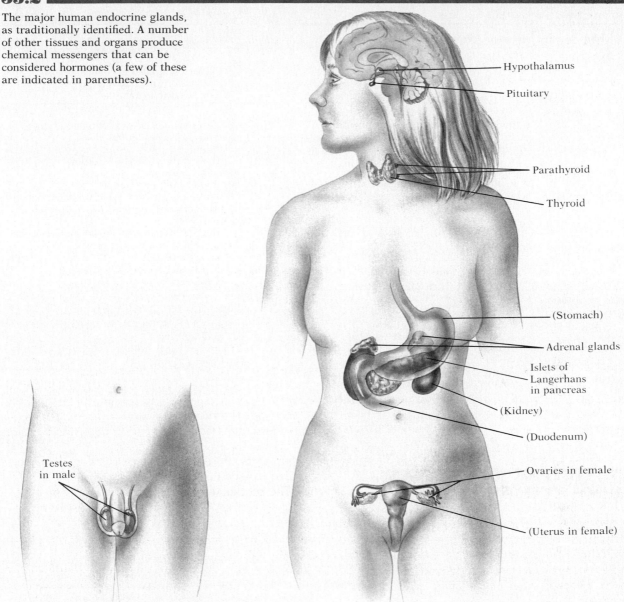

Hypothalamus

Pituitary

Parathyroid

Thyroid

(Stomach)

Adrenal glands

Islets of Langerhans in pancreas

(Kidney)

(Duodenum)

Ovaries in female

(Uterus in female)

Testes in male

hormones that are synthesized in nerve cell bodies in the hypothalamus and are transmitted to the posterior lobe by the nerve cell axons.

The **anterior pituitary** (adenohypophysis) differs greatly from the posterior lobe in structure, function, and origin. Embryologically, it originates in a pocket of ectodermal epithelium on the roof of the mouth. It is a true hormone-synthesizing gland, producing and releasing six hormones. It is also intimately influenced by the hypothalamus. The hypothalamus is drained by a network of capillaries that merge into a short blood vessel, which then travels down the pituitary stalk. There, the blood vessel divides again into a second capillary bed that permeates the anterior pituitary. Here, the hypothalamus secretes incredibly minute amounts of hormones known as **releasing factors.** When these releasing factors reach the glandular cells of the anterior pituitary, they stimulate (and sometimes inhibit) the release of major pituitary hormones.

Therefore, the so-called master gland functions at the bidding of the hypothalamus, which is not actually a gland. Also, the hypothalamus itself is largely under the control of other parts of the brain.

TABLE 35.1

Human endocrine system

Endocrine structure and major hormones	Target	Action
Hypothalamus		
Releasing factors	Anterior pituitary	Stimulate or inhibit hormone release
Oxytocin*	See posterior pituitary	See posterior pituitary
Antidiuretic hormone (ADH)*	See posterior pituitary	See posterior pituitary
Anterior pituitary		
Adrenocorticotropic hormone (ACTH)	Adrenal cortex	Secretes glucocorticoid hormones
	Fat storage regions	Fatty acids released into blood
Growth hormone (GH)	General (no specific organs)	Stimulates growth; amino acid transport; slows carbohydrate utilization
Thyroid-stimulating hormone (TSH)	Thyroid	Secretes hormones
Prolactin	Breasts	Promotes milk production
Follicle-stimulating hormone (FSH)	Ovarian follicles	Stimulates growth of follicle and estrogen production in females, spermatogenesis in males
Luteinizing hormone (LH)	Mature ovarian follicle	Stimulates ovulation, conversion of follicle to corpus luteum, and production of progesterone
	Interstitial cells of testis	Stimulates sperm and testosterone production
Posterior pituitary		
Oxytocin	Breasts	Stimulates release of milk
	Uterus	Contraction of smooth muscle in childbirth and orgasm
Antidiuretic hormone (ADH)	Kidney	Increases water uptake in kidney (decreasing urine volume)
Thyroid		
Thyroxin Triiodothyronine	General (no specific organs)	Increases oxidation of carbohydrates; stimulates (with GH) growth and brain development
Calcitonin	Intestine, kidney, bone	Decreases blood calcium level; increases excretion of calcium by kidney, slows absorption by intestine, inhibits release from bones
Parathyroid		
Parathormone	Intestine, kidney, bone	Increases blood calcium level; decreases excretion of calcium by kidney and speeds absorption by intestine and release from bones
Islets of Langerhans		
Alpha cells: glucagon	Liver	Stimulates liver to convert glycogen to glucose; elevates glucose level in blood
Beta cells: insulin	Cell membranes	Facilitates transport of glucose into cells; lowers glucose level in blood
Delta cells: somatostatin, GH releasing factor	Unknown	Unknown

Hormones of the Anterior Pituitary. Five of the anterior pituitary's hormones influence other endocrine glands. The sixth stimulates body growth. Proper levels of **growth hormone (GH)** in the body are essential to normal growth, but sometimes something goes wrong. Too much GH during the early years of development can produce *gigantism*, or *pituitary giants*. People severely affected by this condition may grow to be seven to nine feet (215–280 cm) tall. Conversely, lower-than-normal GH levels in children results in *dwarfism*, or *pituitary dwarfs*. Pituitary dwarfism is now treatable with GH produced through recombinant DNA techniques (see Chapter 16).

As shown in Figure 35.4, the production of **adrenocorticotropic hormone,** or **ACTH,** is first stimulated by a hypothalamic releasing factor, and is then regulated by a negative feedback control system. The target of ACTH is the cortex (outer layer) of the adrenal gland, which is located on top of the kidney. When stimulated by ACTH, the adrenal cortex secretes an entire battery of hormones. As

TABLE 35.1 (continued)

Endocrine structure and major hormones	Target	Action
Adrenal cortex		
Mineralocorticoids—aldosterone *cortin*	Kidneys	Increased recovery of sodium and excretion of potassium and hydrogen ions; uptake of chloride ion and water
Glucocorticoids—cortisol	General (no specific organs)	Increases glucose synthesis through protein and fat metabolism; reduces inflammation
Sex hormones—androgens and estrogens	General (many regions and organs)	Promotes secondary sex characteristics
Adrenal medulla		
Epinephrine Norepinephrine	General (many regions and organs)	Increases heart rate and blood pressure; directs blood to muscles and brain; "fright or flight mechanism"
Ovaries		
Estrogen	General (many regions and organs)	Development of secondary sex characteristics; bone growth; sex drive (with androgens); regulates cyclic development of endometrium in menstruation; maintenance of uterus during pregnancy
Progesterone (ovarian source replaced by placenta during pregnancy)	Uterus (lining)	
Testes		
Testosterone	General (many regions and organs)	Differentiation of male sex organs in embryo; development of secondary sex characteristics; bone growth; sex drive
Pineal gland		
Melatonin	Uncertain in humans—perhaps hypothalamus and pituitary	May have some influence over hypothalamus or pituitary in cyclic activity
Thymus		
Thymosin	Lymphatic system	May stimulate development of lymphatic tissue
Damaged tissues		
Histamine	Capillaries of damaged area	Increases blood supply and capillary permeability; promotes clotting
Serotonin	Smooth muscles of blood vessels	Constriction—limiting blood loss

*The hypothalamic hormones, oxytocin and ADH, are released into the bloodstream via the posterior pituitary.

the levels of these hormones rise in the blood, they inhibit ACTH production in the pituitary. Besides activating the adrenal cortex, ACTH regulates the metabolism of fats. Under its influence, the body releases fatty acids into the bloodstream for redistribution through the body.

This suggests a word of caution: scientists continually find new targets of well-known hormones. Although a hormone is usually named for the first effect that is discovered, this is rarely the hormone's *only* effect, and is often not even its *principal* effect. Many hormones have multiple, seemingly unrelated targets and corresponding multiple, seemingly unrelated physiological effects.

Thyroid-stimulating hormone (TSH, also known as *thyrotropin*) is another anterior pituitary hormone. It is responsible for stimulating the thyroid to release two thyroid hormones, *thyroxin* and *triiodothyronine*. These thyroid hormones regulate the metabolic rate of the body and influence the growth of the nervous system.

Prolactin promotes milk production in mammals. Toward the end of pregnancy, the blood level of prolactin increases dramatically. But milk is still not produced because it is inhibited by high levels of the sex hormones **estrogen** and **progesterone.** The levels of these sex hormones diminish dramatically at birth, permitting the prolactin to

513

35.3

The hypothalamus, anterior pituitary, and posterior pituitary. Note that the hypothalamus communicates with the anterior pituitary by sending releasing factors through blood vessels. However, hormones of the posterior pituitary are actually produced in neurons of the hypothalamus and carried there via the axons of those neurons.

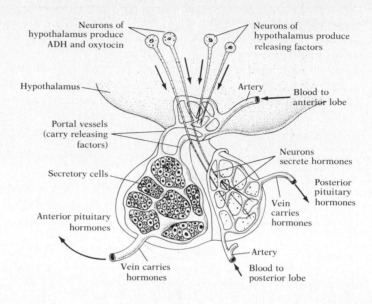

35.4

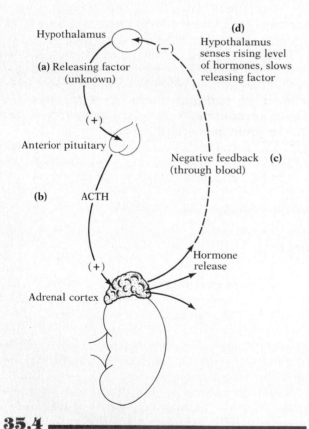

The release of ACTH by the anterior pituitary is controlled by a negative feedback loop. Feedback in this instance involves the rising level of a specific hormone of the adrenal cortex.

stimulate milk production. The actual release of milk is controlled by another hormone, *oxytocin*.

Prolactin is released from the anterior pituitary, but its release is under the control of the posterior pituitary. A common brain neurotransmitter called *DOPA*, having been produced in the hypothalamus, is released from the posterior pituitary into the network of blood vessels that communicate with the anterior pituitary. And there DOPA causes the release of prolactin.

Follicle-stimulating hormone (FSH) and **luteinizing hormone (LH)** are both involved in stimulating the production of gametes and sex hormones in the gonads, and are called *gonadotropins*. These hormones will be considered in Chapter 40.

Hormones of the Posterior Pituitary. Two hormones released by hypothalamic neurons and stored in the posterior lobe are **oxytocin** and **antidiuretic hormone (ADH).** Oxytocin is important to reproduction—it stimulates the contraction of uterine muscle during labor, and after delivery, it helps slow bleeding as the uterus continues to contract. Suckling the baby also stimulates the mother's posterior lobe to release oxytocin (apparently the sensory nerves of the nipples communicate with the brain and, finally, with the hypothalamus). Oxytocin then stimulates the smooth muscle around the milk ducts, and milk flow begins. Interestingly, oxytocin in women is also released during sexual stimulation and orgasm.

Again, the uterus responds by contracting. Researchers studying human sexual behavior suggest that the contractions may cause the uterus to pull in the semen, assisting in fertilization.

A *diuretic* is an agent that increases the water content, and thus the volume, of urine (see Chapter 36). An *antidiuretic* does the opposite. ADH decreases urine volume by withholding water, a part of the body's homeostatic maintenance. The target cells of ADH are the epithelial cells of urine-collecting ducts in the kidneys. ADH is released when the hypothalamus detects an increase in osmotic pressure in the blood, and the target cells respond by shunting water back into the blood, lowering the osmotic pressure to its optimal level.

The Thyroid Gland

The **thyroid gland** is shaped somewhat like a bow tie and is located in an appropriate place—in front of and slightly below the larynx (Figure 35.5). Two of its three hormones, **thyroxin** and **triiodothyronine,** are very similar in structure; they are synthesized from the amino acid *tyrosine.* Thyroxin has four iodine atoms added, and triiodothyronine has three (iodine is an essential mineral in the diet).

The secretion of thyroxin is controlled in a feedback control loop. The hypothalamus sends specific releasing factors to the anterior pituitary, which responds by releasing TSH. TSH causes the thyroid to secrete thyroxin. Thyroxin levels in the blood are monitored by the hypothalamus, which moderates its TSH production accordingly.

Both thyroxin and triiodothyronine influence the rate at which carbohydrates are oxidized by cells (thyroxin occurring in greater quantity). The oxidation rate, called the **basal metabolic rate,** is determined by measuring oxygen consumption for a given time while the subject is at rest. Although thyroxin's effects have been known for many years, just how it works remains a mystery.

Thyroid abnormalities include *hyperthyroidism* (an overactive thyroid) and *hypothyroidism* (the opposite—an underactive thyroid). Hyperthyroidism produces rapid metabolism, accompanied by weight loss, nervousness, and insomnia. Thin, active people are often accused of being "hyperthyroid," but most thin, active people are perfectly normal—they're just thin and active. In instances of true, abnormal hyperthyroidism due to overgrowth of the thyroid gland, the eyes may bulge out noticeably, a condition known as *exophthalmic goiter.*

Hypothyroidism—thyroxin insufficiency—produces a general slowing of the metabolic rate. Hypothyroid adults are usually sluggish and overweight, have low blood pressure, and may have a goiter. Enlargement of the thyroid—*simple goiter*—may also occur. Usually, simple goiter is an adaptive response to insufficient iodine in the diet, but since the availability of iodized salt, few cases have been reported. Hypothyroidism in adults can be successfully treated with thyroxin tablets, but its occurrence in infants and young children can cause serious mental and physical retardation—a condition called *cretinism,* similar in some ways to Down's syndrome. With early diagnosis, cretinism can be controlled with thyroxin.

Calcitonin, the third thyroid hormone, works in concert with a hormone from the *parathyroid glands* to regulate calcium ions in the body.

35.5

The thyroid gland and two of its hormones, thyroxin and triiodothyronine.

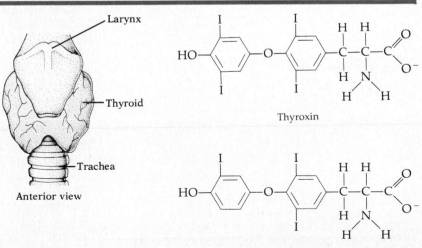

The Parathyroids and Calcium Regulation

The **parathyroid glands** are pea-sized bodies embedded in the tissue of the thyroid (Figure 35.6). The parathyroids secrete **parathyroid hormone** (**PTH,** or *parathormone*—a polypeptide). Parathormone helps raise the calcium levels of the blood, acting as an antagonist of calcitonin (Figure 35.7). The hormones affect such things as bone deposition, ion release and reabsorption in the kidneys, and gut absorption of calcium. Overall, the net effect of parathyroid hormone is to increase the calcium ion (Ca^{++}) concentration in the blood, and the net effect of calcitonin is to decrease it.

Abnormally low levels of parathyroid hormone cause muscle convulsions and, eventually, death. This can occur when the parathyroid glands are destroyed, as sometimes happens in an **autoimmune reaction,** when the body's own immune system mistakenly begins to treat the parathyroid tissue as "foreign" and attacks it. The opposite condition, abnormally high levels of parathyroid hormone, results in a severe decalcification of bone (*osteoporosis*), with the subsequent formation of fibrous cysts in the skeleton. If the condition is severe, death follows.

The Pancreas and the Islets of Langerhans

The **pancreas** is, for the most part, a ducted exocrine gland, since its major secretions are digestive enzymes and sodium bicarbonate, which are released into the small intestines. Scattered through the pancreas, however, are groups of true endocrine cells that secrete their products directly into the bloodstream. These clumps of cells are the is-

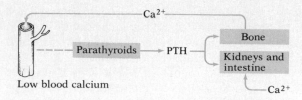
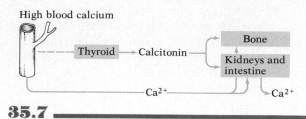

35.7

The thyroid hormone calcitonin and PTH work together to regulate the body's calcium level. When the blood calcium (Ca^{++}) level drops, the level of parathyroid hormone increases. In response, calcium is withdrawn from the bones, its uptake by the intestine increased and its excretion by the kidneys decreased. But when blood calcium is excessive, the thyroid releases calcitonin. Under its influence, the decalcification of bone slows, the intestine decreases its calcium uptake, and the kidneys secrete more calcium into the urine.

lets of Langerhans, or, simply, the **pancreatic islets** (Figure 35.8). Each cluster consists of at least three types of secretory cells, named *alpha, beta,* and *delta.* Alpha cells produce the hormone *glucagon,* while the beta cells secrete the more publicized hormone *insulin.* Each of these polypeptide hormones has a role in the regulation of carbohydrate metabolism (Figure 35.9). Delta cells produce *somatostatin,* a puzzling hormone whose specific action remains unknown.

Glucagon is a polypeptide consisting of a single chain of 29 amino acids. Its principal role is to stimulate the liver to break down *glycogen* (a glucose-storage compound) into glucose. Glucagon is released into the bloodstream when blood glucose levels fall too low, and the glucose that is released from the liver restores the proper level of blood sugar, which in turn slows down the production of glucagon in the pancreatic islets—a classic negative feedback loop.

Insulin, in its active form, consists of 51 amino acids, arranged in two polypeptide chains joined by disulfide linkages (ionic bonding between sulfur side groups). The hormone is large and complex enough to be called a protein. The specific role of insulin is to help glucose move across cell membranes, but it also has other actions: it is involved in fatty acid metabolism and glycogen synthesis, it

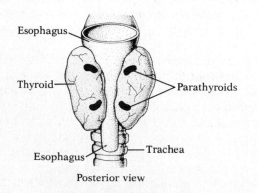

35.6

The tiny parathyroid glands lie embedded in the posterior region of the thyroid lobes.

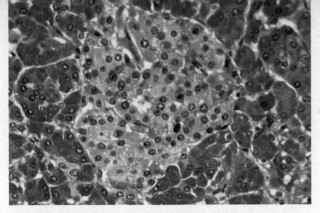

35.8

The islets of Langerhans are clearly distinguishable from the surrounding exocrine tissue. Within the clusters of endocrine tissue are patches of three types of secretory cells that produce the hormones.

LOW BLOOD SUGAR

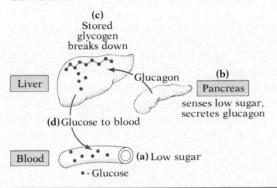

HIGH BLOOD SUGAR

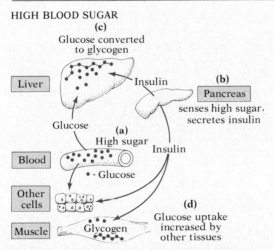

35.9

The control of the blood glucose (sugar) level is of critical importance, since excessively low or high levels can lead to serious problems. The islet cells of the pancreas respond to low blood glucose levels by releasing glucagon. The glucagon is transported to the liver, where it breaks down glycogen to produce glucose. Alternately, a high blood glucose level stimulates the islet cells to release insulin. Insulin clears the sugar from the blood by increasing its uptake in various tissues.

seems to be directly necessary for capillary function, and it stimulates cells, in tissue cultures, to divide. This hormone can affect virtually all the cells of the body. That is, they all have specific insulin receptor sites in their membranes—surface proteins to which only insulin will bind. Once the insulin attaches to such a site, the membrane subsequently becomes more permeable to glucose.

Deficiency in the insulin system produces **diabetes mellitus.** In *juvenile-onset diabetes*, its most severe form, the deficiency is caused by the destruction of beta cells, either by a viral infection or by an autoimmune response. In the more common *adult-onset diabetes*, affected persons have normal levels of insulin, but they may lack enough receptor sites on the membranes of the target cells. In some cases, the membranes may have enough receptor sites but the cells simply fail to respond properly. Injected insulin helps, but too much can lead to further decreases in receptivity, which requires yet more insulin—an unnatural "vicious circle" or *positive* feedback loop (see Chapter 36).

The Adrenal Glands

Ad means upon, and *renal* refers to the kidney. So, in humans, the **adrenal glands** are perched atop the kidneys just as one might suspect. Each adrenal gland is essentially two glands. The outer layer, or *cortex*, produces a number of steroid hormones and has a different origin, structure, and function than the inner layer, or *medulla*. The medulla produces the hormone *epinephrine* (adrenaline), which is a kind of neurotransmitter (Figure 35.10).

The Adrenal Cortex. The hormones of the adrenal cortex fall into three categories according to their functions: **mineralocorticoids, glucocorticoids,** and **steroid sex hormones.** The *mineralocorticoids* regulate minerals. The best known, **aldosterone,** promotes the retention of sodium ions and the release of potassium ions by the kidney. The mineralocorticoids also promote inflammation as part of the body's immune defense reactions. In this role, they oppose—in a cooperative manner—the action of glucocorticoids.

One of the most common glucocorticoids, **cortisol,** is involved in the metabolism of foods, facilitating the conversion of amino acids and fatty acids into glucose. In addition, some glucocorticoids act as anti-inflammatory agents, suppressing inflammation. (A pharmaceutical preparation, *hydrocortisone*, is now available as an "over the counter" drug intended for this purpose.)

Lymphocytes (cells of the immune system) have very specific cortisol receptor sites and a very specific reaction to the hormone: in the presence of

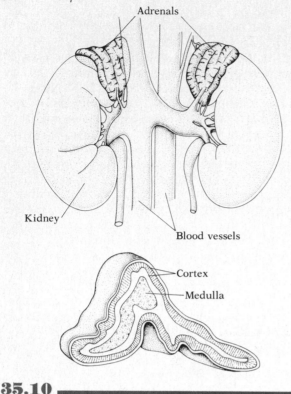

Adrenals

Kidney

Blood vessels

Cortex

Medulla

35.10

The adrenal glands. The adrenal cortex synthesizes a variety of steroid hormones, while the adrenal medulla produces only epinephrine and norepinephrine.

extremely minute quantities, they promptly die. For this reason, cortisol and its derivatives are given in massive quantities to organ transplant recipients and to victims of autoimmune disease in the hope of stifling their immune systems.

The cortical steroids (sex hormones) of the adrenals play an important role in sexual development. In fact, the adrenal cortex makes estrogen and testosterone—the same sex hormones produced by the ovaries and testes—although generally in smaller quantities. Thus they promote secondary sex characteristics, such as beards in men and enlarged breasts in women, and help to maintain reproductive function and libido. The principle adrenal steroid in both men and women is testosterone, with estrogens making up only a minor part of the total output. The effects of sex hormones are described further in Chapters 40 and 41.

The Adrenal Medulla. The adrenal medulla produces two fascinating *amine* hormones: **epinephrine** and **norepinephrine** (commonly known as adrenaline and noradrenaline; *epinephros* in Greek and *adrenal* in Latin both mean "on top of the kidney"). Epinephrine and norepinephrine can cause very specific changes in the body, usually in

response to sudden fright or anger. They reduce blood flow in the capillaries near the body surfaces, causing the skin to pale and reducing bleeding. The blood is diverted to the muscles, which may need to perform some strenuous activity, like getting you out of a car window after an accident. At such times, digestive functions cease. Blood pressure increases, the pupils of the eyes dilate (to see better), and glucose is released from the liver into the bloodstream. Other changes also occur to prepare the body for emergencies, called the "flight-or-fight" responses—the same ones discussed regarding the sympathetic nervous system (Chapter 34). You may also recall that norepinephrine is a neurotransmitter in many sympathetic synapses.

The Ovaries and Testes

The endocrine functions of the ovary and testes are discussed in detail in Chapters 40 and 41, so we'll note just some of the major points here. First, the two hormones of the ovary—estrogen and progesterone—and the principal hormone of the testis—**testosterone**—are all steroids (Figure 35.11).

In addition to their reproductive and behavioral functions, the sex hormones have an important role in skeletal development. The sudden increase of their levels in the blood at the onset of puberty stimulates the lengthening of the long bones and

Estrone
(one of the estrogens)

Progesterone

Testosterone

35.11

The primary sex hormones—estrogens, progesterone, and testosterone—all have steroids. The side groups are responsible for their important functional differences.

causes a marked spurt of growth. Interestingly, it also causes a simultaneous spurt in mental growth, as measured by raw scores on IQ tests.

The timing of the appearance of these hormones is variable; some people are precocious, while some are definitely late bloomers. Toward the end of puberty, the sex hormones promote the final hardening in the long bones, after which no further increase in height usually is possible. Raw IQ scores also stabilize at that time.

Prostaglandins

The prostaglandins are the most recently discovered class of vertebrate hormones—the Nobel Prize was awarded to their discoverers only in 1981. Although some prostaglandins are among the most potent biological materials known, perhaps one reason for their late discovery is that they are not produced by specialized organs. Various prostaglandins are produced by most kinds of tissues.

Prostaglandins may be released by the activity of other hormones or by almost any irritation of the tissues. Some prostaglandins are involved in inflammatory responses and in the sensation of pain. Aspirin inhibits the synthesis of prostaglandins, which is why aspirin is effective against pain, inflammation, and fever.

Prostaglandins also have other actions. For instance, one type causes uterine contractions. Also, blood platelets, which are involved in blood clotting, produce a prostaglandin called **thromboxane** that causes platelets to stick together in clots and can also cause the walls of arteries to contract. Another prostaglandin, **prostacyclin,** has exactly the opposite effects—it prevents clots, keeps blood thin, and prevents arteries from closing. Since prostacyclin is produced by cells that line the blood vessels, prostaglandins may be important in complex ways in maintaining normal circulation.

Prostacyclin synthesis is extremely sensitive to low levels of aspirin. Aspirin can cause bleeding, since it inhibits clotting and arterial constriction, and large doses of aspirin taken by pregnant women close to term has been implicated in serious bleeding within the brains of newborns. So, whereas women shouldn't take aspirin in late pregnancy, what about the rest of us? New studies reveal that habitual aspirin users have far lower rates of arterial disease and heart attacks than nonusers. One large-scale, long-term controlled study is underway, involving some 2000 physician volunteers. Half take one aspirin every other day, and half take a harmless placebo. The results will be monitored carefully for years to come.

CYCLIC AMP AND THE MOLECULAR BIOLOGY OF HORMONE ACTION

Much of our information about the molecular biology of hormone action is very recent; for example, it was only in 1971 that a Nobel Prize was awarded for the discovery of **cyclic adenosine monophosphate (cAMP)** as a participant in hormone activity. Cyclic AMP is so important that it is often referred to as the **second messenger**—the molecular messenger that acts inside the cell.

In light of this, we could refer to the hormones we've been talking about as "first messengers," since it appears that many of them bring their message only as far as the target cell membrane. Within the cell, the actual response is often triggered by cAMP, which apparently then works through what might be called third and fourth messengers. For example, epinephrine, released from the adrenal medulla, is carried by the blood to a target, such as the liver (Figure 35.12). It turns out that the liver cells have very specific receptor sites along their cell membranes. Once fixed to the membrane, epinephrine activates an enzyme known as *adenyl cyclase*, which immediately converts ATP in the cytoplasm to cAMP. The cAMP then triggers the activity of some enzymes and decreases the activity of others; in the case of epinephrine, the result is a decrease in the synthesis of glycogen (stored chains of glucose molecules) and an increase in its rate of breakdown, with a net release of glucose into the blood.

At least nine other hormones are known to stimulate the production of cAMP, utilizing it as a second messenger. But the question arises: How is the activity of so many hormones regulated if they all activate the same second messenger? The answer incorporates two important points. First, cAMP remains in cells. If it circulated freely, it would presumably wreak havoc with body functions. Second, hormones have target cells, and a target cell has a specific binding site for a specific hormone. Thus, no other hormone can bind to that particular site (although a cell may have binding sites for more than one hormone.)

Steroid Hormones: Direct Action at the DNA Level

Not all hormones remain outside of their target cells. The steroid hormones may or may not join with cell-surface receptors—the point is still being argued—but it is certain that they do enter the cell.

35.12

Epinephrine can elevate the blood sugar level by acting on liver cells. Epinephrine first attaches to a receptor site on the cell membrane (a). Its presence activates a membranal enzyme, adenyl cyclase, which converts ATP to cAMP (b). The cAMP activates enzyme complexes that convert glycogen to glucose (c), which is then released into the blood (d).

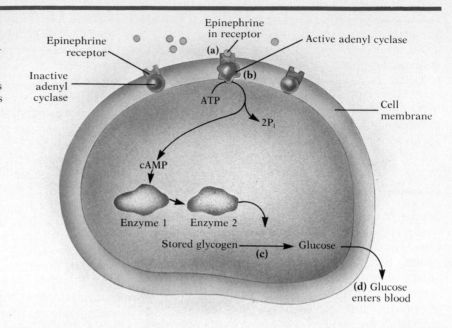

35.13

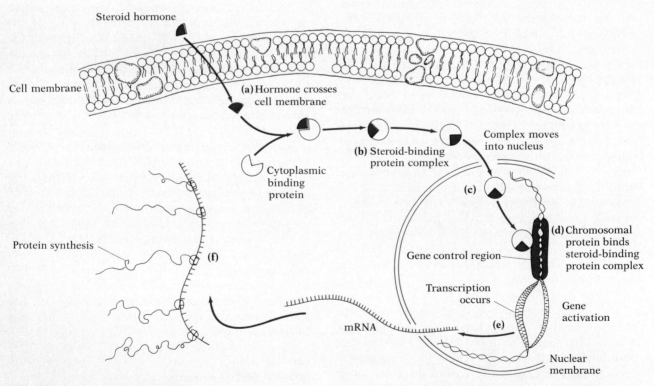

Steroid hormones can operate at the gene level. Once steroids are inside the cytoplasm (a), they are joined by a cytoplasmic binding protein (b) and move directly into the nucleus (c). The whole complex then joins with specific chromosomal proteins along areas of the chromosomes (d) that will then begin transcribing mRNA (e). The mRNA strands then leave the nucleus, where they interact with ribosomes in the usual manner to synthesize proteins (f).

Once inside, the steroid hormones are tightly bound by a **cytoplasmic binding protein.** Then the steroid-binding protein complex moves into the nucleus, where it joins with other proteins that are permanently bound to the chromosomes. In this way, they can act directly on the chromosomes; the whole complex of hormone, cytoplasmic receptor, and chromosomal protein initiates gene activity, with the production of appropriate mRNA and protein (Figure 35.13).

The concept of the chemical messengers called hormones provides us with continuing insight regarding the tightly monitored coordination of various parts of the body. Life can exist only within very precise limits. But because of such intense levels of interaction in the body, organisms need not solely depend on the whims of the environment; they can, through precise mechanisms, change their own internal environments in response to specific and immediate needs.

Summary

The Body's Chemical Messengers

Hormones help coordinate body functions and are effective even in trace amounts. Target tissues have receptor sites that respond only to particular hormones. Once a hormone has activated its target, it is rapidly altered or destroyed. Hormones fall into several major structural classes, including steroids, peptides, modified amino acids, and prostaglandins. Most hormones in vertebrates are produced by the endocrine glands. Invertebrates generally lack specific endocrine glands and produce hormones in the brain and other parts of the nervous system.

Anatomy of the Human Endocrine System

Nine distinct ductless glands, plus numerous other tissues, compose the human endocrine system. (Some ducted glands may also carry hormones.) Pituitary hormones regulate other hormones by negative feedback control, and serve as the connection between the nervous system and the endocrine system. The anterior pituitary, under stimulation from the hypothalamus, produces and releases: (1) growth hormone (GH); (2) adrenocorticotropic hormone (ACTH), involved in the metabolism of fats; (3) thyroid-stimulating hormone (TSH); (4) prolactin, involved in promoting milk production in mammals; and (5) follicle-stimulating hormone (FSH) and (6) luteinizing hormone (LH), both involved in stimulating the production of gametes and sex hormones in the gonads. Hypothalmic neurons release two hormones that are stored in the posterior pituitary: oxytocin (important in milk production and the birth process) and antidiuretic hormone (ADH), which helps maintain the body's water balance.

The thyroid gland produces three hormones: thyroxin, triiodothyronine, and calcitonin. The first two influence the body's basal metabolic rate. Undersecretion of thyroxin results in hypothyroidism, while oversecretion produces hyperthyroidism. Calcitonin lowers blood calcium levels. Parathyroid glands secrete parathyroid hormone (PTH), which helps raise calcium levels in the blood, acting as an antagonist of calcitonin. The interaction of these two hormones affect bones, the kidneys, and digestion.

The pancreas, a ducted exocrine gland, secretes digestive enzymes and sodium bicarbonate into the small intestine. It also contains true endocrine cells, clumped into islets of Langerhans, which secrete hormones such as glucagon and insulin directly into the blood. Glucagon stimulates the liver to break down glycogen into glucose. Insulin helps glucose move across cell membranes, is involved in fatty acid metabolism and glycogen synthesis, aids in capillary functions, and, in tissue culture, stimulates cells to divide. Insulin deficiencies result in diabetes mellitus.

The adrenal cortex produces mineralocorticoids, glucocorticoids, and steroid sex hormones. The most familiar mineralocortocoid, aldosterone, promotes the retention of sodium ions and the release of potassium ions by the kidneys. Cortisol, a glucocorticoid, plays an important role in metabolism. Some glucocorticoids (including cortisol) reduce inflammation and can suppress the immune system. Steroids promote sexual development. The adrenal medulla produces epinephrine and norepinephrine, which function in the "fight or flight" syndrome.

Sex hormones of the ovaries and testes, besides promoting secondary sex characteristics, affect skeletal development and mental growth. Prostaglandins, the most recently discovered hormones, are produced by most kinds of tissues and are involved in inflammatory responses and the sensation of pain. Thromboxane causes blood to clot, while prostacyclin prevents clotting and thins the blood; both are prostaglandins.

Cyclic AMP and the Molecular Biology of Hormone Action

When hormones bind to a cellular receptor site on an organ, a membranal enzyme is activated, converting ATP to cAMP. Cyclic AMP influences enzyme activity within the cell, and is often referred to as the second messenger. In effect, cAMP acts as an intermediary in hormone actions.

Steroid hormones sometimes bind to cytoplasmic binding proteins, and this complex can initiate gene activity inside the cell, causing the production of mRNA and proteins.

Key Terms

hormone
target tissue
receptor site
endocrine gland
endocrine system
steroid
peptide
modified amino acid
prostaglandin
pituitary
negative feedback control
posterior pituitary
anterior pituitary
releasing factor
growth hormone (GH)
adrenocorticotropic hormone (ACTH)
thyroid-stimulating hormone (TSH)

prolactin
estrogen
progesterone
follicle-stimulating hormone (FSH)
luteinizing hormone (LH)
oxytocin
antidiuretic hormone (ADH)
thyroid gland
thyroxin
triiodothyronine
basal metabolic rate
calcitonin
parathyroid glands
parathyroid hormone (PTH)
autoimmune reaction
pancreas
islets of Langerhans (pancreatic islets)
glucagon

insulin
diabetes mellitus
adrenal glands
mineralocorticoids
glucocorticoids
steroid sex hormones
aldosterone
cortisol
epinephrine
norepinephrine
testosterone
thromboxane
prostacyclin
cyclic adenosine monophosphate (cAMP)
second messenger
cytoplasmic binding protein

Review Questions

1. Using an example from the endocrine system, explain how negative feedback control operates. (pp. 510, 515)

2. Explain the difference in the ways in which the hypothalamus exerts its control over the anterior and posterior pituitary. What controls the hypothalamus? (pp. 510–511)

3. List six hormones of the anterior pituitary, and cite a function of each. (pp. 512–514)

4. Name two hormones stored in the posterior pituitary, and state their functions. (pp. 514–515)

5. What are the general effects of overactive or underactive thyroid glands? (p. 515)

6. Summarize the opposing effects of calcitonin and parathyroid hormone on calcium distribution. (pp. 515–516)

7. Where are glucagon and insulin produced? How do their roles differ? (pp. 516–517)

8. List the three classes of hormones of the adrenal cortex and discuss a general role for each class. (pp. 517–518)

9. Using the hormone epinephrine as an example, summarize the second-messenger hypothesis of hormonal action. Include the terms *target cells, receptor sites, adenyl cyclase,* and *cAMP*. (p. 519)

Homeostasis:

Thermoregulation, Osmoregulation, and Excretion

36

Morning comes and your eyes slowly open. As you rustle about, life seems simple and routine. You hardly notice what you are doing. But this is because evolution has not burdened you with the constant awareness of the many processes that enable you to do simple things. While you slept, poisonous nitrogenous substances were washed from the bloodstream. After awakening, you felt certain urges and while one part of your brain was deciding how to satisfy them, another part was coordinating your muscular movements so that you didn't fall flat on your face. And you probably paid no attention to the remarkable fact that you were alive at all; while you slept, various mechanisms were operating that kept your bodily processes within very precise limits. For example, your body temperature fell ever so slightly during the night, but at some point it stabilized and you did not die of hypothermia. When things are going well, your body's activities are kept within certain limits that are conducive to life and good health.

This stability is maintained by processes collectively called *homeostasis*, an important concept that was introduced earlier. In review, homeostasis is the tendency of a system to maintain internal stability by coordinated responses that correct any deviation from that stability. These corrections are made in a number of ways.

THE NATURE OF HOMEOSTATIC MECHANISMS

The body has basically two types of homeostatic responses to changing conditions: physiological and behavioral. *Physiological* responses are made without conscious intervention, and, as we have seen so far, they involve the autonomic nervous system and endocrine system. An animal that has these capabilities does not really have to think much about increasing its metabolic rate to produce more body heat, or about shunting blood into its extremities to cool its body. However, the animal may curl up in a ball to retain more heat, or move into the shade to cool itself. These conscious changes are obviously *behavioral* responses.

Negative and Positive Feedback: A Review

As you may recall from Chapter 35, *negative feedback* is important in hormonal action. Negative feedback involves a stimulus that starts a reaction; as the reaction continues, the stimulus is removed and the reaction ultimately begins to shut itself down. As a simple example, a baby cries when it is hungry; this causes the parent to feed it; the baby soon stops crying. From the baby's point of view, the stimulus was the hunger, and its response was crying, which ultimately stopped the hunger. From the parent's point of view, the stimulus was the crying and the response was feeding the baby, which made the crying stop.

Sometimes such a negative feedback loop fails. What if the baby is crying because of diaper rash, not hunger? If the parent offers unwanted food, the baby cries harder, so the parent tries harder to feed it. This is an example of *positive feedback*, where the stimulus evokes a response that further increases the stimulus instead of decreasing it.

Positive feedback is uncommon in nature, and is often associated with abnormalities. For example, high blood pressure can damage arteries, and the damaged vessel walls can become infused with fatty materials, scar tissue, and cellular growth. This restricts the size of the vessel opening, further increasing blood pressure. And we all know of people who are depressed because they are overweight, and so they overeat because they are depressed, and gain weight because they overeat.

Limitations in Homeostatic Mechanisms

Some homeostatic mechanisms allow more flexibility than others. For example, some marine creatures can exist only within a very narrow range of water salinity (saltiness), but the brine shrimp can thrive within an extremely wide range of salinity. Such homeostatic abilities are not without cost. The shrimp have essentially "invested" in this ability. The metabolic machinery has been channeled away from other specializations as natural selection favored this one. So, although brine shrimp can survive in a freshwater pond or in seawater, they are seldom found in either habitat because, in those relatively stable environments, they cannot effectively compete with species that have specialized for one condition or another. The brine shrimp do best in places such as estuaries, where the variation in salinity could not be tolerated by specialists.

We now come to two more important homeostatic mechanisms that involve multiple, interacting controls. One is *thermoregulation*, the animal's control over its internal temperature. The other is *osmoregulation*, through which the animal controls its body-fluid and mineral-ion balances. The latter is often closely associated with the *excretory system*, which rids the body of nitrogenous wastes.

THERMOREGULATION

Thermoregulation is the ability of an organism to maintain its body temperature either at a constant level or within an acceptable range. Some animals have very little ability to regulate their temperature; some have a moderate ability; and yet others are highly specialized for it.

Why Thermoregulate?

Animals in an environment cooler than their bodies cannot completely avoid heat loss, and since the primary source of heat for animals is their cellular respiratory process (see Chapter 8), we have a paradoxical situation. As the body cools, greater metabolic heat is required. Yet the loss of body heat ordinarily slows all chemical activity, including the respiratory activity required to produce heat. The result, under frigid conditions, is an accelerated (positive feedback) cooling of the animal, unless it can take measures to counteract the phenomenon.

Animals have just a few adaptive options when environmental temperatures fall below optimal levels. Most can attempt to avoid heat loss through behavioral strategies (Figure 36.1), or, as is often the case, the metabolic machinery will simply slow down, sending the animals into a metabolic stupor, their biochemical processes becoming so slow that they become sluggish or immobile. Another option for some animals is to take physiological measures to replace lost metabolic heat and to restrict what heat remains to those parts of the body that are more critical. Keep in mind that behavioral and physiological strategies usually work in concert; in the winter, humans tend to take in more calories *and* put on warmer clothing.

Thermoregulation, of course, also involves the loss of unwanted heat under high environmental temperatures. In fact, problems of coping with overheating are often more difficult than those associated with overcooling. They may also present more severe problems, because physiological damage created by excessive heat is often irreversible, whereas damage done by low temperatures is more likely to be temporary.

Animals that lack efficient metabolic means of adjusting their internal temperatures are **ectothermic** or *poikilothermic* (or, more commonly, "cold-blooded"). Ectotherms adjust their internal temperatures through such behavioral mechanisms as sunbasking. Still, these animals are characterized by their fluctuating internal temperatures.

Endothermic or *homeothermic* (or, more commonly, "warm-blooded") animals tend to maintain rather high, constant internal body temperatures by means of physiological mechanisms. This ability has permitted such animals to explore and establish ecological niches in environments not generally available to ectotherms. In the evolution of birds and mammals (Chapter 29), we saw that the rise of endothermy became important to the success of these groups in the cooler Cenozic era. Ectotherms and endotherms share many regions of the world today, but tend to utilize their resources differently. Mammals and birds, for instance, may forage efficiently in the chilly morning hours, while neighboring reptiles lie motionless, waiting for the sun to increase their metabolic rates.

Endothermy is very expensive. High constant heat requires fuel in the form of food, so endotherms must be efficient food-gatherers. Some ani-

Vertebrate adaptions to cooling external temperatures include a variety of behavioral responses. Humans may pile on clothing and voluntarily increase their muscular activity, a primary source of metabolic heat. Birds tend to crouch into a ball shape, drawing the extremities in. At this time their inner down feathers may be fluffed up, trapping air and improving their insulating quality. Reptiles of temperate regions are baskers. Lacking a physiological means of maintaining warmth, they often use the morning sun to raise their body temperatures. For desert lizards, this presents a problem, since exposing their bodies while in a metabolically sluggish morning condition leaves them vulnerable to predators. The solution for some is to expose only the head at first. Then as the body warms, more of it is exposed. In morning basking reptiles often lie perpendicular to the sun's rays, but later in the day, when heat may become a problem, they tend to orient their bodies in a parallel fashion.

mals are able to survive quite successfully as ectotherms because their lifestyles do not demand a constantly warm body. Such "sit-and-wait" ectothermic predators as frogs, salamanders, lizards, and crocodiles can maintain themselves for very long periods of time with no movement, very little metabolic activity, and no food intake.

Endothermy Reconsidered

The terms *endothermic* and *ectothermic*, therefore, refer to an animal's ability or inability, respectively, to regulate its internal body temperature. The most important ectotherms have traditionally been the invertebrates, fishes, amphibians, and reptiles. The endotherms have been represented by birds and mammals. These clear, classic lines of distinction are now becoming muddled. Many recent studies indicate that there are really no sharp taxonomic dividing lines between endotherms and ectotherms. For example, thermoregulation is common in certain bony fishes, some reptiles, and even

some sharks (Essay 36.1). The platypus, a furry endothermic mammal, has a rather poor ability to regulate its internal temperature. Among the invertebrates, beetles are able to maintain fairly high internal body temperatures by metabolic means.

Thermoregulation in Humans

Humans, like other mammals, maintain internal body temperatures within rather narrow limits. Any consistent variation of more than a few degrees from the optimum usually means trouble. We adjust our body temperature physiologically by varying the rate of metabolic heat production and controlling heat loss or gain from our body surfaces. The two mechanisms work in close harmony through the efforts of the hypothalamus, the body's internal thermostat (Figure 36.2).

The Hypothalamus: A Thermostat. The temperature-regulating portion of the hypothalamus works a bit like an ordinary home thermostat. The

A WARM-BODIED FISH

The bluefin tuna was once believed to be cold-blooded, like many other fishes. Yet it is among the fastest of all bony fishes, and often lives in *very* cold water. This does not seem possible; speed and cold bodies just don't go together. How could an ectotherm generate the metabolic energy needed to swim so fast in its chilling habitat? For one thing, the bluefin tuna is not the "cold fish" we once thought it was. In fact, even in the coldest water its internal temperatures can be quite high, up to nearly 32°C (almost 90°F). This is far better physiological regulation than we (as efficient endotherms) are capable of. How does this fish keep its body warm in frigid surroundings?

Much of the answer seems to be in the bluefin's circulatory system, which is quite different in some ways from that of truly ecto-thermal bony fishes (Figure **a**). In the bluefin tuna, the major arteries leaving the head and warm internal regions, and the veins returning blood from cool external regions, run paired with and parallel to each other, while those of other fishes tend to branch individually. This is the basis for the bluefin's magic ability. The parallel vessels set up the mechanism for a *countercurrent heat exchange*. It works this way: warmer blood leaving the deeper tissues passes cooler blood coming back from the surface. As the two opposing streams pass each other, heat

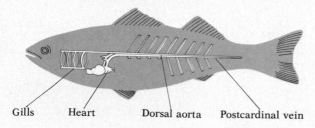

Slow-moving fish (cold-bodied)

Gills   Heart   Dorsal aorta   Postcardinal vein

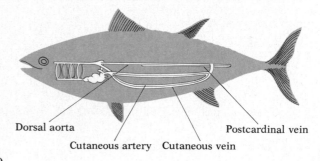

Fast-moving fish (warm-bodied)

Dorsal aorta

Cutaneous artery   Cutaneous vein

Postcardinal vein

(a)

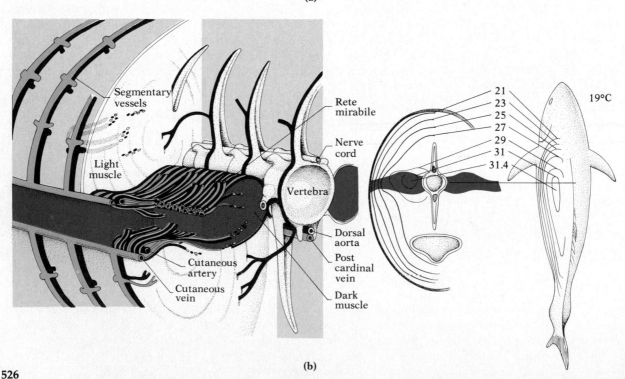

Segmentary vessels

Light muscle

Cutaneous artery

Cutaneous vein

Rete mirabile

Nerve cord

Vertebra

Dorsal aorta

Post cardinal vein

Dark muscle

21
23
25
27
29
31
31.4

19°C

(b)

moves to the cooler returning blood, and so much of the heat never reaches the extremities. In addition, there is another counter-current exchange system—a massive one—serving the swimming muscles of the bluefin tuna, as shown in Figure **b**.

We find two differently colored regions of muscle in the bluefin, light and dark. The dark muscle occurs in a region of higher temperature (as much as 10°C higher than the skin). Its dark color is due to an immense network of blood vessels consisting of parallel arteries and veins. This vascularized region, known as the *rete mirabile* (wonderful net), is a very dense countercurrent heat exchanger and conserver. Because of its arrangement, the *rete mirabile* produces a comparatively warm, lively group of swimming muscles. And that's why the bluefin tuna (and a number of other fast-swimming predatory fish) can swim rapidly in very cold water.

Countercurrent heat exchangers are not uncommon in vertebrates. Birds and mammals (including humans) have similar circulatory arrangements that are, in fact, essential to the maintenance of a constant body temperature. It may seem strange that birds can survive harsh winters, walking about on snow and ice with unprotected feet and legs. Figure **c** shows us how the avian countercurrent heat exchanger works. Notice that the arteries carrying blood to the feet are closely parallel to veins returning blood to the body. Heat from arterial blood passes to cool venous blood in the legs, so the feet remain cold and body heat loss is minimized. ●

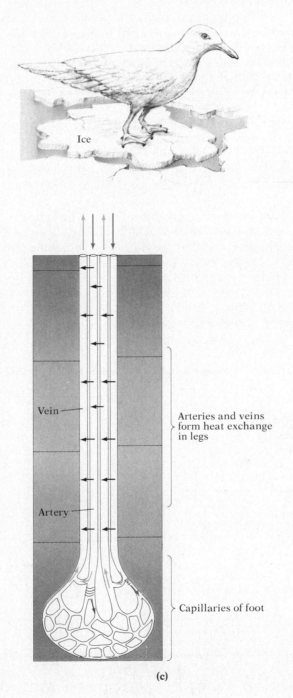

Ice

Vein

Artery

Arteries and veins form heat exchange in legs

Capillaries of foot

(c)

hypothalamus is far more sensitive and precise, however. In fact, physiologists have detected responses in the hypothalamus when blood temperature changed as little as 0.01°C, indicating a sensitivity that surpasses that of some of the best laboratory instruments. The hypothalamus receives information from thermoreceptors in the skin and from its own thermoreceptors, which monitor blood coming from parts of the body (see Figure 36.2).

When the hypothalamus detects a drop in body temperature, it can respond in a number of ways. It can influence the autonomic nervous system to decrease blood flow to the skin, conserving heat. Working through the autonomic nervous system, it can increase heat production by stimulating the adrenal medulla. In response, the gland releases epinephrine into the bloodstream, which increases the conversion of glycogen to glucose in the liver and muscles. This provides the fuel required for increased metabolic activity and heat release. The effects of epinephrine are short-lived, but the hypothalamus can produce a longer lasting increase in metabolism by causing the pituitary to release TSH, which stimulates the thyroid to release its metabolism-elevating hormones (Chapter 35). The result, in both instances, is an increase in body

heat. As body heat increases, the hypothalamus senses it (negative feedback), and eases off on its heat-generating activity.

The Skin and Lungs as Thermoregulators. Two important structures for managing heat loss and gain in humans are the skin and respiratory passages. The skin is beautifully adapted to this function (Figure 36.3). The arrangement of the blood vessels ensures that blood flow to surface capillaries can be increased or decreased, dissipating or conserving heat, respectively. Blood flow in these areas is directly controlled by smooth muscle sphincters (circular muscles) in the tiny arteries leading to the capillary bed. In thermoregulation, as mentioned earlier, contraction of the sphincters is brought about by the hypothalamus, operating through the autonomic nervous system.

When these sphincters close due to cold, blood is kept deep in the warmer parts of the body, and some people feel pain in the fingers, toes, and ears as the temperature in these extremities begins to drop. This is because the blood has been shunted to more vital areas as an adaptive mechanism that sacrifices the less critical parts of the body first.

When excess heat is the problem, the vessels

36.2

The hypothalamus receives thermal information both from thermoreceptors in the skin and by direct sensing of the temperature of blood arriving from the core of the body. Its response to changing temperatures is carried out in two ways: through activation of the autonomic nervous system and the endocrine system. Negative feedback occurs through the continued sensing of blood temperature.

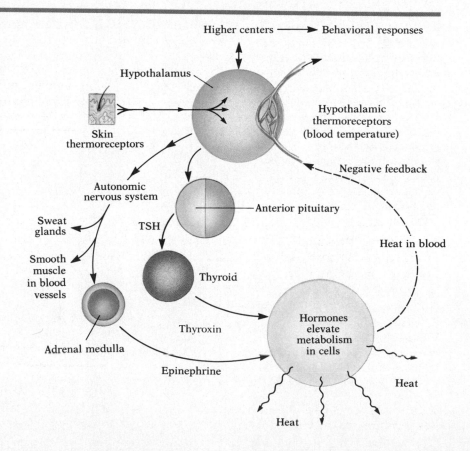

The human skin is an important thermoregulatory organ. Sweat glands secrete water through ducts. The evaporation of the sweat cools the skin. Sebaceous glands secrete oils that keep the hair and skin pliable and waterproof. Capillary beds below the surface can be opened, bringing blood near the skin for cooling, or alternately can be closed, keeping blood in deeper regions and thereby conserving heat. The direction of blood flow is controlled by sphincters (circular valves in the small arteries). Heat and cold receptors are abundant in the skin. Layers of fatty tissue provide heat-retaining insulation.

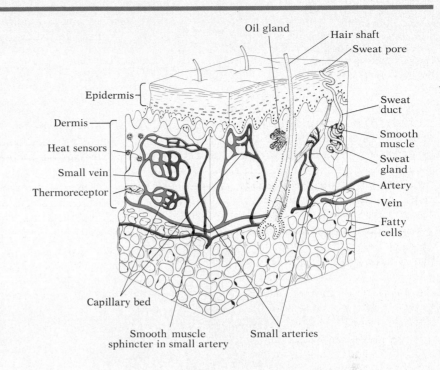

near the skin open and the blood moves away from the internal organs, so that heat is dissipated into the cooler air, especially if aided by the evaporation of perspiration. Humans (and horses) are unusual in this ability to sweat over virtually their entire bodies. Sweat glands in any part of the body at all are present in only a few mammals (in dogs, only on the footpads), and they are entirely lacking in reptiles and birds.

Most mammals can also conserve body heat through **piloerection,** when the hair stands on end. This "fluffing" of the hair traps air near the skin, providing an insulating quality. Each *hair follicle* contains a tiny smooth muscle that is controlled by the autonomic nervous system (see Figure 36.3). When contracted, it elevates the hair shaft to which it is attached. Interestingly, humans have retained this capability. We call the results of this contraction "goose bumps." But piloerection is not important to us in terms of heat conservation; we probably rely more on shivering to generate heat. Our retention of this peculiar ability may be a vestige of the time when the bodies of our forebears had more hair and piloerection was a response to a threat, making them appear larger and more formidable.

Heat loss through breathing is unavoidable, and is an important factor in frigid climates. Air entering the nasal passageways is warmed by blood in the highly vascularized nasal lining, thus protect-

ing the lungs from drastic local heat loss. The nasal passages themselves are then rewarmed by exhaled air. (Physiologists tell us that by the time cold winter air reaches the lungs, it is warmed almost to body temperature.)

Countercurrent Exchanges in Humans. Like other animals, humans have countercurrent heat exchangers (Figure 36.4). The arteries that carry blood to the forearm, for example, lie close to the veins that return blood to the body. This system keeps much of the body's heat from reaching the extremities in a cold environment. However, in warm weather, a shunting artery sends much of the returning blood back through more peripheral veins, thereby cooling the blood.

Humans exist all over the earth and have adapted to a number of different environments, including cold ones. Australian aborigines, to illustrate, commonly sleep naked on the ground. The temperature of their bodies may fall quite low, but not low enough to threaten frostbite. Both Eskimos and Australian aborigines have adapted to survive in cold climates, but they have done so in different ways. In an experiment designed to compare the cold adaptations of aborigines and Eskimos, members of both groups were asked to plunge a hand or foot into iced water. In the aborigine, the flow of blood to the extremity was quickly reduced, thus resulting in conservation of internal body heat. But

Countercurrent heat exchangers are common in human extremities. In the arm, for instance, the larger arteries and veins travel close together deep in the muscle. When the arm is cold, blood returns through the deeper veins, where the countercurrent exchange of heat between the arteries and veins conserves internal body heat. An alternate route for returning blood is through the veins that lie near the surface, just below the skin. When the arm is warm, returning blood follows the surface route, increasing the radiation of heat from the skin.

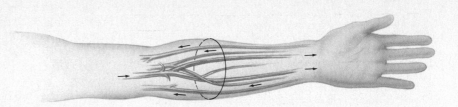

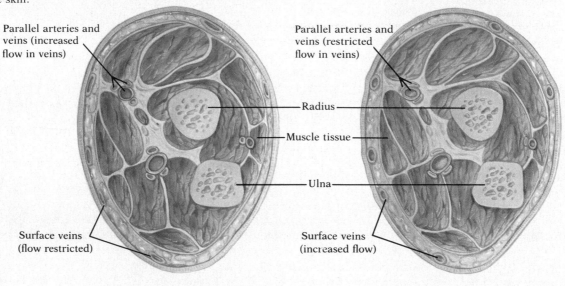

Parallel arteries and veins (increased flow in veins)

Parallel arteries and veins (restricted flow in veins)

Radius

Muscle tissue

Ulna

Surface veins (flow restricted)

Surface veins (increased flow)

(a) Cold conditions

(b) Warm conditions

in the Eskimo, the flow of peripheral blood to the chilled extremity *increased*. The latter reaction obviously wastes more body heat, but it decreases the likelihood of frostbite—a clear danger in the Eskimo's environment.

OSMOREGULATION AND EXCRETION

Thermoregulation is, indeed, an important and fascinating problem for physiologists; and another is **osmoregulation,** or the way that water and ion concentrations are regulated in the cells (and bodies) of animals. It is sometimes said that most cells are about two-thirds water, but to the physiologist, "about" won't do. In fact, for all living things the amount of intracellular water is critical, as is the relative abundance of various ions in the cell fluids.

The problem is to understand how the balance

of water and ions is maintained. In particular, the question centers on the way excess water or ions are removed from the body by *excretion*. **Excretion** refers to the removal of metabolic wastes from the body, particularly the removal of the nitrogenous wastes produced by the metabolism of amino acids. To a great degree, the animal's environment dictates the methods by which nitrogenous wastes are removed.

The Human Excretory System

Because humans are terrestrial creatures, we must conserve water, just like our fellow landlubbers. At the same time, we must wash potentially poisonous nitrogenous wastes from our bodies and regulate such ions as sodium and chloride. Most of nitrogenous waste occurs in the form of **urea,** a relatively harmless byproduct of amino acid metabolism. Both the osmoregulatory and the excretory functions are handled by the kidneys and their associated ducts (with assistance from the lungs and sweat glands).

The Human Excretory Structures. The human excretory system comprises the *kidneys, ureters, bladder,* and *urethra* (Figure 36.5). Each kidney receives a small blood vessel, the **renal artery** (*renal* means "pertaining to the kidney"), which branches directly from the *descending aorta,* a major artery from the heart. (All arteries carry blood from the heart through the rest of the body.) The renal artery is small, but blood passing through it is under extremely high pressure. Blood leaves each kidney through the **renal vein.** (Veins carry blood back to the heart.)

The excretory system removes excess water, excess salts, and urea from the blood. And while the kidneys filter about 180 L of fluid per day, more than 99% of that fluid is recycled back to the blood before the urine (about 1.2 L per day) is formed. At any time, the actual volume and content of the urine depends upon water intake and diet.

The **kidney** (Figure 36.6) has three major regions: the outer *renal cortex,* the *renal medulla,* and the *renal pelvis.* Much of tissue of the three regions is made up of **nephrons,** the filtering units of the kidney, and their associated blood vessels. Each of the one million nephrons in each kidney originates in the renal cortex as an enlarged capsule (or *renal corpuscle*) that is continuous with a lengthy *renal tubule.* Some tubules extend into the medulla, while others are confined to the cortex; all of the tubules eventually join with the tubules of neighboring nephrons to form larger ducts that carry urine into the renal pelvis. Of equal importance are the blood vessels that are closely associated with the nephrons. The nephron carries out its osmoregulatory and excretory functions in three phases: *filtration, reabsorption,* and *tubular secretion.*

The Microscopic Structure of the Nephron. To understand how the nephrons function, we must first take a close look at their microscopic structure. Each aspect of the nephron is significant to its role as an active filter.

A nephron begins as a hollow bulb or cup known as **Bowman's capsule.** From the Bowman's capsule, the nephron forms a slender tubule that is organized into three distinct parts. The first, the **proximal** (near) **convoluted tubule,** gets its name from the twisting route it follows before it is directed downward into the second part, a long, hairpin loop known as the **loop of Henle.** The loop

36.5

The human excretory system consists of the paired kidneys, their associated blood vessels, the renal arteries and veins, the ureters, bladder, and urethra. The system functions in both excretion (the removal of nitrogenous wastes) and osmoregulation (the regulation of body fluids and essential ions).

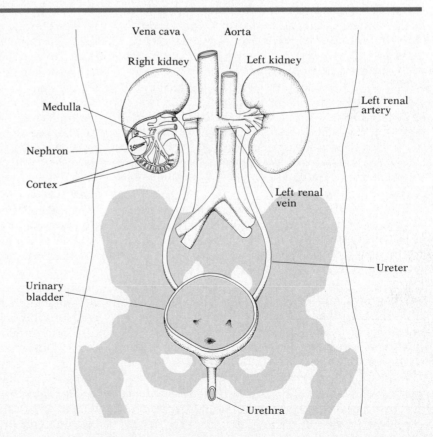

The kidney **(a)** has three major regions: the outer cortex, the medulla, and the renal pelvis. The filtering units of the kidney are the nephrons. These extend from the cortex into the medulla, and their collecting ducts form the cone-shaped pyramids. Urine collects in the spaces of the renal pelvis. Each nephron **(b)** consists of five anatomical regions: the Bowman's capsule, proximal convoluted tubule, loop of Henle, distal convoluted tubule, and collecting duct. Each plays a special role in excretion and osmoregulation. Equally important are the blood vessels serving the nephron. Minute branches of the renal artery enter Bowman's capsule, where they form a tuft of capillaries known as a glomerulus—a major filtering unit. Vessels emerging from the glomerulus form a netlike arrangement over the rest of the nephron before joining with those of other nephrons to eventually form the renal vein and return the blood to the general circulation.

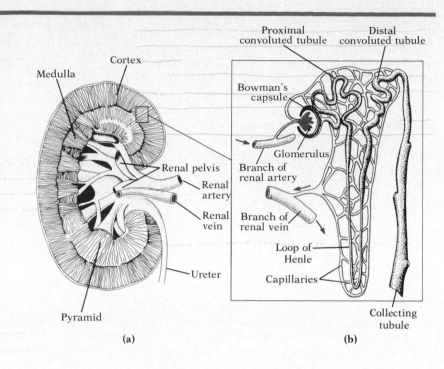

(a)

(b)

of Henle is made up of a *descending limb* that dips down toward (or into) the renal medulla and an *ascending limb* that returns upward. (Such hairpin loops are found in all water-conserving vertebrate kidneys and are extremely prominent in the kidneys of desert-dwelling mammals. This is a good indication that the loop of Henle has something to do with conserving water.) The ascending limb of Henle's loop then gives rise to the last part of the nephron, the **distal** (far) **convoluted tubule.** Like its proximal counterpart, the distal convoluted tubule follows a twisting path. It finally joins a **collecting duct,** which also receives the distal tubules of neighboring nephrons.

Since it is the blood that is filtered, the blood vessels associated with the nephron are of equal importance to its function. The Bowman's capsule contains a dense ball of capillaries known as the **glomerulus,** which arises from a tiny branch of the renal artery (Figure 36.7). The capillaries of the glomerulus, having followed their tortuous route within the Bowman's capsule, rejoin to form a small emerging vessel. This vessel immediately divides again, this time into the **peritubular capillaries,** a network that surrounds the tubule and the collecting duct. Eventually these capillaries will merge into venules (little veins) that join to form the renal vein, through which filtered blood is returned to circulation.

The Filtering Activity of the Nephron. Activity in the nephron occurs in three phases: filtration, reabsorption, and tubular secretion. The first of these, **filtration,** is the task of the glomerulus and Bowman's capsule. Blood entering the glomerulus is under considerable pressure, and the filtering action here is often described as *force filtration.* Significant amounts of the water and small soluble molecules of the blood—including urea—are pushed out of the glomerulus by *hydrostatic pressure* (see Chapter 5). The larger blood elements, such as red blood cells and proteins, are left behind. The fluid that is pressed from the glomerulus into Bowman's capsule is not yet urine, but can be called the *crude kidney filtrate.* It is important to note that force filtration is not very selective of small soluble molecules, so while urea has been removed from the blood, a number of useful solutes have also been removed. These must be returned to the blood prior to the final formation of urine (Figure 36.8).

Immediately following filtration, the vital task of **reabsorption** begins. The blood in the peritubular capillaries surrounding the renal tubule has lost much of its water, so osmotic conditions there prepare it to take in water from the crude kidney filtrate. Through osmosis, the capillaries recover about 80% of the water content of the crude kidney filtrate. Interestingly, about 50% of the urea in the filtrate reenters the blood here as well.

The SEM captures the blood vessels of the nephrons. The arteries branch into arterioles, which form individual glomeruli. Note the vessels leaving the glomeruli to branch out over the rest of the nephron. (From *TISSUES AND ORGANS: a text-atlas of scanning electron microscopy,* by Richard G. Kessel and Randy H. Karton. W. H. Freeman and Company, copyright © 1979.)

In addition, valuable small molecules that had passed through the glomerulus—such blood components as glucose and amino acids—are returned to the blood from the filtrate, via active transport, by the cells lining the tubule. Remaining in the tubular filtrate are miscellaneous toxic substances (any small molecules not specifically reclaimed), urea, some salt, and about 20% of the water. This is far more water than the body can afford to lose.

While reabsorption carries substances out of the filtrate and back into the blood, another process, **tubular secretion,** also occurs in the renal tubule. Selected substances such as hydrogen, ammonium and potassium ions, and creatinine—all metabolic wastes—are actively transported *into* the tubule, where they join the urine. Tubular secretion is essential to the body's acid-base balance.

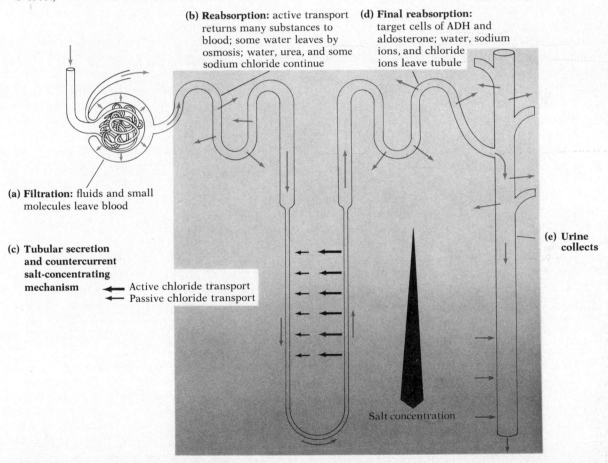

(b) **Reabsorption:** active transport returns many substances to blood; some water leaves by osmosis; water, urea, and some sodium chloride continue

(d) **Final reabsorption:** target cells of ADH and aldosterone; water, sodium ions, and chloride ions leave tubule

(a) **Filtration:** fluids and small molecules leave blood

(c) **Tubular secretion and countercurrent salt-concentrating mechanism**

⟵ Active chloride transport
⟵ Passive chloride transport

(e) **Urine collects**

Salt concentration ⟶

A simplified diagram of activity in the nephron and collecting duct. The upper structures are found in the renal cortex, while the loop of Henle and collecting ducts sometimes pass down into the renal medulla. Urine formation begins with filtration in the renal corpuscle (a). In the proximal convoluted tubule, water is drawn out into the surrounding tissue for reabsorption into the blood (b). Ions enter the surrounding tissue, and some move passively into the descending limb in tubular secretion. This movement from limb to limb sets up a circulation of salt around the loop (c), maintaining the steep osmotic gradient needed to remove excess water from the kidney filtrate. The quantity of water reentering the blood depends on cells lining the collecting ducts; their permeability to water is variable, depending on hormonal control (d) by the hypothalamus. Urine finally passes from the distal convoluted tubule into a collecting duct (e).

In the loop of Henle, the distal tubule, and the collecting ducts, most of the water not removed in the proximal tubule will be returned to the blood. But osmotic conditions have changed, since most of the water left the crude kidney filtrate as it passed through the proximal tubule. Were the loop of Henle a simple tube, the further extraction of water would be difficult, since biological systems usually cannot pump water directly. The solution to this problem is seen in the shape of the loop itself and in its ability to actively transport salt out of the filtrate and into the surrounding extra-cellular space. Where salt goes, water will follow, and in the process the salt is somehow recovered.

The cells of the ascending limb of Henle's loop actively transport salt outward. The ion actually pumped is chloride, but when chloride moves, sodium follows passively. So salt is moved out of the kidney tubule and into the surrounding extra-cellular space. The descending limb does not actively transport salt, but it does permit it to reenter passively, so there is a constant circulation of some of the salt into and out of the two limbs. Because of this ongoing process, the fluid surrounding the tubule becomes hypertonic (in this case, more salty) compared with the fluid in the distal convoluted tubule and collecting ducts. Thus water leaves the nephron because it is flowing from a region of high water (and low salt) concentration to a region of low water (and high salt) concentration. Further active transport moves the salt into the capillary network nearby, where it is again followed by the water. In water-conserving vertebrates, the hairpin loop provides a countercurrent mechanism that concentrates salt in much the same way as parallel arteries and veins concentrate heat.

So the loop has two important functions: to create an osmotic condition that will help in water recovery and to provide a mechanism for recovering salt from the kidney filtrate. In part, the efficiency of water recovery is helped by the fact that the filtrate moves through the salty extracellular space three times: down and up through the loop of Henle, and back down again through the collecting duct. That is essentially how urine is formed. All that remains is for the final product to leave the kidneys through the **ureters** and to enter the **bladder.** From the bladder it leaves the body through the **urethra.**

Just how much water is removed by the kidneys depends, of course, on the person's physiological state. If water intake has been excessive, the urine volume will be considerable and may be quite diluted. If a person is dehydrated, the urine volume may be small but highly concentrated. The amount of salt present in the urine depends upon the intake of sodium chloride in the diet. Of course, the nephron does not control water and salt retention

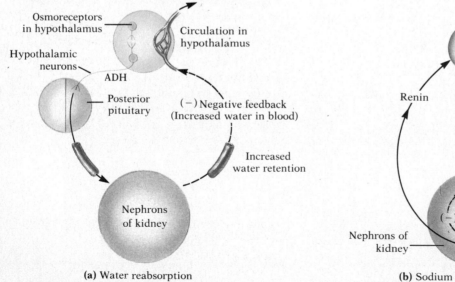

(a) Water reabsorption   **(b)** Sodium chloride reabsorption

36.9

(a) Water reabsorption is controlled in part by the hypothalamus, which secretes ADH via the posterior pituitary. Negative feedback is direct, since the osmoreceptors in the hypothalamus respond to the increased water content of the blood. **(b)** The control of salt reabsorption is more complex. Although aldosterone influences the active uptake of chloride ions by the nephron, release of aldosterone by the adrenal cortex is initiated by renin secretion from the nephron itself. Negative feedback, therefore, is between the salt-sensing cells of the distal convoluted tubule and renin-secreting cells in the glomerular arteriole.

all by itself. Controlling the reabsorption of water and salt, as we saw in the last chapter, involves the intervention of hormones.

Control of the Nephron. One task of the hypothalamus is to measure the *osmotic pressure* (the concentration), of the blood passing through its capillaries. If the osmotic pressure is high (if the blood is low in water), the hypothalamus secretes the hormone ADH into the posterior pituitary, which then releases it into the bloodstream. Its targets are the epithelial cells of the distal convoluted tubule and the collecting ducts of the nephron (Figure 36.9a). The hormone renders those passageways permeable to water, which flows freely from the nephron, to reenter the bloodstream via the capillaries associated with the system. As the proper osmotic pressure becomes reestablished, less ADH is released, the tubules become less permeable, and the urine is more dilute.

The osmotic stimulation of the hypothalamus has another effect: it creates the feeling of thirst. Drinking then causes the blood to become diluted, and the hypothalamus responds accordingly, by decreasing its output of ADH. More urine passes into the renal pelvis, through the ureters, and into the bladder, producing a "conscious" sensation by stimulating the stretch receptors of the bladder.

A similar hormonal mechanism operates to control the retention of sodium chloride (Figure 36.9b). In this case, the hormone is *aldosterone*, a mineralocorticoid (see Chapter 35) that is released by the cortex of the adrenal gland. The link between sodium chloride retention and aldosterone release is indirect and not entirely understood. Apparently, certain cells in the nephron's distal tubule monitor sodium chloride transport, communicating their information to cells in an adjacent small artery that enters the glomerulus (see Figure 36.7). When sodium chloride retention is low, the

arteriolar cells release *renin*, an intermediate hormone, which enters the body's circulation. When renin reaches the adrenal cortex, it stimulates aldosterone release. Aldosterone's target is the distal convoluted tubule, where it increases the rate of active transport of sodium ions out of the nephron; chloride ions follow passively. As active transport increases, renin release slows. The secretion of aldosterone drops, the active recovery of salt is reduced, and the salt content of the urine once again increases. (As mentioned in Chapter 35, aldosterone also increases the excretion of potassium ions.)

Numerous factors can influence water regulation—alcohol, for instance. Alcohol is a diuretic, and increases urine production. If you've ever socialized with people who drink, you may have noticed that their visits to the facilities became more frequent as the evening wore on. In fact, they might have suspected that the output exceeded the input. And they might be right. This is because alcohol suppresses the release of ADH, so the cells of the nephron remain somewhat impermeable to the movement of water back into the blood. Thus, as the blood alcohol level increases, so does the volume of urine. This means, in addition to inconvenient interruptions of brilliant conversations, that alcohol dehydrates our tissues. The most severe effects of this dehydration are felt sometime later: dehydration is partly responsible for something called a hangover.

In this chapter we have seen only a few of the many delicate, interacting, and highly coordinated mechanisms that keep the body's internal environment within the extremely precise limits critical to life. Remember, we live in what is essentially a disruptive environment. To remain organized in the face of such potential disruption requires an uphill battle against a variety of forces. That battle is best fought under optimal conditions, which is what homeostasis is all about.

Summary

The Nature of Homeostatic Mechanisms
Homeostasis is the tendency of a system to maintain internal stability by correcting any deviation from that stability. Homeostatic responses can be physiological—involving the autonomic nervous system and endocrine system—or behavioral, involving conscious changes to new conditions. Physiological and behavioral responses work on positive and negative feedback control.

Homeostatic mechanisms vary in their range of flexibility. Organisms must invest their limited time and energy in specialization, often at the cost of being unable to withstand unusual environmental variations. Two important homeostatic mechanisms are thermoregulation and osmoregulation.

Thermoregulation
Thermoregulation enables an organism to maintain its body temperature at a relatively constant level. Ectothermic ("cold-blooded") animals lack efficient metabolic means of adjusting their internal temperatures. Endothermic ("warm-blooded") animals can maintain a high, constant body temperature by physiological means. Endothermy permits such animals to explore a wider variety of climatic conditions than ectotherms can. But endothermy can be very energetically expensive.

Few clear-cut taxonomic lines can be drawn between endothermic and ectothermic animals. Some fishes possess countercurrent circulatory systems that help them stay warm and active even in extremely cold environments, while some mammals have difficulty maintaining constant body temperatures.

Thermoregulation in humans is controlled largely by the hypothalamus, which acts like an internal thermostat. The hypothalamus detects changes in blood temperature and activates the autonomic nervous system in ways that increase or decrease internal heat production. Humans can regulate body temperature by varying metabolic rates *and* by controlling heat loss or gain from body surfaces. The skin and the respiratory passages are important structures in managing thermoregulation. Humans can cool themselves by perspiring, and can conserve some heat through piloerection. Lungs dissipate body heat through exhalation, while nasal passages warm the air before it enters the lungs. Humans also have countercurrent heat exchangers to warm or cool the blood.

Osmoregulation and Excretion

Osmoregulation involves regulating water and ion concentrations within cells. Excretion is the removal of metabolic wastes from the body.

The human excretory system comprises the kidneys, ureters, bladder, and urethra. The filtering units of the kidney are the nephrons, which carry out osmoregulatory and excretory functions in three phases: filtration, reabsorption, and tubular secretion.

Blood is first force-filtered in the glomerulus, a ball of capillaries within the Bowman's capsule. Then blood in the peritubular capillaries reabsorbs water and other substances from the filtrate in the renal tubule. Tubular secretion involves the active transport, from the peritubular capillaries and surrounding extracellular space, of certain substances *into* the renal tubule. Reabsorption and secretion help concentrate the urine and function in maintaining osmotic conditions and acid-base balances in the blood. The shape of the loop of Henle permits the establishment of a countercurrent mechanism that allows salt and water to be returned to the blood in appropriate amounts.

Hormones influence the reabsorption of water and salt. The hypothalamus responds to increases in osmotic pressure in the blood by secreting ADH into the posterior pituitary. ADH makes the distal convoluted tubules and collecting ducts more permeable to water, so more water is reabsorbed by the blood, reestablishing the proper osmotic pressure. Aldosterone, released by the adrenal cortex, increases the active transport of sodium ions out of the tubule and into the blood, hence influencing the retention of salt in body fluids.

Key Terms

homeostasis	excretion	Bowman's capsule	peritubular capillaries
thermoregulation	urea	proximal convoluted tubule	filtration
ectothermy	renal artery	loop of Henle	reabsorption
endothermy	renal vein	distal convoluted tubule	tubular secretion
piloerection	kidney	collecting duct	ureter
osmoregulation	nephron	glomerulus	bladder
			urethra

Review Questions

1. Compare negative feedback with positive feedback and relate each to the well-being of an animal. (p. 523)

2. Describe the two general ways in which animals thermoregulate, using examples of endotherms and ectotherms. (p. 524)

3. Explain how the blue-fin tuna maintains its warm body temperature, and state why the temperature is important to this particular fish. (pp. 526–527)

4. Discuss the thermoregulatory role of the hypothalamus in humans by describing both heat-generating and heat-dissipating responses. (p. 528)

5. List the major structures of the human excretory system, and describe the system's two main functions. (pp. 530–531)

6. Trace the movement of fluid through the nephron, naming the different parts as you proceed. Include a description of the related blood vessels. (pp. 532–533)

7. Retrace the route of fluids in the nephron, this time including a brief summary of filtration, reabsorption, and tubular secretion. (pp. 532–533)

8. Explain how the loop of Henle functions as a countercurrent mechanism, and how this action aids in water reabsorption. (p. 534)

9. Summarize the actions of ADH and aldosterone in regulating water and ion concentrations. (p. 535)

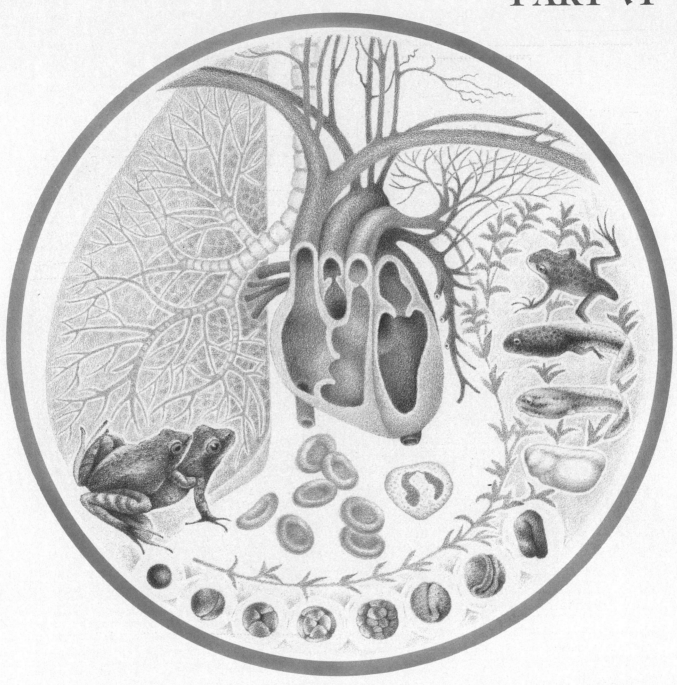

PART VI

Vertebrate Maintenance and Reproduction

Digestion and Nutrition

37

Animals must devote a great deal of time and energy to eating and not being eaten. Humans must join their animal cousins in stalking the earth to search for energy that is stored in the bodies of other living things. We may not always be aware of our endeavor, and we may even try to shield ourselves from it. For example, we can sell real estate and pay someone else to find our food. We can also develop a refined and elaborate ceremony around the process of eating, and insist that our meat be prepared in precisely this way or that. But no matter how delicately we view such matters, the fact remains that the beast that provided our filet once hit the earth with a thud. And, although we feel quite justified in our behavior, we are probably not prepared to offer similar justification in cases where we humans have yielded our stored molecules to the belly of some stronger predator.

Nevertheless, the simple truth is that something alive must die if heterotrophs are to avail themselves of the materials and energy needed to resist entropy. In this chapter we'll see how our bodies handle energy in the form of food, and then we'll focus on that food.

EVOLUTIONARY SPECIALIZATIONS IN THE VERTEBRATE GUT

The vertebrate digestive system follows the usual metazoan tube-within-a-tube plan. It begins at the mouth cavity, in which teeth may be present to tear or grind food as it is manipulated by the tongue. The chewed or "gulped" food passes into a pharynx at the rear of the mouth, and then through a muscular esophagus that squeezes it into a temporary storage organ—the stomach. The stomach empties into the small intestine, which is a major organ of digestion. Here, products of digestion pass through the gut and into the bloodstream. Next, in the large intestine, excess water is absorbed into the blood. The residue of waste is stored in the rectum until it is emptied through the anus. In most vertebrates, the anus empties into another chamber—the cloaca, which accepts solid waste, metabolic waste, and gametes before discharging them into the environment.

Any variation from the usual vertebrate gut (see Chapter 29), as you might expect, would be an evolutionary specialization for some particular diet. For example, as a general rule, the gut is considerably longer in species specialized for plant-eating. This is because plant foods generally take longer to digest. Such elongation increases not only the time food remains in the gut, but the absorptive surface area as well. Such carnivores as sharks, lampreys, and sturgeon have short, straight guts. The surface area of such short guts is increased by a *spiral valve*, a shelflike, spiralling fold in the intestinal wall (see Figure 24.9b).

In no other group has the stomach become so extensive and specialized as in the *ruminants*, such as cattle, deer, giraffes, antelope, and buffalo. They live by eating cellulose-containing plants, but they cannot digest cellulose. In fact, very few animals have this capability. They solve the problem

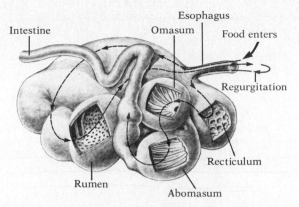

37.1

The four-part stomach of ruminants is specialized for the digestion of cellulose, a mainstay of the animals' diets. Food first enters the *rumen*, where microorganisms digest the cellulose. The food is regurgitated, thoroughly chewed (as a "cud"), and then reswallowed, this time passing into the *reticulum*, then the *omasum*, and finally the *abomasum* (true stomach). During its second transit, the food and microorganisms are digested through chemical processes similar to those of other mammals.

by harboring in the gut immense numbers of protozoa and bacteria, which *can* digest cellulose (Figure 37.1).

Many vertebrate guts have a blind sac where the small intestine joins the large intestine. This is the **cecum,** a pouch that serves as a food-storage organ and as a fermenting vat in a diverse group of mammals, including primates, horses, rabbits, ground squirrels, elephants, conies, and marsupials (Figure 37.2). The cecum allows nonruminants to digest plant materials by retaining them in the bacteria-ridden sac. The human gut has a rather small cecum, from which extends a small, fingerlike pouch, the **veriform appendix,** which is extremely prone to infection (see Figure 37.3).

THE HUMAN DIGESTIVE SYSTEM

As mammalian digestive systems go, ours is rather ordinary. But this allows us to serve us a good representative of our class. As shown in Figure 37.3, the human digestive system includes the mouth, esophagus, stomach, small intestine, and

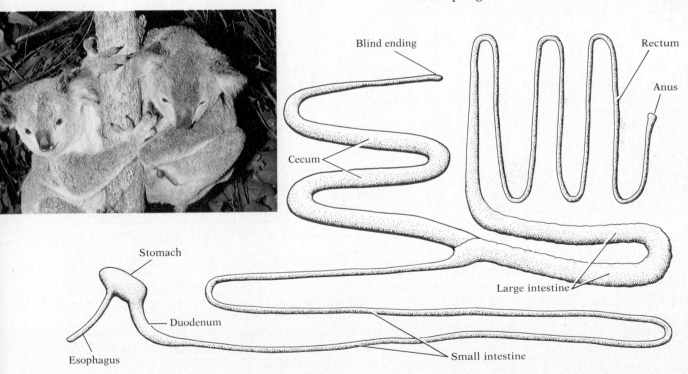

37.2

Many grazing mammals lack the complex four-part stomach of the ruminants, but they can still manage to digest cellulose. Like ruminants, these herbivores utilize the enzymes of microorganisms in digesting cellulose, but the fermentation chamber is the pouchlike cecum found at the union of the small and large intestines. The cecum has reached extreme development in the koala, an Australian marsupial whose diet consists exclusively of eucalyptus leaves. The koala's extraordinary cecum makes up a fifth of its lengthy digestive tract. In humans, the cecum accounts for less than a hundredth of the tract.

The human digestive system is typical of that of many mammals, and is not particularly specialized. It is a muscular tube (some 9 m—30 ft—long when stretched out) with an inner lining that differs from region to region. The system begins with the mouth, which leads to the pharynx and on to the esophagus, a simple, muscular passage to the stomach. The stomach, a muscular sac, stores food and creates an extremely acidic environment where protein digestion begins. Most food digestion and absorption is carried out in the highly coiled small intestine (about 4.5 m long), the lining of which is the most complex in the system. The large intestine, or colon, specializes in absorbing water along with some minerals and useful products of bacterial action. It produces the feces, or digestive wastes. The digestive system includes a number of accessory structures that produce important secretions. These include the salivary glands, the liver, and the pancreas (see Figure 37.11).

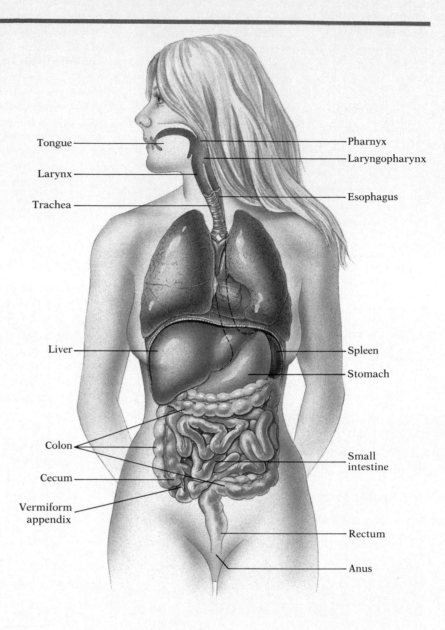

Tongue

Larynx

Trachea

Liver

Colon

Cecum

Vermiform appendix

Pharynx

Laryngopharynx

Esophagus

Spleen

Stomach

Small intestine

Rectum

Anus

large intestine. The organs are held loosely in place by folds of the **peritoneum,** an extensive connective tissue that lines the inner wall of the abdominal cavity as well. The folds carry blood vessels, nerves, and lymphatic vessels—all important to digestion.

The Mouth and Esophagus

The digestive structures of the mouth include the lips, teeth, tongue, pharynx, and salivary glands. In case you're wondering what the lips have to do with eating, they help seal the mouth. (Try eating and swallowing with your lips open.)

The tongue is also surprisingly important in eating. In addition to its role in moving food into position for chewing, swallowing, and sorting out fish bones, it constantly monitors the texture and chemistry of foods. This is a valuable chore, since it tells us about food in time to prevent us from swallowing something we shouldn't. In addition, the tongue can distinguish certain chemicals by specialized chemoreceptors called *taste buds*. These receptors can distinguish four basic tastes: salty, sour, sweet, and bitter (see Chapter 34).

Saliva is produced by three pairs of **salivary glands:** the *parotid, sublingual,* and *submandibular* glands (Figure 37.4). These glands secrete **saliva** through ducts that empty into the mouth. Saliva is about 95% water; the remaining 5% includes ions, lubricating mucus, and an enzyme—**salivary amylase**—that begins starch digestion. This enzyme is probably less important in digestion than in oral hygiene, since it helps break down any starchy food particles caught between the teeth that could encourage bacterial growth.

The **pharynx,** located in the rear of the oral cavity, joins with the nasal cavity to form a common passageway. The pressure-equalizing *eustachian tubes* of the middle ear, an otherwise sealed chamber, also open into the pharynx. Just below the root of the tongue, the pharynx divides, forming the ventral (in front) **larynx** and the dorsal (behind) **laryngopharynx.** During swallowing, the larynx is raised and a flaplike **epiglottis** is pressed against it, directing food into the esophagus (Figure 37.5). If this fails, food will enter the larynx, producing violent choking or coughing spasms.

37.4

Three pairs of salivary glands—the parotids, sublinguals, and submandibulars. The primary salivary secretions, mucus and salivary amylase, are produced in different clusters of cells within each gland. The flow of saliva can be stimulated by the thought or aroma of food, but the greatest flow occurs when food is in the mouth. It is initiated by mechanical stimulation of nerve receptors in the mouth, and by chemical stimulation of the taste buds.

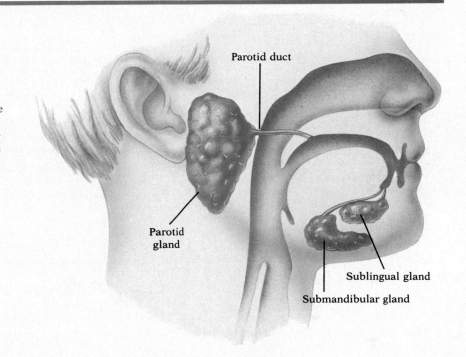

37.5

The important structures of swallowing are the tongue, pharynx, soft palate, epiglottis, larynx, and laryngopharynx. The act is initially voluntary and then becomes involuntary or reflexive. Swallowing begins as the food mass is voluntarily pressed upwards by the tongue against the palate and back towards the pharynx. It is here that the involuntary stages begin. The soft palate elevates, closing off the nasal cavity. The larynx also elevates, bending the epiglottis over the glottis (opening of the larynx) and effectively sealing off the respiratory opening. The food mass then enters the laryngopharynx, where continued reflexive muscular action forces it into the esophagus. The highly complex reflexive part of swallowing is controlled by a neural swallowing center in the medulla.

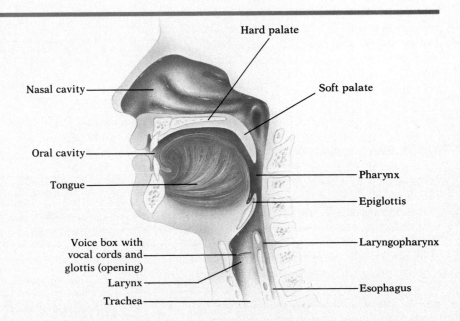

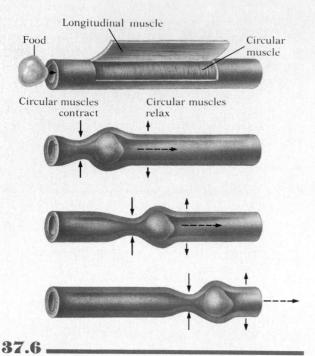

37.6

Peristalsis. Food is moved through the digestive tract through a complex, involuntary act involving the circular smooth muscle layer. As a food mass moves along the gut, the muscle layers ahead relax, while those behind the food reflexively contract, forcing food along. The longitudinal muscles are primarily involved in churning action. The wavelike contractions are under the control of the autonomic nervous system.

The **esophagus** lubricates food and directs it to the stomach. Its upper region contains skeletal (voluntary) muscle; the rest is involuntary, containing circular and longitudinal layers of muscle. Swallowing begins as a voluntary act, but continues as an involuntary one. Food is moved through the esophagus and the remainder of the digestive tract by **peristalsis**—coordinated contractions of smooth muscle (Figure 37.6).

The Stomach

The human **stomach** is essentially a J-shaped sac with a complex lining surrounded by three layers of smooth muscle (Figure 37.7). It has functions other than temporary storage of ingested food. Some digestion is carried on here, and the environment is so acid that it kills such unwanted invaders as bacteria and other potential parasites. (The stomach juices are about pH 1.6–2.4.)

The food in the stomach is thoroughly churned by the muscle layers, so that food is mixed with gastric juices. The food is not squeezed out by their

movements because the stomach is closed at both ends by powerful *sphincter muscles*. Failure of the upper sphincter to close completely during digestion produces heartburn as gastric juices enter the esophagus.

The stomach lining contains glands that produce and secrete the gastric juices (Figure 37.8). **Chief cells** secrete the protein *pepsinogen*, and **parietal cells** secrete *hydrochloric acid* (HCl). The acid is required to activate the pepsinogen, which then forms the digestive enzyme *pepsin*. Other glands secrete *rennin*, an enzyme that helps young mammals to digest milk, and *gastric lipase*, a fat-splitting enzyme.

The stomach is so full of powerful acids and enzymes that it may actually threaten its own lining. One reason we usually don't digest our stomachs is that a layer of *mucin*, an insoluble mucoprotein, forms a coating over the stomach lining. However, such protective measures can fail, as when stress produces an acid imbalance. The result can be *gastric ulcers*, erosions of the stomach lining. Once considered the badge of a hard-driving and successful person, they are now widespread in our population. Fortunately, newly de-

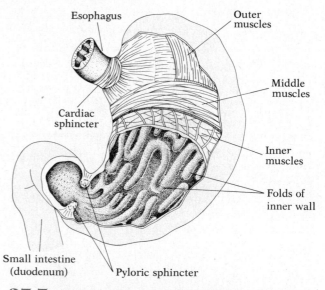

37.7

The human stomach has an average capacity of about one liter. Its walls contain smooth muscle oriented in three directions. During peristalsis, the layers produce powerful writhing and wringing actions. Circular sphincter muscles (the *cardiac sphincter* above and the *pyloric sphincter* below) prevent food from escaping during churning, but the pyloric sphincter must relax to permit food to enter the small intestine. When the stomach is empty, its inner surface is highly folded.

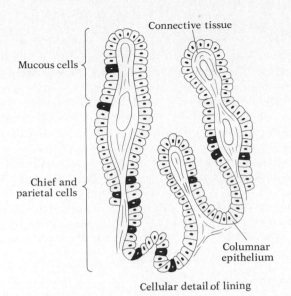

Connective tissue

Mucous cells

Chief and
parietal cells

Columnar
epithelium

Cellular detail of lining

37.8

(left) A longitudinal view of one secretory gland. The uppermost cells secrete mucus. Below these are the chief cells and parietal cells, which secrete pepsinogen and hydrochloric acid, respectively. In the presence of the acid, pepsinogen is converted to the active enzyme pepsin. *(right)* The scanning electron micrograph reveals the lightly pitted surface of the stomach mucosa. The pits are the openings of glands that are lined with the three types of secretory cells. (Photo from *TISSUES AND ORGANS: a text-atlas of scanning electron microscopy*, by Richard G. Kessel and Randy N. Kardon. W. H. Freeman and Company, copyright © 1979.)

veloped drugs can inhibit the acidic secretion of the parietal cells. (One of these drugs, cimetidine, has replaced diazepam—better known by the trade name Valium—as the largest-selling prescription drug in America.)

The Small Intestine

Food, well churned and liquified by stomach action, is then squirted into the upper part of the small intestine, the **duodenum.** The duodenum itself is only about 25–30 cm long, but the **small intestine** is a highly coiled tube about 6 m long. The musculature of the small intestine is similar to that of the esophagus, but its lining, like that of the stomach, is quite intricate and well suited for its tasks. The small intestine completes the process of digestion and absorbs nutrients before it passes the undigested residue to the large intestine.

The lining of the small intestine (Figure 37.9) has an enormous surface area—estimated at 700 m² (about the floor area of four or five three-bedroom houses). The great surface area is produced by four specializations. First of all, the *coiling* permits a longer tube. Second, within the tube, there are numerous *folds* in the lining. Third, the surface of these folds contains tiny fingerlike projections called **villi** (singular, *villus*). It is the villi that give a velvety appearance to gut linings. Finally, the villi themselves are bristling with **microvilli,** fine foldings in the cell membranes that form what is called a *brush border* (Figure 37.10).

The villi, which specialize in food absorption, contain dense capillary beds and saclike vessels called **lacteals.** While most digested foods enter the capillaries, most fats enter the lacteals, extensions of the *lymphatic system.* This system has several functions; one of which is to transport fats away from the intestine, as we will discuss later (see Figure 37.10). Villi contain smooth muscles that enable them to move vigorously, like millions of wiggling fingers, further mixing the food that passes through the small intestine.

It has only been recently discovered that most— perhaps all—nutrients enter the lining of the small intestine through active processes; and, further, that each kind of nutrient probably has its own specific ATP-powered transport mechanism. Recent studies also reveal that many small intestinal enzymes are actually bound to the lining cells and are not free, as was once believed.

The Liver

The upper region of the small intestine, the duodenum, receives secretions from two organs: the liver and the pancreas (Figure 37.11). The **liver** secretes **bile,** which helps break down fats.

The bile is stored in the **gall bladder,** and is released by rather weak muscular contractions triggered by fats in the small intestine. Bile reaches the duodenum through the **common bile duct,** which is joined by the **pancreatic duct** just before it reaches the intestine (see Figure 37.11). The bile carries off metabolic wastes and breaks down fats into tiny droplets. The smaller the droplets, the relatively greater the surface area on which enzymes can act. An obstructed bile duct results in an inability to absorb fats. Surgeons sometimes move the bile duct of a dangerously obese patient to the lower end of the small intestine. The patient, unable to absorb dietary fat, loses weight dramatically.

The Pancreas

The human **pancreas** is a long, glandular organ nestled between the stomach and the duodenum (see Figure 37.11). It secretes *sodium bicarbonate,* which neutralizes the acid that enters from the stomach. In addition, the pancreas secretes a battery of digestive enzymes that act in the digestion and metabolism of fats, carbohydrates, proteins, and nucleic acids. The pancreas is also an endocrine gland. It contains the pancreatic islets, which are made up of clusters of alpha, beta, and delta cells that together produce the important hormones insulin, glucagon, and somatostatin (see Chapter 35).

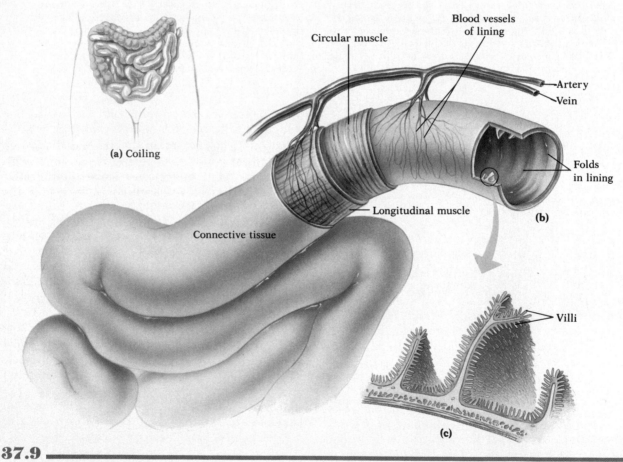

37.9

The surface area of the small intestine is accounted for by coiling **(a),** folding of the lining **(b),** the presence of numerous villi **(c),** and microvilli (not shown). Digested food is actually absorbed through the villi. The small intestine is richly supplied with blood vessels that will carry most of the products of digestion to the liver for storage and modification.

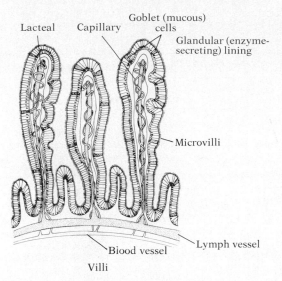

37.10

Villi *(left)* may be from .05 to 1.5 mm long and are densely packed over the intestinal surface, with 100–400 per cm³. The cells covering the villi specialize in absorption, mucus secretion, and digestion. The products of digestion move into a dense capillary bed and a lymph vessel known as a lacteal, both found within each villus. The villi may have highly folded outer membranes, the microvilli *(right)*, as seen in the scanning electron micrograph. These form a brush border that greatly increases the surface area of the small intestine. (Photo from *TISSUES AND ORGANS: a text-atlas of scanning electron microscopy*, by Richard G. Kessel and Randy N. Kardon. W. H. Freeman and Company, copyright © 1979.)

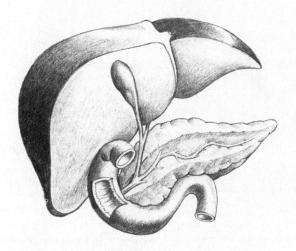

37.11

The liver and pancreas are accessory digestive organs. The liver produces bile, which is important in the emulsification of fats. Bile is stored temporarily in the gall bladder and released when fat is present in the digestive tract. The pancreas produces enzymes that help digest all types of foods. The ducts from both the gall bladder and the pancreas meet to form a common duct that empties into the duodenum of the small intestine.

The Colon

The **colon** (large intestine) absorbs water and minerals, transferring them to the blood, and forms and stores feces before they leave the digestive tract. Nutritionists will argue over the role of the large intestine in digestion. The lining of the colon is glandular, but it secretes only mucus—no enzymes. The mucus protects the colon lining and lubricates it for the passage of feces. Recent evidence indicates that some digestion and absorption of food does occur in the large intestine, and that it may be due solely to the activities of the vast numbers of bacteria that dwell there. You may be surprised to learn that virtually all the material entering the gut is utilized by these numerous and varied bacteria in the large intestine. The result is that feces actually consist almost entirely of living and dead bacteria. *E. coli*, the best known of these tiny organisms, really accounts for only about 1% of the bacteria in the colon.

Intestinal bacteria are quite useful. In fact, an overdose of antibiotics can kill the bacteria, which often results in diarrhea. More importantly, the bacteria provide humans with certain essential vitamins, including vitamin K, biotin, and folic acid. Our relationship with our fecal bacteria is clearly mutualistic.

Chemical Digestion and Absorption

We considered the molecular structure of proteins, fats, and carbohydrates in Chapter 3. Since digestion is the process of breaking these molecules down into smaller particles that can cross membranes and move into the bloodstream, you may want to review the general structure of the large molecules before continuing here.

The bonds of the large molecules are broken through a process called **hydrolysis.** Essentially, this means that enzymes add water to the linkages, disrupting them and yielding molecular subunits. Thus, in digestion, carbohydrates are dismantled into simple sugars; fats, into fatty acids and glycerol; proteins, into their various amino acids; and nucleic acids, into nucleotides. The substrates (the large molecules), the enzymes, and their functions are listed in Table 37.1.

Carbohydrate Digestion.   Simple sugars, such as glucose, can be absorbed "as is" by the intestinal lining. But more complex carbohydrates must first be broken down into simple sugars. Even disaccharides, such as sucrose and lactose, must first be enzymatically split into their component parts. In fact, if sucrose is injected into the blood it will be secreted by the kidneys unchanged, because **sucrase** exists only as a membrane-bounded enzyme of the gut epithelium.

All normal human infants have another membrane-bounded gut enzyme, **lactase,** which splits lactose, a milk sugar. Adults of most human racial groups cease producing lactase, and as a result cannot digest milk sugar. But caucasians have apparently adapted to dairy products over the past few thousands years, and continue producing intestinal lactase after reaching maturity. As adults, they can still digest milk sugar.

TABLE 37.1

Digestive enzymes and their functions

Source and Enzyme(s)	Substrate	Product
Salivary glands		
Salivary amylase	Starch	Glucose
Stomach lining		
Pepsin	Protein	Polypeptides
Rennin	Casein	Insoluble curd
Gastric lipase	Triglyceride	Fatty acids + glycerol
Pancreas		
Trypsin	Peptide linkage	Shorter polypeptides
Chymotrypsin	Peptide linkage	Shorter polypeptides
Ribonuclease	RNA	Nucleotides
Deoxyribonuclease	DNA	Deoxynucleotides
Pancreatic amylase	Starch	Glucose
Pancreatic lipase	Triglyceride	Fatty acids + glycerol
Carboxypeptidase	C-terminal bond	Shorter peptide and one free amino acid
Intestinal lining		
Aminopeptidase	N-terminal bond	Shorter peptide and one free amino acid
Tripeptidase	Tripeptide	Dipeptide + amino acid
Dipeptidase	Dipeptide	Two amino acids
Nuclease	Nucleotide	Pentose + nitrogen base
Maltase	Maltose	Two glucose units
Sucrase	Sucrose	Glucose + fructose
Lactase	Lactose	Glucose + galactose

37.12

Carbohydrate digestion. Starches are long chains of glucose. Their digestion begins with the enzyme amylase, secreted by the salivary glands and the pancreas. The product is maltose, a disaccharide containing two glucose subunits. Maltose is finally broken into glucose by maltase, an enzyme of the small intestine's microvilli.

Amylase in mouth and small intestine

Maltase in small intestine

Starch

Maltose and some short-chain fragments

Glucose

Starch digestion begins in the mouth, where salivary amylase breaks some linkages, producing maltose and some larger fragments (Figure 37.12). In the small intestine, pancreatic amylase converts all starch into maltose, which is finally cleaved into two molecules of glucose by **maltase.**

Fat Digestion.   Fats are first dispersed into tiny droplets by bile salts, and most are then hydrolyzed into fatty acids and glycerol by pancreatic lipase (Figure 37.13). The products then enter the villi. Once inside the cells of the villi, the shorter fatty acid chains move directly into the capillaries for transport to the liver. The longer chains, oddly enough, are reconstructed into fats by the villus cell, and then pass by pinocytosis into the lacteal. The many lacteals empty into lymph vessels that carry the reconstituted fats directly into the circulatory system for distribution throughout the body.

Protein Digestion.   Proteins are the largest and most complex of the food molecules, so it is not surprising that their digestion also is complex. Essentially, protein digestion occurs in three steps, beginning in the stomach. Here, pepsin attacks the molecule, splitting it more or less randomly into peptide fragments of various lengths. The fragments are then subjected to a more specific disruption in the small intestine, where the pancreatic enzymes *trypsin* and *chymotrypsin* break only specific amino acid linkages. This leaves the protein in the form of peptide fragments only two to ten amino acids long. These are finally cleaved, by small intestinal enzymes, into single amino acids. Figure 37.14 reviews protein digestion in greater detail.

Following protein digestion, the amino acids enter capillaries in the villi and are carried directly to the liver, where they are used according to the body's metabolic needs. Many amino acids are simply synthesized into blood proteins (Chapter 39), joining the blood plasma. Others reenter the blood unchanged for distribution to the cells, where they are synthesized into whatever proteins or enzymes the cell needs. Still others are converted into amino acids that are in short supply. The body doesn't store amino acids, so if excesses are present they are *deaminated* (the nitrogen group removed) in the liver cells, and the remaining molecules are converted to glucose or fats to be stored or used for energy needs.

Integration and Control of the Digestive Process

The timing of the release of digestive juices is under at least three types of control: mechanical, neural, and hormonal. The distinctions are not clear-cut, however, since there is important interaction among the three types. For example, salivation can be evoked by thinking of chocolate cake or by chewing some tasteless substance like paraffin. Lemon juice can also stimulate saliva flow. Table 37.2 lists the hormones involved in digestion.

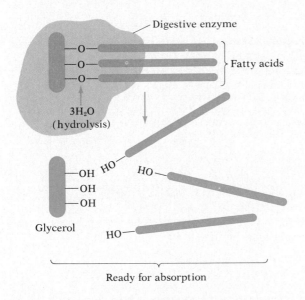

37.13

Triglyceride digestion. The common fats and oils—the triglycerides—contain one subunit of glycerol covalently bonded to three fatty acid chains. For digestion to begin, the fats are first dispersed into fine droplets by the action of bile. The individual molecules are hydrolyzed by the enzyme lipase, which is produced by the stomach and pancreas. The products, free glycerol and fatty acids, are then transported into the villi.

SOME ESSENTIALS OF NUTRITION

Nutrition has become not only an interesting and trendy topic, but a critical one as well, as we are made aware of increasing numbers of contradictory options. Although some of us seem overly obsessed with the subject, at least a certain degree of interest is merited. After all, nutritional information can be useful personally: who would guess that eating too many raw eggs can cause a vitamin deficiency? In addition, a certain level of

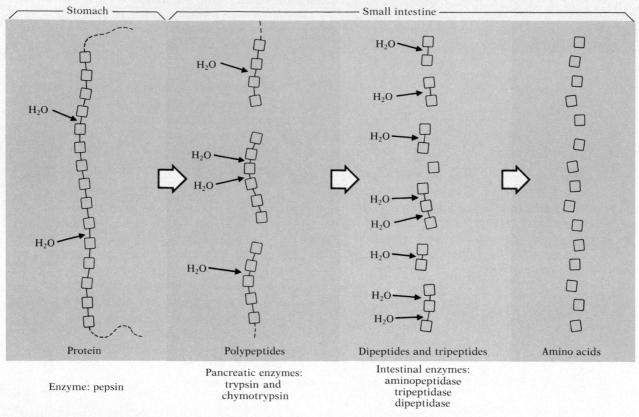

Stomach	Small intestine

Protein

Enzyme: pepsin

Polypeptides

Pancreatic enzymes:
trypsin and
chymotrypsin

Dipeptides and tripeptides

Intestinal enzymes:
aminopeptidase
tripeptidase
dipeptidase

Amino acids

37.14

Proteins contain hundreds—often thousands—of amino acids. The complete digestion of protein to free amino acids requires at least three chemical steps. It begins in the stomach, where the enzyme pepsin hydrolyzes the peptide bonds randomly, producing polypeptide strands of varying length. These strands are next attacked in the small intestine by the enzymes trypsin and chymotrypsin from the pancreas. The en-zymes hydrolyze the peptide bonds of specific amino acids within the strands, producing short fragments of two or three amino acids. Finally, aminopeptidase, tripeptidase, and dipeptidase, enzymes of the intestinal microvilli, break the remaining peptide bonds. The free amino acids are then transported into the capillaries of the villi.

knowledge makes us less vulnerable to false advertising. Also, food is an increasingly critical commodity that may come to play an even larger role in global politics. Now, more than ever, we need to be able to sort fact from fiction in order to use the world's food resources economically.

Unfortunately, interest in food doesn't necessarily equal knowledge of nutrition. Many food faddists are virtually ignorant of the *science* of nutrition. Some food "experts" do not understand that organically grown food is no better for you than that grown with chemical fertilizers; that rose hip vitamin C is no different from synthetic vitamin C produced by bacteria; that large doses of vitamins may be harmful; that dietary protein that exceeds body needs is simply stored as glucose in the liver or is converted to fat on the hips; or that high-protein diets cannot be shown to be beneficial,

and, in fact, can be both fattening and harmful. These statements may be both interesting and confusing, so let's consider diet more closely to understand their relevance.

Carbohydrates

Carbohydrates are common sources of energy, as we saw in our discussion of their use in cell respiration (see Chapter 8). Their usefulness, however, is quite varied and complex.

Once glucose makes its way from the gut into the circulatory system, it is immediately removed and stored as glycogen primarily in the liver. From there it is meted out as glucose according to the body's needs. This keeps the blood glucose level rather constant, with a temporary 10%–20% increase immediately after a high-carbohydrate meal.

TABLE 37.2

Digestive hormones

Hormone	Stimulation	Function
Gastrin	Protein in stomach Vagus nerve (autonomic)	Stimulates release of gastric juice
Enterogastrone	Acid state in intestine Fats in intestine	Inhibits gastric juice release and slows stomach contractions
Secretin	Acid state in intestine Peptides in intestine	Stimulates release of sodium bicarbonate
Cholecystokinin- Pancreozymin	Food entering small intestine	Stimulates secretion of pancreatic enzymes and contraction of gall bladder
Enterocrinin	Stomach materials in intestine	Stimulates intestinal secretions

The skeletal muscles store a considerable amount of glucose as glycogen. During anaerobic activity, glycogen is again broken down into glucose, which is then used as an energy source. Long-distance runners build up muscle glycogen by continually depleting those reserves in long training runs and then building them back to even higher levels. Excess glucose is simply converted into body fat.

Fats

People generally assume that it is good to avoid fats in the diet. But fats are not all bad. In fact, some amount of polyunsaturated fat is essential in the diets of many animals, including humans. Fats have a number of uses. They have twice the energy value of carbohydrates. In addition, they contain the essential fat-soluble vitamins A, D, E, and K. Unsaturated fats are also part of all cell membranes. Some fats can be synthesized in the body; others must be provided in the diet. These are known as **essential fatty acids.**

You are probably aware of the persistent controversy over the connection between saturated fats and cholesterol. You may have even switched to foods with high levels of unsaturated fats—the ones so heavily touted in advertisements for margarine and cooking and salad oils. Essay 37.1 reveals a startling twist to what we have come to accept about saturated fats. Incidentally, if you are trying to cut down on fat intake, keep in mind that some fats can be synthesized not only from excess carbohydrates, but from excess protein as well. For this reason, high-carbohydrate or high-protein diets may defeat their own purpose if the intake of these substances is not carefully measured.

Protein

Protein, an essential nutrient, must be constantly present in the diet since we don't store it well. Although some protein is stored in the liver and muscles, there is a steady turnover of *total* body protein, and we need even more when we are growing. (Low supplies of protein in the first two years of life can produce permanent brain damage.)

When protein is digested, its amino acids are utilized in several ways. For example, they are the building blocks of our own protein; they are used to form nitrogen bases such as those of DNA; they can be oxidized for energy; and they can be stripped of their amino groups and converted to fats and carbohydrates.

Animals generally are able to convert certain amino acids to others. In fact, we can convert 12 of the 20 amino acids we require into others, if necessary. However, the other eight must be supplied in the diet. These are referred to as the **essential amino acids**—a phrase that delights advertising agencies. Actually, all 20 are essential at some level.

The quality of some proteins is lower than that of others, meaning that some kinds are deficient in one or more of the essential amino acids. The synthesis of any protein depends on the presence of all of the required constituent amino acids. This means that the usefulness of any protein in food, for anything other than calories, depends on the relative concentration of its most scarce essential amino acid. In general, animal proteins are of much higher quality than plant proteins. In fact, except for seeds and grains, most plant foods don't have much protein; seeds store proteins that help develop new seedlings, but even these are typically deficient in tryptophan, methionine, and/or lysine. Lysine deficiencies are common among people who rely on corn as their major source of protein, since the major storage protein of corn has no lysine.

Vegetarians, therefore, must select their foods with great care. Legumes, including beans, peanuts, and especially soya products, have fairly high-quality protein. But the best rule is to eat combinations of protein-rich vegetable products, and *know your plants*. An intelligently planned vegetarian diet is unquestionably more healthful than the typical American diet, which includes an excess of animal fats. A well-balanced vegetarian diet that is stretched to include fish as an honorary vegetable will allow many to attain a healthy old age.

Vitamins

Vitamins are also essential in the diets of animals. Biochemists have identified most of them, so we know not only their molecular structures but their precise functions (Table 37.3). There are still a few vitamins, however, that are understood to only a limited extent. All we can say about those is that if you don't have them, you will probably develop some condition or another, usually something unpleasant.

Most vitamins function as *coenzymes*. For example, respiratory enzymes cannot function without the coenzymes NAD and FAD, which are derived from vitamin B_6 and riboflavin, respectively. Shortages of these vitamins can lead to serious illness. Vitamins C and E have a somewhat more general function: both are *antioxidants*, which means that they remove spontaneous free radicals that would otherwise damage our tissues.

Mineral Requirements of Humans

Animals also require a number of inorganic ions that are generally referred to as **minerals.** Those required in the largest amounts include calcium (a major constituent of bone and of many cellular processes), magnesium (necessary for many enzymatic activities), and iron (a component of hemoglobin as well as the chytochromes of the

ESSAY 37.1

CHOLESTEROL AND CONTROVERSY

O Cholesterol is an important constituent of cell membranes. Our livers can make it, but the concentration in our blood depends greatly on how much of it we eat. We actually can't live without it, so how did cholesterol get its unsavory reputation?

The *plaques* that plug arteries in chronic arteriosclerosis are heavily infiltrated with cholesterol. Also, people with abnormally high levels of circulating cholesterol have high rates of arterial and heart disease. It is reasonable to conclude that it is wise to reduce cholesterol intake and to replace saturated (animal and hydrogenated vegetable) fats with unsaturated (nonhydrogenated vegetable) fats. Although many doctors still give this advice, some rather startling new developments may soon change their minds.

In a recent study, a large group of middle-aged men was subdivided into an experimental group and a control group. Members of

the experimental population were put on a diet low in cholesterol and high in unsaturated fats. For instance, they were encouraged to eat special ice cream and plenty of mayonnaise. As expected, their blood cholesterol levels went down. Also, over the years, their rates of arterial disease and heart disease were lower than those of the control population. Case proved? Not quite. Although the death rate from heart attacks was lower in the experimental group, the *total* death rate of the experimental group was significantly *higher* than that of the control group. *The experimental group also had a higher incidence of cancer.*

This was hard to explain. It was suggested that the higher levels of cholesterol in the control group produced healthier cell membranes and that these protected them from cancer. Another more likely possibility is that unsaturated fats are somehow toxic. It is known that unsaturated fats spontane-

ously form *free radicals* (incomplete, or charged, molecules) with highly reactive unpaired electrons. Free radicals tend to react randomly with other molecules. In fact, ionizing radiation of the sort that is known to cause cancer damages cells in a similar way: it creates free radicals that can attack DNA. Ironically, the diet that was designed to suppress one problem may have worsened another.

The results of the study serve as a monumental example of how little we really know about the effects of diet. It chillingly indicates what can happen when we modify our diets because of what seems to be a well-founded scientific opinion. The effects of such a diet change can also be more subtle. Women athletes may have menstrual problems because physical stress and special diets leave them low in blood cholesterol. A generation or two of Americans have avoided cholesterol at every opportunity, and we are only beginning to see the results. ●

TABLE 37.3

Vitamins

Vitamin	Source	Function	Daily requirement	Result of deficiency
A, retinol	Fruits, vegetables, liver, dairy products	Synthesis of visual pigments	1500–5000 IU 3 mg	Night blindness, crustiness about eyes
B_1, thiamine	Liver, peanuts, grains, yeast	Respiratory coenzyme	1–1.5 mg	Loss of appetite, beriberi, inflammation of nerves
B_2, riboflavin	Dairy products, liver, eggs, spinach	Oxidative chains in cell respiration	1.3–1.7 mg	Lesions in corners of mouth, skin disorders
Niacin, nicotinic acid	Meat, fowl, yeast, liver	Part of NAD and FAD cell respiration	12–20 mg	Skin problems, diarrhea, gum disease, mental disorders
Folic acid	Vegetables, eggs, liver, grains	Synthesis of blood cells	0.4 mg	Anemia, low white blood count, slow growth
B_6	Liver, grains, dairy products	Active transport	1.4–2.0 mg	Slow growth, skin problems, anemia
Pantothenic acid	Liver, eggs, yeast	Part of coenzyme A of cell respiration	Unknown	Reproductive problems, adrenal insufficiency
B_{12}	Liver, meat, dairy products, eggs	Red blood cell production	5–6 mg	Pernicious anemia
Biotin	Liver, yeast, intestinal bacteria	In coenzymes	Unknown	Skin problems, loss of hair and coordination
Choline	Most foods	Fat, carbohydrate, protein metabolism	Unknown	Fatty liver, kidney failure, metabolic disorders
C, ascorbic acid	Citrus fruits, tomatoes, potatoes	Connective tissues and matrix antioxidant	40–60 mg	Scurvy, poor bone growth, slows healing, (colds?)
D	Fortified milk, seafoods, fish oils, sunshine	Absorption of calcium	400 IU	Rickets
E	Meat, dairy products, whole wheat	Uncertain	Unknown	Infertility, kidney problems
K	Intestinal bacteria	Blood clotting factors	Unknown	Blood clotting problems

Abbreviations: IU = International units; mg = milligram; μg = microgram.

electron transport chain). Sodium, potassium, and chloride are also needed in fairly substantial quantities in order to replace daily losses; sodium and potassium are involved in nerve cell conduction and osmotic regulation.

Trace Elements. In addition to the various elements that are necessary, in large amounts, for life and good health, there are others that are necessary only in very small amounts. Included are iodine (thyroid hormones), copper (hemoglobin formation and enzyme action), fluorine (protection of teeth), zinc (enzyme action and insulin synthesis), selenium and manganese (enzyme action), and cobalt (red blood cell formation). Newly added to the list of trace elements is silicon, a mineral constituent of rock and one of the commonest elements on the earth. But to be useful to the body silicon must be in a soluble form, as it is in plant fibers. So, getting your "roughage" may be important for more than enhancing bowel regularity. Silicon is now believed to be an important constituent in the elastic walls of arteries, and its absence in diets of highly processed foods may be a significant cause of arterial disease—another strong argument for eating fresh fruits and vegetables.

Summing Up Nutrition

We've seen that low- and high-cholesterol diets are both potentially harmful; that the balance between saturated and unsaturated fats mustn't be tipped too far in either direction; and that too much protein is harmful, but too little is worse. Careless vegetarianism can be dangerous, and so can a diet laden with red meat. One can get sick from having too much vitamin A, or from not having enough. Most people consume too much sodium, but everyone needs a certain amount. Ocean fish can be extremely good for you, unless it is contaminated with high levels of mercury. How can one make intelligent nutritional decisions in the face of such complex scientific evidence?

There is no simple answer. It is clear that most people in developed nations, whatever their diet, eat too much. We must resort to generalities and cliches, such as "moderation in all things," or "variety is the spice of life," or "no one ever suffered from eating sensible amounts of fresh fruits and vegetables." We might stroke our chins in our wisest fashion and say, "get enough roughage." At any rate, it is probably best to avoid diet fads; and to avoid saturated fats—but not fanatically.

Animals have always eaten and digested. But simpler organisms used essentially the same processes long before we appeared. As a result, we have come to know a great deal about foods. Yet it seems that every day, new findings erupt— new notions about nutrition and health. We must, indeed, be prepared to evaluate such discoveries according to the rigid rules of the science of nutrition.

Summary

Evolutionary Specializations in the Vertebrate Gut
The vertebrate digestive system follows the metazoan tube-within-a-tube plan. Herbivores have long guts, while many carnivores have shorter, straighter guts. Ruminants have highly specialized stomachs, and harbor many protozoans and bacteria that can digest cellulose. The small, sac-like cecum allows food to ferment or to be attacked by bacteria, aiding digestion.

The Human Digestive System
The human digestive system includes the mouth, esophagus, stomach, small intestine, and large intestine, which are held loosely in place by the peritoneum. Digestive structures of the mouth comprise the lips, teeth, tongue, pharynx, and salivary glands. Lips and teeth hold, tear, and grind food, while the tongue monitors the chemistry and texture of foods. Three pairs of salivary glands produce water, ions, lubricating mucus, and enzymes that help break down starch. Food passes through the pharynx, where it is directed down the esophagus by peristalsis. The stomach, covered by three layers of smooth muscles and closed at either end by sphincter muscles, stores and churns food and kills many harmful bacteria and potential parasites. Gastric juices contain enzymes that partially digest protein and fats.

Leaving the stomach, liquefied food enters the duodenum, which receives secretions of the liver that help break down fats, while those of the pancreas help break down fats, carbohydrates, proteins, and nucleic acids. In the small intestine, the process of digestion is completed and nutrients absorbed through the villi into the bloodstream and lymphatic system. The colon removes excess water and minerals and transports them into the blood. It also forms and stores feces. Intestinal bacteria in the colon provide essential vitamins to the body.

The chemistry of digestion involves breaking large, complex molecules into smaller particles. Carbohydrates are converted to simple sugars through the actions of lactase, sucrase, salivary amylase, and maltase. Fats are broken down by bile salts and lipase into fatty acids and glycerol. Proteins are converted into single amino acids through the actions of pepsin, pancreatic, and small intestinal enzymes. Mechanical, neural, and hormonal controls cooperatively regulate the release of digestive juices and enzymes.

Some Essentials of Nutrition
Although more is being discovered daily about nutrition, the field is still marked by confusion, fads, and lack of adequate understanding of many of the functions of nutrients.

Carbohydrates are a common source of energy. Glucose is stored in the liver and released as the body needs it. Fats have twice the energy value of carbohydrates and contain some essential vitamins. Some fatty acids can be synthesized in the body, but essential fatty acids must be provided by the diet. The controversy regarding the connection between saturated fats and cholesterol—a known factor in heart disease—is still unresolved. It is now suspected that unsaturated fats spontaneously form free radicals that react randomly with other molecules and may cause cancer.

Protein is particularly important during growth and must be constantly replenished, since the body does not store it well. Amino acids serve as building blocks for more proteins, can be oxidized for energy, and can be converted to fats and carbohydrates. Eight essential amino acids must be supplied by the diet, although the other 12 can be synthesized by the liver.

Most vitamins function as coenzymes that help enzymes perform their proper functions. Other vitamins, such as C and E, act as antioxidants, removing free radicals from the body.

Minerals provide essential ions to the body. Those needed in the largest amounts include calcium, magnesium, and iron. Sodium, potassium, and chloride ions are involved in osmotic regulation and nerve conduction. Trace elements such as iodine, copper, fluorine, zinc, and silicon are also important to good health.

Key Terms

cecum	epiglottis	microvilli	hydrolysis
vermiform appendix	esophagus	lacteal	sucrase
peritoneum	peristalsis	liver	lactase
salivary glands	stomach	bile	maltase
saliva	chief cells	gall bladder	essential fatty acid
salivary amylase	parietal cells	bile duct	essential amino acid
pharynx	duodenum	pancreatic duct	vitamin
larynx	small intestine	pancreas	mineral
laryngopharynx	villi	colon	

Review Questions

1. One of the more interesting vertebrate digestive specializations is seen in the digestion of cellulose by ruminants. Using the cow as an example, trace the movement of food through the four-part stomach and explain where and how cellulose digestion occurs. (Figure 37.1)

2. Beginning with the mouth, list five major parts of the human digestive tract and give a general function for each. (pp. 539–540)

3. Describe the tissue organization of the esophagus, and explain how its smooth muscle portions function in peristalsis. (p. 542)

4. List three digestive enzymes that function in the stomach and describe their functions. (pp. 542, 546)

5. List the four levels of organization (organ to cell) in the small intestine and explain how each con-tributes to the surface area and absorptive properties of the small intestine. (p. 543)

6. Describe the digestive roles of the liver, gall bladder, and pancreas. (pp. 543–544)

7. Briefly discuss the chemical breakdown of carbohydrates, fats, and proteins, listing the final products. In what way is the chemistry of digestion similar for all foods? (pp. 546–547)

8. Why are nutritional scientists changing their minds about unsaturated fats? What evidence supports this shift in emphasis? (Essay 37.1)

9. Specifically, why is it essential that a vegetarian diet include a carefully managed selection of vegetable protein? (pp. 549–550)

10. Summarize the roles of vitamins, minerals, and trace elements in human nutrition. (pp. 550–551)

Gas Exchange in Animals

38

Humans can go without food for weeks, and without water for days. But we can't go without air for more than a few minutes. The need for oxygen is a legacy humans share with all other animals and, for that matter, with most other eukaryotes. When we think of life on other planets, we usually imagine air-breathing creatures like ourselves; our space probes are even programmed to detect oxygen on other planets.

However, we must remember that evolution is opportunistic and life can exist under a variety of conditions. In fact, life probably could not have begun as it did had oxygen been present. But as oxygen became a permanent part of our atmosphere, life forms came to tolerate, utilize, and finally depend on this strange, corrosive gas (see Chapter 20). It's difficult to imagine complex, rational life forms existing under chemical conditions that differ from those on earth, because we have no experience with such systems. For us, the experience of breathing air devoid of oxygen might be very boring at best. But any space traveler visiting earth might well have to protect itself from our deadly gases. This chapter will consider how various animals take oxygen from the air so that it can be used in the metabolic machinery of life.

The process is usually called respiration, but since the term can also refer to cell respiration, it should be noted that the subject here is the physical processes by which gases pass into and out of the body (organismic respiration).

The exchange of gases is quite often a passive process, with oxygen and carbon dioxide simply following the diffusion gradients normally present in the animal. Since oxygen is constantly used in cell respiration, its concentration in the cells and tissues is lower than the concentration outside in the animal's surroundings. Similarly, since carbon dioxide is constantly formed in cell respiration, its concentration in cells and tissues is higher than that in the animal's surroundings. So the exchange of the two gases can be a simple process requiring little, if any, of the animal's energy—at least in simple animals (or any other simple organism). In fact, simple diffusion is important at some level in all organisms. However, as we have emphasized in earlier discussions (Chapters 27–29) larger and more complex animals have evolved specialized structures and specific mechanisms that help move gases into and out of their tissues.

GAS EXCHANGE: AN EVOLUTIONARY PERSPECTIVE

Any consideration of gas exchange must include not only how oxygen enters the animal body, but also how waste gases (such as CO_2) leave the body.

THE RESPIRATORY INTERFACE

If gas is to move into and out of a body, it must cross some boundary. That boundary can be called the **respiratory interface.** This interface—generally a living membrane—must be thin-walled, moist, and of sufficient area to accommodate the animal's physiological needs. A thin membrane, of course, is easier to cross than a thick one, and moistness is essential because gases normally must be dissolved in liquid in order to cross solid barriers easily.

How do animals meet these requirements? As you might expect, the answer varies for different kinds of animals. But three factors appear to be involved in determining the nature of the organism's interface: the size and complexity of the organism, its metabolic needs, and the nature of the surrounding environment (Figure 38.1). The problem of gas exchange cuts across all phylogenetic lines, so our discussion will review some points made in Chapters 27–29.

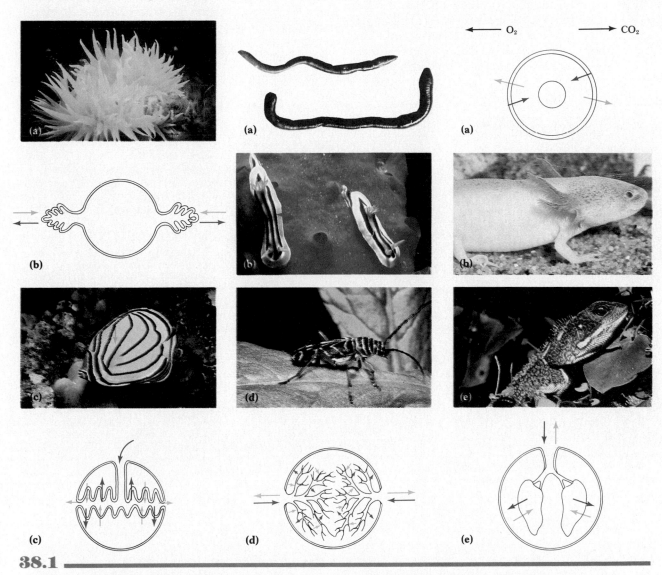

38.1

The precise method by which animals exchange oxygen and carbon dioxide depends upon a number of factors, including their environment and theiry body size and complexity. The simplest type of exchange is found in skin breathers **(a)**, in which thin-bodied aquatic animals like the anemone depend on simple diffusion across two cell layers. The more complex earthworm is also a skin breather, but it succeeds because it lives in a moist environment and has an efficient circulatory system that transports gases throughout its body.

Many aquatic invertebrates and a few aquatic vertebrates utilize the external gill **(b)** for gas exchange.

Included are the colorful nudibranch (a gastropod mollusk) and the "mud puppy," *Necturus*.

The gills of fishes **(c)** are internalized, although they are still essentially outpocketings of the body wall. The efficiency of such gills is increased by a one-way flow of water and a countercurrent blood flow.

Terrestrial insects also have internal respiratory systems. Their tracheae **(d)** branch into thin-walled tubes that penetrate every part of the insect's body.

In terrestrial vertebrates, the internalized lung **(e)** provides the respiratory exchange surface. The exchange is enhanced by efficient circulatory systems in which oxygen is carried primarily by hemoglobin.

Variations in the Vertebrate Interface

Skin breathing—in which gas is exchanged through the body surface itself—is satisfactory for many of the smaller and simpler animals. Skin breathers tend to be aquatic or semiaquatic animals, since their entire surfaces must be moist. Interestingly, some of the more complex, dense-bodied terrestrial animals, such as lungless salamanders (family Plethodontidae), utilize the skin as their major gas exchange surface. (The lungless salamanders also use their vascularized mouth cavity for gas exchange.) Even these animals, however, are restricted to moist, underground, or forest-litter environments; and even for these, desiccation means suffocation. Salamanders enhance this simple exchange with a complex, closed circulatory system that contains oxygen-carrying hemoglobin. Other skin breathers, such as frogs and most of the other salamanders, augment the skin as a respiratory surface with such other structures as lungs or gills.

Most complex aquatic animals require a greater exchange of gas than can be accommodated by the skin, and so they have developed ways to increase the respiratory interface. The most common is the development of gills. **Gills** are feathery, thin-walled extensions of the body wall that are rich in

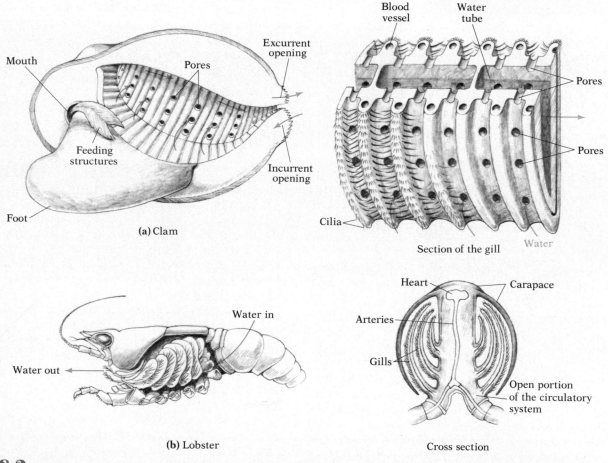

(a) Clam

Section of the gill

(b) Lobster

Cross section

38.2

In certain complex aquatic animals, water is actively passed across large gill structures that are associated with efficient circulatory systems. In the clam **(a)**, cilia constantly sweep water over the gills. Water is drawn in through an incurrent opening; passes over the gills, where gas exchange occurs; and exits through a separate excurrent opening. The feathery gills of the lobster **(b)** are covered by the carapace, a part of the hardened, protective exoskeleton. Rapid flutterings of specialized, paddlelike appendages below the head draw a continuous current of water across the gills from rear to front. The forward direction of water is important; excretory openings near the head release metabolic wastes that could cause problems if carried over the gills. Gas exchange is aided by blood vessels that penetrate each gill filament.

tiny blood vessels. Since the vessels passing through the gills have walls that are only one cell thick, the blood in these areas is very near the surrounding water. Thus, gases are easily exchanged. Gills of one kind or another are found in such animals as marine annelids, mollusks, arthropods, nearly all developing amphibians, and, of course, fishes (Figure 38.2).

Gills reach their greatest complexity in the fishes, where an efficient exchange is provided by a countercurrent flow of water and blood (see Chapter 29). The gills of bony fishes are protected within the gill chambers, which are covered by a tough flap, the *operculum*. Muscular movement of the gill chamber, together with the action of flaps and valves and the rhythmic opening and closing of the mouth area, ensure a one-way flow of water across the gill surfaces.

The Problem with Water.   Gas exchange in a watery environment doesn't present the threat of desiccation faced by terrestrial animals, which must expose a moist membrane to air. But depending on water as a source of oxygen has some serious drawbacks. For one thing, oxygen is not very soluble in water, so the concentration of the gas, even in highly oxygenated water, is rather low. This means that large, active aquatic animals must devote considerable time and energy to moving large volumes of water over their gills.

The solubility of oxygen is inversely proportional to temperature; so, in general, cold water contains more oxygen than warm water. But when even the coldest water is saturated with oxygen, the quantity is less than 1% by volume. This is a paltry amount compared to the oxygen content of air, which is 21% by volume. Furthermore, the diffusion rate of oxygen through water is vastly slower than that through air—300,000 times slower, in fact.

The much greater concentration of oxygen in air may help to explain why natural selection favored the retention of air-breathing in those aquatic vertebrates that returned to the sea. Penguins, whales, seals, and porpoises, for example, and even oceanic turtles and sea snakes, all come to the surface to breathe. As descendants of air-breathing land dwellers, they have undergone many aquatic adaptations, but rarely have these included a means of exchanging gases with the oxygen-poor water.

The Terrestrial Environment.   Most terrestrial vertebrates have solved the problem of keeping their respiratory membranes moist by bringing the respiratory interface inside the body, where it is sheltered from the drying air. In terrestrial vertebrates, the lungs provide the moist internal interface for the exchange of gases. The lungs of most land vertebrates are paired structures consisting of inflatable, highly vascularized, and somewhat spongy tissue (except for in amphibians, in which they are simply hollow sacs). A vast capillary network spreads throughout the lung tissue, and oxygen can either diffuse into the capillaries or, in some species, can be pumped across the membrane at some energy expense. The oxygen is transported from the capillaries of the lung throughout the body by joining temporarily with molecules of hemoglobin, which, in all vertebrates, is contained in red blood cells (*erythrocytes*).

Gas enters and exits the lung through a single, ventral, tubelike structure (the *trachea*) and its branches (the *bronchi*). Various kinds of animals bring air into contact with the lungs in different ways: in amphibians, by swallowing movements; in reptiles and birds, by contraction and expansion of the surrounding body wall; and in mammals, by body-wall movement and contractions of a muscular **diaphragm** (Figure 38.3).

THE HUMAN RESPIRATORY SYSTEM

The human respiratory system (Fig. 38.4) is typical of that of most mammals. Its major parts include the nasal passages and cavity and the larynx, trachea, bronchi, and lungs. Gases are exchanged primarily in the lungs.

Air first enters the system through the nasal passages or the mouth. Within the nasal cavity, it passes over a special nasal epithelium that filters, warms, and moistens it before it enters the lungs. The nasal epithelium has mucus-secreting **goblet cells** scattered among numerous ciliated cells (see Chapter 31). The mucus traps dust and other fine particles, and the ciliated cells sweep the dust-laden mucus toward the throat, where it is swallowed. Bacteria in this mucus are usually killed by harsh stomach acids.

The Larynx

Inhaled air passes through the nasal passages into the pharynx, and from there through the larynx into the trachea. The **larynx**, or *voice box*, contains the opening of the trachea. The vocal cords are

Respiratory movements in vertebrates **(a)** Frogs use a four-stroke system involving throat muscles to ventilate the lungs: (1) the nostrils are opened and the expanding mouth cavity fills with air; (2) the nostrils are closed and the contracting mouth cavity forces air into the lungs (a rare example of positive pressure being created to inflate the lungs); and (3) the nostrils are opened and a contracting mouth cavity expels the air to the outside. Frogs also breath through a simpler method of open-mouthed panting in which gases are exchanged in the mouth cavity only. **(b)** Breathing movemens in some reptiles are simpler. In crocodiles, for example, the body wall is expanded in inspiration, creating a negative pressure in the body cavity with atmospheric pressure forcing air into the lungs. In exhalation, the body wall relaxes creating a positive pressure that forces the air back out. **(c)** Breathing in mammals is similar in principle to that in reptiles, but the presence of the diaphragm permits breathing movements to be concentrated in the thoracic (chest) cavity. The negative, lung-filling pressure is created by drawing the diaphragm back (or down) and elevating the rib cage. The positive, lung-emptying pressure is produced as the diaphragm and rib muscles relax.

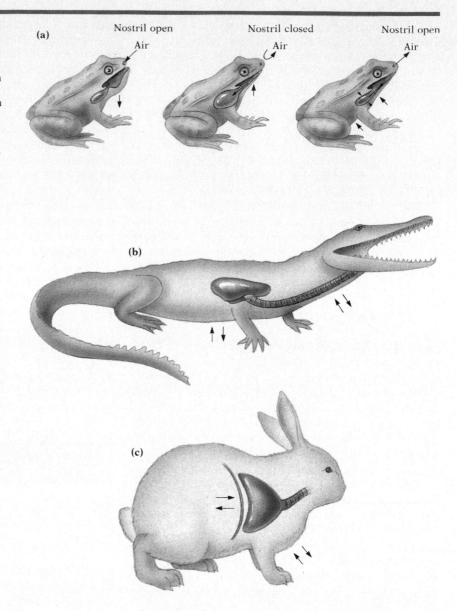

stretched over this opening to form a triangle that narrows to a slit as the cords are tightened (Figure 38.5). During swallowing the larynx is elevated, closing it against the epiglottis. At the same time the vocal cords come together, usually preventing anything from entering the respiratory system below (see Chapter 33).

The Trachea and Bronchial Tree

The **trachea** is essentially a tube that is reinforced by C-shaped rings of cartilage. At the point where the trachea enters the **thoracic cavity** (chest cavity),

it divides into right and left **primary bronchi.** The bronchi enter the lungs, where they branch and rebranch into **bronchioles.** These make up what is called the **bronchial tree** (because it resembles an upside-down tree). The trachea and larger passages of the respiratory tree are lined with an epithelium similar to that of the nasal passages, complete with mucus-secreting and ciliated cells. The moving cilia sweep the mucus film upward, carrying trapped dust particles or other such substances out of the trachea where they, too, are swallowed. In persistent smokers, the cilia may have become paralyzed by the smoke and the chemical toxins it contains, and the epithelium may have permanently degenerated, leaving the lungs vulnerable to a host of intruders. These intruders, of course, include cancer-causing chemicals (Figure 38.6).

The Alveolar Interface

The tiniest branches of the respiratory tree end in grapelike clusters of air sacs called **alveoli** (Figure 38.7). Alveoli are extremely thin-walled and are surrounded by tiny capillaries; here, the atmospheric air is separated from the bloodstream by only one thin layer of flattened epithelial cells. The numerous alveolar clusters provide an enormous total surface area. In fact, our lungs hold some 300 million alveoli, with a combined surface area of nearly 100 m^2 (over 1,000 ft^2)—about the area of a tennis court.

The Lungs and Breathing

Human lungs are roughly triangular, with a broad base. Each lung is enclosed by two layers of baglike membranes, the **pleurae.** The inner pleura is tightly attached to the spongy lung surface; the outer pleura encloses the thoracic (chest) cavity. Inflammation of these sacs produces a condition known as *pleurisy.*

At the base of the lungs is a muscular shelf, the *diaphragm,* that divides the abdominal and thoracic cavities. In its relaxed condition—during expiration—the diaphragm is dome-shaped. During inspiration, the diaphragm is contracted, resulting in lowering and flattening of its dome shape. In addition, the muscles between the ribs contract, causing the rib cage to rise and enlarge. These changes increase the volume of the thoracic cavity. The lungs, which are elastic but muscle-free (except for smooth muscle in some blood vessels), passively inflate. This is because a partial vacuum produced in the thoracic cavity permits the weight of the atmosphere to force air down into the lungs (Figure 38.8). The elastic lungs compress and deflate when the muscles relax and pressures are once again equalized.

Lung Capacity. When we are resting, about 0.5 L of air is moved in and out with each breath—only a small portion of the volume possible. However, when we fill our lungs to their greatest

38.4

The structure and function of the human respiratory system are similar to those of other terrestrial mammals. The air passages include the nostrils, the nasal cavity (and mouth), the pharynx, larynx, trachea, bronchi, and bronchioles. The bronchioles terminate in numerous alveoli, or blind air sacs. The spongy lungs are subdivided into lobes, with three in the right lung and two in the left lung. The muscular, shelflike diaphragm forms the lower body of the thoracic cavity, sealing this region off from the abdominal cavity below.

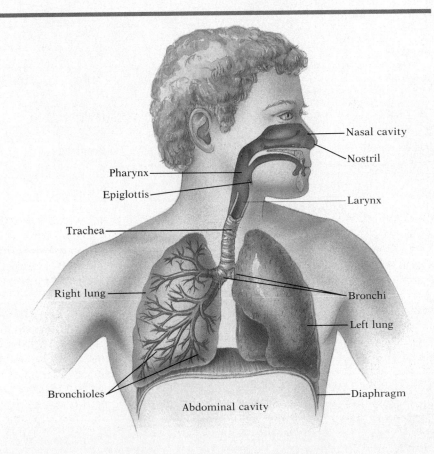

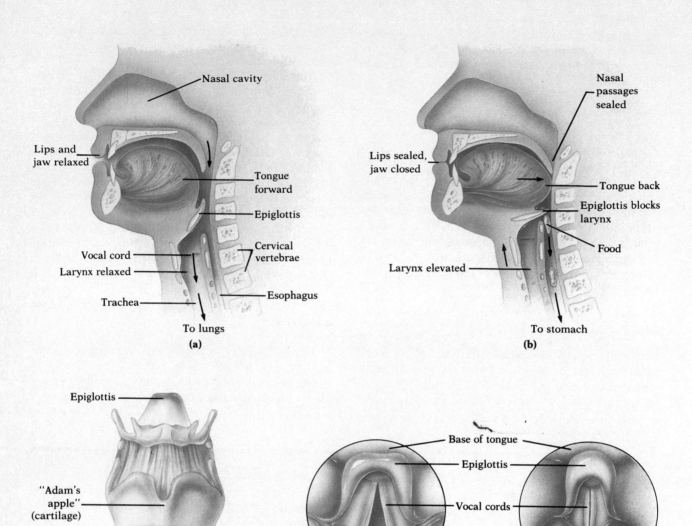

(a)

- Nasal cavity
- Lips and jaw relaxed
- Tongue forward
- Epiglottis
- Cervical vertebrae
- Vocal cord
- Larynx relaxed
- Esophagus
- Trachea
- To lungs

(b)

- Nasal passages sealed
- Lips sealed, jaw closed
- Tongue back
- Epiglottis blocks larynx
- Food
- Larynx elevated
- To stomach

(c) Larynx, frontal view

- Epiglottis
- "Adam's apple" (cartilage)
- Trachea
- Cartilage

(d) Larynx viewed from above

- Base of tongue
- Epiglottis
- Vocal cords
- Glottis
- Breathing
- Voice

38.5

A principal function of the larynx is to guard the entrance of the trachea, preventing foods from entering as they are swallowed **(a).** In swallowing, the larynx is elevated (you can check this with your fingers), and the epiglottis is folded over the respiratory openings, directing food into the esophagus **(b).** The larynx consists of cartilage and muscle. Toward the front is a bulging mass of cartilage, the so-called Adam's apple **(c).** In addition, the larynx houses the vocal cords. As we breathe, the vocal cords form a triangle; but as we speak, the cords tighten to form a slitted opening that varies in breadth to produce different pitches **(d)**

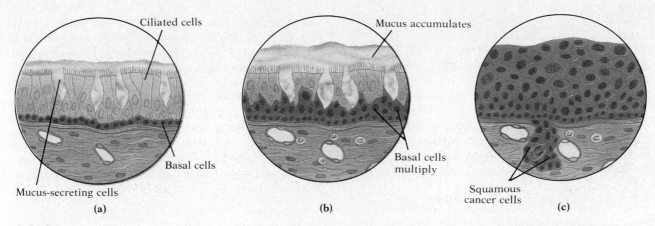

Ciliated cells

Basal cells

Mucus-secreting cells

(a)

Mucus accumulates

Basal cells
multiply

(b)

Squamous
cancer cells

(c)

38.6

The normal ciliated epithelium **(a)** of the respiratory passages includes both ciliated and mucus-secreting columnar cells. The cilia sweep the dust-trapping mucus out of the passages and toward the throat. In the smoker's respiratory lining **(b)**, the cilia become partially paralyzed, and mucus accumulates on the irritated lining. Where an early cancerous state exists, basal cells divide more rapidly and begin to displace normal columnar cells. As the cancer progresses **(c)**, most of the normal columnar cells are replaced by crowded, squamous cancer cells that form a spreading tumor. In advanced cases, clusters of cancer cells may be carried away in the lymphatic system, spreading to other parts of the body.

38.7

The bronchioles terminate in grape-like clusters of alveoli—blind, thin-walled sacs whose surfaces contain extensive capillary beds. Deoxygenated blood, heavily laden with carbon dioxide, enters through the *pulmonary arterioles* and passes through the capillary beds, allowing the waste gas to diffuse into the air-filled spaces of the alveoli. From here they are carried away by exhalation. Simultaneously, oxygen in the alveolar spaces enters the capillary stream, to be carried into the *pulmonary venules* and eventually out of the lungs to the body.

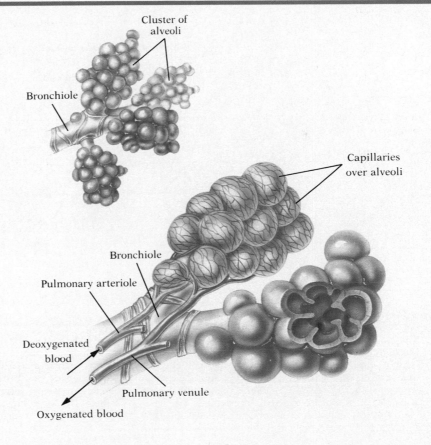

Cluster of
alveoli

Bronchiole

Capillaries
over alveoli

Bronchiole

Pulmonary arteriole

Deoxygenated
blood

Pulmonary venule

Oxygenated blood

extent, that volume (about 4 L) is called the **vital capacity.** (There is a lot of variability among individuals, and between male and female averages. The vital capacity of trained male athletes often exceeds 6 L.) No matter how hard you try, you can't force all the air out of your lungs. There is always about 1.5 L left. This is called the **residual volume.** This air ensures that some carbon dioxide is retained in our circulation with each breath, a factor that can be a matter of life and death.

The Exchange of Gases

The underlying mechanism of gas exchange in the body is diffusion. Several significant physiological mechanisms help this physical process along, but first let's see why diffusion works.

In diffusion, molecules move from regions of greater concentration to those of lesser concentration. There are two general areas in the body where major gradients of oxygen and carbon dioxide exist (Figure 38.9). One is in the body's active tissues, where oxygen is used in cell respiration and carbon dioxide is produced as a waste product. This activity establishes a gradient whereby blood passing through the capillaries of such tissues readily loses oxygen and picks up carbon dioxide. When this blood reaches the alveoli of the lungs, an opposite gradient is encountered. Air within the lung alveoli contains more oxygen and less carbon dioxide than the blood entering the surrounding capillary beds, so a second exchange occurs there.

Hemoglobin and Oxygen Transport.   The key to the efficiency of oxygen transport in vertebrates (and some invertebrates) is a complex protein called **hemoglobin,** which makes up most of the content of red blood cells. The total hemoglobin content is so great that, if it were not compressed in red cells, our blood would be too thick to circu-

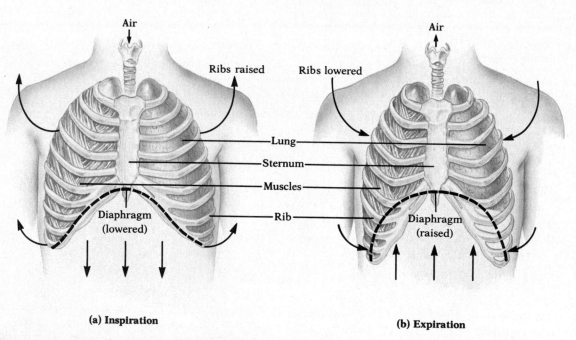

(a) **Inspiration**

(b) **Expiration**

38.8

The combined action of muscles in the rib cage and the diaphragm forces air into and out of the human lung. Inspiration **(a)** occurs when certain rib muscles contract, elevating the ribs and expanding the chest cavity, while the diaphragm contracts, pulling downward. Both actions decrease air pressure in the chest cavity to less than the atmospheric pressure outside. Consequently, air rushes into the respiratory passages and inflates the lungs, which fill the chest cavity. Expiration **(b)** occurs as the rib muscles and diaphragm relax, decreasing the volume of the chest cavity. This produces internal pressure that exceeds the atmospheric pressure, forcing air back out of the shrinking lungs. The lungs have no muscles of their own, but their elasticity assists in expiration.

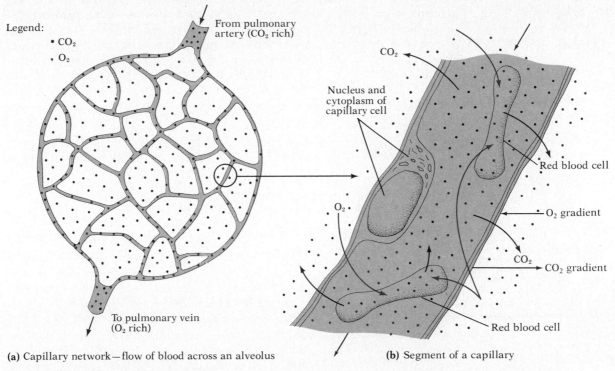

Legend:
- CO₂
- O₂

From pulmonary artery (CO₂ rich)

CO₂

Nucleus and cytoplasm of capillary cell

Red blood cell

O₂

O₂ gradient

CO₂

CO₂ gradient

To pulmonary vein (O₂ rich)

Red blood cell

(a) Capillary network—flow of blood across an alveolus

(b) Segment of a capillary

38.9

Diffusion gradients for oxygen and carbon dioxide in the alveoli and surrounding capillaries **(a)** permit the required exchanges of gases. The higher concentration of carbon dioxide is in the incoming blood, while the higher concentration of oxygen is in the alveolar air space. The reciprocal exchanges occur as blood passes through the capillary bed. In a closer view **(b)**, oxygen enters a capillary, to be taken up by hemoglobin-containing red blood cells. The moving stream of red cells ensures the continuous uptake of oxygen until saturation occurs. Carbon dioxide, in solution in the plasma, escapes across the capillary wall into the alveolar space.

late. Actually, oxygen could be carried in the fluid part of blood plasma without hemoglobin, but the maximum would be only about 0.3 ml of oxygen for each 100 ml of blood. Because of hemoglobin, the blood can carry about 20 ml of oxygen per 100 ml of blood—about 67 times as much!

What precisely is this magical molecule, and how does it work? Hemoglobin is a rather large protein, made of four polypeptide chains and four *heme* groups, each containing an iron atom to which an oxygen can attach (Figure 38.10). But the bonds are reversible. The four oxygen molecules are quickly released under the right conditions. The association and dissociation of O_2 and hemoglobin (Hb) can be written:

$$Hb \ + \ 4O_2 \longleftrightarrow Hb \cdot (4O_2)$$

Hemoglobin   Oxygen   Oxyhemoglobin

This simply means that one hemoglobin molecule plus four oxygen molecules yields one oxy-hemoglobin molecule, and the arrows show that the association is readily reversible. The hemoglobin molecule is able to pick up an entire load of four oxygen molecules in the lung and to release all four in the tissues, where they are needed, before it returns to the lungs for another load.

Carbon Dioxide Transport. Carbon dioxide transport is quite complex. To begin, carbon dioxide is readily soluble in water—in fact, it is some 30 times more soluble than oxygen. Therefore, some of the carbon dioxide picked up by the blood (about 8%) goes into solution in the blood plasma. The rest of the carbon dioxide (92%) enters red blood cells, where it is transported in two ways. Some forms a loose, reversible association with hemoglobin the way oxygen does. However, carbon dioxide does not join the heme groups like oxygen, but reacts with amino acids of the huge protein, forming what is called *carbaminohemoglobin*.

The remaining carbon dioxide entering the red cells reacts with water there to form carbonic acid

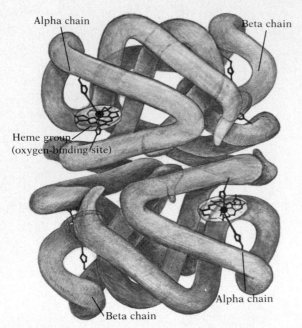

Alpha chain

Beta chain

Heme group (oxygen-binding site)

Alpha chain

Beta chain

38.10

Hemoglobin is a complex, heavyweight protein containing four polypeptides linked into one globular unit. Each hemoglobin macromolecule contains two alpha chains and two beta chains, and the four polypeptides each bear a *heme group*. (A heme group is a complex multiringed structure, containing an atom of iron at its center.) Each heme group is capable of accepting one oxygen molecule, forming *oxyhemoglobin* for transporting oxygen throughout the body. In humans and other vertebrates, vast numbers of hemoglobin molecules are bound to each red blood cell, and the oxygehemoglobin produced when oxygen saturation occurs gives blood its bright red color.

($H_2CO_3^-$). Carbonic acid, in turn, dissociates into hydrogen ions (H^+) and bicarbonate ions (HCO_3^-). This reaction can occur in plasma, but there it is very slow. Red cells, however, contain the enzyme *carbonic anhydrase*, which not only speeds up the formation of carbonic acid but operates reversibly, and can rapidly convert carbonic acid back into carbon dioxide and water. This is quite important, since carbon dioxide must be reformed quickly if it is to leave the body when the blood reaches the lungs.

When carbonic acid dissociates into hydrogen ions and bicarbonate ions in the red cells, the hydrogen ions are *buffered* (rendered neutral) by the protein hemoglobin itself. The bicarbonate ions diffuse out into the plasma, where they are joined by sodium ions, forming sodium bicarbonate ($NaHCO_3$). In addition to providing a means of transporting carbon dioxide, sodium bicarbonate in the blood forms an important part of the body's

buffering system—that is, it helps neutralize any acids or bases that might form, keeping the blood pH near neutral. (The sodium bicarbonate of the blood is identical to commercial baking soda. It is also the main buffering ingredient in many familiar stomach acid neutralizers.) The reactions, so far, are:

1) $CO_2 + Hb \longleftrightarrow$ Carbaminohemoglobin

$$\underset{\text{anhydrase}}{\overset{\text{Carbonic}}{}}$$

2) $CO_2 + H_2O \longleftrightarrow H_2CO_3 \longleftrightarrow H^+ + HCO_3^-$

3) $Na^+ + HCO_3^- \longleftrightarrow NaHCO_3$

As we have said, the reactions described are all reversible, and in each, it is the quantity of carbon dioxide present that dictates the direction—another example of the mass action law at work. So in the active tissues, where carbon dioxide levels are high, the direction of the reactions is toward carbaminohemoglobin and toward the formation of hydrogen and carbonate ions and sodium bicarbonate. But in the capillaries of the alveoli, any free carbon dioxide escapes from the blood, so its concentration decreases. Then in a speedy cascade of reversing chemical events: (1) The carbaminohemoglobin releases its carbon dioxide; (2) the bicarbonate of sodium bicarbonate in the plasma re-enters the red cells; (3) it joins hydrogen ions to form carbonic acid; and (4) with a boost from carbonic anhydrase it is converted back to carbon dioxide and water.

The Bohr Effect.   The **Bohr effect** is named for its discoverer, Christian Bohr, who found that the affinity of hemoglobin for oxygen is influenced by carbon dioxide levels. When CO_2 levels are high, hemoglobin releases oxygen more readily (Figure 38.11). This is an interesting biochemical adaptation. It means that oxygenated blood passing metabolically *inactive* cells does not tend to give up oxygen, even if oxygen levels in those cells are low. But in active cells, where CO_2 levels are high, oxygen is more readily released by hemoglobin. This, of course, corresponds to the oxygen demand in such tissues.

Respiratory Control Mechanisms

We can vary the rate and depth of our breathing, but only up to a point. If your little brother holds his breath to get his way, don't worry. He may begin to lose his rosy complexion, but the ruse

In the Bohr effect, hemoglobin surrenders its oxygen load more readily in the presence of increasing amounts of carbon dioxide. Actually, it is the increasing acidity or lowered pH value, brought about by the formation of carbonic acid as carbon dioxide goes into solution, that encourages the dissociation of oxygen from hemoglobin. In the organism **(a)**, this chemical behavior means that metabolically inactive cells will receive less oxygen than metabolically active ones, regardless of the oxygen gradient. From an adaptive point of view, this peculiar behavior of hemoglobin makes a lot of sense, since the oxygen need is much greater in the active cells. The Bohr effect is readily revealed when the rate of oxygen dissociation from hemoglobin versus carbon dioxide partial pressure is plotted on a graph **(b)**.

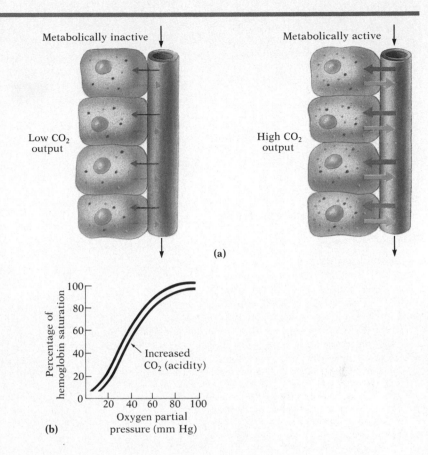

Metabolically inactive

Low CO_2 output

Metabolically active

High CO_2 output

(a)

Percentage of hemoglobin saturation

Increased CO_2 (acidity)

Oxygen partial pressure (mm Hg)

(b)

won't work. No matter how hard he tries, as the CO_2 level in his blood rises, his autonomic nervous system will take over and he will be forced to breathe. On the other hand, we can make ourselves *hyperventilate* by forced, rapid breathing. In this situation, fainting may occur and normal breathing will then be restored. (A word of caution: don't hyperventilate before diving, unless you really know what you're doing. Fainting under water will not restore normal breathing.) In such situations, the body is *not* responding to the levels of oxygen in the blood, but, rather, to the concentration of carbon dioxide.

Breathing movements are coordinated by a respiratory control center deep in the medulla (brainstem). This center is stimulated by impulses from various sensors located in the *aorta* (the large vessel that is the first to receive blood from the heart), the *carotid arteries* in the neck (which can also monitor changes in oxygen), and the *ventricles* (fluid-filled spaces) of the brain. The sensors in the aorta monitor CO_2 and H^+ concentrations in the blood, the carotid arteries do the same but are also able to detect some changes in oxygen level, and the ventricles of the brain monitor changes in the

pH of the cerebrospinal fluid (Figure 38.12). These sensors respond to any change and immediately fire off impulses to the respiratory control center. In addition to controlling breathing movements, these sensors control the total flow of blood to the brain. In response to higher carbon dioxide levels, which are normally associated with the depletion of oxygen, the arteries feeding the brain increase in diameter. When carbon dioxide levels are low, they return to their narrower state.

The brain's respiratory control center, as would be expected, can send impulses to muscles concerned with breathing. Any increase in CO_2—or in the acidity of the blood or that of the cerebrospinal fluid—increases the activity of the respiratory center of the brain. Impulses to the respiratory muscles cause an increase in the breathing rate and depth. Thus CO_2 is exhaled at a greater rate. The blood, then, is quickly restored to its optimal condition. On the other hand, decreases in CO_2 and acidity produce the opposite effect on the respiratory control center, and breathing slows. These mechanisms are quite delicate, and interact to keep the breathing rate constantly adjusted within narrow limits.

The primary respiratory control center is located in the medulla of the brain. Its mission is to continually receive neural input from carbon dioxide-measuring centers elsewhere, and to respond by altering the rate and depth of breathing. These centers, and the medulla, are tinted green in the drawing. Because of the respiratory center's action, the body's oxygen demands can be fulfilled under a variety of conditions, from rest to strenuous activity. The carbon dioxide-sensing centers are located in the ventricles of the brain, the carotid arteries, the aorta, and, to some extent, in the voluntary muscles.

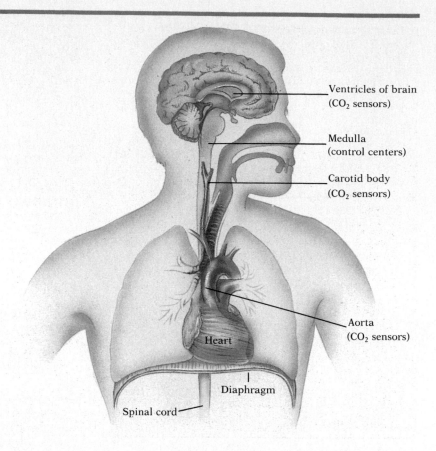

Ventricles of brain (CO_2 sensors)

Medulla (control centers)

Carotid body (CO_2 sensors)

Aorta (CO_2 sensors)

Heart

Diaphragm

Spinal cord

It should be apparent that it is difficult to consider any of the body's major systems alone. We have just witnessed a good example of the interdependence of the body's various systems: in discussing breathing, we had to consider the circulatory system as well as the nervous system. We discuss them separately for the sake of simplicity, but it is important to remember that the body is complex, and its various parts work together as a "harmonious objection to entropy"—another way of describing homeostasis.

Summary

Gas Exchange: An Evolutionary Perspective
The exchange of gases often is a passive process, based on diffusion. Smaller organisms can rely on diffusion to exchange gases, but larger animals have developed specialized organs to facilitate the process.

The Respiratory Interface
The respiratory interface is the boundary that gases must cross if they are to move into and out of the body. It is generally a thin-walled, moist living membrane of sufficient area to accommodate the organism's physiological needs.

Animals accomplish gas exchange in several ways. Smaller and simpler animals use skin breathing, while most larger animals use specialized organs such as gills and lungs. Gills are rich in blood vessels that are only one cell thick, allowing for an easy exchange of gases with water. In bony fishes, the countercurrent flow of water and blood provides for efficient gas exchange, while other marine animals must pump water through gill chambers. Because oxygen is not very soluble in water, some marine animals must come to the surface to get sufficient oxygen for their metabolic needs.

The respiratory membranes of most land animals are within the body, protected from drying air. In terrestrial vertebrates, lungs provide the moist interface. Lungs are paired structures of inflatable, highly vascularized, spongy tissue. Oxygen, which can diffuse into capillaries or be pumped across the membrane, joins temporarily with hemoglobin to be transported throughout the body.

The Human Respiratory System

The human respiratory system includes the nasal passages and cavity, larynx, trachea, bronchi, and lungs. Air enters through the nasal passages and is filtered, warmed, and moistened in the nasal cavity. It then passes through the pharynx and larynx to the trachea, which branches into the right and left primary bronchi. Bronchi, in turn, branch into bronchioles that form the bronchial tree, whose smallest branches end in alveoli. Their thin walls permit the exchange of gases between the blood and the air. The diaphragm, a muscular dome at the base of the lungs, contracts and expands to allow the lungs to inflate and deflate. The greatest extent to which the lungs can be filled is the vital capacity.

Diffusion gradients underlie the mechanism of gas exchange in the body. Blood passing through capillaries in active tissues loses oxygen and gains carbon dioxide. When this blood reaches the lungs, the gradient is reversed. Hemoglobin is the key to efficient oxygen transport and its affinity for the gas is influenced by levels of carbon dioxide in the blood—a phenomenon known as the Bohr effect.

Breathing movements are coordinated by a respiratory control center deep in the medulla. The aorta, carotid arteries, and ventricles of the brain have sensors that monitor carbon dioxide and hydrogen ion levels in the blood, detect changes in oxygen levels, and monitor pH level in the cerebrospinal fluid. Impulses from these vessels stimulate the respiratory control center to speed up or slow down breathing or to change the depth of breathing. Thus, the respiratory system works in close harmony with the circulatory and nervous systems.

Key Terms

respiratory interface	larynx	bronchial tree	hemoglobin
skin breathing	trachea	alveoli	buffering system
gills	thoracic cavity	pleurae	Bohr effect
diaphragm	primary bronchi	vital capacity	
goblet cell	bronchioles	residual volume	

Review Questions

1. Using specific examples, briefly describe four different ways in which animals provide surface area for gas exchange. (p. 555)

2. Explain how the gill organization in fishes permits a countercurrent exchange of carbon dioxide and oxygen. (pp. 556–557)

3. Describe the respiratory epithelium of the nasal cavity and major lung passages, and explain its two functions. (p. 557)

4. Describe the structure of the alveoli. What conditions there make it possible for gas exchange to occur through simple diffusion? (p. 559)

5. Explain the role of the diaphragm, rib muscles, and atmospheric pressure in inspiration. In what way, if any, are these factors involved in expiration? (p. 559)

6. Describe the role of hemoglobin in oxygen transport. In what way is oxygen dissociation related to carbon dioxide levels in tissues (the Bohr effect)? (pp. 562–564)

7. Carbon dioxide is carried by the blood in three ways: in simple solution, as carbaminohemoglobin, and as the bicarbonate ion. Elaborate upon each, using chemical formulas as necessary. How do the enzyme carbonic anhydrase and the law of mass action fit into this chemistry? (pp. 563–564)

8. What is the general role of the medulla in respiration? From what three places does it receive information? (p. 566)

Blood, Circulation, and Immunity

39

Even the crustiest and most jaded biologists may be fascinated by—and perhaps in awe of—something they have undoubtedly seen many times before: the formation of new life. The sight of a living chick embryo (one of the easier vertebrate embryos to watch) cannot help but touch something basic in each of us. Within two days of the onset of development, the minute heart begins to beat. In response, blood cells move through rough-hewn channels (Figure 39.1). This is the developing **circulatory system**. Such early developmental events are typical of vertebrates. In humans, for example, the heart begins to function at about three weeks after conception— even then, the embryo is only the length of the capital letter beginning this sentence.

Why does the circulatory system develop so early, and why is its presence so critical? The answers are found in its functions. First, the circulatory system transports oxygen, carbon dioxide, nutrients, water, ions, hormones, and metabolic wastes. The transport and distribution of these substances are vital to the animal at the beginnings of development and throughout its entire life. Furthermore, this system plays a vital role in supporting the *immune system*, helping to combat bacteria, viruses, and other invaders. We will return to the immune system later in this chapter, and to the development of the human heart in Chapter 41 (where we discuss the fetal circulatory system). Here, we will begin by discussing the structure and function of the adult human's circulatory system.

THE HUMAN CIRCULATORY SYSTEM

The human circulatory system is fairly typical of mammals in general. The system includes the four-chambered heart, the blood vessels—*arteries, arterioles, capillaries, venules,* and *veins*—and, of course, the blood. The system is no stranger to you, since we have discussed its evolutionary history and have often related its functions to those of other vertebrate systems (see Chapter 29). Here we will examine the circulatory system in much more detail, beginning with its vital center, the heart.

The Heart

The four-chambered **heart** is a remarkably efficient organ. Although anatomically it is only one structure, it can be said to function as two separate

of the body) and the **inferior vena cava** (from the lower part of the body). They empty into the right atrium, a thin-walled receiving chamber. When the right atrium contracts, it forces blood into the right ventricle, the thicker-walled chamber below. Contraction of the right ventricle forces blood into the **pulmonary artery,** which branches, carrying blood to both lungs. Freshly oxygenated blood is returned to the heart through the pulmonary veins, first entering the left atrium. (Note that whereas arteries usually carry oxygenated blood, and veins

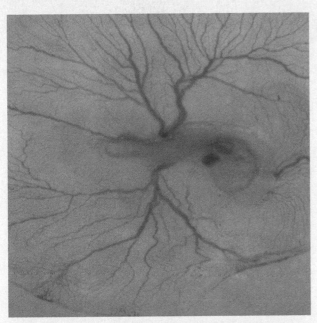

39.1

Although the three-day chick embryo bears little resemblance to what it will eventually become, one of its systems has already begun to function. Within the curve formed by the tiny growing body, the heart appears as a prominent bulge and sends blood cells crowding along tiny vessels in a spasmodic flow. The strong pulses are among the first and most dramatic signs of new life.

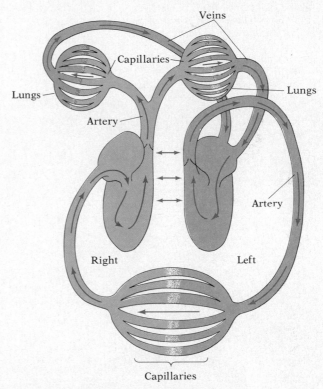

39.2

The four-chambered hearts of birds, mammals, and a few reptiles such as crocodiles are significantly different from those of the other vertebrates. If we emphasize the separation of right and left chambers, the four-chambered heart becomes two pumps in one. The divided heart permits one side to serve the lungs; and the other side, the rest of the body. The "right heart" at the left side of the figure receives deoxygenated blood from the body and pumps it through the lungs, where carbon dioxide is replaced by oxygen. The "left heart" receives the oxygenated blood from the lungs and pumps it to all parts of the body, where oxygen will be exchanged for carbon dioxide before the blood is returned to the "right heart."

pumps (Figure 39.2). The right side, comprising the **right atrium** and the **right ventricle,** receives *deoxygenated* blood by way of **veins** from the body and pumps it to the lungs, where it picks up oxygen and releases carbon dioxide. The *oxygenated* blood returns to the **left atrium,** from which it is pumped to the **left ventricle,** and then, via **arteries,** throughout the body. Thus the oxygenated and deoxygenated blood do not mix. (You may recall that this is not the case with the three-chambered heart of amphibians and reptiles.)

Structures of the Heart. The heart is an enormously powerful muscle (the left side being larger and more powerful than the right), in keeping with the requirements of its task. (This is why many people still believe the heart is located on the left side, and why people swear to all sorts of things with the right hand held over the left lung.) Tracing the flow of blood through this magnificent muscle (Figure 39.3), we begin with the deoxygenated blood returning to the heart from the body. This blood is delivered through two great *veins*, the **superior vena cava** (from the upper part

A cutaway diagram of the heart, illustrating its circulatory pathways. Blood enters the right and left atria almost simultaneously. The superior and inferior venae cavae bring in deoxygenated blood from the body, emptying into the right atrium. Oxygenated blood entering the left atrium comes from the pulmonary circuit via the pulmonary veins. Blood flows from the atria to the ventricles. The contraction of the ventricles sends blood from the right ventricle into the pulmonary arteries (to the lungs), and from the left ventricle into the aorta (to the head and body). Backflow into the right and left atria is prevented by the *tricuspid* and *bicuspid valves*. Blood entering the pulmonary artery and aorta is prevented from flowing back into the ventricles by the *pulmonary semilunar* and *aortic semilunar valves*, respectively (a). The pumping action is summarized in (b).

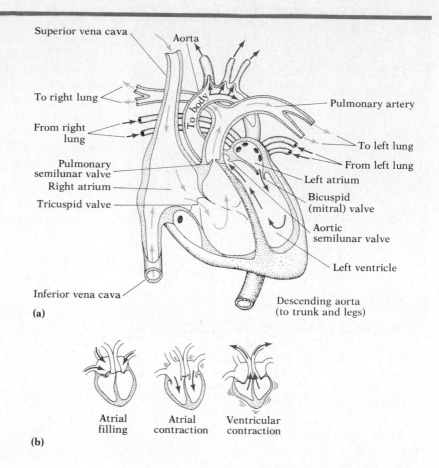

Superior vena cava
Aorta
To right lung
To body
Pulmonary artery
From right lung
To left lung
From left lung
Pulmonary semilunar valve
Left atrium
Right atrium
Bicuspid (mitral) valve
Tricuspid valve
Aortic semilunar valve
Left ventricle
Inferior vena cava
Descending aorta (to trunk and legs)

(a)

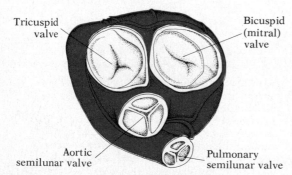

Atrial filling   Atrial contraction   Ventricular contraction

(b)

Tricuspid valve

Bicuspid (mitral) valve

Aortic semilunar valve

Pulmonary semilunar valve

The valves of the heart. The larger valves are between the atria and ventricles. The *bicuspid (mitral) valve* has two flaps of tissue, while the *tricuspid* has three. The valves are supported by the *chordae tendineae*, string-like cords that attach to papillary muscles projecting from the base of the ventricles. When the ventricles contract, these cords are tightened, holding the thin flaps in place as blood surges against them. The aortic and pulmonary semilunar valves have simple but heavy three-part flaps.

usually carry deoxygenated blood, in this case the situation is reversed.)

Incoming oxygenated blood passes from the left atrium to the left ventricle, the extremely thick-walled chamber that must force blood through most of the body. When the left ventricle contracts, blood is forced into the **aorta,** the largest artery in the body.

The Heart Valves.   As the atria and ventricles contract, blood is prevented from flowing backward by four one-way valves (Figure 39.4). The **tricuspid valve** lies between the right atrium and right ventricle, while its counterpart, the **bicuspid valve,** is between the left atrium and left ventricle. The "cusps" are extremely strong, thin-walled membranes that balloon out (like parachutes) and come together as blood in the ventricle starts to back up. Under pressure, the membranes are held in position by tough, tendonous cords *(chordae tendineae)*.

The two other valves, the **pulmonary semilunar valve** and the **aortic semilunar valve,** lie at the base of the pulmonary artery and the aorta, respectively. These valves each consist of three small pockets attached to the inside artery wall. They prevent the backflow of blood from the arteries into the ventricles.

The valves have a great deal to do with the familiar "lub-dup" heart sounds. The first—the "lub"—is produced primarily by the snapping shut of the tricuspid and bicuspid valves as they respond to the two contracting ventricles. The second sound—the "dup"—is the closing of the semilunar valves, which tells us when blood has filled the pulmonary artery and the aorta.

Control of the Heart

The heart is remarkable for its endurance, rhythm, and versatility. It is obviously a tightly regulated organ. It is regulated in two ways: one is intrinsic, coming from within the heart; the other is extrinsic, from without (via hormones and neural impulses).

Intrinsic Control.   We explained earlier (see Chapter 31) that cardiac muscle is intrinsically *contractile;* that is, it contracts without external influences. Even if all nerves serving the heart are severed, for a time it will go on beating quite rhythmically at 70–80 beats per minute.

The **intrinsic heart rhythm** is basically controlled by a specialized group of cells in the right atrium. This control center is technically known as the **sinoatrial (SA) node,** but it is usually called the **pacemaker** (Figure 39.5). The pacemaker generates

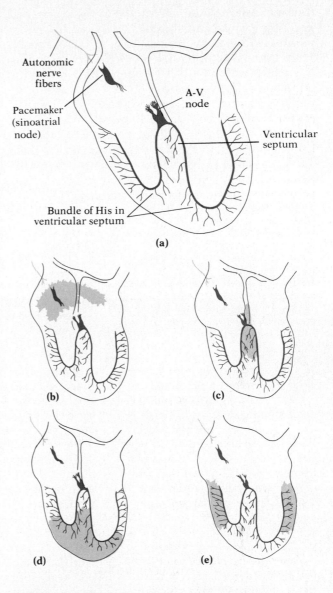

(a)

(b)   (c)

(d)   (e)

39.5

The contraction cycles of the heart originate in the sinoatrial (SA) node, more familiarly known as the *pacemaker* **(a).** Impulses generated in the SA node spread across the atria, causing the atria to contract **(b).** The same impulse reaches a second nodal area known as the *atrioventricular (AV) node.* From this region, the impulse is regenerated and spreads down the *ventricular septum* **(c).** The impulse spreading over the ventricular surfaces initiates the contraction of the ventricles, first at the tip **(d)** and then moving rhythmically upward **(e).** The arrangement of the muscle fibers causes a squeezing and wringing action in the ventricles.

repeated action potentials similar to those of neural impulses. These are transmitted to both atria, which respond by contracting simultaneously. Then the action potential reaches a second node, the **atrioventricular (AV) node,** which relays the impulse to the ventricles. They, too, contract simultaneously. Should the pacemaker fail, the heart rhythm will go awry. In such cases, it may be necessary to install an artificial pacemaker, an electronic device about the size of a pocket watch. Such surgery is now fairly routine (and also rather expensive). Essay 39.1 describes our progress, thus far, in developing a completely artificial heart. (In fact, we hope this information is out of date by the time you read this.)

Extrinsic Control.   While the heart can pump blood without outside influence, it must respond to varying oxygen needs and changing blood pressure in the organs it serves. Input from the nervous system, specifically from its autonomic division, permits the necessary adjustments to be made (see Chapter 34).

You may recall that the heart is innervated by two groups of nerves from the autonomic system—one sympathetic, the other parasympathetic. The parasympathetic nerves slow the heart rate by releasing the neurotransmitter *acetylcholine* into the pacemaker and the cardiac muscle. On the other hand, the sympathetic nerves accelerate the heart rate by releasing the neurotransmitter

ESSAY 39.1
THE ARTIFICIAL HEART

If you are in your 20s, there is an excellent chance that you will have available to you, in your 30s or 40s, a completely artificial heart. We sincerely hope you won't need one, since it's difficult to improve upon the natural model that was part of your original equipment. But if it turns out that you are among the 50,000 people each year who would benefit from such a device, this will all be good news.

Since the development of the first heart-lung machine in the 1930s, there has been a continuing effort to develop a model small enough to fit into the space now filled by the natural heart. To be useful, the artificial heart must also fulfil several other requirements. It must, of course, be relatively maintenance-free and as safe from failure as possible. The selection of materials lining the internal surface of such a device is of vital importance, since many materials tend to stimulate blood-clotting mechanisms. Finally, the artificial heart must be made to adjust its pumping volume to the needs of the body. Ideally, it would contain a computer (microsize) that received input from sensors roughly duplicating those of the body.

From this input, the computer's program would determine the heart response necessary to meet the constantly varying needs of the brain, muscles, skin, digestive system, and reproductive system.

The latest in several generations of artificial heart models comes close to meeting several of these prerequisites. The Jarvik-7 heart (developed by Robert Jarvik, an M.D. and bioengineer at the University of Utah) utilizes a design remarkably similar to that of a natural heart. It contains two ventricle-like pumping chambers, complete with one-way valves. In December of 1982, a Jarvik-7 heart was implanted in 61-year-old Barney B. Clark at the University of Utah Medical Center. The heart was operated by a compressed-air power system, which was connected to the device by tubes emerging from Mr. Clark's abdomen. The world watched attentively as the heart, with only one, quickly repaired mechanical lapse, kept Mr. Clark alive for over three months. (Mr. Clark's death resulted from conditions unrelated to the artificial heart.) Another member of the Utah team has developed a rechargeable battery pack to power the Jarvik-7; the pack is

worn outside the body and is connected to wires that penetrate the chest. A microcomputer is also worn externally.

The Jarvik-7, with a blood-pumping capacity of 45 l per minute, has already proven its potential. More human implants are expected. Also, when experimentally tested in calves, the Jarvik-7 performed well for seven months, and one calf, apparently in good health, put on 50 pounds over the period. There is little reason to believe that the artificial heart, implanted in a human being in reasonably good health, could not perform admirably for even longer periods, and the development of a portable power source means that the recipient would not be confined to a hospital. ●

norepinephine. The release of this **extrinsic neurotransmitter** must be coordinated very precisely to control the heart's response to the body's changing demands. *Epinephrine,* released by the adrenal medulla and carried by the bloodstream, can also elevate the heart rate (see Chapter 35).

The Peripheral Circulation

With the contraction of the ventricles, the blood begins its journey through the body. Now we will see how the circulatory system actually operates, and what goes on in the capillary beds.

The Arteries and Blood Pressure. The arteries, as mentioned earlier, carry blood away from the heart. They are not simple conduits, however; one of their major functions is to maintain blood pressure. The great vessel that receives blood from the left ventricle, the aorta, receives the full impact of the heart's powerful surges. The sudden swell of blood during **systole** (heart contraction) expands the elastic walls of the aorta. As the blood moves from the last contraction of the ventricle onward, the elastic walls of the expanded aorta contract automatically. Therefore, during **diastole** (between contractions, when the ventricle is filling), blood pressure remains high because of the force of the contracting aorta on the remaining blood in the vessel. However, there is some drop in pressure as the ventricles fill. This is called the **diastolic pressure.** A typical **systolic pressure** is 120 mm Hg; a typical diastolic value, 80 mm Hg. The blood pressure in this case would be "120 over 80" (Figure 39.6). (Millimeters of mercury—*mm Hg*—is a standard way of expressing pressure.)

Circulation. As the aorta leaves the heart, it gives rise at once to its first branches, the **coronary arteries,** which go directly to the heart muscle, providing it with nutrients and oxygen. The aorta then curves to the left and forms the *aortic arch*, from which additional arteries arise, their branches extending into the head and arms. From the arch, the aorta proceeds downward, sending branches into viscera, trunk muscles, and the vertebral column. It then divides, in the lower abdomen, to form the major arteries of the legs (Figure 39.7).

The arteries eventually form **arterioles** (small arteries), which branch once again to form **capillaries.** Many arterioles contain smooth muscle sphincters that regulate the flow of blood into the capillary beds (Figure 39.8). The sphincters respond to the autonomic nervous system and to certain hormones. (The role of the arteriolar sphincters of the skin in thermoregulation was discussed in Chapter 36.)

The capillaries are fascinating structures. Some are so small that blood cells must squeeze through them in single file. While the blood is in those

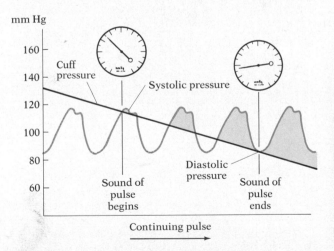

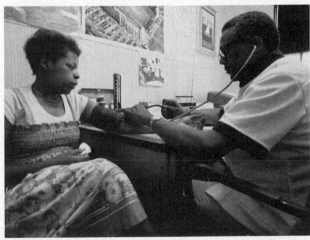

39.6

The sphygmomanometer consists of an inflatable pressure cuff and a pressure gauge or mercury column. The cuff is wrapped around the upper arm and inflated until its pressure exceeds the pressure in the *brachial artery*. As the air in the cuff is gradually released, the first pulse sounds can be detected through a stethoscope. This is the sound of surging blood, which begins as the cuff pressure reaches the highest pressure in the artery. The pressure gauge (or mercury column) at this point will give the systolic pressure in mm Hg. With the continued release of air, the sounds become louder, but then disappear. At this instant the gauge will reveal the diastolic pressure, a point at which the blood surge can no longer be detected.

The largest artery in the body is the aorta, which emerges from the left ventricle, curves to the left, and gives rise to arteries leading to the head and arms. Further down the aorta, paired branches lead to the kidneys, forming the *renal circuit*. The *pulmonary circuit*, originating in the right ventricle, branches into capillary beds in the lungs and pulmonary veins returning to the left atrium. The venous system returns blood to the heart, with veins from the legs merging to form the inferior vena cava in the trunk. As it ascends, the inferior vena cava receives veins from the kidneys and the liver (the *hepatic portal circuit*), along with veins returning from tissues in the trunk, eventually emptying into the right atrium. It is joined there by the superior vena cava, which carries blood from the head and arms.

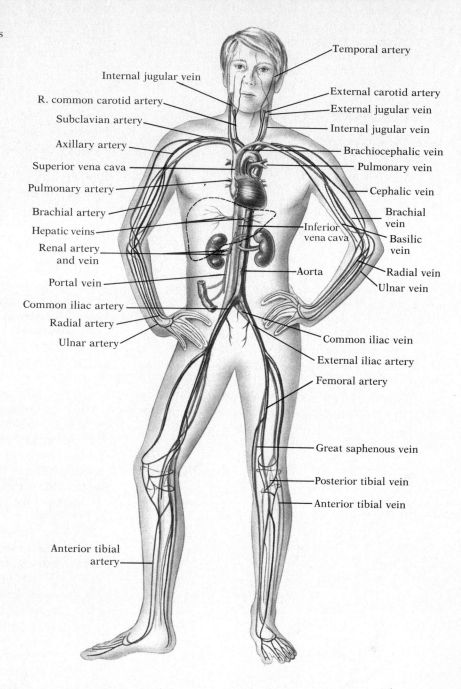

Internal jugular vein
R. common carotid artery
Subclavian artery
Axillary artery
Superior vena cava
Pulmonary artery
Brachial artery
Hepatic veins
Renal artery and vein
Portal vein
Common iliac artery
Radial artery
Ulnar artery

Temporal artery
External carotid artery
External jugular vein
Internal jugular vein
Brachiocephalic vein
Pulmonary vein
Cephalic vein
Brachial vein
Basilic vein
Inferior vena cava
Radial vein
Aorta
Ulnar vein
Common iliac vein
External iliac artery
Femoral artery
Great saphenous vein
Posterior tibial vein
Anterior tibial vein

Anterior tibial artery

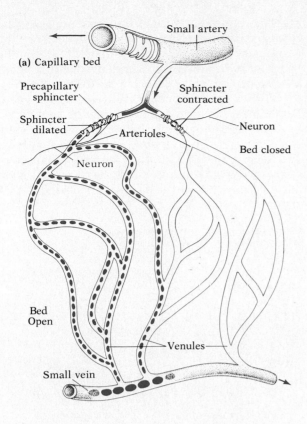

(a) Capillary bed

Small artery

Precapillary sphincter

Sphincter contracted

Sphincter dilated

Neuron

Arterioles

Neuron

Bed closed

Bed Open

Venules

Small vein

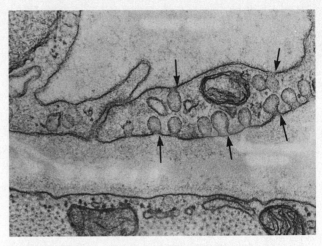

39.9

Capillaries are more than simple, passive tubes. While such substances as water and gases readily diffuse across capillary cells, others must be actively transported. Note the numerous pinocytic vesicles in the cytoplasm of the cells forming the capillaries *(arrows)*. These form around substances to be moved across the capillary walls, drift across the cell, and pump the substances across the membrane on the other side.

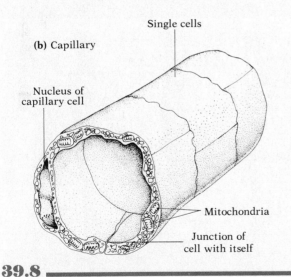

(b) Capillary

Single cells

Nucleus of capillary cell

Mitochondria

Junction of cell with itself

39.8

Capillaries usually occur in highly branched beds **(a)**, and arise from arterioles. They pass through tissue layers and among individual cells. A capillary bed may receive a continuous flow of arterial blood, or the blood may be shunted away to other capillary beds by smooth-muscle sphincters in response to signals from the autonomic nervous system. Unlike larger vessels, capillaries **(b)** are thin walled, consisting of a single layer of cells. Some substances move readily through the capillary walls, while others must be actively transported into and out of the blood.

vessels, it carries out some remarkable and essential tasks. There are so many vessels in a capillary bed that virtually no cell is far from these tiny rivers of life. This is critical, since the cells must draw sustenance from the vessels and deposit metabolic wastes into them.

The capillary wall is formed by a single layer of interlocking cells (see Figure 39.8b). It is so thin that some substances can cross by simple diffusion. The movement of other substances may be encouraged by the high hydrostatic pressure (see Chapter 5) that forces smaller molecules across the thin walls. In addition, some movement is due to active transport in the form of pinocytosis. In this process, fluids and suspended materials are drawn into a pocket formed by the membrane of a capillary cell. The pocket then breaks off, forming a vesicle that is transported across the cytoplasm, and the materials are squeezed out on the opposite side (Figure 39.9).

Veins and the Return to the Heart.   Once the blood has nourished the various tissues of the body and carried away their wastes, it begins its return to the heart. Immediately upon leaving the capillary bed, the blood enters the tiny **venules,** which merge to form the veins. Veins have thinner walls than arteries, but contain the same types of tissues (Figure 39.10).

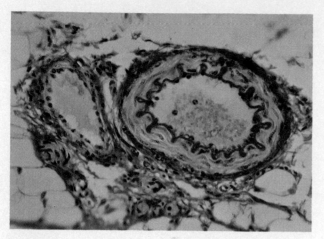

39.10

Both arteries and veins are composed of three layers of tissue, including a smooth inner endothelium, a middle layer of circular smooth muscle and elastic fibers, and an outer layer of collagenous fibers. Arteries and veins differ mainly in the second and third tissue layers. Arteries are generally thicker-walled and muscular, with many more elastic fibers.

Blood has reached the capillary beds under great pressure, forced along by the heart and squeezed by arterial muscles. But in its passage through those profuse and constricting beds, its pressure has been dissipated, and it enters the venules sluggishly. Blood entering the veins moves slowly and must rely on a number of ways to return to the heart. For example, many veins have one-way flap valves that allow the blood to move in only one direction—toward the heart (Figure 39.11). Also, veins in or near skeletal muscles are squeezed when the muscles contract, pushing the blood along, and during breathing, changing pressure in the thoracic cavity helps blood move through the veins there.

Circuits of the Circulatory System

A **circuit,** loosely defined, is an area of the body where some special exchange usually occurs. The **pulmonary circuit** (involving the lungs), where carbon dioxide is exchanged for oxygen, is one such area (see Chapter 38); the *hepatic portal circuit* (involving the liver) is another. In it, blood passing through capillaries in the digestive tract takes up digested food and carries it to the liver (see Chapter 37). The *renal circuit* (involving the kidneys) helps to maintain fluid and ion balances in the blood by excreting excess water and ions (see Chapter 36). The **cardiac circuit** includes the coronary arte-

ries and veins that supply the heart muscle. The coronary arteries receive blood directly from the aorta, just above the point where it leaves the heart, so heart muscle is assured of freshly oxygenated blood. Obviously, such a hard-working muscle needs a good supply of nutrients and oxygen. Sometimes, however, a vessel may be constricted or blocked, killing the tissue it serves and producing cardiac arrest (a "heart attack") (Essay 39.2). The severity of a heart attack and the chances of recovery depend on how much heart muscle actually dies and on how the damage affects the heart's rhythm.

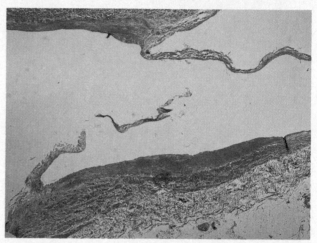

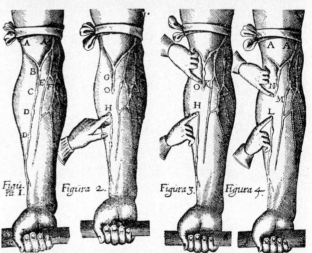

39.11

Veins in the arms and legs have one-way, flaplike valves that help direct the flow of venous blood to the heart **(a).** The valves are important because of the greatly reduced blood pressure in the venous system. William Harvey first demonstrated the valves' presence in the 17th century. (Four of his illustrations **(b)** are shown here.)

THE BLOOD

As we've seen, the blood performs many vital and varied functions. Its volume is substantial, about 5–6 liters in adult males and 4–5 liters in adult females; on the average, blood makes up about 7.7 percent of a person's total body weight. The blood volume includes a generous safety factor, since any healthy adult can lose—or donate—about 1/10 of the total volume (roughly a pint) without ill effects. What is this critical fluid?

The Components of Blood

Structurally, the blood can be divided into two parts, the straw-colored **plasma** (about 55% by volume) and the *formed elements* (about 45%). Formed elements include the *erythrocytes* (red cells), *leukocytes* (white cells), and *platelets* (noncellular bodies important in blood clotting).

Plasma. Blood plasma is about 90% water; most of the remainder is made up of three proteins, *albumin*, *globulin*, and *fibrinogen*. Albumins are important in maintaining osmotic conditions in the blood; globulins function as part of the immune defenses; and fibrinogen operates in blood clotting. Less than 2% of the plasma includes transient ions, hormones, vitamins, and various nutrients, particularly sugars.

Red cells. Erythrocytes (*erythro*, red; *cyte*, cell) are among the smallest and most specialized of our cells. They are only about 8 μm in diameter, and in most mammals take the form of a concave disc (Figure 39.12). Mature erythrocytes lack nuclei, mitochondria, and ribosomes, and function essentially as little bags of *hemoglobin* (see Chapter 38).

Normally there are about 5 million red cells per mm^3 (cubic millimeter) of human blood. Each cell lives about four months, after which it is destroyed in the liver or spleen. So the erythrocytes must be constantly replaced. In adults, new red cells are produced by *stem cells* in the red bone marrow. Their rate of production is controlled by a kidney hormone known as *erythropoietin*, which is released into the blood when cells in the kidney detect a drop in blood oxygen levels—a function of the number of red cells. As the red cell number increases, the stimulus is removed and erythropoietin secretion diminishes (a typical negative feedback mechanism).

ESSAY 39.2
WHEN THE HEART FAILS

At the time the Declaration of Independence was signed, the most common cause of death in this new country was, ostensibly, indigestion. Either the quality of our food has improved since then or, more likely, the problem was misdiagnosis. What the founding fathers and mothers were really suffering from were heart attacks (or heart failure).

What *is* a heart attack? In most instances, the problem is caused by an insufficient blood supply to the heart muscle. The heart attack was once referred to as *coronary thrombosis* ("blood clot in a coronary vessel"). A coronary artery may indeed be blocked by a moving blood clot, but the blockage is more likely to be due to *coronary arteriosclerosis*, a hardening and narrowing of the vessel. A specific form of this condition, *atherosclerosis*, occurs when *plaque* coats the inside of arteries, reducing the inside diameter and restricting blood flow. Plaque is a flaky, crumbly substance that frequently breaks away from artery walls to be carried through the bloodstream, increasing the risk of a blockage. It may break away only partially, forming a flap that blocks blood flow. A blockage near the aorta is particularly dangerous, and most deaths from heart attacks result from such incidents. Blockages farther along in the coronary arteries affect less tissue.

However a vessel is blocked, the muscle deprived of blood soon dies. The death of heart tissue is called *myocardial infarction*. Tissue death is significant because it disrupts the heart rhythm. Impulse conduction and contraction of the heart muscle are precisely coordinated, so a loss of conduction in one area affects the coordinated contraction of the entire heart.

Today, blocked coronary vessels can be routinely repaired in what is known as *coronary bypass surgery*. In this procedure, the damaged artery is removed and replaced by a corresponding length of vein, usually taken from the leg. Double and triple bypass procedures are becoming common, and the prognosis for many heart attack victims is now a long and healthy life. ●

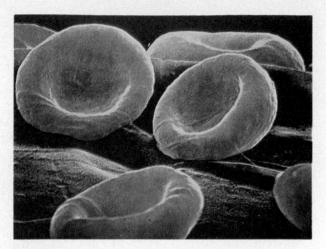

39.12

Red blood cells (erythrocytes) are biconcave discs only 8 μm in diameter. The average adult has about 5 l of blood; at 5 million cells per mm³, that totals some 25 billion red cells (over six times the world's human population).

Platelets and Blood Clotting. Platelets are actually fragments of certain white cells that contain enzymes and other agents that act in blood clotting. The clotting process is quite complex and not completely understood, but there are about 15 participants, some of which act as fail-safe mechanisms to prevent accidental clotting.

When an injury occurs, platelets gather at the wound site, form lengthy extensions, and adhere to collagen fibers, essentially forming a plug. In addition, platelets release *vasoconstrictors*, chemicals that stimulate smooth muscle in nearby blood vessels to contract, slowing the leakage of blood into the wound area. Most significantly, platelets at wound sites release *thromboplastin*, an enzyme that starts a cascading series of reactions that result in the actual clotting events. The final clot contains lengthy fibers of the protein *fibrin* (derived from fibrinogen), which forms a woven pattern in the wound.

THE IMMUNE SYSTEM

The **immune system** operates in close association with the circulatory system. First, it uses the circulatory system as its primary avenue of movement; second, the **leukocytes** (white blood cells) are often the agents that are activated in immune responses.

Our leukocytes are extremely varied and complex. They are produced in the bone marrow from the same undifferentiated stem cells that form the

red blood cells. Unlike the red blood cells, the white cells retain their nuclei and mitochondria. In the blood-forming tissues and certain other organs, some kinds of white blood cells can even divide and produce daughter cells identical to themselves. White blood cells vary in diameter from 9 μm—only slightly larger than an erythrocyte—to 15 μm or more, about the size of most other cells of the body (Figure 39.13).

Under normal conditions there is about one white blood cell for every 700 red blood cells (or about 5000–9000 leukocytes per mm³ of blood).

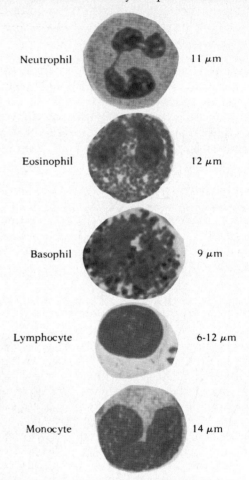

Neutrophil	11 μm
Eosinophil	12 μm
Basophil	9 μm
Lymphocyte	6-12 μm
Monocyte	14 μm

39.13

The white blood cells (leukocytes) are far less numerous than red cells, about 5000–9000 per cubic millimeter in the adult. There are five known types. *Neutrophils* and *monocytes* are phagocytic, engulfing foreign matter, bacteria, and cellular debris from cells destroyed by infection. *Lymphocytes* are undifferentiated; they can differentiate into other white cells and even into red cells, and under certain conditions they can produce antibodies. *Eosinophils* increase in number in the presence of foreign proteins, but no one knows why. *Basophils* are known to secrete serotonin, histamine, and heparin (an anticoagulant). Neutrophils and lymphocytes make up about 95% of the white cells.

Low white cell counts (below 5000 per mm³) indicate damage to elements in the bone marrow that form the white cells. High counts (above 10,000 per mm³) are a sign of infection, or of a more serious condition such as leukemia (in which the count may increase to well over 100,000).

The Work of Leukocytes

All white blood cells are *amoeboid*—that is, they can crawl around amoebalike, the trait that enables them to pass through the walls of capillaries and out into other tissues. They tend to move toward the source of certain hormones, such as those released in response to an infection (Figure 39.14). When not responding to such a call to action, the leukocytes seem to prowl the body randomly, or simply flow with the blood.

Leukocytes function in a number of ways. The **macrophages** that develop from larger white cells known as *monocytes* (see Figure 39.13), for instance, act as scavengers—they engulf, or *phagocytize*, dead cells, worn-out connective tissue matrix, degenerating erythrocytes, and cellular debris. They also attack invading bacteria and viruses.

Killer Cells: A Special Kind of Leukocyte. There is a very peculiar kind of leukocyte called the **natural killer cell.** These cells display a remarkable behavior as they roam the body: they approach other cells, briefly touching them, and then usually move on (rather like security police frisking everyone at a rock concert). Normal cells are allowed to continue unmolested. But should natural killer cells encounter cancerous cells, they immediately attack and destroy them. These killer cells are equally intolerant of virus-infected cells.

Another equally fascinating type of white blood cell is called the **cytotoxic killer cell.** Like the natural killer cell, it does not tolerate the deviance of cancerous or infected cells, and kills them. However, this killer cell differs from the natural killer cell in that it must "learn" which cells to kill. It receives its instructions during the creation of new *antibodies.*

Antibodies: The Body's Silent Weaponry

Antibodies, globular proteins found in the bloodstream, are among the body's most effective lines of defense. They are produced in response to the presence of an **antigen** (foreign substance) such as bacterial or viral surface proteins. Once produced, they respond specifically to that antigen each time it appears. Antibodies will remain in the blood for a long time, continuing to confer immunity against their specific antigen.

39.14

Some leukocytes roam the bloodstream and tissues of the body, attacking invading bacteria. Here, streptococci (spherical bacteria, occurring in rows) are being engulfed by a monocyte, the large amoeboid leukocyte.

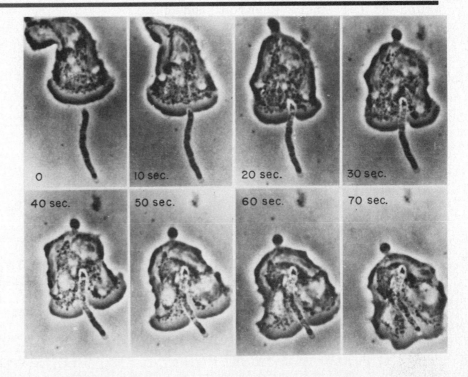

Antibodies are formed by several types of cells, including certain white blood cells called **lymphocytes** (see Figure 39.13). The most familiar types of antibodies are called **immunoglobulins,** each molecule of which consists of four polypeptide chains—two identical *light chains* and two identical *heavy chains.* The four chains, bound together by disulfide (S-S) linkages, form a generalized body "stalk." The stalk is identical within related groups of animals.

In many immunoglobulins, the stalk separates at one end, forming a "Y." It is at the ends of the separated areas that each immunoglobulin becomes distinct, taking on its own specific pattern that renders it effective against only one kind of antigen. These varying parts of the molecule are called *antigen recognition regions* (Figure 39.15a). The configurations of these regions determine the particular antigen to which the molecule can bind. Once formed, some immunoglobulins are released into the blood plasma, while others remain em-bedded in the surface of the lymphocytes that produced them. When an antibody encounters its antigen, it binds to it; the complex then joins others, forming an unwieldy clump (Figure 39.15b). The resulting large, immobile mass is then easily phagocytized by macrophages.

Identifying the Enemy. Now let's return to the macrophage, just after it has engulfed and ingested some foreign cell or virus. Digestion is only partially completed, and some of the invader's molecules form antigenic complexes in the cell membranes. Thus, the macrophage becomes what is called an *antigen-presenting cell.*

The macrophage, with its antigen, then begins to move about tirelessly through the body, touching surfaces with any lymphocyte it encounters. Thus, the foreign substances imbedded in its membrane are presented to countless numbers of these small white blood cells. Usually there is no re-

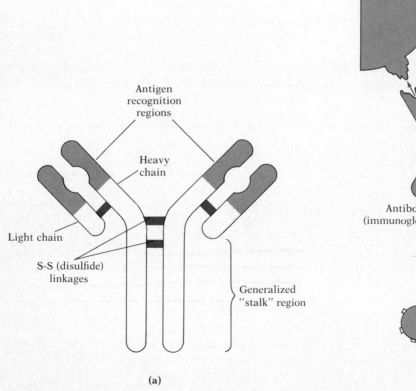

(a)

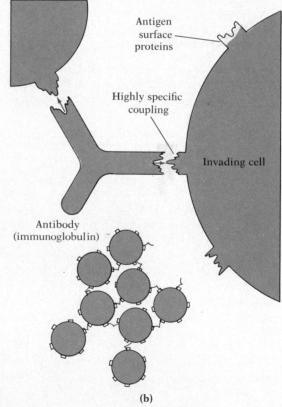

(b)

39.15

(a) Antibodies are immunoglobulins. These proteins consist of two light and two heavy polypeptide chains, connected by disulfide linkages. Each chain has two general regions common to a number of antibodies, and two highly specific antigen recognition regions that bind only to specific antigens. **(b)** When a specific antigen is encountered, the recognition regions of the antibody molecules attach to specific binding sites on the antigen, eventually forming an immobile mass that can be engulfed by phagocytes.

In the ongoing combat against invaders, macrophages bearing captured cell-surface antigens (antigen-presenting cells) seek out lymphocytes with matching antibodies. Once a match is made, the macrophage induces the lymphocyte to begin to reproduce its specific line, resulting in large populations of antibody-bearing cytotoxic killer cells or antibody-secreting cells, both effective against the invaders.

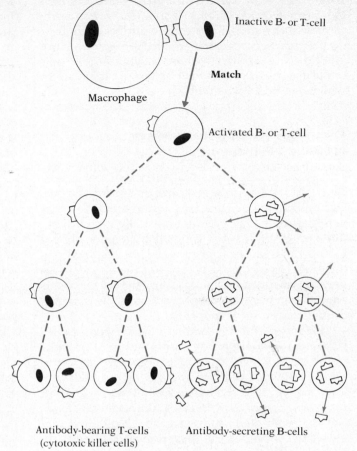

Macrophage

Inactive B- or T-cell

Match

Activated B- or T-cell

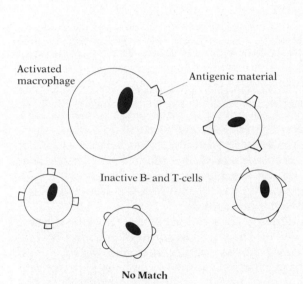

Activated macrophage

Antigenic material

Inactive B- and T-cells

No Match

Antibody-bearing T-cells (cytotoxic killer cells)

Antibody-secreting B-cells

sponse. But eventually—after thousands of failures—the macrophage may find a lymphocyte whose surface antibodies match the structure of the captured foreign molecule.

There are millions of lymphocytes in the body, and perhaps millions of kinds of antibodies on their membranes. An encounter between a macrophage and a lymphocyte that bears a matching antibody is entirely a chance event. When such a match does occur, the lymphocyte begins a series of cell divisions. Each daughter cell divides in turn, and within 10 days or so the lymphocyte with the matching antibody will have literally thousands of descendants, all making that antibody (Figure 39.16). Some will wear the antibody on their surfaces and will become cytotoxic killer cells, destroying any invader bearing the proper antigen. Others will become secretory cells and release antibodies into the bloodstream. These antibodies can coagulate the proteins coating the invading cells, making them "sticky" so that they tend to attach to

solid particles. This renders them easy prey for wandering phagocytic white blood cells.

The cells that carry antibodies on their surfaces and those that secrete antigens are quite different. The first is called a **T-cell** and the second a **B-cell.** Both arise in special cells of the bone marrow, from which they are released into the bloodstream. The T-cells are not yet functional killers, so they move into the thymus (hence the name) where they mature, their cell surfaces changing in a way that prepares them for their special role. When a T-cell is fully mature, it leaves the thymus and begins roaming the bloodstream, where by chance it could meet a macrophage cell.

One may wonder how many specific types of lymphocytes exist. After all, the human body can even make antibodies against crocodile blood. Why would we have evolved antibodies to fight crocodile blood? The immune system obviously "covers all bets" in its preparation for trouble.

The B-cells are a bit of a mystery. They are

formed in the bone marrow along with the T-cells, but no one knows where they go to mature, or how the process takes place. They, too, are preprogrammed to react to only certain antigens, but how they learn to recognize these antigens remains unknown. It is known that in chickens the B-cells mature in the *bursa of fabricus*, a lymphoid organ for which the B-cell was named.

The Primary and Secondary Immune Responses

The immune response involves two distinct steps. The **primary immune response** occurs when a foreign substance or invader is encountered for the very first time. The reaction normally is a bit slow, but usually the invader is finally overcome. Should this sort of invader appear again, the response will be astonishingly swift because of the efficient **secondary immune response.** Let's see why this should be, beginning by describing the sluggish primary immune response.

When an antibody binds to an antigen, the resulting complex interacts with a group of proteins in the plasma known as the *complement*. Once proteins of the complement are joined by an antigen/antibody complex, the proteins begin a series of reactions, some of which cause the feeling we associate with illness. In influenza (the "flu"), the complement stimulates the secretion of *histamine*, dilating blood vessels, increasing local blood flow, and flooding the affected area with white blood cells and oxygen. The histamine also causes redness, the swelling of mucous membranes, and an increase in the flow of mucus. The complement may also cause the release of certain hormones that set even more white blood cells into action.

The complement also induces molecules called *pyrogens* to increase body heat, bringing on fever. It is sometimes a mistake to reduce a low-grade fever by taking aspirin because most harmful bacteria and viruses are inactivated or killed by even a slight increase in body temperature.

The primary immune response is a little slow because it depends on the ability of the macrophage to find a few specific cells and build them into an army. While the army is mobilizing, the invaders may be on a rampage. In time, the primary immune response will be successful and the invader will be defeated. Once the battle is over, the lymphocytes decrease in number and become lost in the crowd. However, they will now exist in greater numbers than before the infection, no matter how inconspicuously; furthermore, they are ready for the next invasion. But they will not be activated until the next time that same type of invader appears, when they will knock out the invader almost immediately.

This rapid reaction, then, is the secondary immune response. It is the reason you don't get measles more than once. And if you've been vaccinated for measles, you may not get the disease at all. This is because being vaccinated with a harmless form of the measles virus triggers a primary response, so if a real invader follows later it will meet the secondary response.

Interferon

Interferon is an antiviral substance manufactured by the cells of most vertebrates in response to viral attack. The term itself comes from *interference phenomenon*, which is what happens when a cell under viral attack becomes resistant to attacks by other viruses. An attacking virus tends to alter a cell's replicating mechanisms, using them to make more viruses that can then infect new cells (see Chapter 20). The interferon helps to block this deadly geometric increase. Furthermore, the interferon manufactured by one cell may cause other cells to become resistant as well.

Interferon does not act against specific viruses, but will inhibit *any* viral attack. Interferon from one species, however, cannot increase resistance to viruses in another species. Thus, in gene-splicing techniques, rapidly multiplying bacteria are induced to make *human* interferon by being "infected" by the human genes that manufacture it.

When it recently became known that interferon could be manufactured by recombinant techniques, hopes in the medical community soared. Interferon seemed to be the answer to everything from cancer to the common cold. But the promises were apparently premature; interferon was simply not the magical cure-all that we hoped. However, in one experiment, not one of eleven volunteers given interferon in a nasal spray caught cold after being exposed to cold viruses, while in the control group, eight of eleven people given plain water spray and exposed to the viruses *did* catch cold.

Three types of interferon are produced by human cells and, as luck would have it, the most promising one in the fight against viruses and cancer, one called *γ-interferon*, has been the most difficult to produce. Recombinant researchers, however, recently announced that they can provide it in large quantities, and inexpensively. The γ-interferon has a different effect from the other two, (called α- and β-interferons). While α- and β-interferons each stimulate the production of about six amino acid chains not normally found in cells, γ-interferon stimulates the production of all twelve of these as well as of four additional ones. Furthermore, it increases the production of eight more chains that normally *do* occur in cells.

Interferon was once expected to be of great use in the control of cancer, and although it is obviously no miracle cure, it may have some useful properties. For example, it reduced tumor size in a number of patients who did not respond to other treatment. In one case, two of three separate cancers discovered in one man completely disappeared after treatment with interferon.

Interferon does have side effects. In some people it triggers cardiac arrhythmias (irregular heartbeats). Interferon may also complicate liver or kidney problems. High doses can even cause confusion, change brain waves, and bring on seizures. Interferon is still considered a useful substance, based on what we know now, and may be a superb form of treatment, as soon as we gain enough information to use it properly.

Attacks against Self

Leukocytes have, perhaps simplistically, been called the body's "police force." In some ways, however, the metaphor is distressingly apt. We do indeed need police officers for protection, but we also know that, on rare occasions, they may overreact and harm the very group they normally protect. Similarly, our protective immune system sometimes may go awry—overreacting not only to "foreign" antigens, but to harmless antigens such as pollen (which causes hay fever), as well. More seriously, leukocytes may even attack the body's own tissues. In such cases, normal body tissues are erroneously identified as "foreign" and are therefore attacked, even to the point of destruction, by misguided leukocytes.

These attacks can produce a number of **autoimmune diseases,** such as rheumatoid arthritis, systemic lupus erythematosus, pernicious anemia, and thyroiditis. Researchers are also taking a second look at familiar illnesses such as certain kinds of diabetes, Addison's disease, and myaesthenia gravis, each of which may be linked to autoimmune problems.

Recently, a new and terrible disease, called *Acquired Immune Deficiency Syndrome (AIDS),* has burst upon the medical scene. It causes the victim's immune system to be suppressed; people with AIDS are susceptible to all sorts of diseases, even very rare ones. In fact, the appearance of rare diseases such as Kaposi's sarcoma and pneumocystis pneumonia assists in identifying the condition in its later stages. One early signal of AIDS is catching a series of lingering, simple colds; other conditions develop as the victim's body becomes increasingly defenseless.

The first cases of AIDS appeared in late 1979. By late 1983, the disease had spread to over 40 states and 20 countries. 95% of AIDS cases are found in certain high-risk groups, primarily among highly promiscuous male homosexuals, Haitians, hemophiliacs, and intravenous drug users. It is not known why these groups, particularly the Haitians, are at risk, and there has been speculation that the disease can be carried in the blood and transmitted in infusions.

Fewer than 14% of AIDS victims survive for three years after diagnosis. No bacteria or virus has been isolated as a definite agent of the disease, and no treatment has been successful. (One hopes that neither of these statements will be true by the time this book is printed.) Intensive research into AIDS is continuing, however, and there are many indications that people in the high-risk groups are actively working to prevent the spread of the disease.

THE LYMPHATIC SYSTEM

The **lymphatic system** is the "secondary circulatory system," and, anatomically, a rather simple one at that. Basically, it is the system of channels through which *lymph* flows. **Lymph** is composed of fluid that has leaked, or been pressed, out of the capillaries by high hydrostatic pressure. The lymph moves between cells, percolating slowly through the body, occasionally collecting into distinct channels. It returns to the bloodstream through ducts entering the large veins near the heart. Because it can enter and leave blood vessels, the lymphatic system is important in maintaining water balance in the blood. We've already mentioned its role in the absorption and transport of digested fats (see Chapter 37), and we will discuss a third function shortly.

Figure 39.17 illustrates the anatomy of the lymphatic system. As you can see, it consists of a large number of *lymph ducts, lymph nodes*, and *lymph vessels.* The lymphatic system lacks a pumping heart, so the fluid is pushed along primarily by the squeezing action of muscles and the normal movement of various organs, as well as the pulsing of

(a) The lymphatic system consists of a number of lymph vessels, nodes, and ducts. The vessels begin as sacs in tissue spaces and join together, forming larger vessels. The lymph vessels or ducts eventually empty into large veins near the heart. **(b)** Fluids are kept moving in one direction by a number of one-way valves, similar to those seen in veins. **(c)** Lymph nodes are located generally throughout the body, but cluster in several regions, including the groin, abdomen, armpits, neck, and head. The nodes are labyrinths through which the lymph passes en route to the ducts. Each node is about 1–2 mm in diameter and has incoming and outgoing vessels.

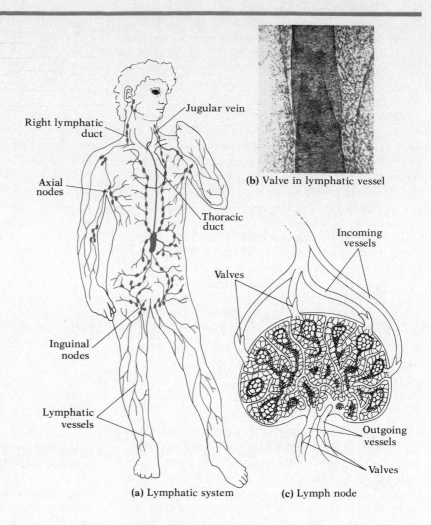

(b) Valve in lymphatic vessel

(a) Lymphatic system

(c) Lymph node

adjacent arteries. The fluid empties into large veins near the heart. A system of check valves prevent the lymph from backing up, so it flows continuously toward the heart.

The **lymph nodes** are scattered throughout the body, but they are concentrated in the neck, armpits, and groin. Each node is a clump of tissue harboring multitudes of lymphocytes. The nodes act as filters of a sort, since foreign materials, bacteria, viral particles, and cancerous cells that have managed to enter the body eventually accumulate in a node, where they are immediately attacked by resident lymphocytes. This, then, is the third function of the lymphatic system—the removal of foreign materials and invading microorganisms from the body's fluids. (The spleen and tonsils aid in this task.) Swollen nodes may be a sign of infection.

The lymphatic system can sometimes fail, and that failure can do us great harm. As the lymphatic system drains the tissues, it may pick up loose cancerous cells. The cancerous cells are usually attacked and killed, but sometimes they survive the attacks and actually begin to divide in the lymph nodes. They can easily spread throughout the body when carried by the lymph fluid. Breast cancer, for instance, often spreads to the nearby axillary (armpit) lymph nodes, causing them to become cancerous. This spread of secondary cancers, or *metastasis*, reduces the victim's chance of survival, even after the primary tumor is removed.

Summary

The Human Circulatory System

The circulatory system transports oxygen, carbon dioxide, nutrients, hormones, water, ions, and metabolic wastes and helps support the immune system. The human circulatory system is composed of the heart, blood vessels (arteries, arterioles, capillaries, venules, veins), and the blood.

Humans have four-chambered hearts. The left atrium and ventricle pump the oxygenated blood, via arteries, throughout the body. Four one-way valves prevent the blood from flowing backward in the heart. Control of the heart's rhythmic contractions is both intrinsic and extrinsic. The sinoatrial (SA) node, or pacemaker, and the atrioventricular (AV) node control heart functions intrinsically. Extrinsic control involves the coordinated action of sympathetic and parasympathetic nerves to speed up and slow down the heart rate.

Systolic pressure and diastolic pressure reflect the emptying and filling of the ventricles as blood enters the aorta. As the aorta leaves the heart, it branches into the coronary arteries and the aortic arch, from which arteries extend into the head, arms, trunk, and legs. Blood eventually travels through arterioles into capillary beds, nourishing tissues and collecting wastes, then returns to the heart via the venules and veins. The circulatory system contains many circuits in which some special exchange occurs. These include the pulmonary, cardiac, hepatic portal, and renal circuits. If vessels in the cardiac circuit are clogged, a heart attack may result, and muscle tissue may be starved of blood and die.

The Blood

Blood is composed of plasma, leukocytes (white blood cells), erythrocytes (red blood cells), and platelets. Plasma is about 90% water and contains the proteins albumin, globulin, and fibrinogen. Red blood cells are produced by stem cells in bone marrow in response to a drop in the level of oxygen in the blood. Platelets are fragments of certain white blood cells and are instrumental in the clotting process.

The Immune System

The immune system operates in close association with the circulatory system. White blood cells are produced by the same stem cells as red cells, but contain nuclei and mitochondria and are amoeboid. Each type of leukocyte has specific functions. Macrophages act as scavengers, phagocytizing cellular debris and attacking invading bacteria and viruses. Natural killer cells destroy cancer cells and virus-infected cells, while cytotoxic killer cells "learn" which cells to kill during the creation of new antibodies.

Antibodies are formed by several types of cells, including lymphocytes. Each antibody is produced in response to a specific antigen, to which it binds, eventually joining other complexes to form a clump that can be easily phagocytized by macrophages. The macrophage presents bits and pieces of the complex to lymphocytes; when a macrophage meets lymphocytes whose surface antibodies match the complex, the B-cells secrete matching antibodies, and the T-cells mature into killer cells, wearing matching antibodies on their surfaces.

The primary immune response is activated when a foreign substance is first encountered, and the much more rapid secondary reponse is triggered when the same invader reappears. At times, the immune system also may react to harmless antigens or to the body's own tissues, resulting i nallergies and autoimmune diseases such as rheumatoid arthritis and pernicious anemia.

The Lymphatic System

The lymphatic system is sometimes called the secondary circulatory system. It transports lymph, a fluid that has been pressed out of the capillaries. The system consists of numerous lymph ducts, nodes, and vessels. The nodes are scattered throughout the body but are concentrated primarily in the neck, armpits, and groin. Lymph is important in filtering foreign substances and abnormal cells from the body's fluids, maintaining the water balance in the blood, and absorbing and transporting digested fats.

Key Terms

circulatory system	bicuspid valve	capillary	antibody
heart	pulmonary semilunar valve	venule	antigen
right atrium	aortic semilunar valve	circuit	lymphocyte
right ventricle	intrinsic heart rhythm	pulmonary circuit	immunoglobulin
vein	sinoatrial (SA) node (pacemaker)	cardiac circuit	T-cell
left atrium	atrioventricular (AV) node	plasma	B-cell
left ventricle	extrinsic neurotransmitter	erythrocyte	primary immune response
artery	systole	platelet	secondary immune response
superior vena cava	diastole	immune system	interferon
inferior vena cava	diastolic pressure	leukocyte	autoimmune disease
pulmonary artery	systolic pressure	macrophage	lymphatic system
aorta	coronary arteries	natural killer cell	lymph
tricuspid valve	arteriole	cytotoxic killer cell	lymph node

Review Questions

1. List three different functions of the human circulatory system. (p. 568)

2. Track the movement of a red blood cell through the heart, beginning with its entrance from the inferior vena cava and ending with its emergence into the aorta. (pp. 569–570)

3. Name, locate, and describe the four heart valves and relate their action to the heart sounds. (p. 571)

4. Explain intrinsic control of the heart muscle. (pp. 571–572)

5. Distinguish between systolic and diastolic pressure and describe the role of arteries in maintaining blood pressure. (p. 573)

6. Describe the structure of a capillary and briefly discuss three mechanisms through which materials enter and leave capillary blood. (p. 575)

7. List the major components of plasma and of the formed elements of blood. (pp. 577–578)

8. What are the specific roles of the immune system's natural and cytotoxic killer cells? (p. 579)

9. Briefly describe how a macrophage makes use of bits of captured foreign matter in stimulating antibody production. (pp. 580–581)

10. What is the general role of an antibody? Describe its molecular structure, pointing out how one specific antibody differs from another. (p. 580)

11. Compare the primary and secondary immune responses, explaining why they differ in reaction time. (p. 582)

12. List three structural components and three functions of the lymphatic system. (pp. 583–584)

Reproduction

The reproductive imperative of all living things is: "Reproduce or your genes will disappear from the population." This expresses nothing more than the unprejudiced arithmetic of evolution, and its meaning is deceptively simple: each generation is made up of the descendants of the reproducers of previous generations. Furthermore, most of the individuals of any generation are derived from the best reproducers of previous generations. Stated another way, natural selection favors traits that result in greater reproductive success. Animals reproduce in a variety of ways, but in this chapter we will consider the reproduction of a representative mammal, *Homo sapiens*.

HUMAN REPRODUCTION

Compared to some mammalian species, the reproductive system of *Homo sapiens* seems rather ordinary. It is, in fact, almost identical to those of the other primates. However, humans do have some unique traits, such as an extremely high level of sexuality, nonseasonal sexual behavior, and, in the male, an inordinately large penis for a primate.

Males

In men, the external genitalia include the **penis** and the paired **testes** (singular, *testis*) suspended in the saclike **scrotum** (Figure 40.1a). The testes in humans and most other mammals develop in the abdomen and descend into the scrotum shortly before birth. The penis itself consists of a cylindrical **shaft** ending in the enlarged **glans**, with the urethral opening at its tip. It is an extremely sensitive organ with an abundance of touch receptors, especially about the glans.

During sexual excitement the penis becomes erect, lengthening and thickening (Figure 40.1b) and curving upward as its spongy *erectile tissues* fill with blood. These changes occur because the flow of arterial blood entering the penis increases, while venous outflow in the penis is retarded. Erection is brought about chiefly through a spinal reflex action, especially in response to touch, but higher brain centers intercede significantly through erotic thought, odors, sounds, and visual images. The conscious centers can act in a strong inhibiting manner as well, so the total neural interaction is a delicate one. When erection occurs, the glans emerges from the *foreskin*, unless the foreskin has been removed by circumcision. Physical stimulation then brings on an *ejaculation*, the release of sperm-bearing semen.

The Testes and Sperm Production. Sperm and male sex hormones are produced in the testes. In many mammals, these dense oval bodies descend during the mating season, and are withdrawn into the safer region of the body cavity when the season ends. But in humans, the testes normally descend permanently, shortly before birth. Their descent into the scrotum is essential, since developing sperm are quite heat sensitive and the scrotum is

(a) The male genitalia, emphasizing the route followed by sperm. (b) The erect penis, showing blood-filled, spongy tissue. (c) Cross-section through the penis showing the major blood vessels and spongy tissue.

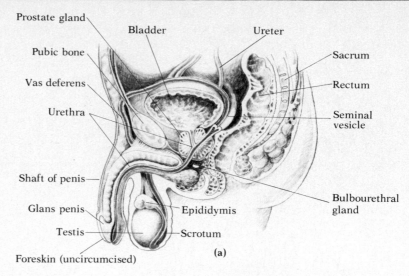

Prostate gland
Bladder
Ureter
Pubic bone
Sacrum
Vas deferens
Rectum
Urethra
Seminal vesicle
Shaft of penis
Glans penis
Epididymis
Bulbourethral gland
Testis
Scrotum
Foreskin (uncircumcised)

(a)

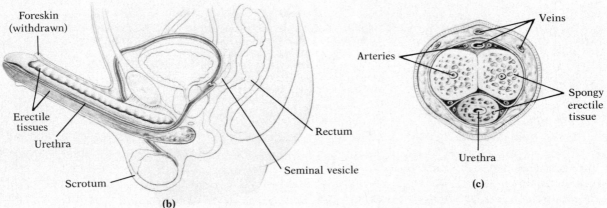

Foreskin (withdrawn)
Veins
Arteries
Erectile tissues
Spongy erectile tissue
Urethra
Rectum
Scrotum
Seminal vesicle
Urethra

(b)

(c)

cooler than the male's higher internal body temperatures. The scrotum can also help regulate the temperature of the testes. In response to heat, its slender muscles relax, permitting the testes to descend away from the body, where it is cooler. Cold causes the scrotum to tighten and contract, drawing the testes closer to the warm body.

The testes contain highly coiled tubes, which form the **seminiferous tubules** and the **epididymis** (Figure 40.2a). The outer walls of the seminiferous tubules contain *interstitial cells* that produce the sex hormone *testosterone*. The sperm are formed from generative cells also in the walls of the seminiferous tubules. After undergoing meiosis (Figure 40.2b), these cells form haploid *spermatids*. These lie embedded in the *Sertoli cells*, where they are nourished and supported as they are transformed into immature sperm. The sperm cannot enter into fertilization, however, before they undergo a final period of maturation in the epididymis. (The structures of sperm and egg cells are discussed in Chapter 41.)

The Sperm Pathway. After the sperm have matured in the epididymis, they are ready for their reproductive role at ejaculation (see Figure 40.2), when they are propelled out of the testes by the wavelike action of smooth muscles and cilia lining the epididymis and **ducti** (or **vasa**) **deferentia** (singular, *ductus deferens*). Each of these paired tubes extends from an epididymis to the urethra.

Near the urethra, the sperm receive fluids from two glands, the **seminal vesicles** and the **prostate gland.** The seminal vesicles add fluid containing fructose (fruit sugar), which provides the sperm with an energy source. The prostate produces an alkaline secretion that gives semen its characteristic thickness and odor. (The increased alkalinity also helps neutralize the vagina's acidic fluids.) The male urethra carries both urine and semen, but during sexual excitement the urine-releasing muscle sphincter below the bladder is involuntarily contracted. Prior to ejaculation, the **bulbourethral glands** secrete clear mucus into the urethra, lubricating it and part of the outer surface of the penis.

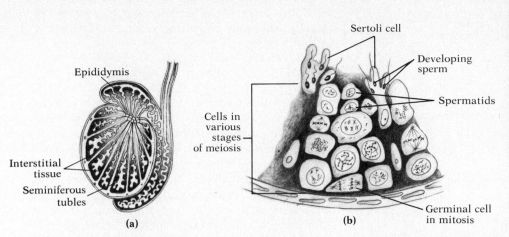

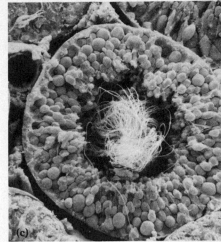

(a)

(b)

(c)

Epididymis

Interstitial tissue

Seminiferous tubles

Cells in various stages of meiosis

Sertoli cell

Developing sperm

Spermatids

Germinal cell in mitosis

40.2

The testis is an oval body containing long, coiled seminiferous tubules that merge above to form the larger epididymis **(a).** Surrounding the tubules are the interstitial cells. A portion of a seminiferous tubule reveals an outer layer of uncommitted cells, followed within by cells in different stages of meiosis **(b).** Bordering the lumen of the tubule are partially formed spermatids, usually surrounded by supporting Sertoli cells. Eventually, spermatids will differentiate into

maturing and inactive spermatozoa, to be swept away by cilia to the epididymis, where the maturation process continues. The scanning electron micrograph of maturing human sperm cells **(c)** reveals the great numbers within the seminiferous tubules. (Photo from *TISSUES AND ORGANS: a text-atlas of scanning electron microscopy,* by Richard G. Kessel and Randy N. Kardon. W. H. Freeman and Company, copyright © 1979.)

Females

In women, the external genitalia are collectively known as the **vulva** (Figure 40.3). The most prominent part is the hair-covered **mons veneris,** a fatty mound overlying the bony pubic arch. Below the mons veneris lie the outer folds of the vulva, the **labia majora** (major lips), which cover a number of sensitive structures. Just within the labia majora are the less prominent, thinner folds of the **labia minora** (minor lips). These join at their upper margins, forming a kind of hood over a small, sensitive prominence, the **clitoris.** The clitoris is derived from essentially the same embryonic tissue as is the glans of the penis. The two are similar in that they are both erectile and have about the same numbers of sensory neurons. In an excited state, the clitoris becomes erect, firm, and highly sensitive.

Enclosed by the labia minora, and near their lower border, lies the vaginal opening, the **introitus.** The introitus may be partially blocked by a membrane known as the **hymen.** The strength of this membrane varies considerably, and its rupture, perhaps by the first intercourse, may produce discomfort and bleeding. The urethral opening in females lies just above the vaginal opening.

Internal Anatomy. The internal anatomy of the human female reproductive system includes the *vagina,* the *uterus,* the *ovaries,* and the *oviducts*

(Figure 40.4). The **vagina,** a distendable tube about 8 cm (3 in) long when relaxed, receives the penis during intercourse and is the passageway through which birth occurs. It is well adapted for both functions, with its highly folded, muscular walls and a lining that secretes a lubricating mucus. The warm, moist interior provides a suitable environment for the vagina's ever-present, acid-producing bacteria, which maintain a pH of 3–4. Should natural flora

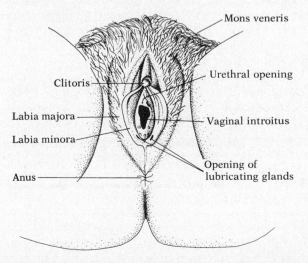

Mons veneris

Clitoris

Urethral opening

Labia majora

Labia minora

Vaginal introitus

Anus

Opening of lubricating glands

40.3

The vulva (external female genitalia).

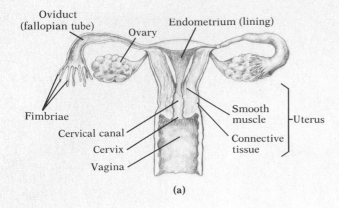

(a)

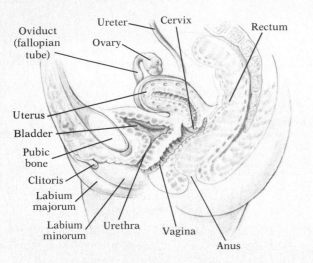

(b)

40.4

(a) The internal reproductive structures in the human female. (b) The scanning electron microscope reveals the numerous cilia that line the oviduct and help move sperm along to the egg. (Photo from *TISSUES AND ORGANS: a text-atlas of scanning electron microscopy*, by Richard G. Kessel and Randy N. Kardon. W. H. Freeman and Company, copyright © 1979.)

be disturbed (as might happen after large doses of antibiotics or excessive douching), other strains of bacteria and some strains of yeast can invade the area and cause infections.

The vagina leads to a soft, muscular, pear-shaped organ, the **uterus,** which is capable of great expansion. The lower tip of the uterus, called the **cervix,** extends slightly into the vagina. The uterus is lined by a soft, vascular *endometrium,* which will receive the embryo should fertilization occur.

The **oviducts,** or *fallopian tubes,* emerge from each side of the upper end of the uterus, extend outward and downward toward the **ovaries,** and terminate in movable, fingerlike *fimbriae.* Although the ovaries produce the eggs, they do not directly connect with the oviducts. Instead, currents produced by the beating fimbriae draw eggs into the oviduct, where they are then swept along toward the uterus by cilia and by muscular contractions.

The Ovary and Egg Production. Like the testes, the ovaries produce both gametes and hormones. Each oval-shaped ovary is about 2.5 cm (1 in) long (Figure 40.5). The egg cells *(oocytes)* are actually produced in the outer tissues, the *germinal epithelium.* In mature women the ovaries contain a total of about 400,000 oocytes, a surprisingly large number considering how few can ever be fertilized. You may recall from our discussion of meiosis (see Chapter 10) that the oocytes are produced during embryonic development; they remain inactive, in prophase of meiosis. A few are activated each month by pituitary hormones. The activated oocytes tend to suppress each other hormonally so that one usually gains a developmental advantage, and it alone matures. The release of mature eggs from the ovary is referred to as **ovulation.**

Fertilization. The egg released at ovulation is swept into the oviduct; if it is to be fertilized, it must encounter sperm in the upper third of that structure. These sperm cells have traveled to this point from near the cervix. They move by the thrust of their own thrashing tails, possibly assisted by orgasmic muscular contractions in the vagina and uterus and by the current produced by the beating of the oviduct's cilia. (The human sexual response cycle is discussed in Essay 40.1.)

The sperm's journey up the oviduct is hazardous, partly because of the distance and the sperm's limited energy reserves but also because of the vagina's acidic environment. Of the millions of sperm released in a single ejaculation, only about 5000 or 6000 ever reach the upper oviduct.

If several thousand sperm cells are already in the oviduct at the very time the egg begins its journey, fertilization is very likely. But there are limitations on the length of time an egg or a sperm can

The outer region of the ovary is the germinal epithelium that contains all of the oocytes, each arrested in prophase I of meiosis. **(a)** Each month, an oocyte becomes surrounded by a cluster of supporting cells—the follicle—and resumes meiosis. **(b, c)** As the cycle continues, the follicle greatly enlarges, becoming fluid-filled, with a number of cells directly surrounding the oocyte itself. **(d)** At midcycle, the oocyte completes meiosis I, and is ejected from the ovary at ovulation. It then proceeds to the oviduct. **(e)** The vacated follicle will form a hormone-secreting body—the corpus luteum. These hormones will support growth in the endometrium for a time, preparing it for the implantation of an embryo if fertilization occurs.

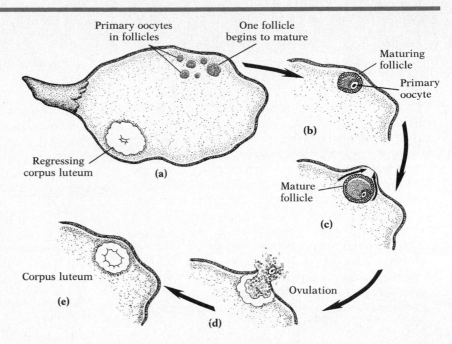

stay alive. Sperm are thought to survive about 48 hours in the female reproductive tract, and eggs from 12–24 hours, so a conservative estimate is that fertilization must occur within 12–24 hours of ovulation. After this, a sperm is likely to reach a dead egg. This means that there are only about two fertile days per month, but estimates vary by a considerable amount.

Hormones and Human Reproduction

Sex hormones undoubtedly play an extremely important role in our lives. They determine not only our sex but our sexual behavior, our sexual development, and our sexual physiology as well. An increasing body of evidence implies that they play a role in our aggressiveness. Their effects are particularly obvious during puberty, when sexual differences between girls and boys are emphasized. At full sexual maturity, these hormones cause the continued production of sex cells as well as an increased sex drive. They begin to wane at about the time we enter our "golden years." The timing appears to be adaptive since a couple who conceived at too late an age might not live long enough to raise their child.

The sex-regulating hormones in both males and females are primarily produced in the pituitary gland and the gonads. The brain's hypothalamus (see Chapter 35) helps to regulate them by sensing the level of gonadal hormones in the blood and increasing or decreasing their secretion by the pituitary through a negative feedback system.

Prompted by the hypothalamus, the anterior lobe of the pituitary releases two hormones into the blood of both males and females: **FSH (follicle-stimulating hormone),** and **LH (luteinizing hormone).** Both are important in human reproduction.

Hormonal Control of Reproductive Behavior in Males. FSH in men causes the seminiferous tubules to increase their meiotic activity and sperm to differentiate. LH stimulates the interstitial tissues that lie in the outer region of the tubules to produce **testosterone,** which also stimulates sperm production (Figure 40.6). Testosterone initiates a number of changes at puberty. The voice deepens (often in an embarrassingly intermittent way), body hair appears, and bones and muscles enlarge, as do the penis and testicles. Sex hormones in males do not ebb and flow in noticeable cycles, but certain stimuli (such as frequent sexual activity) may increase their production. In women, on the other hand, levels of sex hormones rise and fall in dramatic cycles.

Hormonal Control in Females. Let's now focus on the hormones that induce the powerful cycles of women. FSH and LH alter the **ovarian follicles,** the groups of cells surrounding the oocytes. Under the influence of these hormones, the follicles begin to grow, the oocytes resume meiosis, and the ovaries begin to secrete the hormone **estrogen.** Estrogen primarily affects the uterus, where the life-supporting lining, the endometrium, is prepared to receive an embryo—if fertilization occurs. As will be discussed shortly, the cycles of FSH and LH are closely correlated with changes in the uterus at the time of ovulation.

Estrogen is also responsible for the changes that girls undergo at puberty. Worldwide, puberty begins anywhere from nine to 13 years of age (the average age in the United States is now 12.8 years). Estrogen causes the breasts and nipples to enlarge, the hips to broaden, and a layer of fatty tissue to collect under the skin. Less noticeably, estrogen prompts the growth of the uterus, thickens the vaginal lining, and causes enlargement of the vulva. Estrogen cannot be credited for all pubertal changes, however. For example, body hair in women, usually restricted to the armpits and pubic region, is under control of the "male hormone," testosterone, which is produced by the adrenal cortex.

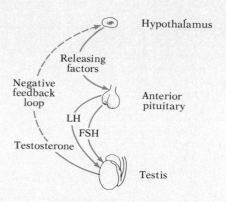

40.6

In males, the hypothalamus stimulates the anterior lobe of the pituitary to release LH and FSH. The first is targeted primarily at the interstitial cells that surround the seminiferous tubules, which respond by producing testosterone. FSH stimulates gamete production, assisted by testosterone. The regulating aspect of male hormonal release is testosterone itself. When blood levels of testosterone rise, the hypothalamus slows its stimulation of the anterior pituitary, which, in turn, reduces its hormonal output.

ESSAY 40.1
THE SEXUAL RESPONSE

Because of the pioneering research efforts of William H. Masters and Virginia E. Johnson of the Reproductive Biology Research Foundation in St. Louis, our knowledge of human sexual behavior is far more precise than it was before. Using volunteers, Masters and Johnson carefully monitored and recorded the physiological changes that occur during intercourse and orgasm.

Masters and Johnson described four phases of sexual response during intercourse (or *coitus*). They labeled them *excitement, plateau, orgasm,* and *resolution*. Excitement (or *arousal*) is characterized in both sexes by increased heart rate, blood pressure, and breathing rate. In women, the response is quite pronounced: the clitoris enlarges and becomes more sensitive, the labia majora elevate and part, and the labia minora redden and increase in size. Meanwhile, secre-

tory glands moisten the vagina. In men, excitement causes the penis to become erect. Secretions of the bulbourethral glands moisten the glans. The scrotum may elevate and become firmer. Now the penis may readily be inserted into the vagina.

During the excitement stage, the plateau phase may be reached. This may last for some minutes and is marked by an increased intensity in the level of pleasure. Either partner may begin involuntary thrusts of the pelvis as various muscles contract. The uterus may elevate and tilt backward at this time. Interestingly, the clitoris may become smaller and recede into its hood, having become exquisitely sensitive to touch.

Orgasm is an intensely pleasurable sensation that accompanies complex contractions of several voluntary and involuntary muscles. In women, the contractions

begin in the pelvic floor and surge through the vagina and uterus. In both men and women, involuntary orgasmic contractions occur at about 0.8-second intervals. In women, the upper part of the vagina may expand as the cervix moves downward (called "tenting"), a response that may help draw semen into the uterus.

In men, orgasm accompanies *ejaculation*, which involves rhythmic, involuntary contractions of the ductus deferentia, seminal vesicles, and prostate gland. The semen, containing its hordes of sperm, is forced into the urethra. The semen may be ejected from the penis in spurts, often propelled with considerable force by powerful muscles at the base of the penis.

Orgasm in men and women is compared in the accompanying figure. The most obvious difference between female **(a)** and male

The Ovarian (Menstrual) Cycle. Puberty in girls is marked by the onset of the **ovarian,** or **menstrual, cycle,** during which the pituitary and ovarian hormones rise and fall—haltingly at first, but they soon reach a cyclic regularity. Together, they initiate conditions leading to the menstrual flow, or "period." The sex drive also may increase sharply at puberty but (fortunately for concerned parents) it will not peak for several more years. Actual fertility, the physical ability to conceive, ordinarily follows the first menstrual flow by about two years.

The ovarian cycle (Figures 40.7 and 40.8) is one of the more fascinating and important aspects of human sexuality. It is closely keyed to two related events: (1) the maturation and release of an egg cell; and (2) the engorgement of the endometrium (uterine lining) with blood and its thickening in preparation for implantation of an embryo. Since these events involve different hormones acting in a highly coordinated and complex way, things can become a bit complicated. For simplicity, let's break this 28-day cycle into two parts, bearing in mind that while the events are clear enough, the causal relationships remain hypothetical.

Days One through Fourteen. The first day ("day one") of the cycle is marked by the onset of *menstruation.* The endometrium, not having received an embryo, begins to slough away, causing several days' bleeding as delicate capillaries rupture. Now the pituitary begins to secrete FSH (and some LH), stimulating the growth of an ovarian follicle and its oocyte. After a few days, the cells of the follicle begin to release estrogen, causing the uterine lining to undergo *growth* and *repair*, beginning the events that prepare the endometrium for an embryo. At about day 14, the estrogen in the blood reaches a critical level that, probably by negative feedback, slows the activity of the hypothalamus (see Figure 40.8a).

As the hypothalamus reduces its stimulation of the pituitary, FSH secretion diminishes and the pituitary dramatically increases the release of LH (see Figure 40.8b). As LH begins to stimulate the ovary, the follicle releases its egg (ovulation). Ovulation

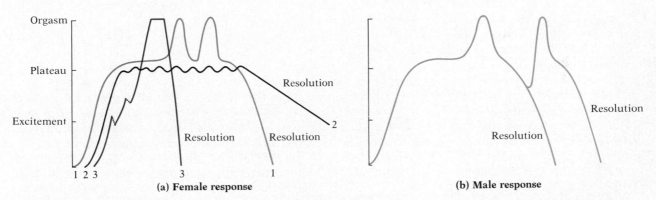

(a) Female response

(b) Male response

(b) orgasm is in the orgasmic peaks. Some women normally experience a single orgasm (*3*), but multiple orgasms are quite commonplace. These may occur as several minor episodes (*2*), or as fewer but more intense ones (*1*). In men, a single orgasm is the rule, followed by at least a partial state of resolution.

Resolution is apparently more pronounced in men than in women. At this time, erection may be lost rapidly, and most men cannot be aroused again for a time. The length of the resolution period is highly variable and usually depends on a number of factors. Resolution is more gradual in women, and immediate rearousal is often possible. This is often a quiet, relaxed, tender time that can provide pleasure of its own.

Keep in mind that this is a generalized account. In the variability of real-life situations, one often finds the idealized description of coitus to be more of a fiction than a reality—although this is one aspect of life where an imperfect reality is vastly preferable to a fictitious perfection. For instance, orgasm is often synchronous for some couples and never synchronous for others, a fact that usually turns out to make very little difference to the people involved. ●

Graphic representation of the menstrual cycle. Note in each case the events of day 14 and of ovulation. Both LH and FSH levels peak at this time, and the follicle reaches maturity. Although estrogen levels peak shortly before day 14, progesterone levels increase *after* ovulation. The endometrium undergoes growth and repair during the first 14 days and reaches its fullest development about a week later. At mid-cycle (day 14) body temperature is slightly elevated. This is a fairly reliable indicator of ovulation, an important part of the rhythm method of birth control.

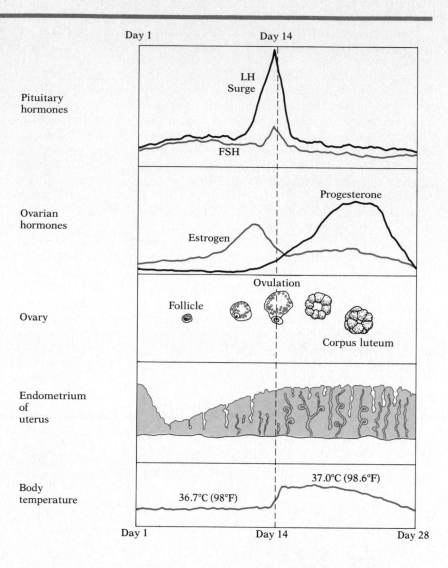

occurs at midcycle, and the event is marked by a slight, temporary rise in body temperature of about 0.3°C (0.6°F). (Awareness of this temperature change is important for women using the rhythm method of birth control.) Normally ovulation occurs on day 14, and by then the endometrium has been growing for about 10 days.

Days Fifteen through Twenty-eight. After ovulation, cells of the vacated follicle undergo change, forming what is called the **corpus luteum** ("yellow body"). Under the influence of LH, the corpus luteum continues to secrete estrogen and begins to secrete *progesterone* (see Figure 40.8c). **Progesterone** and estrogen together help bring the endometrium to a thick, fluid-filled or *glandular state*. An embryo will be about six days old by the time it reaches the uterus. By that time, it will appear to be a hollow ball of cells (see Chapter 41). Should an embryo actually *implant* (attach) in the uterine wall, its membranes will begin to release a hormone that

enters the mother's bloodstream and imitates LH—prompting the continued release of progesterone—a hormone that is present throughout pregnancy—from the corpus luteum.

If fertilization fails to occur, the endometrium will remain receptive until about day 25 or 26. Then the high levels of estrogen and progesterone in the blood trigger another negative feedback loop, causing the hypothalamus to once again reduce its stimulation of the pituitary. Consequently, the release of LH slows, the corpus luteum soon withers, and estrogen and progesterone levels drop. By day 28, the endometrium has deteriorated, and it will soon begin to slough away. The next day is day one of another cycle.

To summarize, pituitary FSH, acting on the ovary, brings about follicle development and estrogen secretion. Estrogen stimulates growth and repair of the endometrium; a rise in estrogen levels, sensed by the hypothalamus at mid-cycle,

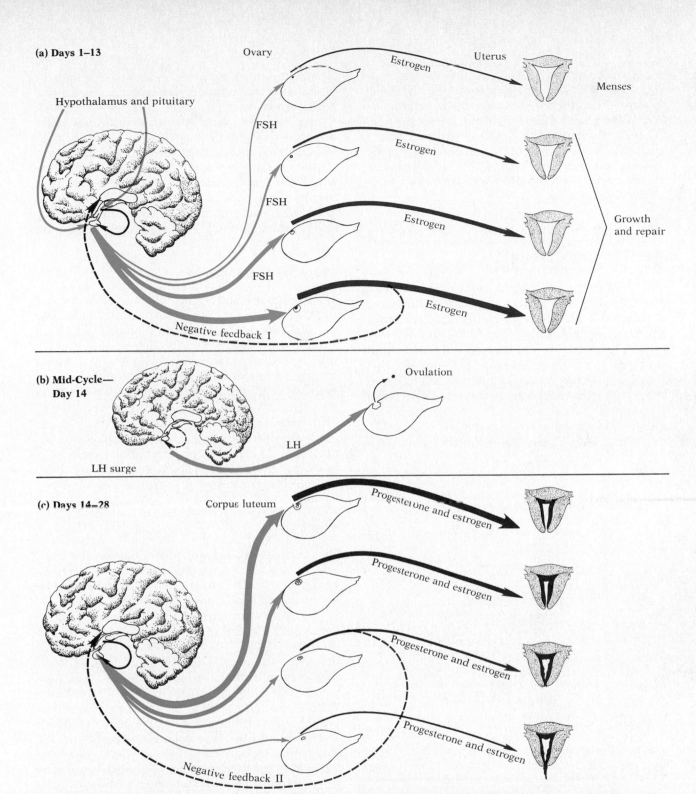

(a) Days 1–13

Ovary

Hypothalamus and pituitary

Estrogen

Uterus

Menses

FSH

Estrogen

FSH

Estrogen

Growth and repair

FSH

Estrogen

Negative feedback I

**(b) Mid-Cycle—
Day 14**

Ovulation

LH

LH surge

(c) Days 14–28

Corpus luteum

Progesterone and estrogen

Progesterone and estrogen

Progesterone and estrogen

Progesterone and estrogen

Negative feedback II

40.8

(a) Hormonal control of the ovarian cycle. From day 1 to 14, FSH and estrogen dominate the cycle, bringing on follicle development and endometrial growth and repair. At mid-cycle **(b)**, negative feedback brings on a pituitary shift to LH secretion. LH stimulates ovulation and the development of a corpus luteum. From day 14 to 28 **(c)**, LH, estrogen, and progesterone dominate the cycle, bringing the endometrium to a fully receptive, glandular state. Without the implantation of an embryo, a second negative feedback event diminishes the hormones and the cycle ends.

brings on a shift to LH secretion by the pituitary. The surge of LH causes ovulation and the development of a corpus luteum, which secretes estrogen and progesterone. The two hormones bring the endometrium to a full state of preparedness. If implantation does not occur, rising levels of the hormones eventually inhibit the hypothalamus, the hormone levels diminish, and the endometrium deteriorates.

BIRTH CONTROL

Birth control has been an important consideration throughout human history. In some cultures it is considered a moral issue; in others, it is almost entirely an economic decision. Some groups today, such as the infamous Auca of Ecuador, sometimes limit their numbers by infanticide. (Normally, they kill only newborn females.) Such drastic behavior in any culture is most common in lean, hard times, when food is scarce and the environment's resources have been nearly exhausted.

By the mid-1970s, in 77% of American marriages

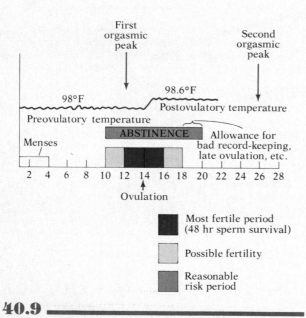

40.9

The rhythm method of birth control is based on sound biological principles. It is logical to assume that there are definite periods of time during the monthly cycle in which conception is highly unlikely. However, when we allow for natural variations in ovarian cycles, errors in recording ovulation, and the question of sperm and egg survival, the so-called safe period becomes shorter. Further, the period of abstinence cuts right through what studies reveal to be a monthly peak of orgasmic response in women.

where the women were in their reproductive years, either the partners were using some form of birth control or one of them had been sterilized. During this time, about 10 or 15 birth control methods were available (Table 40.1).

Since methods of birth control vary so widely, obviously some are better than others, and some may have serious side effects. Some of the more common methods used today are described in Table 40.1; we will give special attention to the rhythm method, the Pill, and intrauterine devices.

The Rhythm Method

The **rhythm method** (Figure 40.9) has been referred to as a "natural" means of birth control, but some say that this distorts the definition of the term. It requires careful attention to daily routine (including recording menstrual periods for several months to establish a baseline). With a good thermometer and attention to detail, women with *very regular* cycles reach a success rate of about 80%. This means that, among women practicing this form of birth control, 20% can reasonably be expected to become pregnant within a year. Expressed another way, each woman can expect to become pregnant every five years.

The Pill

The famed **birth control pill** is among the most widely used, and most effective, of all contraceptives available today. It is now being used by about 100 million women worldwide.

The active substances in the Pill usually are synthetic estrogen and progesterone (or its synthetic form, progestin). They may be used in combination or in sequence. They are slightly more effective in combination, because pills used this way have a slightly greater concentration of hormones. Both sorts of pills work in the same way: they simply override the normal rise and fall of estrogen and progesterone. This inhibits the mid-cycle LH surge, so ovulation does not occur. In a sense, the Pill mimics pregnancy, which also suppresses ovulation by high levels of these two hormones.

From time to time, birth control pills have received unfavorable publicity because of certain limited, but important, side effects. In particular, they have been suspected of increasing the health risk to women with blood-clotting problems, high blood pressure, diabetes, and certain other conditions. This is one reason why a woman's medical history should be carefully studied by her physician before the Pill is prescribed.

TABLE 40.1

Methods of birth control

Method	Application	Effectiveness	Drawbacks
Surgical intervention (by qualified medical persons)			
Abortion (vacuum aspiration, up to 12 wks)	Cervix dilated, embryo and placenta removed by gentle suction	Virtually 100%, hospital stay not required	Psychological effect common; strongly controversial
Abortion (D&C) (up to 12 wks)	Cervix dilated, embryo and placenta removed by scraping	Virtually 100%, hospital stay generally not required	Psychological effect common; 1%–2% have medical complications
Abortion (saline injection, after 16 wks)	Saline (NaCl) solution injected into uterine cavity; labor and expulsion of fetus and placenta ensues	Usually 100%	Psychological effect; some risk from saline poisoning
Sterilization			
Vasectomy	Incisions through scrotum, section of ductus deferens removed and remainder tied off; sperm cannot leave testes	Virtually 100%, now 45% reversible	Some psychological effects occur; increased susceptibility to some disorders suspected, but not proven
Tubal ligation	Incision through abdominal wall, oviducts cut and tied; sperm cannot reach egg	Nearly 100%	Hospital stay generally required; costly; not reversible; newer microtechniques produce less surgical risk
Chemical and/or mechanical intervention (with advice of qualified physician when needed)			
Oral contraceptives ("the Pill")	Combination or sequential estrogen and progestins or progestin alone (minipill); taken daily, prevents ovulation	95%–99%	Costly; must be prescribed and monitored by physician; temporary side effects; greater risk to heavy smokers
Intrauterine devices (IUDs)	Plastic and/or metal devices inserted into uterus; may contain slow-release progestin; prevents implantation	95%–99%	Must be inserted and monitored by physician; temporary discomfort in some; some expulsion; complications if pregnancy occurs; recommended only after at least 1 child
Diaphragm with spermicide	Rubber dome; fits over cervix; blocks sperm; spermicide kills sperm	98% with spermicide and completely regimented use	Must be fitted by physician; strong motivation required; somewhat messy
Condom	Rubber sheath worn over penis; blocks sperm entry	70%–93%, depending on quality and strict usage; safer with spermicide; withdrawal immediately after ejaculation is essential	Requires strong motivation since it is interruptive and some sensation is lost for men; can break; cost fairly high
Spermicide alone (foams, jellies, creams, or suppositories)	Placed in vagina with applicator before each intercourse; kills sperm	About 90% when properly used; otherwise, about 75%	Generally messy and short-lived (newer foams somewhat better); interruptive
Rhythm (natural method)	Intercourse avoided during carefully determined fertile period	Under ideal conditions, about 80%	Requires great motivation; fails when cycles are irregular
Coitus interruptus (withdrawal)	Penis withdrawn just before ejaculation	About 70%	Mental stress for both partners; great self-control required; sperm can leak prior to ejaculation
Douche	Vagina flushed with water or chemical solution (vinegar common) after intercourse	Below 60%	Slightly better than no precautions—in other words, worthless; sperm can enter the cervix within 1–2 seconds after ejaculation
Sponge	Polyurethane sponge saturated with spermicide placed in vagina before intercourse	Believed to be same as diaphragm (98%), but data not yet available; no fitting necessary	Interruptive; reliability not proven; implicated in toxic shock syndrome

NOTE: Experimental innovations still being tested or developed include Silastic implants for slow release of progestin [1–6 years]; long-lasting injections of progestin [3 mos.], now used outside the U.S.; vaccine that brings on menstruation if implantation occurs; morning-after prostaglandin treatment; and male hormonal sperm suppressors.

The debate over the Pill's side effects is by no means resolved, but one point about any danger should be made: in *every* age group, the risks associated with pregnancy are significantly greater than those associated with the Pill. In addition, deaths from complications of pregnancy are highly age-dependent. In the United States, for every 100,000 pregnancies among women between the ages of 15 and 30, there will be about 7 pregnancy-related deaths. But as women grow older the risk increases steadily, until by age 40, there are about 21 deaths per 100,000 pregnancies. By contrast, the number of deaths attributed to the use of the Pill in women under 35 ranges from only 1 to 2 per 100,000, increasing to about 4 per 100,000 as women approach age 40. A number of factors may influence such figures. For example, heavy smoking by users of the Pill greatly increases the risk. Research shows that about 12 of every 100,000 heavy smokers using the Pill at age 40 will die from Pill-related complications.

The IUD

Intrauterine devices (IUDs) are plastic and/or metal devices that are inserted into the uterus and often left for long periods. They are generally recommended for women who have had at least one child. No one yet knows how they work, but they probably prevent implantation of the embryo. Some IUDs are impregnated with synthetic time-released progesterone that interferes with ovulation, as a sort of backup system. The success rate for IUD users is a remarkable 95%–99%.

The primary objection to the IUD is that it may be temporarily uncomfortable. There are also instances of perforation of the uterine wall and infections caused by IUDs. Furthermore, if the device fails and pregnancy occurs, the IUD's presence can cause complications. Still, its failure rate is as low as the Pill's, and its hazards are fewer than those of pregnancy. The overall risk of death from IUD complications is about 1 per 100,000.

Summary

Human Reproduction
Humans, unlike other primates and most mammals, have nonseasonal sexual behavior and a high level of sexuality.

External genitalia in men include the penis and paired testes suspended in the scrotum. The penis consists of a shaft ending in the enlarged glans, with the urethral opening at its tip. Sperm and male sex hormones are produced in the testes, which contain the seminiferous tubules and the epididymis. Mature sperm are propelled out of the testes during ejaculation by the wavelike action of smooth muscles and cilia lining the epididymus and ductus deferentia. The sperm receive fluid from the seminal vesicles and the prostate gland.

In women, external genitalia are known collectively as the vulva. The mons veneris overlies the pubic arch. The labia majora and labia minora below the mons veneris shield the clitoris. The vaginal opening lies within the labia minora, and the vagina itself may be partially blocked by the hymen.

The internal anatomy of the female reproductive system includes the vagina, uterus, ovaries, and oviducts. The vagina leads to the uterus, which is lined with a soft, vascular endometrium that will receive the embryo should fertilization occur. The oviducts, or fallopian tubes, emerge from each side of the upper end of the uterus and terminate in fimbriae that must capture the released egg. The ovaries produce gametes and sex hormones. Several oocytes are activated each month; usually only one matures. For pregnancy to occur, the egg must be fertilized within 12–24 hours after ovulation.

Male and female sex hormones determine gender, sexual behavior, sexual development, and sexual physiology, and may even affect the level of aggressiveness in humans. Sex hormones are produced primarily in the pituitary gland and gonads, and are regulated in part by the hypothalamus through a negative feedback system. Follicle stimulating hormone (FSH) and luteinizing hormone (LH) are released in both men and women. FSH in men causes seminiferous tubules to increase meiotic activity and sperm differentiation. LH causes interstitial tissues to produce testosterone and increases sperm production. Testosterone initiates the maturing of sexual characteristics in boys.

In women, FSH and LH induce the ovaries to begin secreting estrogen, which initiates the maturing of sexual characteristics in girls. Puberty is marked by the onset of the menstrual cycle, a response to the release of an egg and thickening of the endometrium. In the first part of the cycle, the uterus sloughs off the endometrial lining in the form of menstrual blood. In a complex coordination of estrogen, FSH, and LH, ovulation occurs in mid-cycle. If the egg is fertilized, steroid hormones are released that prompt the secretion of progesterone, reducing the levels of estrogen and preparing the endometrium for implantation of the embryo. If the egg is unfertilized, hormone levels drop, and the lining of the uterus begins to slough off on the last day of the cycle.

Masters and Johnson, in their studies of human sexual response, identified four phases of sexual intercourse in humans: excitement, plateau, orgasm, and resolution.

However, expression of these four phases is highly individualized.

Birth Control

Birth control methods commonly used in the United States include the rhythm method, the Pill, and intrauterine devices. The rhythm method requires careful monitoring of daily body temperature to determine times of fertility. Birth control pills use synthetic estrogen and progesterone either in combination or in sequence to inhibit ovulation. Intrauterine devices are inserted into the uterus to prevent implantation of the embryo; they may also inhibit or interfere with ovulation. Both the Pill and the IUD can have serious side effects for some women.

Key Terms

penis	mons veneris	FSH (follicle-stimulating hormone)
testes	labia majora	LH (luteinizing hormone)
scrotum	labia minora	testosterone
shaft	clitoris	ovarian follicle
glans	introitus	estrogen
seminiferous tubule	hymen	ovarian (menstrual) cycle
epididymis	vagina	corpus luteum
ductus (vas) deferens	uterus	progesterone
seminal vesicle	cervix	rhythm method
prostate gland	oviduct	birth control pill
bulbourethral gland	ovary	intrauterine device
vulva	ovulation	

Review Questions

1. Describe the structures of the testes and their roles in sperm production. Include the seminiferous tubules, interstitial tissue, Sertoli cells, and epididymis. (p. 588)

2. Trace the path of sperm from the epididymis through the male reproductive system, naming the structures through which they pass and briefly describing the reproductive functions of each structure. (p. 588)

3. List ten structures of the female reproductive system (external and internal), and state a function of each. (pp. 589–590)

4. Describe hormonal control in males, including the roles of the hypothalamus, pituitary, and testes. (pp. 591–592)

5. Using a simple diagram, identify the four structures involved in hormonal control in females. Use arrows to indicate the direction of control and feedback. (pp. 593–595)

6. List the hormones (and their targets) that function in the first half of the ovarian cycle. How does each target respond? Which of the hormones is involved in negative feedback toward mid-cycle? (pp. 593–594)

7. Describe the mid-cycle shift of pituitary hormones and the effects this shift has on the follicle. (p. 594)

8. Briefly discuss the events in the ovary and uterus during the second half of the ovarian cycle. What brings the cycle to an end? Under what condition will the endometrium remain intact? (pp. 594–596)

9. Develop a calendar illustrating the basis for a natural system of birth control. Take into account the survival times of sperm and egg. (p. 596)

10. List four of the most common methods of birth control (excluding the rhythm method) and explain how each is believed to work. (pp. 596–598)

Development

One of the most fascinating biological moments is that brief instant when sperm and egg join in fertilization. Clearly, that instant triggers a remarkable series of events whose analysis makes us pause in wonder and realize how little we really understand about life. In this chapter we'll try to analyze some of what we *do* know about conception and development, concentrating on humans (but at times including other representative chordates, especially where the developmental detail is more complete). We will see that the newly combined genes in the zygote contain all of the coded instructions needed to produce a new individual, and that by the time development is completed, the tissues, organs, and systems of a new individual will be in place, and they will have established the delicately coordinated interaction that characterizes animal life.

The study of the developmental period is called **embryology** (the study of the embryo). There are three distinct aspects of development: *growth, cellular differentiation,* and *morphogenesis.* **Growth** is simply an increase in size brought about through mitosis and cell division. **Cellular differentiation** is the process whereby cells become different—that is, various cells of an organism become increasingly specialized in shape, chemical makeup, and function. **Morphogenesis** is the emergence of an organism's overall recognizable form and shape as individual organs and structures become increasingly developed. Morphogenesis involves not only the movement, division, and change in shape of specialized cells, but, in some cases, their programmed death. Thus, conceptually, it's one thing to ask how a nerve cell becomes different from a

muscle cell, and another thing to ask how a biceps muscle comes to be different from a triceps muscle.

How do cellular differentiation and morphogenesis actually occur? This is not a rhetorical question, and there is no simple answer. It would seem, after well over a hundred years of working at the problem, that there should be some astounding explanation. But despite our vast experience and powerful new technological breakthroughs, many of the most critical aspects of the problem have not yielded to the incessant probing of biologists.

GAMETES AND FERTILIZATION

The Sperm

Except for a few differences in size and shape, the sperm cells of most animals are essentially similar. Perhaps this similarity stems from their common mission: to move about and penetrate the egg. The principal structures of a sperm are the *head, midpiece,* and *tail* (Figure 41.1). The head contains highly condensed *chromatin* (chromosomal DNA and its related proteins). At the tip of the head is an enzyme-laden *acrosome,* which helps the sperm penetrate the egg. The midpiece contains a curiously shaped, spiralling mitochondrion, along with a centriole and the roots of the microtubules that make up the *flagellum,* or tailpiece. The midpiece provides the sperm's propulsive power. It contains the mitochondria that generate the ATP needed to sustain the action of the flagellum.

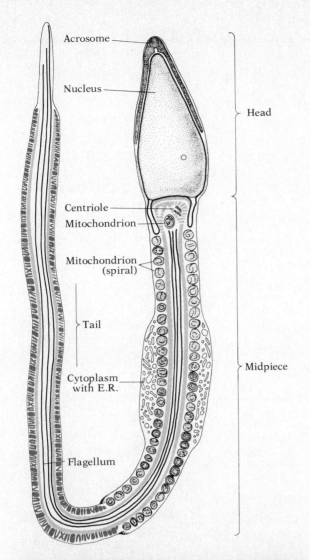

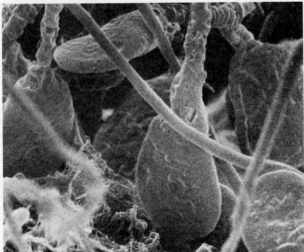

41.1

(*Top*) The human sperm, with its inclusion bodies, is similar to the sperm of other mammals. (Bottom) Scanning electron microscope view.

The Egg

Sperm are much smaller than eggs, but this is not to say all eggs are huge. Humans, like other mammals ranging from mice to whales, produce extremely small eggs, barely visible to the unaided eye (at ovulation the human egg is only about 0.15 mm in diameter—smaller than the period at the end of this sentence). Human egg yolk (the food reserve) is extremely meager in comparison to that of most other vertebrates, but not much yolk is necessary. This is because after a few days of travel through the oviduct, the early mammalian embryo will implant itself in the endometrium and immediately begin drawing nutrients from the mother.

At ovulation, the human egg (Figure 41.2) emerges from the ovary surrounded by a dense covering of follicle cells known collectively as the **corona radiata** ("radiating crown"). Below the corona radiata lies a thick, glassy area, the **zona pellucida** ("clear zone"), which is secreted by corona cells. Finally, below the zona pellucida is the cell membrane, which is called the *vitelline membrane*.

Fertilization

The events of **fertilization,** a complex process in which sperm and egg become joined, are somewhat similar in all animals. Because such echinoderms as sea urchins, sand dollars, and sea stars can be readily induced to shed great numbers of eggs and sperm that survive and function well in the laboratory, fertilization in echinoderms has been intensively studied as representative of the process in animals.

Only recently have we actually been able to observe fertilization in humans. It seems that it should be easy to place a sperm and egg together and to watch them join. In fact, obtaining human sperm is not very difficult. Getting human eggs is another matter entirely, requiring delicate surgery; but now it can be done. In fact, the "test tube" babies that have so captivated the media are the result of such surgery. In test-tube fertilization, viable eggs are removed from a woman, fertilized in the laboratory, and implanted into the uterus. Several hundred children have been conceived this way, but only a few cases have been publicized. (One wonders at all the hubbub. The same procedure—*in vitro* fertilization—has long been done on a mass scale in commercial cattle breeding, where it somehow seems less amazing.)

Under normal conditions, sperm reach the egg somewhere in the upper oviduct, following a chemical attractant produced by the egg. When a

41.2

The human oocyte contains a haploid nucleus and cytoplasm, complete with the usual cellular organelles. The cytoplasm is surrounded by the vitelline membrane, and outside of that is the zona pellucida. The sphere of cells surrounding and penetrating the zona pellucida originates in the follicle and is known as the corona radiata; it is shed at fertilization and the entire oocyte surface changes significantly.

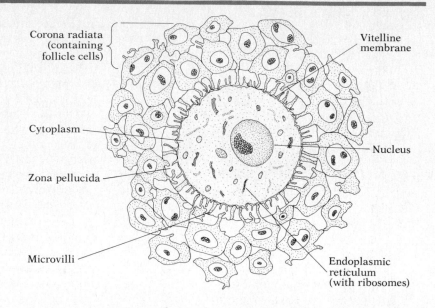

Corona radiata (containing follicle cells)

Cytoplasm

Zona pellucida

Microvilli

Vitelline membrane

Nucleus

Endoplasmic reticulum (with ribosomes)

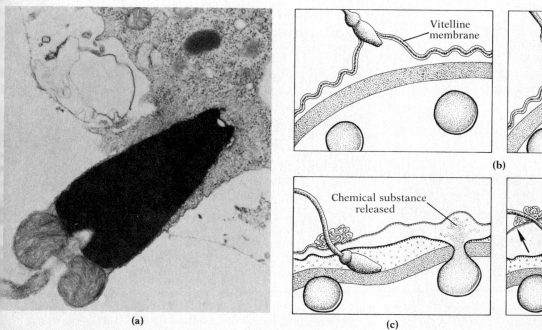

(a)

Vitelline membrane

(b)

Chemical substance released

(c)

Fertilization—membrane rises up

(d)

41.3

Fertilization. In echinoderms, when a sperm head makes contact with the egg (a), the vitelline layer separates from the membrane proper, forming many microvilli—fingerlike projections that surround and snare the sperm head, drawing it into the egg (b). The sperm's entry triggers a chemical response in the egg, transforming the vitelline layer into a fertilization membrane. This sperm barrier rises in a wave over the egg surface, trapping other sperm within (c). The sperm head then enlarges to form the male pronucleus, which will soon fuse with its female counterpart. In humans, fertilization is associated with the completion of meiosis II and the formation of a second polar body (d).

number of sperm reach the neighborhood of the egg, each releases an enzyme from the acrosome that breaks down the corona radiata, allowing contact with the clear zona pellucida. They also produce a substance that causes other sperm to clump and become inactive when their numbers become great enough. Even though only one sperm normally fuses with the egg, thousands are required to supply enough of the enzyme to dissolve the corona radiata.

Once the egg is penetrated by a sperm, a cascade of events suddenly produces a sperm barrier, a tough *fertilization membrane* over the surface of the zygote, rendering it impenetrable to other sperm. After being penetrated by a sperm, the human egg immediately completes its second meiotic division. Two polar bodies are thus produced, a sure sign of successful fertilization (Figure 41.3).

After successful penetration of the zona pellucida and the vitelline membrane, the sperm head enters the egg cytoplasm, leaving its midpiece and tail behind. The sperm nucleus then rapidly swells and becomes rounded. Now called the *male pronucleus*, it migrates to its counterpart in the egg—the haploid *female pronucleus*. During this migration and swelling, both male and female pronuclei complete a round of DNA synthesis in preparation for the first mitosis. Then the two pronuclei fuse to form the diploid zygote nucleus, and development of a new individual is under way.

CLEAVAGE

The zygote now enters its first mitotic division, or **cleavage,** as it is known in the early stages of development. This division produces two cells, which then form four, which form eight, and so on. Mitosis occurs before each round of division. Because there is no cell growth during this period, the cells become smaller with each round of cleavage. The process is slower in some species than in others. For example, although the first cleavage in sand dollars may begin within an hour of fertilization, cleavage in fertilized frog eggs does not begin until after about 90 minutes; and cleavage in human zygotes does not begin until about a day and a half after fertilization.

Patterns of cleavage also vary among different animals. The main variable seems to be the amount of yolk in the fertilized egg. Yolk is an inert material that is inactive in the cleavage process. In fact, it hinders cleavage simply by its inactive bulk (Figure 41.4).

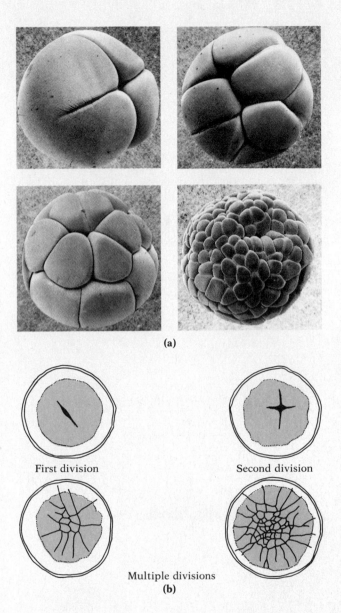

(a)

First division

Second division

Multiple divisions
(b)

41.4

(a) Cleavages in the amphibian embryo begin simply enough, with the first producing two cells of equal size and content. The cleavages following, however, are highly unequal, with smaller cells emerging at the top and larger cells at the bottom. This trend will continue, with the upper cells, or animal pole, dividing much more rapidly than the lower, vegetal pole cells. (b) Early cleavages in the bird egg are quite different from those of the amphibian. The immense yolk of the bird makes complete cell division impossible, so at first, a small group of cells lying at the surface actively divides. This disc of cells will form the embryo proper.

THE EMBRYONIC STAGES

As the young embryonic cells divide, a solid mass of cells (the **morula**) is produced, which develops a cavity (the *blastocoele*) as the embryo reaches the hollow **blastula** stage. Development in human, frog, and chicken embryos is similar in many ways, but the developmental process is still adapted to accommodate the yolk mass. In all three types of embryos, rapidly dividing cells next form a migrating surface wave that rolls under at a designated region, invading the cavity within. This invasion, called **gastrulation,** is a critical developmental event that ushers in the *gastrula* stage.

The Gastrula. The **gastrula** stage is important because it marks the point at which the three em-bryonic *germ layers* first appear. You may recall from our discussions of animal evolution (see Chapter 28) that animals with three germ layers in their embryos are capable of developing complex organs and systems. The important point here is that gastrulation produces the first pronounced embryonic tissue organization, which marks the beginning of the differentiation between internal and external parts of the animal. Figure 41.5 illustrates the differences in gastrulation in frog and chicken embryos.

We learned earlier that the ectoderm will form such parts as the nervous system and skin; the endoderm will form such structures as the lining of the gut, lungs, and most glands; and the other internal organs, as well as bones and muscles, are derived from mesoderm. (Table 41.1 indicates the structures derived from each germ layer.)

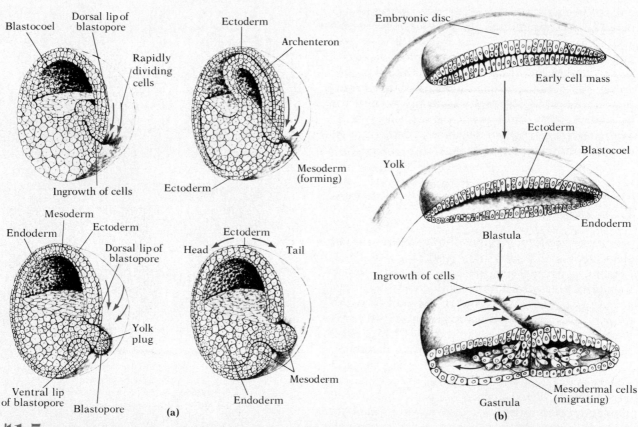

41.5

In the amphibian **(a),** gastrulation begins as a rapidly growing region of the animal pole and progresses inward, forming an invagination (ingrowth into) the blastula. The continued ingrowth displaces the original cavity of the blastula, and subsequently forms a new cavity, the archenteron, or primitive gut. With the continuation of gastrulation, a three-layered embryo forms with outer ectodermal, middle mesodermal, and inner endodermal cell layers. Because of the bulk of the yolk, the bird embryo **(b)** will follow a different pattern of gastrulation. The elongated disc of cells (embryonic disc) contains two layers: an upper ectoderm and a lower mesoderm. The upper layer rises up to produce an elongated blastula cavity. Then an ingrowth of cells begins that is not unlike that seen in the amphibian. It occurs at a midline along the length of the embryo. The ingrowth releases a number of loosely arranged cells, which become the mesoderm of the bird embryo.

TABLE 41.1

Derivatives of the three germ layers

Ectoderm	Mesoderm	Endoderm
Epidermis	Skeleton	Linings of:
Hair	Muscle	Gut
Milk glands	Skeletal	Pancreas
Oil glands	Smooth	Respiratory system
Sweat glands	Cardiac	Pharynx
Mouth lining	Dermis	Liver
Lens of eye	Blood	Urinary bladder
Inner ear	Gonads	
Nervous system	Kidney	
Brain		
Spinal cord		
Spinal nerves		
Adrenal medulla		

NOTE: The germ layers do not generally produce entire structures, but are responsible for their basic format during development. All organs eventually contain tissues derived from all three germ layers.

INDUCTION AND NEURULATION

Soon after gastrulation has occurred, newly formed mesodermal cells coalesce to form a supporting rod along the length of the developing embryo. This is the *notochord*, the structure that gives the chordate phylum its name. In *Branchiostoma*, a cephalochordate (see Chapter 29), the notochord will be the principal internal stiffening rod throughout life; in amphibians and virtually all other vertebrates, it exists only briefly, as its supportive role is taken over by the vertebral column. The notochord has a vital function to perform: it must *induce* the ectodermal cells lying above it to begin the formation of the central nervous system. The events through which the crude outlines of the central nervous system are formed are **neurulation,** and the embryo, at this time, is a **neurula.**

Induction is one of the more fascinating phenomena associated with embryonic development. In induction, one part of the embryo causes another part to proceed along a very specific developmental route. Apparently, some chemical diffuses from the *inducer* (here, the notochord) to the *target* (here, the ectoderm).

In neurulation, the notochord causes the overlying ectoderm to thicken along the dorsal surface of the embryo, forming the *neural plate*. Next, the outer edges of the plate rise up as *neural folds*, increase in size, and curve inward. Then the folds fuse along the embryo, producing the *neural tube*, which will eventually become the dorsal, hollow nerve cord. At the anterior (head) end of the neural tube, the last region to close, there is considerable expansion; here the tube takes on a bulbous form that will become the vertebrate brain (Figure 41.6).

Blocks of mesoderm, called *somites*, will come to lie along either side of the neural tube. They will form the heavy, protective series of bones (the vertebrae) that will protect the sensitive central nervous system.

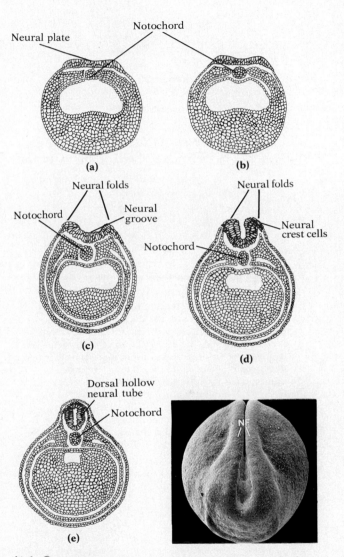

41.6

Neurulation is a remarkable process in the vertebrate embryo, resulting in a clearly recognizable embryo. In the frog, we see the events unfold. **(a)** Ectodermal cells form a thickened plate along the embryo. **(b, c)** The edges then grow, rising up into folds. **(d, e)** These will join above, grow together, and form the dorsal hollow nerve cord. This then sinks below the surface and becomes covered by new ectoderm. With our surface view, we see that the closure of the neural folds first begins at the center, proceeding in both directions, but lagging behind at the anterior end. The folds there become greatly enlarged as they form the crude outlines of the rudimentary brain. (Photo courtesy Carolina Biological Supply)

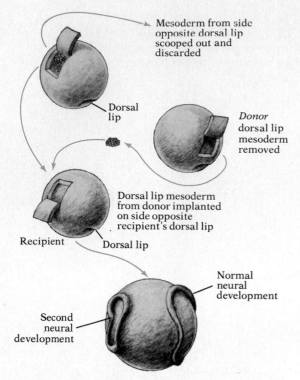

41.7 ───────────────

Spemann transplanted mesoderm from a donor frog embryo to a recipient embryo. Opening an ectodermal flap opposite the dorsal lip of the recipient embryo, he scooped out and discarded the underlying mesoderm. He replaced it with mesoderm from below the dorsal lip ectoderm (the usual site of neurulation) of a donor embryo. The wound healed and the embryo entered its neurulation stage, which proceeded normally, but at the point of the mesodermal transplant, another neurulation process occurred. Spemann reasoned that the mesoderm induced neurulation in the ectoderm—evidence for the *induction theory*.

EXPERIMENTAL EMBRYOLOGY

Much of what we know about normal embryonic development has been known for a long time, but it wasn't until this century that experiments were carried out on embryos in an effort to unveil their many mysteries. A clear breakthrough occurred in the 1920s with the work of Nobel prize winner Hans Spemann.

In a crucial set of experiments, Spemann studied neurulation in the frog embryo, a fascinating phenomenon that had already been observed in great detail. Specifically, Spemann wanted to know what was going on in the germ layers just before neurulation began. What factors prompted the ectoderm's curious change to nerve tissue?

Choosing a region of the gastrula called the *dorsal lip of the blastopore* (the opening formed by the ingrowth of cells during gastrulation), Spemann carried out some amazingly delicate surgery. He first removed some of the ectoderm, then cultured both the damaged embryo and the excised tissue. The embryo failed to develop normally, and the excised tissue formed an undifferentiated blob of cells. This is what you might expect from such damage, but it established that, on its own, ectoderm would not produce anything recognizable.

In the next step (Figure 41.7), Spemann scooped out some mesoderm from below the dorsal lip ectoderm of a *donor* gastrula, and transferred it to a *recipient* gastrula. Operating on the recipient, he lifted a flap in the ectoderm *on the side opposite the dorsal lip* and implanted the dorsal lip mesoderm from the donor. That is to say, he implanted a bit of this material beneath what would normally de-

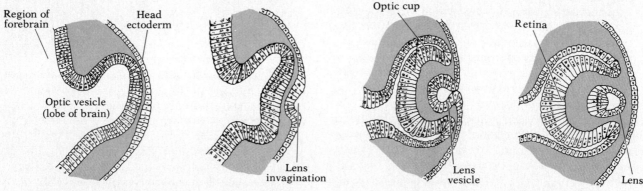

41.8 ───────────────

In the development of the eye in vertebrates (including frogs), an outpocketing of the rudimentary brain grows towards the overlying ectoderm. Upon contact, the ectoderm thickens and begins to grow inward. The brain tissue then begins sinking back, forming the op-

tic cup. The ectodermal invagination continues until a sphere of cells, the rudimentary lens, is formed. The cells within the optic cup will form the retina, while the surrounding layer will form the pigmented tissue of the eye.

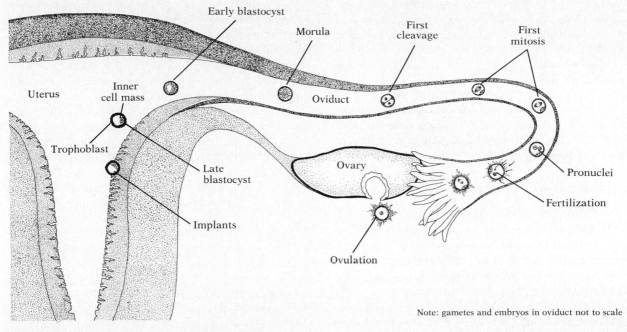

Early blastocyst

Morula

First cleavage

First mitosis

Uterus

Inner cell mass

Trophoblast

Late blastocyst

Implants

Oviduct

Ovary

Ovulation

Pronuclei

Fertilization

Note: gametes and embryos in oviduct not to scale

41.9

After ovulation, the human oocyte is drawn into the oviduct, where fertilization can occur. From the time of fertilization, about six days are required for the transit to the receptive uterus. The first cleavage oc-curs about 36 hours after fertilization, but later divisions occur much faster. When the embryo enters the uterus, it will be a morula. This solid ball of cells will hollow out into a blastocyst.

velop into the amphibian's belly skin. Development proceeded, but amazingly, a second neurulation event occurred at the site of the transplant! In fact, embryos that survived grew a second head. The dorsal lip mesoderm took on a new significance.

Spemann's series of experiments revealed two major points. The obvious one is that the dorsal lip mesoderm can influence development in whatever ectoderm happens to lie over it. An extension of that idea is that different embryonic tissues influence each other reciprocally. This is the influence that came to be known as induction, since one tissue induces changes in another. Since Spemann's initial efforts, many other instances of embryonic induction have been found. An elegant example is the development of the lens of the eye, a case of "triple induction" (Figure 41.8).

Many years were to pass before biologists felt that they had gained the biochemical sophistication and methodology to approach induction from a molecular angle. Spemann's experiments were refined over and over as the search narrowed. Was the mesodermal messenger some kind of hormone? Or was it perhaps an enzyme, or some kind of RNA messenger? Perhaps induction involved just a change in pH and ionic strength. No chemical agent has ever been conclusively identified as *the* inducing agent.

THE EARLY HUMAN EMBRYO

The Support System

Unlike most vertebrates, the mammalian embryo does not need to carry a large food supply or develop heavy protective structures. This is because the embryo is protected within the mother's body and its nutrients are derived from *her* after implantation in the uterus. In order for the embryo to avail itself of the mother's bloodstream as a source of food and oxygen, and as a repository of various wastes, certain very specialized membranes, which form the **placenta**, must arise outside the embryonic body in a particular manner and sequence.

After fertilization of the egg in the oviduct, the first cleavage of the human zygote begins after a delay of about a day and a half. The young embryo technically reaches the morula stage when a ball of 32 cells has formed after five successive divisions (Figure 41.9). Then, as the morula-stage embryo approaches the uterus, other noticeable changes begin to occur.

After additional cell divisions, the ball of cells hollows out, transforming the early embryo into a **blastocyst.** The blastocyst (this stage corresponds to the blastula stage of other chordates) has the appearance of a signet ring. An inner, denser, clump of cells on one side—the *inner cell mass*—is destined to become both the embryo proper and most of the **extraembryonic membranes,** while the single layer forming most of the sphere—the **trophoblast**—is a mammalian specialization for invading the uterine wall and obtaining and providing the first nourishment for the young embryo (Figure 41.10). It is at this time, about six days after fertilization, that the embryo implants itself in the mother's endometrium.

Implantation of the Embryo

As the blastocyst reaches the endometrium (Figure 41.11), the cells of its trophoblast begin secreting hormones that increase the receptivity of the endometrium and signal the mother's hormonal system to continue its secretion of progesterone (progesterone helps prepare the uterus for the embryo's invasion—see Chapter 40). Upon contact, the trophoblast begins probing the uterine surface through cellular projections that penetrate the endometrium (see Figure 41.11b). To facilitate penetration, the trophoblast secretes protein-digesting enzymes that break down uterine tissue, permitting the blastocyst to sink into a blood-filled cavity.

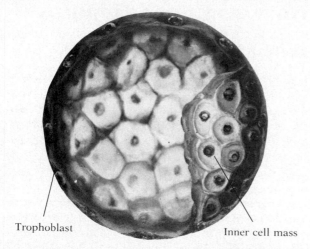

Trophoblast

Inner cell mass

41.10

The human blastocyst is about the same size as the fertilized egg from which it formed, but at the time of implantation it may contain well over 100 cells. Those destined to form the embryo are clustered together into what is called the "inner cell mass," while the remainder form a hollow sphere known as the trophoblast. The trophoblast is unique to mammals and represents an evolutionary step required for the placental mode of development. It is the trophoblast that will form the initial communicating link between embryo and mother when implantation begins.

After this invasion, the trophoblast produces a large number of projections, the **primary chorionic villi,** which greatly increase the exchange surface between embryo and mother (see Figure 41.11c). During this early period, cells from the trophoblast will produce the *chorion,* a layer that will enclose the embryo and its structures. The chorion will later produce **secondary chorionic villi** that will probe deeply into the mother's tissues.

Meanwhile, there have been many changes in the inner cell mass. An outer layer of cells divides rapidly, rising up to form what will become the *amnion.* The remaining cells of the inner cell mass form the **embryonic disc,** which is about two cells thick. At this point, the embryonic disc resembles a shelf and divides the blastocyst into two fluid-filled chambers: the smaller **amniotic cavity** above the disc, and a larger cavity (the *blastocyst cavity*) below (see Figure 41.11c). The fluid-filled amniotic cavity will surround the embryo throughout its development, constantly enlarging to accommodate fetal growth. The *amniotic fluid* will cushion the delicate embryo and help lubricate developing limbs and digits, preventing them from fusing during growth. (The amnion and its fluid are later referred to as the "bag of water"—the one that breaks, announcing the impending birth).

The lower layer of the two-layered embryonic disc, the endoderm, soon behaves in a remarkable way: It spreads outward at the edges and then folds under to form a *yolk sac* (see Figure 41.11c). In the bird egg these same cell movements enclose the yolk mass, but in the human embryo, they enclose clear fluid, forming a third fluid-filled chamber. Blood cells and blood vessels form in the yolk sac, which remains small and becomes increasingly insignificant as the embryo itself grows.

It is at this time, some two weeks into development, that the unstructured, two-layered embryonic disc begins to change rapidly. The disc takes on an elongated slipper shape; a streak (the *primitive streak*) appears down its center; and the mammalian version of gastrulation occurs. Gastrulation is rapidly followed by the formation of a notochord and neurulation. By the third week of development, the neural folds rise up and begin to close, and somites appear at each side (see Figure 41.14a). Progress is rapid, and at 26 days, the brain is outlined, the crude S-shaped heart has formed, and the embryo has elongated, its post-anal tail announcing its vertebrate status. At this time the embryo is about 3.6 mm (1/8 in) long.

As these fast-moving events progress, the **allantois,** the final extraembryonic membrane, also develops. This is important, since it will contribute blood vessels during the formation of the placenta. This is its only function in primates, although in

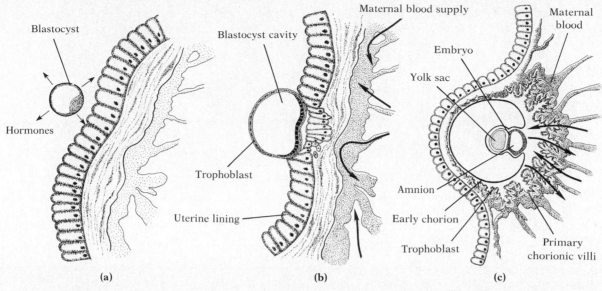

(a) (b) (c)

41.11

Communication between embryo and mother occurs early. The trophoblast **(a)** secretes a hormone, similar to LH, signalling the corpus luteum in the ovary to continue secreting the endometrium-supporting hormone, progesterone. As implantation begins **(b)**, fingerlike growths of the trophoblast penetrate the endometrium, secreting enzymes that will clear a small, blood-filled cavity into which the blastocyst will sink.

During this brief period, the embryo continues to change. The amnion, first of the extraembryonic structures, then begins to balloon out. Later, cells on the opposite side will form a second cavity, the yolk sac, which resides within the trophoblast cavity **(c).** At this time, the embryo itself is represented by an elongated plate, only two cell layers in thickness.

other mammals and in birds and reptiles, it collects wastes and fuses with the chorion to form the *chorioallantois*. The connections between the embryo proper and the extraembryonic membranes narrow somewhat to become the **body stalk** (Figure 41.12). Later, the body stalk will become the **umbilical cord.** Its point of attachment to the embryo is the *umbilicus* ("belly button"). The blood vessels of the allantois become the arteries and veins of the umbilical cord.

With the development of the allantois and the embryo's circulatory system, the placenta emerges. The chorionic villi enlarge and blood vessels penetrate to form extensive capillary beds. The maternal and embryonic blood are separated by only a thin layer of cells, which permits oxygen and growth-supporting substances to be readily exchanged for metabolic wastes.

Despite the great changes that have occurred so far, the embryo will not be clearly recognizable as human until after eight weeks of development (see Figure 41.14d). At that time, it will be about 25 mm (1 in) in length and growing rapidly. The embryo is commonly referred to as a **fetus** from this time until birth. The eight-week-old fetus, de-

cidedly human, floats in a sea of amniotic fluid. As growth progresses, the placenta comes to contain so many blood vessels that it takes on a fibrous appearance. Its exchange surface by now consists of numerous mounds of tissue, each containing many microvilli that drastically increase its surface area; each microvillus contains its own capillaries from the placental vessels (Figure 41.13).

DEVELOPMENT OF THE HUMAN FETUS

Clinically, the 280-day gestation period of human development is divided into three parts called **trimesters.** Most of the significant morphological events occur during the first trimester (Figure 41.14).

Several of the morphological events of the first trimester are quite fascinating. For example, the early heart—one of the first functional organs—begins as a simple tube, which must grow into an S-shape before the atria and ventricles can emerge. The early human embryo even has gill arches at

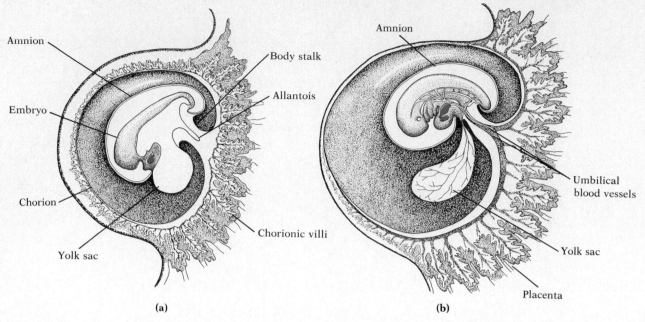

Amnion

Embryo

Chorion

Yolk sac

Body stalk

Allantois

Chorionic villi

(a)

Amnion

Umbilical blood vessels

Yolk sac

Placenta

(b)

41.12

As the embryo continues its development **(a)**, it will undergo the mammalian version of gastrulation. The yolk sac will have enlarged, as will the amnion, now a fluid-filled membrane. Another extraembryonic structure, the allantois, will have appeared, and will contribute to the body stalk. The fingerlike processes that earlier exchanged materials with the endometrium

have now elaborated into far more extensive growths. At about five weeks after conception **(b)**, blood vessels from the embryo—the umbilical veins and arteries—will have branched out into the villi, and the placenta will have formed. The circulatory system is fully functional at this time.

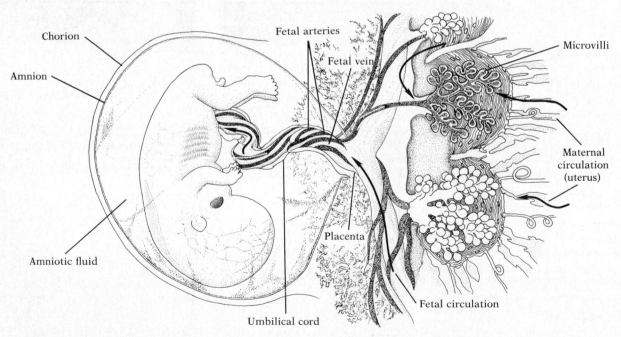

Chorion

Amnion

Amniotic fluid

Fetal arteries

Fetal vein

Placenta

Umbilical cord

Microvilli

Maternal circulation (uterus)

Fetal circulation

41.13

By about the eighth week of life, the embryo takes on a decidedly human form. It is suspended by the body stalk in a pool of amniotic fluid, and the amnion itself has become surrounded by a fourth membrane, the

chorion. The placenta has continued to enlarge as the demands for vital exchanges increase with the embryo's growth.

610

one stage, but each gill arch eventually contributes to the lower jaw, tongue, larynx, middle ear, pharynx, and other final structures—seemingly retracing vertebrate history. The limbs make their appearance as tiny, rounded buds. Their ends go through a paddle-like stage before finger and toe separations occur. The reproductive organs have a unique way of emerging. At about seven weeks, they appear in what is called an "indifferent state"—that is, both sexes are identical. A protrusion called the *genital tubercle* appears; depending on genetic instructions and hormonal output, it will enlarge as the glans penis, or withdraw as the glans clitoris. Folds at either side will emerge as scrotal growth or as labia majora. In males, a groove in the penis will grow together, enclosing the urethra. In females, the groove will differentiate into the labia minora.

By the end of the first trimester, many of the physiological systems will have reached a fairly advanced state of development. The second and third trimester are devoted primarily to continued growth and refinement (see Figure 41.14d and e).

The central nervous system requires all of this time to grow and differentiate, and the bones, which began as beds of cartilage, will continuously take in minerals and harden. These activities place a high demand on the mother's reserves of mineral and protein. Antibodies from the mother cross the placenta during the last month of pregnancy. They will provide the newborn baby with immunity against viral and bacterial infections for a month or two. As the third trimester ends, the fetus, now crowding the mother's abdomen, will weigh about 3200 g (7 lbs) and measure close to 50 cm (19 in) in length.

BIRTH

The birth process has been divided into three stages (Figure 41.15). The first stage involves *dilation* of the cervix, accompanied by a softening of

41.14

Development of the human embryo and fetus. At three weeks (a), many organs have begun to develop, and by five weeks (b) the developing eyes and limbs are apparent. At seven weeks (c), the embryo is almost an inch long. As the fetus enters its third month of development (d), the placenta is beginning to produce hormones, and by 16 weeks of development (e), the placenta is fully developed.

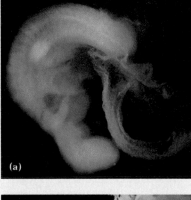
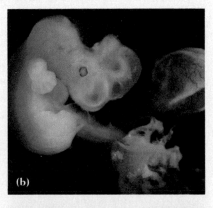
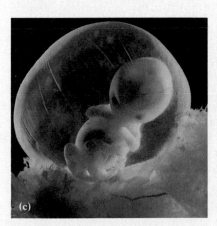
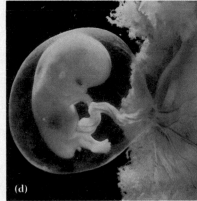
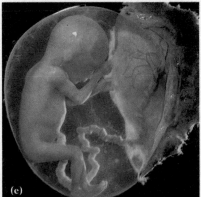

41.15

The birth process. In the first stage of labor, dilation of the cervix occurs and the baby's head eventually crowns *(top)*. The second stage of labor involves the actual expulsion of the fetus *(bottom)*. Expulsion of the placenta—the third stage—follows the birth of the baby.

the cervical tissue. The period of dilation is highly variable, lasting from a few to many hours. It is accompanied by periodic contractions of the uterus called "labor pains." These contractions increase in frequency through the first stage. When they begin to occur every three to four minutes, the head of the fetus *crowns* as it begins to push through the cervical opening. This begins stage two, the *expulsion* of the fetus.

The expulsion process may last from a few minutes to hours. An anesthetic may be required at this time. The pain is highly variable, depending on the mother's emotional state, pain threshold, cultural conditioning, and preparedness.

The final stage of birth is the separation of the placenta and its expulsion from the uterus as the *afterbirth*. In most sophisticated medical facilities, the afterbirth is carefully studied for any abnormalities and for completeness of expulsion.

So now, both the fetus and the placenta have been expelled. What happens to the uterus? Although it has been stretched to some 16 times its former size, it constricts rapidly into a solid ball shape—but total recovery requires five to six

weeks. The contractions help to slow the bleeding at the site of placental detachment.

PHYSIOLOGICAL CHANGES IN THE NEWBORN

Because the baby has been propelled into a harsh new world with startling speed, its systems must be prepared for a new and threatening existence. The vital exchange of gases, for example, formerly provided by the placenta, now must occur independently. The infant's respiratory system must function on its own for the first time.

The circulatory system must also change quickly (Figure 41.16). Oxygenated blood from the placental circulation previously entered the fetus through the umbilical vein, proceeding directly into the vena cava and to the right side of the heart through a hole in the septum between the fetal atria, the **foramen ovale.** Before birth, this opening permitted the blood to flow from the right atrium to the left atrium, thus circumventing the route to the deflated and useless embryonic lungs. In addition, a connecting vessel between the pulmonary artery and aorta, the **ductus arteriosus,** permitted blood from the right ventricle to bypass the lungs and go directly into arterial distribution.

With the baby's first breaths, the ductus arteriosus constricts vigorously, closing that bypass. With the shortcut closed, the blood must move through the rapidly expanding lungs. As a result of this increased pulmonary flow, the volume of blood returning directly to the left atrium suddenly increases. This closes the foramen ovale, which is composed of two overlapping flaps of tissue. If all is well, the foramen ovale will heal completely in about one year.

The first breath of a newborn infant is taken in response to a sudden increase in blood CO_2 when the placental exchange is lost. The rise in CO_2 stimulates the respiratory center of the medulla, with the usual result. The baby will begin to breathe with or without the traditional swat on its rear. However, many physicians believe that the swat can stimulate movement and the expulsion of fluid, speeding up the respiratory process.

Some newly fashionable delivery procedures, by contrast, emphasize birth in a quiet, semidarkened room, no swats, and immediate immersion of the newborn into comfortable lukewarm water.

Lactation

Human mothers, like other mammalian mothers, **lactate.** That is, they produce milk. In fact, they are able to nurse their young immediately after delivery. The breasts, under the influence of estrogen and progesterone, enlarge during pregnancy, and with the delivery, *colostrum* secretion begins. **Colostrum,** a clear, yellowish fluid, differs from milk in that it contains more protein, vitamins, and minerals, and less sugar and fat. It also contains many of the mother's *antibodies,* defenses that can be important to the infant in its first days. The secretion doesn't begin until after birth because the milk-stimulating hormone *prolactin* is suppressed while the progesterone levels of pregnancy are high. A second hormone involved in the production of milk, *oxytocin,* is released in response to suckling.

In a few days, the colostrum is replaced by the whiter, thicker fluid, *milk.* Human milk contains about 700 calories per liter and is sufficient in all required vitamins except vitamin D. In comparison to cow's milk, human milk contains about one-third less casein protein (making it easier to digest), much more milk sugar (lactose), and considerably less calcium and butterfat. It is less acidic, and, interestingly, is bacteria-free.

The processes of fertilization, growth, and development are, indeed, remarkable. Each of us goes through these stages, which may partially explain our fascination with the newcomers to our small planet. A great deal of attention has been focused on ensuring normality through the developmental stages, but this area remains one of the most mysterious and compelling in biology.

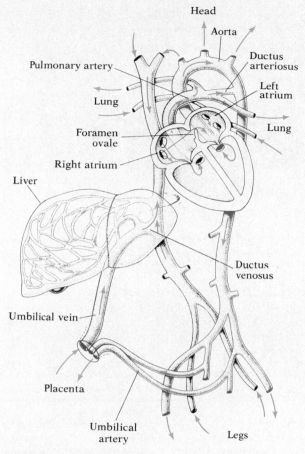

41.16

Parts of the fetal circulatory system change drastically at birth. These involve the umbilical circulation, the foramen ovale of the heart, and the ductus arteriosus, a connecting vessel between the pulmonary artery and the aorta.

Summary

Introduction
Development, a process that begins at conception and continues until death, has three distinct aspects: growth, cellular differentiation, and morphogenesis.

Gametes and Fertilization
Sperm cells are similar in most animals and consist of a chromatin-carrying head, a midpiece containing a mitochondrion, and a whiplike tail. Egg cells contain the yolk and are covered by a corona radiata, zona pellucida, and vitelline membrane. In fertilization, the sperm penetrates the egg and becomes the male pronucleus, which fuses with the haploid female pronucleus to form the diploid zygote nucleus.

Cleavage
Cleavage is the process of early cell division, in which the cells become smaller with each round of mitosis. The rate and pattern of cleavage vary among animals.

The Embryonic Stages
As cell division continues, the embryo goes through a morula stage and a hollow blastula stage. The surface cells then migrate and roll under, invading the cavity in gastrulation. The gastrula stage marks the formation of the germ layers—endoderm, ectoderm, and mesoderm—and the beginning of differentiation between the internal and external parts of the animal.

Induction and Neurulation
In induction, one tissue layer influences the differentiation of another. During neurulation, for example, the notochord, a mesodermal derivative, induces the ectoderm to form the hollow nerve cord.

Experimental Embryology
Using frog gastrulas, Spemann helped explain the role of the mesoderm in inducing the ectoderm to form the early nervous system. Since his experiments, many

other examples of induction have been found, but specific inducing substances have yet to be identified.

The Early Human Embryo

The six-day-old human embryo, a blastocyst, implants in the endometrium. Trophoblast cells secrete hormones that maintain the endometrium and enzymes that break down the uterine tissue, permitting the blastocyst to implant. The trophoblast produces the primary chorionic villi and later the chorion, while the inner cell mass produces the amnion, the yolk sac, the allantois, and the early embryo. The latter two have very limited functions, producing the first blood cells and umbilical vessels in mammals. Gastrulation and neurulation follow, and by the eighth week, the major systems have all formed and the placenta is well developed, connected to the fetus by the umbilical cord. The mature placenta contains numerous villi and microvilli, which provide intimate contact between fetal and maternal circulatory systems.

Development of the Human Fetus

Most of the development of the fetus takes place in the first trimester (three months), when it goes through fertilization, implantation, gastrulation, neurulation, and morphogenesis. The second and third trimesters are devoted in large part to growth and to refinement of the central nervous system and hardening of the bones.

Birth

The birth process occurs in three stages: dilation of the cervix and regular contractions of the uterus, expulsion of the fetus, and separation of the placenta and its expulsion as afterbirth.

Physiological Changes in the Newborn

The newborn's respiratory and circulatory systems must change rapidly to sustain life. Rising carbon dioxide levels in the baby's blood trigger the respiratory response, while the ductus arteriosus and foramen ovale close, forcing the blood to be routed to the left atrium.

The newborn first receives colostrum from the mother, a fluid that contains more protein, vitamins, and minerals and less sugar and fat than milk, as well as the mother's antibodies. After a few days, prolactin and oxytocin are released to stimulate milk production and release, respectively. Human milk is easier to digest and contains more milk sugar than cow's milk, and is bacteria-free.

Key Terms

embryology	morula	blastocyst	body stalk
growth	blastula	extraembryonic membranes	umbilical cord
cellular differentiation	gastrulation	trophoblast	fetus
morphogenesis	gastrula	primary chorionic villi	trimesters
corona radiata	neurulation	secondary chorionic villi	foramen ovale
zona pellucida	neurula	embryonic disc	ductus arteriosus
fertilization	induction	amniotic cavity	colostrum
cleavage	placenta	allantois	

Review Questions

1. Define the three aspects of development. (p. 600)
2. Using simple sketches, describe the structures of sperm and egg cells and identify their functions. (pp. 600–602)
3. Describe the responses of egg cells during fertilization. What is the visual evidence of fertilization in a human egg? (p. 603)
4. Compare cleavage in the frog and bird, and account for the difference in patterns. (pp. 603–604)
5. Describe gastrulation in an amphibian embryo, listing the germ layers formed. Explain their significance to future events. (p. 604)
6. Spemann's experiments led to the theory of embryonic induction. Briefly review his procedure and results, and explain what induction is. (pp. 605–607)
7. Describe neurulation in the amphibian, and indicate how induction is involved. (pp. 606–607)
8. Describe the human embryo six days after fertilization. What is the importance of each part? (p. 608)
9. List four extraembryonic structures in the human embryo, and describe the role of each. Compared to other vertebrates, which of the four has (have) limited functions in the mammal? (pp. 608–609)
10. Briefly describe five important human developmental events of the first trimester. When does the embryo become a fetus? (pp. 609–611)
11. Describe the specific changes that must occur in the circulatory and respiratory systems of a newborn. (p. 612)

PART VII

Behavior and Ecology:

Interrelationships in a Complex Biosphere

The Mechanisms and Development of Behavior

A cheetah crouches in the grass on some African plain. The wary gazelles it stalks are on the lookout, but step by step it stealthily draws near. When the cheetah finally moves, the effect is like the explosion of a granite statue. The gazelles immediately dart off in all directions. The cheetah is the fastest land animal on earth, but in most cases its chase is futile. The gazelles escape.

We have seen such chases before. They are almost standard fare on televised nature programs, although on film, we rarely see the cheetah fail. And think of the countless other animals we have watched on film, many of them species we have never seen in real life (and probably never will). Why do we watch these films? Is it mere curiosity? Why would people in St. Louis watch a film about penguins? Anything they learn from the program is more than they will ever need to know about penguins. Could it be that people are naturally curious about other species because our evolutionary history is inextricably linked to theirs?

For whatever reason, people are interested in animals and how they behave. So here we will take a close look at some of the ways they behave, paying particular attention to the mechanisms and development of the patterns.

INSTINCT

It was long believed that, while humans *learn* their behavior, other animals respond only to unalterable "instincts" stamped into their nervous systems at birth. Since mounting evidence over the years did not support this sweeping generalization, the instinct concept fell into some disrepute. The major questions, however, were largely answered by the work of two Europeans, Konrad Lorenz of Germany and the Dutchman Niko Tinbergen, who did most of his work in England. The two received the 1973 Nobel Prize for their work (along with Karl von Frisch).

Tinbergen and Lorenz called themselves ethologists. **Ethology** is the study of animals under natural conditions, or in laboratory experiments that are designed to discover the role of a behavioral pattern in the wild. The greatest resistance to the ethological approach to the study of behavior came from Americans who called their own approach *comparative psychology* and who concentrated primarily on learning, especially in laboratory rats under extremely artificial conditions.

Considering the confusion, it is hazardous to offer a definition of instinct. For now, we can say that **instinct** has been defined by ethologists as any genetically based, innate pattern that has developed as a result of natural selection. Instinctive behavior can undergo alteration through experience, especially in higher vertebrates, where learning is often a strong behavioral component.

There are theoretically two stages of an instinctive behavior, the **appetitive** and **consummatory stages.** The appetitive part is marked by more or less variable acts that are, to some degree, responsive to environmental cues. As the appetitive stage continues, however, each part is increasingly more stereotyped. Finally, the inflexible, unalterable consummatory act is performed and this leads to a measure of temporary satisfaction. The instinct theory presumes that an animal is born with a predisposition to perform basic behavioral patterns, and that the performance of these patterns usually benefits the animal.

The proper stimulus from the environment is called a **releaser** or **sign stimulus.** Theory has it that an increasing tendency to perform an act builds up in an animal, and that the proper stimulus then "releases" that behavior. The sight of a mouse may cause a hunting cat to crouch, and then the cat's wandering hunting behavior grows increasingly less flexible; each action in the sequence becomes more stereotyped until the cat performs the final consummatory behavior that leads to relief or satiation. In this case, the consummatory behavior consists of swallowing motions.

The theory thus assumes that the *drive* to perform an act usually leads to biological benefit. The releaser triggers a particular set of behavioral patterns by stimulating something in the nervous system; this activates the animal's muscles in such a way that the consummatory pattern is finally performed. No one knows what is activated by the perception of a releaser, but the neural response center has been called the *innate releasing mechanism (IRM).* Each releaser activates an IRM that then controls behavior by activating muscles that produce the instinctive action. The final phase, the consummatory act, brings relief (and the sequence of behavior patterns may not appear again for some time). Now let's consider each of these ideas in more detail.

Fixed-Action Patterns

Many kinds of animals are born with a tendency to perform certain complex behavioral patterns. For example, the first time a tern chick is given a small fish, it jerks its head around in such a way that the fish is swallowed head first, the spines on its back safely flattened. We have all seen tiny kittens teetering around on uncertain legs; even before they have mastered the art of walking, they try to pounce on whatever their bleary eyes can find. What compels them to attempt such a complex act so soon? We will examine why such behavioral patterns are performed later in this chapter, but for now let's just note that many very young animals are capable of quite complex behavioral patterns, and they apparently are born with the tendency and the ability (more or less) to perform them.

A **fixed action pattern** is a precise and identifiable behavior pattern that is innate and characteristic of a given species. Certain fixed-action patterns do not arise until later in an animal's development. They seem to develop and mature, just as physical structures do, and generally appear at about the time they might be useful. For example, vigorous wing flapping and other fixed-action patterns associated with flight normally appear at about the time a young bird is physically ready to begin flying. (Of course, the physical structures associated with flight, such as feathers and flight muscles, also must have matured.) Because some such innate patterns have a delayed onset, researchers once assumed that the animal had learned the behavior. In experiments, however, young birds restrained from wing flapping were still able to fly when the time came and the restraint was removed. (As mentioned, learning *can* have an effect on innate behavioral patterns. Although the ability to fly may be inherent, it can be improved with practice.) (Figure 42.1)

42.1 ━━━━━━━━━━━

A young eagle lands clumsily near an adult. Its fixed-action patterns will later be modified by learning, and its landing will be more graceful.

These acts may require specific movements that are performed in the same way by every member of the species. As an example, a bird may build its first nest by using peculiar sideways swipes of the head to jam twigs into the nest mass. All members of that species use the same motion. And have you noticed that all dogs scratch their ears the same way, by moving the rear leg outside the foreleg? There are numerous other examples; these precise and identifiable patterns exist in a wide range of animals, they are innate (present at birth), and they are characteristic for each species. Thus, *fixed-action patterns* are an important component of instinctive behavior.

Orienting Fixed-Action Patterns

Orienting movements, by which the fixed-action pattern is appropriately positioned and directed, are also components of instinctive behavior. A cat may pounce, but its chances for success are best if it pounces in the direction of the mouse. The scratching motion of a dog is most successful if it is applied directly to the itch. A young bird could get in a lot of trouble by jamming a twig meant for the nest into the wrong place. Orienting obviously has strong environmental components, since orienting cues are derived from the animal's surroundings.

Let's consider some well-documented examples of orienting a fixed-action pattern. The insect-capturing tongue flick of the frog (Figure 42.2) is a fixed-action pattern that does not occur until the frog moves around so that the fly is in the center of

42.3

In a classic experiment, Lorenz and Tinbergen showed that the behavior of a greylag goose rolling an egg back to her nest had two components: fixed and orienting. When they removed the egg while she was retrieving it, she continued the beak-tucking movements (the fixed component) but stopped the slight side-to-side movements that kept the egg moving in a straight line (the orienting component).

the frog's field of vision. This centrally oriented image, then, is what triggers the tongue flick. Once this behavior begins, it cannot be changed; if the fly moves now, the frog misses. The point is that the orienting component is performed according to certain specific environmental cues; it is adjustable. The fixed-action pattern is *not* adjustable; once it starts, it cannot be altered.

In some kinds of behaviors, the orienting and fixed components may be done simultaneously or they may even alternate in very complex ways, making them difficult—if not impossible—to distinguish. In the case of a frog zapping an insect, the two components of the instinctive act are easily distinguishable. But in other cases, careful experimentation may be necessary to separate the two. A simple but remarkable experiment by Lorenz and Tinbergen showed the two components operating together in a way that initially was not apparent. They saw that if an egg of a nesting goose rolls out of the nest, she will roll it back, drawing it along under her chin (Figure 42.3). She keeps the egg rolling in the right direction simply by moving her head from side to side. If the egg rolls to the right, she moves her head to the right as she continues to draw the egg toward her. In the experiment, the egg was removed while the goose was retrieving it. Surprisingly, she continued to draw her head back (the fixed component)—but in a straight line, without the orienting side-to-side movements. This indicated that the fixed-action pattern, once initiated, is independent of additional environmental cues; and that once it starts, it continues.

42.2

A leopard frog orienting to catch a fly. The tongue flick, a fixed-action pattern, is not released until the central nervous system is stimulated by the sight of an insect in the proper position (close and in the midline). The orientation is obvious as the frog shifts its position, but once the tongue flick has started, no adjustment is possible; the act will continue to its completion.

Initiation of Fixed-Action Patterns

Instinctive behavior can be initiated by a number of factors, either internal or environmental. If some predator—perhaps a cheetah (Figure 42.4)—hasn't eaten for a while, it may feel compelled to hunt down some sort of quarry. Hunting, killing, and swallowing all have components of instinctive mechanisms. First, the cheetah may walk about restlessly and then begin a rather random search. Usually she searches where she has had luck stalking prey in the past. (This is, in essence, a highly variable aspect of orientation.) When the prey—say, a hartebeest—is spotted, the cheetah's behavior becomes more stereotyped and predictable. She quickly crouches, raises her head, peers over the grass, and begins creeping forward. She hugs the ground, pausing at each step, just as she always has and just as all the other cheetahs do when stalking prey. As the prey moves, she alters her stalking behavior accordingly, but she continues to use the motions that natural selection has provided. Once her sprint begins, it is always much the same: sets of muscles contract in a coordinated manner as, with each bound, her arched body literally springs back, adding thrust to her rear legs and propelling the graceful body forward. Many different muscles are used in such a sprint, each contracting precisely in turn and staying contracted for a specific time period.

The fixed-action pattern that makes up each bound is performed the same way throughout the species, but at this point, it is still oriented according to the behavior of the prey as it runs this way and that on the grassy African plain. Most prey escape, but since we're making up this story, let's say that this hartebeest is just not having a good day and is caught. The cheetah now orients so as to be able to perform the next fixed-action pattern—knocking down the prey. Before the prostrate animal can rise, the cheetah grabs the helpless beast by the throat and simply holds on, cutting off its air—again, a behavioral trait of all cheetahs. The swallowing movements of the cheetah are fixed-action patterns that never vary, and their performance eventually brings relief from hunger.

In fact, the performance of any fixed-action pattern brings a measure of relief (or loss of motivation), since many animals seem to have a tendency to perform such acts even without a reward such as food. You may have noticed well-fed cats stalking anything from a bird to a ball.

We can derive several points from the hunting behavior of a cheetah. First, the cheetah was motivated to perform a series of instinctive acts. Hunger provided the drive (impetus or motivation). Second, the earlier stages of each instinctive part of the sequence were highly variable, but each became more and more stereotyped until the fixed-action patterns were performed. Third, the

42.4

A hunting cheetah demonstrates instinctive behavior after being motivated by hunger to begin a hunt.

performance of each of these stereotyped patterns provided relief.

In an experiment designed to assess the source of relief in performing one specific consummatory behavior, Russian scientists connected a tube to the esophagus of a dog in such a way that, as it swallowed, the food it ate emptied into a collecting bowl, rather than entering its stomach. After the dog had swallowed a certain number of times, it stopped eating and left the remaining food, not one morsel having entered its stomach. The only difference between the behavior of the experimental animal and that of a control animal was that the experimental dog returned to its food sooner. The implication is that animals may be motivated not by the presence of some commodity, but by the need to perform a fixed-action pattern. Of course, natural selection favors the performance of particular patterns—ones that usually result in the acquisition of something that is rewarding and beneficial to the animal.

Changing Thresholds over Time.   There is some evidence that the desire to perform a fixed-action pattern can increase in a stimulus-deprived animal until the cues that can trigger the performance of the act become increasingly less appropriate, or realistic. In some cases, an instinctive act might even be performed in the absence of an environmental stimulus—just because of an overwhelming urge to do it.

Daniel Lehrman of Rutgers University found that a caged male blond ring dove, when in a courting mood and during a period of isolation from female doves, in time would accept something other than the ideal. When his hormones were running rampant, his urge to bow and coo before a female became overwhelming. When no female appeared, he began to bow and coo to a stuffed model of a female—a model he had previously ignored. When the model was removed and replaced by a rolled cloth, he began to court the cloth; and when this surrogate was removed, the bird directed his attention to a corner of the cage, where he could at least focus his gaze. With the continued absence of a live female dove, the threshold for eliciting the fixed-action courtship pattern became increasingly lower as time went by. It is almost as though there were some sort of building urge (and increasing "energy" that could be released only in a specific way). As this energy increased, the *response threshold*, that is, the minimum stimulus that could elicit a response, decreased to the point at which almost anything would stimulate the dove. This urge, or "energy," is called **action-specific energy,** although neurologic evidence of its existence remains to be found.

Releasers.   As shown in the behavior of the ring dove, an instinctive act is somehow *released* by specific cues either generated internally or perceived in the environment. In the case of the dove, the acceptance of less and less realistic cues was correlated with a rising level of hormones in the blood. In the case of the cheetah, the instinct theory suggests that the hunt started because of the internal prodding of hunger. The stalk was initiated by the sight of a hartebeest, the chase was begun by the sight of a hartebeest within a certain critical distance, and the kill sequence was begun by the proximity to and/or physical contact with a downed hartebeest. Any of the acts may have internally triggered the performance of the next, with each stage having its own orientation and fixed-action pattern until the final, consummating act of swallowing was performed.

You will recall that environmental factors that evoke, or release, instinctive patterns are called releasers. The releaser itself may be only one aspect of a general situation, but that aspect alone can be the cue that signals the existence of an appropriate situation for the release of the instinctive act. For example, a territorial male European robin will attack even a tuft of red feathers at a certain height within his territory (Figure 42.5). Of course, such a response usually is adaptive because tufts of red feathers at that height normally are on the breast of a competitor. So we see that the instinctive act may be triggered by only parts of the total environmental situation.

42.5

A male European robin in breeding condition will attack a tuft of red feathers placed at a certain height in his territory. Since red feathers are usually on the breast of a competitor, it is to his reproductive advantage to behave aggressively at the very sight of them. The phenomenon illustrates that releasers of instinctive behavior need to meet only certain criteria—in other words, to represent only a specific part of the total situation. The model at left is more birdlike than the tuft of feathers, but lacks red coloration.

42.6

Egg size as a supernormal releaser. An oyster-catcher shows a preference for a giant egg rather than a normal egg (foreground) or a herring gull's egg (left).

The effect of a releaser can be increased by exaggerating certain of its aspects. For example, an oystercatcher will abandon its own spotted egg to try to sit on an even *larger* egg with even *more* spots. Such exaggerated and artificial stimuli are called *supernormal releasers* (Figure 42.6). (Tinbergen found what may be the classic example of supernormal releasers—incubating geese that tried to roll volleyballs into their nests.)

We have no idea how releasers work, but it has been suggested that the perception of a releaser sends neural impulses to specific areas or pathways in the central nervous system. Those pathways then send impulses to effectors that orient the animal and stimulate the sequence of muscular contraction that results in a fixed-action pattern. These hypothetical neural centers have been named **innate releasing mechanisms (IRMs).**

It is postulated that many IRMs must be stimulated in order to release a complex pattern. It is suggested that, in some cases, the very performance of a fixed-action pattern may itself serve as a releaser for the next action. In the cheetah, for example, perhaps the act of knocking the hartebeest to the ground is a fixed-action pattern that triggers the killing sequence.

Perspectives on Instinct

Obviously, the term *instinct* has very specific connotations and is often misapplied. For a behavioral pattern to qualify as instinctive, it should meet a number of conditions. For example, does the pattern show an appetitive phase? Is it characteristic of the species? Is it found throughout the species? Will it appear, even in rough form, without practice? Is it stimulated by releasers? Is it useful? Does it ever appear without a stimulus and out of context? Is there a period of satiation immediately following its performance when the threshold for its release is raised?

You have undoubtedly noted that there are certain problems with the classic instinct model. For example, how can an animal perform a complex chain of fixed-action patterns without intervening appetitive patterns? And why haven't the critical parts of the neural apparatus been identified? The instinct concept we've described is probably most useful when accounting for the behavior of insects and the lower vertebrates. It also may help to explain the behavior of other animals when it is not applied too rigidly. In any case, it's the best explanatory model we have.

LEARNING

Now we will leave our consideration of inborn behavior and the ethological theory of instinct. We have seen that natural selection can produce inherent patterns and preferences, and that they can be especially critical in species that have little time or ability to develop critical adaptive behavior patterns. However, animals can come to behave adaptively by individually acquiring information from experience, a process referred to as **learning.** We will see how the ethological and comparative psychological theories have matured, expanded, and merged, so that behavioral scientists generally now agree that adaptive behavior has both innate and learned components. We will shortly discuss a few examples of the results of this union.

Reward and Reinforcement

Before considering some of the ways animals learn, we should be aware that there has been some argument regarding the concept of *reward*, or *reinforcement*. Relevant questions might be: What does an animal seek by expending effort to acquire information? What does it want? How is it rewarded?

In the evolution of *populations*, changes are preserved through their survival value. If the net effect of any genetic change helps an organism to survive, that change is "good," and is retained in the behavioral repertoire. But how does an *individual* ascertain which behavioral patterns to keep in its repertoire? If an act fulfills or relieves a need, then it is considered good. The fulfillment or satiation is the *reward* for having performed that action. The quality of "good" has also been construed as something that lowers motivation. This will surely draw howls from those who subscribe to the "work ethic," but it really only means that a cheetah that has just eaten (received "good") is less motivated to go hunting for a while.

A **reward,** then, is something "good," something that fulfills a need and lowers the motivation to continue the act that led to the fulfillment. (Technically, whereas a reward brings a measure of relief or fulfills a need, **reinforcement** is the process by which the probability of performing an action is increased. It has the advantage of being measurable by noting changes in the animal's behavior, without assuming what goes on in the mind of the animal.)

Instinct and Learning: Acting Together as a Reward. Konrad Lorenz proposed that the performance of a fixed-action pattern is pleasurable and reinforcing, and that this is one way instinct and learning operate together to strengthen the tendency to behave adaptively. He also suggested that the completion of certain acts (such as eating) has a reinforcing effect through *reafference*, or sensory feedback. Consider nest building in crows.

A crow standing at the site of an incomplete nest with a twig in its beak will try to shove the twig into the unfinished nest. It sweeps its head downward and sideways, forcing the twig against the wall of the nest. When it feels the twig meet some resistance, it shoves harder; if the resistance is not strong enough, it shoves again and again. When the twig is wedged more firmly, its resistance increases; this, in turn, increases the bird's efforts until, when the twig sticks fast, the bird con-

ESSAY 42.1
PLAY

Play has been observed in many species of animals and it probably has been subjected, more than any other type of behavior, to the greatest anthropomorphic interpretations. Part of the problem in interpreting play lies in the fact that since humans do it, we think we must understand it. Actually, we really don't know much about play at all.

Play is difficult to define, not least because it may appear in forms that are not recognizable to the human observer. Playlike behavior has been described in fish, but some imagination is required. For instance, "shooters" (*Jaculator*) may squirt water at their aquarium keeper, but this could be because they associate him with food and they tend to shoot at food. It was believed for a time that birds do not play, but in recent years, eider ducks have been seen "shooting the rapids" in Iceland, and a hummingbird was once repeatedly observed to float down a small stream of water that was flowing from a hose.

Ethologists categorize play as a type of learning, and while its importance as such in fish and birds remains to be proven, it does seem to have a role in the behavioral development of many other vertebrates. It can only be expected, to any great degree, in those species for which learning or socialization is important and in those that are behaviorally flexible. Also, play should only be expected in species in which appetitive behavior is not always strongly bound to a consummatory act. In many mammals, for instance, appetitive behavior is actually flexible enough to be broken off without leading to a consummatory act. In fact, play can appear without environmental cues and without being preceded by normal appetitive behavior.

We have all noticed that pet dogs tend to remain playful throughout their entire lives. Consider the fact that, in ordinary appetitive behavior, the animal learns how to overcome obstacles, so that the consummatory act becomes more easily reached as time goes by. But if the consummatory "goal" (such as food) is already

Young red foxes

Female moose with young

summates its activities in what Lorenz describes as an "orgiastic maximum of effort." After the act is finished, the bird loses interest in that twig.

Some species of crows have no innate preference for suitable nest material. At first, young birds of these species will attempt to build a nest with just about anything they can carry, and some of the things they show up with simply won't do. For example, they may bring such unlikely materials as light bulbs or icicles. In such cases, the young bird tries time and again, but a light bulb will not allow it to reach the consummatory stimulus situation, that final push that leads to both relief and biological success. After a failure or two with light bulbs, it choses other material until, in time, it becomes a true connoisseur of twigs. The reinforcement in this kind of learning situation, then, is the re-afferent feedback produced by the performance of a fixed-action pattern.

When experience alters the behavior of an animal, we can say that learning has occurred. However, the importance of learning in the lives of different kinds of animals varies widely. For example, tapeworms probably are not able to learn much. But then, why should we expect differently? Adult tapeworms, after all, live in an environment that is soft, warm, moist, and filled with food. The matter of leaving offspring also requires the simplest of responses (since self-fertilization is common); tapeworms merely lay thousands and thousands of eggs and leave the rest to chance. By contrast, chimpanzees live in variable and often dangerous environments, and they must be able to cope with a number of complex conditions. They are long-lived, highly social, and have very few offspring. This is because each infant must be tended as it gains experience, learning all the while (see Essay 42.1). Learning is important in the world of

---

provided for an animal—by an "owner" or by a parent—the appetitive search may become an end in itself. When this happens, the learning that takes place may not be primarily adaptive in helping to reach the consummatory situation, but instead may be more useful in encouraging the exploration of the environment. So, the adaptiveness of play may not be in helping the animal to learn to reach a goal, but in helping to expand its horizons, in giving it a better overall understanding of its world. This understanding is important to a behavioral process called *insight*—in the simplest terms, insight is learning that occurs through a kind of mental trial and error.

Play also provides practice; when young foxes play at biting each others' necks and knocking each other down, they may be "practicing" being predators. But what about patterns of behavior that appear *only* in play? (Why would a duck shoot the rapids?) There are many accounts of otters racing uphill just to be able to slide down again. To include such be-

havior, the practice theory would obviously have to be modified to include patterns that improve coordination or some other general faculty.

Play has a socializing function in some species. In primate play groups, youthful experiments may be tried, and mistakes go largely unpunished. While playing, young primates can also learn about each others' temperaments and physical abilities, thus setting the stage for later formation of dominance hierarchies.

In many primates and other mammals the incidence of play decreases with age, but the trend is especially evident among males. Reduction in play may reduce the risk of misinterpreted signals among increasingly dangerous peers. Also, young mammals are explorative, curious, and innovative, and are more apt to "test" the environment than adults; adults tend to be more conservative, less explorative, and less playful ●

Juvenile polar bears

Female cheetah and young

the chimpanzee, but when a tapeworm dies, it probably carries very little information to its grave.

The value of learning in animals becomes even more difficult to generalize about when we see "unintelligent" species do some rather remarkable things. We must remind ourselves that natural selection will ensure that animals are able to learn what they need to know, and usually not much more. In some cases, however, animals that are not known for their intelligence are able to perform some rather surprising mental feats in those few areas in which natural selection has blessed them. For example, a bird may be able to locate a nut that it buried with hundreds of others some months ago. That may be on the very day that you can't recall where you left your car.

Let's now take a look at a few of ways in which animals learn, and then see how various behavioral patterns help them adjust more finely to their environment. We will consider three types of learning: *habituation, classical conditioning*, and *operant conditioning*.

Habituation

Habituation is a peculiar kind of learning, and yet probably one of the most important for animals. Essentially, **habituation** involves learning *not* to respond to certain stimuli, particularly those that are irrelevant to an animal's well-being. The first time an animal encounters a stimulus, its response may be immediate and vigorous. But if it encounters the same stimulus again and again, the response gradually diminishes until, finally, the stimulus may be ignored. Habituation is not necessarily permanent, however. If an animal becomes habituated to some sight or sound that then is no longer encountered for a time, the response may reappear when the stimulus is encountered later.

There are several ways in which habituation is important in the lives of animals. For example, a bird learns not to waste energy by taking flight at the sight of every skittering leaf. A reef fish, holding a territory, habituates to its neighbors, whereas a strange fish wandering through the area elicits an immediate attack. Habituation also may help animals flee from furtive, and therefore unfamiliar, predators, while they ignore other, more commonly encountered species that have no reason to hide and intend them no harm.

Classical Conditioning

Classical conditioning was first described in the 1920s by the well-known Russian biologist Ivan Pavlov (Figure 42.7). In classical conditioning, a response to a common stimulus (an **unconditioned stimulus**) can come to be elicited by a normally irrelevant stimulus (a **conditioned stimulus**). Pavlov found that a dog normally salivates at the sight of food, and he built a device to measure the number of drops of saliva generated. He then began a set of experiments in which he presented a dog with a signal light precisely five seconds before food, in the form of meat powder, was mechanically blown into the dog's mouth through a tube. After every few trials, the light was presented *without* being followed by food. (Food followed the light more frequently in some sets of trials than in others.) After each experiment was repeated several times, Pavlov measured the amount of saliva that was secreted when the dog saw only the light. He found that the amount of saliva elicited by the light alone was in direct proportion to the number of previous trials in which the light had been followed by food; the more frequent the rewards, the more the response was reinforced. The food was the unconditioned stimulus; the light was the conditioned stimulus. Salivation in response to food was termed the **unconditioned response,** and salivation brought on by the light alone was called the **conditioned response.**

Pavlov then found that this sort of conditioning, or learning process, also worked in reverse. When a conditioned animal (a dog that associated the light with food) was shown a light that was never followed by food, the conditioned response gradually underwent **extinction;** the dog began to salivate less each time until the response was extinguished (see Figure 42.7).

Other of Pavlov's experiments demonstrated more than the ability to substitute one stimulus for another in eliciting the same response. They also demonstrated two aspects of conditioning now called *generalization* and *discrimination*. **Generalization,** the ability to detect and respond to similar stimuli, was demonstrated when a dog that was conditioned to salivate in response to a green light also responded to a blue or red light. In other words, the dog was able to "generalize" regarding the qualities of lighted bulbs.

Discrimination, the ability to detect and respond to differences among similar stimuli, was demonstrated when, with careful conditioning, it was found that a dog could be taught to respond only to a light with certain properties. Dogs do not see color well, so they are more likely to be responding to differences in light intensity than to variations in color. In any case, if food was consistently presented only with a green light and never with a red or blue light, eventually the dog would respond only to green lights, demonstrating its ability to discriminate.

Operant Conditioning

Operant conditioning differs from classical conditioning in several important ways. In classical conditioning, the reinforcer (or reward, such as food) follows the *stimulus*. In operant conditioning, the reinforcer follows the *response* (Figure 42.8). Also, in classical conditioning the animal has no control over the situation. For example, in Pavlov's experiment all the dog could do was wait for the lights to go on and food to appear. The dog could not make anything happen. In operant conditioning, the animal can determine whether the reward or, in some cases, the stimulus, will appear.

In the 1930s, B. F. Skinner demonstrated operant conditioning with a device known as a *Skinner box*. Once a hungry animal is placed inside a Skinner box, it must perform some action (such as pressing a bar) in order to receive a reward (such as a food pellet from a dispenser). The bar pressing obviously must be learned (Figure 42.9).

When the animal (often a rat or a hamster) is first placed in the box, it usually begins to randomly wander around and investigate its surroundings. As it does so, sooner or later it accidentally presses the bar and a food pellet appears. It doesn't immediately associate the two events, but in time its movements become less random, and it begins to move closer and closer to the bar. Finally, it learns to associate getting food with pressing the bar. After this, it spends most of its time just sitting around, pressing the bar. Operant conditioning, then, is based on the premise that if an action is rewarded, there is an increasing probability that the action will be performed again.

A modified Skinner box can show yet other aspects of behavior. For example, after a pigeon in a Skinner box learns to peck at a bar to receive food, the experiment can be altered so the pecking is rewarded only if the action is performed within a certain interval after a sign that says "Peck" lights up. Soon the pigeon will peck the bar mostly at that time, largely ignoring it until the "Peck" sign is lit. A pigeon will continue to peck for a time after a new sign is presented that clearly says "Don't Peck." The "Peck" sign is always followed by food; the "Don't Peck" sign never is. The result is that the pigeon will begin to ignore the bar when the

---

42.7

Ivan Pavlov **(a)** devised this apparatus **(b)** to demonstrate classical conditioning. Upon presentation of a light, meat powder was blown into the dog's mouth, causing him to salivate. Later, he came to salivate at the sight of a light alone. His salivation, then, was *conditional* on the light. **(c)** Note in the graph on the left that the dog salivated at maximal levels after only seven trials. When the experiment was reversed and food no longer followed the light, the dog stopped salivating after only nine more trials, as shown by the graph on the right.

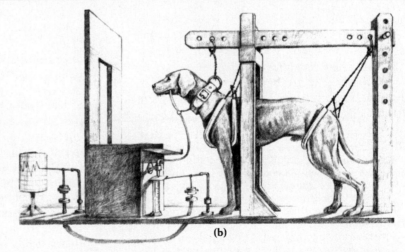

(b)

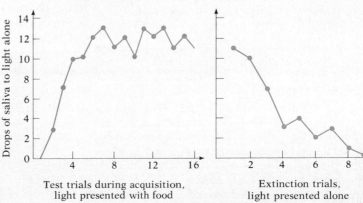

Test trials during acquisition, light presented with food

Extinction trials, light presented alone

(c)

CLASSICAL CONDITIONING

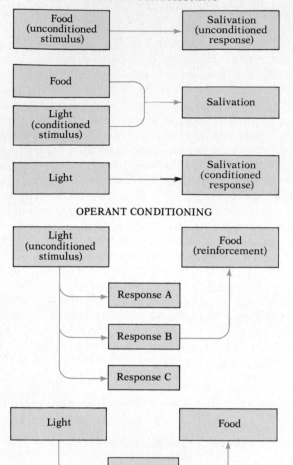

OPERANT CONDITIONING

42.9

A rat in a Skinner box, a device designed to demonstrate operant conditioning. For example, a hungry rat may move randomly, searching for food, until it accidentally presses a bar that delivers a food pellet. Each delivery increases the probability that the rat will press the bar again, until finally the rat learns simply to press the bar each time it wants a pellet.

42.8

The organizational differences between classical conditioning and operant conditioning. In classical conditioning, an unconditioned stimulus becomes paired with a conditioned stimulus. The conditioned stimulus then becomes a substitute for the unconditioned stimulus, in order to produce the unconditioned response. In operant conditioning, when a conditioned stimulus occurs, there is an opportunity for the animal to respond in various ways. However, only the "correct" response is reinforced. Finally, the stimulus produces a specific response.

"Don't Peck" sign is lit. This is another case of discrimination. (Pigeons can also be trained to peck in response to the "Don't Peck" sign—pigeons can't really read.)

Habituation, classical conditioning, and operant conditioning are three examples of kinds of learning in animals. There is no way to know their relative importance in the wild, but it is generally assumed that most acquired behavior patterns in nature are the result of several types of learning.

So, most behaviors have rather complex origins. Some are primarily based in inborn mechanisms, others are largely the result of experience. But it is increasingly apparent that adaptive behavior is often the result of the interaction of both genetic and environmental influences.

Summary

Instinct

Instinct refers to inborn and stereotyped behavior patterns that often include both genetic and learned elements. Fixed-action patterns are specific movements that are innate, and are characteristic for each species. Certain fixed-action patterns may arise later in an animal's development when such actions are likely to be most useful. The orienting component of instinctive behavior is performed according to certain cues and, unlike fixed-action patterns, is adjustable.

Many factors, such as internal or environmental conditions, can initiate instinctive behavior. The performance of fixed-action patterns may be motivated by the *need* to do so, although it is also often associated with achieving some sort of relief. In stimulus-deprived animals, the desire to perform a fixed-action pattern may increase until the behavior is triggered by inappropriate cues, or even when cues are totally absent. This desire, or urge, is referred to in theory as action-specific energy.

Releasers are environmental factors that trigger instinctive patterns of behavior. Exaggerating certain aspects of a releaser can increase its effects. Releasers may be perceived by neural centers called innate releasing mechanisms (IRMs); many IRMs may need to be stimulated to release a complex behavior pattern.

Learning

Learning occurs when experience alters behavior, and is usually a response to a reward or reinforcer. A reward is something that brings a measure of relief or fulfills a need, while reinforcement increases the likelihood that the behavior will be repeated. If the performance of a fixed-action pattern is both pleasurable and reinforcing, instinct and learning may be operating together to enhance adaptiveness. The completion of certain acts may have a reinforcing effect through sensory feedback or reafference. The importance of learning in different animals varies widely; the need for adaptability and flexibility tends to encourage a higher level of learning that enables individuals and species to survive in complex and unpredictable environments.

Habituation, classical conditioning, and operant conditioning are three types of learning. Habituation involves learning *not* to respond to stimuli that may be irrelevant to well-being. The response to such a stimulus diminishes until the stimulus is ignored. Habituation, though not necessarily permanent, can help animals conserve energy by responding only to meaningful environmental stimuli.

In classical conditioning, first described by Pavlov, a response to a common (unconditioned) stimulus can come to be elicited by a normally irrelevant (conditioned) stimulus. Conditioned responses can undergo extinction if the reward or reinforcement is withheld. It was found that animals could generalize about or learn to discriminate among stimuli.

In operant conditioning, the reinforcer or reward follows the response rather than the stimulus. The animal can often determine whether the reward (or even the stimulus) will appear, rather than simply acting as a passive receiver. In a Skinner box, a device used to demonstrate operant conditioning, an animal must learn to perform certain behaviors to earn a reward. Such conditioning can be used to teach an animal to detect subtle differences among stimuli and respond only to very specific conditions. Operant conditioning is based on the premise that an action rewarded is likely to be repeated.

Key Terms

ethology	innate releasing mechanism (IRM)	unconditioned response
instinct	learning	conditioned response
appetitive stage	reward	extinction
consummatory stage	reinforcement	generalization
releaser (sign stimulus)	habituation	discrimination
fixed-action pattern	classical conditioning	operant conditioning
orienting movements	unconditioned stimulus	
action-specific energy	conditioned stimulus	

Review Questions

1. What is the basic difference between the ethological and comparative psychological interpretations of behavior? How does this relate to instinct? (p. 616)

2. Using the hunting behavior of a cheetah, describe appetitive and consummatory behaviors, and provide examples of both orienting and fixed components of a fixed-action pattern. (pp. 619–620)

3. What factor in the greylag goose's egg-retrieving behavior suggests that once fixed-action patterns are initiated, they are independent of additional environmental cues? (p. 618)

4. Using the behavior of the male blond ring dove as an example, explain action-specific energy and its relationship to response threshold. (p. 620)

5. In general, what are releasers, and how do ethologists explain their neural effect? (pp. 620–621)

6. Using nest-building in crows as an example, suggest how the innate aspects of behavior might be modified by experience. (pp. 622–623)

7. Briefly describe the roles of reward and reinforcement in learning. (pp. 621–622)

8. In what way is learning through habituation adaptive and essential to young animals? (p. 624)

9. What are the significant differences between classical conditioning and operant conditioning? (pp. 624–626)

The Adaptiveness
of Behavior

43

An owl sits quietly on the beam of a barn, upright, eyes closed, almost unnoticeable until two mares pass by and one thumps the gate as it looms in the stall door. The owl suddenly lunges forward, feathers abristle and eyes staring widely. The mares walk into the pasture and stand together head to tail, the tail of each swishing across the face of the other. Overhead a crow methodically beats its way toward the nearby woods, a group of small songbirds swooping and diving around it. As evening draws on, the songbirds fall silent as first one kind of insect, then another and another, fills the night with sound. The mares, by now, have eaten, each immediately surrendering her mound of hay as the stallion resolutely approaches, his own hay unfinished.

The animals around us behave as animals will, each according to its tendencies, abilities, and perceptions. We observe them and we often have an explanation for their behavior. It is easy to believe that the owl lunged as a threat, that the horses stood so as to have insects brushed from their faces, and that the songbirds chased the egg-eating crow to protect their young. But there are two problems with such explanations. First, such reasoning suggests that each animal knew its behavior would achieve a desired result. The same effect could be realized if the animal was only responding to a stimulus, according to an inherent set of movements that the stimulus triggered. The second problem is that we cannot know the adaptive response—the benefit—of any behavior without

developing a hypothesis and testing it through careful experimentation. Here we'll see how some kinds of animals behave, and how various behavioral patterns are important to survival.

ARRANGING ONESELF IN SPACE

The earth is a variable place. An animal's environment may abruptly change as it travels from one place to another, or any single place may change over time. Thus, many animals arrange themselves so as to take maximum advantage of the more desirable areas, and others move from one place to another area more appropriate to their needs.

Kinesis and Taxis

The simplest type of spatial adjustment is called **kinesis,** in which the vigor of the animal's movement is proportional to the environmental stimulus, which is usually some form of negative (unpleasant) signal. In simpler terms, this means that an animal is strongly stimulated to move about under undesirable conditions but less so under more favorable conditions. For example, if wood lice are placed in a box with both damp and dry areas, the dryness sends them scrambling, but they slow down or even stop in the damp areas.

A **taxis** is another simple movement, but one influenced by the *direction* of the stimulus. There are a number of taxic responses, as we saw in our discussion of the movement of parts of plants (Chapter 26). Positive *geotaxis,* for instance, results in movement toward the center of gravity; negative *phototaxis* involves movement away from light. The list of such movements is long, and distinguishing between kineses and taxes may be more complex than it seems. For example, *Euglena* move toward a dim light but away from a bright one (Figure 43.1).

43.1

(a) Positive phototaxis. These tubeworms were planted in an aquarium after being stripped of their tubes. As the worms slowly built new tubes, they bent toward the experimenter's light, regardless of the direction from which it came. (b) Kinesis and taxis are not always distinguishable, as is illustrated by the behavior of *Euglena* in the presence of varying intensities of light.

Newly hatched blowfly larvae are positively phototaxic (a response that causes them to leave their dark hatching area), but older larvae that have a chance to move away from the overcrowded hatching area become negatively phototaxic (which enables them to end up in new hiding places). The adults retreat from light (and thus avoid predators). So a taxis may depend upon such diverse factors as the strength of a stimulus and the developmental stage of the animal.

Orientation and Navigation

Some of the most fascinating studies in animal behavior have stemmed from investigations of the remarkable abilities of some animals to know directions and to find far-off places—in some cases, places they have never seen.

Orientation. **Orientation** is simply the ability to face the right direction. It seems a rather unimpressive talent—some worms can do it—but you can't. Humans seem to have little aptitude for orientation if denied our usual clues, such as landmarks. Some of the most fascinating instances of animal orientation are found among birds. We will consider a few pioneering studies initiated in the 1950s by a young German scientist, Gustav Kramer (Figure 43.2).

Kramer found that caged migratory birds became very restless at about the time they would normally begin their migration in the wild. Furthermore, he noticed that as they fluttered around in the cage they tended to launch themselves in the direction they would have migrated. Kramer then devised experiments with caged starlings and found that their movement was, in fact, in the proper migratory direction—except when the sky was overcast. When the starlings couldn't see the sun, there was no clear direction to their restless movements, so Kramer surmised that they were orienting by the sun. To test his hypothesis, he blocked their view of the sun and used mirrors to reflect the sunlight, shifting the apparent position of the sun. The birds did indeed orient according to the position of the new "sun." Subsequent experiments have shown that many birds, particularly daytime migrators, possess the ability to orient by a *sun compass.*

A sense of timing is crucial to such an ability. Birds with **sun-compass orientation** must know not only the normal course of the sun, but also the precise time of day (Figure 43.3). In other words, incredible as it seems, they apparently know where the sun should be at any time of day. Such an ability is obviously largely innate, but in many

Kramer's orientation cage. The birds can see only the sky through the glass roof. The apparent direction of the sun can be shifted with mirrors.

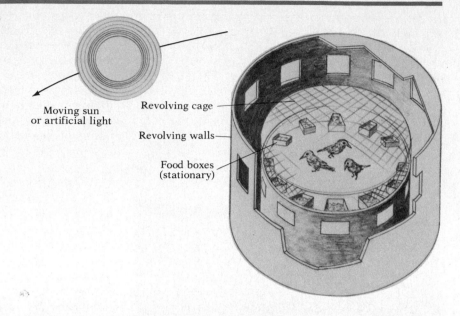

Moving sun or artificial light

Revolving cage

Revolving walls

Food boxes (stationary)

The analysis of sun-compass orientation in starlings tested in Kramer cages. The dots in **(a)** and **(b)** represent directions the birds flew as they tried to migrate. The results in **(a)** show that the birds maintained the same heading even as the sun changed position. In **(b)**, orientation is shifted as the apparent position of the sun is changed by mirrors. In **(c)** the birds were subjected to artificial light-dark schedules that were off by 6 hr (¼ day). The birds shifted their direction by 90° (¼ circle). In **(d)**, an artificial sun was held stationary. The birds then changed their direction at about the same rate the real sun would have moved.

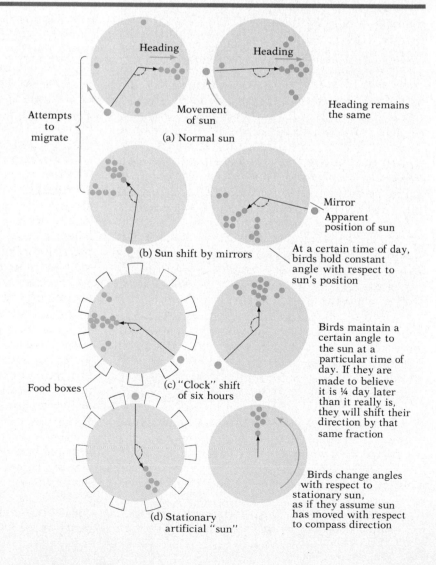

Attempts to migrate

Heading

Heading

Movement of sun

Heading remains the same

(a) Normal sun

Mirror

Apparent position of sun

At a certain time of day, birds hold constant angle with respect to sun's position

(b) Sun shift by mirrors

Birds maintain a certain angle to the sun at a particular time of day. If they are made to believe it is ¼ day later than it really is, they will shift their direction by that same fraction

Food boxes

(c) "Clock" shift of six hours

Birds change angles with respect to stationary sun, as if they assume sun has moved with respect to compass direction

(d) Stationary artificial "sun"

cases it is at least partly learned. In one experiment, a starling was reared entirely under artificial light, and then allowed to see the sun. It was able to orient itself fairly well, although not as well as birds that had seen the sun before. (This would appear to be another example of the interaction of innate behavior, maturation, and learning.) Sun-compass orientation has also been found in a variety of other animals, including insects, fish, reptiles, and even some mammals.

The sun-compass studies raised other questions. What about birds that migrate at night? To test for their ability to orient without the sun, caged night-migrating birds were placed on the floor of a planetarium during their migratory period. A planetarium, of course, is essentially a theater with a domelike ceiling onto which a night sky can be projected for any night of the year. When the planetarium sky matched the sky outside, the birds fluttered in the direction of their normal migration. But when the dome was rotated, the birds changed their direction to match the artificial sky.

Nighttime migrators, too, must be able to precisely measure time, but they may have an even more complex task than daytime migrators. The apparent movement of the stars is much more complex than that of the sun. It seems that birds use a constellation of several stars, whose positions shift at different rates, to "fix" their positions. Birds can also use the stars to correct their migratory course. In one experiment, birds that normally migrate north and south between Western Europe and Africa were shown a planetarium sky with the stars as they would appear at that time over Siberia. The birds, behaving as if they were thousands of miles off course, correctly oriented toward the "east."

Navigation. The ability to orient is indeed remarkable, but **navigation** is a far more complex phenomenon, primarily because it involves not just a certain direction but a particular destination. Navigation involves the ability to start at place A and find place B. The difference between orientation and navigation would become clear if you were blindfolded, driven out into the Mojave desert, and released with only a compass. Finding north would be easy; finding Bakersfield wouldn't be, not even if you had also been given a map— you would need to know your *position* on the map. And, as you sat on a rock, distraught and staring hopelessly at your map, you might notice some birds nonchalantly passing overhead on their way to Argentina. These might even be leaderless adolescent birds that have never made the trip before.

The Adaptiveness of Migration. Birds are probably among the greatest natural navigators on earth. The arctic tern actually flies between the North and South Poles annually, a distance of 18,000 km (11,185 miles). Other species may not travel that far but still show remarkable endurance—such as the geese that fly from James Bay in Canada to Louisiana, apparently without stopping, covering 2700 km (1677 miles) in only 60 hours. And tiny hummingbirds, with their minute food reserves, regularly cross the Gulf of Mexico.

Such seasonal or periodic animal **migrations** are not the exclusive province of birds. Studies of monarch butterflies reveal that some travel as many as 3200 km (about 2000 miles) seasonally. Migrating fish also make legendary journeys. The European eel begins life in the Sargasso Sea, southeast of Bermuda, and then follows the Gulf Stream in a three-year odyssey that carries it to the coastal waters of Europe. The females swim into numerous rivers and streams, spend eight to fifteen years growing, and move back to sea, where they join the males for the return to the Sargasso breeding grounds. The California gray whale makes an annual autumn trek from the frigid waters of the Arctic Ocean and Bering Sea to the warmer coastal waters of southern California. After calves, conceived some 13 months earlier, are born, the group begins its return trip.

Migration is such a common phenomenon in the animal world that it obviously must have powerful adaptive advantages. Focusing on the well-documented data from bird studies, let's briefly consider some of these advantages.

The advantages of going south to warmer climates for the winter, or even of moving from mountains to lower, more protected altitudes, are clear; it's about like coming in out of the rain. But there are also more specific and less blatant benefits to such movements. For example, harsh winter conditions can kill populations of any size, and can throw remaining populations into stronger competition for scarce resources. Migrators returning in the spring may therefore find fewer predators, which may have been killed either by the winter or the sudden disappearance of their prey. Also, nonmigratory (or *resident*) competitors might not have survived the winter, and migratory competitors might not have survived the trip.

One might ask, if the areas to the south are so inviting, why don't the migrators just stay there? Possibly, they leave the tropics because of the great numbers of species there. Tropical residents are well adapted to their environments, and as competition begins to increase in the spring with the appearance of new broods, the visitors would probably not fare well. Also, migrators might return because the annual flush of life in the temperate zone provides predictable and temporarily underexploited resources. Finally, as the breeding season draws on, the days become longer, giving animals more time to find food and rear young.

COMMUNICATION

If you were to come upon a large dog eating a bone, and you walked right up to the dog and reached out as if to take the bone away from it, you might notice several changes in the dog's appearance. The hair on its back might rise, its lips might curl and expose sharp teeth, and it might utter peculiar guttural noises. The dog would be communicating with you. (To see what the message is, grab the bone.)

To make a monumental understatement, **communication** is important in the animal world. We are all aware that animals communicate in many ways and with innumerable adaptive effects. Ultimately, however, the adaptiveness of any behavior

ESSAY 43.1
DECEPTION IN THE ANIMAL WORLD

It was once thought that animal communication is essentially a way for one animal to let another know what it is about to do. Now, however, we are aware that this notion is a bit naive. Communication is more realistically thought of as a kind of "enabling device;" it enables the communicator to increase its likelihood of being successful at survival and reproduction. In other words, communication can enable an animal to more effectively manipulate its environment. In some cases, this manipulation involves deception.

For example, a fish may develop an "eyespot" near its tail while concealing its own eye with a stripe; an animal seeking to head it off moves in one direction while the fish moves off in another. A variety of dangerous species take on common coloration such as yellow and black patterns, as we see in the wasps of the genera *Vespula*, *Bembex*, and *Odynerus*. (This kind of convergent evolution is called *Müllerian mimicry*.) The harmless banded king snake mimics the red, yellow, and black stripes of the dangerous coral snake (an example of *Batesian mimicry*), and is also avoided by predators.

The orchid *Cryptostylis* emits a scent like that of the female Ichneumon wasp. The male wasps thus pollinate the orchids by *pseudocopulation* (shown here). In another example, the *Ophrys* orchids resemble the female black wasp, and they are pollinated as male wasps try to copulate with first one, then another.

The message of some animals such as the ghost crab is "I am not here." Others essentially say "I am

Coral snake

King snake

Bembex

Vespula

Odynerus

depends on its influence on reproductive success. Communication may be directly involved with reproductive success (as when it attracts a mate) or it may be indirectly involved, as when it reduces offspring mortality (for example, by warning offspring of danger). It may also simply help the reproducing animal to live longer, enabling it to mate again. Remember, the evolutionary charge to all living things is "reproduce or your genes will be lost." Communication helps animals to carry out that reproductive imperative.

Deception

It was once thought that communication was essentially a method by which one organism informed another of its situation or intention. But it seems that animals have brought the art of communication a step further—they lie. An animal may lead another animal to "believe" it is about to do one thing, and then do another instead (Essay 43.1). For example, a fish with an "eyespot" on its tail easily escapes a predator that attempts to head

---

something else." The walking stick is an edible insect that resembles an inedible twig. The angler fish seems to be a rock as it lies on the bottom, waving what appears to be a distressed worm near its gaping mouth, ready to snap up whatever curious fish draw near.

In some cases, animals deceive others about their conditions. Belligerent Australian frilled lizards unfurl flaps of skin on their necks, appearing to be larger than they really are. Some birds, such as the common killdeer, feign injury and flutter along the ground in the

"broken wing display," drawing predators away from their nesting areas. A great deal of communication, we see, involves living things deceiving each other in a variety of fascinating, unexpected, and bizarre ways. ●

Ichneumon (male)

Ghost crab

Walking stick

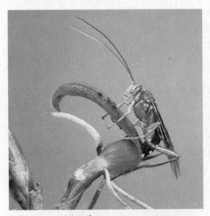

Angler fish

Frilled lizard

Killdeer

it off; it darts in the opposite direction. This deception is in the form of a permanent marking. Other deceptions are behavioral. The dog with the bone, you recall, raised its hackles, which increased its apparent size. As two dogs approach each other in a belligerent manner, they walk stiffly erect, hackles raised, each looking as large as possible. Other animals also deceive: Baby hares may hiss and lunge at an intruder in their burrow as if they were a dangerous species. When some moths are approached by a predator, they quickly open their wings and expose "eyespots," suddenly taking on the appearance of a staring predator. Plants may even deceive animals. Flowers that look and smell like female wasps are pollinated by male wasps that approach them in turn.

Let's consider a few ways communication can influence the behavior (or the probability of behavior) of other animals. That, after all, is what communication is all about. We will consider those inherent communication devices that simply send messages (called **signals**), to other individuals and those that normally function in visually attracting mates or repelling individuals of the same sex **(displays)**.

Visual Communication

Visual communication is particularly important among some fish, lizards, birds, and insects, as well as some primates. Such messages may be transmitted in several ways, such as by color, posture, shape, movement, and timing. As an example, we saw in Chapter 42 that the color red can elicit territorial behavior in European robins. Certain lizards use a head-bobbing version of Morse Code in identifying members of their own species. Some male butterflies are attracted to females by their specific flight movements. Communication by timing is found in fireflies that are attracted to each other through specific flash intervals. (One species flashes at another species' frequency and then eats whatever comes to call, an example of deceptive communication through mimicry.)

Because of the potentially high information content of visual signals, they can be *graded*; that is, they can be of different intensities rather than "on-off, either-or," like many signals (Figure 43.4). Another advantage of visual signals is that the same message may be conveyed by more than one means, say, through both color and posture.

A visual signal can be a permanent part of the animal, as in the coloration of the male pheasant or the striking facial markings of the male mandrill

43.4

An example of graded display. At left, the bird *Fringilla coelebs* is showing a high-intensity threat. The posture at center is a medium-intensity threat, and that below is a low-intensity threat.

(Figure 43.5). These two advertise their maleness at all times, and are continually responded to as males by members of their own species. Visual signals also may be more temporary. For example, the pheasant may strut and the mandrill may glare. Temporary signs may be of different durations, such as the reddened rump of an estrous female chimpanzee or the more short-term signal of a male baboon exposing his long canine teeth as a threat (see Figure 43.5).

Visual signals also have certain disadvantages. For example, a sender that can't be seen can't communicate, and all sorts of things can block vision (such as mountains) or reduce the signal's impact (such as fog). Visual signals are generally useless at night or in dark places (except in light-producing species). Also, distance reduces a signal's impact. As distance increases, the signal must become bolder and simpler, carrying less information.

Sound Communication

Communication by sound is so important in our own species that you may be surprised to learn that, for the most part, it is employed mostly by other vertebrates and arthropods. (They may even influence the evolution of each other's sounds—see Essay 43.2.) The familiar sounds of evening may include the songs of the cricket and the cicada. Insect sounds such as these are usually produced by some sort of friction, such as rubbing the wings together or the legs against the wings. Their message is carried in the *cadence* (or rhythm) rather than in pitch or tone, as is the case with most birds and mammals.

Vertebrates communicate by sound in a number of ways. Some fish may produce sound by frictional devices in the head or by manipulating the air bladder. Land vertebrates, on the other hand, usually produce sound by forcing air through vibrating membranes across the respiratory tract. Vertebrates also communicate by sound in other ways: Rabbits thump the ground, and woodpeckers hammer on hollow trees and on drainpipes early on Sunday mornings.

Most of the amphibians and reptiles do not communicate by sound, but some exceptions are certain species of salamanders that squeak and whistle. (One even barks!) The croaks of male frogs and toads advertise their territories and their size, and females respond to certain qualities of the sounds. Territorial bull alligators can be heard roaring in the remote swamps of the South. Also, Darwin described the roaring and bellowing of mating tortoises when he visited the Galapagos islands.

Sounds may vary in cadence (as we saw with insects), pitch (low or high), volume, and tonal quality. The last is demonstrated when two people hum the same note, yet their voices remain distinguishable. Such differences in sounds can be shown visually by use of a sound *spectrogram.* In effect, this recording translates sound into visual markings. Sound spectrograms enable very precise description and analysis of this type of animal communication.

The function of a sound signal may dictate its traits. A bird calling others to help mob a predator may give low *chuk* sounds that are easy to locate. But when a hawk is spotted overhead, a high-pitched *twee* sound that is hard to locate can warn others without drawing undue attention to the caller. The warning calls of some animals, such as the pica (a rodent), prairie dog, and various primates, vary depending on the *type* of predator that threatens the group.

Sound signals can carry a high information load through variations in frequency, volume, timing, and tonal quality. In addition, sounds are transitory; they don't linger in the environment after they have been emitted. Thus, an animal can stop sending a sound signal should its situation suddenly change—for example, if a predator appears. Further advantages are that an animal doesn't ordinarily have to stop what it is doing to produce a sound, and unlike visual messages, sound can go around or through many environmental obstacles.

The disadvantages of sound communication include its diminished usefulness in noisy environments. Some sea birds that live on pounding, wave-beaten shorelines must rely primarily on visual signaling, while their close relatives in quieter areas signal vocally. Also, sounds grow weaker with distance, and the source of a sound is sometimes difficult to locate.

43.5

A male mandrill *(left)* has permanent markings that advertise his sex, but his signals of anger are temporary and dependent on his mood. It is probably often to his advantage to be perceived as a male, but less frequently advantageous to be perceived as an angry male. A male baboon *(right)* displaying his large canine teeth as a threat signal. These animals are extremely powerful and dangerous.

COEVOLUTION OF HEARING IN BATS AND MOTHS

Noctuid (night-flying) moths are a favorite prey of certain bats. These bats fly swiftly and can turn on a dime to capture their prey on the wing. They avoid obstacles and locate prey by *echolocation* —emitting pulsing, high-frequency sounds that bounce back ("echo") from objects in the environment. These echoes provide the bat with information that allows it to intercept hapless moths. But just as bats have evolved ways of catching moths, noctuid moths have developed ways of avoiding bats. When they are about to encounter a bat, they take evasive measures. As you might suspect when dealing with bats, this is easier said than done, but the moth accomplishes it with a very simple hearing apparatus.

Noctuid moths have two tympana (drumlike hearing organs), one on either side of the thorax (the insect midsection), and each tympanum has only two kinds of sound receptors. One, called the *A1 cell*, is sensitive to low-intensity sounds. The other, the *A2 cell*, responds only to loud sounds. As any sound becomes louder, the A1 cell fires more frequently, responding best to pulses of sound—and it just so happens that bats emit pulses of sound.

In a sense, the moth has beaten the bat at its own game. Its very sensitive A1 neuron is able to detect bat sounds long before the bat is aware of the moth. Not only can the moth detect the distance of the bat, but it can tell whether the bat is coming nearer, since the sound of an approaching bat grows louder. It can also detect the direction the bat is taking. The directional mechanism is simple. If the bat is on the left or right, one or the other tympana will be shielded by the body, and only one A1 cell will fire. If it is directly behind the moth, both A1 cells will fire simultaneously. If the bat is above, the upward beat of the moth's wings will deflect the sound intermittently; bat sounds from below will not be deflected.

What does the moth do with this information? If the bat is quite far away, the moth will simply turn and fly in the opposite direction. The moth probably turns until the A1 cell firing from each tympanum is equalized. When the bat changes direction, so does the moth. Should the faster-flying bat draw within a few meters of the moth, the moth's number is probably up. However, it has one more strategy. As the two approach each other on a collision course, the sounds of the onrushing bat will become very loud, and at this point the A2 cells fire.

As the A2 cells fire, the highly coordinated directional mechanism is inhibited and a new tactic begins. The moth's wings beat in peculiar, irregular patterns or not at all. The insect itself has no way of knowing where it is going as it begins a series of unpredictable loops, rolls, and dives, ideally bringing it near the ground where the echoes of the earth will mask the echoes the bat is receiving.

The noctuid moth's evolutionary response to the bat's hunting behavior serves as a beautiful example of the adaptive response of one organism to another. Also, it shows clearly that the sensory apparatus of any animal is not likely to respond to elements that are irrelevant to its well-being. It is not important for moths to be able to distinguish frequencies of sound, but it is important that they be sensitive to differences in sound volume. ●

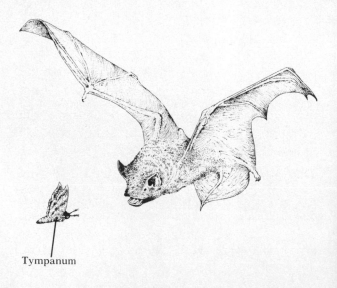

Tympanum

Chemical Communication

You have probably seen ants rushing along, single file, as they sack your cupboard. You may also have taken perturbingly slow walks with a dog that stops to urinate on every bush. In both cases the animals are communicating by means of chemicals. The ants are following chemical trails laid down by their fellows, and the dog is advertising its presence to those who care to know.

Insects make extensive use of chemical signals, and many of the responses elicited by such chemicals follow quite rigid, stereotyped patterns. For example, ants produce an *alarm chemical* if they encounter some sort of threat. When an alarmed ant releases such a chemical, it permeates the area, causing every ant in the vicinity to rush about in a very agitated manner and attack anything foreign.

A chemical produced by one animal that alters behavior in another is referred to as a **pheromone** (*pherein*, to carry; *horman*, to excite). The most powerful pheromone known is a sex attractant called *bombykol* produced by female silkworm moths. Even diluted to one part in a trillion, it can arouse male moths (Figure 43.6).

It was first believed that only insects possessed pheromones and that they triggered only stereotyped, genetically programmed behavior. This notion fell apart when pheromones were found in mammals. It was discovered that if pregnant rats of some species smelled the urine of a strange male, they would abort their fetuses and become sexually receptive. (It was suggested that this trait enabled them to bear the offspring of a "better" male more quickly, one that apparently had displaced the former dominant male.) Another pheromone causes females of most mammalian species to signal their sexual receptivity by scent.

Recent research on human pheromones suggests that women produce a sexual attractant when they are most fertile, and that certain scents produced by males may have a stimulating effect on some females.

Chemical signals are advantageous not only because they can elicit responses in very small amounts, but also because they persist in the environment. This means that the sender and receiver do not have to be precisely situated in either time or space in order to communicate. Also, chemicals can drift around environmental obstacles.

The disadvantages of chemical communication may be due to the same qualities that make them useful. By lingering in the environment, they may alert predators to the communicator's presence. The specificity of chemicals limits their information load, and gradations can be produced only by varying the concentration of the molecules.

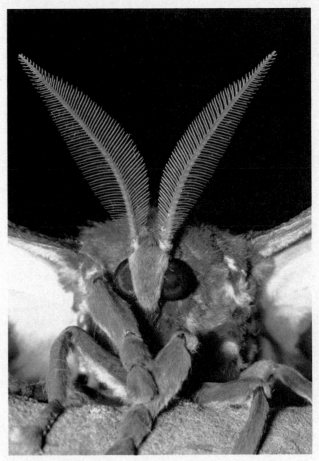

43.6

The antennae of the male Atlas moth are remarkably large, complex, and sensitive. These devices are able to detect minute quantities of sex attractant released by a receptive female. Each large bristle of the antenna has numerous hairs extending outward. Within each is a fluid-filled cavity containing sensory neurons. Chemical substances in the air enter these cavities through pores in the hairs, stimulating the neuron. Impulses thus created are transmitted to the brain.

Why Communicate?

Now that we have some idea of *how* animals communicate, we might wonder *why* they communicate at all. Clearly, there are many reasons, but let's try to organize our ideas a bit. We can begin by considering why it is important to inform other animals of what species you are in.

Species Recognition. Animals tend to inform others of their species affiliation. This may not seem too important—unless one is interested in reproduction (Essay 43.3). Animals have a number of ways to advertise their species. In places where very similar species share the same area, the ritual

ESSAY 43.3
ANIMAL COURTSHIP

The reproductive success of many species of animals involves persuasion: one animal must persuade another to be its mate. Thus courtship behavior has evolved, and its array of manifestations never ceases to amaze even the most jaded biologists. The elaborate ceremonies that have resulted are often beautiful and distinctive, but they all serve the same function—to maximize the reproductive success of the participants.

In some cases, courtship involves only species recognition. These patterns are usually relatively brief, and mating occurs between individuals that need never see each other again. In species in which the male is not important in protection or in feeding the young, the sexes join only to mate, and it is in these species that we generally find the larger, more garish, conspicuous males. In such species, *sexual dimorphism* (different appearances of the sexes) is associated with a different strategy. The males maximize their reproductive success by attracting and inseminating as many females as possible—before predators finally eliminate them. As an example, male wild turkeys (called *toms*)

spread their feathers and strut and gobble in a most impressive way. The hens tend to respond to the appropriate releasers that trigger their sexual behavior.

The courtship ritual is more extended in species in which the male will remain with the female during the nesting period. In these cases, ceremonies may last more than several days; because the participants tend to remain together for long periods of time, they have more invested in the relationship and therefore must be highly selective. (Small sparrows may display to each other for days before making a commitment to mate.) In many of these species (such as the albatross), the males and females may look very much alike. It has

been suggested that, in contrast to males in sexually dimorphic species, the drab male coloration may be an adaptation that reduces the possibilities of predators being attracted to the nest.

Western grebes not only display to each other in elaborate swimming rituals, but may also bring each other gifts of seaweed. In yet other cases, the male may bring food to the female. The advantages of demonstrating this ability are obvious to a reproductive female. In essence, courtship behavior is a means of finding not only a mate, but a healthy mate that has demonstrated the ability to either recognize the appropriate signals or perform the elaborate and often demanding rituals of the species. ●

Western grebes swimming

Turkeys displaying

Albatross courtship . . .

. . . goes on and on

of advertising one's affiliation may be rather elaborate and extended, and mating may be a slow process. After all, mating between individuals that are very similar but of different species will not produce healthy, viable offspring. Where species are so similar that interbreeding could occur, they often develop quite distinct signals and displays that, along with other isolating mechanisms, readily establish species identification (see Chapter 19).

Individual Recognition. It is often important for animals to be able to recognize not only members of their own species, but also individuals within the species. You may have noticed that the gulls at the beach all look alike—at least the adults do. In gulleries, where gulls nest by the thousands, the birds are actually quite able to recognize their own mates by both sight and sound amid the raucous crowd wheeling above. Mate recognition ensures that a pair will attend to the nest that harbors their own offspring, thus increasing their chances of reproductive success. This is particularly important in species where males and females cooperate in rearing the young.

Individual recognition is also important in social species that maintain **dominance hierarchies.** In such species, each individual generally assumes a rank that determines how it will behave toward others. Once animals in a group assume their rank among the others, there will be less fighting over various resources; the subordinate will almost always yield. In any hierarchical group where rank is unknown or not yet established, there is often more fighting, confrontation, and disruption. Rank can be maintained, however, only when each animal can recognize each of the others and therefore respond according to status.

AGGRESSION

The old image of "Nature, red in tooth and claw" apparently has been replaced by the notion that most animals normally get along with their own kind and that humans are the only species that kills its own members. Let's take a closer look at what's happening in the real world.

Fighting

First we'll consider the most obvious form of **aggression**—fighting. You can discount those old films of leopards and pythons battling to the death; it's not likely to happen. After all, what does a python have that a leopard needs badly enough to risk dying for, or vice versa? Fighting is much more likely between animals that compete, so it is most likely to occur between members of the same species. Moreover, if there is competition for mates, fighting is even more likely to occur between members of the same sex within that species.

Fighting may take many forms, but in most species it is stylized—the combatants do not injure each other (Figure 43.7). Such restraint is highly

43.7

In many species, individuals are genetically constrained to fight in relatively harmless ways among themselves. Many of their gestures are not strictly dangerous, but if the fighting establishes dominance so that the loser is deprived of commodities, it can have far-reaching implications. An individual deprived of food, after all, is more likely to fall prey to predators. If an individual is deprived of a mate, the result is genetic death, no matter how long it lives. Most, if not all, of the gestures used in fights between members of the same species are stylized—that is, same-sex combatants will use the same gestures to fight each other throughout the species.

adaptive because, first, no one is likely to get hurt. This may mean the combatants must continue to compete, but competition may be far less risky than serious fighting. Also, since animals tend to breed with those individuals around them, the opponent could well be a relative, and current theory reveals that it is disadvantageous to harm those bearing copies of one's own genes. (We will consider other aspects of this "inclusive fitness" theory later in this chapter.) In any case, the restraint is not purposeful. If there is a reproductive advantage to such behavior, most individuals will behave this way because they are the descendants of generations that behaved in such a way. But notice that the "motive" (adaptiveness) is essentially selfish, not benevolent.

Fighting between members of the same dangerous species is usually harmless and stylized (such "fights" are genetically programmed **rituals,** and are characteristic of the species). Horned antelope may gore an attacking lion, but when they fight each other, they are apparently inhibited from attacking the vulnerable flank of an opponent (see Figure 43.7). Stylized fighting enables the combatants to establish which is stronger, and the weaker is usually permitted to retreat.

On the other hand, all-out fighting may occur between animals that are not able or likely to injure each other seriously, such as hornless female antelope. It may also occur between animals that are so fast that the loser probably can get away without serious injury—house cats, for example.

Fighting, of course, is always dangerous because, even when the fight takes the form of a ritual, accidents can happen, and an injury can lead to retaliation and escalation. Some animals commonly engage in dangerous fighting that often results in death. If a strange rat is placed in a cage with a group of established rats, the group may sniff at the newcomer carefully for a time, but finally the group will attack and kill it. Male guinea pigs and mice may fight to the death. Male sea elephants occasionally kill each other in fights for mating rights. Male lions may kill a stranger from another pride (social group), and hyenas will try to kill any member of another pack. Even gangs of male chimpanzees will occasionally ambush and kill isolated males from other troops.

Territories

Territoriality, the act of animals claiming real estate and defending it against competitors, has intrigued us since it was first described by the ancient Greek philosophers (and because it mirrors our own behavior). However, the notion was largely ignored by the modern scientific community until 1920, when Eliot Howard wrote *Territory in Bird Life,* a book describing his observations of birds expelling each other from certain plots of land. He noticed that one bird might always win fights on one plot of land, but lose to the same opponent on another plot. It seemed as if each bird claimed ownership of a piece of land and would fight particularly well in defense of it. Each bird would immediately attack any intruder of the same species and sex. Of the same species and sex? Obviously, the bird was driving out *competitors.* Members of the same species compete for commodities such as food and nest sites, and members of the same sex compete for mates. So here was a working hypothesis: **Territories** are held against competitors and, once established, reduce competition within that area. Territoriality is also an important factor in population control (as we will see in Chapter 46). Briefly, then, it has been suggested that territories might have the following additional functions: (1) protection against predators, disease, and parasitism; (2) selection of the most vigorous to breed; (3) division of resources among dominant and subordinate individuals; (4) stimulation of breeding behavior; (5) assurance of food supply; and (6) increased efficiency of habitat utilization of a familiar area.

COOPERATION

Cooperation seems to be a much "nicer" concept than aggression, and many of the animal stories of our youth involved animals helping each other in some way. Certainly, cooperation is highly developed in some species, and its complexity and coordination occasionally surpass imagination. But again we must sift fact from fiction.

Cooperative behavior occurs both within and between species. The familiar relationship between the warthog and the tickbird is an example of **interspecific** (between species) **cooperation** (Figure 43.8). The relationship is mutually beneficial; the little bird eats ticks infesting the warthog, while the warthog harbors a wary little lookout. In general, however, cooperation is most highly developed among members of the same species.

Let's consider a few examples of **intraspecific cooperation** (Figure 43.9). Groups of porpoises, for instance, will swim around a female in the throes of birth, driving away any predatory sharks attracted by the blood. They may also carry a wounded comrade to the surface, enabling it to breathe. Their behavior in such cases is highly flexible, constantly adjusted to fit the circumstances. Such flexibility indicates that some aspects of their behavior are not a blind response to innate genetic influences.

Mammals often cooperate in both defensive and hunting behavior. Adult male Himalayan yaks form a circle around the females and young at the approach of danger. They stand shoulder-to-shoulder, their massive horns directed outward—an effective defense against all predators except humans, since the yaks maintain their stance, the only defense they know, even as they are shot one by one. Wolves, African cape dogs, jackals, and hyenas often hunt in packs and may cooperate in bringing down their prey. In addition, members of these species may bring food to others of their group that are unable to participate in the hunt.

Because intelligence is often associated with cooperation, we might expect the highest levels of cooperative behavior among mammals, but in fact social behavior and cooperation are most highly developed in the insects. Their rigid, complex, and highly coordinated behavior patterns are generally considered to be genetically programmed, highly stereotyped, and usually not greatly influenced by learning. One of the more intricate, highly regulated, and cooperative of insect societies is that of honeybees (Figure 43.10).

ALTRUISM

A current theme in modern biology is that animal behavior is essentially selfish and that animals behave in the best interest of their genes, as if they were seeking to perpetuate their kinds of genes.

(Evolutionarily, it doesn't matter whether an animal is actually *trying* to perpetuate its genes, as long as it behaves *as if* it does.)

But we often find seemingly contradictory instances of animals behaving **altruistically.** That is, their behavior results in another being benefited at their own expense. On the surface it would seem that any animal that behaved in such a way would leave fewer descendants by not spending its energies looking after its own reproductive welfare. In time, the genes of altruists might be expected to disappear from the population, replaced by the genes of more selfish individuals.

However, perhaps apparently altruistic behavior persists through generations because it is not so altruistic after all. We know that *reproductive fitness* (reproductive success) is a measure of one's success at leaving his or her *kinds* of genes. Reproductive fitness has traditionally been measured by the number of offspring an individual produces. However, biologists are now aware of the importance of a broader concept known as *inclusive fitness.* **Inclusive fitness** reflects not only the genes one is able to leave in one's own offspring but genes of the same type that are transmitted by one's relatives. We must remember that, not only do our own offspring bear our kinds of genes, but so do our brothers, sisters, cousins, and other relatives, as we know by the rules of simple Mendelian inheritance. So animals can increase reproductive success by assisting relatives who bear the same kinds of genes.

From this we can deduce that in a highly related troop of baboons, a male might fight a leopard to the death in defense of the troop. By the same token, a bird can be expected to give a warning cry

43.8

Interspecific cooperation frequently takes the form of *symbiotic*, or mutually beneficial, relationships. *Symbiosis* is a term that has come to encompass many types of interactions, including *parasitism* (one of the species is harmed), *commensalism* (one species is benefited and the other largely unharmed), and *mutualism* (both species derive some benefit from the association). In the example of the warthog and the tickbird **(a)**, the bird acquires food as it eats ticks that infest the larger animal. Certain ants nest in the thorns of the acacia tree **(b)** and use it for food; the ants are so ferocious that no other pests can attack the tree, and they eat any encroaching vegetation.

(a)

(b)

43.9

Intraspecific cooperation can be seen in a number of species under a variety of conditions. Cormorants and pelicans **(a)** both fish in flocks, driving their prey in front of them until they can all dive in and stand good chances of catching fish near the surface. Yak and muskoxen **(b)** both form defensive circles around more vulnerable females and young in the presence of predators.

43.10

Honeybees tending a queen. These social insects show extremely high levels of cooperation and self-sacrifice. Members of the hive live regimented lives, each with well-defined roles. While the *queen's* role is to lay eggs, the *workers*, all sterile females, begin life as "house bees," preparing cells in the hive to receive food. After a day or so, special *brood glands* develop and they begin to feed larvae. Next they build combs, or become hive *guards*; eventually each becomes a field worker or *forager*, gathering nectar, pollen, or water. The watchword of the hive is efficiency, and this applies to the treatment of males—the *drones*—whose only role in many species is to fertilize a queen. Upon completion of this task, they are quickly stung to death and shoved out of the hive.

when the chance of attracting a predator to itself is not too great, and when the average neighbor is not too distantly related.

Altruism can be carried to extremes in social insects such as honeybees. Since workers are sterile, they can propagate their own genes only by maximizing the egg-laying output of the queen. In some species, the queen is inseminated only once (by a haploid male), resulting in all the workers in a hive being sisters with three-fourths of their genes in common. In such a system, then, almost any sacrifice is worthwhile for its net gain to the hive and to the queen.

SOCIOBIOLOGY

In the mid-1970s an evolutionary concept that had been around for decades in one form or another was revived, reviewed, analyzed, refined, supported, and presented to the public. Since it was a generally familiar concept and was stated very carefully in a professional format, the scientific community was surprised by the turmoil that followed, and has not yet subsided.

The fundamental idea behind **sociobiology** is that social behavior is partly the result of evolutionary processes, and even human behavior is influenced to some degree by natural selection. That idea might have gone unnoticed except for a small group of people who believed that the idea was socially dangerous. They attacked it vigorously, drawing a great deal of attention to an idea they really wanted people to ignore.

In essence, it was feared that a sociobiological explanation of human behavior would lead to a revival of the notion of **biological determinism,** which is the idea that any genetic influence on human behavior cannot be changed. It was argued that the acceptance of such an idea promotes resignation to the status quo and supports such undesirable social patterns as racism and sexism. The opponents of sociobiology generally prefer to believe that culture is the primary molder of our behavior and that we can change any undesirable behavior by education, social programs, or other environmental influences.

Sociobiologists, on the other hand, believe that the discipline holds real promise for building a better society. Perhaps to some it may seem irreverent to suggest that human behavior, to any degree, is preprogrammed through evolution, and that natural selection plays a role in how we treat each other. But sociobiologists argue that if our behavior *is* genetically controlled or influenced to *any* de-

gree, we should know it. They note that we can't hope to find solutions if we don't understand the problem, and that one reason for our notable lack of success in improving society's condition is that we have ignored our biological heritage.

We have seen a number of cases in which evolution has molded social behavior in other species, and we have noted the apparent influence of genetics and natural selection on a trait that we are often proud to exhibit: altruism. Is the ultimate foundation of our altruism different from that of other species? It has been suggested that we are altruistic mainly because in human societies there is a high probability of having the favor returned *(reciprocal altruism).* The idea implies that even our altruism is motivated by selfishness.

Sociobiology, in its refurbished form, is quickly maturing as data now appear from long-term studies and as new researchers approach the problem from many angles. The next few years should be interesting, as sociobiologists tighten their premises, more precisely define their terms, and present us with new approaches to an old idea.

Summary

Arranging Oneself in Space

Animals tend to take maximum advantage of desirable areas, and some travel or migrate to areas appropriate to their needs. Kinesis is movement related to the *strength* of the stimulus, while taxis is movement influenced by the *direction* of the stimulus.

Animals also have the ability to orient themselves and navigate from one area to another with the aid of such environmental cues as the position of the sun or stars. Their behavior is largely innate, but also reflects learning and experience.

Migration is adaptive in a number of ways. Movements to more seasonally benign environments enable migrators to leave areas of reduced commodities. They also leave behind certain predators and parasites and reduce the ease with which they could adapt to a constantly available food supply.

Communication

Communication among animals serves many functions related to reproductive success. Communication may sometimes involve deception, either in the form of permanent markings or in terms of behavioral traits. In some cases, the communication techniques of one animal will produce adaptive changes in another, such as the coevolution of hearing in bats and noctuid moths. Signals simply send messages, while displays typically function in attracting or repelling others.

Visual communication is particularly important among some fish, lizards, birds, insects, and primates. Visual messages can be conveyed through color, posture, shape, movement, and timing. Signals can be graded according to their intensity, communicated through more than one means, and may be either permanent or temporary characteristics of organisms. Visual signals are limited, however, to direct observation.

Communication through sound is used mostly by arthropods and nonhuman vertebrates. Arthropods produce sounds through some type of friction, and messages are carried by cadence. Vertebrates make sounds with frictional devices, by forcing air through vibrating membranes, or by using various nonvocal means. Sound messages can vary in cadence, frequency, pitch, volume, timing, and tonal quality and can carry a high information load, but sound communication is not as effective in noisy environments or over long distances.

Chemical communication involves substances produced by one animal that alter behavior in another. Both insects and mammals use pheromones, which can be employed to mark territory, signal sexual receptivity, warn other animals, or intimidate rivals or predators. Chemical signals are effective in small amounts and persist in the environment, permitting senders and receivers to find one another. However, the signals may also lead predators to their prey.

Communication allows for species recognition and individual recognition, which ensure that mating produces viable, healthy offspring and that, in some cases, mates can join in caring for young. Individual recognition is also important in maintaining dominance hierarchies, in which each member of the group must be able to distinguish the rank and status of the others.

Aggression

Aggression is actually quite a complex behavior. It has been found that fighting is more likely to occur between members of the same species over commodities, or between individuals of the same sex within a species for mates. Fighting is most likely to occur between competitors. It is likely to be a harmless, stylized ritual in dangerous species or sexes. Harmless or evasive animals are more likely to engage in vigorous combat.

Territories can reduce competition within an area; limit populations; protect individuals against predators, disease, and parasitism; aid in the selection of the most vigorous individuals to reproduce; divide resources among dominant and subordinate individuals; stimulate breeding behavior; assure ample food supplies; and increase the efficiency of habitat use.

Cooperation

Cooperative behavior occurs both within a species (intraspecific) and between species (interspecific). Animals often cooperate in defensive and hunting behaviors. Social behavior and cooperation are most highly developed among social vertebrate carnivores and the social insects such as honeybees.

Altruism

When animals behave altruistically, their actions result in another individual being benefited at their own expense. Altruistic behavior may be related to a concept known as inclusive fitness. The results of any altruistic behavior must be a net gain to the group, though individuals may be sacrificed.

Sociobiology

Sociobiology involves studying the effects of natural selection on social behavior. Opponents fear that such study will revive the concept of biological determinism. Sociobiologists, on the other hand, feel that determining which behaviors are genetically preprogrammed will give us a better understanding of human nature and may help us create more humane societies.

Key Terms

kinesis	signal	cooperation
taxis	display	interspecific cooperation
orientation	pheromone	intraspecific cooperation
sun-compass orientation	dominance hierarchies	altruism
navigation	aggression	inclusive fitness
migration	ritual	sociobiology
communication	territory	biological determinism

Review Questions

1. How did Gustav Kramer support his hypothesis regarding the cue used in orientation by caged starlings? What observation suggests that this ability is innate? (p. 629)

2. List four navigational cues known to be used by birds. (p. 631)

3. Give examples of visual communication in insects, fish, lizards, birds, and primates. (pp. 632–634)

4. Describe a general advantage and disadvantage to an individual using each of the following: visual communication, sound communication, and chemical communication. (pp. 634–637)

5. Discuss two ways in which pheromones are used by insects. (p. 637)

6. Using two examples, describe the way in which fighting is typically carried out between individu-

als of the same species. How is this adaptive? Cite an exception. (pp. 639–640)

7. List four specific adaptive advantages of establishing and holding territories. (p. 640)

8. Give two examples of interspecific cooperation and explain how such behavior is adaptive to both species. (pp. 640–641)

9. In which invertebrate group has intraspecific cooperation reached the highest level of organization? Discuss one example. (p. 641)

10. In which instances does altruism become most adaptive? Explain the theoretical basis for this conclusion. (pp. 641–642)

11. Summarize the major proposal of sociobiology. Why has this idea met with such vigorous opposition? (pp. 642–643)

The Biosphere and Its Organization

44

The earth is a very large place. The concept of a small planet may be true in the sense that we can alter vast parts of it, even changing its air or waters. However, any tendency to trivialize the earth's size after a glance at some NASA photo or a coast-to-coast flight can be quickly dispelled by a hike along Alaska's North Slope, an afternoon in a Louisiana woods, or even a walk to the next town. The earth is indeed huge, formidable, fascinating, and very different from one place to the next. Such differences and their effect on the distribution of life on this planet lead us to the broadest of all biological disciplines, ecology.

Ecology (eco, *oikos*; the house) is the study of the interaction between organisms and their environment. *Interaction* implies reciprocity, and the two are indeed reciprocal—they shape each other. The ecologist's task is formidable, since such relationships are immensely complex, and understanding them requires expertise in a number of biological and physical areas. In a real sense, ecology is where the sciences come together. We will begin with a brief look at some rather grand concepts that encompass the biosphere and its physical conditions.

THE BIOSPHERE

The **biosphere** is the thin veil over the earth in which the properties of light, water, and minerals join to permit life. The biosphere includes not only land areas and their subterranean realms, but the waters as well. In essence, on a worldwide basis,

we will examine a great deal of surface area but not much depth. This is because organisms cannot live very far above or below the earth's surface. To be precise, the habitable regions of the earth lie within an amazingly thin layer of approximately 14 miles, from the highest mountains to the deepest ocean trenches. If the earth were the size of a basketball, the biosphere would be about the thickness of one coat of paint. Within these thin limits, the biosphere is a place with very special conditions.

Water

One of the earth's unusual traits is the presence of water in all three states—solid, liquid, and gaseous. We have discussed the role of water in life before, but let's touch again on a few of the basic points. You may recall that much of the biochemistry of life is centered on the peculiar traits of H_2O. In addition, water is resistant to temperature change; it absorbs heat slowly and releases it slowly. Its ability to change from liquid to gas permits it to move rather freely through the biosphere. Its presence in the atmosphere slows the dissipation of radiant heat from the earth's surface, helping the biosphere to remain at a relatively constant temperature.

The Atmosphere

The earth's atmosphere may indeed be wispy and ethereal, but all life depends on this fragile veil. Chemically, it is a protective envelope of gases—

The earth's energy budget. The relative constancy of conditions in the biosphere depends ultimately upon an equilibrium between energy entering and energy leaving. Of the solar energy reaching the upper atmosphere, 30% is immediately reflected back into space. Another 20% is absorbed as heat by water vapor in the atmosphere. The remaining 50% reaches the earth's surface. Most of this energy reenters the atmosphere through evaporation from the earth's waters. The thin arrow represents energy released by organisms.

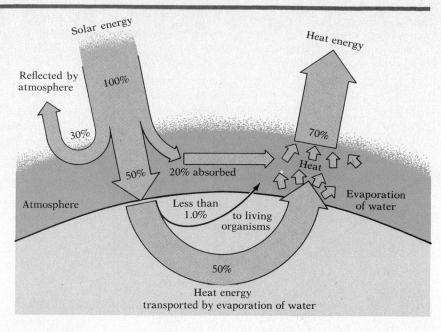

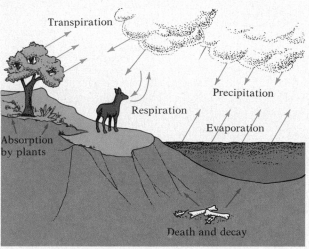

The hydrologic cycle is a constant sequence involving evaporation and precipitation. Living organisms are part of the cycle, as plants absorb water through their roots and release it from their leaves in transpiration. Most organisms carry on respiration, freeing water molecules as a waste product. In the decomposition process, microorganisms complete the breakdown of molecules, returning water to the cycle. The global balance among the world's major water reservoirs—the atmosphere, oceans, continents, and polar ice caps—is usually steady from year to year.

79% nitrogen, 20% oxygen, 0.04% carbon dioxide, and a number of other, quite rare gases. Most of the earth's atmosphere clings close to the planet, not extending more than 5–7 miles high. The atmosphere helps to screen out much of the dangerous ultraviolet radiation that would otherwise make the earth's surface inhospitable to life. It also acts as a gigantic "heat sink," temporarily holding heat close to the earth's surface. While the total energy input from the sun has traditionally been equalled by the escape of radiant energy, this equilibrium, as you may have heard, is now being disrupted by human activities, as we continue to pour CO_2 into the atmosphere (Essay 44.1).

Solar Energy

Solar energy provides the vital energy for photosynthesis, but it has other roles in the pageant of life. Only about half of the incoming solar radiation ever reaches the earth's surface; about 30% is reflected back into space, while 20% is absorbed by the atmosphere. The 50% that does reach earth is absorbed by the land and waters, from which it radiates back into the atmosphere as heat (Figure 44.1). Although the energy reaching the earth's surface eventually escapes back into space, a great deal of work is accomplished during the time it interacts with the biosphere.

Less than one percent of incoming solar energy is used to propel photosynthesis. Most of that energy, instead, is used in shuffling water around.

After all, the heat produced by solar energy is responsible for evaporation from the oceans, lakes, rivers, and, not insignificantly, the leaves of plants. This involves an enormous amount of work. As water is lifted into the atmosphere it loses its heat and condenses, only to fall again to earth, drenching vast areas that would otherwise remain dry and uninhabitable. This constant movement of water is called the **hydrologic cycle** (Figure 44.2).

Climatic Factors

The massive movements of heat and water produce the climates of the earth. These movements are far greater in some areas than in others. For example, much of the solar energy strikes the equatorial regions of the earth fairly evenly, but in the northerly and southerly latitudes the energy varies markedly from one season to the next because of the earth's tilted axis. Without these seasonal fluctuations, the temperate zones we see now would be perpetually frozen.

THE BIOMES AND WATERS OF THE EARTH

The uneven heating of the earth and the variable climate it produces result in an uneven distribution of life over the planet. The distribution, however, has produced rather recognizable areas called biomes. A **biome** is a particular array of plants and animals within a geographic area that has distinctive climatic conditions. Biomes are usually identified by their plant species, which influence the animal life there. The specific plant associations are influenced by climatic factors, particularly by precipitation, temperature, and light.

Life on earth can be grouped into 10 major terrestrial biomes (Figure 44.3), as well as the aquatic realms. Biomes tend to be found at particular latitudes, especially in the Northern Hemisphere. Here, moving northward from the equator, equatorial forests are followed by grasslands and deserts, then temperate forests, northern coniferous forests, and tundra. The effects of altitude can mimic those of latitude (Figure 44.4).

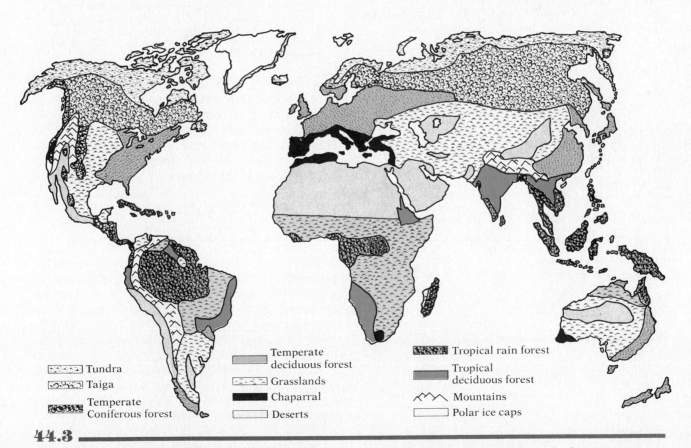

Tundra

Taiga

Temperate Coniferous forest

Temperate deciduous forest

Grasslands

Chaparral

Deserts

Tropical rain forest

Tropical deciduous forest

Mountains

Polar ice caps

44.3

The biomes. Each biome can be identified primarily by its plant life. The plant life has adapted to the specific biome's climatic conditions, including precipitation, availability of light, and, of course, temperature. Both latitude and altitude affect all these variables.

Each biome consists of a number of subunits, called ecological communities, biotic communities, or simply communities. **Communities** consist of populations of plants, animals, and other organisms that interact more or less independently of other such groups. Communities are usually described in their **climax state,** a "steady state" where there is little change and the organisms have established an equilibrium with the physical environment. That is, there is little change in the level of energy tied up in the *biomass* of the organic material. (**Biomass** is the total weight of organisms or organic material in an area at any given time.) As we will see in the next chapter, a great deal of ecology is focused on the community level of organization. We'll now consider the major biomes of the earth, beginning at the equator and moving through the temperate regions toward the poles.

THE TROPICAL RAIN FOREST BIOME

The first biome we encounter is the **tropical rain forest.** Typically, this lush and varied biome receives about 250–450 cm (100–180 in) of annual rainfall. Rain is usually rather evenly distributed throughout the year, although some rain forests

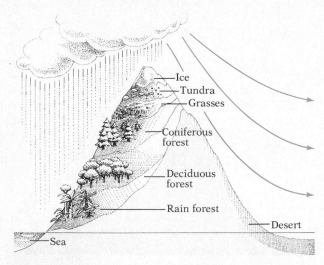

44.4

The altitudinal variation provided by mountains often mimics latitudinal biome distributions. This hypothetical model represents such a distribution in a tropical mountain range. On the other side of the mountain, air masses holding little moisture rush down the slopes and across the barren terrain, leaving typical desert conditions behind as they pick up whatever moisture exists.

44.5

The tropical rain forest as seen from a cleared area reveals its lush growth and hints at its stratification. Most of the animals live in the canopy or subcanopies, rarely descending to the dark forest floor.

experience a short "dry" season. There is little seasonal variation in temperature—often less than the change between day and night temperatures. The largest tropical rain forest is in the Amazon River Basin in South America; the second largest is in the wilds of the Indonesian Archipelago (see Figure 44.3).

Plant and Animal Associations

A tropical rain forest is a verdant and beautiful place. The floor is dark and wet, the damp air ripe with smells. Unlike the situation in most other biomes, no single kind of plant is predominant. Any tree is likely to be a different species from its neighbors; the nearest tree of the same species may even be miles away.

The forest floor is usually shadowed by the nearly continuous leafy *canopy* of trees some 30–45 m tall. Below, smaller trees form rather distinct layers of *subcanopies* (Figure 44.5), interwoven by large numbers of vines. Both trees and vines may be festooned with **epiphytes,** plant species that have evolved an interesting way of competing for sunlight. Epiphytes live on the stems and branches of tall trees in the canopy and do not touch the soil below. They absorb water directly from the surrounding humid air. (One species forms a bucket-like base around its roots that collects water. Any hapless insect falling into the water decomposes, providing the plant with nitrogen.)

The forest floor is often devoid of foliage, but it is teeming with fungal and bacterial decomposers and insect scavengers. The darkness, warmth, and incredible humidity are ideal for rapid decomposition. However, the products of decomposition do not accumulate as *humus* (partially decayed organic material) and enrich the soil as they do in other forests. Instead, they rapidly cycle back into the living plants, leaving the soil notoriously poor. This is a major reason that clearing the tropical rain forests for agriculture is discouraged—any benefits are only short-lived and marginal. Burning the trees cleared from such areas places an added CO_2 burden on the atmosphere (see Essay 44.1), and such clearing alters rainfall patterns, which normally depend partly on the enormous volumes of water recycled through transpiration.

The tropical rain forest harbors an incredible number of animal species, more so than any other terrestrial region. Insects and birds are particularly abundant, as are reptiles, small mammals, and amphibians. Many of the animal species are stratified according to the layers established by the plants, becoming specialists at occupying certain levels of the canopy and subcanopy. In one study of the Costa Rican rain forest, ecologists found 14 ground-foraging species, 59 species occupying the subcanopy, and 69 in the upper canopy. They further found that about two-thirds of the mammals were arboreal (tree dwellers), as were a number of frogs, lizards, and snakes (Figure 44.6).

44.7

Large hooved mammals are prominent among the savanna's herbivore population. On the African plains, predators include the large cats.

THE TROPICAL SAVANNA BIOME

The **tropical savanna** biome is a special kind of grassland that often borders tropical rain forests. Unlike other grasslands, the savanna contains scattered trees or clumps of trees (Figure 44.7). And unlike tropical rain forests, savannas have a prolonged dry season and an annual rainfall of 100–150 cm (40–60 in). The dry season is often marked by frequent and extensive fires, a phenomenon to which plants have had to adapt.

44.6

Animals of the tropical rain forest are generally arboreal, each species specialized for life in specific parts of the canopy and subcanopy.

Plant and Animal Associations

The largest tropical savannas occur in Africa, but they are also found in South America and Australia. In Africa, while grasses are the dominant form of plant life, the strange, misshapen baobab trees, along with palms and colorful acacias, bring relief to the drab landscape. The number and variety of hooved animal species exceeds that of any other biome in Africa, and includes the familiar zebras, wildebeests, giraffes, and antelopes. This is also the domain of such infamous predators as lions and cheetahs. As is happening in many other grassland biomes, much of the natural fauna of the world's tropical savannas is gradually being replaced by domestic cattle.

ESSAY 44.1

CARBON DIOXIDE AND THE GREENHOUSE EFFECT: A DESTABILIZED EQUILIBRIUM

In recent years, atmospheric scientists have become greatly concerned about the increasing levels of carbon dioxide in the air. The CO_2 comes from a variety of sources. As we know, it is produced by the metabolism of most living things. In addition, the enormous amount of carbon dioxide released by the burning of fossil fuels has been a concern for many years (see graphs **a** and **b**), but today we face a new source of CO_2 production—the carbon dioxide that was once part of the living mass of the tropical rain forests. Such forests have always been a great CO_2 *sink* (region of concentration), but they are being cleared at the alarming rate of one percent each year. As they are cleared, the logs are burned and a great concentration of CO_2 is released into the atmosphere. This has all happened quite suddenly, and the earth's waters, which absorb CO_2, have not kept up.

Why the alarm? It has to do with the storage of heat in the atmosphere. One of the physical characteristics of CO_2 gas is that it absorbs the infrared (heat) energy that emanates from the surface of the sunlit earth. So light from the sun passes unhindered through CO_2, radiates from the earth, and warms the CO_2 in the earth's atmosphere. As atmospheric CO_2 increases, the air becomes capable of holding more heat, and so it begins to get warmer.

Since greenhouses maintain their warm temperature in a similar manner—by letting in short-wave light and retaining longer-wave radiation (heat)—the CO_2 phenomenon has been called the *greenhouse effect*. So far, the actual effect seems to have been minor, hypothetically because of geophysical changes that would normally have resulted in a cooling of the earth.

Still, according to the experts, the temperature cycle will eventually reverse, and when it does, the greenhouse effect will be accelerated. Adding to the problem is a steady increase in ocean temperatures. As the oceans warm even a little, their ability to hold CO_2 in solution will decrease. The oceans contain much greater reserves of CO_2 than the atmosphere, and a rise of one or two degrees would unload more of the gas into the air. It has been suggested that a warming earth will result in the melting of the polar ice caps (which has already begun). Not only would this cause ocean levels to rise drastically, but the ice caps play a role in maintaining the energy equilibrium by reflecting solar energy back into space. The greenhouse effect, then, is expected to increase in the coming years, with results that will be varied and far-reaching and that are probably not completely anticipated. ●

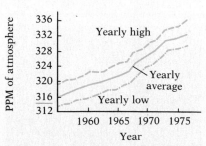

(a) Studies of carbon dioxide content in the atmosphere have been monitored at the Mauna Loa Observatory in Hawaii for many years.

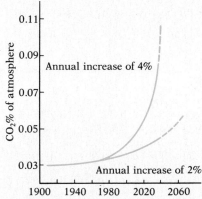

(b) The carbon dioxide problem. The two projected increases in atmospheric concentrations of CO_2 reflect different estimates of future fossil fuel consumption.

THE DESERT BIOME

The **desert** is both a dreaded place and a setting for uncounted fables, but the image most people have of deserts probably reflects only a few of the actual desert biomes. Deserts are actually quite varied places. The world's largest desert is the Sahara, followed by the vast Australian desert. A primary characteristic of the desert is severely limited, seasonal precipitation, usually less than 25 cm (10 in) per year. But while all deserts are dry and most are hot, there are northern deserts where winter snows are common. And all deserts have dramatic day-night extremes in temperature. Without the buffering effect of atmospheric moisture, the desert floor heats rapidly during the day and cools just as rapidly at night. Some of the conditions that produce the desert climate were mentioned in Figure 44.4.

Plant and Animal Associations

Plants adapted to the extremely dry climates of deserts are known as **xerophytes** (*xeric*, dry). In the American desert, perennials such as cactus and other fleshy, water-storing succulents, ocotillo, Joshua tree, creosote bush, sagebrush, and palo verde (Figure 44.8) are adapted to living for long periods with little water. The various cacti have greatly reduced water loss by replacing leaves with spines and producing a thick, waxy cuticle over their photosynthetic stems. Other perennials shed their small leathery leaves and remain dormant throughout the drier seasons. Further, desert plants tend to be widely spaced—partly due to water availability and partly through the chemical inhibition of neighboring plants.

Compared to other plants, leafy desert perennials tend to have fewer and more widely scattered guard cells, and even these are located mostly on the protected underside of their small leaves. Smaller leaves and fewer stomata help in conserving water, but the price is a considerably slower growth rate, since CO_2 uptake and photosynthesis are retarded. Some desert perennials close their stomata during the day and open them at night, storing CO_2 temporarily in intermediate compounds (see Chapter 25).

The tiny but colorful desert annuals reveal another strategy. Their life cycle is short and adapted to the desert's infrequent rainfall. In many species, the tough, resistant seeds require a critical amount of ground water before germinating. If there is not enough water to trigger germination they just sit it out, perhaps for several seasons.

The animals of the desert are primarily arthropods, reptiles, birds, and mammals. Just as plants have had to adapt to the rigors of the desert, so have animals. Animals have the advantage of being able to adapt not only anatomically and physiologically, but behaviorally as well.

Many desert animals avoid the heat by simply staying out of the daytime sun and becoming active at night. Mammals are largely represented by rodents, for which nocturnality has very clear advantages. (Rodents tend to lose water quickly, because of rapid breathing and because small animals have a large surface area relative to their volume.) The kangaroo rat *(Dipodomys deserti)* of the southern California desert is particularly interesting because it *never* drinks. It survives on the water contained in its food and the metabolic water it produces through cell respiration. Its remarkably efficient kidney produces small quantities of highly concentrated urine, but most of the rat's water loss occurs through simple breathing. Even these special

44.8

Both of the North American desert plants shown here (the saguaro, *left*, and the Joshua tree, *right*) have adapted to limited water; such plants are called *xerophytes*. Their thorny epidermis discourages browsing and helps shield the green surfaces from the harsh direct sunlight. Many xerophytes have pulpy water-storing tissues, while others simply slow their metabolic processes and become straggly and leafless between rainy seasons.

Animals in the desert forage in two shifts. The day feeders are fewer in number than the nocturnal species, and include birds such as the roadrunner **(a)** and the desert iguana **(b)**. Even these hardy foragers often remain in shadows at midday. At sundown the second shift begins, as kangaroo rats **(c)** and other rodents start their browsing. This is, of course, an invitation to carnivores like the great-horned owl **(d)**, which go quietly about their deadly business. An intriguing adaptation to desert conditions occurs in the Australian frog *(Cyclorana albogottatus)* **(e)** that survives the dryest season in an underground "cell," retaining water in its skin.

physiological features wouldn't permit desert survival were they not coupled with nocturnality. The rat spends its day in a humid, hair-lined burrow, venturing forth only in the cooler evening.

Of course, predators such as owls and rattlesnakes must follow their prey, so they hunt mostly at night or in the cool of the evening. The relatively few species that are out and about in the daytime—such as the long-legged and swift lizards—are preyed upon by hawks and road runners, which are also adapted to daylight conditions. Even the daytime animals, however, restrict most of their activity to the morning and evening hours (Figure 44.9).

THE CHAPARRAL, OR MEDITERRANEAN SCRUB FOREST, BIOME

The *Mediterranean scrub forest*, or **chaparral** biome (as it is called in California), is rather insignificant among the forests of the world. It does, however, have unique characteristics and its own peculiar plant associations. For example, it is exclusively coastal, found mainly along the Pacific coast of North America and the coastal hills of Chile, the Mediterranean, southern Africa, and southern Australia. This biome is unique in that it consists of broad-leaved evergreens in regions marked by winter rainfall—often as low as 25 cm (10 in)—followed by drought that extends through the summer. The climate is moderated, however, by cooler air from the oceans (Figure 44.10).

During the dry season, the chaparral places the same demands on its inhabitants as does the desert; both plants and animals must adapt to long dry spells. In fact, some species in the two biomes are quite similar. But many of the chaparral plants are adapted to another factor—fire. Fire is a natural phenomenon encouraged by drought, resinous plants, and a deep layer of dry, slowly decomposing litter on the forest floor. Brush fires periodically sweep across the terrain, leaving behind the charred remains of plants and animals. Since the chaparral is made up chiefly of fire-adapted plant species, in most instances recovery is rapid, with shoots sprouting quickly from burned stumps and fire-resistant seeds. Ecologists describe the chaparral as a *fire-disclimax community*, which means that because of fire it never reaches a state of maturity. Virtually every stand of trees is in some state of recovery.

THE GRASSLAND BIOME

In the Northern Hemisphere, **grasslands** can form huge inland plains, such as the North American prairie and the vast Asian steppes. Extensive grasslands also occur in South America (pampas) and in Australia, where their area equals that of the desert (Figure 44.11). There are several similarities between grassland and desert; in fact, grassland often gradually fades into desert. The chief climatic difference between the two is precipitation—grasslands get more rain. The rain, however, is of a seasonal nature, often not sustained or abundant enough to support forests. Another factor that prevents forest penetration is fire, a natural and recurring phenomenon in grasslands.

Plant and Animal Associations

As you might expect, the dominant plants of grasslands are grasses. But since there are many kinds of grasses, grasslands are very different from one place to the next. For example, on the American prairie (at least the part that is still identifiable), the grasses east of the Mississippi may grow nearly 3 m tall, while those in the West rarely exceed ½ m. Again, the difference is principally due to variation in rainfall.

Since rains are commonly seasonal in most grasslands, the plants have developed strategies for drought survival. In lowland regions, roots

44.11

Grasslands, like savannas, support many herbivores. This South American grassland is made up mostly of bunchgrasses, the primary food of llamas, alpacas, and many smaller animals. The llama, a ruminant, is a descendent of camels that crossed from North to South America during the Pleistocene epoch.

may penetrate as far as 2 m below the surface to the permanent water table. Some grasses, however, rely on a vast, spreading diffuse root system. In addition, grasses readily become dormant, reviving when water is once again available. Some grasses produce underground stems (rhizomes) that remain alive after all the foliage has died. This matlike growth, or sod, prevented agricultural intrusion until plowing implements were improved—hence the term "sodbuster."

Grasses are highly efficient at rapidly converting solar energy into the chemical-bond energy of their living matter, so it is not surprising that the grasslands can support large animal populations. Chief among the mammals are the hooved and burrowing types. In North America these include the bison and antelope, animals whose teeth and digestive systems are well adapted to a diet of tough grassland plants. Both groups were drastically reduced in number by hunting and agriculture, and are now seen only in protected areas. (As you are probably aware, there is little virgin grassland in the world today, since most of the grasses have been replaced by grains and other crops.) Burrowers include the prairie dog, gopher, and ground squirrel. These mammals have fared somewhat better than their hooved counterparts, but today they are subjected to relentless hunting and poisoning in cattle-grazing areas.

44.10

The chaparral in southern California may lack the glamour and luster of many other forests, but its plants are tenacious and hardy. These scrubby plants resist an annual drought that would discourage most other plants. Many parts of the chaparral actually qualify as deserts in terms of total precipitation, but they are not called deserts because of their cool, moist marine air.

44.12 ▬▬▬▬▬▬▬▬▬▬▬▬▬▬▬▬▬

The deciduous forest changes its appearance with the seasons. The lovely green hillside of summer will explode in a riot of colors when autumn arrives. Both are in sharp contrast to the starkness of winter. Animals here must adapt to the long cold winters. Many will hibernate, while others simply migrate. The remainder are faced with shortages of food and shelter for the winter months.

THE TEMPERATE DECIDUOUS FOREST BIOME

If you are from east of the Mississippi, you may be well acquainted with the **temperate deciduous forest** biome. (A deciduous forest is one in which trees tend to lose their leaves seasonally.) The temperate deciduous biome extends over much of the eastern United States and northward into southeast Canada. It is also found in Europe and parts of China. Rainfall in the deciduous forest is rather evenly distributed throughout the year, often averaging more than 100 cm (39 in)—enough to support a variety of plant life.

Temperate deciduous forests are usually characterized by marked seasonal changes, but unlike more northerly biomes, they have quite a long growing season. With the onset of winter, much of the water becomes frozen and unavailable to plants, so most perennial deciduous species become dormant (Figure 44.12).

Plant and Animal Associations

The American deciduous forest is generally subdivided into a number of forest types in which certain species dominate. For example, beech and maple forests dominate in the north, while oak-hickory and oak-chestnut complexes are prevalent farther south (mostly oak today, since most chestnuts have been killed by fungi).

The deciduous forests were once the home of the grizzly bear and gray wolf, as well as the mountain lion and black bear. Now these once important predators are restricted to protected areas or, as in the case of the wolf, have been virtually eliminated from all but the more inaccessible areas of the north. Carnivores of the North American deciduous forest today include the less conspicuous bobcat, raccoon, opossum, skunk, and an occasional red fox.

Animals of the deciduous forest adapt to the drastic seasonal changes in a number of ways. Some, primarily birds, migrate to southerly winter habitats. Others lapse into the long chilled stupor called *hibernation*, their metabolism drastically lowered. Yet others—bears, for example—fall into a deep sleep, occasionally rousing themselves for brief foraging expeditions. Some species must simply brave the cold and its food shortages.

THE TAIGA BIOME

The **taiga**, or *northern coniferous forest*, is almost exclusively confined to the Northern Hemisphere. It is made up of great forests of pine, spruce, hemlock, and fir that extend across the North American and Asian continents. Smaller forests are found at higher elevations in many mountain ranges (Figure 44.13). The taiga is unmistakable; there is nothing else like it. It is subject to long, frigid winters and short summer growing seasons. It is difficult to generalize about rainfall because the taiga is so extensive; some places receive large amounts of rain, some very little.

Plant and Animal Associations

Although the taiga is characterized by conifers, communities of poplar, alder, willow, and birch may be found in disturbed places. Furthermore, the taiga is interrupted in places by extensive bogs, or *muskegs*, the remnants of very large ponds. The most common trees are spruce; low-lying shrubs, mosses, and grasses form the spongy ground cover.

Conifers have adapted to their cold environment through reduced needle-like or scale-like leaves that are covered by a waxy secretion. This specialization retards water loss, an important factor since arid conditions are common and ground water is frozen and unavailable throughout most of the year. (One is reminded of the spines and waxy cuticles of desert plants.)

The taiga harbors such large herbivores as moose, elk, and deer. It is also practically the last refuge of both the grizzly and black bears. Wolves still roam here, as do lynx and wolverines (see Figure 44.13). Rabbits, porcupines, hares, and rodents abound, but insect populations aren't as large as they are in deciduous forests. However, there is a disconcerting abundance of mosquitos and flies in some regions during the summer.

The taiga is a continuing target of the lumber industry, as are more southerly coniferous forests. The forests have been partially protected so far by their very size, but the lumber companies seem to be taking whatever they can reach. Their much-publicized replanting programs usually replace mixed forests of genetically diverse and disease-resistant plants with artificially developed and genetically homogeneous trees that are fast-growing and can quickly be reharvested. Biologists are still trying to assess the dangers of such genetic uniformity in a large system.

THE TUNDRA BIOME

Tundra, the northernmost biome, has no equivalent in the Southern Hemisphere (except for a few alpine meadows where similar conditions are found). The annual precipitation is meager, often less than 15 cm (5 in), and much of this falls as snow. During the greater part of the year, much of the moisture is tied up as ice and is unavailable to most forms of life.

The tundra's growing season lasts about two months. During this time, the frozen surface waters thaw and ponds begin to form everywhere. Since the soil remains permanently frozen (*permafrost*) a few feet below, the surface water cannot percolate down. Although the growing season is short, the days are long, permitting an extended *daily* growing period.

Plant and Animal Associations

Tall trees and shrubs are entirely absent from the tundra, except around streams. While the tundra at higher elevations may be composed of only scattered and rather drab plants, in the lower areas growth may be luxurious, dense, and colorful. Pioneering lichens and mosses are common, as are

44.13

The taiga is an extensive biome, found almost exclusively in the Northern Hemisphere. Since the conditions of the taiga are duplicated in high mountains, similar communities are found here. Herbivores of the taiga include large mammals such as the moose and elk. The lynx and grizzly bear are still found in the taiga, protected somewhat from human intervention by the vastness of the territory.

dwarfed versions of some trees, among them willows and birches. Grasses, rushes, sedges, and other low-lying plants complete the summer ground cover (Figure 44.14).

Surprisingly, animal life isn't rare in this peculiar and rugged northern biome. In fact, the tundra supports some rather large herbivores. In North America we find the caribou and musk oxen, and in Europe and Asia, the reindeer. Other animals of the tundra include the ptarmigan, the snowshoe hare, the arctic ground squirrel, and the ever-present, legendary lemmings (see Figure 44.14).

Lemming populations, which can soar in good years, determine the reproductive success of a number of predators, including the arctic wolf. Also, snowy owls and jaegers (large, strong-flying birds) travel great distances to feed on the tiny rodents. How long the migrators stay and how successfully they reproduce depend, for the most part, on the number of lemmings.

Winter comes early in the tundra, and with the rapidly shortening days the migratory animals disappear. The caribou, for example, leave for the forested taiga, where winter food is more plentiful. Those species that remain prepare for survival in a number of ways. Lemmings retreat to food-laden burrows; ptarmigans tunnel into snow banks, to emerge only periodically on foraging expeditions. Since the larger resident herbivores don't hibernate, they must rove the barren, windswept landscape to feed on subsistence foods such as mosses and lichens. The predators follow, feeding on the herbivores. Next summer's insects simply avoid the problem by passing the winter suspended in immature stages.

THE MARINE ENVIRONMENT

Even a casual glance at a globe reveals that most of the earth's surface is oceanic, and the greatest depths of these oceans are deeper than the peaks of the highest mountains are high. The **marine environment** is indeed extensive and complex, containing a vast array of communities. These are divided into two major *provinces:* the deeper, open sea or **oceanic province,** and the shallower seas along the coastlines, the **neritic province.** The marine environment can also be subdivided vertically into the light-penetrating **euphotic zone** and the perpetually dark **aphotic zone** (Figure 44.15).

44.14

In summer, the treeless low tundra becomes a marsh as the snow melts. With little runoff, the landscape becomes dotted with small ponds. Plants include a number of dwarfed trees, grasses, and abundant lichens called reindeer moss. Common herbivores in the tundra include large animals such as musk ox and caribou, and small ones such as birds and lemmings. The lemming is the major prey for several tundra carnivores, including the migratory snowy owl and the arctic fox.

The Oceanic Province

The seas are not uniformly filled with life; in fact, life may be quite sparse in the oceanic province. Nevertheless, because of the vastness of the open seas, the *total* amount of life there is enormous. Much of this life is found in the sunlit euphotic zone, which contains populations of minute plankton, floating and drifting organisms, and *nekton*, the swimmers that feed on the plankton.

Perhaps the greatest mysteries on earth lie in the dark waters of the oceanic province, the depths of the **abyssal region.** The deepest part of the ocean is the famed Marianas Trench, which is 10,680 m (over 6 mi) deep. These mysterious depths are places of tremendous pressure and chilling cold. Nevertheless, the abyss supports a surprising number of peculiar scavengers and predators. Generally lacking a producer population (although we will find an exception in the next chapter), these **benthic** (bottom-dwelling) creatures rely on the continuous rain of the remains of creatures from the euphotic zone above. These tiny corpses will finally settle and contribute to the thick "bottom ooze" of the ocean floor. Tethered cameras miles deep and focused on bait have revealed primitive hagfish, crustaceans, mollusks, echinoderms, and even an occasional shark.

The Neritic Province

In the neritic province, the land masses extend outward below the sea, forming the highly variable *continental shelf.* The neritic province ends at the *continental slope,* where the shelf drops off, often abruptly. In the shallower areas of the shelf, light penetrates to the ocean bottom. Such regions are

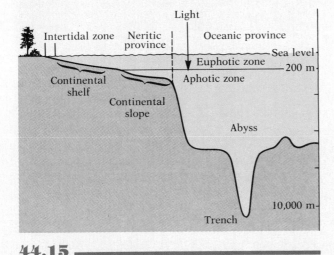

44.15

Organization of the marine environment.

TABLE 44.1

Productivity of organic material

Area of Ocean	Productivity (gC/m²/yr)*	Efficiency (%)
Open (90%)	50	10
Coastal (9.9%)	100	15
Upwellings (0.1%)	300	20

*Measure is grams of carbon (organic material) per square meter per year.

constantly stirred by waves, winds, and tides, which keep nutrients suspended and support many forms of swimming and bottom-dwelling life. Giant kelps and other seaweeds form extensive beds, offering hiding places for many fish.

The greatest productivity of the marine environment is found farther offshore, particularly in the province's colder waters (Table 44.1). Here we find regions of **upwellings,** where deep, nutrient-laden colder waters move to the surface. Little is known about such vertical movement of water in the open sea, but we have a better idea of what causes coastal upwellings. They are generally seasonal and occur when coastal winds blow either seaward or parallel to the coast, moving the surface layers, which are then replaced by deeper layers. This stirring brings up nutrients that would otherwise be forever locked in the bottom sediments. The nutrients can then help support photosynthetic organisms, which provide the base for marine **food chains**—the passage of energy and essential molecules from one group of organisms to the next. (The vast anchovy fisheries off the coast of Peru are dependent upon such upwellings.) Let's look more closely at how the marine food chain is organized.

The Marine Producers. As light passes through the waters of the euphotic zone, its energy is utilized by a variety of microscopic photosynthesizing organisms—chiefly diatoms and dinoflagellates—that are collectively called *phytoplankton.* (Marine ecologists are now studying another type of photosynthesizer in this group that is presently poorly understood but is apparently highly significant. It is composed of minute, flagellated organisms called *nanoplankton.*)

Phytoplankton, along with the larger algae called seaweeds, are the **primary producers** of the sea. This means that energy enters the marine ecosystem via these minute creatures. It has been estimated that 80–90% of the earth's photosynthetic activity is carried on by marine organisms. Thus, the sea's food chain begins with tiny floating plants capturing the sun's energy within their fragile

communities. A diversity of life is possible because here we find a variety of shelters and hiding places, abundant sunlight, and nutrient runoff from the land. However, the coastline also presents a range of problems. The shallowness of the water contributes to violently surging seas, and the periodic flooding and drying can place particularly severe stress on the communities in the tidal areas.

Estuaries, where rivers run into oceans, can produce the problem of changing salinity, while low tides in mud flats require that their inhabitants be burrowers. Along rocky coasts (Figure 44.17), a number of plants and animals have adapted to the surging waves by developing means of holding fast to the rocks. In other cases, animals may seek refuge in burrows, or they may lodge themselves in crevices and on the undersides of rocks. Some mollusks that are exposed to the dry air at low tide can close their shells, and some may hide in deep crevices or take refuge in tidepools.

Among the most fascinating of the shore com-

44.16

The oceanic food chain. Tiny phytoplankton capture the energy of the sun. They are eaten by animals larger than themselves, which are, in turn, eaten by larger animals. At the top are the largest carnivores of the sea. (There are no herbivores in the ocean as there are on land.) Note that each level of the chain consists of far fewer organisms than the one below it.

bodies. The tiny plants are fed upon by animals only a little larger than themselves, the *zooplankton*. A variety of animals, from tiny fish to the great baleen whales, feed upon both sorts of plankton (Figure 44.16).

Shore Communities

The various physical features of the coastline—sandy beaches, rocky shores, bays, estuaries, tidal flats, and reefs—provide for a number of coastal

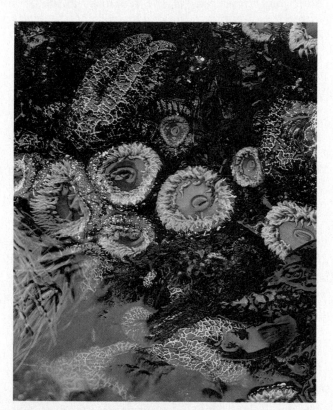

44.17

Rocky tide pools. The rocky coast is home for numerous marine animals. Each organism of the rocky tide pool is adapted in some way to withstand both the surging and pounding of waves and intermittent periods of exposure to the air at low tide. Some live in burrows; others cling to rocks with bristles, suckers, or feet; yet others come in and go out with the tide.

munities are coral reefs. **Coral reefs** are common in tropical and subtropical waters where the temperatures average between 23°C and 25°C. Corals are formed of vast colonies of coelenterates that can secrete heavy walls of calcium carbonate around themselves (Chapter 27). Their irregular growth provides natural refuges for marine animals, including sponges, bryozoans, mollusks (such as the octopus), and many kinds of fishes. Sharks commonly patrol the deep waters alongside the reefs. Where these formations appear along coastlines, they are called *barrier reefs*. The largest is the Great Barrier Reef, which extends for 1200 mi along the east coast of Queensland, Australia.

In this chapter, then, we have seen that the vastness of our "small planet" permits a wide range of environments and a huge array of habitats. Keeping in mind the constant exceptions we encounter in biology, it is possible to categorize the earth's environment according to the arrangement of the life it supports. Such generalization may help us to understand the present status of life on the planet and may also yield clues regarding the historical progression that led to what we see today.

Summary

The Biosphere

Ecology is the study of the interaction between organisms and their environment. The biosphere includes land areas, water habitats, and life-supporting air. The presence of water in the atmosphere slows the dissipation of radiant heat from the earth's surface; the earth's atmosphere also screens out much of the ultraviolet radiation that would otherwise make the earth's surface inhospitable to life, and acts as a gigantic heat sink. Although the energy input from the sun has traditionally been equalled by the escape of radiant energy from the earth's surface, the increased release of CO_2 is changing this balance, a process known as the greenhouse effect. Most of the solar energy reaching the earth propels the hydrologic cycle, resulting in a constant movement of water. Such movement, along with variations in heat, moderates the earth's climate.

The Biomes and Waters of the Earth

The uneven heating of the earth and the variable climate it produces result in the varied distribution of life across the planet. A biome is an array of plants and animals distributed over a geographic area that has distinctive climatic conditions. Life on earth is distributed into 10 major terrestrial biomes, plus the marine and freshwater realms. Each biome consists of communities, which are usually described in their climax states (in which organisms have established a sort of equilibrium with the environment).

The Tropical Rain Forest Biome

Tropical rain forests receive about 250–450 cm (or 100–180 in) of rainfall per year. The great variety of plant species precludes the predominance of any single species. Trees form canopies and subcanopies, while the forest floor supports primarily fungal and bacterial decomposers and insects. The soil is poor because the products of decomposition are washed away or rapidly recycled into living plants. The tropical forest harbors an incredible number of animal species, many of which have become adapted to life in specific layers of the canopies and subcanopies.

The Tropical Savanna Biome

The tropical savanna is a special kind of grassland that often borders on tropical rain forests. It contains scattered trees or clumps of trees and has a prolonged dry season, with an annual rainfall of 100–150 cm (40–60 in). The largest tropical savannas occur in Africa, where grasses are the dominant form of plant life. There are many hooved animals, as well as predators such as lions and cheetahs.

The Desert Biome

Deserts receive less than 25 cm (10 in) of seasonal precipitation per year. They also have dramatic day-night extremes in temperature. Xerophytes have adapted to the dry climate and temperature extremes with waxy cuticles, fewer stomata and leaves, and seeds that can remain dormant for many seasons. Animals adapt by staying out of the sun and being active at night.

The Chaparral, or Mediterranean Scrub Forest, Biome

The chaparral is exclusively coastal and consists of broad-leaved evergreens in regions marked by winter rainfall and summer droughts. Plants and animals have adapted in much the same way as those in desert biomes, with additional plant adaptations for fire.

The Grassland Biome

Grasslands receive more moisture than deserts but resemble them in other respects. Plants must adapt to periods of drought and be resistant to fire; many have vast diffuse root systems or produce rhizomes and stolons that remain alive after foliage has died. Abundant plant life supports a variety of insects, birds, and hooved and burrowing mammals.

The Temperate Deciduous Forest Biome

Temperate deciduous forests cover large sections of the world's landmasses. Precipitation is evenly distributed throughout the year and supports a variety of plant life. The forests have a long growing season, but many deciduous species become dormant in winter. Beech and maple trees dominate northerly American forests, while oak, hickory, and chestnut trees are prevalent farther south. Animals in deciduous forests, a mixture of herbivores and carnivores, adapt to seasonal changes by migrating, by hibernating, or by altering hunting patterns to adjust to food shortages.

The Taiga Biome

The taiga, made up of coniferous forests, is almost exclusively confined to the Northern Hemisphere. It is subject to long, severe winters and short growing seasons. Taiga is marked in places by muskegs, the remnants of large ponds. Conifers have adapted to the climate with needle-like leaves that retain water. The taiga supports large herbivores and a variety of other mammals.

The Tundra Biome

Tundra is the northernmost land biome. During most of the year much of its water is tied up as ice; a few feet below the surface, the soil is permanently frozen. The growing season is short but days are long. Only a few species of plants grow in upper regions, but lichens, mosses, grasses, and some trees grow in lower areas. The tundra can support large herbivores and predators as well as smaller animals. Animals must migrate or otherwise adapt to the long, frigid winters.

The Marine Environment

The extensive marine environment can be divided into neritic provinces along coastlines and oceanic provinces in the deeper open sea. (It can also be divided into euphotic and aphotic zones.) The oceanic province's deep abyssal regions are characterized by tremendous pressure and cold waters, yet support a surprising array of scavengers and predators. The neritic province covers the continental shelf, ending at the continental slope. In shallower areas, suspended nutrients support many forms of swimming and bottom-dwelling life. The most productive areas are farther offshore, in regions of upwellings, where deep, nutrient-laden waters move to the surface. The nutrients help support photosynthesizing organisms (primarily phytoplankton) that are the base of the marine food chain. These primary producers are eaten by zooplankton, which are in turn eaten by many fish and marine mammals.

Coastal communities include sandy beaches, rocky shores, bays, estuaries (where rivers meet the ocean), tidal flats, and reefs. These areas can change dramatically with tides and weather, so the inhabitants have adapted in a number of ways to such forces as pounding waves, changing salinity, and periodic dry conditions.

Key Terms

ecology	desert	neritic province
biosphere	xerophyte	euphotic zone
hydrologic cycle	chaparral	aphotic zone
biome	grassland	abyssal region
community	temperate deciduous forest	benthic
climax state	taiga	upwellings
biomass	tundra	food chain
tropical rain forest	marine environment	primary producer
epiphyte	oceanic province	coral reef
tropical savanna		

Review Questions

1. Describe the use of the solar energy reaching the biosphere. What eventually happens to energy that penetrates the atmosphere? (p. 646)

2. Discuss the general distribution of biomes in the Northern Hemisphere, beginning at the equator and proceeding northward. How can altitude affect biome distribution? (pp. 646–648)

3. List four or five physical factors that help determine the specific biome a region will support. (pp. 646–647)

4. Describe the vertical stratification of life in the tropical rain forests. (p. 648)

5. Briefly describe three specific plant and animal adaptations of the desert biome. (pp. 651–652)

6. Compare the principal climatic conditions of the deciduous forest to those of the tropical forest, and explain the major ways plants and animals have adapted in each. (pp. 648, 654)

7. What large group of organisms composes the primary producers of the marine environment? In what way are these organisms significant to other marine life? (pp. 657–658)

8. Describe the ecological organization of the ocean, naming provinces and zones, and listing characteristics of each. (pp. 656–657)

Ecosystems and Communities

45

In the long eons over which life on this planet has evolved, it has taken innumerable directions. In a sense it has probed every conceivable opportunity, creating niche after niche and diversifying all the while. The result has been a spectrum of life forms that have adapted, not only to the habitats offered by the earth, but also to each other. Thus we find "constellations" of organisms. In order to best understand them and their places in nature, we cannot consider them alone, but rather must see them as part of a system, an interacting group. Let's look at some of the organisms and see how they interact as energy ebbs and flows through often complex webs of life.

Now we will focus more finely on the planet's living systems. Those great and imperfect generalities we call biomes are useful in illustrating the broad principles of the distribution of life, but in order to understand its interactions, we must draw nearer and lose sight of the forest as the trees come into better focus.

In ecology, each unit of interacting organisms and the physical environment of which they are a part is known as an **ecosystem,** a handy operational term that can be applied at just about any level, from the earth itself to a tiny pool of microorganisms. Of course, few researchers would want to consider any such unwieldy system as the earth itself, so most, recognizing that ecosystems can be highly organized, self-contained, and theoretically manageable entities, note that the flow of energy and the cycling of essential substances occur in specific **trophic levels** (those relating to food). And it is often on these trophic levels (producer,

carnivore, or whatever) that research attention is focused. Our plan here is to first discuss the common characteristics of ecosystems, and then learn how they influence biotic communities. We can begin with the concept of energy flow.

ENERGETICS IN ECOSYSTEMS

In the last chapter we saw that about 50% of the solar energy reaching the atmosphere finds its way to the earth's surface. This enormous amount of energy is vitally important in warming the earth and shifting its waters about. But a comparatively small amount (about one-tenth of one percent, as a worldwide average) is captured by photosynthesizers of the earth ecosystem. Meager as it seems, this energy is enough to produce 150–200 billion metric tons of dry organic matter each year. (Since water is not organic and makes up a substantial part of living organisms, such estimates *exclude* its weight.) In more manageable terms, this level of production means that, on the average, each square meter of the earth's surface produces several kg of dry organic matter each year.

Trophic Levels

Let's review a few basic terms regarding the flow of energy through ecosystems. It is first captured by *producers* (photosynthesizers and chemo-synthesizers), or as we described earlier, *primary producers*. From there, energy passes to various *consumers*, organisms that cannot utilize light energy and must rely on others for the organic compounds they require. Dead organisms are fed upon by *reducers*. In the last chapter we referred to *food chains* in the marine ecosystem. There we saw that phytoplankton, the primary producers, were fed upon by zooplankton, which were fed upon by several levels of larger and larger marine creatures. Figure 45.1 traces the flow of energy through several trophic levels. As you would expect, the passage of energy is related to the passage of food molecules.

Producers. The **producers** include plants, algal protists, and phototrophic bacteria. The photosynthesizers use light energy, captured by various pigments, to produce organic materials from carbon dioxide, water, and a few minerals (see Chapter 7). In addition to the photosynthesizers, there are the *chemotrophs*, bacteria that obtain energy from inorganic substances in the earth's crust (see Essay 45.1). The biomass of the earth's producers is about 99% of the total present in the biosphere. (*Biomass*, here, is the total weight of organic matter at any given time.)

Consumers. Consumers include animals, fungi, animal-like protists, and most bacteria. In other words, these are the heterotrophs. (The fungi and bacteria make up a special category, the *reducers*, which we will come to shortly.) Since

some consumers eat producers, others eat other consumers, and some eat both, the flow of energy through the consumers involves several trophic levels. Thus we have *primary consumers*, the herbivores that feed directly on producers; *secondary consumers*, carnivores that feed on primary consumers; and so on through *tertiary*, *quaternary*, and even higher consumer levels (with increasingly rare representatives).

Organizing the trophic levels in this manner is obviously reminiscent of the simple food chains we considered earlier. But in reality, nothing is ever that simple. Most consumers cross trophic levels. For example, there are few true carnivores (sharks and some flies are examples). Consider humans. At how many trophic levels do we feed? Do we have salad with our steak? The steak comes from a herbivore, of course—but what if we eat a tuna sandwich? Tuna eat other carnivores. Because of such complexities, feeding patterns in a community are better represented by **food webs,** such as we see in Figure 45.2.

Reducers. Reducers are vast in numbers but small in size. This becomes apparent when we realize that they are primarily composed of fungi and bacteria. Reducers feed on dead organisms and their wastes by secreting digestive enzymes into their food and then absorbing the breakdown products (Figure 45.3). In so doing, they produce simple by-products such as ammonia, sulfates,

45.1

Energy flowing through ecosystems comes initially from the sun and is first captured by producers in photosynthesis. It then passes, as chemical bond energy in foods, from one consumer to the next and from one trophic level to another. Eventually the energy passes to reducers. Each transfer is about 10% efficient. The remaining energy escapes as heat, a product of the respiratory activities that support the organisms. In a climax community, the light energy captured would be equal to the energy used in respiration.

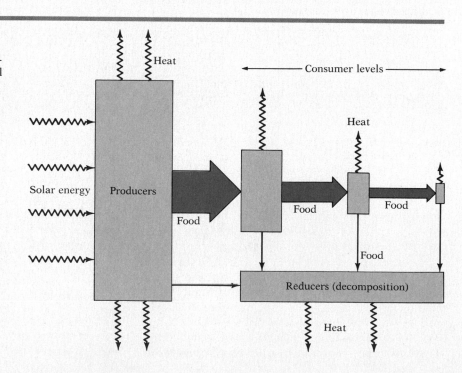

THE OCEANIC RIFT: AN UNUSUAL COMMUNITY

Deep down on the ocean floor, well over a mile beneath the surface, a number of communities thrive in the cold blackness. There are no producers here, but there is life. This is because the constant deluge of organic debris from the food webs above is rich in energy and matter—such sources of nutrients rarely go unexploited in nature. Until 1977, scientists believed that these species were the only inhabitants of benthic communities. But in that year the research submarine *Alvin,* cruising at a depth of 2500 m near the Galapagos islands, came upon a startling sight.

The scientists aboard *Alvin* saw a vent in the seabed spewing forth hot solutions of hydrogen sulfide and carbon dioxide. This in itself was not entirely unexpected, but what they saw nearby was surprising indeed. The waters around the vent were cloudy (a condition later attributed to dense aggregations of bacteria). Enormous, strange tubeworms—blood-red in color, nearly 3 m long, and as thick as a man's wrist—stirred in the turbulent waters. Smaller worm-like animals, arranged in spaghetti-like masses, were found with more familiar filter-feeding crabs, mussels, barnacles, and a variety of other animals common to benthic communities. Large clusters of clams were also found in the vent area; when these foot-long, smooth-shelled bivalves were opened, their flesh was found to be unusually rich in hemoglobin and blood-red in color.

The discovery of the vent communities intrigued the scientific world, and an immediate effort was made to collect and study specimens and to sort out the organization of this bizarre ecosystem. Finally, the pieces of the puzzle began to fit together. It was found that primary consumers in this community do not feed upon detritus falling from above, but are totally independent of life in the upper realms. The source of energy around the vents was found to be the enormous population of chemosynthetic bacteria that crowds the vent opening. These bacteria thrive on the gases boiling forth, using the hydrogen of hydrogen sulfide to reduce carbon dioxide to carbohydrates. The bacteria are also believed to live symbiotically in the skin of the giant tubeworms—animals that have tentatively been classified as *pogonopores,* an obscure phylum of worms that typically lack a mouth and gut.

Unlike other benthic communities, the rift has a seemingly endless supply of food. Oxygen is abundant in the cold abyssal water, so metabolic activity is rapid. The large Galapagos Rift clams, for instance, grow at a rate of 4 cm per year, about 500 times faster than their relatives in other waters. The extraordinary amount of hemoglobin is believed to be an adaptation for times when the oxygen level in the water is low.

At first, scientists aboard *Alvin* believed that the rift community they had discovered was unique. But then new rift communities were discovered, and now it appears that they are quite extensive, cropping up here and there among the innumerable faults in the ocean floor. In fact, in time they may prove to be among the most widespread and richest of marine communities. Rich and active though they are, the rift communities can pass quickly. Like volcanoes, the hot springs eventually die down, leaving behind ghostly monuments of empty shells. But as some vents close, others appear in cracks torn in the sea bottom by the earth's restless, shifting crust. ●

Tube worms

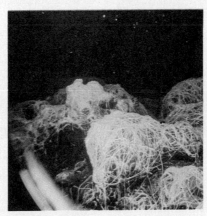
Spaghetti worms

Clam field

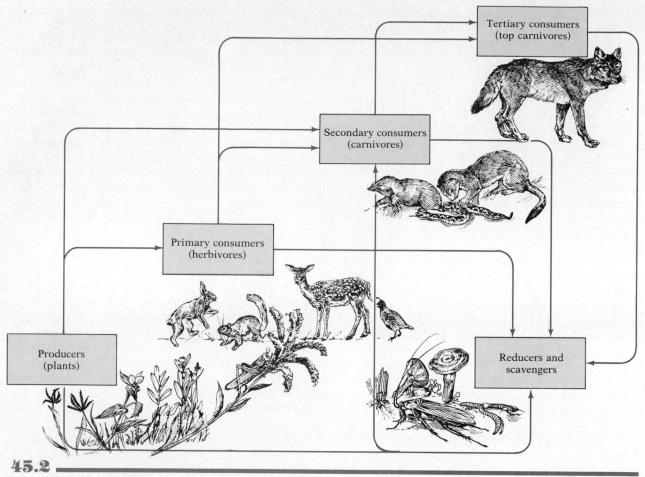

45.2

A simplified food web. Food webs reflect the complex feeding patterns in an ecosystem. The arrows indicate the direction of the flow of energy and matter. In na-ture, some animals feed from more than one trophic level, particularly during shortages when usual food sources become reduced.

45.3

Reducers decompose wastes and the remains of plants and animals, making nutrients available to the ecosystem. Most are microscopic in size, but the bracket fungi that live in fallen trees may be quite large.

nitrites and nitrates, and the usual carbon dioxide and water. Without them the world would be a far different place.

The reducer level is somewhat arbitrary; some ecologists refer to any species that feeds on dead organisms as a reducer. Their list of reducers would include such scavengers or carrion eaters as crows, crabs, jackals, vultures, and veritable armies of beetles and ants.

Trophic Levels as Pyramids

The pioneering ecologist Charles Elton first conceived of the **ecological pyramid** (or *Eltonian pyramid*) as a way of graphically handling some complex data. Essentially, ecological pyramids are an easy way to show the relationships between the different elements in an ecosystem. Their simplicity is deceiving, however, because the data are often hard won. The most common ecological pyramids are the *pyramids of numbers, pyramids of biomass* (weight of the total living matter), and *pyramids of energy.*

Pyramids of Numbers. In pyramids of numbers, counts of individuals at each trophic level provide the data. Consider, for example, a grassland community. The graph of the numbers of individuals at each level produces a typical "stepped" pyramidal shape (as seen in Figure 45.4a), but number pyramids can take a variety of different shapes. For example, if we count trees in a forest and then count the insects, parasites, and birds that feed on the trees, the ecological pyramid can be inverted.

Pyramids of Biomass. Pyramids reveal useful and sometimes surprising information when used to describe the relative biomass of different trophic levels in a community. Obviously, one cannot measure all the individuals in a community, so randomly collected individuals are considered as representative of the entire group. These may be collected in a number of ways, from trapping to intensively collecting in square meters or along extensive lines across the study area. The next step is to sort the organisms according to their trophic levels, then dry and weigh them. Typically, the biomass of the producers is far greater than that of the consumers (Figure 45.4b), and the biomass of any level of consumer is less than that of the level below. As was mentioned earlier, 99% of the earth's biomass is tied up in the primary producer level. Not much of the producer biomass is transferred to the primary consumer level. Of the plant biomass that is eaten by herbivores, some is not actually absorbed but is disposed of in the feces. Of the part that is absorbed and utilized, a considerable amount is used in respiration. The result is that very little of the plant biomass becomes consumer biomass.

Pyramids of Energy. Energy pyramids represent the transfer of calories from one trophic level to the next. While they may not be as radical in appearance as biomass pyramids, they do show the usual "stepped" configuration (Figure 45.4c). The energy transfers from one trophic level to the next show only about 10% efficiency, because about 90% of the energy in the food eaten by consumers is not stored (some of the energy-laden

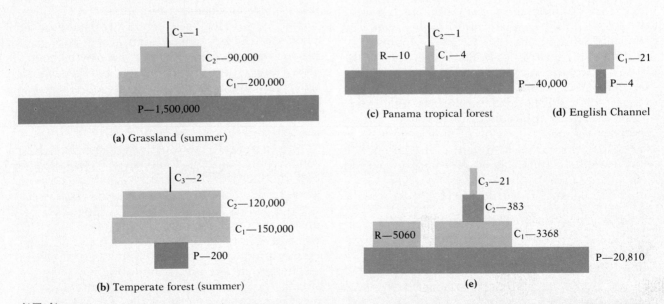

(a) Grassland (summer)

(b) Temperate forest (summer)

(c) Panama tropical forest

(d) English Channel

(e)

45.4

(a) Pyramid of numbers. Plotting the numbers of organisms in each trophic level of a grassland community produces the stepped pyramid. (b) In a forest community the pyramid becomes inverted, since most of the producers (P) are large trees and shrubs. Their numbers are far exceeded by the numbers of consumers (C) they support. The numbers represent counts for each 0.1 hectare (quarter acre). (c) Pyramid of biomass. Measurements of biomass (grams per square meter) in a tropical rain forest reveal a great difference between the producer and consumer levels, where 40,000 g/m² supports a total consumer mass of only 5 g/m². The large reducer and scavenger biomass should be expected in a community where nutrient cycling is very rapid. (d) Pyramids of biomass in the marine environment seem to represent the impossible—the weight of producers is less than that of consumers. (e) An energy pyramid from a freshwater aquatic community at Silver Springs, Florida. Energy flow here is expressed as kcal/m²/year.

molecules are not assimilated at all). Also, we must keep in mind that organisms are not in the business of attending to other trophic levels—food is a commodity for their own metabolism and maintenance. Thus, not all the energy they assimilate is available to the next consumer level.

Humans and Trophic Levels

Energy pyramids may seem abstract, but they can suggest fundamental lessons in economics when they are applied to human populations. We know that humans are basically *omnivores*, capable of feeding at several trophic levels, and obviously the availability of food determines which trophic level is most heavily utilized. As economic conditions worsen, people tend to increasingly shift to lower trophic levels. The poorest people tend to act largely as primary consumers; they eat more plant foods and less meat. The reason is clear—the primary level holds more energy, or calories. To feed people at the secondary level or higher requires costly energy transfers. Since raising cattle, sheep, hogs, and other animal stocks is a wasteful process with little conservation of calories or biomass, meat becomes too expensive (Figure 45.5).

It may seem that the earth could support a much larger population if all humans ate only plant food. It's true that more calories would be available without the energy losses involved in feeding at higher trophic levels. But in spite of the increased calorie supply, there is a problem with nutrition at the herbivore level. Many common plant foods cannot provide certain essential amino acids (especially tryptophan, methionine, and lysine; see Chapter 37), some of which we need in order to form our own proteins. The absence of such essential amino acids from the daily diet can

lead to such infamous protein deficiency diseases as *Kwashiorkor*, a chronic problem in some parts of Africa. The critical amino acids can be provided by plants only if legumes such as soybeans and peas are included in the diet, but this must be done on a daily basis. Humans do not store amino acids very well, and excesses are rapidly converted to fats and lipids or used for energy in a daily turnover.

Energy and Productivity

The rate at which producers in an ecosystem store energy is referred to as the system's **primary productivity,** a concept that has three main aspects: *gross productivity, net productivity,* and *net community productivity.*

Gross productivity is the total rate at which energy is assimilated by producers over a certain period of time. Gross productivity doesn't really tell us how much energy the photosynthesizers are storing or how fast they are growing. After all, plants must expend a considerable amount of the assimilated energy for their own growth and maintenance.

Net productivity, a more useful measurement, takes energy utilization into account. It is determined by subtracting the rate of respiration by photosynthesizers (energy utilization) from gross productivity. In other words, the rate of energy stored minus the rate of energy released equals net productivity. Net productivity is reflected in new growth, seed production, and simple storage of such energy-rich compounds as lipids and carbohydrates.

Net community productivity takes the whole community into consideration, so respiration in both producers and consumers is subtracted from gross productivity. Productivity is expressed in calories or grams (or kilocalories or kilograms) per unit of area over some period of time. Using **GP, NP,** and **NCP** to represent gross, net, and net community productivity, and R_a and R_h to represent respiration in producers (autotrophs) and consumers (heterotrophs), respectively, the three aspects of productivity can be summarized as:

$$GP = \text{Energy assimilated by producers}$$
$$NP = GP - R_a$$
$$NCP = NP - R_h$$

By measuring the net productivity of a community, ecologists can answer such questions as: Is it growing? Has it reached a climax state (full maturity)? Is it declining? Net community productivity occurs only in communities that are growing. As

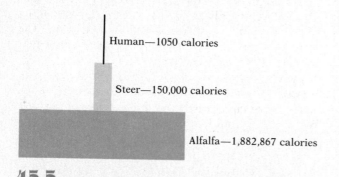

Human—1050 calories

Steer—150,000 calories

Alfalfa—1,882,867 calories

45.5

Where humans live as secondary consumers, energy must first flow from a producer to a primary consumer, and the change entails a considerable loss in the energy level. For each 1000 calories stored by a beef-eating human, the producers will have stored nearly 2 million calories.

TABLE 45.1

Estimated gross primary production (annual basis) of the biosphere and its distribution among major ecosystems

Ecosystem	Area, Millions of km²	Gross Primary Productivity, kcal/m²/yr	Total Gross Production, 10¹⁶ kcal/yr
Marine			
Open ocean	326.0	1,000	32.6
Coastal zones	34.0	2,000	6.8
Upwelling zones	0.4	6,000	0.2
Estuaries and reefs	2.0	20,000	4.0
Subtotal	362.4	—	43.6
Terrestrial			
Deserts and tundras	40.0	200	0.8
Grasslands and pastures	42.0	2,500	10.5
Dry forests	9.4	2,500	2.4
Northern coniferous forests	10.0	3,000	3.0
Cultivated lands with little or no energy subsidy	10.0	3,000	3.0
Moist temperate forests	4.9	8,000	3.9
Fuel-subsidized (mechanized) agriculture	4.0	12,000	4.8
Wet tropical and subtropical (broad-leaved evergreen) forests	14.7	20,000	29.0
Subtotal	135.0	—	57.0
Total for biosphere (round figures; not including ice caps)	500.0	2,000	100.0

SOURCE: From FUNDAMENTALS OF ECOLOGY, 3rd Edition by Eugene P. Odum. Copyright © 1971 by W. B. Saunders Company. Reprinted by permission of Holt, Rinehart and Winston, CBS College Publishing.

they approach the climax state, the rates of energy assimilation and energy use begin to equalize. A net decrease in productivity signals a dying or declining community. The results of productivity studies in several major regions of the earth are summarized in Table 45.1.

Measurements of productivity are of great interest in agriculture, since they reflect crop yields. Plant breeding is often directed at increasing such yields. Among the products of such efforts are the so-called miracle crops that have been particularly important to underdeveloped nations.

NUTRIENT CYCLING IN ECOSYSTEMS

While energy flows through an ecosystem, emerging eventually as heat, the chemical elements essential to life tend to *cycle*. Some of these elements are incorporated into the molecular makeup of the organism, while others are shuffled through complex metabolic pathways and drained of their bond energy. Ultimately, all the molecules will appear either in the organism's waste or in its corpse. They are then subjected to the reducers, which release them into the environment and make them available to yet other organisms. Most of the elements cycle in the form of mineral ions (also called mineral nutrients). Since the cycling of such nutrients involves both geological and biological activity in the ecosystem, the pathways are often called **biogeochemical cycles.**

We can best follow biogeochemical cycles by beginning with producers, because they make use of the simpler ions and molecules. Once they are incorporated into the producers, some of these are passed from one trophic level to the next as food, but they all eventually reach the reducers.

Some biogeochemical cycles can be rather simple, involving only a few steps. For example, some of the water a plant takes in is simply passed to the leaves, where it is released through the stomata, then ready to be taken up again (see Chapter 25). However, the same material can be cycled in a number of ways, and water may become involved in far more circuitous cycles. For example, it may be used in photosynthesis. In this case, the water molecules are broken apart. Oxygen is released into the atmosphere, and hydrogen is used to reduce carbon and form foods. Animals and other consumers may then breathe in the oxygen and use it in cell respiration. The oxygen is later reunited with the hydrogen from food, forming water, which is then released back into the environment. Two other cycles, the *carbon cycle* and the *phosphorus cycle*, are described in Figure 45.6.

(a) The phosphorus cycle. Usable phosphorus in the form of soluble phosphates is found in soil water and in aquatic systems. Some phosphates pass to consumers through the trophic levels, while some are taken in through drinking water. During decomposition, reducers make some phosphates available again, but some locked in animal remains (bones, teeth, shells, etc.) is unavailable for long periods. The loss of phosphates through leaching (from soil water) and through runoff (to the sea) is considerable. Some end up as insoluble phosphorus in deep sediments. A gain in available phosphates occurs through erosion and from pollutants introduced by humans.

(b) The carbon cycle. Carbon dioxide in the atmosphere and waters of the earth is available for cycling. It must enter the trophic levels through producers that fix carbon into organic molecules during photosynthesis. CO_2 is released during respiration by producers, consumers, and reducers, and some is released from the earth's crust through volcanic action. A highly significant amount is released when humans burn fossil fuels.

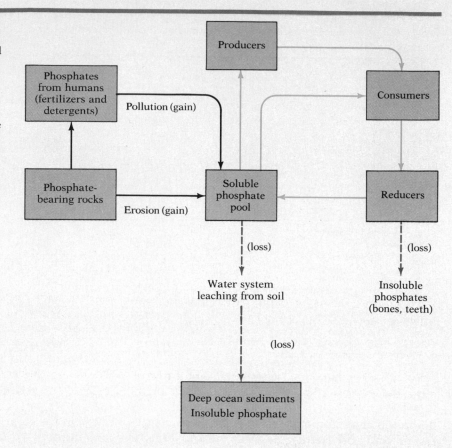

(a) Phosphorus cycle

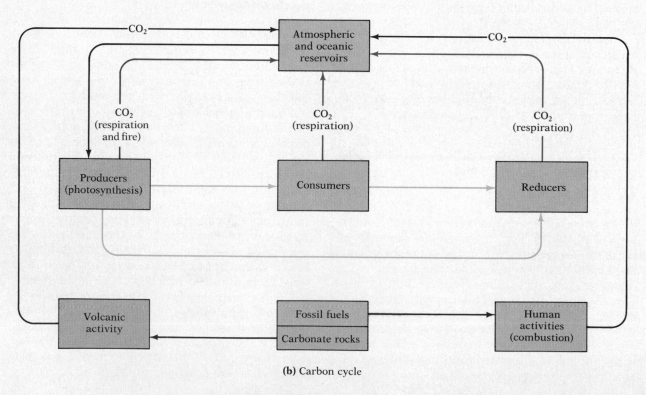

(b) Carbon cycle

The Nitrogen Cycle

One of the best-known biogeochemical cycles is the **nitrogen cycle.** We have referred to the cycle in other contexts, but here let's consider it in more detail. Nitrogen is essential to life, since it is a principal constituent of proteins, nucleic acids, chlorophyll, coenzymes, and several other important kinds of molecules.

Essential nutrients such as nitrogen are generally held in one of two places: **exchange pools,** where they are readily available, and **reservoirs,** where they are less available to living systems. The largest nitrogen reservoir is the atmosphere, about 79% of which is nitrogen gas (N_2). But atmospheric nitrogen as such is not available to the earth's organisms, except to certain nitrogen-fixing bacteria. Plants and most other producers must incorporate nitrogen primarily in the form of nitrate ions (NO_3^-), which are produced by soil and water bacteria over two complex pathways: *nitrogen fixation* and *decomposition*. These ions in the soil and water constitute the major exchange pool of nitrogen.

The Role of Reducers. The details of the nitrogen cycle are summarized in Figure 45.7, using a simple system involving plants, animals, and reducers. As we see, plants take in nitrate ions and incorporate them into their own amino acids, where they are used to make plant protein. The molecules then pass through the consumer levels from herbivore to carnivore, where some of the amino acids are used in the production of the animal's proteins while many of the rest are metabolized. The nitrogen by-product is excreted in urine. Eventually, all organisms and their nitrogen wastes enter the realm of the reducers, where they are broken down into their component parts.

In the next stages, several populations of microorganisms, each with a specific role in the process, begin to handle nitrogen in three major steps: **decomposition** (breakdown of large molecules), **ammonification** (production of ammonia), and **nitrification** (production of nitrites and then nitrates). The nitrates (the end product) can then join the exchange pool, from which they can return to the plant. This may all seem quite efficient, but in fact there are complications that lead to losses.

For example, ammonia (NH_3) reacts rapidly with water, and forms ammonium ions (NH_4^+). These are readily carried out of the producers' reach when water, percolating downward through

45.7

The nitrogen cycle can be viewed as two cycles. The inner cycle includes the uptake of nitrate by producers and its passage as protein, nucleic acid, and other organic molecules through the usual trophic levels. At the reducer level, several major steps are involved in making nitrates available. In the outer cycle, nitrogen enters an ecosystem through the action of nitrogen fixers (although a minor amount of nitrogen fixation has always occurred during lightning storms and, more recently, through the action of sunlight on air pollutants). This input is roughly balanced by nitrogen loss through denitrification, which is carried out by anaerobic soil bacteria. Not seen in the cycle is the extensive human input of synthetic ammonia and nitrates through agriculture. In recent years, the human input has exceeded losses through denitrification.

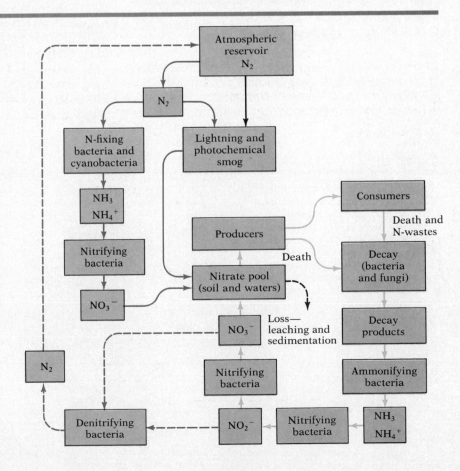

the soil, washes them away. Furthermore, certain anaerobic soil bacteria—the *denitrifiers*—metabolize nitrates, converting them to nitrogen gas that reenters the atmospheric reservoir.

The Role of Nitrogen Fixers. The denitrifiers remove nitrogen from the ecosystem, but the element is never depleted because of the action of **nitrogen fixers.** Nitrogen-fixing bacteria and cyanobacteria are able to utilize atmospheric nitrogen, which they combine with hydrogen, producing ammonia. They release the ammonia that they do not use into the soil or water, where it is converted to nitrites and nitrates by bacteria. In this way, nitrogen lost to denitrification is replaced.

Farmers have used the nitrogen fixers for many years. *Crop rotation* (planting different crops in a rotating sequence) commonly includes such legumes as alfalfa. Nitrogen-fixing bacteria of the genus *Rhizobium* invade the alfalfa roots, which respond by forming cystlike nodules around the bacterial colony (Figure 45.8). In a mutualistic relationship, the bacteria absorb the organic nutrients produced by the plant, and the plant gains usable nitrogen produced by the bacteria.

PRODUCTIVITY IN A FOREST COMMUNITY

In 1969, ecologist George Woodwell and his associates completed a 10-year study of productivity in a scrubby oak-pine forest community near the Brookhaven National Laboratory on Long Island.

Oak-pine forests are common in this area, a product of the disturbance of the great deciduous forests that once graced the rural landscape. Woodwell's study was enormous in scope; it is through such efforts that we are beginning to understand the basic principles of community ecology.

The study began with a detailed description of the structure of the community. The scientists carefully noted what species were present and their relative biomass. From measurements of the biomass, they calculated the gross productivity of the forest. They then set out to determine the community's net productivity. To do this, they had to discover the rate of respiration, which they did by directly measuring the carbon dioxide output of the forest. This is much easier said than done.

One problem was that such measurements must be made in the dark in order to be certain that carbon dioxide uptake during photosynthesis is not a factor. Then, of course, there are the usual breezes in a forest, currents that tend to carry away the CO_2 one is trying to measure. Also, air tends to rise from the warm earth at night. Fortunately, in this case there were frequent nighttime *temperature inversions* (of the sort that produces smoggy days in Los Angeles). In such an inversion, cool surface air becomes trapped close to the ground by warmer layers of air above. The nighttime inversions in the oak-pine forest prevented the usual vertical movement of air and allowed respiratory carbon dioxide to accumulate.

Woodwell and his group concluded that the annual gross productivity of the forest community was 2650 g (about 5.8 lbs) per square meter, while the annual net productivity was 1200 g/m^2. Further

45.8

(a) Root nodules in a leguminous plant. (b) Such nodules contain large colonies of irregularly shaped nitrogen-fixing bacteria from the genus *Rhizobium*. Other nitrogen fixers include the actinomycetes, a group of fungus-like soil bacteria, and cyanobacteria such as *Anabaena*, which associates with the small water plant, *Azolla*, common in rice paddies.

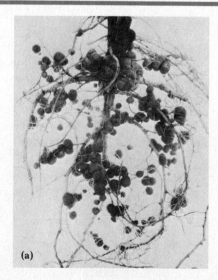
(a)

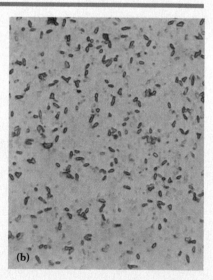
(b)

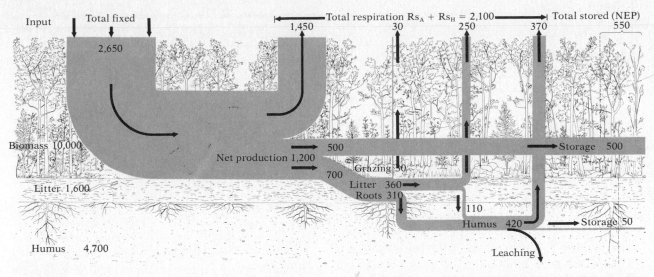

Input   Total fixed

2,650

Total respiration $Rs_A + Rs_H = 2,100$ Total stored (NEP)

1,450   30   250   370   550

Biomass 10,000   500   Storage   500

Net production 1,200

Grazing 50

700

Litter 1,600   Litter   360

Roots   310

110

Humus   420   Storage 50

Humus   4,700

Leaching

45.9

Annual productivity in an oak-pine forest. The flow of energy through the forest community (color) was expressed as grams of organic matter produced annually in each square meter. When corrected for organic

matter consumed during respiration, the net community production was 550 g/m²/yr. This amount is seen as new growth and in the appearance of new organic matter in the soil humus.

tests revealed that the rate at which new organic material was appearing—the net community productivity—(net productivity minus heterotroph respiration)—was 550 g/m²/year (about 1.2 lbs). The forest study is summarized in Figure 45.9.

Similar studies have since been done in other forests, and we now know that, compared to some communities, the net productivity of this forest is modest. Annual net productivity in each square meter of some tropical rain forest communities, for example, can reach several thousand grams. However, the greatest annual productivity is found not in natural communities but in man-made agricultural communities. For instance, in tropically grown sugarcane, an efficient C4 plant (see Chapter 7), the annual net productivity can exceed 9000 g/m², while the productivity of grain fields ranges between 6000 and 10,000 g/m². (Of course, when we consider the energy of fossil fuels used to operate farm machinery and the energy used to manufacture and apply pesticides and fertilizers, net yields fall drastically.) Table 45.2 compares productivity in six quite different ecosystems.

One more observation—perhaps an obvious one—was made by Woodwell. The oak-pine community was growing; it had not reached its climax state. As we mentioned earlier, communities that have reached their climax state have no net community productivity. Their respiratory output equals their photosynthetic output.

THE LAKE: A FRESHWATER COMMUNITY

The freshwater communities of rivers and streams, lakes and ponds are among the best studied on earth. Most of the lakes that grace the earth's surface have been formed rather recently in our geological history. In fact, most northerly lakes were born at the time of the last glacial retreats (10,000 to 12,000 years ago). Lakes are also produced through volcanic activity, as was Crater Lake in Oregon, and through uplifting of the land, which created the lakes of Florida. Lake Baikal in Russia, the world's deepest at 750 m (2460 ft), is especially ancient; it was formed in the Mesozoic.

Limnologists (*limne;* pool or lake), ecologists who study freshwater communities, have divided lakes into zones, each with its own physical features and each harboring a characteristic array of life. The zones are called *littoral, limnetic,* and *profundal* (Figure 45.10). Although the terminology is different, the organization is similar to that of the marine environment (see Chapter 44).

Life in the Lake Zones

The **littoral zone** is the area where light penetrates to the bottom of the lake. Producers in the littoral

TABLE 45.2

Annual production and respiration as kcal/m²/year in growing and climax ecosystems

	Alfalfa Field (USA)	Young Pine Plantation (England)	Medium-aged Oak-Pine Forest (NY)	Large Flowing Spring (Silver Springs, FL)	Mature Rain Forest (Puerto Rico)	Coastal Sound (Long Island, NY)
Gross primary production	24,400	12,200	11,500	20,800	45,000	5,700
Autotrophic respiration	9,200	4,700	6,400	12,000	32,000	3,200
Net primary production	15,200	7,500	5,000	8,800	13,000	2,500
Heterotrophic respiration	800	4,600	3,000	6,800	13,000	2,500
Net community production	14,400	2,900	2,000	2,000	Very little or none	Very little or none

SOURCE: Adapted from FUNDAMENTALS OF ECOLOGY 3rd Edition by Eugene P. Odum. Copyright © 1971 by W. B. Saunders Company. Reprinted by permission of Holt, Rinehart and Winston, CBS College Publishing.

zone include a variety of free-floating and rooted plants that form a progression of types as the water deepens. Some rooted plants break the lake's surface; others are completely submerged. As in marine waters, freshwater producers include numerous species of photosynthetic bacteria, protists, and algae. Together, these form the *phytoplankton* (Figure 45.11). Consumers in the littoral zone include animal-like protists, snails, mussels, aquatic insects, and insect larvae. Salamanders and frogs also prefer the littoral zone, as do both herbivorous and carnivorous fish and turtles. And here we find a number of wading birds and birds that step gingerly along the mats of broad-leaved plants.

The **limnetic zone** is the open water, but includes only the depths penetrated by light. Almost all the producers here are microscopic. They include the phytoplankton that extend from the littoral zone, along with flagellated algal forms such as *Euglena* and *Volvox*. In northern lakes, phytoplankton populations undergo seasonal *blooms* during which their productivity exceeds that of the plants of the littoral zone. These blooms are a response to available nutrients, sufficient light, and favorable temperatures, and often follow a bloom of nitrogen-fixing cyanobacteria. The primary consumers are the zooplankton, composed largely of tiny crustaceans. Their great numbers are made up of only a few species, whose populations rise and fall in response to the numbers of producers. At the higher consumer levels we find principally the lake fishes, which consist mainly of plankton-feeding species and the carnivorous species that feed upon them. The food web of the limnetic zone is often simple and direct (Figure 45.12).

The **profundal zone** begins where light ceases to penetrate the lake waters, and it extends to the muddy, sediment-rich lake floor. There are, of course, no producers here. Life is represented mainly by reducers such as bacteria and fungi, and by a few detritus-feeding clams and worm-like insect larvae. All of the profundal species are adapted to periods of very low oxygen concentrations. The sparse life here is critical to the organisms above, because reducers convert deposits formed of corpses raining from above into mineral nutrients. The distribution of these nutrients throughout the lake depends, as in marine environments, on the vertical movement of the waters.

Thermal Overturn and Lake Productivity

There is no aerobic (oxygen-using) life in the deeper waters of the tropical Lake Tanganyika, but temperate Lake Baikal, which is about 300 m deeper, supports aerobic life at every depth. The difference is the amount of **thermal overturn**, the vertical movement of water masses brought on by seasonal temperature changes. Thermal overturns

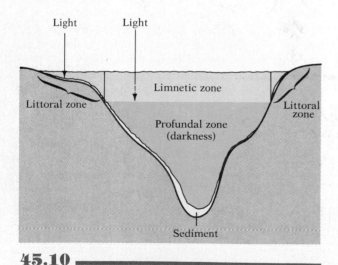

45.10

Lake zonation. Each zone differs in its physical conditions and inhabitants.

45.11

Producers of the littoral zone include **(a)** bottom-rooted, aquatic plants such as cattails, bulrushes, and arrowheads living nearer the shore, and floating water lilies and pond weeds farther out. **(b)** Microscopic producers (phytoplankton) include many filamentous and single-celled green algae, along with diatoms and cyanobacteria. **(c)** Primary consumers include the familiar freshwater snails, bottom-dwelling water mites, crustaceans, insect larva, and nymphs. **(d)** Smaller aquatic predators (secondary and tertiary consumers) of the littoral zone include the diving beetles, water scorpions, and nymphs of the damsel and dragon flies. There are also larger carnivorous species such as fish, frogs, and wading birds.

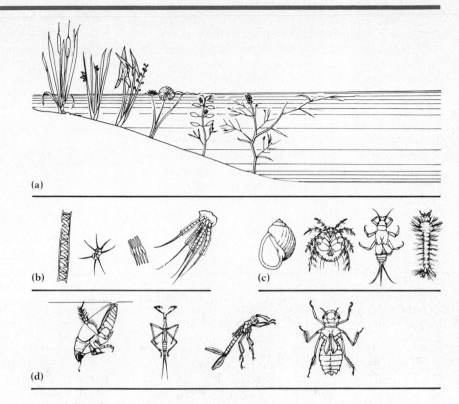

45.12

The limnetic zone producers **(a)** encompass several species, including phytoplankton common to the littoral zone. **(b)** The zooplankton include rotifers as well as crustaceans of principally two groups, the "cyclops" (one-eyed) copepods and the strange, flattened cladocerans. **(c)** The plankton support predatory insects and plankton-straining fishes, which in turn are fed upon by larger fishes **(d)** such as bass and pike.

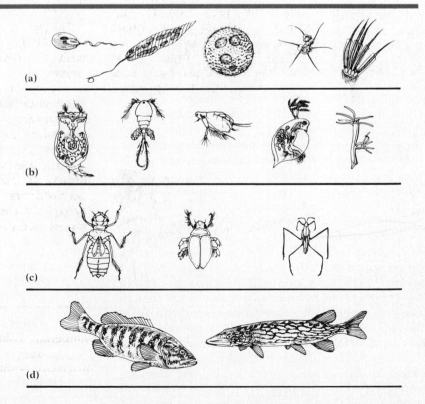

carry dissolved oxygen to the lake depths and bring nutrients to the surface. The seasons, of course, are more marked in temperate regions.

Thermal overturn in temperate lakes occurs in the fall and spring, when surface waters undergo drastic changes in temperature. It is a peculiar characteristic of water that, as its temperature decreases, its density increases—it gets heavier—until it reaches 4°C. Below 4°C water's density *decreases* sharply, and at 0°C (the freezing point) it is at its lightest. The effects of changes in temperatures and density are seen in Figure 45.13, where each season's conditions are described.

The conditions that prevent overturn in Lake Tanganyika are similar to those that occur in temperate-zone lakes during the summer. A temperature gradient exists between top and bottom waters. The lighter, warmer upper waters may be well mixed by wind action, but they cannot move into the dense, colder waters below. The result is that many temperate-zone lakes have three distinct summer temperature regions. There is an upper warm-water region, the *epilimnion* (upper lake), and a lower cold-water region, the *hypolimnion* (lower lake), each with relatively constant temperatures throughout. Between the two is a region called the **thermocline,** where temperatures drop as depth increases. Typically, oxygen depletion begins just below the thermocline.

COMMUNITIES OVER TIME: ECOLOGICAL SUCCESSION

As time passes, communities change. In some cases they grow and their biomass increases. In other cases more energy is burned in respiration than is produced; we consider these communities to be declining. Even when biomass and energy are stabilized, the community may be changing. Sometimes the change produces a sequence of organisms within the community itself, resulting in a process known as **ecological succession.**

As populations within a community alter the environment, they set the stage for invasions by different species. The result is that the community takes on new traits, and with new species altering the environment in their own manner, the change goes on. Ecological succession is somewhat predictable and sequential, although ecologists are finding it less so than they once believed. Not only do invasions by unexpected, opportunistic species break up the orderly progression, but unanticipated physical changes—perhaps a period of drought—can alter the usual events of succession.

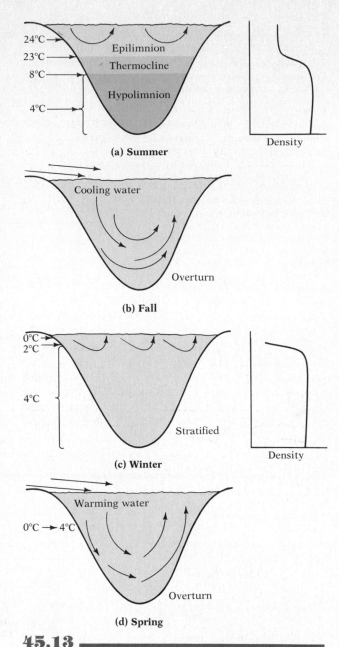

(a) Summer

(b) Fall

(c) Winter

(d) Spring

45.13

(a) In summer the highest water temperature is in the epilimnion and the lowest is in the hypolimnion. Between the two, a steep temperature gradient, or thermocline, occurs. Movement in the less dense epilimnion cannot disturb the denser cooler layers below, so overturn cannot occur. **(b)** In the fall, cooling surface waters approach 4°C (maximum density), sink to the bottom, and permit a wind-driven overturn to occur. **(c)** In winter, the summer temperature gradient is reversed, with the coldest temperatures at the surface (no thermocline forms), yet the density gradient is roughly similar to that of summer, preventing overturn. **(d)** In early spring, warming surface waters reach 4°C (maximum density) and sink, starting another wind-driven overturn.

Ecological succession occurs in two fundamental ways. **Primary succession** occurs where no community previously existed, such as on rocky outcroppings, newly formed deltas, sand dunes, emerging volcanic islands, and lava flows. (The volcanic slopes of Mount St. Helens are presently a good place for studying primary succession.) **Secondary succession** occurs where a community has been disrupted. We find it, for example, where a neglected farm is reverting to the wild, or in a forest community that has been subjected to *clear cutting,* the controversial lumbering practice in which all trees are removed.

Primary Succession

In primary succession (Figure 45.14), the first organisms to invade are usually hardy, drought-resistant species, often called **pioneer organisms.** For example, lichens are often the first to invade rocky outcroppings, held fast by their tenacious, water-seeking fungal component while the algal component provides food as its chloroplasts are exposed to the sun. Lichens gradually erode the rock surface as they probe into tiny crevices and help pry them open. Sand then accumulates in tiny fissures, and the bodies of dead lichens add to the humus. Soil is being born, and with it come opportunities for such plants as grasses and mosses to establish themselves.

The plant roots penetrate the rocky crevices, ex-

erting a remarkable pressure, prying at the rocks and gradually widening the fissures. By now certain insect and reducer populations will also have established themselves. As these early plants gain a toehold, the lichens that made their penetration possible give way; they cannot compete with the emerging plants for light, water, and minerals. Similarly, when the grasses and mosses have contributed significantly to the soil-building efforts, they will be replaced by fast-growing shrubs, as new kinds of animals continue to invade.

Primary succession in bare rock outcroppings is an extremely slow process, often requiring hundreds of years. But once the soil has formed, the process can accelerate. Studies of succession from sand dune to climax forest community on the shores of Lake Michigan indicate that this transition took about 1000 years.

Secondary Succession

In secondary succession, the same principles apply, but events occur at a more rapid pace. Soil is often already in place, eliminating the long soil-building stages of primary succession. In deserted farms, grasses, shrubs, and saplings are often the first to appear, along with a variety of "weeds." The species we call weeds are usually imported—carried accidentally into a region. In balanced, well-adapted communities that are undisturbed, weeds are held in check, but since they tend to be

45.14

Primary succession from a bare rock outcropping to a fir-birch-spruce community. Pioneering lichens and mosses begin the soil-building process, followed by the invasion of increasingly larger plants until a forest climax community develops.

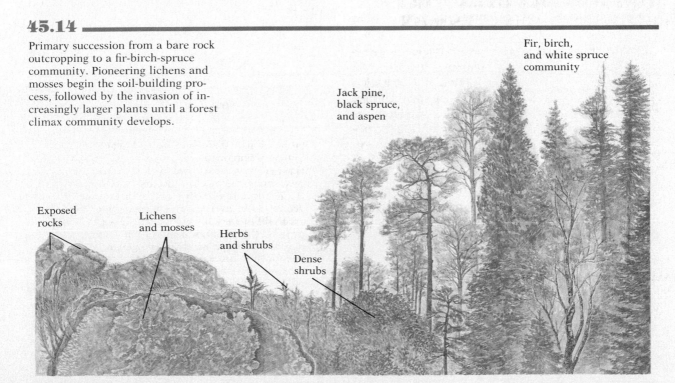

Exposed rocks

Lichens and mosses

Herbs and shrubs

Dense shrubs

Jack pine, black spruce, and aspen

Fir, birch, and white spruce community

fast-growing, opportunistic plants, they quickly invade disturbed communities. (Even the tumbleweed is an import; the large, ball-shaped plant is a native of Russia. Vacant lots in Southern California are often home to the wild oat and mustard, natives of the Mediterranean region.)

As secondary succession progresses, the initial invaders are eventually replaced by plants from the surrounding community. Larger, faster-growing trees block the sunlight, and a new generation of shade-tolerant shrubs emerges below the canopy. Eventually the lines between the area in succession and the surrounding community begin to blur (Figure 45.15).

The time involved in secondary succession varies widely. In grassland communities, for example, succession to a climax community may take only 20–40 years. At the other extreme, fragile tundra may require hundreds of years to recover from a disturbance—if it ever recovers at all. Wagon tracks made more than 100 years ago are still clearly visible in this delicate biome.

Succession in the Freshwater Aquatic Community

Just as terrestrial communities undergo succession, so do freshwater ones. Limnologists refer to the process as **eutrophication.** A determining factor in the rate at which eutrophication occurs is the availability of nutrients. Lakes and ponds that are rich in nutrients and high in productivity are called *eutrophic* (true foods), while those that have a very limited nutrient supply and little productivity are called *oligotrophic* (few foods). The general trend in freshwater bodies is toward eutrophication, but if any essential nutrient becomes unavailable the trend can be quickly reversed.

As eutrophication progresses, organic materials are produced, so sediments increase and the depth of the water decreases. Littoral-zone plants crowd the shores of eutrophic lakes, extending farther and farther across the water. They are followed by increasing numbers of water-tolerant shore plants (Figure 45.16). Unless the trend is interrupted, the lake will eventually convert to a marsh, and with the invasion of terrestrial plants from the surrounding community the last traces of the lake will be lost. Interestingly, the ancient oligotrophic Lake Baikal has shown alarming indications of eutrophication, but not through natural means. Wastes from the human community along its shores are artificially fertilizing the water and enabling the rapid production of organic material.

Eutrophication is ordinarily an extremely slow process in lakes. Its progress is typically checked by a scarcity of two nutrients, phosphates and nitrates. In recent years, however, these nutrients have become readily available as humans dump sewage into water systems or permit the runoff of surface water from heavily fertilized farms or cattle feedlots. The addition of phosphates to laundry detergents has also added a heavy burden to natural water systems. The sudden increase of nitrates and phosphates in fresh waters produces unprecedented algal blooms, a first step in eutrophication through pollution.

45.15

The stages of secondary succession are revealed in a series of photos taken in the same section of the Bitterroot National Forest in Montana over a 70-year period—**(a)** 1909, **(b)** 1925, **(c)** 1937, and **(d)** 1979.

45.16

Eutrophication. **(a)** Early in succession, aquatic plants begin to spread from the edges of the pond. **(b)** Eventually these plants extend across the open water. **(c)** As the pond's waters disappear, invading marsh grasses, cattails, and sedges replace the floating plants, converting the pond into a marsh.

ECOSYSTEMS AND HUMAN INTERVENTION

The impact of humans on natural communities is profound, and our ability to alter such systems grows as our technological abilities increase. Even as we learn about the effects of our previous alterations, we continue to manipulate the intricate and myriad factors that contribute to the equilibrium of ecosystems. Of course, we are aware of our impact to some degree, and we often make well-intentioned, if unsuccessful, efforts to set things right. Our efforts often falter simply for lack of basic information. The bottom line seems to be that we just don't know how to live in harmony with the ecosystems of which we are a part; our technology has far outstripped our basic understanding of our environment. As we turn to the scientific community for answers, ecologists will play an increasingly important role in changing the ways in which we interact with the biosphere.

Summary

Energetics in Ecosystems

Ecosystems are defined as units of interacting organisms and the physical environment of which they are a part. Organisms in an ecosystem or community fall into three broad trophic levels: producers, consumers, and reducers. Nearly all producers derive energy from the sun. Consumers obtain energy by feeding on producers or on one another. Consumers can be primary (herbivores), secondary (carnivores feeding on herbivores), or of even higher trophic levels. Reducers decompose dead organisms and wastes.

Ecological pyramids graphically illustrate trophic levels on the basis of various data such as numbers, biomass, or energy transfers. Transfers of energy from one trophic level to another are usually very inefficient.

Primary productivity has three main aspects: gross productivity (the rate at which energy is assimilated by producers over a certain time period); net productivity (gross productivity minus the producers' rate of energy release); and net community productivity (respiration—energy release—in both producers and consumers is subtracted from gross productivity). Net community productivity occurs only in communities that are growing; as they approach the climax state, rates of energy assimilation and energy use begin to equalize.

Nutrient Cycling in Ecosystems

Energy flows through ecosystems, eventually emerging as heat, but essential chemicals continue to cycle. The pathways are known as biogeochemical cycles.

The nitrogen cycle involves exchange pools (in which nitrate ions in soil and water are available to producers) and reservoirs (in which nitrogen is less available to living systems, such as in the atmosphere). Plants incorporate nitrate ions into their amino acids; these molecules then pass from herbivores to carnivores; eventually, the molecules enter the realm of the reducers, which break them down into component parts. Then several populations of microorganisms handle the molecules in three steps: decomposition, ammonification, and nitrification. The end products can join the exchange pool and be taken up by plants. Nitrogen is never depleted in the ecosystem because of the action of nitrogen fixers.

Productivity in a Forest Community

In a 10-year study of an oak-pine community, scientists measured biomass and determined gross productivity. To determine net community productivity, they measured the forest's CO_2 output. The net productivity, measured in grams per square meter per year, was found to be lower than that of tropical rain forests, for example. The greatest annual productivity is found in man-made agricultural communities.

The Lake: A Freshwater Community

Lakes, like terrestrial communities, have producers, consumers, and reducers, with nutrients and gases cycling through the trophic layers. Lake ecosystems can be divided into littoral, limnetic, and profundal zones. Littoral zones, where light penetrates to the bottom, include shorelines and shallow waters where sunlight and nutrients are abundant. Plants form a progression from the shore outward. Limnetic zones, in which there is still light, can support many types of producers and consumers. The profundal zone is the deepest level, where light ceases to penetrate the water. Although few producers are found there, it is rich in nutrients filtering down from above and supports a large population of bacteria and fungi.

Thermal overturn, the vertical movement of water masses brought on by seasonal climatic changes, carries dissolved oxygen to lake depths and brings nutrients to the surface. Many temperate-zone lakes have a warm epilimnion, a cold hypolimnion, and a thermocline between the two (in summer).

Communities Over Time: Ecological Succession

Sequential change in communities is known as ecological succession. Primary succession occurs where no community previously existed, and pioneer organisms can take hold. The action of wind, water, and plant growth slowly builds soil and prepares the area for grasses and shrubs. Secondary succession follows primary succession or occurs in areas where the original community has been disrupted. Succession gradually produces a community that remains stable as long as environmental conditions remain the same.

Eutrophication in freshwater systems is similar to succession in terrestrial communities. The availability of nutrients often determines the speed of change and development. Eutrophic lakes are high in productivity, while oligotrophic lakes are less productive and change more slowly. Although eutrophication is usually a slow process, high levels of nitrates and phosphates cause algae to multiply rapidly, which depletes the community of oxygen and results in rapid conversion to marshland.

Ecosystems and Human Intervention

Humans have a profound impact on natural communities. We often learn about the effects of our growing technology only after irreversible changes have been made.

Key Terms

ecosystem
trophic level
producer
consumer
food web
reducer
ecological pyramid
primary productivity
gross productivity
net productivity

net community productivity
biogeochemical cycles
nitrogen cycle
exchange pool
reservoir
decomposition
ammonification
nitrification
nitrogen fixers
littoral zone

limnetic zone
profundal zone
thermal overturn
thermocline
ecological succession
primary succession
secondary succession
pioneer organism
eutrophication

Review Questions

1. Prepare a simple sketch of energy flow through an ecosystem, including the producer, consumer, and reducer levels and the approximate percent energy transfers. What eventually happens to all absorbed energy? (pp. 661–662)

2. Compare biomass and energy pyramids. How can a biomass pyramid become inverted? Can this happen to an energy pyramid? (p. 665)

3. Considering what humans eat, suggest what foods might appear on your plate if you were eating at the primary, then secondary, consumer levels. (p. 662)

4. Give several examples of reducers. Of what special ecological significance are they? (pp. 662, 664)

5. Explain the relationships among gross, net, and net community productivity. (p. 666)

6. Explain how the following fit into the nitrogen cycle: decomposers, animals, nitrogen fixers, denitrifiers, nitrifiers, and plants. (pp. 669–670)

7. Compare productivity in the Long Island oak-pine community to that in a tropical rain forest. In what communities do we find the greatest productivity? How is such productivity possible? (pp. 670–671)

8. Compare the three lake zones. Where is the greatest diversity of life found? Which zone lacks a primary producer? (pp. 671–672)

9. Explain why climatic change is so important to the levels of nutrients and oxygen available throughout the lake depths. (pp. 672–674)

10. Describe the typical events of primary and secondary succession. Explain, with examples, how one group of organisms paves the way for the next. (pp. 675–676)

Populations and How They Change

46

Informed people all over the world are becoming increasingly concerned about human population growth. Their concern is understandable; as a species, we have never been in this situation before. The earth has never supported so many humans, and our numbers are growing by the second. We can't begin to predict our future or even guess intelligently at our fate. Our best-educated guesses have been foiled time and again because our population seems to have a disconcerting lack of respect for the rules.

Or perhaps there are few "rules" when it comes to humans. Perhaps other species are more predictable, which is why we study them to learn how populations behave—about what causes them to change, grow out of control, or dwindle away. Let's see if there are fundamental principles of population behavior, and if they apply to us.

POPULATION GROWTH PATTERNS

The story of population changes can be told by two simple curves, the **J-shaped curve** and the **S-shaped curve**. First, consider the J-shaped curve (Figure 46.1).

Let's suppose a few reproductive organisms are placed in an ideal environment with unlimited resources. Under such conditions they can be expected to reproduce at their maximum rate. Since there are only a few to start with, their numbers may rise slowly at first (say, from two to four, to eight, and so on). However, as new reproducers are added to the population, not only will the *numbers increase*, but the **population growth rate** will increase as well. Consider the way interest is compounded in your savings account. As you make weekly deposits, of course, your savings grow by simple addition. But interest is also added to your savings; new interest paid is based on the *total* amount—the money you deposited and the interest it has earned. Not only do your savings increase, but the *rate* of their growth also increases. This pattern is known as **exponential (or geometric) growth**.

The maximum rate at which any population can increase under ideal conditions is called its **reproductive potential** (or **biotic potential**); such an increase would produce the J-shaped curve. Most species never reach their biotic potential, or reach it only briefly, because environmental conditions are rarely ideal. The expanding population encounters environmental situations that impede growth. These factors collectively are called **environmental resistance**.

A clear example of geometric growth occurs when a small number of bacteria are introduced into a rich laboratory culture medium. Under ideal conditions the familiar *E. coli*, a champion reproducer, will divide every 20 minutes. At this rate, after 24 hours one bacterium would have given rise to 40 septillion descendants. But even as simple as *E. coli*'s growth requirements are, such a rapidly expanding rate of increase could not be sustained. Probably sometime midway through the 24-hour period, the waste produced by the bacteria would increase and the resources supporting such phenomenal growth would be reduced to a

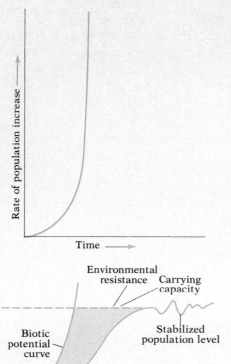

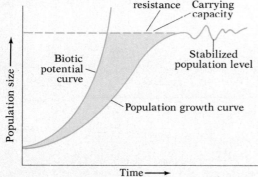

46.1

The J-shaped growth curve (*top*) is produced by unhindered population growth when species reproduce at or near their biotic potential. When the rate of increase slows and eventually stabilizes at the carrying capacity, the S-shaped curve (*bottom*) results.

point where the biotic potential could no longer be reached.

Even if conditions were ideal and the population reached its reproductive potential, the increase could not go on forever. After all, our planet is a finite world; there *are* limits. The size of a population that any environment can support indefinitely is called its **carrying capacity**.

Populations, then, are likely to encounter environmental resistance that depresses their growth rate so that their biotic potential is never achieved. As the rate of increase slows, a gentler slope is produced—the more realistic S-shaped curve (see Figure 46.1). As the population more gradually reaches the environment's carrying capacity, its growth rate decreases until it stabilizes and fluctuates around the population size that the environment can support, sometimes rising slightly above it and sometimes dropping beneath it.

Rapidly growing populations sometimes **overshoot** the environment's carrying capacity so drastically that their numbers cannot be sustained. In some cases, the population may suddenly begin to drop, and may drop well below the original carrying capacity. Such a rapid decline is known as a **population crash** (Figure 46.2). A crash can be due to a number of factors, such as a rapid depletion of resources or damage to the environment. Obviously, populations can be influenced by both *biotic* (living) factors as well as *abiotic* (nonliving) ones (we will say more about this later). Populations can overshoot the carrying capacity and abuse the environment while their numbers are high—to such a degree that they then could lower the carrying capacity of the environment for many species, resulting in an even more severe crash. For example, the elephants crowded into reserves in East Africa have destroyed acres of the slow-growing trees (such as acacias and baobabs) on which they feed, and scientists believe that the area will never recover.

In some cases, population crashes are part of the normal cycle of life. For example, they occur commonly in areas with markedly different seasons. Consider populations that increase each spring and summer, only to dwindle with the approaching rigors of winter. Winter is a harsh season that temporarily lowers the environment's car-

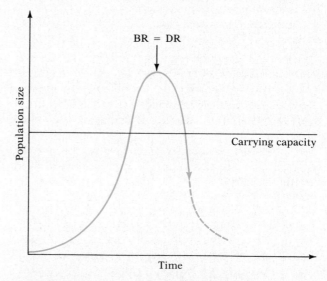

46.2

A crash can be expected when a rapidly growing population temporarily expands well above the environment's carrying capacity. A number of factors may then act to quickly reduce the population's numbers to well below the original carrying capacity. The relationship between the birth rate (BR) and the death rate (DR) is seen in each portion of the growth curve.

rying capacity. Species that have evolved under such fluctuating conditions have adapted in a number of ways: by becoming less vulnerable (for example, laying on fat), by migrating, by hibernating, by altering social patterns (huddling, for instance), or by simply making the best of it (as deer do). The seasonal return of warm weather restores the carrying capacity to higher levels, and populations normally respond by increasing their numbers quickly.

Populations tend to grow, remain static, or decline in accordance with the relative number of births and deaths (if we discount migration, the movement of individuals into and out of populations). Births and deaths are usually expressed in terms of the **crude birth rate** and the **crude death rate**: the number of each per unit of population over some specified period of time (Figure 46.3, and see Table 47.3). The difference between the two is the rate of natural increase.

The rate of natural increase *(r)* is determined by simply subtracting the death rate from the birth rate *(b − d)*. So *r* can be a positive number, zero, or a negative number, depending on whether the birth rate is greater than, equal to, or less than the death rate. In 1981 the estimated crude birth rate of humans was 28 per 1000 and the crude death rate was 11 per 1000; thus the rate of natural increase was 17. This translates into an annual growth rate of 1.7%, a number that alarms many people, since it means a doubling time for the human population of just 41 years.

Life Span and the Population

Information about life span and age are important factors in characterizing a population and predicting its course. How many individuals in a population are below, within, or beyond the reproductive age? How long is the life span? These questions are extremely important in determining probable future trends in our own population. For example, 1980 censuses revealed that 37% of the earth's humans were below 15 years of age. That is, most were not yet of reproductive age. And most of these people were statistically likely to live through their reproductive period and beyond.

Death now claims people later in life than ever before. But this information in itself is not particularly useful. In order to make meaningful predictions, we need to know which age groups are most vulnerable—that is, subjected to the greatest mortality. In many natural populations, death occurs quite frequently in the very young. But once an individual has survived the rigors of early life, the probability of living to old age increases. Obviously, mortality increases again in the aging seg-

ment of the population. **Survivorship curves** indicate the probability of living out the normal life span for every age category. Survivorship curves for five types of animals are shown in Figure 46.4.

Adaptive Strategies for Populations

It has been suggested that populations tend to adopt different reproductive "strategies," depending on the characteristics of the group and its niche. The extremes of this adaptive range are referred to as **r-selection** and **K-selection**. (*K* refers to carrying capacity and *r* refers to natural rate of increase.) The reproductive strategy of any group of animals theoretically falls somewhere along the r-K spectrum.

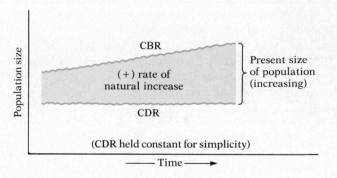

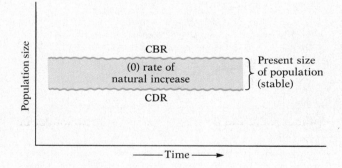

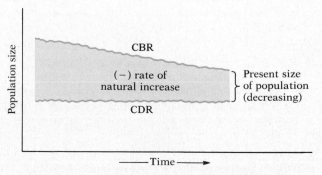

46.3

The rate of natural increase (shaded area) in a population is the difference between the crude birth rate (CBR) and crude death rate (CDR).

Ecologists consider tapeworms to be an extreme case of r-selected animals. These species maximize their reproductive output by simply producing as many offspring as possible (with as little investment in any single one as possible). They may blindly lay thousands of eggs, leaving the rest to chance. A good deal of their energy, then, goes into simply manufacturing their offspring, and no energy or time is spent in caring for them.

At the other extreme are the K-selected species. These may produce few offspring, but any they do produce receive a great deal of their parents' attention. Chimpanzees are good examples: even the most prolific individuals have only a few offspring, but the females tend them carefully until they can survive independently, often a matter of several years. The father may make his investment in other ways, such as defending the group that includes his offspring. The longer developmental periods of K-selected species give them time to prepare for the rigors of a competitive world.

Another way of viewing r- and K-selection is to keep in mind that maximizing the *quantity* of offspring (r-selection) rather than the *quality* (K-selection) is particularly adaptive where conditions

TABLE 46.1

Some characteristics of r- and K-selection

	r-selection	K-selection
Climate	Variable and/or unpredictable	Fairly constant and/or predictable
Mortality	Density independent	Density dependent
Survivorship	High mortality when young; high survivorship afterwards	Either little mortality until a certain age, or constant death rates over a period of time
Intraspecific and interspecific competition	Variable, lax	Usually keen
Selection favors	Rapid development; high rate of population increase; early reproduction; small body size; single reproduction	Slower development; greater competitive ability; delayed reproduction; larger body size; repeated reproductions
Length of life	Usually less than one year	Usually more than one year
Leads to	Productivity	Efficiency

SOURCE: Adapted from E. R. Pianka, "On r- and K-selection." *American Naturalist* 104: 592–97 (1970).

are unpredictable. The advantage of producing numerous offspring if conditions are unstable or unpredictable is the increased probability that more of them will encounter conditions that enable them to mature. Most of the offspring will be lost, but the parental investment in them is low so the loss is minimized. K-selected species can be expected under more stable or predictable conditions in which the likelihood is high that a properly prepared offspring will survive. Table 46.1 lists the traits that characterize r- and K-selected species. Do you see why each trait is listed where it is?

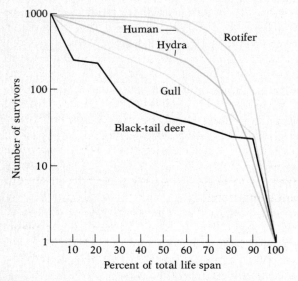

46.4

Survivorship curves for five species, each beginning with a population of 1000 (vertical axis). Points along each line represent the percentage of the life span reached as the populations age (horizontal axis). In blacktail deer, a species that experiences a high death rate among its young, the numbers drop off rapidly, with the average individual achieving only 6% of its potential life span. The average human and rotifer survive the rigors of early life to complete about 66% of their potential life spans, while the average *Hydra* and gull complete about 37% and 24%, respectively.

INFLUENCES ON POPULATIONS

Thus far, we have lumped the various factors that tend to reduce populations under the catchall term of *environmental resistance*. Now let's take a closer look at some of these factors and how they operate. First, populations are controlled in two major ways.

Density-Independent and Density-Dependent Controls

In some cases, populations are controlled by factors that have nothing to do with their size or density. Such factors are said to exert **density-independent control.** As an example, the parching sun does not respond to the density of corn plants in a field; it kills them all. Such controls are almost always abiotic—physical forces such as weather patterns or geological events (Figure 46.5). Just as density-independent effects can reduce population numbers, they can also increase them. Spring rains may cause all the flowering annuals of the desert to germinate at once. As long as the rains are heavy and there is no competition for the water, the flowering is density-independent. But if there is competition for that water (or any other resource), then we see **density-dependent control** of the population. Obviously, the more competition one has (that is, the denser the population), the more one is harmed and the less likely one is to reproduce maximally. Thus, crowding can reduce populations through density-dependent effects.

Interestingly, crowding can also exert density-dependent effects that *increase* population sizes. For example, some prey animals confuse predators by their sheer numbers; as they dash away, those in larger groups (with greater density) are more

likely to foil a pursuer than those in smaller groups. So we see that both density-independent and density-dependent effects can operate to either raise or lower population density.

More about Biotic Controls

The most common forms of density-dependent population control involve the interactions of living things. So let's have a closer look at some ways in which populations can be controlled by *biotic* influences.

Our examples of biotic controls will include the following five cases:

1. Competition within and between species
2. Territoriality and dominance hierarchies
3. Self-poisoning
4. Disease and parasitism
5. Predator-prey relationships

Competition Within and Between Species. There is currently some argument among biologists regarding the importance of **competition** in the utilization by two or more individuals (or species) of the same limiting resource in nature. But where it exists there can be little doubt that competition is keenest between individuals of the same species, and it may well be magnified within individuals of the same sex. After all, these organisms are the most similar and so tend to use the same resources. Two lionesses may compete for the choicest part of a downed zebra, but while this seems to fit our definition of competition, the loser in such cases will probably not die from lack of food. Competition probably has its greatest effect on populations when essential commodities are in short supply. Competition, by the way, is not often expressed in bloody battles. Instead, it frequently takes the form of a quiet but relentless attempt to gain some resource at the expense of another individual. Plants may compete for water, minerals, and sunlight (Figure 46.6). Certain desert plants produce shallow root systems that tend to crowd out other plants of the same species that might have competed for scarce water.

Most field research is centered on competition between members of different species. The notion is that two competing species can affect each other's population levels in their zones of interaction by denying commodities, such as food, to each other.

It is believed that if the level of competition were overly intense—say, if both species attempted to interact with the environment in identical ways (to occupy the same niche)—one species would simply replace the other in the area of overlap. In the wild the situation is often not so desperate.

46.5

The effects of natural disasters, such as fire, flood, landslide, and volcanic eruption, are usually density-independent. That is, population density has little to do with their effects.

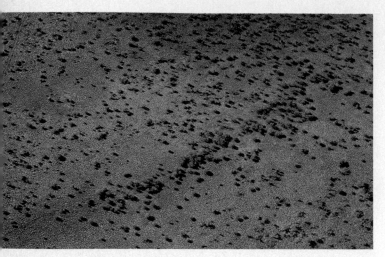

46.6

In the desert, population density within a plant species may be determined by water availability, so individuals form a well-spaced pattern. In other instances, plants discourage competition for water by secreting toxic substances from the root cells.

In fact, very similar species often coexist as neighbors without apparent undue conflict. This is because, over long periods of adjustment, they have adapted to each other by subdividing the niche. The result is that similar species that would appear to be strongly competitive have instead become specialists, each species exploiting only a narrow part of the environment and generally ignoring or avoiding the other species.

Probably the classic study of such specialization was performed by the American ecologist R. H. MacArthur (Figure 46.7). He found that five species of North American warblers coexisted in the same spruce tree groves, and he wondered if they were simply *sharing* the same food resources. It turns out that the sharing is minimized. Careful observation revealed that each species tends to feed in a different part of the tree. Thus, the different species MacArthur studied reduced competition among themselves by becoming specialists. But at the same time, by restricting themselves to certain feeding areas the warblers effectively reduced their food supply. This reduction could be expected to have an influence on their numbers.

Territoriality and Dominance Hierarchies. Territoriality in birds was first discussed in the writings of the ancient Greek philosophers. Territorial birds occupy an area—a **territory**—and defend it, particularly against intruders of the same species and sex. As we have seen, territoriality has a number of advantages. A territory may reserve a

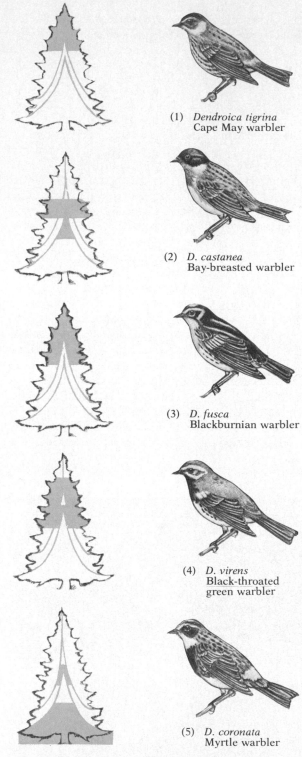

(1) *Dendroica tigrina*
Cape May warbler

(2) *D. castanea*
Bay-breasted warbler

(3) *D. fusca*
Blackburnian warbler

(4) *D. virens*
Black-throated
green warbler

(5) *D. coronata*
Myrtle warbler

46.7

Five species of the North American warbler often use the same spruce trees for feeding and nesting, but each species tends to use a specific zone. The darkened areas indicate where each species spends at least half of its feeding time. By exploiting different parts of the tree, the species avoid competition and can thus occupy the same habitat.

food supply and a nest site; it enables the territorial animal to become very familiar with a specific area; and it advertises that the territory holder is a healthy and able animal. In some species of birds, the males must have a good territory in order to attract females; even a splendid male cannot attract a mate if he holds an inferior territory. If good territories are in short supply, those birds unable to acquire one will not be able to reproduce. In such species, the availability of attractive territories affects population size (see Chapter 43).

Dominance hierarchies, or pecking orders (Figure 46.8), can also be important in regulating populations. In hierarchical groups, the dominant individuals have freer access to resources than subordinate individuals do. The rankings may be established by combat, play, or by formal threats and confrontation without contact. While dominance hierarchies encourage stability by decreasing the likelihood of confrontation, this social structure is also important in the way such populations change. For instance, when food is scarce, the low-ranking individuals are the first to starve, since higher-ranking individuals have priority for commodities. However, it is assumed that the subordinate's chances are better if he seeks other resources rather than challenges a superior.

Self-Poisoning. Almost all species produce toxic (poisonous) material of some kind. In some cases it is simply waste, but in other instances it may be used for some other purpose—defense,

46.9

The sandy, grass-free zone bordering the cluster of purple sage is a product of volatile growth-inhibiting chemicals released by the sage.

for example. Toxic wastes can have a drastic influence in reducing population growth. Those that cannot escape their own wastes may well be poisoned by them. (Bacteria growing in a petri dish will finally die of their own waste.) On the other hand, toxins are used in various ways by certain species. Some ecologists have suggested that certain bacteria render food rotten and therefore unpalatable to most other organisms. They then live for a time steeped in their own wastes, but with their decomposing food reserved for themselves. No self-respecting animal would touch it.

Some plants manufacture poisons that they use in interesting ways. Some, for instance, secrete toxins from their roots that retard root growth in other plants. The poisons they make may also inhibit their own growth somewhat, as well as the development of their offspring, but the behavior is basically adaptive in that it reduces the population size and also the level of competition for water and minerals (Figure 46.9).

And what about the poisons we humans discharge into the environment? Are we in danger of poisoning ourselves? The answer is a definite yes (Figure 46.10), but we are not yet decreasing our population to any significant degree by such behavior. The problem with analyzing the effect our

46.8

Complex social interaction characterizes the macaques, providing a measure of both safety and order. Individuals and subgroups are organized in a hierarchy, with dominant members receiving first priority in feeding and reproduction.

46.10

Residents of Times Beach, Missouri, were recently forced to vacate their community when it was learned that the area was contaminated by the highly toxic industrial waste dioxin. Such events, the product of negligent toxic-waste disposal, are becoming all too commonplace.

wastes may have on us lies essentially with our cleverness. We have found ways to escape the usual checks on population growth. Also, we have managed to manufacture chemicals so complex and alien to the planet that we have no way to predict their long-range effects. The earth and its inhabitants have never been exposed to anything even remotely like them.

Disease and Parasitism. Among the most important density-dependent regulators of many populations are **disease** and **parasitism.** One reason is that increased density means greater proximity, which in turn facilitates the transmission of diseases and parasites. Also, disease and parasitism work hand in hand in times of hunger and starvation, helping to eliminate any weakened individuals. In some instances, disease helps to reduce a population by increasing the incidence of predations. For example, a two-week-old caribou can already outsprint a full-grown wolf, and healthy adult caribou seldom fall prey to wolves. But caribou are susceptible to a laming hoof disease, and it is these lamed animals that a wolf is likely to cull out of a herd. So both factors can influence population size, and it has been suggested that their effects might benefit their prey by removing the weak and sick.

Predator-Prey Relationships. There is little doubt that predators can influence the numbers of their prey. If a lion eats a zebra, that's one less zebra. But in the long run, the effect of a predator on its prey (and vice versa) may be quite complex. Predators normally do not—and probably cannot—eliminate their prey species altogether (barring human intervention, of course). This is because of their *reciprocal* effects—the influence of each species on the other.

The conventional explanation for the reciprocal influence is that under natural conditions, a feedback principle governs the interaction of predator and prey. As a prey species multiplies, it provides more food for predators. As a result, the well-fed predators increase in number. Their numbers do not rise immediately, however, because it takes time for the energy derived from food to be converted into successful reproductive efforts. When the number of predators finally does rise, they begin to exert increasing pressure on the prey. But as they begin to kill off the prey, they find themselves with less food, and so their own numbers fall, due perhaps to less successful reproductive efforts or perhaps to outright starvation. Again, the response lags a bit. Because of such lags, the prey

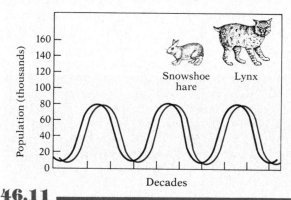

46.11

A theoretical relationship exists between the numbers of a prey population and its primary predator. As the prey population increases, the increased food supply is reflected in an increase in the predator population. The resulting pressure on the prey depresses its numbers. After enough time elapses for food reduction to influence the predator's reproductive output, its population decreases. The model is admittedly simplistic, and there is only limited evidence from nature to verify it at this time.

population may be well on the road to recovery before the predator population begins to rise again (Figure 46.11).

Humans as Predators. Most of the delicate, self-regulating interactions between predator and prey are lost when modern humans go on the hunt. The reason is apparently simple: We have removed many of the regulatory influences of natural selection. With other species, natural selection plays a more vital role. In nature, as the predator population evolves better ways of catching its prey, the prey population responds by evolving better ways of foiling the predators. The predators must then improve their methods further, and so on. But humans don't wait for evolution to produce better hunting abilities; we improve our technology instead. For example, when fisheries began noting smaller catches, the fishing industry didn't let up and allow the fish populations to recover. In fact, it did precisely the opposite—it developed new means of locating and catching fish. With their increased efficiency, the fisheries put even greater pressure on the dwindling prey population. Furthermore, because the human population is growing at a dizzying rate, the demand for food from our oceans steadily increases.

We see, then, that the size and density of populations are influenced by a wide range of factors, from simple abiotic influences to the complex and interacting biotic factors. We are aware of some of the forces operating on populations, but we are still woefully short of understanding the underlying, fundamental principles of population change. It is in our best interest to continue research in the area of population biology, however, because such informationis likely to become critical in the coming years as our own population continues to grow. We will examine this phenomenon in the next chapter.

Summary

Population Growth Patterns

Population growth patterns can be represented by J-shaped and S-shaped curves. The J-shaped curve illustrates exponential growth, in which the population growth rate increases steadily as more reproductive organisms are added to the group. The maximum rate at which any population can increase under ideal conditions is called its reproductive (or biotic) potential. Environmental resistance affects populations and limits their numbers so that their biotic potential is never maintained. The lower rate of population increase produces the S-shaped curve. The number of individuals any environment can support indefinitely is its carrying capacity.

Some populations grow so rapidly that they overshoot their environment's carrying capacity and experience a population crash. Biotic and abiotic factors can affect carrying capacities, and in areas with markedly different seasons, population crashes can be part of the normal cycle of life.

The difference between crude birth rate and crude death rate in a population reflects its rate of natural increase (deaths are subtracted from births). Life spans are important in predicting a population's course. Survivorship curves are used to indicate the probability of living out the normal life span for every age category in a population.

r-selected species maximize their reproductive output by producing as many offspring as possible; they do not invest time or energy in caring for offspring after they are produced. K-selected species produce few offspring but invest large amounts of time and energy in nurturing them through their developmental periods. In r-selected species, the sheer quantity of offspring helps to ensure reproductive success in unstable or unpredictable conditions. K-selected species ensure the quality of offspring, who are more likely to survive in stable or predictable environments.

Influences on Populations

Environmental factors affecting populations can be density independent (usually abiotic, such as weather patterns) or density dependent (most commonly biotic). Biotic controls involve the interaction of living things, and include competition within and between species, territoriality and dominance hierarchies, self-poisoning, disease and parasitism, and predator-prey relationships. Competition is strongest among members of the same species, and is often intensified among members of the same sex within a species. Competition between species can affect each species' population levels, particularly if the species compete heavily. However, some competitors subdivide the niche.

Territoriality and dominance hierarchies can affect populations by increasing the success of some individuals at the expense of others. Some organisms produce toxic substances that limit their own reproductive potential somewhat, but serve to keep competing species at bay as well. Both disease and parasitism can decrease population growth directly or indirectly. Predator-prey relationships are often quite complex, with the numbers of one population constantly influencing the numbers of the other.

Key Terms

J-shaped curve
S-shaped curve
population growth rate
exponential (geometric) growth
reproductive (biotic) potential
environmental resistance
carrying capacity
overshoot

population crash
crude birth rate
crude death rate
survivorship curve
r-selection
K-selection
density-independent control

density-dependent control
biotic control
competition
territory
dominance hierarchy
disease
parasitism

Review Questions

1. What do crude birth and death rates have to do with the rate of natural increase? (p. 681)

2. Draw a generalized population growth curve, integrating the ideas of biotic potential, geometric increase, environmental resistance, and carrying capacity. Give several examples of environmental resistance. (pp. 679–680)

3. Cite examples and compare the reproductive strategies of r-selected and K-selected species. Which, if either, is more successful in the long run? Explain your answer. (p. 682)

4. Distinguish between density-dependent and density-independent population control mechanisms. Give an example of a biotic, density-independent factor and of an abiotic, density-independent factor. (p. 683)

5. Compare competition among members of the same species and among different species. What often occurs between species that share the same niche? (pp. 683–684)

6. Explain how territoriality and dominance hierarchies are adaptive in some species. (pp. 684–685)

7. The graph representing rising and falling snowshoe hare and lynx populations suggests a natural feedback system at work. How might this happen? (Figure 46.11)

8. Characterize the current state of human predation. In what way does such behavior appear to be nonadaptive? (p. 687)

The Human Population

47

Now we turn our attention to a set of numbers that has stimulated a great deal of concern and controversy in recent years: 4.5, 30, 12, 1.8, 39, and 35. A look at the world population data in Table 47.1 shows that the numbers represent, respectively, the number of people on the earth in 1980 (in billions), our crude birth rate, crude death rate, percentage of annual growth, population doubling time (in years), and percentage of people below the age of 15. These numbers tell us the status of our own population, and they are indeed disturbing.

Let's take a closer look at the implications of these numbers. The need to know about the history and current status of the human population becomes apparent when we realize that the population of the world will have doubled between the time most of today's college students were born and the year 2000 A.D. As our numbers increase, we continue to accelerate our demands on the earth's increasingly scarce resources, and we continue to waste what we have and foul our environment.

The gloom and doom statistics are abundant, and anyone who is at all interested has probably heard enough of them by now. But just in case, here is one more: There are 25 more humans living now than there were 10 seconds ago when you began reading this paragraph. By tomorrow at this time 211,000 will have been added, and by next year, 77 million. That is equivalent to the population of Mexico—and most of them will live in a style similar to that of the average citizen of that struggling nation.

We can generate such statements all day, but once we understand the problem, do we wallow in depression or simply look away? Or do we join the ranks of hopeful and determined people who are willing to tackle some of these obstacles? In order to be of real help (and even to vote intelligently), we need to understand the nature of the problem.

We'll begin by delving into the history of our numbers. Throughout most of our history populations remained fairly stable, but in the past 50,000–100,000 years we have experienced three significant growth surges (Figure 47.1).

THE HISTORY OF HUMAN POPULATIONS

Let's begin our overview with a look at the early population of *Homo erectus*, an ancestor that lived about one million years ago. Small bands roamed distant, grassy plains, one or another of the group stopping occasionally to dig at a root or pick at the soft parts of an insect. The hominid population,

TABLE 47.1

World population data: 1970 and 1980.

Region	Year	Total (millions)	Crude Birth Rate	Crude Death Rate	Annual % Inc.	Doubling Time (years)	% Below 15 Yrs. of Age
World	1970	3632	34	14	2.0	35	37
	1980	4471	30	12	1.8	39	35
Africa	1970	344	47	20	2.6	27	44
	1980	478	46	19	2.8	25	45
Asia	1970	2045	38	15	2.3	31	40
	1980	2604	32	12	2.0	35	47
North	1970	228	18	9	1.1	63	20
America	1980	252	15	8	0.7	100	23
Latin	1970	283	38	9	2.9	24	42
America	1980	364	36	9	2.8	25	40
Europe	1970	462	18	10	0.8	88	25
	1980	484	14	10	0.4	175	20
Nations of Special Interest							
United	1970	205	17.5	9.6	1.0	70	30
States	1980	228	15.0	7.0	0.8	88	25
Soviet	1970	243	17.9	7.7	1.0	70	28
Union	1980	266	18.0	10.0	0.8	88	26
People's	1970	760	34.0	15.0	1.8	39	?
Rep. of	1980	1027	26.0	9.0	1.7	41	32
China (estimate)							
India	1970	554	42.0	17.0	2.6	27	41
	1980	663	34.0	15.0	1.9	37	41

SOURCES: Population Reference Bureau and the Environmental Defense Fund.

estimated to have been about 125,000 at that time, was not having much impact on the environment.

Later, the earliest humans roamed the land as hunters and gatherers, and were undoubtedly subject to the same density-independent controls that influence populations of herbivores and carnivores today (Figure 47.2a). Infants and children probably suffered high mortality rates, but such losses were quickly replaced in a species where fertility was not a seasonal event. The average life span is estimated to have been 30 years; the high infant mortality rate was probably counterbalanced by some people living much longer (Table 47.2).

The First Population Surge

The first growth surge in the human population was probably due to the development of increasingly efficient tools. With them, early people could more effectively modify and exploit their environment. In addition, humans—inveterate wanderers—had by then penetrated and established themselves on all of the continents. By 10,000 years ago, the earth probably supported about 5 million people. (Estimates of these early

human populations are based on limited data, partly from anthropological studies of surviving primitive cultures.)

The Second Population Surge

About 10,000 years ago (some say 8000), the human population began its second growth surge, this time with more authority. With the development of agriculture and the domestication of animals came increasing densities of local populations. There was less need to roam the countryside in search of food; in fact, there was a great need to stay put and tend the fields and livestock (Figure 47.2b). With the storage of surplus food, winter and drought no longer exacted such a great toll on human life.

With the increased quantity and dependability of the food supply, humans probably experienced a lower death rate, particularly among the young. Furthermore, there was quite possibly an increase in the birth rate because of better nutrition. Large families may have been encouraged because they meant more hands to till the fields. But life was by no means simple, since the crops were subjected to the inconsistencies of weather and to infestation by insects and other herbivores whose own numbers responded to the novel food supply.

The unprecedented population growth of the early days of agriculture did not continue at its initial soaring rate, but settled into a steadier, more gradual climb. Yet between the advent of agriculture and the time of Christ, the human population rose from 5 million to about 133 million. By 1650 A.D., it had reached an estimated 500 million.

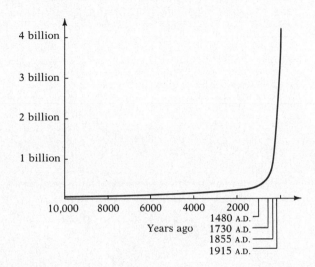

(a)

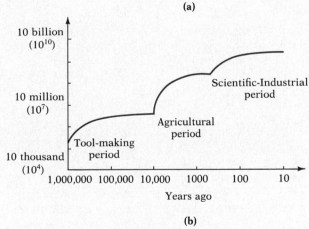

(b)

47.1

Two ways of viewing human population history. **(a)** The arithmetic plot clearly reveals the near vertical rise of the J-shaped curve, a danger signal to most species. Hidden in the gradually rising line preceding this is the earlier population surge brought on by the switch from hunting and gathering to agriculture. The logarithmic plot **(b)**, where time is compressed, shows three growth surges. These surges are the products, respectively, of advances in hunting and gathering technology, the rise of agriculture, and the recent era of health-care practices.

TABLE 47.2

Estimated average life span in human populations

It seems that our life span, as a group, was fixed by evolutionary processes early in our history. Our attempts at increasing our longevity probably have resulted only in our coming closer to reaching the limits set by our physical constitutions. The examination of the remains of our primitive ancestors shows that many of the conditions we associate with old age affected them in much the same way that they affect us today. Also, in classic Rome, a person who lived to the age of 75 was more likely to reach 90 than someone in the United States today. (However, it might be argued that that is because it took a sturdier constitution to reach 75 in those days.)

Population	Years
Neanderthal	29.4
Upper Paleolithic	32.4
Mesolithic	31.5
Neolithic Anatolia	38.2
Austrian Bronze Age	38
Classic Greece	35
Classic Rome	32
United States, 1900–1902	48
United States, 1950	70
United States, 1977	72

SOURCE: Adapted from ''The Probability of Death'' by E. S. Deevey. Copyright © 1950 by Scientific American, Inc. All rights reserved. Reprinted by permission.

History reveals that on a regional level this growth was interrupted many, many times by the decimating effects of disease, famine, and war. These are largely density-dependent and closely interrelated factors. A severe example of the effects of disease occurred in the 14th century, when one-fourth of Europe's population was killed by the ''Black Death''—the bubonic plague. Such other diseases as typhus, influenza, and syphilis also took their toll on the crowded and incredibly filthy towns of the medieval period.

Interestingly, the loss of such numbers is insignificant in view of population growth today. At today's population growth rate, for example, the number of deaths from the 14th-century bubonic plague could be recouped in one year, while the number of people killed in all the wars of the last 500 years could be replaced in about six months.

The Third Population Surge

The third population growth surge began in Europe in the mid-17th century, after the unexplained decline of the plague (perhaps only those who were naturally immune were left alive). A number of explanations have been advanced to account for this third surge. For one thing, the crowded populations of Europe expanded into the New World, with its array of opportunities and unexploited resources. More significantly, people were becoming aware of the causes of disease (Figure 47.3). By the 19th century public sanitation programs had begun, vaccines were developed, and rapid advances in food storage and transportation technologies led to a marked increase in food supplies. Between 1750 and 1850 the population of Europe doubled; that of the New World increased fivefold.

Populations were surging in other nations as well, for reasons that are not completely understood. In China, the most heavily populated nation at that time, agriculture had made great gains, and a long period of comparative political stability followed the overthrow of the Ming dynasty in 1644. India, however, had known little rest from turmoil and periodic famines (Figure 47.4). In 1770, the worst famine of all reportedly killed half the population of Bengal. African populations are believed to have remained stable until about 1850, when the impact of imported European medical advances began to depress the death rate.

The third surge has continued into modern times, and the rate of the rise has constantly accelerated. This is due largely to a host of innovations in industry, agriculture, and public health. Many of these innovations arose in industrialized, developed countries and were exported to heavily populated developing regions.* In the developed nations, famine was all but eradicated with the

Developed nations are those that have a slow rate of population growth; a stable, industrialized economy; a low percentage of workers employed in the agricultural sector; a high per capita income; and a high degree of literacy. *Developing* nations have the opposite traits. Of course, many countries have intermediate conditions, and some have a combination—a privileged upper class and a poor lower class.

47.2

(*Top*) The hominids of one million years ago, probably *Homo erectus*, are believed to have lived as hunters and gatherers, wandering their territory in a perpetual search for food. They probably utilized a variety of plant foods, along with grubs and other insect larvae and whatever small game they could kill. Their impact on the environment was relatively limited. (*Bottom*) Even these meager efforts at agriculture, some 10,000 years ago, effectively raised the carrying capacity of the environment for humans. Agriculture's effect was to create the first population boom, as humans became less subject to the limitations of hunting and gathering.

In the late 1700s, Edward Jenner used pus scrapings from relatively harmless cowpox sores to develop an effective vaccine against smallpox. While his efforts were amazingly successful, they were not without public controversy, as we see in this 18th-century cartoon.

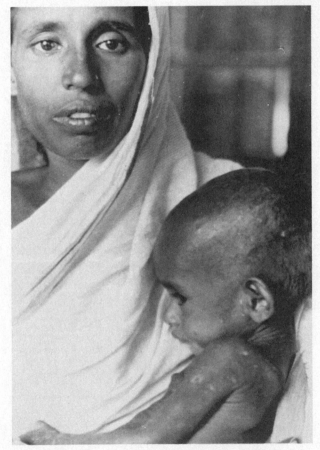

Until recent times, India's massive population has been periodically subjected to drastic food shortages, often the product of cyclic drought. During these periods, famine spread quickly through the nation, striking city dwellers particularly hard.

advent of pesticides, chemical fertilizers, and high-yield crops. Potential disease epidemics were routinely controlled by vaccines, antibiotics, and insecticides.

In summary, we can note that the human population grew from about 5 million at the dawn of agriculture to 500 million by 1650. In the next 200 years the world population doubled, reaching 1 billion. (**Doubling time** is the number of years required for a population to double in numbers.) Between 1850 and 1930 the numbers doubled again, to 2 billion. The next doubling took only 45 years, and in 1975 our world population stood at 4 billion. By 1970, thoroughly alarmed population experts were predicting another doubling, to 8 billion, by the year 2000—a span of only 35 years.

THE HUMAN POPULATION TODAY

To the surprise of nearly everyone, the rate of natural increase in the world population slowed toward the end of the 1970s, and that deceleration continues today (see Table 47.1). (Note the implications of the word *rate*. The occupants of a car approaching a cliff at 30 miles per hour might take little comfort in knowing that its rate is slowing and it will be traveling at only 15 miles per hour by the time it goes over the cliff.)

At the end of 1980, demographers estimated the world's population to be near 4.5 billion. The annual growth rate had fallen slightly and the doubling time had increased to 39 years. These data

TABLE 47.3

Basic population arithmetic

$$\text{Crude birth rate} = \begin{array}{l}\text{number of births per year}\\ \text{per 1000 population}\end{array}$$

$$\left(\text{determined by: } \frac{\text{total births}}{\text{midyear population}} \times 1000\right)$$

$$\text{Crude death rate} = \begin{array}{l}\text{number of deaths per year}\\ \text{per 1000 population}\end{array}$$

$$\left(\text{determined by: } \frac{\text{total deaths}}{\text{midyear population}} \times 1000\right)$$

$$\begin{array}{l}\text{Rate of natural}\\ \text{increase (or}\\ \text{decrease)}\end{array} = \text{crude BR} - \text{crude DR}$$

$$\text{Percent annual growth} = \frac{\text{rate of natural increase}}{10}$$

$$\begin{array}{l}\text{Doubling time}\\ \text{(approximately)}\end{array} = \frac{70}{\text{percent annual growth}}$$

(example: % annual growth in the world in

1980 was 1.7: $\frac{70}{1.7} = 41.18$ years

SOURCE: From LIVING IN THE ENVIRONMENT, Third Edition by G. Tyler Miller, Jr. Copyright © 1982 by Wadsworth, Inc. Reprinted by permission of Wadsworth Publishing Co., Belmont, Calif. 94002.

suggest some headway in our attempts to control our population, which can be at least partially attributed to changing attitudes of women toward their role in society, changes in preferences in family size, advances in methods of birth control, and the liberalization of abortion laws in developed nations.

Growth in the Developing Regions

The new data generated a measure of relief and even a growing optimism. But it turns out that the depressed growth rates occurred primarily in the most developed nations, those that could best support increased populations, such as the United States, Japan, Western Europe, and the Soviet Union. Most poorer, developing nations of the world show few signs of controlling their populations. The annual rate of growth in those regions (excluding China) is an ominous 2.4% and the doubling time is 29 years. (The method of calculating doubling time is shown in Table 47.3.) While the crude birth and death rates in the U.S. in 1980 were 15 and 7 per thousand, respectively, those rates in Africa were 46 and 19. Further, the doubling time in Africa is an alarmingly brief 25 years. How do you suppose these shifting population trends will affect political, social, and economic stability in the near future? What effects are they having now?

At first glance, the news from Latin America seemed hopeful: In the past few years there has been a decrease in the crude birth rate. But again, the numbers are misleading. In this region, the birth rate is already four times the death rate. Furthermore, many Latin American nations already troubled by political unrest and dismal economic ditions face a doubling time about the same as Africa's.

Asia has traditionally troubled demographers because so little is known about it and yet it has enormous reproductive potential. (It is instructive to keep in mind that well over half of the people walking the earth today are Asians, and one in every four humans alive today is Chinese.) Within the last decade the birth rate in China (reportedly) declined somewhat, without an equivalent fall in the death rate. Perhaps partly because of this shift in China, the doubling time for Asian populations has increased from 31 to 35 years. Massive birth control programs in China and several other Asian nations have been instrumental in the declining birth rates. Similar efforts in India have been somewhat successful, but India's annual increase is still close to 2% and its doubling time is only 37 years. (Doubling times in a number of nations are shown in Table 47.4.)

The small successes Asia is currently enjoying, however, may be swamped by another problem, one of momentum. Specifically, 47% of these people are under the age of 15 and have yet to enter the breeding population. Asia could well be in for another population explosion.

It is difficult if not impossible to predict what the future holds, but there are ways of making educated guesses. Let's gaze into the crystal ball of demography and see how populations are forecast.

THE FUTURE OF THE HUMAN POPULATION

Our track record in predicting population growth is not very impressive; demographers in the U.S. were taken by surprise by the baby boom of the 1950s, and they are still trying to explain the latest downward trend. However, increasingly sophisticated and precise calculations show some promise of improving the accuracy of our projections.

Fertility Rate

Two of the indicators of future population trends are the general fertility rate and the total fertility rate (Figure 47.5). The **general fertility rate** is the number of live births per thousand women in the reproductive age bracket (15–44 in the U.S. and

TABLE 47.4

Doubling time in selected nations

% Annual Growth	Doubling Time (yrs)	Nation		
		(Africa)	**(Eurasia)**	**(Latin America)**
4	23 or less	Algeria; Ghana; Kenya; Nigeria	Iran; Iraq; Syria	Ecuador; El Salvador; Guatemala; Honduras; Nicaragua; Venezuela
3	23–35	Chad; Congo; Ethiopia; Niger; Somalia; S. Africa	Afghanistan; Burma; India; Lebanon; N. Korea; Pakistan; Philippines	Bolivia; Brazil; Mexico; Panama; Paraguay; Peru
2	35–69		China; Iceland; Indonesia; Israel; Norway; Poland; S. Korea; Taiwan; Thailand	Argentina; Chile; Uruguay
		(All nations)		
1	70 +	Australia; Canada; Japan; New Zealand; U.S.A.; U.S.S.R.	Most of Europe (E. Germany: 6930 years) (Luxembourg: 3465 years) (Sweden: 1555 years)	

15–49 in certain other nations). The general fertility rate gives us a clear idea of what is happening in terms of family size, but like the crude birth and death rates, it comes after the fact. The **total fertility rate,** on the other hand, is a *prediction* of the average number of children women will have over their reproductive lifetimes.

Such predictions are based on information from many sources, including economists, government agencies, churches, family planning groups, and the like. But they are also based on an unusual variable in science: *attitude*. The attitude of American women in their reproductive period toward domestic life and family size changed radically in the 1960s and '70s (as did that of women in many developed nations). Women began to assume new roles in industrialized societies. They entered new

areas of the work force, challenged male enclaves, demanded rights and privileges previously reserved for men, and placed less emphasis on children. Their new attitudes were duly noted by the demographers, who then predicted a reduced rate of population growth. But such trends can change quickly, and if attitude is an important variable in forecasting population sizes, demographers must remain current. In any case, measuring attitudes is a very risky business.

Population Structure

Knowing the age structure of any population is critical to understanding growth patterns and making predictions. One way to portray such data is by

47.5

Fertility studies in the U.S. between 1925 and 1980. The two plots include the general fertility rate (scale on the right) and total fertility rate (scale on the left). The depression years are seen as a valley, followed by a reproductive peak—the "baby boom" years—that came after World War II. The recent valley, following the boom years, is good news to those alarmed by population growth. But keep in mind that attitudes towards family size can change and that women born in the baby boom years are still in the reproductive period of life.

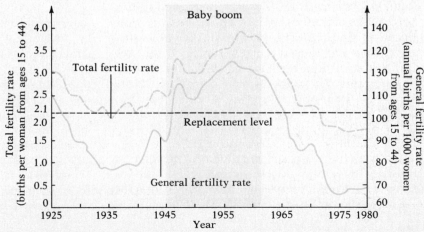

695

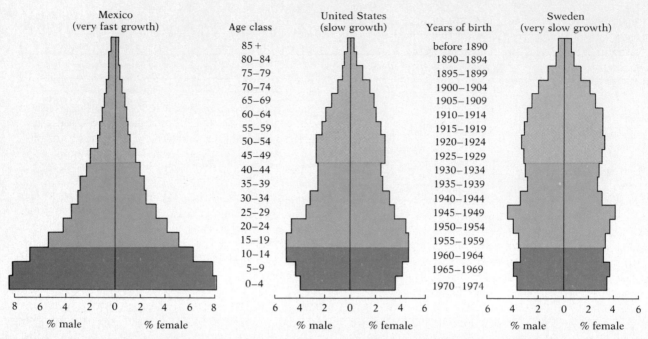

Mexico (very fast growth)	Age class	United States (slow growth)	Years of birth	Sweden (very slow growth)
	85 +		before 1890	
	80–84		1890–1894	
	75–79		1895–1899	
	70–74		1900–1904	
	65–69		1905–1909	
	60–64		1910–1914	
	55–59		1915–1919	
	50–54		1920–1924	
	45–49		1925–1929	
	40–44		1930–1934	
	35–39		1935–1939	
	30–34		1940–1944	
	25–29		1945–1949	
	20–24		1950–1954	
	15–19		1955–1959	
	10–14		1960–1964	
	5–9		1965–1969	
	0–4		1970–1974	

47.6

Age structure pyramids (1977) for Mexico, the United States, and Sweden reveal important differences between developing countries and those that are more economically advanced. Future growth rates can be predicted by studying the lowest levels of the pyramids, since these include females that have yet to reproduce. The middle region of a pyramid contains the reproducers and the labor force. These individuals have the burden of supporting both the lower and the upper levels, a burden whose size can be estimated by a look at the bases and tops of the pyramids. From the U.S. pyramid, find the region representing the depression, the post-World-War II baby boom, and your own generation. Where do the serious burdens fall?

age structure pyramids. In Figure 47.6, you can see how such pyramids are formed. Note the marked differences in the shapes of such pyramids between developed and developing nations. In developed areas, recent population increases have been comparatively slow, so the base is not very wide. Also, people tend to live longer and thus to occupy the upper levels in greater proportions. In developing nations, on the other hand, the rate of increase is still expanding, swelling the lower levels. Obviously, these lower levels are important to population forecasting since they represent future reproducers. Finally, such shapes illustrate that people in developing regions have fewer health advantages and are more likely to die sooner, resulting in a marked decrease in the upper third of these regions' age brackets.

Demographic Transition

There is an interesting relationship between a country's developmental progress and its population structure: As nations undergo economic and technological development, their population growth tends to decrease. According to the theory of **demographic transition,** nations go through several developmental phases, the earliest of which is characterized by high birth and death rates and slow growth. As they begin to develop, the birth rate remains high but the death rate falls. The result is that the population begins to grow rapidly. Then as industrialization peaks, the birth rate falls and begins to approximate the death rate. The population enters a fluctuating equilibrium state (Figure 47.7).

One major prediction based on the theory of demographic transition is that population growth in developing parts of Asia, Africa, and Latin America will slow as they become further industrialized. But can the answer to the enigma of world population growth be that simple? Not quite. First, it is the developed nations that must pay the enormous costs of such a massive industrialization program, and this could place a great burden on their own economics. (Also, who needs more competition in the marketplace?) Second, there are severe risks in encouraging developing countries to go through such transitions. For example, if massive development programs stall in the second and most difficult phase, soaring populations will preclude the third stage and send the hopeful developing nation into a deadly population spiral. Thus, any such developmental program must be approached with extreme caution.

Growth Predictions and the Earth's Carrying Capacity

The fundamental question of how large the human population can become is irrevocably tied to what the earth can support—its human carrying capacity. If we have learned anything from population studies of other species, it is that this capacity cannot be exceeded for long without severe risk—for example, risk to the environment. Any such damage would lower the environment's carrying capacity and set the stage for a devastating population crash.

The range of estimates of the earth's human carrying capacity is enormous. In other words, the experts cannot agree. Some population biologists believe that we have already exceeded our limits

and that our present population represents a drastic overshoot. At the other end of the spectrum are the optimists who believe the human population can increase to 50 billion and still survive easily. (Biologists don't take this latter estimate very seriously.)

Recent estimates by more moderate population experts suggest that the human population could be sustained *temporarily* at 8–15 billion. From here, they suggest, our numbers could gradually decrease to new, more stable levels. If we fail to restrain ourselves when we reach the higher numbers, we can expect not a gradual decrease in numbers but a massive increase in our death rate—a dieback or crash. It has been calculated that such a crash might kill 50–80% of the human population. Population biologist Paul Ehrlich, writing in 1977, emphasized that this is probably the way our population will stabilize. The dieback, says Ehrlich, will likely be due to a combination of famine, war, disease, and ecological disruption. With the exception of war (which is rare among other species) these are common density-dependent controls.

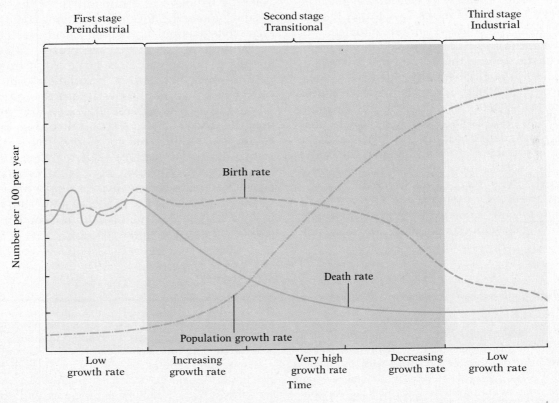

47.7

According to the theory of demographic transition, nations or regions go through three population phases. Obviously, many developing third-world nations are in the second, transitional stage, where falling death rates bring about rapid population increases.

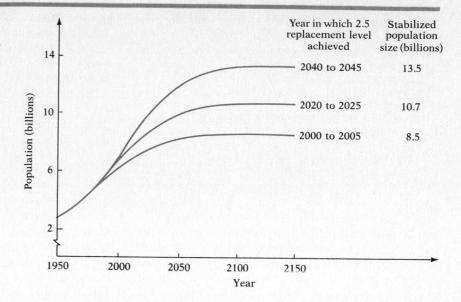

World population according to three estimates of when ZPG will be achieved. The upper level is probably the most realistic.

Year in which 2.5 replacement level achieved	Stabilized population size (billions)
2040 to 2045	13.5
2020 to 2025	10.7
2000 to 2005	8.5

To leave the subject on a note of cautious optimism, we reiterate that world population growth is slowing down somewhat and that some of the more heavily populated nations have recently joined this trend. Further, it is within the power of the world's family of nations to see that the decreasing trend is continued and accentuated. Our goal, if we are to avoid chaos, is ZPG—**zero population growth,** where the crude birth rate equals the crude death rate. This is also called the **replacement level.** Essentially, it means that each couple simply replaces itself, by having only two children. (The popular belief that the United States has achieved this goal is inaccurate.) Because of the burgeoning numbers of young people, the future size of the world's population depends largely upon when ZPG is reached (Figure 47.8).

ZPG is admittedly utopian, but it is not impossible. Some population experts maintain that many slow-growing developed nations are now reaching the goal of ZPG and that others can do so within a few decades. The trend toward family planning and use of birth control is increasing, and one hopes that efforts to stimulate such interest in developing nations will continue. Under the best of circumstances, the developing nations could reach some state of population stability in about 50 years.

The bottom line is that we must assume our species is not special; it is not exempt from the natural laws that govern population control in other species. Our only special feature is our mental capacity. We have the ability to analyze, predict, imagine, and finally to *choose.* Of course, we can choose by deciding not to choose, not to take a stand, not to be involved. But the time for that luxury is past. We must now learn as much as possible about the nature of overpopulation, apply ourselves to solving the problem, and stand ready to be accountable for our actions when we are judged by future generations.

Summary

The History of Human Populations
In the past 50,000–100,000 years, the human population has experienced three significant growth surges. The first growth surge probably occurred with the development of increasingly efficient tools, with which people could more effectively modify and exploit the environment. Around 10,000 years ago, the second growth surge coincided with the development of agriculture and the domestication of animals; humans probably began to experience a lower death rate, and possibly a higher birth rate. This growth was interrupted numerous times by a variety of factors such as disease, famine, and war. In the mid-17th century, the third population surge began, possibly because of expansion into the New World, the introduction of sanitation programs and sophistication of medical practices, advances in the preservation of food, and political stability in some areas. Between 1650 and 1850, the world population doubled

(from 500 million to 1 billion). There were 2 billion people by 1930, and 4 billion by 1975; in 1970, some predicted that there would be 8 billion people on earth by the year 2000.

The Human Population Today

The rate of natural increase of the world's population slowed in the late 1970s, and is continuing to decelerate. The doubling time of the human population has increased, primarily in developed nations that could theoretically support increased populations. Developing nations, however, show few signs of controlling their populations. Some developing nations, such as China, have instituted major birth-control propaganda programs to stem their high rates of natural population increase.

The Future of the Human Population

Future population trends can be estimated by evaluating the general fertility rate (the number of live births per thousand women of reproductive age) and the total fertility rate (a prediction of the average number of children women will have). Predictions such as these are based on data and on attitudes (which are difficult to measure). Understanding growth patterns and predicting future trends also involves the use of age structure pyramids, which reflect the numbers of people at various age levels in a population.

A country's developmental progress and its population structure are related in an interesting way; as development increases, population growth tends to decrease. Several developmental phases occur, according to the theory of demographic transition, with the earliest characterized by high birth and death rates, the next by high birth rates and lower death rates, and the next by low birth and death rates, which reflect a fluctuating equilibrium state. This theory is the basis for the prediction that population growth in developing parts of Asia, Africa, and Latin America will slow as those areas become further industrialized. Programs based on the theory must be approached cautiously, however.

The basic issue in human population studies is the carrying capacity of the earth. Estimates vary greatly, and some population biologists believe that humans have already exceeded the carrying capacity and are in a phase of overshoot. A population crash could result in stabilization—or the population could gradually decrease, possibly through zero population growth programs, through which we could reach our replacement level.

Key Terms

doubling time
general fertility rate
total fertility rate
age structure pyramids

demographic transition
zero population growth
replacement level

Review Questions

1. Describe the innovations that brought about the first two great population surges in human history. (p. 690)

2. List the three major causes of death during the Middle Ages. Were these density dependent or density independent? Explain. (p. 691)

3. List three innovations that may explain the most recent human population growth surge, and explain how each may have affected the birth rate and the death rate. (p. 693)

4. What is the status of human population growth today? Specifically, where is growth most rapid? What are some of the possible political and social ramifications of this? (p. 694)

5. Describe two ways of visualizing fertility. Which requires the most conjecture? (pp. 694–695)

6. Briefly predict the future of human population growth according to the theory of demographic transition. Upon what specific observations is this theory based? What are some of the theory's pitfalls? (pp. 696–697)

7. With simple drawings, depict the population age structure for Mexico, the United States, and Sweden. What future conditions can we predict according to the base of the diagram? According to the top? (p. 696)

8. What are experts telling us about the earth's carrying capacity? Should human numbers be maintained at our current level? Explain. (pp. 697–698)

APPENDIX A
Geologic Timetable

Eras (years since start)	Periods	Extent in millions of years	Geological events
Cenozoic	**Quaternary**		
	Holocene (present)	last 10,000 years	
	Pleistocene	.01–2	4 ice ages, glaciation in N. Hemisphere; uplift of Sierras
	Tertiary		
	Pliocene	2–6	Continued uplift; drastic cooling
	Miocene	6–23	More uplift in Rockies, isthmus of Panama formed; climate drying
	Oligocene	23–36	Mountain uplift in Europe, Asia; volcano action in Rockies
	Eocene	35–54	Inland seas diminished
65,000,000	Paleocene	54–65	Continents formed, separations continuing
Mesozoic	Cretaceous-Paleocene discontinuity	65	Asteroid collides with earth; dust obscures sun (recent hypothesis)
	Cretaceous	65–135	Two major land forms (Laurasia and Gondwana); continental separation occurs through era; Rockies forming, other continents low, seas over Europe
	Jurassic	135–197	Continued mountain building, most continents low, inland seas
225,000,000	Triassic	197–225	Mountain building in North America (Pangaea); continental drift begins
Paleozoic	Permian	225–280	Very cool; mountain building, glaciation in south, seas drain, Appalachians formed
	Carboniferous	280–345	Lowlands, shallow seas, coal swamps, mountain building in E and W N. America (Pangaea)
	Devonian	345–405	Landscape varies, Appalachians forming
	Silurian	405–425	Flattened landscape, some mountains; shallow seas, lowlands
	Ordovician	425–500	
570,000,000	Cambrian	500–570	Steady increase in temperature
Precambrian		1000	Cooling; atmosphere has become oxidizing rather than reducing
		2000	Low-lying, vast, inland seas; tropical climate with little latitudinal variation
Origin of earth, 4.5–5.7 billion years		3000	Oxygen production
		4000	Oldest rock formation, crust hardening
		4500	Chemical evolution; solar system forms

Classification of Organisms

THE PROKARYOTES

Single-celled organisms, tough cell wall, no membrane-bounded organelles or organized nucleus. Circular DNA, not joined with protein. Reproduction mostly by fission; some by conjugation. Any flagella solid and rotating.

KINGDOM ARCHEBACTERIA Unique, proteinaceous cell walls. Cell membrane with branched fatty acids. Mostly anaerobic; includes methanogens, halophiles, and thermophiles (Chapter 20).

KINGDOM EUBACTERIA ("true" bacteria): Cell walls of peptidoglycan, membranes with straight-chain fatty acids; includes many pathogens, free-living reducers, phototrophs, and chemotrophs. Found in coccus, bacillus, and spirochaete forms, occurring singly, in clusters, or in chains. The cyanobacteria are colonial, with membranous photosynthetic lamellae, and can fix nitrogen (Chapter 20).

THE EUKARYOTES

All other organisms. Membrane-bounded cellular organelles, linear chromosomes join protein. Cell division by mitosis and meiosis, sexual reproduction common. Any flagella or cilia are microtubular. Single-celled, colonial, and multicellular.

KINGDOM PROTISTA Includes photosynthetic, plantlike (algal) and heterotrophic, animal-like (protozoan) forms. Primarily single-celled or colonial (Chapter 21).

PHYLUM PYRROPHYTA (1100 species; "fire algae," the dinoflagellates): Single-celled, flagellated, chitinous cell walls, phototrophic.

PHYLUM EUGLENOPHYTA (800 species; euglenoids): Single-celled, flagellated, flexible body wall, phototrophs or heterotrophs reproduce mitotically.

PHYLUM CHRYSOPHYTA (11,500 species; yellow-green and golden-brown algae): Single-celled or colonial, glass walls, phototrophic.

PHYLUM MASTIGOPHORA (2500 species; flagellated protozoans): Single-celled, heterotrophic.

PHYLUM SARCODINA (11,500 species; amoeboid protozoans): Single-celled, phagocytic heterotrophs; includes marine radiolarians and foraminiferans.

PHYLUM SPOROZOA (6000 species; nonmotile protozoans): Single-celled, parasitic spore formers.

PHYLUM CILIOPHORA (7200 species; ciliated protozoans): Single-celled, extremely complex and diverse heterotrophs.

PHYLUM ACRASIOMYCOTA (26 species; cellular slime molds): Heterotrophic, individual amoebae that live alone or join to form multicellular plasmodia.

PHYLUM MYXOMYCOTA (450 species; acellular slime molds): Heterotrophic, form multinucleate feeding plasmodia.

KINGDOM FUNGI Multicellular heterotrophs, including reducers and parasites. Extracellular digestion. Mycelial organization that may or may not include cell walls. Either sexual or asexual spores; primarily haploid with brief diploid stage (Chapter 21).

PHYLUM OOMYCETES (475 species; water molds): Flagellated fungi, many parasitic.

PHYLUM ZYGOMYCETES (600 species; bread molds): Mycelium without cell end walls; simple sexual zygospore.

PHYLUM ASCOMYCETES (30,000 species; sac fungi): Extensive mycelium with cell end walls. Complex sexual dikaryotic asci, ascospores produced through meiosis. Many species symbiotic with cyanobacteria or algae, forming *lichens*.

PHYLUM BASIDIOMYCETES (25,000 species; club fungi): Extensive mycelium with cell end walls. Large, combasidiocarp in which basidiospores are produced.

PHYLUM DEUTEROMYCETES (also, *Fungi Imperfecti*) (25,000 species): Various fungi with no known sexual stage.

KINGDOM PLANTAE Primarily nonmotile, multicellular organisms with dense cell walls of cellulose. Specialized tissues and organs. Most phototrophic. Alternating generations (Chapter 22).

NON-VASCULAR PLANTS

DIVISION RHODOPHYTA (4000 species; red algae): Coastal seaweeds, floridean or carageenan as storage carbohydrates.

DIVISION PHAEOPHYTA (1000 species; brown algae): Coastal seaweeds and kelps, fucoxanthin pigments, laminarin and mannitol storage carbohydrates. Often large, some with vascular tissue.

DIVISION CHLOROPHYTA (7000 species; green algae): Single-celled, colonial, and multicellular, pigments mostly chlorophylls and carotenoids, usually aquatic.

DIVISION CHAROPHYTA (250 species; stoneworts): Freshwater alga with apical growth, calcareous cell walls.

DIVISION BRYOPHYTA (16,000 species; mosses, liverworts, hornworts): Multicellular, nonvascular, terrestrial. Simple aerial spore, motile sperm, predominant gametophyte. Generally small with little supportive tissue.

VASCULAR PLANTS

DIVISION TRACHEOPHYTA (vascular plants): Vascular tissue in roots, stems, and/or leaves. Predominant sporophyte; some with distinct generations.

CLASS PSILOPHYTA (4 species; whisk ferns): Simple, with few surviving species. Vascular stem, scalelike leaves. Aerial spore, motile sperm, distinct sporophyte and gametophyte.

CLASS LYCOPHYTA (1000 species; club mosses): Vascular roots, stems, and leaves. Usually with aerial spore, motile sperm, and distinct sporophyte and gametophyte.

CLASS SPHENOPHYTA (12 species; horsetails): One surviving genus, upright vascular stems, prominent nodes and tiny, scalelike nonphotosynthetic leaves. Aerial spore, motile sperm, and distinct sporophyte and gametophyte.

CLASS PTEROPHYTA (11,000 species; ferns): Most with aerial spore, motile sperm, predominant sporophyte, photosynthetic gametophyte, and vascular roots, stems, and leaves.

VASCULAR PLANTS WITH SEEDS

SUBDIVISION SPERMATOPHYTES (seed plants): Gametophytes develop within sporophyte tissue, male and female spores produced, and microspores released within pollen grains. Embryo develops within seed that includes stored foods and protective seed coats.

SUPER CLASS GYMNOSPERMAE (naked seeds)

CLASS CYCADOPHYTA (100 species; the cycads): Palmlike leaves, exposed seeds, wind-dispersed pollen, flagellated sperm within pollen tube.

CLASS GINKGOPHYTA (1 species; ginkgo): Trees with fan-shaped leaves, exposed seeds, wind-dispersed pollen, motile sperm within pollen tube.

CLASS CONIFEROPHYTA (500 species): Usually large trees with needlelike or scalelike leaves. Evergreens, exposed seeds borne upon cones, nonmotile sperm.

CLASS GNETOPHYTA (71 species): Gymnosperms with angiosperm features: xylem vessels, pollen cones. Exposed seeds, nonmotile sperm.

SUPERCLASS ANGIOSPERMAE (flowering plants): Flowers present, seeds enclosed by fruit, xylem vessels present. Nonmotile sperm.

CLASS DICOTYLEDONEAE (200,000 species; the dicots): Diverse, net-veined leaves, secondary growth common, floral parts in fours, fives, or multiples of these, two cotyledons.

CLASS MONOCOTYLEDONEAE (50,000 species; the monocots): Diverse, parallel-veined leaves, secondary growth rare, floral parts in threes or multiples of threes, one cotyledon.

KINGDOM ANAMALIA
Multicellular, heterotrophic eukaryotes. Specialized tissues, most with organ systems. Most highly responsive. Diploid except for gametes. Fertilization without intervening haploid life cycle. Small, flagellated sperm and large stationary egg typical (Chapters 27–30).

SUBKINGDOM PARAZOA animals of flagellate origins, simple developmental progression.

PHYLUM PORIFERA (5000 species; the sponges): Forms tissues. Nonmotile adults, filter feeding, skeletal elements of calcium carbonate, silicon dioxide, or spongin. Asexual reproduction by budding, sexual reproduction by fertilization of internalized egg (Chapter 27).

SUBKINGDOM METAZOA Animals of ciliate origin; includes all animals except Porifera.

RADIATE, ACOELOMATE PHYLA
(radial symmetry, no coelom, diploblastic)

PHYLUM COELENTERATA (9000 species): Radial body of two cell layers, saclike gastrovascular cavity, tentacles and stinging cells. May alternate between medusa and polyp stages, or only one stage may be present. Three classes: Hydrozoa (hydroids), Scyphozoa (jellyfish), Anthozoa (corals and anemones) (Chapter 27).

PHYLUM CTENOPHORA (90 species; comb jellies): Radial body of two cell layers. Tentacles with glue cells (Chapter 27).

BILATERAL, ACOELOMATE PHYLA
(bilateral symmetry, no coelom triploblastic)

PHYLUM PLATYHELMINTHES (13,000 species; flatworms): Flattened body, branching gastrovascular cavity, dense bodies with many cell layers. Three classes: Turbellaria (free-living planarians), Trematoda, and Cestoda (parasitic flukes and tapeworms) (Chapter 27).

THE BILATERAL, PSEUDOCOELOMATE PHYLA
(bilateral symmetry, pseudocoelom)

PHYLUM ASCHELMINTHES (12,000 species named—estimated half million unnamed; the roundworms and rotifers): Class Nematoda (roundworms) includes free-living and parasitic species; slender body, pseudocoelom (not completely mesodermally lined), tube-within-tube body plan (complete gut). Class Rotifera (rotifers), free-living, minute, with complex organ systems (Chapter 27).

PHYLUM NEMATOMORPHA (230 species; horsehair worms)

PHYLUM RYNCHOCOELA (650 species; proboscis or ribbon worms)

THE BILATERAL, COELOMATE, PROTOSTOME PHYLA
(bilateral symmetry, true coelom, embryologically "mouth-first" animals)

PHYLUM ANNELIDA (9,000 species; segmented worms): Body subdivided into repeating segments, true coelom, well-developed digestive system, closed circulatory system. Three classes: Oligochaeta (earthworms), Hirudinea (leeches), and Polychaeta (marine worms) (Chapter 28).

PHYLUM PRIAPULIDA   (9 species; proboscis worms)

PHYLUM POGONOPHORA   (100 species; beard worms)

PHYLUM SIPUNCULA   (300 species; peanut worms)

PHYLUM TARTIGRADA   (350 species; water bears)

PHYLUM ARTHROPODA   (800,000 to 1,000,000 species; "jointed-footed" animals): Paired, jointed appendages with chitinous exoskeleton, varied segmentation, wide distribution (Chapter 28).

> **Subphylum Chelicerata** Six pairs of appendages, four pairs being legs, with paired chelicerae (fangs). Three classes: Meristomata (horseshoe crabs), Arachnida (spiders, ticks, scorpions, mites, daddy-longlegs), and Pycnogonida (sea spiders).

> **Subphylum Mandibulata** Most with three pairs of walking legs, mandibles, compound eyes, antennas, some with wings. Four classes: Crustacea (aquatic with crusty exoskeleton, gills). Chilopoda (centipedes), Diplopoda (millipedes), and Insecta (insects—commonly three pairs of legs, wings at some time, three-part body, specialized mouth parts).

PHYLUM ONYCOPHORA   (70 species; *Peripatus):* Possessing both annelid and arthropod characteristics.

PHYLUM MOLLUSCA   (47,000 species): Controversial classification—segmentation and coelom may not exist. Diversification through modifications of head, foot, mantle, and radula. Includes seven classes: Aplacaphora (solenogasters—wormlike, radula only clear characteristic), Monoplacophora (*Neopalina*, deep-sea form, believed to be extinct), Scaphopoda (tooth shells), Polyplacophora (chitons), Bivalvia (bivalves: two shells—clams, etc.), Gastropoda (snails, slugs), and Cephalopoda (octopus, squid—rather intelligent, fast, predators, foot subdivided into tentacles. Covering mantle, large brain, keen eyesight (Chapter 28).

PHYLUM BRACHIOPODA   (250 species; lampshells): Appear similar to bivalves, but shell mounted differently, lopophore (ring of ciliated tentacles) present (Chapter 28).

PHYLUM PHORONIDA   (18 species): Lopophore present.

PHYLUM ECTOPROCTA   (4000 species; moss animals or bryozoans): Lopophore present.

THE BILATERAL, COELOMATE, DEUTEROSTOME PHYLA
(bilateral symmetry, true coelom, embryologically "mouth second")

PHYLUM ECHINODERMATA   (6000 species): Spiny, skinned animals, five-part radial symmetry as adults, bilateral larvae, endoskeleton, water vascular system. Five classes: Crinoidia (sea lilies), Holothuroidia (sea cucumbers), Echinoidea (sea urchins, sand dollars), Asteroidea (sea stars, basket stars), and Ophiuroidea (serpent stars, brittle stars) (Chapter 28).

PHYLUM HEMICHORDATA   (80 species; acorn worms): Gill slits show relatedness to chordates (Chapter 28).

PHYLUM CHORDATA   (43,000 species): Gill slits, notochord, postanal tail, dorsal hollow nerve cord all present at some time (Chapters 28–30).

> **Subphylum Urochordata**   (1300 species; sea squirts): chordate characteristics seen mainly in bilateral.

> **Subphylum Cephalochordata**   (28 species; lancelet): fishlike body, permanent notochord and gill slits, filter feeder.

> **Subphylum Vertebrata**   (41,700 species; the vertebrates): Vertebral column of bone or cartilage, heads well developed, ventral heart, dorsal aorta, two pairs of limbs. Seven classes: the fishes: Agnatha (jawless fishes), Chondrichthyes (cartilagenous fishes: sharks, rays, chimera), and Osteichthyes (bony fishes). Also, Amphibia (frogs, toads, salamanders), Reptilia (reptiles), Aves (birds), and Mammalia (mammals).

Careers in Biology

Biology is the study of life; that's a pretty wide-ranging definition. Active work in the field can encompass everything from finding a cure for cancer to protecting tropical rain forests. It can mean helping humanity to reach the stars or understand the ocean depths. When you design an experiment that turns out right, "you've discovered a piece of the truth," as one biologist puts it. We hope that this text has given you a greater appreciation of the miracle of your own life and of the many plant and animal lives around (and inside) you. The frontiers of science are expanding every day, and important work is being done in every area of biology.

To get an idea of the types of careers open to biology majors, consider that in 1980, 33% of life scientists were engaged in research and development for universities, government agencies, and private industry; 20% held management or administrative positions; 20% were college instructors; and 27% worked as consultants to business or government or in technical or service positions (*Occupational Outlook for College Graduates*, 1980). Most life scientists work in fields that relate to biology, agriculture, or medicine. It has been estimated that more than 11,000 life science graduates will be needed to fill various positions *each year* until 1995. They will focus on such areas of growing biological and social concern as aging, disease, food supplies, waste disposal, pollution, genetic engineering, and even criminal behavior. The following list just begins to illustrate the variety of career opportunities in the life sciences.

Agronomist	Nurse
Archeologist	Optometrist
Bacteriologist	Osteopath
Bioillustrator	Paramedic
Biostatistician	Park ranger or warden
Brewmaster	Pharmacist
Dentist	Physical or occupational
Dietitian	therapist
Environmental planner or	Physician
manager	Plant pest control inspector
Field ecologist	Range manager
Food processing manager	Recreation manager
Forester	Resource policy analyst
Forest products technolo-	Science writer
gist	Teacher
Greenhouse manager	Veterinarian
Horticulturist or gardener	Waste disposal engineer
Laboratory immunologist	Water quality controller
Marine scientist or engineer	Wildlife conservation and
Medical technologist	management specialist
Museum curator	

For further information, consult with the life science departments at your school, read the following booklets, or write to the organizations listed here.

From Superintendent of Documents, U.S. Government Printing Office, Washington, DC 20025:

> *Federal Career Directory: A Guide for College Students*
> *Occupational Outlook Handbook Bulletin 1550* (annual editions)
> *Biological Scientists: Occupational Outlook Bulletin 1550–8*
> *Careers in the U.S. Department of the Interior, Publication #3*

From American Medical Association, 535 N. Dearborn, Chicago, IL 60610:

> *Helping Hands: Horizons Unlimited in Medicine*

Each of these groups publishes a career booklet, all of which can be obtained from: Federation of American Societies for Experimental Biology, 9650 Rockville Pike, Bethesda, MD 20014:

> American Association of Immunologists
> American Institute of Nutrition
> American Physiological Society
> American Society of Biological Chemists
> American Society for Experimental Pathology
> American Society for Pharmacology and Experimental Therapeutics

Write to these organizations for additional information.

American Association for the Advancement of Science
1515 Massachusetts Ave., N.W.
Washington, DC 20005

American Institute of Biological Sciences
1401 Wilson Blvd.
Arlington, VA 22209

American Society of Cell Biology
c/o Nancy Bucher, M.D.
Huntington Laboratories
Massachusetts General Hospital
Boston, MA 02114

American Society of Plant Physiologists
9650 Rockville Pike
Bethesda, MD 20014

American Society of Zoologists
Box 2739
California Lutheran College
Thousand Lakes, CA 91360

Biosciences Information Service
2100 Arch St.
Philadelphia, PA 19103

Botanical Society of America
New York Botanical Garden
Bronx, NY 10458

Ecological Society of America
c/o Ralph Good
Biology Department
Rutgers University
Camden, NJ 08102

Genetics Society of America
P.O. Box 6018
Rockville, MD 20850

American Society for Microbiology
Publications Office
1913 I St., N.W.
Washington, DC 20006

Glossary

Pronunciation Key

The pronunciation of each word appears just after the word. The letters and signs used are pronounced as in the words below. The mark ′ is placed after the syllable with the primary or heavy accent; the mark ′ is placed after the syllable with the secondary, or lighter accent.

a	hat	o	hot	th	thin
ā	age	ō	open	TH	then
ä	far	ô	order	z	zero, breeze
ch	child	oi	oil	zh	measure
e	let	ou	out	ə	represents:
ē	equal	u	cup		a in about
ėr	term	ů	put		e in taken
i	it	ü	rule		i in pencil
ī	ice	s	say, yes		o in lemon
ng	long	sh	she		u in circus

A band (ā′ band) a band of striated muscle corresponding to the region of myosin filaments.

abscisic acid (ab sis′ik as′id) hormone that causes leaves to separate from a plant.

absorption spectrum (ab sôrp′shən spek′trəm) a graph indicating the wavelengths of light absorbed by a molecule.

accessory pigments (ak ses′ər ē pig′mənts) the carotenes, a family of pigments that aid in absorbing light energy in the light-harvesting antennas.

acetyl CoA (ə sē′tl kō ā′) an intermediate compound in cell respiration, to which most fuels are converted before entering the Krebs (citric acid) cycle.

acid (as′id) a proton donor that yields hydrogen ions in water; a compound capable of neutralizing bases and of lowering the pH of solutions.

actin (ak′tən) a cytoplasmic protein and a constituent of muscle, known in both globular and fibrous forms. See also *myofilaments*.

action potential (ak′shən pə ten′shəl) in a neuron, a traveling, depolarizing wave; a short-lived change in membrane potential that produces a neural impulse or, in a muscle, contraction. Compare *resting potential*.

action spectrum (ak′shən spek′trəm) a graph relating light-induced biological activity (for example, carbon fixation or oxygen release in photosynthesis) to the wavelengths of visible light (or to other electromagnetic energy).

active site (ak′tiv sīt) the part of an enzyme that interacts directly with the substrate molecule.

active transport (ak′tiv tran′spôrt) transport of a substance across the cell membrane, usually against the concentration gradient, that requires energy.

adaptation (ad ap tā′shən) any alteration in the structure or function of an organism that is maintained by natural selection, through which the organism becomes better able to survive and reproduce in its environment.

adaptive radiation (a dap′tiv rā′dē ā′shən) evolutionary divergence of two or more species from an ancestral form with the establishment of new, more specialized niches.

adenine (ad′n ēn) a purine, one of the nitrogenous bases found in both DNA and RNA, as well as in ATP and several coenzymes.

ADP (adenosine diphosphate) (ə den′ə sēn′ dī fos′ fāt) a compound of adenine, ribose, and *two* phosphate groups; a degraded form of ATP.

adhesion (ad hē′zhən) the attraction between two dissimilar substances, such as a solid and a liquid.

aerobic (er′ō′bik) *adj.* requiring oxygen.

aggregate fruit (ag′rə git früt) a fruit developing from multiple carpels of the same flower.

allantois (ə lan′tō is) one of the extraembryonic membranes; in birds and reptiles it serves as a repository for the embryo's nitrogenous wastes.

allele (ə lēl′) a particular form of a gene at a gene locus.

allopatric speciation (al′ə pat′rək spē′shē ā′shən) formation of new species from populations that are geographically separated. Compare *sympatric speciation*.

allotetraploid (al′ə tet′rə ploid) *adj.* derived from the hybridization of two distinct species, carrying the full diploid chromosome complements of both. See also *autotetraploid, polyploid, tetraploid*.

alternation of generations (ôl tər nā′shən uv jen′ə rā′shənz) The existence in the life cycle of an individual of a haploid (1N) gametophyte stage that alternates with a diploid (2N) sporophyte stage. The haploid gametophyte produces gametes by *mitosis;* upon fertilization, the diploid sporophyte emerges. It produces haploid spores through *meiosis*, starting a new gametophyte generation.

alveolus (al vē′ə ləs) (pl. *alveoli*) one of the air sacs that occur in grapelike clusters at the ends of bronchioles in the vertebrate lung. Alveolar walls contain dense capillaries where gas exchange occurs.

amino acid (ə mē′nō as′id) **1.** any organic molecule of the general formula R–CH(NH2)COOH, having both acidic and basic properties. **2.** any of the 20 molecular subunits that make up protein.

amnion (am′nē ən) the innermost extraembryonic membrane of reptiles, birds, and mammals.

amoeboid movement (ə mē′boid müv′mənt) cellular movement by pseudopods; movement whereby regions in the cell soften and the liquid cytoplasm flows into those regions. See also *phagocytosis*.

anabolism (ə nab′ə liz′əm) metabolic activity that results in the chemical building up of molecules. See also *catabolism*.

anaerobic (an′ə rō′bik) *adj.* in the absence of oxygen.

anaerobic fermentation (an′ə rō′bik fėr′men tā′shən) part of cell respiration: the enzymatic breakdown of glucose, in the absence of oxygen, to form alcohol and carbon dioxide or other energy-rich waste products.

analogue (an′l og) in comparative morphology, a structure similar to another in form or function but derived from different evolutionary or embryonic precursors (for example, the wings of an insect and a bird).

anaphase (an′ə fāz) **1.** the stage of mitosis or meiosis II in which the centromeres divide and separate and the two daughter chromosomes travel to opposite poles of the cell. **2.** anaphase I of meiosis, the stage at which the chromosomal tetrads part and the homologous centromeres of each pair travel to opposite poles of the spindle.

angiosperm (an′jē ə spėrm′) a plant in which the seeds are enclosed in an ovary; a flowering plant.

annual plant (an′yü əl plant) a plant that completes its life cycle —germination, growth, reproduction, and death—within a year. Compare *biennial, perennial*.

annual rings (an′yü əl ringz) the concentric rings seen in the cross-section of a woody stem, each of which corresponds to one season's growth.

antagonist (an tag′ə nist) one of a pair of skeletal muscles (or one of two groups of muscles) whose actions cooperatively oppose one another.

anterior (an tir′ē ər) in bilateral organisms, toward the head end. Compare *posterior*.

anther (an′thər) in a flower, the pollen-producing organ of the stamen.

antheridium (an′thə rid′ē əm) (pl. *antheridia*) in plants, a male reproductive organ that produces and stores motile sperm.

antibody (an′ti bod′ē) a protein molecule of the immune system that can recognize and bind to a foreign substance or invader (such as a bacterium or virus). See also *immunoglobulin*.

anticodon (an′ti kō′don) a region of a tRNA molecule consisting of three sequential nucleotides that will have a matching codon in mRNA.

antigen (an′tə jen) **1.** any large molecule, such as a cell-surface protein or carbohydrate, that stimulates the production of specific antibodies or that binds specifically with such antibodies. **2.** any antibody-specific site on such a molecule.

anus (ā′nəs) the posterior opening of the digestive tract (gut), through which digestive wastes are eliminated.

aorta (ā ôr′tə) in vertebrates, the principal or largest artery; it carries oxygenated blood from the heart to the body.

aphotic zone (ā′fō′tik zōn) "without light"; in a body of water, the depth to which light never penetrates.

apical meristem (ā′pə kəl mer′ə stem) the undifferentiated tissue at the stem and root tip that contributes cells for primary growth.

appendicular skeleton (a′pen dik′yə lər skel′ə tən) in vertebrates, bones of the pectoral and pelvic girdles and of the appendages. Compare *axial skeleton*.

arboreal (är bôr′ē əl) *adj.* dwelling in trees.

Archebacteria (är′kə bak tir′ē ə) one of the two prokaryote kingdoms (or phyla in some schemes); it contains primitive bacteria such as methanogens (methane producers), thermophiles (heat lovers), and acidophiles (acid lovers). See also *Eubacteria*.

archegonium (är kə gō′nē əm) (pl. *archegonia*) the female (egg-producing) reproductive structure in the gametophytes of ferns and bryophytes.

arteriole (är tir′ē ōl) a small artery, usually giving rise directly to capillaries.

arteriosclerosis (är tir′ē ō sklə rō′sis) a chronic disease characterized by thickening, hardening, and loss of elasticity of the arterial walls.

artery (är′tər ē) a vessel carrying blood away from the heart, toward a capillary bed.

artificial selection (är′tə fish′əl si lek′shən) the intentional selection (by humans) of domesticated animals or plants for breeding according to desired characteristics. See also *natural selection*.

ascus (as′kəs) (pl. *asci*) in ascomycetes, the sac in which meiosis occurs and in which four or eight ascospores are subsequently formed.

asters (as′tərz) paired, radiating mitotic structures, each consisting of microtubules and microfilaments radiating like a "starburst" from a centriole. Asters are formed during mitosis and meiosis in all animal and in many other eukaryotic cells.

atherosclerosis (ath'ər ō sklə rō'sis) a form of arteriosclerosis characterized by fatty deposits (plaques) in the inner lining of the arterial walls.

atom (at'əm) the smallest indivisible unit of an element still retaining the element's characteristics.

atomic mass (ə tom'ik mas) the average mass of the atoms of an element; also called *atomic weight*.

atomic nucleus (ə tom'ik nü'klē əs) the central part of an atom containing the protons and neutrons, most of the mass of an atom.

atomic number (ə tom'ik num'bər) the number of protons in an atomic nucleus, specific to each element.

ATP (adenosine triphosphate) (ə den'ə sēn' trī fos'fāt) a common molecule involved in many biological energy-exchange reactions; it consists of the nitrogenous base adenine, the sugar ribose, and *three* phosphate groups joined by two energy-rich bonds.

autoimmune disease (ô'tō imyün' də zēz') an abnormal condition in which the organism's immune system attacks and destroys one or more of the organism's own tissues.

autonomic nervous system (ô'tə nom'ik nèr'vəs sis'təm) the system of nerves and their ganglia arising from the brain and spinal cord and controlling involuntary functions, chiefly in the internal organs. Compare *somatic nervous system*.

autosome (ô'tə sōm) any chromosome other than a sex (**X** or **Y**) chromosome.

autotetraploid (ô tə tet'rə ploid) *adj.* having four homologues of each chromosome type, derived from chromosomal duplication without cell division in a diploid organism. See also *allotetraploid, polyploid, tetraploid*.

autotroph (ô'tə trof) an organism capable of using simple compounds (such as carbon dioxide) as its only source of carbon, and sunlight or simple inorganic compounds as its only source of energy. See also *chemotroph* and *heterotroph*.

axial skeleton (ak'sē əl skel'e tən) in vertebrates, the skull, vertebral column, and bones of the chest. Compare *appendicular skeleton*.

axon (ak'son) the extension of a neuron that conducts nerve impulses away from the cell body.

bacillus (bə sil'əs) **1.** an aerobic, rod-shaped, spore-producing bacterium of the genus *Bacillus*. **2.** any rod-shaped bacterium.

bacteria (bak tir'ē ə) (sing. *bacterium*) prokaryotes; minute, single-celled and colonial organisms from the kingdom *Archebacteria* or *Eubacteria*, often associated with disease ("germs").

bacteriophage (bak tir'ē ə fāj) a virus that infects and disintegrates bacteria.

bark (bärk) the portion of a stem outside of the wood consisting of cambium, phloem, cortex, epidermis, cork cambium, and cork; everything from the vascular cambium outward.

Barr body (bär bod'ē) a dark-staining feature in the nuclei of the cells of female mammals, representing the condensed **X** chromosome.

basal body (bā'səl bod'ē) a structure found beneath each eukaryotic flagellum or cilium, consisting of a circle of nine short triplets of microtubles.

basal metabolic rate (bā'səl met'ə bol'ik rāt) a measure of oxygen consumption per minute per kilogram of an individual at rest.

base (bās) **1.** *(a)* a compound that reacts with an acid to form a salt; *(b)* a substance that releases hydroxide ions (OH⁻) when dissolved in water; **2.** a nitrogenous base (purine or pyrimidine) of nucleic acids.

base pairing (bās par'ing) the specific manner in which the nitrogenous bases of nucleic acids pair up and form hydrogen bonds: adenine always opposes thymine (A-T or T-A) and cytosine always opposes guanine (C-G or G-C).

basidiocarp (bə sid'ē ō kärp') the spore-producing organ in the *Basidiomycetes*; a mushroom.

basidium (bə sid'ē əm) (pl. *basidia*) the meiotic cell of *Basidiomycetes* such as mushrooms; it produces basidiospores by budding.

B-cell (bē'sel) a lymphoid cell that matures in the bone marrow (mammals) or bursa of Fabricius (birds) and later circulates in the blood; involved in the immune response, especially in the production of free antibodies. See also *T-cell*.

berry (ber'ē) a simple fruit, including a fleshy ovary and one or more carpels and seeds.

biennial (bī en'ē əl) a flowering plant that lives for two years, producing flowers and seed in the second. Compare *annual, perennial*.

bilateral symmetry (bī lat'ər əl sim'ə trē) having left and right sides that are approximate mirror images; having a single plane of symmetry.

bile (bīl) a bitter-tasting, highly pigmented, alkaline liquid secreted by the liver, containing bile salts and bile pigments, that functions in fat digestion.

binomial system (bī nō'mē əl sis'təm) the tradition (introduced by Linnaeus) that each organism is given a Latin taxonomic name consisting of a generic term and a specific term (genus and species).

biome (bī'ōm) an array of plants and animals distributed over a geographic area that has distinctive climatic conditions.

bipedal (bī ped'əl) *adj.* "two-footed"; walking on two feet.

blastocyst (blas'tə sist) the hollow, blastulalike embryonic stage in a mammal, including the inner cell mass and the trophoblast.

blastula (blas'chə lə) an early embryonic stage in mammals, consisting of a single layer of cells that forms a hollow ball enclosing a central cavity, the blastocoel.

body stalk (bod'ē stôk) in embryology, the connection between the early embryo and the extraembryonic tissues; later the body stalk becomes the umbilical cord.

Bohr effect (bôr ə fekt') the accelerated release of oxygen by hemoglobin when carbon dioxide is present.

bronchiole (brong'kē ōl) a minute airway in the lung that is a small branch of a bronchus and part of the respiratory tree.

bronchus (brong'kəs) (pl. *bronchi*) either of the two main branches of the trachea.

bryophyte (brī'ə fīt) a moss, liverwort, or hornwort of the division *Bryophyta*.

buffer (buf'ər) a solution of chemical compounds capable of neutralizing both acids and bases, thus resisting change in pH.

bulk flow (bulk flō) The movement of water or another liquid brought about by pressure or gravity, generally from areas of greater water potential to areas of lesser water potential.

bundle sheath (bun'dl shēth) one or more layers of compactly arranged parenchyma cells that enclose the small veins in a leaf.

calorie (kal'ər ē) **1.** *small calorie* (calorie proper), the amount of heat (or equivalent chemical energy) needed to raise the temperature of one gram (roughly one milliliter) of water of 1˚C. **2.** *large calorie, kilocalorie* (1000 small calories), the heat needed to raise the temperature of a kilogram of water by 1˚C.

Calvin cycle (kal'vən sī'kəl) the biochemical cycle in photosynthesis in which carbon dioxide, with the aid of NADPH and ATP, is fixed into carbohydrate.

cambium (kam'bē əm) undifferentiated meristematic tissue in a plant, including *cork cambium, procambium*, and *vascular cambium*.

capillary (kap'ə ler'ē) small blood vessels (with walls one cell thick) in which exchanges between the blood and tissues occur. Capillaries are located between arterioles and venules.

carbohydrate (kär'bō hī'drāt) a class of organic compounds with the empirical formula $(CH_2O)_n$, characterized by many –OH and –H side groups and an aldehyde or ketone group; sugars, starches, cellulose, and chitin.

cardiac muscle (kär'dē ak mus'əl) specialized involuntary muscle of the heart whose fibers are striated and branching.

carnivore (kär'nə vôr) an organism that eats animals.

carotene (kar'ə tēn) a red or orange pigment, found in most plants as an accessory photosynthetic pigment.

carpel (kär'pəl) in flowers, a simple pistil, or a single member of a compound pistil; one sector or chamber of a compound fruit.

cartilage (kär'tl ij) a firm, elastic, flexible, translucent type of connective tissue; in development, a precursor of bone formation.

Casparian strip (ka sper'ē ən strip) a waxy, waterproof strip on cell walls of root-tip endoderm that permits some active control of water uptake by directing incoming water through the cytoplasm of the endodermal cells.

catabolism (kə tab'ə liz'əm) metabolic activity that results in the chemical breakdown of molecules and the release of their energy. See also *anabolism*.

catalyst (kat'list) an agent that greatly accelerates a chemical reaction, while not being permanently altered itself.

cell (sel) the structural unit of life, consisting of metabolically active cytoplasm and hereditary macromolecules (DNA and RNA), the entire complex enclosed in a semipermeable membrane. See also *eukaryote* and *prokaryote*.

cell body (sel bod'ē) the region of a neuron containing the cell nucleus and most of the cytoplasm and organelles.

cell cycle (sel sī'kəl) the typical cycling events in the life of a cell, including the G1, S, G2, and M phases.

cell division (sel də vizh'ən) in a general sense, both nuclear (mitosis or meiosis) and cytoplasmic division; more specifically, the division of cytoplasm. See also *cytokinesis*.

cell membrane (sel mem'brān) the semipermeable membrane that surrounds all cells and consists of a double layer of phospholipids, with proteins, glycoproteins, and glycolipids interspersed in a mosaic arrangement; also called *plasma membrane*.

cellular differentiation (sel'yə lar dif'ə ren shē ə'shən) during development, the commitment of immature cells or tissues to a specific morphological and functional type.

cell wall (sel wôl) the semi-rigid enclosure of a plant, fungal, algal, or bacterial cell that gives it support and a definite shape.

central dogma (sen'trəl dôg'mə) the proposition that all biological information is encoded in DNA, transmitted through DNA replication, transcribed into RNA, and translated into protein. (The term was coined by Francis Crick.)

central nervous system (sen'trəl nèr'vəs sis'təm) in vertebrates, the brain and spinal cord, to which sensory impulses are transmitted and from which motor impulses are sent.

centriole (sen'trē ōl) a paired, microtubular organelle in animals, protists, fungi, and lower plant cells; absent (or invisible) in the cells of seed plants.

centromere (sen'trə mir) the specialized region of a chromosome to which spindle fibers are attached; also called *kinetochore*.

cephalochordate (sef′ə lə kôr′dāt) "head cord animal"; a lancelet (*Branchiostoma*) of a chordate subphylum in which the notochord persists throughout life and extends through what would be the head if it had one.

cerebellum (ser′ə bel′əm) the double walnut-shaped portion of the hindbrain that coordinates voluntary movement, posture, and balance.

cerebrospinal fluid (sə rē′brō spī′nl flü′id) a cushioning fluid that surrounds the spinal cord and the ventricles of the brain.

cerebrum (sə rē′brəm) the anterior portion of the vertebrate brain; the largest portion in humans, consisting of two *cerebral hemispheres* and controlling many localized functions, among them voluntary movement, perception, speech, memory, and thought.

CF1 particle (pär′tə kəl) an enzyme-containing body on the outer surface of the thylakoid, where the energy of the electrochemical proton gradient is put to work in chemiosmotic phosphorylation.

C4 plant (sē fôr′ plant) a plant in which carbon dioxide is fixed into four-carbon compounds in leaf mesophyll cells, transported to the bundle sheath cells, and released and concentrated for the Calvin cycle in chloroplasts there. Compare *C3 plant*.

Chargaff's rule (chär′gofs rül) Chargaff determined that, in the DNA of all species tested, the amount of adenine present was always equal to the amount of thymine, and the amount of cytosine equal to the amount of guanine.

charging enzyme (chärj′ing en′zīm) any of a group of specific enzymes that covalently link amino acids to their appropriate tRNAs, thus charging the tRNAs.

chemical bond energy (kem′ə kəl bond en′ər jē) the potential energy invested in the formation of a chemical bond or released, and available for work, upon its dissolution.

chemiosmosis (kem′ē oz mō′sis) the process in mitochondria, chloroplasts, and aerobic bacteria in which an electron transport system uses the energy of photosynthesis or oxidation to pump hydrogen ions across a membrane, resulting in an electrochemical proton concentration gradient, or chemiosmotic differential, that can be used to produce ATP.

chemiosmotic differential (kem′ē oz mot′ik dif′ə ren′shəl) the electrochemical proton gradient produced by the active transport and sequestering of protons in the chloroplast or mitochondrion, whereby an electrical or pH gradient is established. The great free energy of the differential is used to power ATP synthesis.

chemiosmotic phosphorylation (kem′ē oz mot′ik fo′sfər ə la′shən) the phosphorylation (production) of ADP using the free energy of the chemiosmotic differential in the CF1 and F1 particles.

chemoreceptor (kēm′ō ri sep′tər) a neural receptor sensitive to a specific chemical or class of chemicals.

chemotroph (kem′ə trōf) an organism that lives on the energy of inorganic chemical reactions. See also *autotroph* and *heterotroph*.

chiasmata (ki ag′mə tə) (sing. chiasma) after repulsion during prophase I of meiosis, X-shaped points of residual connection between homologous chromatids; they are believed to represent prior crossover events.

chitin (kīt′n) a structural carbohydrate that is the principle organic component of arthropod exoskeletons.

chlorophyll (klôr′ə fil) a green photosynthetic pigment found in chloroplasts and in photosynthetic prokaryotes. It occurs in several forms, *Chlorophyll a, b,* and *c*.

chloroplasts (klôr′ə plasts) photosynthetic organelles (plastids) common in plants and algal protists; numerous internal membranous thylakoids containing photosystems with chlorophyll, electron/proton transport systems, and CF1 particles.

cholesterol (kə les′tə rol′) a common steroid occurring in all animal fats; a vital component of cell membranes; an important constituent of bile for fat absorption; a precursor of vitamin D; and a controversial dietary constituent.

chorion (kōr′ē on) 1. the tough covering of insect eggs. 2. the outermost extraembryonic membrane of birds, reptiles, and mammals; it contributes to formation of the placenta in placental mammals.

chorionic villi (kôr′ē on′ik vil′ī) highly branched and pouched growths of the placenta, where the fetal and maternal blood are separated by a membrane's thickness.

chromatid (krō′mə tid) in a G2 chromosome, one of the two identical chromosome replicas held together by the centromere prior to cell division.

chromatin (krō′mə tən) the substance of chromosomes—a molecular complex consisting of DNA, histones, and nonhistone chromosomal proteins.

chromatin net (krō′mə tən net) the netlike appearance of chromatin in the interphase nucleus.

chromosome (krō′mə sōm) 1. in eukaryotes, a linear DNA molecule (or two DNA molecules when replication has occurred), one centromere, and associated proteins. 2. in prokaryotes, a naked, circular DNA molecule (lacking in protein). 3. the DNA or genetic RNA molecule of a virus.

cilia (sil′ē ə) (sing. *cilium*) fine, hairlike, motile organelles found in groups on the surface of some cells; shorter and more numerous than flagella, but similar in structure, they exhibit coordinated oarlike movement.

circulatory system (sèr′kye lə tôr′ē sis′təm) the system consisting of blood-forming organs or tissues, vessels, the heart, and blood; also called *vascular system*.

cistron (sis′tron) a sequence of DNA specifying the sequence of a polypeptide chain; also called *structural gene*.

citric acid cycle (sit′rik as′id sī′kəl) see *Kreb's cycle*.

cleavage (klē′vij) cytoplasmic division of a zygote and young embryo.

cline (klīn) 1. a simple geographic gradient, or regular change, in a given character. 2. a regular change in allele frequency over geographic space.

cloaca (klō ā′kə) the common cavity into which the intestinal, urinary, and reproductive canals open in all vertebrates except placental and marsupial mammals.

clones (klōnz) a group of genetically identical organisms derived from a single individual by asexual reproduction.

closed circulatory system (klōzd sèr′kye lə tôr′ē sis′təm) a circulatory system in which the blood elements remain in blood vessels and do not leave to percolate through tissue spaces. Compare *open circulatory system*.

coacervates (kō as′ər vāts) Droplets of protein or other substances that form spontaneously in colloidal suspensions, surrounding themselves with a lipid shell; important to some theories of the origin of life.

coccus (kok′əs) (pl. *cocci*), any spherical bacterium (principally eubacteria).

codominance (kō dom′ə nəns) the individual expression of both alleles in a heterozygote.

codon (kō′don) 1. a series of three nucleotides in mRNA that specify a particular amino acid (or chain termination) in protein synthesis. 2. the colinear, complementary series of three nucleotides or nucleotide pairs in the DNA from which mRNA codon is transcribed. Also called *code group*.

coelom (sē′ləm) *true coelom*: a principal body cavity, or one of several such cavities, between the body wall and gut, entirely lined with mesodermal epithelium; compare *pseudocoelom*.

coenzyme (kō en′zīm) a small organic molecule required for an enzymatic reaction in which it is often reduced (for example, NAD, NADP, or FAD).

coevolution (kō ev′ə lü′shən) evolutionary change in one species that is influenced by the activities of another (for instance, the behavior of a predator and its prey).

cohesion (kō hē′zhən) the attraction between molecules of a single substance.

coleoptile (kō′lē op′təl) in the embryos and young shoots of grasses, a specialized tubular leaf structure that completely encloses and protects the plumule during emergence.

colinearity (kō lin′ē ar′ə tē) the principle that the linear arrangement of nucleotides in DNA corresponds to the linear arrangement of nucleotides in RNA, which in turn corresponds to the linear arrangement of amino acids in a polypeptide.

collagen (kol′ə jən) a common, tough, fibrous animal protein occurring principally in connective tissues.

collenchyma (kə leng′kə mə) in plants, a strengthening tissue; a modified parenchyma consisting of elongated cells with greatly thickened cellulose walls.

commensalism (kə men′sə liz′əm) a symbiotic relationship in which one partner benefits while the other is neither helped nor hurt. Compare *mutualism, parasitism*.

community (kə myü′nə tē) in ecology, an assemblage of interacting populations forming an identifiable group within a biome (for example, a sage desert community or a beech-maple deciduous forest community).

compact bone (kom′pakt bōn) dense, hard bone with spaces of microscopic size.

companion cell (kəm pan′yən sel) in plants, a nucleated cell adjacent to a sieve tube member and believed to assist it in its functions.

competitive exclusion (kəm pet′ə tiv ek sklü′zhən) the observation that if two different species occupy the same *ecological niche*, one will be displaced; also called *Gause's law*.

complement (kom′plə mənt) a group of blood proteins that interact with antibody-antigen complexes to destroy foreign cells.

complete dominance (kəm plēt′ dom′ə nəns) the expression of a gene with the complete lack of expression of its allele.

complete flower (kəm plēt′ flou′ər) a flower that has all of the usual floral parts present.

compound (kom′pound) in chemistry, a pure substance of a single molecular type consisting of two or more elements in a fixed ratio.

compound eye (kom′pound ī) an arthropod eye consisting of many simple eyes closely crowded together, each with an individual lens and a restricted field of vision, so that a mosaic image is formed.

conditioned stimulus (kən dish′ənd stim′yə ləs) in animal behavior, an environmental situation or condition that is normally irrelevant to a desired behavior but can come to stimulate the behavior. See also *unconditioned stimulus*.

conjugation (kon′jə gā′shən) sexual reproduction in which organisms (usually single-celled) fuse to exchange genetic material; in ciliates, a temporary cytoplasmic fusion of pairs, accompanied by meiosis and the exchange of haploid nuclei.

connective tissue (kə nek′tiv tish′ü) one of the primary animal tissues, of mesodermal origin, with scattered cells and abundant extracellular substance or interlacing fibers, usually including collagen.

consummatory behavior (kən sum′ə tôr′ē bi hā′vyər) a part of instinctive behavior that involves highly stereotyped (invariable) behavior and the performance of a fixed-action pattern (for instance, swallowing food).

continental drift (kon′tə nen′tl drift) the slow movement of the continents relative to one another on the earth's surface. See also *plate tectonics.*

continuous variation (kən tin′yü əs ver′ē ā′shən) continuous gradation in the expression of a trait where two or more pairs of alleles contribute to such expression (for example, height and skin color in humans).

contractile vacuole (kən trak′təl vak′yü ōl) an organelle of many freshwater protists that maintains the cell's osmotic equilibrium by bailing excess water through an active, ATP-powered process; also called a *water vacuole.*

control (kən trōl′) a standard of comparison in a scientific experiment; a replica of the experiment in which a possibly crucial factor being studied is omitted.

convergent evolution (kən vèr′jənt ev′ə lü′shən) the independent evolution of similar structures in distantly related organisms; often found in organisms that occur in similar ecological niches, such as marsupial moles and placental moles.

cork (kôrk) in plants, secondary tissue produced by the *cork cambium,* consisting of cells that become heavily suberized and die at maturity, resistant to the passage of moisture and gases; the outermost layer of bark.

corpus callosum (kôr′pəs kə lō′səm) a broad, white neural tract that connects the cerebral hemispheres and correlates their activities.

corpus luteum (kôr′pəs lü′tē əm) "yellow body"; a temporary endocrine body that develops in the ovarian follicle after ovulation; it secretes estrogen and progesterone, which maintain the endometrium. It continues secretion if pregnancy occurs, and regresses quickly if it does not occur.

cortex (kôr′teks) **1.** (animals) the outer layer or rind of an organ, such as the *adrenal cortex.* Compare *medulla.* **2.** (plants) the portion of stem between the epidermis and the vascular tissue.

cotyledon (kot′l ēd′n) a food-storing structure in dicot seeds, sometimes emerging as first leaves; a food-digesting organ in most monocot seeds; first leaves in a gymnosperm embryo; also called *seed leaf.*

covalent bond (kō vā′lənt bond) a relatively strong chemical bond in which an electron pair is shared by two atoms, simultaneously filling the outer electron shells of both.

cranial nerve (krā′nē əl nèrv) in humans, one of 12 pairs of major nerves that emerge directly from the brain and pass through skull openings to the body's periphery.

cranium (krā′nē əm) **1.** the skull. **2.** the part of the skull enclosing the brain.

crista (kris′tə) (pl. *cristae*) a shelflike fold of the inner mitochondrial membrane, containing numerous electron transport systems and F1 particles.

crossing over (kros′ing ō′vər) **1.** the exchange of chromatid (DNA) segments by enzymatic breakage and reunion during meiotic prophase. **2.** a specific instance of such an exchange: a crossover.

crude birth rate (krüd bèrth rāt) the number of live births per 1000 individuals in the population at midyear.

crude death rate (krüd deth rāt) the number of deaths per 1000 individuals in the population at midyear.

C3 plant (sē thrē′ plant) a plant in which carbon dioxide is fixed into carbohydrates directly in the Calvin cycle. Compare *C4 plant.*

cutin (kyüt′n) in plants, a fatty substance secreted into the outer epidermal cell walls of leaves and young stems, where it forms the cuticle.

cyanobacterium (sī′ə nō bak tir′ē əm) a photosynthetic eubacterium that uses water as a source of protons and whose cells exhibit membranous chlorophyll-containing lamellae; many are capable of nitrogen fixation; also called *cyanophyte* and *blue-green alga.*

cyclic AMP (cAMP) (sik′lik ā em pē) ("second messenger") adenosine monophosphate; synthesized in response to certain hormones arriving at the cell membrane, it stimulates further activity in the target cell.

cytochrome (sī′tə krōm) iron-containing enzymes or carrier proteins found in electron/hydrogen transport chains in the thylakoid and mitochondrion.

cytokinesis (sī′tō ki ne′səs) division of the cell cytoplasm following mitosis or meiosis.

cytoplasm (sī′tə plaz′əm) in eukaryotes, that region of the cell between the cell membrane and nuclear membrane, including the cytoplasmic organelles and matrix.

cytosine (sī′tə sēn′) a pyrimidine, one of the four nucleotide bases of DNA and RNA.

cytoskeleton (sī′tə skel′ə tən) the supporting framework within the cell; it consists of the *microtrebecular lattice, microtubules,* and *microfilaments.*

dehydration linkage (dē′hī drā′shən ling′kij) a covalent bond formed between two compounds by the removal of one oxygen atom and two hydrogens, which form water.

deletion (di lē′shən) in genetics, **1.** the removal of any segment of a chromosome or gene. **2.** the site of such a removal after chromosome healing—a mutation. **3.** the deleted chromosome.

dendrite (den′drīt) an extension of a neuron that receives impulses and conducts them toward the cell body.

denitrification (dē nī′trə fə kā′shən) the process by which microorganisms, chiefly anaerobic bacteria, convert nitrates and nitrites to nitrogen gas, resulting in a loss of soil fertility.

depolarization (dē pō′lər ə zā′shən) in neural transmission, a loss of polarization that is characteristic of the resting state; a shift in the neuron from a polarized condition (positively charged exterior and negatively charged interior) to a nonpolarized condition as a neural impulse is generated. See also *action potential.*

deuterostome (dü′tə rə stōm′) a bilateral animal (for example, an echinoderm or chordate) whose anus arises from the first embryonic opening (blastopore) and whose mouth arises later as a second embryonic opening; compare *protostome.*

diaphragm (dī′ə fram) **1.** in mammals, a dome-shaped, muscularized body partition that separates the chest and abdominal cavities and is involved in breathing movements. **2.** a birth control device; a thin rubber cup with a springlike rim that, when inserted to cover the cervix, acts as a physical barrier to sperm.

diastolic pressure (dī′ə stol′ik presh′ər) the blood pressure between the heart's contractions. See also *blood pressure* and *systolic pressure.*

dicotyledon (dī kot′l ēd′n) a flowering plant (angiosperm) of class *Dicotyledonae,* characterized by seeds with two cotyledons; also called *dicot.*

differential (dif ə ren′shəl) the difference in pH or concentration of a solute in two fluids, especially on either side of a semipermeable membrane; also called *pH* or *concentration differential.* See also *chemiosmotic differential.*

differentiation (dif′ə ren′shē ā′shən) in development, the poorly understood process whereby a cell or cell line becomes structurally or physiologically specialized.

diffusion (di fyü′zhən) the random movement of molecules of a gas or solute under thermal agitation, resulting in a net movement from regions of higher concentration to regions of lower concentration.

digestion (də jes′chən) the hydrolytic cleavage (adding of water), through enzyme action, of complex food molecules into the molecular subunits, permitting absorption to occur.

diploid (dip′loid) *adj.* having a double set of genes and chromosomes, one set originating from each parent. Compare *haploid, polyploid.*

directional selection (də rek′shə nəl si lek′shən) selection favoring one extreme of a continuous phenotypic distribution (for example, the darkest of several colors present).

disaccharide (dī sak′ə rīd′) a carbohydrate consisting of two simple sugar subunits (for example, sucrose and lactose).

disruptive selection (dis rup′tiv si lek′shən) selection that through changing or cycling conditions shifts back and forth, favoring first one end of a phenotypic range and then another.

divergent evolution (də vèr′jənt ev′ə′lü′shən) evolutionary change away from the ancestral type, with selection favoring differences in newly arising species.

DNA (deoxyribonucleic acid (de ok′sə rī′bō nü kle′ik as′id) a double-stranded nucleic acid polymer; the genetic material of all organisms (except RNA viruses).

DNA polymerase (pol′ə mə rās′) any of several enzymes or enzyme complexes that catalyze the replication of DNA.

DNA repair system (ri per′ sis′təm) a complex of enzymes that identifies and repairs any primary lesions (spontaneous changes) in the nucleotide bases of DNA.

dominance hierarchy (dom′ə nəns hī′ə rär′kē) behavioral interactions established in a troop, flock, or other species group in which every individual is dominant to those lower on the order and submissive to those above; also called *pecking order.*

dominant (dom′ə nənt) **1.** a phenotypic trait that is always expressed when a certain allele is present. **2.** *dominant allele:* one that expresses a given phenotypic trait, whether homozygous or heterozygous.

dorsal (dôr′səl) *adj.* situated near or at the back of an organism with bilateral symmetry.

dorsal hollow nerve cord (dôr′səl hol′ō nèrv kôrd) a characteristic neural structure of chordates, which in vertebrates forms the *brain* and *spinal cord.* "Hollow" refers to the presence of (fluid-filled) foldings and cavities.

double helix (dub′əl hē′liks) the configuration of the native DNA molecule, which consists of two antiparallel strands wound spirally around each other.

doubling time (dub′ling tīm) the number of years required for a population to double in size.

drupe (drüp) in plants, a simple fleshy fruit, usually with a single seed, derived from one carpel (for example, olive, peach, cherry).

ecological niche (ē′kə loj′ə kəl nich) the position or function of an organism in a community of plants and animals; the totality of adaptations, specializations, tolerance limits, functions, biological interactions, and behaviors of a species.

ecological succession (ē′kə loj′ə kəl   sək sesh′ən) the gradual progression or change in the species composition of a community; the progression of one community into another.

ecosystem (ē′kō sis′təm) in ecology, a unit of interaction among organisms and between organisms and their physical environment.

ectoderm (ek′tə dèrm′) in animal development, the outermost of the three primary germ layers of the embryo; the source of all nerve tissue, sense organs, the outer skin, and associated organs of the skin.

ectothermy (ek′tə thèrm′ē) a condition in which the body temperature cannot be metabolically regulated, but reaches equilibrium with the temperature of the surroundings.

effector (ə fek′tər) any structure that elicits a response to neural stimulation (for example, a muscle or gland).

electromagnetic spectrum (i lek′trō mag net′ik spek′trəm) the range of electromagnetic radiation, from low-energy, low-frequency radio waves to high-energy, high-frequency gamma rays.

electron (i lck′tron) one of the three common constituents of an atom; its mass is 1/1837 of a proton's and its electrostatic charge is −1.

electron acceptor (i lek′tron ak sep′tər) a molecule that accepts one or more electrons in an oxidation-reduction reaction (and thus becomes reduced), for example a cytochrome or coenzyme.

electron carrier (i lek′tron kar′ē ər) a molecule that behaves cyclically as an electron acceptor and an electron donor; a common constituent of electron transport systems.

electron donor (i lek′tron dō′nər) a molecule that loses one or more electrons to an electron acceptor in an oxidation-reduction reaction (and thereby becomes oxidized).

electron orbit (i lek′tron ôr′bit) 1. the state of an electron as determined by its energy as it moves within an atom. 2. the space within which an electron pair moves in an atom. Also called *electron orbital.*

electron shell (i lek′tron shel) 1. the space occupied by the orbits of a group of electrons of approximately equal energy. 2. an energy level of a group of electrons in an atom.

electron transport system (i lek′tron tran′spôrt sis′təm) a series of cytochromes and other proteins, bound within a membrane of a thylakoid, mitochondrion, or prokaryote cell, that passes electrons and/or hydrogen atoms in a series of oxidation-reduction reactions that result in the net movement of hydrogen ions across the membrane.

element (el′ə mənt) a substance that cannot be separated into simpler substances by purely chemical means.

elongation (ē′long ā′shən) growth by lengthening; in plant development, the expansion in one direction of stem or root cells under turgor and the subsequent growth in length of the plant.

embryo sac (em′brē ō sak) in flowering plants, the mature megagametophyte after division into six haploid cells and one binucleate cell, enclosed in a common cell wall.

embryology (em′brē ol′ə jē) the scientific study of early development in plants and animals.

endergonic (en′dər gon′ik) *adj.* relating to a chemical reaction that requires an input of energy from some outside source and in which the products contain greater energy than the reactants (for example, the synthesis of ATP from ADP and P$_i$); compare *exergonic.*

endocrine gland (en′dō krən gland) a discrete gland that secretes hormones directly into the blood; also called a *ductless gland.*

endocytosis (en′dō sī tō′sis) the process of taking food or solutes into the cell (into vacuoles) by engulfment (a form of active transport); see also *phagocytosis,* compare *exocytosis.*

endoderm (en′dō dèrm′) the innermost of the three primary germ layers of a metazoan embryo and the source of the gut epithelium and its embryonic outpocketings (in vertebrates, the liver, pancreas, and lung); also called *entoderm.*

endodermis (en′dō dèr′mis) a single layer of cells around the stele of vascular plant roots that forms a moisture barrier—its lateral cell walls are pressed tightly together and waterproofed, forming the Casparian strip.

endometrium (en′dō mē′trē əm) in mammals, the tissue lining the cavity of the uterus; it responds cyclically to ovarian hormones by thickening in preparation for the implantation of an embryo, and is shed as the menstrual flow.

endoplasmic reticulum **(ER)** (en′dō plaz′mik ri tik′yə ləm) extensive and dynamic membranes of the cell cytoplasm, usually a site of synthesis, packaging and transport. *Rough endoplasmic reticulum:* with bound ribosomes, the site of protein synthesis. *Smooth endoplasmic reticulum:* without bound ribosomes, the site of synthesis of nonprotein materials.

endoskeleton (en′dō skel′ə tən) a mesodermally derived supporting skeleton, inside the organism and surrounded by living tissue, as in vertebrates.

endosperm (en′dō spèrm′) a nutritive tissue of seeds, formed around the embryo in the embryo sac.

endospore (en′dō spôr) a resistant, thick-walled spore formed from a bacterial cell; see also *spore.*

endothermy (en′dō thèrm′ē) a condition in which animals regulate their body temperature through the metabolism of cellular fuels, usually maintaining it at some constant optimal level.

energy (en′ər jē) the capacity or potential to accomplish work (with work defined as the movement of matter); it exists in several forms, including heat, chemical, electrical, magnetic, and radiant (electromagnetic).

entropy (en′trə pē) in thermodynamics, the energy in a closed system that is not available for doing work; also a measure of the randomness or disorder of such a system; see also *energy* and *free energy.*

enzyme (en′zīm) a protein that catalyzes chemical reactions.

epicotyl (ep′ə kot′l) in the embryo of a seed plant, the part of the stem above the attachment of the cotyledon(s).

epidermis (ep′ə dèr′mis) 1. in plants, the outer protective cell layer in leaves and in the primary root and stem. 2. in animals, the outer epithelial layer of the skin.

epinephrine (ep′ə nef′rən) a hormone with numerous effects produced by the adrenal medulla and by nerve synapses of the autonomic nervous system; also called *adrenaline.*

epistasis (i pis′tə sis) the masking of a trait ordinarily determined by one gene locus by the action of a gene or genes at another locus.

epithelium (ep′ə thē′lē əm) a basic animal tissue type, which covers a surface or lines a canal or cavity; it serves to enclose and protect.

erythrocyte (i rith′rō sīt) a hemoglobin-filled, oxygen-carrying, circulating blood cell; enucleate in mammals, but with a physiologically inactive, condensed nucleus in other vertebrates; also called *red blood cell.*

Eubacteria (yü′bak tir′ē ə) "true bacteria"; the better-known prokaryote kingdom, containing many familiar human pathogens and important soil and water bacteria. See also *Archebacteria.*

eucoelomate (yü se′lə māt) any animal possessing a true coelom (body cavity lined with mesodermally derived tissue); also called *coelomate.*

eukaryote (yü′kar′ē ōt) a cell or organism with cells containing a membrane-bound nucleus, chromosomes complexed with histones, and other proteins and membrane-bounded cytoplasmic organelles. Compare *prokaryote.*

euphotic zone (yü fō′tik zōn) the area of a body of water that receives sufficient light for photosynthesis to occur.

eutrophic (yü trō′fik) *adj.* pertaining to fresh waters, rich in nutrients essential to plant and algal growth, thus rich in life and usually in rapid ecological succession. Compare *oligotrophic.*

evolution (ev′ə lü′shən) 1. any gradual process of formation, growth, or change. 2. descent with modification. 3. long-term change and speciation (division into discrete species) of biological entities. 4. the continuous genetic adaptation of organisms or populations through mutation, hybridization, random drift, and natural selection.

excretion (ek skrē′shən) the removal of cellular metabolic wastes from the body.

exergonic (ek′sər gon′ik) *adj.* describing a chemical reaction that releases energy, with the products containing less free energy than the reactants. Compare *endergonic.*

exocytosis (ek′sō sī tō′sis) the process of expelling material from vacuoles through the cell membrane. Compare *endocytosis.*

exoskeleton (ek′sō skel′ə tən) an external skeleton or supportive covering (as in arthropods, where it consists of chitin).

experimental variable (ek sper′ə men′tl ver′ē ə bəl) a crucial factor whose effect is being tested by an experiment; the one factor that is different between the experiment and the control.

expressed sequence (EXON) (ek spres′d sē′kwəns/ek′son) the nucleotide sequences that remain in a messenger RNA molecule after tailoring and thus are expressed in a polypeptide. Compare *intervening sequence (INTRON).*

extraembryonic membrane (ek′strə em′brē on′ik mem′brān) any of several external life-supporting structures produced by the vertebrate embryo (for example, amnion, chorion, allantois, and yolk sac).

facilitated diffusion (fə sil′ə tā′tid di fyü′zhən) diffusion of molecules across a cell membrane assisted by a reversible association with carrier molecules; it differs from active transport in that no energy is expended and net movement follows the concentration gradient.

FAD, FADH2 flavin adenine dinucleotide, a coenzyme that is a hydrogen carrier in metabolism. FAD+ is the oxidized form and FADH2 is the reduced form.

feedback (fēd′bak′) the return of part of the output of a system back to the input, which regulates or affects the system's functioning. In *negative feedback,* the amount of output is sensed by the system and acts in an inhibiting manner, slowing activity and thus reducing output; in *positive feedback,* the output stimulates activity, further increasing the flow of output.

fertilization (fèr′tlə zā′shən) the sexual process whereby gametes or gamete nuclei are united.

fetus (fē′təs) in vertebrates, an unborn or unhatched individual past the embryo stage; in humans, a developing, unborn individual past the first eight weeks of pregnancy.

filament (fil′ə mənt) 1. a long fiber. 2. see *muscle fiber.* 3. in flowers, the slender stalk of the stamen, on which the anther is situated.

filter feeder (fil′tər fē′dər) an animal that obtains its food by filtering minute organisms from a current of water.

first law of thermodynamics (thėr'mō dī nam'iks) the physical law that states that energy cannot be created or destroyed.

fitness (fit'nəs) **1.** the state of being adapted or suited (for instance, to the environment). **2.** *relative fitness* or *Darwinian fitness:* the relative expectation of survival and reproduction of an individual or a specific genotype, compared with that of the general population or a standard genotype.

flagella (flə jel'ə) (sing. *flagellum*) **1.** long, whiplike, motile eukaryote cell organelles projecting from the cell membrane; longer and fewer in number than cilia, they propel the cell by undulations. **2.** analogous, nonhomologous organelles of bacteria consisting of a solid, helical protein fiber that passes through the cell wall and propels the cell by rotating like a propeller.

flower (flou'ər) sexual reproductive organ of an angiosperm (flowering plant).

fluid mosaic model (flü'id mō zā'ik mod'l) a description of the cell membrane as a phospholipid bilayer that has a fluidlike core and contains an assortment of specifically oriented proteins, with some proteins extending through to both surfaces and other proteins specific for either the inner or the outer surface.

F1 particle (pär'tə kəl) an ultramicroscopic mitochondrial organelle attached to the inner surface of the crista; the site of chemiosmotic phosphorylation.

food chain (füd chān) a sequence of organisms in an ecological community, each of which is a food for the next higher organism, from the primary producer to the top predator.

force filtration (fôrs fil trā'shən) hydrostatic pressure within the glomerulus of the nephron that forces small molecules and ions out of the blood into Bowman's capsule, from where they enter the tubule as crude kidney filtrate.

forebrain (fôr'brān) **1.** the anterior of the three primary divisions of the vertebrate embryonic brain. **2.** the parts of the adult brain developed from embryonic forebrain.

founder effect (foun'dər ə fekt') the chance assortment of genes carried out of the original population by colonizers (or founders) who subsequently give rise to a large population.

frame-shift mutation (frām'shift muÿ tā'shən) an insertion or deletion of a nucleotide which results in a frame change and the misreading during translation of all mRNA codons "downstream."

free energy (frē en'ər jē) potential energy, available for use in work.

fruit (früt) the mature, seed-bearing ovary of a flowering plant; it may be swollen and sweet or starchy.

fungus (fung'gəs) (pl. *fungi*), an organism of the kingdom *Fungi*, including yeasts, mushrooms, molds, mildews, part of the lichen symbiosis, rusts, smuts, sac fungi, puffballs, water molds, and sometimes the slime molds.

gametes (gam'ēts) Haploid cells that unite in sexual reproduction, producing a diploid zygote; typically, the haploid sperm or egg cell.

gametophyte (gə mē'tō fīt) in plants with alternation of generations, the haploid form, in which gametes are produced. Compare *sporophyte*.

ganglion (gang'glē ən) a mass of nerve tissue containing the cell bodies of neurons.

gap junction (gap jungk'shən) dense structure that physically connects membranes of adjacent cells along with channels for cell-to-cell transport.

gastrovascular cavity (gas'trō vas'kyə lər kav'ə tē) the cavity of coelenterates, ctenophores, and flatworms, which opens to the outside only via the mouth and functions as a digestive cavity and crude circulatory system; also called *coelenteron*.

gastrula (gas'trü la) a young metazoan embryo consisting of three germ-tissue layers, with an inner cavity (archenteron) opening out through a blastopore.

gastrulation (gas'trə lā'shən) the process of cellular ingrowth by ectoderm whereby a blastula becomes a gastrula.

Gause's law (gous'əs law) see *competitive exclusion*.

gene (jēn) (variously defined) **1.** the unit of heredity that controls the development of a hereditary character. **2.** a continuous length of DNA with a single genetic function. **3.** a *cistron* or *structural gene*, that is, the sequence of DNA coding for a single polypeptide sequence.

gene cloning (jēn klōn'ing) technique whereby pieces of DNA from any source are spliced into plasmid DNA, cultured in growing bacteria, purified, and recovered in quantity. See also *recombinant DNA*.

gene flow (jēn flō) the exchange of genes between popluations through migration, pollen dispersal, chance encounters, and the like.

gene linkage (jēn ling'kij) the presence of several genes physically linked on the same chromosome.

gene pool (jēn pül) all the genetic information of a population considered collectively.

general fertility rate (jen'ər əl fėr til'ə tē rāt) the average number of live births per 1000 females in their reproductive years (in the U.S., women 15–44).

genetic code (jə net'ik kōd) the specific groupings of nucleotides in DNA and RNA that specify the order of amino acids in a polypeptide or protein. Each of the 64 codons (sequences of three nucleotides in DNA or RNA) specifies an amino acid or chain termination in protein synthesis.

genetic drift (jə net'ik drift) changes in gene frequencies through chance rather than through natural selection. See also *founder effect* and *population bottleneck*.

genetic engineering (jə net'ik en'jə nir'ing) modern techniques of gene management, including gene cloning; gene splicing; amino acid, DNA, and RNA nucleotide sequencing; and gene synthesis.

genetic recombination (jə net'ik rē'kom bə nā'shən) the exchange and subsequent recombination of genes during crossing over in meiosis I.

genotype (jēn'ə tīp) **1.** the genetic constitution of an organism (specific genes present). **2.** *total genotype:* the sum total of genetic information of an organism.

geographic isolation (jē'ə graf'ik ī'sə lā'shən) the continued separation of portions of a species population by geographic or geological barriers, for instance, by newly formed rivers.

geotropism (jē'ot'rə piz'əm) in plants, a growth response to gravity; *positive geotropism:* the tendency of a growing root tip to turn downward; *negative geotropism:* the tendency of a growing shoot to turn upward.

germination (jėr'mə nā'shən) **1.** the end of dormancy in a seed, when water is absorbed and digestion of stored materials and growth of the embryo begin. **2.** spore germination, the end of dormancy in a spore.

germ layer (jėrm lā'ėr) any of the three layers of cells formed at gastrulation: *ectoderm*, *endoderm*, and *mesoderm*.

gill (gil) **1.** in animals, a thin-wallled organ of great surface area, for obtaining oxygen from water. **2.** in fungi, the thin, flattened structures on the underside of a mushroom (basidiocarp) that bear the spore-forming basidia.

gill slits (gil slitz) a chordate characteristic, permanent openings into the pharygeal cavity of primitive chordates; associated with gills in fishes and represented only as transitory structures in the embryos of terrestrial vertebrates; also called *pharyngeal gill slits*.

glial cells (glē'əl selz) numerous nonconducting supporting cells of the central nervous system that may play some role in information storage; also called *neuroglia*.

glomerulus (glə mer'ə ləs) (pl. *glomeruli*) the mass or tuft of capillaries in a Bowman's capsule.

glucose (glü'kōs) a six-carbon sugar, occurring in an open chain form or either of two ring forms; the subunit of many carbohydrate polymers; also called *dextrose, blood sugar, corn sugar,* and *grape sugar*.

glycogen (glī'kə jən) animal starch, a highly branched polysaccharide consisting of alpha glucose subunits; a storage carbohydrate in the liver and muscles of animals.

glycolysis (glī'kol'ə sis) the enzymatic, anaerobic breakdown of glucose in cells, yielding ATP (from ADP), and either lactic acid; alcohol and CO_2; or pyruvate and NADH.

Golgi body (gōl'jē bod'ē) a membranous structure found especially in the cytoplasm of secretory cells, involved in the packaging of cell products from the endoplasmic reticulum into secretion granules; also called *Golgi complex* or *Golgi apparatus*.

gonad (gō'nad) in animals, the structure responsible for producing gametes and often sex hormones; an ovary or testis.

granum (grā'nəm) (pl. *grana*) a stack of thylakoid disks in a chloroplast.

grassland biome (gras'land bī'ōm) one of the natural biomes of the earth, characterized by perennial grasses, limited seasonal rainfall, and great numbers of herbivorous mammals, birds, and insects.

guanine (gwä'nēn') one of the nitrogenous bases of RNA and DNA.

guard cell (gärd sel) in the plant leaf or stem, one of a pair of crescent-shaped cells that form a stoma (pore) and whose changes in turgor regulate the size of stomatal opening.

guttation (gə tā'shən) the normal exuding of moisture from the tip of a leaf or stem in certain plants, presumably due to root pressure.

gymnosperm (jim'nə spėrm') a nonflowering seed plant of the group *Gymnospermae*, producing seeds that lack fruit; included are conifers, cycads, gnetophytes, and ginkgos.

half life (haf līf) in radioisotopes, the time it takes for half of the atoms in a sample to undergo spontaneous decay.

haploid (hap'loid) *adj.* having a single set of genes and chromosomes. Compare *diploid, polyploid*.

Hardy-Weinberg law (här'dē wīn'bėrg lô) a statement of the genotype frequencies expected given allele frequencies in a population of randomly mating diploid individuals; also called *binomial law*.

Haversian system (hə vėr'shən sis'təm) a Haversian canal together with its surrounding, concentrically arranged layers of bone, canaliculi, lacunae, and osteocytes.

heat of activation (hēt uv ak'ti vā'shən) the energy output needed before an exothermic chemical reaction can proceed.

hemizygous (hem'ə zī'gəs) *adj.* the condition of X-linked genes in males, which are neither homozygous nor heterozygous.

hemoglobin (hē'mə glō'bən) a protein, a respiratory pigment consisting of one or more polypeptide chains, each associated with a heme (iron-containing) group.

hemophilia (hē'mə fil'ē ə) uncontrolled bleeding in humans due to the lack of a necessary blood-clotting constituent; a genetic disease caused by recessive alleles at either of the two sex-linked loci; also called *bleeders' disease*.

hermaphrodite (hər maf'rə dīt) an individual animal or plant with both male and female reproductive organs.

heterotroph (het'ər ə trof) an organism that requires organic compounds as an energy and/or carbon source (for example, all animals and fungi).

heterozygous (het'ər ə zī'gəs) *adj.* having two different alleles, commonly a dominant and a recessive, for a specific trait (n.: *heterozygote*).

hindbrain (hīnd'brān') **1.** the posterior of the three primary divisions of the embryonic vertebrate brain. **2.** the parts of the adult brain derived from the embryonic hindbrain, including the *cerebellum*, *pons*, and *medulla oblongata*.

holdfast (hōld'fast') a rhizoidal base of a seaweed, serving to anchor it to the ocean floor.

homeostasis (hō'mē ə stā'sis) the tendency toward maintaining a stable internal environment in the body of a higher animal through interacting physiological processes involving negative feedback control.

homeothermic (hō'mē ə thér'mik) capable of maintaining a stable high internal body temperature independently of the environment; also called *warm-blooded, endothermic*.

homologous (ho mol'ə gəs) *adj.* **1.** similar because of a common evolutionary origin. **2.** derived from a common embryological source; e.g., the *glans clitoridis* and the *glans penis*. **3.** *homologous chromosomes*: pair members, which have the same kinds of genes in the same order and which pair in meiosis.

homologue (hom'ə log) either of the two members of each pair of chromosomes in a diploid cell.

hormone (hôr'mōn) a chemical messenger transmitted in body fluids or sap from one part of the organism to another, producing a specific effect on target cells and regulating physiology, growth, differentiation, or behavior.

hydrogen bond (hī'drə jən bond) a weak electrostatic attraction between the positively polar hydrogen of a side group and a negatively polar oxygen of another side group.

hydrologic cycle (hī'drə loj'ik sī'kəl) the cyclic evaporation and condensation of the earth's waters, driven by heat in the atmosphere; also the biogeochemical cycling of water through photosynthesis and respiration between the living and nonliving environment; also called the *water cycle*.

hydrolysis (hī drol'ə sis) the enzymatic reaction of a compound with water so that the compound is split and water is added in place of the preexisting bond, an —OH group going to one subunit and an —H group going to the other; also called *hydrolytic cleavage*.

hydrophilic (hī'drə fil'ik) *adj.* "water loving"; pertaining to the tendency of polar molecules or their polar side groups to mix readily with water.

hydrophobic (hī drə fō'bik) *adj.* "water fearing"; pertaining to the tendency of nonpolar molecules or their nonpolar side groups to dissolve readily in organic solvents but not in water; resisting wetting.

hydrostatic pressure (hī'drə stat'ik presh'ər) the pressure exerted in all directions within a liquid at rest.

hypertonic (hī'pər ton'ik) *adj.* having a higher osmotic potential (for instance, higher solute concentration) than the cytoplasm of a living cell (or other reference solution).

hypha (hī'fə) (pl. *hyphae*) one of the individual filaments that make up a fungal mycelium.

hypocotyl (hī'pə kot'l) the part of the plant embryo below the point of attachment of the cotyledon.

hypothesis (hī poth'ə sis) a conjecture that is set forth as a possible explanation for some observation or phenomenon and that serves as a basis for experimentation or argument. Compare *theory*.

hypotonic (hī'pə ton'ik) *adj.* having a lower osmotic potential (for instance, lower solute concentration) than the cytoplasm of a living cell (or other reference solution).

immune response (i myün' ri spons') the array of physiological and developmental responses against a foreign substance or organism invading the body, including phagocytosis, antibody production, complement fixation, lysis, agglutination, and inflammation.

immunoglobulin (i myü'nō glob'yə lən) a protein antibody produced by T-cells in response to specific foreign substances; it consists of four subunits that are joined through disulfide linkages and have specific antigen binding sites.

imperfect flower (im pér'fikt flou'ər) any flower lacking in stamen (male) or carpel (female) reproductive structures.

implantation (im'plan tā'shən) in mammalian reproduction, the invasion of the uterine endometrium and attachment therein of the mammalian embryo (blastocyst).

incomplete flower (in'kəm plēt' flou'ər) a flower lacking in one or more of the four major floral parts (sepals, petals, stamens, carpels).

incomplete penetrance (in'kəm plēt' pen'ə trəns) a variability in the expression of a dominant allele where it may not be expressed or may be only partially expressed (for example, polydactyly).

independent assortment (in'di pen'dənt ə sôrt'mənt) Mendel's second law: the inheritance of one pair of factors (alleles) in an individual will occur independently of the simultaneous inheritance of a second pair of factors (alleles) (except where gene linkage groups occur. See *linkage group*.)

indeterminate life span (in'di tér'mə nit līf span) potentially endless life span in organisms such as perennial plants, where aging does not appear to occur.

induction (in duk'shən) the influence on the direction of differentiation and development that one embryonic tissue has on another.

inductive reasoning (in'duk'tiv re'zn ing) reasoning that moves from the specific to the general, reaching a conclusion based on a number of observations. Compare *deductive reasoning*.

initiation (i nish'ē ā'shən) the first steps in the translation of the genetic code; the beginning of polypeptide synthesis.

initiation complex (i nish'ē ā'shən kom'pleks) the physical association of a messenger RNA, two ribosomal subunits, and methionine-charged transfer RNA required to begin synthesis of a polypeptide.

insertion (in sèr'shən) **1.** in genetics, the addition of extra genetic material into a chromosome, gene, or other DNA sequence; *base insertion*: the insertion of a single base pair into a DNA sequence. **2.** in anatomy, *muscle insertion*: the distal attachment of a tendon or muscle (for instance, the attachment on the part to be moved). Compare *origin*.

interneuron (in'tər nûr'on) a neuron of the central nervous system that makes connections between sensory and motor neurons.

interphase (in'tər fāz) all of the cell cycle between successive mitoses; included are G1, S, G2 phases. See also *meiotic interphase*.

interspecific competition (in'tər spi sif'ik kom'pə tish'ən) competition between or among different species. See also *competitive exclusion, intraspecific competition*.

intervening sequence (INTRON) (in'tər vēn'ing sē'kwəns/in'tron) nonexpressed portions of messenger RNA, removed from the message by tailoring prior to translation. Compare *expressed sequence (EXON)*.

intraspecific competition (in'trə spi sif'ik kom'pə tish'ən) competition among members of the same species. See also *interspecific competition*.

intrinsic heart rhythm (in trin'sik härt riTH'əm) rhythmic contraction of the heart originating through the inherent capacity of cardiac muscle to contract without outside influence.

inversion (in vèr'zhən) the transposition of a portion of a chromosome following breakage and repair, altering the relative order of gene loci.

invertebrate (in vèr'tə brit) any animal lacking a vertebral column.

in vitro (in vi'trō) "in glass"; in a test tube or other artificial environment.

in vivo (in vi'vō) "in life"; in the living body of a plant or animal.

ion (ī'on) any electrostatically charged atom or molecule.

ion gates (ī'on gāts) controllable pores in a neuron that open to admit sodium or potassium ions during a neural impulse.

ionic bond (i on'ik bond) a chemical attraction between ions of opposite charge.

ionization (ī'ə nə zā'shən) **1.** the dissociation of a molecule into oppositely charged ions in solution. **2.** the creation of ions by the energy of ionizing radiation.

ionizing radiation (ī'ə nīz'ing rā'dē ā'shən) energetic radiation that produces ions in air and free hydroxyl radicals in water, the latter being responsible for induced mutation and tissue damage; included are X-rays, gamma rays, and streams of charged particles from the breakdown of radioactive isotopes.

islets of Langerhans (ī'lits uv läng'ər häns) clumps of alpha, beta, and delta endocrine cells in the pancreas, which secrete *insulin, glucagon*, and *somatostatin*, respectively.

isogametes (ī'sō gam'ēts) gametes that are identical in size and appearance, such as the (+) and (−) isogametes of *Chlamydomonas*. See also *mating types*.

isotonic (ī'sə ton'ik) *adj.* having the same osmotic potential (e.g., the same concentration of solutes) as the cytoplasm of a living cell or other reference solution.

isotope (ī'sə tōp) a particular form of an element in terms of the number of neutrons in the nucleus. See also *radioisotope*.

J-shaped curve (jā'shāp d kėrv) a plot of population growth where growth approaches the biotic potential of the species and generally exceeds the environment's carrying capacity. Compare *S-shaped curve*.

karyotype (kar'ē ō tīp) **1.** a mounted display of enlarged light photomicrographs of the chromosomes of an individual, arranged in order of decreasing size. **2.** the total chromosome constitution of an individual. **3.** the chromosomal makeup of a species.

kidney (kid'nē) in vertebrates, paired excretory organs serving to excrete nitrogenous wastes and regulate the balance of body ions and fluids.

kinetic energy (ki net'ik en'ər jē) energy associated with motion (accomplishing work).

Krebs cycle (krebz sī'kəl) in cell respiration, the biochemical pathway in the mitochondrion where pyruvate, newly converted to acetyl CoA, is combined with oxaloacetate and sequentially oxidized and decarboxylated, thereby, producing CO_2, reducing NAD^+ and FAD^+ to NADH and $FADH_2$, producing a small amount of ATP, and ending up with oxaloacetate again; also called the *citric acid cycle*.

K-selection (kā'si lek'shən) reproductive strategy of a species adapted to a fairly constant environment, with a small number of offspring and considerable parental care. Compare *r-selection*.

lactase (lak'tās) a digestive enzyme that hydrolyzes lactose to glucose and galactose; absent in most non-Caucasian adults.

lamella (lə mel'ə) (pl. *lamellae*) **1.** within chloroplasts, membranes that extend between grana (stacked thylakoids). **2.** one of the bony concentric layers (ringlike in cross-section) that surround a Haversian canal in bone. **3.** any thin, platelike structure.

larva (lär'və) in insects, a developmental stage following the egg and preceding the pupa, during which the immature insect is usually very active and voracious.

larynx (lar'ingks) in terrestrial vertebrates, the expanded part of the respiratory passage at the top of the trachea; in mammals it contains the vocal chords and constitutes a resonating *voice box*.

lateral line organ (lat'ər əl līn ôr'gən) in nearly all fish, a canal-like sensory organ containing a line of pitted openings and believed to be responsive to water currents and vibrations; distantly homologous to the mammalian inner ear.

leaf hairs (lēf harz) hairlike projections from leaf epidermal cells, generally those on the underside of the leaf.

leukocyte (lü'kə sīt) a vertebrate white blood cell.

lichen (lī'kən) a combination of a fungus and an alga growing in a symbiotic relationship.

ligament (lig'ə mənt) a tough, flexible, but inelastic band of connective tissue that connects bones or supports an organ in place. Compare *tendon*.

ligase (lig'ās) an enzyme that joins broken DNA strands or Okazaki fragments; used in gene-splicing technology.

light-dependent reaction (līt'di pen'dənt rē ak'shən) the part of photosynthesis directly dependent on the capture of photons; specifically the photolysis of water, electron and proton transport, and the chemiosmotic synthesis of ATP and NADPH; also called *light reaction*.

light-harvesting antenna (līt'här'və sting an ten'ə) part of a photosystem; clustered chlorophyll a, chlorophyll b, carotene molecules, and an associated reaction center. Functions in absorbing light energy and shunting it to the reaction center.

light-independent reactions (līt'in'di pen'dənt rē ak'shən) the part of photosynthesis not immediately requiring light; specifically the fixation of CO_2 into carbohydrate using the NADPH and ATP produced by the light reactions; also called *Calvin cycle* and *dark reaction*.

limnetic zone (lim net'ik zōn) the open waters of a lake beyond the littoral zone, but including only the depths through which light penetrates and in which photosynthesis can occur.

linkage group (ling'kij grüp) a group of gene loci located on the same chromosome; ultimately an entire chromosome.

lipid (lip'id) an organic molecule that tends to be more soluble in nonpolar solvents (such as petroleum products) than in polar solvents (such a water).

lobe-finned fish (lōb'find fish) any fish with fleshy pectoral and pelvic fins, including lungfishes and crossopterygians.

locus (lō'kəs) (pl. *loci*) specific place on a chromosome where a gene is located; also called *gene locus*.

long-day plant (lòng'dā plant) a plant that begins flowering at some specific time before the summer solstice when day length exceeds night; flowering is triggered by a critical, established period of darkness. Compare *short-day plant*.

lymph (limf) watery intercellular fluid in the lymphatic system.

lymphatic system (lim fat'ik sis'təm) the system of lymphatic vessels and ducts and lymph nodes that serves to redistribute excess tissue fluids and to combat infections.

lymphocyte (lim'fə sīt) any of the several varieties of similar-looking leukocytes involved in the production of antibodies and in other aspects of the immune response. See also *B-cell*, *T-cell*.

Lyon effect (lī'ən ə fekt') the mosaiclike gene expression of X-linked genes in human females (some cells in a tissue express a trait while others do not), resulting from the random inactivation of one X chromosome in each cell of the human female embryo.

lysosome (lī'sə sōm) a small, membrane-bounded cytoplasmic organelle, generally containing strong digestive enzymes or other cytotoxic materials.

macromolecule (mak'rō mol'ə kyül) any large biological polymer, such as a protein, nucleic acid, or complex polysaccharide (for example, cellulose or glycogen).

macronutrient (mak'rō nü'trē ənt) a plant nutrient required in relatively substantial quantities, e.g., nitrogen, phosphorus, potassium, sulfur, magnesium, and calcium. Compare *micronutrient*.

macrophage (mak'rō fāj) a large phagocyte, one of the leukocytes.

mammal (mam'əl) any member of the vertebrate class *mammalia*, most of which are characterized by the presence of hair, a muscular diaphragm, milk secretion, and placental development.

marsupial (mär sü'pē əl) a mammal of the subclass *Metatheria*; usually the female has a pouch (*marsupium*); included are the kangaroo, wombat, koala, Tasmanian devil, opossum, and wallaby.

mass action (mas' ək'shən) the law that, in reversible chemical reactions, the rate and net direction of the reaction depend on the relative concentrations of the reactants and products.

mating types (māt'ing tīps) genetically different clones or strains of fungi, protists, and certain plant algae, where sexual reproduction can occur between clones (mating types), but not within a clone; males and females do not exist.

mechanism (mek'ə niz'əm) the theory that everything in the universe, including biological phenomena, can be explained by physical law (*materialism*).

mechanoreceptor (mek'ə nō ri sep'tər) a sensory neuron specialized in detecting touch or pressure against the skin or hair; also called a *touch receptor*.

medulla (mi dul'ə) **1.** the inner portion of a gland or organ. Compare *cortex*. **2.** *medulla oblongata*: a part of the brainstem developed from the posterior portion of the hindbrain and tapering into the spinal cord.

medusa (mə dü'sə) the motile, free-swimming jellyfish form of coelenterate. Compare *polyp*.

megaspore (meg'ə spôr) a single large cell with one haploid nucleus; it is formed after meiosis of a megaspore mother cell in plants, and the female gametophyte develops from it by mitosis.

meiosis (mī ō'sis) in all sexually reproducing eukaryotes, the process of chromosome reduction, in which a diploid cell or diploid cell nucleus is transformed into four haploid cells or four haploid nuclei (the usual manner of sperm and egg production); also called *reduction division*.

meiotic interphase (mī ot'ik in'tər fāz) the period, which may be prolonged or so brief as to be virtually nonexistent, between telophase I and prophase II of meiosis, during which there is no DNA replication.

Mendel's first law (Men'dlz fèrst lô) segregation: the law that heterozygous alleles separate in gamete formation, each allele going to approximately half the gametes produced.

Mendel's second law (Men'dlz sek'ənd lô) independent assortment: the law that during meiosis and gamete production, alleles on one pair of chromosomes separate from each other independently of the way a second pair of alleles separates on some other pair of chromosomes.

menstrual cycle (men'strü'əl sī'kəl) the cycle of hormonal and physiological events and changes involving growth of the uterine mucosa, ovulation, and the subsequent breakdown and discharge of the uterine mucosa in menstruation (menses); the cycle averages 28 days; also call the *ovarian cycle*.

meristem (mer'ə stem) see *apical meristem*.

mesoderm (mes'ə'dèrm') the middle layer of the three primary germ layers of the gastrula, giving rise in development to the skeletal, muscular, vascular, renal, and connective tissues, and to the inner layer of skin and the epithelium of the coelom (*peritoneum*).

messenger RNA (mRNA) (mes'n jər) **1.** in prokaryotes, RNA directly transcribed from an operon or structural gene and containing one or more contiguous regions (cistrons) specifying a polypeptide sequence. **2.** in eukaryotes, RNA transcribed from a structural gene, tailored and usually transported to the cytoplasm; it contains a single contiguous region specifying a polypeptide sequence.

metabolic pathway (met'ə bol'ik path'wā') a sequence of enzymatic reactions through which a metabolite passes before the formation of the final product or products.

metabolism (mə tab'ə liz'əm) the chemical changes and processes of living cells, including anabolism and catabolism.

metaphase (met'ə fāz) the stage of mitosis or meiosis in which the centromeres of the chromosomes are brought to a well-defined plane in the middle of the mitotic spindle prior to separation in anaphase.

metaphase plate (met'ə fāz plāt) the equatorial plane of the mitotic spindle on which the centromeres are oriented in mitosis.

Metazoa (met'ə zō'ə) all animals other than *Parazoa* or phylum *Porifera* (sponges); that is, all animals whose bodies are composed of cells differentiated into tissues and organs and who usually have a digestive cavity lined with specialized cells.

methanogen (me than'ə jən) a methane-generating archebacterium.

micronutrient (mī'krō nü'trē ənt) an element necessary for plant growth but needed only in extremely small quantities; also called *a trace element*. Compare *macronutrient*.

microspore (mī'krə spôr') in seed plants, one of the four haploid cells formed from meiosis of the microspore mother cell; it undergoes mitosis and differentiation to form a pollen grain.

microtrabecular lattice (mī'krō trə bek'yə lər lat'is) in the cell cytoplasm, a weblike system of microtubules and microfilaments that form a cytoskeletal framework upon which many organelles are suspended.

microtubule (mī'krō tü'byül) a cytoplasmic hollow tubule composed of spherical molecules of tubulin, found in the cytoskeleton, the spindle, centrioles, basal bodies, cilia, and flagella.

microvilli (mī'krō vil'ī) (sing. *microvillus*) **1.** tiny fingerlike outpocketings of the cell membrane of various epithelial secretory or absorbing cells, such as those of the kidney tubule epithelium and the intestinal epithelium **2.** cellular projections formed in the placenta and containing capillaries. Also called *brush border*.

midbrain (mid'brān') **1.** the middle of the three primary divisions of the vertebrate embryonic brain. **2.** the parts of the adult brain derived from the embryonic midbrain.

midrib (mid′rib′) the large central vein of a dicot leaf, containing vascular and supporting fibrous tissue.

mineral nutrient (min′ər al nü′trē ənt) an inorganic compound, element, or ion needed for normal plant growth.

mitochondrion (mī′tə kon′drē ən) (pl. *mitochondria*) a threadlike, self-replicating, membrane-bounded organelle that is found in every eukaryotic cell and functions in oxidative chemiosmotic phophorylation.

mitosis (mī tō′sis) cell division or nuclear division in eukaryotes, involving chromosome condensation, spindle formation, precise alignment of centromeres, and the regular segregation of daughter chromosomes to produce identical daughter nuclei.

mitotic apparatus (mī tot′ik ap′ə rat′əs) in lower plants, the centrioles, mitotic spindle, spindle fibers, and asters; in higher plants, the spindle and spindle fibers.

mitotic spindles (mī tot′ik spin′dlz) a highly organized system of microtubules involved in the organization and proper separation of chromosomes during mitosis and meiosis.

mole (mōl) in chemistry, the quantity of a substance whose weight in grams is equal to the substance's molecular weight, or Avogadro's number: 6.023×10^{23} molecules of a substance.

molecular biology (mə lek′yə lər bī ol′ə jē) a branch of biology concerned with the ultimate physiochemical organization of living matter; the study of biological systems using biochemical methods.

molecule (mol′ə kyül) a unit of chemical substance consisting of atoms bound to one another by covalent bonding.

moneran (mə nir′ən) *adj.* refers to the bacteria or prokaryotes. (older term).

monocotyledon (mon′ə kot′l ēd′n) a flowering plant of the class *Monocotyledonae*, characterized by seeds with only one cotyledon (for example, grasses, palms, orchids, lilies): also called *monocot*.

monosaccharide (mon′ō sak′ə rīd) the basic molecular carbohydrate subunit; a simple sugar (e.g., glucose, fructose).

morphogenesis (môr′fō jen′ə sis) the emergence of final form and structure in the embryo.

morula (môr′yü lə) an early embryonic state consisting of a ball of cells.

motile (mō′tl) *adj.* moving or able to move by itself.

motor neuron (mō′tər nür′on) a neuron that innervates muscle fibers; impulses from it cause the muscle fibers to contract.

multiple alleles (mul′tə pəl ə lēls′) the alleles of a gene locus when there are more than two alternatives in a population.

multiple fruits (mul′tə pəl früts) a cluster of fused individual fruits, derived from a cluster of flowers (for instance, pineapple).

muscle fiber (mus′əl fī′bər) in skeletal muscle, one of the multinucleate cells, which takes the form of a long, contractile cylinder.

mutagen (myü′tə jən) a chemical or physical agent that causes mutations.

mutant (myüt′nt) an individual bearing a mutation; a new or abnormal type of organism produced by mutation.

mutation (myü tā′shən) any abnormal, heritable change in genetic material.

mutualism (myü′chü ə liz′əm) a mutually beneficial association between different kinds of organisms; a form of symbiosis in which both partners gain fitness. Compare *commensalism, parasitism.*

mycelium (mī sē′lē əm) (pl. *mycelia*) the mass of interwoven hyphae that forms the vegetative body of a fungus.

myelin (mī′ə lən) a soft, white, somewhat fatty material that forms a myelin sheath around certain nerve axons and is derived from the cell membranes of Schwann cells; the white matter of the brain and spinal cord.

myofibril (mī′ə fī′brəl) a tubular subunit of muscle fiber structure, consisting of many myofilaments organized into *sarcomeres*, the contractile units.

mylofilaments (mī′ə fil′ə mənts) the highly organized fibrous proteins of striated muscle, including the thin, movable *actin myofilaments* and the thicker, stationary *myosin myofilaments.*

myosin (mī′ə sən) a protein involved in cell movement and structure, especially in muscle cells. See also *myofilament, sarcomere.*

myosin bridge (mī′ə sən brij) the globular head of the fibrous protein myosin; it forms an ATP-activated, movable connection between myosin and actin and is responsible for muscle contraction.

NAD (nicotine adenine dinucleotide) (nik′ə tēn′ ad′n ēn′ dī′nü′lē ətīd) a coenzyme that is a hydrogen carrier in respiration (also NAD^{+}) *NADH*, also $NADH + H^{+}$, is the reduced form of NAD. *NADP*, nicotine adenine dinucleotide phosphate, is a similar hydrogen carrier in photosynthesis.

natural selection (nach′ər əl si lek′shən) the differential survival and reproduction in nature of organisms having different heritable characteristics, resulting in the perpetuation of those characteristics and/or organisms that are best adapted to a specific environment; also called *survival of the fittest.*

negative feedback (neg′ə tiv fēd′bak′) see *feedback.*

nematocyst (nem′ə tə sist) one of the minute stinging cells of the coelenterates, consisting of a hollow thread coiled within a capsule and an external hair trigger.

nephridium (ni frid′ē əm) an excretory organ found in annelids, occurring—paired—in each body segment and typically consisting of a ciliated funnel draining through a convoluted, glandular duct to the exterior.

nephron (nef′ron) a single excretory unit of a kidney, consisting of a glomerulus, Bowman's capsule, proximal convoluted tubule, loop of Henle, distal convoluted tubule, and collecting duct that discharges into the renal pelvis.

neritic province (ni rit′ik prov′əns) the coastal sea from the low-tide line to a depth of 100 fathoms; generally waters of the continental shelf.

nerve (nèrv) a number of neurons following a common pathway, covered by a protective sheath and supporting tissue.

nerve tissue (nèrv tish′ü) tissue that is naturally excitable or irritable, that is, capable of conducting neural impulses.

net community productivity (net kə myü′nə tē prō′duk tiv′ə tē) in ecology, the rate at which a biotic community gains in biomass or stored energy; determined by subtracting the total energy released in respiration by producers and consumers over a specified period from the total energy incorporated by producers over that period.

net productivity (net prō′duk tiv′ə tē) in ecology, the rate at which producers store energy or biomass; determined by subtracting the rate of energy release or biomass use during respiration by producers from the rate of energy or biomass incorporation.

neuromuscular junction (nùr′ō mus′kyə lər jungk′shən) the synapse between a neural motor end plate and a muscle fiber.

neuron (nùr′on) a cell specialized for the transmission of nerve impulses; it consists of one or more branched *dendrites*, a *nerve cell body* in which the nucleus resides, and a terminally branched *axon*; also called *nerve cell.*

neurotransmitter (nùr′ō tranz mit′ər) a short-lived, hormonelike chemical (such as acetylcholine) that, when released from an axonal knob into a synaptic cleft, crosses the space to stimulate the next neuron to transmit a nerve impulse. See also *synapse, synaptic cleft.*

neurula (nùr′ə lə) an early vertebrate embryo, slightly older than a gastrula, in which the neural tube has formed.

neurulation (nùr′ə lā shən) the development of a neurula from a gastrula; equivalently, the development of the neural plate, neural folds, and neural tube.

neutralist (nü′trə list) a population geneticist or evolutionary theorist who argues that a substantial proportion of the protein and DNA changes in evolution have been due to selectively neutral mutations fixed by random drift.

neutron (nü′tron) one of the two common constituents of an atomic nucleus; it has no charge and no effect on chemical reactions. See also *proton.*

niche (nich) see *ecological niche.*

nitrification (nī′trə fə kā′shən) the chemical oxidation of ammonium salts into nitrites and nitrates by the action of soil bacteria.

nitrogen cycle (nī′trə jən sī′kəl) the cyclic transfer of nitrogen compounds from producer to consumer to reducer and back to producer, through food webs; it also includes the gain of nitrogen compounds through nitrogen fixation and lightning and their loss through denitrification.

nitrogen fixation (nī′trə jən fik sā′shən) the chemical change of nitrogen from the stable, generally nonusable form of atmospheric nitrogen (N_2) to soluble and more readily utilized forms such as nitrates; usually by the action of cyanobacteria and other nitrogen-fixing bacteria, but sometimes by lightning, automobile engines, or the industrial preparation of synthetic fertilizers.

nondisjunction (non′dis jungk′shən) the failure of homologous chromosomes to segregate properly in meiosis, resulting in daughter cells with extra or missing chromosomes.

norepinephrine (nôr′ep′ə nef′rən) a compound that serves as a synaptic neurotransmitter and as an adrenal hormone; also called *noradrenaline.*

normal distribution (nôr′məl dis′trə byü′shən) the idealized, symmetrical distribution taken by a population of values centering on a mean, when departures from the mean are due to the chance occurrence of a large number of individually small independent effects; often approached in real populations; also called *bell-shaped curve.*

notochord (nō′tə kôrd) a turgid, flexible rod running along the back beneath the nerve cord and serving as a body axis; it exists in all chordates at some point in development, but is replaced in most vertebrates by the vertebral column.

nuclear membrane (nü′klē ər mem′brān) in all eukaryotes, the double membrane surrounding the nucleus and separating the nuclear contents from the cytoplasm.

nucleic acid (nü klē′ik as′id) either DNA or RNA; DNA is a double polymer of deoxynucleotides and RNA is a single polymer of nucleotides.

nucleolus (nü klē′ə ləs) (pl. *nucleoli*) a dark-staining body of RNA and protein found within the interphase nucleus of a cell; the site of synthesis and storage of ribosomes and ribosomal materials.

nucleotide (nü′klē ə tīd) **1.** a compound consisting of a nitrogenous base and a phosphate group linked to the 1′ and 5′ carbons of ribose, respectively; the repeating subunit of RNA. **2.** *deoxynucleotide*; a compound consisting of a nitrogenous base and a phosphate group linked to the 1′ and 5′ carbons of deoxyribose, respectively; the repeating subunit of DNA.

nucleus (nü′klē əs) in all eukaryote cells, a prominent, usually spherical or elipsoidal double membrane-bounded sac containing the chromosomes and providing physical separation of the DNA and the cytoplasm.

oceanic province (ō′shē an′ik prov′əns) the open sea, as distinguished from the neritic province.

Okazaki fragment (ō′ka za′kē frag′mənt) in DNA synthesis, the original form of a newly synthesized single strand; a polynucleotide of some 200–300 bases, incorporated through use of the enzyme ligase.

olfactory (ol fak′tər ē) *adj.* pertaining to the sense of smell, as detected by *olfactory receptors* in the mouth or nasal cavity and interpreted by *olfactory centers* in the brain. See also *Jacobson's organ.*

oligotrophic (ol′ə gō trof′ik) *adj.* a lake rich in dissolved oxygen and poor in plant and algal nutrient requirements; producer growth is thus held in check, and the lake ages very slowly. Compare *eutrophic.*

omnivore (om′nə vôr) "eating everything"; an organism that feeds on both animal and plant material.

oncogenes (ong′kə jēnz) segments of DNA that are capable of transforming their normal cell hosts into cancer cells.

oocyte (ō′ə sīt) an egg cell before maturation: *primary oocyte;* a diploid cell precursor of an egg meiosis: *secondary oocyte;* an egg cell after formation of the first polar body.

oogenesis (ō′ə jen′ə sis) the meiotic process that results in the production of an egg cell or ovum.

open circulatory system (ō′pən sėr′kyə lə tôr′ē sis′təm) a circulatory system in which the vessels open into intercellular spaces, through which the blood percolates before returning to the heart. Compare *closed circulatory system.*

operant conditioning (op′ər ənt kən dish′ən ing) learning through conditioning in which the reward or reinforcement follows a particular response that is desired over other possible responses.

operon (op′ə ron) in bacteria, the functional genetic unit of a set of inducible or repressible enzymes, including the inhibitor locus and a contiguous stretch of DNA that contains the promoter, operator, and usually the cistrons of several genes.

opposable thumb (ə pō′zə bəl thum) in primates, a thumb that can touch any of the other four fingertips on the same hand or paw.

organ (ôr′gən) a distinct structure that consists of a number of tissues and carries out a specific function.

organelle (ôr′gə nel′) a functionally and morphologically specialized part of a cell.

organ system (ôr′gən sis′təm) a number of organs participating jointly in carrying out a basic function of life (e.g., respiration, excretion, reproduction, digestion).

orientation (ôr′ē ən tā′shən) the directing of bodily position according to the location of a particular stimulus.

origin (ôr′ə jin) 1. evolutionary ancestry. 2. the nonmoving, skeletal base to which a muscle or tendon attaches; compare *insertion.*

osmoregulation (oz′mō reg′yə lā shən) in aquatic organisms, the homeostatic regulation of the osmotic potential in spite of fluctuations in the salinity of the environment.

osmosis (oz mō′sis) the movement of water across a membrane from an area of high water potential to an area of lower water potential, when the difference was brought about by different solute concentrations.

osmotic potential (oz mot′ik pə ten′shəl) a property of a solution equal to the osmotic pressure that would occur if it were rigidly confined and separated from pure water by a semipermeable membrane; also called *water potential.*

osmotic pressure (oz mot′ik presh′ər) the actual hydrostatic pressure that builds up in a confined fluid because of osmosis.

ovarian follicle (ō var′ē ən fol′ə kəl) the cluster of cells in which a mammalian oocyte matures, and which later gives rise to a corpus luteum.

ovary (ō′vər ē) 1. in animals, the (usually paired) organ in which oogenesis occurs and eggs mature. 2. in flowering plants, the enlarged, rounded base of a pistil, consisting of a carpel or several united carpels, in which ovules mature and megasporogenesis occurs.

overshoot (ō′vər shūt′) the hyperpolarization that occurs as a neuron recovers from an action potential; the brief period during which the net positive charge outside the neuron exceeds that found during the resting or common polarized state; also called *refractory period.*

oviduct (ō′və dukt) a tube, usually paired, for the passage of eggs from the ovary toward the exterior or to a uterus, often modified for the secretion of a shell or protective membrane; in humans it is also known as a *fallopian tube.*

oviparous (ō vip′ər əs) *adj.* producing eggs that develop and hatch outside the mother's body. Compare *ovoviviparous, viviparous.*

ovoviviparous (ō′vō vī vip′ər əs) producing eggs that are fertilized internally and develop within the mother's body but without any direct connection to the maternal circulation; the young are released shortly before hatching or after hatching. Compare *viviparous, oviparous.*

ovulation (ov′yə lā′shən) the release of one or more eggs from an ovary.

ovule (ō′vyül) in seed plants, an oval body in the ovary that contains the female gametophyte and consists of the embryo sac surrounded by maternal tissue.

oxidation (ok′sə dā′shən) 1. the loss of electrons from an element or compound. 2. *dehydrogenation:* the loss of hydrogens from a compound. 3. the addition of oxygen to an element or compound. 4. a multistep process in which oxygen is added or hydrogens or electrons are removed (e.g., the oxidation of glucose).

oxidative phosphorylation (ok′sə dā′tiv fos′fər ə lā′shən) the production of ATP from ADP and Pi in a process requiring oxygen, as in the mitochondrion, although oxygen is not directly involved.

palisade parenchyma (pal′ə sād′ pə reng′kə mə) a tissue of a lengthy, vertically arranged photosynthetic cells in the leaf, forming a closely packed layer (or layers) just below the upper epidermis.

paradigm (par′ə dīm) a broad, major concept in science, usually representing a new way of viewing natural phenomena (e.g., the theory of relativity in physics, continental drift in geology, the central dogma or theory of evolution through natural selection in biology).

parasitism (par′ə sī′tiz′əm) a symbiotic relationship in which an organism of one kind (the parasite) lives in or on an organism of another kind (the host) generally to the host's detriment. Compare *commensalism* and *mutualism.*

parasympathetic division (par′ə sim′pə thet′ik də vizh′ən) that part of the autonomic nervous system whose nerves emerge from the brain and lower spinal cord, and whose action generally slows activity in the viscera. Compare *sympathetic division.*

Parazoa (par′ə zō′ə) phylum *Porifera,* the sponges, included with the *Metazoa* in the animal kingdom but not directly related to any other animal groups.

parenchyma (pə reng′kə mə) a basic plant tissue type, consisting typically of thin-walled cells and commonly specializing in photosynthesis and storage.

partial dominance (pär′shəl dom′ə nəns) where neither of a pair of alleles is totally dominant and the combined expression of two alleles in the heterozygote produces an intermediate trait (for example, in the blossoms of four o'clocks, red × white = pink).

passive transport (pas′iv tran′spôrt) movement of fluids, solutes, or other materials without the expenditure of ATP energy (for example, by diffusion) especially across a membrane.

pecking order (pek′ing ôr′dər) see *dominance hierarchy.*

pentaradial symmetry (pen′tə rā′dē əl sim′ə trē) a modified radial symmetry in which there are five repeated radial parts; seen in echinoderm adults.

peptide (pep′tīd) a short chain of amino acids linked by peptide bonds, most often seen as a partial digestion product of a protein or polypeptide.

peptide bond (pep′tīd bond) the dehydration linkage formed between the carboxyl group of one amino acid and the amino group of another; also *peptide linkage,* a covalent bond.

peptidoglycan (pep′tə dō glī′kən) chemical material of the cell wall in eubacteria; it consists of sugars and short peptide strands cross-linked by strands of the amino acid glycine.

perennial (pə ren′ē əl) in plants, a species that lives for an indefinite number of years. Compare *annual, biennial.*

perfect flower (pėr′fikt flou′ər) a flower that contains both carpel (female) and stamen (male) sexual parts.

pericycle (per′ə sī′kəl) a layer of tissue that sheaths the stele of the root and is associated with the formation of lateral roots.

periderm (per′ə dėrm′) in plant stems and roots, a protective layer of secondary tissue replacing the epidermis; it is derived from epidermal cells and consists of cork, cork cambium, and underlying parenchyma.

peripherial nervous system (pə rif′ər əl nėr′vəs sis′təm) in vertebrates, all neurons outside the central nervous system.

peristalsis (per′ə stal′sis) successive waves of involuntary contractions passing along the walls of the esophagus, intestine, or other hollow muscularized tube, forcing the contents onward.

peritoneum (per′ə tə nē′əm) the smooth, transparent membrane lining the abdominal cavity of a mammal. *Peritoneal cavity;* the principle body cavity (abdominal coelom) of a mammal.

permafrost (pėr′mə frôst) in arctic and high-altitude tundra, the permanently frozen layer of soil and/or subsoil.

permeable (pėr′mē ə bəl) *adj.* of membranes; having pores or openings that permit liquids or gases to pass through; also *semipermeable, selectively permeable, impermeable.*

petal (pet′l) one of the usually white or brightly colored leaflike elements of the corolla of a flower.

petiole (pet′e ol) the small stalk that emerges from the stem of a plant and supports the leaf.

pH a common measure of the acidity or alkalinity of a liquid (actually, the negative logarithm of the hydronium ion concentration of a solution); pH values of less than seven (the neutral point) indicate acidity, and values greater than seven indicate alkalinity.

phagocite (fag′ə sīt) 1. any leukocyte that engulfs particles. 2. any cell that characteristically engulfs foreign matter.

phagocytosis (fag'ə sī tō'sis) engulfment of solid materials into the cell and the subsequent pinching off of the cell membrane to form a digestive vacuole.

pharynx (far'ingks) **1.** in most vertebrates, the cavity between the mouth and the esophagus (it contains the gills in fishes). **2.** an analogous region in the alimentary canals of various invertebrates, including some in which it is eversible and toothed.

phenotype (fē'nə tīp) the final effect of the total interaction of genes with each other and with the environment, expressed in the individual.

pheromone (fer'ə mōn) a substance that is released into the environment by one individual and affects the behavior of another (for example, an alarm chemical in ants, a sex attractant in moths).

phloem (flō'em) a complex vascular tissue of higher plants that consists of sieve tubes, companion cells, and phloem fibers, and functions in transport of sugars and other nutrients.

phosphate (fos'fāt) common phosphorus- and oxygen-containing group or its free ion; part of ATP, nucleic acids, and coenzymes.

phospholipid (fos'fō lip'id) any of a class of phosphate-esterified lipids, including *lecithins, cephalins,* and *sphingomyelins;* a major component of cell membranes.

phosphorylation (fos'fər ə lā'shən) the enzymatic addition of a phosphate group to a compound, for example, the addition of phosphate to ADP to produce ATP and water.

photon (fō'ton) a "packet" (quantum) of electromagnetic radiant energy; a unit of light energy.

photoperiodism (fō'tō pir'e ə diz'əm) the response of an organism to the length of daylight or dark periods (photoperiods), involving sensitivity to the onset of light or darkness and a capacity to measure time.

photorespiration (fō'tō res'pə rā'shən) in C3 plants, the addition of oxygen rather than carbon dioxide to ribulose bisphosphate and the subsequent loss of Calvin cycle components, brought about under brightly lighted, very dry conditions when stoma close and carbon dioxide levels fall.

photosynthesis (fō'tō sin'thə sis) in phototrophic organisms, the organized capture of light energy in photosystems and its transformation into chemical bond energy in carbohydrates (glucose and other compounds).

photosystem (fō'tō sis'təm) in the thylakoid: light-harvesting antennas and electron/hydrogen transport systems, both of which function in the light reactions of photosynthesis; also *photosystem I (P700)* and *photosystem II (P680).*

phototroph (fō'tō trōf) an autotrophic organism that derives its energy initially from light; a photosynthetic organism.

phototropism (fō to'trə piz'əm) the growth response of a plant to light; it may be positive (growth toward) as in stems or negative (growth away) as in roots.

phylogenetic tree (fī'lō jə net'ik trē) a branching, treelike graphic representation of the interrelations and evolutionary history of a group of organisms, indicating the relative order of successive divisions of the line of descent.

phytochrome (fī'tō krōm) a red-light-sensitive protein complex of certain plant cell membranes; it is involved in many light-induced phenomena, including flowering, leaf formation, and seed germination.

phytoplankton (fī'tō plangk'tən) in the aquatic environment (marine and fresh waters), minute photosynthesizing organisms such as diatoms; the base of the marine food chain.

piloerection (pī'lō i rek'shən) the lifting up of hair by tiny involuntary muscles in response to cold or fright; bristling.

pioneer organism (pī'ə nir' ôr'gə niz'əm) during ecological succession, a type of organism specialized for the initial invasion of an uninhabited or seriously disturbed area (e.g., a rocky outcropping, landslide, or burned-out region).

pistil (pis'tl) in flowering plants, the female reproductive structure, composed of one or more carpels and ovaries, and a style and a stigma. See also *carpel.*

pith (pith) thin-walled parenchymous tissue in the central strand of a stem's primary growth; the dead remains of such tissue at the center of a woody stem.

placenta (plə sen'tə) **1.** in mammals other than monotremes and marsupials, the organ formed by the union of the endometrium and the extraembryonic membranes of the fetus; it provides for nourishment of the fetus, elimination of waste products, and the exchange of dissolved gases. **2.** in flowering plants, the part of the ovary that bears and nourishes the ovule.

plasma (plaz'mə) the fluid matrix of blood tissue; it is 90% water and 10% various other substances, including plasma proteins, ions, and foods.

plasmid (plaz'mid) in bacteria, a small ring of DNA that occurs in addition to the main bacterial chromosome and is transferred from host to host; also used in recombinant DNA techniques.

plastid (plas'tid) any of several forms of self-replicating, semiautonomous plant cell organelles, including *chloroplast,* specialized for photosynthesis; *chromoplast,* specialized for pigmentation; and *leucoplast,* specialized for starch storage.

platelets (plāt'lits) minute, fragile noncellular discs present in the vertebrate blood; upon injury they are ruptured, releasing factors that initiate blood clotting and wound healing.

plate tectonics (plāt tek ton'iks) the movement of great land and ocean floor masses (plates) on the surface of the earth relative to one another, occurring largely in the Cenozoic era; also called *continental drift.*

point mutation (point myü'tā shən) a mutation involving a minor change in a DNA sequence, such as a base substitution, addition, or deletion.

polar body (pō'lər bod'ē) a very small, functionless daughter cell produced by the highly unequal cleavage during meiosis I and II in oogenesis.

polarization (pol'lər ə zā'shən) the process in which the outside of a resting neuron becomes positively charged relative to the inside, through the action of sodium/potassium ion exchange pumps.

pollen grain (pol'ən grān) the male gametophyte of a seed plant; it contains a generative nucleus and a tube nucleus and is enclosed in a hardened, resistant case.

pollen sac (pol'ən sak) one of two or four chambers in an anther in which pollen develops and is held.

pollen tube (pol'ən tüb) a tube that extends from a germinating pollen grain and grows down through the style to the embryo sac, into which it releases sperm nuclei.

pollination (pol'ə nā'shən) the transfer of pollen from one plant to another; in flowering plants, from a stamen to a stigma, preceding pollen tube growth and fertilization.

polygenic inheritance (pol'ē jen'ik in her'ə təns) inheritance involving many interacting variable genes, each having a small effect on a specific trait.

polymer (pol'ə mər) a molecule made up of a string of more or less identical subunits (for example, starch, nucleic acid, polypeptide).

polyp (pol'ip) the typical attached, nonswimming form of coelenterate. Compare *medusa.*

polypeptide (pol'ē pep'tīd) a strand of amino acids linked by peptide bonds, longer than a peptide but not usually a complete, functional protein. See also *protein.*

polyploid (pol'ē ploid) *adj.* having more than two complete sets of chromosomes per cell. See also *allotetraploid, autotetraploid, tetraploid.*

polyribosome (pol'ē rī'bə sōm) several ribosomes simultaneously transcribing the same messenger RNA strand; also called *polysome.*

polysaccharide (pol'ē sak'ə rīd') a polymer of sugar subunits.

pome (pōm) simple fleshy fruit, formed in its outer portions by the floral parts themselves (for example, apple, pear).

population bottleneck (pop'yə lā'shən bot'l nek') a period of time when the size of a population becomes small, resulting in a random change in gene frequencies; see also *genetic drift.*

population crash (pop'yə lā'shən krash) the usually rapid depletion of a population that has exceeded the carrying capacity of its environment.

positive feedback (poz'ə tiv fēd'bak) see *feedback.*

posterior (po stir'ē ər) in bilateral organisms, toward the tail or anal end (in humans toward the back). Compare *anterior.*

potential energy (pə ten'shəl en' ər jē) energy stored in chemical bonds, nonrandom organization, elastic bodies, elevated weight, or any other static form in which it can theoretically be transformed into another form or into work.

predator (pred'ə tər) an animal that actively seeks out and kills other animals for food.

primary consumers (prī'mer'ē kən sü'mərs) in ecology, herbivores.

primary growth (prī'mer'ē grōth) the initial growth or elongation of a plant stem or root, resulting primarily in an increase in length and the addition of leaves, buds, and branches. *Primary growth pattern:* the distinctive pattern of xylem, phloem, and other tissues in primary growth. Compare *secondary growth.*

primary immune response (prī'mer'ē i myün' ri spons') the relatively slow response of the immune system upon its first contact with an invading organism or foreign protein. Compare *secondary immune response.*

primary phloem (prī'mer'ē flō'em) phloem developed from apical meristem—that is, the phloem of primary growth.

primary producers (prī'mer'ē prə dü'sərz) in ecology, plants, algae, or other photosynthetic (or chemosynthetic) organisms that form the base of a food chain.

primary root (prī'mer'ē rüt) the root of a plant that grows through the production of primary tissues.

primary succession (prī'mer'ē sək sesh'ən) the succession of vegetational states that occurs as an area changes from bare earth to a climax community.

primary xylem (prī'mer'ē zī'lem) in primary growth, xylem produced by procambium rather than vascular cambium.

procambium (prō kam'bē əm) in plants, the primary tissue that gives rise to primary xylem and primary phloem.

profundal zone (prə fun'dl zōn) the depths of a lake that are perpetually dark because sunlight does not penetrate to them.

progeny testing (proj'ə nē test'ing) determination of an organism's genotype by crossing it with a known recessive homozygous individual and observing the resulting offspring.

prokaryote (prō kar'ē ōt) any organism of the kingdom *Archebacteria* or *Eubacteria;* its cells lack a membrane-bounded nucleus and membrane-bounded organelles. Compare *eukaryote.*

prophase (prō fāz) The first stage of mitosis or meiosis, characterized by the condensation of chromosomes.

proprioceptor (prō′prē ə sep′tər) a sensory receptor that responds to changes in body position, muscle tension, or internal chemistry.

protein (prō′tēn′) one of the molecules of life, a functional macro-molecule consisting of one or more polypeptides, often joined by disulfide linkages and frequently including one or more prosthetic groups.

proteinoids (prō′tə noidz) minute spheres of protein that form spontaneously when proteins are placed in solution; possible precursors to the first cellular life.

prothallium (prō thal′ē əm) the fern gametocyte, typically a small, flat, green thallus with rhizoids; it bears numerous antheridia and/or archegonia; also called *prothallus*.

protocell (prō′tə sel′) in the origin of life, a hypothetical cell containing the simplest organization and chemical substances needed to carry on life.

protoderm (prō′tə dèrm) primary meristematic tissue; it gives rise to the epidermis of roots, stems, and leaves.

proton (prō′ton) **1.** one of the two particles composing the atomic nucleus in ordinary matter; it has an electrostatic charge of $+1$ and a mass 1837 times that of an electron; its numbers determine the chemical properties of the atom. Compare *electron, neutron.* **2.** a hydrogen ion.

proton pump (prō′ton pump) an active transport system that uses energy to move hydrogen ions (protons) from one side of a membrane to the other against a concentration gradient, as in chemiosmosis.

protostome (prō′tə stōm) an animal in which the mouth derives from the first embryonic opening (the blastopore). Compare *deuterostome.*

pseudocoelom (sü′də sē′ləm) in nematodes and rotifers, the body cavity between the body wall and the intestine that is not entirely lined with mesodermal epithelium; the gut is entirely endodermal and thus not muscularized.

pseudopod (sü′də pod) "false foot"; any temporary protrusion of the protoplasm of a cell serving as an organ of locomotion or engulfment.

pulmonary circuit (pul′mə ner′ē sèr′kit) the passage of venous blood from the right side of the heart through the pulmonary arteries to the capillaries of the lung, where it is oxygenated and from which it returns by way of the pulmonary veins to the left atrium of the heart.

punctuated equilibrium (pungk′chü ā′tid ē′kwə lib′rē əm) a theory stating that evolution does not proceed in a gradual manner but rather in sudden bursts of activity, followed by very long time intervals during which little evolutionary activity is seen.

pupa (pyü′pə) in insects, the period of development between the larval and adult stages, during which time extensive body transformations occur prior to the emergence of the adult; the pupa generally is enclosed in a hardened pupal case or cocoon.

purine (pyür′ēn) a nitrogenous, double-ringed base of DNA or RNA consisting of 5-membered and 6-membered rings (e.g., adenine, guanine).

pyrimidine (pir′ə mid′ēn) a nitrogenous, single-ringed base of DNA or RNA consisting of a six-membered ring (for example, cytocine, uracil, thymine).

radial symmetry (rā′dē əl sim′ə trē) circular or spherical body symmetry where a radius cut through any part will intersect the same body parts (e.g., jellyfish, comb jelly).

radioisotope (rā′dē ō ī′sə tōp) an unstable isotope that spontaneously breaks down with the release of ionizing radiation; also called *radioactive isotope.*

radula (raj′ù lə) in all mollusks except bivalves, a toothed, chitinous band that slides backward and forward, scraping and tearing food and bringing it into the mouth.

rapid eye movement (REM) sleep (rap′id ī müv′mənt slēp) that part of sleep characterized by a high degree of relaxation in the voluntary muscles, but rapid movement of the closed eyes and considerable alpha activity registering on an electroencephalogram.

reabsorption (rē′ab sôrp′shən) in the kidney, the return of water, ions, amino acids, sugars, and other valuable substances from the crude kidney filtrate back into the blood following force filtration.

reaction center (rē ak′shən sen′tər) the part of a light-gathering antenna in which light-activated chlorophyll *a* transfers an electron to the electron transport system. See also *photosystem.*

receptor site (ri sep′tər sīt) a specific site on a cell membrane that usually consists of protein and is capable of recognizing and binding with a specific hormone or other informational molecule.

recessive allele (ri ses′iv ə lēl′) an allele that is not expressed or masked by a dominant allele in a heterozygote.

recombinant DNA (rē kom′bə nənt dē en ā) general term for laboratory manipulation of DNA; includes gene splicing and gene cloning.

reducer (ri dü′sər) in ecology, a fungus or bacterium that breaks down dead organisms into small molecules.

reducing power (ri düs′ing pou′ər) the relative ability of a substance to transfer electrons or hydrogen to some other substance in an oxidation/reduction reaction.

reduction (ri duk′shən) of a substance, the addition of electrons or hydrogen atoms.

reflex arc (rē′fleks ärk) the simplest form of a complete neural reaction—involving a sensory neuron, interneuron, and motor neuron—where the integration of information involves only the spinal cord.

reinforcement (rē′ən fôrs′mənt) the process by which the probability of performing an action is increased.

releaser (sign stimulus) (ri lēs′ər/sīn stim′yə ləs) a stimulus that acts as a cue, releasing a certain behavior in an animal.

releasing factors (rē lēs′ing fak′tôrz) highly specific chemical substances produced in the hypothalamus and transported through the blood to the anterior pituitary, where each type stimulates that gland to release a specific hormone.

replication (rep′lə kā′shən) DNA synthesis: the process whereby a DNA helix is unwound, the hydrogen bonds between adjacent nitrogen bases broken, and a new strand assembled through base pairing along each old strand.

replication fork (rep′lə kā′shən fôrk) the point at which unwinding proteins separate the two DNA strands in the course of DNA replication.

repressible operon (ri pres′ə bəl op′ə ron) an operon governing a synthetic pathway; it is generally active but can be inactivated by the presence of its normal metabolic product in the medium.

repressor protein (ri pres′ər prō′tēn′) in bacterial operons, a protein that binds the operator and prevents transcription either when bound to an inducing molecule (inducible operon) or when not bound (repressible operon).

reproductive isolation (rē′prə duk′tiv ī′sə lā′shən) **1.** the state of a population in which there is no mating between members of the group and members of other groups, and no immigration or emigration of individuals. **2.** the state of a population or species in which successful mating outside the group is biologically impossible becaue of anatomical mating barriers, hybrid inviability, or hybrid sterility.

respiration (res′pə rā′shən) **1.** breathing. **2.** the process by which an organism supplies oxygen to its tissues and removes carbon dioxide. **3.** *cell respiration*: any ATP-yielding metabolic activity occurring in living matter.

resting potential (res′ting pə ten′shəl) the charge difference across the membrane of a neuron or muscle fiber while it is not transmitting an impulse. Compare *action potential.*

restriction enzyme (ri strik′shən en′zīm) in bacteria, a defensive enzyme that recognizes and cuts out specific, short, viral DNA sequences, thus protecting the cell against most viruses; useful in experimental DNA manipulation.

retrovirus (ret′rō vī′rəs) an infectious DNA sequence that inserts itself into the genome, copies itself into RNA, then copies itself into DNA, which can then reinsert itself into new genomes; it represents a rare instance of RNA producing DNA.

reverse transcriptase (ri vèrs′ tran skrip′tās) an enzyme of certain RNA viruses that copies RNA sequences into single-stranded and double-stranded DNA sequences in a minor reversal of the central dogma; also called *RNA-dependent DNA polymerase.*

rhizoid (rī′zoid) **1.** a rootlike structure that serves to anchor the gametophyte of a fern or byrophyte to the soil. **2.** a portion of a fungal mycelium that penetrates its food medium.

rhizome (rī′zōm) an underground, horizontal plant stem that is often thickened by deposits of reserve food material, produces shoots above and roots below, and is distinguished from a true root in possessing leafy, nodes, and usually scalelike leaves.

rhodopsin (rō dop′sən) the light-sensitive protein pigment of retinal rods that bleaches in the presence of light, somehow starting an action potential, and is restored in darkness; also called *visual purple.*

ribosomal RNA (rRNA) (rī′bə sō′məl är en ā) the RNA that forms the matrix of ribosome structure; it consists of a large, an intermediate, and two relatively small sequences.

ribosome (rī′bə sōm) a cytoplasmic organelle consisting of ribosomal RNA and protein; it occurs in two subunits and is involved in polypeptide synthesis.

RNA (ribonucleic acid) (rī′bō nü klē′ik as′id) a single-stranded nucleic acid macromolecule consisting of adenine, guanine, cytosine, and uracil; it is divided functionally into rRNA (ribosomal RNA), mRNA (messenger RNA), and tRNA (transfer RNA).

RNA polymerase (är en ā pol′ə mə rās′) the enzyme or enzyme complex catalyzing transcription.

rod (rod) one of the numerous long, rod-shaped sensory bodies in the vertebrate retina; it contains many membrane layers bearing visual pigments, and is responsive to faint light but not to variations in color. Compare *cone.*

root (rüt) the portion of a seed plant that functions as an organ of absorption, anchorage, and sometimes food storage, and differs from the stem in lacking nodes, buds, and leaves.

root apical meristem (rüt ā′pə kəl mer′ə stem) region of undifferentiated tissue just above the root cap; it gives rise to primary growth in the root.

root cap (rüt kap) a protective mass of parenchymal cells that covers the root apical meristem.

root hair (rüt her) one of the many tiny tubular outgrowths of root epidermal cells, especially just behind the root apex, that function in absorption.

root tip (rüt tip) the actively growing end of a primary or secondary root, where root apical meristem is found.

r-selection (är'si lek'shən) the reproductive strategy seen in disruptive environments, where the organism produces large numbers of offspring but offers little if any parental care. Compare *K-selection.*

saliva (sə lī'və) a viscous, colorless, mucoid fluid secreted into the mouth by ducted salivary glands.

saltatory propagation (sal'tə tôr'ē prop'ə gā'shən) the skipping movement of an impulse from one node of a myelinated neuron to another.

sap (sap) the watery fluid transported by phloem that circulates dissolved sugars, other organic compounds, and mineral nutrients from one part of the plant to another.

sarcomere (sär'kə mir) the contractile unit of striated muscle bounded by Z line partitions; it consists of actin filaments bound to the Z line partitions and myosin filaments regularly interspersed between them.

sarcoplasmic reticulum (sär'kō plaz'mik ri tik'yə ləm) a membranous, hollow tubule in the cytoplasm of a muscle fiber, similar to the *endoplasmic reticulum* of other cells; calcium ions are sequestered here when the muscle is at rest.

Schwann cell (shwän sel) one of the many cells that constitute the myelin sheath, wrapped around the axon of a myelinated neuron.

scientific method (sī'ən tif'ik meth'əd) a research methodology in which a problem is identified, relevant data are gathered, hypotheses are formulated, and predictions are made and tested through experimentation or additional observation.

scutellum (skyü tel'əm) in monocots, the cotyledon in its specialized form as a digestive and absorptive organ.

secondary consumer (sek'ən der'ē kən sü'mər) a carnivorous animal that feeds upon herbivores or primary consumers.

secondary growth (sek'ən der'ē grōth) growth in dicot plants that results from the activity of secondary meristem, producing chiefly an increase in the diameter of stem or root. See *primary growth.*

secondary immune response (sek'ən der'ē i myün' ri'spons) the more rapid production of antibodies and conquest of an invader during a second or subsequent infection. Compare *primary immune response.*

secondary succession (sek'ən der'ē sək sesh'ən) ecological succession occurring in a disturbed community.

secondary xylem (sek'ən der'ē zī'ləm) xylem produced by the vascular cambium during secondary growth.

secondary phloem (sek'ən der'ē flō'əm) phloem produced by the vascular cambium during secondary growth.

second law of thermodynamics (sek'ənd lô uv thèr'mō dī nam'iks) the statement that all systems proceed toward entropy and that all chemical transformations are imperfect—that is, energy is lost as it goes from one form to another.

second messenger (sek'ənd mes'n jər) an intracellular chemical compound that transfers a hormonal message from the cell membrane to the nucleus or cytoplasm.

seed (sēd) the fertilized and ripened ovule of a seed plant, comprising an embryo, including one or two cotyledons, and usually a supply of food in a protective seed coat; it is capable of germinating under proper conditions and developing into a plant.

segmentation (seg'mən tā'shən) the condition of being divided into segments, originally repetitions of nearly identical parts (e.g., annelids), but frequently followed in evolution by the specialization of different segments, as seen in arthropods and vertebrates.

sensory (sen'sər ē) *adj.* **1.** pertaining to the senses. **2.** receptive of stimuli. **3.** conveying nerve impulses from a sense organ to the central nervous system.

sex chromosome (seks krō'mə sōm) an X or a Y chromosome, or a chromosome involved in determining sex.

sex-influenced trait (seks'in'flü əns d trāt) a genetic trait that can occur in either sex but is more common in one (for instance, breast cancer in women, ulcers in men).

sex-limited trait (seks'lim'ə tid trāt) a variable trait that affects members of one sex only (e.g., prostate cancer in men, endometriosis in women).

sex-linked (seks'lingk d) *adj.* pertaining to genes located on the X or Y chromosome, and inherited in sex-linked patterns; any genes linked to sex-determining genes.

sexual dimorphism (sek'shü əl di môr'fiz'əm) differences—in size, color, anatomy, etc.—between the sexes.

shoot (shüt) the plant stem and foliage.

shoot apical meristem (shüt ā'pə kəl mer'ə stem) undifferentiated tissue at the stem tip that produces primary growth in the stem.

short-day plant (shôrt'dā plant) a plant that begins flowering after the summer solstice and in which flowering is triggered by periods of dark longer than some innately determined minimum. Compare *long-day plant.*

sickle cell (sik'əl sel) an abnormal, crescent-shaped erythrocyte associated with *sickle-cell anemia*; a severe recessive condition attributable to homozygosity for an allele producing sickle-cell hemoglobin; *sickle-cell trait:* the heterozygous condition for the allele specifying sickle-cell anemia.

sieve tube (siv tüb) in phloem, a thin-walled tube consisting of an end-to-end series of enucleate, living cells joined by sieve plates; a channel through which sap flows.

sign stimulus See *releaser.*

simple fruits (sim'pəl früts) fruits derived from a single carpel or several fused carpels.

skeletal muscle (skel'ə təl mus'əl) muscle attached to the skeleton, under direct and conscious control; striated with multinucleate unbranched fibers; also called *voluntary muscle, striated muscle.* Compare *cardiac muscle, smooth muscle.*

skin breather (skin brē'тнər) any organism in which a significant proportion of the exchange of respiratory gases occurs through a vascularized moist skin (for example, earthworms, most amphibians).

sliding filament theory (slīd'ing fil'ə mənt thē'ər ē) the widely accepted explanation of skeletal muscle contraction in which actin myofilaments in the sarcomere are actively drawn through myosin myofilaments, thus shortening the contractile unit.

smooth muscle (smüтн mus'əl) the muscle tissue of the glands, viscera, iris, piloerectors, and other involuntary structures; it consists of masses of uninucleate, unstriated, spindle-shaped cells, usually occurring in thin sheets; also called *involuntary muscle.*

sociobiology (sō'sē ō bī ol'ə jē) the area of biology concerned with the genetic basis of human individual and group behavior.

sodium/potassium exchange pump (sō dē əm pə tas'ē əm eks chānj pump) a membrane active transport mechanism that utilizes ATP energy to move sodium ions out of the cell and potassium into it.

somatic nervous system (sō mat'ik nèr'vəs sis'təm) the voluntary or conscious part of the peripheral nervous system. Compare *autonomic nervous system.*

sorus (sôr'əs) (pl. *sori*) one of the clusters of sporangia on the underside of a fern frond.

speciation (spē'shē ā'shən) an evolutionary process by which new species are formed, often by the division of one species into two.

species (spē'shēz) the major subdivision of a genus, regarded as the basic category of biological classification; related individuals that resemble one another through recent common ancestry and that share a single ecological niche; in sexual organisms, a group whose members are potentially able to breed with one another but unable to breed with members of any other group.

specific heat (spi sif'ik hēt) the heat, expressed in calories, required to raise the temperature of 1 gram of some substance 1° C; a way of considering the quantity of heat that various substances are capable of holding (for example, water has great specific heat).

spermatogenesis (spèr'mə tō jen'ə sis) the meiotic process resulting in the production of haploid sperm.

spindle (spin'dl) a system of microtubules present in the cell during mitosis and meiosis, resembling the spindle of a primitive loom; it serves in the separation of chromosomes during the division processes.

spindle poles (spin'dl pōlz) the two points of origin of the mitotic apparatus; they represent the microtubular organizing centers and contain the centrioles in cells where these bodies appear.

spiral valve (spī'rəl valv) a helical fold of the intestinal wall in the short intestine of sharks and certain bony fishes; it slows the passage of food and provides additional absorptive surface.

spirochaete (spī'rə kēt') any of an order of slender, corkscrew-shaped bacteria.

spongy bone (spun'jē bōn) bone with a network of thin, hard walls and numerous spaces; it is spongelike in appearance.

spongy parenchyma (spun'jē pə reng'kə mə) in a leaf, the loosely arranged photosynthetic tissue, containing many air spaces, below palisade parenchyma.

sporangium (spə ran'jē əm) a structure in which spores are produced; it is found in algae, fungi, bryophytes, and ferns.

spore (spôr) a minute unicellular reproductive or resistant body, specialized for dispersal, for surviving unfavorable environmental conditions, and for germinating to produce a new vegetative individual when conditions improve.

sporophyte (spôr'ə fīt) in plants having an alternation of generations, a diploid individual capable of producing haploid spores by meiosis; the prominent form of ferns and seed plants. Compare *gametophyte.*

S-shaped curve (es'shāp d kèrv) a plot of population growth where growth is rapid at first but then slows when *environmental resistance* is met, and levels off at some point near or below the *carrying capacity.* Compare *J-shaped curve.*

stabilizing selection (stā'bə līz ing si lek'shən) selection against both extremes of a continuous phenotype, favoring an intermediate optimum.

stamen (stā'mən) the male reproductive structure of a flower, consisting of a pollen-bearing anther and the filament on which it is borne.

stele (stē'lē) in roots and stems of vascular plants, a central cylinder containing vascular tissue.

steroid (ster'oid) any of a class of lipid-soluble compounds, some of which are hormones, consisting of four interlocking saturated hydrocarbon rings and their side groups; included are *cholesterol, estrogen, testosterone, cortisol,* and others.

stigma (stig'mə) in flowers, the top, slightly enlarged and often sticky end of the style, on which pollen grains adhere and germinate.

stipe (stīp) the stemlike structure in red or brown algae that supports the blades or blade.

stoma (stō'mə) (pl. *stomata*) one of the minute pores in the epidermis of leaves, stems, and other plant organs; it is formed by the concave walls of two *guard cells* and allows the diffusion of gases into and out of intercellular spaces.

stroma (strō'mə) the enzyme-containing fluid region that surrounds the thylakoids of a chloroplast.

stromatolite (strō mat'ə līt) a macroscopic living or fossil geological structure of layered domes of deposited material, attributed to the presence of shallow-water photosynthetic prokaryotes.

style (stīl) the stalk of the pistil in a flower, connecting the stigma with the ovary.

suberin (sü'bər in) a complex fatty substance of cork cell walls and other waterproofed cell walls.

substitution (sub'stə tü'shən) in genetics, a DNA mutation in which one nucleotide is replaced or modified by another.

substrate (sub'strāt) a substance acted upon by an enzyme.

sun compass (sun kum'pəs) a behavioral mechanism utilizing the angle of the sun and the time of day to compute direction for navigation.

survivorship curve (sər vī'vər ship kėrv) a graph with numbers of individuals plotted on the X axis, and percentage of total life span completed plotted on the Y axis; it is useful in comparing periods of greatest mortality in several different species.

symbiosis (sim'bē ō'sis) the living together in intimate association of two species; it includes three categories: *mutualism* (both organisms gain); *commensalism* (one gains at little or no expense to the other); and *parasitism* (one gains at the expense of the other).

symbiosis hypothesis (sim'bē ō'sis hī poth'ə sis) the hypothesis that the eukaryotic cell evolved from the mutualistic union of various prokaryotic organisms, one of which gave rise basically to the cytoplasm, nucleus, and motile membranes; a second to mitochondria; a third to chloroplasts and other plastids; and a fourth to cilia, eukaryotic flagella, basal bodies, centrioles, the spindle, and all other microtubule structures.

sympathetic division (sim'pə thet'ik də vizh'ən) that portion of the autonomic nervous system whose nerves emerge only from the spinal cord and function to speed up the usual pace of the visceral organs served. Compare *parasympathetic division*.

sympatric speciation (sim pat'rik spē'shē ā'shən) speciation in populations that are not geographically separated. Compare *allopatric speciation*.

synapse (sin'aps) 1. *n.* the junction between the axon of one neuron and the dendrite or cell body of another; it must be crossed by neural impulses. 2. *v.i.* the pairing together of homologous chromosomes during zygotene of prophase I in meiosis.

synaptic cleft (si nap'tik kleft) the minute space between the synaptic knob of one neuron and the dendrite or cell body of another; neurotransmitters are released into it when nerve impulses are transmitted between cells.

synaptonemal complex (sə nap'tə nē'məl kom'pleks) in crossing over, a complex structure composed of protein and RNA and formed between sister chromatids in meiotic prophase to accomplish the specific zipperlike pairing of homologous chromosomes.

systolic pressure (si stol'ik presh'ər) the highest arterial blood pressure of the cardiac cycle. Compare *diastolic pressure*.

taiga (tī'gə) a subarctic forest biome dominated by spruce and fir trees; it is found in Europe and North America and at high altitudes elsewhere.

taxis (tak'sis) the movement of an organism toward or away from a stimulus.

taxonomy (tak son'ə mē) the science of identifying, naming, and classifying organisms.

T-cell (tē'sel) a lymphocyte of a variety that matures in the thymus, produces immunoglobulins bound tightly to its exterior surface, and interacts in complex ways with other types of cells in the immune system; it eliminates foreign cells it encounters; also called a *cytotoxic killer cell*.

telophase (tel'ə fāz) the stage of mitosis or meiosis in which new nuclear membranes form around each group of daughter chromosomes, the nucleoli appear, and the chromosomes decondense; at this time the cell membrane and cytoplasm usually divide to form two daughter cells.

temperate deciduous forest (tem'pər ət di sij'ü əs fôr'ist) a forest biome of the temperate zone, in which the dominant tree species and most other trees are deciduous and are bare in winter months.

tendon (ten'dən) a tough dense cord of fibrous connective tissue that is attached at one end to a muscle and the other to that part of the skeleton that moves when the muscle contracts. Compare *ligament*.

termination (tėr'mə nā'shən) in translation, the end of polypeptide synthesis, when "stop" codons on the messenger RNA are encountered by the ribosome, which releases the polypeptide and comes apart into its subunits.

territory (ter'ə tôr'ē) the space defended by a territorial animal.

tertiary consumer (tėr'shē er'ē kən sü'mər) a carnivorous animal that feeds on secondary consumers, which in turn feed on herbivores.

test cross (test krôs) the cross of a dominant individual with a homozygous recessive individual to determine whether recessive alleles exist.

tetraploid (tet'rə ploid) having four complete sets of chromosomes in each cell. Compare *allotetraploid, autotetraploid, polyploid*.

theory (thē'ər ē) 1. a coherent group of general propositions used as principles of explanation for a class of phenomena (for example, *Darwin's theory of the origin of species*). 2. a more or less verified explanation accounting for a body of known facts or phenomena. Compare *hypothesis*.

thermal overturn (thèr'məl ō'vər tėrn') the seasonal overturn of lake waters brought about by changing surface temperatures that increase the density of surface waters, allowing them to sink, thereby disrupting the thermocline and permitting a windblown revolving of water. See also *thermocline*.

thermocline (thèr'mō klīn) in a body of water, a temperature gradient where the temperature changes rapidly as a function of depth; thermoclines act as barriers to the vertical movement of water.

thermodynamics (thèr'mō dī nam'iks) 1. the branch of physics that deals with the interconversions of energy as heat, potential energy, kinetic energy, radiant energy, entropy, and work. 2. the processes and phenomena of energy interconversions.

thermoreceptor (thèr'mo ri sep'tər) a sensory receptor that responds to temperature or changes in temperature.

thermoregulation (thèr'mō reg'yə lā'shən) an animal's control over its internal temperature: the behavioral or physiological mechanisms that maintain a body at a particular temperature in an environment with a fluctuating temperature.

thylakoid (thī'lə koid) the membranous structure of chloroplasts consisting of a *thylakoid membrane*, containing light-harvesting antennas and the photosynthetic electron transport chain; an inner lumen that collects protons during active photosynthesis; and CF1 particles, the sites of chemiosmotic phosphorylation.

thymine (thī'mēn') a pyrimidine, one of the four nitrogenous bases of DNA.

tissue (tish'ü) a group of contiguous cells of similar origin, structure, and function. Compare *organ*.

total fertility rate (tō'tl fər til'ə tē rāt) a projection of the average number of children women aged 14–44 will bear.

totipotency (tə tip'ə tən sē) the condition of a cell whereby it retains the potential to undergo development and differentiation along any of the specialized lines genetically possible for that species.

trachea (trā'kē ə) (pl. *tracheae*) 1. in land vertebrates, the air passage between the lungs and the larynx, usually stiffened with rings of cartilage; it divides to form the bronchi. 2. one of the air-conveying tubules in the respiratory system of an insect, millipede, or centipede.

tracheid (trā'kē əd) a long, tubular xylem element that functions in support and water conduction; distinguished from *xylem vessels* by having tapered, closed ends and communicating with other tracheids through pits.

transcription (tran skrip'shən) the process of RNA synthesis as the RNA nucleotide sequence is directed by specific base pairing with the nucleotide sequence of the transcribed strand of DNA.

transcription complex (tran skrip'shən kom'pleks) enzymes essential to the process through which DNA is transcribed into RNA, including unwinding proteins and RNA polymerase.

transfer RNA (tRNA) (tran'sfèr är en ā) in the synthesis of polypeptides, a class of RNA molecules with the task of identifying and bonding with specific amino acids and then, on the ribosome, identifying and bonding with corresponding sites on the messenger RNA.

transformation (tran'sfər mā'shən) the direct incorporation of a DNA fragment from its medium into a bacterium's own chromosome.

translation (tranz lā'shən) polypeptide synthesis as it is directed by mRNA and assisted by ribosomes and tRNA; the transfer of linear information from a nucleotide sequence to an amino acid sequence according to the genetic code.

translocation (tranz'lō kā'shən) 1. the step in protein synthesis in which a transfer RNA molecule moves (translocates) from one ribosomal tRNA attachment site (pocket) to the other. 2. in chromosomes, the breakage and improper (nonhomologous) rejoining of chromosome segments. 3. the movement of solutes through the phloem from one part of a plant to another.

transpiration (tran'spə rā'shən) the evaporation of water vapor from leaves.

transpiration pull (tran'spə rā'shən pùl) the pulling of water up through the xylem of a plant using the energy of evaporation, the water potential gradient in the leaf, and the tensile strength of water.

triglyceride (trī glis'ə rīd') a nonpolar, hydrophobic lipid consisting of three fatty acids, covalently bonded to one molecule of glycerol.

trisomy 21 (trī'sō mē) a severe human congenital pathology attributable to the presence of three rather than two homologues of chromosome 21; also called *Down's syndrome*.

trophic level (trof'ik lev'əl) relating to nutrition; a level in a food pyramid.

tropical rain forest (trop'ə kəl rān fôr'ist) a tropical woodland biome that has an annual rainfall of at least 250 cm and often much more; it is typically restricted to lowland areas and characterized by a mix of many species of tall, broad-leaved evergreen trees that form a continuous canopy, with vines and woody epiphytes, and by a dark, nearly bare forest floor.

tropical savanna (trop'ə kəl sə van'ə) a biome that is primarily grassy but frequently interrupted by groves of drought-resistant trees; in the African continent, it occurs between tropical rain forest and desert.

tropism (trō'piz'əm) growth toward or away from an external stimulus, in plants usually accomplished by differential cell elongation in the stem or root. See also *geotropism, phototropism*.

true-breeding (trü'brē'ding) *adj.* an organism or strain that when mated with individuals like itself produces offspring like itself; specifically, it is homozygous for the genes in consideration.

T-system (tē'sis'təm) in muscle tissue, a system of tubular vesicles on the surface of the contractile units, thought to be important in spreading an action potential over a fiber and in sequestering calcium ions during recovery.

tubular secretion (tü'byə lər si krē'shən) in the nephron, the active transport of certain substances from the crude filtrate back into the blood.

tubulin (tü'byə lin) a protein consisting of two dissimilar polypeptides making up the subunits of microtubules.

tundra (tun'drə) a biome characterized by level or gently undulating treeless plains of the arctic and subarctic that support dense growth of mosses and lichens as well as dwarf herbs and shrubs; it is underlain by permafrost and seasonally covered by snow.

turgor (tèr'gər) the normal state of turgidity and tension in living plant cells, created by the uptake of water through osmosis, *turgor pressure*: the actual hydrostatic pressure developed by the fluid of a turgid plant cell.

unconditioned stimulus (un'kən dish'ənd stim'yə ləs) the normal or usual stimulus that produces a certain predictable behavior. Compare *conditioned stimulus*.

unwinding enzymes (un wīnd'ing en'zīms) nuclear enzymes that aid in opening the DNA helix so that replication or transcription can occur.

upwelling (up'wel'ing) in oceans, the wind-driven rise of deep water layers to the surface; associated with the circulation of mineral nutrients and a consequent increase in productivity and biomass.

urea (yūr'ē ə) a highly soluble nitrogenous compound that is the principle nitrogenous waste of the urine of animals.

uterus (yü'tər əs) **1.** in female mammals, a muscular, vascularized, mucous-membrane-lined organ for containing and nourishing the developing young prior to birth and for expelling them at birth. **2.** an enlarged section of the oviduct of various vertebrates and invertebrates modified to serve as a place of development for the young or eggs.

vacuole (vak'yü ōl) a general term for any fluid-filled, membrane-bounded body within the cytoplasm of a cell. See also *contractile vacuole*.

vascular cambium (vas'kyə lər kam'bē əm) the cylinder of meristematic tissue that in secondary growth produces xylem on its inner side and phloem on its outer side, thus contributing to growth in circumference.

vascular plant (vas'kyə lər plant) a plant with xylem and phloem; a tracheophyte.

vascular rays (vas'kyə lər rāz) in woody stems, radiating, spoke-like lines of parenchyma and collenchyma tissue that conduct materials laterally and help relieve pressure caused by expansion during circumferential growth.

ventral (ven'trəl) in bilateral animals, toward the belly; downward, opposite the back. Compare *dorsal*.

ventral nerve cord (ven'trəl nèrv kôrd) a common feature of many invertebrate phyla, the main longitudinal nerve cord of the body; it is solid and paired, with a series of ganglionic masses.

venule (ven'yül) a small vein.

vertebrates (vèr'tə brāts) animals in the subphylum *Vertebrata*, phylum *Chordata*; animals with vertebral columns or backbones.

vessel (ves'əl) a conducting tube in a dicot formed in the xylem by the end-to-end fusion of a series of cells (vessel elements) followed by the loss of adjacent end walls and of cell cytoplasm. Compare *tracheid*.

virus (vī'rəs) a noncellular, parasitic organism transmitted as DNA or RNA enclosed in a membrane or protein coat, often together with one or several enzymes; it replicates only within a host cell, using host ribosomes and enzymes of synthesis.

viscera (vis'ər ə) the internal organs within the body cavity, e.g., heart, lungs, intestines, liver.

vital capacity (vī'tl kə pas'ə tē) the maximum amount of air that can be exhaled after a fully forced inhalation.

vitalism (vī'tl iz'əm) an untestable doctrine that ascribes the functions of a living organism to a *vital principle* or *vital force* distinct from chemical and physical forces; no longer taken seriously.

vitamin (vī'tə mən) an organic substance taken in with food that is essential to the metabolic activity of an organism, usually because it supplies part of a coenzyme not made by the organism.

viviparous (viv'ə par'əs) *adj.* producing live young from within the uterus; during development nourishment is supplied by the mother's tissues, usually via a placenta. Compare *oviparous, ovoviviparous*.

water potential gradient (wô'tər pə ten'shəl grā'dē ənt) the difference in the potential energy of water between a region of greater water potential and a region of lesser water potential. Because of gravity, pressure, or an osmotic gradient, water moves down its water potential gradient.

water vascular system (wô'tər vas'kyə lər sis'təm) a system of vessels in echinoderms that contains sea water and is used as a hydraulic system in the movement of tentacles and tube feet.

wood (wùd) the hard, fibrous xylem of secondary growth, especially that of the central stem of a tree; it consists of lignified cellulose cell walls.

xylem (zī'lem) one of the two complex tissues in the vascular system of plants; it consists of the dead cell walls of vessels, tracheids, or both, often together with sclerenchyma and parenchyma cells; it functions chiefly in water conduction and strengthening the plant. See also *tracheid, vessel*, compare *phloem*.

Z line (zē' līn) in striated muscle, the partition between adjacent contractile units to which actin filaments are anchored.

zygospore (zī'gə spôr) a diploid fungal or algal spore formed by the union of two similar sexual cells; it has a thickened wall and serves as a resistant resting spore.

zygote (zī'gōt) a cell formed by the union of two gametes; a fertilized egg.

Suggested Readings

The readings listed here are of two types. For each Part of the book, relevant texts and other primary sources are listed first, then a selection of recent *Scientific American* articles is given. Further articles are listed and annotated in each chapter of the Instructor's Manual.

Part I

Alberts, B. et al. 1983. *Molecular Biology of the Cell.* New York: Garland Publishing Co.

Calvin, M., ed. 1973. *Organic Chemistry of Life; Readings from Scientific American.* San Francisco: W.H. Freeman Co.

The Chemical Basis of Life: An Introduction to Molecular and Cell Biology: Readings from Scientific American. Intro. by P.C. Hanawalt and R.H. Haynes. 1973. San Francisco: W.H. Freeman Co.

Darwin, C. 1859. *On the Origin of Species through Natural Selection.* A facsimile of the first edition. Cambridge, Mass: Harvard University Press.

de Beer, G. 1965. *Charles Darwin: A Scientific Biography.* New York: Doubleday.

Lehninger, A.L. 1975. *Biochemistry: The Molecular Bases of All Structures and Functions.* 2d ed. New York: Worth.

Life: Origin and Evolution: Readings from Scientific American. Intro. by C.E. Folsome. 1979. San Francisco: W.H. Freeman Co.

Moorehead, A. 1969. *Darwin and the Beagle.* New York: Harper and Row.

Porter, E. 1971. *Galapagos.* New York: Ballantine.

Weissmann, G., and Clairborne, R., eds. 1975. *Cell Membranes: Biochemistry, Cell Biology and Pathology.* New York: HP Publishing Co.

Scientific American articles. San Francisco: W.H. Freeman Co.

de Duve, C. 1983. "Microbodies in the Living Cell." *Scientific American,* May.

Dustin, P. 1980. "Microtubules." *Scientific American,* August.

Hayflick, L. 1980. "The Cell Biology of Aging." *Scientific American,* January.

Porter, K.R., and Tucker, J.B. 1981. "The Ground Substance of the Living Cell." *Scientific American,* March.

Shulman, R. G. 1983. "NMR (nuclear-magnetic-resonance) Spectroscopy of Living Cells." *Scientific American,* January.

Part II

Avery, O.T. et al. 1944. "Studies on the Chemical Nature of the Substance Inducing Transformation of Pneumococcal Types." *Journal of Experimental Medicine* 79:137. (Classic early experiment on identifying DNA)

Chedd, G. 1981. "Genetic Gibberish in the Code of Life." *Science 81,* November.

Dawkins, R. 1976. *The Selfish Gene.* New York: Oxford University Press.

Gilbert, L.E., and Ravin, P.H. 1975. *Coevolution of Plants and Animals.* Austin Tex.: University of Texas Press.

Joravsky, D. 1970. *The Lysenko Affair.* Cambridge, Mass.: Harvard University Press. (A penetrating look at science under the influence of Soviet politics)

Lack, D. 1947. *Darwin's Finches.* Cambridge: Cambridge University Press.

Lewin, R. 1983. "A Naturalist of the Genome." *Science* 222:402.

Mendel, G. 1965. "Experiments in Plant Hybridization (1865)." Translated by Eva Sherwood. In *The Origin of Genetics.* edited by C. Stern and E. Sherwood. San Francisco: W.H. Freeman Co.

Menosky, J.A. 1981. "The Gene Machine." *Science 81,* July/August.

Messelson, M., and Stahl, F.W. 1958. "The Replication of DNA in *E. coli.*" *Proceedings of the National Academy of Sciences* (U.S.). 44:671.

Rensberger, B. "Tinkering with Life." *Science 81,* November.

Scientific American Editors. 1978. *Evolution: A Scientific American Book.* San Francisco: W.H. Freeman. Co.

Shine, I., and Wrobel, S. 1976. *Thomas Hunt Morgan: Pioneer of Genetics.* Lexington: University of Kentucky Press.

Strickberger, M.W. 1976. *Genetics.* 2d ed. New York: Macmillan.

Volpe, P. 1981. *Understanding Evolution.* 4th ed. Dubuque, Iowa: Wm. C. Brown.

Watson, J.D. 1968. *The Double Helix.* New York: Atheneum.

Watson J.D., and Crick, F.H.C. 1953. "Molecular Structure of Nucleic Acids: A structure of deoxyribose nucleic acid." *Nature* 171:737. (This is the one that started it all: the most influential single paper in scientific history.)

Scientific American articles. San Francisco: W.H. Freeman Co.

Aharonowitz, Y., and Cohen, G. 1981. "The Microbiological Production of Pharmaceuticals." *Scientific American,* September.

Anderson, W.F., and Diacumakos, E.G. 1981. "Genetic Engineering in Mammalian Cells." *Scientific American,* July.

Bishop, J.M. 1982. "Oncogenes." *Scientific American,* March.

Brill, W.J. 1981. "Agricultural Microbiology." *Scientific American,* September.

Chambon, P. 1981. "Split Genes." *Scientific American,* May.

Chilton, M. 1983. "A Vector for Introducing New Genes into Plants." *Scientific American,* June.

Cohen, S.N., and Shapiro, J.A. 1980. "Transposable Genetic Elements." *Scientific American,* February.

Gilbert, L.E. 1982. "The Coevolution of a Butterfly and a Vine." *Scientific American,* August.

Grivell, L.A. 1983. "Mitochondrial DNA." *Scientific American,* March.

Hopwood, A. 1981. "The Genetic Programming of Industrial Microorganisms." *Scientific American,* September.

Howard-Flanders, P. 1981. "Inducible Repair of DNA." *Scientific American,* November.

Kornberg, R.D., and Klug, A. 1981. "The Nucleosome." *Scientific American,* February.

Lake, J.A. 1981. "The Ribosome." *Scientific American,* August.

Novick, R.P. 1980. "Plasmids." *Scientific American,* December.

Pestka, S. 1983. "The Purification and Manufacture of Human Interferons." *Scientific American,* August.

Part III

Alexopoulos, C.J. 1962. *Introduction to Mycology.* New York: Wiley.

Baker, H.G. 1963. "Evolutionary Mechanisms in Pollination Biology." *Science* 139:877.

Fox, G.E. et al. 1980. "The Phylogeny of Prokaryotes." *Science* 209:457.

Galston, W.W., and Davies, P.J. 1970. *Control Mechanisms in Plant Development.* Englewood Cliffs, N.J.: Prentice-Hall.

Lehner, E., and Lehner, J. 1973 *Folklore and Odysseys of Food and Medicinal Plants.* New York: Tudor.

Ravin, P.H. et al. 1981. *Biology of Plants,* 3d ed. New York: Worth.

Salle, A.J. 1973. *Fundamental Principles of Bacteriology.* 7th ed. New York: McGraw-Hill.

Sporne, K.R. 1971. *The Mysterious Origin of Flowering Plants.* Burlington, N.C.: Carolina Biological Supply Co.

Went, F.W. 1963. *The Plants.* Life Nature Library. New York: Time, Inc.

Scientific American articles. San Francisco: W.H. Freeman Co.

Blakemore R.P., and Frankel, R. B. 1981. "Magnetic Navigation in Bacteria." *Scientific American,* December.

Eigen, M. et al. 1981. "The Origin of Genetic Information." *Scientific American,* April.

Groves, D.I.; Dunlop, J.S.R.; and Buick, R. 1981. "An Early Habitat of Life" *Scientific American,* October. (Stromatolites)

Kaplan, D.R. 1983. "The Development of Palm Leaves," *Scientific American,* July.

Ptashne, M.; Johnson, A.D.; and Pabo, C.O. 1982. "A Genetic Switch in a Bacterial Virus." *Scientific American,* November.

Shepart, J.F. 1982. "The Regeneration of Potato Plants from Leaf-Cell Protoplasts." *Scientific American*, May.

Simons, K.; Garoff, H.; and Helenius, A. 1982. "How an Animal Virus Gets into and out of Its Host Cell." *Scientific American*, February.

Woese, C.R. 1981. "Archebacteria." *Scientific American*, June.

Part IV

Animal Engineering. Intro. by D.R. Griffin. 1974. San Francisco: W.H. Freeman Co.

Cornejo, D. 1982. "Night of the Spadefoot Toad." *Science 82*, September.

Johanson, D.C., and Edey, M.A. 1981. "Lucy: The Inside Story." *Science 81*, March.

Johanson, D.C., and White, T.D. 1979. "A Systematic Assessment of Early African Hominids." *Science*, 203:321.

McMenamin, M.A.S. 1982. "A Case for Two Late Proterozoic—Earliest Cambrian Faunal Province Loci." *Geology*, June.

Rensberger, B. 1981. "Facing the Past." *Science 81*, October. (Neanderthal man)

Storer, T.I. et al. 1979. *General Zoology*, 6th ed. New York: McGraw-Hill.

Scientific American articles San Francisco: W.H. Freeman Co.

Langston, Jr., W. 1981. "Pterosaurs." *Scientific American*, February.

Mossman, D.J., and Sarjeant, W.A.S. 1983. "The Footprints of Extinct Animals." *Scientific American*, January.

Roper, C.F.E., and Boss, K.J. 1982. "The Giant Squid." *Scientific American*, April.

Rukang, W., and Shenglong, L. 1983. "Peking Man." *Scientific American*, June.

Russell, D.A. 1982. "The Mass Extinctions of the Late Mesozoic." *Scientific American*, January.

Part V

Landau, B.R. 1980. *Essential Human Anatomy and Physiology*. 2d ed. Glenview, Ill.; Scott, Foresman and Co.

Oppenheimer, J.H. 1979. "Thyroid Hormone Action at the Cellular Level." *Science* 203:971.

Sperry, R. 1982. "Some Effects of Disconnecting the Cerebral Hemispheres." *Science* 217:1223.

Kolata, G. 1982. "New Theory of Hormones Proposed." *Science* 215:1383.

Scientific American articles. San Francisco; W.H. Freeman Co.

Bloom, F.E. 1981. "Neuropeptides." *Scientific American*, October.

Hudspeth, A.J. 1983. "The Hair Cells of the Inner Ear." *Scientific American*, January.

Llinas, R.R. 1982. "Calcium in Synaptic Transmission." *Scientific American*, October.

Morell, P., and Norton, W.T. 1980. "Myelin." *Scientific American*. May.

Newman, E.A., and Hartline, P.H. 1982. "The Infrared 'Vision' of Snakes." *Scientific American*, March.

Schmidt-Nielsen, K. 1981. "Countercurrent Systems in Animals." *Scientific American*, May.

Van Dyke, C., and Byck, R. 1982. "Cocaine." *Scientific American*, March.

Wurtman, R.J. 1982. "Nutrients That Modify Brain Function." *Scientific American*, April.

Part VI

Katchadourian, H. 1974. *Human Sexuality: Sense and Nonsense*. San Francisco: W.H. Freeman Co.

Landau, B.R. 1980. *Essential Human Anatomy and Physiology*. 2d ed. Glenview, Ill: Scott, Foresman and Co.

Money, J., and Ehrhardt, A.A. 1972. *Man and Woman, Boy and Girl: The Differentiation and Dimorphism of Gender Identity from Conception to Maturity*. Baltimore: Johns Hopkins University Press.

Rugh, R., and Shettles, L.B. 1971. *From Conception to Birth: the Drama of Life's Beginnings*. New York: Harper and Row.

Shell, E.R. 1982. "The Guinea Pig Town" *Science 82*, December. (Framingham, Mass.)

Shodell, M. 1983. "The Prostaglandin Connection." *Science 83*, March.

Weisman, I.L. et al. 1978. *Essential Concepts in Immunology*. Menlo Park, Calif.: Benjamin Cummings.

West, S. 1983. "One Step Behind a Killer" *Science 83*, March. (AIDS)

Scientific American articles. San Francisco: W.H. Freeman Co.

Beaconsfield, P. et al. 1980. "The Placenta." *Scientific American*, August.

Buisseret, P.D. 1982. "Allergy." *Scientific American*, August.

Degabriele, R. 1980. "The Physiology of the Koala." *Scientific American*, July.

Jarvik, R.K. 1981. "The Total Artificial Heart." *Scientific American*, January.

Leder, P. 1982. "The Genetics of Antibody Diversity." *Scientific American*, May.

Lerner, R.A. 1983. "Synthetic Vaccines." *Scientific American*, February.

Moog, F. 1981. "The Lining of the Small Intestine." *Scientific American*, November.

Rose, N.R. 1981. "Autoimmune Disease." *Scientific American*, February.

Winfree, A.T. 1983. "Sudden Cardiac Death: A Problem of Topology." *Scientific American*. May.

Zucker, M.B. 1980. "The Functioning of Blood Platelets." *Scientific American*, June.

Part VII

Brown, J.L. *The Evolution of Behavior*. New York: W.W. Norton.

Gould, J.L. 1982. *Ethology: The Mechanisms and Evolution of Behavior*. New York: W.W. Norton.

Mech, L.D. 1970. *The Wolf: The Ecology and Behavior of an Endangered Species*. Garden City, New York: Natural History Press.

Odum, E.P. 1983. *Basic Ecology*. Philadelphia, Penn.: Saunders.

Ricklefs, R.E. 1978. *Ecology*, 2d ed. Newton, Mass.: Chiron Press.

Scientific American Editors. 1970. *Biosphere: A Scientific American Book*. San Francisco: W.H. Freeman Co.

Skinner, B.F. 1938. *The Behavior of Organisms: An Experimental Analysis*. New York: Appleton-Century-Crofts.

Trivers, R.L. 1971. "The Evolution of Reciprocal Altruism." *Quarterly Review of Biology* 46:35.

Wallace, R.A. 1979. *Animal Behavior: Its Development, Ecology, and Evolution*. Glenview, Ill.: Scott, Foresman and Co.

———. 1979. *The Genesis Factor*. New York: William Morrow.

Wilson, E.O. 1975. *Sociobiology, The New Synthesis*. Cambridge, Mass.: Harvard University Press.

———. 1978. *On Human Nature*. Cambridge, Mass.: Harvard University Press.

Scientific American articles. San Francisco: W.H. Freeman Co.

Alkon, D.L. 1983. "Learning in a Marine Snail." *Scientific American*, July.

Beddington, J.R., and May, R.M. 1982. "The Harvesting of Interacting Species in a Natural Ecosystem." *Scientific American*, November.

Cloud, P. 1983. "The Biosphere." *Scientific American*, September.

Hauser, P.M. 1981. "The Census of 1980." *Scientific American*, November.

Heinrich, B. 1981. "The Regulation of Temperature in the Honeybee Swarm." *Scientific American*, June.

Ingersoll, A.P. 1983. "The Atmosphere." *Scientific American*, September.

Lloyd, J.E. 1981. "Mimicry in the Sexual Signals of Fireflies." *Scientific American*, July.

Partridge, B.L. 1982. "The Structure and Function of Fish Schools." *Scientific American*, July.

Revelle, R. 1982. "Carbon Dioxide and World Climate." *Scientific American*, July.

Illustration Acknowledgments

Unless otherwise acknowledged, all photos are the property of Scott, Foresman and Company.

Contents in Brief Part I(1)/Hugh Spencer Part I(r)/From *Scanning Electron Microscopy in Biology: A Student's Atlas on Biological Organization* by R.G. Kessel and C.Y. Shih. © Springer–Verlag 1974 Part II(1)/Drs. Y. Daskal and H. Busch. In *The Cell Nucleus, Chromatin, Part C*, ed., H. Busch. ©1978 by Academic Press, Inc. Part II(r)/Courtesy of Tsuyoshi Kakefuda/National Institutes of Health Part III(1)/Manfred Kage/Peter Arnold Inc. Part III(r)/John Ebeling Part IV(1)/Kim Taylor/Bruce Coleman Ltd. Part IV(r) M. Philip Kahl Part V(1)/Ed Reschke Part V(r)/From *Living Images* by Gene Shih and Richard Kessel. Reprinted courtesy of Jones and Bartlett Publishers, Inc., Boston, MA Part VI(1)/Ed Reschke Part VI(r)/Nilsson, Lennart. 1974 *Behold Man*. Boston: Little, Brown and Co. Part VII(tl)/George J. Sanker/DRK Photo Part VII(r)/Wayne Lankinen/DRK Photo Part VII(bl)/John Ebeling

Chapter 1 1.1/"Galileo Before the Holy Office" by Robert Fleury. Louvre, Paris 1.2/NASA 1.6/"Charles Darwin, Age 30" by George Richmond R.A. Royal College of Surgeons of England 1.8/"HMS Beagle" by Owen Stanley. National Maritime Museum, London 1.9/© Robert Rattner 1.11/John Dawson Page 16/Wolfgang Kaehler (t, cr, bl); George H. Harrison (cl, br) Page 17/Tui De Roy Moore (bl); George H. Harrison

Chapter 3 3.4(a)/Brown, R.M., and Willison, J.H.M. 1977. In *International Cell Biology 1976-1977*, ed., B.R. Brinkley and K.R. Porter, pp. 267-283. © 1977 by The Rockefeller University Press 3.9/National Institutes of Health

Chapter 4 Page 53 (t)/Dr. Morton/American Society for Microbiology Page 53 (b)/Dr. Daniel Branton 4.4/Courtesy of Dr. J. David Robertson 4.5/Dr. Daniel Branton 4.7a/Courtesy of Dr. Emma Shelton 4.7b/Dr. Daniel Branton 4.9/Courtesy of D. James Morré, Purdue University 4.12a/Hugh Spencer 4.12b/Courtesy Abbott Laboratories 4.13a/Courtesy Abbott Laboratories 4.14/Courtesy of Donald Larson 4.16a/Bouck, G.B. 1971. *J. Cell Biology* 50:362-384. Reproduced by copyright permission of The Rockefeller University Press. 4.16b/Dr. G.B. Bouck 4.17/Turner, F.R. 1968. *J. Cell Biology* 37:370. Reproduced by copyright permission of the Rockefeller University Press. 4.18/(br)/Macmillan Science Co., Inc.

Chapter 6 6.1/Marty Stouffer/Animals Animals 6.2/David R. Frazier 6.3/Stephen J. Krasemann/DRK Photo 6.4/U.P.I.

Chapter 7 7.1/G.R. Roberts 7.9/Charlton Photos 7.10/Photo by Dr. W.W. Thomson. Courtesy of Dr. R.M. Leech, University of York

Chapter 9 9.3/Courtesy of Dr. Henry L. Nadler, Children's Memorial Hospital, Chicago Page 123/Drs. Y. Daskal and H. Busch. In *The Cell Nucleus, Chromatin, Part C*, ed., H. Busch. © 1978 by Academic Press, Inc. 9.4/Paulson, J.R., and Laemmli, U.K. *Cell* 12:817-828. © 1977 M.I.T. Page 125/Courtesy of Dr. Henry L. Nadler, Children's Memorial Hospital, Chicago 9.6/Dr. Andrew S. Bajer 9.7/Courtesy of Drs. B.R. Brinkley and J. Cartwright 9.9/Giménez-Martin, G., de la Torre, C., and López-Sàez, J.F. In *Mechanisms and Control of Cell Division*, ed. T.L. Rost and E.M. Gifford, Jr., pp. 267-283. © 1977 by Dowden, Hutchinson and Ross, Inc.

Chapter 10 10.2/Jean-Marie Luciani, Courtesy Pasteur Institute, Paris 10.3/Professor M. Westergaard. In *DNA, Chromatin and Chromosomes* by E.M. Bradbury, N. Maclean and H.C. Matthews. © 1981 by Blackwell Scientific Publications 10.4/James L. Walters

Chapter 11 11.1/Culver Pictures

Chapter 12 12.9/Courtesy of Dr. Murray L. Barr Page 170/Courtesy of the New York Public Library, Astor, Lenox and Tilden Foundations

Chapter 13 13.4/Blakeslee, A.F. 1914. *J. of Heredity* 5:512 13.5/© Walter Chandoha 13.6(t)/Keystone Press Agency 13.6(b)/Wide World

Chapter 14 14.4/NASA 14.5/Dr. Lee D. Simon 14.7/X-ray diffraction photograph of DNA, B-form, taken by Rosalind Franklin late in 1952. From J.D. Watson, *The Double Helix*, p. 168. New York: Athenum. © 1968 by J.D. Watson. 14.12/Courtesy of Tsuyoshi Kakefuda/National Institutes of Health

Chapter 15 15.2/Miller, O.L., Jr., and Beatty, B.R. 1969. *Science* 164:955-957. 15.5/Lake, J.A. 1981. *Scientific American* 245:84 15.11/Courtesy of Steven L. McKnight and O.L. Miller, Jr.

Chapter 16 16.2/Dr. T.F. Anderson/Institute for Cancer Research, Philadelphia

Chapter 17 17.1/Charlton Photos 17.2/Everett C. Johnson 17.5/Wide World

Chapter 18 18.1/© Walter Chandoha 18.3/Dr. H.B.D. Kettlewell 18.5/National Institutes of Health 18.6/Blakeslee, A.F. 1914. *J. of Heredity* 5:512 18.10/Jeff Foott 18.11/Milt & Joan Mann/Cameramann international

Chapter 19 19.2/M. Philip Kahl 19.3/Daniel L. Feicht 19.5a/Dr. E.R. Degginger 19.5b/Nadine Orasona/Tom Stack & Associates 19.6/C.A. Morgan 19.6a/James Tallon/Outdoor Exposures 19.6b/Sonja Bullaty 19.10/U.S. Department of Agriculture 19.12/© Robert Rattner 19.13/Melinda Berge/Photographers, Aspen (Tasmanian devil); Erwin & Peggy Bauer (sloth); Douglas Baglin/Animals Animals (rabbit bandicoot); Stephen J. Krasemann/DRK Photo (hare); Gary Milburn/Tom Stack & Associates (glider); Wayne Lankinen (flying squirrel); Melinda Berge (Tasmanian devil); Annie Griffiths (wolverine); Hans & Judy Beste/Tom Stack & Associates (numbat); Loren McIntyre (anteater); G.R. Roberts (short-nosed bandicoot); Hans & Judy Beste/Animals Animals (long-nosed bandicoot); Leonard Lee Rue III/Tom Stack & Associates (rat) 19.14(l)/Dr. E.R. Degginger 19.14(r)/Pete Carmichael 19.16(l)/Richard Ellis 19.16(r)/Dr. E.R. Degginger

Chapter 20 20.1/U.C.S.D. Photo 20.2/Dr. Sidney W. Fox. In Fox and Dose, "Molecular Evolution and the Origins of Life." 20.3/Dr. A. Oparin, Bakh Institute of Biochemistry, Moscow 20.7/© Rick Smolan 20.8/Dr. J.D. Zeikus 20.9/Dr. R. Wyckoff/National Institutes of Health 20.10(tl)/Dr. Tony Brain/Science Photo Library 20.10 (tc)/The Upjohn Company 20.10(tr,bc)/Biophoto Associates 20.10 (bl)/Armed Forces Institute of Pathology 20.10(br)/Beecham Laboratories, Division of Beecham, Inc. 20.11/Drs. Maria Costa and George B. Chapman, Georgetown University 20.12(t)/U.S. Dept. of Health 20.12(b)/Centers for Disease Control 20.13a,c/Biophoto Associates 20.13b/Tom Adams 20.13d/Courtesy of D.L Findley, P.L. Walne and R.W. Holton, University of Tennessee, Knoxville. From *J. Psychology* 6:182–188. 1970. 20.14/Courtesy Woods Hole Oceanographic Institution 20.15a/Courtesy Robley C. Williams 20.15b/Gene M. Milbrath, Ph.D./U.S.D.A. 20.15c/Courtesy of R.F. Bils 20.16/Courtesy of Drs. Ari Helenius, Kai Simon and Henrik Garoff

Chapter 21 21.2(l)/Tom Adams 21.2(c)/Brian Parker/Tom Stack & Associates 21.2(r)/Tom Stack & Associates 21.3/Dr. Paul E. Hargraves 21.4/Biophoto Associates 21.4(cr)/Dr. Paul E. Hargraves 21.5/Frieder Sauer/Bruce Coleman Ltd. 21.7(l)Centers for Disease Control 21.7(r)/Dr. J.A.L. Cooke/Animals Animals 21.8/Dr. Kwang W. Jeon 21.9a/Biophoto Associates 21.9b/Manfred Kage/Peter Arnold Inc. 21.9c/M. Walker/N.H.P.A. 21.10(t)/William Patterson/Tom Stack & Associates 21.10(c)/Brian Parker/Tom Stack & Associates 21.10(bl)/Manfred Kage/Peter Arnold Inc. 21.10(br)/Eric V. Gravé 21.12/Loomis, William F., *Dictyostelium discoideum: A Developmental System*. © 1975 by Academic Press, Inc. 21.16a/Loren A. McIntyre 21.16b/Runk/Schoenberger from Grant Heilman Photography 21.16c/Robert P. Carr 21.16d/U.S. Department of Agriculture 21.17/G.R. Roberts 21.18(t)/Eric V. Gravé 21.18(b)/Pramer, D. 1964. *Science* 144:382-388 21.19(l)/G.R. Roberts 21.19(r)/D. Wilder

Chapter 22 22.2/Howard Hall 22.3/Howard Hall 22.5/Biophoto Associates 22.6a/Macmillan Science Co., Inc. 22.6b/Jeffrey L. Rotman 22.7a/G.R. Roberts 22.7b/Macmillan Science Co., Inc. 22.10a/Walter Dawn 22.10b/Robert P. Carr 22.10c/G.R. Roberts 22.11/Steve Lissau 22.12(bl)/From *Living Images* by Gene Shih and Richard Kessel. Reprinted courtesy of Jones and Bartlett Publishers, Inc., Boston, MA 22.12(br)/G.R. Roberts 22.14a/A.J. Belling, New York University 22.15a,b/G.R. Roberts 22.15c/M. Philip Kahl 22.16/Harald Sund

Chapter 23 Page 330(l,r)/Dr. E.S. Ross Page 330(c)/Robert P. Carr Page 331(1)/Dr. E.S. Ross Page 331(c)/Oxford Scientific Films/Animals Animals Page 331(d)/Dr. Merlin D. Tuttle, Milwaukee Public Museum 23.2/G.R. Roberts Page 334a,c/John Ebeling Page 334b/© Mark Weidling Page 334d/Don & Pat Valenti Page 334e/Steve

Lissau   Page 335f/Dr. E.S. Ross   Page 335g/Dr. Timothy Plowman Page 335h/John Ebeling   Page 335i,j/Robert P. Carr   Page 338(tl,r)/ G.R. Roberts   Page 339(c)/Robert P. Carr   Page 340(tl,bc)/G.R. Roberts   Page 340(bl)/John Ebeling   Page 341(tl)/John Shaw   Page 341(tr,br)/Robert P. Carr

Chapter 24   24.7/Biophoto Associates   24.8/U.S. Department of Agriculture   24.10/Biophoto Associates   24.13/Biophoto Associates 24.14a/John Ebeling   24.14b/Grant Heilman Photography   24.15(r)/ From *Living Images* by Gene Shih and Richard Kessel. Reprinted courtesy of Jones & Bartlett Publishers, Inc., Boston, MA.

Chapter 25   25.1/Chuck Place   25.2/U.S. Department of Agriculture 25.6/G.R. Roberts   25.7/Biophoto Associates   25.9/Paul P. Kormanik, U.S.D.A., F.S.

Chapter 26   26.2/U.S. Department of Agriculture   26.5/Biophoto Associates   26.8a/G.R. Roberts   26.8b/Zig Leszczynski/Earth Scenes 26.9a,b/Derek Fell   26.9c/Dr. Timothy Plowman

Chapter 27   27.5/Jeffrey L. Rotman   27.7/Kim Taylor/Bruce Coleman Ltd.   27.8/William H. Amos/Bruce Coleman Inc.   27.9a/Jeffrey L. Rotman   27.9b/Oxford Scientific Films/Animals Animals   27.9c/ Douglas Faulkner/Sally Faulkner Collection   27.9d/U.S. Naval Photographic Station, Washington, D.C.   27.10/G.R. Roberts   27.11/U.S. Department of Agriculture   27.13(l)Tom Adams   27.13(r)/U.S. Department of Agriculture   27.14/Eric V. Gravé

Chapter 28   28.3a/Jeffrey L. Rotman   28.3b/U.S. Department of Agriculture   28.3c/Jane Burton/Bruce Coleman Inc.   28.6a/Douglas Faulkner/Sally Faulkner Collection   28.6b/Carson Baldwin/Animals Animals   28.6c/M. Philip Kahl   28.6d/M. Ederegger/DRK Photo 28.6e/Maria Zorn/Animals Animals   28.6f/K.G. Preston-Maflam/ Animals Animals   28.6g/John Ebeling   28.7/Robert P. Carr   28.8/Dr. L.M. Beidler   28.10/David Scharf   28.11a/Jeff Foott/Bruce Coleman Ltd.   28.11b/Jeffrey L. Rotman   28.11c,d,e/Howard Hall   28.12/ Douglas Faulkner/Sally Faulkner Collection   28.13a,e/Howard Hall 28.13b,c/Jeffrey L. Rotman   28.13d/Douglas Faulkner/Sally Faulkner Collection   28.14(t)Douglas Faulkner/Sally Faulkner Collection 28.14(b)Jeffrey L. Rotman   28.16/Jeffrey L. Rotman

Chapter 29   29.1/Heather Angel/Biofotos   29.4c/Jeffrey L. Rotman 29.4d/Dr. Wolf H. Fahrenbach   29.7/Peter Scoones/Seaphot   29.9a/ C.A. Morgan   29.9b/Dr. E.S. Ross   29.9c/George H. Harrison 29.11a/Dr. E.S. Ross   29.11b/Don and Pat Valenti   29.11c/Joe McDonald/Bruce Coleman Inc.   Page 433/C.A. Morgan   29.12/James P. Rowan/Click, Chicago Ltd.   29.14(tl,bl)/G.R. Roberts   29.14(tc,r)/ William Boehm   29.14(bl)/Wolfgang Bayer Productions   29.15/ Paläontologisches Museum, Museum für Naturkünde an der Humboldt-Universität, Berlin, DDR   29.16/Courtesy of Dr. Carl Welty 29.19/Hans Reinhard/Bruce Coleman Inc.

Chapter 30   30.2/Loren A. McIntyre   30.3/M. Philip Kahl   30.4/Joy Spurr/Bruce Coleman Inc.   30.8/Field Museum of Natural History

Chapter 31   31.1/Ed Reschke   31.2/Ed Reschke   31.3(b)/Ed Reschke 31.5(tr)From *Living Images* by Gene Shih and Richard Kessel. Reprinted courtesy of Jones and Bartlett Publishers, Inc., Boston, MA   31.8/Ed Reschke   31.11(a)/G.F. Gauthier/Photo Researchers 31.11(b)/Biology Media/Photo Researchers

Chapter 32   32.1/Marty Stouffer/Animals Animals   32.4/Dr. Cedric S. Raine   32.10/Dr. John Heuser

Chapter 33   33.1/Prepared by Rufus B. Weaver, M.D., 1888./Courtesy of Dr. Peter S. Amenta, Hahnemann University, Philadelphia, Pa. 33.3/Manfred Kage/Peter Arnold Inc.   33.12/Dan McCoy/Rainbow 33.13/Courtesy DREAMSTAGE Scientific Catalog. © J. Allan Hobson and Hoffmann–LaRoche Inc.

Chapter 34   34.3/Nilsson, Lennart. 1974. *Behold Man.* Boston: Little, Brown and Co.   34.8/Courtesy of Dr. Edwin B. Lewis

Chapter 35   35.8/Ed Reschke

Chapter 36   36.1(t)/U.W. Green Bay photo by Mike Brisson   36.1(bl)/ Robert P. Carr   36.1(br)/Wolfgang Kaehler

Chapter 37   37.2/G.R. Roberts

Chapter 38   38.1(tl)/U.S. Naval Photographic Station, Washington D.C.   38.1(tr)/U.S. Department of Agriculture   38.1(mc)/Jeffrey L. Rotman   38.1(cr)/G.R. Roberts   38.1(bl)/Douglas Faulkner/Sally Faulkner Collection   38.1(bc)/D. Wilder   38.1(br)/William Boehm

Chapter 39   39.1/Jerome Wexler   39.4/Armed Forces Institute of Pathology   Page 572/University of Utah Medical Center   39.6/ Richard Stromberg/Chicago   39.9/D.W. Fawcett/Photo Researchers 39.10/Ed Reschke   39.11a/Biophoto Associates   39.12/Nilsson, Lennart. 1974. *Behold Man.* Boston: Little, Brown and Co.   39.13/ Biophoto Associates   39.14/James D. Hirsch, Rockefeller University 39.17/Ed Reschke

Chapter 41   41.1/Nilsson, Lennart. 1974. *Behold Man.* Boston: Little, Brown and Co.   41.3/Anderson, E.J. *J. Cell Biol.* 37:514–539. Reproduced by copyright permission of the Rockefeller University Press. 41.4a/Dr. L.M. Beidler   41.10/Russ Kinne/Photo Researchers 41.14/Nilsson, Lennart. 1974. *Behold Man.* Boston: Little, Brown and Co.; Nilsson, Lennart. 1977. *A Child Is Born.* New York: Delacorte Press   41.15/Maternity Center Association

Chapter 42   42.1/Stephen J. Krasemann/DRK Photo   42.2/Charles G. and Rita Summers   Page 622/Stephen J. Krasemann/DRK Photo Page 623(l)/Erwin and Peggy Bauer   Page 623(r)/Wolfgang Bayer Productions   42.7/The Bettmann Archive   42.10/Courtesy Charles Pfizer and Co., Inc.

Chapter 43   43.1a/John Beach/Wildlife Picture Agency   43.1b/Brian Parker/Tom Stack & Associates   Page 632(t,c)/Dr. E.R. Degginger Page 632(b)Dr. E.S. Ross   Page 633(tl)/J.A.L. Cooke/Oxford Scientific Films/Animals Animals   Page 633(tc)/Stephen J. Krasemann/DRK Photo   Page 633(tr)/D. Wilder   Page 633(bl)/Jeffrey L. Rotman   Page 633(bc)/John Chellman/Animals Animals   Page 633(br)/Don and Pat Valenti   43.5(l)/George H. Harrison   43.5(r)M. Philip Kahl   Page 636/Dr. Merlin D. Tuttle, Milwaukee Public Museum   43.6/M.P.L. Fogden/Bruce Coleman Inc.   43.7(l)/Stefan Meyers/Animals Animals 43.7(c)/Stephen J. Krasemann/DRK Photo   43.7(r)/Wolfgang Bayer Productions   Page 639(tl)/Robert C. Fields/Animals Animals   Page 639(tr)/John Ebeling   Page 639(b)/Candace Bayer/Wolfgang Bayer Productions   43.8(l)/Leonard Lee Rue III/Animals Animals   43.8(r)/ Loren A. McIntyre   43.9(l)/Lynn M. Stone   43.9(r)/Stephen J. Krasemann/DRK Photo   43.10/Stephen Dalton/NHPA

Chapter 44   44.5/Loren A. McIntyre   44.6/Loren A. McIntyre   44.7/ Dr. E.S. Ross   44.8(l)/John Shaw   44.8(r)/James Tallon/Outdoor Exposures   44.9a/Wyman Meinzer   44.9b/John Gerlach/DRK Photo 44.9c/Bob & Clara Calhoun/Bruce Coleman Inc.   44.9d/William Boehm   44.9e/Dr. E.S. Ross   44.10/Tom McHugh/Photo Researchers 44.11/Loren A. McIntyre   44.12/Lynn M. Stone   44.13(tl)/George J. Sanker/DRK Photo   44.13(tr)/Wayne Lankinen/DRK Photo   44.13-(bl)/John Ebeling   44.13(bc)/Stephen J. Krasemann/DRK Photo 44.14/Stephen J. Kraseman/DRK Photo   44.14(bl)/Varin-Visage/ Jacana   44.17/Phil Degginger

Chapter 45   Page 633(l)/Dudley Foster/WHOI   Page 633(c)/James Childress, UC-SB/WHOI   Page 633(r)/Alvin External Camera/WHOI 45.3/G.R. Roberts   45.4/From FUNDAMENTALS OF ECOLOGY 3rd Edition by Eugene P. Odum. Copyright © 1971 by W.B. Saunders Company. Reprinted by permission of Holt, Rinehart and Winston, CBS College Publishing   45.8(b)/Walter Dawn   45.15/Bitterroot National Forest, U.S. Forest Service   45.16/John Ebeling

Chapter 46   46.5/U.P.I.   46.6/G.R. Roberts   46.8/Zig Leszczynski/ Animals Animals   46.9/Muller, C.H. 1966. *Bulletin of the Torrey Botanical Club* 93:332-351   46.10/Gilbert Dupuy/Black Star

Chapter 47   47.3/James Gillray/The Bettmann Archive   47.4/Wide World   47.5, 47.6, 47.7, 47.8 From LIVING IN THE ENVIRONMENT, Third Edition by G. Tyler Miller, Jr. Copyright © 1982 by Wadsworth, Inc. Reprinted by permission of Wadsworth Publishing Co., Belmont, Calif. 94002.

Index

The Metric System

Metric Prefixes

(units: gram, meter, and liter are common suffixes)

Prefix	Multiple	Symbol
(greater than one)		
deka	10	da
hecto	10^2	h
kilo	10^3	k
mega	10^6	M
(less than one)		
deci	10^{-1}	d
centi	10^{-2}	c
milli	10^{-3}	m
micro	10^{-6}	μ
nano	10^{-9}	n
pico	10^{-12}	p

Metric Length

1 meter	$\times$	10	=	dekameter (10m)
(the unit)		100	=	hectometer (10^2 m)
		1,000	=	kilometer (10^3 m)
		1,000,000	=	megameter (10^6 m)

1 meter	$\div$	10	=	decimeter (10^{-1} m)
		100	=	centimeter (10^{-2} m)
		1,000	=	millimeter (10^{-3} m)
		1,000,000	=	micrometer (10^{-6} m)
		1,000,000,000	=	nanometer (10^{-9} m)
		1,000,000,000,000	=	picometer (10^{-12} m)
		10,000,000,000	=	Angstrom (Å) (10^{-10} m) (an older unit of measurement)

Metric Weights or Masses

1 gram (the unit) $\times$ 1,000 = kilogram

1 gram	$\div$ 1,000	=	milligram (mg) (10^{-3} g)
	1,000,000	=	microgram (μg) (10^{-6} g)
	1,000,000,000	=	nanogram (ng) (10^{-9} g)
	1,000,000,000,000	=	picogram (pg) (10^{-12} g)

Metric-English Conversions

Length

English (USA)	= Metric
inch	= 2.54 cm, 25.4 mm
foot	= 0.30 m, 30.48 cm
yard	= 0.91 m, 91.4 cm
mile (statute) (5,280 ft)	= 1.61 km, 1609 m
mile (nautical) (6077 ft, 1.15 statute mi)	= 1.85 km, 1850 m

Metric	= English (USA)
millimeter	= 0.039 in
centimeter	= 0.39 in
meter	= 3.28 ft, 39.37 in
kilometer	= 0.62 mi, 1,091 yd, 3,273 ft

Weight

English (USA)	= Metric
grain	= 64.80 mg
ounce	= 28.35 g
pound	= 453.60 g, 0.45 kg
ton (short—2000 lb)	= 0.91 metric tons (907 kg)

Metric	= English (USA)
milligram	= 0.02 grains (0.000035 oz)
gram	= 0.04 oz
kilogram	= 35.27 oz., 2.20 lb
metric ton (1000 kg)	= 1.10 tons

Volume

English (USA)	= Metric
cubic inch	= 16.39 cc
cubic foot	= 0.03 m³
cubic yard	= 0.765 m³
ounce	= 0.03 l (30 ml or cc)*
pint	= 0.47 l
quart	= 0.95 l
gallon	= 3.79 l

Metric	= English (USA)
milliliter	= 0.03 oz
liter	= 2.12 pt
liter	= 1.06 qt
liter	= 0.27 gal

1 liter $\div$ 1,000 = milliliter or cubic centimeter (10^{-3}l)
1 liter $\div$ 1,000,000 = microliter (10^{-6}l)

*Note: 1 ml = 1 cc